Ius Comparatum – Global Studies in Comparative Law

Volume 45

As globalization proceeds, the significance of the comparative approach in legal scholarship increases. The IACL / AIDC with almost 800 members is the major universal organization promoting comparative research in law and organizing congresses with hundreds of participants in all parts of the world. The results of those congresses should be disseminated and be available for legal scholars in a single book series which would make both the Academy and its contribution to comparative law more visible. The series aims to publish the scholarship emerging from the congresses of IACL / AIDC, including: 1. of the General Congresses of Comparative Law, which take place every 4 years (Brisbane 2002; Utrecht 2006, Washington 2010, Vienna 2014, Fukuoka 2018 etc.) and which generate (a) one volume of General Reports edited by the local organizers of the Congress; (b) up to 30 volumes of selected thematic reports dealing with the topics of the single sections of the congress and containing the General Report as well as the National Reports of that section; these volumes would be edited by the General Reporters of the respective sections; 2. the volumes containing selected contributions to the smaller (2-3 days) thematic congresses which take place between the International Congresses (Mexico 2008; Taipei 2012; Montevideo 2016 etc.); these congresses have a general theme such as "Codification" or "The Enforcement of Law" and will be edited by the local organizers of the respective Congress. All publications may contain contributions in English and French, the official languages of the Academy.

More information about this series at http://www.springer.com/series/11943

Académie Internationale de Droit Comparé
International Academy of Comparative Law

Eva-Maria Kieninger
Editor

Security Rights in Intellectual Property

Springer

Editor
Eva-Maria Kieninger
Faculty of Law
University of Würzburg
Würzburg, Germany

ISSN 2214-6881 ISSN 2214-689X (electronic)
Ius Comparatum – Global Studies in Comparative Law
ISBN 978-3-030-44190-6 ISBN 978-3-030-44191-3 (eBook)
https://doi.org/10.1007/978-3-030-44191-3

This Springer imprint is published by the registered company Springer Nature Switzerland AG.
The registered company address is: Gewerbestrasse 11, 6330 Cham, Switzerland

Contents

Contributors

Venetia Argyropoulou European University of Cyprus, Faculty of Law, Nicosia, Cyprus

Nicolas Binctin Université de Poitiers, Poitiers, France

Jan Jakob Bornheim University of Canterbury, Christchurch, New Zealand

Moritz Brinkmann Institut für deutsches und internationales Zivilverfahrensrecht, Rheinische Friedrich-Wilhelms-Universität Bonn, Bonn, Germany

Iván Heredia Cervantes Universidad Autónoma de Madrid, Madrid, Spain

Élise Charpentier Faculté de droit, Université de Montréal, Montréal, QC, Canada

Andreas Chr. Christoforou Nicosia, Cyprus

Răzvan Dincă University of Bucharest, Law School, Bucharest, Romania

Christian Dorfmayr University of Vienna, Department of European, International, and Comparative Law, Vienna, Austria

Th. C. J. A. (Dick) van Engelen Maastricht University, Maastricht, The Netherlands

Hano Ernst University of Zagreb, Faculty of Law, Zagreb, Croatia

Beata Giesen Faculty of Law and Administration, University of Lodz, Department of Civil Law, Lodz, Poland

Igor Gliha University of Zagreb, Faculty of Law, Zagreb, Croatia

Yuriko Haga Kanazawa University, Kanazawa, Japan

Megumi Hara Gakushuin University, Tokyo, Japan

Robert G. Howell Faculty of Law, University of Victoria, Victoria, BC, Canada

Teemu Juutilainen Faculty of Law, University of Turku, Turku, Finland

Dionysia Kallinikou National and Kapodistrian University of Athens, Athens, Greece

Sadulla Karjiker Anton Mostert Chair of Intellectual Property Law, Stellenbosch University, Stellenbosch, South Africa

Eva-Maria Kieninger Julius-Maximilians-Universität Würzburg, Würzburg, Germany

Pierrina Koriatopoulou National and Kapodistrian University of Athens, Athens, Greece

Pavel Koukal Masaryk University, Faculty of Law, Brno, Czech Republic

Su-Hua Lee College of Law, National Taiwan University, Taipei, Taiwan

Gea Lepik University of Tartu, School of Law, Department of Private Law, Tartu, Estonia

Jasmine Malekzadem University of Ghent – UGent, Gent, Belgium

Patrick Masiyakurima University of Leicester, Leicester, UK

Sheelagh McCracken University of Sydney Law School, Sydney, NSW, Australia

Laura Murguía-Goebel Faculty of Law of the Julius-Maximilians-Universität Würzburg, Würzburg, Germany

Simone Lahorgue Nunes Levy and Salomão Advogados, Rio de Janeiro, Brazil

Ergun Özsunay Istanbul University Law Faculty (Em.), Istanbul, Turkey

Murat R. Özsunay Istanbul Bar Assoc. Apprentice Training Center (SEM), Istanbul, Turkey

Helena Pullmannova Masaryk University, Faculty of Law, Brno, Czech Republic

David Rüther Institut für deutsches und internationales Zivilverfahrensrecht, Rheinische Friedrich-Wilhelms-Universität Bonn, Bonn, Germany

Marco Ricolfi Turin University, Department of Law, Torino, Italy

Radu Rizoiu University of Bucharest, Law School, Bucharest, Romania

Michel Séjean Université Bretagne Sud, Lorient, France

Bianca Scraback Institut für deutsches und internationales Zivilverfahrensrecht, Rheinische Friedrich-Wilhelms-Universität Bonn, Bonn, Germany

Matthias E. Storme Catholic University of Leuven – KU Leuven, Leuven, Belgium

Tatiana Eleni Synodinou Law Department, University of Cyprus, Nicosia, Cyprus

Romana Matanovac Vučković University of Zagreb, Faculty of Law, Zagreb, Croatia

Security Rights in Intellectual Property: General Report

Eva-Maria Kieninger

Abstract The general report gives an insight into the main legal and economic challenges for the creation and perfection of security rights in intellectual property rights. It highlights the differences among legal systems in relation to the transferability of those rights and their collateralisation. An overview of the creditor's remedies in the event of the debtor's default and insolvency as well as some basic information on the costs of creating security rights in IPR's complete the comparative survey.

1 Introduction

1.1 Economic Importance

In 2002, introducing his seminal comparative work on security interests in intellectual property, *Howard Knopf* noted that "not long ago, intellectual property was seen as a footnote, a mere boiler plate or other afterthought aspect of most corporate transactions. Often now, it is the whole point of the most important deals taking place. [. . .] The mergers of AOL and Time-Warner, Seagram and Vivendi, and BCE and CTV are all about intellectual property." However, he continued: "odd as it seems in the face of the staggering sums of money being paid essentially for patents, copyright and trademarks through share prices, the use of intellectual property as collateral in what should be routine exercises in corporate finance, is beset with structural uncertainty."[1] The literature that has been published since 2002 and the

[1] Knopf (2002), pp. 1 and 3 *et seq.*

E.-M. Kieninger (✉)
Julius-Maximilians-Universität Würzburg, Würzburg, Germany
e-mail: kieninger@jura.uni-wuerzburg.de

E.-M. Kieninger (ed.), *Security Rights in Intellectual Property*, Ius Comparatum – Global Studies in Comparative Law 45,
https://doi.org/10.1007/978-3-030-44191-3_1

national reports prepared for this project[2] both show that not much has changed. As a conclusion to a recently published 600-page monograph, *Peter Picht* states that intellectual property rights are still only used as collateral reluctantly and on a small scale.[3] If they are used, then this is mostly done in the context of an "all-asset" security right.

On the other hand, there is unanimous support for the proposition that security rights in intellectual property (IP) rights[4] could be economically valuable, if not even crucial, for SMEs.[5] This is particularly true for start-ups, which are often very innovative and creative, but have limited access to corporate financing, relying instead on capital markets. Therefore, they need to focus on bank loans; however, they do not own traditional collateral such as land or equipment.[6] For Germany, *Maximilian Decker* has noted that 60% of technology-driven SMEs finance themselves with private equity and have very limited access to bank loans, which are the traditional means of corporate financing in Germany. In over 70% of the cases in which banks refused to lend money to SMEs in the area of research and development, the reason was a lack of collateral. *Decker* concludes that the market for IP rights as collateral is dramatically underdeveloped.[7]

1.2 *Main Legal and Economic Challenges*

The following paragraphs set out some of the main legal and economic obstacles to taking security interests in IP rights. Whereas some could be overcome or at least mitigated by law reforms and international standardization (see below, Sects. 1.2.1 and 1.2.3), others are inherent in the subject itself (Sects. 1.2.2 and 1.2.4) and are therefore hardly susceptible to reform.

1.2.1 Secured Transactions Law Not Sufficiently Adapted to IP Rights

As will be shown in greater detail in Sect. 3, the question whether it is at all possible to transfer or collateralize IP rights is, in most jurisdictions, governed by IP law,

---

[2]The national reports (except the report on the United States of America) will be published in Kieninger E-M (ed) (2019), Security Rights in Intellectual Property. The information on US law in the present general report relies on the unpublished report prepared for this project by *Neil Cohen*.

[3]Picht (2018), p. 602.

[4]In this contribution, the notion of intellectual property (IP) is used in a broad sense, including not only copyright (= intellectual property in a narrow sense), but also industrial property, such as patents, designs, and trademarks. Many jurisdictions have separate enactments for these different types of IPRs and may also use different (i.e. broader or narrower) terminology.

[5]Small and medium-sized enterprises.

[6]See Denoncourt (2017), pp. 1, 4 *et seq.* Knopf (2002), pp. 1, 5.

[7]Decker (2012), pp. 2 *et seq.*

which is mostly statutory law (see Sect. 3.1.2). Only in some jurisdictions do the general principles of property law or even secured transactions law also play a role (see for greater detail Sects. 3.1.1 and 3.1.3 below).

On the other hand, it is mainly secured transactions law that governs the question which security rights can be created (see for details Sect. 3.2). However, in general, secured transactions law has not been specifically designed for or adapted to IP rights. In most jurisdictions, it has been developed for tangible assets and has only been extended to intangible assets like receivables. The fact that IP rights are very often registered and are limited in territorial scope to the jurisdiction for which they have been created and in which protection is sought (*lex protectionis*) has so far not been taken into account in the development of secured transactions law. Also, IP registration might take place at a different level of the state structure than notice filing under secured transactions law: IP registries may be organized federally or even supranationally (e.g. EU), whereas notice filing or registration as a mode of perfection under secured transactions law may have to be carried out at the level of the individual state or province. Tensions, uncertainties, and high transaction costs might be the result.[8] A notable exception is Australia, whose secured transactions law is one of the most modern and advanced in the world.

With respect to unregistered rights such as copyright or unregistered trademarks, registration as a means of perfecting security rights might not even be available, which is an obvious hindrance in legal systems that, as a matter of principle, require registration for the effectiveness of security rights *erga omnes*; see, for example, the Italian[9] and Finnish reports in this project.[10]

An inherent difficulty lies in the fact that IP rights might prove unreliable: third parties may successfully challenge the very existence of the IP right. The grantor may prove not to be the owner and thus, given the fact that legal systems regularly do not provide for a bona fide acquisition of security rights in IP rights,[11] the secured party will have acquired nothing at all.

The shortcomings of unreformed and unmodern national secured transactions law may add further difficulties.[12] For instance, in systems that use ownership as security, no junior security right can be created. The rules relating to pledges and usufruct are also often outdated, especially when it comes to enforcement.[13] In many jurisdictions, the legal characterization of licences as either mere obligatory rights or

---

[8]See Ballagh (2017) Secured Financing with Intellectual Property: Managing Uncertainties, www.ballaghedward.ca (Law Office, Hamilton, Ont.) noting: "The standard legal advice is sometimes called the 'belts and suspenders' approach. Where feasible, parties are advised to register their security interests on both the federal and the provincial registers in *all* the relevant jurisdictions [i.e. provinces]," cited in Howell (2019), Section 2.2.

[9]See in this volume Ricolfi (2019), Section 2.2.

[10]See in this volume Juutilainen (2019), Section 4.3.

[11]But see in this volume Storme and Malekzadem (2019), Section 27, on the possibilities of bona fide acquisition.

[12]On the following, see in this volume Brinkmann et al. (2019), Section 5.

[13]See, for example, Dorfmayr (2019), Section 7.1.1 on judicial enforcement.

absolute rights is unresolved, creating difficulties when it comes to the use of licences as collateral and their classification for the purposes of secured transactions law. In sum, the English reporter describes secured transactions law over IP rights as "complex and disadvantageous" due to the double registration system and to the distinction and unclear relationship between legal and equitable interests.[14]

The fact that IP rights have hitherto only rarely been used as collateral, resulting in a lack of case law in this area, further adds to the legal uncertainty.[15]

1.2.2 Life Cycle of an IP Right

IP rights are time-limited rights and can lose their value rather fast, especially in the technology sector. While this is generally also true for tangible property such as inventory, security rights over inventory tend to be created over a certain class of goods (rather than specific pieces), so that more modern species of the same kind of product can be covered by a single security agreement over time. In contrast, the life cycle of a loan may easily surpass the life cycle of an IP right.[16]

1.2.3 The Problem of Evaluation

Another problem lies in the difficulty of evaluating IP rights and—consequently—the value of a security right over an IP right. Obviously, such an evaluation is necessary in order for the parties to assess the economic impact of a potential security right: To what extent will the sale or use of the IP right cover the advanced credit? Is the security right worth the transaction costs? Can it have any influence on the interest rate?

As the national reports in this project prove once more, the problem of evaluation is central to the use of IP rights as a basis for obtaining credit. With respect to nearly all jurisdictions covered, this difficulty is mentioned as one of the main reasons why IP rights are not used more regularly as collateral. Not only is there an inherent difficulty in fixing a certain sum of money to an IP right, given the great variety of these rights, but there is also no widely recognized—let alone internationally standardized—method of evaluation. For Germany alone, *Decker*[17] counts no less than 30 different procedures for evaluating IP rights and laments the lack of any standards. According to the Australian reporter for the present project,[18] "leading practitioners, pointing to difficulties inherent in valuing intellectual property given in

---

[14]See in this volume Bornheim (2019), Sections 9 and 10.

[15]Cf. Dorfmayr (2019), Section 10; see in this volume Karjiker (2019), Section 3.1.1.

[16]See in this volume Brinkmann et al. (2019), Section 1, citing Bill Gates: "Intellectual property has the shelf life of a banana."

[17]Decker (2012), p. 486.

[18]For the following, see McCracken (2019), Section 4.4. *et seq.*

particular the lack of a standard market, observe that there are differing valuation methods for intellectual property, that can produce vastly different valuations."

Presently, three main approaches to evaluation can be distinguished: (i) the cost approach, which looks at the cost of creating the IP; (ii) the market approach, which, for its practical application, requires an active marketplace (which is often lacking) for the relevant kind of IP right; and (iii) the income approach, which looks at the estimated financial benefits that the IP right can produce.[19]

Considering the variety here, it comes as no surprise that the different methods lead to huge differences in outcome. One obvious way forward would be the development of at least national (better: international) standardized methods of evaluation.[20]

An even more pressing problem involving evaluation arises when a jurisdiction adopts a very strict view on excessive collateralization or oversecurity. This used to be the case in Germany (prior to 1997, when a particular judgment of the united civil law chambers of the BGH was passed)[21] and still seems to be the case in Estonia.[22] If courts hold that a security agreement is void in its entirety once the collateral's value exceeds the amount of the debt by a certain percentage, correct evaluation of the collateral becomes crucial for the whole transaction. It is not surprising if parties refrain from including a type of collateral that carries such a fatal risk in their security arrangement.

1.2.4 Problems Connected to Enforcement

Decreasing Value of the Collateral

Another difficulty lies in the fact that the parties need to evaluate the collateral at the time of (or immediately prior to) the conclusion of the security agreement; however,

---

[19]See Howell (2019), at fn. 53, citing Weston Anson, *Want to Value Your Intellectual Property? Here are Three Approaches*. Available at www.ipinbrief.com/three-approaches-to-value-IP/. Weston Anson is the Chairman of CONSOR, *Ibid*. Howell (2019), continues on to discuss the pros and cons of the different approaches and their suitability for secured transactions, citing David Ullmann (lawyer) and Sheldon Title (accountant), "How to Seize Something You Can't Touch: A Review of Issues and Process with the Foreclosure of Intellectual Property Assets", *Annual Review of Insolvency Law 2014* ed. Janis P. Sarra, available on *WestlawNext*, Canada. In the same vein, see in this volume Brinkmann et al. (2019), Section 4.1; Decker (2012), pp. 490 *et seq*.; Argyropoulou et al. (2019), at fn. 36. The French report makes a twofold distinction between static and dynamic approaches; see in this volume Séjean and Binctin (2019), Section 3.1.2.1 and Section 3.1.2.2. See in this volume Murguía-Goebel (2019), Section 3.3, listing an "option-based method" as an additional, fourth method.

[20]See in greater detail Decker (2012), pp. 490 *et seq*. See also in this volume Murguía-Goebel (2019), Section 3.3, pointing to the OECD guidelines for the valuation of intangible assets.

[21]See in greater detail in this volume Brinkmann et al. (2019), Section 3.2.1.

[22]See in this volume Lepik (2019), Section 9.

the value may differ greatly at the time of enforcement.[23] For example, if the business is insolvent, its trademark may decrease in value or even become worthless.[24] With tangible property or intangibles, this difficulty may also exist (e.g. the inventory or the equipment of an insolvent company may also be worth less than that of a going concern), but generally speaking, the receivables of a company, its immovable property, and, to a certain extent, its movables are not as directly dependent on the commercial soundness of the company as a whole as its IP rights are. In sum, there is a danger that a security right in IP rights may be worth the least when it is needed the most (i.e. upon the insolvency of the grantor).[25]

Liquidity of the Market

Another problem is the frequent lack of a liquid market for IP rights once enforcement is sought through sale or licensing.[26] Often, there are very few businesses which can possibly make use of the patent, design, or trademark. Trademarks are often only of interest to the direct competitor. But, of course, more liquid markets may develop in the future.[27]

2 The Limited Role of International Uniform Law for Security Rights in IP

2.1 Uniform Law on Intellectual Property

There is a wealth of international treaties in the area of IP rights[28]; for patents, these include the Paris Convention for the Protection of Industrial Property of 1883 (as amended by the Stockholm Act of 1967; 195 contracting parties) and the Patent Cooperation Treaty of 1970 (last amended in 2001; 152 contracting parties); for trademarks, these include the "Madrid System," consisting of the Madrid Agreement Concerning the International Registration of Marks of 1891 (last amended in 1979; 55 contracting parties) and the Madrid Protocol of 1989 (101 contracting parties); and for copyright, these include the Berne Convention for the Protection of Literary and Artistic Works of 1886 (last amended in 1971; 185 contracting parties).[29] The

---

[23]Decker (2012), pp. 497 *et seq.*

[24]Cf. Dorfmayr (2019), Section 10.

[25]See in this volume Brinkmann et al. (2019), Section 1.

[26]Decker (2012), pp. 489 *et seq.*

[27]Decker (2012), pp. 503 *et seq.* with examples.

[28]See the list of administered treaties on the website of the World Intellectual Property Organization, http://www.wipo.int/treaties. Accessed May 8, 2018.

[29]See on these texts Dorfmayr (2019), Section 1.2 with further references.

effect of these treaties and of the TRIPS Agreement is that the structure of IP law, at least, is rather uniform around the world.

At a regional level, the European Patent Convention has existed since 1973 (EPC),[30] but so far, it has only unified the procedure leading to the granting of the European patent. Once such a patent has been created, its content, the remedies for its infringement, its transferability, etc. continue to be governed by national Member States' laws; therefore, this type of patent only creates a so-called "bundle of national patents." The Community Patent Convention, which would have created a uniform and autonomous European patent, is no longer on the political agenda. Instead, the European Union has created the "European unitary patent" through secondary legislation based on so-called "enhanced collaboration" (Arts. 326 ff TFEU).[31] With its ratification of the Unified Patent Court Agreement, which forms part of the European Patent Package, on April 26, 2018, the UK has only very recently paved the way for the European unitary patent to become operational in the first half of 2019.[32]

The EU has created a number of genuinely supranational "Community" or "European Union" IP rights through regulations, most notably the European Union trademark and the Community design, which are administered by the European Union Intellectual Property Office in Alicante, Spain.[33]

Yet these instruments, as far as our topic is concerned, at most provide uniform substantive rules on the transferability of IP rights and formal requirements for the effectiveness of transfers (e.g. writing or registration). These issues will be examined in greater detail in Sect. 3.2 ("Transferability and Collateralization of IP Rights Under Supranational Law"). Examples are the EU Trade Mark Regulation,[34] which, in its Art. 22, explicitly states that "(1) An EU trade mark may, independently of the undertaking, be given as security or be the subject of rights in rem" and "(2) At the request of one of the parties, the rights referred to in paragraph 1 or the transfer of those rights shall be entered in the Register and published"; and the Community Design Regulation (CDR), which contains an almost identical provision in Art. 29 CDR: "(1) A registered Community design may be given as security or be the

[30]The revised texts of the Convention and its protocols, which entered into force on December 13, 2007, and the Implementing Regulations, in force since May 1, 2016, are available on the website of the European Patent Office: http://www.epo.org/law-practice/legal-texts/html/epc/2016/e/ma0.html. Accessed May 8, 2018. See the detailed treatment on the European Patent Convention in Dorfmayr (2019), after fn. 19.

[31]Reg. (EU) No. 1257/2012 and Reg. (EU) No. 1260/2012, in force since January 20, 2013. Yet, their applicability depends on the entering into force of the Convention on a European Patent Court; see Art. 18 section 2 of the Reg. (EU) No. 1257/2012.

[32]See www.epo.org/law-practice/unitary/unitary-patent/start.html. Accessed June 19, 2019.

[33]Regulation (EU) 2017/1001 of the European Parliament and of the Council of June 14, 2017 on the European Trade Mark (codification), OJ L 154, 16.6.2017, p. 1; Council Regulation (EC) No. 6/2002 of December 12, 2001 on Community Designs, OJ L 3, 5.1.2002, p. 1.

[34]Regulation (EU) 2017/1001 of the European Parliament and of the Council of June 14, 2017 on the European Union Trade Mark (Codification), OJ L 154, 16.6.2017.

subject of rights in rem. (2) On request of one of the parties, the rights mentioned in paragraph 1 shall be entered in the register and published."

Otherwise, the international instruments do not contain specific substantive rules on security rights in IP rights, which is, of course, a direct consequence of the lack of internationally uniform or harmonized secured transactions law. The only international instrument providing for a uniform international security interest, i.e. the Cape Town Convention together with its asset-specific protocols,[35] does not touch upon IP rights.

2.2 *Soft Law on Secured Transactions*

There are many international and supranational efforts to promote the modernization and harmonization of secured transactions law; see foremost the UNCITRAL Legislative Guide on Secured Transactions, as well as the UNCITRAL Model on Secured Transactions and its supplement on security rights in IP.[36] In addition, there are also regional projects, such as the Model Inter-American Law on Secured Transaction, the OHADA Uniform Act on Security Interests, and the Model Law of the European Bank for Reconstruction and Development (EBRD) for Central and Eastern European states. Last but not least, the academic project of a Draft Common Frame of Reference (DCFR) for European private law contains draft rules on secured transactions in its Book IX. Some of these texts have been quite influential for law reform in some countries around the world,[37] but they have not yet led to a harmonized approach to secured transactions law in general, or, more specifically, to the use of IP rights as collateral.

3 IP Rights as Collateral: Transferability in General

The most fundamental question is whether the different IP rights existing in each jurisdiction are at all capable of being the subject-matter of a security interest. In other words, can a party with an interest in or ownership of the IP right create a consensual right[38] to secure an obligation? If yes, which type(s) of security rights are

[35]For the texts of these instruments, see www.unidroit.org.

[36]See below Section 6.2, with references.

[37]See generally Macdonald (2009), p. 745. See in this volume Murguía-Goebel (2019), Sections 2.1 and 2.3; see also in this volume Shieh and Lee (2019), Section 5 (on a bill introducing the floating charge following the recommendations in the UNCITRAL texts). For Belgium, see Dirix (2015), p. 273.

[38]Meaning a right created by way of a transaction between the creditor and the debtor, as opposed to a right which arises by operation of law without any agreement between the parties, such as a statutory lien or a privilege.

available (e.g. security interest, pledge, mortgage, security ownership, charge, lien, etc.)? The following chapters try to summarize the national answers and to highlight some peculiarities. In general, they focus on rights in patents, design rights, trademarks, and copyright. National rights are contemplated under Sect. 3.1, while genuinely supranational rights such as the EU trademark and the Community design are covered in Sect. 3.2. The types of security rights available are set out in Sect. 4.

3.1 Collateralization of IP Rights Under National Law

Whether IP rights can be used as collateral depends first on their classification as transferable property. For the most part, IP rights, especially registered rights such as patents and trademarks, are considered to be transferable or assignable and therefore are able to be collateralized.

3.1.1 General Taxonomy of Property Law

The possibility of using an IP right as collateral can flow from its general classification as personal, movable, or intangible property in the sense of the general principles of property law. Thus, in Belgium, IP rights are considered to be "movable and intangible assets," and as such are capable of being the subject of those security rights that exist for movable, intangible assets.[39] In Brazil, the collateralization of IP rights flows from their characterization as "movable assets."[40] In South Africa, there is a debate about whether IP rights should be classified as moveable or immoveable property, but with respect to most IP rights, statutory law explicitly characterizes them as moveable property.[41]

The classification as possible collateral can also rest on more specific provisions that are to be found in secured transactions law. Thus, in the Common Law provinces of Canada, the decisive definition is contained in the Personal Property Security Acts (PPSAs) of each province, typically using expressions such as "intangibles, meaning personal property other than goods" or "personal property, including choses in action, that is not goods."[42] These provisions are interpreted as including the usual IP rights, such as patents, copyright, industrial designs, and trademarks, and might even extend to domain names, but do not include trade secrets, whose proprietary nature is doubted.[43]

---

[39] Storme and Malekzadem (2019), Section 6, at fn. 13.

[40] Lahorgue (2019), Section 2.

[41] See in this volume Karjiker (2019), Section 2.

[42] See Howell (2019), Section 2.1.

[43] See Howell (2019), Section 2.1.

Transferability or assignability might in some jurisdictions be accorded to IP rights even though they do not fit well into the general taxonomy of property law. A notable example is English law,[44] where, generally speaking, property is divided into "choses in possession" and "choses in action," and where it must therefore be discussed how IP rights can be accommodated within this dichotomy in view of the fact that the Patent Act explicitly states that patents are *not* choses in action. A pragmatic approach simply adds IP rights as a third category under the name of "other incorporeal property." In any event, it is not subject to doubt that IP rights can be collateralized under English law.[45] A second example for this kind of difficulty is Cypriot law, where the category of movables under which IP rights are to be subsumed seems to be unclear.[46] A third example is Austrian law, where IP rights are difficult to classify within the dichotomy of "true property rights," which as a matter of principle can only exist in tangible goods, and "relative rights" (claims). As the Austrian reporter points out, patents are seen as being equivalent to "true property rights" but, in contrast, trademarks are considered to be mere claims.[47]

3.1.2 Specific Statutory Provisions

Mostly, however, the transferability and suitability of IP rights to be used as collateral flows from specific statutory provisions, typically to be found in respective IPR acts. This is the case for example in Australia,[48] Germany,[49] France,[50] the United States, South Africa,[51] Mexico,[52] Spain,[53] Taiwan,[54] Japan,[55] Turkey,[56]

[44]For the following, see in this volume Bornheim (2019), Section 2.4.1.

[45]See in this volume Bornheim (2019), Section 2.4.1.

[46]See Argyropoulou et al. (2019), Section 2.

[47]Dorfmayr (2019), Section 2.1. See also McGuire (2008), pp. 219 *et seq.* McGuire's conclusion (at p. 222) is that "the determination of the legal nature of intellectual property rights according to the dichotomy 'property' or 'right' does not solve the problem of determining the proper transfer rules."

[48]McCracken (2019), Section 3.1.

[49]See in this volume Brinkmann et al. (2019), Section 2.

[50]See in this volume Séjean and Binctin (2019), Section 2.1 and the references to incorporeal intellectual property.

[51]See in this volume Karjiker (2019), Section 2. In addition, South African law allows the common law "cession" of IP rights; see in this volume Karjiker (2019), Section 2.

[52]See in this volume Murguía-Goebel (2019), Section 3.1.

[53]See in this volume Heredia Cervantes (2019), Section 2.

[54]See in this volume Shieh and Lee (2019), Section 2.1.1.

[55]See in this volume Hara and Haga (2019), Section 3.1.

[56]See in this volume Özsunay and Özsunay (2019), Section 1.2.

Greece,[57] and Finland.[58] In the Netherlands,[59] the general rule on transferability in Article 3:83(1) Burgerlijk Wetboek (B.W.) is limited to "ownership rights, limited property rights and claims"; this means that IP rights are only transferable pursuant to Article 3:83(3) B.W. if the law specifically provides for it. Therefore, under Dutch law, only IP rights that have a statutory basis may be transferred. Those which are only recognized by courts, such as certain rights to publicity, cannot be subject to a proprietary transaction.

3.1.3 Interplay Between Secured Transactions Law and IP Law

Ideally, statutory sources on secured transactions law and on IP rights should be in harmony concerning the possibilities and different ways of using IP rights as collateral. However, in some federal states such as the US and Canada, the existence of detailed and sophisticated rules in both areas of the law, which, however, are placed on different jurisdictional levels (i.e. state/provincial and federal) can create considerable legal uncertainties and give rise to litigation. The reports on Canadian law[60] give a thorough insight into these complexities. At the other end of the spectrum, Australia has successfully avoided these difficulties by enacting the Personal Property Security Act (PPSA) at the federal level.

3.1.4 Preliminary Rights

Transferability is not necessarily linked to the IP right having finally come into existence (e.g. through registration). In some instances, proprietary rights may already exist when the process leading up to the registration of the IP right has not yet fully been completed. These preliminary stages may already carry considerable value and hence may be able to be used as collateral. For example, the German Patent Act, § 6, mentions the right to the patent and the right to have the patent granted as preliminary rights which exist at least once an application has been filed with the Patent Office. These preliminary rights are hence able to be used as collateral.[61] In Australia, applications for the registration of a patent or trademark are not considered property under general principles, but in practice, they are nonetheless treated as such by parties to secured transactions.[62] In contrast,

[57] See in this volume Kallinikou and Koriatopoulou (2019), Section 2.

[58] See in this volume Juutilainen (2019), Section 3.

[59] For the following, see in this volume van Engelen (2019), Section 2.1.

[60] See report on Howell (2019), after fn. 26; Charpentier (2019), after fn. 32 and after fn. 56.

[61] See in this volume Brinkmann et al. (2019), Section 3; Decker (2012), pp. 18 *et seq*. In the same vein, see in this volume Heredia Cervantes (2019), Section 2; Matanovac Vučković et al. (2019), Section 2.3.

[62] McCracken (2019), Section 4.

legislation in Taiwan explicitly prohibits the use of “the right to apply for IP protection” as collateral, since it is not certain that the application will be successful.[63] Japanese law distinguishes between different types of security rights: while a patent application may be the subject of a security assignment, using the creation of a pledge in such a way is legally prohibited.[64]

3.1.5 Exceptions to the General Transferability of IP Rights

There are a number of notable exceptions to the general proposition that classic IP rights such as patents, trademarks, and copyright are transferable and capable of being collateralized: under German law, copyright cannot be transferred according to sec. 29 subsec. 2 German Copyright Act. The same is true for Austria (pursuant to Article 23 Austrian Copyright Act),[65] the Czech Republic,[66] and Croatia.[67] With this rule, these jurisdictions are out on a limb compared to the other jurisdictions covered in this general report.[68] However, there are still various ways to use copyright as the basis for secured financing: the claims (e.g. royalties) stemming from a licence can be subjected to a security assignment[69]; a security right can be created in the licence of the IP right[70]; or a security licence can be given to the lender, who will in turn sublicense the copyright back to the borrower—see Sect. 5 below for more detail.

[63]See in this volume Shieh and Lee (2019), Section 2.1.2.1.

[64]See in this volume Hara and Haga (2019), Section 3.1(1).

[65]Dorfmayr (2019), Section 2.1.

[66]See in this volume Koukal and Pullmannova (2019), Section 1.1, referring to Art. 26 Czech Copyright Act.

[67]Matanovac Vučković et al. (2019), at fn. 58.

[68]Copyright can be assigned as “personal or moveable property” under English law—see in this volume Bornheim (2019), Section 2.4.2. Under French law: *Le droit d'auteur* is subject to the general rules on proprietary security; see in this volume Séjean and Binctin (2019), Section 2.1. South Africa: The Copyright Act explicitly provides that copyright is transmissible as movable property; see in this volume Karjiker (2019), Section 2.4. Japan: see in this volume Hara and Haga (2019), Section 3.2. Finland: Copyright may theoretically be used as collateral, but since Finland does not have a register for copyright and yet nevertheless requires some sort of publicity (either through registration, dispossession, or notification) for a security right to be perfected, it is argued that, consequently, copyright cannot be used as collateral; see in this volume Juutilainen (2019), Section 4.3.

[69]In this case, the grantor of the security right is the holder of the IP right and the licensor.

[70]See in this volume Brinkmann et al. (2019), Section 3, and, from a comparative point of view, Koziol (2011), passim. In this case, the grantor of the security right is the licensee.

3.2 *Transferability and Collateralization of IP Rights Under Uniform Supranational Law*

The following chapter only covers genuinely uniform supranational IP rights, such as the EU trademark. It does not cover IP rights where only some aspects are unified or harmonized, such as the European patent or copyright under the Berne Convention.

3.2.1 EU Trade Mark Regulation

The European Union Trade Mark Reg.[71] in part provides for uniform rules on transferability and collateralization in its Arts. 19 ff. Following subsection 1 of Art. 20, an EU trademark can be transferred separately from any transfer of the undertaking, but under subsec. 2, a transfer of the whole of the undertaking will usually include the trademark if there is no agreement to the contrary. Subsection 3 requires the assignment of the trademark to be in writing, otherwise the transfer will be void. Finally, Art. 22(1) explicitly states that an EU trademark may be given as security, independently of the undertaking. Transfers of or security rights in trademarks shall be entered in the register and published pursuant to Art. 20 (5) and Art. 22(2), respectively. Third-party effects depend on registration according to Art. 27. An application for an EU trademark can already be treated as transferable property and as collateral—see Art. 28.

Obviously, these rules do not cover every aspect of a transfer or grant of a security right in an EU trademark. Hence, as a fallback rule, Art. 19 EU Trade Mark Reg. contains a conflicts rule providing for the application of the national law of the Member State in which the proprietor has his seat or domicile on the relevant date, or, if he has no seat, the national law of the Member State where he has an establishment.[72] Whether this rule refers to the substantive law of the relevant Member State or to its conflicts rules is subject to debate.[73] Another difficulty and possible source of legal uncertainty lies in the fact that the proprietor's seat may

[71]Regulation (EU) 2017/1001 of the European Parliament and of the Council of June 14, 2017 on the European Trade Mark (codification), OJ L 154, 16.6.2017, p. 1.

[72]See Art. 19 EU Trade Mark Reg.: "Unless Articles 20 to 28 provide otherwise, an EU trade mark as an object of property shall be dealt with in its entirety, and for the whole area of the Union, as a national trade mark registered in the Member State in which, according to the Register: (a) the proprietor has his seat or his domicile on the relevant date; (b) where point (a) does not apply, the proprietor has an establishment on the relevant date. 2. In cases which are not provided for by paragraph 1, the Member State referred to in that paragraph shall be the Member State in which the seat of the Office is situated. 3. If two or more persons are mentioned in the Register of EU trade marks as joint proprietors, paragraph 1 shall apply to the joint proprietor first mentioned; failing this, it shall apply to the subsequent joint proprietors in the order in which they are mentioned. Where paragraph 1 does not apply to any of the joint proprietors, paragraph 2 shall apply."

[73]See McGuire (2008), p. 230, in whose view the rule refers to the conflicts rules at the seat.

change.[74] Therefore, this conflicts solution is regarded as being less satisfactory in comparison with uniform European rules on the transfer and collateralization of EU trademarks (which, however, do not yet exist).[75]

3.2.2 Community Design Regulation

The Community Design Regulation (CDR)[76] follows two different concepts of design protection. First, a Community design might be filed and subsequently registered with the EUIPO ("registered Community design," Art. 1 para 2 (b) CDR).[77] In this case, an examination that confirms compliance with formal requirements (Art. 45 *et seq.* CDR) is followed by registration in the Community design register (Art. 48 CDR) and publication in the Community design bulletin (Art. 49 CDR). On the other hand, the Community Design Regulation accords limited protection to designs that are not registered with the EUIPO and are only made available to the public within the Community ("unregistered designs," Art. 1 para 2 (a) and Art. 11 CDR).[78]

Registered Community designs can be transferred and collateralized; see Art. 27 ff. Community Design Regulation (CDR). Some general issues are regulated in the CDR itself, such as the possibility of transferring a registered Community design or of creating a security right over it. For issues that are not regulated in the CDR, Art. 29 CDR provides for the applicability of the national law of the Member State in which the holder of the Community design has his seat or domicile, or, failing this, an establishment. This conflicts rule is identical to Art. 19 EU Trade Mark Regulation, discussed above at the end of Sect. 3.2.1.

Given the fact that both genuinely supranational IP regulations fail to provide substantive rules on the kinds of security rights available and on the creation and perfection of these rights, instead merely calling for the application of the national law at the holder's seat, the discussion in Sect. 4 and following will only give an overview of national secured transactions law as relating to national IP rights. Unless stated otherwise, this information also applies to European Union IP rights.

---

[74]McGuire (2008), p. 230.

[75]McGuire (2008), pp. 230 *et seq.*

[76]Council Regulation (EC) No. 6/2002 of December 12, 2001 on Community Designs, OJ L 3, 5.1.2002, p. 1.

[77]A registered Community design may also be obtained on the grounds of an international application subject to the rules of the Hague Agreement Concerning the International Deposit of Industrial Designs, which has not been ratified by Austria, but has been ratified by the European Union; see Horn and Grünwald (2015), p. 187.

[78]Dorfmayr (2019), after fn. 26.

4 IP Rights as Collateral: Which Security Rights Are Available?

As stated earlier, the answer to the question which types of security interests can be taken in IP rights mainly depends on secured transactions law, which is not unified or harmonized internationally and which in most cases is not specially designed to cover IP rights. While some jurisdictions apply the rules relating to security rights over tangibles, others follow the rules on security over intangibles in general or on security over claims. A third group of states has specific provisions on security interests in IP rights in some or all of the states' statutes on general IP law (e.g. England and Wales).[79]

However, the main difference lies between those jurisdictions that are based on a uniform, functional approach and employ notice filing as the most important method of perfection (Art. 9 UCC-type secured transactions law, such as in—obviously—the United States of America, Canada, and Australia), and those jurisdictions that do not follow a functional and uniform approach, but instead know different types of security rights, some of which are based on the model of a limited real right (i.e. pledge, charge, and mortgage) and some of which are based on ownership (i.e. security ownership, security assignment, and retention of title). Under the second, non-functional approach, the classification of different types of collateral is typically of greater importance when it comes to the possibility of creating a security right than it is under the functional approach.

4.1 Jurisdictions with a Functional Approach to Security Rights

In the US, there is only one type of security right available: the "security interest" as defined in state law enacting Art. 9 UCC § 1-201(b)(35). The definition is functional and covers all interests in any personal property "that secures payment or performance of an obligation," regardless of its form. A growing number of jurisdictions around the world have shaped their secured transactions law along the lines of the American model.

In the course of the 1990s, the Common Law provinces and territories of Canada all enacted their PPSAs, modelled after Art. 9 UCC.[80] The respective definitions of "intangibles" or "personal property" that can become the subject of a functionally defined "security interest" all include IP rights such as patents, copyright, industrial

[79]See in this volume Bornheim (2019), Section 2.4.2.

[80]See Howell (2019), at fn. 17; in Québec, the relevant provisions are to be found in the Civil Code. They are likewise inspired by Art. 9 UCC; see Charpentier (2019), after fn. 5.

designs, trademarks, etc.[81] The Australian PPSA 2009 likewise follows a functional approach and defines "security interest" as "an interest in personal property provided for by a transaction that, in substance, secures payment or performance of an obligation". Therefore, any property interest having a security function is reclassified as an "in substance security interest," regardless of whether it is treated as a charge, mortgage, conditional sale, or assignment under general law.[82]

Belgium has only recently seen a major reform of its secured transaction law (i.e. the Pledge Act, in force since January 1, 2018). It has been inspired by the UNCITRAL Legislative Guide on Secured Transactions and by Book IX of the DCFR, which are in turn both basically modelled on Art. 9 UCC. Yet the functional approach as pursued by the Belgian legislator is somewhat attenuated.[83] Retention of title is still kept as a separate category, partly following its own rules. Likewise, the system of so-called "privileges" (a kind of statutory lien) has been retained. Therefore, there are still a variety of different security rights, each following its own rules (e.g. retention of title, termination with proprietary effect, seller's lien, and fiduciary transfer).[84] Security rights in IP rights, which were difficult to create under the old law, have now received a more favourable legal basis.

4.2 *Jurisdictions Without a Functional Approach to Security Rights*

Within this group, a further distinction can be made between jurisdictions that have recently undergone a major reform of secured transactions law (Sect. 4.2.1) and those that have not (Sect. 4.2.2).

4.2.1 Modernized Systems

French law regards IP rights as intangibles (*bien incorporels*), but due to the fact that the *Code civil* only contains specific provisions on charges over claims (*créances*), charges over IP rights are treated as charges over tangibles.[85] Since the *Code de la propriéte intellectuelle* declares copyright, designs, trademarks, etc. to be transferrable (*transmissible*), these rights are also regarded as being transferrable by way of a pledge or charge (*nantissement*). In addition, full ownership of an IP right can be used as security if it is either retained (*réserve de propriété*) or transferred as a

---

[81]Howell (2019), at fn. 19.

[82]For details, see McCracken (2019), Section 3.2. *et seq.*

[83]The Belgian report itself calls the new system "functional"—see Storme and Malekzadem (2019), at para 6—and so this characterization is followed here.

[84]See Storme and Malekzadem (2019), para 7 *et seq.*

[85]See in this volume Séjean and Binctin (2019), Section 2.1.

fiduciary security (*fiducie-sûreté*). Thus, the full range of security devices created or reformed through the new French secured transactions laws of 2006 and 2009 is also available for IP rights.

The Netherlands stands somewhat in between the groups under Sects. 4.1 and 4.2, since it has not opted for a functional approach in its general secured transactions law, but, due to the fact that Dutch courts have denied the possibility of mortgaging IP rights and due to the abolition of the security transfer of ownership in the 1992 Dutch Civil Code (Burgerlik Wetboek, B.W.), the only security right available for IP rights is in fact the pledge (Art. 3:227 B.W.).[86] Thus, with respect to security rights in IP, Dutch law can be described as following at least a unitary approach.

Mexico underwent a series of reforms between 2000 and 2014 that left the country with one of the most modern secured transactions registry systems. However, the substantive law has not developed into a similarly functional system. This is partly because Mexico is a federation in which large areas of private law are left to the legislative power of the 32 individual states.[87] In addition, although it has adopted a notice filing system, Mexico has not opted for a functional and unitary approach; instead, it has retained the distinction between commercial pledges (possessory and non-possessory) and security trusts, with each following its own rules.[88] IP rights can be the subject of either a non-possessory pledge or a security trust.

In the Czech Republic, security rights over IP rights are regulated by the law on security rights in movables, which forms part of the new Civil Code that entered into force on January 1, 2014. The Civil Code has not adopted a functional/unitary approach, and it adheres to the traditional dichotomy between pledges (liens) and security transfers. In this respect, it resembles the traditional systems; however, with respect to enforcement, it is modern insofar as it allows out-of-court enforcement through the sale of the collateral.[89]

Croatian law has undergone various reforms[90] that have left it with a functional[91] but non-unitary system. With the exception of copyright, IP rights can be encumbered either through a charge or by way of a security assignment; these two are treated equally as a matter of principle.

4.2.2 Traditional Systems

German secured transactions law has mostly been created through court practice and academic literature. The Civil Code and the Insolvency Act only provide for a handful of rather general rules, none of which are specifically adapted to creating

---

[86] See in this volume van Engelen (2019), Section 2.2.1.

[87] See in this volume Murguía-Goebel (2019), Section 2.

[88] See in this volume Murguía-Goebel (2019), Section 3.1.

[89] See in this volume Koukal and Pullmannova (2019), at fn. 62.

[90] See the critical appraisal by Matanovac Vučković et al. (2019), at fn. 31, with further references.

[91] Matanovac Vučković et al. (2019), at fn. 56.

security rights in IP. The pledge is the only security right in movable (tangible and intangible) property that the German Civil Code regulates in detail. However, due to the fact that a pledge in corporeal movables necessitates a transfer of possession that cannot be replaced by mere constructive possession, fiduciary ownership and retention of title are used in practice. IP rights are regarded as intangibles, and thus they can be assigned as security or pledged. With general intangibles such as claims, the pledge is hardly used due to the requirement of giving notice to the account debtor. The security assignment, for which no notice is necessary, is preferred in practice. However, with respect to IP rights, it seems that both the pledge and the security assignment are used. Usufruct, which otherwise only plays a minor role in secured transactions law, is also an option with respect to IP rights.

Japanese law resembles German law in that case law has come to recognize the security assignment as a second proprietary security right in addition to the pledge, which is regulated by the Civil Code.[92]

In Austria,[93] IP rights that are transferable (which is the case for all IP rights except copyright) can be pledged or be the subject of a security transfer of ownership or a security assignment, depending on whether they are regarded as tangible or intangible movable property. Since both transactions follow the same rules, the distinction is of merely theoretical interest.

In Taiwan, only the pledge (which is regulated by the Civil Code) is available.[94] It is created through a simple agreement between the parties, without any further formal requirements. For its effectiveness against third parties, it needs to be registered in the relevant IP registries. The date of registration will also determine priority.

In Brazil, the parties have the choice between a pledge, a fiduciary transfer, and a usufruct, each of which follow its own specific rules.[95]

4.3 *Jurisdictions with Specific Statutory Provisions for Security Over IP Rights*

Under English law, IP rights are considered to be pure intangibles; thus, only non-possessory security rights such as charges or mortgages can exist. While the Copyright, Designs and Patents Act 1988 (UK) declares such rights to be assignable, they are also regarded as "mortgageable by way of assignment."[96] However, there are also a number of statutory provisions which specifically mention the possibility

[92]See in this volume Hara and Haga (2019), Section 3.1(2).

[93]See Dorfmayr (2019), Section 2.2.2.

[94]See in this volume Shieh and Lee (2019), Section 3.1.1.

[95]Lahorgue (2019), Sections 2 and 3.1.

[96]See in this volume Bornheim (2019), Section 2.4.2.

of charging or mortgaging IP rights, such as the Trade Marks Act and the CDPA 1988 in relation to registered designs.[97]

Cypriot law resembles English law in that its enactments on IP law recognize the transferability of IP rights and that, therefore, even if their status within the different categories of property law is somewhat unclear, IP rights can in fact be used as collateral. Possible security rights include the Common Law lien (a right to retain possession), the security assignment of the IP right (which seems to be theoretically possible but is not practised because, inter alia, the Cypriot IP registries do not allow for the registration of security rights), and the charge (which in practice mostly takes the form of a floating charge). A pledge can only be constituted by granting possession, which, under Cypriot law, cannot (like in many other jurisdictions) be substituted by registration. As a result, the pledge is not a suitable security right for IP rights.[98]

Italian law provides an interesting example of a jurisdiction where security rights in registered IP rights are specifically provided for—see Art. 140 Italian Industrial Property Code (IIPC) (Legislative Decree No. 30 of 2005), which states that "security rights over industrial property titles may be created only as collateral for money credits."[99] However, since the rule does not specify the kind of security right that can be created (i.e. whether it is a pledge pursuant to Art. 2784 ff. *Codice civile* or a mortgage under Art. 2808 ff. *Codice civile*), it is debated which kind of security right is meant in Art. 140 IIPC.[100] The question has not yet been settled by the courts as IP rights are only rarely used as security in practice outside of the special field of movie financing. Moreover, Art. 140 IIPC only relates to registered IP rights. Unregistered copyright, which can be assigned under Italian law, can nevertheless not be transferred by way of security, since this kind of transaction is generally prohibited by Art. 2744 *Codice civile* (the ban on the so-called *pactum commissorium*). Therefore, one must resort to the pledge of rights pursuant to Art. 2806 *Codice civile*. However, pledges of unregistered copyright or of other unregistered rights such as trademarks and designs can only take effect *inter partes* since no mode of perfection is available. As the Italian reporter notes, it is therefore unsurprising that "secured financing based on specific copyright protected works has not taken off in this country."

South African law is particularly complex, as there are several ways to create security rights in IP. In the first way, the respective IP statutes (relating to trademarks, patents, and designs) provide for the "hypothecation" of these rights as the result of a "pledge" in which physical transfer of possession is replaced by registration. A second manner involves a possible security cession of the IP right, which has the advantage of not requiring registration. A third method is the creation of a

[97]See in this volume Bornheim (2019), Section 2.4.2.

[98]Argyropoulou et al. (2019) (after fn. 23) gives a detailed account of how this problem can be circumvented through the creation of a special purpose vehicle and a pledge of the shares.

[99]See in this volume Ricolfi (2019), fn. 4, with translation into English.

[100]For the detailed analysis, see in this volume Ricolfi (2019), Section 2.1.

"notarial bond," which does have to be registered and can be created either over specific assets (a "special bond") or over all of the movable property of the debtor (a "general bond").[101]

In Spain, the relevant IP acts explicitly state that IP rights can be given as security. However, according to the predominant view, the parties can nevertheless only create a chattel mortgage (*hipoteca mobiliaria*).[102]

In Estonia, the Law of Property Act explicitly states that all registered IP rights (i.e. patents, trademarks, designs, etc.) can be subjected to a registered security right.[103] As an alternative, the respective IP enactments also allow for the security transfer of these rights.[104]

5 Licences and Royalties as Collateral

First, one needs to distinguish between the use of licences and royalties as collateral on the one hand and the use of a licence as a substitute for a security right (strictly speaking) on the other. In the latter scenario, instead of granting a security right in the IP right, the grantor/holder of the IP right might grant the secured party a "security licence," which gives the secured party the ability to use the IP right only in case of default. In order to enable the grantor to continue to exploit the IP right before default, the secured party will sublicense his rights back to the grantor. This scheme is primarily used where IP rights cannot be transferred or collateralized, as is the case in Germany and Austria in relation to copyright,[105] but it is also used elsewhere, such as in Cyprus.[106]

However, licences can also be used as collateral by the licensee.[107] There are two main issues connected to this kind of secured transaction. The first involves the fact that the licence will be created through a contract between the holder of the IP right (the licensor) and the licensee, who receives a right to use/exploit the IP right. The holder of the IP right is the debtor of the licensee, who in turn becomes the grantor of the security right. Jurisdictions may require the consent of the licensor (as a

[101] Karjiker (2019), under Section 3 contains a detailed account of all three kinds of security rights in all types of IP rights that can exist under South African law.

[102] See in this volume Heredia Cervantes (2019), Section 2.

[103] Lepik (2019), at fn. 7.

[104] See in this volume Lepik (2019), Section 2.2.

[105] See in this volume Brinkmann et al. (2019), Section 3.5.1; Koukal and Pullmannova (2019), Section 2; Matanovac Vučković et al. (2019), at fn. 59 *et seq.* Furthermore, see Koziol (2011), *passim* (covering Germany, Austria, and Japan).

[106] See Argyropoulou et al. (2019), text before fn. 33.

[107] For example, see in this volume Heredia Cervantes (2019), Section 2; Hara and Haga (2019), Section 3.1(1); Dincă and Rizoiu (2019), Section 2.

third-party debtor) for the transfer or creation of a security right in the licence.[108] Also, the terms of the licensing agreement might restrict or even prohibit the (security) transfer or creation of a security right in the licence.[109]

The second issue relates to the question if and under what conditions a licence or certain kind of licence can be classified as a proprietary right so that, in terms of secured transactions law, it should be treated as intangible property rather than as a mere claim or obligatory right. In Canada, the proprietary nature of a licence was recognized in the famous *Contech* case, which opened up the possibility of characterizing this security right as a Purchase Money Security Interest (PMSI), giving it so-called "super-priority."[110] In Germany, there is a (mainly academic) debate whether exclusive licences amount to a right in rem.[111]

Royalties stemming from a licence are usually claims for the payment of money and may thus be used as collateral in the same way as other receivables.[112] The French report stresses that creating a security right in the income generated by the exploitation of IP rights might be economically more attractive and legally more common than creating a security right in the IP right itself.[113] In Belgium, the creation and perfection of a security right in royalties is possible without any registration: "control" of the grantee is sufficient and already flows from the grantee's entitlement to notify the debtor.[114]

In systems where the security right is automatically extended to the proceeds of the collateral, conflicts of priority can arise between a security right in royalties and a security right in the respective IP right from which the royalties flow as "proceeds." Belgian law solves this conflict by referring to the time at which the respective rights were created.[115]

---

[108] See in this volume Brinkmann et al. (2019), fn. 235 with further references; Dorfmayr (2019), Section 2.2.5 with further references.

[109] See in this volume Brinkmann et al. (2019), Section 2.5.

[110] *Contech Enterprises, Inc.* v. *Vegherb, LLC* (2015) (*Contech*), see Howell (2019), at fn. 23.

[111] See in this volume Brinkmann et al. (2019), Section 2.5; Picht (2018), pp. 158 *et seq.*

[112] See Dorfmayr (2019), Sections 2.4 and 3.2.7; Storme and Malekzadem (2019), Section 23; see in this volume van Engelen (2019), Section 2.3; see in this volume Ricolfi (2019), Section 3.1.1; McCracken (2019), Section 4.1; see in this volume Hara and Haga (2019), Section 3.1.(1); Matanovac Vučković et al. (2019) , text before fn. 64.

[113] See in this volume Séjean and Binctin (2019), Section 2.5. See also Charpentier (2019), at fn. 45.

[114] Storme and Malekzadem (2019), Section 23 at the end.

[115] See Storme and Malekzadem (2019), Section 28.

6 Creation ("Attachment"), Perfection, and Priority, Including Requirements as to Form, Registration, and Publicity

With respect to creation, perfection, and priority, again, a main dividing line lies between jurisdictions that follow a functional and unitary approach (e.g. the US, Canada, and Australia) and jurisdictions where various or multiple types of security rights exist, with each type following its own rules for creation and perfection. In the first group, creation (or "attachment" in the terminology of Art. 9 UCC) typically only requires a written document, whereas perfection usually requires registration or notice filing. Priority is typically determined by the "first-to-file" rule, with tailored exceptions, such as those for PMSIs (Purchase Money Security Interests). In the second, non-functional/non-unitary group, rules on creation, perfection, and priority will typically vary according to the type of security right chosen by the parties. After the end of the Soviet regime, many of the Central and Eastern European states saw major reforms in their secured transactions laws (see the reports on Estonia, Croatia, and Romania), which were often inspired by the Model Law of the European Bank for Reconstruction and Development[116] and the UNCITRAL Legislative Guide on Secured Transactions. Yet although both of these models advocate a functional approach, some legislators opted for a mixture between traditional and modern (registrable) security rights, creating, as the reporters for Croatia state, a "complex system of security interests as a consequence of [. . .] historical development and of rapidly and erratically introducing a myriad of novel property interests into an emerging system of property law."[117]

The following summary also takes note of the fact that not all jurisdictions distinguish between "creation" and "perfection." Most of them, however, differentiate between effectiveness *inter partes* and effectiveness *erga omnes.*

With respect to priority in insolvency, most reports focus on priority rules that are specific to security rights. However, it must be kept in mind that where the realization of the security right takes place within the insolvency proceedings (which is the rule in most jurisdictions), a number of specific groups of insolvency creditors will take precedence over any secured creditor.[118]

The following paragraphs concern what in English terminology is called a "fixed charge," i.e. a security right relating to specific assets. "All-asset" security rights are looked at separately in Sect. 7.

[116]Cf. Dahan and Simpson (2004), pp. 98 *et seq.*

[117]See Matanovac Vučković et al. (2019), at fn. 31.

[118]See in this volume, for example, Murguía-Goebel (2019), Section 3.4 (the detailed list).

6.1 *Functional Approach*

6.1.1 Functional and Unitary Approach

The main issue with the modern Art. 9 UCC-type systems lies in the fact that notice will have to be filed under secured transactions law in order to perfect the security interest, but at the same time, the transaction might also need to be registered in an IP register, since it involves an IP right. Where the two bodies of law are placed on different jurisdictional levels (i.e. state/provincial and federal), transaction costs will rise, especially when the different bodies of law are not (sufficiently) coordinated. Parties might be forced to use what the Canadian report terms the "belts and suspenders" approach: "Where feasible, parties are advised to register their security interests on both the federal and the provincial registers in *all* the relevant jurisdictions."[119]

In the United States, an Art. 9 UCC single functional security interest is available for all IP rights. Creation presupposes that the grantor has the power to dispose of the IP right, and it requires a written document. The main issue under US law concerns the question whether registration of the security right in the federal IP registers supplants filing under secured transactions law, which is state law. As a matter of principle, IP law is federal and takes precedence over state law. According to statutory IP law (which is older than Art. 9 UCC), "assignment" includes the granting of security rights, mortgages, etc. Therefore, security rights can be entered in the IP registers. As for the question whether registration in the IP registers "supplants" filing under the UCC, there is neither a statutory provision nor a Supreme Court decision on this matter, so this area is surprisingly unclear. For security rights over patents and trademarks, filing is held to be sufficient, but registration with the Patent and Trademark Office (PTO) is often also undertaken as a precautionary measure. In contrast, federal registration with the Copyright Office (CO) pre-empts the need to file under Art. 9 UCC; however, it seems to be good practice to do so. Of course, with unregistered copyright, there can be no pre-emption of filing under the Art. 9 UCC system, so filing with the UCC filing office suffices. But since filing against an unregistered copyright does not provide security in case the copyright holder does in fact register his copyright (and the security interest therein) with the CO, many lenders will request that borrowers register their copyright with the CO before advancing credit on this basis. Under US law, priority in relation to a subsequent lien creditor and trustee in bankruptcy follows the first-to-file rule. With respect to priority in relation to a buyer or transferee of an IP right, the problem lies in the fact that registration with the PTO, although not necessary for perfection, might be necessary to prevent bona fide

[119]See Ballagh M (2017) Secured Financing with Intellectual Property: Managing Uncertainties, www.ballaghedward.ca (Law Office, Hamilton, Ont.), noting: "The standard legal advice is sometimes called the 'belts and suspenders' approach. Where feasible, parties are advised to register their security interests on both the federal and the provincial registers in *all* the relevant jurisdictions [i.e. provinces]," cited Howell (2019), Section 2.2.

acquisition free of encumbrance by a buyer of the IP right. With respect to copyright, the rules pertaining to registration in the copyright register may take precedence over Art. 9 UCC. Therefore, the transfer or assignment of a copyright can be registered within one month of its creation and can thus retroactively take priority over a later security right, even if the earlier right was not visible in the register.

The relationship between IP rights legislation and registration at the federal level on the one hand and the PPSAs at the provincial level on the other is also a major issue in the Canadian Common Law provinces and in Québec. Federal IP law at least partly regulates the assignment and licensing of IP rights, but at the same time, the functional definition of security rights under the PPSAs and the rules on hypothecs in the Civil Code of Québec lead to the concurrent application of provincial secured transactions laws. As the reporters for Common Law Canada and Québec show in great detail, the exact delimitation of the applicability of federal and provincial legislation in this area is highly disputed and still awaits an appellate analysis.[120] Generally speaking, this issue is relevant for the assignment of IP rights and for licences, whereas charges and mortgages are outside the context of federal legislation. Where federal IP rights legislation comes into play, it seems that ownership and the power of the grantor to dispose are dependent upon the entry of the grantor's interest in the IP right in the national IP register, whereas perfection as a requirement for priority under provincial secured transactions legislation is determined by the first-to-file rule.[121]

By enacting the PPSA as a federal piece of legislation, Australia has successfully avoided the abovementioned difficulties. In addition, Australian legislation explicitly addresses the priority issue between legislation relating to IP and enactments on secured transactions. As the reporter states, although "it is possible for security rights in both patents and trade marks to be registered, both the Patents Act and the Trade Marks Act expressly state that the recording in the relevant register of a PPSA security interest does not affect a dealing with the patent or registered trade mark. They also make clear that the registers do not provide prima facie evidence of security interests. These provisions reflect a legislative intention that the PPSA is the sole governing legislation for security interests and, in particular, for resolving priority disputes."[122]

However, the filing of notices of secured transactions over IP rights still seems to involve some complexities connected to the different categories of collateral under which IP rights might be subsumed.[123] In addition, and quite interestingly, the Australian PPSA not only distinguishes between "attachment" and "perfection," but also uses "enforceability against third parties" as a separate category that is a step between attachment and perfection. "Attachment" requires the power to dispose and the giving of value, but does not necessarily require a written security agreement

[120]Howell (2019), Section 2.3. at fn. 33 ff; Charpentier (2019), at fn. 53 *et seq.*

[121]Howell (2019), Section 4.

[122]See McCracken (2019), Section 5.4.

[123]McCracken (2019), Section 4.1. *et seq.*

(however, written form may be required by IP legislation).[124] "Enforceability against third parties" is regularly achieved through a written security agreement, whereas for perfection, the effective registration of a financing statement in the Personal Property Securities Register is needed. Only perfection gives the security right its maximal effectiveness, which includes effects in relation to the trustee in bankruptcy.

As to the issue of priority, Australia follows the usual rule of notice filing systems; thus, as a general default rule (i.e. subject to subordination agreements between the parties), it is the time of perfection that determines the order of priority between two perfected security interests and between a perfected interest and the trustee in bankruptcy.[125]

6.1.2 Functional But Non-unitary Approach

Belgian secured transactions law has just undergone a thorough reform and can today be regarded as one of the most modern systems in the EU.[126] With regard to the technique of filing, the Belgian reform has been influenced by Book IX of the Draft Common Frame of Reference and by the UNCITRAL Legislative Guide on Secured Transaction, which in turn have drawn inspiration from Art. 9 UCC.[127] Nevertheless, Belgian law still distinguishes between retained rights, granted rights, and privileges by operation of law and is characterized here as a functional but non-unitary system. Also, Belgium has opted for a system of transaction filing rather than notice fling.[128]

Article 7 of the new Belgian Pledge Act specifically mentions IP rights as potential collateral but gives precedence to specific statutes relating to IP rights. Thus, it is doubtful whether the IP-specific requirements concerning the form of security agreements prevail over the more elaborate requirements concerning the form and content of security arrangements in the new Pledge Act.[129] Another source of doubt and difficulties lies in the fact that the Belgian legislator has failed to specify whether a pledge of IP rights still needs to be registered in the IP-specific registers for third-party effectiveness, or whether filing in the new general pledge register

---

[124]See in greater detail McCracken (2019), Section 5.1.

[125]For exceptions (e.g. for PMSIs), see McCracken (2019), Section 6.1.2. *et seq.*; for the circumstances in which the buyer of an IP right takes it free of encumbrance, see McCracken (2019), Section 6.2. *et seq.*

[126]The new Pledge Act came into force on January 1, 2018. On this Act, see Dirix (2015) and the bibliography in Storme and Malekzadem (2019).

[127]See Dirix (2015), p. 273.

[128]Storme and Malekzadem (2019), para 17.

[129]Storme and Malekzadem(2019), para 16.

(available online) will suffice.[130] This unresolved question also plays a role with regard to priority, especially vis-à-vis a bona fide purchaser.[131]

Finnish secured transactions law can also be categorized as a functional but non-unitary system, providing for not only pledges but also security transfers and security assignments of IP rights in the relevant IP enactments. A written agreement and an entry in the relevant IP registry are generally required, yet this is problematic for copyright since no such registry exists.[132] Priority is, as a matter of principle, determined by the date of creation, not the date of registration; however, a second pledgee or transferee who in good faith registered his security right before the first pledgee or transferee will take priority.[133]

Croatia has also adopted a functional[134] but non-unitary system. Although it formally distinguishes between charges and security assignments,[135] the rules relating to charges also apply to security assignments.[136] Following the general principles of property law, Croatian law does not differentiate between creation and perfection.[137] Basically, the security right is created by a notarial deed and needs to be registered in the relevant IP register in order to attach (if the collateral is a registered IP right).[138] As a matter of principle, the date of registration decides priority issues.[139]

Similarly, Romanian law subjects all security rights that can be created over IP rights to the rules on "movable hypothecs,"[140] but has retained various aspects based on ownership, such as conditional sale and retention of title.[141] However, as far as IP rights are concerned, only the movable hypothec is available. Romanian law has adopted the distinction between attachment and perfection and has also introduced a notice filing system,[142] including uniform rules on priority.[143] Unfortunately, it has also imported the dichotomy between secured transactions registries and IP registries, as well as the unresolved question whether registration in the former suffices with respect to perfecting security rights in IP.[144]

---

[130] See in detail Storme and Malekzadem (2019), para 19.

[131] See in detail Storme and Malekzadem (2019), para 27.

[132] See in this volume Juutilainen (2019), Section 4.3.

[133] See in this volume Juutilainen (2019), Section 5.

[134] Matanovac Vučković et al. (2019), at fn. 56.

[135] Matanovac Vučković et al. (2019), at fn. 32.

[136] Matanovac Vučković et al. (2019), at fn. 56.

[137] Matanovac Vučković et al. (2019), Section 3.2.

[138] See Matanovac Vučković et al. (2019), after fn. 68 for details.

[139] See Matanovac Vučković et al. (2019), after fn. 88.

[140] See in this volume Dincă and Rizoiu (2019), Section 2.

[141] See in this volume Dincă and Rizoiu (2019), Section 2.

[142] See in this volume Dincă and Rizoiu (2019), Section 3.3.

[143] See in this volume Dincă and Rizoiu (2019), Section 4.

[144] See in detail in this volume Dincă and Rizoiu (2019), Section 3.3.

6.2 Non-functional Approach

The following section distinguishes between those non-functional jurisdictions that have seen at least some reform of secured transactions law in recent decades and those where the rules of the civil codes, dating back to the eighteenth and nineteenth centuries, are still more or less the foundation of modern secured transactions law.

6.2.1 Modernized Systems

French secured transactions law underwent two major reforms, one in 2006 and one in 2009, through which fiduciary or security ownership (*fiducie-sûreté*) was introduced in French law for the first time. This reform has added some general security rights, such as the *gage commun* and the *fiducie-sûreté*, to the existing range; however, it did so without abandoning the pre-existing range of very specific security rights.[145] Two of these are of special importance in the present context: the *nantissement de logiciel* (software) and the *nantissement cinématographique*, which has existed since 1944[146] and is now regulated by the *Code du cinéma et de l'image animée* of 2009.[147]

French law does not use the terminology "creation" and "perfection," but distinguishes between effectiveness *entre les parties* and *opposabilité aux tiers*. A mere written agreement is sufficient for effectiveness between the parties. An exception is the *fiducie-sûreté*, where registration in the *registre national de fiducie* (which is not open to the public) is a condition for its validity.[148] Otherwise, registration is only a condition for the effectiveness of the security interest against third parties. Registration needs to be effected in the various IP registers.[149] In the case of a *nantissement cinématographique*, the security right has to be entered into the *Registre public du cinéma et de l'audiovisuel*.[150]

Dutch law does not distinguish between creation and perfection. A pledge (which is the only available security right for IP rights) is created by "the mere execution of the deed of pledge," which is a written document that can be in electronic form and does not require the involvement of notaries. Registration of the pledge in the relevant IP register is necessary, but is also sufficient for third-party effectiveness.[151]

In Mexico, the parties may choose between pledging the debtor's property via a non-possessory pledge, which can attach all categories of movable property (present and future), including intangibles, or a security trust, which transfers title to the

[145]For a general appraisal of the French reform, see Leavy (2007), pp. 101 *et seq.*

[146]See Loi de 22.2.1944; cf. Fargeaud (1963), pp. 71 *et seq.*

[147]See in this volume Séjean and Binctin (2019), Section 3.2.2.

[148]See in this volume Séjean and Binctin (2019), Section 3.2.2.1.

[149]See the details in this volume Séjean and Binctin (2019), Section 3.2.2.

[150]See in this volume Séjean and Binctin (2019), Section 3.2.2.3.

[151]See in this volume van Engelen (2019), Sections 3.1 and 3.2.

trustee/creditor and comes with a more efficient foreclosure procedure.[152] Both security rights must be laid down in a written contract (if the debt surpasses a certain amount, a notarial deed will also be necessary) and must be registered both in the IP registry and in the secured transactions registry—but it should be noted that the IP registry will make an automatic entry in the secured transactions registry.[153] As a general rule, it is the time of registration which determines priority.

As stated earlier, many Eastern European states have seen some reform in their secured transactions laws in recent decades, but these have had very different outcomes. Some countries have retained a non-unitary, non-functional approach. In Estonia, for example, secured transactions involving IP rights are partly regulated by general property law, partly by IP law. As the Estonian report sets out in great detail,[154] the requirements concerning form and registration depend first on the security right chosen (i.e. pledge or security transfer) and second on the type of IP right. Generally speaking, Estonian law requires a written security agreement and registration in the relevant IP registry.

6.2.2 Traditional Systems

Under German law, generally speaking, no separate category of "perfection" exists. Once a right *in rem* is effectively created, it is also effective *erga omnes*.[155] For IP rights of national origin, nothing more than an agreement between the parties is needed in order to assign an IP right by way of security or to pledge it. A written document is only needed as far as European law applies (i.e. for an EU trademark or Community design). In practice, however, security agreements are always in writing.[156] A registration of the pledge is possible (in the relevant IP registers), but it does not have any effect with respect to German IP rights.[157] With respect to EU rights, registration protects the pledgee or assignee against third parties, who might otherwise take the IP right free from encumbrance.[158] The acquisition of a security right in an IP right under German national law always requires the power of disposal on the side of the grantor. But there is some academic debate around the possibility of the bona fide acquisition of security rights in European IP rights from a registered non-holder.[159] Priority between different holders of proprietary rights is (as is normal in German secured transactions law) determined by the time of creation through agreement, with the consequence that the order of priority is not visible for

[152]See in this volume Murguía-Goebel (2019), Section 3.1.
[153]See in this volume Murguía-Goebel (2019), Section 3.1 at the end.
[154]See in this volume Lepik (2019), Section 3.
[155]See in this volume Brinkmann et al. (2019), fn. 113.
[156]See in this volume Brinkmann et al. (2019), Section 3.1.1.
[157]See in this volume Brinkmann et al. (2019), Section 3.1.1.
[158]See in this volume Brinkmann et al. (2019), Section 3.1.1.
[159]See in this volume Brinkmann et al. (2019), fn. 160, with further references.

third parties—this is, of course, a major shortcoming of German secured transactions law.[160] The use of ownership in lieu of a security right (strictly speaking) does not allow for the creation of junior rights in the same property. It also gives rise to concerns about over-collateralization, which the German Supreme Court has solved by giving the secured creditor a duty to release collateral when certain limits have been reached.[161]

Like German law, Austrian law does not distinguish between creation and perfection; however, in contrast to German law, Austrian law always requires a valid underlying obligation (*titulus*) for the valid transfer or creation of a proprietary right. In addition, effective creation requires a *modus*—an "appropriate act of publicity." Pledges and security transfers of patents, utility models, and protected designs have to be entered in the relevant registers, and this entry in turn requires a notarized deed.[162] For trademarks, there is some debate as to whether registration is an absolute must, or whether this can be replaced by a so-called "book entry" (*Buchvermerk*).[163] The underlying assumption of a distinction between creation and perfection in the European IP regulations creates some tensions with Austrian domestic law.[164]

Also, in Greece, no distinction is made between creation and perfection. Both require an agreement which must either be in notarized form or be contained in a written document with an officially certified date. For its effectiveness *inter partes* as well as *erga omnes*, the security right must also be entered in the relevant IP registry.[165]

The same is true in the Czech Republic: pledges and security transfers (which are infrequently used with respect to IP rights) both have to be entered in the relevant IP registries to gain effectiveness *inter partes* as well as *erga omnes*. However, with respect to trademarks that are pledged as part of a business enterprise, the law provides that registration is to be made in the pledge registry instead of the trademark registry.[166] In any event, registration leads to constructive notice of the security right. Interestingly, as a default rule, the grantor remains entitled to transfer the collateral, but parties to the security agreement can exclude the grantor and this agreement can also be registered.[167]

In Japan, there is a marked difference between the security assignment, which was developed by case law, and the pledge, which is regulated by statute. The difference is especially prominent in enforcement, where the parties to a security

---

[160] Kieninger (2008), p. 182.

[161] See in greater detail in this volume Brinkmann et al. (2019), Section 3.2.1.

[162] Dorfmayr (2019), Section 3.2.1.

[163] Dorfmayr (2019), Section 3.2.2.

[164] Dorfmayr (2019), Section 3.2.4.

[165] See in this volume Kallinikou and Koriatopoulou (2019), Section 3.

[166] The reporters from the Czech Republic note that this rule is "without any substantial justification or proper reasoning"; see in this volume Koukal and Pullmannova (2019), Section 4.

[167] See in this volume Koukal and Pullmannova (2019), Section 2.

assignment are free to agree upon the enforcement method, but the pledgee is bound to follow the statutory rules and sell the IP right by public auction. With respect to creation and perfection, both security assignments and pledges of IP rights need to be registered in the relevant IP registries (only). The date of registration determines priority.

The law in England and Wales (which so far has not adopted a unitary, functional system) has in fact adopted the distinction between attachment and perfection, at least in the description of secured transactions law. As the English reporter notes, attachment gives rise to more than a merely obligatory relationship between the debtor and the creditor; thus, an unperfected security interest would still be a proprietary right in relation to an unsecured creditor outside insolvency.[168] Attachment presupposes ownership of or legal title to the collateral; a legal mortgage also needs to be in writing.[169] It is a special feature of English law that where the requirements of a common law mortgage are not met, an equitable interest may still be created.[170] The dichotomy between registration requirements stemming from secured transactions law and those flowing from IP law is also present in English law. Under the Companies Act 2006, so-called "company charges" need to be registered with the Companies House in order to be perfected. On the relationship between the registration of security rights in IP rights in specialized IP registers and such registration in the Company Registry, the reporter for England and Wales notes that "it is argued that the priority rules of the IP registries should entirely displace the notice function of the company register."[171]

In contrast, charges (whether fixed or floating) over IP rights cannot be entered in IP registries in Cyprus; instead, they need to be registered in the companies register (if created by a company) in order to be perfected.[172] Assignments of patents and trademarks are registrable in IP registries, but seem not to be used for security purposes.[173]

In Italy, it is highly debated whether the registration of a security right in the appropriate IP register is merely a mode of perfection, or whether it is a requirement for the creation of a security right *inter partes*. As the Italian reporter shows, the second view dominates, especially in IP literature; however, a literal reading of the respective provisions speaks in favour of the first view.[174] Priority is governed by the sequence of (valid) registrations, validity requiring, inter alia, a notarized deed and payment of the registration fee.[175]

---

[168]See in this volume Bornheim (2019), Section 3.1.1.3.

[169]For a detailed account of English IP legislation on this point, see in this volume Bornheim (2019), Section 3.2.1.

[170]See in this volume Bornheim (2019), Section 3.1.1.3.

[171]See in this volume Bornheim (2019), Section 4.2.

[172]Argyropoulou et al. (2019), Section 5.

[173]Argyropoulou et al. (2019), text after fn. 24.

[174]For a detailed account of this debate, see in this volume Ricolfi (2019), Section 3.1.4.

[175]See in this volume Ricolfi (2019), Sections 3.1.5 and 3.1.6.

In Spain, the only available security right over IP rights is the chattel mortgage (*hipoteca mobiliaria*).[176] The security agreement must be contained in a notarial deed, which has to give specific information on the collateral and the secured debt—otherwise, it is void.[177] Interestingly, it must only be registered in the "Registry of Movable Goods," not in the IP registry; however, note that registration in the IP registry is necessary for the creation of the security right since there is no creation by a non-holder.[178] Priority is determined by the date of registration on the movable property registry.

In Brazil, all security agreements, whether they take the form of a pledge, fiduciary transfer, or usufruct, have to be in writing and have to be registered in the Registry of Deeds and Documents in order to be effective against third parties. In addition, security rights in patents, trademarks, and industrial designs have to be registered in the *Instituto Nacional da Propriedade Industrial*.[179]

6.3 Concluding Remarks

It seems quite obvious that, independent of the distinctions between functional/non-functional systems and notice/transaction filing systems, the dualism of the registration of security rights in the relevant IP registers and the registration (or other form of publicity) of secured transactions is the most common source of uncertainty and conflict in jurisdictions. Typically, registers for IP rights are older than secured transaction registers; some of them are organized on a different level (e.g. supranational instead of national, federal instead of state/provincial, etc.) than the secured transaction registers. A major step towards facilitating borrowing against IP rights would be to solve this conflict and either create a single system of publicity or create clear and comprehensive rules on the relationship between both registration systems. Mexico has the interesting solution of simply providing that the registration of a security right in a specialized IP registry will automatically lead to an entry in the secured transactions registry.[180]

---

176 See in this volume Heredia Cervantes (2019), Section 2.

177 See in this volume Heredia Cervantes (2019), Section 3.

178 See in this volume Heredia Cervantes (2019), Section 3.

179 Lahorgue (2019), after fn. 23.

180 See in this volume Murguía-Goebel (2019), Section 3.2.

7 Security Over IP Rights as Part of an Enterprise Charge

In practice, IP rights are most often only used as collateral together with a security right in the enterprise holding the IP right as a whole.[181] Apart from the value of the IP right in itself, a major reason for this is the concern that otherwise, a secured creditor might not be able to sell the business or its products in the event of default. In such cases, it is not the IP right itself which is viewed as valuable collateral; rather, the possible lack of rights in the IP right is regarded as a potential hindrance to the economic exploitation of the business, especially regarding the sale of the tangible assets of the business. Another motive for including IP rights in enterprise charges is the concern that otherwise, third-party creditors could take a security right in individual IP rights and thus gain priority over the holder of an enterprise charge. The German reporters, after having conducted 120 interviews with IP practitioners, conclude that security rights over IP rights are very rare, "except as additional collateral in situations where all of the debtor's assets are encumbered, such as in the context of project financing. In such a situation, security rights over IP rights might serve as a shield against seizure of the IP right by other creditors rather than a sword (against the debtor)."[182] Since foreclosures by other creditors could have ruinous effects on the success of the project, the creditor will try to anticipate such a seizure by taking any IP rights as collateral (e.g. by way of a security assignment) and thus frustrate the drastic effects of a third party's foreclosure.

Charges over the assets of an enterprise or company as a whole ("enterprise charges") can take very different forms, depending on the jurisdiction. Functional and unitary legislation—such as Art. 9 UCC; the PPSAs of the Canadian Common Law provinces, Australia, and New Zealand; and, following the US model in this respect, Mexican law—allow security agreements that cover all present and future property of the debtor. There are minor differences in the way this intention needs to be expressed. In the US, the different property types of Art. 9 have to be listed, with IP rights falling into the category of "general intangibles." Other jurisdictions, such as Australia, allow so-called "general security agreements" or "all PAP [present and after-acquired property] agreements."[183]

[181]For example, see in this volume Brinkmann et al. (2019), Section 1; see also in this volume Juutilainen (2019), Section 9. In contrast, the Mexican report states that although legislation explicitly caters for a floating lien on IP assets, practice in Mexico still shies away from it; see in this volume Murguía-Goebel (2019), Section 3.5.

[182]Brinkmann et al. (2019), Section 1.

[183]See the detailed description in McCracken (2019), Section 6.3 *et seq.*

Other jurisdictions, such as France, England, Scotland,[184] Cyprus,[185] South Africa,[186] Japan, Finland,[187] and Romania,[188] allow security rights over the assets of a company. While the English floating charge (and its Romanian legal transplant[189]) is special in the way it treats the charge that is only attached to individual assets in the event of crystallization,[190] the French *nantissement sur fonds de commerce* can be described as a fixed charge over specific assets of a company, including certain IP rights.[191] Brazilian law allows for a charge over the assets of a corporation, including its IP rights, through the issuance of debentures.[192] Japanese law distinguishes between an "enterprise mortgage," which resembles the English floating charge and can only be created by a stock company in order to secure corporate bonds, and a "foundation mortgage," which was inspired by German law and whose main collateral consists of immovables. Enterprise mortgages include IP rights but are practically never used because they are subordinate to other security rights over the same assets.[193]

A third group of jurisdictions does not explicitly provide for enterprise charges; rather, it upholds the principles of specialty and specificity, according to which proprietary rights can only exist in specific, determined assets, not in a group of assets. Yet some members of this group of jurisdictions (e.g. Germany) have been able to accommodate an all-asset security transfer of ownership or assignment by lowering their requirements to mere determinability.[194]

A fourth group of jurisdictions provides for an enterprise charge but only extends it to unregistered IP rights such as copyright. This is the case in Estonia.[195] In Italy, the specific legislation that enables companies to secure credit through a special

---

[184] See in this volume Masiyakurima (2019), Section 5.

[185] Argyropoulou et al. (2019), Section 6.

[186] See in this volume Karjiker (2019), Section 5 on the "general notarial bond."

[187] See in this volume Juutilainen (2019), Section 6. The Finnish system is interesting from a comparative point of view: first, because the creation involves signing a "promissory note," and second, because only 50% of the value of the encumbered assets can be used to pay off the mortgagor with priority over unsecured creditors.

[188] See in this volume Dincă and Rizoiu (2019), Section 5.

[189] See in this volume Dincă and Rizoiu (2019), Section 5.

[190] See in this volume Bornheim (2019), Sections 5.1.1 and 5.1.2. The Common Law provinces of Canada seem to follow this concept; see Howell (2019), Section 5.

[191] See in this volume Séjean and Binctin (2019), Section 5. The same was true for Belgium before January 1, 2018; see Storme and Malekzadem (2019), para 20 (*gage sur fonds de commerce*). Under the new Act, Belgian law still allows for the pledge of an enterprise, but considers the individual assets to be attached; see Storme and Malekzadem (2019), para 21.

[192] Lahorgue (2019), Section 5.

[193] See in this volume Hara and Haga (2019), Sections 3.1.(3), 3.1.(4) and 4.

[194] See in general Bülow (2017), pp. 482 *et seq*. For the similar situation in Austria, see Dorfmayr (2019), Section 5; however, Austrian law seems more reluctant to accept all-asset security rights. The Turkish approach, on the other hand, seems to resemble German law; see in this volume Özsunay and Özsunay (2019), Section 5.

[195] See in this volume Lepik (2019), Section 5.

enterprise charge is only applicable to financial institutions (as lenders). Again, this charge only covers unregistered IP rights.[196]

In a fifth group of jurisdictions, the creation of an enterprise charge or a functional equivalent is not possible at all; see the Netherlands,[197] Spain,[198] Greece,[199] Croatia,[200] and Taiwan. Nevertheless, it should be noted that a bill introducing the floating charge is currently being discussed in Taiwan.[201]

8 The Legal Relationship Before Default

Usually, secured transactions law is not particularly interested in the mutual rights of the parties before default. However, where IP rights are used as collateral, a number of interesting and practically relevant matters arise, such as the right to use the IP right through production or licensing and the right (or even duty) to defend the IP right against infringements.[202] In order to uphold the IP right, the regular payment of fees or the use of the right may be necessary.[203]

As a matter of principle, mutual rights and obligations will be governed by the security agreement,[204] which in many states is subject to the principle of good faith and fair dealing.[205] The Australian and Canadian Common Law reports contain useful examples of the typical content of such an agreement.[206] Under non-unitary secured transactions systems, the mutual rights and obligations will additionally depend on the category of security right that the parties have created.[207] The German, Italian, South African, and Croatian reports contain thorough examinations of typical arrangements.[208] The degree to which parties enjoy contractual freedom in structuring their respective rights and obligations of course differs from one jurisdiction to another. For example, while the Italian reporter stresses that most statutory

---

[196] See in this volume Ricolfi (2019), Section 2.3.

[197] See in this volume van Engelen (2019), Section 5.

[198] See in this volume Heredia Cervantes (2019), Section 3.

[199] See in this volume Kallinikou and Koriatopoulou (2019), Section 5.

[200] Matanovac Vučković et al. (2019), Section 5.

[201] See in this volume Shieh and Lee (2019), Sections 2.2.4 and 5.

[202] See in detail Picht (2018), pp. 304 *et seq.*

[203] See e.g. in this volume Séjean and Binctin (2019), Section 6.1.

[204] See in this volume Karjiker (2019), Section 6. In Japan, the security agreement is the only source for the mutual rights and obligations. For pledges, there are some rules contained in the respective IP enactments; see in this volume Hara and Haga (2019), Section 6.

[205] For example, see in this volume Juutilainen (2019), Section 7.

[206] McCracken (2019), Section 7.1 *et seq.*; Howell (2019), Sections 6.1 and 6.2.

[207] See, for example, Lahorgue (2019), Section 6.

[208] See in this volume Brinkmann et al. (2019), Section 3.6; see in this volume Ricolfi (2019), Section 3.1.7; see in this volume Karjiker (2019), Section 6; Matanovac Vučković et al. (2019), Section 6.

provisions do not involve issues of public policy, thus allowing ample room for party autonomy,[209] it is not possible for the parties under Estonian law to limit the right of the pledgor of an IP right to dispose of it.[210] Generally speaking, if jurisdictions following a non-functional approach distinguish substantially between pledges and security transfers, the parties to the latter seem to enjoy a greater degree of freedom of contract.[211]

In some modern secured transactions laws, the legislator has provided specific default rules—see, for example, the new Romanian Civil Code of 2009[212] and the new Belgian Pledge Act, in force since January 1, 2018.[213] In the absence of specific legislative rules, either general principles or rules of secured transactions law will provide the outer limits of party autonomy, as well as default rules. Usually, if the purpose of the secured transaction is to lend and borrow money, it is in the interest of both parties that the security provider continue to manage the IP rights, exploit the rights, pay the fees, sue for infringement, etc.[214] A bank will not be in a position to carry out most of these managerial tasks.[215] As for entitlement to bring an infringement action, the English High Court already held 100 years ago[216] that in equity, the mortgagor retains equitable ownership and is therefore entitled to sue in case of infringement.[217] Where the pledge of the IP right transfers the right to use it to the pledgee, the parties may create a sublicence to enable the grantor to continue with the exploitation of the IP right.[218]

---

[209] See in this volume Ricolfi (2019), Section 3.1.7.

[210] See in this volume Lepik (2019), Section 6.1. However, the pledgee's written consent is required for the transfer of a trademark; see in this volume Lepik (2019), Section 6.1.

[211] For example, see in this volume Lepik (2019), Section 6.

[212] For a detailed account, see in this volume Dincă and Rizoiu (2019), Section 6.

[213] Storme and Malekzadem (2019), paras 29 *et seq.* In Turkey, the rights and obligations under security agreements on movables and claims before default are laid down in detail in the Civil Code; see in this volume Özsunay and Özsunay (2019), Section 6. The Estonian reporter also gives a detailed account of the statutory rules relating to the pre-default relationship in case of a pledge; see in this volume Lepik (2019), Section 6.1.

[214] See also in this volume Heredia Cervantes (2019), Section 6. In Japan, any authorization of the pledgee to use the IP right must be expressly granted by contract; see in this volume Hara and Haga (2019), Section 6.1.

[215] See the detailed discussion of the parties' interests in this volume Ricolfi (2019), Section 3.1.7.

[216] *Van Gelder Apsimon & Co v Sowerby Bridge United District Flour Society* (1890), 44 Ch D 374 (CA) [*Van Gelder*].

[217] See in greater detail in this volume Bornheim (2019), Section 6. In the Netherlands, in contrast, it is the pledgee who has to sue the infringing party; see in this volume van Engelen (2019), Section 6.1.

[218] See Dorfmayr (2019), fn. 128.

9 Remedies of the Secured Creditor Outside Insolvency (Enforcement)

Rules on enforcement go to the heart of secured transactions law.[219] If the secured party is not able to realize the value of the collateral in a sufficiently speedy and low-cost manner, the whole transaction tends to lose much of its commercial effectiveness. Quick and effective enforcement is, as a matter of principle, also in the interest of the debtor (unless the collateral is, for example, his family home), since it will help to reduce or extinguish his debt. Nevertheless, debtors need safeguards against any enforcement that is arbitrary; is contrary to good faith and fair dealing; or gives a surplus to the creditor. Key policy questions in this area cover the extent to which private, out-of-court enforcement should be allowed and the extent to which the parties should be free to set enforcement mechanisms in the security agreement. Considerations specific to IP concern the effect of enforcement on licences[220] and the role of IP registries in the context of enforcement.

Jurisdictions can again be grouped according to whether they are modern or unreformed; unitary or non-unitary; or functional or non-functional. As a general rule, the more recent a secured transactions law, the more it tends to opt for contractual freedom and out-of-court enforcement.

9.1 *Unitary and Functional Systems*

In the unitary and functional systems (e.g. the US, Australia, and the Canadian Common Law provinces), no material distinction is made between enforcement outside insolvency and enforcement in insolvency. As a general rule, enforcement is flexible, allowing for the disposition of the collateral without the necessity of judicial proceedings. There are no special rules on the enforcement of security rights in IP that would differ from the rules applicable to other types of collateral. Generally, the secured party can either retain (i.e. take the collateral "on [his] own account") or dispose of the IP rights by sale or through a licence.

Romania provides a contrast to this. Although it has imported a secured transactions law based on a functional approach and notice filing into its new Civil Code, it has partly retained traditional rules on enforcement, such as the prohibition of the *pactum commissorium*.[221] In addition, the US-inspired self-help remedies are not

[219]For a general overview (from a European perspective), see Dirix (2008), pp. 223–241.

[220]See, for example, in this volume Brinkmann et al. (2019), Section 3.5.3.

[221]See in this volume Dincă and Rizoiu (2019), Section 7.1.

applicable to security rights in intangibles.[222] The lack of clear enforcement rules is the main obstacle to the use of IP rights as collateral in Romania.[223]

9.2 Non-unitary Systems

In this group, enforcement rules tend to differ from one type of security right to another.[224] The degree of flexibility also depends on the time at which the enforcement rules were enacted: the older the law, the stricter it tends to be. Thus, under Austrian law, judicial enforcement is still the rule, following statutory rules on pledges.[225] The secured creditor first has to sue for performance and obtain an execution title; then, execution is carried out through the licensing, leasing, or sale of the IP right. Out-of-court enforcement is only possible when this has been previously agreed upon and within the framework of the mandatory debtor protection rules.[226] For example, a forfeiture clause (*pactum commissorium/pacte commissoire*) is prohibited. In the same vein, Dutch law only allows for a foreclosure sale by public auction (in case of a patent or plant variety, this auction has to be carried out by a notary); other means of selling the pledged property require a court order.[227] South African law joins these two jurisdictions in requiring a court order for the realization of a pledge, hypothecation, or cession of IP rights.[228] The same is true for Spanish and Croatian law, except where the (commercial) parties to the secured transaction have agreed on an out-of-court procedure in the notarial deed; in this case, the realization can be handled by a notary and the sale can be conducted through a public auction.[229] In Brazil and Estonia, we find a marked difference between a pledge and a fiduciary transfer: with the former, a court order is necessary (unless agreed otherwise by the parties) and the *pactum commissorium* is prohibited; with the latter, the fiduciary transferee becomes full owner upon default and can realize the collateral accordingly.[230]

Under German law, the remedies available to the secured party heavily depend on the type of security chosen. Where the parties choose a pledge, they are bound to the

[222] See in this volume Dincă and Rizoiu (2019), Section 7.2.

[223] See in this volume Dincă and Rizoiu (2019), Section 10.

[224] See, for example, the detailed account of the different remedies available to the secured creditor in enforcement and insolvency given by the South African reporter: Karjiker (2019), Section 4.

[225] See in this volume Dorfmayr (2019), Section 7.1.1.

[226] See Dorfmayr (2019), Section 7.1.2.

[227] Van Engelen (2019), Section 7.1.

[228] See in this volume Karjiker (2019), Sections 4.1 and 7.

[229] See in this volume Heredia Cervantes (2019), Section 7.1.c; Section 2; Matanovac Vučković et al. (2019), at fn. 108.

[230] Lahorgue (2019), Section 7.1.; see in this volume Lepik (2019), Section 7.1 for pledges and Section 7.2 for security transfers.

rather strict and outdated rules on enforcement in the Civil Code (i.e. no *pactum commissorium*, sale only by public auction). If the parties have chosen a security assignment, security licence of the IP right, or security usufruct, they enjoy a greater freedom of contract and can also include elements such as a forfeiture clause. Also, in England and Wales, remedies depend on the agreement between the parties and on the type of security interest chosen. The creditor of a mortgage can apply to a court for a foreclosure order, transferring legal title to the creditor. Where the mortgage is in deed form, the creditor can appoint a receiver, who will then take over the assets and realize them. Italy is yet another example of a jurisdiction where the choice between different security devices is significant when it comes to enforcement. In case of a pledge, the collateral may be seized and sold, or even acquired by the creditor in satisfaction of the debt under further conditions. Mortgages are more complex (see Artt. 555 ff. of the Italian Civil Procedure Code) since they were originally primarily designed for immovables. In its IP legislation, Italy has also adopted some IPR-specific rules on enforcement that involve the IP registry.

Belgium and France provide examples of modern, non-functional or non-unitary approaches to secured transactions law. In Belgium, out-of-court enforcement can be agreed upon by the parties as long as they act in good faith. The new Pledge Act contains default rules in Arts. 47 to 56. In France, the secured party can obtain a court order ordering either the sale of the assets or the handing over of the collateral to the creditor as payment. An agreement on a *pactum commissorium* is also possible. In case of retention of title, the creditor can ask for the restitution of the collateral. Another example of a modern jurisdiction is Mexico, which provides for a non-judicial enforcement procedure when the debt and its enforceability are not disputed and there is agreement on the delivery of the collateral.[231] In Taiwan, a *pactum commissorium* is possible if it is registered.[232]

10 Remedies of the Secured Creditor in Insolvency

Once the security right in the IP right has been created and (if applicable) perfected, and therefore enjoys priority against the insolvency administrator (or trustee in bankruptcy), each jurisdiction's general rules on the enforcement of security rights in insolvency apply, including the powers of the administrator to avoid or set aside the transaction where it has granted unjustified preferential treatment to a certain creditor (the so-called *actio pauliana*). Once again, in non-unitary/non-functional systems, the rights and remedies of the secured party may depend on the kind of security right created.[233] However, special questions relating specifically to security

[231]See in this volume Murguía-Goebel (2019), Section 3.7.1.2.1.

[232]See in this volume Shieh and Lee (2019), Section 3.3.

[233]For example, see in this volume Brinkmann et al. (2019), Sections 3.1.4, 3.2.4, 3.3.3, 3.4.3 and 3.5.3.

in IP rights may arise where the IP right has been licensed to a third party (the licensee) and a security right has been created either in the licence (the licensee being the debtor/grantor in the secured transaction) or in the royalties (the licensor and holder of the IP right being the grantor/debtor in the secured transaction).[234] The Italian report contains a detailed account of the rights of the insolvency administrator in either scenario.[235] In Germany, the effects on the licence are largely unclear and hotly debated among scholars. One key issue is the question whether a licence (at least an exclusive one) amounts to a right in rem. If this is the case, the preponderant view seems to be that the trustee cannot terminate the licence unilaterally.[236]

11 Practical Use of Security Rights in IP and Costs

11.1 Costs

The reporters list the following as factors that need to be taken into account in assessing the cost of creating and perfecting a security interest in IP rights:

- costs for legal advice (which are generally estimated to be rather high, since the area is complex and not sufficiently covered by case law and standardized practice), including documentation
- notarial fees, where there is a need for a notarial deed or a signature certified by a notary
- registration fees for IP registries
- registration fees for the secured transactions register
- register tax, stamp duty tax, or "state fee"

The reports give individual information on the cost of registration in IP or secured transactions registries, as well as on the cost of notarial documentation. The cost of obtaining legal advice seems to play an important role, but is very hard to estimate.

11.2 Frequency of Transactions

The reporters were asked to give some information on how common secured transactions involving IP rights are based on the number of entrances in registries, expert interviews, personal experience, or (if no other source of information was available) a personal estimate. The following summary only gives a rough idea; for all details

[234] On this topic see also Koziol (2011), pp. 115 *et seq.*

[235] See in this volume Ricolfi (2019), Section 5.

[236] See in this volume Brinkmann et al. (2019), Section 3.5.3.

and the methodology pursued by each reporter, the reader is referred to the national reports themselves.

- Australia: rare with respect to single IP rights, but common practice with respect to security rights over "all present and future property"
- Austria: rare
- Brazil: uncommon
- Czech Republic: rare[237]
- Croatia: rare
- Cyprus: very rare[238]
- England and Wales: rare and coincidental
- Estonia: uncommon
- Finland: uncommon[239]
- France: common with respect to trademarks
- Germany: very rare
- Greece: it is "not easy to obtain credit by granting a security right over IP rights"
- Italy: very rare (except for security interest in copyright in movies)
- Japan: IP rights are never used as collateral, except in the case of copyright in movies
- Mexico: uncommon
- Netherlands: only done as part of security rights over "all assets"
- Romania: quite commonly used, but only as part of an enterprise charge
- Scotland: rare
- South Africa: far from being a common practice, except for the enterprise charge ("notarial bond" or security cession); the hypothecation of trademarks is also becoming more common
- Spain: IP is not seen as suitable collateral (except for rights over "cinematographic works")
- Taiwan: only trademarks are (sometimes) used as collateral
- Turkey: rare
- US: common, especially in the case of "all-asset" security rights

[237]The Czech reporters give some figures taken from the registry for the period of 2014–2016. While the number of registrations of security rights over patents and utility models rests between 1 and 9 per year, security rights over trademarks occur more often (i.e. between 112 and 379 per year). There are around 50 enterprise charges involving patents per year; see in this volume Koukal and Pullmannova (2019), Section 9, table 2.

[238]The reporters for Cyprus note that "guidelines issued by the Central Bank of Cyprus for banking institutions suggest that goodwill and other intangible assets must be valued at zero percent for the purpose of determining a loan amount"; see in this volume Argyropoulou et al. (2019), Section 9.

[239]Juutilainen (2019), Section 9, counts a total of only 131 security rights over national patents, 61 security rights over European patents, and 262 security rights over trademarks for the entire period of 1996–2019.

12 Reform and Harmonization Projects

12.1 *National Reform Proposals*

In Scotland, the Law Commission has proposed a new act on secured transactions over tangible and intangible property, which would move Scotland in the direction of a notice filing system.[240] In Taiwan, the government and industries have recognized the importance of enterprise charges in fostering security rights in IP and therefore aim to introduce the floating charge, following recommendations in the UNCITRAL texts.[241] However, generally speaking, security rights in IP rights do not seem to rank high on the political agenda for most countries.

12.2 *International Proposals*

As part of its project on secured transactions, UNCITRAL added a supplement on security rights in intellectual property to its Legislative Guide on Secured Transactions in 2010.[242] The Model Law on Secured Transactions, based on the Legislative Guide and adopted in 2016,[243] contains a limited number of asset-specific rules relating to intellectual property. These rules mainly try to address potential conflicts between the security rights in assets and the intellectual property rights linked to those assets. Thus, Article 17 provides that: "A security right in a tangible asset with respect to which intellectual property is used does not extend to the intellectual property and a security right in the intellectual property does not extend to the tangible asset." In the same vein, Article 34, para. 6 states that "subject to the rights of a secured creditor with a security right in intellectual property in accordance with article 50, the rights of a non-exclusive licensee of an intangible encumbered asset licensed in the ordinary course of the licensor's business are not affected by the security right, provided that, at the time of the conclusion of the licence agreement, the licensee does not have knowledge that the licence violates the rights of the secured creditor under the security agreement." Article 99, paragraph 1, which is part of the chapter on private international law, follows the traditional *lex protectionis* approach, and hence subjects the creation, effectiveness against third parties, and priority of a security right in intellectual property to the law of the state in which the intellectual property is protected. Nonetheless, paragraph 2 gives the parties the

---

[240]See https://www.scotlawcom.gov.uk/files/5514/9987/1139/Moveable_Transactions_Scotland_Bill_-_consultation_draft_-_bill_-__July_2017.pdf; see in this volume Masiyakurima (2019), Section 11.

[241]See in this volume Shieh and Lee (2019), Section 5.

[242]Available at http://www.uncitral.org/pdf/english/texts/security-lg/e/10-57126_Ebook_Suppl_SR_IP.pdf.

[243]See http://www.uncitral.org/uncitral/en/uncitral_texts/security/2016Model_secured.html.

ability to create a security right in intellectual property (also under the law of the state in which the grantor is located) and to make it effective under that law against third parties other than another secured creditor, a transferee, or a licensee. Paragraph 3 provides that the law applicable to the enforcement of a security right in intellectual property is the law of the state in which the grantor is located.

13 Some Tentative Conclusions

As already stated at the beginning of this chapter, there are a number of non-legal obstacles to the use of IP rights as collateral that cannot be alleviated through law reform, such as the potentially dramatic loss of value suffered by those rights upon the owner's insolvency; the difference in the life cycle of a typical bank loan and that of an IP right; and the lack of liquid markets in enforcement.

However, there are other, legal issues where law reform can lead to better access to credit based on IP rights as collateral. One example of such a reform involves better coordination between IP registries and the use of registration as a mode of perfection under secured transactions law (i.e. notice filing)—see the best practice example of Australia. Furthermore, it goes without saying that the prohibition of the transfer of certain IP rights such as copyright in German and Austrian law, which makes collateralization impossible, could be removed.[244] In fact, in many jurisdictions, copyright presents specific difficulties, especially when it is unregistered. For example, some jurisdictions deny the possibility to charge copyright if the security right cannot be entered in an IP registry. On the other hand, the existence of special enactments on charges over copyright in movies show that these difficulties, which are often of a purely technical nature, may be overcome.

Another important issue is the matter of enterprise charges or "all-asset" security rights: where they exist, IP rights can more easily be part of a larger transaction and thus add to the overall value of the collateral. One way to promote security in IP is to allow for the creation of a charge over all of the assets (or certain parts of them) of a company.[245]

On a more general note, the reports show that the lack of statutory law specifically directed toward the admissibility of security rights in IP and their creation, perfection, and priority is a major hindrance to the development of a financing practice that relies on IP rights as collateral. While courts around the world have managed to create case law on secured transactions with respect to movables and even receivables in the absence of comprehensive, unambiguous statutory law, this seems not to

[244]See also in this volume Juutilainen (2019), Section 4.3, on the problem that security rights in copyright should be registered from the perspective of secured transactions law, but cannot be registered due to the lack of a copyright registry.

[245]See in this volume Shieh and Lee (2019), Section 5, on a bill aiming to introduce the floating charge.

have happened in the field of IP rights. Given the existing non-legal risks highlighted at the beginning of this chapter, in practice, people seem unwilling to take the additional risk of legal uncertainty. This in turn prohibits the development of case law. Clear statutory law seems to be the only way to end this vicious circle.

Another point which is mentioned in several reports is the disproportionally high transaction costs, especially where notaries and several registries have to be involved. Small and medium-sized enterprises in particular are thus prevented from using IP as collateral.[246] It goes without saying that jurisdictions that require the creation of separate security interests for each and every asset instead of allowing an "all-asset" clause or an enterprise charge add considerably to these transaction costs.

The national segmentation of IP registration and secured transactions law presents yet another obstacle for companies that hold IP rights in various countries and/or seek to obtain financing internationally. As the Italian reporter notes, citing a speech made by WIPO's Director General F. Gurry[247]: "A way out has been proposed in the last decade: to set up a global digital register for all copyrighted works for which rightholders intend to have the full copyright protection. One of the goals of the global digital register would be to finally enable a registration of all transactions concerning copyrighted works, including securities, which would be conditional for the creation and perfection of the secured transaction. The technical feasibility of the project has been endorsed by the UN agency responsible for IP. The idea is finding support from research institutions operating in the field."[248] On this optimistic note, the general report comes to a close.

References

Argyropoulou V, Christoforou A, Synodinou T-E (2019) Security rights in intellectual property in Cyprus. In: Kieninger E-M (ed) Security rights in intellectual property. Springer, Heidelberg

Bornheim JJ (2019) Security rights in intellectual property in England and Wales. In: Kieninger E-M (ed) Security rights in intellectual property. Springer, Heidelberg

Brinkmann M, Rüther D, Scraback B (2019) Security rights in intellectual property in Germany. In: Kieninger E-M (ed) Security rights in intellectual property. Springer, Heidelberg

Bülow P (2017) Recht der Kreditsicherheiten, 9th edn. CF Müller, Heidelberg

Charpentier É (2019) Les sûretés sur la propriété intellectuelle au Québec (Canada). In: Kieninger E-M (ed) Security rights in intellectual property. Springer, Heidelberg

Dahan F, Simpson J (2004) The European bank for reconstruction and development's secured transactions project. In: Kieninger E-M (ed) Security rights in movable property in European private law. Cambridge University Press, Cambridge, pp 98–116

Decker M (2012) Geistiges Eigentum als Kreditsicherheit. Mohr Siebeck, Tübingen

[246] For example, see in this volume Murguía-Goebel (2019), Section 3.8.

[247] The Future of Copyright, Sydney, February 25, 2011, available at www.wipo.int/about-wipo/en/dgo/speeches/dg_blueskyconf_11.html (accessed June 27, 2019).

[248] Ricolfi (2019), Section 7.

Denoncourt J (2017) IP debt finance and SME's: revealing the evolving conceptual framework drawing on initiatives from around the world. In: Kono T (ed) Security interests in intellectual property. Springer, Singapore, pp 1–38
Dincă R, Rizoiu RA (2019) Security rights in intellectual property in Romania. In: Kieninger E-M (ed) Security rights in intellectual property. Springer, Heidelberg
Dirix E (2008) Remedies of secured creditors outside insolvency. In: Eidenmüller H, Kieninger E-M (eds) The future of secured transactions in Europe. De Gruyter, Berlin, pp 223–241
Dirix E (2015) Das neue belgische Gesetz zu den Mobiliarsicherheiten. Zeitschrift für Europäisches Privatrecht (ZEuP) 2015:273–287
Dorfmayr C (2019) Security rights in intellectual property in Austria. In: Kieninger E-M (ed) Security rights in intellectual property. Springer, Heidelberg
Fargeaud P (1963) Le gage sans dépossession comme instrument de crédit et le Marché Commun. Librairie du Journal des Notaires et des Avocats, Paris
Hara M, Haga Y (2019) Security rights in intellectual property in Japan. In: Kieninger E-M (ed) Security rights in intellectual property. Springer, Heidelberg
Heredia Cervantes I (2019) Security rights in intellectual property in Spain. In: Kieninger E-M (ed) Security rights in intellectual property. Springer, Heidelberg
Horn C, Grünwald A (2015) Gewerblicher Rechtsschutz II. Verlag Österreich, Vienna
Howell R (2019) Security rights in intellectual property in Canada (Common Law). In: Kieninger E-M (ed) Security rights in intellectual property. Springer, Heidelberg
Juutilainen T (2019) Security rights in intellectual property in Finland. In: Kieninger E-M (ed) Security rights in intellectual property. Springer, Heidelberg
Kallinikou D, Koriatopoulou P (2019) Security rights in intellectual property in Greece. In: Kieninger E-M (ed) Security rights in intellectual property. Springer, Heidelberg
Karjiker S (2019) Security rights in intellectual property in South Africa. In: Kieninger E-M (ed) Security rights in intellectual property. Springer, Heidelberg
Kieninger E-M (2008) Die Zukunft des deutschen und europäischen Mobiliarkreditsicherungsrechts. Archiv für civilistische Praxis (AcP) 208(2):182–226
Knopf H (2002) Security interests in intellectual property: an international comparative approach. In: Idem (ed) Security interests in intellectual property. Thomson/Carswell, Toronto, pp 1–93
Koukal P, Pullmannova H (2019) Security rights in intellectual property in the Czech Republic. In: Kieninger E-M (ed) Security rights in intellectual property. Springer, Heidelberg
Koziol G (2011) Lizenzen als Kreditsicherheiten, Zivilrechtliche Grundlagen in Deutschland, Österreich und Japan. Mohr Siebeck, Tübingen
Lahorgue S (2019) Security rights in intellectual property in Brazil. In: Kieninger E-M (ed) Security rights in intellectual property. Springer, Heidelberg
Leavy J (2007) France. In: Sigman HC, Kieninger E-M (eds) Cross-border security over tangibles. Selier European Law Publishers, Munich
Lepik G (2019) Security rights in intellectual property in Estonia. In: Kieninger E-M (ed) Security rights in intellectual property. Springer, Heidelberg
Macdonald R (2009) Transnational secured transactions reform: Book IX of the Draft Common Frame of Reference in Perspective. Zeitschrift für Europäisches Privatrecht (ZeuP):745–782
Masiyakurima P (2019) Security rights in intellectual property in Scotland. In: Kieninger E-M (ed) Security rights in intellectual property. Springer, Heidelberg
Matanovac Vučković R, Ernst H, Gliha I (2019) Security rights in intellectual property in Croatia. In: Kieninger E-M (ed) Security rights in intellectual property. Springer, Heidelberg
McCracken S (2019) Security rights in intellectual property in Australia. In: Kieninger E-M (ed) Security rights in intellectual property. Springer, Heidelberg
McGuire M-R (2008) Intellectual property rights: "property" or "right"? The application of the transfer rules to intellectual property. In: Faber W, Lurger B (eds) Rules for the transfer of movables: a candidate for European harmonisation or national reform? Sellier European Law Publishers, pp 217–237

Murguía-Goebel L (2019) Security rights in intellectual property in Mexico. In: Kieninger E-M (ed) Security rights in intellectual property. Springer, Heidelberg
Özsunay E, Özsunay MR (2019) Security rights in intellectual property in Turkey. In: Kieninger E-M (ed) Security rights in intellectual property. Springer, Heidelberg
Picht PG (2018) Vom materiellen Wert des Immateriellen – Immaterialgüterrechte als Kreditsicherungsmittel im nationalen und internationalen Rechtsverkehr. Mohr Siebeck, Tübingen
Ricolfi M (2019) Security rights in intellectual property in Italy. In: Kieninger E-M (ed) Security rights in intellectual property. Springer, Heidelberg
Séjean M, Binctin N (2019) Security rights in intellectual property in France. In: Kieninger E-M (ed) Security rights in intellectual property. Springer, Heidelberg
Shieh M-Y, Lee S-H (2019) Security rights in intellectual property in Taiwan, Republic of China. In: Kieninger E-M (ed) Security rights in intellectual property. Springer, Heidelberg
Storme ME, Malekzadem J (2019) Security rights in intellectual property in Belgium. In: Kieninger E-M (ed) Security rights in intellectual property. Springer, Heidelberg
Van Engelen TCJA (2019) Security rights in intellectual property in The Netherlands. In: Kieninger E-M (ed) Security rights in intellectual property. Springer, Heidelberg

Security Rights in Intellectual Property in Australia

Sheelagh McCracken

Abstract This Chapter explores how consensual security rights over intellectual property (IP) operate in Australia under the *Personal Property Securities Act 2009* (Cth) (PPSA). While outlining the various types of IP recognised in Australia, the Chapter focuses on copyright, patents and registered trade marks. As personal property within the scope of the *PPSA*, these are each available as collateral. Moreover, some dealings with them may also constitute security interests within the expanded statutory definition of that term, albeit lacking a security function. The Chapter examines how security arrangements over IP are typically structured in Australia as part of more general security interests over present and future acquired property and give rise to property and contractual rights for both the secured party and the grantor. It also analyses how a security interest must attach, be enforceable against third parties and perfected in order for the secured party to obtain optimal protection, while identifying the circumstances in which that secured party must nonetheless yield to third parties claiming a higher ranking priority or a right to take free of the security interest. Remedies available to the secured party in the event of a debtor's default are also briefly considered.

1 Introduction

On 30 January 2012 Australia transformed its historical common law regime governing secured transactions relating to personal property by implementing the *Personal Property Securities Act 2009* (Cth) (*PPSA*). This relatively new legal framework is intended to provide "more certain, consistent, simpler and cheaper

S. McCracken (✉)
University of Sydney Law School, Sydney, NSW, Australia
e-mail: Sheelagh.McCracken@sydney.edu.au

E.-M. Kieninger (ed.), *Security Rights in Intellectual Property*, Ius Comparatum – Global Studies in Comparative Law 45,
https://doi.org/10.1007/978-3-030-44191-3_2

arrangements for personal property securities for the benefit of all parties".[1] Although it is in part modelled on legislation developed in Canada and New Zealand (and hence may be said to be derived from Article 9 of the US *Uniform Commercial Code*), it has nonetheless been described judicially as[2]:

> ..ultimately something of an amalgam of the legislative experience in these jurisdictions rather than a direct transportation of any particular legislative regime into Australia.

This Chapter explores how security rights are taken over intellectual property in Australia under the *PPSA*.[3] After outlining in Sect. 2 the principal intellectual property rights recognised in Australia, the Chapter analyses in Sect. 3 the available categories of security rights. It then examines in Sect. 4 how security transactions are typically structured and analyses in Sect. 5 how the secured party may obtain the 'optimal' level of statutory protection,[4] enabling that secured party in due course to enforce its security rights—not only against the grantor but also third parties, such as other secured parties or persons seeking to buy or lease the collateral from the grantor. The priority position of the secured party vis-à-vis those third parties is assessed in Sect. 6, while the remedies available to the secured party on default by the debtor are considered in Sect. 7. Section 8 concludes.

2 Outline of Intellectual Property Rights

In Australia intellectual property rights cover a range of rights, most of which are created under statute rather than at common law. They may also be protected by statute, generally now under Commonwealth[5] legislation.[6]

---

[1]Replacement Explanatory Memorandum to the Personal Property Securities Bill 2009 (Cth), Outline.

[2]*Samwise Holdings Pty Ltd v Allied Distribution Finance Pty Ltd* [2018] SASCFC 95, [39]. A review commissioned by the Commonwealth Government pursuant to *PPSA* s 343 (the Whittaker Report) has identified the need for further reform before these goals are fully achieved: Commonwealth of Australia (2015), paras 1.1–1.7.

[3]The law is generally stated as at 14 September 2018, the date to which this Chapter is revised.

[4]*Hamersley Iron Pty Ltd v Forge Group Power Pty Ltd (in liq) (recs & mgrs apptd)* (2017) 52 WAR 90, [108].

[5]Australia is a federation of six states, with two federal territories. The power of the Commonwealth Government to legislate in respect of intellectual property arises from the *Commonwealth of Australia Constitution Act* s 51(xviii), which confers powers to make laws for the 'peace, order, and good government of the Commonwealth with respect to. . .copyrights, patents of inventions and designs, and trade marks;..'. Additional powers may be sought under the more general powers with respect to 'trade and commerce with other countries, and among the States' (s 51(i)) and 'external affairs' (s 51(xxix)).

[6]The author gratefully acknowledges the very helpful comments of Dr. Fady Aoun of the University of Sydney Law School on Sect. 2.

2.1 Categories

This Chapter focuses on the three most common and widely recognised forms of intellectual property—copyright, patents and registered trade marks.

While copyright arises automatically on the creation of the relevant work and is protected under the *Copyright Act 1968* (Cth) (*Copyright Act*), patents and registered trade marks are granted or created through registration, and that grant or creation, as well as their protection, are governed respectively by the *Patents Act 1990* (Cth) (*Patents Act*) and the *Trade Marks Act 1995* (Cth) (*Trade Marks Act*).

- *Copyright* is the exclusive right to do certain acts in relation to a work. Depending on the type of work, these may include acts to reproduce, publish, perform in public, communicate to the public, make an adaptation and enter into a commercial rental arrangement.[7] The work may be a literary, dramatic or musical work, or an artistic work or, under the latter arrangement, a computer program. Copyright also comprises exclusive rights with regard to sound recordings, films, television and sound broadcasts and published editions.[8] Depending on the medium, these may include rights to make a copy, cause the recording, film or broadcast to be seen or heard in public and communicate them to the public.
- A *patent* confers 'exclusive rights, during the term of the patent, to exploit the invention and to authorise another person to exploit the invention.'[9]
- A *trade mark* is 'a sign used, or intended to be used, to distinguish goods or services dealt with or provided in the course of trade by a person from goods or services so dealt with or provided by any other person.'[10] Once registered, it too confers exclusive rights, being (as of the date of registration)[11] rights to use the trade mark and authorise its use by others.[12] It also gives the right to obtain statutory relief in the event of infringement.

In addition to these rights are registered designs; circuit layouts and plant breeders' rights, which are respectively created and protected under the *Designs Act 2003* (Cth) (*Designs Act*), and protected under the *Circuit Layouts Act 1989* (Cth) (*Circuit Layouts Act*) and the *Plant Breeder's Rights Act 1994* (Cth) (*PBR Act*).

---

[7] *Copyright Act* s 31.

[8] *Copyright Act* ss 85–88.

[9] *Patents Act* s 13(1).

[10] *Trade Marks Act* s 17.

[11] Registration generally takes effect from the filing date for the application for registration: *Trade Marks Act* s 72.

[12] *Trade Marks Act* s 20.

- A *design* is defined by reference to a product, which is 'a thing that is manufactured or hand made'.[13] It is 'the overall appearance of the product resulting from one or more visual features of the product.'[14]
- A *circuit layout* is 'a representation, fixed in any material form, of the three-dimensional location of the active and passive elements and interconnections making up an integrated circuit.'[15]
- *Plant breeder's rights* are specified exclusive rights to do, or license others to do, specified acts with regard to propagating material of a particular plant variety.[16]

The phrase 'intellectual property' has no fixed legal meaning in Australia. It has been described in broad general terms as[17]:

> ...a generic term for the various rights or bundles of rights which the law accords for the protection of creative effort – or, more especially, for the protection of economic investment in creative effort.

Typically also discussed under this rubric are matters such as confidential information, particularly in the form of know-how and trade secrets, unregistered trademarks and technological developments such as domain names.

2.2 *Pre-Requisites*

Pre-requisites for existence vary according to the type of intellectual property. Copyright, which is not registrable, subsists from the creation of a work, while patents depend for their legal grant on registration. While a trade mark can exist prior to registration and may be protected under common law through, for example, an action in tort for passing off, registration is critical to obtaining exclusive statutory rights.

2.2.1 Existence

Under the *Copyright Act*[18] copyright subsists in an original literary, dramatic musical or artistic work by an author who is an Australian citizen or resident and where, in the case of a published work, it was first published in Australia.[19]

---

13 *Designs Act* ss 5–6.

14 *Designs Act* s 5.

15 *Circuit Layouts Act* s 5.

16 *PBR Act* s 11.

17 Stewart et al. (2018), [1.1].

18 *Copyright Act* s 8 makes clear that copyright subsists only under that legislation, subject to the prerogative rights of the Crown under s 8A.

19 *Copyright Act* s 32.

Generally, the author is the owner of the copyright,[20] although this may be qualified (subject to agreement) in relation to newspapers, periodicals, photographs, portraits or engravings and in circumstances where the work is made under a service contract.[21] Copyright typically lasts for 70 years from the end of the year of an author's death.[22]

Copyright also subsists in sound recordings and films where the maker is an Australian citizen or resident or a company incorporated under Australian legislation and the recordings and films are made or first published in Australia.[23] It subsists in broadcasts made in Australia, either under a statutory licence or by one of the two national broadcasters, the Australian Broadcasting Corporation (ABC) or the Special Broadcasting Service Corporation (SBS).[24] Generally, ownership of this copyright is in the maker[25] and typically lasts for 70 years from the end of the year of the first publication of the recording or film or for 50 years from the end of the year of the broadcast.[26]

2.2.2 Registration

A patent which confers the relevant exclusive rights is granted by the Commissioner of Patents by registering prescribed particulars in the Register of Patents.[27] The patent dates from the date of 'filing of the relevant complete specification' or a date otherwise determined under regulations.[28] The term is 20 years in the case of a standard patent and 8 years in the case of an innovation patent, with the possibility only of a limited extension in the case of standard patents relating to pharmaceutical substances.[29]

Although a trade mark may be registered or unregistered, the exclusive rights conferred by statute are only conferred on the registered owner of a registered trade mark.[30] Registration generally has effect from the 'filing date in respect of the

---

[20] *Copyright Act* s 35(2).

[21] *Copyright Act* s 35((3)–(6).

[22] *Copyright Act* s 33. In respect of certain works which have not been published, performed or broadcast before the author's death, time starts to run from the date of first publication, performance or broadcast.

[23] *Copyright Act* ss 89–90. It may subsist more generally in a recording or film by an Australian.

[24] *Copyright Act* s 91.

[25] *Copyright Act* ss 97–99. In the case of recordings and films made pursuant to an agreement for their making, ownership may be made subject to the agreement.

[26] *Copyright Act* ss 93–95.

[27] *Patents Act* s 61 (standard patent), s 62 (innovation patent).

[28] *Patents Act* s 65.

[29] *Patents Act* ss 67, 68, Part 3. See ss 7 and 18 for differences between a standard patent and an innovation patent, the latter involving an 'innovative' as distinct from 'inventive' step.

[30] *Trade Marks Act* s 20.

application for registration.'[31] It expires 10 years after that filing date, but may be renewed prior to the expiry.[32]

Both the patentee and the registered owner of the registered trade mark are said to deal with the patent and trade mark as absolute owner. Such dealings are generally subject only to rights appearing in the respective registers to be vested in another.[33] Excluded, however, from those rights affecting dealings is a recorded interest that is a security interest under the *PPSA*, described under both the *Patents Act* and the *Trade Marks Act* as a 'PPSA security interest'.[34]

Equities are enforceable against the patentee or registered owner (except to the 'prejudice of a purchaser in good faith for value'). They do not, however, include those that are PPSA security interests.[35]

2.3 Registration Systems

There are national registers for registration of patents and trade marks, which are prima facie evidence of registered particulars.[36] Registrations are primarily of ownership and are maintained by IP Australia, which is an Australian Government agency within the Department of Industry, Innovation and Science responsible for administering certain intellectual property rights and legislation including trade marks and patents.[37] The registers are:

- The Register of Trade Marks,[38] which shows particulars of trade marks. The trade mark is registered in the name of the person making the application and in respect of the goods and/or services specified.[39] Interests in, or rights over, registered trade marks including licences can be registered, on proof to the Registrar's reasonable satisfaction of the applicant's entitlement.[40]

[31] *Trade Marks Act* s 72, unless a registration application is also made in other countries prescribed by the regulations.

[32] *Trade Marks Act* ss 72(3), 75.

[33] *Patents Act* s 189; *Trade Marks Act* s 22. See Sect. 2.3 for a description of the registers.

[34] *Patents Act* s 189(2A), s 3 and Schedule 1; *Trade Marks Act* s 22(2A), s 6. PPSA security interest means a security interest within the *PPSA*, other than a transitional security interest which is essentially a security interest created before the commencement of the *PPSA* on 30 January 2012. See Sect. 3.2 for discussion of these security interests.

[35] *Patents Act* s 189(3), (4); *Trade Marks Act* s 22(3), (4).

[36] *Patents Act* s 195; *Trade Marks Act* s 210. This does not, however, apply to PPSA security interests: *Patents Act* s 195(3); *Trade Marks Act* s 210(4).

[37] See https://www.ipaustralia.gov.au/about-us.

[38] *Trade Marks Act* s 207.

[39] *Trade Marks Act* s 69.

[40] *Trade Marks Act* s 113.

- The Register of Patents,[41] which is a register of standard and innovation patents in force.[42] The patentee is the 'person for the time being entered in the Register as the grantee or proprietor of a patent.'[43] Registration particulars are set out in regulations and make provisions for licences to be registered.[44]

Copyright, by contrast, is not registrable. It is currently administered by the Department of Communications and the Arts.

3 Categories of Security Rights

3.1 Ability to Create a Consensual Security Right

A party with an interest in intellectual property may create a consensual security right, provided two criteria are satisfied. First, the particular intellectual property must be recognised under general law[45] as property. Second, the party seeking to create the security right must have the legal capacity to enter into the underlying contractual transaction and to deal with the property.

Property As a security right is itself a property interest, it presupposes the existence of property over which the security right may be taken. Copyright and registered trade marks, as well as the statutorily conferred exclusive rights to a patent, are all expressly declared by legislation to be personal property and each is expressly acknowledged as capable of assignment.[46] Interestingly, while applications for registration of a patent and trade mark are not considered property under general law, commentators nonetheless report a practice whereby secured parties are treating them as property and registering financing statements, with a view to protecting purported security rights over them.[47] Although it is sometimes difficult to determine under general law whether a licence amounts to property, the *PPSA* makes clear that certain types of licences, including an intellectual property licence

---

[41] *Patents Act* s 186.

[42] *Patents Act* s 187.

[43] *Patents Act* s 3, Schedule 1.

[44] Patents Regulations 1991, Regulation 19.1.

[45] The term 'general law' is used in this Chapter as a synonym for 'common law' in the sense of non-statutory law viz. common law and equity, as it is the term used by the *PPSA*, the primary statute regulating security interests over intellectual property: see Sect. 3.2. *PPSA* s 10 defines 'general law' as 'the principles and rules of the common law and equity'.

[46] *Copyright Act* s 196(1); *Patents Act* s 13(2); *Trade Marks Act* ss 21, 106. The latter statute also makes clear that a registered trade mark can be assigned without goodwill.

[47] Gunning et al. (2016), para 19.35. This practice appears to have developed as a result of applications being themselves allocated serial numbers for the purposes of registration under the *PPSA*, as discussed in Sect. 4.1. For discussion of financing statements, see Sect. 5.3.

as defined by the *PPSA*, may be personal property for the purposes of the *PPSA*.[48] Specific rights arising in the context of intellectual property, such as contractual rights arising under the licence and including debts, are also property at general law.

Legal Capacity Both an individual and a corporation are recognised under Australian law as having legal personality and hence potentially the legal capacity to enter into a transaction providing for a security right.[49] Individuals have capacity if they are over the age of 18 and of sound mind. Corporations typically encountered in the commercial sector are constituted under the *Corporations Act 2001* (Cth) (*Corporations Act*) and have the capacity of a natural person, which includes the power to enter into contracts.[50] Each may act through agents. Each may also hold property.

3.2 Types of Security Rights

The type of security rights available depends in the first instance on whether the particular property sought to be secured falls within the definition of 'personal property' under the *PPSA*. If it does so fall, a more extensive range of rights than under general law become available as 'security interests'.

Personal Property Copyright, patents and registered trade marks all fall within that statutory definition, being property that is neither land nor rights statutorily declared not to be personal property for the purposes of the *PPSA*.[51] Moreover, they are not removed from the legislative scope by *PPSA* s 8(1) which excludes certain property and certain interests in property.[52] Hence the taking of security over each of these three types of intellectual property is generally regulated by the *PPSA*. Other related rights are likely also to be personal property within the legislative scope; for example, contractual rights under a licence, including debts created by a licensee's obligation to make a payment such as a fee or a royalty. As foreshadowed in Sect. 3.1, a licence (including an intellectual property licence), is expressly stated to be personal property, provided that it is transferable by the licensee.[53]

The *PPSA* itself contains a definition of intellectual property, which is explored in more detail in Sect. 4.1. While generally the property discussed in this Chapter will fall within that specific definition, an asset beyond its scope would still potentially be

[48] *PPSA* s 10 'licence', 'intellectual property licence', 'personal property'. For conditions, see Sect. 3.2.

[49] See generally McCracken et al. (2017), Ch. 11, 'Capacity and Authority to Borrow and to Grant Security'.

[50] *Corporations Act* s 124.

[51] *PPSA* s 10 'personal property'.

[52] *PPSA* s 8.

[53] *PPSA* s 10 'personal property', 'licence'. The desirability of this limitation has been questioned by the Whittaker Report (at para 4.4.3).

regulated by the *PPSA* so long as it was within the definition of personal property. In other words, intellectual property as defined in the *PPSA* is simply a sub-category of intangible personal property and does not preclude other property from being intangible personal property.

Security Interests In addressing security rights, the *PPSA* adopts the generic term 'security interest'.[54] Under *PPSA* s 12 that term is used expansively to cover not only property interests which function as security,[55] but also certain additional property interests which lack such a function but are nonetheless encompassed within the scope of the definition for policy reasons.[56] Courts and commentators typically refer to these property interests as respectively an 'in substance security interest' and a 'deemed security interest'. The categories are, however, not mutually exclusive, as an interest which is a deemed security interest may have a security function.

3.2.1 Primary Definition of Security Interest

The primary definition of 'security interest' is set-out in *PPSA* s 12(1):

> …an interest in personal property provided for by a transaction that, in substance, secures payment or performance of an obligation (without regard to the form of the transaction or the identity of the person who has title to the property).

Hence any property interest having that function and arising out of a transaction[57] is classified as a security interest. It is an 'in substance security interest'.

PPSA s 12(2) offers examples of different types of transactions potentially falling within this definition of a security interest in s 12(1). Those most relevant[58] to intellectual property are a charge, a mortgage, a 'conditional sale agreement (including an agreement to sell subject to retention of title)' and an assignment.

These transactions differ in form under general law. Under the retention of title arrangement, title to the personal property does not pass until payment. Title is thus reserved, rather than granted. By contrast, a charge is typically understood in terms

---

[54]*PPSA* s 10 defines 'interest' to include 'a right in the personal property'. 'Security interest' is hereafter used in this Chapter to mean security rights.

[55]See Sect. 3.2.1.

[56]See Sect. 3.2.2.

[57]Although this term is not defined in the Dictionary in *PPSA* s 10, courts have interpreted it as signifying a consensual arrangement: see, for example, *Dura (Australia) Constructions Pty Ltd v Hue Boutique Living Pty Ltd* (2014) 49 VR 86.

[58]A pledge is not available as it requires possession and hence is restricted to property that has a physical manifestation: *Palgo Holdings Pty Ltd v Gowans* (2005) 221 CLR 249. A lease is not available as it is defined by reference to goods. Hire purchase is typically also understood as confined to goods. Some categories overlap. Section 12(2) refers, for example, to an assignment and a transfer of title.

of a grant of an interest and as meaning an appropriation of property for the satisfaction of an obligation,[59] while a mortgage is an assignment or transfer of title by way of security.[60] Although the mortgage and charge are interests recognised under general law as operating by way of security, their attributes are changed by the *PPSA*. Once they are determined to be security interests within the scope of the *PPSA*, they are each described and regulated for the most part simply as a 'security interest'.[61]

More problematic is the scope of an 'assignment' where that assignment is not a mortgage but rather an outright transfer subject to a reversionary interest. Commentators give the example of an assignment where title reverts on a failure by an assignee to pay royalties.[62] The view is expressed that what is sometimes termed an 'assignment back clause' is indeed a security interest where it is structured so as to secure an obligation.[63]

Section 12(2) is not an exclusive list of transactions amounting to a security interest under the *PPSA*. Other property interests which in a particular transaction perform a security function could fall within s 12(1), such as an equitable interest under a trust of the particular intellectual property. A licence, however, is not of itself a security interest.[64]

3.2.2 Expanded Definition of Security Interest

Of the three additional property interests recognised in *PPSA* s 12(3) as a 'security interest' despite their lack of a security function, one is relevant to the treatment of intellectual property; namely, the interest of a transferee—either under a transfer of chattel paper or under a transfer of an account.

[59] See, for example, *Beconwood Securities Pty Ltd v Australia and New Zealand Banking Group Ltd* (2008) 246 ALR 361. It is sometimes described as an equitable assignment, but the stronger view is that such a description is inaccurate: see, for example, Tolhurst (2016), para 3.17.

[60] *Palgo Holdings Pty Ltd v Gowans* (2005) 221 CLR 249; *Beconwood Securities Pty Ltd v Australia and New Zealand Banking Group Ltd* (2008) 246 ALR 361. The transfer may take place at law or in equity.

[61] Nonetheless, it is common practice to note the particular form of the interest in the charging clause. See, for example, *Hamersley Iron Pty Ltd v Forge Group Power Pty Ltd (in liq) (recs & mgrs apptd)* (2017) 52 WAR 90. This becomes important, for example, to enforcement of remedies conferred by the security agreement: see Sect. 7. Sometimes the *PPSA* itself draws distinctions: see generally Loxton (2012).

[62] Pemberton and Chatwood (2010), p. 194. See also Shtein and Wong (2015), p. 20 referring to an assignment of copyright to a software distributor on the basis that copyright reverts on breach of a distribution agreement. The interest of the assignor must amount under the particular arrangement to an interest in property.

[63] Swinson and Howley (2010), Ch. 4.9, para 150.

[64] *PPSA* s 12(5)(a).

Chattel paper The term 'chattel paper' includes[65]:

> ...one or more writings that evidence a monetary obligation and ... a security interest in specific intellectual property or a specific intellectual property licence.

Chattel paper is, however, an American concept introduced under Article 9 of the US *Uniform Commercial Code*[66] that was unknown to Australian law until the implementation of the *PPSA*. The Whittaker Report has recommended that it should be removed from the *PPSA*.[67]

Account An account is defined as a certain type of debt.[68] Relevantly for dealings with intellectual property, it includes:

> ...a monetary obligation...that arises from....disposing of property...by...licence...or granting a right, or providing services, in the ordinary course of a business of granting rights or providing services of that kind...

Hence a liability to make a royalty payment under the terms of a licence may be an account.

Transfer Although the meaning of the term 'transfer' within the *PPSA* is sometimes ambiguous,[69] it appears at least to refer to a transfer of title and hence would cover a sale of an account or chattel paper, with the relevant interest being that of ownership. The purchaser as transferee of the account or chattel paper is thus deemed to have a security interest.

3.2.3 Security Interests as Purchase Money Security Interests

Some security interests may be classified by the *PPSA* as a 'purchase money security interest' (PMSI). This is not a further type of security interest, but rather a label indicating that a security interest may be accorded what is often described as 'super-priority'.[70] Those interests of particular relevance to intellectual property are security interests which secure all or part of the purchase price and those which are taken by a financier ('a person who gives value') for the purpose of enabling the grantor to acquire rights where the value is actually applied for that purpose.[71] Colloquially referred to as a 'seller's PMSI' and a 'lender's PMSI', they are discussed in the context of the priority rules in Sect. 6.

---

[65]*PPSA* s 10.

[66]Gilmore (1965), pp. 378–379.

[67]Whittaker Report, para 4.3.3, Recommendation 15.

[68]*PPSA* s 10 'account'. See also *Hamersley Iron Pty Ltd v Forge Group Power Pty Ltd (in liq) (recs & mgrs apptd)* (2017) 52 WAR 90.

[69]Whittaker Report, para 7.1. See Whittaker (2013), and Loxton et al. (2018b).

[70]See Sect. 6.1.2.

[71]*PPSA* s 14(1), (2).

3.2.4 Conceptualisation of Security Interests

While *PPSA* ss 12(2) and 12(3) make clear that various property interests are created under the transactions and brought within the legislative scope as 'security interests', there is documented debate within Australia as to how those interests should be conceptualised.[72] This impacts directly on any response to the seemingly straightforward question of what security rights are available. If they are all conceptualised in the same way as, for example, a charge, the answer is one. If they are not so conceptualised, the answer is open-ended—namely, however many property interests are capable of performing a security function, together with those property interests specified in s 12(3).

The debate has to-date centred primarily on a transaction involving under general law a retention of title to goods by the secured party and the delivery of legal possession to the grantor. Conceptualising the interest of the secured party as a 'charge' requires the grantor to be treated as (or deemed to be) the owner of the goods and the secured party as (or deemed to be) a chargee. There is, however, no explicit statutory direction in the *PPSA* that title pass from the owner as secured party to the grantor, resulting in the secured party obtaining a mere encumbrance.

Dealings with intellectual property and related rights are affected by this debate. Conceptualisation of the statutory security interest as a charge leads some commentators to conclude by analogy that under title *transfer* arrangements such as a mortgage, for example, 'title to the collateral remains in the grantor—even if the security agreement is in the form of a mortgage.'[73]

4 Typical Structure of Transactions

Leading practitioners observe that it is 'rare' in Australia for a security interest to be taken over intellectual property alone rather than as part of a security interest over all present and future property.[74] As it is regular business practice to grant a security interest over all present and future property to banks (generally referred to as a General Security Agreement (GSA),[75] or an All PAP),[76] intellectual property is typically an inherent part of the personal property offered by way of security. The same commentators have emphasised that, in the absence of intellectual property as

[72]Whittaker Report, para 5.1.2; Annexure C, 2d. In response, see Loxton et al. (2018a, b, c).

[73]Duggan and Brown (2016), paras 3.3, 3.4.

[74]Gunning et al. (2016), para 19.55.

[75]This adopts Canadian and New Zealand usage under equivalent legislation.

[76]This is an Australian term referring to all present and after-acquired property and arising from terminology used in the registration process.

part of the collateral, a security interest over business assets may prove worthless due to difficulties in the business operating without access to those rights.[77]

Nonetheless, where the particular intellectual property or licence is of high-value or is the principal asset of the grantor, a security interest is likely to be taken over it directly under what is sometimes termed a Specific Security Agreement (SSA). The general law terminology of mortgage or charge may also still be found, although the secured party's interest is nonetheless a 'security interest' by reason of the definition of 'security interest' in *PPSA* s 12.[78]

A security interest may be structured in conjunction with a security interest over goods. In those circumstances, the *PPSA* applies to the intellectual property rights (including rights exercisable under an intellectual property licence) as it applies to the goods, if the exercise of the rights relating to the goods 'necessarily involves an exercise of the intellectual property rights'[79] and a security interest over the intellectual property rights has also been taken.[80]

Outright transfers of chattel paper or accounts are typically structured as sales.

4.1 Type of Collateral

The collateral may typically take one or more of several forms of personal property[81]:

- the intellectual property, being the copyright, the registered trade mark or the exclusive rights to the patent;
- an intellectual property licence, defined as 'an authority or licence (within the ordinary meaning of that term) to exercise rights comprising intellectual property';[82]
- royalties payable under an intellectual property licence[83];
- other specific contractual rights arising under such a licence, whether in favour of the licensor or licensee.

---

[77]Gunning et al. (2016), para 19.55.

[78]See Sect. 3.2.1.

[79]*PPSA* s 105(1).

[80]The Whittaker Report points out that illustrations provided in the Replacement Explanatory Memorandum to the Personal Property Securities Bill 2009 overlook the requirement in *PPSA* s 105(1)(b) for a security interest over the intellectual property rights: Whittaker Report, para 9.3.4.3.1.

[81]See Sect. 3.1 regarding a practice of taking security interests over applications for registration.

[82]*PPSA* s 10 'intellectual property licence'.

[83]Under the *Resale Royalty Right for Visual Artists Act 2009* (Cth), an artist may have a 'right to receive resale royalty on the commercial resale of an artwork: ss 6, 12. Such a resale royalty right cannot be used as collateral as it is made inalienable: s 33.

Classification of personal property within the *PPSA* is important, as different rules may apply according to the classification. As noted at Sect. 3.1, the intellectual property itself and the intellectual property licence are examples of intangible property. Intangible property is a residual category of personal property under the *PPSA*, being personal property that is not goods, financial property or an intermediated security.[84]

The classification becomes complex as the *PPSA* contains a definition of 'intellectual property', which is a sub-category of intangible property and to which it applies special rules.[85] The reason for this further statutory definition is unclear. The Whittaker Report has recommended that it be removed from the *PPSA*, so that the legislation can 'keep pace with the general law meaning, as it might develop over time.'[86]

The definition as it currently stands includes copyright, trade marks and patents, albeit expressed in somewhat different terms:

> . . .
>
> (b) the right to exploit or work an invention, or to authorise another person to exploit or work an invention, for which a patent is in effect under the *Patents Act 1990*;
>
> (c) the rights held by a person who is the registered owner of a trade mark that is registered under the *Trade Marks Act 1995*;
>
> . . .
>
> (f) the right under the *Copyright Act 1968* to do an act comprised in the copyright in a literary, dramatic, musical or artistic work or a published edition of such a work, or in a sound recording, cinematograph film, television broadcast or sound broadcast...

The definition also includes more broadly:

> (g) a right under or for the purposes of a law of a foreign country that corresponds to a right mentioned [above]

as well as:

> the right to be a party to proceedings in relation to such [rights].[87]

Other *PPSA* classifications of collateral are also important, not only once again for the application of particular rules but also for the completion of the electronic financing statement which is required for an 'effective registration' and hence

[84] *PPSA* s 10 'intangible property'.

[85] See, for example, *PPSA* ss 105, 106. The fact that property regarded as intellectual property under general law falls outside this definition does not preclude that property from being the object of a security interest. A security interest is taken over personal property and personal property includes not only that intellectual property but other property falling outside that definition. It would be classified simply as 'intangible property'. See generally Sect. 3.2.

[86] Whittaker Report, para 9.3.4.2, Recommendation 377.

[87] The Whittaker Report has recommended deletion of this right in the absence of any 'cogent explanation' for it: para 9.3.4.2.2, Recommendation 379. It would not, however, typically be assignable under general law.

perfection of a security interest.[88] Examples of particular relevance to intellectual property are 'serial numbered property'; 'consumer or commercial property'; 'inventory'; and 'proceeds'.

Serial numbered property is property bearing a 'serial number by which the regulations require, or permit, the collateral to be described in a registration.'[89] The relevant regulations are the Personal Property Securities Regulations 2010. Serial numbered property includes patents and trade marks and licences over each.[90]

Consumer property is personal property held by an individual 'other than. . . .held in the course or furtherance, to any degree, of carrying on an enterprise to which an ABN has been allocated'.[91] All other personal property is commercial property.[92] Leading Australian practitioners note that 'most intellectual property' granted in Australia would be commercial property.[93] It is possible for it to be 'inventory' in specified circumstances,[94] in particular when 'in the course or furtherance. . . of an enterprise to which an ABN has been allocated. . .[it] is held. . . for sale. . . or. . . to be provided under a contract for services. . .'.

Proceeds Identifying property as 'proceeds' is critical, given that a security interest attaches to proceeds automatically on a dealing with the collateral giving rise to proceeds, unless there is contrary provision in the security agreement.[95] Proceeds generally refers to 'identifiable or traceable personal property' derived from a direct or indirect dealing with the collateral (or collateral proceeds), provided that the grantor has an interest in them (or the power to transfer rights in them to the secured party).[96] More specifically, where the collateral is intellectual property or an intellectual property licence, 'proceeds' expressly additionally includes[97] a licensor's right 'to receive payments under any licence agreement in relation to the collateral'. Of course, a security interest over all present and future property catches property that would be proceeds as future property and thus as original collateral.

---

[88] See Sect. 5.3.

[89] *PPSA* s 10 'serial number'.

[90] See Personal Property Securities Regulations 2010 ('PPS Regulations'), Schedule 1, Part 2, 2.2. In a financing statement, they must be described by serial number when they are consumer property and may be so described when they are commercial property. See PPS Regulations [2.2(3)] for how they are described—for a patent or a trade mark, it is essentially the patent or trade mark number issued by IP Australia or if there is no number, the application number issued by IP Australia. In the case of a patent, a PCT number is used where neither of the numbers have been issued. PCT number is defined in (4) to indicate a certain international application number or in its absence, a specified international publication number.

[91] *PPSA* s 10. ABN is an abbreviation for Australian Business Number, which is a number identifying a business and is obtained through registration on the Australian Business Register.

[92] *PPSA* s 10.

[93] Gunning et al. (2016), para 19.20.

[94] *PPSA* s 10.

[95] *PPSA* s 32(1)(b).

[96] *PPSA* s 31(1), (1)(a), (3).

[97] *PPSA* s 31(1)(d).

4.2 Parties

The person who has a security interest is generally termed under general law a secured creditor, with the person granting the security interest being typically described as a debtor or a borrower. In relation to transactions such as mortgage and charge the relevant terms are mortgagee and mortgagor; chargee and chargor. Under a retention of title arrangement by way of sale the parties are the vendor and the purchaser.

Under the *PPSA*, and seemingly on account of the range of transactions brought within the legislation, the terms used are rather the 'secured party' and the 'grantor', the latter being defined generally as the 'person who has the interest in the personal property to which a security interest is attached'.[98] The Australian legislation differentiates between the grantor and the debtor, with the grantor not necessarily a debtor.

4.3 Extent of Rights

Under the transaction, both secured parties and grantors have property rights, as regulated under the *PPSA*. They also have contractual rights arising out of their security agreement, some of which may be circumscribed by the *PPSA*.

4.3.1 Property Rights: Secured Party

The secured party has, or obtains, an interest in the personal property. Examples of differing bundles of rights under varying transactions are found in *PPSA* s 12(2), although not all arise in the context of intellectual property and related rights. Such collateral has no physical manifestation and can thus, for example, not be made the object of a pledge.[99] Section 12(2) envisages the secured party's interest as either title (whether transferred or retained) or a lesser bundle of rights, such as a charge.

Australian courts have yet to conceptualise the secured party's interest in the context of intellectual property transactions. As noted at Sect. 3.2.4, arguments based on similar legislation in other jurisdictions, in particular the common law provinces of Canada and New Zealand, suggest that a security interest arising under PPS-style legislation may be conceptualised as a charge, even in circumstances where the secured party retains title under the transaction. Although there is no explicit direction to that effect in the *PPSA*, that treatment has been recognised

[98] *PPSA* s 10.

[99] See Sect. 3.2.1.

judicially in Australia in the context of a lease of goods where the lessee was regarded as the owner,[100] but the outcome remains the object of debate.[101]

Also open to debate, and linked to the conceptualisation discussion, is the role of *PPSA* s 112, which purports to limit the enforcement of a secured party's rights and remedies by reference to the grantor's own ability to deal. This is discussed in the context of remedies in Sect. 7.

Seemingly less controversial, however, is the categorisation of the secured party's interest as a legal interest by reason of its statutory attributes, although Australian courts have yet to pronounce on this.[102] What they have recognised is that the interest is a fixed interest attaching to property on satisfaction of the criteria for attachment set out in *PPSA* s 19(2).[103]

A secured party may find the scope of its security interest curtailed in certain circumstances. For example,

- a secured party obtaining a security interest through a transfer of an account or chattel paper takes subject to certain rights of the account debtor whether arising under the underlying contract or through other equities, such as set-off[104];
- a secured party enforcing remedies under *PPSA* Chapter 4 may (as noted above) find its powers limited by reference to the grantor's own ability to deal by operation of *PPSA* s 112, although the scope of this provision is unclear and is discussed in the context of remedies in Sect. 7;
- where the collateral is a licence granted by the owner of copyright, successors in title to the grantor—such as a secured party—are bound to the same extent as the grantor under *Copyright Act* s 196(4);
- in the event of intellectual property being transferred after the grant of a security interest in a licence of that intellectual property in circumstances in which the licensee continues to hold the licence, then the security agreement providing for that security interest binds every successor in title to the licensor—such as a secured party—to the same extent as it was binding on the licensor under *PPSA* s 106.[105]

---

[100] *Re Maiden Civil (P&E) Pty Ltd; Albarran v Queensland Excavation Services Pty Ltd* (2013) 277 FLR 337, although the proposition was made obiter. See generally Sect. 3.2.4.

[101] See Loxton et al. (2018a, b, c).

[102] This categorisation has been accepted in relation to equivalent legislation in Canada: see, for example, *Bank of Montreal v Innovation Credit Union* [2010] 3 SCR 3, [42].

[103] *Hamersley Iron Pty Ltd v Forge Group Power Pty Ltd (in liq) (recs & mgrs apptd)* (2017) 52 WAR 90. This applies even where the security interest is expressly described as a 'floating charge'. For attachment criteria, see Sect. 5.1.

[104] *PPSA* s 80. *Hamersley Iron Pty Ltd v Forge Group Power Pty Ltd (in liq) (recs & mgrs apptd)* (2017) 52 WAR 90.

[105] The Whittaker Report noted, and agreed with, opinions that this section was 'unlikely to be engaged', given that a licensor is not generally bound by a security interest granted by a licensee. It recommended its removal from the legislation unless good reasons for its retention could be advanced: Whittaker Report, para 9.3.4.4, Recommendation 381.

4.3.2 Property Rights: Grantor

The grantor may have ownership of the intellectual property or of rights under the licence, whether as licensor or licensee. It may have a lesser interest such as an equitable interest, if for example the grantor is the beneficiary under a trust. Where the grantor's rights are less than ownership, this raises the question, discussed in Sect. 5.1, whether those rights are sufficient to enable the security interest to attach to the particular personal property or only to the lesser rights in the property.

4.3.3 Contractual Rights: Secured Party and Grantor

Contractual rights exist under the 'security agreement' entered into by the parties. The agreement may[106] provide for security interests in after acquired property and for future advances. It is acknowledged by *PPSA* s 18 as 'effective according to its terms'. The *PPSA* thus generally recognises parties' autonomy, although there are some qualifications.[107]

The security agreement may provide a licence to deal. It may also contain[108] rights and remedies to be exercisable in the event of default either in addition to or, less likely, in substitution for the statutory remedies of disposal and retention set-out in *PPSA* Chapter 4.

The parties may provide in the security agreement for a prohibition on transfer of the collateral or for a declaration of a transfer as a default. However, the *PPSA* enables the collateral to be transferred by consent between the grantor and the transferee or by operation of law.[109]

4.4 Mechanisms to Evaluate Intellectual Property as Security

The extent to which the ability to grant a security interest over the intellectual property facilitates access to credit depends on an assessment of the value of the intellectual property.

Leading practitioners, pointing to difficulties inherent in valuing intellectual property given in particular the lack of a standard market, observe[110]:

> There are differing valuation methods for intellectual property, that can produce vastly different valuations.

---

[106]*PPSA* s 18(2), (4) respectively. 'Security agreement' is defined generally as 'an agreement or act by which a security interest is created, arises or is provided for': *PPSA* s 10.

[107]*PPSA* s 257.

[108]*PPSA* s 110. See Sect. 7.

[109]*PPSA* s 79.

[110]Gunning et al. (2016), para 19.40.

IP Australia[111] lists a range of common valuation methods, including 'relief from royalties; excess profits or notional maximum royalties payable; capitalisation of earnings; net present value of incremental cash flows; gross profit differential; premium sales price; comparable market transactions; cost-based; brand strength; real options'.[112] IP Australia also points to various accounting standards,[113] noting the current absence of a single comprehensive standard devoted to intellectual property.

It is also difficult to estimate the costs involved in creating or enforcing security rights over the intellectual property as they depend on a range of factors which vary according to the complexity of the particular transaction and the extent to which legal and other professional advice is sought.

5 Steps for Making Security Rights Effective

The *PPSA* draws on three distinct concepts for determining the effectiveness of a security interest: 'attachment', 'enforceability against third parties' and 'perfection'. Attachment makes the security interest enforceable against the grantor,[114] while enforceability against third parties, as the name suggests, makes it enforceable against persons other than the grantor.[115] Both attachment and enforceability against third parties are generally pre-requisites to perfection.[116]

Perfection has been judicially described as offering the 'optimal protection' under the *PPSA*.[117] Failure to perfect renders the secured party vulnerable in a priority dispute with another secured party[118]; subject to a buyer taking free of the security interest,[119] and most significantly, susceptible to losing the security interest on an insolvency event such as the bankruptcy of an individual grantor or the administration or liquidation of a corporate grantor.[120]

Perfection thus enhances the secured party's status as against third parties. It is critical nonetheless to appreciate that pre-insolvency lack of perfection does not

[111]See Sect. 2.3.

[112]IP Australia, 'Auditing your IP', available at www.ipaustralia.gov.au.

[113]IP Australia, 'Auditing your IP', available at www.ipaustralia.gov.au. It identifies 'AASB 138: Intangible Assets; AASB136: Impairment of Assets; Accounting Interpretation 132: Intangible Assets website costs'.

[114]*PPSA* s 19.

[115]*PPSA* s 20.

[116]*PPSA* s 21(1)(b). See *PPSA* s 21(1)(a) for confirmation that perfection can occur automatically by legislative force in various provisions, either absolutely or for a temporary period.

[117]*Hamersley Iron Pty Ltd v Forge Group Power Pty Ltd (in liq) (recs & mgrs apptd)* (2017) 52 WAR 90, [108].

[118]*PPSA* Part 2.6. See Sect. 6.

[119]*PPSA* Part 2.5. See Sect. 6.

[120]*PPSA* s 267, subject to s 268.

preclude the security interest from being enforceable as against the grantor and third parties. Perfection is also clearly relevant to the relationship between the secured party and the grantor. The vesting of the unperfected security interest in the grantor on a relevant insolvency event dramatically alters that relationship, rendering the previously secured party an unsecured creditor.

5.1 Attachment

A security interest attaches to the collateral and becomes enforceable by the secured party against the grantor on satisfaction of the two criteria set out in *PPSA* s 19(2). Each criterion for attachment is set out in the alternative. Neither require writing,[121] making it possible for a security interest under an oral agreement to be enforceable against the grantor.

The more straightforward requirement is that value must be given by the secured party or the grantor must do an act by which the security interest arises. Value is defined to include not only consideration sufficient to support a contract, but also an antecedent debt or liability.[122] A typical example of where a secured party gives value is where it makes a loan, while a relevant act by the grantor would include execution of a security agreement.

The other requirement is that the grantor must have 'rights in the collateral' or 'the power to transfer rights in the collateral to the secured party'.[123] While rights obviously include ownership of the collateral, it is not clear what lesser rights other than possession might be sufficient for the security interest to attach to the whole of the collateral (as distinct from simply to the lesser rights themselves). Where the rights amount to legal possession of the goods, the *PPSA* provides in some circumstances for that possession to be sufficient to enable the security interest to attach to the goods.[124] The strict wording of s 19(2) enables an argument to be developed that a lesser interest in particular property might also be sufficient to enable that security interest to attach to the whole of that property, but that remains to be explored by the courts.[125]

---

[121]One court has suggested obiter a further implied requirement; namely that there should be a security agreement: *Dura (Australia) Constructions Pty Ltd (in liq) v Hue Boutique Living Pty Ltd* (2014) 292 FLR 114.This is clearly not required by the actual wording. The fact that the term 'transaction' in s 12(1) requires an agreement between the parties may be sufficient: see Whittaker Report, para 5.1.4.

[122]*PPSA* s 10.

[123]*PPSA* s 19(2)(a).

[124]*PPSA* s 19(5).

[125]Loxton et al. (2018a).

The fact that a security interest attaches on the occurrence of these two events means that the security interest is a fixed interest.[126] While it is possible to provide in the security agreement for attachment to be deferred to a later time, this does not preclude the security from being a fixed interest. Such drafting does not make the security interest operate as a floating charge.

As noted in Sect. 4.1 a security interest is expressed in *PPSA* s 32 to attach automatically to proceeds on a dealing with the collateral giving rise to proceeds, in the absence of contrary agreement.

In the context of intellectual property, a further issue may arise by reason of the requirements in Commonwealth intellectual property legislation for certain formalities for assignments of the property. An assignment may be expressed to be ineffective where it is not done in writing and signed, either by the assignor alone, or by both assignor and assignee. The *Copyright Act*, for example, provides[127]:

> An assignment of copyright (whether total or partial) does not have effect unless it is in writing signed by or on behalf of the assignor.

The *Patents Act* requires writing and a signature by (or on behalf of) both the assignor and assignee.[128]

These provisions are problematic where the security interest has been created through a transfer of title to the copyright or patent rights. If the grantor purports to grant a security interest by way of transfer of title, does a failure to comply with these legislative requirements preclude the transfer from being effective as a security interest?

The point of intersection between the *PPSA* and other federal and state statutes is an area of some uncertainty. Section 254 confirms that the *PPSA* is not an exhaustive code and that both general law and statutes may operate concurrently with the *PPSA* to the extent that they are capable of so doing. Determining their capability can, however, prove difficult. While the *PPSA* does contain some provisions relating to the resolution of inconsistencies, its treatment is not comprehensive. No express statutory direction is given on this particular issue. Nonetheless, in circumstances where the assignment forms the security agreement,[129] s 257 (in conjunction with s 18) suggests compliance with the formalities in the *Copyright Act* and the *Patents*

[126] *Hamersley Iron Pty Ltd v Forge Group Power Pty Ltd (in liq) (recs & mgrs apptd)* (2017) 52 WAR 90.

[127] *Copyright Act* s 196(3).

[128] *Patents Act* s 14(1). Cf. *Trade Marks Act* s 109 which rather requires an assignment of a registered trade mark to be recorded on the register.

[129] 'Security agreement' includes 'an act by which a security interest is created, arises or is provided for': *PPSA* s 10.

Act is required by making the security agreement subject to the operation of Commonwealth statutes. The point has not yet been explored by the courts. Nor is there any mention in the Whittaker Report.[130]

5.2 Enforceability against Third Parties

While the *PPSA* does not define third parties for the purposes of making the security interest enforceable against third parties under *PPSA* s 20, those likely to be considered within this category are those with a competing claim such as other secured parties and those buying or leasing the property from the grantor who are seeking to acquire the property free of an existing security interest. Also included are unsecured creditors.

Insolvency officials fall within the scope of third parties where they are, for example, a trustee in bankruptcy appointed on the bankruptcy of an individual under the *Bankruptcy Act 1966* (Cth). On bankruptcy, the general property of the bankrupt vests in the trustee.[131] By contrast, on liquidation of a corporation under the *Corporations Act*,[132] a liquidator only assumes custody and control of the property. Hence the liquidator is not distinct from an insolvent corporate grantor and is unlikely to be a third party for the purposes of the *PPSA*.

For a security interest over intellectual property or an intellectual property licence, royalties, other rights, or goods to be enforceable against third parties, there must be a security agreement with the appropriate coverage.[133] This means that the security agreement, defined[134] as including 'an agreement... by which a security interest is created, arises or is provided for', has to be evidenced in writing that is either signed by the grantor or adopted or accepted by an act (or omission) of a grantor which reasonably appears to demonstrate the grantor's intention to so adopt or accept.[135] Writing includes electronic recording and can be constituted by more

[130] *PPSA* s 258 does not appear to apply. Canadian commentators suggest avoiding equivalent conflict under Canadian legislation by recharacterising the security interest as a charge: Cuming et al. (2012), p. 715. However, as noted in Sects. 3.2.4 and 4.3.1, recharacterisation in Australia remains a matter of some debate.

[131] *Bankruptcy Act 1966* (Cth) s 58.

[132] *Corporations Act* s 474.

[133] *PPSA* s 20(1)(b)(iii). Alternative means of possession and control are generally not available in the context of intellectual property or related rights as they are not susceptible to possession or control. Possession generally requires the collateral to have a physical manifestation, in the absence of statutory direction: *Knauf Plasterboard Pty Ltd v Plasterboard West Pty Ltd (in liq) (recs & mgrs apptd)* (2017) 254 FCR 559 (but see PPSA s 24(5) for possession of electronic chattel paper). Control is only available with respect to very limited forms of collateral: *PPSA* s 21(2)(c).

[134] *PPSA* s 10.

[135] *PPSA* s 20(2)(a). See *Citadel Financial Corporation Pty Ltd v Elite Highrise Services Pty Ltd (No 3)* [2014] NSWSC 1926.

than one document.[136] There must also generally be an adequate description of the property, unless that property is proceeds.[137]

Where the security interest in the intellectual property rights is accompanied by a security interest in goods perfected by registration and the exercise of the secured party's rights 'necessarily involves an exercise of the intellectual property rights', the description of the goods in the security agreement or in the registered description of the goods (or indeed under a notice issued under the *PPSA*) is taken under *PPSA* s 105 for the purposes of the *PPSA* to include a description of the intellectual property rights or of an intellectual property licence which is required in order to exercise those rights. The Whittaker Report describes this provision as 'a source of confusion and uncertainty' and recommends its deletion.[138]

5.3 Perfection

The status of perfection is generally achieved through the taking of a perfecting step under *PPSA* s 21. Perfection can however be achieved automatically 'by force of the Act'. In the context of intellectual property and related rights, this is most likely to arise in the context of perfecting security interests over proceeds.[139]

Where a security interest is both attached and enforceable against third parties in compliance with *PPSA* ss 19, 20, perfection with respect to intellectual property is typically achieved through a secured party making an effective registration on the Personal Property Securities Register ('PPSR').[140] A single registration can perfect more than one security interest.[141] Registration may be made prior to the attachment

[136] *PPSA* s 10 'writing'. *Carrafa, Goutzos & Lofthouse (liq of Relux Commercial Pty Ltd) (in liq) v Doka Formwork Pty Ltd* [2014] VSC 570.

[137] *PPSA* s 20(6).

[138] Whittaker Report, para 9.3.4.3, Recommendation 380. It views it as inconsistent with Recommendation 243 of the *UNCITRAL Legislative Guide on Secured Transactions, Supplement on Security Rights in Intellectual Property* (2011), which advises that security rights in tangible assets should not extend to the intellectual property and vice versa. *PPSA* s 105 does however contemplate security interests over both the goods and the intellectual property.

[139] *PPSA* s 33(1)(a) perfects a security interest in proceeds if the security interest in the original collateral is perfected by a registration that describes the proceeds in accordance with the regulations.

[140] *PPSA* s 21(1)(b), s 21(2)(a). Once again, the alternative methods of taking possession and control are not available, as intellectual property is generally not capable of possession or control (subject to PPSA s 24(5) regarding possession of electronic chattel paper).

[141] *PPSA* s 21(4).

of the security interest to the collateral,[142] although a person must have reasonable grounds to believe that they are (or will become) a secured party.[143]

Effective registration requires completion of an electronic financing statement containing prescribed data.[144] At this stage the classification of collateral as consumer or commercial and serial numbered (discussed in Sect. 4.1) becomes important. To the extent that the intellectual property is classified as commercial rather than consumer property, the secured party has the option to include the serial numbers of trade marks and patents (and licences). Clearly, if the intellectual property is the primary form of collateral in a particular transaction, the secured party will do so as failure to take such action leaves the secured party vulnerable to a claim by a buyer to take free of its security interest under *PPSA* s 44.[145] If however the intellectual property is simply part of an overall security package and represents only some of the assets under a GSA, then a secured party deciding whether to register the serial numbers will typically assess the risk of buyers taking free against the value and significance of those particular assets.

Defects in a financing statement can lead to the loss of perfection where they are 'seriously misleading' or there is otherwise a particular defect said to make registration ineffective, such as the grantor's details being incorrect and hence precluding a search from disclosing the registration.[146] Where the collateral is required by the regulations to be described as consumer property, it must be described by the serial number. This covers patents and trademarks (and licences over them).[147]

Where the grantor is a company and subject to regulation by the *Corporations Act*, there is a time limit within which registration should be made; essentially 20 business days after the security agreement comes into force.[148]

Standard fees for registering a financing statement on the PPS Register are prescribed. As at the date of writing, the fees are as follows[149]:

---

[142] *PPSA* s 21(3).

[143] *PPSA* s 151. There is a civil penalty if this requirement is breached.

[144] *PPSA* s 153.

[145] See Sect. 6.2.

[146] *PPSA* ss 164, 165. The example of the error in the grantor's details assumes the collateral is not required to be described by serial number e.g. commercial property. See generally *Re OneSteel Manufacturing Pty Ltd (admins apptd)* (2017) 93 NSWLR 611.

[147] PPS Regulations, Schedule 1, Part 2 [2.2]. See Sect. 4.1 for discussion of 'consumer property'.

[148] *Corporations Act* s 588FL, subject to s 588FN. *Re Accolade Wines Australia Ltd* [2016] NSWSC 1023. See also *Re Carpenter International Pty Ltd* (2016) 307 FLR 37. Failure to comply may lead to the security interest vesting in the company if the company becomes insolvent within 6 months of the date of registration. The Whittaker Report has recommended that s 588FL be repealed: Recommendation 362.

[149] See https://www.ppsr.gov.au/fees. There are additional fees for amending a financing statement. It is not possible to estimate the costs involved in creating or enforcing security rights as they depend on a range of factors which vary according to the complexity of the particular transaction and the extent to which legal and other professional advice is sought.

- $6.80 where the duration is 7 years or less;
- $34 where the duration is more than 7 years but less than or equal to 25 years;
- $119 where the financing statement has no stated end time.

5.4 Registration in an Intellectual Property Register?

While both the *Patents Act* and the *Trade Marks Act* provide primarily for a register of owners,[150] each permit other interests to be registered.

In the case of trade marks, registration may be as an assignee or person to whom the trade mark has been transmitted[151] or as a person who has applied to the Registrar for the recording of interests in or rights to registered trade marks.[152] (That record is neither proof nor evidence of the person's entitlement to the interest or right.)[153] For patents, details of the particulars on the Register are prescribed by the regulations.[154] Patents Regulations 1991, Regulation 19.1 includes particulars of 'an entitlement as mortgagee, licensee or otherwise to an interest in a patent' as well as a 'transfer of an entitlement to a patent or licence, or to a share in a patent or licence.'[155]

Hence it is possible for security interests in both patents and trade marks to be registered. Nonetheless, both the *Patents Act* and the *Trade Marks Act* expressly state that the recording in the relevant register of a PPSA security interest does not affect a dealing with the patent or registered trade mark.[156] They also make clear that the registers do not provide prima facie evidence of security interests.[157] These provisions reflect a legislative intention that the *PPSA* is the sole governing legislation for security interests and, in particular, for resolving priority disputes.[158]

Nonetheless, value is perceived in enabling registration for other purposes. The Commonwealth Government has pointed, for example, to enabling secured parties 'to receive notifications, [be] given an opportunity to be heard, or [be] given the opportunity to make submissions under sections 84(2), 84A(4), 84A(5) and 111 of the Trade Marks Act.'[159] With respect to patents, commentators point to the benefit

---

[150] See Sect. 2.3.

[151] *Trade Marks Act* s 109.

[152] *Trade Marks Act* Part 11, s 113. See Davison et al. (2016), para 4.19.

[153] *Trade Marks Act* s 116.

[154] *Patents Act* s 187.

[155] Patents Regulations 1991, Regulation 19.1(2) requires proof of entitlement to the 'reasonable satisfaction of the Commissioner'.

[156] *Patents Act* s 189(2A); *Trade Marks Act* s 22(2A). See Sect. 2.2.2.

[157] *Patents Act* s195; *Trade Marks Act* s 210. See Sect. 2.3.

[158] See Explanatory Memorandum to the Personal Property Securities (Consequential Amendments) Bill 2009 Schedule 2, paras 18, 20, 22, 24 with respect to patents; paras 36, 38, 41, 48 with respect to trade marks.

[159] Explanatory Memorandum to the Personal Property Securities (Consequential Amendments) Bill 2009 Schedule 2, para 35.

of receipt of notifications and the requirement under *Patents Act* s 103 for the written consent of registered mortgagees to any amendment to a patent specification.[160]

Registration on both registers was recommended by commentators from the outset.[161] Moreover, it is reportedly becoming common practice to conduct periodic searches to keep abreast of changes which may require the financing statement to be updated.[162]

6 Priorities

The *PPSA* sets out a comprehensive, albeit not exhaustive, set of rules for determining the ranking of claims. Competing claimants may be either other secured parties or persons purporting to buy (or lease) from the grantor. The *PPSA* distinguishes the rules applicable to these categories of claimants, both as a matter of substance and of terminology. The former raises the question of 'priority between security interests'; the latter, 'taking personal property free of security interests'. This distinction between 'priority' and 'taking free' is reflected in the structure of the *PPSA*, with the differing provisions dealt with in separate parts of the legislation.[163] For the purposes of this Chapter, both sets of rules are dealt with under this general heading of priorities.

It is important in both sets of rules to determine the status of the security interest—perfected or unperfected. An unperfected security interest is generally more vulnerable than a perfected security interest. This raises a further question of whether there is a particular time at which priority has to be determined and after which it is no longer possible to alter the priority outcome through perfection. The Whittaker Report has recommended that priority should be determined when security interests 'come into conflict'.[164]

The status of perfection can also be relevant in other conflict situations. A common example[165] is where the grantor becomes insolvent and a conflict arises between the holder of the unperfected security interest and the insolvency official. If unperfected on insolvency events such as bankruptcy, administration or liquidation, the security interest generally vests in the grantor.[166] If, however, the security

[160]Swinson and Howley (2010), para 4.9.1350.

[161]See, for example, Chambers (2011). For some emerging concerns regarding trade marks, see Burrell and Handler (2016).

[162]Swinson and Howley (2010), para 4.9.1500.

[163]See *PPSA* Part 2.5 for taking free rules, and Part 2.6 for priority rules.

[164]Whittaker Report, para 7.7.1, Recommendation 220. There is as yet no Australian case law on this point.

[165]Another example is the position of the execution creditor, who is given priority over an unperfected security interest in particular circumstances: *PPSA* s 74.

[166]*PPSA* s 267. There is an exception under s 268 for security interests constituted by a transfer of chattel paper or a transfer of an account where those transfers have no security function.

interest is perfected, any further challenge would have to be mounted under the relevant insolvency legislation or under the general law, to the extent such rules are able to operate concurrently under *PPSA* s 254. A liquidator of a corporate grantor might claim, for example, that the grant of the security interest was an uncommercial transaction and should thus be set-aside.[167]

6.1 *Priority Vis-à-Vis Other Secured Parties*

Priority rules determining which of two secured parties is to prevail are typically determined by the application of default rules set-out in *PPSA* s 55. These apply if the *PPSA* 'provides no other way of determining that priority', such as by affording 'super-priority' to purchase money security interests in certain circumstances or by preferencing a perfected secured party of a transferor over a perfected secured party of a transferee. They are also subject to the secured party making a subordination agreement.[168]

6.1.1 Default Rules

Where one security interest is perfected and the other is unperfected, the perfected security interest has priority.[169] That is the outcome whether the perfected security interest was created before or after the unperfected security interest, and seemingly[170] also whether in the latter situation the holder of the perfected security interest knew of the existence of the unperfected security interest.

Where both security interests are unperfected, the determining factor becomes the order of attachment.[171] The *PPSA* is silent as to the outcome if both unperfected security interests relate to future property and hence attach to that property at the same time when the grantor obtains rights in the property (assuming value was given by both secured parties or the grantor had done the act by which the security interest arose).[172] While the Replacement Explanatory Memorandum suggests that such

[167] *Corporations Act* s 588FB. See generally McCracken et al. (2017), paras 14.390–14.470.

[168] *PPSA* s 61.

[169] *PPSA* s 55(3).

[170] While *PPSA* s 55(3) does not deal expressly with this situation, its language does not suggest any qualification.

[171] *PPSA* s 55(2).

[172] See Sect. 5.1.

security interests should rank equally,[173] an alternative approach is for priority to be determined by reference to the date of the security agreement.[174]

If both security interests are perfected, priority is determined by the order of the priority time.[175] Assuming that there has been no break in the perfection of the competing security interests,[176] the order with respect to security interests perfected by registration is the earlier date of registration.[177]

Default rules are displaced in a number of situations. In the context of intellectual property, they would be displaced primarily in two situations[178]:

- where one or more of the perfected security interests is a purchase money security interest ('PMSI');
- where the grantor transfers the collateral to a transferee who has granted (or will grant) a security interest in the transferred collateral.

6.1.2 PMSIs

The security interest may qualify as a purchase money security interest under s 14. The relevant circumstances where the collateral is intellectual property are two-fold—where the security interest is taken in collateral[179]:

- 'to the extent that it secures all or part of its purchase price' (seller's PMSI);
- 'by a person who gives value for the purpose of enabling the grantor to acquire rights in the collateral, to the extent that the value is applied to acquire those rights' (lender's PMSI).

The fact that the particular security interest has PMSI status is however not of itself sufficient to confer super-priority. To obtain that, various procedural requirements must be satisfied.

To gain priority over a perfected non-PMSI given by the same grantor, the PMSI must comply with s 62. If it is in inventory, it has to be perfected by registration at the time the PMSI attaches to the inventory. If it is not inventory, it has to be perfected

[173] Replacement Explanatory Memorandum to the Personal Property Securities Bill 2009, Ch. 2, para 110.

[174] This is recommended by the Whittaker Report, para 7.7.2 Recommendation 221.

[175] *PPSA* s 55(4).

[176] *PPSA* s 55(6); s 56.

[177] *PPSA* s 55(5)(a). If a security interest is perfected by force of the Act, it is the earlier of the date of that automatic perfection and the date of registration: s 55(5)(c).

[178] See Sects. 6.1.2 and 6.1.3. Intellectual property is incapable of control (see *PPSA* s 21(2)(c)) and hence incapable of attracting the overriding priority afforded to security interests over property perfected by control under *PPSA* s 57.

[179] See Sect. 3.2.3. PPSA s 14(2) excludes an interest in original collateral that is chattel paper.

by registration within 15 business days of the day of attachment.[180] In both cases, the registration (through the financing statement) must state that it is a PMSI.[181]

A seller's PMSI prevails over a lender's PMSI given by the same grantor under s 63, provided that the requisite time limits are complied with. If the collateral is inventory, the seller's PMSI must be perfected by the time of attachment. If it is not, then the relevant time is within 15 business days of attachment.

6.1.3 Transferred Collateral

In circumstances where the grantor of a security interest transfers collateral to a transferee, as in the case of a sale of the intellectual property, and a priority dispute arises as between a secured party of the transferor and that of a transferee, the perfected security interest given by the transferor has priority over the perfected security interest given by the transferee.[182]

6.2 *'Priority' Vis-a-Vis Other Third Parties*

The *PPSA* provides protection to other third parties such as buyers from the grantor who seek to take the intellectual property free of an existing and continuing security interest. This protection is found in the taking free rules under Part 2.5.[183]

A preliminary issue is whether the particular security interest has actually continued in the collateral. It is only if it continues that the buyer must bring itself within the taking free rules.

Generally, a security interest continues in the particular collateral where there is a dealing giving rise to proceeds.[184] A purchase from the grantor would give rise to proceeds, those proceeds taking the form of both the promise to make payment as well as the actual payment.[185] The security interest will not continue, however, where the secured party has either authorised the disposal or agreed that the dealing would extinguish the security interest.[186]

If the security interest does continue and thus remains a fixed interest in the collateral, then the buyer will seek to take free under the general taking free rules. There are a number of grounds available. Of most relevance in the context of

[180] *PPSA* s 62(2)(b)(ii); s 62(3)(b)(ii).

[181] *PPSA* s 62(2)(c); s 62(3)(c).

[182] *PPSA* ss 66–67, assuming that the transferor-granted interest has been continuously perfected since the transfer. See s 68 for determining priority if the perfection has not been continuous.

[183] See generally Boxall (2011).

[184] *PPSA* s 32(1).

[185] See Sect. 4.1.

[186] *PPSA* s 32(1)(a)(i), (ii).

intellectual property are the following circumstances where 'buyers'[187] are said to take free:

- where the security interest is unperfected, provided that the buyer has given value[188];
- where the secured party's registration has not described the intellectual property by its serial number, provided that the buyer does not hold as inventory[189];
- where the property is sold in the ordinary course of the seller's business of selling property of that kind, provided that the buyer does not hold as inventory and has no actual knowledge that the sale breaches the security agreement.[190]

6.3 Priority Status of 'Enterprise Charges'

As noted in Sect. 4, companies may create a security interest over all their present and future property, which is a fixed interest.[191] There are no additional prerequisites or costs. This type of security interest, sometimes described in other jurisdiction as an 'enterprise charge', is subject under the *PPSA* to the same rules for determining priorities within the *PPSA* as against other secured parties—by reference to the fact of perfection and, if both competing security interests are perfected, the order of priority time or, if both are unperfected, the date of attachment.[192] Future advances have the same priority.[193]

As a matter of practice, this security interest is likely to find itself postponed to competing security interests which are PMSIs and which have complied with procedural requirements.[194] While it could itself be a PSMI in relation to part of the collateral, the secured party's ability to obtain PMSI status is dependent on the value being actually applied for the acquisition of the rights.[195]

---

[187]The provision also benefits 'lessees', although this is of no relevance to intellectual property which is intangible and incapable of lease. For an argument that these terms 'buyers and lessees' should encompass not only an assignee but also a licensee, see Coburn (2014).

[188]*PPSA* s 43. See s 43(2) for an exception to this rule.

[189]*PPSA* s 44. It is argued that s 105 gives protection where a secured party's exercise of rights in relation to goods 'necessarily involves an exercise of the intellectual property rights' and the obligation secured by the security interest in the goods is also secured by a security interest attached to the intellectual property rights: Swinson and Howley (2010), para 4.9.1200.

[190]*PPSA* s 46.

[191]*PPSA* s 19(2). *Hamersley Iron Pty Ltd v Forge Group Power Pty Ltd (in liq) (recs & mgrs apptd)* (2017) 52 WAR 90. See Sect. 5.1.

[192]See Sect. 6.1.1.

[193]*PPSA* s 58.

[194]See Sect. 6.1.2.

[195]*PPSA* s 14. See Sect. 6.1.2.

This security interest is also subject to the same taking free rules.[196] Again as a matter of practice, an issue arises in the context of intellectual property. As the intellectual property may be serial numbered property, an assessment has to be made as to whether that property should be expressly identified as serial numbered property in the financing statement, so as to preclude the operation of a buyer taking free of the security interest under *PPSA* s 44.[197]

It is in the context of insolvency, however, where this security interest becomes vulnerable to a loss of priority. This is despite the fact that it is perfected and thus does not vest in the grantor on insolvency and that it may have priority as against other competing third parties. Its vulnerability arises if it amounts to a security interest over circulating assets under the *PPSA* and thus a 'circulating security interest' under the *Corporations Act*, being a security interest that has attached to a circulating asset to which the grantor has title.[198]

The extent of the loss of priority depends on the type of insolvency regime. The substantive distinction between the various corporate insolvency officials in Australia—liquidator, receiver, voluntary administrator—was well summarised judicially in the following terms[199]:

> The role of a liquidator is to get in the assets of the company that is being wound up, dispose of those assets and out of the proceeds discharge the debts due to creditors (pro rata if there is a deficiency) and pay the balance (if there be a balance) to the contributories. When this task is complete the company is finished. This is in marked contrast to the role of a party-appointed receiver or an administrator. A party-appointed receiver takes control of the company's assets (and sometimes manages its business), but for the single purpose of discharging the debt due to his appointer, the secured creditor. The receiver holds any surplus he has secured for the benefit of the company. On his retirement the company continues in existence. An administrator does little more than take over the running of the company, and then only for a relatively short period. This enables the creditors to decide the company's fate.

A circulating security interest is, for example, subordinate to certain employee's claims in a liquidation,[200] certain debts in a receivership where the receiver is appointed under a circulating security interest[201] as well as to an administrator's right of indemnity in respect of liabilities incurred in the course of a voluntary administration.[202] It is also vulnerable in a liquidation if it was created within

---

[196] See Sect. 6.2.

[197] See Sect. 6.2. See also Sects. 4.1 and 5.3.

[198] *Corporations Act* s 9, s 51C for definition of 'circulating security interest'; *PPSA* s 10, s 340 for definition of 'circulating asset'. 'PPSA security interest' in s 51C excludes a transitional security interest: see *Corporations Act* s 9, s 51.

[199] *Beconwood Securities Pty Ltd v Australia and New Zealand Banking Group Ltd* (2008) 246 ALR 361, [60].

[200] *Corporations Act* s 556, 561.

[201] *Corporations Act* s 433.

[202] *Corporations Act* ss 443D, 443E.

6 months of the liquidation as it is made void against the liquidator in certain circumstances.[203]

A company incorporated under the *Corporations Act* has the express power to 'grant a circulating security interest over the company's property.'[204] The difficulty lies in working out what are the circulating assets for this purpose to trigger the statutory preferential claims.[205]

Whether personal property is a circulating asset under the *PPSA* depends on one of two questions being satisfied[206]:

- Does the personal property fall within one of 6 specified categories, including certain accounts, an ADI account (other than a term deposit); currency, inventory; and a negotiable instrument?[207] or
- If not, has the secured party 'given the grantor express or implied authority for any transfer of the personal property to be made, in the ordinary course of the grantor's business, free of the security interest'?[208]

Most relevant to intellectual property in the former case is an account arising from granting a right or providing services in the ordinary course of a business of granting rights or providing services of that kind. The intellectual property is less likely to be inventory, which in this context has its ordinary meaning, or an account that is the proceeds of inventory.

7 Remedies

A secured party who has an in substance security interest[209] is given important remedies under *PPSA* Chapter 4. Remedies may also be conferred under the security agreement, as the *PPSA* expressly states that it does not 'derogate from' rights and remedies in a security agreement.[210]

---

[203] *Corporations Act* s 588FJ.

[204] *Corporations Act* s 124(1)(f).

[205] See *Re Amerind Pty Ltd; Commonwealth of Australia v Byrnes & Hewitt* (2018) 54 VR 230.

[206] *PPSA* s 340, subject to s 340(4A) which excludes an account or chattel paper where the security interest is provided for by a transfer of an account or chattel paper.

[207] The asset will, however, not be a circulating asset if an effective registration discloses control of the asset by the secured party and the secured party does have control: *PPSA* s 340(2).

[208] *PPSA* s 340(1)(b). An asset is not caught 'merely because the secured party has given express authority to transfer specific personal property, or a specific class of personal property, free of a security interest': s 340(4).

[209] *PPSA* s 109 excludes deemed security interests from the remedial regime unless they do secure payment or obligation. Hence a transfer of chattel paper or an account that has no security function is excluded.

[210] *PPSA* s 110. Remedies available through the security agreement might include sale, foreclosure (though it can only be exercised if the security interest is a mortgage) and receivership.

The security agreement is said to be effective according to its terms. It is dependent for its scope on those terms and for its operation on general contractual rules.[211] Hence the drafting of the security agreement is very important. Also important are the terms of any licence. In the case of a licence, a secured party generally exercises its rights subject to the terms and conditions of the licence. *PPSA* s 112 restricts a secured party from seizing, purchasing or disposing of a licence other than in accordance with its terms and conditions and with any other statutory requirements.[212]

7.1 Mutual Rights and Obligations Prior to Default

A security agreement would typically include[213] power for the secured party to exercise rights such as to renew registrations or pursue infringers; to restrict the ability to grant a licence, at least without consent; to collect royalties prior to default; and to take steps to preserve the intellectual property. Commentators proffer detailed questions that the parties should resolve prior to entering into the secured transaction,[214] many of which would be appropriate to record in the security agreement.

If the security agreement contains a prohibition on transfer, that does not preclude the collateral from being transferred, whether by consent as between the grantor and the transferee or by operation of law.[215] The secured party's rights under the security agreement (or otherwise) such as the right to 'treat a prohibited transfer as an act of default' are stated not to be prejudiced.[216]

7.2 Enforcement Under the PPSA

The statutory remedies in *PPSA* Chapter 4 are cumulative[217] and should be exercised 'honestly; and. . .in a commercially reasonable manner'.[218] It is possible to exclude certain statutory remedies.[219] They are in any event not available where a receiver is

[211] *PPSA* ss 18, 254, subject to s 257. See Sect. 4.3.3.

[212] *PPSA* s 112(3). See *Re Maiden Civil (P&E) Pty Ltd; Albarran v Queensland Excavation Services Pty Ltd* (2013) 277 FLR 337.

[213] See, for example, UNCITRAL (2011), Ch VI [222]-[226].

[214] Swinson and Howley (2010), para 4.9.1500. See also Gunning et al. (2016), paras 19.65–19.70.

[215] *PPSA* s 79(1).

[216] *PPSA* s 79(2).

[217] *PPSA* s 114.

[218] *PPSA* s 111.

[219] *PPSA* s 115.

appointed to a corporate grantor.[220] If a grantor is an individual, consumer provisions contained in the National Credit Code apply.[221] There are special rules for enforcing security interests over an account or chattel paper, enabling a secured party to give a notice to make payment to it.[222]

Remedies are in principle the same outside insolvency as in insolvency, assuming that the corporate grantor is not in receivership. This statement also presupposes that the security interest is perfected. As noted in Sect. 5, a security interest which is unperfected at the time of the grantor's insolvency generally vests in the grantor. A secured party generally stands outside the insolvency regime, unless there are grounds for a liquidator setting it aside as, for example, an uncommercial transaction or other 'voidable transaction'.[223]

The enforcement process under the *PPSA* may be triggered by a default by the debtor.[224] There is no requirement that the secured party should be first ranking, although a higher ranking secured party can take over the enforcement process.[225]

Where there is default under the security agreement by the debtor, the secured party is entitled to seize.[226] As intellectual property is intangible property, that seizure may be made through the giving of a notice to the grantor and where the property is a licence, by notice either to the licensor or the licensor's successor.[227] That seizure is however subject to the terms and conditions of the licence and any applicable statute.[228]

The secured party is required after seizure under s 123 or otherwise either to dispose of the collateral or to take action to retain it.[229] Disposal and retention are the two principal statutory remedies. The order for distribution of proceeds is set out in s 140, reflecting commercial expectations that higher ranking interests are paid first.

Disposal Disposal generally means sale, but in the case of intellectual property it includes the alternative of disposal by licence.[230] Where sale is the preferred method, the secured party may make a private or public sale and owes a duty to any other secured party and the grantor to exercise all reasonable care to obtain at least the market value or, if there is no such value, the best price reasonably obtainable in the

[220] *PPSA* s 116.

[221] Regulations may deal with the interrelationship, and with when compliance with the National Credit Code may be taken as compliance under the *PPSA*: *PPSA* s 119.

[222] *PPSA* s 120.

[223] See McCracken et al. (2017), paras 14.440–14.450.

[224] *PPSA* s 123.

[225] *PPSA* s 127.

[226] *PPSA* s 123(1).

[227] *PPSA* s 123(2). Alternatively, the parties may agree upon another method: s 123(3).

[228] *PPSA* s 112(3). *Re Maiden Civil (P&E) Pty Ltd; Albarran v Queensland Excavation Services Pty Ltd* (2013) 277 FLR 337.

[229] *PPSA* s 125.

[230] *PPSA* s 128.

circumstances.[231] It is possible for the secured party to purchase the collateral itself, provided no objection is received from the grantor or a higher ranking secured party.[232] The secured party must purchase by public sale and at a price that is at least the market value.[233]

The disposal under s 128 enables the person taking the collateral to take it free of the grantor's interest, the secured party's interest, as well as any security interest held by a lower ranking secured party.[234]

The power to dispose by licence is required to be exercised 'in accordance with the terms and conditions of the security agreement.'[235] That exercise is also expressly made subject to the terms and conditions of the licence and any statute.[236]

Retention The alternative remedy is retention, which enables a secured party to take the property on its own account.[237] The exercise of this remedy is subject to the secured party giving notice to certain persons, including the grantor and to no objection being made.[238] It becomes entitled to take steps to have title pass to it, enabling it to take free of the interests of the grantor, itself as secured party and lower ranking security interests.[239] Importantly, the effect of the exercise of this remedy is to extinguish the debt or obligation secured by the security interest.[240] If an objection is received, the secured party must sell.[241]

Grantor's rights The grantor's statutory rights are twofold. Up until the time of disposal, it may redeem the collateral by satisfying the obligation and making payment of expenses relating to the enforcement.[242] It can reinstate the security agreement until either disposal or retention by paying amounts in arrears and expenses and remedying other defaults, but this right can only be exercised once during the life of the security agreement.[243]

---

[231] *PPSA* ss 128(2), 131. Procedural requirements include the obligation to give notice of disposal (s 130) and to provide a statement of account (s 132).

[232] *PPSA* ss 129, 130. In certain circumstances notice is dispensed with: s 130(5).

[233] *PPSA* s 129(3).

[234] *PPSA* s 133.

[235] *PPSA* s 128(4).

[236] *PPSA* s 128(6).

[237] *PPSA* s 134.

[238] *PPSA* s 134(2).

[239] *PPSA* s 136(1), (2). See also s 141.

[240] *PPSA* s 136(5).

[241] *PPSA* s 137. The alternative of lease is not available where the collateral is intangible property.

[242] *PPSA* s 142. This assumes that it has not agreed after default not to redeem. Other secured parties also have a right to redeem but subject to the grantor's right.

[243] *PPSA* s 143.

8 Conclusion

At a general level, a security interest over intellectual property, an intellectual property licence and related rights such as royalties raises the same general legal and practical issues as other security interests arising under the *PPSA*, which have been documented by the Whittaker Report. The *PPSA* is a complex statute. Determining whether a particular transaction has the requisite security function when it is structured as an outright transfer can, for example, prove problematic in legal terms, while describing and valuing the collateral can prove challenging in practical terms.

Amendments to the *Patents Act* and the *Trade Marks Act* in the wake of the introduction of the *PPSA* to make clear that security interests over patents and trade marks are governed by the *PPSA* are generally recognised as having improved the previous overlapping statutory regimes. Commentators have praised the Australian approach as an advance on the position in Canada and the US, observing that[244]:

> In both those countries, rationalising the interaction between secured transactions law and intellectual property law has proved to be a major challenge, at least partly because the secured transactions laws are a provincial (state) responsibility, while the intellectual property laws are a federal responsibility and it is difficult to coordinate reforms at both levels. A by-product of Australia's decision to enact a federal PPSA was that it resolved the coordination problem.

There are nonetheless still some areas of concern, notably in relation to the formalities for effective assignments of copyright and patents, as discussed in Sect. 5.1.

Assessing the risk of omitting serial numbers in financing statements and thereby potentially enabling buyers to take free of a security interest appears to be a perennial issue where a security interest over intellectual property is proposed. Other practical considerations have been raised by commentators, which go to the inherent nature of intellectual property, such as the validity and maintenance of a patent.[245] Also typically of general concern are the terms and conditions of the licence which may render the licence unsatisfactory collateral, such as a restriction on transfer (which could preclude the licence from being personal property for the purpose of the *PPSA*, given the statutory definition of licence) or termination on insolvency.[246]

In 2015 the Whittaker Report made 394 recommendations with respect to the *PPSA*, observing[247]:

> There is no one single step that by itself will produce a major improvement to the Act. Rather, improvement needs to come from the making of many small changes.

Many of those recommendations, if implemented, will obviously have some impact on the current process of taking security over intellectual property, but in

[244] Duggan and Brown (2016), para 2.39. See Swinson (2002) for analysis of the position pre-*PPSA*.
[245] See, for example, Gunning et al. (2016), paras 19.65–19.70.
[246] Swinson and Howley (2010), para 4.9.1000.
[247] Whittaker Report, para 1.3.

doing so will not differentiate between intellectual property and other forms of personal property as collateral.

Several of the recommendations are, however, directed specifically at intellectual property and appear intended to enhance the process of taking security over this form of collateral. Recommendations 377–381 are as follows:

377 That the definition of 'intellectual property' in s 10 be deleted;
378 That careful consideration be given to the manner in which the term 'intellectual property' is used in the Act, and if there are provisions in which the breadth of the term should be limited to registered intellectual property, that those provisions be amended accordingly;
379 That the definition of 'intellectual property' in s 10 be amended, if it is retained, by deleting the text '(including the right to be a party to proceedings in relation to such a right)', unless a good reason can be identified for retaining it;
380 That s 105 [intellectual property relating to goods] be deleted;
381 That Government ask stakeholders whether s 106 [licences and transfers of intellectual property] should be retained and, if no good reasons are put forward for retaining s 106, that it be deleted.

As at the date of writing, the Australian Government is yet to announce its formal response to the Whittaker Report. Any changes to the *PPSA* in relation to intellectual property should be examined in the context of overall reform to intellectual property. In August 2017, the Government issued its response to a public inquiry on Intellectual Property Arrangements conducted by the Productivity Commission, an Australian Government agency.[248] The Government expressed its wish[249]:

> …to ensure that the intellectual property (IP) system provides appropriate incentives for innovation, investment and the production of creative works while ensuring it does not unreasonably impede further innovation, competition, investment and access to goods and services.

Maintaining harmony between the various legal frameworks is consistent with UNCITRAL's approach which regards the promotion of secured credit without interference with the goals of intellectual property law as a key objective in developing a modern secured transactions regime.[250]

References

Boxall A (2011) Personal property securities act 2009 (Cth): some consequences for buyers of personal property. Commer Law Q 25(1):15–24

248 Commonwealth of Australia (2016), p. 2.
249 Commonwealth of Australia (2017), p. 3.
250 UNCITRAL (2011), Introduction, paras 49–50.

Burrell R, Handler M (2016) Registering security interests over trademarks in Australia: theory and practice. In: Calboli I, de Werra J (eds) The law and practice of trademark transactions: a global and local outlook. Edward Elgar, pp 197–220
Chambers K (2011) Update-security interests in intellectual property under the new PPS regime. Aust Intellect Prop Law Bull 24(6):171–173
Coburn T (2014) Security interests affecting IPRs: finding your way around the PPSA. Aust Intellect Prop Law Bull 27(10):289–291
Commonwealth of Australia (2015) Review of the Personal Property Securities Act 2009 (Mr Bruce Whittaker (Chairman)) (the Whittaker Report)
Commonwealth of Australia (2016) Intellectual Property Arrangements, Productivity Commission Inquiry Report, Overview and Recommendations, No 78
Commonwealth of Australia (2017) Australian Government Response to the Productivity Commission Inquiry into Intellectual Property Arrangements
Cuming R, Walsh C, Wood R (2012) Personal property security law, 2nd edn. Irwin Law, Canada
Davison M, Monotti A, Wiseman L (2016) Australian intellectual property law, 3rd edn. Cambridge University Press, Melbourne
Duggan A, Brown D (2016) Australian personal property securities law, 2nd edn. LexisNexis Butterworths, Chatswood
Gilmore G (1965) Security interests in personal property, Vol 1. Little, Brown & Co, Boston: reprinted (1999) LawBook Exchange, New Jersey
Gunning P, Lange M, Swinson J (2016) The PPSA and security interests over intellectual property. In: King & Wood Mallesons, Australian finance law, 7th edn. Thomson Reuters, Pyrmont, pp 649–659
Loxton D (2012) New bottle for old wine? The characterisation of PPSA security interests. J Bank Financ Law Pract 23(3):163–181
Loxton D, McCracken S, Boxall A (2018a) PPSA models: a minimalist approach. Commer Law Q 32(1):3–31
Loxton D, McCracken S, Boxall A (2018b) Chains of leases: aligning PPSA models with commercial expectations. Commer Law Q 32(2):3–13
Loxton D, McCracken S, Boxall A (2018c) PPSA models: easy as ABCD? Commer Law Q 32 (3):52–70
McCracken S, Stumbles J, Tolhurst G, Dixon O (2017) Everett & McCracken's banking and financial institutions law, 9th edn. Thomson Reuters, Sydney
Pemberton S, Chatwood R (2010) Using your IP to get finance? Implications of the personal property securities act 2009 for IP lawyers and their clients. Aust Intellect Prop Law Bull 22 (10):190–197
Shtein O, Wong K (2015) Personal property securities act (PPSA) – key points for intellectual property (IP) practitioners. Aust Intellect Prop Law Bull 28(1):18–23
Stewart A, van Caenegem W, Bannister J, Liberman A, Lawson C (2018) Intellectual property in Australia, 6th edn. LexisNexis Butterworths, Sydney
Swinson J (2002) Security interests in intellectual property in Australia. Bond Law Rev 14 (1):86–131
Swinson J, Howley J (2010) Intellectual property. In: Wappett C, Edwards S, Whittaker B (eds) Personal property securities in Australia, LexisNexis (looseleaf collection, 1st edn, current to July 2015) Australia, 115,001–115,268
Tolhurst G (2016) The assignment of contractual rights, 2nd edn. Hart, Oxford
UNCITRAL Legislative Guide on Secured Transactions, Supplement on Security Rights in Intellectual Property (2011) United Nations, New York
Whittaker B (2013) Dealings in collateral under the personal property securities act 2009 (Cth) – in search of a "harmonious whole". J Bank Financ Law Pract 24(3):203–219

Security Rights in Intellectual Property in Austria

Christian Dorfmayr

Abstract The national report aims to give an overview on the possibilities and limits of the use of IP rights as collateral for secured transactions in Austria. The report shows that IP rights are in principle a suitable object for secured transactions, although the legal situation with regard to the creation and enforcement of security rights in IP rights is not always clear. Overall, it can be seen that IP right-based secured transaction are associated with considerable additional costs, that the significance of IP rights for secured transactions is currently limited, and that a revision of the current law regime is not imminent.

1 Overview on Intellectual Property Rights Under Austrian Law

1.1 Introduction

Traditionally, intellectual property rights (IPRs) are characterized by Austrian legal doctrine as subjective rights granted by statute and relating to intellectual creations, i.e. intangible goods.[1] The field of intellectual property rights encompasses the areas of industrial property rights on the one hand (see Sect. 1.2) and copyright on the other hand (see Sect. 1.3).[2] As "absolute rights," IPRs are effective against third parties and entitle the proprietor to exclude anyone from uses prescribed by the law

[1]Schönherr (1982), p. 2; Walter (2008), p. 1 et seq.; Wiebe (2018), p. 31.

[2]Grünwald (2015), p. 5; Kucsko (2003), p. 98 et seq.; Schönherr (1982), p. 1 et seq.

C. Dorfmayr (✉)
University of Vienna, Department of European, International, and Comparative Law, Vienna, Austria
e-mail: christian.dorfmayr@univie.ac.at

E.-M. Kieninger (ed.), *Security Rights in Intellectual Property*, Ius Comparatum – Global Studies in Comparative Law 45,
https://doi.org/10.1007/978-3-030-44191-3_3

with respect to the subject matter (*ius excludendi*).[3] IPRs are subject to the "principle of enumeration," which means that the range of permissible types of IPRs is limited to those enacted by the legislator (*numerus clausus* of IPRs).[4] Within the Austrian constitutional distribution of powers, legislative and administrative matters of intellectual property fall exclusively within the competences of the Austrian federation (the *Bund*) and not of the individual federal states (the *Länder*), as laid down in section 10 para 1 subparas 6 and 8 of the Austrian Federal Constitutional Act.[5]

1.2 Industrial Property

1.2.1 Trademarks

Trademarks protected by the Austrian Trademark Act (ATMA)[6] are defined as signs, such as words (including names), designs, letters, numbers, sounds or the shape of goods or of their packaging which can be displayed in the Trademark Register. However, such signs are subject to trademark protection only where they are capable of distinguishing the goods and services of one undertaking from those of other undertakings (section 1 ATMA). According to section 2 para 1 and section 19 para 1 ATMA, trademarks are acquired upon registration in the Austrian Trademark Register administered by the Austrian Patent Office (APO, section 16 para 1 ATMA) following a positive assessment as to their legality by the APO (section 20 para 1 ATMA). The registration process is initiated upon a written application (section 16 para 2 ATMA).

An Austrian trademark may also be acquired as a result of an international registration under the Madrid Agreement Concerning the International Registration of Marks (hereinafter the Madrid Agreement)[7] or the Protocol Relating to the Madrid Agreement (hereinafter the Madrid Protocol)[8] based on a trademark registered ("basic registration") or applied for ("basic application") in a country that is a member of the Madrid Union ("country of origin").[9] In this case, an Austrian

[3]Kucsko (2003), p. 95; Some authors and the Austrian Supreme Court (*Oberster Gerichtshof*), however, emphasize the existence of a corresponding right of the proprietor to exclusively use the intangible good, see e.g. Schönherr (1982), p. 11 and Supreme Court 15.10.2002, 4 Ob 209/02 t.

[4]Kucsko (2003), p. 95.

[5]*Bundes-Verfassungsgesetz*, Federal Law Gazette 1930/1, as last amended by Federal Law Gazette I 2020/24.

[6]*Markenschutzgesetz 1970*, Federal Law Gazette 1970/260, as last amended by Federal Law Gazette I 2018/91.

[7]*Madrider Abkommen über die internationale Registrierung von Fabrik- oder Handelsmarken*, Federal Law Gazette 1970/45, as last amended by Federal Law Gazette I 2008/2.

[8]*Protokoll zum Madrider Abkommen über die internationale Registrierung von Marken*, Federal Law Gazette III 1999/32, as last amended by BGBl III 2019/173.

[9]Art. 1 para 2 Madrid Agreement; Art. 2 para 1 Madrid Protocol.

trademark may be granted as a result of a procedural cooperation between the competent office in the country of origin, the International Bureau of the World Intellectual Property Organization (WIPO) and the APO. Since the Madrid System merely aims to facilitate the registration process,[10] an international registration under the terms of the Madrid Agreement and the Madrid Protocol does not result in the acquisition of an "international" or "transnational" trademark as such, but rather a bundle of national trademarks. Thus, if Austria is a designated country for which an international trademark application has been filed under the Madrid System, the international registration made by the International Bureau and followed by a grant of protection by the APO has the same effect as a national trademark registration directly processed by the APO.[11]

The European Union trademark (hereinafter the EU trademark) under the European Union Trade Mark Regulation (EUTMR)[12] is a genuine supranational trademark that is effective throughout the European Union (Art. 1 para 2 EUTMR), which includes Austria. The existence of two different trademark regimes which are effective for the Austrian territory requires coordination, which is why both the EUTMR and the ATMA provide "conflict rules."[13] The essential protection requirements of the EUTMR are identical to those of the ATMA ("signs . . . capable of: (a) distinguishing the goods or services of one undertaking from those of other undertakings; and (b) being represented on the Register of European Union trade marks [...]", Art. 4 EUTMR). In order to register an EU trademark, an application has to be filed with the EU Intellectual Property Office (EUIPO, Art. 30 para 1 and Art. 2 para 1 EUTMR). Following an examination procedure (Art. 41 et seq. EUTMR) and any (unsuccessful) opposition procedure (Art. 46 et seq. EUTMR), the EU trademark is recorded in the Register of EU Trademarks (Art. 51 EUTMR) and thereby obtained (Art. 6 EUTMR).

---

[10]Engin-Deniz (2017), p. 2171.

[11]Supreme Court 10.5.1950, 1 Ob 167/49 and 171/50; Supreme Court 8.7.2003, 4 Ob 128/03 g; Grünwald (2015), p. 203; Ullrich (2013), § 2 para 104.

[12]Regulation (EU) 2017/1001 of the European Parliament and of the Council of June 14, 2017 on the European Union Trade Mark, OJ L 154, 16.6.2017, p. 1.

[13]The proprietors of an earlier national trademark may therefore file opposition against the registration of an EU trademark that is identical or similar to (and likely to be confused with) a national trademark (Art. 8 para 1, Art. 8 para 2 a (ii, iii) EUTMR). After registration, the EU trademark may be declared invalid upon application (Art. 60 para 1 a EUTMR). An earlier EU trademark, on the other hand, gives rise to the opposition and declaration of invalidity of an Austrian trademark with a lower priority (section 2 para 3, section 29a et seq. ATMA).

1.2.2 Patents and Utility Models

Patents that are subject to the Austria Patent Act (APA)[14] and utility models according to the Austrian Utility Models Act (AUMA)[15] both seek to protect inventions in all fields of technology that are capable of industrial application (section 1 para 1 APA, section 1 para 1 AUMA). While the APA requires "true inventiveness" in the sense that the invention is not obvious to a person skilled in the art (section 1 para 1 APA), only an "inventive step" is required for the grant of protection under the AUMA (section 1 para 1 AUMA). Unlike with patents (section 99 APA), the registration of a utility model under the AUMA does not require a substantive examining procedure by the APO (section 18 para 1 AUMA) and comes with a six-month grace period with regard to the novelty requirement (section 3 para 4 AUMA). Apart from that, the maximum period of protection differs.[16] After a successive (formal and/or substantive) examination by the APO, patents and utility models are recorded in their respective registers (Patent Register, see section 101c para 2 APA; Utility Model Register, see sections 22 and 24 AUMA). Patents and utility models become legally effective upon the publication of the registration in the patent or utility model gazette (section 101c para 2 APA, sections 6 and 23 AUMA).

Patents under the Austrian Patent Act may also be obtained as a result of an international application under the Patent Cooperation Treaty (PCT)[17]: after the first phase, in which a centralized (preliminary) international examination ("international phase") is carried out at the International Bureau of the WIPO, the centralized registration procedure transforms into various national application procedures ("national phase"). When Austria is a designated country of an international patent application, the "national phase" is administered by the APO as per the rules of the Austrian Patent Act.[18]

In addition, patent protection in Austria can also be obtained by filing a European patent application according to the European Patent Convention (EPC).[19] The

[14] *Patentgesetz 1970*, Federal Law Gazette 1970/259, as last amended by Federal Law Gazette I 2018/37.

[15] *Bundesgesetz über den Schutz von Gebrauchsmustern*, Federal Law Gazette 1994/211, as last amended by Federal Law Gazette I 2018/37.

[16] Patents: 20 years from the date of the patent application (section 28 para 1 APA); utility models: 10 years from the end of the month in which the application was filed (section 6 AUMA).

[17] *Vertrag über die Internationale Zusammenarbeit auf dem Gebiet des Patentwesens*, Federal Law Gazette 1979/348, as last amended by Federal Law Gazette III 2019/189.

[18] See e.g. Burgstaller (2009), p. 20 et seq.

[19] *Übereinkommen über die Erteilung europäischer Patente*, Federal Law Gazette 1979/350, as last amended by Federal Law Gazette I 2008/2; as a matter of fact, the issue of conflicting national patents and European patents is addressed by neither the Austrian Patent Act nor the European Patent Convention. As novelty of the invention is a substantial prerequisite for patent protection under the Austrian Patent Act (section 1 para 1 APA) as well as under the European Patent Convention (Art. 52 para 1 EPC), an opposition claim (sections 102 et seq. APA; Art. 100 et seq. EPC) or a declaration of invalidity (section 48 APA) may be filed or sought by the holder of the earlier patent.

European Patent Office (EPO), which centrally conducts grant and opposition proceedings, grants European patents that are effective in all designated contracting states. However, a European patent generally grants (only) the same rights and has the same effect as a national patent granted in the designated State (Art. 2 para 2 and Art. 64 para 1 EPC). The European patent has therefore been described as being like a bundle of national patents, connected only through the centralized granting act.[20] European patents are to be recorded in the European Patent Register (Art. 127 EPC; see also section 7 of the Patent Conventions Implementation Act (PCIA)[21]). The European patent becomes effective upon the date of publication of the mention of the grant in the European Patent Bulletin (Art. 97 para 3 EPC).

Based on an application for a European patent, a proprietor of a European patent may in the future file a request for unitary effect as per the Unitary Patent Regulation (UPR)[22] up to "one month after the mention of the grant is published in the European Patent Bulletin" (Art. 9 para 1 g UPR[23]). Upon registration of the unitary effect in the Register for Unitary Patent Protection, the proprietor obtains a supranational patent with unitary effect in all participating Member States (Art. 3 UPR), including Austria.

1.2.3 Designs

Under the Austrian Design Protection Act (ADPA),[24] the appearance (i.e. design) of a product, as well as aspects of this appearance, may be protected provided that the product design "is new and has individual character" (section 1 para 1 ADPA). In order for a design to be registered, a written registration application has to be filed with the APO (section 11 ADPA). Following a formal examination by the APO,[25] the design is entered in the Austrian Design Register (section 18 ADPA) and published in the Austrian Design Gazette (section 17 ADPA). The design becomes legally effective on the day of registration (section 6 ADPA).

---

[20] See e.g. Supreme Court 19.11.2009, 17 Ob 24/09 t.

[21] *Bundesgesetz über die Einführung des Europäischen Patentübereinkommens und des Vertrages über die internationale Zusammenarbeit auf dem Gebiet des Patentwesens*, Federal Law Gazette 1979/52, as last amended by Federal Law Gazette I 2013/126; additionally, a German translation of the European patent has to be filed with the APO—see section 4 et seq. PCIA.

[22] Regulation (EU) No. 1257/2012 of the European Parliament and of the Council of December 17, 2012 Implementing Enhanced Cooperation in the Area of the Creation of Unitary Patent Protection, OJ L 361, 31.12.2012, p. 1.

[23] See also Rule 6 of the Decision of the Select Committee of the Administrative Council of the EPO of December 15, 2015 Adopting the Rules Relating to Unitary Patent Protection (SC/D 1/15), OJ EPO 2016, A 39.

[24] *Bundesgesetz vom 7. Juni 1990 über den Schutz von Mustern*, Federal Law Gazette 1990/497, as last amended by Federal Law Gazette I 2018/37.

[25] The APO does not enquire whether the design fulfills the criteria of novelty and individuality (section 16 para 1 ADPA).

Additionally, the design of a product is subject to protection within the entirety of the European Union (which includes Austria) where the design fulfills the requirements laid down by the Community Design Regulation (CDR).[26] While the subject-matter ("appearance [. . .] of a product", Art. 3 (a) CDR) and the requirements for protection (novelty and individual character, Art. 4 para 1 CDR) of the unitary Community design correspond with the rules of the Austrian Design Protection Act,[27] the Community Design Regulation follows two different types of design protection. Under the first, a Community design application is filed and subsequently registered with the EUIPO ("registered Community design", Art. 1 para 2 (b) CDR).[28] In this case, a positive examination as regards the formal requirements (Art. 45 et seq. CDR) is followed by registration in the Community design Register (Art. 48 CDR) and publication in the Community Designs Bulletin (Art. 49 CDR). Under the second, the Community Design Regulation provides limited protection for designs which have not been registered but have been made available to the public ("unregistered designs", Art. 1 para 2 (a) CDR).

1.3 Copyright

Under the Austrian Copyright Act (ACA),[29] the author of a work in the field of literature, music, fine arts or cinema enjoys protection of his or her work (*Schöpferprinzip*, section 10 ACA), provided that the work represents a unique and original creation[30] (section 1 para 1 ACA). The author is not only entitled to a number of exclusive exploitation rights (section 14 et seq. ACA), but also enjoys a certain amount of protection of his or her moral rights (section 19 et seq. ACA). Unlike industrial property (Sect. 1.2 *supra*), copyright protection is not subject to registration; instead, it comes into existence after the work has been realized and made perceptible to the human senses.[31]

In addition to the protection of works, the Austrian Copyright Act grants a variety of "neighbouring rights" to performing artists (section 66 et seq. ACA), producers of

[26]Council Regulation (EC) No. 6/2002 of December 12, 2001 on Community Designs, OJ L 3, 5.1.2002, p. 1, as amended by Council Regulation (EC) No. 1891/2006 of December 18, 2006, OJ L 386, 29.12.2006, p. 14.

[27]A design registered by the APO might therefore be declared invalid where it is in conflict with a prior Community design (section 23 para 1 subpara 2 and 3 ADPA, section 1 para 5 ADPA) and vice versa (Art. 25 para 1 (b) and (d) CDR).

[28]A registered Community design may also be obtained on the grounds of an international application subject to the rules of the Hague Agreement Concerning the International Deposit of Industrial Designs, which has not been ratified by Austria but has been by the European Union; see Horn and Grünwald (2015), p. 187.

[29]*Bundesgesetz über das Urheberrecht an Werken der Literatur und der Kunst und über verwandte Schutzrechte*, Federal Law Gazette 1936/111, as last amended by Federal Law Gazette I 2018/105.

[30]See also the case law of the European Court of Justice (ECJ) on the interpretation of the term "work" under Directive 2001/29/EC, most recently ECJ 12.9.2019, C-683/17, note 29 et seq.

[31]See e.g. Supreme Court 11.2.1997, 4 Ob 17/97 x; ECJ 12.9.2019, C-683/17, note 32 et seq.; Walter (2008), p. 168 et seq.

photographs and motion pictures (section 73 et seq. ACA), producers of phonograms (section 76 ACA), broadcasting companies (section 76a ACA), publishers of posthumous works (section 76b ACA), and producers of databases (section 76c et seq. ACA).

2 Categories of Security Rights in Intellectual Property Rights Under Austrian Law

2.1 Preliminary Remarks: Nature of IPRs

The question whether IPRs are to be considered true "property" rights or merely "relative rights" (claims) under Austrian civil law doctrine is a difficult[32] yet inevitable question for this report. On the one hand, the wording of the Austrian Civil Code (ACC)[33] seems to give a clear-cut answer: Since "everything that differs from the person and serves for the use of men is called property in the legal sense" (section 285 ACC), mere rights (such as claims and IPRs) are covered under the broad definition of "property."[34] On the other hand, it is well established that both a number of the provisions of the ACC property rules and the general principles of property law (*Sachenrecht*) derived from the systematics of the Austrian Civil Code may only be applied to tangible goods.[35] This understanding is reflected in the set doctrine that the assignment of claims (section 1392 et seq. ACC), although "property" within the meaning of section 298 ACC, is not subject to the property transfer rules of the Civil Code which would require the performance of a formal transfer act (section 427 ACC). Instead, this assignment occurs merely upon consensus between the parties.[36] When it comes to *security rights in claims*, however, the performance of a formal transfer act that provides for the publicity of the secured transaction as prescribed by section 452 ACC is deemed necessary (see also Sect. 2.2.1 *infra*).[37]

It is worth pointing out that the ambiguous nature of IPRs (whether "true property rights" or mere claims) leads to a different accentuation and choice of words within IPR doctrine. There is a tendency in patent law to emphasize the nature of the patent as a "true property right" as the transfer of a patent requires a formal act of transfer

[32]See McGuire (2008), p. 217.

[33]*Allgemeines bürgerliches Gesetzbuch*, Collection of Judiciary Laws 1811/946, as last amended by Federal Law Gazette I 2020/16.

[34]This is expressly confirmed in section 298 ACC, where mere rights are to be considered "movable property rights".

[35]Iro (2016), p. 2; Kisslinger (2011), § 292 para 9; Koziol et al. (2018), p. 266.

[36]Ertl (2002), § 1392 para 1 et seq.; Neumayr (2017), § 1392 para 5; Welser and Zöchling-Jud (2014), p. 135.

[37]See e.g. Supreme Court 30.4.2014, 3 Ob 34/14 t; Ertl (2002), § 1392 para 3; Neumayr (2017), § 1392 para 7; Welser and Zöchling-Jud (2014), p. 140 et seq.

(i.e. a register entry, as per section 43 para 1 APA).[38] In trademark law, on the other hand, reference is typically made to the rules of assignment of claims as sections 11 and 28 ATMA suggest the possibility of transferring the trademark by mere consensus between the parties.[39] Supported by the fact that copyright as such is not transferable *inter vivos* (section 23 para 3 ACA), certain principles of property law such as the distinction between "title" and "mode of acquisition" (Sect. 3.1 *infra*) are considered to be inapplicable in the area of copyright law.[40]

2.2 *Categories of Security Rights in IPRs: Pledge and Ownership Transfer/Security Assignment*

2.2.1 Preliminary Remarks

Under Austrian law, IPRs may be used as collateral in secured transactions through either a) a pledge of the IPR or b) a transfer of the IPR for security purposes.[41] According to the Austrian Civil Code, a pledge (*Pfandrecht*)[42] is a limited right *in rem* which is granted to a creditor in order to be satisfied by an asset in case the secured obligation is not fulfilled at the agreed time (section 447 ACC). As any *tradeable asset* may be used as a pledged asset (section 448 ACC), mere rights are as a general rule covered by section 448 ACC and may therefore be pledged.[43] When it comes to the use of the "ownership" of an IPR for security purposes, it is to be noted that such a transaction may, due to the ambiguous nature of IPRs (Sect. 2.1 *supra*), be regarded as either a security transfer of this ownership (*Sicherungsübereignung*) or a security assignment (*Sicherungszession*). As both types of transactions are subject to the principle of publicity and therefore an "act of publicity" (*Publizitätsakt*) is necessary for the secured transaction to become legally effective (section 452 ACC),[44] this distinction does not come with practical implications.

---

[38] See e.g. Supreme Court 12.2.1991, 4 Ob 173/90; Burgstaller (2009), p. 145 et seq. (nevertheless referring to the acquirer of the patent as the "assignee" on p. 147); Lang (1999a), p. 101 et seq.; Weiser (2016), p. 282 et seq. and p. 297; see also Thiele (2018), § 22 para 3.

[39] Engin-Deniz (2017), p. 538; Grünzweig (2017), § 11 para 2; Salomonowitz (2013), § 11 para 8.

[40] Supreme Court 23.11.1999, 4 Ob 274/99 v; OGH 18.10.1994, 4 Ob 93/94; Walter (1995), p. 101.

[41] As for the non-existent possibility to use patents (or, for that matter, utility models or registered designs) in "retention of title" constructions, see Lang (1999a), p. 107 et seq.

[42] Although "pledge" may not be the accurate term to describe a non-possessory security right in an IPR, I will nevertheless continue to use this term as Austrian law does not linguistically distinguish between possessory pledges and non-possessory liens on mere rights. As a matter of fact, the possessory pledge is the legislative prototype when it comes to the *Pfandrecht*.

[43] Koziol et al. (2018), p. 414; Wolkerstorfer (2016), § 448 paras 31 and 42.

[44] As for the security transfer of ownership in property, see e.g. Supreme Court 9.12.2008, 5 Ob 168/08 d; Koziol et al. (2018), p. 451 et seq. with further references; as for security assignments, see e.g. Supreme Court 30.4.2014, 3 Ob 34/14t.

Both concepts rely on the same legal structure and principle: the secured creditor assumes "ownership" and is therefore fully capable of transferring the (property) right to third parties; however, he or she is legally bound by the grantor of the security right to do so only upon the default of the debtor. Both security transfer of ownership and security assignment therefore rely on the concept of a fiduciary agreement.[45]

2.2.2 Security Rights in Austrian IPRs

As for national trademarks, patents, utility models, and designs, the legal wording of the underlying laws explicitly states that these IPRs can be pledged (section 28 para 1 ATMA; section 34 APA; section 11 AUMA; section 21 ADPA). Since all these rights are in principle transferable (section 11 para 1 ATMA; section 33 para 2 APA; section 10 para 1 AUMA; section 10 para 1 ADPA), a transfer may also be carried out for security purposes.[46] In the area of copyright, a distinction has to be made between copyright and the rights of a performing artist on the one hand, and all other neighbouring rights on the other hand: the legal status of authors and performing artists as such is not transferable *inter vivos* (section 23 para 3 ACA; section 68 para 4 ACA) and their exploitation rights are not subject to compulsory enforcement (i.e. execution) for monetary claims, as explicitly stated in the law (section 25 para 1 ACA; section 68 para 4 ACA).[47] It has therefore been concluded that copyright (and the legal position of performing artists) as such cannot be used as collateral.[48] However, the aforementioned limitations do not apply to the neighbouring rights of producers of photographs and motion pictures (section 74 para 7 ACA); producers of phonograms (section 76 para 6 ACA); broadcasting companies (section 76a para 5 ACA); or producers of databases (section 76d para 5 ACA). Exploitation rights relating to these neighbouring rights may therefore in principle be used as collateral.[49]

---

[45]See e.g. Iro (2016), p. 244 et seq.; Koziol et al. (2018), pp. 452, 455 et seq.

[46]For trademarks, see Engin-Deniz (2017), p. 541; Koch (2011), p. 465; Salomonowitz (2013), § 11 para 74 et seq.; for patents, see Koch (2011), p. 469; Lang (1999b), p. 477; Lang (1999a), p. 101 et seq.; for utility models, see Koch (2011), p. 475; for design protection, see Appl (2018), p. 120; Horn and Grünwald (2015), p. 164; Koch (2011), p. 475.

[47]Nevertheless, see the exception regarding the copyright-based exploitation rights of film producers, which can be transferred *inter vivos* and are subject to compulsory enforcement (section 40 para 1 ACA).

[48]Koch (2011), p. 476; Wolkerstorfer (2016), § 448 para 42.

[49]Wolkerstorfer (2016), § 448 para 42.

2.2.3 Security Rights in "International" and Supranational IPRs

Since the Madrid System and the PCT merely aim to facilitate the registration process of a "bundle" of national IPRs, neither instrument provides substantive rules relating to security rights in the respective IPRs.[50] The same is true for European Patents as per the EPC.[51] Consequently, these issues are regulated by the national trademark and patent law provisions of the designated States.

As for supranational EU trademarks and registered Community designs, the regulations explicitly mention that these may be given as security or be the subject of rights in rem (Art. 22 para 1 EUTMR; Art. 29 para 1 CDR) they may also be transferred (Art. 20 para 1 EUTMR; see also Art. 28 CDR).[52] However, the types of security interest provided for and the conditions under which they may arise are governed by the law applicable to the EU trademark or the Community design as an "object of property," as described under Article 19 EUTMR and Article 27 CDR.[53] These questions are therefore, in principle, regulated fully and for the entire EU by the law of the seat, domicile, or establishment of the proprietor of the trademark or design. This strategy of making reference to national IPR law has also been taken up by the unitary patent system: in the absence of provisions regarding the use of a unitary patent as collateral, such aspects are regulated by the law applicable to the unitary patent as an object of property (Art. 7 UPR: law of residence or (principle) place of business on the date of filing of the European patent application). Where Art. 7 UPR, Art. 19 EUTMR, and Art. 27 CDR make reference to Austrian law, a security right as set out above (Sect. 2.2.2 *supra*) may be crated in the IPR.

2.2.4 Security Rights in IPR Applications

Additionally, an IPR may be used as collateral before it comes into existence: since not only patents and trademarks but also patent and trademark applications can be transferred pursuant to the clear wordings of the Austrian Patent Act and the Austrian Trademark Act (section 33 para 2 APA,[54] section 28a ATMA[55]), patent and trademark applications are tradable in the sense of section 448 ACC and can

[50]Koch (2011), p. 470 (regarding the PCT).

[51]Kolle (2019), Art. 2 para 15.

[52]According to a decision by the Office for Harmonization in the Internal Market (Fourth Board of Appeal) 13.9.2010, R 357/2010-44 (*Carborundum*) note 12, the security transfer of an EU trademark falls within the scope of application of Art. 20 (transfer) and not Art. 22 (securities and rights in rem) of the EUTMR; see also Schennen (2017), Art. 17 para 13; for registered designs, see Ruhl (2019), Art. 28 para 10.

[53]Ruhl (2019), Art. 29 para 4; Schennen (2017), Art. 19 para 4.

[54]Friebel and Pulitzer (1971), p. 296 et seq.; Koch (2011), p. 472 et seq.; Lang (1999b), p. 476.

[55]This was argued in legal literature even before section 28a ATMA was introduced (effective as of Jan. 19, 2019)—see Engin-Deniz (2017), p. 541; Kucsko (2003), p. 384; Salomonowitz (2013), § 11 para 73.

therefore be pledged. The same is true for utility model and design protection applications.[56] As for supranational IPRs, the transfer and rights in rem provisions cited in Sect. 2.2.3 *supra* apply *mutatis mutandis* to EU trademark applications and registered Community design applications (Art. 28 EUTMR; Art. 34 CDR). In the field of international IPRs, a statement on transferability and the possibility of use as security can be found in Art. 71 EPC, where it is expressly stated that a European patent application may either be transferred or—depending on the law of the designated State (Art. 74 EPC)[57]—be the subject of a right in rem (see also Rule 23 EPC Implementing Regulation[58]). When it comes to international patent and trademark applications, it seems correct to assume that these issues are also governed by the law of the designated State,[59] as neither the PCT nor the Madrid treaties provide for substantive law rules in this regard.

2.2.5 Security Rights in IPR Licences

While IPR licences[60] (including copyright licences) may in principle be used as collateral under Austrian law,[61] the transfer or pledging of an IPR licence nonetheless requires the consent of the IPR proprietor in certain cases. As a rule,[62] the transfer of a copyright licence that qualifies as an exclusive exploitation right (*Werknutzungsrecht*)[63] is only possible with the author's consent, which may only be refused for important reasons (section 27 para 2 ACC). Therefore, the pledging of an exclusive exploitation right would be subject to the author's approval as well.[64] Whether the transfer and pledging of a non-exclusive exploitation authorization (*Werknutzungsbewilligung*) requires the approval of the author as well is, however,

---

[56]Koch (2011), p. 475.

[57]Grabinski (2019), Art. 71 para 5; Heinrich (2019), Art. 74 EPÜ para 5; Lang (1999a), p. 115.

[58]Decision of the Administrative Council of December 12, 2002 Adopting the Implementing Regulations to the European Patent Convention 2000, OJ EPO 2003/2, as amended by the Decision of the Administrative Council of December 7, 2006.

[59]Lang (1999a), p. 130 regarding PCT applications.

[60]More precisely put: the rights of a licensee to use the IP as stipulated by the licensing contract within the framework of statutory law.

[61]Koch (2011), p. 478 et seq.; Koziol (2011), p. 99 et seq.; Lang (1999a), p. 70; more restrictive: Koppensteiner (2012), p. 210.

[62]However, this rule does not apply to the majority of licences relating to cinematographic works (see section 40 para 2 ACA), to computer programs (section 40c ACA) and database works (section 40c ACA), and is not applicable to neighbouring rights licenses, with the exception of licences granted by a performing artist (section 68 para 4 ACA).

[63]In the field of copyright licences, a distinction is made between exclusive rights to exploitation (*Werknutzungsrechte*) and non-exclusive exploitation authorizations (*Werknutzungsbewilligung*) under Austrian law—see section 24 para 1 ACA.

[64]Koch (2011), p. 478; Koziol (2011), p. 100 et seq.

uncertain.[65] The transfer (and pledging) of a patent licence generally requires the consent of the patent proprietor (section 38 APA). However, with respect to trademark, registered design and utility model licences, there are no indications of IPR proprietor consent requirements under Austrian law.[66]

2.3 *Granting of Licences for Security Purposes*

In theory, not just existing licences may be used as collateral: the act of granting a licence itself may be used for security purposes as well (the so-called "security licence"). If agreed upon, the creditor is entitled to monetize the licence through its sale or through the granting of sub-licences in the event of default.[67] A security licence may be granted by either a licensee entitled to grant sub-licences or the IPR proprietor. It has, however, been argued that in the field of copyright, the act of granting a security licence may not be in line with the publicity requirement under section 452 ACC.[68] In a decision rendered by the Supreme Court concerning a contract that might be interpreted as a copyright-based security licence agreement,[69] the court did not address the requirement of publicity. As the facts of the case leave room for interpretation and the security licence was established by means of a copyright licence (i.e. in an area of IPR law where no distinction is made between "title" and "mode of acquisition"), the legal situation remains rather unclear in this regard.

2.4 *Monetary Claims Against Licensees as Collateral*

In addition, the monetary claims of a licensor against a licensee arising from a licence agreement may be pledged or assigned in accordance with the general rules of the Civil Code. However, it should be noted that, in the absence of an agreement, the pledging of an IPR does not automatically extend to monetary claims against a licensee. This is because claims of this kind may be considered to be "civil fruits" (i.e. monetary proceeds) of the pledged asset (the IPR),[70] which the law does not generally regard as being covered by the pledge agreement.[71]

[65] Büchele (2017), § 28 para 13 et seq. with further references.

[66] Koch (2011), p. 478; Salomonowitz (2013), § 14 para 70, however, advocates for a consent requirement for trademark licences by analogy to section 38 APA.

[67] Koziol (2011), p. 107 et seq. with further references; Walter (2008), p. 783.

[68] Koch (2011), p. 476 et seq.

[69] Supreme Court 23.11.1999, 4 Ob 274/99 v.

[70] Lang (1999a), p. 69 et seq.

[71] See e.g. Supreme Court 24.11.2005, 3 Ob 261/05 m; Wolkerstorfer (2016), § 457 para 7 with further references.

3 Creation and Third-Party Effectiveness of Security Rights

3.1 Title and Mode of Acquisition

Under Austrian civil law, unlike under Art. 9 UCC, no distinction is made between the creation of a security right (i.e. effectiveness between the parties to the transaction) on the one hand and the third-party effectiveness of a security right on the other hand.[72] Therefore, the third-party effectiveness of a security right is the legal consequence of the lawful creation of a security right.[73] The creation of a security right (pledge or security transfer) requires the existence of a valid "title" in accordance with section 451 para 1 ACC—that is to say, it requires legal grounds, which in most cases consist of a valid agreement between the grantor and the creditor.[74] Furthermore, a formal acquisition act (*modus*) has to take place which "allow [s] everyone to easily recognize that a pledge has been created" (section 452 ACC) or that a security transfer has been effected. This should enable creditors to see whether and to what extent a creditor's liability fund has already been reduced by security interests.[75] Accordingly, the creation and third-party effectiveness of a security right in an IPR requires the performance of an appropriate act of publicity.[76]

3.2 The Mode of Acquisition Required to Establish a Security Right

3.2.1 Patents, Utility Models, and Protected Designs

Patents, utility models, and protected designs are designed as "pure" registration rights, in the sense that pledges and IPR transfers only become effective upon their entry in the relevant register (section 43 para 1 APA; section 32 para 1 AUMA; section 22 para 1 ADPA). In order to initiate the registration process, a written application has to be filed by an involved party (section 43 para 5 APA; section 32 para 4 AUMA; section 22 para 5 ADPA). In addition, a copy of the underlying document (the pledge or security agreement) has to be submitted and the original document has to either be a "public document" or include the signature (verified by a notary or court) of the IPR proprietor. Where the IPR has not been pledged but

---

[72]As for supranational IPRs, see Sect. 3.2.4.

[73]Faber (2012), p. 348; Koziol (2013), p. 370; Wolkerstorfer (2016), § 451 para 2.

[74]For a pledge, this agreement is referred to as a "pledge agreement" (*Pfandbestellungsvertrag*); the underlying agreement of a security transfer is referred to as a "security agreement" (*Sicherungsabrede*), see Iro (2016), pp. 182, 244, 247; Koziol et al. (2018), pp. 417, 453.

[75]See e.g. Böhler (2012), p. 125 with further references.

[76]Koch (2011), *passim*; Koziol (2013), p. 368; Lang (1999a), pp. 22, 102.

transferred (for security purposes), the submission of concurring declarations from the parties is sufficient (section 43 para 6 APA, section 32 para 2 AUMA, section 22 para 2 ADPA).

3.2.2 Trademarks and Copyright (Neighbouring Rights)

The Austrian Trademark Act does not provide an express rule on the mode of acquisition as far as the creation of a security right in an Austrian trademark is concerned. Although it is possible to register a pledge or a trademark transfer (section 28 para 1 ATMA), there is no provision comparable to section 43 para 1 APA which would provide that the registration has constitutive effect.[77] It has therefore been deduced that the entry in the Trademark Register primarily serves to "make visible" the pledge or the transfer of the trademark—i.e. it merely has declaratory effect.[78] Given that there are no alternatives to obtaining publicity, it is nevertheless assumed in the literature that the security right in the trademark is not created and effective until it is registered in the Trademark Register.[79] According to some scholars, a note in the trademark proprietor's business books should be sufficient as an alternative.[80] In order to register the pledge or the transfer of the trademark, a written application is necessary (section 28 para 1 ATMA). The document requirements correspond to those in the Austrian Patent Act (section 28 para 2 ATMA). With regard to international trademarks under the Madrid System, it has been suggested by scholars[81] that a pledge shall become effective upon registration in the International Register in accordance with Rule 20 of the Common Regulations under the Madrid Agreement.[82]

In the field of copyright and neighbouring rights, it remains unclear whether publicity is required and if so, how publicity may be obtained, where neighbouring rights or exploitation rights as such are transferrable (as for copyright and neighbouring rights licences, see Sect. 3.2.5 *infra*). As far as can be seen, these questions have not yet been discussed in the literature.

---

[77]While section 28 para 5 ATMA refers to certain paragraphs of section 43 APA (paras 3, 4 and 7), no reference is made to section 43 para 1 APA.

[78]Austrian Patent Office (Board of Appeal) 24.10.1991, Bm 9-12/89; Grünzweig (2017), § 28 para 2; Salomonowitz (2013), § 11 para 71.

[79]Hinteregger (2012), § 448 para 13; Koch (2011), p. 466; Madl (1991), p. 329; Wolkerstorfer (2012), p. 188 et seq.; Engin-Deniz (2017), p. 636 however assumes that the entry in the Trademark Register is only relevant in terms of third-party effectiveness.

[80]Grünzweig (2017), § 28 para 2; Salomonowitz (2013), § 11 para 71.

[81]Koch (2011), p. 467; Engin-Deniz (2017), p. 636; Wolkerstorfer (2012), p. 190.

[82]*Gemeinsame Ausführungsordnung zum Madrider Abkommen über die internationale Registrierung von Marken und zum Protokoll zu diesem Abkommen*, Federal Law Gazette III 1997/109, as last amended by Federal Law Gazette III 2017/21; in case of a security transfer of the trademark, however, Rule 25 para 1 a (i) of the Common Regulations seems to be the more suitable provision.

3.2.3 IPR Applications

At present, some uncertainty still exists as to how publicity can be obtained where the pledging or security transfer of an IPR application is envisaged by the parties. As far as patent applications are concerned, it has been suggested that either notifying the APO or lodging a request with the APO to transfer the patent application should suffice.[83] With regard to trademark applications, diverging views could be found in trademark literature.[84] However, the most recent amendment of the Austrian Trademark Act[85] creates the legal basis for a suitable publicity act by introducing a new section 28a, according to which the transfer or pledging of a trademark application may be entered in the register at the written request of one of the parties concerned.

3.2.4 Supranational IPRs and IPR Applications

With regard to the treatment of supranational IPRs as objects of property, a uniform approach is applied to the EU trademark and the registered Community design: at the request of one of the parties, a security right (Art. 22 para 2 EUTMR, Art. 29 para 2 CDR) or the transfer of the registered IPR (Art. 20 para 4 EUTMR, Art. 28 (a) CDR) may be "entered in the Register and published." The registration of the security right or the transfer triggers the third-party effectiveness of the underlying legal acts (Art. 27 para 1 EUTMR, Art. 33 para 2 CDR).[86] For EU trademarks or registered Community designs that are also subject to Austrian law "as an object of property" (Art. 19 EUTMR, Art. 27 CDR), the implicit distinction between creation and third-party effectiveness of the security interest made under the EUTMR and the CDR does in the majority of cases not affect the outcome: entry in the relevant register is required under national and supranational trademark and design law in order to achieve third-party effectiveness.[87] However, according to the EUTMR and the CDR, and in contrast to Austrian trademark and design law, effectiveness is also stipulated towards a third party who had actual knowledge of the underlying transaction (Art. 27 para 1 EUTMR, Art. 33 para 2 CDR). Overall,

---

[83]Koch (2011), p. 473; Lang (1999b), p. 477, Lang (1999a), pp. 50 et seq., 104 et seq.; as for EPC patents, registration in the European Patent Register in accordance with Rule 22 ("Registration of Transfers") and Rule 23 ("Registration of Other Rights") of the EPC Implementing Regulation provides the necessary publicity.

[84]Koch (2011), p. 467: notification of the APO or request for transfer should be carried out; Salomonowitz (2013), § 11 para 73: database registration with the APO or note in the applicant's business books should be undertaken; Engin-Deniz (2017), p. 541 and p. 636: mere consensus between the parties should suffice.

[85]*Bundesgesetz, mit dem das Markenschutzgesetz 1970 geändert wird*, Federal Law Gazette I 2018/91.

[86]In the case of unregistered designs, the third-party effectiveness of a security interest is subject to the law applicable according to Art. 27 CDR (Art 33 para 1 CDR).

[87]For national trademarks, this is only true if registration is the sole possible mode of acquisition.

the question arises as to how the concept of third-party effectiveness under the EUTMR and the CDR relates to the Austrian "principle of publicity" (an indispensable prerequisite for third-party effectiveness *and for the creation* of the security right) where EU trademarks or registered Community designs are also subject to Austrian law as objects of property.[88]

In order to register the security right or transfer, documents specified in Art. 20 para 5 and Art. 26 EUTMR and Art. 23 et seq. of the Community Design Implementing Regulation[89] have to be submitted. The transfer of an EU trademark has to be done in writing and requires the signature of the parties (Art. 20 para 3 EUTMR). The abovementioned rules apply mutatis mutandis to the pledging or security transfer of an EU trademark or Community design application (Art. 28 EUTMR, Art. 34 CDR).

Under the unitary patent system, there are no provisions concerning the third-party effectiveness of patent transactions; therefore, such effectiveness is subject to the law applicable to the unitary patent as an object of property (Art. 7 UPR). Where Art. 7 UPR refers to Austrian law, a security right may be acquired upon entry in the (yet-to-be-established) Register for unitary patent protection (Art. 15 of the Rules Relating to Unitary Patent Protection). As Rule 20 para 2 (b) of the Rules Relating to Unitary Patent Protection makes reference to Rule 22 and Rule 23 of the EPC Implementing Regulations, security rights in a patent with unitary effect may be registered on these grounds. In order to register the security right, documents have to be submitted (Rule 22 para 1 and Rule 23 para 1 of the EPC Implementing Regulations).

3.2.5 Pledging and Security Transfer of Licences

For the pledging or the security transfer of licences, it has been suggested in literature that the notification of the licensor is a suitable method.[90] This way, potential lenders are able to enquire with the licensor as to whether the licensing

[88]Koch (2011), p. 467 argues that prior to the act of registration, the security interest has neither been established (created) nor become effective; therefore, there is no valid legal "act" in terms of Art. 27 para 1 EUTMR, Art. 33 para 2 CDR of which a third party may have knowledge. This interpretation is strongly influenced by an Austrian point of view, which puts more emphasis on the importance of the "publicity act" and favours the application of domestic law rules (based on Art. 19 EUTMR, Art. 27 CDR) over an extensive interpretation of the substantive law rules laid down in the regulations themselves. Among German scholars, it is argued that security rights are in principle established and effective upon mere consensus, and Art. 27 EUTMR and Art. 33 CDR are perceived to be an exemption to this rule; see Schennen (2017), Art. 23 para 5; Taxhet (2018), Art. 27 UMV para 4. The latter opinion seems to be more compatible with the *Carborundum* decision of the OHIM (R 357/2010-44).

[89]Commission Regulation (EC) No. 2245/2002 of October 21, 2002 Implementing Council Regulation (EC) No. 6/2002 on Community Designs, OJ L 341 of 17.12.2002, p. 28, as amended by Commission Regulation (EU) 876/2007 on July 24, 2007, OJ L 193 of 25.7.2007, p. 13.

[90]Koch (2011), p. 479; Koziol (2013), p. 368 et seq.

law is encumbered or not. It is, however, questionable whether the mere notification of the licensor suffices in situations where the licence was entered in the relevant register. For these situations, it has been argued that the security right is only validly created and effective upon registration.[91] Nevertheless, the wording of the IPR laws does not expressly provide for the possibility of registering the pledge of a licence. Where a registered licence is transferred for security purposes, the registration of the new licensor could nevertheless serve as a suitable act of publicity.

3.2.6 Security Licences

The questions of whether an "act of publicity" is required for the granting of a license for security purposes in all areas of IPRs and how publicity can be obtained in such cases are not finally clarified and hardly discussed.[92] As of today, the question remains as to whether the aforementioned decision of the Supreme Court[93] can be used to support the argument that such a security right can be created without any publicity requirements having been met.

3.2.7 Pledging and Security Transfer of Monetary Claims

The pledging or security assignment of monetary claims arising from licence agreements follows the general rules for the security assignments and pledges of claims. Under Austrian law, it is therefore necessary either to notify the third-party debtor (i.e. the debtor of the licence fee) or to record the pledge or assignment in the licensor's business books.[94]

4 Priorities

4.1 *Priorities with Respect to the Insolvency Administrator*

4.1.1 Preferential Claims

Where a security right (i.e. pledge or security transfer) has been created and become effective, the secured creditor is entitled to preferential satisfaction from the IPR or licence in the insolvency proceedings of the grantor of the security right. For this

[91]Koziol (2011), p. 367; Wolkerstorfer (2016), § 448 para 42.

[92]Koziol (2013), p. 369; Koch (2011), p. 477.

[93]Supreme Court 23.11.1999, 4 Ob 274/99 v.

[94]See e.g. Supreme Court 30.4.2014, 3 Ob 34/14 t; Koziol et al. (2018), pp. 422 et seq., 456; Neumayr (2017), § 1392 para 7.

purpose, the collateral remains nonetheless part of the insolvency estate and in this capacity is, in principle (see Sect. 7.2 *infra*), subject to administration and realization by the insolvency administrator. Secured creditors are, however, to be satisfied preferentially from the proceeds of the collateral (*Absonderungsrecht*), according to section 48 and section 10 para 3 Austrian Insolvency Act[95] (AIA), and the collateral is considered a "separate estate" (*Sondermasse*). Only the surplus resulting from the liquidation proceeds of the separate estate becomes part of the common insolvency estate (section 48 para 2 AIA), which is available to unsecured creditors, including creditors of claims against the estate (*Massegläubiger*, see section 46 et seq. AIA) and mere insolvency creditors (*Insolvenzgläubiger*, see section 51 AIA). Where the separate estate is not sufficient to cover the secured claim, the secured creditor also participates in the insolvency proceedings as an insolvency creditor for the extent of the loss (section 103 para 3 AIA, section 132 AIA).[96]

The enforcement of a preferential claim is nonetheless subject to restrictions. First, it must be noted that in situations where fulfilling the secured (preferential) claim could endanger the continued business of the insolvent grantor's enterprise, the satisfaction of this claim may not be demanded before six months have passed following the opening of insolvency proceedings. However, this exception does not apply where the fulfillment of the secured claim is essential in order to avert serious personal or economic disadvantages for the secured creditor (section 11 para 2 AIA). The second restriction is that the default interest rate for secured interest claims is capped for a period of six months after the opening of the insolvency proceedings (section 48 para 1 AIA). Third, secured interest claims that accrue following the opening of insolvency proceedings and that are not covered by the realization proceeds of the "separate estate" cannot be asserted as insolvency claims (section 132 para 6 AIA).

4.1.2 Termination of Licence Agreements

The insolvency-specific and mandatory (section 25b para 1 AIA) reasons for terminating contracts that are laid down in sections 21–25 AIA are a particular threat to the continued existence of a licence as collateral in the event of insolvency. For licence agreements, the application of either the *lex generalis* on mutually unfulfilled contracts[97] (section 21 AIA) or the special rules on lease contracts (sections 23 and

[95] *Bundesgesetz über das Insolvenzverfahren*, Law Gazette of the Austrian Empire 1914/337, as last amended by Federal Law Gazette I 2020/24.

[96] See also Dellinger et al. (2018), p. 90 et seq.

[97] Whereas the obligation of the licensor to tolerate the use of the IPR is never fully "fulfilled" during the term of the licence agreement (see Supreme Court 8.9.2009, 4 Ob 135/09 w; see also section 32 para 1 ACA), for section 21 AIA to apply, the obligations of the licensee must be partially unfulfilled as well. This is the case in particular where an upright license payment obligation exists, see e.g. Burgstaller (2016), p. 59.

24 AIA) might be considered.[98] In legal literature, a distinction is made depending on whether the licence agreement in question includes elements that are typical of a lease agreement. Where this is the case, only the provisions on lease contracts shall apply (section 23 et seq. AIA). However, in cases where the licence agreement includes elements that are atypical of a lease agreement, such as the licensee's contractual duty to exploit the licence, section 21 AIA should be applicable.[99] The Supreme Court applied section 21 AIA in two cases,[100] but did not rule out the applicability of section 23 et seq. AIA where the elements of a lease agreement predominate.[101] From the perspective of an insolvency administrator, the application of section 21 is more advantageous since the provision grants the insolvency administrator a right of withdrawal from the contract, regardless of whether the insolvent debtor is the licensor or the licensee of the contract. By contrast, section 23 AIA only grants the insolvency administrator of the insolvent lessee (licensee) a specific termination right, whereas the administrator of an insolvent lessor enters into the lease agreement without being granted an insolvency-specific right to terminate the contract (section 24 AIA).

In the event that a licence is pledged, transferred, or granted for security purposes, there is therefore a risk for the secured party that the insolvency administrator of the insolvent licensor will terminate the licence agreement pursuant to section 21 AIA. The insolvency of the licensee constitutes a risk as well where the licence has been pledged[102]: in this instance, the insolvency administrator of the licensee would be entitled to withdrawal or termination, irrespective of the qualification of the licence contract with regard to sections 21 and 23 AIA (see also section 32 para 2 ACA[103]). The question has therefore been raised whether the obligation to maintain the collateral (see Sect. 6 *infra*), which in principle also affects the insolvency administrator, renders the exercise of a termination or withdrawal right by the insolvency administrator unlawful.[104]

---

[98] Gamerith (2000), Vor §§ 21–26 KO para 1; Höller (2013), § 14 para 156; Höller (2017), § 32 para 8 et seq.; Rathauscher (1999), p. 7; according to Koziol (2011), p. 124, licences entered in the Patent Register and licences with "absolute" effect should to be treated as easements, which are not subject to contract withdrawal or termination in accordance with sections 21 et seq.

[99] Höller (2013), § 14 para 163; Höller (2017), § 32 para 17; Rathauscher (1999), p. 82 et seq.; Widhalm (2001), p. 208; Widhalm-Budak (2017), § 21 IO para 61.

[100] Supreme Court 16.12.2010, 17 Ob 18/10 m; Supreme Court 8.9.2009, 4 Ob 135/09 v.

[101] Supreme Court 8.9.2009, 4 Ob 135/09 v.

[102] Where the licence has been transferred to the creditor as a security, the right to withdraw from or terminate the contract would, in this author's opinion, not come into effect, as the transfer of the licence causes the new licensee to take over the contractual position of the former licensee; see Supreme Court 8.9.2009, 4 Ob 135/09 w and Büchele (2017), § 28 para 3 with further references.

[103] Section 32 para 2 ACA stipulates that *the author* has a withdrawal right against an insolvent licensee who was contractually granted the exclusive right to reproduce and distribute the work of the author. However, section 32 para 2 ACA only applies in scenarios where the reproduction of the work has not yet begun at the time that insolvency proceedings are opened.

[104] Koziol (2011), p. 141 et seq.; Koch (2011), p. 480 et seq.

4.2 *Priorities with Respect to Other Parties, Taking Rights in the Same IPR*

Possible conflicts between secured creditors and other persons exercising rights in the same IPR have rarely been discussed in case law and legal literature. There is therefore a high degree of legal uncertainty in this area of the law. The legal basis for solving these problems seems to be clearest in patent, utility model, and design law, which will therefore serve as the starting point of this chapter.

4.2.1 Security Rights in Patents, Utility Models, and Registered Designs

Priorities with Respect to the Acquirer of the IPR

The effective pledge of a patent, utility model, or registered design does not prevent the IPR owner from disposing of the IPR—unlike in the case of a security transfer of the IPR.[105] As a right in rem, the (registered) pledge is attached to the IPR and passes to the acquirer as an encumbrance of the IPR (section 44 APA; section 32 para 4 AUMA; section 22 para 5 ADPA). Due to the nature of the registers, it has been argued that a good faith, burden-free acquisition of the IPR (*gutgläubiger lastenfreier Erwerb*) is not possible.[106] This is why any potential conflict between a pledgee and a new acquirer will be resolved in favour of the pledgee. The Austrian law on patents, utility models, and designs should thus guarantee a high degree of legal security for the secured party in this respect.[107]

[105]Supreme Court 30.4.1996, 4 Ob 2083/96 v; Constitutional Court 13.10.1986, B-699-707/85.

[106]Friebel and Pulitzer (1971), pp. 348, 363; Lang (1999a), p. 25 et seq.; this seems to be true with regard to security interests in a registered IPR; however, see Supreme Court 12.2.1991, 4 Ob 173/90, according to which "the lack of registration of the licence in the Patent Register only harms the licensee vis-à-vis a party *who relied on the Patent Register*"; see also Thiele (2018), § 22 para 25. As far as registered Community designs are concerned, it should be noted that a good-faith, burden-free acquisition of the IPR is conceivable under Art. 33 para 2 CDR where the acquirer had no actual knowledge of the unregistered pledge or security transfer. Whether a non-registered pledge or security transfer constitutes a valid legal "act" in terms of Art. 33 para 2 CDR may, however, be disputed where the registered Community design is subject to Austrian law as an "object of property"; see Koch (2011), p. 467.

[107]Where the IPR has been transferred for security purposes, the debtor is no longer the proprietor of the IPR. Consequently, the APO will reject any request for transfer to a new acquirer made by the former proprietor.

Priorities with Respect to Other Creditors and Licensees in Execution Proceedings

As far as the granting of a pledge is concerned, the fact that the IPR may be used for several secured transactions as an existing pledge does not prevent the IPR proprietor from granting further pledges with regards to the same collateral.[108] In contrast, the concept of a security transfer is designed to merely grant a single security right in the collateral.[109] Where several pledges have effectively been created in the same IPR, their priority (rank) depends on when the publicity act (mode of acquisition) has been performed. Therefore, the date of entry in the register is decisive.[110] Where multiple pledges exist, every pledgee (including subordinate ones) may, in principle, realize the property right according to the rules of the Austrian Enforcement of Judgements Act (AEJA)[111] when the secured claim is due.[112] Following the realization of the IPR, the secured creditors are nevertheless to be satisfied according to their priority (rank) from the proceeds of realization.[113]

The situation is similar where an unsecured creditor of the IPR proprietor takes enforcement action against an encumbered patent, utility model, or design. In this case, too, a pledgee may not prevent the execution of the property right; however, they are entitled to preferential satisfaction from the proceeds of the right's realization (section 258 AEJA). In this regard, the legal position of a secured creditor to whom an IPR has been transferred for security purposes differs from that of a (mere) pledge creditor. This is because the former may file opposition against the enforcement actions of a third party on the grounds of section 37 AEJA, given that the transferred IPR is no longer considered to be part of the creditor's liability fund.[114]

In addition to a conflict between various (secured) creditors, there may also be a conflict between a secured creditor and a licensee. This could occur in the event of an enforced sale of the IPR, where a licence in this IPR has to be taken over by the executive purchaser and therefore may reduce the amount of proceeds to be generated from the sale of the property right. According to the clear legal wording of the relevant legislation, however, only licences that have been entered in the relevant register are effective against third parties and must therefore be assumed by an acquirer of the IPR (section 43 para 2 and section 44 APA; section 32 para 4 AUMA;

---

[108] Iro (2016), p. 209 et seq.; Koziol et al. (2018), p. 439.

[109] Faber (2012), p. 347; Iro (2016), p. 245.

[110] More precisely: the date of receipt of the application by the APO, if the application leads to registration (section 43 para 3 APA; section 32 para 4 AUMA; section 22 para 5 ADPA).

[111] *Gesetz vom 27. Mai 1896, über das Exekutions- und Sicherungsverfahren (Exekutionsordnung)*, Law Gazette of the Austrian Empire 1896/97, as last amended by Federal Law Gazette I 2020/16.

[112] Iro (2016), p. 211.

[113] Sections 332 para 2, section 286 para 3 AEJA (enforced auction); section 334 para 2, section 125 AEJA (enforced receivership); section 340 para 2, section 125 AEJA (enforced lease).

[114] See e.g. Supreme Court 10.6.1981, 3 Ob 31/81; Koziol et al. (2018), pp. 453, 456.

section 22 para 5 ADPA).[115] In principle, this rule also applies where the right is acquired by way of an enforced sale (auction). However, according to legal literature, in this case, the further existence of the licence will ultimately depend on the priority of the registered licence and the amount of proceeds generated by the sale (sections 150 and 227 para 1 AEJA).[116]

4.2.2 Security Rights in Trademarks

The majority of the remarks in regard to patents, utility models, and designs can be applied *mutatis mutandis* to national trademark law. The rank order principle in particular also applies in trademark law (section 28 para 5 ATMA makes reference to section 43 para 3 APA). However, the fact that the role of the national trademark register and related matters have not yet been conclusively clarified is a particular problem.[117] Despite the fact that registration in the national trademark register is merely declaratory (see Sect. 3.2.2 *supra*), the secured creditor may well be fully protected against a later purchaser if it is assumed that a good faith, burden-free acquisition[118] (or in general, a good faith acquisition[119]) is not possible under Austrian trademark law. In this case, the security interest will continue to exist against a later purchaser. Apart from that, the outcome of a conflict between a creditor taking a security right in a trademark and a licensee of the same trademark is also uncertain where the trademark is subject to an enforced sale (auction). In this regard, a solution similar to the one under patent law has been offered.[120]

4.2.3 Security Rights in Licences

Where a licence is pledged in favour of several creditors, the priority of the pledge is to be determined in accordance with the general principles of civil law and therefore depends on when the security right is effectively acquired by the creditor.[121] In addition to the concerns addressed above, the question arises whether security interests in licences continue to exist in the case of a non-executive sale of the underlying IPR. According to the wording of the law, they do continue to exist for

[115] See also Friebel and Pulitzer (1971), pp. 305, 351 with references to earlier case law; see, however, Supreme Court 12.2.1991, 4 Ob 173/90.

[116] Friebel and Pulitzer (1971), p. 296; Suman (1904), p. 175, cited in Lang (1999a), p. 90.

[117] As for the role and function of the EU Trademark Register, see Sect. 3.2.4.

[118] Supreme Court 3.5.2000, 4 Ob 109/00 h; Supreme Patent and Trademark Senate 26.3.2008, Om 12/07.

[119] Koppensteiner (2012), p. 198, fn. 2; Schönherr (1982), p. 23.

[120] Höller (2013), § 14 para 176 et seq.; Koziol (2011), p. 128, however, argues that the trademark purchaser who has actual knowledge of the unregistered licence acquires the trademark subject to the non-registered licensee's right.

[121] Iro (2016), p. 209; as for the mode of acquisition, see Sect. 3.2.5.

patent, utility model, and design licences where the licence has been registered (see section 'Priorities with Respect to Other Creditors and Licensees in Execution Proceedings' *supra*). They also continue for EU trademark licences and Community design licences that have been registered or that were known to the acquirer (Art. 27 para 1 EUTMR; Art. 33 para 2 CDR). However, whether a national trademark licensee is entitled to succession protection is uncertain. Following the notion that an exclusive licence constitutes a "quasi right in rem" or an "absolute right,"[122] parts of Austrian trademark law literature assume that an exclusive trademark licence generally conveys succession protection.[123] In the area of copyright law, succession protection is granted to a licensee who is entitled to the non-exclusive use of a protected work (*Werknutzungsbewilligung*) against a licensee to whom an exclusive exploitation right (*Werknutzungsrecht*) in the same work is subsequently granted or transferred (section 24 para 2 ACA).

5 Enterprise Charges

While the legal institute of the enterprise charge is unknown to Austrian civil law, the contractual creation of a set of comprehensive security rights is possible; however, it is a complex endeavour due to Austrian property law principles: an enterprise within the meaning of "a permanently established organization pursuing independent business activities" (section 1 para 2 of the Austrian Commercial Code[124]) usually consists of a variety of tangible and intangible goods.[125] Due to the principle of specialty *(Spezialitätsgrundsatz)* in property law, according to which the creation and transfer of property rights is only possible for individual objects, an enterprise as such cannot be the object of a security interest.[126] The granting of security interests in all objects belonging to an enterprise therefore requires the observance of the relevant acquisition modes in order for the respective collateral to be pledged or transferred (physical or symbolic transfer for movables; entry in the land register for immovable property; entry in the IPR register for most IPRs; notification of the third-party debtor for claims, etc.).[127] Since IPRs are not perceived

[122]Supreme Court 15.2.2000, 4 Ob 29/00 v; Supreme Court 17.8.2000, 4 Ob 178/00 f; Supreme Court 15.10.2002, 4 Ob 209/02 t.

[123]Hiti (2003), p. 10; Koppensteiner (2012), p. 208; Schönherr (1982), p. 30.

[124]*Bundesgesetz über besondere zivilrechtliche Vorschriften für Unternehmen (Unternehmensgesetzbuch - UGB)*, Law Gazette of the German Empire 1897, p. 219, as last amended by Federal Law Gazette I 2019/63.

[125]Koziol et al. (2018), p. 279 et seq.

[126]Supreme Court 19.12.1984, 3 Ob 113/84; Wolkerstorfer (2016), § 447 para 14.

[127]Iro (2016), p. 178; Wolkerstorfer (2012), p. 123.

to be ancillary assets (see section 458 ACC) to immovable property, they are not covered by a mortgage on immovables used for the purposes of an enterprise.[128]

6 Rights and Obligations Before Default

The contracting parties to the pledge/security agreement are subject to a number of mutual rights and obligations before the secured claim becomes due. On the one hand, the pledgee is not entitled to use the pledged asset without the proper approval of the pledger (section 459 ACC) due to the merely satisfactory function of the pledge.[129] An ancillary agreement according to which the pledgee is entitled to the usufruct of the pledged asset is deemed to be void (section 1372 ACC). In addition, not only the creditor (sections 459, 1369 ACC) but also the grantor is obliged to maintain and safeguard the collateral to the fullest extent possible.[130] Therefore, the latter has to provide a substitute pledge in the event of a culpable deterioration or destruction of the pledged asset (section 458 ACC). On these grounds, the proprietor of the IPR is liable to compensate the creditor in the event that the encumbered IPR was waived (surrendered) by the proprietor.[131] In certain cases, the grantor may also be obliged to act actively. For example, if a trademark is pledged, the grantor is obliged to ensure that the IPR is put to "genuine use" (section 33a ATMA; section 18 EUTMR) and pay the necessary renewal fees[132] in order to safeguard the continued existence of the collateral.[133]

7 Enforcement

7.1 Enforcement Outside Insolvency Proceedings

7.1.1 Judicial Enforcement

According to section 461 ACC, a pledge entitles the pledgee to demand judicial realization of the pledged asset, whereby the court must act in accordance with the

[128]Higher Regional Court Linz 15.1.1962, 1 R 4.

[129]As the main purpose of a security transfer is to establish a right to preferential satisfaction rather than a right to use the IPR, the parties to a security agreement will generally agree on the relicensing of the IPR until the secured claim becomes due; see Koch (2011), p. 468; Koziol (2011), p. 110 et seq.; Lang (1999a), p. 102; Salomonowitz (2013), § 11 para 76.

[130]See e.g. Supreme Court 29.8.2017, 6 Ob 228/16 x.

[131]Friebel and Pulitzer (1971), p. 291.

[132]Where the grantor fails to pay the fee, the creditor is entitled to do so instead; see Koziol (2011), p. 112 et seq.

[133]Koch (2011), pp. 468, 479 et seq.; Wolkerstorfer (2012), pp. 182, 190.

Civil Procedure Act and the Enforcement of Judgements Act. The same applies where the collateral has been transferred for security purposes rather than being pledged.[134] The pledgee must first obtain an execution title by filing suit for performance (*Leistungsklage*). In the next step, the creditor can apply to the competent court for enforcement, which is to be carried out in accordance with the provisions on "enforcement against other property rights" (section 330 et seq. AEJA). After the enforcement court has approved judicial enforcement proceedings, the IPR or licence is seized (Art. 331 AEJA), transforming the contractual security interest into an enforceable "right of satisfaction" and depriving the grantor of the power to dispose of the seized object.[135] In the case of patents, utility models, and designs, seizure is effected by the entry of a judicial pledge in the relevant IPR register.[136] Trademarks, however, are seized upon a court order that prohibits the grantor of the security right from disposing of the trademark (section 331 para 1 AEJA)[137]; where licences are involved, the licensee and the licensor are addressed by this court order (*Doppelverbot*).[138] The seizure is finally followed by realization of the collateral, and although the creditor may apply for a certain type of liquidation, the execution court decides at its own discretion on the type of realization used (section 331 para 2 AEJA).[139] According to the Enforcement of Judgements Act, the primary forms of enforcement "against other property rights" are enforced receivership (section 334 AEJA) and enforced leasing (section 340 AEJA).[140] In both cases, the creditor is satisfied from the proceeds of future licensing agreements. In enforced receivership, a separate administrator is appointed who has to conclude (sub)licence agreements and collect due licence claims. Where it seems more advantageous (in particular due to the lower cost), enforced leasing can be ordered instead (section 340 para 1 AEJA). Here, (sub)licensing takes place without intervention by an administrator on the basis of court-approved licensing terms.[141] The creditor may, however, also obtain satisfaction from the proceeds of a sale of the IPR or licence where the court orders an open market sale or an auction.[142] According to a decision of the Supreme Patent and Trademark Senate, another option for enforcement

[134]Supreme Court 7.11.1951, 3 Ob 574/51; Fidler (2016), § 461 para 82 with further references.

[135]Friebel and Pulitzer (1971), p. 292; Rechberger and Oberhammer (2009), p. 76 et seq.

[136]Frauenberger (2014), § 331 EO para 50 et seq.; Friebel and Pulitzer (1971), p. 292; Neumann and Lichtblau (1976), p. 2462 et seq.; Oberhammer (2015), § 331 para 61.

[137]Supreme Patent and Trademark Senate 25.10.2000, Om 3/2000; Austrian Patent Office (Board of Appeal) 24.10.1991, Bm 9-12/89.

[138]Oberhammer (2015), § 331 EO para 62; Neumann and Lichtblau (1976), p. 2463; more restrictive: Frauenberger (2014), § 331 EO para 50 et seq.

[139]Supreme Patent and Trademark Senate 25.10.2000, Om 3/2000.

[140]Supreme Court 19.11.2008, 3 Ob 207/08 z; Friebel and Pulitzer (1971), p. 291.

[141]Frauenberger (2014), § 340 EO para 2; Oberhammer (1999), p. 378.

[142]Frauenberger (2014), § 332 EO para 2; Oberhammer (2015), § 332 EO para 2; an auction should, however, only take place where another type of enforcement cannot be carried out at all, or can only be carried out at disproportionately high costs (section 332 para 1 AEJA), see Supreme Court 19.11.2008, 3 Ob 207/08 z.

against trademarks is the transfer of the trademark to the creditor, by analogy to section 303 para 1 AEJA (judicial transfer of receivables), whereby the creditor takes on the legal position of the grantor of the security right in order to seek satisfaction.[143]

7.1.2 Out-of-Court Enforcement

Where collateral has been fully transferred to a creditor for security purposes, the creditor can effectively dispose of the collateral out of court by virtue of full ownership[144] and may do so where the security agreement allows this. In the case of a pledged asset, however, no statutory right exists that would enable the pledge creditor to demand out-of-court enforcement of IPRs and licences.[145] The pledgee may therefore only do so where this has been agreed with the grantor of the security right.[146] Such an agreement must be compatible with the mandatory provision of section 1371 ACC, which only refers to pledge agreements in its wording, but is nevertheless also applicable to security agreements[147] and security licence agreements.[148] Section 1371 ACC limits the possibility of extrajudicial enforcement in various ways. For one, it renders invalid any contractual provision according to which the collateral falls to the creditor upon the due date of the secured obligation. It also prohibits any agreement under which the secured creditor may sell or retain the collateral at his discretion, or even sell or keep the collateral at a price determined in advance (section 1371 sentence 2 ACC). According to case law, however, an out-of-court sale agreement is permissible at all times where the grantor's legitimate interests are effectively protected. This is the case where the out-of-court sale has to be made at a price based on objective criteria (price estimated by an expert) or where the grantor is given the opportunity to name a (higher bidding) buyer.[149]

143 Supreme Patent and Trademark Senate 25.10.2000, Om 3/2000.

144 Eccher and Riss (2017), § 361 para 6; Salomonowitz (2013), § 11 para 77. However, the creditor may only do so if he is entitled to take such action under the security agreement; see e.g. Apathy (2011), p. 299.

145 The statutory right to seek out-of-court enforcement (section 466a et seq. ACC) only concerns tangible property; see Koch (2011), p. 469; Wolkerstorfer (2012), pp. 186, 190.

146 Oberhammer and Domej (2017), Vor §§ 461-466e para 2; Fidler (2016), Vor §§ 461 para 37; Koch (2011), p. 469.

147 See e.g. Supreme Court 3.11.2005, 6 Ob 183/05 p.

148 Supreme Court 23.11.1999, 4 Ob 274/99 v.

149 See e.g. Supreme Court 15.1.2002, 5 Ob 295/01 w with further references.

7.2 *Enforcement in Insolvency Proceedings*

When it comes to preferential claims in insolvency proceedings, the insolvency administrator has several options. The administrator is entitled to pay the secured debt and thus extinguish the security interest (section 120 para 1 AIA), but may also sell the secured property either in court (section 119 ACA) or out of court (section 120 para 2 AIA). If the administrator chooses the latter option, the secured creditor has the right to appeal to the insolvency court on the grounds that a court sale (auction) would be considerably more advantageous for him or her (section 120 para 2 AIA). However, the secured creditor may also seek or continue to seek judicial enforcement[150] against the collateral, as preferential claims remain unaffected by the opening of insolvency proceedings (section 11 para 1 AIA) and are not covered by the bar of trial which is triggered upon the commencement of insolvency proceedings (section 6 para 2 AIA). In such cases, however, the competent execution court may stay the execution proceedings begun by the secured creditor if the insolvency administrator has already envisaged extrajudicial realization of the collateral (section 120a para 1 AIA).[151]

8 Costs

The costs associated with the creation of a security interest in an IPR or in a licence depend on each individual case. In addition to expenses for legal advice in advance (the amount of which depends on the respective contractual agreement), fees for registration in the respective register may come into play. Where a pledge or a transfer of ownership is entered in the national patent, utility model, design or trademark register, it amounts to EUR 125.00 (EUR 85.00 for the registration as per section 28 para 1 subpara 4 of the Patent Office Fees Act,[152] plus an additional EUR 40.00 according to section 14 TP (*Tarifpost*) 10 para 1 subpara 7 Austrian Act on Fees[153]). The fee for the registration of a right in rem in an EU trademark is EUR 200.00 (Annex I A 26 EUTMR) and so is the fee for the registration of a right in rem

[150] As of today, it is uncertain whether an agreement on out-of-court enforcement of the collateral is insolvency-proof in the sense that it is binding not only upon the grantor of the security right but also upon the insolvency administrator. If this is the case, the secured creditor may seek out-of-court enforcement even after the opening of insolvency proceedings; see Fidler (2016), Vor §§ 461-466e para 38; Oberhammer and Domej (2017), Vor §§ 461-466e para 9.

[151] However, the stay is not to be granted where the continuation of the execution proceedings is indispensable for the secured creditor to avert serious economic disadvantages (section 120a para 1 AIA).

[152] *Bundesgesetz über die im Bereich des Patentamtes zu zahlenden Gebühren und Entgelte*, Federal Law Gazette I 2004/149 as last amended by Federal Law Gazette I 2018/89.

[153] *Gebührengesetz 1957*, Federal Law Gazette 1957/267, as last amended by Federal Law Gazette I 2020/23.

in or transfer of a registered Community design.[154] The registration of a transfer or of "other rights" regarding a European patent application[155] or a unitary patent[156] amounts to EUR 100.00.

An additional cost factor is involved in the requirement to obtain a notarized or court-certified signature in order to register a pledge, as provided for in national IP laws (see Sect. 3.2.1 *supra*). The fees for signature certification in general depend on the amount of the secured claim and therefore increase with it. However, the fees for notarial certification[157] are capped at the top, unlike those for judicial certification.[158] Where the IPR is transferred for security purposes (and not merely pledged), a fee for the establishment of the document of the underlying legal transaction (*Rechtgeschäftsgebühr*) is charged in accordance with section 33 TP 21 of the Austrian Act on Fees.[159]

The costs of judicial enforcement depend to an even greater extent on the individual case. In addition to costs that may be incurred for legal advice, there are also costs for the remuneration of qualified experts, whom judges normally need to consult.[160] Further costs include execution fees,[161] any auctioning or open market sale costs, and, if applicable, the remuneration of a forced administrator (section 113 et seq. AEJA). A prevailing creditor may, however, demand reimbursement of the costs incurred in enforcement proceedings and enforce the reimbursement claims together with the secured claim, provided that these costs were necessary for the realization of the secured claim (section 74 AEJA; section 41 Code of Civil

[154] Points 17 and 18 of the Annex to the Commission Regulation (EC) No. 2246/2002 of December 16, 2002 on the Fees Payable to the Office for Harmonization in the Internal Market in Respect of the Registration of Community Designs, OJ EC L 341 of 17.12.2002, p. 54, as amended by Commission Regulation (EC) No. 877/2007 of July 24, 2007.

[155] Decision of the President of the EPO Dated December 13, 2013 Revising the Office's Fees and Expenses (republication), OJ EPO 2016/2 (supplementary publication), p. 19 et seq.

[156] Art. 5 of the Decision of the Select Committee of the Administrative Council of December 15, 2015 Adopting the Rules Relating to Fees for Unitary Patent Protection (SC/D 2/15), OJ EPO 2016, A 40.

[157] The fees for notarial certification are prescribed in section 25 para 1 of the *Bundesgesetz vom 8. November 1973 über den Notariatstarif*, Federal Law Gazette 1973/576, as last amended by Federal Law Gazette I 2017/40.

[158] The fees for judicial certification are laid down in Tarifpost 11 (a) *Bundesgesetz vom 27. November 1984 über die Gerichts- und Justizverwaltungsgebühren*, Federal Law Gazette 1984/501, as last amended by Federal Law Gazette I 2019/81.

[159] Arnold and Arnold (2011), § 33 TP 21 paras 6 and 7 with further references; Graf and Pronbauer (2016), p. 208; Twardosz (2015), § 33 TP 21 paras 14 and 31 with further references.

[160] The fees of the court-appointed expert are regulated by the *Bundesgesetz vom 19.2.1975 über die Gebühren der Zeugen und Zeuginnen, Sachverständigen, Dolmetscher und Dolmetscherinnen, Geschworenen, Schöffen und Schöffinnen*, Federal Law Gazette 1975/136, as last amended by Federal Law Gazette I 2019/44.

[161] *Bundesgesetz über die Vollzugsgebühren*, Federal Law Gazette 2003/31, as last amended by Federal Law Gazette I 2018/58.

Procedure[162]). The extent to which a lawyer's costs are reimbursable is determined in accordance with the Austrian Lawyers' Tariff Act.[163]

9 Practical Usefulness

The practical usefulness of IPRs and licences does not appear to be very great for the purposes of secured transactions in Austria. Among the various possible applications, the pledging of trademarks is most likely to play a role in the restructuring of companies where the insolvent company uses all its assets that have not yet been used as collateral to secure credit. Even in such cases, however, it is unlikely that the trademark is ever realized, either because there is hardly any prospect of successful realization due to its low value, or because the bank later releases the collateral to facilitate the entry of an investor. Unlike in other countries, in Austria, the use of exploitation rights (section 40 para 1 ACA) and (exclusive) licences (*Werknutzungsrechte*) for secured transactions does not play a major role in the domestic film industry which relies to a considerable extent on public subsidies and public financing (e.g. *Österreichischer Filmfonds (ÖFI), Filmfonds Wien, Filmstandort Austria, Fernsehfonds Austria, Österreichischer Rundfunk*).[164]

This assessment, which is based on discussions with various experts from the field of credit security practice, seems to coincide with the statistical surveys of the APO, which up until 2003 included the annual number of pledges entered in the Patent Register and the Designs register.[165] In view of the fact that these numbers include pledges registered during court-ordered enforcement procedures (see Sect. 7.1.1 *supra*), the number of pledges registered annually up until 2003 can in fact be described as rather low.[166] Nevertheless, the increasing importance of IPRs and licences for secured credit in the future has been emphasized in Austrian literature.[167]

[162]*Gesetz vom 1. August 1895, über das gerichtliche Verfahren in bürgerlichen Rechtsstreitigkeiten*, Law Gazette of the Austrian Empire 1895/113, as last amended by Federal Law Gazette I 2018/109.

[163]*Rechtsanwaltstarifgesetz*, Federal Law Gazette 1969/189, as last amended by Federal Law Gazette I 2020/19.

[164]In the recent past, however, financiers of larger Austrian film projects have begun to demand so-called "*completion guarantees*" ("*completion bonds*"). These guarantees usually include a takeover clause according to which the completion guarantor (usually an insurance company) has the right to assume the role of the film producer or to substitute the film producer for the purpose of completing the film. For this purpose, all copyrights and neighbouring rights necessary for the production and exploitation of the film are assigned to the guarantor in the event of a takeover.

[165]Unfortunately, the number of pledges registered concerning trademarks and utility models was never recorded statistically.

[166]Between 1997 and 2003, an average of 24 pledges per year was registered in the Patent Register. No pledges were registered at all in relation to Austrian registered designs during this period.

[167]Koziol (2011), p. 1 et seq.; Salomonowitz (2013), § 11 para 67.

10 Legal and Practical Difficulties

The relative insignificance of IPRs and licences in the field of secured transactions is likely due to several factors. One point of criticism voiced by practitioners is that IPRs sometimes lose value rather quickly (e.g. patents and utility models due to technical progress), which can be a particular problem for loans with long maturities. In addition, IPRs are not recognized risk mitigation techniques that can reduce the equity ratio required for lending under the Capital Requirements Regulation.[168]

In regard to trademarks in particular, it has also been noted that a security right in a trademark which does not extend to the associated products is only rarely of value. In addition, a company's impending insolvency might have an impact on its economic reputation and, as a result, on the value of the trademark.

11 Law Reform

Among the more recent law reform efforts, the work of the *Ludwig Boltzmann Institut für Rechtsvorsorge und Urkundenwesen* is of note. In 2003, the institute set up a working group which dealt with the general question whether an amendment to the law of secured transactions introducing a register for security rights in movable property (*Register für Mobiliarsicherheiten*) would be useful, and examined how such a register could best be structured.[169] The result of the working group's activities was a series of recommendations which were largely oriented towards the previous status quo, thus adhering to the existence of different categories of security rights (retention of title, pledge, security transfer of ownership, etc.). Therefore, the focus of the working group was on the creation of a new register as an additional means of obtaining publicity (section 452 ACC). As far as security rights in IPRs were concerned, it was recommended that security rights in patents should be excluded from the scope of the register and thus continue to be entered in the Patent Register. The creation of security rights in exclusive exploitation rights (*Werknutzungsrechte*) under the Austrian Copyright Act, on the other hand, was to take place upon entry in the new register.[170] However, it remained unclear whether the creation of security interests in trademarks or licences (other than exclusive copyright licences) would also be possible by means of entry in the new register.[171]

The preparatory work of the Ludwig Boltzmann Institute was subsequently taken up by the Federal Ministry of Justice, which also set up a working group. In this

---

[168]Regulation (EU) No. 575/2013 of the European Parliament and of the Council of June 26, 2013 on Prudential Requirements for Credit Institutions and Investment Firms and Amending Regulation (EU) No. 648/2012, OJ L 176, 27.6.2013, p. 1.

[169]Schauer (2006), p. 267.

[170]Schauer (2006), p. 268 (recommendation 2.3.4); Lukas (2007), p. 267.

[171]Koziol (2013), p. 374.

context, however, it became clear that there was no consensus on the basic aim of a potential amendment to the Austrian law on secured transactions.[172] Meanwhile, the reform efforts announced in the middle of the 2000s have come to a standstill: while the government program for 2007–2010 still made reference to the intended establishment of a register for secured transactions,[173] the two subsequent government programs no longer contained any plans for a revision of the current legal situation. In the government program 2017–2022,[174] the "revision of parts of property law" was again considered.

References

Apathy P (2011) Die Sicherungsübereignung. In: Apathy P, Iro G, Koziol H (eds) Österreichisches Bankvertragsrecht, vol 9. Springer, Vienna, pp 277–301

Appl C (2018) Musterschutzrecht. In: Wiebe (ed) Wettbewerbs- und Immaterialgüterrecht, 4th edn. Facultas, Vienna, pp 91–124

Arnold W, Arnold N (2011) Rechtsgebühren, 9th edn. Facultas, Vienna

Böhler E (2012) Allgemeiner Teil des Kreditsicherungsrechts. In: Apathy P, Iro G, Koziol H (eds) Österreichisches Bankvertragsrecht, vol 8, 2nd edn. Springer, Vienna, pp 1–204

Büchele M (2017) § 28. In: Kucsko G, Handig C (eds) Urheber.recht – Systematischer Kommentar zum Urheberrechtsgesetz, 2nd edn. Manz, Vienna

Burgstaller P (2009) Patentrecht und Technologietransfer. Verlag Medien und Recht, Vienna

Burgstaller P (2016) Urheber- und Patentlizenzen in der Insolvenz. Ecolex 2016:57–60

Dellinger M, Oberhammer P, Koller C (2018) Insolvenzrecht – Eine Einführung, 4th edn. Manz, Vienna

Eccher B, Riss O (2017) § 361. In: Koziol H, Bydlinski P, Bollenberger R (eds) ABGB Kurzkommentar, 5th edn. Verlag Österreich, Vienna

Engin-Deniz E (2017) Markenschutzgesetz und weitere kennzeichenrechtliche Bestimmungen, 3rd edn. Verlag Österreich, Vienna

Ertl G (2002) § 1392. In: Rummel P (ed) Kommentar zum ABGB, vol 1, 3rd edn. Manz, Vienna

Faber W (2012) Das Mobiliarsicherungsrecht des DCFR: Perspektiven für eine Reform in Österreich bzw. in Europa (Teil I). JBl 2012:341–358

Fidler P (2016) Vor §§ 461, § 461, Vor §§ 461-466e. In: Fenyves A, Kerschner F, Vonkilch A (eds) Großkommentar zum ABGB (Klang), §§ 447 – 530, 3rd edn. Verlag Österreich, Vienna

Frauenberger U (2014) §§ 331, 332, 340. In: Deixler-Hübner A, Burgstaller A (eds) Exekutionsordnung – Kommentar, updated commentary. LexisNexis, Vienna

Friebel L, Pulitzer O (1971) Österreichisches Patentrecht – Das materielle Recht, 2nd edn. Heymann, Cologne

Gamerith H (2000) Vor §§ 21–26 KO. In: Bartsch R, Pollak R, Buchegger W (eds) Österreichisches Insolvenzrecht, vol 1, 4th edn. Springer

Grabinski K (2019) Art 71. In: Ehlers J, Kinkeldey U (eds) Europäisches Patentübereinkommen, 3rd edn. C.H. Beck, Munich

[172] Lukas (2007), p. 268.

[173] Lukas (2007), p. 269 referring to *Regierungsprogramm 2007-2010*, p. 149.

[174] Zusammen. Für unser Österreich. Regierungsprogramm 2017-2022, p. 43. https://www.bundeskanzleramt.gv.at/documents/131008/569203/Regierungsprogramm_2017%e2%80%932022.pdf/b2fe3f65-5a04-47b6-913d-2fe512ff4ce6. Accessed Jan 9, 2019.

Graf S, Pronbauer L (2016) Die Zessionsgebühr bei Markenübertragungen. ÖBl 2016:208–218
Grünwald A (2015) Gewerblicher Rechtsschutz I – Markenrecht mit Mustern und Formularen. Verlag Österreich, Vienna
Grünzweig C (2017) Österreichisches, europäisches und internationales Markenrecht – Praxiskommentar zum Markenschutzgesetz. LexisNexis, Vienna
Heinrich P (2019) Art 74 EPÜ. In: Fitzner U, Lutz R, Bodewig T (eds) Beck'scher Online-Kommentar Patentrecht, 13th edn. C.H. Beck, Munich
Hinteregger M (2012) § 448. In: Schwimann M, Kodek G (eds) ABGB Praxiskommentar, vol 2, 4th edn. LexisNexis, Vienna
Hiti K (2003) Zur Drittwirkung von Marken- und Patentlizenzen. ÖBl 2003:4–11
Höller W (2013) § 14. In: Kucsko G, Schumacher C (eds) Marken.schutz – Systematischer Kommentar zum Markenschutzgesetz, 2nd edn. Manz, Vienna
Höller W (2017) § 32. In: Kucsko G, Handig C (eds) Urheber.recht – Systematischer Kommentar zum Urheberrechtsgesetz, 2nd edn. Manz, Vienna
Horn C, Grünwald A (2015) Gewerblicher Rechtsschutz II – Patent-, Gebrauchs und Geschmacksmusterrecht mit Mustern und Formularen. Verlag Österreich, Vienna
Iro G (2016) Sachenrecht, 6th edn. Verlag Österreich, Vienna
Kisslinger M (2011) § 292. In: Fenyves A, Kerschner F, Vonkilch A (eds) Großkommentar zum ABGB (Klang), §§ 285 – 352, 3rd edn. Verlag Österreich, Vienna
Koch B (2011) Kreditsicherheiten an Gesellschaftsanteilen, Immaterialgütern, Internet-Domains. In: Apathy P, Iro G, Koziol H (eds) Österreichisches Bankvertragsrecht, vol 9. Springer, Vienna, pp 435–483
Kolle G (2019) Art 2. In: Ehlers J, Kinkeldey U (eds) Europäisches Patentübereinkommen, 3rd edn. C.H. Beck, Munich
Koppensteiner H-G (2012) Markenrecht – Österreichisches und Europäisches Wettbewerbsrecht, 4th edn. LexisNexis, Vienna
Koziol G (2011) Lizenzen als Kreditsicherheiten – Zivilrechtliche Grundlagen in Deutschland, Österreich und Japan. Mohr Siebeck, Tübingen
Koziol G (2013) Sicherungsrechte an Immaterialgüterrechten und Register für Mobiliarsicherheiten. In: Perner S, Riss O (eds) Festschrift für Gert Iro zum 65. Geburtstag. Jan Sramek Verlag, Vienna, pp 365–379
Koziol H, Welser R, Kletečka A (2018) Bürgerliches Recht, vol 1, 15th edn. Manz, Vienna
Kucsko G (2003) Geistiges Eigentum – Markenrecht, Musterrecht, Patentrecht, Urheberrecht. Manz, Vienna
Lang S (1999a) Patente, Patentanmeldungen und Erfindungen als Kreditsicherungsmittel. Verlag Österreich, Vienna
Lang S (1999b) Patente, Patentanmeldungen und Erfindungen als Kreditsicherungsmittel. Ecolex 1999:475–479
Lukas M (2007) Vom UNCITRAL Legislative Guide on Secured Transactions zu einem Mobiliarpfandregister in Österreich. ÖBA 2007:262–269
Madl P (1991) Pfandrecht an Marken. Ecolex 1991:329–330
McGuire M-R (2008) Intellectual property rights: "property" or "right"? The application of the transfer rules to intellectual property. In: Faber W, Lurger B (eds) Rules for the transfer of movables: a candidate for European harmonisation or national reforms? Sellier De Gruyter, Berlin, pp 217–237
Neumann G, Lichtblau L (1976) In: Heller L, Berger F, Stix L (eds) Kommentar zur Exekutionsordnung, vol 3, 4th edn. Manz, Vienna
Neumayr M (2017) § 1392. In: Koziol H, Bydlinski P, Bollenberger R (eds) ABGB Kurzkommentar, 5th edn. Verlag Österreich, Vienna
Oberhammer P (1999) Das Mietrecht als Gegenstand der Zwangsvollstreckung. Wobl 1999:376–384
Oberhammer P (2015) §§ 331, 332, 340. In: Angst P, Oberhammer P (eds) EO – Kommentar zur Exekutionsordnung, 3rd edn. Manz, Vienna

Oberhammer P, Domej T (2017) Vor §§ 461-466e. In: Kletečka A, Schauer M (eds) ABGB-ON - Kommentar zum Allgemeinen bürgerlichen Gesetzbuch, updated online commentary. Manz, Vienna
Rathauscher S (1999) Bestandrechte und Konkur. Orac, Vienna
Rechberger W, Oberhammer P (2009) Exekutionsrecht, 5th edn. Facultas, Vienna
Ruhl O (2019) Art 28, 29. In: Ruhl O, Tolkmitt J (eds) Gemeinschaftsgeschmacksmuster – Kommentar, 3rd edn. Carl Heymanns Verlag, Cologne
Salomonowitz S (2013) §§ 11, 14. In: Kucsko G, Schumacher C (eds) Marken.schutz – Systematischer Kommentar zum Markenschutzgesetz, 2nd edn. Manz, Vienna
Schauer M (2006) Arbeitsgruppe "Register für Mobiliarsicherheiten"– Abschluss der Tätigkeit und Empfehlungskatalog. NZ 2006:267–272
Schennen D (2017) Art 17, 19, 23. In: Eisenführ G, Schennen D (eds) Unionsmarkenverordnung, 5th edn. Carl Heymanns Verlag, Cologne
Schönherr F (1982) Gewerblicher Rechtsschutz und Urheberrecht – Allgemeiner Teil. Manz, Vienna
Suman J (1904) Kommentar zum österreichischen Patentgesetz. M Breitenstein, Vienna
Taxhet M (2018) Art 27 UMV. In: Kur A, Bomhard V, Albrecht F (eds) Markenrecht – Markengesetz, Verordnung über die Unionsmarke (UMV), 2nd edn. C.H. Beck, Munich
Thiele C (2018) § 22. In: Thiele C, Schneider T (eds) MuSchG und Muster-RL – Österreichisches und Europäisches Design- und Musterschutzrecht, vol 1. Verlag Österreich, Vienna
Twardosz B (2015) Gebührengesetz, 6th edn. Manz, Vienna
Ullrich R (2013) § 2. In: Kucsko G, Schumacher C (eds) Marken.schutz – Systematischer Kommentar zum Markenschutzgesetz, 2nd edn. Manz, Vienna
Walter M (1995) OGH 18.10.1994, 4 Ob 93/94 (annotation). MR 1995:101–106
Walter M (2008) Handbuch Österreichisches Urheberrecht, vol 1. Verlag Medien und Recht, Vienna
Weiser A (2016) Patentgesetz, Gebrauchsmustergesetz – Kurzkommentar, 3rd edn. Manz, Vienna
Welser R, Zöchling-Jud B (2014) Bürgerliches Recht, vol 2, 14th edn. Manz, Vienna
Widhalm K (2001) Die Rechte des Urhebers, Masseverwalters und Dritten im Konkurs und Ausgleich des Werknutzungsberechtigten. ÖBl 2001:205–214
Widhalm-Budak K (2017) § 21 IO. In: Konecny A (ed) Kommentar zu den Insolvenzgesetzen, updated commentary. Manz, Vienna
Wiebe A (2018) Einführung. In: Wiebe (ed) Wettbewerbs- und Immaterialgüterrecht, 4th edn. Facultas, ViennaWal, pp 27–38
Wolkerstorfer T (2012) Das Pfandrecht des Unternehmers – Aktuelle Praxisprobleme und Lösungen. Manz, Vienna
Wolkerstorfer T (2016) §§ 447, 448, 451. In: Fenyves A, Kerschner F, Vonkilch A (eds) Großkommentar zum ABGB (Klang), §§ 447 – 530, 3rd edn. Verlag Österreich, Vienna

Security Rights in Intellectual Property in Belgium

Matthias E. Storme and Jasmine Malekzadem

Abstract This chapter provides an overview of security rights in intellectual property and some related topics under Belgian law; as it was written as a national report for the Congress of the International Academy of Comparative Law, it tries to deal with the subtopics that were identified by the General Reporter (Eva-Maria Kieninger). In Sect. 1, we give a very short overview of the assets within the scope of the contribution (i.e. the intellectual property rights recognized in Belgian law) and, where relevant, the system of publicity (i.e. registration) for such rights. In Sect. 2, we discuss the proprietary security rights in IP and in associated assets (i.e. royalties) that are recognized in Belgian law, as well as how they are created and perfected; we also add security rights in related assets, namely royalties. In Sect. 3, we discuss the rules governing conflicting rights in the same asset (i.e. priorities), in Sect. 4 we look at the rights of the parties (irrespective of a default) in relation to the secured debt. Finally, in Sect. 5, we discuss the enforcement of security rights in IP.

1 Overview of IP Rights

Federal Law In Belgium, intellectual property law is a matter of federal law. As Belgium is a Member State of the EU, the law of intellectual property is evidently to a large extent implementing EU law. Moreover, uniform Benelux (Belgium, the Netherlands, and Luxemburg) law also plays an important role.

Insolvency law and the law on security rights are also a federal matter, apart from a few exceptions not relevant for this report. Both the law on security rights in movables and the law on insolvency have been recodified recently in Belgium, the

M. E. Storme (✉)
Catholic University of Leuven – KU Leuven, Leuven, Belgium
e-mail: matthias.stormr@kuleuven.be

J. Malekzadem
University of Ghent – UGent, Gent, Belgium
e-mail: Jasmine.Malekzadem@ugent.be

E.-M. Kieninger (ed.), *Security Rights in Intellectual Property*, Ius Comparatum – Global Studies in Comparative Law 45,
https://doi.org/10.1007/978-3-030-44191-3_4

first by the Act of July 11, 2013 on security interests in movable property,[1] introducing Title XVII of Book III into the Civil Code, hereinafter referred to as the (new) "Pledge Act".[2] These new rules on security rights (contained in the Pledge Act) entered into force on January 1, 2018. Secondly, a new Insolvency Act has entered into force on May 1, 2018.[3]

Categories Intellectual property rights (hereinafter referred to as "IP rights") are traditionally divided into two categories in Belgian doctrine: (i) copyrights and (ii) industrial property rights.[4] The category of copyrights contains: traditional works of literature, music, and art, as well as audiovisual works, and even computer programs and databases. The category of industrial property rights contains, among other things: patents, including supplementary protection certificates; plant breeders' rights; designs; trademarks; trade names; names of origin; and topographies of integrated circuits ("chips"). Whether domain names are also IP rights are disputed, according to some authors they are mere rights to performance of service obligations; whether they can be pledged if thus qualified depends on the effect of the no-assignment clauses and other clauses that are typically found in the service contract with the domain registration provider.

Copyright According to Belgian law, copyright does not need to be registered for its creation. Every type of work by an author is protected simply by way of expression (Article XI.165 §1 Code of Economic Law, hereinafter "CEL").[5] The only requirement is that the work must have a concrete form and should be original.

---

[1]Act of July 11, 2013 on security interests in movable property, Belgian Official Gazette of August 2, 2013, www.ejustice.just.fgov.be/cgi_loi/change_lg.pl?language=fr&la=F&cn=2013071122&table_name=loi.

[2]For more information about the new Pledge Act, see: Storme (2017), Dirix (2013), Cattaruzza (2013), Georges (2013), Grégoire (2014), Derijcke (2013), Baeck and Kruithof (2014), del Corral (2014), Becue (2014) and Baeck (2015).

[3]Act of August 11, 2017 introducing Book XX on Insolvency in the Code of Economic law, Belgian Official Gazette of August 11, 2017.

[4]See for more information: Corbet et al. (1995), p. 246; Gielen and Hagemans (2011); Gotzen and Janssens (2016); Vanhees (2015).

[5]Since January 1, 2015, Belgian legislation on IP rights has mostly been codified in the new Code of Economic Law (hereinafter referred to as "CEL").

Article XI.165 CEL:

> § 1er. L'auteur d'une œuvre littéraire ou artistique a seul le droit de la reproduire ou d'en autoriser la reproduction, de quelque manière et sous quelque forme que ce soit, qu'elle soit directe ou indirecte, provisoire ou permanente, en tout ou en partie.
>
> Ce droit comporte notamment le droit exclusif d'en autoriser l'adaptation ou la traduction.
>
> Ce droit comprend également le droit exclusif d'en autoriser la location ou le prêt.
>
> L'auteur d'une œuvre littéraire ou artistique a seul le droit de la communiquer au public par un procédé quelconque, y compris par la mise à disposition du public de manière que chacun puisse y avoir accès de l'endroit et au moment qu'il choisit individuellement.
>
> L'auteur d'une œuvre littéraire ou artistique a seul le droit d'autoriser la distribution au public, par la vente ou autrement, de l'original de son œuvre ou de copies de celle-ci.

Registration Requirement for Other IP Rights In contrast, patents, trademarks, and designs have to be registered before they can enjoy any specific protection.

- Belgian patents must be registered with the Belgian Office for Intellectual Property ("*Dienst voor de Intellectuele Eigendom*" or "*DIE*"/"*L'Office belge de la Propriété intellectuelle*" or "*OPRI*") (Articles XI.14, XI.26 and XI.29 CEL).[6] According to Article 74 European Patent Convention,[7] European patents (being a bundle of national patents) must be registered with the European Patent Office and follow the national law regarding the registration of pledges. The parallel uniform EU patent is not yet in force.
- Trademarks and design rights are uniformly governed by Benelux law and necessarily relate to the territory of the three Benelux countries. Benelux trademarks and Benelux designs must be registered with the Benelux Office for Intellectual Property in The Hague (Articles 2.2, 2.5.1, 3.5.1, and 3.9.1 of the Benelux Convention for Intellectual Property of February 25, 2005 (hereinafter "BCIP")).[8] In addition to Benelux trademarks and designs, it is possible to obtain EU trademarks and designs. Such trademarks and designs must be registered with the European Union Intellectual Property Office (EUIPO) in Alicante (Articles 25 and 46 Regulation No 207/2009 of February 26, 2009 on EU trademarks[9] and Article 35.1 Regulation No 6/2002 of December 12, 2001 on Community designs).[10]

> La première vente ou premier autre transfert de propriété de l'original ou d'une copie d'une œuvre littéraire ou artistique dans l'Union européenne par l'auteur ou avec son consentement, épuise le droit de distribution de cet original ou cette copie dans l'Union européenne.

[6]See for the French text of the CEL: www.ejustice.just.fgov.be/cgi_loi/change_lg.pl?language=fr&la=F&cn=2013022819&table_name=loi.

[7]European Patent Convention of December 13, 2007, publication June 2016, https://documents.epo.org/projects/babylon/eponet.nsf/0/F9FD0B02F9D1A6B4C1258003004DF610/$File/EPC_16th_edition_2016_en.pdf. See also Keur (2016), pp. 144–145.

Article 74 European Patent Convention:

> Sauf si la présente convention en dispose autrement, la demande de brevet européen comme objet de propriété est soumise, dans chaque Etat contractant désigné et avec effet dans cet Etat, à la législation applicable dans ledit Etat aux demandes de brevet national.

[8]Benelux Convention for Intellectual Property of February 25, 2005, published in the Belgian Official Gazette on April 26, 2006 (hereinafter referred to as "BCIP"), www.ejustice.just.fgov.be/cgi_loi/change_lg.pl?language=fr&la=F&cn=2005022553&table_name=loi. English translation at https://www.boip.int/wps/wcm/connect/www/8e563086-0af6-4839-a639-3b39ead93fc1/01-BCIP-na+protocol2010+EN-clean.pdf?MOD=AJPERES.

[9]Regulation no. 207/2009 of the Council of February 26, 2009 on the EU Trademarks, data.europa.eu/eli/reg/2009/207/oj, as amended by the Regulation no. 2015/2424 of the European Parliament and the council on December 16, 2015, data.europa.eu/eli/reg/2015/2424/oj.

[10]Regulation no. 6/2002 of the Council of December 12, 2001 on Community designs, data.europa.eu/eli/reg/2002/6/oj.

Property Law of IP: Limited Proprietary Right in IP Intellectual property rights are movable and intangible assets.[11]

As such, they are an object of property law—more specifically, of ownership (a concept that Belgian law also applies to intangibles)—and of certain limited proprietary rights, such as the rights of usufruct and pledge. These dismemberments of ownership of IP rights can, in their turn, also be the subject of security rights. Thus, a right of usufruct in an IP right can be pledged.

As for licences, their nature is debated in Belgian law.[12] According to traditional doctrine, a licence is not a proprietary right; rather, it is merely a personal right of the same nature as rights arising out of rental or lease contracts. There are nevertheless good arguments for qualifying licences as proprietary rights (and dismemberments of ownership) of the same nature as rights of pledge or usufruct, as patents, trademarks, and design rights have to be registered in exactly the same way as rights of pledge or usufruct. Moreover, trademarks and design rights are governed by uniform Benelux laws and licences are proprietary rights according to dominant opinion in the Netherlands.

The rules on property of IP rights are basically the same as for other forms of (intangible) property; the general principles of property law apply (such as the *numerus clausus*; the principles of transferability and seizability; the anteriority principle; the principle of specialty; etc.), and IP rights can be transferred and pledged according to the rules on property in general. The transfer of an IP right, just like the transfer of any other asset, requires that the right be conveyed to an acquirer who is entitled to acquire (*causa adquirendi*) by an alienator who has the authority to dispose of the asset, and such a transfer will have effect only if the asset is specified and in existence. *Infra*, we will discuss in what cases an acquirer in good faith is protected despite the lack of authority of the alienator. As we will see, the rules for pledging an IP right are based on the rules for transfer of property.

2 Security Rights in IP, Including Their Creation and Perfection

General and Structure IP rights are movable and intangible assets.[13] Therefore, according to Belgian (common) law, only security rights regarding movable intangibles can be created in IP rights. The topic of "security rights over intellectual property" has not been much discussed within Belgian doctrine and jurisprudence.[14] Under Belgian practice before January 1, 2018 and to the best of our knowledge,

[11] De Page (1975), nrs. 620–622; Storme (2000), pp. 329–331; Sagaert (2014), pp. 83–84.

[12] See for the debate in Belgium Vanbrabant (2013), p. 1090 et seq.

[13] De Page (1975), nrs. 620–622; Storme (2000), pp. 329–331; Sagaert (2014), pp. 83–84.

[14] A limited amount of publications: Van Hoof (1995); Struelens (2002); Heremans and Muyldermans (2003), nr. 17; Dirix and De Corte (2006), nrs. 469–470, 515; Malekzadem

only the common pledge (which includes the pledge of a business or enterprise) was used, mostly for registered IP rights. The new Pledge Act creates more security as to the validity of security rights over IP rights, including unregistered IP rights (*cf. infra* Sect. 2.2).

We distinguish these security rights according to the way they come into existence. They include: retained rights (Sect. 2.1), granted rights (Sects. 2.2 and 2.3), and privileges by operation of law (Sect. 2.4). We conclude with a section on security rights in the "fruits," *i.e.* in royalties (Sect. 2.5). Although this means that there is not one single security right in IP, the system is nevertheless a functional system: these categories follow from the nature of things and are not dependent on the way parties frame their transactions. The label given by the parties does not matter. The distinction between retained security rights (Sect. 2.1) and granted security rights (Sect. 2.2) corresponds to the distinction in systems recognized as functional (such as the American system) between a purchase money security interest and another security interest. The second difference is based on the fact that certain rights to performance (i.e. claims) are by operation of law secured by a security interest (by a seller's lien and privilege for preservation costs) and that creditors who desire stronger protection (such as a guarantee for other rights to performance) will have to stipulate a security right in their relationship with the acquirer of the IP (i.e. reservation of title), *c.q.* the pledgor as owner of the IP (i.e. right of pledge).

2.1 Retained Security Rights

To begin with, security rights can come into existence in the favour of a transferor of an IP right as a right retained by the transferor, especially in case of sale. Under Belgian law, a transferor is already protected by operation of law, but he can strengthen his protection by stipulating a reservation of title.

Retention and Termination with Proprietary Effect In relation to tangible movables, Belgian law distinguishes between the position of the transferor before the factual delivery of the thing and the position of the transferor after (that is, whether the transferee (*i.e* the buyer, etc.) is already in factual possession or not). Before such delivery, the transferor's right to suspend the performance of his obligation and his right to terminate the underlying contract for (fundamental) non-performance have proprietary effect (even in case of insolvency proceedings opened against the transferee). Where the (obligatory) right to suspend has proprietary effect, we call it a "right of retention" (*retentierecht, droit de rétention*[15]). The same rule applies in

(2009); Delmotte and Goldschmidt (2011); Delmotte and Goldschmidt (2012); Malekzadem (2012); Vanbrabant (2013); Masson (n.d.-a, b).

[15]In the field of tangible movables, there are two situations called "right of retention" that are very different in nature, the one case being the right of a transferor to retain the goods in anticipation of a

favour of assignors of intangibles, especially rights to performance, where the notification of the debtor of the assigned right plays the same demarcative role.

This can be applied *mutatis mutandis* to IP rights, where the registration of the transfer of the right plays the same role: as long as the transfer of an IP right is not registered in the relevant specific IP register, the transferor's right to suspend the performance of his obligation and his right to terminate the underlying contract for (fundamental) non-performance thus have proprietary effect. After "loss of possession," only the security rights described in the following paragraphs remain. As there is no specific register for copyright, the agreement transferring copyright should in this context be deemed to be the moment of delivery, at least when the transferee is entitled to exercise this right (and thus is already in control).

Seller's Lien After delivery (*i.e.* dispossession), respectively—where it applies—notification or registration, according to the Belgian Civil Code (art. 20, 5° Act on Privileges and Mortgages in the Civil Code), a seller of movable goods, including IP rights, has, by operation of law (without the need to stipulate it), a lien (*i.e.* "special privilege") on the asset sold. This lien secures the unpaid price and its "accessory rights" such as costs and interest for late payment. However, it does not cover penalty clauses or other debts that the buyer has.

Reservation of Title Transferors can strengthen their position as secured creditors by stipulating a reservation of title *(eigendomsvoorbehoud/réserve de propriété)*. By virtue of the Act of July 11, 2013 introducing the new Pledge Act in the Civil Code, reservation of title is basically governed by the Civil Code (art. 69 and 70 of the Pledge Act in the Civil Code), as well as a few restrictive rules in the Insolvency Act (Art. XX.194 CEL, Book XX of the CEL constituting the new Insolvency Act introduced by the Act of August 11, 2017). In general, a clause of reservation of title has proprietary effect on the condition that it was stipulated in writing[16] at the moment of delivery at the latest (see *supra* for what this means in relation to IP rights). Except in cases that are not relevant for IP rights, registration of the reservation of title is not required. It can apply irrespective of the classification of the contract (whether the transfer takes place on the basis of a sale or another type of contract—see Art. 69 III Pledge Act). It is also beyond any doubt that the rules under the new Pledge Act also apply in principle to intangible assets, including IP rights.[17]

The position of a transferor is slightly stronger with reservation of title than without it: the transferor may simply claim back the asset (when this is done in accordance with contractual conditions), and he will continue to have the right after

possible termination of the transfer contract, the other case being the right of a creditor in possession of the asset to suspend restitution until the payment of a debt closely connected to the asset, where the right is thus a right of pledge by operation of law.

[16]In case of a consumer contract, it must also be accepted in writing by the consumer—Art. 69 II Pledge Act.

[17]E.g. Sagaert (2017), p. 38.

the transferee has already transferred the asset to a third party (save for the protection of bona fide third-party purchasers).

In case of bankruptcy, the right to reclaim the goods must be exercised within a short period after bankruptcy (art. XX.194 II CEL) and the insolvency administrator may retain the asset by paying the outstanding price—and only the price, not any other outstanding debts (art. XX.201 II CEL). In cases other than bankruptcy, reservation of title can probably also be used as a security for outstanding debts other than the purchase price (the text of the new Pledge Act is not very clear on this point).

Application to the Creation of a Licence Insofar as a licence would be qualified as a proprietary right under Belgian law, these devices apply *mutatis mutandis* when the IP holder issues a licence for a price.

2.2 *Security Rights Granted to a Creditor*

General For movables in general, security rights can be granted to a creditor either as a right of pledge (*pand/gage*) based on a contract of pledge, or through dispossession leading to an implied right of pledge by operation of law (usually referred to as either "right of retention" or "lien").[18]

In the field of IP rights, only the first mode is relevant, and thus only the contractual pledge will be discussed here, with the exception of statutory privileges. These will be discussed under Sect. 2.4.

For the sake of clarity, the following terms will be consistently used below:

- "(Right of) pledge" refers to the security interest (unless otherwise specified) (*pandrecht/droit de gage*);
- "Pledgor" refers to the security provider (*pandgever/constituant du gage*); and
- "Pledgee" refers to the security taker (*pandhouder/créancier gagiste*).

Fiduciary Transfer Although the fiduciary transfer of ownership of an IP right as a security seems to be valid as such, we will not discuss it separately, as under Belgian law, such a security transfer has the same effects as a pledge (it is *converted* into a pledge); this follows from case law on fiduciary assignments (especially Court of Cassation December 3, 2010[19]), and was codified in Article 62 of the new Pledge

---

[18]As for rights to performance as intangibles, the second method does not apply, but there are a number of other devices for creating a security right over such rights by operation of law, such as so-called "direct actions." See also Section D.

[19]Cass. December 3, 2010, concl. Dubrulle, *Pas.* 2010, 3094 = *Dr. banc. fin.* 2011, 120, note Peeters = *NjW* 2010, 834, note Sagaert = *RW* 2010-11, 1177 note Fransis = *RGDC* 2011, 497, note Georges = *TBH/RDC* 2011, 866, note Grégoire and Czupper: the assignment of a credit as a security "*can never bring more to the creditor, in case of concursus creditorum, than a pledge right on such credit, and that the assignee of the credit can therefore not exercise (enjoy) more rights than those enjoyed by the holder of a pledge*".

Act, which provides that "*the assignment of a credit as a security vests the assignee only with a pledge on the assigned credit*". Although this judgment and provision relate to rights to performance, there is no reason why they would not equally apply to other intangible assets, such as IP rights.

Old Law Until December 31, 2017, no general (civil or commercial) provision specifically defined any security interest over IP rights. Furthermore, it was debatable whether IP rights could be pledged according to common legislation. This uncertainty arose from the former Article 2076 of the Belgian Civil Code, which required dispossession of the encumbered goods.[20] With respect to intangible assets such as IP rights, this condition was problematic. Indeed, it is not possible to simply hand over an IP right to a creditor. Some legal scholars suggested that the registration of a pledge in the relevant intellectual property register was to be considered a kind of dispossession, as it could be argued that if certain formalities could meet the objectives of the requirement to hand over the encumbered good, such formalities would suffice and there would be no further need to hand over the concerned good to the creditor.[21] Nevertheless, there was no certainty in this respect, in particular because nothing would prevent the right-holder from continuing to exploit—and, in that sense, possess—his IP right after such registration.

Before the introduction of the new Pledge Act, there was, however, already specific legislation providing a system of registration for pledges relating to patents, trademarks, or designs, in particular: (i) the specific legislation on IP rights and (ii) the specific legislation on the pledge of a business. However, this specific legislation only relates to the registration of pledges, which grants them proprietary effect; it does not determine the regime of the pledge, such as: (i) the creation/validity of a pledge of IP rights, (ii) the rights and obligations of the pledgor and the pledgee, (iii) the exercise and eviction of the pledge, *etc.*

As mentioned above, the matter was recodified by the Act of July 11, 2013 on security interests in movable property, introducing the "Pledge Act," which entered into force on January 1, 2018.

New Law: Pledge in General Article 7 of the new Pledge Act now expressly provides the right to grant pledges over IP rights.[22] More generally, dispossession is

---

[20] Article 2076 Civil Code: "*Dans tous les cas, le privilège ne subsiste sur le gage qu'autant que ce gage a été mis et est resté en la possession du créancier, ou d'un tiers convenu entre les parties*".

[21] Malekzadem (2012), pp. 81, 87.

[22] Article 7 Pledge Act:

> Le gage peut avoir pour objet un bien mobilier corporel ou incorporel, un bien meuble par nature qui est devenu immeuble par destination ou un ensemble déterminé de tels biens, à l'exception des navires et des bateaux et bâtiments immatriculés au sens du livre II du Code de commerce.
>
> Sauf disposition restrictive dans la convention de gage, le gage ayant pour objet un fonds de commerce comprend l'ensemble des biens qui composent le fonds de commerce.
>
> Sauf disposition restrictive dans la convention de gage, le gage ayant pour objet une exploitation agricole comprend l'ensemble des biens qui servent à l'exploitation.

no longer a validity requirement for rights of pledge; it is only one possible way of giving the right of pledge proprietary effect. Such an *erga omnes* effect can now also be obtained by registering the right of pledge in the new general, national, and online Belgian register for pledges on movables (the "pledge register"). This possibility does not exist for pledging rights of performance (*i.e.* claims) (Article 20 Pledge Act). As for the practical functions of the pledge register, the Pledge Act has been implemented by the Royal Decree of September 14, 2007, which implemented the articles of Title XVIII of the Belgian Civil Code concerning the national pledge register.[23] Any registration is effective for a period of 10 years, but can be renewed (Article 35 Pledge Act).

Art. 7 VI of the Pledge Act states that the provisions of the Pledge Act apply to IP rights only insofar as they are not incompatible with rules that specifically regulate IP rights. The legislator has, however, not given any indication as to how this compatibility should be determined. In the following paragraphs, we give an overview of the rules on the creation and perfection of a right of pledge of an IP right, taking into account this general rule.

New Law: Creation of a Right of Pledge As with any transfer of property or creation of a proprietary right on the basis of a contract, Belgian law requires:

- A valid underlying (contractual) obligation as the entitlement that justifies the transfer or creation (causal rather than abstract system of property law);
- That the transfer or creation be performed through the consent of the grantor, which is presumed to have already been given in the underlying contract (unless the parties postpone the proprietary effect); and
- The authority of the grantor to dispose of the encumbered IP right, unless the acquirer is protected by the rules regarding the protection of third-party purchasers (see *infra* Sect. 3).

As for the formation and validity of the underlying contract of pledge that entitles the pledgee to acquire the right of pledge, the Pledge Act imposes formal requirements for any pledge granted by a consumer and these rules also apply to pledges over IP rights (as these rules are not incompatible with the specific rules on IP rights). The underlying pledge agreement must be in document form and signed by both

---

Si le constituant du gage est un consommateur au sens de l'article I.1, 2°, du livre Ier du Code de droit économique, la valeur du bien gagé ou des biens gagés ne peut excéder le double de l'étendue du gage telle que fixée par l'article 12.

Seuls les biens cessibles en vertu de la loi peuvent être donnés en gage.

Les dispositions du présent Chapitre ne sont applicables aux gages ayant pour objet des droits de propriété intellectuelle que dans la mesure où elles ne sont pas incompatibles avec d'autres dispositions régissant spécifiquement de tels gages.

[23] Published in the Belgian Official Gazette of September 26, 2017.

parties (Article 4 Pledge Act),[24] and it must also indicate the value of the assets pledged (an element that is not required for pledges by a non-consumer).[25]

The requirements for the effectiveness of the right of pledge in relation to third parties or in case of insolvency (namely, publicity requirements) do not apply as regards (i) the validity and formation of the underlying contract and (ii) the creation of the right of pledge between the parties.[26]

Nevertheless, Art. 4 I Pledge Act provides that even for a pledge by a non-consumer, the contract of pledge can only be proven in writing and the writing must indicate (a) the encumbered assets, (b) the secured debts, and (c) the ceiling or maximum amount for which the assets are encumbered. As, based on other provisions of the Pledge Act, this general rule does not apply when there is dispossession of the pledged asset (art. 40 I Pledge Act), the question arises whether it applies to a pledge of IP rights that has already been registered in the specific register for such IP rights (which is possible for patents, trademarks, and design rights), as such registration has traditionally been considered a mode of dispossession. The specific rules for the registration of a pledge in the specific registers do nevertheless also require a written document, but do not specify its content. More specifically, they do not require the indication of a ceiling.[27] This requirement is not incompatible with the specific rules and thus, in our opinion, continues to apply.

It must also be noted that the first two content requirements are understood in a very flexible way:

- As for the indication of the encumbered assets, it follows from Article 7 I Pledge Act that the assets should *not* be indicated individually and that a general description is sufficient. In case future IP rights are included, the proprietary right of pledge will evidently only attach when the right exists, but no new pledge agreement (or new registration) is required.
- As for the indication of the secured debts, it is possible to stipulate an *omnibus* pledge, *i.e.* a pledge securing all present and future debts towards the pledgee.

---

[24] Article 4 Pledge Act:

La mise en gage est prouvée par un écrit contenant la désignation précise des biens grevés du gage, des créances garanties et du montant maximum à concurrence duquel les créances sont garanties.

Si le constituant du gage est un consommateur au sens de l'article I.1, 2°, du livre Ier du Code de droit économique, la validité de la convention requiert qu'un écrit soit rédigé, selon le cas, conformément au prescrit de l'article 1325 ou de l'article 1326.

L'écrit visé à l'alinéa 2 mentionne, aux fins de l'application de l'article 7, alinéa 4, la valeur du bien gagé ou des biens gages.

[25] For details, see: Steennot (2017), p. 125 et seq.

[26] Article 2 Pledge Act:

Sous réserve de l'article 4, alinéa 2, le gage est constitué par la convention conclue entre le constituant du gage et le créancier gagiste.

[27] For patents, see the Royal Decree of December 2, 1986, which implemented the rules of Art. XI.50 and XI.51 CEL.

New Law: Effectiveness of a Right of Pledge for IP Rights Without a Specific Register The Pledge Act provides, for movables in general, two ways to make a right of pledge effective towards third parties with competing rights, make it effective in insolvency proceedings (*i.e.* perfected), and give it a "ranking":

- Through dispossession (called "control" for intangibles such as rights to performance (*i.e.* claims)); or
- Through registration in the pledge register (Article 15)[28] (as mentioned above, this is not possible for rights to performance (*i.e.* claims)).

The Pledge Act has not abolished the ability to make a pledge in registered IP rights effective through registration in the specific register. As this double regime raises specific questions for these rights, we must first analyse the case where such a specific register does not exist. This is the case for copyright in Belgium in particular, as there is no specific register for copyright. In addition, the Pledge Act does not provide for a form of dispossession for intangibles other than rights to performance (*i.e.* claims), which makes it very doubtful that copyright can be pledged through dispossession (*cf. supra*).

Thus, the only safe method for making the pledge effective is registration according to the new Pledge Act.

Registration according to the Pledge Act takes place in the national online pledge register (Article 26) set up by the Belgian Finance Ministry. The register is open for consultation (Article 34). Entries in the register can be made directly by the secured creditor, who has to notify the debtor (Article 29). Registration requires the existence of a pledge agreement. As a consequence, advance filing is not possible. "Transactional filing" was chosen instead of mere "notice filing."[29] However, it is a notice filing in the sense that the pledge agreement itself does not have to be registered. Article 30 Pledge Act determines the data that has to be entered for the registration of

[28]Article 15 Pledge Act:

Le gage est opposable aux tiers par un enregistrement dans le registre des gages effectué conformément à l'article 29, alinéa 1er.

L'enregistrement dans le registre des gages est exclu pour une mise en gage de créances.

L'identification erronée du constituant du gage prive d'effet l'enregistrement sauf si une recherche dans le registre à partir de l'élément d'identification correct permet de retrouver l'inscription, sans préjudice de l'article 29, alinéa 2.

L'identification erronée du créancier gagiste ou de son représentant tel que visé à l'article 3ou la désignation erronée des biens grevés du gage privent d'effet l'enregistrement sauf si elles n'induisent pas gravement en erreur une personne raisonnable effectuant une recherche, sans préjudice de l'article 29, alinéa 2.

La désignation erronée des créances garanties ou du montant maximal à concurrence duquel elles sont garanties ne prive pas d'effet l'enregistrement, sans préjudice de l'article 29, alinéa 2.

Le rang du gage est déterminé par l'ordre chronologique de son enregistrement.

Le Roi fixe les modalités d'application du présent article.

[29]See also Borchard (2016).

a right of pledge—namely, information regarding the identity of the parties (pledgor and pledgee), the encumbered assets, the secured debts, and the ceiling.

The person filing the notice is liable for any incorrect entries (Article 29) and the pledgee can ask the creditor to remove any incorrect information (Article 33).

The registration expires after 10 years, unless renewal (valid for another 10 years) takes place during the first period (Article 35). Once the entry expires, it no longer appears on the register. Registration is done in the name of the pledgor or an agent of the pledgor (*e.g.* a security agent) (Article 3 Pledge Act). The pledgee may delete the entry at any time. He is obliged to do so if the secured debt is paid. In case of a dispute between the parties, only the court can order the deletion of the registration.[30]

---

[30]Articles 25-35 Pledge Act:

Art. 25. Tiers-acquéreurs

"L'enregistrement au registre des gages exclut l'application de l'article 2279 à l'égard d'ayants cause à titre particulier du constituant du gage qui agissent dans le cadre de leur activité professionnelle."

Art. 26. Registre des gages

"L'enregistrement d'un gage et d'une réserve de propriété s'effectue dans le Registre national des Gages, appelé registre des gages, conservé à l'administration générale de la Documentation patrimoniale du Service public fédéral Finances

Le registre des gages est un système informatisé destiné à l'enregistrement et à la consultation de gages et de réserves de propriété, à la modification, au renouvellement, à la cession ou à la radiation de l'enregistrement de gages ou de réserves de propriété et à la cession de rang d'un gage enregistré.

Le Roi règle les modalités de fonctionnement du registre des gages.

L'Administration Générale de la Documentation Patrimoniale du service public fédéral Finances est le responsable du traitement au sens de la loi du 8 décembre 1992 relative à la protection de la vie privée à l'égard des traitements de données à caractère personnel et est chargé de l'application des dispositions de cette loi.

Les articles 27, 28, 32, 33, 34, 35, 36 et 37 s'appliquent par analogie à l'enregistrement de la réserve de propriété."

Art. 29. Enregistrement

"§ 1 Le créancier gagiste est habilité en vertu de la convention de gage à enregistrer son gage en inscrivant dans le registre des gages les données visées à l'article 30 telles que celles-ci figurent dans l'écrit visé à l'article 4, en conformité avec les modalités fixées par le Roi après avis de la Commission de la protection de la vie privée.

Le créancier gagiste répond de tout dommage qui résulterait de l'enregistrement de données erronées.

Le créancier gagiste informe par écrit le constituant du gage de l'enregistrement.

§ 2. Le vendeur est habilité, en vertu de la convention dans laquelle figure la clause de réserve de propriété, à enregistrer ladite

réserve de propriété en inscrivant dans le registre des gages les données visées à l'article 30 telles que celles-ci figurent dans l'écrit visé à l'article 69, en conformité avec les modalités fixées par le Roi après avis de la Commission de la protection de la vie privée.

Le vendeur est responsable de tout dommage qui résulterait de l'enregistrement de données erronées. Le vendeur informe l'acheteur par écrit de l'enregistrement."

Art. 31. Consultation

"§ 1er. En ce qui concerne un gage enregistré, les données suivantes sont consultables:

1° le numéro d'enregistrement;

Registration of a right of pledge does not protect the pledgee in the event that the pledgor lacks authority: it does not equal "(dis)possession" and the Pledge Act does not equal such registration with dispossession. Older rights will thus prevail over the right of pledge. Whether *bona fide* acquisition is possible on other grounds is discussed further under Sect. 3. On the other hand, registration of the pledge in the pledge register may to some extent protect the pledgee against later acquisition of rights in the asset by third parties, as it prevents a pledge registered in the pledge register at a later time from having priority and prevents professional acquirers of the asset or rights in the asset from acquiring in good faith. However, it does not

---

2° l'identité du créancier gagiste ou du représentant visé à l'article 3;
3° l'identité du constituant du gage;
4° le cas échéant, l'identité du mandataire du créancier gagiste ou du représentant visé à l'article 3;
5° la désignation des biens grevés du gage ayant fait l'objet de l'enregistrement;
6° la désignation des créances garanties ayant fait l'objet de l'enregistrement;
7° le montant maximal à concurrence duquel les créances sont garanties et qui a fait l'objet de l'enregistrement;
8° la déclaration du créancier gagiste, du représentant visé à l'article 3 ou de leur mandataire selon laquelle le créancier ou représentant est responsable de tout dommage qui résulterait de l'inscription de données erronées;
9° la date de l'enregistrement.
§ 2. En ce qui concerne une réserve de propriété enregistrée, les données suivantes sont consultables:
1° le numéro d'enregistrement;
2° l'identité du vendeur;
3° l'identité de l'acheteur;
4° le cas échéant, l'identité du mandataire du vendeur;
5° la désignation des biens vendus ayant fait l'objet de l'enregistrement;
6° la désignation du prix d'achat non payé ayant fait l'objet de l'enregistrement;7° la déclaration du vendeur ou de son mandataire que le vendeur est responsable de tout dommage qui résulterait de l'inscription de données erronées;
8° la date de l'enregistrement."
Art. 33. Données erronées
"Le constituant du gage a le droit de requérir du créancier gagiste la radiation ou la modification de données erronées."
Art. 35. Durée et renouvellement
"L'enregistrement du gage expire après dix ans. Dès ce moment, le gage cesse d'être consultable dans le registre des gages.

Ce délai peut toutefois être renouvelé pour des périodes successives de dix ans.

Le renouvellement est effectué par un enregistrement dans le registre préalablement à l'expiration du délai de dix ans et selon les modalités fixées par le Roi après avis de la Commission de la protection de la vie privée.

Ce renouvellement peut être total ou partiel et peut, le cas échéant, s'accompagner d'une diminution du montant maximal garanti et/ou de l'importance des biens donnés en gage.

Le renouvellement mentionne le numéro d'enregistrement de l'enregistrement à renouveler.

La mention d'un enregistrement renouvelé indique également la date de l'enregistrement initial.

Le créancier gagiste informe par écrit le constituant du gage du renouvellement de l'enregistrement."

necessarily protect against non-professional acquirers, as they have no duty to consult the pledge register (art. 25 Pledge Act). Again, this question is discussed further under Sect. 3.

Note that insofar as a licence would be qualified as a proprietary right, the rules for pledging licences are not those for pledging rights to performance; rather, they are those for pledging IP rights.

Costs The cost of registering in the general pledge register and the cost of consulting the pledge register have been determined by the abovementioned Royal Decree of September 14, 2017. The cost of registration is, depending on the secured amount, between 20.00 euros (for secured amounts under 10,000.00 euros) and 500.00 euros (for secured amounts of 500,000.00 euros or more). The cost of renewal is the same as the cost of original registration. The cost of a modification is 60% of the registration cost. A consultation of the pledge register costs 5.00 euros.

Effectiveness of a Right of Pledge for IP Rights with a Specific Register Before the pledge register existed, Belgian law already had or knew specific legislation providing a system of registration for pledges in the IP registers relating to patents, trademarks, and designs. This specific legislation only relates to the registration of the pledge in the IP right register; it does not determine the regime of the pledge. Registration in the IP right register based on this specific legislation is required not for the validity of the (pledge) agreement, but for its effectiveness towards third parties.

The main rules in this specific legislation, relevant for our topic, are the following:

(1) The pledge of a Belgian patent must, just like the patent itself and its transfer, be registered with the Belgian Office for Intellectual Property (see *supra*) in order to be enforceable towards third parties (Articles XI.50 and XI.52 CEL).[31] Thus, the Belgian Office for Intellectual Property (Art. XI.52 §1 CEL) needs to be notified of the pledge, and will enter the information in its register according to the receipt date (Art. XI.50 CEL *juncto* Art. XI.52 §2 CEL). The Belgian Patent Act does not determine who is liable to carry out this notification (whether the pledgor, the pledgee, or both). The notification is achieved by providing the following: (i) a copy of the pledge agreement, or (ii) any other official document regarding the pledge, or (iii) an extract of these documents, together with (iv) a proof of payment of taxes (Art. XI.50 §3 of the CEL).

(2) The pledge of a Benelux trademark or design right must, just like the IP right itself and its transfer, be registered in the register of the Benelux Office for Intellectual Property in The Hague (Article 2.33 *c.q.* 3.27 BCIP) in order to be effective against third parties. The notification requires an extract of the pledge agreement or declaration signed by the pledgor and pledgee.[32]

---

[31] Clerix et al. (2016), pp. 361–362.

[32] Article 2.33 BCIP:

(3) With regards to EU trademarks and design rights, Articles 19 and 23 of the Regulation No 207/2009 of February 26, 2009 on EU trademarks (as amended by Regulation 2015/2424) and Articles 29, 32, and 33 of the Regulation No 6/2002 of December 12, 2001 on Community designs provide for similar provisions. The registration has to be made in the register administered by EUIPO (previously OHIM).[33]

La cession ou autre transmission ou la licence n'est opposable aux tiers qu'après l'enregistrement du dépôt, dans les formes fixées par règlement d'exécution et moyennant paiement des taxes dues, d'un extrait de l'acte qui la constate ou d'une déclaration y relative signée par les parties intéressées. La disposition de la phrase précédente s'applique aux droits de gage et aux saisies.

Article 3.27 BCIP:

La cession ou autre transmission ou la licence n'est opposable aux tiers qu'après l'enregistrement du dépôt, dans les formes fixées par règlement d'exécution et moyennant paiement des taxes dues, d'un extrait de l'acte qui l'a constaté ou d'une déclaration y relative signée par les parties intéressées. La disposition de la phrase précédente s'applique aux droits de gage et aux saisies.

[33]Articles 19 and 23:

Art. 19 Right in rem

"1. A EU trademark may, independently of the undertaking, be given as security or be the subject of rights in rem.

2. At the request of one of the parties, the rights referred to in paragraph 1 or the transfer of those rights shall be entered in the Register and published;

3. An entry in the Register effected pursuant to paragraph 2 shall be cancelled or modified at the request of one of the parties."

Art. 23 Effects vis-à-vis third parties

"1. Legal acts referred to in Articles 17, 19 and 22 concerning a EU trademark shall have effects vis-à-vis third parties in all the Member States only after entry in the Register. Nevertheless, such an act, before it is so entered, shall have effect vis-à-vis third parties who have acquired rights in the trademark after the date of that act but who knew of the act at the date on which the rights were acquired.

2. Paragraph 1 shall not apply in the case of a person who acquires the EU trade mark or a right concerning the EU trademark by way of transfer of the whole of the undertaking or by any other universal succession.

3. The effects vis-à-vis third parties of the legal acts referred to in Article 20 shall be governed by the law of the Member State determined in accordance with Article 16.

4. Until such time as common rules for the Member States in the field of bankruptcy enter into force, the effects vis-à-vis third parties of bankruptcy or like proceedings shall be governed by the law of the Member State in which such proceedings are first brought within the meaning of national law or of conventions applicable in this field."

Articles 29 and 33 Regulation No 6/2002 of December 12, 2001 on Community designs:

Art. 29 Rights in rem on a registered Community design

"1. A registered Community design may be given as security or be the subject of rights in rem.

2. On request of one of the parties, the rights mentioned in paragraph 1 shall be entered in the register and published."

Art. 33 Effects vis-à-vis third parties

Given the abovementioned rule of Art. 7 VI Pledge Act, the question is whether a right of pledge of such IP rights can also be perfected by registering it in the general pledge register. The parliamentary documents on the new Pledge Act do not give any clarification in this regard.

Under the old law, it was already possible to register a right of pledge of an enterprise as a whole (*fonds de commerce, handelszaak*) in the mortgage register (now for movables replaced by the pledge register), and when the enterprise comprised trademarks, designs, or patents, it was deemed possible to make the pledge of these rights effective against third parties through such registration.[34] This pleads in favour of the interpretation that the new rule recognizes the effectiveness of a right of pledge once it is registered in the general pledge register, without registration in the specific IP right register. Nevertheless, such an interpretation causes serious difficulties, as will be discussed under Sect. 3. It would have been much simpler to explicitly provide that a pledge of such IP rights can be made effective against third parties only by registering it in the specific IP right register.

The main rules concerning registration in the pledge register have been discussed *supra* under "New Law - Effectiveness of a Right of Pledge for IP Rights Without a Specific Register": they are general rules that do not distinguish by IP right type and are therefore not repeated here.

2.3 *Enterprise Charges*

Pledge of an Enterprise: Old Law Before the entry into force of the new Pledge Act, a pledge without dispossession was organized specifically for the general pledge of a business or enterprise (*pand op de handelszaak/gage sur fonds de commerce*) under the Business Pledge Act of October 25, 1919. Article 2, paragraph 1 of that Act listed the "assets" of the business that were automatically included by

"1. The effects vis-à-vis third parties of the legal acts referred to in Articles 28, 29, 30 and 32 shall be governed by the law of the Member State determined in accordance with Article 27.

2. However, as regards registered Community designs, legal acts referred to in Articles 28, 29 and 32 shall only have effect vis-à-vis third parties in all the Member States after entry in the register. Nevertheless, such an act, before it is so entered, shall have effect vis-à-vis third parties who have acquired rights in the registered Community design after the date of that act but who knew of the act at the date on which the rights were acquired.

3. Paragraph 2 shall not apply to a person who acquires the registered Community design or a right concerning the registered Community design by way of transfer of the whole of the undertaking or by any other universal succession.

4. Until such time as common rules for the Member States in the field of insolvency enter into force, the effects vis-à-vis third parties of insolvency proceedings shall be governed by the law of the Member State in which such proceedings are first brought under the national law or the regulations applicable in this field."

[34]E.g. Kh. (Commercial Court) Kortrijk January 12, 2011, *RW* 2011-12, 284.

granting a pledge on the business, *i.e.* "*the clients, the signboard, the business house, the trademarks, the leases, the movable and the equipment of the storehouse*". This enumeration was not limitative so that the contracting parties could provide a larger enumeration of assets, including, for example, patents, designs, and copyrights. Such a pledge could only be granted in favour of an acknowledged credit institution/bank within the EU (Article 7 of the Business Pledge Act). The pledge of the business had to be registered with the pledged business' local mortgage registry office (*hypotheekkantoor/bureau de conservation des hypothèques*) to be effective towards third parties and in the case of insolvency procedures (Articles 3 and 4 of the Business Pledge Act). This institution was to some extent the model for the general "registry pledge" in the new Pledge Act.

Pledge of an Enterprise: New Law Under the new Pledge Act, there is no longer a specific regime for pledging a business or enterprise. Art. 7 of the Pledge Act provides that a pledge can encumber either a single asset or a whole category of assets. Article 7 II states that "*the pledge of a business relates to all the goods that constitute the business, except for restrictive clauses in the pledge agreement*". This implies that when a pledge of a business is granted, this pledge also covers IP rights, unless agreed otherwise.

When a business is pledged under the new Pledge Act, this does not really constitute a floating charge with the characteristics that are typical of floating charges in other legal systems. Thus, in case of conflicting rights in certain assets of the business, the conflict has to be solved for each asset separately. On the other hand, as in the case of a floating charge, the pledgor retains the authority to dispose of the assets "in the ordinary course of business" (Article 21 Pledge Act, see *supra*).

2.4 Other Security Rights by Operation of Law

Other Specific Privileges To be thorough, we can refer to some specific privileges that are created by statutory law and that are in theory applicable to IP rights, such as the privilege for costs incurred for the preservation of an IP right.[35]

2.5 Security Rights in Royalties

Contractual Pledge of Royalties Where the IP right is licensed to a licensee, this will normally give rise to rights to payment of royalties (hereinafter abbreviated as "royalties"). These rights/royalties can also be encumbered by security rights, which can encumber rights to performance in general—there are no special rules for

[35]See also Dirix and De Corte (2006), p. 172.

pledges of royalties that differ from the rules for pledges of receivables or rights to performance in general.[36]

In principle, royalties can thus be pledged separately according to these rules. This also requires:

- A valid underlying (contractual) obligation as the title of the creation of a right of pledge (causal rather than abstract system of property law),
- Performed by consent of the pledgor as to the creation of a right of pledge, which is presumed to be given in the underlying contract (unless parties postpone the proprietary effect); and
- the authority of the pledgor to dispose of the encumbered rights, unless the acquirer is protected by the rules regarding the protection of third-party acquirers.

As for the formation and validity of the underlying contract of pledge, the formalities are slightly less strict than they are for the pledge of other movables: the written document is only required as evidence (even for pledgors who are consumers) and does not have to mention the value of the pledged asset (Article 61 Pledge Act) (see the rules on these requirements in general *supra*).

Moreover, no publicity is required for the effectiveness or perfection of such a right of pledge: registration in the pledge register is excluded by the Pledge Act (Article 20) and the "control" required for effectiveness is purely fictitious: it does not require a notification to the debtor/licensee (which would equal dispossession); instead, it merely requires the entitlement to notify (which follows from the contract of pledge unless otherwise agreed).

Pledge by Operation of Law What is, however, important, is the fact that Belgian law grants a right of pledge of these royalties by operation of law to the pledgee of the IP right itself. Article 9 of the Pledge Act provides that a right of pledge automatically attaches to both the fruits of the pledged asset and to any right to payment that compensates a loss of value of the pledged asset. Applied to IP rights, this means that the pledge of an IP right automatically extends to a pledge of the royalties, unless a third party has already acquired rights in the royalties before the IP right itself was pledged.

3 Conflicting Rights in IP and Priorities

Principles and Conflict Rules The security rights discussed in this report are proprietary rights and follow the general rules that apply to conflicts between property rights under Belgian law. They can be summarized in four rules:

[36]For the pledge of rights to performance in general, see: Storme (2017), p. 227 et seq.

(i) The starting point is that the older right has priority over the younger (*i.e.* the principle of anteriority) (*anterioriteitsbeginsel/principe d'antériorité*); however, "older" must be verified in relation to the specific asset. Thus, the rights of the unpaid seller in the asset sold are necessarily older than any right the buyer grants to a third party, even if this is based on a contract concluded before the buyer bought the asset (*nemo dat quod non habet*); this is true for both reservation of title and for the privilege of the unpaid seller and is confirmed in Article 58 Pledge Act.[37] The criterion is not whether the security is a purchase money security, but the effect is similar: in case the unpaid seller is paid by a third person granting credit, that person is subrogated (*cessio legis*) in the seller's right to payment and the security rights securing that right pass to the subrogated creditor.

(ii) Nevertheless, third-party acquirers will have priority over older rights when they have acquired in good faith and first fulfilled the publicity requirements. Good faith is to be judged at the time when one acquires the right (and not at the time of publicity) and relates to the absence of the authority to dispose. We will discuss the publicity required for good faith acquisition *infra*. As long as there is no conflict with the administration of an insolvent estate, an older but unregistered right will prevail over a younger right acquired in bad faith, even if the younger right is registered (*i.e.* published) first (for patents: Article XI.50 §5 CEL[38]; for Benelux trademarks and design rights: Article 2.33 *c.q.* 3.27 BCIP).

(iii) In case of *concursus* (*e.g.* the opening of insolvency proceedings, including seizure, or the liquidation of a legal person), the ranking of rights of pledge is equally determined by publicity (in case of IP rights with a specific register, this applies not only to the rights of pledge, but also to ownership transferred).

(iv) Finally, when there is a security right securing a claim for costs for the preservation of the asset, the order of priority is reversed, and the youngest

[37] Article 58 Pledge Act:

Art. 58. Super priorité

"Un gage basé sur un droit de rétention pour une créance en conservation de la chose prime tous les créanciers gagistes.

Sous réserve de l'alinéa 1er, le vendeur impayé qui s'est réservé la propriété, le vendeur privilégié et le privilège du sous-traitant priment les créanciers gagistes sur ces biens."

[38] Articles XI.50 and XI.52 CEL:

Art. XI.50. § 6:

"La cession ou mutation n'a d'effet à l'égard de l'Office et n'est opposable aux tiers qu'après l'inscription de sa notification au registre et dans les limites qui résultent de l'acte ou du document visés au paragraphe 3. Toutefois, avant l'inscription de la notification, la cession ou mutation est opposable aux tiers qui ont acquis des droits après la date de la cession ou de la mutation, mais qui avaient connaissance de celle-ci lors de l'acquisition de ces droits."

Art. XI.52. § 2:

"L'article XI.50 §§ 3 à 6, est applicable par analogie aux droits réels visés au paragraphe précédent."

costs have priority over the older ones (*inter alia* Article 57 Pledge Act,[39] but the rule is more general).

Specific Problems: Authority to Dispose When applying these rules, two specific questions arise. Both are linked to the organization of publicity: one is raised by the plurality of publicity mechanisms and the other concerns the evaluation of good faith; they will be discussed under "Specific Problems - Plurality of Registers".

A third question relates to the notion of authority to dispose. When is this requirement "fulfilled"?

(i) First of all, there is authority to dispose despite the existence of an older right in the asset if the holder of the older right has authorized the transaction granting a conflicting younger right.
(ii) Furthermore, the Pledge Act provides that the pledgor who has pledged an asset retains the authority to dispose of it "in the ordinary course of business" (Article 21 Pledge Act). A later transferee thus takes the asset free from the security right if the transfer took place in the ordinary course of business. This rule is especially important for goods in case the pledgor trades in such goods. However, it is difficult to imagine that it can ever apply to the sale of IP rights, except in the form of a licence: granting a licence may be an ordinary course of business, but selling a pledged IP right is usually not.
(iii) Even if a licence could be considered to be a proprietary right (a possible conception), the owner of an IP right that has already been pledged still has the authority to license the right in the ordinary course of business. This is understandable, as under Belgian law, the "fruits" of such a licence, such as the royalties, are automatically encumbered with a right of pledge in favour of the pledgee of the right itself (Article 9 Pledge Act, discussed *supra*).

Specific Problems: Plurality of Registers Regarding the first and second questions, a problem arises if one accepts that a right of pledge of an IP right for which there is a specific IP right register can nevertheless also be registered in the general pledge register. It arises because these registers are independent from each other and do not automatically connect to or update each other. Registrations will not necessarily occur simultaneously.

---

[39] Article 57 Pledge Act:

Art. 57. Règle d'antériorité

"Le droit de gage a priorité sur tous les droits plus récents sur les biens gagés, sans préjudice des articles 21 à 26 du Titre XVIII du Livre III du présent Code.

S'il y a plusieurs créanciers gagistes, leur ordre de rang est déterminé selon la date de l'enregistrement ou de la prise en possession.

Les créanciers gagistes qui ont procédé à l'enregistrement ou ont reçu la possession le même jour occupent le même rang.

Si les biens gagés sont devenus immeubles, l'ordre de rang entre le créancier gagiste et un créancier hypothécaire ou privilégié sur les immeubles est déterminé selon la date de l'enregistrement et celle de l'inscription de l'hypothèque ou du privilège."

The question is more specifically whether a registration in the general pledge register not only assures the effectiveness of the pledge in case of insolvency, but is also sufficient for a bona fide purchaser to acquire priority over older rights. This is not at all evident, since for other movable assets, the registration in the general pledge register does not have this effect. For tangibles, possession is required in order to acquire *a non domino* (Article 2279 CC), and for rights to performance (where a pledge cannot be registered in the general pledge register), the debtor must be notified of that right. The Pledge Act does not create an additional mode of acquiring *a non domino*, whereas the specific laws on IP rights organizing specific registers do, to some extent (as a land register does this for rights in immovables). Registration in the specific IP right register thus equals "possession," whereas registration in the general pledge register for tangible assets does not necessarily do the same.

As for the requirement of good faith, one can deduce from the legislation (Art. 25 Pledge Act) that professional acquirers should consult both registers, whereas a non-professional acquirer has no duty to consult the general pledge register.

If one accepts that pledges of patents, trademarks, and designs can be registered in the general pledge register despite the existence of a specific IP right register, and that the Pledge Act does not create an additional mode of acquiring *a non domino*, the result will be the following in case there are two acquirers of conflicting rights in the same IP right (conflicting proprietary rights can be ownership, a pledge, usufruct and, in my opinion (*cf. supra*), also a licence; however, only a right of pledge can be registered in the pledge register—the other rights can only be registered in the specific IP right register):

- If the first acquirer registers first in the specific IP right register and later the second acquirer registers first in the general register, the first acquirer prevails.
- If the first acquirer registers first in the general pledge register and later the second acquirer registers first in the specific IP right register, a non-professional second acquirer will prevail if he was in good faith at the moment of acquisition (for pledge rights, at the moment the underlying pledge contract was concluded). As the first right was already registered at the time the second was acquired, a professional second acquirer cannot be in good faith, as he should have consulted the general pledge register; however, the same is not necessarily true for a non-professional acquirer (Art. 25 Pledge Act).
- If the second acquirer registers first in the specific IP right register and later the first acquirer registers first in the general pledge register, the second acquirer gets priority if he was in good faith at the time of acquisition.
- If the second acquirer registers first in the general pledge register and later the first acquirer then registers first in the specific IP right register, the first acquirer will prevail.

This solution, which requires a reasoning that is based on the analogical application of certain rules but is not found explicitly in the legislation, is in line with the recommendations in the UNCITRAL Legislative Guide, IP Supplement 2011. The only time that it will not apply is in cases where the older right of pledge is overruled on the basis of the ordinary course of business rule, discussed supra.

Conflicting Rights in Royalties As explained *supra*, the pledgee of an IP right has by operation of law a right of pledge of the royalties as "fruits" of the encumbered asset. This may conflict with a separate right of pledge granted to another creditor.

First of all, it is possible for the licence to be granted before the IP right is pledged. In principle, the pledgee of the IP right has to respect the licence as an older right (see the conflict rules *supra*), as well as a right of pledge of the royalties out of the licence; the right to such royalties out of a licence that has already been granted is considered to be an existing right rather than a future one, even if it is conditional. The right of pledge of the pledgee of the royalties is not overruled by a later pledging of the IP right itself. The outcome could, however, be different if the licence is not recognized as proprietary; the pledgee of the IP right could then disregard the licence as a mere obligatory right.

If the licence is granted after the pledging of the IP right, a later pledging of the royalties would have to give priority to the right of pledge of the royalties that the pledgee of the IP right has on the basis of Article 9 Pledge Act.

Finally, if the licence is granted after the pledge of the IP right, but the holder has already pledged future rights to performance in advance, including future rights to royalties from a licence contract that has not yet been concluded, the right of pledge of the royalties cannot attach as long as the right to royalties does not exist; in addition, based on Article 9 Pledge Act, the right of pledge of the pledgee of the IP right itself has priority over the right of pledge of the royalties. In Belgian doctrine, this is also explained as an effect of "real subrogation" taking place and overriding rights already granted in future assets.

4 Rights Before Default

Regarding the Right to Use the IP Right Articles 17 and 22 of the Pledge Act[40] expressly provide the possibility for the pledgor to use the encumbered assets, yet

---

[40]Articles 16 and 22 Pledge Act:

Art. 16. Obligations du constituant du gage

"Le constituant du gage doit veiller aux biens grevés en bon constituant.

Le créancier gagiste a le droit d'inspecter les biens grevés à tout moment."

Art. 22. Sanction

"La clause en vertu de laquelle le créancier gagiste peut se faire remettre tout ou partie des biens grevés sur sa simple demande est réputée non écrite.

Si le constituant du gage manque gravement à ses obligations, le juge peut, sur demande du créancier gagiste, ordonner que les biens grevés lui soient remis ou qu'ils soient placés sous séquestre judiciaire.

La disposition frauduleuse ou le déplacement frauduleux des biens grevés est passible des peines prévues par l'article 491 du Code pénal."

add that this use should be "*reasonable*" and "*in conformity with the destination*" of the encumbered goods. These precisions echo the obligation prescribed to the pledgor "*to take care of the encumbered goods as a good pledger would*" ("*en bon constituant*," referring to the common French expression "*en bon père de famille*"—*cf.* Art. 16 of the Pledge Act).

However, Article 42 of the Pledge Act provides that "*the pledgee may not use the encumbered goods unless and to the extent that it is necessary for their preservation*".

On the basis of Article 21 of the Pledge Act (see *supra*), the pledgor has the right to grant licences "in the ordinary course of business," unless otherwise agreed.

Regarding the Maintenance of the IP Right In principle, the pledgor is responsible for the maintenance and defence of the encumbered IP right. Indeed, according to Article 16 of the Pledge Act, the pledgor must take care of the encumbered property as a decent pledgor and the pledgee is entitled to inspect the encumbered property at any time. Even though the scope of obligations of a "*decent pledgor*" is neither specified nor clear, one might assume that a decent pledgor is responsible for actively maintaining the IP right and, therefore, for paying all taxes regarding the validity of the patent, renewing the trademark, and actively using it in order to avoid revocation or termination as long as the pledge is in force.

Pursuant to Article 9 of the Pledge Act, the pledgor and, where appropriate, the pledgee are accountable to each other regarding claims that can subrogate the encumbered property and regarding proceeds issuing from the encumbered goods. Even though this provision might seem difficult to apply to IP rights, it confirms the assumption that the pledgor is responsible for the maintenance and defence of the IP right and that the pledgee, where appropriate, can also be held accountable. For the sake of clarity, it is recommended that both the pledgee and the pledgor enter into an agreement in which they specify their rights and obligations regarding the encumbered property (*e.g.* regarding renewal, defence, expiration, revocation *etc.*) in order to prevent the pledgee from losing his security.

As concerns more specifically the right to take legal action and/or obtain damages for infringement to the encumbered IP rights, the intervention of the pledgee is not stipulated by statutory law. Indeed, the legal texts provide that the IP right owner, possibly accompanied by the licensee and/or, in some cases, the usufructuary,[41] reserves the right to exercise the infringement action, but they do not expressly address the situation of the pledgee.

It must, however, be noted that as long an IP right is encumbered, the pledgee has the right to not see this IP right disappear. Therefore, each specific IP right regulation

[41]*Cf.* Art. 2.32.4-5 BCIP; Art. 22.3-4 Regulation No. 207/2009 for EU trademarks; Art. 3.26.4-5 BCIP; Art. 3.23-4 of Regulation 6/2002 for Community designs, and Art. XI.60 §2 CEL.

expressly provides that the owner of an encumbered IP right may not waive his IP right or request revocation of its registration without the pledgee's prior consent.[42]

Inspection Right Article 16, al. 2 of the Pledge Act provides that "*the pledgee has the right to inspect the pledged goods at any time*", particularly to ensure that "*the pledger takes care of the pledged goods as a good pledger would*" (al. 1). This "*right of inspection*" thus enables the pledgee to ensure that the pledgor respects, for example, his obligations to maintain and/or renew the encumbered IP right. Should the pledgor fail to do this, it is accepted that the pledgee must be allowed to pay the maintenance fees instead of the pledgor (and ask for reimbursement).

Right to the Proceeds Article 9 provides that, "*unless otherwise agreed, the pledge extends to the proceeds produced by the encumbered goods*". According to the preparatory work of the new Pledge Act, it appears that this provision was adopted with reference to Recommendation 19 of the UNCITRAL Legislative Guide on Secured Transactions:

> The law should provide that, unless otherwise agreed by the parties to a security agreement, a security right in an encumbered asset extends to its identifiable proceeds (including proceeds of proceeds) (p. 98).

The word "proceeds" referred to in Recommendation 19 is defined as follows:

> whatever is received in respect of encumbered assets, including what is received as a result of sale or other disposition or collection, lease or licence of an encumbered asset, proceeds of proceeds, natural and civil fruits or revenues, dividends, distributions, insurance proceeds and claims arising from defects in, damage to or loss of an encumbered asset (p. 11–12).

While it may seem clear that royalties from licences granted in respect of the encumbered IP right will in principle be encumbered by the pledge, many questions remain unanswered regarding the exact scope of Article 9. Does it mean that during the agreed duration of the pledge, the pledgor either cannot collect the royalties or has to keep them on a separate account? Can the pledgor make reasonable use of the royalties in order to, for example, pay the maintenance and/or renewal fees of the encumbered IP right and/or reimburse the secured debt? To date, in the absence of a clear answer to this question, it is recommended that the parties expressly settle the fate of the current and future royalties that will be perceived by the pledgor during the duration of the pledge.

---

[42] *Cf.* Art. 50.3 of Regulation No. 207/2009 for EU trademarks and Art. 51.4 Regulation No. 6/2002 for Community designs ("*Surrender shall be entered only with the agreement of the proprietor of a right relating to the EU trade mark/Community design and which is entered in the Registry*").

Cf. Art. 2.25.2 BCIP and Art. 3.21.3 BCPI ("*If a licence has been registered, cancellation of the trademark/design registration can only be done at the joint request of the trademark/design holder and the licensee. The preceding sentence also applies in case of registration of a pledge*").

Cf. Art. XI.55 §6-§8 CEL ("*If rights of usufruct, pledge or licence have been registered, the patent cannot be surrendered, in whole or in part, without the consent of these rights holders*").

Accessory Character A pledge is an accessory right and can secure all types of obligations. If the secured claim is transferred to a third party, the security right also passes to the transferee.

5 Enforcement

Seizure: Pledge by Consumer Generally speaking, the pledgee can only take action in the event of default.[43]

Where the pledgor is a consumer, the enforcement is governed by the mandatory rules of Article 46 Pledge Act. The pledgee needs authorization from a judge in order to enforce the right of pledge. The judge will grant authorization either to sell the asset by auction (through a bailiff) or by private sale, or to appropriate the asset for the value determined by an expert. In the case of private sale, the pledgee is not allowed to acquire the IP right himself.

Seizure: Pledge by Non-consumer Where the pledgor is not a consumer, there is freedom of contract regarding the mode of enforcement (art. 47 VI Pledge Act), save for the mandatory liability of the pledgee when enforcement takes place contrary to good faith and fair dealing or in an economically irresponsible way. Judicial control takes place only *a posteriori*.

The Pledge Act contains default rules in Articles 47 to 56. Thus, the pledgee is entitled to sell the asset, either by auction through a bailiff or by private sale, or to lease the asset (*c.q.* license the IP right). In the case of private sale, the pledgee is still not allowed to acquire the right himself (Article 52). Before requesting the sale of the underlying IP right, the pledgee should verify that his security right is effective and enforceable against third parties. If not, there is a risk that the purchaser of the IP right will be entitled to ignore his rights. Further detailed default rules can be found in Article 48 and ff of the Pledge Act.

In case of default, the pledgee may also appropriate the asset himself in accordance with clauses in the contract. Such clauses must provide that the value of the encumbered IP right will be estimated by an expert (Article 53),[44] unless the clauses have been agreed after default. In view of the aforementioned, it is advisable to

---

[43]For a general overview of the rules on enforcement under the new Pledge Act, see Malekzadem (2017), p. 163 et seq.

[44]Articles 51-53 Pledge Act:

Art. 51. Vente

"Le créancier gagiste peut charger un huissier de justice de la vente publique ou de gré à gré ou de la location des biens grevés."

Art. 52. Vente au créancier gagiste

"Le créancier gagiste n'a pas le droit de se porter acheteur en cas de vente de gré à gré."

Art. 53. Appropriation par le créancier gagiste

"Si le débiteur est en défaut de paiement, le constituant du gage peut autoriser l'appropriation par le créancier gagiste des biens grevés du gage.

carefully draft the pledge agreement, in order to accurately define the rights of the pledgee in the event that the pledgor does not fulfil his obligations, including in the case of an insolvent pledgor.

One of the practical problems is that, at least for certain types of IP rights, such as patents, the market value is much lower if the acquirer cannot also purchase additional know-how or other IP rights that are necessary for the proper use of the patent. However, pledging know-how as such does not seem to be possible under Belgian law; thus, in practice, it is necessary for the business as a whole to be pledged in order for the real value of the pledged IP rights to be enjoyed.

Collecting the Royalties Pledged Regarding the right of pledge of royalties, the pledgee is, in principle, entitled to collect the royalties from the debtor of the royalties (art. 67 I Pledge Act) and to set the proceeds off using the outstanding secured debt of the owner of the royalties. Where there are several pledgees, only the first has this right (art. 67 III Pledge Act). However, if a creditor other than the pledgee seizes the royalties, the debtor of the royalties has to pay them to the bailiff, who will distribute the proceeds according to the ranking of the debts of the owner of the royalties (art. 67 IV Pledge Act).[45]

Insolvency Proceedings Against the Pledgor When insolvency proceedings such as bankruptcy are opened against the pledgor, an insolvency administrator is appointed with the authority to dispose of the assets according to the applicable rules of procedure.

An unpaid seller with reservation of title can still, within a short period of time, revendicate his asset (art. XX.194 II CEL); however, as mentioned above, the insolvency administrator may retain the asset by paying the outstanding price—and only the price, not any other outstanding debts (art. XX.201 II CEL).

Une telle convention peut également être conclue lors de la conclusion de la convention de gage ou à un moment ultérieur, lorsque la convention prévoit que la valeur des biens sera déterminée par un expert au jour de l'appropriation et, pour les biens qui sont négociés sur un marché, par référence au prix de ce marché."

[45]Art. 67 Pledge Act:

Art. 67. Droit de recouvrement du créancier gagiste

"Sauf convention contraire, le créancier gagiste est fondé à exiger, par la voie judiciaire et extrajudiciaire, l'exécution de la créance gagée. A cet égard, le créancier gagiste peut exercer tous les droits accessoires de la créance.

Le créancier gagiste impute les montants perçus sur la créance garantie lorsque celle-ci est exigible et verse le solde au constituant du gage.S'il y a plusieurs créanciers gagistes, le pouvoir prévu aux alinéas 1er et 2 revient uniquement au créancier gagiste ayant le rang le plus élevé.

Si une voie d'exécution ou une saisie conservatoire a été pratiquée sur la créance gagée, le tiers-débiteur est tenu de payer entre les mains de l'huissier de justice, lequel procède conformément aux articles 1627 et suivants du Code judiciaire.

Si la créance garantie n'est pas encore exigible, le créancier gagiste verse les montants perçus sur un compte bancaire distinct ouvert à cet effet, avec l'obligation de verser le solde au constituant du gage lorsque la créance garantie a été exécutée."

The exercise of other security rights, especially pledges, by the secured creditors (*i.e.* pledgees) themselves is temporarily suspended in case of bankruptcy (for details, see art. XX.121 CEL) in order to give the insolvency administrator the chance to sell the business as a going concern or as a whole. Of course, the pledgee retains his priority regarding the proceeds if the pledged asset is sold by the insolvency administrator.

When a judicial reorganization procedure is opened, the exercise of security rights is also suspended, except for a right of pledge that encumbers merely specific rights to performance (e.g. a right of pledge only encumbering the royalties from a specific licence) (art. XX.52 CEL).

References

Baeck J (2015) Het nieuwe pandrecht. RW 2015–2016:1209–1222

Baeck J, Kruithof M (eds) (2014) Het nieuwe zekerheidsrecht. Intersentia, Antwerpen

Becue P (2014) De wet van 11 juli 2013 met betrekking tot de hervorming van zakelijke zekerheden op roerende goederen (nieuwe Pandwet). T. Verz 2014:352–386

Borchard WM (2016) Intellectual property as security. http://www.cll.com/OnMyMindBlog/Intellectual_Property_as_Security. Accessed 23 Mar 2019

Cattaruzza J (2013) Les grands axes de la réforme des sûretés mobiliers. Bank Fin. R 2013:183–194

Clerix A, Pede V, D'Halleweyn N, Kraft H, Callens P, Beck M (2016) Octrooien in België: Een praktische leidraad. die Keure, Brugge

Corbet J, Flamee M, Gevers F (1995) Intellectuele eigendomsrechten. Biblo, Kalmthout

De Page H (1975) Traité élémentaire de droit civil belge, V, Bruylant, Brussel nos. 202 en 620-622

Del Corral J (2014) Zekerheidsrechten. Stand van zaken. NJW 2014:578–596

Delmotte B, Goldschmidt E (2011) Financiering op basis van intellectuele eigendom, eindelijk rechtszekerheid? T.Fin.R 2011:61–71

Delmotte B, Goldschmidt E (2012) Intellectuele eigendom als bron van financiering. Over het lot van merken, modellen en licenties bij faillissement, het belang van zekerheidsrechten en de nieuwe opportuniteiten onder het Belgisch recht. Bull.BMM 2012:74–79

Derijcke W (2013) La réforme des sûretés réelles mobilières. TBH 2013:691–722

Dirix E (2013) De hervorming van roerende zakelijke zekerheden. Kluwer, Mechelen

Dirix E, De Corte R (2006) Zekerheidsrechten. In: Beginselen van Belgisch Privaatrecht, vol 12. Kluwer, Mechelen

Georges F (2013) La réforme des sûretés mobilières. Rev.dr.ULg 2013:319–368

Gielen CH, Hagemans N (2011) Kort begrip van het intellectuele eigendomsrecht. Kluwer, Mechelen

Gotzen F, Janssens M-C (2016) Wegwijs in het intellectueel eigendomsrecht. Vanden Broele, Brugge

Grégoire M (2014) La modification du Code civil en ce qui concerne les sûretés réelles mobilière. In: Georges F (ed) Insolvabilité et guaranties. Larcier, Brussel, pp 9–32

Heremans T, Muyldermans D (2003) Domeinnamen in het Belgisch vermogensrecht. IRDI 2003:13–19

Keur A (2016) Intellectuele eigendomsrechten als verhaalsobject: verhaal van vorderingen door uitwinning van IE-rechten in Nederland. Boom Juridisch Uitgeverij, Utrecht

Malekzadem J (2009) Beslag op domeinnamen. Een eerste verkenning. RW 2009–2010:1498–1506

Malekzadem J (2012) Beslag en inpandgeving van onlichamelijke roerende goederen, in het bijzonder de intellectuele eigendomsrechten. In: Storme ME (ed) Themis Beslag- en Insolventierecht 2012. Acco, Leuven, pp 69–93

Malekzadem J (2017) De uitwinning van pandrechten na de hervorming. In: Storme ME (ed) Roerende zekerheden na de pandwet. Intersentia, Antwerpen, pp 157–178

Masson L (n.d.-a) Inpandgeving intellectuele rechten. Commentaar voorrechten en hypotheken loose-leaf collection., nr. II.B

Masson L (n.d.-b) Le gage de droits intellectuels. Comm.Priv., loose-leaf collection., Issue 25, 87–93

Sagaert V (2014) Goederenrecht. In: Beginselen van het Belgisch privaatrecht, vol 5. Kluwer, Mechelen

Sagaert V (2017) Het eigendomsvoorbehoud (en retentierecht) onder de Pandwet. In: Storme ME (ed) Roerende zekerheden na de pandwet. Intersentia, Antwerpen, pp 29–62

Steennot R (2017) De bescherming van de consument bij pandovereenkomsten. In: Storme ME (ed) Roerende zekerheden na de pandwet. Intersentia, Antwerpen, pp 125–155

Storme ME (2000) De drievoudige gelaagdheid van schuldvorderingen en hun bescherming. In: Cousy H, Dirix E, Stijns S, Stuyck J, van Gerven D (eds) Liber Amicorum Walter Van Gerven. Kluwer, Deurne, pp 329–331

Storme ME (2017) Zekerheidsrechten op schuldvorderingen (op naam). In: Storme ME (ed) Roerende zekerheden na de pandwet. Intersentia, Antwerpen, pp 223–299

Struelens P (2002) Pandovereenkomsten op computerprogramma's en databanken. Een zakelijke zekerheidsovereenkomst toegepast op enkele intellectuele rechten. IRDI 2002:12–15

Van Hoof J (1995) Overdracht van intellectuele rechten en voorwerp van zekerheden. In: Vlaams Pleitgenootschap bij de balie te Brussel (ed) Intellectuele Eigendomsrechten. Biblo, Kalmthout, pp 122–147

Vanbrabant B (2013) Les droits intellectuels dans le patrimoine. Doctoral thesis, Université de Liège

Vanhees H (2015) Basiswetteksten inzake het recht van de intellectuele eigendom. Intersentia, Antwerpen

Security Rights in Intellectual Property in Brazil

Simone Lahorgue Nunes

Abstract This chapter addresses transactions related to intellectual property ("IP") where IP rights serve as a security for the credit. Since there is no specific statutory provision in Brazil regulating security over IP rights, this chapter will address the general rules that are relevant to this matter in the country. Among other topics, this chapter encompasses an overview of IP rights in Brazil; the categories of security rights; the structure of the related transactions; the priorities of a security right in insolvency processes; enterprise charges; rights before default; enforcement; typical costs; and legal and practical challenges in this matter.

1 Overview of IP Rights

There are two main legal regimes in Brazil for the recognition, registration, and protection of intellectual property rights: industrial property and copyright.[1] IP is regulated solely by federal statute and by certain administrative regulations issued by federal agencies; no supranational laws (other than international treaties ratified by Brazil) or state/local/provincial laws apply.

1.1 Industrial Property

Industrial property is basically regulated by Law No. 9 279 of May 14, 1996 (the "Law on Industrial Property" or "LIP" and encompasses patents, industrial designs,

[1]The Brazilian system follows the French-based Civil Law "*droit d'auteur*" system, as opposed to the Common Law copyright system. The term "copyright" will be used in all references to authors' rights for the purposes of consistency with the other jurisdictions.

S. L. Nunes (✉)
Levy and Salomão Advogados, Rio de Janeiro, Brazil
e-mail: slahorgue@levysalomao.com.br

E.-M. Kieninger (ed.), *Security Rights in Intellectual Property*, Ius Comparatum – Global Studies in Comparative Law 45,
https://doi.org/10.1007/978-3-030-44191-3_5

trademarks, and geographical indications. Industrial property rights must be registered with the National Institute of Industrial Property ("*Instituto Nacional da Propriedade Industrial*"—the "INPI").

A patent is an exclusive right over either an invention or a utility model, as per Article 6[2] of the Law on Industrial Property. The patent owner's consent is required for the production, use, sale or import of the patented product, as provided for by Article 42[3] of the Law on Industrial Property.

The requirements for obtaining a patent are: novelty; inventive act or activity; and industrial applicability.

- *Novelty* (Articles 11 and 12 of the LIP): The invention or utility model introduces a feature that has not been in existence on the market previously—that is, something more than the state of the art.[4] The term "state of art" means the highest level of general development of a product or industry at the relevant time and may be understood as everything made accessible to the public before the date upon which the patent application is filed with the INPI.
- *Inventive act or activity* (Articles 13 and 14 of the LIP): The invention or utility model is not derived in an evident or obvious way from the state of the art from the standpoint of an expert in that specific area/industry.
- *Industrial applicability* (Article 15 of the LIP): The invention or utility model can be used or produced in any type of industry.

The following items are not patentable in Brazil pursuant to Article 10 of the LIP: (i) discoveries, scientific theories, and mathematical methods; (ii) purely abstract conceptions; (iii) commercial, accounting, financial, educational, advertising, drawing (i.e. random selection), and inspection/supervision schemes, plans, principles, or methods; (iv) literary, architectural, artistic, and scientific works, or any aesthetic creation; (v) computer programs *per se*; (vi) presentation of information; (vii) game rules; (viii) surgical techniques and methods, as well as therapeutic or diagnostic methods, for use on humans or animals; and (ix) all or parts of natural living beings and biological materials found in nature, even if isolated therefrom, including the genome or germplasm of any natural living being and natural biological processes.

A trademark is a sign[5] that identifies goods or services sold or supplied by a certain business. The trademark has to be (a) distinctive, in the sense that it enables one to differentiate the relevant good or service from competing businesses' identical

---

[2]*Article 6: "The author of an invention or a utility model shall be granted the right to obtain the patent that ensures property thereof, under the conditions set forth in this Act."*

[3]*Article 42: "A patent confers on its holder the right to prevent a third party from, without such holders' consent, producing, using, offering for sale, selling or importing for the aforementioned purposes: (I) any product that is the object of the patent; (II) any process or product directly obtained through a patented process."*

[4]Article 11 of the LIP: "*An invention and a utility model are considered to be new if they are not part of the state of the art.*"

[5]Article 122 of the LIP: "*Any distinctive, visually perceivable, sign that is not included in legal prohibitions may be registered as a trademark.*"

or similar goods or services, and (b) new. Trademark registrations in Brazil follow the "first to file" principle.

An industrial design is defined under Article 95 of the Law on Industrial Property as "*the ornamental plastic form of an object or the ornamental set of lines and colors which may be applied to a product, providing a new and original visual result in its external configuration and that may serve as a model for industrial manufacturing*".

A geographical indication may be either an indication of source or an appellation of origin and seeks to protect signs identifying the geographical origin of goods whose characteristics or reputation is connected with or attributable to this origin.

There are other kinds of IP assets protected by specific statutes and not strictly considered to be "industrial property," like integrated circuit layout designs (regulated by Law No. 11 484 of May 31, 2007—the "IC Designs Act") and plant varieties (regulated by Law No. 9 456 of April 25, 1997). Integrated circuit layout designs are registrable with the INPI and plant varieties are registrable with the National Service for the Protection of Plant Varieties, which is a branch of the Ministry of Agriculture.

1.2 Copyright

Copyright is basically regulated by Law No. 9 610 of February 19, 1998 (the "Copyright Act"), which protects intellectual works that are "*creations of the mind, expressed by whatever means and supported by whatever medium, tangible or intangible, known or susceptible of invention in the future*" (Article 7). The remainder of Article 7 lists several examples of works protected under the copyright regime, such as the text of literary, artistic, or scientific works, sermons, speeches, choreographies, musical compositions, audiovisual works, paintings, sculptures, and photographs.

Copyright protection is not conditional upon registration, as set forth by the Berne Convention for the Protection of Literary and Artistic Works, which was ratified in Brazil pursuant to Decree No. 75 699 of May 6, 1975[6] and the Copyright Act.[7]

[6]*Article 5: "(1) Authors shall be entitled to, as to the works in respect of which they are protected under this Convention, in countries of the Union other than the country of origin, the rights that those countries' respective laws currently grant, or may grant in the future, to their nationals, as well as the rights specially granted by this Convention. (2) The entitlement to and the exercise of these rights shall not be subject to any formality; such entitlement and such exercise shall be independent of the existence of protection in the country of origin of the work. Consequently, apart from the provisions of this Convention, the extent of protection as well as the procedural means afforded to the author to protect its rights shall be governed exclusively by the laws of the country where protection is claimed."*

[7]*Article 18: "The protection of the rights to which this Act applies does not depend on registration."*

Nevertheless, it is possible to register certain works with public bodies, as follows[8]: (i) written works with the National Library, (ii) audiovisual works with the National Film Agency (Ancine),[9] (iii) visual arts with the National School of Fine Arts of the Federal University of Rio de Janeiro, (iv) music with the School of Music of the Federal University of Rio de Janeiro, and (v) drafts, sketches, and three-dimensional works relating to geography; engineering; topography; architecture; park and garden planning; stage scenery; and science with the Federal Council of Engineering and Agronomy or the Federal Council of Architecture and Urbanism, as the case may be. This registration creates a rebuttable presumption as to the authorship of the works.

Copyright in Brazil encompasses authors' rights and neighbouring (related) rights.

With regard to authors' rights, the Copyright Act distinguishes between economic and moral rights,[10] in the sense that the latter are inalienable and cannot be waived.[11] The most notable moral right is the right to the paternity of the artistic work—please see Sect. 3, item 2 of this chapter for further comments on moral rights.

Neighbouring or related rights are certain rights granted to performers, producers of phonograms, and broadcasting companies.

1.3 Software

Software is protected under Law No. 9 609 of February 19, 1998 (the "Software Act").

Pursuant to the Software Act, the IP protection of software is not conditional upon prior registration and is regulated under the legal regime applicable to copyright, provided that the specific provisions of the Software Act are observed[12]; it is

---

[8]*See* Article 19 of the Copyright Act and Article 17 of Law No. 5 988 of December 14, 1973 (the former copyright act, which has been superseded by the Copyright Act except for its Article 17).

[9]The primary purpose of registering a Brazilian audiovisual work with Ancine is not related to IP protection. It is related to the organization of the Brazilian audiovisual market and to taxation (the so-called "Condecine tax"), as provided for by Executive Order No. 2 228-1 of September 6, 2001 and by Law No. 12 485 of September 11, 2011. However, such registration may be understood as creating a rebuttable presumption concerning the paternity of Brazilian audiovisual works.

[10]Article 22 of the Copyright Act: "*The moral and economic rights in the work shall belong to the author who created it.*"

[11]Article 27 of the Copyright Act: "*Moral rights are inalienable and irrevocable.*"

[12]*Article 2: "The regime of IP protection of software is the one applicable to literary works under copyright law in force in the country, pursuant to the terms of this Act.*

(...)

§ 3. The protection of the rights to which this Act applies does not depend on registration."

nevertheless possible to register the source code and the object code with the INPI to facilitate proof of ownership of the software.[13]

Note that when software is embodied in hardware and any other technological device, the creation/invention connected with this technology may be protected under both the copyright and industrial property regimes—the latter regarding the tangible part of such technology.

1.4 Supranational IP Rights

There are no supranational IP rights in Brazil and no supranational authorities are empowered by Brazilian law to register IP rights granted under Brazilian law.

That being said, Brazil is a signatory party to and has ratified the major international conventions on intellectual property, as follows:

(i) the Paris Convention for the Protection of Industrial Property (as revised at Stockholm in 1967), pursuant to Decree No. 1 263 of October 10, 1994;
(ii) the Berne Convention for the Protection of Literary and Artistic Works, ratified pursuant to Decree No. 75 699 of May 6, 1975;
(iii) the Rome Convention for the Protection of Performers, Producers of Phonograms, and Broadcasting Organizations, ratified pursuant to Decree No. 57 125 of October 19, 1965;
(iv) the Universal Copyright Convention (as revised at Paris in 1971) ratified pursuant to Decree No. 76 905 of December 24, 1975; and
(v) the Agreement on Trade-Related Aspects of Intellectual Property Rights ("TRIPS"), ratified pursuant to Decree No. 1 355 of December 30, 1994.[14]

[13]The INPI enacted (a) Normative Instruction No. 071/2017 on April 28, 2017 to provide for the applicable rules and procedures for software registration and (b) Resolution PR No. 61 on March 18, 2013 to regulate the filing of applications for the registration of software and the procedures for numbering these applications.

[14]The Paris, Berne, and Rome conventions are administered by the World Intellectual Property Organization ("WIPO"). The Universal Copyright Convention is administered by the United Nations Educational, Scientific and Cultural Organization ("UNESCO"). The TRIPS Agreement is an international agreement among the member nations of the World Trade Organization ("WTO") that was negotiated at the end of the Uruguay Round of the General Agreement on Tariffs and Trade, spanning from 1986 to 1994. WIPO, UNESCO and the WTO are specialized agencies of the United Nations.

2 Categories of Security Rights

The United Nations Commission on International Trade Law ("UNCITRAL") groups IP-related secured transactions in two separate categories. The first one encompasses "*transactions in which the intellectual property rights themselves serve as security for the credit (that is, the rights of an owner, the rights of a licensor or the rights of a licensee)*". The second encompasses the collateralization of receivables associated with certain IP rights. This chapter addresses only the former category and not the latter.[15]

There is no specific statutory provision in Brazil regulating security over IP rights. IP rights are considered movable assets pursuant to Article 3 of the Copyright Act, Article 5 of the Law on Industrial Property, and, in broader terms, Article 83, III of Law No. 10 406 of January 10, 2002 (the "Civil Code"). As a result, IP rights may be secured pursuant to the regime applicable to security rights over movable assets in general.

As a general rule, security rights may be created over immovable or movable assets. Some security rights are applicable to both kinds of assets and others only to movable or only to immovable assets.

As an exception, we understand that it is not possible to create security rights over geographical indications due to their collective and local nature: Article 182 of the LIP sets forth that "*The use of the geographical indication is limited to those producers and service providers who are located in that venue, and with respect to appellations of origin it is also mandatory that quality requirements be satisfied*".

The main security interests that may be contractually placed over IP rights are the pledge ("*penhor*"), fiduciary transfer ("*alienação fiduciária*"), and usufruct ("*usufruto*"), all of which are rights *in rem* (opposable against any third party). These interests are regulated chiefly by the Civil Code, the Law on Industrial Property and specific statutory laws governing fiduciary transfers, as explained later on.

3 Structure of Transactions: Attachment and Perfection

3.1 General Remarks

Secured transactions over IP rights are not common in Brazil. Their basic structure entails the lender being granted a security right over the relevant IP right owned by the borrower. A summary of the main security interests that may be placed over IP assets under Brazilian law is as follows:

[15] United Nations Commission on International Trade Law (2011). See especially paragraph no. 35.

- Pledge[16]: By means of a pledge, a pledgor gives a good to the pledgee (i.e. the creditor) as a security for a debt. The pledgor retains ownership of the relevant IP right. Brazilian scholars recognize the possibility of creating pledges of intangible assets.[17]
- Fiduciary transfer: The IP right owner (i.e. the debtor or a third party) transfers temporary ownership of the IP right to the creditor, to be either cancelled upon repayment of the debt or consolidated in favour of the creditor upon default.[18] Fiduciary transfers in general are subject to the provisions of the Civil Code, while fiduciary transfers in the context of the National Financial System (i.e. financing granted by banks and other financial institutions duly registered with the Brazilian Central Bank) are regulated by Law No. 4 728 of July 14, 1965, Law 10 931 of August 2, 2004, and Decree-law No. 911 of October 1, 1969. The main difference between those two regimes is that collateralization under the Civil Code regime is limited to non-fungible (i.e. not freely interchangeable) movable assets; other than that, there are more similarities than differences between them.[19]
- Usufruct: The owner retains formal ownership of the IP asset ("*nua-propriedade*"), while the benefits from it are transferred to the creditor ("*usufruto*"); such "benefits" encompass the rights to possess, use, administer, and earn profit from the asset. The transferee ("*usufrutuário*") acts in his or her own interest and not in the interest of the owner ("*nu-proprietário*") or of any third party. This mechanism is ordinarily used in the context of succession/estate planning to benefit the transferee rather than to secure indebtedness.

For further comments on contractual and proprietary rights related to each of these three security interests, please see Sect. 6 of this chapter.

3.2 Specific Remarks on Copyright

As previously mentioned, the copyright regime encompasses economic and moral rights.

[16]Article 1 431 et seq. of the Civil Code.

[17]"*Rights can also be pledged, because the pledge, as modern doctrine acknowledges, is one of the few in rem rights that can be created over intangible assets.*" Gomes (2012), p. 366.

[18]Article 1 361 of the Civil Code: "*Fiduciary transfer is the terminable ownership of a non-fungible movable good that a debtor transfers to a creditor to serve as collateral.*"

[19]Fiduciary transfer was developed in the context of the financial and capital markets to foster the acquisition of consumer goods such as vehicles, but its use has been widespread. The broadened scope of this security interest was affirmed long ago by the Superior Court of Justice upon issuing the Uniform Precedent ("*Súmula*") No. 28: "*The fiduciary transfer agreement may encumber a good that already was debtor's property.*"

Moral rights are inalienable and cannot be waived. Therefore, the creditor cannot exercise any moral right stemming from copyright and their collateralization is void. Even if the debtor (i.e. the author of the work) defaults and his or her assets are sold/ liquidated, such moral rights will continue to be held by the debtor regardless of the kind of security interest placed over them.

The list of moral rights under Article 24 of the Copyright Act is as follows: (i) to claim authorship of the work at any time; (ii) to have the author's name, pseudonym, or conventional sign appear or be announced as such when the work is used; (iii) to keep the work unpublished; (iv) to ensure the integrity of the work by objecting to any modification or any act that may have an adverse effect upon the work or be prejudicial to the author's reputation or honour in his or her capacity as the author; (v) to amend the work either before or after it has been used; (vi) to withdraw the work from circulation or to suspend any kind of use that has already been authorized where the circulation or use of the work may harm the author's reputation or image; and (vii) to have access to the sole copy or a rare copy of the work that is lawfully in a third party's possession with a view to preserving the memory of the work by means of a photograph or similar item, or an audiovisual process (provided that the least possible inconvenience is caused to the third party, who must in any event be indemnified for any damage suffered).

3.3 Mechanisms to Evaluate IP Rights

Brazilian law does not provide for mechanisms to evaluate IP rights granted as collateral. Pronouncement No. 4 of the Brazilian Accounting Pronouncements Committee ("CPC")[20] contains guidelines for the appraisal of companies' intangible assets that may be useful for this purpose.

In most cases, the debtor and the creditor agree in writing on a valuation criterion (e.g. the income approach, market approach, or cost approach) and usually hire an independent firm to carry out the appraisal.

M·CAM International, a finance firm for global innovation and intangible asset management, uses a system which determines the value for IP assets by assessing three main considerations: "*1. How long will the company and the targeted marketplace be depending on the innovations protected by the IP assets? As innovations can be rendered obsolete by newer technologies, it is important to determine whether the innovations are early or late in the technology lifecycle. 2. How active is the market for intangibles similar to those serving as collateral? What form does the activity take (e.g., licensing, cross-licensing, purchases and sales of similar IP)? Do these transactions represent cash expenditures or in-kind purchases? 3. Do secondary markets for the innovations serving as collateral exist and what are the*

[20]CPC is the Brazilian standard-setting body engaged in the study, development and issuance of accounting standards, interpretations and guidance for Brazilian companies.

sizes of those markets? That is, are there other applications of the innovations outside of its original intended field of use? For example, can the owner transfer the IP for a laser missile guidance system to the manufacturer of a high precision surgical device?"[21]

As there is no specific domestic regulation with regard to this matter, considerations such as these or any others that have an economic rationale behind them may be used in order to evaluate IP rights in Brazil.

3.4 Effectiveness of Security Rights

Each pledge,[22] fiduciary transfer,[23] or usufruct[24] of IP rights must be set forth in a written contract. This contract must have sufficient information on the debt, maturity, interest rate (if any), and collateral, and must be registered with the Registry of Deeds and Documents to be opposable against third parties.[25] This requirement applies to every kind of IP right that may be given as a security.

If the grantor of the security right in the IP right is not identical to the debtor of the secured debt, then the former must join the credit agreement as an intervening party.

If the secured IP right is a trademark, patent, industrial design, or integrated circuit layout design, then the security interest must be recorded with the INPI as well, pursuant to Articles 136, II and 59, II of the Law on Industrial Property and Article 42 of the IC Designs Act. In such cases, these security rights will produce effects with regard to third parties after publication in the INPI's Industrial Property Gazette (Articles 60 and 137 of the LIP and Article 43 of the IC Designs Act).

---

[21]Burton et al. (2014).

[22]Article 1 432 of the Civil Code: "*The pledge agreement shall be registered by any of the parties; the common pledge agreement shall be registered with the Registry of Deeds and Documents*". Article 1 452 of the Civil Code: "*The pledge of rights is constituted upon registry of the deed or private contract with the Registry of Deeds and Documents.*"

[23]Article 1 361 first paragraph of the Civil Code: "*The fiduciary ownership is constituted upon registry of the relevant agreement, be it a deed or a private contract, with the Registry of Deeds and Documents (...).*"

[24]Article 129 of Law No. 6 015 of December 31, 1973.

[25]Notarial services at federal level are regulated by Article 236 of the Constitution and by Law No. 6 015/73. Such services are provided by notaries and registrars, whose activities are also regulated by state laws and overseen by state authorities.

3.5 Registration of Security Rights

Security rights can be registered with the INPI. The registration makes the security interest produce effects with regard to third parties, which is necessary for the creditor to benefit from the legal priorities granted by each kind of security interest.

Note that although copyright protection does not require any registration, the agreements under which security interests may be placed over copyright must be registered with the Registry of Deeds and Documents to be opposable against third parties.

4 Priorities in Insolvency Processes

Law No. 11 101 of February 9, 2005 (the "Business Insolvency Act" or "BIA") contemplates three types of insolvency processes[26]:

- Judicial reorganization ("*recuperação judicial*"): This is a debtor-in-possession proceeding in which an administrator is appointed by the court to oversee the debtor's activities, the debtor presents a restructuring plan to be voted upon by the creditors, and the creditors are divided into a maximum of four classes (namely, labour/employment, secured debt, unsecured debt, and small enterprise). None of the classes necessarily have priority over the others as claims will be repaid according to the approved plan (the plan may, for example, place small enterprises ahead of secured creditors for payment).
- Liquidation ("*falência*"): The debtor is removed from the management of the business immediately upon adjudication and an administrator is appointed to manage the estate. The administrator finds and sells all assets of the estate and then uses the money to pay the estate's creditors according to a ladder of priorities.
- Pre-pack ("*recuperação extrajudicial*"): The debtor strikes a deal with secured and/or unsecured creditors out of court in advance and may submit it for court homologation. If the deal is supported by the creditors whose claims amount to more than 60 percent of the sum of all claims and it is submitted to the court, then it binds the creditors of the remaining claims upon homologation. No administrator is appointed. Pre-packs are rare in Brazil.

The priority rights granted to creditors secured by a pledge, fiduciary transfer, or usufruct of IP assets vary according to the type of process, as explained below.

[26]Personal bankruptcy ("*insolvência civil*") is regulated by Law No. 5 869 of January 11, 1973. Financial institutions, insurers, pension funds, and credit cooperatives are subject to industry-specific statutes. Neither of those cases is addressed in this chapter.

4.1 Pledge

The creditor's claim will be affected by a judicial reorganization filing and will be payable according to the restructuring plan approved by the creditors. As a rule, all secured creditors must be treated equally under the *pari passu* principle. The debtor may sell, transfer, or assign his or her assets as laid out in the plan, but a pledge over any such assets may not be cancelled or changed without prior consent from the relevant secured creditor (Article 50, paragraph 1 of the BIA). However, we note that the Superior Court of Justice has recently found that in certain cases the majority of the creditors may vote to suppress the security over an asset and this will be binding upon the relevant secured creditor.[27]

The creditor's claim will be affected by a liquidation filing as well. Pursuant to Articles 83 and 84 of the Business Insolvency Act, the estate's administrative expenses and labour/employment claims are the only claims payable ahead of secured claims. The priority of secured claims is limited to the liquidated value of the collateralized asset (i.e. the purchase price paid to the estate by the buyer of the asset); any claim in excess of this value will be deemed an unsecured claim. Note that it is possible to create multiple pledges of a single IP right, thereby creating tiers of priority. A second- or third-tier pledgee may not necessarily benefit from such priority in practice if payment to the first-tier pledgee has exhausted the asset's liquidated value.

The creditor's claim may or may not be affected by a pre-pack filing, depending on the scope of the restructuring plan and, if pledgee has not supported the plan, on whether debtor has garnered the support of more than the creditors whose claims amount to more than 60% of the sum of the secured claims. Assuming that the pledgee's claim has been affected, the same rule applicable to judicial reorganization applies and the debtor may not cancel or change the pledge without the pledgee's prior consent (Article 163, paragraph 4 of the BIA).

4.2 Fiduciary Transfer

Claims secured by the fiduciary transfer of an IP right will not be affected by any insolvency proceedings, on the grounds that ownership is deemed to have been fully transferred to the creditor and fully consolidated into creditor's property upon default; consequently, the asset no longer belongs to the debtor or to his or her estate.

The creditor must be paid out by the proceeds of the sale of the IP right—the creditor may not continue to own the IP right after the debtor has defaulted. Any outstanding balance will be deemed an unsecured claim upon reorganization, liquidation (Article 83, VI, b of the BIA), and, if applicable, pre-pack. Unlike with a

[27] Appeal No. Resp 1,532,943-MT, 3rd Chamber, Justice Marco Aurélio Bellizze, ruled on September 13, 2016.

pledge, there can be no different tiers of fiduciary transfer as ownership of the asset is temporarily transferred to the creditor upon signature of the agreement (and vests in full upon default).

Note that if the underlying IP right is essential for the conduct of the debtor's business as a going concern during reorganization, then a 180-day stay (extendable on a case-by-case basis) will apply and the security may not be enforced during the stay period.

4.3 *Usufruct*

The right to benefit from an IP asset encumbered with usufruct is not affected by any insolvency filings, although the asset may be sold at any time (i.e. ownership may be transferred freely and the usufruct is opposable against the transferee).

5 Enterprise Charges

5.1 *Possible Structures*

The creditor and the debtor may agree to place security interests over all of the debtor's IP rights, but a list must be produced and individual filings must be made with the relevant bodies (the INPI and/or the Registry of Deeds and Documents, as discussed above) instead of a single, indistinct charge being made over all of the IP rights.

In addition, universal and floating charges have not been set forth in statute in Brazil, except in one relevant case: a corporation, whether publicly traded or not, may issue debentures with a floating charge over all of its assets (including its IP rights) pursuant to Article 58, first paragraph of Law No. 6 404 of December 15, 1976 (the "Corporations Act"); no specific prerequisites apply to IP rights other than those that apply to any issuance of debentures by a Brazilian corporation in general. The ensuing comments refer to this specific case.

5.2 *Costs*

Debentures are a type of commercial paper similar to notes/bonds. The cost of issuing debentures depends on whether the issuance is private or public and on the amount involved. The main costs are associated with the registration of the indenture with the Registry of Deeds and Documents and the Central of Custody and Financial Liquidation of Securities ("Cetip").

The cost of registering the indenture with the Registry of Deeds and Documents varies from state to state and, ordinarily, according to the amount of the issuance. In the state of Rio de Janeiro, for example, an initial amount of BRL 600.00 is charged and then an additional BRL 100.00 is charged for each BRL 100,000.00 of the issuance. In the state of São Paulo, the cost ranges from BRL 1000.00 to BRL 17,000.00 (all figures have been rounded up for the sake of simplicity).

Cetip charges 0.0050% on the amount of issuance, starting at BRL 15,000.00 and going up to BRL 99,000.00.[28] Cetip also charges monthly fees for holding the debentures in its custody.

The indenture must be registered with the relevant state Commercial Registrar. The cost of such a registration is around BRL 500.00.

5.3 Priority

Pursuant to Article 58, first paragraph of the Corporations Act, the floating charge grants debenture holders a general statutory privilege over the debtor's assets upon insolvency. Floating charges are not rights *in rem*, and thus the underlying claims are not deemed to be secured claims upon insolvency.

The claim will be deemed unsecured upon judicial reorganization (Articles 26, III and 41, III of the BIA).

As for liquidation, claims with general statutory privilege are on the fifth tier of priority: they are payable behind administrative expenses (which are not subject to the ladder of priorities) and are followed by labour/employment claims, secured claims, taxes, and claims with specific statutory privilege (e.g. construction liens, mechanics' liens, and the like), and are payable ahead of unsecured claims and equity.

Priority upon pre-pack is contingent upon the scope of the restructuring (to the extent that the debentures may or may not be affected by it) and the content of the plan.

Note that a debenture-related floating charge is not very common in Brazil, as creditors tend to favour collaterals over specific assets (e.g. *in rem* guarantees) instead. A likely reason for this could be the unfavourable treatment this type of charge receives under the Business Insolvency Act.

[28] In accordance with the price table available at https://www.cetip.com.br/comunicados-documentos/unidadetitulos/tabela-de-precos. Accessed May 5, 2017.

6 Rights Before Default

6.1 Pledge

Pursuant to Article 1 433 of the Civil Code, the pledgee is entitled to: (i) keep possession of the asset; (ii) refuse to return the asset until he or she has been reimbursed for reasonable expenses incurred without his or her fault; (iii) be indemnified for losses due to defects in the asset; (iv) foreclose on the pledge in court, or to arrange for an out-of-court sale of the asset if this has been set forth in the pledge agreement or if the pledgor has otherwise empowered the pledgee to do so; (v) profit from the asset while it is in pledgee's possession; and (vi) proceed with an early asset sale, contingent upon prior court authorization, if there is reasonable risk that the pledged asset will perish or deteriorate (the pledgor may prevent the sale by properly replacing the asset or providing another collateral).

If pledgor is a third party, then he or she is not required to replace the asset if the asset is lost, damaged, or devalued without the pledgor's fault (unless provided otherwise in the pledge agreement).

Pursuant to Article 1 434 of the Civil Code, the pledgee cannot be forced to return the pledged asset or any part thereof until the debt has been repaid in full. The pledgor may ask the court to authorize the sale of just a portion of the asset or, if the pledge has been placed on more than one asset, of just one asset or a selection of the assets, to the extent necessary to repay the debt.

There is an important caveat with respect to the foregoing: although Article 1 431[29] of the Civil Code expressly sets forth that possession of the asset will be assigned to the pledgee upon execution of the pledge agreement, intangible assets such as IP rights may be subject to different rules. The Civil Code provisions have been structured to properly address the pledge of tangible assets only. Such an asset should remain in the creditor's custody until the debt is repaid—by keeping possession of the pledged asset, the creditor is in a safer position, with more certainty regarding the conservation of the asset if enforcement of the collateral becomes necessary. It is our understanding that this rule should only apply to IP rights as an exception because (i) they are intangible and non-perishable from a physical standpoint, so the transfer of their possession would not enhance the creditor's protection,[30] and (ii) usually the debtor needs to use the IP that he or she owns to conduct business in the ordinary course.[31] Given the unique features of IP rights, we understand that the parties have the ability to establish in a contract that the pledgor

[29] *Article 1 431: "A pledge is constituted by the effective transfer of possession of a movable thing that is susceptible of conveyance, made by debtor or someone on its behalf to creditor or its representative, as a debt collateral*".

[30] Exception is made for works of art such as paintings and sculptures.

[31] The sole paragraph of Article 1 431 sets forth that in rural, industrial, and mercantile pledges and in pledges of vehicles, the debtor will retain possession of the goods and must safeguard and maintain them. The solution proposed for IP rights would therefore not be inconsistent with the law.

will remain in possession of the asset and may continue using it over the course of the pledge (unless, of course, the creditor must enforce it or insolvency ensues).

Pursuant to Article 1 430 of the Civil Code, if the proceeds of the sale of the pledged asset have not been sufficient to repay the debt, the pledgor will remain liable for the outstanding amount.

Pursuant to Article 1 435 of the Civil Code, the pledgee must, in his or her capacity as the possessor of the asset, (i) keep it in custody and indemnify the pledgor for any loss or deterioration for which the pledgee is at fault; (ii) defend possession of the asset, including in court if necessary (see our previous comments on the possession of IP rights by the pledgee); (iii) offset the profits stemming from the asset (e.g. royalties) against custody and maintenance expenses, interest, and principal of the financing, in that order; (iv) return the asset to the pledgor upon repayment of the debts, together with the profits; and (v) deliver any proceeds of the sale of the pledged asset in excess of the debt to pledgor in case of enforcement of the pledge in or out of court.

The following rules apply to the profits stemming from the pledged asset (e.g. royalties and licence fees): (i) the pledgee is entitled to keep them "*as long as the asset is in his possession*" (see our previous comments on the possession of IP rights by the pledgee) (Article 1 433, V); (ii) if the pledgee keeps those profits, he or she must offset them against custody and maintenance expenses, interest, and principal of the financing, in that order (Article 1 435, III); and (iii) upon repayment of the debt, the pledgee must return the asset to the pledgor, together with the related profits (Article 1 435, IV).[32]

Accordingly, Francisco Eduardo Loureiro states that "*the appropriation of the profits derives from the law, regardless of any agreement to that effect between the parties, but this can be provided otherwise by agreement. Creditor only retains possession of the profits and, upon termination of the pledge, it must return them to owner together with the pledged asset. It may, however, choose to offset the profits against expenses related with the assets, interest and principal of the collateralized obligation, successively*".[33]

Therefore, the royalties received while the pledge is in force can be used to repay the principal of the financing (once the custody and maintenance expenses and interest have been paid). It is advisable for the agreement between the debtor and the creditor to address this issue in a detailed fashion.

The pledgee may not retain property or possession of the pledged asset in case of default and any clause to the contrary will be void[34] (this constitutes a prohibition of agreement of forfeiture or "*pacto comissório*"): the asset must be sold in the event of a court proceeding or an out-of-court enforcement. The forfeiture clause is

---

[32]Caio Mário da Silva Pereira states that "*if the pledged good generates profits, it shall be returned together with its profits that have not been received yet by the debtor during the [pledge] agreement*". da Silva Pereira (2017), p. 11.

[33]Loureiro (2018), p. 1 467.

[34]*See* Article 1,428 of the Civil Code.

forbidden by most Western jurisdictions for two reasons: to protect the weak debtor from the creditor's greedy exploitation and to avoid the assets given as collateral being appropriated by the creditor without regard to their actual market value.[35] Note that after the maturity date, the asset may be delivered to the creditor as payment in kind if the parties so agree.

6.2 *Fiduciary Transfer*

While ownership over the IP asset is temporarily transferred to the creditor, the debtor keeps direct possession over the course of the collateral agreement pursuant to Article 1 361, second paragraph of the Civil Code[36] and Article 66 of Law No. 4 728/65. The debtor must ensure that the asset is well preserved while the security interest is in force.

As Article 1 214 of the Civil Code sets forth that the good faith possessor is entitled to earn profits from the asset, we understand that the debtor will earn such profits (e.g. royalties).

In case of default, the debtor must deliver the asset to the creditor (Article 1 363, II of the Civil Code), who must sell it in or out of court and use the sale proceeds to discharge the debt (including interest and other charges); afterwards, the creditor must return any surplus to debtor.[37]

As is the case with pledges, (a) any clause in fiduciary transfer agreements authorizing the creditor to keep property or possession of the pledged asset upon default will be void (this constitutes a prohibition of agreement of forfeiture or "*pacto comissório*") and (b) after the maturity date, the asset may be delivered to the creditor as payment in kind if the parties so agree (Article 1 365 of the Civil Code).

6.3 *Usufruct*

Title to the asset and the power to sell it or otherwise dispose of it are the only rights that remain with the debtor/owner, whereas the creditor/beneficiary is entitled to all of the benefits derived from the asset (e.g. royalties or licence fees) (Article 1 394 of the Civil Code).

The beneficiary must ensure that the asset is well preserved and bear the associated costs, such as taxes (Article 1 403 of the Civil Code).

---

[35]Loureiro (2018), p. 1 464.

[36]Article 1 361, second paragraph of the Civil Code: "*Upon constitution of fiduciary transfer, possession shall be split and debtor shall become the direct possessor of the good.*"

[37]*See* Article 2 of the Decree-law No. 911/69 and Article 1 364 of the Civil Code.

During the term of the usufruct, the beneficiary's rights are not affected by a transfer of ownership to a third party or by foreclosure on the asset.

The parties may also agree that any prospective sale of the asset be subject to prior approval from the creditor.

7 Enforcement[38]

Brazilian law does not contain specific provisions regarding the enforcement of IP-related security interests upon default outside or in insolvency. The following comments address the general applicable rules.

7.1 *Outside Insolvency*

The pledgee may carry out an out-of-court sale of the asset upon default, provided that this has been expressly agreed upon in the underlying contract or that the pledgee has been duly empowered by the pledgor to do so (Article 1 433, IV of the Civil Code). Otherwise, the pledgee must enforce the pledge agreement in court to have the asset's fair value appraised by a court-appointed expert. The pledgee must then either (a) sell the asset via a public or private auction subject to court oversight ("*alienação*") or (b) offer to acquire the asset at its fair value ("*adjudicação*"). If any debt remains outstanding afterwards, then the creditor may pursue other assets belonging to the debtor to the extent necessary.

As for fiduciary transfers, the creditor will become the full owner of the asset upon default and must sell it either in or out of court to a third party and use the sale proceeds to discharge the debt (including interest and other charges). The creditor must then return any surplus to debtor (Article 2 of Decree-law No. 911/69).

As for usufruct, please see Sect. 6.3 of this chapter.

7.2 *In Insolvency*

Claims secured by pledge may not be pursued against the debtor either upon judicial reorganization or upon liquidation, and the collateral may not be enforced by the creditor. The creditor may nonetheless seek to challenge the list of creditors if his or her claim has been listed as unsecured debt and/or has been listed for an incorrect

[38]This section does not apply to usufructs given their very nature: the debtor retains only formal ownership of the asset, while the creditor may profit from it directly; thus, there is no need to enforce usufructs.

amount. Other than that, the creditor will have the general right to petition to the court if the debtor has acted to hurt creditor's interests (e.g. through fraudulent conveyances, failure to present books and records in court periodically, etc.).

As regards reorganizations specifically, the creditor has the right to vote to either approve or reject the restructuring plan. His or her claim must be paid in accordance with the approved restructuring plan. If the debtor fails to make any payment laid out in the plan within the first two years following the court homologation, then the creditor may seek to have the reorganization promptly converted to liquidation (Article 61, first paragraph of the BIA). If the debtor defaults on any payment after the first two years, then the creditor may sue to enforce the plan in court (Article 62 of the BIA).

As regards liquidations, assets will be collected, evaluated, and sold by the judicial administrator. Pursuant to Article 140 of the Business Insolvency Act, there is a preferential order for the sale of assets upon liquidation: (i) the transfer of the whole business; (ii) the separate transfer of each branch and business unit; (iii) the sale of assets that comprise a specific branch or unit; and, finally, (iv) the piecemeal sale of assets. An auction process is mandatory (Article 142). The proceeds will be used to pay administrative expenses first, then the actual claims against the debtor as tiered according to the ladder of priorities—that is, labour/employment claims first, secured claims (which include those involving the pledge of IP assets) second, and then finally the remaining claims. The proceeds are prorated among all of the creditors within each tier.

Note that labour/employment claims and other comparable claims (e.g. attorney fees) have statutory priority in all cases, and taxes are also granted statutory priority in certain cases. Therefore, if any such cross-claim is filed, that claimant will be entitled to the sale proceeds ahead of the secured creditor.

As for fiduciary transfers on insolvency, please see Sect. 4.2 of this chapter.

8 Typical Costs

It is not possible to assess the costs for legal advice, either with respect to the drafting/perfection/registration of the transaction or with respect to its enforcement, since those costs will vary depending on the structure and complexity of the deal and on the billing practices of the counsel retained by each party, among other factors.

Costs for notarial deeds are covered in Sect. 5 of this chapter.

With regard to enforcement, there will be costs related to court costs and to legal assistance in filing lawsuits. Court costs vary from state to state, but are usually charged based on the value of the claim, with a minimum and a maximum threshold. For instance: in São Paulo, initial costs range from BRL 150.00 to BRL 80,000.00; in Rio de Janeiro, they range from BRL 250.00 to BRL 40,000.00. Note that there will be court costs related to other matters, such as filing appeals and retaining court-appointed experts to appraise the asset value.

9 Practical Usefulness

Secured transactions involving IP rights are not common in Brazil, especially with regard to certain assets protected by copyright.

For instance, there are not many transactions under which security interests are placed over audiovisual works. A likely reason could be that registration is not mandatory for the acknowledgement of the paternity of the work (which sometimes leads to disputes on such paternity) and this industry is characterized by a high level of informality in Brazil, which involves risks such as off-balance-sheet liabilities.

SMEs do not seem to obtain credit on better terms in Brazil by virtue of securing their IP rights than standard credit facilities and collaterals.

10 Legal and/or Practical Difficulties

The main difficulties involved in taking security rights over IP rights are related to the valuation of IP rights; the creation of legal structures that provide creditors with the cash flow stemming from IP rights; and, for works under the copyright regime, the limitations imposed by authors' moral rights (which can be exercised by them at any time and thus may negatively affect the guarantee) on the use of the assets and on the exercise of economic rights stemming from those assets.

Also with regard to copyright, although Brazil exports different types of works of art, the domestic industry is not yet duly organized. From a legal standpoint, this affects the quality of the IP assets produced in this sector.

As for assets protected by industrial property, they can be subject to variations in their economic value; for instance, the market value of an important drug patent could be substantially reduced if the drug is replaced with a new one. As another example, antitrust concerns or public health policies could lead to the risk of a compulsory licence in respect of a patent being granted.

11 Law Reform

A bill[39] was introduced at the House of Representatives in 2013 for allowing IP rights to be used as collateral for government-backed financing if they are owned by so-called "strategic defence businesses" (i.e. businesses in the defence sector that are duly enrolled with governmental authorities and meet certain standards) or by domestic businesses and non-profit entities dedicated to research and innovation. Its statement of justification (i.e. preamble) recognizes that from a strictly legal standpoint, such authorization is not necessary; nevertheless, it states that enacting

[39] House Bill No. 6 454/2013.

a statute that expressly allows such transactions will encourage them and expedite the bureaucratic credit approval process within governmental bodies.[40] The bill's legislative process has been stayed and it is uncertain whether it will be resumed.

References

Burton BW, Bienias E, Quinn CK (2014) Financing Alternatives for Companies: Using Intellectual Property as Collateral. https://www.srr.com/article/financing-alternatives-companies-using-intellectual-property-collateral#sthash.XO9IaFyh.dpuf. Accessed 10 Dec 2018

da Silva Pereira CM (2017) Instituições de Direito Civil, Vol IV, 25th edn. Forense, Rio de Janeiro

Gomes O (2012) Direitos Reais, 21th edn. Updated by Luiz Edson Fachin. Forense, Rio de Janeiro

Loureiro FE (2018) Livro III - Do direito das Coisas. In: Coordenador Ministro César Peluso (ed) Código Civil Comentado, 12th edn. Manole, Barueri/SP

United Nations Commission on International Trade Law (2011) UNCITRAL Legislative Guide on Secured Transactions – Supplement on Security Rights in Intellectual Property. United Nations Publication. http://www.uncitral.org/pdf/english/texts/security-lg/e/10-57126_Ebook_Suppl_SR_IP.pdf. Accessed 10 Dec 2018

[40]"*One might argue that, in theory, there would be no need for legislation authorizing official development agencies to accept intellectual and industrial property rights as collaterals. If it is not forbidden, it would be automatically authorized. However, we are aware that the financing policy of the development agencies tends to be very conservative, especially when it comes to the choice of collaterals of the transaction. It can be very risky for a manager to accept as collateral less traditional assets in financing operations (….). The scope of the legislation, therefore, would be to make clearer the rule that, provided that there is a rational analysis of how enforceable the collateral based on intangible assets is, such as patents, nothing should hinder credit approval by official development agencies. This would avoid contestations by supervision bodies about the reasonableness of collaterals based on intangible assets per se.*"

Security Rights in Intellectual Property in Canada: Common Law

Robert G. Howell

Abstract Nine provinces and three territories are common law jurisdictions in Canada. The province of Quebec is a civil law jurisdiction. This paper considers the scope of rights under *Personal Property Security Acts* (PPSA) over *Intellectual Property Rights* (IPRs) from a common law jurisdictional perspective, focusing on the PPSA provisions of two common law provinces, British Columbia and Ontario. PPSA legislative measures are not uniform in detail across all Canadian common law jurisdictions, but there is similarity in principle and concept.

PPSA legislation is a provincial legislative constitutional power. This is in contrast with the predominantly federal legislative constitutional source of IPRs in a context where some federal IPR legislation addresses *ownership* and *priorities* upon assignment or, where applicable, licensing of the IPR. The result is a bifurcation of federal and provincial measures in Security Interests over IPRs involving assignment and, sometimes, licensing. However, as both federal and provincial legislative measures can co-exist and can both be complied with, there is likely no application of principles of constitutional paramountcy.

There are, however, issues of court jurisdiction between federal and provincial courts. While the Supreme Court of Canada and the provincial Superior Courts (Trial and Appellate) can determine all matters concerning IPRs and Security Interests under PPSA, the Federal Court is the more usual choice for IPR litigation, especially involving patent, industrial design, registered trademark, plant breeder rights and integrated circuit topographies under the relevant IPR legislation. Yet the Federal Court has no direct jurisdiction over provincial PPSA. However, PPSA issues may be seen as *incidental* to the substantive IPR issues and thereby give jurisdiction indirectly. This is sensible but the scope of this approach awaits appellate analysis

I acknowledge the research assistance initially of Ms. Emily Compton and Mr. Karl Doering (both UVic 2018) and subsequently Ms. Jin-Zhi Pao (UVic 2019), and the secretarial assistance of Ms. Gail Rogers and Ms. Colleen Chong.

R. G. Howell (✉)
Faculty of Law, University of Victoria, Victoria, BC, Canada
e-mail: rhowell@uvic.ca

E.-M. Kieninger (ed.), *Security Rights in Intellectual Property*, Ius Comparatum – Global Studies in Comparative Law 45,
https://doi.org/10.1007/978-3-030-44191-3_6

and may be limited. Yet, should a determination require enforcement beyond an *in personam* order, only the Federal Court has jurisdiction to directly vary or rectify a federal IPR registry.

All of these matters are considered in this paper together with a discussion of key IPR and PPSA elements, including valuation methodology and priorities between parties and the position of a Trustee in Bankruptcy. Law reform possibilities are included.

1 Overview of IPRs

Canadian IPRs are predominantly of federal jurisdiction and statutory in nature.[1] However, in two key contexts provincial common law provides the basis for protection. These latter areas are *trade secrets* protected primarily by the breach of confidence (equity) proceeding; and *unregistered trademarks* protected by the passing off (tort) proceeding.

The federal statutory IPRs are:

(i) Patents (*Patent Act*, 1985)
(ii) Copyright (*Copyright Act*, 1985)
(iii) Industrial Design (*Industrial Design Act*, 1985)
(iv) Registered Trademarks (*Trademark Act*, 1985)
(v) Plant Breeders' Rights (*Plant Breeders Rights Act*, 1990)
(vi) Integrated Circuit Topographies (*Integrated Circuit Topography*, 1990)

All of these federally based IPRs, except copyright, require application, governmental examination, and the grant of an exclusivity under the applicable legislation. The scope of exclusivity is limited nationally to Canada, i.e. each represents a grant of national dimension and can be infringed only within Canada and is remedial before the federal and provincial courts of Canada. Copyright is the exception and is protected universally on the basis of "national treatment" within member countries of the applicable international conventions.[2] Copyright exclusivity is available upon creation of a "work" by a citizen or resident of Canada or other treaty country at the time of creation; or if the work or subject matter is first published within a treaty country. The prospect of application of private international law (conflict of laws) has been discussed elsewhere by the writer.[3] Importantly, since 2004, copyright can no longer be established, in the component of "originality", by merely "sweat of the brow" or simply "industriousness". The Supreme Court of Canada adopted a test of "skill and judgment", described as falling between the traditional "sweat of the

[1]For a comprehensive survey of Canadian IPRs see Vaver (2011).

[2]For a list of IPR treaties, including copyright treaties, that Canada is party to, see Canadian Intellectual Property Office, *IP Treaties* at http://www.ic.gc.ca/eic/site/cipointernet-internetopic.nsf/eng/wr02322.html.

[3]Howell (2016).

brow" and the U.S. test of "creativity". The court defined "skill" as: "the use of one's knowledge, developed aptitude or practiced ability in producing the work"; and "judgment" as "the use of one's capacity for discernment or ability to form an opinion or evaluation by comparing different possible options in producing the work".[4] There is, therefore, an (albeit minimal) element of "copyrightability" that must be met before protection is available.

A Canadian copyright may be registered, and gain certain presumptions regarding ownership as well as procedural and litigational advantages, but registration is not a prerequisite to gaining protection.

As noted, the IPRs of unregistered trademark and trade secret are protected by provincial common law. Protecting unregistered trademarks, the tort of passing off is not limited to trademarks *per se* but covers a broad indicia of public recognition of a business or product. The proprietary designation is not afforded to the mark or other indicia, but rather to the concept of business *goodwill* to which the mark or other indicia of identification relates.[5] The elements of passing off have been stipulated by the Supreme Court of Canada as:

> the existence of goodwill, deception to the public due to a misrepresentation and actual or potential damage to the public[6]

In addition, the *Trademark Act* (1985), section 7(b) provides a federal statutory tort similar to passing off in the following terms:

> 7. No person shall ... (b) direct public attention to his goods, services or business in such a way as to cause or be likely to cause confusion in Canada at the time he commenced so to direct attention to them, between his goods, services or business and the goods, services or business of another [.][7]

Presumably, the proprietary focus under this provision is similarly the plaintiff's business goodwill. Although there is no express evidential or elemental requirement of establishing goodwill, as there is for passing off, the existence of goodwill is inherent in the finding of confusion.

As to trade secrets, Canadian courts have been reluctant to adopt a proprietary theory, preferring a *relational* perspective between the parties, emphasizing that a *relationship of confidence* is established when information is received in circumstances that reasonably give rise to an obligation of confidence.[8] A proprietary analysis of trade secrets is more appropriate if the subject matter is well defined,

---

[4] *CCH Canadian Ltd. v. Law Society of Upper Canada* (2004), para 16.

[5] See *A.G. Spalding & Bros.* v. *A.W. Gamage Ltd.* (1915) (the seminal case); *Erven Warnink BV* v. *J. Townend & Sons (Hull) Ltd.*, (1979) followed in *Consumers Distributing Co.* v. *Seiko Time Canada Ltd.* (1984), and *Ciba-Geigy Canada Ltd.* v. *Apotex Inc.* (1992).

[6] *Ciba-Geigy Canada Ltd. v. Apotex Inc.* (1992), p. 132.

[7] *Trademarks Act*, RSC 1985, c. T-13 (as amended). With respect to a section 7(b) proceeding see *Kirkbi AG and Lego Canada Inc.* v. *Ritvik Holdings Inc.* (2005) confirming the constitutional validity of this provision as a "stand alone" statutory tort.

[8] See *Cadbury Schweppes Inc.* v. *FBI Foods Ltd.* (1998), currently the leading Canadian case concerning breach of confidence.

demarcated and contained and, of course, not publicly known. In such circumstances it possesses a "quality of confidence" which would not necessarily exist for a mere collection of information that affords an advantage to a competitor of not having to be collected afresh. The Supreme Court of Canada appears to have recognized the difficulty of characterizing trade secrets by providing for "remedial flexibility" and, when appropriate, allowing a proprietary remedy (such as the constructive trust) for breach of confidence (trade secret) proceedings without the requisite of first establishing a proprietary status to the information.[9] As will be noted later, this lack of a firm proprietary characterization for trade secrets may hamper the establishing of an effective security interest in a trade secret.

However, the requisite detail and identification does exist, and has been recognized as proprietary, in an item closely related to IPRs—namely, a domain name. The leading Canadian decision is *Tucows.Com Co.* v. *Lojas Renner SA* (2011) (*Tucows*) where the Court of Appeal for Ontario afforded proprietary status to a domain name in the particular context of establishing personal jurisdiction in Ontario. The Supreme Court of Canada declined leave to appeal.[10] The proprietary characterization will apply in contexts beyond the enabling of jurisdiction in a province. Although the precise scope and application is yet to be determined,[11] the value attaching to particular domain names might constitute a collateral within a Security Interest. Andrew Cochran, writing prior to *Tucows* and focusing on earlier indications, provides an analysis of a domain name as a Security Interest.[12]

Yet, the position is more complicated. It is one thing to recognize a proprietary status for a particular purpose (such as in the context of *Tucows*, the taking of jurisdiction), but quite another to assume that the property appellation is to be applied across all contexts in some manner of universality without further consideration. Domain names are issued by registries under the control of the Internet Corporation for Assigned Names and Numbers (ICANN).[13] Geographic, or second tier, domain names are issued within national jurisdictions and in Canada this function is performed under the oversight of the Canadian Internet Registry Authority (CIRA). All applicants to any registry, whether first tier or second tier, must complete a Registrant Agreement. It includes submission to the ICANN operated Uniform Domain Name Dispute Resolution Policy ("UDRP") as an alternative, but

[9]See *Lac Minerals Ltd.* v. *International Corona Resources Ltd.* (1989), where a majority awarded the proprietary constructive trust with respect to a relationship involving a breach of confidence, but falling short of a fiduciary relationship.

[10]See *Tucows* (2011). Leave to Appeal to SCC denied [2011] SCCA No. 450. Rule 17.02(a) of the *Ontario Rules of Civil Procedure* afforded jurisdiction "in respect of real or personal property in Ontario". See also Scassa and Deturbide (2012), pp. 273–274.

[11]For example, what will constitute the infringement of a domain name—essentially an address—but of significant value in a context similar to trademark law.

[12]Cochran (2004).

[13]Howell (2011), pp. 153–162.

not a substitute for, adjudication in a court,[14] and ordinarily will contain a provision defining or regulating the nature of a domain name. The CIRA Registrant Agreement contains the following clause:

> **3.2 No Proprietary Right.** The Registrant acknowledges and agrees that a Domain Name is not property and that a Domain Name Registration does not create any proprietary right for the Registrant, the Registrar of Record or any other person in any name used as a domain name or in any Domain Name Registration. The entry of a domain name in the Registry and/or in the "WHOIS" database shall not be construed as evidence of ownership of any Domain Name Registration. The Registrant shall not in any way transfer or purport to transfer a proprietary right in any Domain Name Registration or grant or purport to grant as security or in any other manner encumber or purport to encumber any Domain Name Registration.

This clause was noted in 2013 by a UDRP Dispute Panel, though the dispute did not itself concern security interests.[15] The writer has suggested elsewhere that an agreement of this nature will likely preclude a proprietary interest between the contracting parties, but not necessarily between a registrant (holder) and a third party who may be interfering with the domain name.[16] However, a clause in the above terms would expressly prohibit the granting of a security or an encumbrance by a registrant.

2 Security Rights

2.1 *Provincial PPSA*

The nine provinces and three territories of common law in Canada have enacted *Personal Property Security Acts* (PPSA)[17] All reflect the principle of a taking and perfecting of a "Security Interest" over personal property (i.e. other than land) of a person or other juristic entity obligated to the holder of the Security Interest. The seminal source of Canadian PPSA was Article 9 of the United States *Uniform Commercial Code* (UCC). For present purposes references to PPSA will be to the enactments of the provinces of British Columbia and Ontario. Attention is, however, drawn to Howard Knopf's (ed) substantial work in 2002 comprising 17 contributing

[14]Rule 18, UDRP, enables a UDRP Panel to suspend or terminate a UDRP process in the event of the initiation of court proceedings.

[15]See CIRA Domain Name Dispute re *ArcelorMittal SA* v. *NETNIC Corp. Protective Registration Services*, BCICAC File DCA 1430-CIRA Jan. 29, 2013, para 33.

[16]Howell (2019).

[17]See PPSA (1996) as amended; PPSA (1990) as amended; PPSA (2000) amended; PPSA (1993) as amended; PPSA (1993) as amended; PPSA (1995–96) as amended; PPSA (1993) as amended; PPSA (1995–96) as amended; PPSA (1997) as amended; PPSA (2002) as amended; PPSA (1994 as amended; PPSA (1994) as amended.

chapters from authors in Canada and globally focusing comparatively in application and policy on this topic. It presents a substantial Canadian emphasis.[18]

The definitions of "Security Interest" are:

British Columbia (PPSA, 1996)	**Ontario** (PPSA, 1990)
"means (a) an interest in goods, chattel paper, investment property, a document of title, an instrument, money *or an intangible* that secures payment or performance of an obligation . . ." (emphasis added).	"means an interest in personal property that secures payment or performance of an obligation"

The term "intangible" is defined as:

British Columbia	**Ontario**
"means *personal property* other than goods, chattel paper, a document of title, an instrument, money and investment property, and *includes a licence*" (emphasis added)	"means all *personal property, including choses in action*, that is not goods, chattel paper, documents of title, instruments, money or investment property" (emphasis added)

These, and similar provisions in other PPSA are commonly regarded as including all the earlier noted categories of IPRs, but the writer would reserve reaching this conclusion with respect to trade secrets where Canadian courts have focused on relational personal liability in preference to a proprietary theory (*Cadbury Schweppes Inc.* v. *FBI Foods Ltd.* (1998)). Likewise the location of property in the business goodwill with respect to IPRs in unregistered marks and other indicia, may require more specific identification when focusing a Security Interest.[19]

The scope of Security Interest would encompass all types of security, including pledge, mortgage, security ownership, charge and lien so long as there is a securing of an obligation of payment or performance. Security situations concerning IPRs have focused on *assignment, licence, purchase money security interests* and *charging collaterally*. In this context, note is made that British Columbia (and elsewhere) specifically includes a *licence* as proprietary in itself within the definition "intangible property". Ontario does not. Classical common law analysis would consider a licence to be merely an *in personam* consent to use and is revocable at will.[20] Within IPR analysis a licence has been treated as proprietary in a leading British Columbia case, *Contech Enterprises, Inc.* v. *Vegherb, LLC* (2015) (*Contech*). The development from "mere permission to use" to *proprietary* interest has been recently analyzed in British Columbia in a context of copyright.[21] The steps are: (i) Mere

[18]Knopf (2002). A number of the contributing chapters are referenced herein independently in the text, footnotes and bibliography.

[19]Any difficulty in this context might be overcome by focusing the Security Interest on the *goodwill* pertaining to the particular mark or indicia.

[20]Ziff (2010), p. 347.

[21]See *Ankenman Associates Architects Inc.* v. *0981478 BC Ltd* (1917), paras 22 to 31 citing academic texts.

permission to use, being non-proprietary, revocable at will by the licensor and not within a Security Interest. (ii) A licence granted under a contract involving the giving of valuable consideration by the licensee to the licensor. This arrangement will create an *equitable interest* in the copyright in favour of the licensee. Revocability will be determined accordingly to the terms of the contract. Such a licence is not proprietary. It is purely contractual. (iii) A licence that grants an interest in the copyright. Such a licence is proprietary and may be the subject of a Security Interest.

Contech, is a landmark case decided by the British Columbia Court of Appeal and favourably endorsed academically.[22] Contech carried on business in the province of British Columbia. It had granted general security agreements (GCAs) to various financiers. It later agreed to purchase all the assets (mainly IPRs) of Vegherb. Only part of the purchase price was paid at the time of the agreement. The remainder (over $2 million) was to be paid by installments. Vegherb's IPRs were licensed to Contech with title remaining in Vegherb, constituting a Purchase Money Security Interest (PMSI) that was registered and perfected under British Columbia's PPSA. Contech defaulted in installment payments to Vegherb. It filed for a commercial reorganization under the federal *Bankruptcy and Insolvency Act* (1985) (BIA). The BC Court of Appeal rejected a reorganization whereby Contech would keep the IPRs and Vegherb would simply share with the financiers holding GCAs. Rather, the asset (IPR) purchase by Contech from Vegherb over time with a licence of the IPRs constituted a PMSI and gave, under BC PPSA a "super-priority"[23] applied to a PMSI that encompassed IPRs.[24] Siebrasse and Duggan point out that this distinguishes PPSA (Canada) from Article 9 in the U.S. UCC where a PMSI cannot be granted for IPRs but only for "goods and software".[25]

2.2 Security Related Federal IPR Provisions

The federal legislation for *copyright* and *patent* protection, as well as exclusive rights under the *Plant Breeders' Rights Act,* contain security related "priority" provisions that may present a conflict between federal legislative measures and provincial PPSA raising the potential of a federal paramountcy or pre-emption.[26] From a practice perspective, filings both federally and provincially are completed. Ballagh[27] notes "The standard legal advice is sometimes called the 'belts and suspenders' approach. Where feasible, parties are advised to register their security

[22] Siebrasse and Duggan (2016).

[23] See BC PPSA (1996), s. 34(1)(b).

[24] If the situation had been a general bankruptcy distribution rather than a commercial reorganization the position would have been different.

[25] Siebrasse and Duggan (2016), pp. 28–29.

[26] Hatzikiriakos (2006), p. 139.

[27] Ballagh (2017).

interests on both the federal and the provincial registers in *all* the relevant jurisdictions [i.e. provinces]".

The federal *Copyright Act* contains the following provisions:

(i) Section 13(4) to (7)

Assignments and licences

(4) The owner of the copyright in any work may assign the right, either wholly or partially, and either generally or subject to limitations relating to territory, medium or sector of the market or other limitations relating to the scope of the assignment, and either for the whole term of the copyright or for any other part thereof, and may grant any interest in the right by licence, but no assignment or grant is valid unless it is in writing signed by the owner of the right in respect of which the assignment or grant is made, or by the owner's duly authorized agent.

Ownership in case of partial assignment

(5) Where, under any partial assignment of copyright, the assignee becomes entitled to any right comprised in copyright, the assignee, with respect to the rights so assigned, and the assignor, with respect to the rights not assigned, shall be treated for the purposes of this Act as the owner of the copyright, and this Act has effect accordingly.

Assignment of right of action

(6) For greater certainty, it is deemed always to have been the law that a right of action for infringement of copyright may be assigned in association with the assignment of the copyright or the grant of an interest in the copyright by licence.

Exclusive licence

(7) For greater certainty, it is deemed always to have been the law that a grant of an exclusive licence in a copyright constitutes the grant of an interest in the copyright by licence.

(ii) Section 57(3)

When assignment or licence is void

(3) Any assignment of copyright, or any licence granting an interest in a copyright, shall be adjudged void against any subsequent assignee or licensee for valuable consideration without actual notice, unless the prior assignment or licence is registered in the manner prescribed by this Act before the registering of the instrument under which the subsequent assignee or licensee claims.

With respect to an exclusive licence, a majority of the Supreme Court of Canada has determined that such a grant is effective against even the owner of the copyright.[28] An assignee or licensee with an interest in the copyright can obtain a registration of the copyright.[29] The original instrument (or a certified copy) of the assignment or licence must be provided to the Registrar who may allow other

[28]See *Euro-Excellence Inc.* v. *Kraft Canada Inc.* (2007), paras 75 and 118–123. Three (perhaps four) justices considered that a licence, even if exclusive, had to be distinguished from an assignment and therefore gave no rights against the owner of the copyright. See paras 28–37 and 52.

[29]See *Copyright Act* s. 55(1) and (2) (for "works") and s. 56(1) and (2) (for "other subject matter").

evidence of the assignment or licence that is to the Registrar's satisfaction.[30] Section 57(3) determines priorities at a federal level.

The federal *Patent Act*, sections 50 and 51 provide:

Patents to be assignable

50(1) Every patent issued for an invention is assignable in law, either as to the whole interest or as to any part thereof, by an instrument in writing.

Registration

(2) Every assignment of a patent, and every grant and conveyance of any exclusive right to make and use and to grant to others the right to make and use the invention patented, within and throughout Canada or any part thereof, shall be registered in the Patent Office in the manner determined by the Commissioner.

Attestation

(3) No assignment, grant or conveyance shall be registered in the Patent Office unless it is accompanied by the affidavit of a subscribing witness or established by other proof to the satisfaction of the Commissioner that the assignment, grant or conveyance has been signed and executed by the assignor and by every other party thereto.

When assignment void

51 Every assignment affecting a patent for invention ... is void against any subsequent assignee, unless the assignment is registered as prescribed by those sections, before the registration of the instrument under which the subsequent assignee claims.

Section 52(2) above provides for both an *assignment* and an *exclusive licence* and mandates that such be registered in the Patent Office. Section 51 addresses priorities, but only with respect to *assignment*.

The federal *Plant Breeder's Rights Act*, section 31(1) requires notification to the Commissioner of Plant Breeders' Rights of any assignment of those rights and section 31(3) provides for priorities as follows:

Unregistered assignment void against subsequent assignee

31(3): An assignment of plant breeder's rights is void against a subsequent assignee thereof for valuable consideration without notice who is registered as the holder of the rights unless, before the subsequent assignee is so registered, the person to whom that assignment is made is registered as holder of the rights.

The remaining categories of IPRs—trademarks, industrial designs and integrated circuit topographies—are legislatively enabled for assignment or licence,[31] but without any federal legislative stipulation of priorities. All Security Interests in these categories are, therefore, provincial PPSA. However, notice, with details, is required to be registered federally for designs.[32] Any securities related consequences of a failure to attend to such registration is not provided.

[30]See *Copyright Act*, s. 57(1)(a).

[31]See *Industrial Design Act*, s. 13(1), (2) and (3); *Integrated Circuit Topography Act*, s. 7(1)(2); and *Trademarks Act*, ss. 48 and 50.

[32]See *Industrial Design Act*, s. 13(1) and (3). With respect to an integrated circuit topography, a transfer or licence of a topography must be recorded on the register by the Registrar "on being

2.3 Federal and Provincial Relationship

The relationship between federal "securities related provisions" and provincial PPSA awaits appellate analysis across a broad range of issues. As noted earlier, a federal pre-emption or paramountcy has been suggested, at least in some circumstances.[33] In *Contech*, the recent landmark British Columbia case, pre-emption was not argued, nor presented. Siebrasse and Duggan correctly note that the facts, given earlier, did not cause "a direct conflict with paramount federal legislation".[34] This is an essential requirement. The constitutional dimensions of federal paramountcy are narrow, requiring that federal and provincial laws present an express contradiction so that it is impossible to comply with both or that a federal purpose is frustrated.[35]

In a securities situation involving priorities there can be compliance with both federal and provincial legislation. If both are not complied with an outcome in priorities may be different, but this does not mean that there is an inconsistency between federal and provincial laws. For example if the facts in *Contech* are hypothetically changed to a situation where subsequently to granting a licence of its IPRs to Contech as part of a PMSI, Vegherb had given a further licence (or an assignment) to a third party who registered this licence or assignment with the federal Copyright Office under the provisions set out above and Contech had not made a prior such registration federally, then the licences to Contech would be presumptively void under section 57(3), *Copyright Act* against the subsequent assignee or licensee, producing a different outcome but one resulting from a failure to comply with section 57(3), *Copyright Act*, rather than from any inconsistency between federal and provincial laws. Indeed, in 1991 the Federal Court in *Poolman* v. *Eiffel Productions SA* interpreted section 57(3) as being simply presumptive of ownership without replacing the general provincial laws concerning Security Interests and priorities in general.[36]

Essentially, therefore, Security Interests in IPRs throughout common law Canada invokes both federal and provincial jurisdictions and infrastructures with the analysis focused on the scope of application of each. IPRs are not the only areas of interface between federal and provincial securities laws. Banking, shipping, and railways are other areas. In 1999, Professor Roderick Wood addressed these areas (not of direct concern in this report) as well as IPRs. Wood laments the federal usage of *form* for categories of "assignment" and "licence" as opposed to the more recent and flexible *substance* approach in PPSA of simply determining whether a transaction amounts

furnished with evidence of the transfer of grant [of a licence]", *Integrated Circuit Topography Act*, s. 21(1). Registration of assignment or licence is seemingly optional for the assignee or licensee.

[33]Hatzikiriakos (2006), p. 139.

[34]Siebrasse and Duggan (2016), p. 27.

[35]Hogg (2007–2017) Vol. 1, ch. 16.3(a) and (b).

[36]*Poolman* v. *Eiffel Productions SA* (1991), para 24.

to a security upon the completion of an obligation.[37] Yet, this categorization of "assignment" or "licence" (of an interest in the IPR) is the essence of the limitation of the scope of federal involvement and will require to be interpreted. Wood correctly notes that Canadian constitutional pre-emption by paramountcy does not ordinarily include a negative pre-emption of the whole field by an expression of only a partial context of application. Rather, there is a *concurrency* of jurisdiction.[38] It is required that both federal and provincial legislative measures be enacted validly within a federal and a provincial legislative "head of power" jurisdiction.[39] Valid enactment requires that the federal and the provincial enactment are, in "pith and substance", within a head of power for that level of government. If one is not, then that is conclusive before reaching any issue of paramountcy. The validly enacted legislation prevails.[40]

Copyright and Patent have an express federal legislative jurisdiction and Plant Breeders' Rights are likely within the federal "Trade and Commerce" jurisdiction.[41] Likewise, the regulation of security interests in property is validly provincial.[42] The scope and content of these and other federal heads of power for intellectual property matters have received little judicial interpretation.[43] It is, therefore, possible to argue these federal heads ought to be limited in pith and substance to the substantive dimensions of these subject areas, but not to include the setting of priorities for assignment or licences. In effect this would conclude that the setting of priorities is not, in pith and substance, an issue of "copyrights" or "patents" or "plant breeds", but instead is an issue of personal property security and, therefore, exclusively a matter of provincial PPSA. The IPR would simply be a particular type of asset. This argument, however, is difficult to sustain as the substance of an IPR includes the ability to assign or licence the IPR and a logical extension of this is to set priorities.

---

[37]Wood (2000), p. 100, section V, "Security Interests in Intellectual Property." Wood examines a number of subject areas within federal legislative jurisdiction. Section V concerns intellectual property rights.

[38]Wood (2000), p. 106.

[39]Hogg (2007–2017), vol. 1, ch. 15.5 and 16.1.

[40]Hogg (2007–2017), ch. 16.1.

[41]See *Constitution Act* (1867), s. 91 (22) ("Patents of Invention and Discovery"), 91(23) ("Copyrights") and 91(2) ("The Regulation of Trade and Commerce").

[42]*Constitution Act, 1867*, s. 92 (13) ("Property and Civil Rights in the Province").

[43]The federal "Copyrights" head of power (s.91 (23) *ibid*) has been considered with respect to (1) the inclusion of moral rights within this head of power; and (2) the levying of a fee on blank audio-recording media to cover "private copying" of lawfully acquired recordings. In both instances the legislative inclusion within the head of power has been upheld, See *Snow v. The Eaton Centre Ltd.* (1982), (re moral rights) and *Private Copying Collective v. Canadian Storage Media Alliance* (2005) at paras 32–38 (re the levy on blank audio-recording media). There has been academic challenge to the inclusion within the head of power of technological protection measures. See de Beer (2005), pp. 89–124. However, the present writer would find technological protection measures to be within the head of power. See Howell (2011), pp. 265–268.

Priority provisions would, therefore likely meet the relevant constitutional test of being sufficiently integrated into the legislation.[44]

Security Interests outside of assignment or licence (e.g. a charge or mortgage as collateral securing an obligation and being therefore a Security Interest) cannot possibly invoke a federal paramountcy as these situations are outside of the contexts in federal legislation. Provincial PPSA is, therefore, the *exclusive* source of security for these interests.

However, security transactions involving assignment and (in some instances) licence of IPRS (at least for copyright, patents and plant breeder rights where federal priorities are stipulated, and, possibly, also for industrial designs) will present a potential mixture of federal and provincial priorities and will require registration both federally and provincially (PPSA), as is the practice of practitioners. This potential mix of federal and provincial security interests is illustrated as follows:

1. A owns copyright and gives a licence to B in the copyright to secure an obligation.
2. A subsequently gives a licence to C in the copyright to secure an obligation. C would gain priority over B if B has not registered its licence in the federal Copyright Office.
3. A subsequently gives D a charge over its copyright. Both B and C would lose priority to D if B and C have not each registered their interest under provincial PPSA.

For informational purposes the federal offices will accept copies of Security Interests beyond the context of the federal legislation.[45] This is a useful practice and may afford notice, but cannot avoid PPSA filing for priority.

British Columbia PPSA (and those of some other provinces) expressly excludes from PPSA matters covered by federal legislation, as follows:

[44]The Supreme Court of Canada has stipulated the following test: First, the impugned provision must be characterized in isolation from the whole of the legislation. Second, the statute as a whole must be validly within the particular head of power, and third, the impugned provision must be sufficiently integrated into the legislation. See *Kirkbi AG v. Ritvik Holdings, Inc.* (2005), paras 14 to 32 in a trademark context.

[45]See: (1) Re Copyright—Government of Canada, Canadian Intellectual Property Office, at https://www.ic.gc.ca/eic/site/CIPOinternet-internetopic.nsf/eng/wr00054.html noting "Other Documents: The Canadian Intellectual Property Office (CIPO) will also record other documents that relate to a copyright such as a change of name … or a security agreement"; (2) Re Patent—Manual of Patent Office Practice, ch. 6, para 6.04, at https://s3.ca-central-1.amazonaws.com/manuels-manuals-opic-cipo/MOPOP_English.html; (3) Re Trademarks—Innovation, Science and Economic Development Canada—Security Agreements at https://www.ic.gc.ca/eic/site/cipointernet-internetopic.nsf/eng/wr00228.html; and Re Industrial Designs—Industrial Design Office Practices, para 15.1 at https://www.ic.gc.ca/eic/site/cipointernet-internetopic.nsf/eng/wr00276.html#n15. See also Ballagh (2017), p. 2 noting: "Although security agreements are accepted for recordal on all federal registers, it is not mandatory".

> a security agreement governed by an Act of the Parliament of Canada that deals with rights of parties to the agreement or the rights of third parties affected by a security interest created by the agreement . . .[46]

Ontario PPSA does not expressly include such a limitation. Yet, whether by way of reliance on an express statutory exclusion as in British Columbia, or by judicial interpretation of the inter-relationship of federal and provincial legislative measures, the scope of application of the federal enactments must be interpreted and will prevail within that scope of application, leaving provincial PPSA to cover the residue.

Professor Ronald Cuming noted early in the commentaries on IPRs and PPSA that unlike PPSA, the federal legislative sources do not contain any requirement that an assignee (or, where applicable, licensee) "perfect" the secured interest against the debtors trustee in bankruptcy.[47] This requires further explanation because the federal IPR legislation does not address the interests of a trustee in bankruptcy or other third party interest beyond the relationship between the holders of successive assignments or (if applicable) licences. However, *within this limited context*, no notion of "perfection" exists. Accordingly, a trustee in bankruptcy of one of the parties in the string of successive assignments would ordinarily not receive a greater title than that of the bankrupt. So that if the bankrupt party has not registered his or her assignment, the trustee in bankruptcy would be bound by this omission. The writer would interpret Professor Cuming to this effect. However, further evaluation is necessary in a transaction that involves more than this limited scenario.

Before leaving the federal IPR statutes note should be made of the criticism of federal registries as difficult to search, incomplete and involving distinctly separate registries between the categories of IPRs.[48]

3 Security Transactions and Valuation

Assignment and, in some contexts, licensing of IPRs has been noted above to involve unresolved issues of federal and provincial legislative jurisdiction, but *charging* or *mortgaging* an IPR as a collateral securing an obligation is entirely provincial exclusively within PPSA principles. Yet, there are many gaps in statutory and case law development. *Contech* in the British Columbia Court of Appeal has provided certainty in the context of licensed IPRs in a Purchase Money Security Interest (PMSI) transaction. Major difficulties are, however, presented in the choice of mechanisms to assess the worth or value of an IPR.

A preliminary step is to recognize recent studies by independent Canadian institutes that find Canadian commercialization to be more fledgling in comparison

---

[46]See BC PPSA (1996) s. 4(b).

[47]Cuming (1995), p.10, footnote 18.

[48]Ballagh (2017).

with that in the United States and other developed countries. The studies seek to promote, indeed push, Canadian innovation companies and other stakeholders to embrace innovation and intellectual property. In September 2016, the Intellectual Property Institute of Canada (IPIC) published its submission to the federal portfolio *Innovation, Science and Economic Development Canada*.[49] While acknowledging significant Canadian academic research innovation, IPIC notes:

> However, much of our world-class research and innovation stalls at the pre-commercialization stage due to an inability of Canadian innovators to move concepts to a commercially-ready stage, and a lack of Canadian receptor capacity willing to invest in early-stage commercial development. As a result, an "innovation gap" exists in Canada that results in many early-stage technologies languishing without commercial development, or being taken up and commercialized by foreign countries. In either case, there is little economic benefit to Canada.[50]

To the same effect, an earlier commentary recommends a taxation incentive on *commercialising* or *exploiting* of research and development (R&D) rather than on generating R&D itself.[51] In this circumstance of lower innovative commercialization there is less of an IPR valuation infrastructure in Canada. The United States and Europe have many more specialist IPR asset consulting and valuation firms (Forbes Ranking). This said, Canadian law firms have provided "IP Audits" to their clients for several years and Canadian accounting and valuation firms (often as part of a global firm) have provided valuation services.[52]

Three approaches to valuation have been identified in the United States:

(i) A *Cost Approach* that looks at historical cost or future replacement cost of the IPR;
(ii) A *Market Approach* that can operate when "a truly active marketplace exists and actual comparable transactions can be found"; and
(iii) An *Income Approach* that looks at the estimated financial benefits that the IPR can produce and is described by Anson as the most common.[53]

From the perspective of a Security Interest securing an obligation, either a market approach or an income approach would be a logical methodology. A market approach (re-sale) is usual for a tangible asset, but a tangible asset ordinarily is more capital than income focused. The primary objective of IPRs is to earn income.

---

[49]*Innovation, Science and Economic Development Canada* (ISED), constitutes a federal governmental portfolio that comprises seventeen federal departments and agencies. ISED has the mandate "to further the [federal] government's goal of building a knowledge based economy in all regions of Canada". The first listed objective is to promote "innovation through science and technology". See https://www.ic.gc.ca/eic/site/icgc.nsf/eng/h_00022.html. A pdf of ISED's Departmental Plan 2017–2018 is available at the site.

[50]IPIC (2016), pp. 9–10.

[51]C.D. Howe Institute (2013).

[52]Many international firms on the Forbes Ranking, *ibid.*, have Canadian offices. See also BDO Canada at https://www.bdo.ca/en-ca/services/advisory/valuations/overview/.

[53]Anson (2012).

For example, in PMSTs, as in *Contech*, the purchaser is likely using or be going to use the IPRs producing an immediate income objective.[54] Gordon Smith, again in a United States context, but from economic, business and investment perspectives, also emphasizes an income approach for intellectual property assets.[55] However, in a security transaction involving IPRs as collateral to a lender (e.g. a bank or financial institution) use of the IPRs in the transaction is unlikely, so a market approach focused on capital or resale value is likely the more appropriate methodology, so long as a market exists for the IPRs.

Overall, however, a substantial similar measure exists between an income approach and a market approach given that the market value or sale price will likely depend upon the income worth of the IPRs to a buyer. Canadian commentators David Ullmann and Sheldon Title, involved in corporate restructuring and insolvency, discuss the three methods of valuation of IPRs, that is the *cost*, *market* and *income* approaches. They note the market approach to consider:

> transactions involving comparable forms of intellectual property and related licensing arrangements and royalty rates [and continuing] [v]alue is calculated by comparing the price at which similar property has been exchanged on the market.

This requires a marketplace of "comparable data" and "a sales process" to establish prices, but that at the core of the price setting exercise is the cash flow (income) worth of the IPRs comparatively with that of other similar IPRs in the particular marketplace. It is the comparison of market prices that distinguishes a market approach from an income approach *simpliciter*. As with Anson, Ullmann and Title note the income approach to be "the most widely used method", but conclude that this is often reflective of IPRs for "solely internal purposes.[56]

Ullmann and Title also acknowledge the subjective and assumptive nature of IPR valuation and provide examples in a context of corporate restructuring where relatively speculative assessments of IPR value have to date been accepted by Canadian courts.[57]

---

[54]The writer, however, is not aware of the actual valuation methodology used in this case.

[55]Smith (2002), pp. 309–313.

[56]Ullmann and Title (2014), section III, 3, "Approaches to Valuing Intellectual Property", (ii) "The Income Approach".

[57]Ullmann and Title (2014)—"Case Study: Ambercore" noting in insolvency proceedings in Ontario a court ordered requirement of IPR valuation. The US New Jersey firm, Astrina Capital (*astrina.com*) was retained by the Receiver. The court accepted a "valuation letter" short of a comprehensive valuation. The authors also discuss Nortel's patents valuation at 500% less than what the patents gained at auction less than two months after the valuation. *Ibid.* at section VII—"Conclusion".

4 Priorities

The general setting of priorities with respect to a trustee in bankruptcy (or other specified representative of creditors upon an insolvency) under the federal *Bankruptcy and Insolvency Act* (1985) is determined by provincial PPSA in respect of matters within PPSA. As noted earlier, the federal IPR provisions are limited strictly to the *context and stipulated event(s)* in the federal statutes, that is *between holders of assignments* (or, as applicable, licences) when a prior assignment (or, where applicable, a licence) is not registered under the federal enactment. The position with respect to these purely federal dimensions is first considered. No directly relevant authority exists.

4.1 Federal IPR Provisions

Also as noted earlier, to the extent that federal IPR statutes govern issues of ownership between persons, no mechanism of "perfection" exists. It is simply "presumptive ownership" between the two or more holders involved, determined simply by federal IPR registration. However, it is also noted that a trustee in bankruptcy might not gain a better title than that of a bankrupt assignee who failed to register an interest with a relevant federal IPR registry.

Bankruptcy itself is a federal jurisdiction governed by the *Bankruptcy and Insolvency Act* (1985). This enactment defines "property" as:

> property means *any type of property*, whether situated in Canada or elsewhere, and includes money, goods, *things in action*, land and every description of property, whether real or personal, legal or equitable, as well as obligations, easements and every description of estate, interest and profit, present or future, vested or contingent, in, arising out of, or incident to property (emphasis added)

IPRs are definitely included ("any type of property", "things in action"). Part IV deals with "Property of the Bankrupt". Section 71 vests the property in the trustee. This is subject to the rights of "secured creditors", defined in section 2 as (in part):

> secured creditor means a person holding a mortgage, hypothec, pledge, charge or lien, on or against the property of the debtor . . . or a person whose claim is based on, or secured by, a negotiable instrument held as collateral security [various inclusions]

The first question, therefore, is whether a federal registration under an IPR enactment creates in the registrant the status of a "secured creditor". The answer is no, it does not. As noted earlier, the IPR provisions are likely seen as presumptive ownership provisions. Furthermore, an assignment or licence is not directly within the definition "secured creditor" in the BIA noted above. Accordingly, registration under the federal IPR enactments will not in itself protect a registrant from the assignment to, and priority of, the trustee in bankruptcy under the BIA.

The second question, however, is whether a bankrupt party in a line of assignees (or, where applicable, licencees) *has any property* in an assigned (or licensed) interest if the federal IPR enactments have not been complied with. This has been described as the *limited context* in which the federal IPRs operate. Here the presumptive ownership provisions may deny property in an assignment to an earlier unregistered (federal IPR) bankrupt assignee and, therefore, mean there is no property to pass to the trustee in bankruptcy.

4.2 Provincial PPSA

Within the provincial PPSA structure a Security Interest in a collateral is subordinated to a trustee in bankruptcy [or other specified representative of creditors] if the Security Interest is not "perfected". The relevant provision of PPSA legislation in British Columbia and Ontario (by way of example) are as follows:

4.3 British Columbia PPSA

Subordination of unperfected security interests

20: A security interest

. . .

(b) in collateral is not effective against

(i) a trustee in bankruptcy if the security interest is unperfected at the date of the bankruptcy, or

(ii) a liquidator appointed under the *Winding-up and Restructuring Act* (Canada) if the security interest is unperfected at the date that the winding-up order is made.

4.4 Ontario PPSA

Unperfected security interests

20(1): Except as provided in subsection (3), until perfected, a security interest,

. . .

(b) in collateral is not effective against a person who represents the creditors of the debtor, including an assignee for the benefit of creditors and a trustee in bankruptcy;

Similar provisions exist in other Canadian common law PPSA. Perfection is effected in the manner stipulated in PPSA according to the type of asset. In both British Columbia and Ontario these perfection requirements are set out in Part 3 [III] of the respective PPSAs similarly to other provinces. It is beyond the scope of this report to address all types of assets in their requirements for perfection. However, the *general* (i.e. non-specific) provisions that would be applicable to IPRs with respect to British Columbia and Ontario are:

(i) B.C. Section 25

> [R]egistration of a financing statement perfects a security interest in collateral

(ii) Ontario Section 23

> Registration perfects a security interest in any type of collateral[58]

The subordination of an unperfected Security Interest to a trustee in bankruptcy was confirmed by the Supreme Court of Canada in *Giffen (Re)* (1998), a proceeding from British Columbia. The proceeding did not involve IPRs. The respondent had leased a motor vehicle to a company which then leased it to an employee. The lessor was not a party to the lease from the company to the employee, but was involved by receiving the deposit from the employee and was entitled to receive installment payments direct from the employee, at rates that it had set, if the company ceased to make the payments under the lease between the lessor and the company. The lessor had reserved its ownership of the vehicle, even though both the lessor and the company were noted in the vehicle registration as owners. A trustee in bankruptcy was appointed for the company.

The trustee in bankruptcy succeeded. The lessor did not have the status of a secured creditor because the Security Interest had not been perfected and PPSA. Section 20(b)(i) determines that a Security Interest not perfected at the date of a bankruptcy is not effective against a trustee in bankruptcy. To be perfected the Security Interest must first "attach" to a creditor's security entitlement (PPSA (1996), PPSA (1990)), meaning it must come into effect between a debtor and creditor who has given value and secured the obligation of the debtor to pay the creditor.[59] Second, all other steps required for perfection must have been completed.[60] In this context section 25 provides: "registration of a financing statement perfects a security interest in collateral".[61] The term "financing statement" is defined.

The trial judge had found in favour of the trustee in bankruptcy under the above provisions. The BC Court of Appeal reversed on the basis that *ownership* had been retained by the lessor and had not passed to the bankrupt company, so that there was no "property" to pass to the trustee in bankruptcy. The Supreme Court of Canada found that a combination of provincial PPSA [section 20(b)(i)] and the federal BIA rendered the actual location of ownership to be irrelevant. The court also accepted the constitutional interrelationship of the federal BIA and provincial PPSA.[62]

---

[58]The term "collateral" is defined as "personal property that is subject to a security interest" (B.C. and Ontario, s. 1).

[59]See generally ss 12, 12.1 and 13 PPSA (1996) and s. 11(2) PPSA (1990).

[60]See PPSA (1996) s. 19(b) and PPSA (1990) s. 19(b).

[61]In Ontario, in the context of a lease of a motor vehicle or goods, perfection similarly occurs upon the filing of a "financing statement". See PPSA (1990) ss. 25(5) and 27(4).

[62]*Giffen (Re)* (1998), para 15 et seq.

Might this analysis in *Giffen (Re)* apply to IPRs and federal IPR registrations as assignments (or licences where applicable) as discussed in Sect. 2.3 above? Recall, there it was concluded that registration under federal IPR legislation did *not* itself give the registrant any status as a secured creditor under BIA, but that the federal IPR legislation could determine *ownership* and might, thereby, mean a federally unregistered bankrupt assignee might not have property to pass to a trustee in the bankruptcy. It is suggested that in the narrow context of interests between simply successive assignees (or, where applicable, licensees) PPSA section 20(b)(i) and *Giffen (Re)* ought to have no application. The federal IPR provisions should prevail. However, an assignment or licence of an IPR that is merely a component of a larger scheme or transaction that is a Security Interest, being "an intangible that secures payment or performance of an obligation" and one that is capable of constituting the holder a "secured creditor" under BIA, then the analysis in *Giffen (Re)* and section 20 (b)(i) BC PPSA ought to apply to this more broadly defined transaction requiring registration and perfection under PPSA if an assignment to the trustee in bankruptcy is to be avoided as a "secured creditor". It is noted by way of example that section 2 (1)(b) of BC PPSA and section 2(a)(ii) Ontario PPSA specifically include within a security interest an *assignment* that "secures payment or performance of an obligation".

4.5 Purchase Money Security Interests (PMSI)

With respect to priorities in a PMSI transaction, recall the earlier discussion concerning PMSIs and the recent British Columbia case of *Contech* and the "super-priority" afforded by PPSA even as against a trustee in bankruptcy.

5 Enterprise or Floating Charge

An enterprise or floating charge is provided for under provincial PPSA. Section 2(1), PPSA (BC) provides that the act applies to:

(a) to every transaction that in substance creates a security interest, without regard to its form and without regard to the person who has title to the collateral, and
(b) without limiting of paragraph (a), to a chattel mortgage, a conditional sale, a *floating charge*, a pledge, a trust indenture, a trust receipt, an assignment, a consignment, a lease, a trust, and a transfer of chattel paper if they secure payment or performance of an obligation. (emphasis added)

Likewise, section 2 PPSA (Ontario) stipulates that the act applies to:

(a) every transaction without regard to its form and without regard to the person who has title to the collateral that in substance creates a security interest including, without limiting the foregoing,

(i) a chattel mortgage, conditional sale, equipment trust, debenture, *floating charge*, pledge, trust indenture or trust receipt (emphasis added)

The essence of a floating charge is its application to fluctuating or changing assets of a debtor entity. For example, "stock in trade" by its nature is fluid or in flux. It is acquired, sold, and more is acquired for further sale. The concept of a floating charge is, however, of less significance under Canadian PPSA provisions than was the position under former securities legislation where the date of "attachment" determined priorities. As a floating charge did not at the outset "attach" to a particular item until a specified time or upon defined events in the security agreement those events had to be sufficiently identified before the charge became "fixed" to the relevant asset. Today, PPSA provides for priorities upon "perfection" of the Security Interest and this may be achieved simply upon "registration of a financing statement".[63] Recognizing this the Supreme Court of Canada has noted "The PPSA legislation treats *all* charges, including floating securities, as fixed charges" and gives a creditor a proprietary interest over a collection of assets both existing and future.[64]

IPRs will be included in the milieu of enterprise assets that can be subject to a floating charge either over *all* enterprise assets or specifically over all IPRs, although there has been no judicial determination to this effect with respect to IPRs either as part of all assets of an enterprise or as a specifically identified asset. No conflict exists between federal enactments and provincial PPSA as the floating charge is simply that—a "charge" and thereby outside the scope of federal IPR legislative measures concerning assignment or (where applicable) licence of IPRs. The flexibility afforded by a floating charge is most appropriate to a milieu of IPRs because IPRs are not static assets. Terms of exclusivity will expire; key elements (e.g. distinctiveness of origin of a trademark) may or may not continue to be met for particular IPRs. Conversely, the enterprise will ordinarily be continuing its innovation and development of new IPR items.

6 Rights Before Default

The mutual rights and obligations in Security Interests with respect to IPRs before default is determined by the terms of the security agreement between the parties. In all transactions of encumbrance of IPRs the lender or creditor is not in possession of the IPR, but has a financial interest in the IPR that needs to be protected by ensuring the continuing value of that IPR. A security agreement should contain provisions that will achieve this objective, but each agreement will depend on the specific IPR and the context of the particular security arrangement.

[63]See PPSA (BC) s. 25 and PPSA (Ontario) s. 23. See to this effect *674921 BC Ltd.* v. *New Solutions Financial Corporation*, 2006 BCCA 49, [2006] 50 B.C.L.R. (4th) 201, paras 2–4.

[64]*Bank of Montreal v. Innovation Credit Union (2010),* para 47.

6.1 Rights of Lender Not in Possession of Collateral

In general, a borrower/owner of encumbered (charged) IPRs ordinarily ought to agree to:

(i) Ensure that all maintenance fees payable to IP registries are paid on time so that the validity of the registration is maintained and that all steps are taken to ensure the continued validity of the IPR. For example, if the IPR is a trademark, the holder must properly use the trademark to maintain its registrability and to preserve the distinctiveness of the mark;

(ii) In consultation with the lender/mortgagee, to prosecute any infringement of the IPR by a third party to preserve the optimal value of the market royalty payments and, therefore, the market value of the IPR itself;

(iii) Except with the agreement of the lender/mortgagee, grant no subsequent assignment or licence of the IPR, unless licensing the IPR is part of the borrower's/mortgagor's business and that the licensing of the IPR (to produce royalties) is the objective in the particular instance;

(iv) Provide the lender/mortgagor with periodic financial, operational and valuation reports and information.

Although there is no legislative provision or judicial authority specifically related to IPRs in this context, two sources of law should be considered. First, the equitable jurisdiction with respect to "waste" of an asset is exercisable between mortgagee and mortgagor and would, in principle, exist for all encumbered assets[65] including IPRs. Second, general PPSA provisions (section 17 below) affording protection similar to that of "equitable waste" to a borrower who is not in possession of the collateral may also guide an interpretation of "waste" for a lender.

6.2 Rights of a Borrower Not in Possession of Collateral

Consider, for example, section 17, BC PPSA as follows:

17 (1) In this section, **"secured party"** includes a receiver.

[65]Waste at common law is focused on relationships of limited holders (life estates, leases) and ultimate holders (in fee by remainder or reversion) of land. However, in equity (developed by Chancery) waste (referred to as "equitable waste") was applied in many relationships where one party has possession while the other has ownership or future or potential possessory interests. The relationship of mortgagor and mortgagee of land is a common example. The principle can apply equally to chattels and in an early security related case (pre PPSA) was applied to a "crop payment purchase" of land—the buyer being given possession and being subject to a covenant to crop the land and provide the vendor of the land with payment by way of half the crop. The court found that this implied "good husbandry" which was not achieved and waste was applied. See *Welst v. Smith* (1926), para 11.

(2) A secured party must use reasonable care in the custody and preservation of collateral in the possession of the secured party and, unless the parties otherwise agree, in the case of an instrument or chattel paper, reasonable care includes taking necessary steps to preserve rights against other persons.

(3) Unless otherwise agreed, if collateral is in the secured party's possession,

(a) reasonable expenses, including the costs of insurance and payment of taxes or other charges incurred in obtaining, maintaining possession of and preserving the collateral, are chargeable to the debtor and secured by the collateral,
(b) the risk of loss or damage to the collateral, unless caused by the negligence of the secured party, is on the debtor to the extent of any deficiency in insurance coverage,
. . .
(c) the secured party must keep the collateral identifiable, but fungible collateral may be commingled.

(4) Subject to subsection (2), a secured party may use the collateral

(a) in the manner and to the extent provided in the security agreement,
(b) for the purposes of preserving the collateral, or
(c) in accordance with an order of a court in the manner directed.[66]

Of course, section 17 applies directly to collateral *in possession* of the secured party. IPRs cannot be physically possessed but an IPR can be controlled and utilized. It is simply a different nuance to which the court can analogise in equity. A borrower's interests would arise usually in a context where the borrower has made an *assignment* of an IPR to a lender for a period of time to secure an obligation of repayment or other performance. In this situation the borrower's interests would include an obligation to reassign the IPRs upon repayment of the loan or advance. The borrower would, accordingly, have similar concerns to those set out above to preserve and protect the IPR.

Except as specifically provided otherwise, section 17 "to the extent that it gives rights to the debtor or imposes obligations on the secured party [cannot] be waived or varied by agreement or otherwise."[67]

7 Enforcement

A secured party seeking to enforce a Security Interest under PPSA on default of the debtor or encumbered party, would ordinarily *seize* the collateral while also complying with procedures stipulated in PPSA.[68] IPRs (as collateral) like all intangible property cannot be seized. Therefore, some change of ownership in an IPR registry will ordinarily need to be effected.[69] Of course, if the secured party already holds the

[66]Section 17, Ont. PPSA (1990) is broadly similar.

[67]See PPSA (1996), s. 56(3).

[68]See PPSA (1996), ss. 55–67 and Ontario PPSA (1990), ss. 58–66.

[69]Registration is not necessary for a valid copyright. However, voluntary registration may have occurred and may need correction. Also registration of an assignment or licence may need correction.

IPR by way of assignment then this would likely have already been done. If this is not the case (i.e. the secured party being the holder of a licence or charge), the debtor or a trustee in bankruptcy or other receiver would need to effect this in favour of the secured party. If this is not forthcoming the secured party would have to seek an order of the court requiring *in personam* compliance.

Recent examples of this have occurred with respect to domain names. In *Tucows*, the Court of Appeal for Ontario expressly held that relief by way of a declaration could be given but in part declared "that [the defendant] is not entitled to the transfer of the domain name". Subsequently at trial in a further case, *Mold.ca.inc* v. *Mouldservices.ca.inc* (2013), an Ontario court made a change of ownership order by declaration in the following terms:

> [The defendant] shall forthwith:
>
> a. transfer and convey the Domain Names to the plaintiffs and deliver up all account information and passwords in his possession, power or control relating to the Domain Names;
> b. transfer all rights of access, administration and control for and over the Domain Names to the plaintiffs; and
> c. direct the applicable domain name registrar(s) to transfer all rights of access, administration and control for and over the Domain Names to the plaintiffs.[70]

These declarations were directed *in personam* and such orders could equally be made with respect to ownership change of an IPR. Any registry change is made by the party so ordered. An *in personam* order simply declares rights and obligations between the particular parties.

More difficulty would be experienced if the party so ordered decides not to obey the order. Could an *in rem* order, directed to a registry of the IPR, be made to effect the change on the register? The difficulty here is conflicting jurisdiction between provincial courts with subject jurisdiction over provincial PPSA and the Federal Court, *with no specific PPSA jurisdiction*, but with *exclusive* jurisdiction to vary an entry in an IPR registry. Consider the *Federal Courts Act* (1986), section 20(1)(b) as follows:

> The Federal Court has exclusive original jurisdiction, between subject and subject as well as otherwise,
>
> . . .
>
> (b) in all cases in which it is sought to impeach or annul any patent of invention or any certificate of supplementary protection issued under the *Patent Act*, or to have any entry in any register of copyrights, trade-marks, industrial designs or topographies ... made, expunged, varied or rectified.[71]

To the same effect see *Industrial Design Act* (1985), section 22(1), (3) and (4); *Trademarks Act* (1985), section 57(1); and *Patent Act* (1985), section 52.

---

[70]See Simpson (2014), McKiernan (2014), p. 10 discussing this proceeding.

[71]See *Decosol (Canada) Itee* v. *PVR Co.* (1973), paras 20–22 and para 2 (in the dissent) reaffirming this position.

These sections are quite explicit. A provincial court, where PPSA issues are determined, could not by declaration effectively order a variation of a federal IPR registry. In acknowledging this the Ontario Superior Court has, however, cautioned that the Federal Court exclusivity is narrow and cannot take away matters traditionally within provincial court jurisdiction but the notes expressly:

> [T]he authority of the Federal Court in relation to patents of invention under the current arrangement is exclusive as to the *in rem* remedy, namely the universal determination of the intrinsic value of patents and the registration thereof.[72]

The position as to the Federal Court engaging upon PPSA and the provisions of common law and equity is discussed in the Conclusion of this report.

8 Conclusion and Law Reform

The infrastructure of security interests in IPRs in Canada is one of bifurcation between federal measures in most categories of IPRs on the one hand and provincial PPSA measures in Security Interests over property including *intangibles* or *choses in action* on the other. Today's informationally focused economy presents IPRs as business assets of substantial market value in potential royalty payments from their usage through assignment and licence to third parties. The key functions of assignment and licence in these circumstances are encompassed within the federal IPR legislative measures. This includes a determination of relational ownership between originators, assignees and licensees. This includes a prioritizing of these interests by registration in applicable federal registries and may invoke issues of constitutional paramountcy in the event of conflict with provincial PPSA measures. However, these federal and provincial legislative measures can co-exist and can both be complied with, removing any likelihood of a constitutional paramountcy issue.

Provincial PPSA measures operate in a much broader context than simply assignment and licensing and related ownership interests. PPSA is concerned with assets, tangible or intangible, that are used in a variety of ways, particularly by mortgage or charge, *to secure payment or performance of an obligation* to a third party who usually has provided financing to an innovator or user. However, these Security Interests may also include situations of assignment or licence. If so, the interrelationship of federal (IPR) and provincial (PPSA) legislation must be considered.

Federal IPR measures are likely limited to a context of assignment or licensing *simpliciter*, that is without further security dimension. In this limited context federal IPR legislation may determine ownership interests, but do not grant any status as a secured creditor against a trustee in bankruptcy under BIA. This can be achieved only by perfection under PPSA.

---

[72] *Roche Palo Alto LLC v. Apotex Inc.* (2005), paras 4 and 5.

The Supreme Court of Canada and the provincial Superior Courts (Trial and Appellate) can hear all matters concerning both IPRs and Security Interests under PPSA. However, many federal statutory IPR disputes (particularly patent, industrial design and registered trademark) are heard by the Federal Court of Canada. This Court has jurisdiction to deal with the registration and ownership provisions of the federal legislation noted above, but lacks specific jurisdiction to determine provincial PPSA. The advantage of a Federal Court order in an IPR determination is the "Canada-wide" application of the order. Provincial Superior Court orders apply in only the particular province. However, provincial PPSA is the dominant and primary focus of securities in property, including IPRs. This may be inconvenient if proceedings involve both specialized IPR substantive issues that the Federal Court is better positioned to determine and security interests requiring these to be heard separately by a provincial court. Furthermore, only the Federal Court has jurisdiction to vary or rectify a federal IPR registry. The granting of an "incidental" jurisdiction to the Federal Court to determine a securities issue in the course of the substantive hearing might, therefore, be sensible in terms of allocation of scarce judicial resources. The Federal Court has utilized a jurisdictional theory of including common law or equitable matters that are *incidental* to IPR matters and is enabled in this respect by the *Federal Courts Act*, section 20(2) providing concurrent jurisdiction to apply common law or equity in respect of a core IPR jurisdiction.[73] The question has always been how far into common law or equitable issues should the court go *incidentally* to the IPR core. A significant move into PPSA issues has been made in a context of federal shipping law. First, with respect to ownership of a ship subject to a Security Interest under PPSA Ontario, the Federal Court upheld jurisdiction,[74] and second, more broadly, the Federal Court gave a detailed examination of its jurisdiction and concluded both statutorily and under case authority, that the Federal Court could "take cognizance of the Ontario PPSA" in exercising its jurisdiction in federal maritime law and noting the expression "'incidental' [to] not mean unimportant".[75]

Within the federal context an improvement would be the combination of registries, currently distinct and separate for each relevant category of IPR, into one IPR registry covering all relevant IPRs. In addition, a requirement of filing a copy of all PPSA security interests and perfections in such a registry would be useful from an informational perspective. This would be entirely achievable from an electronic filing perspective. The registries (federal and provincial) would simply need coordination with, perhaps, some integration.

---

[73]See e.g. *Titan Linkabit Corp.* v. *SEE See Electronics Engineering Inc.* (1992); *Kraft Canada Inc.* v. *Euro Excellence Inc.* (2004), para 25. For sub. proc. (not on this point) see *Kraft Canada Inc.* v. *Euro Excellence Inc.* (2005), *Kraft Canada Inc.* v. *Euro Excellence Inc.* (2007) and *R.L.P. Machine & Steel Fabrication Inc.* v. *Ditullio*, (2001).

[74]See *General Motors Acceptance Corp. of Canada Ltd.* v. *Furjanic* (1994).

[75]*Ballantrae Holdings Inc.* v. *"Phoenix Sun" (The)*, (2016) concluding at paras 144 and 145.

This leads to a larger question as to the extent to which all issues, including assignment and licensing *simpliciter* should be left exclusively to provincial PPSA administration. The federal IPR statutes could be limited to substantive IPR issues without the need for federal registries for assignment or licences. This presents a "clean solution" but there would be difficulties in drawing the demarcation and assignment and licences are logically part of the substance of an IPR and likely are properly within federal constitutional authority. A more logical demarcation is to leave ownership issues between owners, assignees and licensee *without more* to the federal legislation; but allocating all transactions that *secure payment or performance of an obligation*, even if by assignment or licence, to provincial PPSA.

In 2000 the Uniform Law Conference of Canada (ULCC) reported on many subject areas of federal constitutional allocation that also involved some interplay with Security Interests under provincial PPSA. A brief assessment with respect to IPRs was included, but without any conclusive recommendation for reform. The two options of making all issues exclusively federal (one federal registry for all Security Interests in IPRs) or, conversely, requiring all security related matters to be dealt with exclusively at a provincial level were noted (Uniform Law Conference of Canada, Part V, Intellectual Property). Earlier reform proposals include an initiative by the National Intellectual Property Section of the Canadian Bar Association in 1998 discussing a draft *Intellectual Property Security Act* comparatively between the laws of selected Commonwealth countries and which today can be seen in the assessment and evaluation by Fuhrer and Bourne in Knopf's 2002 work.[76] Also in Knopf, Walsh reflects on federal and provincial alternatives in this context.[77]

Constitutional dimensions will likely mean a bifurcated approach will continue, but there is scope for improvement and refinement. An enhancement of jurisdiction of the Federal Court would also seem to be desirable given the significant involvement of that court in matters concerning IPRs.

Finally, there is the issue of IPR valuation. Currently, this is very imprecise, yet the nature of IPRs is such that precision is impossible. Perhaps some element of consistency by experienced valuers is all that might be hoped for in an essentially speculative context. Speculation ought not, however, extend to the proper provision of security protection.

[76] Fuhrer and Bourne (2002).

[77] Walsh (2002).

References

Anson W (2012) Want to Value Your Intellectual Property? Here are Three Approaches. Retrieved online from: www.ipinbrief.com/three-approaches-to-value-IP/. Accessed Apr 2019

Ballagh M (2017) Secured Financing with Intellectual Property: Managing Uncertainties. Retrieved online from: https://www.ballaghedward.ca/uploads/pub_uploads/valuation-and-perfection-of-security-in-ip-2-.pdf. Accessed Apr 2019

Canadian Bar Association, National Intellectual Property Section (1998) CBA Annual Meeting in St. John's, Newfoundland, Draft Intellectual Property Security Act preserved by Fuhrer and Bourne (2002). In: Knopf H (ed) Security Interests in Intellectual Property. Thomson/Carswell, Toronto

C.D. Howe Institute (2013) Improving the Tax Treatment of Intellectual Property Income in Canada, Commentary No. 379 (Pantaleo N, Poschmann F, Wilkie S). Retrieved online from: www.cdhowe.org/sites/default/files/attachments/research_papers/mixed/Commentary_379_O.pdf. Accessed Apr 2019

Cochran AB (2004) A chose by any other name: domain names as a security interest. Can J Law Technol 3(2):65–79

Cuming RC (1995) Security interests in intellectual property. College of Law, University of Saskatchewan, SCLESI Seminar on Intellectual Property. Retrieved online from: http://library.lawsociety.sk.ca/inmagicgenie/documentfolder/AC0462.pdf. Accessed Apr 2019

De Beer J (2005) Constitutional jurisdiction over paracopyright laws. In: Geist M (ed) In the public interest: the future of copyright law. Irwin Law Inc., Toronto

Fuhrer JM, Bourne TC (2002) The draft intellectual property security act revisited. In: Knopf H (ed) Security interests in intellectual property. Thomson/Carswell, Toronto

Government of Canada, Canadian Intellectual Property Office (IPIC) (2016) Intellectual Property and Canada's Innovation Agenda", submission to Innovation, Science and Economic Development, Canada (ISED). Retrieved online from: www.ipic.ca/download.php?id=1517 (pdf). Accessed Apr 2019

Government of Canada, Innovation, Science and Economic Development, Canada (ISED). Retrieved online from: www.ic.gc.ca/eic/site/icgc.nsf/eng/h_00022.html. Accessed Apr 2019

Hatzikiriakos K (2006) Secured transactions in intellectual property. LexisNexis/Butterworths, Markham

Hogg P (2007) Constitutional law of Canada, 5th edn. Carswell/Thomson-Reuters, Toronto. Looseleaf updated, Release 1, 2017

Howell R (2011) Canadian telecommunications law. Irwin Law Inc, Toronto

Howell R (2016) Intellectual property rights and private international law: a tangled web. Intellect Prop J 28:187

Howell R (2019) The nature and scope of property in a domain name. In: Goudreau M, Wilkinson M (eds) New paradigms in the protection of inventiveness, data and signs. Yvon Blais, Montreal

Knopf H (2002) Security interests in intellectual property. Thomson/Carswell, Toronto

McKiernan M (2014) Ruling Confirms Web Addresses and Personal Property Law. Times, June 2, 2014. p 10

Scassa T, Deturbide M (2012) Electronic commerce and internet law in Canada. CCH Canadian Limited, Toronto

Siebrasse N, Duggan A (2016) Intellectual property dealings and the PPSA: *Contech Enterprises Ltd. v. Vegherb, LLC*. Intellect Prop J 28:21–32

Simpson J (2014) Property in Domain Names: Registration Doesn't Always Mean Ownership Shift Law Blog (January 12, 2014). Retrieved online from: https://www.shiftlaw.ca/ip-law-toronto-blog/property-in-domain-names-registration-doesnt-always-mean-ownership.html. Accessed Apr 2019

Smith GV (2002) Business, economic and valuation issues. In: Knopf H (ed) Security interests in intellectual property. Thomson/Carswell, Toronto

Ullmann D, Title S (2014) How to seize something you can't touch: a review of issues and process with the foreclosure of intellectual property assets. Ann Rev Insolvency Law, 55–96. Available on WestlawNext, Canada

Uniform Commercial Code, American Law Institute with The National Conference of Commissioners on Uniform State Laws, Official Text and Comments 2014–2015 edition (2015). Retrieved on line from: https://www.ali.org/publications/show/uniform-commercial-code/. Accessed Apr 2019

Uniform Law Conference of Canada (ULCC) – Federal Security Interests Research Study, Part V, Intellectual Property. Retrieved on line from: https://www.ulcc.ca/en/annual-meetings/341-2000-victoria-bc/civil-section-documents/338-federal-security-interests-research-study-and-report-2000?showall=&start=22. Accessed Apr 2019

Vaver D (2011) Intellectual property law, copyright-patents-trade-marks, 2nd edn. Irwin Law Inc, Toronto

Walsh C (2002) Federal or provincial regulation of security interests in Canadian intellectual property: the conflict of laws dimension. In: Knopf H (ed) Security interests in intellectual property. Thomson/Carswell, Toronto

Wood RJ (2000) The nature and definition of federal security interests. Can Bus Law J 34:65–113

Ziff BH (2010) Principles of property law, 5th edn. Carswell, Toronto [The latest edition is 7th edn (2019)]

Case Law

674921 B.C. Ltd. v. Advanced Wing Technologies Corp/New Solutions Financial Corporation (Cross Appeal), 2006 BCCA 49, [2006] 50 B.C.L.R. (4th) 201

A.G. Spalding & Bros. v. A.W. Gamage Ltd. (1915), 32 RPC 273 (HL)

Ankenman Associates Architects Inc. v. 0981478 BC Ltd, 2017 BCSC 333, (1917) 145 C.P.R. (4th) 279 (BCSC)

ArcelorMittal SA v. NETNIC Corp. Protective Registration Services, BCICAC File DCA 1430-CIRA Jan. 29, 2013

Ballantrae Holdings Inc. v. "Phoenix Sun" (The), 2016 F.C. 570

Bank of Montreal v. Innovation Credit Union, 2010 SCC 47, [2010] 3 S.C.R. 3

Cadbury Schweppes Inc. v. FBI Foods Ltd. (1998), [1999] 1 S.C.R. 167

CCH Canadian Ltd. v. Law Society of Upper Canada, [2004] 1 S.C.R. 339, 2004 SCC 13

Ciba-Geigy Canada Ltd. v. Apotex Inc. (1992), [1992] 3 S.C.R. 120, 44 CPR (3d) 289

Consumers Distributing Co. v. Seiko Time Canada Ltd. (1984), [1984] 1 S.C.R. 583, 1 CPR (3d) 1

Contech Enterprises Inc. v. Vegherb, LLC (2015), 2015 BCCA 99, 74 B.C.L.R. (5th) 86

Decosol (Canada) Itee v. PVR Co. (1973), 13 C.P.R. (2d) (QBCA)

Erven Warnink BV v. J. Townend & Sons (Hull) Ltd., [1979] AC 731 (HL)

Euro-Excellence Inc. v. Kraft Canada Inc. (2007), 2007 SCC 37, [2007] 3 S.C.R. 20

General Motors Acceptance Corp. of Canada Ltd. v. Furjanic (1994), 79 F.T.R. 172 (FCTD)

Giffen (Re), [1998] 1 S.C.R 91

Kirkbi AG and Lego Canada Inc. v. Ritvik Holdings Inc. (2005) 2005 SCC 65, [2005] 3 S.C.R. 302

Kraft Canada Inc. v. Euro Excellence Inc. (2005), 2005 FCA 427, [2006] 3 F.C.R. 91, 2006 FC 453

Kraft Canada Inc. v. Euro Excellence Inc., 2004 FC 652, [2004] 4 F.C.R. 410

Lac Minerals Ltd. v. International Corona Resources Ltd. (1989), [1989] 2 S.C.R. 574, 61 D.L.R. (4th) 14

Mold.ca.inc v. Mouldservices.ca.inc (Unreported, Sup. Ct. Justice, Ont. Court File No. CV-13-480391: December 30, 2013). This case is not reported in any digital or non-digital reporter series or database

Poolman v. Eiffel Productions SA (1991) 35 C.P.R. (3d) 384 (FCTD)

R.L.P. Machine & Steel Fabrication Inc. v. Ditullio, 2001 FCT 245

Roche Palo Alto LLC v. Apotex Inc., 2005 O.J. No. 4948; (2005), 45 C.P.R. (4th) 248

Titan Linkabit Corp. v. SEE See Electronics Engineering Inc. (1992) 44 C.P.R. (3d) 469 (FCTD)
Tucows.Com Co. v. Lojas Renner SA., 2011 ONCA 348, 106 O.R. (3d) 561 (Ont.CA). Leave to appeal to SCC denied, [2011] SCCA No. 450
Welst v. Smith (1926), [1927] 1 W.W.R. 280, [1927] 1 D.L.R. 448 (Sask. K.B.)

Legal Acts

Bankruptcy and Insolvency Act, R.S.C. 1985, c. B-3 as amended
Constitution Act, 1867 c. 3
Copyright Act, R.S.C. 1985, c. C-42 as amended
Industrial Design Act, R.S.C. 1985, c. I-9 as amended
Integrated Circuit Topography Act, S.C. 1990, c. 37 as amended
Patent Act, R.S.C. 1985, c. P-4 as amended
Personal Property Security Act, Nunavut S.N.W.T. 1994, c. 8 as amended
Personal Property Security Act, R.S.A. 2000, c P-7
Personal Property Security Act, R.S.B.C. 1996, c. 359 as amended; R.S.O. 1990
Personal Property Security Act, R.S.Y. 2002, c. 169 as amended
Personal Property Security Act, S.M. 1993, c. 14 as amended
Personal Property Security Act, S.N. 1995-96, c. 13 as amended
Personal Property Security Act, S.N.B. 1993, c.P-7.1 as amended
Personal Property Security Act, S.N.S. 1995-96, c. 13 as amended
Personal Property Security Act, S.N.W.T. 1994, c. 8 as amended
Personal Property Security Act, S.P.E.I. 1997, c.33 as amended
Personal Property Security Act, S.S. 1993, c, P-6.2 as amended
Plant Breeders Rights Act, S.C. 1990, c. 20 as amended
Trademark Act, R.S.C. 1985, c. T-13 as amended

Les sûretés sur la propriété intellectuelle au Québec (Canada)

Élise Charpentier

Abstract Le Parlement du Canada a adopté plusieurs lois relatives à la propriété intellectuelle, dont la *Loi sur les brevets*, la *Loi sur les marques de commerce*, la *Loi sur le droit d'auteur*. Ces lois ne comportent aucune disposition explicite relative aux sûretés et la question de savoir si ces lois jouent un rôle en la matière se pose toujours. Au Québec, c'est dans le *Code civil du Québec* qu'on trouve les principales règles relatives à la propriété et aux droits civils. Ce Code est le fruit d'une réforme qui, en matière de sûretés, visait à simplifier les différents régimes existants. Le droit privé québécois s'appliquant dans un contexte nord-américain, on notera que le régime juridique applicable à l'hypothèque mobilière s'inspire, en partie, de l'article 9 du *Uniform Commercial Code*.

Au Canada, la Constitution partage les pouvoirs entre le législateur fédéral et ceux des provinces[1]. La propriété intellectuelle relève de l'autorité législative exclusive du parlement du Canada, alors que les provinces ont juridiction sur les transferts de

Ce texte reprend le rapport présenté lors du Congrès de l'Académie internationale de droit comparé (Fukuoka, 2018). L'auteur remercie Rosemarie Sarrazin, assistante de recherche, de son inestimable apport.

[1] Au sujet des rapports entre la législation fédérale et celles des provinces canadiennes, voir le texte de Robert G. Howell dans le présent ouvrage. On notera que la *Loi d'interprétation* prévoit que «Le droit civil et la common law font pareillement autorité et sont tous deux sources de droit en matière de propriété et de droits civils au Canada et, s'il est nécessaire de recourir à des règles, principes ou notions appartenant au domaine de la propriété et des droits civils en vue d'assurer l'application d'un texte dans une province, il faut, sauf règle de droit s'y opposant, avoir recours aux règles, principes et notions en vigueur dans cette province au moment de l'application du texte» (art. 8.1., L.R.C., 1985, c. I-21).

É. Charpentier (✉)
Faculté de droit, Université de Montréal, Montréal, QC, Canada
e-mail: elise.charpentier@umontreal.ca

E.-M. Kieninger (ed.), *Security Rights in Intellectual Property*, Ius Comparatum – Global Studies in Comparative Law 45,
https://doi.org/10.1007/978-3-030-44191-3_7

propriété et les droits civils[2]. On distingue traditionnellement la propriété intellectuelle des contrats qui s'y rapportent.

1 La propriété intellectuelle: aperçu

En droit canadien, le brevet est défini comme un droit exclusif octroyé par l'État pour une invention, il n'existe donc pas sans formalité ; la marque de commerce est un droit qui prend naissance lorsqu'une personne utilise une combinaison de mots, de sons ou de dessins pour distinguer des produits et services offerts sur le marché ; et le droit d'auteur est un droit qui existe dès la création d'une œuvre littéraire, artistique, dramatique ou musicale originale. Le brevet est donc bien différent de la marque de commerce ou du droit d'auteur. En effet, la propriété intellectuelle d'une invention dépend de l'obtention d'un brevet, tandis que propriété intellectuelle d'une marque de commerce ou d'un droit d'auteur existe dès qu'une personne utilise la marque ou crée l'œuvre, ils peuvent toutefois être enregistrés afin d'assurer leur protection. L'*Office de la propriété intellectuelle du Canada* est l'organisme canadien responsable de l'administration et du traitement de l'ensemble demandes relatives à la propriété intellectuelle, ainsi que la gestion des registres de brevets, de marques de commerce et de droit d'auteur.

1.1 Brevets

En vertu de la *Loi sur les brevets,* le brevet emporte «le droit, la faculté et le privilège exclusif de fabriquer, construire, exploiter et vendre à d'autres, pour qu'ils l'exploitent, l'objet de l'invention, sauf jugement en l'espèce par un tribunal compétent »[3]. La loi pose une présomption selon laquelle la personne qui dépose la demande est l'inventeur et a droit au brevet[4]. La notion de brevet est intimement liée à celle d'« inventeur » qui a été définie par la jurisprudence comme suit: « [...] l'inventeur est la personne ou les personnes qui ont conçu la réalisation, le procédé, la machine, fabrication ou composition de matières, ainsi que tout perfectionnement de l'un d'eux, "présentant le caractère de la nouveauté et de l'utilité"»[5]. Quant à l'objet du brevet, il doit s'agir d'une invention, ce qui exclut les « simples principes scientifiques ou conceptions théoriques»[6], l'invention que le requérant souhaite

[2]*Loi constitutionnelle de* 1867 (R.-U.), 30 & 31 Vict., c. 3, reproduite dans L.R.C. (1985), app. II, no 5, art. 91 et 92. À ce sujet voir Lord and Moyse (2013), n° 8-12.

[3]Art. 42 *Loi sur les brevets*, L.R.C. 1985, c. P-4 (ci-après « L.B. »).

[4]Art. 27(1) L.B.

[5]*Apotex Inc.* c. *Wellcome Foundation Ltd.*, [2002] 4 R.C.S. 153, n° 96.

[6]Art. 27(8) L.B.

breveter doit être nouvelle, non évidente et utile[7]. Le droit exclusif du titulaire du brevet se caractérise par son exclusivité et par le fait qu'il est limité dans le temps : il prend naissance à la date de dépôt de sa demande pour une durée de 20 ans[8].

Lors du dépôt d'une demande de brevet, le requérant ne doit pas avoir divulgué l'invention au public ou, si cela a été fait, il doit s'assurer de sa déposer demande dans les 12 mois suivant la divulgation[9]. Les documents qui doivent accompagner la demande et les droits payables sont énoncés aux *Règles sur les brevets*[10].

Le système canadien reconnaît, par ailleurs, la possibilité de faire une demande de brevet par le biais du *Traité de coopération en matière de brevets*[11]. Ce traité, dont le Canada est signataire[12], prévoit qu'un requérant peut faire une demande au niveau international afin d'uniformiser les procédures administratives, et ensuite compléter les formalités de chaque pays dans lequel il souhaite obtenir un brevet[13].

1.2 Marques de commerce

La notion de marque de commerce est définie comme « un mot, plusieurs mots, une phrase, un dessin, ou une combinaison de ces éléments, ou même des sons servant à caractériser les produits ou les services d'une personne ou d'un organisme et à les distinguer de ceux que d'autres offrent sur le marché »[14]. L'article 4 de la *Loi sur les marque de commerce* précise qu'«[u]ne marque de commerce est réputée employée en liaison avec des produits si, lors du transfert de la propriété ou de la possession de ces produits, dans la pratique normale du commerce, elle est apposée sur les produits mêmes ou sur les emballages dans lesquels ces produits sont distribués, ou si elle est, de toute autre manière, liée aux produits à tel point qu'avis de liaison est alors donné à la personne à qui la propriété ou possession est transférée »[15]. En ce qui a trait aux services, l'emploi est défini ainsi : « Une marque de commerce est réputée employée en liaison avec des services si elle est employée ou montrée dans l'exécution ou l'annonce de ces services »[16].

En droit canadien, la marque de commerce existe dès lors qu'elle est employée, sans autre formalité[17]. Le titulaire de la marque de commerce est donc la première

---

[7]Dumont et Shahinian (2017), n° 1.

[8]Art. 44 L.B.

[9]Art. 28.2(1) L.B.

[10]*Règles sur les brevets*, DORS/96-423 (Gaz. Can. II), art. 27(1).

[11]Voir http://www.wipo.int/treaties/fr/registration/pct/.

[12]Voir http://www.wipo.int/export/sites/www/treaties/fr/documents/pdf/pct.pdf.

[13]Voir, entre autres, les art. 3 et 29 du *Traité de coopération en matière de brevets*.

[14]Lucas (2014), n° 16.

[15]Art. 4 *Loi sur les marques de commerce*, L.R.C. 1985, c. T-13, (ci-après « L.M.C. »).

[16]*Id.*

[17]Art. 3 L.M.C.

personne à l'avoir utilisée. Cette antériorité est primordiale, puisque si une personne n'étant pas la première à utiliser une marque de commerce l'enregistre, cet enregistrement peut être radié à la demande du premier utilisateur[18].

L'enregistrement de la marque de commerce n'est pas nécessaire afin que cette dernière existe. Il permet de protéger la marque de commerce vis-à-vis des tiers et garantir au propriétaire son exclusivité puisque l'enregistrement donne naissance à une présomption de titularité du droit. Il procure d'autres avantages, comme l'exclusivité de l'utilisation de la marque de commerce au Canada pour une durée de 15 ans (renouvelables dans la mesure où elle est utilisée)[19]. L'enregistrement de la marque de commerce est soumis à des conditions et la demande doit contenir certaines informations[20].

1.3 Droit d'auteur

Le droit d'auteur peut porter sur une oeuvre littéraire, une oeuvre artistique, une oeuvre musicale, une oeuvre dramatique, une oeuvre audiovisuelle ou cinématographique, ou encore une compilation[21]. Le droit protège le mode d'expression de l'idée, c'est-à-dire l'oeuvre, pas sur l'idée elle-même[22]. Il existe durant la vie de l'auteur, et demeure pour les 50 ans suivant le décès de ce dernier[23].

La *Loi sur le droit d'auteur* établit que l'auteur est le premier titulaire du droit d'auteur[24]. La notion d'auteur n'est pas définie dans la loi, la doctrine et la jurisprudence définissent l'auteur comme « celui qui donne l'empreinte de sa personnalité à une oeuvre, qui exerce son talent et son jugement pour créer une oeuvre originale»[25].

L'enregistrement n'est pas une condition *sine qua non* de l'existence du droit d'auteur[26]. Cependant, il permet de protéger l'auteur dans la mesure où il entraîne une

---

[18]L.M.C. Art. 17 (1) L.M.C.

[19]Art. 46(1) L.M.C.
Art. 45(1) L.M.C.
Art. 45(3) L.M.C.

[20]À ce sujet voir Carrière (2017). Voir, entre autres, les article 16 et 30 L.M.C.

[21]Art. 13(3) *Loi sur le droit d'auteur*, L.R.C. 1985, c. C-42 (ci-après « L.D.A. »). La loi pose certaines exceptions à ce principe. Ainsi, l'employeur est le premier titulaire du droit lorsque l'auteur est un salarié qui crée son oeuvre dans le cadre de son emploi, mais si l'auteur est un journaliste, il conserve néanmoins le droit d'interdire sa publication ailleurs que dans un journal (voir *Robertson* c. *Thomson Corp.*, [2006] 2 R.C.S. 363.).

[22]Lord et Moyse (2013), n° 30; *Pelchat* c. *Zone 3 inc.*, 2013 QCCS 78.

[23]Art. 6 L.D.A.

[24]Art. 13(1) L.D.A.

[25]Lucas (2014), n° 2; *CCH Canadienne Ltée* c. *Barreau du Haut-Canada*, [2004] 1 R.C.S. 339, n° 16.

[26]Azzaria (2017), n° 51.

présomption que celui qui a enregistré l'oeuvre en premier en est l'auteur[27]. L'enregistrement du droit d'auteur est soumis à des conditions et la demande doit contenir certaines informations[28].

2 Catégories de sûretés applicables aux différents droits intellectuels

Au Canada, les lois sur la propriété intellectuelle, comme la *Loi sur les brevets*, la *Loi sur les marques de commerce* et la *Loi sur le droit d'auteur*, ne créent pas de sûreté particulière susceptible de grever la propriété intellectuelle[29]. En conséquence, la question de savoir si la personne titulaire d'un droit intellectuel, ou d'une licence d'exploitation d'un tel droit, peut le grever d'une sûreté conventionnelle pour garantir une obligation dépend des règles qui se trouvent dans les lois des provinces. Le Québec connaît deux types de sûretés conventionnelles : l'hypothèque et la propriété-sûretés. Dans le contexte de la propriété intellectuelle, l'hypothèque est le seul mécanisme « intéressant » puisque la propriété-sûreté pose d'importants problèmes[30].

Le *Code civil du Québec* définit l'hypothèque comme «un droit réel sur un bien, meuble ou immeuble, affecté à l'exécution d'une obligation; elle confère au créancier le droit de suivre le bien en quelques mains qu'il soit, de le prendre en possession ou en paiement, de le vendre ou de le faire vendre et d'être alors préféré sur le produit de cette vente suivant le rang fixé dans le présent code»[31].

L'hypothèque peut grever autant un bien immeuble qu'un bien meuble[32]. En principe, tous les biens peuvent être hypothéqués, aucun droit patrimonial n'est exclu sur la base de sa nature physique ou juridique. Ainsi, l'hypothèque peut tout aussi bien grever un droit réel, qu'un droit personnel. L'hypothèque mobilière peut

[27] Azzaria (2017), n° 52.

[28] Afin d'enregistrer une oeuvre et de protéger son droit, l'auteur doit remplir le formulaire de l'OPIC (Office de la propriété intellectuelle du Canada, *Le guide du droit d'auteur*, en ligne: <http://www.ic.gc.ca/eic/site/cipointernet-internetopic.nsf/fra/h_wr02281.html#preparingApplicationRegistration> (consulté le 16 mai 2017)).

[29] À ce sujet voir, entre autres, Lèger (1993), p. 403; Wood (2000), p. 65.

[30] Outre ceux qui se posent dans le cadre d'un litige avec un tiers au sujet du droit intellectuel, on pense, par exemple, à la situation où le titulaire d'une marque de commerce cède ses droits à un créancier afin de garantir le remboursement d'un prêt : l'article 50 LMC impose au créancier-titulaire de la marque des obligations de contrôle de l'emploi. Voir Payette (2015), n° 1374 et seq.; Zimmerman et al. (1991), p. 74.

[31] Art. 2660 C.c.Q.

[32] Art. 2665 al. 1 C.c.Q.

donc porter sur un brevet[33], une marque de commerce[34] et un droit d'auteur puisque les droits de propriété intellectuelle sont des biens meubles[35]. D'ailleurs, l'article 2684 C.c.Q. - qui énumère, de manière non limitative[36], les biens susceptibles d'être grevés d'une hypothèque sur une universalité de biens[37] - fait expressément référence aux brevets et marques de commerce[38]. C'est d'ailleurs généralement par le biais de ce mécanisme que la propriété intellectuelle est grevée d'une sûreté, comme le souligne Louis Payette : «[h]abituellement perçue par les prêteurs comme un complément d'importance relative aux actifs intangibles d'une entreprise, la propriété intellectuelle a traditionnellement fait l'objet de sûretés la grevant accessoirement à ces autres biens»[39]. La personne physique ou morale titulaire de droits intellectuels peut donc grever d'une hypothèque chacun de ses droits ou l'universalité de ceux-ci[40].

L'exploitation de plusieurs entreprises dépend des licences d'exploitation dont elles sont titulaires. Si d'un point de vue économique, une licence est un actif, de celui du droit privé, elle est un meuble (une créance), en principe susceptible d'être hypothéqués. Toutefois, contrairement à l'hypothèque consentie par le titulaire du droit intellectuel, la licence est souvent sujette à plusieurs restrictions qui pourraient limiter la possibilité de l'hypothéquer ou les droits conférés au titulaire de l'hypothèque[41]. Par ailleurs, le titulaire d'un droit intellectuel qui a accordé une licence d'exploitation peut hypothéquer les revenus qu'il reçoit en contrepartie[42].

---

[33]Outre le brevet lui-même, la demande de brevet a une valeur également, et elle peut donc faire l'objet d'une hypothèque (en ce sens, Payette (2002), n° 78).

[34]L'hypothèque grevant une marque de commerce peut être consentie sans que la marque ait été préalablement enregistrée à l'OPIC par le propriétaire de la marque (voir Payette (2015), n° 1424).

[35]Payette (2002), n° 1.

[36]*Id.* Voir aussi *Collège d'enseignement général et professionnel de Trois-Rivières* c. *Leblanc et Lafrance inc.*, [2001] R.J.Q. 2659. (C.S.).

[37]L'article 2666 C.c.Q. précise que : «L'hypothèque grève soit un ou plusieurs biens particuliers, corporels ou incorporels, soit un ensemble de biens compris dans une universalité».

[38]Art. 2684 C.c.Q.:

> Seule la personne, la société ou le fiduciaire qui exploite une entreprise peut consentir une hypothèque sur une universalité de biens, meubles ou immeubles, présents ou à venir, corporels ou incorporels.
>
> Celui qui exploite l'entreprise peut, ainsi, hypothéquer les animaux, l'outillage ou le matériel d'équipement professionnel, les créances et comptes clients, <u>les brevets et marques de commerce</u>, ou encore les meubles corporels qui font partie de l'actif de l'une ou l'autre de ses entreprises et qui sont détenus afin d'être vendus, loués ou traités dans le processus de fabrication ou de transformation d'un bien destiné à la vente, à la location ou à la prestation de services (nous soulignons).

[39]Payette (2015), n° 1344.

[40]Art. 2683 C.c.Q.

[41]À ce sujet voir Payette (2002), n° 93.

[42]Art. 2710 C.c.Q. À ce sujet voir Payette (2015), n° 1380 et seq.

3 Structure des opérations

3.1 Formation du contrat

L'hypothèque conventionnelle étant un contrat, elle doit respecter les conditions d'existence prévues au *Code civil du Québec* pour les contrats[43]. Bien que les contrats soient en principe consensuels et que l'hypothèque conventionnelle soit un contrat, ce contrat est formaliste. C'est-à-dire que sa formation dépend de l'accomplissement de formalités déterminées par le législateur. Les formalités imposées par le législateur varient en fonction de la nature immobilière ou mobilière de l'hypothèque.

Or, l'hypothèque mobilière sans dépossession doit simplement être constituée par écrit[44]. Le contenu de cet écrit est, en partie, imposé par le législateur qui exige une désignation du bien grevé[45] et l'indication la somme pour laquelle elle est consentie[46].

3.2 Publicité – Opposabilité

La publicité d'une hypothèque mobilière sans dépossession ayant pour objet un brevet, une marque de commerce ou un droit d'auteur se fait par une inscription des droits au *Registre des droits personnels ou réels mobiliers*[47]. La publicité des droits joue un rôle déterminant en matière hypothécaire. Elle rend l'hypothèque opposable aux tiers[48], même si un tiers connaît l'existence d'une hypothèque, elle ne peut pas lui être opposée si elle n'est pas publiée[49]. Sans publicité, l'hypothèque peut être valide, mais ses effets sont alors très limités : elle produit ses effets entre le propriétaire du bien grevé et le titulaire de l'hypothèque seulement.

La question se pose toutefois de savoir si cette inscription suffit lorsque l'hypothèque grève un brevet, une marque de commerce ou un droit d'auteur. L'incertitude résulte du fait que les lois fédérales sur la propriété intellectuelle ne font pas directement référence aux sûretés accordées, mais contiennent des dispositions relatives aux cessions ou aux transferts des droits. Ainsi, les cessions de brevets

---

[43]Voir les art. 1385 et suiv. C.c.Q.

[44]Art. 2696 C.c.Q.

[45]Art. 2697 C.c.Q.

[46]Cette règle s'applique même si l'hypothèque garantit l'exécution d'une obligation dont la valeur ne peut être déterminée ou est incertaine. Art. 2689 C.c.Q.

[47]Art. 2934 C.c.Q.: «La publicité des droits résulte de l'inscription qui en est faite sur le registre des droits personnels et réels mobiliers ou sur le registre foncier, à moins que la loi ne permette expressément un autre mode».

[48]Art. 2663, 2941, al.1 C.c.Q.

[49]L'art. 2963 C.c.Q. le prévoit expressément: «L'avis donné ou la connaissance acquise d'un droit non publié ne supplée jamais le défaut de publicité».

et de droits d'auteur doivent être enregistrées pour être opposables aux cessionnaires subséquents[50]; alors que la *Loi sur les marques de commerce* indique seulement que le registraire inscrit le transfert d'une marque de commerce[51]. Par ailleurs, la *Loi sur le droit d'auteur* contient une référence un peu surprenante à l'existence d'une hypothèque. En effet, son article 59(1) se lit comme suit : «Tout acte de cession d'un droit d'auteur ou toute licence concédant un intérêt sur un droit d'auteur peut être exécuté, souscrit ou attesté en tout lieu dans un pays signataire ou dans un pays partie à la Convention de Rome ou au traité de l'OIEP par le cédant, le concédant ou le débiteur hypothécaire, devant un notaire public, un commissaire ou autre fonctionnaire ou un juge légalement autorisé à faire prêter serment ou à certifier

---

[50] Art. 50 L.B.:

(1) Tout brevet délivré pour une invention est cessible en droit, soit pour la totalité, soit pour une partie de l'intérêt, au moyen d'un acte par écrit.

(2) Toute cession de brevet et tout acte de concession ou translatif du droit exclusif d'exécuter et d'exploiter l'invention brevetée partout au Canada et de concéder un tel droit à des tiers sont enregistrés au Bureau des brevets selon ce que le commissaire établit.

Art. 51 L.B.:

Toute cession en vertu des articles 49 ou 50 est nulle et de nul effet à l'égard d'un cessionnaire subséquent, à moins que l'acte de cession n'ait été enregistré, au terme de ces articles, avant l'enregistrement de l'acte sur lequel ce cessionnaire subséquent fonde sa réclamation.

Art. 57 L.D.A.:

(1) Le registraire des droits d'auteur enregistre, sur production du document original ou d'une copie certifiée conforme ou de toute autre preuve qu'il estime satisfaisante et sur paiement de la taxe dont le montant est fixé par les règlements ou déterminé conformément à ceux-ci, l'acte de cession d'un droit d'auteur ou la licence accordant un intérêt dans ce droit.

(2) [Abrogé]

(3) Tout acte de cession d'un droit d'auteur ou toute licence concédant un intérêt dans un droit d'auteur doit être déclaré nul à l'encontre de tout cessionnaire du droit d'auteur ou titulaire de l'intérêt concédé qui le devient subséquemment à titre onéreux sans connaissance de l'acte de cession ou licence antérieur, à moins que celui-ci n'ait été enregistré de la manière prévue par la présente loi avant l'enregistrement de l'instrument sur lequel la réclamation est fondée.

[51] Art. 48 L.M.C.:

(1) Une marque de commerce, déposée ou non, est transférable et est réputée avoir toujours été transférable, soit à l'égard de l'achalandage de l'entreprise, soit isolément, et soit à l'égard de la totalité, soit à l'égard de quelques-uns des services ou produits en liaison avec lesquels elle a été employée.

(2) Le paragraphe (1) n'a pas pour effet d'empêcher qu'une marque de commerce soit considérée comme n'étant pas distinctive si, par suite de son transfert, il subsistait des droits, chez deux ou plusieurs personnes, à l'emploi de marques de commerce créant de la confusion et si ces droits ont été exercés par ces personnes.

(3) Le registraire inscrit le transfert de toute marque de commerce déposée, une fois que lui ont été fournis une preuve du transfert qu'il juge satisfaisante et les renseignements qu'exigerait l'alinéa 30g) dans une demande, par le cessionnaire, d'enregistrer cette marque de commerce.

des documents en ce lieu, qui appose à l'acte sa signature et son sceau officiel ou celui de son tribunal» (nous soulignons). Il semble bien que pour Louis Payette, cet article n'est pas déterminant puisqu'il ne traite que des formalités à respecter[52].

Outre la diversité des règles qu'elles établissent, ces lois ne définissent pas les notions de «cession» et de «transfert». On peut donc se demander si elles s'appliquent à la constitution d'une sûreté[53]. Autrement dit, ces notions sont-elles suffisamment larges pour englober une sûreté visant la propriété intellectuelle ? On ne trouve, malheureusement, aucune décision judiciaire établissant clairement la portée de ces notions.

La question se pose de savoir si l'enregistrement d'une hypothèque au registre de l'*Office de la propriété intellectuelle du Canada* suffit à la rendre opposable. Pour que ce soit le cas «on devait englober les 'sûretés' dans le concept de 'cession' entretenu par la loi, alors le créancier bénéficiaire de la sûreté ne serait pas autorisé à rattacher à cet enregistrement d'autres effets que ceux qu'y rattache la Loi sur le droit d'auteur. Or, la Loi sur le droit d'auteur dit simplement qu'un cessionnaire de bonne foi et à titre onéreux, dont la cession est enregistrée conformément à cette loi, est en droit d'ignorer une cession antérieure du même droit effectuée au profit d'un tiers si cette cession n'a pas été ainsi enregistrée. La loi fédérale ne dit aucunement que la cession - ou possiblement la sûreté - devient opposable aux tiers à la condition d'être enregistrée au registre tenu par l'Office de la propriété intellectuelle»[54]. Inversement si l'hypothèque est publiée conformément au *Code civil du Québec* mais non enregistrée à l'*Office de la propriété intellectuelle du Canada*, il faudrait, pour pouvoir considérer l'hypothèque inopposable «surmonter un obstacle de taille. En effet, l'article 57 (3) n'entre en jeu qu'en faveur d'une personne de bonne foi. La Loi sur le droit d'auteur ne définit pas ce qu'est la 'bonne foi'; en la circonstance, le *Code civil du Québec* — que la loi fédérale sur l'interprétation invite à appliquer supplétivement le fait. L'article 2943 C.c.Q. dispose en effet qu'une inscription au

[52]Payette (2015), n° 1417.

[53]Cette question a été abordée par la Cour d'appel de l'Alberta dans l'arrêt *Colpitts* c. *Sherwood*, [1927] 3 D.L.R. 7 (C. A. Alb.). On a toutefois justement observé que cet arrêt ne pose par un principe général. Voir Fraser Milner Casgrain (2000):

> «L'arrêt Colpitts portait sur un litige quant au droit de préférence d'un cessionnaire subséquent d'un brevet ayant effectivement connaissance d'un acte de cession antérieur qui n'avait par ailleurs pas été enregistré. Le tribunal a considéré que la cession consentie à titre de sûreté était en fait une cession assujettie à l'enregistrement prévu en vertu des dispositions de la Loi sur les brevets. Le tribunal statua que le cessionnaire subséquent qui avait connaissance de la cession ne jouissait pas d'un droit de préférence par rapport au cessionnaire antérieur dont la cession n'avait pas été enregistrée. Ce qui est particulier à cette affaire, c'est que toutes les parties impliquées dans les diverses transactions étaient pourtant au courant des actes dressés à cet égard. Il ne s'agissait pas d'une situation où le tribunal devait trancher un litige impliquant un cessionnaire ayant eu connaissance de l'existence d'un cessionnaire subséquent après avoir enregistré une cession. En d'autres termes, la décision rendue dans l'arrêt Colpitts semblerait raisonnable dans les circonstances en l'espèce, mais cette conclusion ne devrait pas être considérée comme étant un principe d'application générale».

[54]Payette (2007), p. 12.

Registre des droits personnels et réels mobiliers crée une présomption de connaissance du droit inscrit sur un bien chez celui qui acquiert des droits dans ce bien et, d'autre part, l'empêche de plaider de bonne foi s'il n'a pas consulté le registre»[55]. Quoiqu'il en soit, la Cour d'appel du Québec a déjà jugé que «ces enregistrements [à l'*Office de la propriété intellectuelle du Canada*] ne conféraient aucune valeur juridique comme telle, de sorte que la priorité d'enregistrement ne donnait aucun droit supérieur»[56].

La question de la publicité, de l'opposabilité, des sûretés relatives à la propriété intellectuelle demeure entière, mais elle ne semble pas poser de graves problèmes puisqu'en pratique, les hypothèques grevant un brevet, une marque de commerce ou un droit d'auteur sont inscrites conformément au *Code civil du Québec* et enregistrées à l'*Office de la propriété intellectuelle du Canada.*

4 Droits du titulaire de l'hypothèque

L'hypothèque ne dépouille pas le constituant. Il continue de jouir de ses droits et peut en disposer, quoique sans porter atteinte aux droits du créancier hypothécaire[57]. S'il détruit ou détériore le bien hypothéqué, ou en diminue sensiblement la valeur et que le créancier en subit une perte, celui-ci peut recouvrer des dommages-intérêts compensatoires[58]. Comme le souligne un auteur, l'«[...]absence d'exploitation de la propriété intellectuelle constitue par conséquent une violation de cette disposition, dans la mesure où les lois relatives à la propriété intellectuelle font de cette exploitation une condition de conservation du droit. De la même manière, l'inertie face à la contre-façon par un tiers pourrait entraîner une diminution de valeur [...]»[59].

À partir du moment où le débiteur est en défaut le créancier hypothécaire peut exercer les droits qu'il a sur le bien hypothéqué, c'est-à-dire qui peut prendre possession du bien hypothéqué pour l'administrer[60], le prendre en paiement[61], le

[55]Payette (2007), p. 13; vois aussi Payette (2015), n° 1412.

[56]*Banque Mercantile du Canada* c. *Télé-Métropole International Inc.*, J.E. 96-1135 (C.A.) p. 6; voir aussi Sotiriadis et Danis (2002), p. 593; El Sissi (1996), p. 52.

[57]Art. 2733 C.c.Q.: «L'hypothèque ne dépouille ni le constituant ni le possesseur qui continuent de jouir des droits qu'ils ont sur les biens grevés et peuvent en disposer, sans porter atteinte aux droits du créancier hypothécaire.».

[58]Art. 2734 C.c.Q.: «Ni le constituant ni son ayant cause ne peuvent détruire ou détériorer le bien hypothéqué, ou en diminuer sensiblement la valeur, si ce n'est par une utilisation normale ou en cas de nécessité.».

[59]Payette (2015), n° 1387.

[60]Art. 2773 C.c.Q.: «Le créancier qui détient une hypothèque sur les biens d'une entreprise peut prendre temporairement possession des biens hypothéqués et les administrer ou en déléguer généralement l'administration à un tiers. Le créancier, ou celui à qui il a délégué l'administration, agit alors à titre d'administrateur du bien d'autrui chargé de la pleine administration.».

[61]Art. 2783 C.c.Q.: «Le créancier qui a pris le bien en paiement en devient le propriétaire à compter de l'inscription du préavis. Il le prend dans l'état où il se trouvait alors, mais libre des hypothèques publiées après la sienne.».

faire vendre sous contrôle de justice[62] ou le vendre[63]. Avant d'exercer un droit hypothécaire, le créancier doit toutefois en informer le débiteur et toute autre personne contre laquelle il entend exercer son droit[64].

Dans ce contexte, si plusieurs créanciers sont titulaires d'une hypothèque sur le bien, il faut déterminer le rang de chacun. À cet égard, même si on considère que l'enregistrement de l'hypothèque dans les registres des brevets, des marques de commerce et des droits d'auteurs est nécessaire afin de la rendre opposables à certaines personnes, il ne permet pas d'établir le rang des droits. Selon certains, l'affaire *Poolman* c. *Eiffel Productions SA*[65] établit que « le rang de la sûreté devait être déterminé conformément aux dispositions de la loi provinciale. La décision du tribunal dans cet arrêt indique que les tribunaux s'en remettront aux lois provinciales sur les sûretés mobilières lorsqu'il y a lieu de déterminer les droits de préférence entre des actes de cession concurrents»[66]. En droit civil québécois, les droits prennent, en principe, rang suivant la date où ils ont été publiés[67]. C'est le cas lorsque l'hypothèque mobilière sans dépossession grève du brevet, une marque de commerce ou un droit d'auteur, et ce, peu importe qu'elle grève un bien en particulier ou une universalité de biens, incluant des biens futurs puisque l'article

---

[62]Art. 2791 C.c.Q.: «La vente a lieu sous contrôle de justice lorsque le tribunal désigne la personne qui y procédera, détermine les conditions et les charges de la vente, indique si elle peut être faite de gré à gré, par appel d'offres ou aux enchères et, s'il le juge opportun, fixe, après s'être enquis de la valeur du bien, une mise à prix.».

[63]Art. 2784 C.c.Q.: «Le créancier qui détient une hypothèque sur les biens d'une entreprise peut, s'il a présenté au bureau de la publicité des droits un préavis indiquant son intention de vendre lui-même le bien grevé et, après avoir obtenu le délaissement du bien, procéder à la vente de gré à gré, par appel d'offres ou aux enchères.».

[64]Ce mécanisme a notamment pour but de protéger le propriétaire du bien hypothéqué et les tiers – le créancier exerce son droit en quelques mains que le bien se trouve (art. 2654, 2660 C.c.Q.), il peut donc l'exercer contre le débiteur ou une autre personne - qui ont intérêt à ce que celui-ci soit conservé dans le patrimoine de son propriétaire. Le préavis est une mesure d'ordre public, le débiteur ne peut pas y renoncer. L'absence de préavis est d'ailleurs fatale (*Amyot* c. *Banque nationale du Canada*, [2004] R.J.Q. 2385 (C.A.)).

L'information du débiteur et, le cas échéant, de cette autre personne se fait par la signification du préavis qui est par la suite inscrit au *Bureau de la publicité des droits* (art. 2757 C.c.Q.). Le *Code civil du Québec* requiert non seulement la signification d'un préavis, il en détermine le contenu. Ainsi l'article 2758 C.c.Q. précise que le préavis doit dénoncer le défaut du débiteur et informer le débiteur ou le tiers de son droit de remédier à ce défaut. Il doit aussi indiquer le montant de la créance, le droit hypothécaire que le créancier désire exercer et le bien qui fera l'objet du recours hypothécaire. Enfin, le préavis doit sommer la personne à qui il est adressé de délaisser le bien dans le délai prévu par la loi. Ce délai est de 20 jours losrqu'il s'agit d'un bien meuble.

Avant l'expiration du délai imparti pour délaisser le bien, les créanciers ne peuvent exercer leurs droits hypothécaires (art. 2749 C.c.Q.).

[65](1991) 35 C.P.R. (3d) 384 (C.F.P.I.).

[66]Fraser Milner Casgrain (2000).

[67]Art. 2945 al. 1 C.c.Q.: «À moins que la loi n'en dispose autrement, les droits prennent rang suivant la date, l'heure et la minute inscrites sur le bordereau de présentation ou, si la réquisition qui les concerne est présentée au registre foncier, dans le livre de présentation, pourvu que les inscriptions soient faites sur les registres appropriés.».

2954 C.c.Q. prévoit que «[l]'hypothèque mobilière qui, au moment où elle a été acquise, l'a été sur le meuble d'autrui ou sur un meuble à venir, prend rang à compter du moment où elle a été publiée [. . .]».

En principe, ces règles s'appliquent même en cas d'une faillite. Au terme de la *Loi sur la faillite et l'insolvabilité*[68], une loi fédérale, le titulaire d'une hypothèque est considéré comme un créancier garanti[69]. Dans ce contexte, le titulaire de l'hypothèque peut, en principe, exercer les recours prévus au *Code civil du Québec,* il peut faire valoir ses droits[70]. Le syndic peut toutefois, en certaines circonstances s'adresser au tribunal afin que les droits du créancier garanti soient suspendus[71].

---

[68]*Loi sur la faillite et l'insolvabilité*, LRC 1985, c B-3 (ci-après «L.F.I.»).

[69]Voir la définition du terme «créancier garanti» à l'art. 2 L.F.I.:

> Personne détenant une hypothèque, un nantissement, une charge, un gage ou un privilège sur ou contre les biens du débiteur ou sur une partie de ses biens, à titre de garantie d'une dette échue ou à échoir, ou personne dont la réclamation est fondée sur un effet de commerce ou garantie par ce dernier, lequel effet de commerce est détenu comme garantie subsidiaire et dont le débiteur n'est responsable qu'indirectement ou secondairement.

[70]Art. 69.3 L.F.I.:

> (1) Sous réserve des paragraphes (1.1) et (2) et des article 69.4 et 69.5, à compter de la faillite du débiteur, ses créanciers n'ont aucun recours contre lui ou contre ses biens et ils ne peuvent intenter ou continuer aucune action, mesure d'exécution ou autre procédure en vue du recouvrement de réclamations prouvables en matière de faillite.
>
> (1.1) Le paragraphe (1) cesse de s'appliquer à tout créancier le jour de la libération du syndic.
>
> (2) Sous réserve des articles 79 et 127 à 135 et du paragraphe 248 (1), la faillite d'un débiteur n'a pas pour effet d'empêcher un créancier garanti de réaliser sa garantie ou de faire toutes autres opérations à son égard tout comme il aurait pu le faire en l'absence du présent article, à moins que le tribunal n'en décide autrement. Tout report ordonné à cet égard doit toutefois être conforme aux règles suivantes : a) dans le cas d'une garantie relative à une dette échue à la date où le failli est devenu tel ou qui le devient dans les six mois suivants, l'exercice des droits du créancier ne peut être reporté à plus de six mois après cette date; b) dans le cas d'une garantie relative à une dette qui ne devient échue que plus de six mois après la date où le failli est devenu tel, l'exercice des droits du créancier peut être reporté à plus de six mois après cette date — mais en aucun cas au-delà de la date à laquelle la dette devient exigible en vertu de l'acte ou de la règle de droit instituant la garantie — seulement si tous les versements d'intérêts en souffrance depuis plus de six mois sont acquittés et si tous les autres manquements de plus de six mois sont réparés, et seulement tant qu'aucun versement d'intérêts ne demeure en souffrance, ou tant qu'aucun autre manquement ne reste sans réparation, pendant plus de six mois.
>
> (2.1) L'ordonnance visée au paragraphe (2) ne peut avoir pour effet d'empêcher le créancier garanti de réaliser la garantie financière ou d'effectuer à l'égard de celle-ci toute autre opération.

[71]*Id.*

5 Conclusion

Les incertitudes dont est empreint régime juridique actuel relatif aux hypothèques ayant pour objet un brevet, une marque de commerce ou un droit d'auteur sont telles que certains auteurs estiment qu'une réforme devrait être mise de l'avant. Il est permis de s'interroger sur la nécessité d'une telle réforme dans le contexte où la pratique a su adopter une solution simple (l'inscription de la sûreté au *Registre des droits personnels et réels mobiliers* et son enregistrement à l'*Office de la propriété intellectuelle du Canada*) afin de protéger les droits de créanciers hypothécaires. On doit en effet reconnaître que les problèmes pratiques que posent les incertitudes sont apparemment peu nombreux.

Ouvrages cités

Azzaria G (2017) Notion d'oeuvre originale et conditions générales de protection. Dans: JurisClasseur Québec, coll. Propriété intellectuelle, fasc. 4. LexisNexis, Montréal
Carrière L (2017) Traitement administratif des marques de commerce: bases d'enregistrement et priorité. Dans: JurisClasseur Québec, coll. Propriété intellectuelle, fasc. 14. LexisNexis, Montréal
Dumont A, Shahinian SS (2017) Brevetabilité et définition de l'invention. Dans: JurisClasseur Québec, coll. Propriété intellectuelle, fasc. 23. LexisNexis, Montréal
El Sissi RH (1996) Security Interests in Copyright. I.P.J. 10:35–59
Fraser Milner Casgrain (Juin 2000) Les sûretés fédérales, Etude pour La Commission du Droit du Canada. https://www.ulcc.ca/fr/reunions-annuelles/342-2000-victoria-bc-reunions-annuelles/documents-de-la-section-civile-2000/339-droit-commercial-les-suretes-federales-2000
Léger JA (1993) Partage des compétences législatives en matière de droit d'auteur et de droit civil au Canada. CIPR 10:403–431
Lord F, Moyse P-E (2013) Principes et justifications de la propriété intellectuelle. Dans: JurisClasseur Québec, coll. Propriété intellectuelle, fasc. 1. LexisNexis, Montréal
Lucas F (2014) Propriété intellectuelle et titularité. Dans: JurisClasseur Québec, coll. Propriété intellectuelle, fasc. 2. LexisNexis, Montréal
Payette L (14 mai 2007) Exploitation sous licence: impact des droits des créanciers du donneur de licence, Texte d'une présentation faite lors d'un colloque sur les droits d'auteur organisé par ALAI Canada
Payette L (2002) Les sûretés et la propriété intellectuelle. Dans: Développements récents en droit de la propriété intellectuelle, Service de la formation permanente, Barreau du Québec, vol 177. Éditions Yvon Blais, Cowansville, pp 1–60
Payette L (2015) Les sûretés réelles dans le Code civil du Québec, 5e édn. Éditions Yvon Blais, Cowansville
Sotiriadis BH, Danis C (2002) La *prise de garanties* en matière de propriété intellectuelle. CPI 14 (2):581–604
Wood RJ (2000) The nature and definition of Federal Security Interests. C.B.L.J 34:65–113
Zimmerman CS, Bertrand L, Dunlop L (1991) Intellectual Property in Secured Transactions. CIPR 8:74–125

Security Rights in Intellectual Property in Croatia

Romana Matanovac Vučković, Hano Ernst, and Igor Gliha

Abstract This Chapter surveys the Croatian law on secured transactions involving intellectual property. As Croatia has been an emerging market since the early nineties and an EU member since mid-2013, the Croatian legal system has been challenged by simultaneous developments in areas of both secured transactions law and IP law. These developments have unfortunately resulted in two complex systems, which remain closed in and burdened by their own idiosyncrasies. As in other developed jurisdictions (with notable exceptions, such as in the US), secured transactions over IP in Croatia remain rare and fraught with significant legal risks and uncertainties. As noted by Professor Kieninger in her general analysis in this volume, it is, however, clear that there is a growing market and global need for such transactions, particularly in the early financing of SMEs, to which Croatian law will be unable to stay immune or unresponsive. Given that it requires significant changes in order to achieve clarity and to develop a streamlined version of secured credit involving IP, Croatian law will most certainly have to be revamped, hopefully finding inspiration in competitive comparative models presented in other chapters. This offers a silver lining to its current somewhat erratic and still immature non-unitary system of secured transactions.

1 Overview of IP Rights

1.1 Introduction

The legal protection of intellectual property rights in the Republic of Croatia has a long history. It might be said that the modern era of this protection began at the end of the nineteenth century, when the modern laws on copyright, patents, and trademarks entered into force, based on the pillars of the Paris Convention and the Berne

R. Matanovac Vučković · H. Ernst (✉) · I. Gliha
University of Zagreb, Faculty of Law, Zagreb, Croatia
e-mail: romana.matanovac.vuckovic@pravo.hr; hernst@pravo.hr; igliha@pravo.hr

E.-M. Kieninger (ed.), *Security Rights in Intellectual Property*, Ius Comparatum – Global Studies in Comparative Law 45,
https://doi.org/10.1007/978-3-030-44191-3_8

Convention. Today, the Republic of Croatia is well integrated in the system of the international registration of industrial property rights administered by WIPO, such as the PCT system and the Madrid system, and in the European patent system administered by the EPO. It is also a party to all of the relevant international agreements and treaties in the field of intellectual property rights.[1] Croatian laws are also completely harmonized with the European standards in this field.

Registration procedures for patents, trademarks, and industrial designs are conducted by the State Intellectual Property Office (SIPO).[2] SIPO also keeps national registers of patents, trademarks, and industrial designs.

1.2 Patents

The subject matter of patent protection and the legal protection of inventions under the Patent Act[3] (ZP) in general comply with the standards provided in the European Patent Convention and the Patent Cooperation Treaty and implement the *acquis communautaire* of the European Union in the field of patents.[4]

A patent is an exclusive right which protects the owner's interest in the commercial exploitation of an invention. A patent may be registered for any invention in any field of technology if the invention is new, involves an inventive step, and is eligible for industrial application.[5] It is possible to recognize a patent for an invention that includes computer programs (e.g. computer-implemented inventions), as well as patents for inventions in the field of biotechnology.

The right to patent protection belongs to the inventor, i.e. the person who created the invention in the course of creative work, and it includes the rights to submit a patent application and to acquire patent protection.[6] The right to patent protection can be subject to legal transactions, including secured transactions.[7] A patent application confers on the applicant a priority right, as from the filing date. In a case where two or more inventors who worked independently created the same invention, the ZP recognises the first-to-file principle.[8] Also, a published patent application confers on the applicant temporary rights according to which he or she

[1] A full list of the international treaties and agreements in the field of industrial property to which the Republic of Croatia is a party is available at http://www.dziv.hr/hr/zakonodavstvo/medjunarodni-ugovori/.

[2] See www.dziv.hr.

[3] Zakon o patentu [Patent Act], Narodne novine (NN) 173/03, 87/05, 76/07, 30/09, 128/10, 49/11, 76/13, 46/18.

[4] See generally Matanovac Vučković (2007a), pp. 12–14; Matanovac Vučković (2007b), pp. 3–78; Adamović (2007), pp. 146–173.

[5] ZP art. 5(1).

[6] ZP art. 12(1). See also Matanovac Vučković (2011), p. 684.

[7] See ZP art. 62.

[8] ZP art. 22(1). See also Matanovac Vučković (2011), p. 683.

may claim damages from any third party commercially using the invention that is the subject matter of the application. The right deriving from the patent application can also be subject to legal transactions, including secured transactions.[9]

Within 6 months from the date of publication of the patent application, the applicant may file a request for the grant of the patent based on a substantive examination, or a request for the grant of the patent without any substantive examination (i.e. a consensual patent).[10] SIPO performs a full substantive examination of the application in order to conclude whether the invention is new, involves an inventive step, and is eligible for industrial application.[11] Once it has established that the application complies with these requirements, SIPO issues a decision on the grant of the patent and enters the patent in the register.[12] The patent right can be the subject of legal transactions, including secured transactions.[13]

The registration of the patent confers on its owner the exclusive right to exploit the invention. The duration of the patent protection is 20 years from the filing date of the application.[14]

At the request of the patent owner, SIPO can issue a Supplementary Protection Certificate (SPC)[15] if the basic patent was granted for medicinal products intended for humans or animals or for plant protection products, provided that the placement on the market of these products must be previously authorized. The rights conferred by the SPC have the same effects as those conferred by patents and run for a period equal to the length of time between the date of filing of the patent application and the date of issuance of the marketing authorization, but no longer than 5 years. The right derived from the SPC is also subject to legal transactions, including secured transactions.[16]

1.3 Trademarks

The legal protection of registered trademarks in the Trademark Act[17] (ZŽ) complies with standards provided in international conventions and agreements, such as the Madrid Agreement and the Madrid Protocol, and implements the *acquis*

[9]See ZP art. 62a.

[10]ZP art. 36. Prior to the 2007 ZP Amendments, it was possible to register a patent based on the results of a substantive examination conducted in a foreign patent office which had contractual arrangements in this respect with SIPO. See generally Adamović and Sučić (2006), pp. 63–67.

[11]ZP art. 37.

[12]ZP art. 48(1), 48(7), and 49(1).

[13]See ZP art. 62a.

[14]ZP art. 70(1).

[15]See ZP Heading Xa.

[16]See ZP art. 62a.

[17]Zakon o žigu [Trademark Act], NN 173/03, 76/07, 30/09, 49/11, 46/18.

communautaire in the field of trademarks, including the European Union trademark system.[18] In Croatia, only registered trademarks are recognized.[19]

Any sign which is capable of being represented graphically can be registered as a trademark if it is capable of distinguishing the goods or services of one undertaking from the same kind of goods or services of another undertaking.

The trademark registration procedure is initiated by filing a trademark application with SIPO. A trademark application gives the applicant a priority right as from the filing date.[20] A trademark application can be subject to legal transactions, including secured transactions.

After receiving the trademark application, SIPO determines whether there are absolute or relative grounds for refusal. If there are no grounds for refusal, the trademark is registered and published.[21,22] The registration of the trademark confers on its owner the exclusive right to exploit the trademark with respect to the goods or services for which it is registered in the course of trade and commerce. The duration of the trademark protection is 10 years as from the filing date of the application[23] and it can be renewed an indefinite number of times.[24] A registered trademark can be subject to legal transactions, including secured transactions.

1.4 Copyright and Related Rights

The subject matter of copyright in the Copyright and Related Rights Act[25] (ZAPSP) complies with the standards provided in the Berne Convention, Rome Convention, WCT, and WPPT and implements the *acquis communautaire* of the European Union in the field of copyright.[26]

Croatian copyright law, like other copyright laws on the European continent, differentiates between copyright and related rights, such as rights of performers, phonogram producers, film producers, broadcasting organizations, publishers, and producers of databases.

---

[18] See generally Matanovac Vučković (2007a), pp. 12–14; Matanovac Vučković (2007b), pp. 3–78; Matešić (2007), pp. 174–188.

[19] ZŽ art. 4.

[20] ZŽ art. 17(1).

[21] ZŽ arts. 32 and 34.

[22] See also Matanovac and Rački Marinković (2006), p. 174; Zlatović (2008), pp. 358–359; Dika (2007), p. 622.

[23] ZŽ art. 43.

[24] ZŽ, art. 44.

[25] Zakon o autorskom pravu i srodnim pravima [Copyright and Related Rights Act], NN 167/03, 79/07, 80/11, 125/11, 141/13, 127/14, 62/17, 96/18.

[26] See generally Matanovac Vučković (2007b), pp. 3–78.

The holder of the copyright is the author and the object of the copyright is his or her work. The author is a person who created a work eligible for copyright protection. A copyrighted work is defined as an original intellectual creation in the literary, scientific, or artistic domain that has an individual character, irrespective of the manner and form of its expression or its type, value or purpose.[27] This general definition of a copyrighted work embraces all possible types and categories of works. In addition to the original expressions of works, alterations of works, such as translations, adaptations, musical adaptations, and other alterations, are also protected.

Copyright shall protect the personal and intellectual ties of the author with his or her work (i.e. the moral rights) as well as his or her economic interests in respect of the copyrighted work (i.e. the economic rights). According to the ZAPSP and in theory, copyright is a single and inseparable right. Because of its strictly personal component, copyright cannot be transferred in legal transactions during the lifetime of an author and only rights of exploitation can be granted. It is an unwaivable, non-transferable, and inalienable single right.[28]

Under the ZAPSP, the economic component of copyright consists of an open list of exclusive rights. It is specifically stated that the author is entitled to do with his or her copyrighted work and the benefits thereof as he or she pleases, unless otherwise provided by law.[29] Copyright is one indefinite right and the particular economic interests emanating from it, such as the exclusive right of reproduction (i.e. the right of multiplication), the exclusive right of distribution (i.e. the right to put into circulation), the exclusive right of communication of the work to the public, and the exclusive right of alteration are only emanations of the single, exclusive copyright. The author is entitled to remuneration for each and every use of his or her work, unless otherwise provided by law or contract.[30]

The owners of related rights regularly do not have an indefinite, exclusive power over the subject matter of the rights' protection. They only have the exclusive rights that are enumerated in the ZAPSP and defined as a definite set of exclusive rights and rights to remuneration. Only performers have both moral and economic interests; therefore, the rights of performers will fall under the same legal regime that pertains to the availability of legal transactions for copyrighted works. However, since other related rights do not have a moral component, they can be subject to legal transactions, including secured transactions.

[27]ZAPSP art. 5(1).

[28]See ZAPSP art. 42(29(1), 43(1), 44, 49 and 50.

[29]See ZAPSP art. 18.

[30]See ZAPSP art. 13(3). See Viši privredni sud Hrvatske [High Commercial Court of Croatia], Pž-694/82 (1982) (if an author receives an agreed pecuniary reward for composing and recording stage music, he or she does not lose the right to claim special remuneration for every performance of his or her copyrighted work).

2 Categories of Security Rights

2.1 *Introduction*

Croatian law contains a complex system of security interests as a consequence of its historical development and of rapidly and erratically introducing a myriad of novel property interests into an emerging system of property law.[31] For the purposes of this study, there is no need to review security interests in tangible personal property, as intellectual property rights are intangible. Security interests in intangibles consist of two basic varieties: (a) the charge, and (b) the assignment by way of security.[32]

Charge The charge is one of the five categories of property rights and it authorizes the creditor to satisfy his or her secured claim from the value of the encumbered property. Generally, all rights that are suitable for the satisfaction of a creditor's claim may be charged.[33] Charges are inseparable from the collateral, meaning they follow the encumbered right[34] and may not be transferred to another right.[35] Charges are also inseparable and accessory to the secured claim, and encumber the collateral as long as the claim exists either in its entirety or in part.[36] The claim may be a present claim[37] or a future claim,[38] with at least the maximum secured amount clearly defined.[39] The collateral secures the principal as well as costs and interest.[40] Charges afford the creditor priority over all competing claims, unless otherwise provided by statute.[41] Priority is generally determined by the time of creation.[42]

A voluntary charge is created through a contract stipulating that the debtor will transfer a right by way of security to the creditor and that the creditor will return this right to the debtor once the claim ceases.[43] The charge agreement may not stipulate

---

[31] See generally Ernst (2012), p. 32.

[32] See generally Gavella (2007), pp. 99–462 (discussing charges); Gavella (2007), pp. 469–551 (discussing fiduciary transfers); Dika (2007), pp. 746–783 (discussing judicial and notarial charges); Dika (2007), pp. 784–821 (discussing judical and notarial fiduciary transfers).

[33] ZV art. 298(2).

[34] ZV art. 299(1).

[35] ZV art. 299(2). Exceptionally, if the right ceases and is replaced by another right such as a claim in tort, the replacement claim will serve as collateral. ZV art. 301(4).

[36] ZV art. 301(5). The charge will be transferred automatically if the claim is assigned or otherwise transferred. ZV art. 303(1).

[37] ZV art. 301(1).

[38] ZV art. 301(2).

[39] ZV art. 301(1).

[40] ZV art. 301(3).

[41] ZV art. 302(1).

[42] ZV art. 302(3).

[43] ZV art. 307.

that the creditor will acquire the right upon default[44] or simply sell it.[45] Negative pledge clauses are void.[46] The creation of a charge requires registration if the right is created by registration, as a general rule.[47] If this general rule is applied to IP rights, this means that charges over IP rights created by registration must be registered in order to attach, but this can be modified by special rules on some IP rights (see *infra*). The charge agreement does not generally need to be in writing, unless specifically required by another law. A charge created in a simple written form will be valid under the provisions of the Ownership and Other Property Rights Act[48] (ZV).

The most common version of a charge is one executed as a notarial deed or on court record (the notarial version being used almost exclusively due to its speediness). Article 300 of the Enforcement Act[49] (OZ) does not cover intellectual property directly, but refers to "other valuable rights." Both the collateral and the secured claim must be specified in the contract. The claim may be a present claim or a future claim with a defined maximum secured amount.[50] The collateral must be specified, which should not prove difficult for intellectual property rights as they are easily documented. The collateral may belong to either the debtor or to a third party.[51]

The benefit of the notarially or judicially created charge is that it is immediately enforceable upon default. The creditor can skip litigation and proceed to the enforcement of the security interest by requesting a writ of execution[52] with priority relating back to the time the interest was created.[53] These charges must always be registered (see *infra*).[54]

Security Assignment The security assignment (fiduciary transfer) of rights is an alternative to the charge, although it is used somewhat less frequently than the charge. The transfer is executed in a fashion similar to the charge, most often by notarial deed or court record.[55] There are no special rules regarding intellectual property, hence intellectual property rights are simply treated as "rights." Security assignments of rights are separately identified under the OZ, but are treated

[44]ZV art. 307(4).
[45]ZV art. 307(5).
[46]ZV art. 307(4).
[47]ZV art. 310.
[48]Zakon o vlasništvu i drugim stvarnim pravima [Ownership and Other Property Rights Act], NN 91/1996, 68/1998, 137/1999, 22/2000, 73/2000, 114/2001, 79/2006, 141/2006, 146/2008, 38/2009, 153/2009, 90/2010, 143/2012, 152/2014.
[49]Ovršni zakon [Enforcement Act], NN 112/2012, 25/2013, 93/2014, 55/2016, 73/2017.
[50]OZ art. 302(2).
[51]See OZ art. 306.
[52]OZ art. 305(1).
[53]OZ art. 305(4).
[54]See OZ art. 300.
[55]See OZ art. 310.

functionally[56] since all rules concerning charges (as opposed to ownership) are applicable to security assignments, unless otherwise provided by statute.[57]

Charges and security assignments are treated differently depending on the underlying collateral, with industrial property rights and related rights on the one hand and copyright on the other, as discussed further below. The reason for the different approaches stems from varying conceptual approaches (i.e. copyright is treated as a single unitary right with separate economic and moral components).

2.2 Copyright and Related Rights as Collateral

Copyright cannot be sold, donated, or assigned in whole or in part, but can be inherited as a whole and divided in case of heir partition.[58] Copyright cannot be attached in enforcement. Only economic benefits acquired through the use of the copyrighted work may be attached.[59] The only available transaction *inter vivos* is to create rights to exploit the copyrighted work. Furthermore, the author may allow someone else to manage his or her right by contract (e.g. a collective management organization or agency). Finally, in addition to contractual arrangements, the author may issue a simple, unilateral authorization to use the copyrighted work.[60] Such a right may be created as an exclusive or non-exclusive right, restricted in terms of content, duration, and territory.[61] Therefore, copyright as a whole or in part cannot be subject to transactions *inter vivos* and so cannot be attached or used as collateral in any form.[62] This is because if attachment is unavailable, there is no way of attaching a charge or carrying out an assignment by way of security.

However, a right of exploitation of a copyrighted work, being a new right that the author derives (i.e. creates) from his or her copyright, may be transferred to others with the prior authorization of the author, or without such authorization if the right is included in the transfer of a business or a part of a business.[63] Such a right of exploitation can be created as an exclusive right that includes the rights of unlimited reproduction, distribution, communication to the public in any way, and alteration of the copyrighted work. Furthermore, it can be created as being temporally or spatially unrestricted. If the exploitation right is construed as an exclusive and unlimited right in terms of content, territory, and duration, the user of the work (i.e. the holder of the right of exploitation) may exploit the work in practically any way possible and reap

---

[56]See generally, Ernst (2011).

[57]ZV art. 297(2).

[58]ZAPSP art. 42.

[59]ZAPSP art. 43(1).

[60]ZAPSP art. 44(1).

[61]ZAPSP art. 44(2).

[62]See generally Gliha (2004), pp. 97–112; Kunda and Matanovac Vučković (2010), pp. 85–131.

[63]See ZAPSP art. 47(1).

all of the economic benefits derived from it, while the author may only exercise rights stemming from the moral, personal component of copyright. The creation of a right of exploitation can be done with or without compensation and this right may be judicially attached. Therefore, it can also be subject to security interests. The right of exploitation may also be called a licence, although this term is not used in Croatian legal vocabulary or in the ZAPSP.

Economic benefits derived from the exploitation of a copyrighted work may also be subject to security rights as receivables. The author or the holder of the right of exploitation has the right to reap economic benefits from the exploitation of the copyrighted work and these benefits are in fact receivables that may be transferred, attached, or used as collateral.

The same regime applies to the related rights of performers, as these rights, under the ZAPSP, also include both a moral and an economic component. Hence, the related rights of performers cannot be transferred *inter vivos*. It is possible to transfer or encumber the right to exploit an artistic performance in the same way as is described above for the right of exploitation of a copyrighted work. Furthermore, receivables for the payment of economic benefits derived from exploiting an artistic performance may also be transferred or encumbered.

Conversely, other related rights do not have a moral component to them and are freely alienable, may be attached, and may be used as collateral.[64] Receivables for the payment of economic benefits derived from exploiting the subject matter of related rights may also be transferred, attached, and used as collateral. It is also possible to create an exploitation right in the subjects protected by related rights, which may also be transferred, attached, and used as collateral.

In summary, the following rights may be used as collateral:

(i) related rights of phonogram producers
(ii) related rights of videogram (film) producers
(iii) related rights of broadcasting organizations
(iv) related rights of publishers
(v) related rights of database producers
(vi) rights of exploitation of copyrighted works
(vii) rights of exploitation of performances
(viii) rights of exploitation of phonograms
(ix) rights of exploitation of videograms
(x) rights of exploitation of broadcasted signals
(xi) rights of exploitation of publications
(xii) rights of exploitation of databases
(xiii) receivables derived from the exploitation of copyright and related rights

[64] ZAPSP arts. 133(2), 139(2), 143(3), 145(2), and 146(2).

2.3 Industrial Property Rights as Collateral

Industrial property rights are, in principle, freely alienable, and may be transferred to others in whole or in part, licensed, attached, and used as collateral. There are no statutory restrictions on alienating such rights, but such alienation should be carried out in accordance with the nature of the right in question and the purpose of the protection granted by this right.

In case of both patents and trademarks, transfers and encumbrances are available for rights arising before registration. Due to the fact that the registration relates back to the filing date of the application or the date of the priority right, if so requested, the application right may be freely transferred, although all such transfers remain conditional upon registration. If the application does not lead to registration, the application right ceases when SIPO denies the registration. All of the effects of the transfer or encumbrance of the application right are thus cancelled retroactively. On the other hand, if the application right does result in registration, it is transformed into a registered patent or trademark. All pre-registration transfers or encumbrances are automatically transformed into transfers or encumbrances of the registered right.

If we apply such reasoning to patents, the following situations can be discerned. With respect to an invention, there are four rights that may be subject to security. The right to a patent is created at the time of the invention and includes the right to apply for registration, as described above. With the filing of a patent application, the right to an invention ceases and is transformed into a temporary patent application right. Once the patent has been registered, the patent application right is transformed into a patent right, relating back to the date of the application or to the priority date, if so requested. The same applies to consensual patents. Finally, certain patents (but not consensual patents) may be extended via Supplementary Protection Certificates, as is the case with pharmaceutical patents and patents for plant protection products. Once registration lapses, the patent right may thus be transformed into a Supplementary Protection Certificate right.

There are only two steps (i.e. phases), and thus two rights available for security, with respect to trademarks: the trademark application right and the registered trademark.

Both patents and trademarks may be subject to licensing agreements, and the licence may also be used as collateral. The licence may be issued during the application phase; hence, the application right may be subject to a licence.

Finally, economic benefits derived from the use of the invention or the trademark may also be used as collateral. These are receivables for the payment of economic benefits and are treated as such.

In conclusion, the following rights are available as collateral:

(i) rights to a patent
(ii) patent application rights
(iii) registered patents
(iv) consensual patents
(v) Supplementary Protection Certificate rights

(vi) trademark application rights
(vii) registered trademarks
(viii) patent licences
(ix) trademark licences
(x) receivables from the use of inventions and trademarks

Note that rights to a patent, patent application rights, trademark application rights, and consensual patents are conditional rights. The actual value of patent or trademark application rights or rights to a patent becomes clear and makes sense only after registration. On the other hand, consensual patents protect an invention without undergoing a full examination procedure, meaning that there is still the possibility that an interested party might request that such a procedure be conducted, thus jeopardizing the existence of the right. This, however, does not prohibit the encumbrance of the right.[65]

There are no special rules on international patent applications under the PCT or on international trademark registration under the Madrid Agreement. Both the international patent application and the international trademark application have the same effects as national registrations, and the same rules discussed above apply to them. European patent applications and European patents have the same effects as national patent applications and national patents, and the same rules discussed above also apply.

With respect to EU trademarks, supranational rules contained in the European Union Trade Mark Regulation[66] apply. These rules stipulate the laws applicable to the disposition of European trademarks and the effects thereof.[67] The disposition of European trademarks with an effect on the entirety of the EU territory is governed by the national rules of a particular Member State. Which law will apply in a particular case depends on the seat or domicile of the person registered as the proprietor in the EUIPO register. If there is no such seat or domicile, the law of the Member State where the proprietor has an establishment applies. If there is no such establishment, Spanish law applies, because the EUIPO seat is in Spain. It is possible for Croatian law also to apply; however, it would be applied in accordance with the principle of EU trademarks having unitary effects across the entirety of the EU territory. Note, however, that Reg. art. 19 cannot be applied to all instances where an EU trademark is transferred because we must distinguish between the effects of transactions (i.e. transfers or encumbrances), their contractual aspects, and their property (in rem) effects. In this respect, Reg. art. 19 does not exclude national rules on private international law—in fact, it underlines their importance.

Finally, note that the applicable law is determined by reference to the domicile, seat, or establishment "on the relevant date." It is possible for the proprietor of the EU trademark to change his or her domicile, seat, or establishment location, and such

[65] ZP arts, 62(2), 62a(4); ZŽ art. 42.

[66] Regulation (EU) 2017/1001 of the European Parliament and of the Council of June 14, 2017 on the European Union Trade Mark, 2017 OJ (L 154) 1 (EU) (hereinafter: Regulation).

[67] Regulation art. 19.

addresses may change to territories outside the EU. The applicable law changes accordingly. However, there will be no change to the applicable law once the transaction has been carried out, meaning that the origin situs law will apply irrespective of a later change of domicile, seat, or establishment location.

Under both Croatian and EU law, a trademark is non-accessory, meaning it can be transferred independently of the underlying business, and neither system of law requires that the trademark be used before registration or that any statement of intent to use the trademark be filed with the application. However, if a registered trademark remains unused for a period of 5 years, it may be revoked. A misleading trademark may also be revoked. Therefore, trademarks which have become unused or misleading due to transfers or encumbrances may also be revoked.

With respect to the potential application of Croatian law, it can be concluded that charges and security assignments under Croatian law are available. The same applies to the use of EU trademark licences and receivables from EU trademark use as collateral. The effects of such dispositions are then identical to the effects of national security interests over trademark application rights or registered trademarks.

3 Structure of Transactions: Attachment and Perfection

3.1 Typical Structures

A typical charge transaction will involve drafting a contract in-house (or having one drafted by an attorney) and then submitting this draft to a notary for review, or having the notary draft the contract directly. The same applies to security transfers. There are no typical secured transactions with respect to intellectual property, as these transactions are considered extremely unusual and uncommon. There is no available case law on such transactions.

3.2 Attachment and Perfection

General Rules on Attachment and Perfection Croatian general property law does not distinguish between attachment and perfection, (i.e. between the creation of a security right *inter partes* and its effects against third parties). The starting point for this non-discriminatory position lies in the fact that a security right is a property right which *ex hypothesi* affects third parties. Consequently, there cannot be a security right that only has a relative effect. This does not imply that Croatian law does not accept the effects of a pledge or similar contract because the law envisages the primary obligation of the parties to create a security interest in the collateral. However, no security interest (as a property right) exists in the period between the execution of such a contract and its performance. The parties are simply obligated to perform the contract in terms of creating the right; once the right has been created, the applicable provisions of property law govern the transaction, for the most part.

As mentioned earlier, a charge in an intangible is created either through assignment by way of security or through registration. Under general property law, assignment applies to non-registrable rights,[68] while registration applies to rights created through registration.[69] Rights created through registration do not attach unless they are registered; however, there are exceptions with respect to some intellectual property rights, as discussed below.

For rights not created through registration, registration is sometimes nevertheless required. With respect to notarial and judicial charges, OZ Article 300 specifies that for "other valuable rights", registration is the method of creating a charge over such rights.[70] This means that the method of creating and perfecting a charge depends on the form of the security interest chosen by the parties. All notarial and judicial charges will be registered, while non-registrable rights may be also charged through simple contracts. Similarly, for judicial and notarial security assignments, OZ Article 313(3) specifies that the transfer "is deemed complete" once the assignment has been executed and the transfer has been registered in the register prescribed by statute. Either the notary[71] or the court[72] is responsible for "taking all necessary measures" for attachment and perfection.

Therefore, charges are both created and perfected by way of registration if the charge is registrable, according to the Act on the Register of Judicial and Notarial Security Interests Over Movables and Intangibles[73] (ZU).[74] As security interests, security assignments attach and are usually perfected by way of registration.[75] Note, however, that rights and receivables may be assigned by way of security even without registration, as per the Obligations Act[76] (ZOO).[77]

The general public register for movable tangibles and intangibles is a register run by the Financial Agency (FINA). This register was created by the Act on the Register of Judicial and Notarial Security Interests Over Movables and Intangibles. Obviously, this register was principally designed for judicially or notarially created security interests (both charges and security assignments).[78] Unfortunately, the

---

[68]ZV art. 310(1).

[69]ZV art. 310(2).

[70]OZ art. 300(1)(9).

[71]OZ art. 307(1).

[72]OZ art. 303(1).

[73]Zakon o upisniku sudskih i javnobilježničkih osiguranja tražbina vjerovnika na pokretnim stvarima i pravima [Act on the Register of Judicial and Notarial Security Interests Over Movables and Intangibles], NN 121/05.

[74]ZU art. 17.

[75]ZU art. 18.

[76]Zakon o obveznim odnosima [Obligations Act], NN 35/2005, 41/2008, 125/2011, 78/2015.

[77]Croatian law does not follow UCC Art. 9 which notably includes sales of accounts.

[78]See ZU art. 6(1) (listing registrable rights).

register does not support the registration of non-judicial or non-notarial charges. However, due to the fact that judicial and notarial security interests are overwhelmingly more popular in practice, the number of non-registrable transactions is most likely negligible.

Registration is a quasi-judicial procedure. The creditor submits a request for registration together with the necessary documents (i.e. the security agreement[79] and proof of right). The registrar is limited in its capacity to determine either the actual existence of the right (i.e. collateral) or its holder. For registered rights, the creditor must submit a certificate from the relevant registry as proof of right.[80] The debtor is prohibited (i.e. estopped) from challenging the security interest after registration based on the fact that he or she lacks rights in the collateral.[81] However, a third party who claims that he or she is the lawful right-holder may challenge the security interest, either immediately or during execution.[82] A separate remedy in the form of an action to expunge is also provided for registrations that have become final.[83] Registration is not a substitute for a lack of rights. The registrar issues orders granting or denying registration.[84] An order may be appealed through a formal objection to the local municipal court.[85]

Trademarks A charge over a national trademark is created by contract. The charge is registrable in the SIPO register (following creditor application) and SIPO publishes the charge in its official gazette. Priority exists only after registration and so registration provides effect against other bona fide creditors,[86] but the right is created irrespective of registration. This means that the charge exists irrespective of registration and is perfected against all third parties even without registration if these parties had or ought to have had notice of the security interest.

Patents A charge over a national patent is also created by contract. The charge is also registrable in the patents register, following creditor application. The effect of registration is, as with trademarks,[87] to determine priority. Hence, the charge exists irrespective of registration and is perfected against all third parties without registration if they knew or ought to have known of the interest.

---

[79] ZU art. 24(1).
[80] ZU art. 24(2).
[81] ZU art. 20(1).
[82] ZU art. 21(1)-(2).
[83] See ZU art. 34.
[84] See ZU art. 26.
[85] See ZU art. 30.
[86] ZŽ art. 40(3).
[87] ZP art. 62a(2).

4 Priorities

Priorities are generally determined by the date of perfection, which often coincides with the date of creation. Priorities depend on both the possibility of registration and the type of register. For registrable charges, priorities are determined by the date of filing of the registration application. All judicial and notarial charges and security assignments are registrable with the FINA (or another register) and the date of filing determines priority.[88] Trademark and patent charges and security assignments, unless executed in notarial or judicial form, don't have to be registered, but registration will determine priority.

For registrable charges, an earlier registered charge will have priority over a later registered or unregistered charge. A later registered charge will not trump an earlier unregistered charge if the earlier charge was not registrable. An earlier unregistered charge will trump a later unregistered charge. For registrable security assignments, a registered security assignment will preclude further security assignments and charges. Several registered charges may encumber the same right, but only a single security transfer may be made (further registration applications will be dismissed[89]). An unregistered security assignment will also trump later security assignments and charges if this first assignment was not registrable.

For trademarks and patents, the situation is not entirely clear, but it seems that an earlier registered charge will trump later registered charges; however, an earlier unregistered charge will not trump a later registered or unregistered charge if the later charge was made without notice because all patent and trademark charges may be registered.

Under non-bankruptcy law, charges have priority over unsecured claims. However, some claims have super-priority—namely, taxes and other public fees for the last year relating to the collateral, if any.[90] Costs and interest have the priority of the principal.[91]

Under bankruptcy law, covered by the Bankruptcy Act[92] (SZ), charge holders have priority over unsecured creditors to enforce their charge in bankruptcy, but are junior to debts of the estate.[93] Charges are enforced in bankruptcy and all pending executions are transferred to the bankruptcy court.[94] The bankruptcy trustee will sell the collateral by applying the rules on judicial execution.[95] Unlike enforcement law,

[88]ZU art. 13(1).

[89]ZU art. 13(2).

[90]OZ art. 113.

[91]OZ art. 167(3).

[92]Stečajni zakon [Bankruptcy Act], NN 71/2015, 104/2017.

[93]SZ arts. 154-157.

[94]SZ art. 169(6).

[95]SZ art. 249.

bankruptcy law recharacterizes all security assignments as charges and treats them accordingly.[96]

5 Enterprise Charges

Croatian law does not recognize "enterprise charges" as such, but it does recognize a special kind of "floating security" that is essentially a security interest in inventory. This interest is created as a notarial or judicial security over a group of *tangibles*. Even though it is termed a "floating charge," it is not equivalent to the English floating charge. The Croatian floating charge is defined spatially, as it can be created over all tangibles located inside a designated space. The interest will automatically terminate once the tangible is removed from the designated area,[97] so the transferee can take it free and clear of the interest. There are no similar provisions for intangibles and due to the specific character of these provisions, they cannot be analogously applied to intangibles.

6 Rights Before Default

There are no special rules for intellectual property rights, so general secured transactions law applies. Unfortunately, the general rules on secured transactions do not provide any special rules on rights before default with respect to intangible collateral such as intellectual property rights; rather, it only stipulates the rules on tangible property.[98] Due to the fact that the right is transferred in case of both charges and security assignments, it would seem that the creditor, not the debtor, would exercise the right. However, due to the nature of intellectual property and the secured transaction, this does not seem to be an acceptable interpretation. At the very least, the parties should be able to structure the transaction by contractually agreeing that the debtor would remain authorized to exercise the right, irrespective of the charge or assignment. For receivables, the ZV provides that the creditor must take every measure to preserve the claim and to receive interest payments or other periodic payments, as well as the principal once it becomes due.[99] All received payments are set off against the secured claim if it is due; otherwise, they must be deposited with the court.[100] The OZ provides the same for notarially and judicially created charges:

---

[96] SZ art. 150(1), and 153(1)(1).

[97] ZU art. 38(4).

[98] ZV art. 333.

[99] ZV art. 334(1)-(3).

[100] ZV art. 334(4).

the creditor must take every measure to preserve the claim[101]; collect interest payments and other periodic payments[102]; and collect payment on the debt itself once it becomes payable. All collected payments are set off against the creditor's claims, plus costs and interest.[103]

In case of judicial or notarial security assignments, it is the debtor who is expressly designated to continue to exercise the right transferred as security.[104] The parties may stipulate otherwise[105]; however, in such a case, the parties must also stipulate methods for calculating the benefits for the secured party, which are automatically set off against the secured claim.[106]

7 Enforcement

Charges are generally enforceable judicially.[107] Extrajudicial enforcement is available if the debtor has agreed in writing to such enforcement; however, in commercial contracts such enforcement is always available unless explicitly excluded.[108] Hence, due to the commercial nature of intellectual property transactions, it will usually be available. The creditor must sell the collateral at public auction, unless stipulated otherwise.[109] This means that the contract may contain rules on extrajudicial enforcement that the creditor must follow. If these rules are breached, the creditor is liable for damages.[110]

The judicial enforcement of charges is carried out via execution.[111] A writ of execution will order that the IP right be seized,[112] prohibiting the debtor from further dispositions,[113] and will order an expert appraisal[114] and judicial sale.[115] An auction is not mandatory unless the right is of significant value and can be expected to sell at

[101]OZ art. 320(1)(1).
[102]OZ art. 320(1)(2).
[103]OZ art. 320(1)(3).
[104]OZ art. 315(1).
[105]OZ art. 315(1).
[106]OZ art. 315(3).
[107]ZV art. 336(2).
[108]ZV art. 337(2).
[109]ZV art. 337(3).
[110]ZV art. 337(7).
[111]See Ernst and Matanovac Vučković (2013a, b).
[112]See OZ art. 138.
[113]OZ art. 142.
[114]*See* OZ art. 145.
[115]*See* OZ art. 149.

a price higher than the appraisal price.[116] The minimum sales price is half of the appraised value.[117]

Security assignments are enforced differently from charges. In case of a simple security transfer, there are no special rules on enforcement and the situation is unclear. The assignment will most likely be recharacterized as a charge[118] and then enforced as such. Special rules do exist for notarial and judicial security assignments. The creditor is authorized to sell the collateral after default,[119] but only via a notary.[120] Alternatively, the creditor may seek unrestricted rights, which essentially removes all restrictions imposed on the creditor due to the transfer having been for security purposes only. In order to remove these restrictions, the creditor must follow a strict process defined by statute. First, the creditor must contact the debtor via a notary and ask him or her to notify the creditor, via the same notary, whether he or she requests that the collateral be sold.[121] If the debtor does request that it be sold, he or she must list the lowest acceptable price for the sale and name a notary willing to conduct the sale.[122] The price listed must be no less than equal to the secured claim, plus costs and interest.[123] The creditor must order a sale under the defined terms and the notary must attempt the sale in the following 3 months.[124] If the attempted sale fails (e.g. because there is no potential buyer found or the required price was not offered), the creditor is "deemed to have acquired the right in full" for the price equalling the secured claim together with costs, interest, and taxes.[125] The outcome is identical if the debtor fails to respond to the creditor's initial request.[126]

The debtor may also request that the creditor sell the collateral or that the creditor become the unrestricted holder of the encumbered right for the price equalling the secured claim together with costs, interest, and taxes.[127] If the creditor agrees or does not respond, the notary will issue a certificate in the following 15 days.[128]

In case the debtor becomes insolvent, charge holders and security assignees are treated the same. The bankruptcy trustee will sell the collateral and, after the sale, pay into the estate an amount to cover the costs (this is normally 10% of the proceeds).[129]

[116] OZ art. 149(4).
[117] OZ art. 150(1).
[118] ZV art. 297(2).
[119] OZ art. 316(1).
[120] OZ art. 316(3).
[121] OZ art. 322(1).
[122] OZ art. 322(2).
[123] OZ art. 322(3).
[124] OZ art. 322(6).
[125] OZ art. 322(7).
[126] OZ art. 322(7).
[127] OZ art. 325(1).
[128] OZ art. 325(4).
[129] See SZ arts. 253-254.

8 Typical Costs

The cost of a secured transaction involving intellectual property will vary and usually depends on the value of the transaction. Typically, a secured transaction will be part of a larger, complex transaction (e.g. a loan) and will almost certainly require legal services. The services of an attorney are paid as per a tariff.[130] Furthermore, the transaction will most likely be executed in the form of a notarial deed or be notarized, which will incur notarial fees, dependent upon the value of the secured claim. The registration itself will incur a registration fee of approximately EUR 35.

9 Practical Usefulness, Legal, and Practical Difficulties

Security interests in intellectual property are rare. There are many reasons for this, the main ones being the lack of detailed rules, the complexity of the transaction, and the lack of generally accepted rules for appraising intellectual property. The examples that could be found are patent charges, including consensual patents. Banks will usually not provide any better terms for granting these types of security interests than they will for other secured loans.

As for collective management societies, both authors and SMEs use future receivables that the author or SME will have against the collective management society. The amount of such receivables is unknown, but due to the fact that payments are made on a yearly basis for the previous year, usually only short-term loans between the collective management society and its members will be collateralized with such receivables. The terms of such loans are not publicly disclosed.

10 Law Reform

There are currently no proposals for law reform in this area, and none seem to be planned. Because these issues are primarily viewed as issues of secured transactions law, any law reform project would require an overhaul of that body of law. A special regime for intellectual property rights that would deviate significantly from general principles would most likely not be welcomed, particularly bearing in mind the existing complexity of Croatian secured transactions law. However, a major overhaul of secured transactions law might enable a thorough analysis of the exceptions required for intellectual property.

[130]See Tarifa o nagradama i naknadi troškova za rad odvjetnika, NN 142/2012, 103/2014, 118/2014, 107/2015.

References

Adamović J (2007) Novela Zakona o patentu iz 2007. In: Matanovac R (ed) Prilagodba hrvatskog prava intelektualnog vlasništva europskom pravu. Narodne novine, Zagreb, pp 146–173

Adamović J, Sučić T (2006) Načini stjecanja patenta te utjecaj prakse Europskog patentnog ureda na postupak potpunog ispitivanja u Republici Hrvatskoj. In: Matanovac R (ed) Hrvatsko pravo intelektualnog vlasništva u svjetlu pristupa Europskoj uniji. Narodne novine, Zagreb, pp 53–91

Dika M (2007) Građansko ovršno pravo. Narodne novine, Zagreb

Ernst H (2011) Funkcionalizam u mobilijarnom osiguranju. Dissertation, University of Zagreb

Ernst H (2012) Underregulation, overregulation, and misregulation of security interests in Croatian law. In: Jessel-Holst C, Meyer T, Josipović T, Petrić S, Dabovska Anastasovska J, Kostić Mandić M, Povlakić M, Radivojević Z, Stanković E (eds) New perspectives of South East European Private Law, South East European post-doctoral colloquium in private law – proceedings, Zagreb, September 2012. Centre for South East European law school network, Skopje, p 32

Ernst H, Matanovac Vučković R (2013a) Prava na izumu koja mogu biti predmet ovrhe – hrvatska, europski i međunarodna perspektiva. Nova pravna revija 4(2):23–38

Ernst H, Matanovac Vučković R (2013b) Ovrha na žigu - kako premostiti podnormiranost? Zbornik Pravnog fakulteta Sveučilišta u Rijeci 34:173–208

Gavella N, Josipović T, Gliha I, Belaj V, Stipković Z (2007) Stvarno pravo, vol 2. Narodne novine, Zagreb

Gliha I (2004) Raspolaganje autorskim pravom (i srodnim pravima). Zbornik Hrvatskog društva za autorsko pravo 2004(5):97–112

Kunda I, Matanovac Vučković R (2010) Raspolaganje autorskim pravom na računalnom programu – materijalnopravni i kolizijskopravni aspekti. Zbornik Pravnog fakulteta Sveučilišta u Rijeci 34(Suppl. 1):85–131

Matanovac R, Rački Marinković A (2006) Registri prava intelektualnog vlasništva. In: Josipović T (ed) Hrvatsko registarsko pravo. Narodne novine, Zagreb, pp 153–200

Matanovac Vučković R (2007a) Novele zakona o pravima industrijskog vlasništva kao rezultat druge faze usklađivanja s pravnom stečevinom Europske unije u području prava intelektualnog vlasništva. Informator 2007(5586):12–14

Matanovac Vučković R (2007b) Zbirka propisa u području prava intelektualnog vlasništva. Narodne novine, Zagreb

Matanovac Vučković R (2011) Hrvatska i Makedonija u europskom patentnom sustavu. Zbornik Pravnog fakulteta u Zagrebu 61:675–694

Matešić S (2007) Novela Zakona o žigu iz 2007. In: Matanovac R (ed) Prilagodba hrvatskog prava intelektualnog vlasništva europskom pravu. Narodne novine, Zagreb, pp 174–188

Zlatović D (2008) Žigovno pravo. Vizura, Zagreb

Security Rights in Intellectual Property in Cyprus

Venetia Argyropoulou, Andreas Chr. Christoforou, and Tatiana Eleni Synodinou

Abstract The present chapter explores the type of security rights that may be created over intellectual property in the Republic of Cyprus. The chapter begins with a general overview of IP rights recognised in Cyprus, focusing on patents, trademarks, and copyright. Thereafter, the chapter examines the categories of security rights that can be created over IP in Cyprus. The Chapter draws a distinction between security rights over tangible and intangible property, aiming to demonstrate the distinct features of IP that make traditional security interests over tangible property unsuitable for securing interests over IP. This is important as Cypriot law does not specifically regulate security interests over IP rights and therefore it falls in the hands of practitioners to properly recognize the type of security interest best suited for their IP transactions. Thereafter, the Chapter examines such security interests that are mostly used in IP transactions in Cyprus and studies the structure of such transactions and any creation or perfection requirements. Lastly, the final parts of this chapter deal with enforcement issues and provide practical tips for practitioners. Importantly, the Chapter offers a comparative view between English law practice in security interests over IP rights and the practice in the Republic of Cyprus, allowing for useful conclusions.

V. Argyropoulou
European University of Cyprus, Faculty of Law, Nicosia, Cyprus
e-mail: v.argyropoulou@euc.ac.cy

A. C. Christoforou
Nicosia, Cyprus

T. E. Synodinou (✉)
Law Department, University of Cyprus, Nicosia, Cyprus
e-mail: synodint@ucy.ac.cy

E.-M. Kieninger (ed.), *Security Rights in Intellectual Property*, Ius Comparatum – Global Studies in Comparative Law 45,
https://doi.org/10.1007/978-3-030-44191-3_9

1 General Overview of IP Rights in Cyprus

Intellectual property (IP) protects immaterial goods that are the product of a creative or mental activity.[1] The types of intellectual property in Cyprus are: (a) patents,[2] (b) trademarks,[3] (c) copyright and related rights,[4] (d) industrial designs and utility models,[5] (e) geographical indications,[6] and (f) plant varieties.[7]

For the purposes of this chapter, we will mainly focus on patents, trademarks, and copyright. In order to be protected, all forms of intellectual property must fulfill certain substantial conditions, which will be examined below.

1.1 *Patents*

Patents are exclusive rights which are granted to the owner of a new invention. A patent prevents others from making, using, importing, or selling the invention without the patent owner's (i.e. the patentee's) permission.

An invention can be patented if it falls within the scope of patentable subject matter. According to section 5 of Law No. 16(I)/1998, a patent cannot be granted for: "(a) discoveries, scientific theories and mathematical methods; (b) aesthetic creations; (c) schemes, rules and methods for performing mental acts, playing games or doing business, and programs for computers [;] and (d) presentation of information." The Law also states that "[a] patent shall not be granted in respect of an invention [whose publication or exploitation] would be contrary to public order or morality".

Under Article 2(2) European Patent Convention (EPC), the European patent shall, in each of the Contracting states for which it is granted, have the effect of and be subject to the same conditions as a national patent granted by that state, unless the EPC provides otherwise.

Section 64 of the Patents Law of 1998 (No. 16(I)/1998) states that any European patent application shall be registered in the Registrar of Companies and Official Receiver (DRCOR) of the Republic of Cyprus. According to section 65, patent rights may only become effective from the date on which a translation of the claims made by the applicant in one of the official languages of the Republic is published by the Registrar of Companies and Official Receiver. When the European Patent Office grants a European patent designating Cyprus, the patent proprietor shall register a

[1] Kur and Dreier (2013), p. 2.

[2] Patents Law of 1998 (No. 16(I)/1998).

[3] Trade Marks Law, Cap. 268.

[4] Copyright Laws 1976 to 1993 (No. 59/1976).

[5] Law No. 4(I)/2002.

[6] Appellation of Origin and Geographical Indications for Agricultural Products and Foodstuffs Law 2006 (No. 139(I)/2006).

[7] Protection of New Varieties of Plants Law 2004 (No. 21(I)/2004).

translation of the patent in one of the official languages of the Republic of Cyprus in the Registrar of Companies and Official Receiver. If the translation is not registered, the patent shall be deemed to be void from the outset.[8]

Article 139 (3) of the EPC states that "*Any Contracting State may prescribe whether and on what terms an invention disclosed in both a European patent application or patent and a national application or patent having the same date of filing or, where priority is claimed, the same date of priority, may be protected simultaneously by both applications or patents*". The law of Cyprus does not provide for simultaneous protection. According to section 71 of the Patents Law of 1998, to the extent that it protects the same invention, the national patent ceases to have effect from the date on which (a) the period for filing the notice of opposition to the European patent expires without such notice having been filed, (b) the opposition proceedings are finally closed and the European patent has been maintained, or (c) the national patent is granted, providing that this date falls after the date provided in either (a) or (b). Under Article 168 of the EPC, "*[a]ny Contracting State may declare in its instrument of ratification or accession, or may inform the Government of the Federal Republic of Germany by written notification at any time thereafter, that this Convention shall be applicable to one or more of the territories for the external relations of which it is responsible. European patents granted for that Contracting State shall also have effect in the territories for which such a declaration has taken effect.*" The territorial field of application pursuant to Article 168 of the EPC is the territory of the Republic of Cyprus.[9]

1.2 Trademarks

Trademarks are signs which individualize the goods or the services of a given enterprise and distinguish them from the goods or services of other parties. Not all signs are registrable as trademarks.

According to section 2 of the Trade Marks Law, "trademark" means a mark consisting of any signs capable of being represented (particularly by words, including the name of a person; pictures; letters; numbers; the shape of the goods or their packaging; or any combination thereof) which by their very nature distinguish the goods or services of an undertaking from those of other undertakings where that mark is used or intended to be used for the purposes of such discrimination. Signs cannot be registered as trademarks if they do not have a distinctive character or if they consist exclusively of signs or indications which may serve in trade to designate

[8]Section 66 of the Patents Law of 1998.

[9]European Patent Office (EPO) (2015) National law relating to the EPC, European patent applications and patents: law and practice of the EPC contracting states. http://documents.epo.org/projects/babylon/eponet.nsf/0/18152865EA06F0C0C1257F62005E1E6D/$File/National_law_relating_to_the_EPC_17th_edition_en.pdf. Accessed Mar 28, 2019.

the kind, quality, quantity, intended purpose, value, geographical origin, time of production, or other characteristics of the goods or services. Furthermore, the following also cannot be registered as trademarks: marks consisting solely of signs or indications which have become customary in everyday language or in the legitimate and established practice of the trade; trademarks consisting solely of (i) the shape imposed by the very nature of the goods, (ii) the shape of the goods necessary to achieve a technical result, or (iii) the shape giving substantial value to the goods; marks which could mislead the public, in particular as to the nature, quality, or geographical origin of the goods or services; marks which are unacceptable or void under Article 6*bis* of the Paris Convention for the Protection of Industrial Property; marks that include a sign of great symbolic importance, in particular a religious symbol; marks for which the application for registration was made in bad faith by the applicant; and any scandalous design or any sign that is contrary to public policy or morality.[10]

Community trademarks can co-exist with national trademarks.[11] So, it is possible a priori to register the same sign as a community trademark and as national—i.e. Cypriot—trademark.[12] Community trademarks and national trademarks are mutually exclusive[13] and they "should be taken into consideration against each other as earlier rights constituting relative grounds for refusal or invalidity."[14]

In relation to transitional law, Article 142 a [of the Community Trademark Regulation (CTMR)] provides that *all pending CTM applications and registered CTMs are, as of 1 May 2004, extended automatically to the new Member States but may not be refused or declared invalid on absolute or relative grounds which would become applicable merely as a result of the accession of new Member States.*

> On the other hand, the CTM applications filed on or after 1 May 2004 are not subject to this [rule] and may be refused upon opposition, or declared invalid, on account of an earlier national right existing in a new Member State, provided that that earlier right is 'earlier' in the comparison of the two filing or priority dates.[15]

1.3 Copyright and Related Rights

Copyright protects creative and artistic works. Under Law No. 59/1976, in order to be protected, a work has to be original in the sense that it is the "author's own intellectual creation". This criterion, following the Common Law copyright

[10]Section 13 of the Trade Marks Law.

[11]See Recital 6 of the Community Trademark Regulation (CTMR).

[12]Kur and Dreier (2013), p. 162.

[13]Kur and Dreier (2013); See Section 14 of the Trade Marks Law.

[14]Gödölle (2009).

[15]Opposition Guidelines (2004), Part 7, Transitional rules relating to enlargement. http://euipo.europa.eu/en/mark/marque/pdf/part_7-EN.pdf. Accessed Mar 28, 2019.

tradition, has been interpreted by Cypriot courts as an objective one. Thus, a work it is protected if it has not been copied from another work.[16] Another condition for the granting of protection is that the work has to be fixed in some form. No formalities are required for the protection to be awarded. Mere ideas are not protected by copyright law.[17] Performances are protected in Cyprus by a neighbouring right. There are no special prerequisites for protecting a performance (for example, the performance does not have to be original or creative).[18]

Apart from copyright, whose protection is granted without the need for registration, all the other forms of intellectual property need to be registered in order to obtain protection. The registration of all forms of intellectual property takes place at the DRCOR of the Republic of Cyprus.

Cyprus has been a Member of the European Union since 2004 and all EU supranational IP rights are applicable to Cyprus. Cyprus is also member of the EPC and of the Patent Cooperation Treaty (PCT). There are no supranational IP rights in relation to copyright and related rights. As regards interferences between national and supranational IP rights concerning patents and trademarks, the IP laws of Cyprus provide several rules, discussed below.

2 Categories of Security Rights Over IP in Cyprus

Under Cypriot law, it is recognized, at least in theory, that any asset, tangible or intangible, may be taken as a security right to secure any commercial transaction allowed by law. This asset may be mortgaged, pledged, charged, assigned, made subject to a lien, or otherwise encumbered. At this point and for the purpose of establishing the status of IP rights in terms of property type, it is essential to indicate that under Cypriot law, there is no express indication describing what category the aforementioned rights may be fall into. IP rights are intangible (i.e. incorporeal) property and are not a chose in possession, but a chose in action. This means that intellectual property cannot be physically possessed.[19] In light of the continental law division between movable and immovable property, intellectual property shall logically fall within the category of movable property, even if there is not a uniform definition of what movable property can consist of under Cypriot law. Indeed, "movable property" can have several meanings depending on the statute, while "immovable property" has the same definition and is duly defined in all statutes using the meaning given by section 2 of the Immovable Property (Tenure, Registration, and Valuation) Law, Cap. 224, as amended. So, the Compulsory

[16]See: Supreme Court of Cyprus, *Socratous v. Gruppo Editoriale Fabbri – Bompiani and others, (1997).*

[17]Section 3(3)(a) of Law No. 59/1976.

[18]See: Synodinou and Jougleux (2010), pp. 15–20.

[19]Bridge (2002), p. 5.

Expropriation (Amendment) Law of 1962 (No. 15/1962), as amended, defines "movable property" as any type of tangible object that is not immovable property and it includes all of the rights or interests in such objects. Furthermore, the Trustees Law, Cap. 193, as amended, indicates that "movable property" means any property of any description that is not immovable property. The only statute that explicitly refers to IP rights as property is the recent Leasing Law of 2016 (No. 72(I)/2016), which indicates that "property" means movable or immovable property, including intellectual property rights, that is subject to leasing. Moreover, Cyprus' Copyright Laws 1976 to 1993 (No. 59/1976), as amended, section 12(1) describes copyright as movable property.

The Cypriot legal system is a mixed one with a strong Common Law influence, but also a significant continental law influence in relation to certain legal domains, one of these domains being land law.[20] In this context, mortgages can be acquired only in relation to land and not in relation to moveable or intangible property.[21] Indeed, IP rights cannot be mortgaged under Cypriot law, since such a security interest would only involve legal interests created over immovable property, not immovable property. An exception to this principle would be the registration of a mortgage on an aircraft or ship; however, such a security interest is expressly defined in the relevant laws involving such property. There is no statute or case law known to the authors of this chapter that involves the possibility of mortgaging IP rights.

Generally, the most common types of security devices given for movable property in Cyprus are a registered charge; pledge; floating charge over the asset or assets in question; assignment; and common law lien. As will be explained below, regardless of the theoretical approach concerning the application of such interests to movable property, there are practical difficulties in the actual registration and enforcement of security interests over intangible property such as IP rights.

2.1 Common Law Lien

A common law lien applies were a creditor retains possession of the movable property belonging to the debtor until the amount due has been paid. This right will not give the right to the creditor to sell or otherwise make any other transaction with the property and the lien will be eliminated if the creditor gives away possession of the property. A lien over movable property will not create a cause of legal action; rather, it will be grounds for defence against a lawsuit.[22] Immediately, the question arises as to how intangible assets such as IP rights may be "possessed" by a creditor

[20]See on this issue: Synodinou (2013).

[21]In contrast, under UK law, it is possible to mortgage certain intangible assets, since a broad definition of is given for the term "mortgage". For example, section 30 of the UK Patents Act 1977 provides that any patent or patent application may be mortgaged.

[22]See on this issue: Poetis (2012), Chapter B.

by virtue of a lien. For example, it has been argued successfully that architects have a lien over their architectural drawings, should a client decide not to pay the architect's fees. It has also been established under Cyprus' Copyright Laws 1976 to 1993 (No. 59/1976), as amended, that, pursuant to section 3(1)(a)(iv), works of architecture are protected as artistic works. Having said that, it must be decided that the lien over the architectural drawings must cover the means by which the drawings will be delivered (i.e. printed copy or otherwise) per se and not the right over them. In other words, the copyrightable right over the drawings cannot be transferred in any physical sense; hence, no lien right would be applicable to it. Similarly, the English courts (which have a persuasive authority in the Cypriot legal system) in *Your Response Ltd v Datateam Business Media Ltd [2014] EWCA Civ 281*, which concerned an electronic database that is also copyrightable, affirmed the above approach by deciding that a service provider of an electronic database cannot exercise a common law lien over the database in relation to his outstanding fees. The structured information contained in a database (i.e. the intangible part of the right) is not treated as property and thus it is not possible to transfer possession in any physical sense. The case in question concerned the application of a common law lien over a database in the absence of any contractual provisions. On that point, the Court noted that transfers of intangible property, in electronic or other forms, are usually covered by contracts that may, if the parties wish, expressly provide for liens. In view of the above and in the absence of any case law from a Cypriot court or any express statutory provisions to the contrary, we are of the opinion that common law liens cannot be exercised over intangible property (i.e. over IP rights).

2.2 Pledge

In the same vein as above, a pledge is a security right that requires possession of the property in question and grants the right of possession (but not any right of ownership) to the pledgee (i.e. the creditor) until the pledgor's obligation has been performed. Cyprus' Contract Law, Cap. 149, as amended, section 130, describes a pledge as the bailment of goods as security for the payment of a debt or performance of a promise. Section 106(1)(a) describes "goods" as every kind of movable property and includes bills of exchange; promissory notes; bonds (whether in customary form or not), other than those secured by a mortgage of immovable property; and share certificates or share warrants for shares in a company. The difference between the lien and the pledge is that the pledgee (i.e. the creditor) has the additional right to retain the goods pledged as collateral or to sell the goods for the amount owed to him.[23]

Again, a pledge requires possession of the property; therefore, this right cannot be exercised over IP rights as they are and is limited to the physical medium on which

[23] *Pothonier v Dawson (1816) Holt N.P.383.*

an IP right is recorded and/or stored. In other words, IP rights will not be regarded as property or "goods" in order for a pledge to be used as a security right.

Bearing in mind the above difficulties concerning the creation of a pledge of IP rights, it is common for intellectual property companies (of any kind or type) to incorporate a separate private limited liability company as a subsidiary or, depending on the preferred structure, as a holding company. Then, they assign all of their IP rights to the newly incorporated company. This new company, having only IP rights as assets, will provide an exclusive licence to the original company for its entire portfolio. With this structure, the new company will be able to pledge its shares to a banking institution to obtain financing, if needed. The pledge of share certificates is expressly allowed by Cyprus' Contract Law, Cap. 149, section 138(d).

2.3 Assignment: Licence

Assignments involve the complete transfer of the title of ownership of a property as part of a transaction and by way of providing security to a third person. Assignment by way of providing security to a creditor will involve the transfer of rights and the benefits over these rights to the creditor, with the debtor reserving his right to claim back his property upon repayment of his obligations.

There is no doubt that the IP rights in question (i.e. copyright, trademarks, and patents) are to be regarded as "property of the creator," which means the inventor—a legal or physical person. Having said that, Cyprus' Copyright Laws 1976 to 1993 (No. 59/1976), as amended, section 12(1) indicates that copyright shall be transferable as movable property through assignment, testamentary disposition, or operation of law. Furthermore, in section 12(5), it is mentioned that such assignment or the granting of any licence for a copyright must be in writing in order to be valid.

Although it is not explicitly mentioned in the main body of the statute under a separate heading, Cyprus' Patents Law of 1998 (No. 16(I)/1998), as amended, will allow for assignment in a more or less conclusive way. The owner's proprietary interest is recognized in section 27(1), which stipulates that the owner of the patent shall have the right to prevent third parties from performing without his authorization a number of actions. Concerning the assignment procedure, section 3(2) indicates that the Registrar's "register shall include such matters constituting or relating to the patent as are prescribed and entries of all corrections, amendments, assignments, transmissions or other matters that the Registrar is empowered or required by this Law to record." Moreover, Cyprus' Patent Law Regulations of 1999, as amended, Regulation 5(2) provides that for an assignment agreement to be allowed to be submitted to the Registrar, then the patent registration number must be visible, as well as the date that the ownership of the patent will change and the names and signatures of the assignor and the assignee. At this point, it must be clarified that no additional details will be required by the Registrar, nor will it be necessary to provide the financial aspects of the assignment or the purpose for which the assignment is taking place.

As for trademarks, Cyprus' Trade Marks Law, Cap. 268, as amended, section 57 (2) indicates that "equities in respect of a trade mark may be enforced in like manner as in respect of any other personal property." Moreover, section 3(1) states that the Trade Marks Registrar shall keep a register with all registered trademarks, together with "the names, addresses and descriptions of their proprietors, notifications of assignments and transmissions, the names, addresses and descriptions of all registered users, disclaimers, conditions, limitations, and such other matters relating to the registered trade marks as may be described." Consequently, according to section 24 (1), "[n]otwithstanding any rule of law or equity to the contrary, a registered trade mark shall be, and shall be deemed always to have been, assignable and transmissible either in connection with the entire or the remainder goodwill of a business or otherwise." In this respect, "where a person becomes entitled by assignment or transmission to a registered trade mark, he shall make application to the Registrar to register his title, and the Registrar shall, on receipt of the application and on proof of title to his satisfaction, register him as the proprietor of the trade mark in respect of the goods or services in respect of which the assignment or transmission has effect, and shall cause particulars of the assignment or transmission to be entered in the register."[24]

It is worth mentioning that the Law makes a distinction between the assignment of a trademark with its goodwill and the assignment of the trademark rights only. Therefore, should a trademark be assigned, then this factor must be clearly mentioned in the application.

Again, as with patents above, the Registrar will not assess in detail the transaction between the assignor and the assignee or the licensor and the licensee. The assignment agreement may be limited, mentioning merely that the consideration for the transaction was a "fee," and it only needs to include the involved party names and the trademark details. Likewise, should a trademark owner decide to give a licence to third party, then the affidavit ("case report") accompanying the application only needs to refer to the involved party names; their details; the trademark in question; and the classes involved in the licence, together with its nature and duration. No further details are required, nor does any agreement need to be attached (save where such an agreement is mentioned in the affidavit above).[25]

In view of what is mentioned above, it appears that, at least theoretically, all three IP rights may be used to secure an obligation through an assignment and/or licence. For example, a trademark may be assigned by way of security to the creditor and in turn the creditor may license the right to use the trademark back to the debtor until full repayment is made.

Despite the possibility of using the assignment/licence scheme to provide security for an obligation, it is very rare if not unlikely for a banking institution in Cyprus to proceed with this scenario. A reason for this might be the fact that the laws and

[24] Section 24(1) Trade Marks Law, Cap. 268.

[25] As for assignments, the relevant provisions in terms of procedure are Regulations 64–73 of the Trade Mark Regulations of 1951–2015; in regard to licences, see Regulation 86.

regulations governing the abovementioned IP rights do not provide Cyprus' Intellectual and Industrial Property Authority with the means to record a creditor's security interest over a registered IP right in the actual register and/or in the official IP rights folder. It is also implicit that under Cyprus' Copyright Laws 1976–1993, copyright protection is automatically created and there is no means of registering this right; thus, there is no way to register a potential security. Moreover, Cyprus' register of registered IP rights will not indicate to an interested third party whether the IP right in question is being used as a security for credit facilities or for any related transactions. It is noted that according to Cyprus' Intellectual and Industrial Property Authority, no request to enter a record under this scheme has ever been recorded by a perspective creditor.

2.4 Charges

A charge over IP rights is created when the owner agrees to give to a creditor a right in the IP rights in question as security for a loan or other obligation. The IP rights will basically remain charged until the repayment of the loan or discharge of the obligation. Depending on the type of the charge, the owner may be able to deal freely with the IP rights until the charge "crystallizes" for the benefit of the creditor.

Under Cypriot law, security can be taken over future or exchangeable assets through an equitable fixed or floating charge. While fixed charges restrict the freedom of the security provider (i.e. the chargee) in the sense that he cannot dispose of the charged asset, floating charges usually give the chargee complete freedom to dispose of the charged asset.[26] A charge will not result in the granting of a proprietary interest over the property, but it will allow the chargee (i.e. the creditor—the person in whose favour the charge has been granted) to acquire the property for the purpose of recovering any amount due. Charges over IP assets must be in writing in order to be valid.[27] There are no statutory or common law requirements in relation to the wording of a charge, but it is prudent to expressly mention that the IP is charged as a continuing security for the loan and other obligations set out in the underlying financing documentation.[28]

The legal basis for creating a charge is found in Cyprus' Companies Law, Cap. 113, as amended, section 90, where it is stated that every charge, every assignment thereof, and every amendment or change to the particulars of the charge or the assignment thereof that is "created after the fixed date by a company registered in the

[26]Worthington (2010), pp. 1–10.

[27]Halsbury's Laws of England (1996), §§ 824, 825, 827 and 830. See also: Marios Kallias as the Receiver and Manager of companies PAK Estates Limited and Andri Georgiou (Coiffure) Limited v 1. Antri Georgiou and others, Case No.: 3587/2010, Court of First Instance, District Court of Nicosia, 16/07/2010.

[28]Bromfield and Runeckles (2006), p. 344.

Republic and being a charge to which this section applies shall, so far as any security on the company's property or undertaking is conferred thereby, be void against the liquidator and any creditor of the company, unless the prescribed particulars of the charge [and every assignment thereof] together with the instrument, if any, duly stamped [. . .] are delivered to or received by the registrar of companies for registration [. . .] [within the prescribed period]."

The above section is duly applicable to the creation of a charge "on [a company's] goodwill, on a patent or a licence under a patent, on a trade mark or on a copyright or a licence under a copyright" (section 90(2)(g), Companies Law, Cap. 113).

As for the validity and thus the legality of the certificates and/or the information provided by the Registrar of Companies of Official Receiver concerning any related matter, Cyprus' Evidence Law, Cap. 9, section 35 provides that "A document which is publicised as part of a public or ecclesiastical registry may be admissible as evidence without any need to provide further evidence." For the purposes of this Law, "public authority" means any governmental department and "registry" means any registry in any format.

Moreover, pursuant to Cyprus' Companies Law, Cap. 113, section 365 (3), "[a] copy of, or extract from, any document kept and registered at the office for the registration of companies, certified to be a true copy under the hand of the registrar or other officer duly authorised by him (whose official position it shall not be necessary to prove), shall in all legal proceedings be admissible as evidence as of equal validity with the original document."

Upon the registration of the charge pursuant to section 90 of Cyprus' Companies Law, Cap. 113, the Registrar of Companies shall issue a certificate "of the registration of any charge registered pursuant to this Part, stating the amount thereby secured, and the certificate shall be conclusive evidence that the requirements of this Part as to registration have been complied with." (Cyprus' Companies Law, Cap. 113, section 93(2)).

Although the creation of such a charge is expressly allowed by law, creditors and/or banking institutions in the Republic of Cyprus rarely use IP rights as the sole security for granting credit. Nonetheless, when used in this way, this category of security right (which includes the floating charge discussed below) is the most common and will typically involve trademarks and patents. As for copyright, to the extent of the filing Registrar's knowledge, no such charge has ever been recorded.

The possibility of setting up a floating charge over a company's assets, including any IP rights, will be thoroughly discussed in Question 5 below.

As a general comment, it must be pointed out that IP rights are not given sufficient attention and/or value so that prospective creditors (which are mostly banking institutions) can rely on them to secure an obligation. Although this is not a common transaction, the day-to-day workings of Cyprus' Registrar of Companies has shown that when IP rights are used as a security right (outside of any of the other bilateral agreements mentioned above between IP right-holders and creditors), such a security will take the form of a charge (most often a floating charge).

As described earlier, the legal basis for the creation of a floating charge stems from the Companies Law, Cap. 113. This raises the question whether charges can be created over the property of individuals. This question has regretfully not been answered by either Cypriot law or the Cypriot courts. However, if they were to offer a response to this question, it seems as though it would be suitable to refer to the practice followed in England, as English courts have not recognized a floating charge over the assets of an individual.

This refusal to recognize such a floating charge is not related to the differences between the nature of a company and that of an individual; instead, the reasons are technical, relating to the language of the Bills of Sale Act 1878, as amended. Indeed, as per Shalom Lerner "*Under this Act, a debtor who charges personal chattels must provide a detailed description of the charged assets. The Act does not apply to charges created by companies. This enabled the Courts of Equity to recognize a company's debenture, even if the chattels were only generally described in the debenture instead of specifically described as the Act requires. As mentioned, in order to create a charge over the assets of an individual, the individual must annex to or write on the bill of sale a schedule containing an inventory of the personal chattels comprised in the bill. Therefore, an individual cannot create a floating charge over his assets*".[29]

Similarly, a floating charge is unlikely to award the same protection and have the same legal effects when it relates to the property of an individual.

Another related way to use an IP right is through leasing. Pursuant to the provisions of a relatively new Cypriot law—that is, the Leasing Law of 2016 (No.72(I)/2016)—and pursuant to a written agreement that is not a loan, a lessee (i.e. the person who uses the property) can obtain exclusive possession of a certain property (which can include an IP right) from the lessor (i.e. the owner of the property) in exchange for the payment of an agreed amount. This also gives the lessee the right to purchase the property while the leasing agreement or its renewal are in effect.

This is very encouraging and is likely the first time that IP rights have been expressly described as property in a Cypriot statute concerning a commercial transaction; nevertheless, it is the authors' opinion that this Law is mainly directed at forms of (movable and immovable) property that are not IP rights.

3 Structure of Transactions

Cypriot law does not specifically regulate security interests over IP rights. Therefore, security over such rights will be governed by the general commercial law principles that govern security over intangible movable property. Hence, IP rights, to the extent that this is compatible with their nature, will be treated alike, as there are no specific

[29] Lerner (1998), p. 3.

securities that pertain to only one type of IP right. Thus, whether the security relates to a patent, trademark, or copyright (either registered and unregistered), the available transactions are the same and can be divided into two main categories: (1) those where the IP rights alone constitute the security for financing, and (2) those where the IP rights form the collateral for the financing together with other rights or assets.[30]

The former category includes the following transactions[31]: (i) assignments, (ii) licences, (iii) fixed charges, and (iv) joint ownership. The latter category, on the other hand, includes floating charges on all of the assets of a company. As mentioned above, there are additional security transactions available for movable tangible property, such as the pledge or possessory lien, but Cyprus, in line with English Common Law, does not make security interests that require the security taker to have possession of the secured asset available for IP rights.

We shall now examine transactions of the first category (i.e. where IP rights alone form the security).

3.1 Assignment

An assignment is an agreement for the transfer of the rights, title, and interest pertaining to all or part of the rights stemming from IP rights (with the exception of moral copyright, which, in line with English law, is non-assignable[32]). As indicated above, all IP rights can be assigned through an assignment agreement, which should specify the IP rights being assigned. The assignment may be permanent or limited to a specific period and it may be limited to some of the acts that the IP owner has the (exclusive) right to control. The content of the agreement is not specifically provided for by law; instead, the parties may freely negotiate and agree on the appropriate type(s) of security interest and the rights and obligations of the parties.

The validity and enforceability of the security will depend on the security agreement's compliance with the common law and with the provisions of the Contract Law, Cap. 149. An assignment operates as security in two ways: in combination with a charge or in combination with a licence agreement.

As regards an assignment in combination with a charge, a charge can be granted over any type of registered or unregistered IP and can either be fixed over a specific asset or float over all of the assets of a company. Although fixed charges are not common for IP, they are nonetheless a flexible tool as they grant to the lender a

[30]UNCITRAL Legislative Guide on Secured Transactions—Supplement on Security Rights in Intellectual Property, paras 35 et seq.

[31]Neocleous and Chrysaphinis (2018), pp. 11–15.

[32]Davies et al. (2010), Vol. 1, p. 192.

beneficial (but not legal) interest in the secured IP.[33] In such cases, the charge is signed at the same time as the loan agreement as a separate agreement between the lender and the borrower and/or guarantor, by virtue of which the IP is charged as continuing security for the loan and other obligations set out in the underlying loan agreement. The content of the charge may be freely negotiated between the parties, but ideally the charge will be granted with full title guarantee and the guarantee that the IP is free from any encumbrances, other charges, or other rights that are exercisable by third parties. In such cases, to facilitate the enforcement of the charge, the borrower will grant the lender power of attorney to enter into an assignment agreement with a third-party purchaser. Therefore, the lender will satisfy his claim against the IP holder through the sale and assignment of the IP. This structure could apply even without or separately from a charge, but in such cases, attention should be paid to the wording of the assignment to ensure that the assignment is contingent upon a default on the loan agreement.

As regards an assignment in combination with a licence agreement, an assignment agreement is signed between the lender and the borrower and enables the IP to be transferred to the lender. The lender in turn licenses the right to use the trademark back to the borrower. In such cases, the assignment agreement provides for re-assignment once full repayment has been made.

3.2 Licence

In addition to the abovementioned use of the licence agreement, this agreement can also be used on its own. In such cases, the borrower grants the lender an exclusive licence agreement for the duration of the underlying financing agreement so that the lender can monetise the IP and in so doing obtain profits for the repayment of the loan. The extent of such rights varies according to the wording of each agreement, but in most cases the lender is granted a revocable, limited, exclusive, non-transferable, non-assignable, royalty-free licence to use, reproduce, display, and commercially exploit the IP. Compulsory licences, which are available in a very limited manner according to the Patents Law of 1998, could be a hindrance to this right. To obtain a non-voluntary licence, one must demonstrate that the patent owner has been contacted, but that it has not been possible to get a licence from him within a reasonable time and with reasonable terms.[34] Furthermore, the applicant for a non-voluntary licence must prepare a plan demonstrating the need to use the licence.

[33]Bromfield and Runeckles (2006), p. 345.

[34]Markides (2009).

3.3 Fixed Charge

Charges do not award legal title to the lender; rather, they only award beneficial title. In case of default, unless power of attorney to assign the IP has been granted to the lender, the most appropriate remedy is to appoint a receiver who takes control of the property for the purpose of selling it, satisfying the debt, and handing the balance, if any, over to the lender. A provision for the appointment of such a receiver should be included in the agreement creating the charge.

3.4 Co-ownership

In such cases, the investor finances the development of the IP in exchange for co-ownership. Co-ownership therefore awards both the lender and the borrower proprietary shares in the IP. Co-ownership can result from the assignment of IP rights to two or more persons. According to Cypriot law, collective ownership of property takes the form of "tenancy in common," whereby each owner owns an undivided share of the property.[35] Under Cypriot law, co-owners have the following rights[36]: (i) right to unlimited use at will: Each joint owner has the right to an equal, undivided share in the IP and the right to exploit the IP for his own benefit, without accounting for the other joint owners (ii) right to exploit: Each joint owner has the right to exploit their own IP right, but cannot do so in a way that is detrimental to the rights of the other joint owners (iii) right to transfer: each joint owner is entitled to license or assign his interest in the IP without the consent of the other co-owners.

One important issue regardless of which form of transaction is chosen is the issue of accurately evaluating the IP value. The valuation process is a subjective area involving a high degree of technical complexity. To choose the best suitable valuation process, one must cross-check all of the approaches and obtain expert legal and valuation advice, as it is likely that IP valuations will be challenged. Consequently, the experience and credibility of the value will be of paramount importance.

[35]IPR Helpdesk (2009).

[36]See Demetriades (2016), p. 75.

4 Creation and Perfection of Security Transactions Over IP Rights in Cyprus

The conditions for the validity of security transactions over IP rights are set out in the Cypriot Contract Law, Cap. 149, which in general governs the conditions for contracts' validity. According to this Law, each of the above agreements has to be made with the free consent of parties who are competent to contract for a lawful consideration and with a lawful object and also has to be made in such a manner that it is not declared void under sections 24-30 of the Cypriot Contract Law, Cap. 149. From the Contract Law, Cap. 149, we can deduce that there is no need to record a security interest in a register as it is considered to exist upon its creation and is effective against third parties.[37]

Below, we shall examine whether there are any specific conditions for validity or for the registration of the transactions that have already been mentioned.

4.1 The Validity of Assignments

4.1.1 Assignment of Patents

As stated above, the assignment of a patent refers to the patent holder's transfer of the rights of the patent, either wholly or partially, to the assignee, who acquires the right to make use of the patent and to bar others from making, using, or commercially exploiting the invention.[38] "The assignment can be either exclusive or [non-exclusive]. The exclusivity can be further limited, for example exclusivity to a territory or market or line of products." The Patents Law does not specifically regulate assignment. Therefore, in the absence of provisions to the contrary, the assignment of a patent is created upon the conclusion of an assignment agreement, which should be in writing as it is filed with the register of patents. Following the execution of the assignment agreement, it should be recorded with the Registrar of Patents. As per Patent Regulation No. 6(2), the following must be provided for such a registration[39]:

1) A request for recordal on the prescribed form;
2) A deed of assignment in Greek or with a Greek translation, signed by both the assignor and the assignee and mentioning "at least the serial number and date of

[37] WIPO/IP/FIN/GE/09/7 Annex 1 Geneva (2009), p. 144. https://www.wipo.int/edocs/mdocs/copyright/en/wipo_ip_fin_ge_09/wipo_ip_fin_ge_09_7_annex.doc.

[38] Chakravarty (2009), p. 515.

[39] Vernout et al. (2016), p. Cyprus-8.

the patent application or of the patent, the title of the invention and the names, addresses, nationalities, and signatures of the assignor and assignee"[40];
3) Power of attorney from the assignee; and
4) Payment of the fees.

4.1.2 Assignment of Trademarks

Registered trademarks may be assigned only by the registered proprietor through a written assignment agreement between the proprietor (i.e. the assignor) and the assignee, of their own volition. Such an assignment can take place with or without the goodwill of the business and in respect of all or part of the goods or services for which the trademark is registered.

In accordance with the Trademark Regulation No. 72 for the assignment and transfer of registered trademarks, the following must be provided for recordal[41]:

(1) A request for recordal on the prescribed form;
(2) An original or certified copy of the deed of assignment, signed by the assignor and the assignee;
(3) A power of attorney signed by the assignee; and
(4) Payment of the required fee.

It should be noted that until the certificate of the registration of the trademark has been issued, the trademark may be assigned. In this case, the assignment will be recorded, but the Registrar's certificate of the assignment will not be issued.

For certification marks, assignment can be completed only with the special consent of the Registrar. This provision intends to ensure that certification marks are not separately assigned to different persons, as the simultaneous use of the same or a similar mark by different persons in respect of the same goods or services would lead to confusion and deception.[42]

4.1.3 Assignment of Copyright

As stated above, the Copyright Laws 1976 to 1993 (No. 59/1976), as amended, allow for the assignment of copyright; however, for such an assignment to be valid, it must be in writing. Copyright is transmissible by assignment as movable property. An assignment of copyright may be limited so as to apply only (a) in relation to some of the acts which the copyright owner has the exclusive right to control, (b) for part of the period for which the copyright subsists, or (c) to a specified country or other geographical area. No particular form of assignment is required and there is no need

[40]Patent Regulations of 1998. http://www.wipo.int/wipolex/en/text.jsp?file_id=126101. Accessed Mar 29, 2019.

[41]Vernout et al. (2016).

[42]Kailasam and Vedaraman (2003), p. 465.

for a specific assignment agreement to be made between the parties; rather, the assignment may be part of any agreement or deduced from any document. Oral assignments are not valid. There is no need or way to register such an assignment.

4.2 *Validity of Licensing*

4.2.1 Licensing of Patents

There are no formalities linked to the validity of a patent licence, nor is there any provision relating to the recording of voluntary licences.

4.2.2 Licensing of Trademarks

The procedure for the licensing of a trademark is provided for in the Trade Marks Law and in the Trade Mark Regulations. Trade Marks Law section 29(1) provides that a third person, not the trade or service mark owner, "may be registered as a registered user [. . .] in respect of all or any of the goods or services in respect of which [the mark] is registered", subject to any conditions or instructions imposed at the time of registration. As per section 29(4) of the Trade Marks Law, for the proper completion of the registration of a person or firm as a registered user, the application for registration needs to be made by the trademark owner and the registered user of the mark together and it must be accompanied by "information, verified by Statement of Case and Statutory Declaration, which must state the following (in summary)[43]:

(1) particulars of the [licence agreement];
(2) the degree of control by the proprietor over the permitted use;
(3) whether the [licence will be exclusive];
(4) the mark or marks in respect of which the application is made;
(5) any conditions or restrictions proposed [. . .];
(6) whether the [licence] is to be for an indefinite or a limited period and, if the latter, its duration; and
(7) any other documents, information or evidence the Registrar may require."[44]

4.2.3 Licensing of Copyright

As indicated above, section 12 of the Copyright Laws 1976 to 1993 (No. 59/1976) provides that an exclusive licence of a copyright must be in writing to be valid. A

[43]Vernout et al. (2016).

[44]Neocleous (2013), p. 37-Cyprus.

non-exclusive licence to do an act that is controlled by copyright may be written or oral, or may be inferred from conduct. Similarly, as with assignments, there is no particular form requirement for licences.

4.3 Validity of Charges

As mentioned above, the registration of charges in Cyprus is regulated by the Companies Law, Cap. 113, sections 90(1) and 90(2) in particular. The aforementioned provisions provide the necessary procedures that should be followed for the registration of charges. Based on the provisions in sections 90(2) and 90(1), charges can encumber goodwill, a patent, a licence under a patent, a trademark, a copyright, or a licence under a copyright.

According to section 90(1), charges need to be registered with the Registrar of Companies, and failure to register such charges renders them invalid. In fact, such registration needs to take place within 21 days from the date of the charge's creation if the charge is created in Cyprus. If the charge is created outside of the Republic of Cyprus (this includes property situated outside of Cyprus), then the period of registration is extended to 42 days from the date of the charge's creation. The registration can be made either by the company whose IP has been charged or by any interested person. Finally, "every company is obliged to maintain at the registered office of the company a register of charges and include all charges with all the necessary details. In case an officer of the company [knowingly] and willfully authorises or allows the omission of any entry required to be made following the provisions of the Law, he/she will be liable to a fine of up to €427."[45]

4.4 Validity of Joint Ownership

Joint ownership is not a common practice in Cyprus. Instead, to achieve a similar effect, it is common to use a special purpose vehicle ("SPV") as the owner of the IP. The shares of the SPV are jointly held by the lender and the borrower and the rights of each shareholder are specifically provided for in the company's articles of association.

One contentious point between IP law and the law of secured financing is registration.[46] For example, under Cypriot law, copyright is not registrable and copyright protection automatically vests in the owner. Thus, security over copyright is not registered in Cyprus, as there is no copyright register in Cyprus.[47] But even in

[45]Chambers (2016).

[46]Campbell (2010), p. 533.

[47]Lipton (2011), p. 290, referring to England.

cases where IP law requires the registration of IPs and relevant registers exist, these registers are meant to document the creation of IP rights, not the registration of security rights over them as part of the owners' commercial dealings.[48]

Therefore, although Cyprus maintains registers of trademarks and patents, these registers are made for filing transactions (e.g. the creation, modification, and assignments of patents), and not for registering encumbrances. In fact, section 3 of the Patents Law of 1998 (No. 16(I)/1998), as amended, does not seem to grant the patents' Registrar powers to accept notice of such things and no relevant forms exist on the Registrar's website for this purpose. That being said, the assignment of patents is registrable.

Similarly, the Trade Marks Law, Cap. 268 provides for the registration of the creation, assignment, license, and transfer of trademarks but not for the registration of charges. Hence, the recordal of a security interest in IP has no effect upon its priority against later competing assignments.[49] As indicated above, charges are registrable and should be filed with the Registrar of Companies within a specific deadline to be valid. Additionally, to the extent that an IP right (regardless of the nature of this right) belongs to a Cypriot company, Cyprus' Companies Law, Cap. 113 provides that all charges created by a company over its assets must also be registered in its register of charges, which is part of the company's statutory books.[50] This reference to "charges" is very widely interpreted to refer to any form of encumbrance over the company's property. As the Law does not differentiate between tangible and intangible assets, charges over a Cypriot company's IP rights are registrable in the company's registry of charges as indicated above. Therefore, failure to carry out this registration would not invalidate the charge, but it would make the directors liable to a fine.

5 Priorities

As indicated above, except for charges, security transactions over IP do not operate as encumbrances in the traditional manner. Therefore, an assignment of IP rights has the effect of a transfer of the owner's rights, title, and interest in the respective IP rights.[51] Hence, once IP rights are assigned, they are alienated from the property of the assignor (i.e. the previous IP owner) and form part of the property of the assignee.[52] Thus, the bankruptcy or insolvency of the assignor will not have an impact on the assigned IP rights (to the extent that these were fully and validly assigned). In case of the bankruptcy or insolvency of the assignee, the IP rights will

---

[48]Campbell (2010), p. 534.

[49]WIPO/IP/FIN/GE/09/7 Geneva (2009), p. 144.

[50]Sections 98-100 of the Companies Law, Cap. 113.

[51]European IPR Helpdesk, Assignment of intellectual property rights.

[52]With the exception of moral rights in copyright, which remain with the author of the work.

be part of the assignee's property and will be distributed in accordance with the Bankruptcy Law, Cap. 5 or the Companies Law, Cap. 113. If this is a case of co-ownership, no priority rights are awarded, but the co-owners may be able to make an offer to buy the insolvent party's shares and interest in the IP from the liquidator or bankruptcy trustee.

We shall now examine the effects of insolvency on licences and charges.

In relation to licensing, regretfully, both the Bankruptcy Law, Cap. 5 and the laws pertaining to patents, trademarks, and copyright are silent on the effects of bankruptcy and insolvency. Hence, it is questionable whether a licence agreement will remain valid once the insolvency process starts. As Cypriot law is silent on this issue, the licence agreement entered into between the parties will be of paramount importance. It is common for such licence agreements to contain provisions giving either party the right to terminate the licence in the event of the other party's insolvency. Without such a provision, it must be stated that the appointment of an administrator or liquidator will not in itself lead to the termination of a licence, as the effect of administration or liquidation is that the person who has become insolvent is no longer able to administer his property on his own, but the commercial agreements may be continued by the administrator or liquidator. In fact, a licence will only automatically terminate upon the insolvency of the licensee, rather than that of the licensor.[53] In case of the licensor's bankruptcy or insolvency, it is likely that the liquidator or bankruptcy trustee will endeavour to sell the IP right as a going concern, although nothing bars the liquidator or bankruptcy trustee from terminating the IP licence.

Insofar as charges are concerned, the following chain of priority applies when an order for distribution of assets has been issued[54]:

- actual expenses and the remuneration of the liquidator
- rights of the liquidator
- expenses of the applicant creditor
- priority debts such as government taxes, duties, etc.
- note holders of floating charges
- unsecured debts
- any deferred debts

Thus, holders of floating charges will be satisfied before any unsecured creditors, while among the various holders of charges, the priority of earlier registration can be invoked against subsequent registrations and the charge that was registered first will prevail against later charges.

[53]Worden and Smyth (2013).

[54]Sections 291 and 300 of the Companies Law, Cap.113.

6 Floating Charges in Cypriot Law

Cypriot law allows for a floating charge to exist over a company or a company's assets.[55]

In brief, a floating charge is a type of a security interest which "floats" over the related (present or future) assets of a company until an event of default occurs or until the company enters into liquidation.[56] At that point, the floating charge "crystallizes"—in other words, it becomes attached to all of the assets in question. It basically offers the secured creditor the remedy of realizing any assets subject to the charge (as if this had been a fixed charge from the beginning) and, if the floating charge covers all of the assets of the company, of appointing a receiver and a manager, and taking control of the company's business with the purpose of eliminating the debt. Should the assets of the company include IP rights, then the creditor via the receiver will be able to manage and/or sell those rights with a view to discharging and/or limiting the debt.

The floating charge was described in Halsbury's Laws of England, as follows: "*The terms 'floating charge' and 'floating security' mean a charge or security which is not to be put into immediate operation, but is to float so that the company is to be allowed to carry on its business. It contemplates, for instance, that book debts may be extinguished by payment, and other book debts may come in and take the place of those which have disappeared. While a specific charge is one which without more, fastens on ascertain and definite property or property capable of being ascertain and defined, a floating charge moves with the property which it is intended to affect until some event occurs or some act is done which causes it to settle and fasten on the subject of the charge within its reach and grasp. It is of the essence of a floating charge that it remains dormant until the undertaking charged ceases to be a going concern, or until the person in whose favour the charge is created intervenes. His right to intervene may be suspended by agreement, but if there is no such agreement, he may exercise his right whenever he pleases after default.*"[57]

Moreover, as to the effect of a floating charge, it is stated in Halsbury's Laws of England that: "*A floating security being only a charge on the assets for the time being, the company may in the ordinary course of business, unless it is otherwise agreed and until the security becomes fixed, sell, let, mortgage, or otherwise deal with any of its assets, and pay dividends out of profits, just as if the floating charge had not been created. Where a company has created a floating charge on its undertaking and assets and has reserved power to mortgage its property, it cannot in general create another general floating charge over all the assets to rank in priority to or pari passu with the first floating charge; but where the company has*

[55] Section 90(2)(d) of Companies Law, Cap. 113.

[56] See: *Re Yorkshire Woolcombers Association ([1903] 2 CH 28.*

[57] Halsbury's Laws of England (1996), § 824.

reserved power to charge specific assets, it may create a floating charge on those assets in priority to the general floating charge."[58]

Having said that, and as it is adamantly clear that IP rights are to be regarded as property which can be a part of a company's assets, it is thus possible for IP rights to be included in an agreement creating a floating charge.

The instrument creating the floating charge will normally refer to the assets included in the charge, the circumstances in which the floating charge will crystallize, and the right to appoint a receiver. As regards the assets covered by the floating charge, it is common practice for banking institutions in Cyprus to use wording that will cover the entire property of a company (whether present or future), including its goodwill, other intangible property, and any book debts, for an unlimited amount. This also includes interest, expenses, commissions, and other expenditures that the company might owe from time to time.

It must be mentioned that the reason why banks include the above wording in relation to "*[g]oodwill and other intangible property*" is merely a legal issue and nothing more: the banks merely intend to make it crystal clear that the assets involved in the floating charge will cover everything (i.e. both tangible and intangible property). In any case, even during the initial drafting of the agreement setting up the floating charge, banks do not usually have the intention of enforcing the charge against such types of property. This topic will be explained further below.

Upon calculating the value of a company for the purpose of creating a floating charge, a bank will take into consideration every aspect of the company, especially when the company in question is operating in a particular field or its stock has a limited market or industry. Nevertheless, pursuant to express guidelines set out by Cyprus' Central Bank,[59] goodwill and other intangible assets will be estimated as zero percent of the overall value of the charge. This means that, should the bank ever decide to enforce its rights under the floating charge, the company will be facing financial difficulties and thus at that point its goodwill will have no value at all.

As mentioned earlier, such charges will be void against the liquidator and any creditor of the company unless the required particulars of the charge, together with a duly stamped certified copy of the legal instrument creating the charge, are delivered to Cyprus' Registrar of Companies and Official Receiver within 21 days of the instrument's singing date.[60] If the agreement was concluded/signed outside of Cyprus, then the aforementioned deadline is extended to 42 days (no further extension will be given without a court order).

Although the Registrar might accept the agreement for submission if it is not duly stamped, it is highly advisable to always have the agreement stamped before Cyprus' Revenue Stamp Authority. The stamp duty for doing so is as follows. For agreements concerning an amount up to €170 000, then, excluding the first €5 000, the stamp duty is €1.50/€1 000. For an amount exceeding €170 000 then the stamp duty

[58]Halsbury's Laws of England (1996), § 825.

[59]The relevant document is unpublished.

[60]Section 92 of Companies Law, Cap. 113.

is €2/€1 000. Additionally, Form HE24E from Cyprus' Registrar of Companies must be submitted along with a fee which is calculated based on the security amount. For amounts of €0–€17 086.01, the fee is €140; for €17 086.01–€34 172.03, the fee is €240; for €34 172.03–€85 430.07, the fee is €380; for €85 430.07–€170 860.14, the fee is €540; and for €170 860.14 and over, the fee is €640. To fast-track the procedure, there is an additional fee of €20.

In regard to the priority given to a general charge holder, sections 89 and 300 of Cyprus' Companies Law, Cap. 113, as amended, are relevant.

Section 89(1) indicates that, "*[w]here either a receiver is appointed on behalf of the holders of any debentures of the company secured by a floating charge, or possession is taken by or on behalf of those debenture holders of any property comprised in or subject to the charge, then, if the company is not at the time in course of being wound up, the debts which in every winding up are under the provisions of Part V relating to preferential payments to be paid in priority to all other debts, shall be paid out of any assets coming to the hands of the receiver or other person taking possession as aforesaid in priority to any claim for principal or interest in respect of the debentures.*"

Section 300(1) states that "[i]n a winding up, there shall be paid in priority to all other debts": (a) "all Government [and local] taxes and duties due from the company [at the date of liquidation] and having become due and payable within twelve months before that date and, in the case of assessed taxes, not exceeding [...] one year's assessment"; (b) any salary plus benefits due to employees; (c) compensation payable as the result of an accident to employees; and (d) any other amount payable to employees.

A floating charge will then follow the abovementioned preferential debts.

The general rule is that, unless there is an agreement between the creditors to the contrary, charges over the same asset have priority over one another depending on the date and sometimes time of recordal by the Registrar. A fixed charge has priority over all other charges. It is self-evident that with the exception of preferential debts (as per section 300 above), all registered secured debts will have priority over unsecured debts. Similarly, should there be insufficient funds to cover such debts in full, then within each category of claim, creditors will rank equally and shall receive equal proportions.

At this point, it must be noted that section 303 of the Companies Law, Cap. 113 states that: "*Where a company is being wound up, a floating charge on the undertaking or property of the company created within twelve months of the commencement of the winding up shall, unless it is proven that the company immediately after the creation of the charge was solvent, be invalid, except to the amount of any cash paid to the company at the time of or subsequently to the creation of, and in consideration for, the charge, together with interest on that amount at the rate of five per cent per annum or such other rate as may for the time being be prescribed by order of the Accountant-General.*"

7 Rights Before Default

As mentioned above, the only genuine security interests over IP rights in Cyprus are fixed and floating charges, while assignments, licences, and joint authorship are ways of using IP by way of quasi-security rights. Since charges are created by contract, the obligations and the rights of the debtor and of the creditor should normally be defined in the contract. The debtor whose IP is charged with a fixed or a floating charge does not have the right to enforce or to enjoy the income/profit of the charged IP right prior to default.[61]

Depending on whether the charge is fixed or floating, the creditor will have less or more control over the IP asset. Indeed, preventing the debtor from freely disposing of assets that are subject to a fixed charge is an integral part of the nature of a fixed charge. In the case of IP, this could mean that the debtor should be prohibited from granting licences to third parties to use the secured IP rights without the consent of the creditor.[62] If such restrictions are not expressly stipulated by the parties, the charge might be interpreted by courts as being a floating charge.[63]

The floating charge does not attach immediately to the IP asset and it does not give the creditor control over the asset until the specific event of default occurs and the charge is crystallized. Thus, the debtor will continue his business as usual and will have freedom to deal with the IP asset, for example through the granting of licences.[64] In this context, the creditor can assign the IP asset to a third party and the latter will acquire it without the charge. The use and the commercialization of the IP asset through licensing can be subject to certain contractual restrictions agreed by the parties. The nature of a floating charge makes it unsuitable as a method of taking security over IP, since if contractual restrictions have not been agreed upon, borrowers can potentially sell off any commercially valuable IP at any time before the charge crystallizes.[65] Therefore, logically, the creditor may seek to place some restrictions and obligations on the debtor in order to ensure that the value of the IP asset is maintained. Usually, a balance has to be found between the interest of ensuring the value of the IP asset and the interest of taking into account the IP asset's real or anticipated commercial value. For example, a general obligation to maintain patents and patent applications without any right to allow unimportant patents to lapse or to abandon patent applications could have the consequence of unnecessary patenting costs being incurred. In this respect, the debtor would seek to reserve the right to allow trademarks and patents to lapse or to abandon them where there are reasonable grounds to believe that they are no longer of value.[66]

---

[61]Matheson et al. (2016), p. 7.

[62]Matheson et al. (2016), p. 3.

[63]See: *National Westminster Bank v Spectrum Plus Ltd [2005] UKHL 41.*

[64]Matheson et al. (2016), p. 6.

[65]Bromfield and Runeckles (2006), p. 345.

[66]Marshall and Caldwell (2014).

The debtor and the creditor can also agree in the contract that creates the charge (and/or in the contract of assignment, and/or in the licence) for the debtor to offer a warranty in case of the expiration, revocation, or annulment of IP rights that are subject to registration (i.e. patents, trademarks, and design rights) and in case a third party challenges the copyright ownership of the debtor.

8 Enforcement of Charges in Cyprus

This chapter will be limited to explaining the enforcement of charges only. The reason for this is that a charge is the only feasible type of security right that might be used in regard to IP rights by a creditor in Cyprus. The use of the assignment/ licensing scheme to secure an obligation will not require the enforcement of the IP right should there ever be a default, since the IP right in question will already be registered/owned by the creditor; thus, it will not be regarded as part of the debtor's assets.

Before explaining the enforcement of charges in situations outside or in insolvency, it must be noted that as regards the rights and obligations of creditors during the liquidation of a company, Cyprus' Companies Law, Cap. 113 adopts the same regulations as it does for insolvency procedures against physical persons.[67]

For this purpose, section 251(2)(a) of the Companies Law, Cap. 113 states that "*where a company is liquidated by the Court, any person who claims to be a creditor of the company, wishing to recover the debt owed to him, in whole or in part, must submit a prove of debt declaration before the liquidator within 35 days from the date of publication of the liquidation order in the official gazette of the Republic.*" Moreover, section 251(13) of the same statute clarifies that "*[i]f a secured creditor realizes his security, he may prove for the balance due to him, after deducting the net amount realized.*" In addition, "*[i]f a secured creditor surrenders his security he may prove for his whole debt as if he was an unsecured creditor.*"

In other words, if the amount owed to the secured creditor is covered by the security, then it would not be wise for this creditor to surrender his security and let himself be part of the unsecured creditors list. Generally speaking, if the security fully covers the amount owed to a secured creditor (with priority over other secured creditors of the same asset), then it will make no difference whether the company is outside or in liquidation.

In view of the above, it is once again noteworthy that when a floating charge is involved, this security interest will float over a specific asset or over all of the assets of the company (depending on the actual wording of the agreement) until an event of default takes place or until the company enters into liquidation.

Having said that, it is the authors' view that the enforcement of the charge will generally follow the same procedural rules; thus, for the purpose of this chapter,

[67] Section 298B of the Companies Law, Cap. 113.

there is no need to distinguish between cases of default outside insolvency and cases of default in insolvency.

In the vast majority of situations, a creditor with a charge over the assets of a company may appoint a receiver to basically take possession of the assets concerning the charge and discharge the debt from the proceeds. Should the security right be a floating charge covering the entire assets of the company, including goodwill and other intangible assets, then the creditor may appoint a receiver and manager to take possession of the company's business and applicable property; carry on the company's business; and sell any of its assets with a view to satisfying the debt.

Usually, the procedure for appointing a receiver will not involve a judicial review. In other words, the agreement creating the charge can allow a receiver to be appointed directly by the creditor of the company. Upon appointment of the receiver, the Registrar of Companies must be notified as per section 97(1) of the Companies Law, Cap. 113. The status of the receiver and manager was duly discussed in the case *Ninos Hadjirousos as the receiver of company Y. Liasides Developers Ltd* (2011) 1 JSC 1703,[68] where it was decided that a receiver and manager must be regarded as the representative of the debenture holder and thus of the creditor who appointed him. The appointment of the receiver will not affect the existence of the company or its legal status. The status of receivership must not be associated with liquidation; however, if the floating charge covers the company's assets, then the director's duties (not his status) will be suspended.

Despite the fact that there are no codified guidelines as to the way the receiver has to act during the receivership, section 337(1) of Companies Law, Cap. 113 states that "*a receiver or manager of the property of a company appointed under the powers contained in any instrument may apply to the Court for directions in relation to any particular matter arising in connection with the performance of this functions, and on any such application the Court may give such directions, or may make such order declaring the rights of persons before the Court or otherwise, as the case may be.*"

Case law in regard to the appointment, rights, and obligations of a receiver and manager is rather lacking; nevertheless, after the 2013 banking crisis in Cyprus, there has been quite a rapid increase of decisions by courts of first instance discussing this subject. In all of these decisions, the courts are following the guidelines laid down by English courts.

In relation to the enforcement of a charge concerning only IP rights by way of appointing a receiver, it has to be mentioned that such a case has never been recorded with Cyprus' Registrar of Companies and Official Receiver. Nevertheless, pursuant to the provisions of Cyprus' Companies Law, Cap. 113, it must be concluded that the procedures that need to be followed will be the same as with any type of property. However, due to the lack of precedent, the Registrar will first have to seek legal advice from Cyprus' Attorney General's Office.

---

[68] *Supreme Court of Cyprus, Ninos Hadjirousos as the receiver of company Y. Liasides Developers Ltd (2011) 1 JSC 1703.*

9 Costs and Practical Usefulness

The only types of security rights used over IP rights (among the overall assets of a company) are charges, pursuant to section 90(2)(g) of the Companies Law, Cap. 113, and floating charges, pursuant to section 90(2)(d) of the same law. Both types will involve submitting to the Registrar of Companies and Official Receiver the same form (HE24E), together with the legal instrument creating the charge in question. Again, the agreement shall be stamped as indicated in Question 5 above and the submission fees will follow the same scale.

The fees for enforcing a charge (including a charge over IP rights) cannot really be determined. Other than the very standard fees—such as for Registrar's Form HE35 for notification of the receiver's appointment (€20 + €20 acceleration fees), Form HE37 pertaining to the receiver's income accounts and payments (€20 + €20 acceleration fees), and, in the end, Form HE38 in regard to the discharge of the receiver (€20 + €20 acceleration fees)—one cannot predict what fees will be incurred due to situations that might arise during the receivership. It is very common during receiverships in Cyprus for receivers to bring legal actions against third parties (i.e. debtors of the company) or even to defend the interests of the company in lawsuits (as defendants). Moreover, there is very often the need to carry out bookkeeping tasks or perform audit checks. The employee factor is also a very important one, since most floating charges concern all assets in addition to the entire business, leaving no actual "managing" to the directors of the company. Such costs, which will also involve legal fees, cannot be calculated since every receivership is based on its own facts and data.

The receiver's fee for conducting his task is agreed between the parties (meaning the creditor and the receiver) and no fixed fee is applicable.

Unfortunately, there is no data for transactions concerning the provision of IP rights as security for an obligation. As indicated in another part of chapter, the most frequent security rights used by creditors are charges and floating charges (for movable property). However, this does not necessarily mean that IP rights are the essence of these security rights. On the contrary, the Charges Division of the Registrar of Companies has confirmed that IP rights are very rarely used as security rights.

It is the authors' opinion that it would be very difficult, if not impossible, for an SME to obtain credit by granting a security right over just an IP right. This is also supported by the fact that the guidelines issued by the Central Bank of Cyprus for banking institutions suggest that goodwill and other intangible assets must be valued at zero percent for the purpose of determining a loan amount. The whole situation would be different if, for example, a Cypriot pharmaceutical company, owning patented products in Cyprus and abroad, concluded several long-term licence agreements with distributors. But in this instance the creditor would not assess the value of the IP right per se, but the value of the contract in terms of the licence proceeds.

10 Legal and/or Practical Issues

In conclusion, the need to protect intellectual property rights is sadly not a priority for Cypriot businesses. The country also lacks heavy industry, which could increase the need to protect new and evolving technologies. However, Cyprus is a major exporter for several branded products and a considerable number of Cypriot companies do have a presence in various countries abroad. The surprising aspect of this is that, despite the fact that most of the exported products could involve IP rights, the companies in question do not make any effort to protect their interests from that perspective. In addition, through experience, it has been noted that although Cyprus is one of the most attractive jurisdictions in the world for setting up a so-called "intellectual property box tax regime,"[69] there is still no interest in involving IP rights in a more commercial way.

Security transactions over IP are not frequent in Cyprus and common practice seems to suggest that financial institutions are reluctant to grant financing on the sole security of intangible IP Rights. Indeed, in addition to the difficulties caused by the regulatory framework and the unclear evaluation process, using IP rights as security involves several inherent commercial risks. For example, the registration of either a trademark or patent is not undisputable proof of its validity, as the law allows for deregistration in various instances (e.g. following a challenge for non-use, a challenge for similarity after registration, etc.); in these cases, the creditor could even be found liable for damages for infringement.[70] It is to this end that for the vast majority of financing transactions, financial institutions will request multiple securities involving both tangible and intangible assets, mostly in the form of floating charges over the entire property of an enterprise. In this sense, IP rights can assist in granting security, but it is unlikely that only immovable property will ever suffice for securing financing. This is because of the transparency deficit concerning the valuation of IP rights and the non-developed registration system. It is because of these practical difficulties that "creditors are often hesitant in accepting information products as loan security, even if they are protected as 'property' under patent or company laws".[71]

As the law stands now, the Cypriot legislator has neglected to deal in detail with IP rights in general. The legislation, which was adopted several years ago, does not meet the needs and expectations of a modern commercial transactions system over IP.

To better safeguard investors' rights and promote the use of IP as security, the following suggestions could be taken into account.

---

[69]The intellectual property box tax regime or "IP box" can be regarded as a special tax scheme/regime that was introduced by several countries to promote research and development by taxing specific IP rights differently from other commercial income.

[70]Lipton (2011), p. 24

[71]Lipton (2000), p. 24.

First, a specific reference to the use of IP rights as an applicable form of security could be included only in the laws about registered IP. Since registration cannot be provided for copyright law, it would be inconsistent with the whole function of copyright to establish registration only when copyright is used a security.

The second suggestion has to do with the submission of agreements. While the law expressly provides for the registration of assignments, licences and joint ownership of trademarks, patents, and designs, this registration is limited to a mere reference to the existence of the transaction, without any legal requirement to submit the agreement itself. It would be wise for the law to require that the text of the agreement be submitted. However, due to the confidential nature of such transactions, access to this document should be restricted.

References

Bridge MG (2002) Personal property law. Clarendon law series, 3rd edn. Oxford University Press, Oxford

Bromfield V, Runeckles J (2006) Taking security over intellectual property: a practical overview. Eur Intellect Prop Rev 28:344–348

Campbell D (ed) (2010) Comparative law yearbook of international business, vol 32. Wolters Kluwer, Alphen aan den Rijn

Chakravarty S (2009) Importance of assignment agreements under intellectual property laws in India. J Intellect Prop Rev 14(6):513–522

Chambers M (2016) Registration of charges in Cyprus. https://www.chambers.law/registrations-of-charges-in-cyprus/. Accessed 29 Mar 2019

Davies G, Garnett K, Harbottle G (eds) (2010) Copinger and Skone James on copyright, 16th edn. London, Sweet and Maxwell

Demetriades D (2016) Cyprus. In: Howie M, Smith Freehills H (eds) The International Comparative Legal Guide (ICLG) to real estate 2016: a practical cross-border insight into real estate law, 11th edn. Global Legal Group, London

European IPR Helpdesk, Assignment of intellectual property rights. https://www.iprhelpdesk.eu/taxonomy/term/182. Accessed 29 Mar 2019

European Patent Office (EPO) (2015) National law relating to the EPC, European patent applications and patents: law and practice of the EPC contracting states, 17th edn. http://documents.epo.org/projects/babylon/eponet.nsf/0/18152865EA06F0C0C1257F62005E1E6D/$File/National_law_relating_to_the_EPC_17th_edition_en.pdf. Accessed 29 Mar 2019

Gödölle I (2009) Regional conference on the coexistence of the community and national trade mark systems in Europe. Budapest. http://www.hipo.gov.hu/English/RC/Godolle_I_text.pdf. Accessed 29 Mar 2019

IPR Helpdesk (2009) Joint ownership in intellectual property rights. http://www.innovaccess.eu/sites/default/files/jointownershipinintellectualpropertyrights_0000000649_00.xml.pdf. Accessed 29 Mar 2019

Kailasam KC, Vedaraman R (2003) Law of trademarks and geographical indications. Wadhwa and Company, Nagpur

Kur A, Dreier T (2013) European intellectual property law, texts, cases & materials. Edward Elgar, Cheltenham

Lerner S (1998) The registration of company charges against real property under Israeli law. In: Ziegel JS (ed) New developments in international commercial and consumer law: proceedings of the 8th Biennial Conference of the International Academy of Commercial and Consumer Law. Hart Publishing, Oxford, pp 205–228

Lipton JD (2000) Security over "Information Products". AIPJ 11:23–39

Lipton JD (2011) Security interests in intellectual property. In: De Lacy J (ed) Personal property security law reform in the UK: comparative perspectives. Routledge-Cavendish, London, pp 285–307

Lord Hailsham of St. Marylebone (ed) (1996) Halsbury's laws of England, Vol. 7/3, 4th edn. Butterworths, London

Markides H (2009) IP in business transactions: Cyprus. Thomson Reuter's Practical Law. https://uk.practicallaw.thomsonreuters.com/3-385-2707?transitionType=Default&contextData=(sc.Default)&firstPage=true&bhcp=1. Accessed 29 Mar 2019

Marshall J, Caldwell R (2014) Taking security over patents. TaylorWessing. https://united-kingdom.taylorwessing.com/synapse/march14.html. Accessed 29 Mar 2019

Matheson S, Osha J, Verschuur AM, Inui Y, Laakkonen A, Nack R (2016) Report for UK, study question (general) – security interests over intellectual property. In: AIPPI General Secretariat (ed) AIPPI Yearbook III (2016). AIPPI, Zurich, p 4

Neocleous A (2013) Cyprus. In: Arnold, Siedsma (eds) Manual for the handling of applications for patents, designs and trademarks throughout the world. Wolters Kluwer, Alphen aan den Rijn, Supplement No. 149

Neocleous E, Chrysaphinis G (2018) Cyprus. In: Campbell D (ed) International secured transactions. Thomson Reuters, Nicosia, Chapter 11

Opposition Guidelines (2004) Part 7, transitional rules relating to enlargement, http://euipo.europa.eu/en/mark/marque/pdf/part_7-EN.pdf. Accessed 28 Mar 2019

Poetis AP (2012) The right to a lien in Cyprus. Nicosia

Synodinou T (2013) Real property in Cyprus, in search of an identity. Jahreshefte der Internationalen Juristenvereinigung Osnabrück (IJVO) 18(2013):23–42

Synodinou T, Jougleux PH (2010) La propriété intellectuelle dans l'environnement académique: approche comparative du système légal français et chypriote. Nicosia

UNCITRAL Legislative Guide on Secured Transactions – Supplement on Security Rights in Intellectual Property. http://www.uncitral.org/pdf/english/texts/security-lg/e/10-57126_Ebook_Suppl_SR_IP.pdf. Accessed 29 Mar 2019

Vernout R, Kyriacou M, Livera R (2016) Cyprus. In: Arnold, Siedsma, Neocleous (eds) Manual on industrial property, Supplement No. 168. Kluwer Law International, Alphen aan den Rijn

Worden T, Smyth N (2013) The impact of insolvency on licensors and licensees in the life sciences sector. https://united-kingdom.taylorwessing.com/synapse/march13.html. Accessed 29 Mar 2019

Worthington S (2010) An "Unsatisfactory Area of the Law" fixed and floating charges yet again. Int Corp Rescue 7(4):1–10

Case Law

Marios Kallias as the Receiver and Manager of companies PAK Estates Limited and Andri Georgiou (Coiffure) Limited v 1. Antri Georgiou and others, Case No.: 3587/2010, Court of First Instance, District Court of Nicosia, 16/07/2010

National Westminster Bank v Spectrum Plus Ltd [2005] UKHL 41

Pothonier v Dawson (1816) Holt N.P.383

Re Yorkshire Woolcombers Association ([1903] 2 CH 28

Supreme Court of Cyprus, Ninos Hadjirousos as the receiver of company Y. Liasides Developers Ltd (2011) 1 JSC 1703

Supreme Court of Cyprus, Socratous *v*. Gruppo Editoriale Fabbri – Bompiani and others, (1997)

Your Response Ltd v Datateam Business Media Ltd [2014] EWCA Civ 281

Legal Acts

European Patent Office (EPO) (2015) National law relating to the EPC, European patent applications and patents: law and practice of the EPC contracting states, 17th edition, http://documents.epo.org/projects/babylon/eponet.nsf/0/18152865EA06F0C0C1257F62005E1E6D/$File/National_law_relating_to_the_EPC_17th_edition_en.pdf
Opposition Guidelines, Part 7, Transitional rules relating to enlargement, http://euipo.europa.eu/en/mark/marque/pdf/part_7-EN.pdf
Patent Regulations of 1998, http://www.wipo.int/wipolex/en/text.jsp?file_id=126101
Patents Law of 1998 (No. 16(I)/1998)
Protection of New Varieties of Plants Law 2004 (No. 21(I)/2004)
Recital 6 of the Community Trademark Regulation (CTMR)
Trade Marks Law, Cap. 268
Law No. 4(I)/2002
Copyright Laws 1976 to 1993 (No. 59/1976)
Appellation of Origin and Geographical Indications for Agricultural Products and Foodstuffs Law 2006 (No. 139(I)/2006)
WIPO/IP/FIN/GE/09/7 Geneva (2009)

Security Rights in Intellectual Property in the Czech Republic

Pavel Koukal and Helena Pullmannova

Abstract This chapter provides general information on the legal regulation of security rights over intellectual property under the law of the Czech Republic. The issue discussed is divided into two main parts.

The authors begin by providing a short overview of the national and EU protections for intellectual property and emphasize that the ability to use intellectual property assets as security is determined primarily by the transferability of the IP rights. Therefore, it is necessary to make a distinction between personal (moral) rights and economic rights, since only economic rights are transferable.

The authors conclude that under Czech law, the most relevant and commonly used security rights are the pledge; the transfer of a right as a security; and the prohibition against encumbrance and/or alienation. Furthermore, the authors discuss the creation, accessorial nature, and perfection of these rights. A few remarks are also made regarding the valuation of the intangible assets. Finally, the frequency with which security right transactions are registered by the Industrial Property Office of the Czech Republic is considered.

1 Overview of Intellectual Property Protection in the Czech Republic

In Czech law, the legal protection of intellectual property can be divided[1] into:

(A) Industrial property rights;
(B) Rights related to industrial property rights;
(C) Copyright; and
(D) Rights related to copyright and neighbouring rights.

[1] Vojčík (2012), pp. 33–35; Vojčík (2016), pp. 20–21; Telec (1994), p. 42.

P. Koukal (✉) · H. Pullmannova
Masaryk University, Faculty of Law, Brno, Czech Republic
e-mail: pavel.koukal@law.muni.cz; helena.pullmannova@law.muni.cz

E.-M. Kieninger (ed.), *Security Rights in Intellectual Property*, Ius Comparatum – Global Studies in Comparative Law 45,
https://doi.org/10.1007/978-3-030-44191-3_10

The protection of industrial property (e.g. patents, trademarks, and registered industrial designs) is generally linked to a formal act. These rights require the filing of an application, followed by registration in the industrial property register. In the Czech Republic, the application is filed with the Industrial Property Office in Prague (hereinafter "IPO" or "Industrial Property Office"). If a new plant variety is registered, the application is submitted to the National Plant Variety Office, which is a part of the Central Institute for Supervising and Testing in Agriculture seated in Brno.

Copyright, rights related to copyright, neighbouring rights, and the so-called "unregistered Community design" exist without the necessity of registration (for example, through the creation of a work of art or publishing of a design).

Intellectual property rights are rights of an absolute nature (*erga omnes*), as opposed to, for example, the right to the protection against unfair competition, which is a relative right (*inter partes*).[2] Intellectual property protection is limited to the territory of the Czech Republic (as per the principle of territoriality), with the exception of EU trademarks and Community designs, which constitute EU supranational protection and provide unitary protection within the whole territory of the EU.

With regard to the transferability of rights, intellectual property rights are divided into: (i) personal (moral) rights (the right to the attribution of authorship of the invention; the right to the attribution of authorship of the design; and the moral rights of authors and performing artists, such as the right to the attribution of authorship, the divulgation right, and the integrity right) and (ii) economic rights (patents, trademarks, industrial designs, the economic rights of authors, and rights related to copyright).

Personal (moral) intellectual property rights are not transferable. Economic rights are generally transferable. One exception is the economic rights of authors/ performing artists, which are not transferable during the life (*inter vivos*) of the author/performing artist but are inheritable [Art. 26 (2) of Act No. 121/2000 Coll., on Copyright and Rights Related to Copyright and on Amendment to Certain Acts, as amended; hereinafter "Copyright Act"].[3] They can be transferred only through a "constitutive transfer" (i.e. by granting a licence).[4] Another exception is the rights related to the so-called "collective trademark" (see further).

[2]Telec and Tůma (2007), p. 67; Koukal (2016), pp. 450–466.

[3]The English translation available at: http://www.wipo.int/wipolex/en/text.jsp?file_id=137175. Accessed Jan 10, 2019.

[4]The legal regulations regarding licence contracts are set forth in Art. 2358-2389 Civil Code (Act. No. 89/2012 Coll., Civil Code, as amended; the English translation available [online] at: http://obcanskyzakonik.justice.cz/images/pdf/Civil-Code.pdf. Accessed Jan 10, 2019). The Copyright Act is applicable as a *lex specialis* in relation to the Civil Code. "Copyright law forms, together with other rights to the results of intellectual creative activity and together with other special proprietary rights, a sub-system of substantive civil law". Decision of the Czech Supreme Court from 2007-04-30, File No. 30 Cdo 739/2007.

The effects of the transfer of industrial property rights are conditional upon the execution of the registration in the registry of the Industrial Property Office or National Plant Variety Office.

1.1 Copyright

Copyright law is governed by the first section of Copyright Act.

The duration of the moral rights of the author and that of the economic rights of the author are different.[5] The transferability of rights *inter vivos*[6] is expressly prohibited for both categories of author's rights. These rights cannot be affected by the execution of a decision [Art. 26 (1) Copyright Act]. Only the right to use the copyrighted work can be licensed to another person. However, claims arising from the exercising of economic rights (such as claims arising from licence agreements) can be transferred and might be subject to security rights without restrictions.[7]

The rules mentioned above also apply to the moral and economic rights of performing artists.

In contrast, the rights related to copyright (e.g. the right of the phonogram producer to his recording; the right of the audio-video producer to his recording; the right of the radio or television broadcaster to his broadcast; the publisher's right to a previously unpublished work whose property rights have expired; and the publisher's right to reward) are transferable [Art. 76 (5), Art. 80 (4), Art. 84 (3) Copyright Act] *inter vivos* and also *mortis causa*. Similarly, the database maker's right is transferable [Art. 90 (6) Copyright Act].[8] Therefore, these rights may serve as the subject matter of a security.

1.2 Trademarks

Trademarks are regulated by Act No. 441/2003 Coll., on Trademarks and on Amendments to Act No. 6/2002 on Judgements, Judges, Assessors and State

[5]Moral rights last only for the period of the author's life (limited post-mortal protection is vested to close relatives to the author, legal persons associated with the author, or the relevant collecting society [Art. 11 (5) Copyright Act]). Economic rights last for the period of the author's life and for 70 years after his death [Art. 27 (1) Copyright Act].

[6]The transfer of rights upon the death of the author (*mortis causa*) is permissible; the general rules of the inheritance law regulated by the Civil Code are fully applicable. Telec and Tůma (2007), pp. 314–315.

[7]Telec and Tůma (2007), pp. 157–158, 309–314.

[8]Telec and Tůma (2007), pp. 678–680, 689–690, 708–710, 732–734.

Judgement Administration and on Amendments to Some Other Acts (Act on Courts and Judges), as amended [hereinafter "Trademarks Act"].[9]

The trademark owner is endowed with exclusive economic rights (Art. 8 ff. Trademarks Act). Since trademark rights are of an economic (proprietary) nature (i.e. the Trademarks Act does not grant the owner any moral rights) only, they are freely transferable and can be the subject matter of security rights and/or be affected by the levy of execution (Art. 15, Art. 17 Trademarks Act).[10] A transfer of the trademark can be done independently from a transfer of the business enterprise for all or for selected classes of products/services for which the trademark has been registered [Art. 15 (1) Trademarks Act]. The trademark can also be licensed (Art. 18 Trademarks Act)[11]; however, collective trademarks are an exception (Art. 39 Trademarks Act).

1.3 Patents

The patent regulation can be found in Act No. 527/1990 Coll., on Inventions and Rationalisation Proposals, as amended (hereinafter "Patents Act"), and in the Regulation of the Industrial Property Office No. 550/1990 Coll., on Proceedings in Matters of Inventions and Industrial Designs, as amended.[12]

Patent rights as well as the right to a patent (i.e. the right to file a patent application) are fully transferable[13] (Art. 15 Patents Act), can be given as a security, and can also be licensed [Art. 14 (1) Patents Act].

1.4 Industrial Designs

Industrial designs are regulated by Act No. 207/2000 Coll., on the Protection of Industrial Designs, as amended (hereinafter "Industrial Designs Act").[14]

---

[9]The English translation available at: https://www.upv.cz/en/legislation/national/codes.html. Accessed Jan 10, 2019. The trademark legislation has been amended in 2019, depending on the implementation of Directive (EU) 2015/2436 of the European Parliament and of the Council of December 16, 2015, to approximate the laws of the Member States relating to trademarks.

[10]Horáček et al. (2015), pp. 160–167.

[11]Horáček et al. (2015), pp. 168–171.

[12]The English translation is available at: https://www.upv.cz/en/legislation/national/codes.html. Accessed Jan 10, 2019. Czech patent legislation is fully compatible with the principles contained in the European Patent Convention.

[13]Chloupek et al. (2017), pp. 137–140. However, the inventor's right of authorship of the invention is not waivable or transferable, given that it is a personal (moral) right.

[14]The English translation is available at: https://www.upv.cz/en/legislation/national/codes.html. Accessed Jan 10, 2019.

Even though industrial design protection also provides a personal (moral) right (namely, the right to the attribution of the authorship of the design; Art. 35 (2c) Industrial Designs Act) which is not transferable, the owner of the industrial design is not limited in the legal transactions that he can make in relation to the registered industrial design: he can freely transfer his rights, provide the registered design as a security, or grant a licence (Art. 30 to 32 Industrial Designs Act). The design rights can also be affected by the levy of execution [Art. 31 (2) Industrial Designs Act].

1.5 Supranational IP Rights

European trademarks registered according to Council Regulation No. 207/2009[15] on the Community Trade Mark, as amended by Regulation No. 2015/2424, and Community designs (both registered or unregistered) protected by the Council Regulation No. 6/2002[16] on Community Designs are objects of industrial property which exist independently of the national protection (Art. 96 Regulation No. 6/2002; Recital Nos. 7 and 8 Regulation No. 2017/1001). The European regulation is not a substitute for the national protection. The aim of the European protection is only to overcome the territorial limits of the national protection of trademarks and industrial designs within the EU.

The same is also applicable for the European patent, which is granted by the European Patent Office on the basis of the European Patent Convention. The European patent consists of a set of national patents that exist separately in individual countries where the European patent has been validated.

There will be a similar relationship between the national patent protection and the future concept of the uniform European patent regulated by Regulation No. 1257/2012.[17] This European patent with uniform effect will be independent of national patents [Recital 26, Art. 7 (4) Regulation No. 1257/2012].

Community designs, EU trademarks, and the European patent are all fully transferable and hence can be the subject matter of security rights.

[15]The English codified version has been promulgated by Regulation (EU) 2017/1001 of the European Parliament and of the Council of June 14, 2017 on the European Union Trade Mark. The English version is available at: http://eur-lex.europa.eu/legal-content/EN/TXT/?uri=CELEX:32017R1001. Accessed Oct 21, 2018.

[16]The English version is available at: https://eur-lex.europa.eu/legal-content/EN/ALL/?uri=CELEX%3A32002R0006. Accessed Oct 21, 2018.

[17]Regulation (EU) No. 1257/2012 of the European Parliament and of the Council of December 17, 2012 Implementing Enhanced Cooperation in the Area of the Creation of Unitary Patent Protection, available at: https://eur-lex.europa.eu/legal-content/EN/TXT/?uri=CELEX:32012R1257. Accessed Oct 21, 2018.

2 Categories of Security Rights Over Intellectual Property and the Structure of Secured Transactions

Intellectual property rights can generally serve as objects of security on the basis of contractual rights, both in the form of relative rights (i.e. obligations) and in the form of proprietary rights (i.e. rights in rem). However, only economic intellectual property rights can serve as objects of security rights. Personal (moral) rights, such as the right to the attribution of authorship of the copyrighted work or of the invention, are non-transferable and thus they cannot serve as the subject matter of security rights.

Even though economic rights are generally eligible to be the subject matter of security rights, this would not apply to economic rights of authors and performing artists that are not transferable. Therefore, the economic rights of authors and performing artists cannot serve as the subject matter of security rights because the Copyright Act prohibits their transferability *inter vivos* [Art. 12 (2) Copyright Act].[18] The same rule shall be applied *mutatis mutandis* to designations of origin, and geographical indications.[19]

Only the legal forms of protection (e.g. patents, industrial designs, trademarks, etc.) can serve as objects of security rights, not the intangible assets (i.e. inventions, technical solutions, designs, signs, works of art, or artistic performances) themselves. Even though the Civil Code is based on a broad concept of legal objects (Art. 496 Civil Code),[20] intangible assets cannot be transferred due to their intangible nature.

The Civil Code stipulates that "[a]ny marketable thing may be pledged" [Art. 1310 (1) Civil Code]. Absolute economic rights (e.g. trademarks, patents, and registered industrial designs) and possibly relative economic rights (i.e. claims) can serve as typical subjects of security rights. Both a licence contract (Art. 2358 ff. Civil Code),[21] as it is a "set of relative rights," and monetary claims arising from licence or franchising agreements can also be used as security.[22]

---

[18]Telec and Tůma (2007), pp. 169–170.

[19]Art. 2, 8, 23, and 24 of the Act No. 452/2001 Coll., on the Protection of Designations of Origin and Geographical Indications and on the Amendment to the Act on Consumer Protection, as amended. The English translation available at: https://www.upv.cz/en/legislation/national/codes.html. Accessed Oct 21, 2018.

[20]"(1) A corporeal thing is a controllable part of the external world having the character of an independent object. (2) Incorporeal things are rights whose nature allows it, and other things without corporeal substance" (Art. 496 Civil Code).

[21]Macek (2014), pp. 597–606; Koukal (2017), p. 1033.

[22]Telec and Tůma (2007), pp. 312–313.

The same conclusions apply for the supranational forms of IP protection (i.e. the EU trademark and the Community designs). EU trademarks or Community designs can be the subject matter of a security right, especially a pledge.[23]

Security rights are regulated in Czech law by the Civil Code. Security rights can be either proprietary or personal.[24] The security rights of a personal nature (i.e. suretyships, financial guarantees, and promissory notes), as well as those security rights which are only applicable to tangible movable assets (e.g. earnests, hand pledges, retention rights, or agreements on deductions from wages or other income), are irrelevant for intellectual property rights, and therefore will not be discussed any further.

The most relevant and most commonly used security rights are the pledge[25] (Art. 1309 ff. Civil Code) and the transfer of a right as a security (Art. 2040 ff. Civil Code). Since the new Civil Code entered into force (on January 1, 2014), a "prohibition to encumber or alienate a thing" can be also negotiated (Art. 1761 Civil Code).

The most frequently used form of security transaction involving intellectual property is a pledge (Art. 1309 ff. Civil Code). The transferable economic rights can only serve as a collateral (see the explanation above). The pledge is a security right that is absolute in nature and therefore is attached to the collateral (of a patent, trademark, registered design, etc.), even if it has been transferred. If the debt has not been repaid, then the pledge-holder[26] (pledgor) can sell the collateral.

Both cash and non-cash obligations can be secured by a pledge. As a general principle, a pledge on an industrial property right becomes effective upon the date of its registration in the appropriate register (for trademarks, patents, or industrial designs).[27]

When a debt is secured by a pledge, the pledgor is entitled to satisfy his claims from the sale of the pledged intellectual property right if the debtor fails to satisfy the debt properly and in due time [Art. 1309 (1) Civil Code]. The pledgee (i.e. the debtor) shall refrain from anything that could impair the collateral or cause the protection to expire. For example, the pledgee (i.e. the debtor) is required to keep the protection (e.g. patent, trademark, etc.) in force for the entire duration of the debt.

---

[23]Art. 29 of the Council Regulation (EC) No. 6/2002; Art. 19 of the Council Regulation (EC) No. 207/2009 as amended by the Regulation No. 2015/2424; Art. 22 of the Regulation of the European Parliament and of the Council No. 2017/1001.

[24]Kindl (2016), pp. 55–56.

[25]In this chapter, we use the following terminology: by "pledge" we mean the form of the security right, and by "collateral" we mean the subject matter that has been given as a security (such as a trademark, patent, or industrial design).

[26]We use the term "pledgor" to refer to the person who has the benefit of the pledge and is the creditor in the obligatory relationship with the debtor.

[27]Art. 17 (3) Trademarks Act; Art. 31 (1) Industrial Designs Act. The Civil Code provides the general rule that "a pledge on a right which is registered in a public register is created by the registration in this register, unless otherwise provided by another legal regulation" (Art. 1316 Civil Code).

Similarly, the debtor must refrain from anything that could jeopardize the existence of the legal protection. If the subject matter of the pledge is a trademark, the debtor must refrain from any activity which would lead to the trademark becoming generic and thus would allow the trademark protection to be challenged by third parties seeking revocation of the protection (Art. 31 Trademarks Act). If the debtor is a small entrepreneur or a consumer, it is not possible for the contracting parties to negotiate the forfeiture [Art. 1315 (3) Civil Code].

On the other hand, the pledgor has no statutory right to restrict the pledgee with respect to the transferability of the pledged intellectual property right. The law stipulates that for the transfer of the collateral, the consent of the pledgor is not required. As a result, we see that together with the establishing of the pledge, the contracting parties also generally agree on the special prohibition of the transfer (Art. 1761 Civil Code),[28] which gives the pledgor the explicit right to prevent the transfer of the pledged trademark.

For the "transfer of a right as a security" (Art. 2040 to 2044 Civil Code), the debtor or a third party temporarily transfers the right to the intellectual property rights to the creditor. A transfer of a right as a security is presumed to be a transfer with a "resolutive condition" that the debt will be discharged. If a transfer of a right as a security concerns an asset registered in a public register (i.e. the registers for patents, trademarks, or industrial designs), the temporary transfer of the right as a security is also registered there. Unless the debt is paid in time, the conditional transfer becomes unconditional and the transferee becomes the full, unlimited owner of the transferred right. However, transfers of a right as security are not frequently used in connection with intellectual property rights.

The last security right which is used in practice is the "prohibition to encumber or alienate a thing" (Art. 1761 Civil Code). Without the consent of the creditor, the debtor cannot transfer the right to the collateral, or the right to establish a security right over intellectual property rights. Since the pledgor has no statutory right to restrict the pledgee as regards the transferability of the pledged asset, the prohibition against alienation is usually set up at the same time that the pledge is established.

3 Collateral Valuation Methods

The subject matter of the pledge is valued by the general methods used for asset valuation. Even though the contracting parties may agree on the method of the valuation or even on the value of the trademark as such [Art. 1359 (1) Civil Code],[29]

[28]"A prohibition to encumber or alienate a thing has effect only between the parties, unless it has been established as a right in rem. Such a prohibition is valid if it has been established for the duration of a trust, succession by fideicommissum, representation or for another specific and reasonable period in such an interest of a party which deserves legal protection" (Art. 1761 Civil Code).

[29]Richter (2013), pp. 1115–1116.

the value must correspond to the price at which the asset would be sold at a given place and time under comparable circumstances, i.e. the "usual price" [Art. 1365 (1) Civil Code]. If insolvency proceedings have already been initiated, special rules apply (see below).

If the transfer of intellectual property rights as a security (Art. 2040 Civil Code) has been agreed upon, the law does not set explicit rules on the valuation of the subject matter of the secured obligation. It is therefore up to the contracting parties to decide how the asset should be valuated (the rule of the "usual price" must be applied as well).

For the valuation of debt-securing assets (i.e. trademarks, patents, know-how, trade secrets, designs, etc.), the general methods used for the valuation of intangible assets should be used. They are as follows[30]:

- The actual costs method;
- The purchasing costs method;
- The market price method[31];
- The income method, where the value is based on forthcoming income (royalties); and
- The selling analogy method,[32] which is based on comparisons with intellectual property transactions carried out in similar circumstances.

A crucial aspect for a precise valuation is the appropriate identification of the subject matter that is being valued (i.e. whether it is a trademark or a patent, who the owner is, the range of the absolute rights, the territorial scope of the protection, the duration of the protection, etc.).[33] If a patent is being valuated, we must pay special attention to the product quality and to the requirements of future investments (especially when pharmaceutical inventions are concerned). For a trademark, we must also focus on the actual duration of the protection in the past, consumer awareness of the trademarked products, the volume of advertising, etc.

The valuation is usually carried out by the expert. However, this is not a requirement prescribed by the law, with the exception of when intangible investments in the company's capital are to be valued.[34] In such cases, the intangible asset must be valued by any expert selected from a list of court experts.

---

[30]Svačina (2010), pp. 57, 76, 97, 134.

[31]"The market value is the estimated amount of money for which the asset would be possibly exchanged at the valuation date between the willing buyer and the seller, when both parties act freely and in an informed and reasonable manner."; Svačina (2010), p. 75.

[32]Svačina (2010), pp. 134–153.

[33]Svačina (2010), pp. 62.

[34]Art. 143, 251, 478, 573 Act No. 90/2012 Coll., on Business Corporations, as amended. The English translation available at: http://obcanskyzakonik.justice.cz/images/pdf/Business-Corpora tions-Act.pdf. Accessed Jan 10, 2019.

4 Registration of the Security Rights in the IP Registries and in the Pledge Register

The Trademark Register, Patent Register, and Industrial Design Register are public registers and therefore the transfer of rights and establishing of security rights must be registered in them. The setting up of a pledge, the transfer of a right as a security, and the prohibition against alienation or encumbrance are subject to the registration principle.

When a pledge on industrial property is established, the law stipulates that the pledge agreement has legal effects following its registration in the public register [Art. 17 (3) Trademarks Act, Art. 31 (1) Industrial Designs Act, Art. 1316 Civil Code]. In contrast to the legal regulations on the transfer of industrial rights or on the licencing of a trademark, industrial design, or patent,[35] the law does not explicitly distinguish between the *inter partes* and *erga omnes* effects of the pledge. For this reason, the pledge on industrial property rights takes effect either among the parties involved or against third parties upon its entry into the public register (Art. 1316 Civil Code). These findings apply to the transfer of a right as a security (Art. 2041 Civil Code) as well.

However, if a trademark is pledged as part of a business enterprise, the pledge is established through registration in the Pledge Register [Art. 1319 (2) Civil Code], not in the Trademark Register.[36] Subsequent registration of the pledge in the Trademark Register only has a declaratory effect.

This rule does not apply to industrial designs or patents. Registration in the Industrial Design Register or Patent Register has a constitutive effect and the pledge is created only when it is entered in either of these registers, not when it is entered in the Pledge Register. The legal regulations on trademarks differ from and the regulations on patents and industrial designs in this respect without any substantial justification or proper reasoning.

If a pledge is established on the royalties arising from licence agreements, the security right is created once the contract becomes effective [Art. 1335 (2) Civil Code]. The pledge becomes effective against the licensee from the moment that the pledgee (i.e. the licensor) notifies the licensee of its existence, or from the moment that the pledge is proven to the licensee by the pledgor [Art. 1336 (2) Civil Code]. If

[35] If industrial property rights are transferred, the contract is legally binding among the parties at the moment of the conclusion of the contract [Art. 1745, 570 (1) Civil Code]. However, the effectiveness *erga omnes* (against third parties) takes effect upon the registration of the transfer in the registry [Art. 14 (2), Art. 15 Industrial Designs Act; Art. 30 (1), Art. 32 (3) Patents Act; Art. 15 (3), Art. 18 (3) Trademarks Act].

[36] The pledge which is established on a set of assets or on a business enterprise arises on the basis of registration with the Pledge Register, which is maintained by the Notarial Chamber of the Czech Republic. The pledge must be in the form of a notarial deed [Art. 1314 (2) Civil Code]. The security does not exist until after registration. However, the Pledge Register is not a public register that is freely accessible to the public and that everyone can inspect.

the royalties have become due, the pledgor has the right to claim royalties directly from the licensee.

5 Priorities of Secured Creditors

When a right to an asset is registered in any of the registers for trademarks, industrial designs, or patents,[37] everyone is expected to be familiar with the existence of the secured right since ignorance of this registered information is not excused. If several pledges are set up on the same intellectual property right, the moment when they are submitted for registration [Art. 982 (1) Civil Code] determines their order. Similarly, when a pledge on intellectual property is entered into the public register, it takes precedence over any pledge or other security right that is not registered in the public register (Art. 981 Civil Code).

The order of the rights of secured creditors (Art. 981, 982, 2016 Civil Code)[38] is determined by (i) when each creditor began to claim his rights, and (ii) when the right to the secured asset was established. The order of the secured creditors is therefore as follows: (i) the creditors secured with a proprietary right (*right in rem*) that has been registered in the public register, (ii) the creditors secured with a proprietary right (*right in rem*) that has not been registered in the public register, (iii) the creditors secured with contractual collateral (secured rights *inter partes*), and (iv) unsecured creditors. Within each category, earlier rights have priority over younger rights. If a pledge was not registered in the public register (such as in the case where a trademark has been pledged as part of a business enterprise and the parties did not submit a request for registration in the Trademark Register), the pledgor whose right was registered in the public register would be in a better position since he would be preferably satisfied.

However, if insolvency proceedings have been initiated against the debtor, the special rules for insolvency proceedings stipulated by in Insolvency Act[39] would apply instead of the general rules contained in the Civil Code.

All creditors must enter the insolvency proceedings if they wish to satisfy their claims. Secured creditors who do not enter the insolvency proceedings within 2 months after the date that the court declared bankruptcy over the debtor's assets lose their right to satisfy their claims through the sale of the secured asset [Art. 167 (4) Insolvency Act].

If insolvency proceedings have been initiated, the order of the creditors is as follows: first, the so-called "priority claims"[40] (Art. 168 Insolvency Act) and the

---

[37]However, not in the Pledge Register, which is not considered to be a public register.

[38]Richter (2014), pp. 1252–1254.

[39]Act No. 182/2006 Coll., on Bankruptcy and Settlement, as amended (the English translation is not available).

[40]E.g. costs of insolvency proceedings, the remuneration of the bankruptcy liquidator, taxes, or fees.

"claims equal to priority claims"[41] (Art. 169 Insolvency Act) are satisfied by the bankrupt debtor's assets; next, the rights of secured creditors are satisfied. The order of the secured creditors in relation to a single secured asset (e.g. a pledged trademark) is determined by when their rights were created [Art. 167 (1) Insolvency Act).[42]

If the sale of the security is not sufficient to fully satisfy the debt owed to the secured creditor, the remaining debt is satisfied from the bankrupt debtor's other assets and the secured creditor is satisfied together with the unsecured creditors. If there is anything left over, it will be used to satisfy the subordinated claims (Art. 172 Insolvency Act).[43]

If the creditor's claim is not fully satisfied through the insolvency proceedings, the claim does not cease to exist (Art. 244 Insolvency Act); rather, it becomes enforceable title, which will allow the creditor to enforce the claim if the debtor's asset position improves in the future.

6 Enterprise Charges

The security over the business enterprise that corresponds to the notion of the "floating charge" usually takes the form of a pledge.

A pledge on a business enterprise is created upon its registration in the Pledge Register [Art. 1319 (2) Civil Code). As already mentioned above, the moments when a pledge is created on some industrial property rights (which are parts of business enterprises) differ significantly without substantial justification or proper reasoning. The registration of the right in the Industrial Design Register or Patent Register has a constitutive effect and the pledge is created only once it is entered in this register. However, when the pledge is established over a trademark, the registration of the pledge in the Trademark Register is only declaratory. Thus, the moment of the formation of the pledge differs based on the type of industrial property that is part of the business enterprise.

The position of the third parties' rights and of the rights of the liquidator of the bankruptcy assets is the same as regards the debtor's other assets.

The usual costs involved in establishing of a pledge over a business enterprise are connected to the notarial deed [Art. 1314 (2) (a) Civil Code].

---

[41] E.g. unpaid employee wages, receivables of the state, or outstanding alimony.

[42] Richter (2014), pp. 1252–1254.

[43] A subordinated claim is a claim which, according to the wording of the contract, should be satisfied only after the satisfaction of another creditor's claim.

7 Enforcement of the Security Rights

Outside of insolvency, we can speak about the enforcement of security rights only in respect of the pledge, since the "transfer of a right as a security" and the "prohibition to encumber or alienate a thing" are enforced directly by the Industrial Property Office, which administers the register of industrial property rights. If the transfer of a right as a security becomes unconditional, the Industrial Property Office deletes the notification in the register. Similarly, the Industrial Property Office must request the creditor's consent for the alienation or encumbrance of an industrial property right if these types of security rights have been established by the contracting parties.

The pledgor has the right to satisfy himself through the collateral in whatever manner was agreed in writing as per the conditions stipulated in the Civil Code (e.g. through the sale or retention of the asset). As a general rule, before the debt is due, any agreement stipulating that the pledgor can sell the collateral in any manner or that he may retain the collateral for an arbitrary or predetermined price is prohibited [Art. 1315 (2) Civil Code]. However, when the debt is not paid properly or on time, the pledgor may satisfy his claim in a manner that has been agreed in writing with the pledgee [Art. 1359 (1) Civil Code]. Another possibility is for the pledgor to satisfy his claim from the proceeds gained from the sale of the asset at a public auction (or from a sale administered by a court). If it has been stipulated that the pledgor may sell the pledged asset in a way other than at a public auction, this will also be binding upon the legal successor to the pledgee (Art. 1360 Civil Code).

A pledgor shall notify the pledgee of the beginning of the pledge's enforcement in writing [Art. 1362 (1) Civil Code]. If a pledge is registered in a public register (such as the Patent Register, Trademark Register, or Industrial Design Register) or a collateral in the Pledge Register (e.g. when a trademark is pledged as part of a business enterprise), the pledgor shall submit the information about the enforcement of the pledge to the Industrial Property Office. The pledgor must wait 30 days after the notification is registered in the register before he may sell the pledged asset [Art. 1364 (2) Civil Code].

If insolvency proceedings are initiated, the creditor will usually be satisfied through the sale of the asset outside of a public auction. However, the liquidator of the bankruptcy must agree on the method of selling the intellectual property with the creditors' committee (Art. 286 Insolvency Act). It is only possible for the collateral to be sold for a usual price as determined by an expert or for a price based on the pledgee's accounting if the creditors' committee and the insolvency court consent.

8 Typical Costs of Secured Transactions

The costs involved in the preparation of the security agreement may differ depending on the category of the intellectual property right; it is not possible to quantify them in general. However, when the intellectual property right is subject to a pledge as a part

Table 1 Part XI. section No. 127 letter c) of the Administrative Fees Act

	Patent	Trademark	Industrial design
Registration of a pledge or registration of a transfer of a right as a security	CZK 600 (EUR 23)	CZK 600 (EUR 23)	CZK 600 (EUR 23)

of a business enterprise, the pledge agreement has to be concluded in the form of a notarial deed. The costs related to the notarial deed and the subsequent registration in the Pledge Register are usually 0.2% of the value of the asset.

The costs of registering in the Patent Register, Trademark Register, or Industrial Design Register are regulated by the Administrative Fees Act.[44] These fees (see Table 1) are due upon the filing of the application for the registration of the right.

However, any changes to the listed security rights (such as changes to the attachments to the pledge agreement, changes to the name of the pledgor, etc.) are recorded free of charge because they are not included in the list of fees which is set by the Administrative Fees Act. Similarly, the prohibition to encumber or alienate industrial property rights and the registration of an industrial property right as a part of a business enterprise are carried out by the Industrial Property Office free of charge.

9 Frequency of Security Transactions Over Industrial Property

In practice, security transactions over intellectual property rights rarely occur. Creditors (usually banks) generally do not have any interest in securing debts using intellectual property rights because they do not represent a sufficiently liquid form of security.

The statistical data on the issue that is shown in the Table 2 was provided by the Industrial Property Office and covers the past 3 years.

According to the information provided by the Industrial Property Office, not a single transfer of a right as a security has yet been registered for any of the abovementioned categories of industrial property rights.

The pledge is the most often used form of security over industrial property rights. The records on pledges also indicate that the debt is usually either paid on time or is refinanced in a short term. The Industrial Property Office was notified of only 44 cases of enforcement of a pledge in 2014 and just 1 case in 2015.

[44] Act No. 634/2004 Coll., on Administrative Fees, as amended. The English translation is available at: https://www.upv.cz/en/legislation/national/related-legislation.html. Accessed Jan 10, 2019.

Table 2 Number of registrations of security transactions in the industrial property registries

Change in the relevant register	Year	Industrial property right	Quantity
Request for the registration of a pledge	2014	Patent	3
		Utility model	4
		Validated European patent	1
		Trademark	303
	2015	Patent	3
		Utility model	9
		Industrial design	1
		Validated European patent	1
		Trademark	112
	2016	Patent	1
		Industrial design	3
		Validated European patent	2
		Trademark	379
Request for the registration of a prohibition to encumber or alienate a thing	2014	Trademark	169
	2015	Trademark	71
	2016	Trademark	150
Request for the registration of a prohibition against establishing a pledge (i.e. the application specifically mentions just the prohibition against establishing a pledge and does not mention the other security rights)	2014	Trademark	3
	2015	Trademark	52
	2016	Trademark	147
Request for the registration of a prohibition against the alienation of rights (i.e. the application concerns just the prohibition against alienation and does not concern encumbrance)	2015	Trademark	1
Request for the registration of a security right over industrial property rights as part of a business enterprise	2014	Patent	50
		Utility model	2
	2015	Trademark	13
	2016	Patent	53
		Utility model	1

List of Cases

Decision of the Czech Supreme Court from 2007-04-30, File No. 30 Cdo 739/2007.

List of Laws

Administrative Fees Act	Act No. 634/2004 Coll., on Administrative Fees, as amended. The English translation available [online] at: https://www.upv.cz/en/legislation/national/related-legislation.html
Business Corporations Act	Act No. 90/2012 Coll., on Business Corporations, as amended. The English translation available [online] at: http://obcanskyzakonik.justice.cz/images/pdf/Business-Corporations-Act.pdf
Civil Code	Act. No. 89/2012 Coll., Civil Code, as amended; the English translation available [online] at: http://obcanskyzakonik.justice.cz/images/pdf/Civil-Code.pdf
Copyright Act	Act No. 121/2000 Coll., on Copyright and Rights Related to Copyright and on Amendment to Certain Acts, as amended; the English translation available [online] at: http://www.wipo.int/wipolex/en/text.jsp?file_id=137175
Designations of Origin and Geographical Indications Act	Act No. 452/2001 Coll., on the Protection of Designations of Origin and Geographical Indications and on the Amendment to the Act on Consumer Protection, as amended. The English translation available [online] at: https://www.upv.cz/en/legislation/national/codes.html
Industrial Designs Act	Act No. 207/2000 Coll., on the Protection of Industrial Designs, as amended; The English translation is available [online] at: https://www.upv.cz/en/legislation/national/codes.html
Insolvency Act	Act No. 182/2006 Coll., on Bankruptcy and Settlement, as amended (the English translation is not available).
Patents Act	Act No. 527/1990 Coll., on Inventions and Rationalisation Proposals, as amended; The English translation is available [online] at: https://www.upv.cz/en/legislation/national/codes.html
Trademarks Act	Act No. 441/2003 Coll., on Trademarks and on Amendments to Act No. 6/2002 on Judgements, Judges, Assessors and State Judgement Administration and on Amendments to Some Other Acts (Act on Courts and Judges); The English translation available [online] at: https://www.upv.cz/en/legislation/national/codes.html

References

Chloupek V, Hartvichová K, Hejl P, Jarolímková A, Malý J (2017) Patentový zákon. Komentář. C. H. Beck, Praha

Horáček R, Biskupová E, De Korver Z (2015) Práva na označení a jejich vymáhání (Zákon o ochranných známkách, Zákon o ochraně označení původu a zeměpisných označení, Zákon o vymáhání práv z průmyslového vlastnictví). Komentář, 3rd edn. C. H. Beck, Praha

Kindl M (2016) Zajištění a utvrzení dluhů. C. H. Beck, Praha

Koukal P (2016) Soukromoprávní ochrana a vymáhání průmyslových práv v České republice. In: Vojčík P, Filičko V, Koromház P (eds) Košické dni súkromného práva I. Univerzita Pavla Jozefa Šafárika, Košice, pp 450–466

Koukal P (2017) § 2364. In: Pražák Z, Fiala J, Handlar J (eds) Závazky z právních jednání podle občanského zákoníku. Komentář k § 1721-2893 OZ. Leges, Praha, p 1033

Macek J (2014) § 2358. In: Hulmák M et al (eds) Občanský zákoník VI. Závazkové právo. Zvláštní část § 2055–3014. Komentář. C. H. Beck, Praha, pp 597–606

Richter T (2013) § 1359. In: Spáčil J et al (eds) Občanský zákoník III. Věcná práva § 976-1474. Komentář. C. H. Beck, Praha, pp 1115–1116

Richter T (2014) § 2016. In: Hulmák M et al (eds) Občanský zákoník V. Závazkové právo. Obecná část § 1721–2054. Komentář. C. H. Beck, Praha, pp 1252–1254

Svačina P (2010) Oceňování nehmotných aktiv. Ekopress, s. r. o., Praha

Telec I (1994) Tvůrčí práva duševního vlastnictví. Masarykova univerzita and Doplněk, Brno

Telec I, Tůma P (2007) Autorský zákon. Komentář. C. H. Beck, Praha

Vojčík P (2012) Právo duševného vlastníctva. Vydavatelství a nakladatelství Aleš Čeněk, Plzeň

Vojčík P (2016) Teorie právní ochrany nehmotných statků. Metropolitní univerzita Praha, o. p. s., Praha

Security Rights in Intellectual Property in England and Wales

Jan Jakob Bornheim

Abstract In this contribution, the author analyses the interaction between secured transaction law and intellectual property law in England and Wales. The interaction between these two areas of law is complex and not well-coordinated.

English secured transaction law can be categorized as formal as opposed to functional, meaning that the effects of a security interest differ depending on what form this security interest takes. Different attachment, perfection and priority rules apply depending on whether the security interest is a legal or an equitable security interest.

The rules relating to the attachment and perfection of a security interest, particularly a legal security interest, will depend on the rules applying to the specific intellectual property right—they are a function of intellectual property law, not secured transactions law; these rules differ between different intellectual property rights. The statutory provisions applying to the different intellectual property rights take little account of common law and equity property rules and lead to a differential treatment of security interests depending on what type of property constitutes the object of security.

A number of intellectual property rights are registrable in a specific registry, depending on the type of intellectual property. In that case, registration of the security interest in the relevent intellectual property right registry influences priority.

Floating charges are security interests in present and future property that allow the debtor to retain the right to deal with the property in the ordinary course of business. In practice, only businesses will grant a floating charge. Floating charges add an additional layer of complexity to the priority framework, as the otherwise applicable priority rules are modified by the rules in relation to floating charges. As well, floating charges by an incorporated business trigger an additional registration requirement in the company register that is not synchronised with the specific intellectual property law registration system.

J. J. Bornheim (✉)
University of Canterbury, Christchurch, New Zealand
e-mail: janjakob.bornheim@canterbury.ac.nz

E.-M. Kieninger (ed.), *Security Rights in Intellectual Property*, Ius Comparatum – Global Studies in Comparative Law 45,
https://doi.org/10.1007/978-3-030-44191-3_11

1 Overview of Intellectual Property Rights

Intellectual property law in the United Kingdom is uniformly based on statute, meaning that the relevant statutes or European regulations apply throughout the entire United Kingdom. The main intellectual property rights (IPRs) available in British law are copyright, design rights, trade marks, and patents.

Of these IPRs, copyright only exists domestically. The existence of copyright is a function of domestic law,[1] but the statute and case law is influenced by European directives and international treaties. In addition to copyright, British law recognizes related rights: different performers' rights,[2] the database right,[3] technological protection measures, rights management information, the public lending right, and the droit de suite. Of these adjacent rights, the first two are property rights. More precisely, a number of performers' rights[4] and the *sui generis* database right[5] are property rights. The statements on copyright apply *mutatis mutandis* to these rights. In relation to the *sui generis* database right, the application of the relevant copyright law principles is expressly legislated,[6] whereas in relation to performer's rights, the relevant provisions follow a structure parallel to the copyright provisions. For the purpose of this analysis, the discussion of copyright includes the *sui generis* database right and the performer's rights listed in s 191A *Copyright, Designs and Patents Act 1986* (UK), but the relevant performer's right sections will be indicated where necessary.

Designs rights can exist as domestic rights[7] or as EU design rights.[8] Both exist in a registered form and in an unregistered form. Just like design rights, trade marks can exist as domestic trade marks[9] or as EU trade marks.[10] At the time of writing of this chapter (mid-January 2019), it is unclear whether the UK will ratify the *Draft*

---

[1]Namely the *Copyright, Designs and Patents Act 1986* (UK).

[2]*Copyright, Designs and Patents Act 1986* (UK), ss 180–205B.

[3]*Database Regulation 1986*, ss 12–25.

[4]*Copyright, Designs and Patents Act 1986* (UK), s 191A ("The following rights conferred by this Chapter on a performer – reproduction right (section 182A), distribution right (section 182B), rental right and lending right (section 182C), making available right (section 182CA), – are property rights").

[5]*Database Regulation 1986*, s 13(1) ("A property right ("database right") subsists, in accordance with this Part, in a database if there has been a substantial investment in obtaining, verifying or presenting the contents of the database.").

[6]*Database Regulation 1986*, s 23 ("The following provisions of the 1988 Act: sections 90 to 93 (dealing with rights in copyright works); sections 96 to 98 (rights and remedies of copyright owner); sections 101 and 102 (rights and remedies of exclusive licensee); apply in relation to database right and databases in which that right subsists as they apply in relation to copyright and copyright works.").

[7]*Copyright, Designs and Patents Act 1986* (UK) and *Registered Designs Act, 1949* (UK).

[8]*Community Design Regulation.*

[9]*Trade Marks Act 1994* (UK).

[10]*EU Trade Mark Regulation (2017 Recast).*

Withdrawal Agreement to enable an orderly withdrawal of the UK from the European Union. If it does, art 54 *Draft Withdrawal Agreement* provides that the holders of an EU IPR will also become holders of the equivalent UK right, but as a result of the UK's withdrawal from the EU, EU IPRs will lose their effect in relation to the UK.

Patents can exist as domestic patents[11] or as European patents.[12] The European Patent Organisation itself is an institution indepent of the EU. European patents are in essence a bundle of individual national patents with a unified application system. In addition to the *Convention on the Grant of European Patents*, the UK has ratified the *UPC Convention.*[13] The combined effect of the *UPC Convention* and the accompanying *Unitary Patent Protection Regulation* is to set up a unitary patent and a unified patent court in participating EU Member States. However, the *UPC Convention* is the subject of a constitutional challenge in Germany, delaying the German ratification.[14] As a result, neither can the *UPC Convention* enter into force nor can the *Unitary Patent Protection Regulation* have any effect. While the future relation between the UK and the EU is uncertain at the time of writing of this chapter, it is already clear that the *UPC Convention* will not enter into force before the UK's withdrawal.[15] It is uncertain whether or not the UK can participate in the UPC system after its withdrawal.[16]

2 Categories of Security Rights

2.1 Security Rights, Other Property Rights, and Personal Rights

Unlike IP law, property law, including secured transaction law, is not uniform throughout the United Kingdom. English secured transactions law follows a formal approach. This approach is characterized by a distinction between certain title-based transactions and secured transactions in which the creditor receives a right less than full ownership of the collateral.[17] The qualifier "certain" is necessary because the prototypical English security interest, the mortgage, does in fact involve a transfer of title.

[11] *Patents Act 1977* (UK).

[12] *Convention on the Grant of European Patents.*

[13] See EU, Council (2018), *passim.*

[14] Legal Tribune Online (2017), *passim.*

[15] *UPC Convention*, art 89(1) provides that the agreement only enters into force four months after the ratification by, amongst others, the three Member States with the largest number of European patents in effect. This includes Germany.

[16] See Lamping and Ullrich (2018), *passim.*

[17] Goode (2013), para 1.04. See also Bridge et al. (1999), *passim.*

2.2 Categories of Security Rights

Formalism in English secured transaction law goes further than a distinction between title-based and pure security interests in that English law has thus far not adopted a unitary security interest; a unitary security interest would mean that there is only one security interest governed by a unitary set of rules allowing minor variations. Instead, English law recognizes four different types of consensual security interests created by agreement between parties; these are the pledge, the contractual lien, the mortgage, and the charge.[18] The first two, pledge and lien, are possessory security interests.[19]

A mortgage is a transaction by virtue of which the secured creditor, the mortgagee, receives title to the collateral.[20] In the case of intangibles, the transfer can take the form of an assignment or a novation. (Novation being the substitution of creditors of a debt and thus not relevant for the present analysis.[21]) The transfer of the asset is conditional; if the debtor repays their debt, the mortgagee is under an obligation to re-transfer the asset back to the mortgagor.[22] The mortgagor's right to regain the asset is recognized as an property right, the mortgagor's "equity of redemption."[23] However, if the debt is not paid, the mortgagee has the right to appropriate the asset to pay the debt.[24] In that case, the mortgagor no longer has any equitable entitlement to the asset. The differences between a mortgage and an outright transfer of title are a function of the fact that the mortgage is a security interest. A security interest has three specific differences that set it apart from an outright transfer of title. First, a security interest is connected with an underlying obligation. If there is no corresponding obligation, the transfer cannot be a security interest. Second, the security interest is defeasible if the obligation is fulfilled. Third, the security interest extends only as far as is necessary to secure the obligation. If there are any surplus profits, the mortgagor is entitled to this surplus.[25]

The final security interest is the charge. Unlike a mortgagor, the chargor retains title, but with "a clog on [their] ownership in favour of the [chargee]."[26] The charge

---

[18]See *Re Cosslett (Contractors) Ltd.* (C.A. Civ.), 508, per Millett LJ; Goode (2013), paras 1.05, 1.46; Tosato (2011), p. 94.

[19]Goode (2013), para 1.08.

[20]Goode (2013), para 1.54; Tosato (2011), p. 95. Thomas (2017), p. 222 suggests that it is also a necessary requirement that the mortgagee receive a right to possession, but this does not seem to be the generally accepted definition of a legal mortgage and it is unclear what this requirement adds other than denying the existence of legal mortgages for all pure intangible assets.

[21]See Goode (2013), para 1.54.

[22]See Goode (2013), para 1.54; Tosato (2011), p. 95.

[23]Bridge et al. (1999), p. 589, there note 72.

[24]See Goode (2013), para 1.56.

[25]See Goode (2013), para 1.36, ref'g to *Re George Inglefield Ltd.* (C.A.).

[26]See Goode (2013), para 1.11. See also Tosato (2011), p. 95, calling it a "a 'shadow' cast over the collateral until the obligation is discharged or the security is realized."

is effective against purchasers of the asset and is thus a property right, but as an equitable interest, it is susceptible to defeat by the *bona fide* rule.[27]

2.3 Legal and Equitable Security Rights

In addition to the distinction between the different forms of security, a further distinction needs to be made between legal and equitable security interests in English law. Whether an interest is defined as legal or equitable is not a mere linguistic issue. The characterization will influence the applicable priority rules. The principle, examined in more detail below, is that an equitable interest is defeasible by a *bona fide* purchaser for value without notice whereas a legal interest is protected by the *nemo dat quod non habet* rule.[28] In addition to yielding different results, legal and equitable interests also differ in the requirements necessary for their creation. Different rules apply to the attachment of legal or equitable interests.[29] Specific registration requirements for company security interests, including equitable interests, have reduced the importance of the distinction between legal and equitable interests without negating it entirely. Registration of a company security interest can be a perfection requirement notwithstanding the equitable nature of the interest.[30] Registration can also constitute notice, defeating the *bona fide* rule and thus impacting priority.[31]

The mortgage is a legal interest where the legal title is transferred to the mortgagee; equitable mortgages and almost all charges are equitable interests. The reason for the latter characterization is that at law, only the transfer of full title is a recognized transaction,[32] and a charge only transfers a conditional right to appropriate the asset for the satisfaction of the debt. However, because any mortgage includes the right to appropriate the asset for the satisfaction of the outstanding debt,[33] any equitable mortgage is said to be a charge at the same time, and thus the word "charge" is sometimes used to include equitable mortgages or even all mortgages.[34] In this text however, the word "charge" is used in the stricter sense unless there is an indication to the contrary.

[27] See Goode (2013), para 1.11. See Sects. 2.3 and 4.1.2.

[28] Goode (2013), para 1.12. See Sect. 4.1.

[29] See subsection "Attachment of a Legal Security Interest" within Sect. 3.1.1.

[30] See subsection "Attachment of a Legal Security Interest" within Sect. 3.1.1.

[31] Goode (2013), para 1.12. The priority scheme is discussed in Sect. 4.

[32] See Sect. 3.1.1. The rule has been modified in relation to certain classes of property, see subsection "Transfer of Title" within Sect. 3.1.1.

[33] See Sect. 6.

[34] Goode (2013), para 1.56.

2.4 *Availability of Security Rights for IP Rights*

2.4.1 The Place of IPRs in Personal Property Law

IPRs can be used as security in English law, but they fit uncomfortably into the common law system of property. A straightforward taxonomy in English law consists of a division of personal property into "choses in possession" and "choses in action"; the first type of property is tangible and in principle susceptible to possession, whereas the latter is intangible.[35] IPRs are not susceptible to possession, which in English law is single and exclusive.[36] In principle, intellectual property rights are incorporeal property and as such can be used as collateral for a security interest.[37] To be more precise, intellectual property rights are pure intangibles as they are not represented by a document. The fact that there are registration requirements or formal requirements relating to the assignment of some IPRs does not change the pure intangible nature of IPRs.[38] If there were a simple two-fold characterization of personal property it would easily follow that IPRs are choses in action, but this is not the case. The characterization of IPRs as choses in action has been an ongoing debate in English law.[39] The issue is put in particularly sharp focus in relation to patents. The *Patents Act 1977* (UK) provides that patents are not choses in action,[40] but some commentators classify it as such anyways.[41] The alternative suggestion is thus a threefold characterization: choses in possession, choses in action, and other incorporeal property.[42]

However, regardless of whether IPRs are choses in action, or whether the taxonomy of English personal property law is threefold, IPRs, including patents, are assignable and thus can be mortgaged.[43] Despite the exclusion of patents from the class of choses in action, the mortgagee of a patent receives the same rights as the mortgagee of any other personal property.[44] It is thus unclear what the statute means

---

[35]See e.g. Sheehan (2017), p. 2. See also Elphinstone (1893), *passim*.

[36]Tosato (2011), p. 95. See also Pollock and Wright (1888), *passim*.

[37]See Thomas (2017), pp. 221–222.

[38]See Tosato (2011), p. 95, there note 19.

[39]Tosato (2011), pp. 94–95. See Brodhurst (1895), *passim*; *Colonial Bank v. Whinney* (C.A.), 283–284; Elphinstone (1893), *passim*; Sweet (1894), *passim*; Sweet (1895), *passim*; Williams (1894), *passim*; Williams (1895), *passim*. But see Holdsworth (1920), pp. 1013–1014, pointing out that IPRs are originally conceptually closer to real property, and that their treatment as choses in action and thus as personal property is an historical accident.

[40]*Patents Act 1977* (UK), s 30(1) ("Any patent or application for a patent is personal property (without being a thing in action), and any patent or any such application and rights in or under it may be transferred, created or granted in accordance with subsections (2) to (7) below.").

[41]See the table in Sheehan (2017), p. 2.

[42]Elphinstone (1893), p. 312; Tosato (2011), pp. 94–95.

[43]See Tosato (2011), p. 95.

[44]*Van Gelder Apsimon & Co v. Sowerby Bridge United District Flour Society* (C.A.). See also Thomas (2017), p. 222.

when it defines patents as not being choses in action.[45] For the purpose of this analysis, not much hinges on the potential distinction between IPRs and choses in action, but it does create uncertainty as to the application of general rules on choses in action to IPRs, one case of which will be discussed below.[46]

Possessory security interests—pledge and lien—cannot be created in pure intangibles, including intellectual property, for want of possession of these assets;[47] however, where a security interest in intangibles is erroneously described as a lien by the parties, it can be re-characterized as a charge.[48] Presumably, this applies to intellectual property as a subspecies of intangible property as well.

2.4.2 Security Interests in Particular IPRs

Using IPRs as security is specifically provided for by statute in relation to a number of IPRs. Unfortunately, the wording used throughout the statutes is not consistent. The *CDPA 1986* does not specifically mention the use of copyright, related rights, and domestic design rights as security. Rather, it only provides that the rights are assignable at law. In relation to copyright, the statute provides that copyright is "transmissible by assignment, by testamentary disposition or by operation of law, as personal or moveable property."[49] It is thus mortgageable by way of assignment.[50] The same provision exists for performers' rights.[51] In relation to registered designs[52]

---

[45]Cf. Thomas (2017), pp. 221–222, describing patents as "functionally" equivalent to choses in action.

[46]Namely, the application of the writing requirements for assignments in the *Law of Property Act, 1925* (UK), s 136 to registered designs.

[47]See Goode (2013), paras 1.05, 1.08, 1.48, 1.59; Tosato (2011), p. 94.

[48]*Re Lehman Brothers International (Europe)* (Ch. D.), para 34–46, per Briggs J; Goode (2013), para 1.53.

[49]*Copyright, Designs and Patents Act 1986* (UK), s 90(3).

[50]Thomas (2017), p. 224.

[51]*Copyright, Designs and Patents Act 1986* (UK), s 191B(1) ("A performer's property rights are transmissible by assignment, by testamentary disposition or by operation of law, as personal or moveable property.").

[52]*Registered Designs Act, 1949* (UK), s 2(2) ("Where a design becomes vested, whether by assignment, transmission or operation of law, in any person other than the original proprietor, either alone or jointly with the original proprietor, that other person, or as the case may be the original proprietor and that other person, shall be treated for the purposes of this Act as the proprietor of the design.") and s 19(1) ("Where any person becomes entitled by assignment, transmission or operation of law to a registered design or to a share in a registered design, or becomes entitled as mortgagee, licensee or otherwise to any other interest in a registered design, he shall apply to the registrar in the prescribed manner for the registration of his title as proprietor or co—proprietor or, as the case may be, of notice of his interest, in the register of designs.").

and unregistered domestic design rights,[53] the statute provides for the assignment and mortgaging (in the case of registered designs) of the IPR, but does not mention charges. On the other hand, neither statute contains a prohibition against the creation of an equitable charge.

In relation to domestic trade marks and patents, the statute provides for the use of the IPR as security both by way of mortgage as well as by way of charge. In the case of trade marks, Section 24(4) *Trade Marks Act 1994* (UK) provides in a straightforward fashion that trade marks can be mortgaged by way of assignment or charged.[54] A trade mark application can also be the subject of security interest.[55] In the case of patents, the statute is slightly less straightforward. Patents can be mortgaged by virtue of the *PA 1977*.[56] Section 130 *PA 1977* in turn defines the term "mortgage" as including the term "charge."[57] Bently and Sherman seem to suggest it should therefore also be possible to create a *legal* charge in patents.[58] But the act does not say anything about the legal or equitable nature of either mortgages and charges, and it is thus doubtful whether the drafters of the statute intended to deviate from the common law rules against legal charges. A patent application can also be the subject of security interest.[59] It is worthwhile pointing out that before the modern *PA 1977*, there are a few cases from the nineteenth century in which patents were used as mortgages, underlining the fact that their potential use as security is as much a function of common law as it is of statute.[60]

European design rights[61] and trade marks[62] can both be used as security. In both cases, the relevant regulations contain a provision that the substantive property law is

---

[53]*Copyright, Designs and Patents Act 1986* (UK), s 222(1) ("Design right is transmissible by assignment, by testamentary disposition or by operation of law, as personal or moveable property.").

[54]*Trade Marks Act 1994* (UK), s 24(4) ("The above provisions apply to assignment by way of security as in relation to any other assignment.") and s 24(5) ("A registered trade mark may be the subject of a charge (in Scotland, security) in the same way as other personal or moveable property."). See also Thomas (2017), p. 223.

[55]Thomas (2017), p. 223.

[56]*Patents Act 1977* (UK), s 30(2) ("Subject to section 36(3) below, any patent or any such application, or any right in it, may be assigned or mortgaged."). See also Bently and Sherman (2014), p. 645.

[57]*Patents Act 1977* (UK), s 130 ("'[M]ortgage', when used as a noun, includes a charge for securing money or money's worth and, when used as a verb, shall be construed accordingly[.]").

[58]Bently and Sherman (2014), p. 645.

[59]Thomas (2017), p. 223.

[60]See *Brown v. North* (C.A.); *New Ixion Tyre and Cycle Co v. Spilsbury* (C.A.); *Steers v. Rogers* (H.L.). See also Tosato (2011), p. 93, pointing out that these cases were "isolated" and "not common practice."

[61]*Community Design Regulation*, art 29(1) ("A registered Community design may be given as security or be the subject of rights *in rem.*" [Emphasis original).

[62]*EU Trade Mark Regulation (2017 Recast)*, art 22(1) ("An EU trade mark may, independently of the undertaking, be given as security or be the subject of rights *in rem.*" [Emphasis original]).

the law of a Member State.[63] In practice, the most common scenario is that the use of a European IPR will be governed by the law of the Member State in which the holder is domiciled. European patents are also treated in a manner akin to the corresponding domestic IPR.[64]

3 Attachment and Perfection

3.1 General Rules of Attachment and Perfection

3.1.1 Attachment

Concept of Attachment

Attachment makes the security interest binding between the parties, but not between all third parties. Attachment is enough to make the interest binding on an unsecured non-insolvency creditor. Once the interest has attached, the grantor can no longer deny the creditor's *in rem* right in the specific asset. Perfection, on the other hand, makes the security interest enforceable against all third parties except those with higher priority.[65]

Attachment of a Legal Security Interest

General Requirements for the Attachment of a Legal Security Interest

The transfer of a legal security interest has five requirements: (1) there must be an agreement to transfer legal title to the creditor, (2) the IPR must be identifiable, (3) the transferor must have the right in the IPR to grant security, (4) the interest must secure an obligation, and (5) any contractual condition must be complied with.[66] The first and the last requirement warrant a closer look.

Transfer of Title

The requirement of a valid transfer of a legal interest at law can be further specified as follows: At common law, the transferor (or their principal in case of agency) must have the legal title to the asset at the time of the transfer; the security interest must be created by a present transfer of an existing asset; the transfer must be to the creditor;

[63] *Community Design Regulation*, art 27; *EU Trade Mark Regulation (2017 Recast)*, art 19. See also Bariatti (2010), pp. 403–404.
[64] See Bariatti (2010), pp. 400–401.
[65] See Goode (2013), para 2.02. On perfection see Sect. 3.1.2. On the priority scheme see Sect. 4.
[66] See Goode (2013), paras 2.03, 2.07.

and where any statutory requirements exist for the transfer of title, they must be complied with.[67] The requirement that the legal title be transferred applies at common law; it has been modified by statute in relation to maritime liens or a charge in land, but not in relation to IPRs.[68] From the foregoing, it follows that, of the security interests that can exist in relation to intellectual property (i.e. the mortgage and the charge), only the mortgage can exist as a legal interest. This is because the charge is defined as an interest that consists of less than an outright transfer of the title asset; therefore, by definition, the charge can never meet the requirement "transfer of legal title" that is necessary to be characterized as legal.[69]

Attachment of an Equitable Security Interest

The requirements for the creation of a legal mortgage do not all apply to the creation of an equitable security interest. First, the attachment of equitable mortgages and charges does not require the present transfer of the legal title to a present interest in the asset in compliance with statutory formalities; equity regards as done what ought to be done—even where formality requirements are not complied with.[70] Second, the transferor can transfer less than full legal title.[71] Whereas equity will overcome some shortcomings of the legal transfer, there are still requirements relating to the security agreement in order to create a valid security interest: The agreement must be clear about the intent of the parties to create the security, it must be clear about the time of the attachment, and it must identify the assets to which it relates rather than leaving them up to an act of appropriation by the debtor. If these requirements relating to the agreement and the other four requirements (requirements [2]–[5]) for attachment[72] are met, the agreement suffices to create a security.[73]

Formality Requirements

Where the creation of a legal mortgage fails because formality requirements are not complied with, an equitable mortgage is created instead.[74] This statement is not reversible, however: compliance with formality requirements is a necessary criterion

---

[67]Goode (2013), para 1.12.

[68]See Goode (2013), para 1.55. Regarding the legal charge in land see *Law of Property Act, 1925* (UK), s 85(1): "A mortgage of an estate in fee simple shall only be capable of being effected at law either by a demise for a term of years absolute, subject to a provision for cesser on redemption, or by a charge by deed expressed to be by way of legal mortgage[.]."

[69]See also Tosato (2011), p. 95.

[70]Goode (2013), para 1.19, 2.04.

[71]See subsection "Transfer of Equitable Title" within Sect. 3.1.1.

[72]See Sect. 3.1.1.

[73]Goode (2013), paras 2.04, 2.11.

[74]Tosato (2011), p. 95.

for legal characterization, but not sufficient for it. Thus, for example, the fact that an equitable security interest can be registered does not transform such an interest into a legal interest once it is registered.[75]

Sometimes, in application of s 53(1)(c) *Law of Property Act, 1925* (UK),[76] it is argued that unlike the creation of an equitable interest, the transfer of any such equitable interest must be in writing. This would mean that the equitable owner of an IPR could only grant an equitable mortgage by assignment in writing,[77] whereas the legal owner can grant an equitable mortgage without complying with any formality requirements. This somewhat surprising result appears to be based on a misreading of the relevant statutory section. Section 53(1)(c) *LPA, 1925* in fact applies only to land.

Present Transfer or Future Transfer

The promise to transfer an asset in the future is not sufficient to create a legal mortgage,[78] but it is sufficient for the creation of an equitable mortgage.[79] Based on the maxim that equity regards as done what ought to be done, there is no difference between an equitable mortgage and an agreement for an equitable mortgage or between a charge and an agreement for a charge.[80]

Transfer of Future Property

A present transfer of future property is usually not sufficient to create a legal mortgage, but it is sufficient for the creation of an equitable mortgage.[81] The reason for this is that at common law, with limited exceptions, future property cannot be

[75]Goode (2013), para 1.12.

[76]*Law of Property Act, 1925* (UK), s 53(1)(c) ("Subject to the provision hereinafter contained with respect to the creation of interests in land by parol [. . .] a disposition of an equitable interest or trust subsisting at the time of the disposition, must be in writing signed by the person disposing of the same, or by his agent thereunto lawfully authorised in writing or by will.").

[77]See Garnett et al. (2013), paras 5.195, 5.201; *Wang Industrial Co v. Takmay Industrial Co Ltd.* (Hong Kong C.A.); *Roban Jig & Tool Co Ltd. v. Taylor* (C.A. Civ.); Garnett et al. (2013), paras 5.195, 5.201, all relying on *Law of Property Act, 1925* (UK), s 53(1)(c) respectively the Hong Kong equivalent, the now repealed *Law Amendment and Reform (Consolidation) Ordinance*, s 6(1)(c).

[78]Goode (2013), para 2.11.

[79]See Goode (2013), paras 1.56, 2.11.

[80]Goode (2013), para 2.04.

[81]*Holroyd v. Marshall*. See Goode (2013), para 2.12 and Thomas (2017), p. 222, ref'g to *Gorringe v. Irwell India Rubber and Gutta Percha Works* (C.A.); *William Brandt's Sons & Co v. Dunlop Rubber Co Ltd.* (H.L.); *Swiss Bank Corp. v. Lloyds Bank Ltd.* (H.L.), 613; *Baxter International Inc. v. Nederlands Produktielaboratorium voor Bloedtransfusiapparatuur BV* (Engl. and W. Pat.).

assigned.[82] A charge, always being an equitable interest, can be granted over present or future property.[83]

Where an interest in future property is created, attachment is postponed until the transferor acquires the property.[84] At the same time, the interest itself is deemed to be a present interest.[85] This is important for issues such as priority, where priority follows the first-in-time rule,[86] or deadlines for registration.[87]

Transfer of Equitable Title

Where the mortgagor only transfers the equitable title rather than the legal title to the mortgagee, the result is an equitable mortgage; it is referred to as such, rather than as a trust—the "security trust" has no separate conceptual identity from an equitable mortgage.[88]

3.1.2 Perfection

Concept of Perfection

Perfection relates to the process by which the creditor makes the security interest enforceable against an unlimited group of third parties. An unperfected security interest is enforceable against the transferor and a limited class of third parties, namely unsecured creditors outside insolvency.[89] A perfected security interest is enforceable against everybody, including the liquidator, the administrator and all other creditors ("creditors" here means secured creditors,[90] execution creditors,[91] and unsecured creditors[92]). Perfection and priority are related, but distinct questions.[93] It is possible to have a perfected security interest that is enforceable against an unlimited class of parties, but to lose out in a specific priority contest against a specific higher-ranking creditor. Equitable security interests are not unperfected by

---

[82]See Harrison (1952), *passim* on the restrictions against assignments of future property.

[83]Tosato (2011), p. 95.

[84]Goode (2013), para 2.13.

[85]Goode (2013), para 2.13.

[86]See Sect. 4.

[87]Goode (2013), para 2.13.

[88]Goode (2013), para 1.57.

[89]Goode (2013), para 2.23.

[90]*Re Monolithic Building Co* (C.A.).

[91]*Victoria Housing Estates Ltd. v. Ashpurton Estates Ltd.* (C.A. Civ.), 123, per *curiam.*

[92]Goode (2013), para 2.16, 2.23; Gullifer and Raczynska (2016), p. 282.

[93]Cf. Goode (2013), para 2.16.

mere virtue of being equitable rather than legal interests. They are still enforceable against third parties,[94] subject to equity-specific priority rules.[95]

Company Security Interests Registration Requirements

Any security interest—or, in the terminology of the act, any "company charge"—created by a company is registrable under s 859A *Companies Act 2006* (UK).[96] Registration under the *Companies Act 2006* is a perfection requirement. Where a security interest has to be registered in the company registry, it is unenforceable if it is not registered there, even if it is registered in the specialist registries.[97] An unregistered company security interest is valid not only against unsecured creditors, but also against outright purchasers of the property.[98] If a company is registered in the United Kingdom, any security interest created by it is registrable even if it comprises property situated outside the United Kingdom.[99] This raises a conflict-of-laws issues as the validity and third-party effects of property rights are generally governed by the *situs* of the property.

Registration of the security interest requires that the transferor or any person with interests in the charge (usually the chargee or its agent) must deliver to the registrar a statement of particulars and a certified copy of the charge instrument within 21 days of the creation of the charge. Delivery can be electronic or in paper format. The particulars must identify chargor and chargee and whether the charge is fixed or floating; if floating, they must identify whether the terms include a negative pledge clause; if fixed, they must identify whether the charged assets include any land, ship, aircraft or intellectual property required to be registered in the United Kingdom.[100] The particulars allow any third parties to decide whether they want to inspect the entire charge document.[101]

In addition to the company registry, there are also a number of specialist registers, including IPR registers. Registration of the security interest in those registers is not a perfection requirement.[102] These registers are addressed below.[103]

---

[94]See Goode (2013), para 1.19.

[95]See Sect. 4.1.

[96]See Gullifer and Raczynska (2016), pp. 273–274. The *Companies Act 2006* (UK) refers to security interests as charges, regardless of whether they are charges or mortgages.

[97]Goode (2013), para 5.24.

[98]As was the case under the previous version of the *Company Act*. See *Stroud Architectural Systems Ltd. v. John Laing Construction Ltd.* (Engl. and W. Ref.). See also Goode (2013), para 2.23; Gullifer and Raczynska (2016), p. 284.

[99]Goode (2013), para 2.22.

[100]*Companies Act 2006* (UK), s 859D [Text ommitted due to length].

[101]On the registration process see Goode (2013), paras 2.23–2.24; Gullifer and Raczynska (2016), pp. 276–277.

[102]Goode (2013), paras 2.16, 2.21, 2.32; Tosato (2011), p. 98.

[103]See Sect. 4.2.

3.2 *Attachment and Perfection Relating to IPRs*

As mentioned above, the creation of a mortgage requires a transfer of the legal or equitable title of the mortgaged property. Applying this requirement to IPRs, formality requirements relating to the assignment of title are often cited as an obstacle for the effective creation of a mortgage in IPRs.[104] It should be noted that while there are requirements relating to the assignment of IPRs, they relate to the assignment, but not to the agreement to assign. Thus, these requirements affect the creation of a legal mortgage, but do not generally impede the creation of an equitable mortgage.[105]

3.2.1 Attachment and Perfection Relating to Domestic IPRs

The common law rules on attachment and perfection determine how security in IPRs can be taken. Because a legal mortgage is created by transfer of legal title, the attachment and perfection requirements in relation to the creation of a legal security interest in IPRs is a function of the law relating to the assignment of the IPRs. The law in that area displays a very heterogenous approach.

Copyright is assignable in writing.[106] This includes future copyright.[107] Thus, mortgages can be easily created, including legal mortgages in future copyright.[108] This is an exception from the general rule against the creation of a legal mortgage in future property.[109] The exception is limited in scope, however: by virtue of its wording, it only applies to copyright that has not yet come into existence, not to copyright that already exists but is not currently owned by the assignor. In other words, an assignor hoping to acquire an already-existing copyright can only assign their future copyright in equity, while the potential author of a future work can assign their future copyright at law. The assignment of copyright at law must be in writing,

---

[104]Thomas (2017), pp. 222–223; Tosato (2011), p. 95.

[105]This differs from the situation in relation to land, where *Law of Property Act, 1925* (UK), s 53(1)(b) is a form requirement affecting the creation of equitable interests.

[106]*Copyright, Designs and Patents Act 1986* (UK), s 90(3) ("An assignment of copyright is not effective unless it is in writing signed by or on behalf of the assignor.").

[107]*Copyright, Designs and Patents Act 1986* (UK), s 91(1): "Where by an agreement made in relation to future copyright, and signed by or on behalf of the prospective owner of the copyright, the prospective owner purports to assign the future copyright (wholly or partially) to another person, then if, on the copyright coming into existence, the assignee or another person claiming under him would be entitled as against all other persons to require the copyright to be vested in him, the copyright shall vest in the assignee or his successor in title by virtue of this subsection." See *Performing Right Society Ltd. v. B4U Network (Europe) Ltd.* (Ch. D.); Bently and Sherman (2014), p. 294 and Thomas (2017), p. 224.

[108]Tosato (2011), pp. 99–100.

[109]See subsection "Transfer of Future Property" within Sect. 3.1.1.

but courts have accepted the equitable assignment of copyright.[110] An equitable mortgage in copyright might thus be created where the legal formalities for transfer are not complied with.[111]

There is an additional potential problem in relation to the assignment of copyright: at common law, there is a requirement that the property in which security is taken be identifiable where the subject matter of the transaction is susceptible to division into units that are capable in law of being separately owned and transferred.[112] Copyright of complex works can presumably be divided legally into copyrights in parts of the work. The author of a book has a copyright in each chapter and each passage. This creates a potential uncertainty regarding the possibility of using copyright in complex works as collateral. Performers' rights must be assigned in writing.[113] Future performers' right are assignable like copyright.[114]

The assignment of unregistered design rights must be made in writing.[115] There is no specific provision dealing with form requirements for registered design rights. While the High Court found that the assignment must be in writing *Copyright of Designs Act, 1842* (UK),[116] the Court's reasoning relied on the fact that registration of the assignment required written proof of the assignment. The current *Registered Designs Act, 1949* (UK) however only provides that "proof of title" must be made to the "satisfaction" of the registrar.[117] Nevertheless, it is still assumed that assignments of registered designs must be in writing.[118] The fact that s 136 *LPA, 1925* provides that the assignment of choses in action must be in writing seems to support this approach, but it is not necessarily self-evident that registered designs are choses in action if patents are definitely not.[119] The law is regrettably unclear on this point. Registration of the assignment of a registered design is not a form requirement, but a

---

[110]The leading case is *Performing Right Society Ltd. v. London Theatre of Varieties Ltd.* (H.L.), noting that an assignment of future copyright were at the time invalid at common law, but valid in equity. It is unclear whether the assignment would have been formally valid.

[111]Garnett et al. (2013), para 5.201.

[112]Goode (2013), para 2.06. See also Goode (2003), *passim*.

[113]*Copyright, Designs and Patents Act 1986* (UK), s 191B(3) ("An assignment of a performer's property rights is not effective unless it is in writing signed by or on behalf of the assignor.").

[114]*Copyright, Designs and Patents Act 1986* (UK), s 191C(3) ("If on the rights coming into existence the assignee or another person claiming under him would be entitled as against all other persons to require the rights to be vested in him, they shall vest in the assignee or his successor in title by virtue of this subsection.").

[115]*Copyright, Designs and Patents Act 1986* (UK), s 222(3) "An assignment of design right is not effective unless it is in writing signed by or on behalf of the assignor.").

[116]*Copyright of Designs Act, 1842* (UK). *Jewitt v. Eckhardt* (Ch. D.).

[117]*Registered Designs Act, 1949* (UK), s 19(3).

[118]See *e.g. Ifejika v. Ifejika*, paras 25–26, per Patten LJ, who goes from finding that *Registered Designs Act, 1949* (UK), s 2(2) imposes no form requirement for legal assignments to a discussion of an equitable assignment without giving reasons for rejecting a legal assignment. See also Bently and Sherman (2014), p. 751.

[119]See Sect. 2.4.1.

potential priority point.[120] The future assignment of the prospective ownership of an unregistered design right follows the same principle as the assignment of future copyright.[121]

The assignment of trade marks must be in writing.[122] Unlike copyright, future trade marks are not assignable.[123] Thus, a legal mortgage cannot be created in future trade marks.[124] There is no form requirement relating to the creation of a charge. Registration is not a form requirement for either type of security.[125]

Unlike the other UK statutes, the *PA 1977* specifically provides for form requirements relating to the use of patents as security, not just in relation to assignment. The wording of the act has the potential effect of making the creation of security in patents more cumbersome than the creation of security in other IPRs. According to the wording of the statute, the creation of a mortgage in a patent requires that the mortgage be in writing and signed by the parties.[126] Registration is not a requirement for the creation of a legal mortgage.[127] Unlike copyright, future patents are not assignable.[128] Thus, a legal mortgage cannot be created in future patents.[129] The statute does not clearly spell out whether the form requirement also applies to the creation of equitable mortgages and charges. Given that it defines the term "mortgage" as encompassing "charges,"[130] however, it would seem to follow that the

[120]Bently and Sherman (2014), p. 752.

[121]*Copyright, Designs and Patents Act 1986* (UK), s 223(1) ("Where by an agreement made in relation to future design right, and signed by or on behalf of the prospective owner of the design right, the prospective owner purports to assign the future design right (wholly or partially) to another person, then if, on the right coming into existence, the assignee or another person claiming under him would be entitled as against all other persons to require the right to be vested in him, the right shall vest in him by virtue of this section.").

[122]*Trade Marks Act 1994* (UK), s 24(3) ("An assignment of a registered trade mark, or an assent relating to a registered trade mark, is not effective unless it is in writing signed by or on behalf of the assignor or, as the case may be, a personal representative. Except in Scotland, this requirement may be satisfied in a case where the assignor or personal representative is a body corporate by the affixing of its seal.").

[123]See Tosato (2011), p. 95.

[124]Thomas (2017), p. 223; Tosato (2011), p. 95.

[125]Cf. Bently and Sherman (2014), p. 1098.

[126]*Patents Act 1977* (UK), s 30(6) ("Any of the following transactions, that is to say (a) any assignment or mortgage of a patent or any such application, or any right in a patent or any such application; (b) any assent relating to any patent or any such application or right; shall be void unless it is in writing and is signed by or on behalf of the assignor or mortgagor.").

[127]Cf. Beale et al. (2012), para 14.61; Bently and Sherman (2014), p. 645. But see Thomas (2017), p. 222, who argues it is unclear whether registration is necessary, but there is no further argument as to why. Later, he states "[r]egistration of a patent mortgage is not compulsory, nor is it a perfection requirement" (Thomas 2017, p. 225). If registration is not necessary for perfection, it is hard to see why it would be required for attachment, as perfection presupposes attachment.

[128]See Tosato (2011), p. 95.

[129]Thomas (2017), p. 223; Tosato (2011), p. 95.

[130]*Patents Act 1977* (UK), s 130. See text in footnote 57.

requirement applies to equitable interests as well.[131] While it is not impossible for statutes to provide for specific form requirements in relation to equitable transactions,[132] this would mean that equitable security interests in patents are the only equitable security in IPR to which specific form requirements apply for attachment. This potentially matters as it would mean that in relation to patents, registration becomes a perfection point, whereas in relation to other IPRs, registration only determines priority in a competition between a registered and an unregistered purchaser.[133]

3.2.2 Attachment and Perfection Relating to EU IPRs

In relation to European trade marks and design rights, registration of the security interest is expressed as a perfection requirement, and an unregistered right cannot be set up against third parties without notice.[134] Yet it is unclear whether a trustee in bankruptcy is a third party as regards the perfection function of EU IP registries.[135]

4 Priorities

4.1 General Priority Rules

4.1.1 Priority Rules in a Contest of Two Legal or Two Equitable Interests

The priorities of mortgages and charges are governed by the rules of general property law and equity.[136] Between two parties claiming to have the better legal title, the *nemo dat quod non habet* rule applies: a transferor having transferred the legal interest in an asset to a first transferee cannot transfer to a second transferee a title that is better than or on par with the title transferred to the first transferee.[137] A similar rule applies in relation to competing equitable interests. In a contest between

[131]Making this point in relation to equitable assignments of patents Thomas (2017), p. 222.

[132]For example, *Law of Property Act, 1925* (UK), s 53(1)(b) provides that a trust in land must be created in writing.

[133]See Sect. 4.2.

[134]*Community Design Regulation*, art 33(2); *EU Trade Mark Regulation (2017 Recast)*, art 27 (1) See Bariatti (2010), pp. 405–406; Bently and Sherman (2014), p. 1101.

[135]Cf. Bently and Sherman (2014), p. 1101.

[136]These rules have been summarized in *Macmillan Inc. v. Bishopsgate Investment Trust Plc. (No. 3)* (Ch. D.), 999–1005, per Millet J.

[137]Goode (2013), para 5.04.

two parties claiming an equitable interest in the property, the earlier interest defeats the latter interest.[138]

4.1.2 Bona Fide Purchaser of Legal Title for Value Without Notice

Where a priority contest takes place between the holder of an equitable interest and the subsequent purchaser of a legal interest, the first-in-time rule is modified and the purchaser of the legal interest might win: an equitable interest is defeated by the subsequent purchase of the legal title where the purchaser is a *bona fide* purchaser for value without notice.[139] This is known as "overreaching." The purchaser must have notice at the time they give value, not at the time they acquire the legal interest.[140]

4.1.3 Registration of Company Security Interests and Notice

In relation to company security interests, the order of registration is irrelevant as regards priority, and the first-in-time rule applies as long as interest is perfected by registration in time.[141] However, registration of a company security interest has two potential priority implications. First, registration of a company security interest gives notice for the purpose of the *bona fide* purchaser rule,[142] but there is no further effect of registration. A company security interest registration is primarily a perfection requirement, not a priority point. A potential priority contest could thus arise between different security interests, all of which are unregistered but are registrable in the company register. The treatment of these priority contests is unsettled.[143] Where there is a contest between a registered company security interest and an unregistered one, the registered security interest wins.[144] Second, company security interest also potentially constitutes notice for the purpose of the application of the tacking rules, but it is unclear to what extent this is the case.[145]

---

[138]Goode (2013), para 5.04.

[139]Goode (2013), paras 5.07, 5.09.

[140]*Bailey v. Barnes* (C.A.); *Taylor v. Russell* (H.L.). See Goode (2013), para 5.09.

[141]Goode (2013), para 5.16.

[142]Goode (2013), para 5.15. On the *bona fide* rule see "4.1.2 Bona Fide Purchaser of Legal Title for Value without Notice."

[143]See *Re Monolithic Building Co* (C.A.), 662, per Lord Cozens-Hardy MR and Goode (2013), para 5.26.

[144]Goode (2013), para 5.28.

[145]Goode (2013), para 5.22.

4.1.4 Priority in Insolvency

In liquidation, British insolvency law operates on the assumption that assets subject to a security interest do not form part of the insolvent's estate; rather, they belong to the secured creditor.[146] The secured creditor's right to the asset is consequentially not viewed as a question of insolvency ranking; instead, the asset subject to the security is simply unavailable to the other creditors.[147] This means that unless there is a statutory provision to the contrary allowing the liquidator to include these assets in the insolvent's estate (*e.g.* rules on fraudulent conveyances), the liquidator will not be able to use these assets to satisfy the other creditors.

[146]See *Re Pyle Works (No.1)* (C.A.), 577–578, per Cotton LJ; Goode (2011), para 6.45; *Buchler v. Talbot*, para 15, per Lord Nicholls.

[147]See *e.g.* Palmer and Morse (2017), para 15.441, making no reference to the ranking of a fixed charge in insolvency.

4.2 Priority Relating to IP Rights

In relation to patents,[148] domestic trade marks,[149] and registered designs,[150] registration in the specialized IP registries is a priority point.[151] The effect of registration is that a registered security interest wins over an unregistered security interest, and earlier registration prevails over later registration.[152] Registration of the security also provides notice, meaning that where the security interest is equitable, the subsequent purchaser of the legal title in the IPR cannot overreach the equitable interest.

The registration of security interests in IPRs raises a number of issues. First, it is unclear if and to what extent the general priority rules continue to apply if there is a

[148]For patents, this is a function of *Patents Act 1977* (UK), s 33(1) ("Any person who claims to have acquired the property in a patent or application for a patent by virtue of any transaction, instrument or event to which this section applies shall be entitled as against any other person who claims to have acquired that property by virtue of an earlier transaction, instrument or event to which this section applies if, at the time of the later transaction, instrument or event (a) the earlier transaction, instrument or event was not registered, or (b) in the case of any application which has not been published, notice of the earlier transaction, instrument or event had not been given to the comptroller, and (c)in any case, the person claiming under the later transaction, instrument or event, did not know of the earlier transaction, instrument or event."), s 33(2) ("Subsection (1) above shall apply equally to the case where any person claims to have acquired any right in or under a patent or application for a patent, by virtue of a transaction, instrument or event to which this section applies, and that right is incompatible with any such right acquired by virtue of an earlier transaction, instrument or event to which this section applies.") and s 33(3)(b) ("This section applies to the following transactions, instruments and events: [. . .] (b) the mortgage of a patent or application or the granting of security over it[.]"). See *Finecard International Ltd. v. Urquhart Dyke & Lorri* (Ch. D.), para 15, per Smith J. See also Goode (2013), para 5.16 and Bently and Sherman (2014), p. 646.

[149]*Trade Marks Act 1994* (UK), s 25(2)(c) ("The following are registrable transactions: [. . .] the granting of any security interest (whether fixed or floating) over a registered trade mark or any right in or under it[.]") and s 25(3) ("Until an application has been made for registration of the prescribed particulars of a registrable transaction (a) the transaction is ineffective as against a person acquiring a conflicting interest in or under the registered trade mark in ignorance of it[.]"). See also Goode (2013), para 5.16; Thomas (2017), p. 223; Tosato (2011), pp. 96–97. The situation was different under *Trade Marks Act, 1938* (UK), s 28(6), which contained a prohibition against "traficking in trade marks." See *American Greetings Corp's Application (Holly Hobbie)* (H.L.).

[150]*Registered Designs Act, 1949* (UK), s 19(4) ("Subject to any rights vested in any other person of which notice is entered in the register of designs, the person or persons registered as proprietor of a registered design shall have power to assign, grant licences under, or otherwise deal with the design, and to give effectual receipts for any consideration for any such assignment, licence or dealing: Provided that any equities in respect of the design may be enforced in like manner as in respect of any other personal property.") and s 19(1) ("Where any person becomes entitled by assignment, transmission or operation of law to a registered design or to a share in a registered design, or becomes entitled as mortgagee, licensee or otherwise to any other interest in a registered design, he shall apply to the registrar in the prescribed manner for the registration of his title as proprietor or co-proprietor or, as the case may be, of notice of his interest, in the register of designs."). See Goode (2013), para 5.16.

[151]Bently and Sherman (2014), p. 646; Thomas (2017), p. 225.

[152]Tosato (2011), pp. 97–98.

conflict between two security interests not registered in the special registries.[153] Second, the IP registries do not allow filing a priority notice that would secure priority before the security itself is filed. Third, it is unclear to what extent notice of an unregistered security interest defeats reliance on the register.[154]

Fourth, the fact that registration determines priority means that the rank of legal mortgages is no longer determined by the first-in-time rule, which is unusual for legal interests.[155] Consequently, it is argued that registration is a form requirement, meaning that where the form requirement is not met, the interest is an equitable interest.[156] Tosato, on the other hand, suggests that the registration of security interests in IP is only a priority point and does not determine the legal or equitable nature of the interest at all; his argument appears to be that, because registration governs priority, the legal or equitable nature of the unregistered interest should not matter.[157] While this true, because of the first issue, the argument is potentially only valid to the extent that the contest is between a registered and an unregistered purchaser. It can be added that exceptions to the *nemo dat* rule governing priority at law exist elsewhere in English law. A similar mechanism applies to sales of goods, where priority of competing legal titles is determined by possession.[158]

Fifth, insofar as the company registry provides notice, a potential conflict may arise between the priority function of the specialized registers and the notice provided by the company registry.[159] This issue would be put in particularly sharp focus if one were to characterize IPR security interests not registered in the IP

[153]Cf. Goode (2013), para 5.16, there note 64, ref'g to *Fraser v. Oystertec Plc.* (Pat.); and *Finecard International Ltd. v. Urquhart Dyke & Lorri* (Ch. D.).

[154]Thomas (2017), pp. 225–226.

[155]Tosato (2011), p. 98.

[156]See Goode (2013), para 1.12 and Davies (2006), p. 567, suggesting that "since the Patents Act and the Trade Marks Act do not actually establish a compulsory system of registration, legal interests are treated as equitable interests because they have no effect against a subsequent interest holder who does not have actual notice of their existence."

[157]Tosato (2011), p. 98.

[158]*Sale of Goods Act 1979* (UK), s 24 ("Where a person having sold goods continues or is in possession of the goods, or of the documents of title to the goods, the delivery or transfer by that person, or by a mercantile agent acting for him, of the goods or documents of title under any sale, pledge, or other disposition thereof, to any person receiving the same in good faith and without notice of the previous sale, has the same effect as if the person making the delivery or transfer were expressly authorised by the owner of the goods to make the same.") and s 25(1) ("Where a person having bought or agreed to buy goods obtains, with the consent of the seller, possession of the goods or the documents of title to the goods, the delivery or transfer by that person, or by a mercantile agent acting for him, of the goods or documents of title, under any sale, pledge, or other disposition thereof, to any person receiving the same in good faith and without notice of any lien or other right of the original seller in respect of the goods, has the same effect as if the person making the delivery or transfer were a mercantile agent in possession of the goods or documents of title with the consent of the owner."). These provisions allow certain people in possession of goods to transfer a better title to the goods than they have without given the authority to do that by the holder of the higher-ranking title.

[159]See Sect. 4.1.3.

registries as equitable and the special IP priority rules as particular applications of the general priority rules.[160] In a priority contest between an equitable chargee and a subsequent purchaser of a legal interest, the creditor of an equitable interest not registered in the IP registries but registered in the company registry could claim that the registration of the equitable charge constituted notice. To solve this problem, it is argued that the priority rules of the IP registries should entirely displace the notice function of the company register.[161] This approach in turn would then raise a sixth issue; namely, whether the company registry could still play a role in relation to a priority contest between to unregistered IPR security interests.

5 Enterprise Charges

5.1 *The Floating Charge*

5.1.1 Concept of the Floating Charge

English law allows for the creation of a floating charge.[162] The floating charge is a present security interest in a fund of assets, but it is unattached to a specific asset.[163] Whether a charge is a floating charge or a fixed charge depends on the intention of the parties.[164] The hallmark of a floating charge is not so much that it entails all present and after-acquired property, but that the chargor retains the ability to dispose of assets encompassed by the floating charge in the course of their business.[165]

A floating charge can in principle be created by incorporated businesses or by unincorporated businesses or individuals. In practice, the latter occurrence is rare because a charge in tangible personal property by an unincorporated entity or individual is currently covered by the *Bills of Sale Act, 1878* (UK).[166] As such, it

[160]See above text at footnote 156.

[161]See Tosato (2011), p. 99.

[162]*Re Panama, New Zealand & Australian Royal Mail Company*; *Re Yorkshire Woolcombers Association* (C.A.).

[163]*Evans v. Rival Granite Quarries, Ltd.* (C.A.), 999, per Buckley LJ. See also Goode (2013), para 4.03.

[164]See *Agnew & Kevin James Bearsley v. The Commissioner of Inland Revenue (Re Birtwhistle)* (N.Z.), para 34, per Lord Millett. For further details see Goode (2013), para 4.05.

[165]*Re Yorkshire Woolcombers Association* (C.A.), 294, per Vaughan Williams LJ; *Siebe Gorman & Co. Ltd. v. Barclays Bank Ltd.* (Ch. D.). This aspect has not been overruled by *National Westminster Bank plc v. Spectrum Plus Limited*. See Goode (2013), paras 1.10, 4.01–4.04, 4.08, 4.11.

[166]*Bills of Sale Act, 1878* (UK), s 4: "The expression 'bill of sale' shall include bills of sale, assignments, transfers, declarations of trust without transfer, inventories of goods with receipt thereto attached, or receipts for purchase moneys of goods, and other assurances of personal chattels, and also powers of attorney, authorities, or licenses to take possession of personal chattels as security for any debt, and also any agreement, whether intended or not to be followed by the

can only be granted in presently owned property.[167] A charge in debts must be in the form of a bill of sale. Otherwise, it is void in insolvency.[168] However, no such restriction applies to floating charges in IPRs. Thus, individuals can grant floating charges in IPRs. However, the above-mentioned restrictions mean that most floating charges are granted by companies; consequently, most case law relates to floating charges granted by companies.

Due to the fact that the floating charge is designed to attach to future property in the asset class, it generally takes the form of an equitable interest,[169] but the characterization of the chargee's interest is not discussed because most classes of assets do not allow the creation of a legal mortgage in future property. Turner argues that "a fixed charge in the form of a legal mortgage coupled with a power for the chargor to deal with charged assets is not a 'floating charge,' even though that arrangement might be economically equivalent to one."[170] However, it is not entirely clear from this passage whether his argument is not simply based on the facts for most assets, due to the prohibition against future assignments, an automatic replacement mechanism is not possible.[171] There is arguably no reason why the floating charge cannot be a legal mortgage in cases where the law allows a legal mortgage in future property.[172] The question may be important for those IPRs that

execution of any other instrument, by which a right in equity to any personal chattels, or to any charge or security thereon, shall be conferred[.]."

[167] *Bills of Sale Act (1878) Amendment Act, 1882* (UK), s 5: "Save as herein-after mentioned, a bill of sale shall be void, except as against the grantor, in respect of any personal chattels specifically described in the schedule thereto of which the grantor was not the true owner at the time of the execution of the bill of sale."

[168] *Insolvency Act 1986* (UK), s 344(1) and s 344(2): "(1) The following applies where a person engaged in any business makes a general assignment to another person of his existing or future book debts, or any class of them, and is subsequently adjudged bankrupt. (2) The assignment is void against the trustee of the bankrupt's estate as regards book debts which were not paid before the presentation of the bankruptcy petition, unless the assignment has been registered under the Bills of Sale Act 1878."

[169] See subsection "Transfer of Future Property" within Sect. 3.1.1.

[170] Turner (2006), p. 207, ref'g to *Swiss Bank Corp. v. Lloyds Bank Ltd.* (C.A. Civ.), 466–467, per Buckley LJ.

[171] For example, in *Gordon Mackay & Co., Ltd. v. Capital Trust Corp., Ltd.*, 384–385 Duff J writes that "I have not been able to satisfy myself that you cannot have a floating security by way of mortgage. Nobody doubts that you can have a mortgage of after acquired property: the statute, indeed, recognizes that itself. You can have, for example, a valid mortgage of chattels to be afterwards brought upon certain premises. As soon as the property is brought there and identified, the *equitable* right of the mortgagee attaches." [Emphasis added.] In that case, the class of assets contemplated was one in which no legal assignment of future property was permissible.

[172] The possibility of a floating charge by way of legal mortgage is potentially mentioned in Goode (2013), para 5.42, there note 188, ref'g to *Taylor v. M'Keand* (C.P.D.) and *Payne v. Fern* (Q.B.D.) as possible examples of floating charges by way of a legal mortgage; however, it is also possible that these are supposed to be examples of a fixed charge over a class of assets. The text is unclear at that point.

can be assigned in advance, as it would be possible to set up an asset class entailing only IPRs that can be assigned in advance.

5.1.2 Concept of Crystallization

Upon crystallization, the floating charge attaches to the specific items of property included in the class of assets to which the floating charge relates; the chargor loses their power to dispose of the property.[173] Crystallization does not create a new charge and thus triggers no registration requirements in the company registry.[174] Decrystallization is also possible, but it is uncertain whether that triggers registration requirements, *i.e.* whether the decrystallized floating charge needs to be registered anew.[175] The parties can agree on any specified event, including a choice by the creditor, as the crystallizing event.[176] Unless the parties have agreed otherwise, crystallization affects the entire class of assets subject to the charge.[177] Where a company ceases trading, the floating charge crystallizes unless the parties agree otherwise,[178] including if this is due to the liquidation of the company.[179]

5.2 Attachment and Perfection of the Floating Charge

In relation to attachment and perfection, the general rules apply. This means that a floating charge granted by a company must be registered. Furthermore, at the moment the floating charge crystallizes, priority will depend on the proper registration of the resulting fixed security interest in any IPRs subject to the floating charge. This means that if security interests in the IPRs are not registered individually for each IPR at the moment of crystallization, the charge in them has low priority.

---

[173]There is some debate on what crystallization actually means and the nature of the floating charge, see Goode (2013), paras 4.06, 4.31; Nolan (2004), *passim*; Worthington (1996), pp. 78–86.

[174]Goode (2013), para 4.31.

[175]See Goode (2013), para 4.63; Grantham (1997), *passim*; Tan (1998), *passim*.

[176]*Fire Nymph Products Ltd. v. Heating Centre Pty Ltd.* (N.S.W. C.A.); *Re Woodroffes (Musical Instruments) Ltd.* (Ch. D.); *Re Brightlife Ltd.* (Ch. D.); *Covacich v. Riordan* (H.C.); *DFC Financial Services Ltd. v. Coffey* (P.C.); *Re Manurewa Transport Limited* (S.C.); *Deputy Commissioner of Taxation (Cth) v. Horsburgh (No 2)* (S.C.). See Goode (2013), paras 2.09, 4.52–4.54, 4.56–4.57.

[177]*Evans v. Rival Granite Quarries, Ltd.* (C.A.), 998, per Fletcher Moulton LJ; *Robson v. Smith* (Ch. D.), 126, per Romer J; *Re Caroma Enterprises Ltd.* (Alta. Q.B.); *Evans v. Rival Granite Quarries, Ltd.* (C.A.), 1000, per Buckley LJ. See Goode (2013), para 4.49.

[178]*Re Crompton* (Ch. D.), 964–965, per Warrington J; *Re Brightlife Ltd.* (Ch. D.), 212, per Hoffman J; *Re Real Meat Co Ltd.* (Ch. D.), 260–261, per Chadwick J. See also Goode (2013), para 4.34.

[179]Goode (2013), para 4.34.

5.3 *Priority of the Floating Charge*

Priority questions relating the interaction of a floating charge and other legal or equitable interests, including other security interests and other floating charges, are in principle governed by general priority rules.[180] A crystallized floating charge takes precedence over all other interests according to the general priority rules and subject to law preferences. However, the priority rules are subject to the retained power of the chargor to deal with the property.[181] This means that a subsequent purchaser in the course of the business defeats the floating chargee's interest.[182] Where the transfer of the asset exceeds the grantor's retained power, the *bona fide* purchaser of a legal interest for value without notice will prevail if floating charge is in the form of an equitable interest.[183] However, it should be kept in mind that a floating charge might potentially take the form of a legal mortgage in relation to copyright and related rights.[184] In that case, the *bona fide* purchaser exception would not apply.[185] Similar to enforcement outside of insolvency, the appointment of a liquidator[186] or an administrator[187] relegates the floating chargee's interest to the interests of preferential creditors.

6 Rights Before Default

The reciprocal rights and obligations arising due to the creation of a security interest are mostly the result of the agreement between the parties creating the interest, subject to the following principles. The creation of a legal mortgage in IPRs leads to a split between legal title and equitable entitlement: legal title is transferred to the

---

[180] See Sect. 4.

[181] Goode (2013), para 5.40.

[182] Goode (2013), para 5.40.

[183] See Goode (2013), para 5.42.

[184] See Sect. 5.1.1.

[185] That appears to be the point made by Goode (2013), para 5.42, there note 188, ref'g to *Taylor v. M'Keand* (C.P.D.) and *Payne v. Fern* (Q.B.D.); otherwise, the reference to priority rules for legal interests in the context of floating charge priority rules would be inexplicable.

[186] *Insolvency Act 1986* (UK), s 175(2)(b) ("(1) In a winding up the company's preferential debts (within the meaning given by section 386 in Part XII) shall be paid in priority to all other debts. (2) Preferential debt (a) rank equally among themselves after the expenses of the winding up and shall be paid in full, unless the assets are insufficient to meet them, in which case they abate in equal proportions; and (b) so far as the assets of the company available for payment of general creditors are insufficient to meet them, have priority over the claims of holders of debentures secured by, or holders of, any floating charge created by the company, and shall be paid accordingly out of any property comprised in or subject to that charge.").

[187] *Insolvency Act 1986* (UK), ss Schedule B1; para 65(2), applying s 175 to a distribution by an administrator.

mortgagee, whereas the mortgagor retains the equity of redemption. This leads to a number issues, as the mortgagor will be the one who has an interest in exercising the rights arising from the IPR in relation to third parties (*e.g.* infringement actions or in dealings with the IP registry).[188] These issues were addressed in relation to patents by the High Court in *Van Gelder Apsimon & Co v. Sowerby Bridge United District Flour Society*: In that case, the claimant had transferred a patent by way of mortgage and then brought an action based on the patent. The defendant claimed that the claimant would thus not be entitled to sue. Relying on general property law principles, the Court found that it is a principle of equity that the mortgagor retains the equitable ownership of the mortgaged property and can thus rely on this ownership to show a cause of action.[189] In *Van Gelder*, it was found that the IPO registers assignments by way of mortgage differently from outright assignments, allowing a distinction between the equitable proprietor and the mortgagee. This is still current practice at IPO; however, there is no specific statutory basis for doing so.[190] In relation to mortgaging trade marks similar issues arise: the renewal of registration or filing of a relative ground for refusal are better left to the mortgagor than to the mortgagee.[191] Tosato argues that the IPO's current practice of distinguishing between equitable patent proprietor and mortgagee should be extended to trade marks as well.[192] The issues arising from a split of legal and equitable title resulting from the creation of a legal mortgage can also be avoided by opting for an equitable mortgage or for the creation of charge. This can potentially impact priority, although this only applies in relation to unregistered security interests in registrable IPRs.[193] The *Patent Rules 2007* (UK) are also unclear whether a charge as distinct from a mortgage in a patent can be registered, but there are good arguments why this should be possible.[194]

As stated initially, the creation of a mortgage or a charge means that the chargee receives the right to appropriate the asset to the satisfaction of the outstanding debt.[195] Where the chargor of a fixed charge—i.e. a mortgage or a charge—disposes of the property, the chargee can in principle follow their security interest into the hands of the third-party purchaser, subject to the rules of perfection and priority. In case of a floating charge, following requires crystallization.[196] If the chargee is unable to follow their interest into the hands of the purchaser, they can instead trace their interest into the proceeds the chargor has received in lieu of the

---

188 Tosato (2011), pp. 96–97.
189 See Tosato (2011), p. 96.
190 Tosato (2011), p. 96.
191 Tosato (2011), p. 96.
192 Tosato (2011), pp. 96–97.
193 See Sect. 4.
194 See Thomas (2017), p. 223.
195 See Sect. 2.2.
196 See Goode (2013), para 4.06.

property.[197] In case of a fixed charge, the interest in the traceable proceeds will constitute a new charge, unless the fixed charge was drafted to include the traceable proceeds.[198] However, the new charge does not require company registration, because the new charge is not created by the company.[199] In the case of a floating charge, whether or not the original floating charge entails the traceable proceeds is determined by the definition of the class of assets subject to the floating charge.[200] The grantor of a security has a right to redeem the property. Any restrictions on this right of redemption are potentially void.[201] Upon crystallization, the floating chargee enjoys the same rights as a fixed chargee.

7 Enforcement

7.1 Enforcement Outside Insolvency

The rights conferred to the creditor for the enforcement of the security interest will depend on the agreement between the parties. Typically, the creditor will be given the right to take possession of the charged assets, to sell them, or to appoint a receiver, who will realize the asset on the creditor's behalf.[202] Where the security interest is a mortgage, the creditor can apply to the court for a foreclosure order, transferring legal title to the creditor (where the mortgage is equitable) and extinguishing the mortgagor's equity of redemption.[203] A court can deny the foreclosure application and order the sale of the asset instead.[204] If a charge or mortgage is made in deed form, the transferee has a statutory power to appoint a receiver, regardless of the content of the agreement.[205] The receiver will take over

---

[197] See Goode (2013), paras 1.64, 1.67.

[198] See Goode (2013), para 1.68.

[199] See Goode (2013), para 1.68.

[200] See Goode (2013), para 1.68.

[201] Goode (2013), para 1.37.

[202] Goode (2013), para 4.65. Goode argues that where a charge agreement includes these self-help rights, the agreement is properly characterized as a legal or equitable mortgage, not a mere charge, see Goode (2013), para 1.55, there note 238.

[203] Goode (2013), para 4.65.

[204] *Law of Property Act, 1925* (UK), s 91(2) ("In any action, whether for foreclosure, or for redemption, or for sale, or for the raising and payment in any manner of mortgage money, the court, on the request of the mortgagee, or of any person interested either in the mortgage money or in the right of redemption, and, notwithstanding that (a) any other person dissents; or (b) the mortgagee or any person so interested does not appear in the action;and without allowing any time for redemption or for payment of any mortgage money, may direct a sale of the mortgaged property, on such terms as it thinks fit, including the deposit in court of a reasonable sum fixed by the court to meet the expenses of sale and to secure performance of the terms.").

[205] *Law of Property Act, 1925* (UK), s 101(1) ("A mortgagee, where the mortgage is made by deed, shall, by virtue of this Act, have the following powers, to the like extent as if they had been in terms

the assets and realize them, and the proceeds will be used to pay the chargee. Once the transferor of the security interest loses the right to use the collateral, any fruits of the asset belong to the transferee.[206] Thus, licence fees generated from an IPR being used as collateral will also be appropriated to the satisfaction of the debt once the creditor has taken over the asset. If there is a surplus on the realization of the assets, the grantor has an equitable right to the surplus proceeds.[207] As a result, where licencing fees are sufficient to satisfy the debt, the debtor's equity of redemption should allow them to regain the asset before it is sold off.

Once the floating charge crystallizes, the floating chargee has the same rights that are available to the fixed chargee. In addition, the chargee of a floating charge will usually be given the power to appoint a receiver. They can make an application for the appointment of a receiver regardless of whether the floating charge has crystallized,[208] and regardless of whether there has been a default.[209] The floating chargee can also apply for an injunction enjoining the chargor from disposing of the assets.[210]

7.2 *Enforcement Inside Insolvency*

The chargee of a fixed charge may be given the power to apply for the appointment of an administrator.[211] In administration, the administrator will try to keep the company going. An administrator disposing of assets subject to a fixed charge requires leave from the court.[212] The fixed chargee or other creditors can also apply for a winding-up order, putting the company into liquidation. Because assets subject to a fixed charge do not form part of the insolvent's estate,[213] the liquidator who sells of these assets is under a duty to hand over the proceeds to the secured creditor.

---

conferred by the mortgage deed, but not further (namely): [. . .] A power, when the mortgage money has become due, to appoint a receiver of the income of the mortgaged property, or any part thereof; or, if the mortgaged property consists of an interest in income, or of a rentcharge or an annual or other periodical sum, a receiver of that property or any part thereof[.]") and s 205(1)(xvi) ("'Mortgage' includes any charge or lien on any property for securing money or money's worth[. . . .]").

206 Goode (2013), para 1.65, ref'g to *Tucker v. Farm & General Investment Trust* (C.A.), where the point is made more broadly: fruits of property belong to the person entitled to the possession.

207 Goode (2013), para 1.37.

208 *Hubbuck v. Helms* (Ch. D.); *Edwards v. Standard Rolling Stock Syndicate* (Ch. D.); *Re Victoria Steamboats Ltd.* (Ch. D.); *Re London Pressed Hinge Co Ltd.* (Ch. D.).

209 *Re London Pressed Hinge Co Ltd.* (Ch. D.).

210 Goode (2013), para 4.06.

211 Goode (2013), para 4.65.

212 Goode (2013), para 4.10.

213 See Sect. 4.1.4.

The floating chargee has similar rights to the fixed chargee when putting the company into administration or liquidation. A floating chargee is given the power to appoint an administrator out of court under a "fast-track" procedure not available to other creditors if their security interest covers substantially the whole of the company's property either by virtue of one floating charge or alone or by virtue of a combination of several fixed and/or floating charges, and if they have a contractual power to appoint an administrator.[214] Similar to enforcement outside of insolvency, the appointment of a liquidator[215] or an administrator[216] relegates the floating chargee's interest to the interests of preferential creditors. An administrator disposing assets subject to a floating charge does not require any leave from the court.[217] Further, a certain sum is ringfenced for unsecured creditors from assets subject to the floating charge.[218] If a charge is created as floating charge, this relegation applies regardless of later crystallization.[219] This even applies if the asset was only acquired after crystallization.[220] In effect, empirically the floating chargee will realize very little, if any, value in insolvency, and the floating charge's main value lies in the chargee's power to control the company management.[221]

---

[214] *Insolvency Act 1986* (UK), ss Schedule B1; para 14.

[215] *Insolvency Act 1986* (UK), s 175(2)(b) ("(1) In a winding up the company's preferential debts (within the meaning given by section 386 in Part XII) shall be paid in priority to all other debts. (2) Preferential debt (a) rank equally among themselves after the expenses of the winding up and shall be paid in full, unless the assets are insufficient to meet them, in which case they abate in equal proportions; and (b) so far as the assets of the company available for payment of general creditors are insufficient to meet them, have priority over the claims of holders of debentures secured by, or holders of, any floating charge created by the company, and shall be paid accordingly out of any property comprised in or subject to that charge.").

[216] *Insolvency Act 1986* (UK), ss Schedule B1; para 65(2), applying s 175 to a distribution by an administrator.

[217] Goode (2013), para 4.10.

[218] *Insolvency Act 1986* (UK), s 176A(2) ("The liquidator, administrator or receiver (a)shall make a prescribed part of the company's net property available for the satisfaction of unsecured debts, and (b)shall not distribute that part to the proprietor of a floating charge except in so far as it exceeds the amount required for the satisfaction of unsecured debts.").

[219] *Insolvency Act 1986* (UK), s 251 ("'[F]loating charge' means a charge which, as created, was a floating charge [. . .]."); *Companies Act 2006* (UK), s 754(1) ("This section applies where debentures of a company registered in England and Wales or Northern Ireland are secured by a charge that, as created, was a floating charge."). See Goode (2013), para 5.68.

[220] *Inland Revenue Commissioners v. Goldblatt* (Ch. D.).

[221] See Mokal (2003), *passim*.

8 Typical Costs

The nominal costs associated with security interests in IPRs are low. The registration of a security interest in a trade mark[222] or patent[223] at the UK IPO costs £50. The registration of a security interest in a registered design right is free.[224] Other than that, the costs associated with creating or enforcing security in IPRs are the same as any other asset. There is no statutory guidance regarding the content of a security interest. Transaction costs are therefore potentially high, because the details of the content of the security interest must be negotiated between the parties.[225] The registration of a company charge at the company registry costs £23.[226] There are no costs relating to other form requirements and notarization is not necessary. In principle, the costs of enforcement of security interests in IPR are the same as the enforcement of other security interests. Where the security is realized by the appointment of a receiver, the receiver will take their fees from the money realized by selling of the asset. Where the liquidator of the company acts as receiver of property that is subject to a fixed charge and thus not part of the estate, they will usually only agree to do so in return for the chargee agreeing to reimburse them for the fees.

9 Practical Usefulness

Given a number of unresolved issues relating to use of IPRs as security that are summarized in the next section, secured financing in IP in England is rare and coincidental.[227] It has been described as complex and disadvantageous by practitioners[228] and as being "ripe for reform."[229] The reasons for this will be summarized in the next section.

---

[222] UK, Intellectual Property Office (2019), "Form 24: Application to record or amend a security interest."

[223] UK, Intellectual Property Office (2018b), "Form 21: Application to register or give notice of rights."

[224] UK, Intellectual Property Office (2018a), Form DF12A "Record/cancel a change of ownership, licence or security."

[225] See generally Merrill and Smith (2000), *passim*.

[226] Companies House Form MR1: Particulars of a charge. https://www.gov.uk/government/uploads/system/uploads/attachment_data/file/537724/MR01_v2.1.pdf. Accessed July 4, 2017.

[227] See Thomas (2017), p. 224; Tosato (2011), p. 93. Edenborough (2009), *passim* points out that in insolvency, IPRs will often be the last remaining valuable unencumbered assets.

[228] Thomas (2017), p. 224.

[229] Secured Transactions Law Reform Project (2016), para 3.29.

10 Difficulties of the Current Regime

As the foregoing analysis shows, taking security in IPRs in England and Wales is subject to a number of issues. A general problem with security interests in English law is the maintained distinction between equitable and legal security interests and the impact that this has on the priority rules. These are put in sharper focus in relation to IPRs for a number reasons. First, there are different form requirements between different IPRs. Second, depending on the IPR, different rules relating to the assignment of future property apply. This means that the option of creating a legal interest in future property depends on the type of the IPR. A third issue is the conceptual distinction between tangibles and intangibles; this creates problems of financing where parties try to take security in goods that combine tangible and intangible aspects.[230] Fourth, as seen above, the creation of a legal mortgage leads to a split of legal and equitable title, leading to potential issues where the mortgagor needs to act as the titular holder of the affected IPR.[231] The *Van Gelder* principle potentially may apply to unregistered IPRs because there is, by definition, no register that distinguishes between outright assignment and mortgage.[232] One way to circumvent the issues arising from the split of legal and equitable entitlement in cases of IPR mortgages is to combine the mortgage with an exclusive licence back to the mortgagor.[233] Another way would be to an equitable mortgage or charge instead of a legal mortgage. In these cases, the grantor would retain legal title to the IPR. However, it might be argued that there are no problems in relation to the granting of legal mortgages in unregistered IPRs. The identification of a problem turns the *Van Gelder ratio* upside down. In *Van Gelder*, the Court reasoned that the general property law principle is that in equity, the mortgagor must be treated as owner of the collateral and at issue was whether the *Patents, Designs, and Trade Marks Act, 1883* (UK)[234] created an exception to that.[235] It was not an issue whether a third party must have notice of the retained equitable ownership. The Court rejected any negative impact of s 87 *Patents, Designs, and Trade Marks Act, 1883* on the rights of the mortgagor, the equitable owner of the patent, because the registry practice of distinguishing between mortgagee and outright assignee negated any impact the

---

[230]Thomas (2017), p. 215.

[231]See Sect. 6.

[232]See Tosato (2011), p. 97, making this argument in relation to copyright.

[233]Thomas (2017), p. 224; Tosato (2011), pp. 97, 100.

[234]*Patents, Designs, and Trade Marks Act, 1883* (UK).

[235]*Patents, Designs, and Trade Marks Act, 1883* (UK), s 87 read as follows: "The person for the time being entered in the register of patents, designs, or trade marks, as proprietor of a patent, copyright in a design or trade mark, as the case may Sect. 87. be, shall, subject to any rights appearing from such register to be vested in any other person, have power absolutely to assign, grant licenses as to, or other- wise deal with, the same, and to give efifectual re- ceipts for any consideration for such assignment, license, or dealing." But it went on to say that the foregoing only applies "[p]rovided that any equities in respect of such patent, design, or trade mark may be enforced in like manner as in respect of any other personal property."

statute might have on the general property law principles. This approach is supported by *Hardacre v. Armstrong*,[236] in which the Court held that the equitable proprietor of a copyright should be entitled to bring a claim.[237] However, *Hardacre v. Armstrong* involved a case in which the equitable owner of the copyright was merely beneficially entitled because the copyright was not registered (which was necessary at that time). It is thus not relevant as regards modern unregistered IPRs.[238] In other words, without a rule that provides that the mortgagor of a copyright loses their rights deriving from copyright, the mortgagor of an unregistered IPR should retain full equitable ownership and any rights deriving from their ownership. However, the issue of whether the *Van Gelder* principle extends to unregistered IPRs remains unresolved. Fifth, an issue arises because the double registration regime: the two registries are not synchronized and there is thus an additional burden on chargor and chargee.[239] The statutory framework also does not clarify the relationship between the registers and their respective notice and priority functions.[240] On the other hand, in relation to copyright, it is possible that security interest is unregistered. There is no time limit for registration, meaning that a number of old security interests can be attached to the IPR and the first in time to register would win out.[241] As priority can also depend on actual notice, factual disputes and priority circles might result.[242]

11 Reform

The Law Commission has suggested a repeal of the *Bills of Sale Act, 1878* and the *Bills of Sale Act (1878) Amendment Act, 1882* (UK) and the enactment of a *Goods Mortgages Act*.[243] This proposal has been adopted by the Queen's Speech after the 2017 general election,[244] but was then shelved after consultation.[245] The *Goods Mortgages Act* would not have applied to security interests in intangible property.[246]

[236] *Hardacre v. Armstrong* (K.B.D.).

[237] This argument is made by Garnett et al. (2013), para 5.201.

[238] See Tosato (2011), p. 97.

[239] Tosato (2011), pp. 98–100. See also Thomas (2017), p. 231.

[240] See Sect. 4.2.

[241] Tosato (2011), p. 98; Townend (1997), p. 182.

[242] Tosato (2011), p. 98.

[243] Law Commission (2016), *passim*.

[244] UK, Her Majesty's Government (2017), *passim*.

[245] UK, Her Majesty's Treasury (2018), *passim*.

[246] See Law Commission (2016), para 4.33, excluding security interests in IPR from the scope of the proposed *Goods Mortgages Act* because "[i]t is already possible for individuals to grant security over intangible goods, such as shares and intellectual property rights. As the Bills of Sale Acts do not apply to intangible goods, it is in fact easier for individuals to use them as security."

The suggested reforms were thus very targeted, and had been criticized as being motivated by "a drive for short-term solutions [. . .] hamstring[ing] the prospect of a wider modernisation in this area,"[247] a criticism that was also raised in the consultation process.[248]

The Secured Transactions Law Reform Project and the City Law Society are both working in the area of secured transaction law reform. The Secured Transactions Law Reform Project has announced that the matter of security interests in IPRs will be the subject of a discrete study.[249] Areas where reform is seen as desirable include the differential treatment of IPRs[250]; the unclear priority scheme[251]; the doubling of registration requirements[252]; the introduction of a notice-filing system either generally[253]; or particularly in relation to IPR security interests[254]; the notice effect of registration[255]; the distinction between fixed and floating charges[256]; and the formalist approach to security interests.[257]

References

Bariatti S (2010) The law applicable to security interests in intellectual property rights. J Priv Int Law 6:395–416

Beale H, Bridge MG, Gullifer L, Lomnicka E (2012) The law of security and title-based financing, 2nd edn. Oxford University Press, Oxford

Bently L, Sherman B (2014) Intellectual property law, 4th edn. Oxford University Press, Oxford

Bridge MG, Macdonald RA, Simmonds RL, Walsh CE (1999) Formalism, functionalism, and understanding the law of secured transactions. McGill Law J 44:567–664

Brodhurst S (1895) Is copyright a chose in action? Law Q Rev 11:64–75

Davies I (2006) Secured financing of intellectual property assets and the reform of English personal property security law. Oxford J Legal Stud 26:559–583

Edenborough M (2009) The mis-treatment of intellectual property rights in insolvency. Butterworths J Int Bank Financ Law 24:397

Elphinstone HW (1893) What is a chose in action. Law Q Rev 9:311–315

EU, Council (2018) Agreement on a unified patent court (upc). https://www.consilium.europa.eu/en/documents-publications/treaties-agreements/agreement/?id=2013001. Accessed 10 Jan 2019

[247] Gullifer and Raczynska (2016), pp. 287–290.

[248] See UK, Her Majesty's Treasury (2018), *passim*.

[249] Secured Transactions Law Reform Project (2016), *passim*.

[250] Gullifer and Raczynska (2016), p. 294; Tosato (2011), pp. 101–102.

[251] Goode (2013), para 2.33; Gullifer and Raczynska (2016), pp. 284, 293.

[252] Gullifer and Raczynska (2016), pp. 294–295.

[253] Gullifer and Raczynska (2016), pp. 292–293.

[254] Davies (2006), p. 580; Tosato (2011), pp. 103–104.

[255] Goode (2013), para 2.33; Gullifer and Raczynska (2016), p. 284.

[256] Gullifer and Raczynska (2016), p. 290.

[257] Gullifer and Raczynska (2016), p. 290.

Garnett K, Davies G, Harbottle G (2013) Copinger and Skone James on copyright, 17th edn. Sweet & Maxwell, London
Goode RM (2003) Are intangible assets fungible? Lloyd's Maritime Commer Law Q, 379–388
Goode RM (2011) Principles of corporate insolvency law, 4th edn. Sweet & Maxwell, London
Goode RM (2013) Goode on legal problems of credit and security, 5th edn. Sweet & Maxwell, London
Grantham RB (1997) Refloating a floating charge. Comp Financ Insolvency Law Rev, 53–66
Gullifer L, Raczynska M (2016) The English law of personal property security: under-reformed. In: Gullifer L, Akseli O (eds) Secured transactions law reform: principles, policies and practice. Hart, Oxford, pp 271–296
Harrison WN (1952) The legal assignment of future goods. Univ Queensl Law J 2:42–48
Holdsworth WS (1920) The history of the treatment of choses in action by the common law. Harv Law Rev 33:997–1030
Lamping M, Ullrich H (2018) The impact of Brexit on unitary patent protection and its court. Max Planck Institute for Innovation & Competition Research Paper. https://papers.ssrn.com/sol3/papers.cfm?abstract_id=3232627. Accessed 9 Jan 2019
Law Commission (2016) Bills of sale. LAW COM, London
Legal Tribune Online (2017) Kurz vor der Ausfertigung: BVerfG stoppt EU-Patent. Legal Tribune Online. http://www.lto.de/recht/nachrichten/n/bverfg-stoppt-eu-einheits-patent-verfassungsbeschwerde/. Accessed 10 Jan 2019
Merrill TW, Smith HE (2000) Optimal standardization in the law of property: the *numerus clausus* principle. Yale Law J 110:1–70
Mokal R (2003) The floating charge: an elegy. In: Worthington S (ed) Commercial law and commercial practice. Hart, Oxford, pp 479–509
Nolan RC (2004) Property in a fund. Law Q Rev 120:108–126
Palmer FB, Morse G (2017) Priority of distribution of assets. In: Palmer FB, Morse G (eds) Palmer's company law. Sweet & Maxwell, London
Pollock F, Wright RS (1888) An essay on possession in the common law. Clarendon Press, Oxford
Secured Transactions Law Reform Project (2016) Policy paper April 2016. https://www.law.ox.ac.uk/sites/files/oxlaw/field/field_document/str-general-policy-paper-april-2016.pdf. Accessed 24 Nov 2016
Sheehan D (2017) The principles of personal property law, 2nd edn. Hart, Oxford
Sweet C (1894) Choses in action. Law Q Rev 10:303–317
Sweet C (1895) Choses in action. Law Q Rev 11:238–240
Tan CH (1998) Automatic crystallisation, de-crystallisation and convertibility of charges. Comp Financ Insolvency Law Rev, 41 et seq
Thomas S (2017) Security interests in intellectual property: proposals for reform. Legal Stud 37:214–247
Tosato A (2011) Security interests over intellectual property. J Intell Prop Law Prac 6:93–104
Townend DMR (1997) Intellectual property as security interests: technical difficulties presented in the law. Int Pharm Q, 168–195
Turner PG (2006) Charge characterisation in English law: a settled debate? Sing J Legal Stud 2006:200–212
UK, Her Majesty's Government (2017) Queen's speech 2017: Background notes. https://www.gov.uk/government/uploads/system/uploads/attachment_data/file/620838/Queens_speech_2017_background_notes.pdf. Accessed 28 June 2017
UK, Her Majesty's Treasury (2018) Consultation outcome: Goods Mortgages Bill. https://www.gov.uk/government/consultations/goods-mortgages-bill. Accessed 10 Jan 2019
UK, Intellectual Property Office (2018a) Design forms and fees. https://www.gov.uk/government/publications/design-forms-and-fees/design-forms-and-fees. Accessed 24 Aug 2017
UK, Intellectual Property Office (2018b) Patent forms and fees. https://www.gov.uk/government/publications/patent-forms-and-fees/patent-forms-and-fees. Accessed 24 Aug 2017

UK, Intellectual Property Office (2019) Trade mark forms and fees. https://www.gov.uk/government/publications/trade-mark-forms-and-fees/trade-mark-forms-and-fees. Accessed 29 June 2017
Williams TC (1894) Is a right of action in tort a chose in action? Law Q Rev 10:143–157
Williams TC (1895) Property, things in action, and copyright. Law Q Rev 11:223–237
Worthington S (1996) Proprietary interests in commercial transactions. Clarendon Press, Oxford

International Treaties

UPC Convention, 2018, OJ, c C175
Convention on the Grant of European Patents
Draft Withdrawal Agreement

Legislation

European Union

Community Design Regulation [2002] OJ L3/1
EU Trade Mark Regulation (2017 Recast) [2017] OJ L 154/1
Unitary Patent Protection Regulation [2012] OJ L361/1

Hong Kong

Law Amendment and Reform (Consolidation) Ordinance, c 25

United Kingdom

Bills of Sale Act, 1878a, 41 & 42 Vict., c 31
Bills of Sale Act (1878b) Amendment Act, 1882, 45 & 46 Vict., c 43
Companies Act 2006, 2006, c 46
Database Regulation 1986, 1997, S.I., c 3032
Copyright of Designs Act, 1842, 5 & 6 Vict., c 100
Copyright, Designs and Patents Act 1986, 1988, c 48
Insolvency Act 1986, 1986, c 45
Law of Property Act, 1925, 15 & 16 Geo. V, c 20
Patent Rules 2007, 2007
Patents Act 1977, 1977, c 37
Patents, Designs, and Trade Marks Act, 1883, 46 & 47 Vict., c 57
Registered Designs Act, 1949, 12, 13 & 14 Geo. VI, c 88
Sale of Goods Act 1979, 1979, c 54
Trade Marks Act, 1938, 1 & 2 Geo. VI, c 22
Trade Marks Act 1994, 1994, c 26

Cases

Australia

Deputy Commissioner of Taxation (Cth) v. Horsburgh (No 2), [1984] V.R. 773, 70 F.L.R. 182 (S.C.)
Fire Nymph Products Ltd. v. Heating Centre Pty Ltd. (1992), 7 A.C.S.R. 365, 10 A.C.L.C. 629 (N.S.W. C.A.)

Canada

Re Caroma Enterprises Ltd. (1979), 108 D.L.R. (3d) 412 (Alta. Q.B.)
Gordon Mackay & Co., Ltd. v. Capital Trust Corp., Ltd., [1927] S.C.R. 374, [1927] D.L.R. 1150

Hong Kong

Wang Industrial Co v. Takmay Industrial Co Ltd. (1979), [1980] F.S.R. 303 (Hong Kong C.A.)

New Zealand

Agnew & Kevin James Bearsley v. The Commissioner of Inland Revenue (Re Birtwhistle), [2001] UKPC 28, [2001] A.C. 710, [2001] W.L.R. 454 (N.Z.)
Covacich v. Riordan (1993), [1994] N.Z.L.R. 502 (H.C.)
DFC Financial Services Ltd. v. Coffey, [1991] N.Z.L.R. 513 (P.C.)
Re Manurewa Transport Limited, [1971] N.Z.L.R. 909 (S.C.)

United Kingdom

American Greetings Corp's Application (Holly Hobbie), [1984] W.L.R. 189, [1984] All E.R. 426 (H.L.)
Bailey v. Barnes, [1894] Ch. 25 (C.A.)
Baxter International Inc. v. Nederlands Produktielaboratorium voor Bloedtransfusiapparatuur BV (1997), [1998] R.P.C. 250 (Engl. and W. Pat.)
Re Brightlife Ltd. (1986), [1987] Ch. 200, [1987] W.L.R. 197, [1986] All E.R. 673 (Ch. D.)
Brown v. North (1882), 9 Q.B.D. 52 (C.A.)
Buchler v. Talbot, [2004] UKHL 9, [2004] A.C. 298, [2004] W.L.R. 582, [2004] All E.R. 1289
Colonial Bank v. Whinney (1885), 30 Ch. D. 261 (C.A.)
Re Cosslett (Contractors) Ltd. (1997), [1998] Ch. 495, [1998] W.L.R. 131, [1997] All E.R. 115 (C.A. Civ.)
Re Crompton, [1914] Ch. 954 (Ch. D.)
Edwards v. Standard Rolling Stock Syndicate (1892), [1893] Ch. 574 (Ch. D.)
Evans v. Rival Granite Quarries, Ltd., [1910] K.B. 979 (C.A.)
Finecard International Ltd. v. Urquhart Dyke & Lorri, [2005] EWHC 2481, [2006] F.S.R. 27 (Ch. D.)
Fraser v. Oystertec Plc., [2003] EWHC 2787, [2004] B.C.C. 233, [2004] F.S.R. 22 (Pat.)

Re George Inglefield Ltd. (1932), [1933] Ch. 1 (C.A.)
Gorringe v. Irwell India Rubber and Gutta Percha Works (1886), 34 Ch. D. 128 (C.A.)
Hardacre v. Armstrong (1905), 21 T.L.R. 189 (K.B.D.)
Holroyd v. Marshall (1862), 10 H.L. Cas. 191, 11 E.R. 999
Hubbuck v. Helms (1887), 56 L.T. 232, 3 T.L.R. 381 (Ch. D.)
Ifejika v. Ifejika, [2010] EWCA Civ 563, [2010] F.S.R. 29
Inland Revenue Commissioners v. Goldblatt (1971), [1972] Ch. 498, [1972] W.L.R. 953, [1972] All E.R. 202 (Ch. D.)
Jewitt v. Eckhardt (1878), 8 Ch. D. 404 (Ch. D.)
Re Lehman Brothers International (Europe), [2012] EWHC 2997, [2014] B.C.L.C. 295 (Ch. D.)
Re London Pressed Hinge Co Ltd., [1905] Ch. 576 (Ch. D.)
Macmillan Inc. v. Bishopsgate Investment Trust Plc. (No. 3) (1993), [1995] W.L.R. 978, [1995] All E.R. 747 (Ch. D.)
Re Monolithic Building Co, [1915] Ch. 643 (C.A.)
National Westminster Bank plc v. Spectrum Plus Limited, [2005] UKHL 41, [2005] A.C. 680, [2005] W.L.R. 58, [2005] All E.R. 209
New Ixion Tyre and Cycle Co v. Spilsbury, [1898] Ch. 484 (C.A.)
Re Panama, New Zealand & Australian Royal Mail Company (1870), 5 L.R. Ch. App. 318
Payne v. Fern (1881), 6 Q.B.D. 620 (Q.B.D.)
Performing Right Society Ltd. v. B4U Network (Europe) Ltd., [2012] EWHC 3010, [2013] Bus. L.R. 664, [2013] F.S.R. 19 (Ch. D.)
Performing Right Society Ltd. v. London Theatre of Varieties Ltd. (1923), [1924] A.C. 1 (H.L.)
Re Pyle Works (No.1) (1890), 44 Ch. D. 534 (C.A.)
Re Real Meat Co Ltd. (1995), [1996] B.C.C. 254 (Ch. D.)
Roban Jig & Tool Co Ltd. v. Taylor (1978), [1979] F.S.R. 130 (C.A. Civ.)
Robson v. Smith, [1895] Ch. 118 (Ch. D.)
Siebe Gorman & Co. Ltd. v. Barclays Bank Ltd. (1978), [1979] Lloyd's Rep. 142 (Ch. D.)
Steers v. Rogers, [1893] A.C. 232 (H.L.)
Stroud Architectural Systems Ltd. v. John Laing Construction Ltd. (1993), [1994] B.C.C. 18 (Engl. and W. Ref.)
Swiss Bank Corp. v. Lloyds Bank Ltd., [1980] W.L.R. 457, [1980] All E.R. 419 (C.A. Civ.)
Swiss Bank Corp. v. Lloyds Bank Ltd. (1981), [1982] A.C. 584, [1981] W.L.R. 893, [1981] All E.R. 449 (H.L.)
Taylor v. M'Keand (1880), 5 C.P.D. 358 (C.P.D.)
Taylor v. Russell, [1892] A.C. 244 (H.L.)
Tucker v. Farm & General Investment Trust, [1966] Q.B. 421, [1966] W.L.R. 1241, [1966] All E.R. 508 (C.A.)
Van Gelder Apsimon & Co v. Sowerby Bridge United District Flour Society (1890), 44 Ch. D. 374 (C.A.)
Victoria Housing Estates Ltd. v. Ashpurton Estates Ltd. (1982), [1983] Ch. 110, [1982] W.L.R. 964, [1982] All E.R. 665 (C.A. Civ.)
Re Victoria Steamboats Ltd. (1896), [1897] Ch. 158 (Ch. D.)
William Brandt's Sons & Co v. Dunlop Rubber Co Ltd., [1905] A.C. 454 (H.L.)
Re Woodroffes (Musical Instruments) Ltd. (1985), [1986] Ch. 366, [1985] W.L.R. 543, [1985] All E.R. 908 (Ch. D.)
Re Yorkshire Woolcombers Association, [1903] Ch. 284 (C.A.)

Security Rights in Intellectual Property in Estonia

Gea Lepik

Abstract This paper provides a theoretical overview of and practical guidance on the use of intellectual property (IP) rights as security in Estonia. It begins with an overview of the different IP rights in Estonia and the categories of security rights that can be granted over them. Like in other European countries, there are both non-registered and registered IP rights in Estonia. The different types of IP rights can be categorized as either copyright and related rights or as industrial property rights. In addition to national IP rights, EU-wide IP rights such as EU trademarks and Community designs also have effect in Estonia. The main ways to create a security right over an IP right are by establishing a pledge over IP rights or by transferring the IP rights as security. An IP right may be encumbered with a pledge through the establishment of a registered security over movables (for registered IP rights) or a pledge of rights (for non-registered IP rights). In addition, non-registered IP rights can also form part of a general commercial pledge, which is established over the entire movable property of an enterprise.

The paper then examines the creation and effect of the relevant security rights. With regard to the creation of security rights, the structure and content of the necessary transactions are described, as well as the conditions for the perfection of the security rights. The effect of the security rights is analysed, starting from the rights of the security holder before default and continuing on to the priority of different security rights and the enforcement of the different types of security rights. In analysing the issues of enforcement, distinction is made between enforcement in bankruptcy proceedings and enforcement outside insolvency. The practical issue of the costs of creating and of enforcing the relevant security rights is also addressed.

The paper ends with an overview of the theoretical problems and practical difficulties involved in taking security over IP rights, trying to explain the relative unpopularity of this method of securing debts in Estonia. At the time of writing, there were no proposals for a law reform relating to security over IP rights either in Estonia

G. Lepik (✉)
University of Tartu, School of Law, Department of Private Law, Tartu, Estonia
e-mail: gea.lepik@ut.ee

E.-M. Kieninger (ed.), *Security Rights in Intellectual Property*, Ius Comparatum – Global Studies in Comparative Law 45,
https://doi.org/10.1007/978-3-030-44191-3_12

or at the EU level. However, the need for reform in Estonia is expected to be considered at the time of drafting an Industrial Property Code in the near future.

1 Intellectual Property Rights in Estonia

Two main categories of intellectual property (IP) rights exist in Estonia. These are copyright and related rights, and industrial property rights.

1.1 Copyright and Related Rights

Copyright protects original works in the literary, artistic, or scientific domain. To be protected, a work must be expressed in an objective form and be capable of being perceived and reproduced in this form either directly or by means of technical devices (§ 4(2) of Copyright Act (CA)). A work is considered original if it is the author's own intellectual creation (*Ibid*). As Estonia is a Member State of the EU, the judgments[1] of the Court of Justice of the European Union (CJEU) must be taken into account in determining whether a work fulfills the originality criteria. Copyright in a work is created with the creation of the work (CA § 7(1)); registration or deposit of the work or completion of other formalities is not required for the creation or exercise of copyright (CA § 7(3)).

There are four categories of related rights in Estonia. These are the rights of performers, producers of phonograms, broadcasting service providers, and producers of the first fixation of a film. Certain related rights are also granted to a person who, after the expiry of copyright protection, for the first time lawfully publishes or lawfully directs at the public a previously unpublished work, and to a person who carries out a critical or scientific publication of a work unprotected by copyright.

In addition, the makers of databases are granted *sui generis* protection over their databases to protect investments made by them.[2] A *database* is defined as "a collection of works, data, or other economics arranged in a systematic or methodical way and individually accessible by electronic or other means". The definition of a database does not cover computer programs used in the making of the database or the operation thereof (CA § 75^2). The maker of a database is a person who has made a substantial investment (evaluated either qualitatively or quantitatively) in the collecting, obtaining, verification, arranging, or presentation of data which constitutes the content of the database (CA § 75^3(1)). If a database fulfills the relevant

---

[1] In particular, C-5/08 *Infopaq International* [2009] ECR I-06569; C-145/10 *Painer* [2011] ECR I-12533.

[2] See Chapter VIII^1 of the CA.

criteria, particularly the originality requirement, it may also be eligible for copyright protection.

1.2 Industrial Property Rights

The second category of IP rights comprises of various rights which require registration with the competent authority (in Estonia this is the Patent Office) in order to be created. The main available national industrial property rights are patents and utility models for inventions, trademarks, industrial designs, and the layout designs of integrated circuits. It is also possible to receive protection for plant varieties and geographical indications.

Inventions can be protected either through a patent or a utility model in Estonia. Patents are either national patents, granted by the Estonian Patent Office under the national Patent Act (PA), or European patents, which are granted by the European Patent Organization under the Convention on the Grant of European Patents (EPC). While the conditions and processes for granting these patents differ, their legal force, particularly the rights they give to the owner of the patent, is governed by national patent law in both cases. Under both the PA and the EPC, an invention must be novel, involve an inventive step, and be industrially applicable in order to be eligible for protection (see PA § 8, EPC Arts 52–57). In the future, the European patent with unitary effect will also have effect in Estonia.[3]

An alternative to patent protection is the utility model. Utility models are registered at the Patent Office in accordance with the Utility Models Act (UMA). While the conditions for the grant of a utility model are very similar to those for the grant of a patent (see UMA § 5(1) and § 7), there are some important differences. Primarily, the procedure of granting a utility model does not involve an official examination by the Patent Office, and the lack of novelty or of an inventive step is not a basis for refusing to register a utility model (see UMA § 21(5)). Although the Patent Office carries out a search of the state of the art as regards the invention (UMA § 21(1^1) and § 21^1) and draws up a search report, the report only has an informative meaning (UMA § 21^1(6)). This makes the proceedings quicker and less costly for the applicant, but there is often a higher likelihood of (successful) challenges to the validity of a utility model than there is for a patent.

A sign used to distinguish the goods and services of a person can be registered as a trademark. In Estonia, legal protection is granted to (i) trademarks which are registered with the Patent Office in accordance with the Trade Marks Act (TMA); (ii) trademarks with a registration (valid in Estonia) that has been entered in the International Register of the Bureau pursuant to the Madrid Protocol; and (iii) trademarks which are well known in Estonia within the meaning of Article 6 *bis*

[3] The law ratifying the Agreement on a Unified Patent Court was adopted by the Parliament of Estonia on June 26, 2016. The ratification instrument was submitted on August 1, 2017.

of the Paris Convention for the Protection of Industrial Property. European Union trademarks granted by the EUIPO also have effect in Estonia.

In order to be registered as an Estonian trademark, a sign must satisfy certain primary conditions: it must be a sign,[4] it must be capable of being represented in the register in a manner which enables the competent authorities and the public to determine the clear and precise scope of the legal protection afforded to the trademark, and it must be capable of distinguishing the goods or services of a person from other similar types of goods or services of other persons (see TMA § 3 and § 6). In addition to these basic conditions, there must be no circumstances which preclude the legal protection of a sign. These circumstances are divided into absolute (e.g. the sign is indistinctive, descriptive, or customary in language or business practices (see TMA § 9)) and relative (i.e. there is an earlier right which prevents legal protection from being granted to the sign (see TMA § 10)) grounds for refusal of protection.

The two-dimensional or three-dimensional design of a product can be protected by an industrial design. Industrial designs acquire legal protection by registration in the register of industrial designs pursuant to the procedure provided for in the Industrial Designs Protection Act (IDPA, see § 5(2)). Legal protection is granted to industrial designs which are new, have an individual character, and may be used for manufacturing industrial or handicraft products (IDPA § 5(1)). Registered and unregistered Community designs also have effect in Estonia.

It is possible to register with the Patent Office and gain protection through a layout design of an integrated circuit in accordance with the Layout-Designs of Integrated Circuits Protection Act (LDICPA). For the purposes of this act, an *integrated circuit* "means a product, in its final form or intermediate form, in which the elements, at least one of which is an active element, and some or all of the interconnections are integrally formed in or on a piece of material and which is intended to perform an electronic function" (LDICPA § 4). The *layout design of an integrated circuit* "means the three-dimensional disposition, however expressed, of the elements, at least one of which is an active element, and of some or all of the interconnections of an integrated circuit, or such reproduction of three-dimensional disposition prepared for an integrated circuit intended for manufacture" (LDICPA § 5).

In order to be granted protection, the layout design of an integrated circuit "[must be] original and [must not have] been commercially exploited in any part of the world for more than two years prior to the filing [. . .] for registration" (LDICPA § 8 (1)). "Layout-designs of integrated circuits are original if they are the result of their creators' creative activities and are not commonplace among experts creating and manufacturing layout-designs of integrated circuits at the time of their creation" (LDICPA § 8(2)).

Protection in accordance with the Geographical Indications Protection Act (GIPA) is granted to geographical indications "used to designate goods and services

[4]In determining whether something constitutes a *sign*, the case law of the CJEU is observed, e.g. C-321/03 *Dyson* [2007] ECR I-00687.

of natural, agricultural, handicraft or industrial origin, except the geographical indications and designations of origin for agricultural products, foodstuffs and alcoholic beverages protected at Community level" (GIPA § 1(1)). "Geographical indication means: (1) the name of or a reference to a geographical area which indicates the specific geographical origin of a good or service if the given quality, reputation or other characteristic of the good or service so identified is essentially attributable to the geographical area where the good is produced, processed or prepared for sales or where the service is rendered; (2) another word, phrase or symbol that, resulting from long-term and consistent use, has become essentially attributable to the geographical area where the good is produced, processed or prepared for sales or where the service is rendered" (GIPA § 3(1)). Geographical indications are granted legal protection through registration in the state register of geographical indications pursuant to the procedure provided for in GIPA (§ 5(1)).

It is also possible to protect plant varieties by registering them in the relevant register in accordance with the Plant Propagation and Plant Variety Rights Act (PPPVRA). A variety means "a plant grouping within a single botanical taxon of the lowest known rank which is defined by the expression of the characteristics resulting from a given genotype or combination of genotypes, is distinguished from other plant groupings by the expression of at least one of the said characteristics and is considered as a unit with regard to its suitability for being propagated unchanged" (PPPVRA § 2(1)). In order to be protectable, a variety must be distinct, uniform, and stable and must bear a suitable variety denomination (PPPVRA § 10, see further §§ 11–15).

National trademarks and EU trademarks exist in parallel. The conditions and procedures for the granting of rights arising from a national trademark and the consequences of infringing such a trademark are set down in the TMA, while the EU trademark is governed by Regulation (EU) 2017/1001 of the European Parliament and of the Council of 14 June 2017 on the European Union trade mark.[5] Nothing in Estonian law prevents the registration of a single sign as both a national and an EU trademark. For the purposes of ascertaining the existence of relative circumstances which prevent granting protection to a national trademark, earlier EU trademarks which have been registered or filed for registration are taken into consideration (TMA § 11(1)(6–7).

National patents and European patents valid in Estonia exist in parallel. While the procedures and conditions for the granting of the former are governed by the PA, those for the granting of the latter are governed by the EPC. However, after a patent has been granted, a national patent and a European patent valid in Estonia have the same legal force and are governed by the national PA. It is not possible to gain protection for a single invention through both a national patent and a European patent valid in Estonia: "[w]here a European patent in which the Republic of Estonia is indicated as the designated state and a national patent having the same filing date or, where priority has been claimed, the same priority date, have been granted to the

[5]OJ L 154, 16.6.2017, pp. 1–99.

same person or his or her legal successor, the legal effect of the national patent shall cease to exist to the extent that the invention is covered by the European patent as of the day: (1) of expiry of the term for filing an opposition to the European patent, provided that no opposition has been filed to the European patent, or (2) on which a final decision to maintain the European patent, resulting from the opposition procedure, enters into force" (§ 12(1) of Implementation of Convention on Grant of European Patents Act (ICGEPA)). If an application for such patent is pending in the Estonian Patent Office, it "shall be rejected to the extent that the invention is covered by the European patent" (ICGEPA § 12(2)). The prohibition on simultaneous protection does not apply to utility models (ICGEPA § 12(3)). Nevertheless, once the system of unitary European patents becomes effective, it will be possible to protect an invention through both an Estonian patent and a European patent with unitary effect.

2 Categories of Security Rights Over IP in Estonia

There are two main ways to create a consensual security right over an IP right: encumber the IP right with a pledge; or transfer the right as a security. As an alternative to transferring the IP right itself, it is possible to transfer specific rights related to it (e.g. a claim for licence fees arising from a licence agreement).

2.1 Pledge Over IP Rights

A pledge is a right of security that gives the person for whose benefit the pledge is established the right to satisfaction of the claim secured by the pledge out of the pledged property, unless the obligation is appropriately performed (§ 276(1) of Law of Property Act (LPA), see also LPA § 297(1)). The person whose right is encumbered with a pledge is called the pledgor (*pantija*), and he/she can be either the debtor of the secured claim or a third person (LPA § 278). The person in whose favour the pledge is established is called the pledgee (*pandipidaja*; LPA § 281, § 299). As a property right, a pledge is an absolute right, i.e. it is effective towards all persons and continues to exist even when the pledged IP right has been transferred. The pledgee is not entitled to acquire the pledged right, but the pledge grants him/her a priority of satisfaction of his/her claim before other creditors in enforcement and bankruptcy proceedings. In some cases (e.g. for a "pledge of rights"), the pledge gives the pledgee a statutory right to sell the pledged property in order to get satisfaction for the secured claim.

Any claim with a monetary value can be secured by a pledge. This includes not only financial claims, but also all other claims which can be financially evaluated, such as a claim for compensation of damages. It is also possible to secure conditional and future claims. The secured claim must be sufficiently determined—that is to say, when the claim arises it must be possible to ascertain whether it was intended to be secured or not. In addition, it is possible to secure the debt of a third person. The establishment of pledges is widely used in practice for securing different obligations, particularly credit claims.

The two main ways of encumbering an IP right with a pledge are through establishing a "registered security over movables" (for registered IP rights—see below, Subsection (a)) or a "pledge of rights" (for non-registered IP rights—see below, Subsection (b)). In addition, non-registered IP rights can also form part of a so-called general "commercial pledge," which is established over the entire property of an enterprise (see below, Subsection (c)).

(a) According to LPA § 297(1), "[a] patent, trade mark, industrial design, utility model, variety, [or] layout-design of an integrated circuit [. . .] which is entered in a register [. . .] may be encumbered with a registered security over movables" (hereinafter "registered security"). This is confirmed in TMA § 24(1), PA § 14 (2^1), and UMA § 13(4). The Supreme Court has referred to the wording of LPA § 297(1) and emphasized that a registered security can only be established in an object which is entered in a register, the data of which is public and the maintenance of which is regulated pursuant to the procedure provided by law.[6] As the register of plant varieties in Estonia does not comply with these conditions (the maintenance of this register is not regulated by law), doubts have been expressed in legal literature over whether plant varieties can be the object of a registered security, even though they are explicitly mentioned in LPA § 297(1).[7] The registered security is governed by specific provisions in the LPA. To the extent that these specific provisions do not apply, the general provisions on pledges in the LPA and the Ship Property Law Act (SPLA) apply. Based on the case law of the Supreme Court, in case of gaps in this regulation, the provisions on mortgages (e.g. in the LPA and in the Land Register Act) may also be applied by analogy.[8]

(b) An alternative form of pledge that could be used for pledging IP rights is the pledge of rights. A proprietary right may be the object of a pledge if it is transferable and if the pledging of that specific right is not prohibited by law (LPA § 277(1) and § 314(1)). This means that in principle, those IP rights which are transferable could be the object of a pledge of rights. There is no provision in the law which would explicitly exclude the possibility of encumbering registered IP rights with a pledge of rights or even with both a pledge of rights and a registered security at the same time. However, the prevailing opinion in literature

[6]Judgment No. 3-2-1-116-10 of December 11, 2013 of the Civil Chamber of the Supreme Court, paras 29–30.

[7]Volens (2014), § 297, Sec. 3.2.2.c.

[8]Judgment No. 3-2-1-116-10 of January 5, 2011 of the Civil Chamber of the Supreme Court, para 31; Volens (2014) § 298, Sec. 3.b.

is that for registered IP rights which are entered in a public register and which can be encumbered with a registered security, the more specialized option of creating a registered security interest replaces the more general concept of a pledge of rights and thus encumbering such IP rights with a pledge of rights is not possible.[9] The pledge of rights should still be available for non-registered IP rights, such as copyright and related rights, as well as for those registered IP rights that do not meet the requirements of establishing a registered security (e.g. plant varieties—*see (a) above*). Nevertheless, it is not possible to establish a pledge over non-transferable rights such as moral rights.

In addition to specific provisions on the pledge of rights in the LPA, the provisions on the possessory pledge (i.e. the pledge of things) and the general provisions on pledges apply to the pledge of rights unless otherwise provided by law (LPA § 314(2)).

(c) A commercial pledge is a pledge of (almost) the entire movable property of an undertaking registered in the commercial register in accordance with the Commercial Pledges Act (CPA). However, a commercial pledge does not extend to those things and rights, such as IP rights, which can be encumbered with a registered security, even if no such security has been established.[10] Thus, a commercial pledge can only extend to those IP rights which can be the object of a pledge of rights. If a pledge has already been established on an IP right, the commercial pledge will not extend to it (see CPA § 2(3)(2)).

There is an important difference between a registered security and commercial pledge on the one hand, and a pledge of rights on the other hand. The first two forms of pledges are non-accessory, meaning that their validity does not depend on the existence of a secured claim. The pledge of rights, however, is accessory, meaning that its validity depends on the existence of a secured claim (see LPA § 297(3), CPA § 1(2)).

A court may establish a judicial registered security over movables as an involuntary form of security to secure a claim satisfied on the basis of a judgment (PLA § 297^2(2)). This type of security is also entered in the register pursuant to the general procedure (PLA § 297^2(3)). The provisions concerning the registered security apply to the judicial registered security (PLA § 297^2(1)).

[9]Volens (2014), § 297, Sec. 3.4.4. An argument in favour of this conclusion is that when registered IP rights are encumbered with a pledge, the law always requires the pledge to be entered in the relevant register (§ 31(1) of the Principles of Legal Regulation of Industrial Property Act (PLRIPA)).

[10]CPA § 2(3)(2) and LPA § 314(2); see also Volens (2014), § 297, Sec. 3.4.5; Judgment No. 3-2-1-41-05 of May 11, 2005 of the Civil Chamber of the Supreme Court, para 43; Judgment No. 3-2-1-133-13 of December 11, 2013 of the Civil Chamber of the Supreme Court, para 32.

2.2 *Transfer of IP Rights as Security*

As an alternative to encumbering an IP right with a pledge, it is possible to transfer the right as a security (e.g. see TMA § 50^1, PA § 45, UMA § 42, and IDPA §§ 73–73^1). It is also possible to transfer a pending application, as well as the right to apply for an IP right (e.g. see PA §§ 43–44, UMA §§ 41–42, and IDPA §§ 71–72). In case of copyright and related rights, only the economic rights can be transferred, whereas moral rights are inalienable (e.g. see CA § 11(2)–(3), § 48(1)).

3 Structure of Transactions: Attachment and Perfection

3.1 *Structure of Secured Transactions Over IP Rights*

3.1.1 Pledge Over IP Rights

For the establishment of a pledge over an IP right to secure a debt, the following agreements are concluded or usually exist:

- Real right contract on the establishment of a pledge (*pledge contract*)—an agreement between the pledgor and the pledgee concerning the establishment of a pledge. This agreement creates the pledge (in case of a pledge of rights) or is the basis for entering a pledge in the relevant register (in case of a registered security or commercial pledge) and it determines the content, including the monetary value, of the pledge right.
- For a pledge of rights, the pledge contract must generally be in writing (LPA § 315(2)). For a registered security, there is no general requirement of form. Nevertheless, it is arguable that a general provision in LPA § 282(2) applies, according to which an agreement for the establishment of a pledge must be entered into in writing if the value of the pledged thing exceeds 50 euros. In any case, since the pledge contract has to be submitted to the Patent Office together with a request to make an entry in the relevant register concerning the pledge, the contract needs to at least be in a form which can be reproduced in writing.[11] A specific requirement of form has been established for trademarks, which requires the agreement for the establishment of a pledge to be notarized (TMA § 24(2)).
- Secured contract—the contract under which the secured claim arises (typically a credit agreement). Typically, this contract also stipulates the obligation of the debtor to secure the performance of his/her obligation by providing a security.

[11]For patents, it is stated on the webpage of the Patent Office that a written pledge contract should be appended to the application for making an entry in the register concerning the registered security. The Estonian Patent Office. https://www.epa.ee/et/toimingud-eesti-patendiregistris/pandi-registreerimine. Accessed May 1, 2020.

The secured contract does not have to be between the pledgor and the pledgee; rather, it can also be between third persons.

- Security contract (*tagatiskokkulepe*)—the contract in which the pledgee and the pledgor determine which claims are secured by the pledge.

In the case of a registered security, all three contracts are independent—that is to say, the validity of one does not depend on the validity of the others (i.e. it is a non-accessory pledge). There is no need for a secured claim in order for the registered security to exist, and the registered security does not automatically cease to exist when the secured debt is satisfied (PLA § 297(3)). The pledge of rights, however, is a non-accessory form of pledge, which means that the security contract cannot be separated from the real right contract on the establishment of a pledge. Thus, a pledge of rights cannot exist without a valid security contract. Usually, the security contract and the pledge contract are concluded together and in the same document.

Additional optional agreements:

- Upon establishing a registered security, the pledgor and the pledgee may also conclude a notarized agreement on immediate compulsory enforcement. Such an agreement prescribes that the owner of the IP right encumbered with a registered security be subject to immediate compulsory enforcement for the satisfaction of the secured claim, without the pledgee having to obtain a court judgment in order to get satisfaction for his claim from the pledged IP right (§ 2(1)(19) of the Code of Enforcement Procedure (CEP)).
- Furthermore, the parties may conclude other agreements whereby they change or specify the rights and obligations arising from their legal relationship as pledgor and pledgee, particularly obligations to provide information or to refrain from certain acts and their liability for failing to perform their obligations. Such agreements are not entered in the register.
- In case a third person has encumbered his/her IP rights with a pledge, this usually occurs under an agreement with the debtor, such as an authorization agreement.

3.1.2 Transfer of IP Rights as Security

For transferring a registered IP right (i.e. a trademark, patent, utility model, industrial design, variety, or integrated circuit), a transfer agreement is required and an entry needs to be made in the relevant register following a request to make such an entry (TMA § 50^1, PA § 45, UMA § 42, and IDPA §§ 73–73^1). For transferring a non-registered IP right, the conclusion of a transfer agreement is sufficient. The agreement for transferring copyright (i.e. the economic rights in the work) must be concluded in written form (CA § 49(1)). Either in the same document as the transfer agreement or in an additional one, the parties should also agree on the conditional obligation of the transferee to transfer the IP right back to the transferor upon satisfaction of the debt. There are no requirements of form for this agreement and it is not entered in the relevant register. The parties to these agreements are normally the debtor and the creditor, but they can also be a third person. If a third person is securing the debt of a debtor, this usually occurs under an agreement with the debtor, such as an authorization agreement.

3.2 *Perfection of Security Rights*

3.2.1 Pledge Over IP Rights

Registered Security

For the creation of a registered security over an IP right, a pledge contract must be concluded between the owner of the IP right (i.e. the pledgor) and the pledgee and an entry concerning the registered security must be made in the relevant register (LPA § 299(1)). The pledge contract must reflect the intention of the parties to establish a registered security, and it must specify the monetary value of the registered security. There are no other requirements as to its substance. In order to make an entry concerning the registered security in the relevant register, a request must be made to the registrar (i.e. the Estonian Patent Office—see PLRIPA § 7)[12] (LPA § 297^3(1)). In the TMA, it is further specified that a written request from the proprietor of the trademark or the pledgee is needed and it must be submitted together with a notarized agreement for the establishment of a pledge (TMA § 50^6(1)–(2)).

The existence of a secured claim and/or a security contract determining which claims are secured by the pledge is not a precondition for the validity of a registered security (LPA § 297(3)). A registered security can be valid as a property right even if it does not secure any claims. Its scope is determined by the monetary value of the pledge (LPA § 299(2)). However, if a secured claim exists, the amount of the claim and the date of its satisfaction are among the information that needs to be entered in the register (PLRIPA § 31(1)).

Between the parties, the secured contract may establish and thus create a legal obligation for the debtor to secure the satisfaction of his/her debts by establishing a pledge for the benefit of the creditor. Such an agreement constitutes a contractual obligation to conclude a pledge contract. As a property right, a registered security is effective between the parties and against third parties from the moment that it is entered in the relevant register on the basis of the pledge contract (LPA § 297(1), § 299). In order to transfer an IP right encumbered with a registered security, the written consent of the pledgee is required (see TMA § 50^1(4), IDPA § 19(3)).

[12] Registered securities over industrial property rights are entered in their respective registers: the register of patents, the register of utility models, the register of European patents valid in Estonia, the register of integrated circuits, the register of trade and service marks, and the register of industrial designs (PLRIPA § 1(2) and § 15(2)(5)). These registers are maintained by the Patent Office (PLRIPA § 7).

Pledge of Rights

In order for a pledge of rights to be validly created, there has to be a contract on the establishment of a pledge (i.e. a pledge contract) between the owner of the IP right and the pledgee, as well as a secured claim and a valid security contract determining which claims are secured by the pledge. No entries in registers are required. In case future claims are secured, they must be sufficiently determined—that is to say, it has to be possible to ascertain the type and legal basis of the secured claims.

The pledge contract must be concluded in writing (LPA § 315(2)). There is no requirement of form for the security contract. However, since the validity of a pledge of rights depends on the existence of a secured claim (given that such a pledge is an accessory security), a requirement of written form can be understood from the law (see LPA § 315(2)–(2^1)).[13]

Once a pledge of rights has been established, it is effective between the parties and against third parties. A pledgee also obtains a right of security if the pledgor is not entitled to establish a pledge, unless the pledgee did not act in good faith when establishing the pledge (LPA § 282^1(1)). A pledgee acted in bad faith if the pledgee knew or ought to have known when establishing the pledge that the pledgor had no right to encumber the IP right with a pledge (LPA § 282^1(2)).

A claim secured by a pledge has priority over all other claims with respect to the pledged property (LPA § 280). Several pledges of rights can be established on the same IP right (LPA § 277(3)). If an IP right is encumbered with several rights of security, the ranking of the rights of security is specified according to when they were created (LPA § 281(1), § 314(2)). If a pledged IP right is encumbered with the right of a third person, a new right of security will obtain a higher ranking than that right, unless the pledgee knew or ought to have known about the existence of the other right at the moment of obtaining the new right of security (LPA § 282^1(4)).

A pledge of rights is not extinguished upon the transfer of the encumbered IP rights unless the pledgee becomes the owner of the pledged IP rights (LPA § 286(1), § 314(2)).

3.2.2 Transfer of IP Rights as Security

The transfer of a registered IP right (i.e. trademark, patent, utility model, industrial design, variety, or integrated circuit) is effective between the parties and against third persons after a transfer agreement has been concluded and an entry concerning the transfer has been made in the relevant register (see TMA § 50^1, PA § 45, UMA § 42, and IDPA §§ 73–73^1).

The transfer of economic rights in a non-registered IP right is effective after a written transfer agreement has been concluded (see CA § 49(1)). Any agreement concerning the obligation of the transferee to transfer the IP right back to the original

[13] Kõve (2014), § 279, Sec. 3.3.3.

owner after the debt has been satisfied is only effective between the parties themselves. If transferring the IP right back has become impossible (e.g. the transferee has transferred it to a third party), then the original owner can no longer require that this obligation be performed (§ 108(2)(1) of the Law of Obligations Act (LOA)); instead, he/she must use other remedies (e.g. claim for compensation of damages).

3.3 Registering of Security Rights

3.3.1 Pledge Over IP Rights

Registered Security

A registered security over a patent, trademark, industrial design, utility model, variety, or layout design of an integrated circuit is entered in the relevant registry. The registered security becomes effective only after an entry concerning it has been made in the registry. This ensures the publicity of the security right and provides information to the creditors of the pledgor.

Pursuant to LPA § 297[1], only the information required by law is entered in the register with regard to the registered security. The nature of this information is specified in LPA § 299(2) and PLRIPA § 31(1); in the case of trademarks, this is further clarified in § 56 of the regulation of the Minister of Justice dated January 3, 2012 and titled "Trade Marks Regulation." No substantive provisions can be found on registered security in other laws or regulations on industrial property rights. The norms referred to above require the following information to be entered in the register: the name of the pledgee, the monetary value of the registered security, the amount of the claim secured by the pledge, and the term given for the satisfaction of this claim.

An entry in the register is made following a request submitted by the owner of the IP right or the person who is intended to become the pledgee (LPA § 297^3, TMA § $50^6(1)$). Although a request from either one of these parties is sufficient, the intention of both the owner of the IP right and the future pledgee to establish a registered security must be reflected in the pledge contract (i.e. the real right contract establishing the pledge) (LPA § 299(1)).[14] For trademarks, the request must be in writing (TMA § $50^6(1)$); however, no requirements of form have been set by law for other industrial property rights. The pledge contract (i.e. the real right agreement for the establishment of the pledge) must be appended to the request (see TMA $50^6(2)$). In case the registered security is to be entered with a higher ranking than that of an existing right of security, the consent of the pledgee who is forced to fall lower in the ranking is also needed.

[14]Volens (2014), § 297^3, Sec. 3.2. et seq.

An entry in the register can be amended if the relevant information changes; for example, when the pledge is transferred to a legal successor of the pledgee (see TMA § 24(3)), or when the monetary value or ranking of the registered security changes. In order to amend an entry at the request of the proprietor of the IP right, the consent of any person whose right (entered in the register) might be prejudiced by the amendment of the entry is required. In the case of trademarks, this consent must be notarized (TMA § 50^6(8)).

An entry concerning a registered security is deleted from the register upon termination of the claim or upon waiver of the pledge by request. Specific provisions are provided in the TMA that indicate that the entry is automatically deleted from the register upon termination of the claim (see TMA § 50^6(6)), although in practice the entry is deleted on the basis of a request. These provisions also require that the request of the pledgee to waive the pledge be accompanied by a notarized request for waiver of the pledge (TMA § 50^6(7)). For the deletion of an entry concerning a registered security at the request of the proprietor of a trademark, the notarized consent of the pledgee is required (TMA § 50^6(8)).

Once effective (i.e. entered in the register), the registered security is effective between the parties themselves and against third parties, giving the pledgee priority over competing claimants to get satisfaction for his/her claim out of the pledged IP rights. In case the same IP right is encumbered with several registered securities, the priority of the pledgees is determined by the ranking of their right of security. In order to have the ranking changed, a request must be filed with the Patent Office, together with the agreement of the persons whose rights will change in ranking (e.g. see TMA § 50^5(5)).

Pledge of Rights

Pledges of rights over non-registered IP rights are not entered in any register.

3.3.2 Transfer of IP Rights as Security

Only the transfer of an IP right and the change of its ownership are entered in the relevant register. The fact that a transfer is done with the purpose of securing a debt and that the transferee may be required to transfer the IP right back to the original owner upon satisfaction of the claim is not reflected in the register.

4 Priorities of Security Rights

4.1 Pledge Over IP Rights

Out of the bankruptcy estate, payments relating to the bankruptcy proceedings (e.g. the costs of the proceedings, including remuneration of the trustee—see

Bankruptcy Act (BA) § 146(1), § 148, § 150) are made first. After that, the claims of the creditors are satisfied based on their ranking (see BA § 153). Accepted claims secured by pledges rank highest (BA § 153(1)(1)). These claims are "satisfied first to the extent of the money received from the sale of the pledged object from which the payments [relating to the bankruptcy proceedings (see BA § 146(1))] [. . .] have been deducted" (BA § 153(2)). A pledgee is required to participate in covering the expenses relating to the bankruptcy proceedings, up to a maximum amount of 15% of the proceeds received from the sale of the pledged object (*Ibid*). In case of several pledgees of rights in the same IP right, "[t]he expenses [of the bankruptcy proceedings] are divided between [them] in proportion to the share of the proceeds of the sale of the pledged object" (BA § 153(3)).

The order of priority of other parties holding pledges of the same IP right is determined by the ranking of their rights, which in turn is determined by when the rights of security were created. In the case of a registered security, the ranking is determined by the time of entry in a register (LPA § 300(1)). If different applications to register pledges are submitted concurrently for the same object, they are granted the same ranking (PLA § 300(2)). However, this rule "[does] not apply if the persons concerned have agreed on a different [. . .] ranking of rights and an entry has been made in the register concerning such agreement" (PLA § 300(3)). The claims secured by a pledge are satisfied first in bankruptcy proceedings out of the money received from the sale of the pledged object, and "[t]he expenses [of the bankruptcy proceedings] are divided between [them] in proportion to the share of the proceeds of the sale of the pledged object" (BA § 153(3)). "If a claim secured by a pledge is not satisfied in full out of the money received from the sale of the [pledged object], the rest of the claim shall be satisfied together with [other claims in the second ranking]" (BA § 153(4)). "Claims of a lower ranking are satisfied after the claims of the preceding ranking have been satisfied in full" (BA § 153(5)). "If the estate is not sufficient for satisfying all the claims of the same ranking, the claims shall be satisfied in proportion to the sizes of the claims" (BA § 153(6)).

4.2 *Transfer of IP Rights as Security*

If an IP right has been transferred to a creditor as security for a debt, it is regarded as an object belonging to a third person and is not included in a bankruptcy estate (see BA § 123(1)). Thus, proceeds from its sale cannot be used to cover any expenses relating to the bankruptcy proceedings.

Since an IP right is transferred as security only once, the question of priority with respect to other parties holding rights in the same IP right does not arise.

5 Enterprise Charges

5.1 IP Rights as Part of a Security Right Over All Assets

Pursuant to CPA § 1(1), "[a]n undertaking registered in the commercial register may establish a pledge registered in the commercial pledge register on the undertaking's movable property [as] security for a claim (commercial pledge), without the undertaking transferring possession of the pledgeable property." "The provisions concerning registered security over movables in the [LPA] apply to a commercial pledge unless otherwise provided for in [the CPA]" (CPA § 1(3)).

"A commercial pledge extends to all [encumberable] movable property of a company or movable property relating to the economic activity of a sole proprietor" "which belongs to [the] undertaking at the time the pledge entry is made and [. . .] which the undertaking acquires after the pledge entry is made" (CPA § 2(1)–(2)). However, a commercial pledge does not extend to certain categories of property, including "property on which another class of registered security over movables [. . .] may be established [emphasis added]" (CPA § 2(3)(1)). It follows that registered IP rights (i.e. patents, utility models, trademarks, industrial designs, or integrated circuits) cannot be part of a commercial pledge. Nevertheless, IP rights which cannot be encumbered with a registered security (particularly copyright and related rights) can be part of a commercial pledge to the extent to which they can be encumbered with a pledge of rights (i.e. only the economic rights). However, if a pledge of rights has already been established on an IP right, a commercial pledge will not extend to this IP right (CPA § 2(3)(2) by analogy).

5.2 Establishing a Commercial Pledge

"In order to establish a commercial pledge, an undertaking (pledgor) enters into a commercial pledge contract with the pledgee. [The] contract must set out: (1) the business name and registry code of the pledgor; (2) the name and personal identification or registry code of the pledgee; (3) the amount of the pledge; [and] (4) other information provided by law" (CPA § 4(1)). "A commercial pledge contract must be authenticated by a notary" (CPA § 4(2)). "[The] pledge is created [. . .] after a corresponding entry is made in the commercial pledge register" following a request for such (CPA § 4(3)).

In order to make "an entry concerning a commercial pledge in the commercial pledge register, a state fee shall be paid in the amount of 0.2 per cent of the value of the pledge [. . .] but not less than 32 euros and not more than 2560 euros" (§ 70(1) of the State Fees Act (SFA)).

5.3 *Priority of a Commercial Pledge*

"In the event of compulsory execution [...], a pledgee may demand the settlement of a claim out of the property encumbered with a commercial pledge to the extent of the amount of the pledge according to the ranking of the pledge" (CPA § 10(1)).

"If a claim for payment is made on the encumbered property for the settlement of a claim which is not secured by a commercial pledge or for the settlement of a claim of [another] commercial pledgee [with a lower ranking], the pledgee may demand the settlement of [his/her] claim from funds received from [the] sale of the property [...], even if the pledgee's claim is not yet collectable, ahead of the creditor for whose benefit the collection is made" (CPA § 10(4)). However, "if the property remaining after settlement of the other claim constitutes the full security for the pledgee", "[t]he pledgee cannot demand the settlement of [his] claim" (*Ibid*).

In the event of "bankruptcy, a pledgee may demand the settlement of a claim out of the property encumbered with a commercial pledge to the extent of the amount of the pledge according to the ranking of the pledge" (CPA § 10(1)). For a more detailed overview of the enforcement of a pledge in bankruptcy proceedings, see Section 7.

6 Rights Before Default

6.1 *Pledge Over IP Rights*

The establishment of a pledge creates a legal relationship between the pledgee and the owner of the pledged IP right. For both registered security and pledges of rights, this relationship is regulated by the PLA. In the case of registered security, §§ 23–28 of the SPLA apply as well.

The existence of a pledge does not deprive the owner of the IP right of his rights, and he/she continues to be entitled to use and dispose of them. Any agreement between the pledgee and the holder of the IP right which limits the right of the holder to dispose of (including to transfer) the object of the pledge is invalid (SPLA § 28). The pledge does not give the pledgee the right to use the IP right; rather, it only gives him/her "the right to demand compulsory execution [of the secured claim] by compulsory auction" if the secured claim is not satisfied (LPA § 302(1) for registered security; LPA § 288(1) and § 314(2) for pledge of rights).

The main obligation of the pledgor is to refrain from acts which would decrease the value of the pledged IP right and from acts which would otherwise negatively affect the pledgee. The pledgor has a duty to ensure that the encumbered IP right is preserved and that the value of the security is maintained (SPLA § 23 for registered security).

There are no direct obligations arising from the pledge for the pledgee. Nevertheless, there may be an obligation arising from the security contract to refrain from initiating enforcement proceedings for the sale of the pledged IP right without a collectable and enforceable claim. Also, in case the pledgor is a third party and not the debtor, the pledgee has a duty arising from the general principle of good faith to inform the owner of the pledged IP right of the debt and of the presumed compulsory sale of the pledged object in order to allow him/her to pay the debtor's debt.

Parties can add or specify their rights and obligations upon mutual agreement. However, the law does not foresee the possibility of entering such additional agreements in the register and thus making them part of the pledge right. The infringement of such agreements can lead to the possible use of contractual remedies, including claims for compensation of damages.

6.1.1 Rights and Obligations of the Parties in Specific Situations

Deleting the Encumbered IP Right from the Register The consent of the pledgee is not required in order to delete the encumbered IP right from the register, except in the case of trademarks. According to § 19(3) of the TMA, a trademark "cannot be surrendered if the trade mark is encumbered with a pledge". No such requirement arises from other relevant industrial property laws. Pursuant to the general rules in § 299^2 of the LPA, "[t]he registrar notifies the pledgee immediately of deletion of the pledged object from the register" and "makes a notation under the registered security [. . .] concerning the deletion of the pledged object." A registered security does not extinguish upon deletion of the pledged object from the register. (LPA § 299^2(1) and (2))

Transferring the Encumbered IP Right The written consent of the pledgee is required for the transfer of an encumbered trademark (TMA § 50^1(4)). Upon transfer of the pledged object, the legal position of the pledgor (including his/her rights and obligations) are transferred to the acquirer.

Encumbering the IP Right with Additional Pledges As a general principle, "several pledges may be established on one and the same object of pledge for the benefit of one or several creditors" (LPA § 277(3)). The pledgee and the pledgor can agree otherwise, but this agreement will not have effect against third parties and it will not make the additional encumberment of the IP right invalid. Violation of such an agreement can, however, lead to the use of contractual remedies against the pledgor.

Changing or Increasing Claims Secured by an IP Right In order to increase the amount secured by the pledge, the pledgor and the pledgee can agree on an amendment to the security contract. The maximum amount of the security is determined by the monetary value of the pledge that has been entered in the register; this can be changed by amending the pledge contract and making a corresponding entry in the register. Thus, any other pledgees with lower rankings must always consider the possibility that the amount that is secured for claims can be increased or replaced within the limits of the value of the pledge without their consent.

Assignment of the Secured Claim When the claim secured by the pledge is transferred, "[s]ecurity given to secure a claim and rights arising from accessory obligations which are related to the claim [. . .] shall transfer to the new obligee upon assignment of the claim." It is presumed that "the person assigning the claim [is also obliged] to transfer the security and the rights arising from accessory obligations which are not related to the claim" (LOA § 167(1)). This means that while a pledge of rights is automatically transferred with a claim (see LPA § 289 and § 314(2)), a registered security must be transferred to the new pledgee separately. However, the assignor and assignee of the claim may agree that securities are not transferred upon assignment of the claim.

6.2 Transfer of IP Rights as Security

If an IP right is transferred to a creditor, even only as security, the transferee becomes the new owner of the IP right and is entitled to exercise all of the rights arising from it. This includes use of the object of the IP right, licensing, and disposing of the right. However, the parties can contractually limit the rights of the transferee in the transfer agreement; for example, by agreeing that the transferee should not license or transfer the IP right unless the debtor fails to perform his/her obligations. The parties can also agree on the obligation of the transferee to transfer the IP right back to the debtor/transferor once the debtor has performed his/her obligations.

In the case of copyright and related rights, the only rights which are transferred are the economic rights. If the debtor/transferor is the author of the work or the creator of the object of the related rights, the creditor/transferee must refrain from violating his/her moral rights.

7 Enforcement of Security Rights Over IP

7.1 Pledge Over IP Rights

7.1.1 General Issues

The satisfaction of a secured claim takes place with the sale of the encumbered object, either voluntarily by the proprietor or in enforcement or bankruptcy proceedings. The pledgee does not have a personal claim against the pledgor and cannot demand the satisfaction of his claim from the pledgor's other property. "Any agreement entered into before [the secured claim] falls due whereby the pledgee acquires the object encumbered with the [pledge] for satisfaction of the [secured claim] is void" (LPA § 302(2) for registered security; LPA § 292(3), § 314(2) and § 319^2(2) for pledge of rights; TMA § 25(3) for trademarks specifically). The law does not forbid such an agreement between the pledgee and the pledgor after the secured claim falls due.

The pledge only extends to the pledged property. The law of pledge does not entitle the pledgee to the satisfaction of his/her claims from any advantages receivable from the use of the object (including licence fees). Extending the scope of the pledge to include licence fees is also not possible. However, a similar result could be achieved by encumbering the right to licence fees with a parallel pledge of rights or by agreeing on a conditional assignment of claims for licence fees under a licence contract.

7.1.2 Outside Insolvency

There are two main ways to enforce a pledge over IP rights outside insolvency. The first is a voluntary satisfaction of the claim from the pledged IP rights (both registered security and pledge of rights). Subject to the agreement of the pledgor and the pledgee, it is possible for the pledgor to sell the encumbered object voluntarily (or for it to be sold at a so-called *voluntary auction* outside of enforcement proceedings) to a third person, and the revenue is used to satisfy the secured claims (this is a so-called *free sale*). The pledgee may also purchase the pledged object, in which case the purchase price is deemed to be paid by the pledgee to the extent of the debt. In the case of voluntary sale of the pledged object, all rights with which the object is encumbered remain effective, unless the pledge is extinguished on agreement.

The second, more common way to enforce a pledge is through satisfaction of the claim from the pledged IP rights in enforcement proceedings. This option is further described below.

Registered Security over Industrial Property Rights

"If a claim secured by a registered security [. . .] is not performed, the pledgee has the right to demand compulsory execution [through the sale of the encumbered IP rights at a] compulsory auction" (LPA § 302(1), see TMA § 25(1)–(2)). "An object encumbered with a registered security [. . .] is sold by public auction pursuant to the procedure provided by law on the basis of an execution document" (LPA § 302 (3)). Such a document can be:

- A court judgment which confirms the existence of the secured right and declares the pledgee's right to the realization of the pledge (CEP § 2(2)(1)). The required court judgment can be obtained on the basis of a claim made by the pledgee against the owner of the encumbered property (i.e. pledgor), whereby the pledgee requests that the pledgor tolerate compulsory execution from the pledged property in the manner and scope specified in the judgment.

- In case the pledgee and the owner of the encumbered IP right concluded a notarized agreement on immediate compulsory enforcement before the secured claim fell due (CEP § 2(2)(19)), the pledgee may turn to a bailiff to initiate enforcement proceedings for compulsory execution even without a court judgment.

In order to claim payment on the encumbered property in enforcement proceedings, the property must first be seized (CEP § 52(1), see also § 110). As of seizure, the pledgor is prohibited from disposing of the property and any "disposition in violation of the restraint on disposition is void" (CEP § 54(1)–(2)). "A notation concerning [this] prohibition [is entered in the relevant register and it] prohibits the making of entries to the respective extent in the register without the application or consent of a bailiff" (CEP § 54(3)).

The bailiff will sell the object of the pledge at a public electronic auction (CEP § 78(1)), which is conducted in an electronic online auction environment (CEP § 81 (1)). "If an electronic auction cannot be conducted [...], an auction may be conducted orally" (CEP § 78(2)). If a public oral auction is organized, the bailiff decides "the place of the oral auction, taking account of the possibilities to sell a thing and the costs relating to the auction" (CEP § 81(2)). "If the price of [the object of the pledge] pursuant to the instrument of seizure is up to 2000 euros, a bailiff may authorise the [Estonian Chamber of Bailiffs and Trustees in Bankruptcy] to sell the [property]" (CEP § 78(3)).

"The starting price of a thing at an auction is the price which is based on its valuation and set out in an instrument of seizure" (CEP § 82(1)). The bailiff has limited grounds for changing the starting price and must ask for the opinion of the claimant and the debtor in this respect (CEP § 82(2)–(3)). "Upon failure of an auction,[15] a claimant may demand that a repeated auction be organised" (CEP § 100(1)). For the repeated auction, the "bailiff may reduce the price of things, but not more than by 25 per cent compared to the starting price of the previous auction, after asking the opinion of [the] debtor and [the] claimant concerning the reduction of the price" (CEP § 100(5)). "The price of the things shall not be reduced more than 70 per cent compared to the starting price at the first auction" (*Ibid*).

The procedure of the public auction is regulated by the CEP. The pledgee and the pledgor may also participate in the public auction. If the thing is sold to the pledgee, the monetary value of the pledgee's claim is set off against the selling price (see LPA § 294(3) for pledge of rights).

"On the basis of an application of [the] claimant [(i.e. the pledgee) or the] debtor [(i.e. the pledgor)], [the] bailiff may sell [the seized thing] in a manner different from an oral or electronic auction if the auction has failed or it can be presumed that the thing cannot be sold at an auction or the revenue presumably received from the thing at an auction is significantly smaller as compared to the revenue received when the thing is sold in any other manner" (CEP § 101(1)). "Upon sale in another manner,

[15] See CEP § 99(1) for grounds for failure of an auction.

[the] bailiff may discount the assets, but not more than 50 per cent compared to the value set out in [the] instrument of seizure, after requesting the opinion of [the] debtor [(i.e. the pledgor)] and [the] claimant [(i.e. the pledgee)] concerning the discount" (CEP § 101(4)). The bailiff may also sell the encumbered thing to the claimant (i.e. the pledgee). "In such case, the claim [. . .] shall be set off and the purchase price is deemed to be paid by [the] debtor to [the] claimant to the extent of the debt" (CEP § 101(5)).

Pledge of Rights

Pursuant to CEP § 128, "[e]nforcement proceedings are permitted in respect of proprietary rights of an author if the author has commenced the exercise thereof and the work has been published with the consent of the author. Transfer of proprietary copyrights to a third person is also deemed to be exercise, regardless of the fact whether the third person has commenced to exercise the right." "A claim for payment may be made on an inalienable right in the manner determined by a bailiff if the exercise of the right can be transferred to another person and unless otherwise provided by law" (CEP § 127(1)). Although related rights are not expressly mentioned in these provisions, the same principles should apply by analogy.

In general, the enforcement proceedings for demanding compulsory execution from proprietary rights of copyright or related rights are similar to such proceedings when they involve registered industrial property rights. However, unlike in the case of registered security, here the pledgee of a pledge of rights also has a statutory right to sell the pledged right (LPA § 319[6], § 294). This means that the pledgee can sell the object of the pledge and obtain satisfaction for his/her claims from the revenue of the sale without the consent of the pledgor and without the need to obtain an enforcement instrument (e.g. a court judgment) and initiate enforcement proceedings. A pledged thing is normally sold by public auction, the time and place of which must be made known to the pledgor and third persons who have rights in the pledged thing (LPA § 294(1)–(2)). "The pledgee and the pledgor may also participate in the public auction", and "[i]f the thing is sold to the pledgee, the monetary value of the pledgee's claim shall be set off against the selling price" (LPA § 294(3)). "The pledgee and the pledgor may agree to sell the pledged thing in a [different] manner", provided that any third persons whose rights in the pledged thing would extinguish upon the sale of the thing give their consent (LPA § 294(4)). "The obligation of a pledgor shall be deemed performed to the extent of the money received from [the] sale of the pledged thing from which the necessary sale expenses have been deducted" (LPA § 295(1)). "The money remaining after payment of the sale expenses and satisfaction of the claim of the pledgee shall be returned to the pledgor" (LPA § 295(2)).

Extent and Priority of Satisfaction of Claims

The claims which are secured by the pledge are determined by the security contract. As a general rule, in addition to the main claim, a pledge secures collateral claims relating to the secured claim, including interest and penalties (LPA § 279(4)). "Procedure expenses, expenses relating to the sale of the thing and expenses necessary for the preservation of [the] pledged object which are incurred by the pledgee are also secured by the pledge" (LPA § 279(6)). According to SPLA § 37, a registered security extends to: the main claim; unpaid interest for the last 3 years before the sale of the pledged property in a compulsory auction or before declaration of bankruptcy; late interest penalties; and expenses incurred when enforcing the debt. The parties can limit the extent of the secured claim in the security contract. Claims are secured up to the amount of the monetary value of the pledge—that is to say, the monetary value of the pledge determines the maximum extent to which the pledgee is entitled to get satisfaction for his/her claims from the pledged property.

In enforcement proceedings, a claim is "satisfied together with the fine for delay and other collateral claims the extent of which [is determined in the] enforcement instrument" (CEP § 56(1)). Before distribution of the revenue received from enforcement proceedings, the enforcement costs (including bailiff's fees and necessary sale expenses) are deducted from the revenue (CEP § 174(2)). Thereafter, the claims are satisfied out of the revenue in accordance with a distribution plan (CEP § 174(3)). First, "the collectable collateral claims and [then] the principal debt and the interest calculated after seizure are deleted from the debt of [the] debtor" (CEP § 56(2)).

In case an IP right is encumbered with several pledges, "[c]laims are satisfied according to the ranking of [these] pledges unless otherwise provided by law" (LPA § 302(4)). "Claims secured by pledges with one and the same ranking are satisfied in proportion to the amount of the claims" (LPA § 302(5)). The rankings are determined according to the time of creation of the rights of security (LPA § 281(3)). "The ranking of a registered security [...] is determined by the time of entry in a register" (LPA § 300(1)). The claim of the pledgee with a low-ranking pledge can only be satisfied from the revenue if there is money left after satisfying the claims of the pledgees with higher rankings (see LPA § 302(4)–(5); and CEP § 105(1) and § 106).

Upon the sale of an IP right in enforcement proceedings by a bailiff, the security rights which have the same ranking as or a higher ranking than the security being enforced are preserved, while the rights with a lower ranking are extinguished. The same applies for both a registered security and a pledge of rights (see CEP § 104 and § 158). To protect their rights, the other pledgees have the following options:

- In addition to the pledgee who initiated the enforcement proceedings, other pledgees holding security rights in the same IP right can participate in the proceedings and in the distribution of the revenue from the sale of the encumbered property for the satisfaction of their claims. A pledgee who is not the claimant in the proceedings "may submit an application to a bailiff in which [that

person] applies for the preferred satisfaction of his or her claim from the revenue, regardless of whether or not his or her claim has fallen due" (CEP § 108(1)).
- "A person whose right is extinguished by compulsory enforcement may, before the sale of [the] thing, submit an application to a bailiff in which [that person] applies for compensation for the extinguished right out of [the] revenue" (CEP § 108(2)).

"A bailiff shall distribute the revenue received from the sale of [the thing] between claimants and other persons entitled to participate in the revenue in the order of creation of the rights of security" (CEP § 105(1)). However, the entitled persons can agree on a different order for distribution of the revenue (*Ibid*).

7.1.3 In Bankruptcy Proceedings

In case of the bankruptcy of the pledgor, the claims secured by a pledge are satisfied together with other creditors' claims from the money received from the sale of the bankruptcy estate (see BA § 44, §§ 135–137 and § 139). A precondition for satisfying a claim in bankruptcy proceedings is that both the claim and the right of security are accepted. Thus, even a claim secured by a pledge must be filed—that is to say, the trustee must be notified and the claim must be defended in the bankruptcy proceedings (see BA § 93(1)) and § 100(1)). Even if enforcement proceedings for the realization of the pledge are already pending, they must be terminated when the bankruptcy of the pledgor is declared, and the secured claim must be submitted for defence in the bankruptcy proceedings. Pursuant to § 103(4) of the BA, "claims satisfied by a court or arbitration decision which has entered into force [and] rights of security accepted by a court or arbitration decision which has entered into force [. . .] are deemed to be accepted without defence" (BA § 103(4)).

As a general rule subject to some exceptions (see BA § 133(2)–(4)), "[a] trustee may commence the sale of the bankruptcy estate after the first general meeting of creditors unless the creditors have decided otherwise at the meeting" (BA § 133(1)). The bankruptcy estate is sold pursuant to the Code of Enforcement Procedure, taking into account the specifications prescribed by the Bankruptcy Act (BA § 135(1)). "If an object included in the bankruptcy estate is encumbered with a [pledge], the trustee shall sell the encumbered object within three months [. . .] as of the time when the trustee was entitled to commence the sale of the bankruptcy estate" (BA § 140).

As a rule, the "[b]ankruptcy estate is sold by auction pursuant to the procedure provided by the [CEP]" (BA § 136(1)). "The starting price of assets shall be determined by the trustee and approved by the bankruptcy committee" (BA § 136 (2)). "At a repeated auction, a trustee may reduce the starting price of the assets by 50 per cent", while any further reductions can only be made with the consent of the bankruptcy committee (BA § 136(3)). Exceptions to the general rule are as follows:

- "With the consent of the trustee, a debtor who is a natural person may sell the [. . .] rights included in the bankruptcy estate himself or herself" (BA § 135(2)).

- "[The] general meeting of creditors may require the trustee by a precept to sell the assets without an auction if the sale of assets in another manner is more profitable" (BA § 137(1)). "If [the] general meeting does not issue [such a precept] [...], [the trustee may sell the estate] without an auction in a more profitable manner with the consent of the bankruptcy committee" (BA § 137(2)).

Extent and Priority of Satisfaction of Claims

Out of the bankruptcy estate, first the payments relating to the bankruptcy proceedings (e.g. the costs of the proceedings—see BA § 146(1), § 148, § 150) are made. After that, the claims of the creditors are satisfied based on their rankings (see BA § 153). Accepted claims secured by a pledge constitute the highest ranking (BA § 153(1)(1)). These claims are "satisfied first to the extent of the money received from the sale of the pledged object from which the payments [relating to the bankruptcy proceedings (see BA § 146(1))] [...] have been deducted" (BA § 153 (2)). A pledgee is required to participate in covering the expenses relating to the bankruptcy proceedings, up to a maximum amount of 15% of the proceeds received from the sale of the pledged object (*Ibid*). "If a pledged object has been encumbered with several rights of security, the claims shall be satisfied according to the rankings of the [...] security out of the money received from the sale of the pledged object [and t]he expenses [from the bankruptcy proceedings] are divided between the pledgees in proportion to the share of the proceeds of sale of the pledged object" (BA § 153(3)).

"If a claim secured by a pledge is not satisfied in full out of the money received from the sale of the [pledged object], the rest of the claim shall be satisfied together with [other claims in the second ranking, unless the] bankrupt has pledged the assets thereof in order to secure the debt of a third person" (BA § 153(4)). "Claims of a lower ranking are satisfied after the claims of the preceding ranking have been satisfied in full" (BA § 153(5)). "If the estate is not sufficient for satisfying all the claims of the same ranking, the claims shall be satisfied in proportion to the sizes of the claims" (BA § 153(6)).

Recovery of Security

The concept of the "recovery" of transactions or actions has been established in Estonian bankruptcy proceedings with the aim of preventing the debtor from intentionally damaging the creditors by diverting his/her property. In certain cases specified in the Bankruptcy Act, the court can "revoke transactions which were concluded or other acts which were performed by the debtor before the declaration of bankruptcy and which damage the interests of the creditors" (BA § 109(1)).

Among other bases of recovery, "a court shall revoke the grant of security if the security was granted:

(1) during the period from the appointment of an interim trustee until declaration of bankruptcy;
(2) in order to secure an obligation which had arisen within six months before the appointment of an interim trustee if the debtor was not required to grant such security at the time when the obligation arose or if the debtor was insolvent at the time of granting the security and the person in whose favour the security was granted was or should have been aware of the insolvency;
(3) within two years before the appointment of an interim trustee if the security was granted in favour of a person connected with the debtor unless the person or the debtor proves that the debtor was solvent at the time of granting the security". (BA § 114(1))

"Grant of security shall not be recovered if the security was granted in order to secure a loan or any other credit agreement and after granting the security the debtor came into possession of the amount of money corresponding to the value of the security pursuant to the secured contract, except in the case specified in [Subsection (3) above]" (BA § 114(2)). In order to revoke the grant of security, usually the security contract is revoked by the court.

7.1.4 In Reorganization and Debt Restructuring Proceedings

In case a company is likely to become insolvent, a possible way to prevent actual insolvency and future bankruptcy proceedings is to reorganize the company. Pursuant to § 2 of the Reorganisation Act (RA), "[t]he reorganisation of an enterprise means the application of a set of measures in order for an enterprise to overcome economic difficulties, to restore its liquidity, improve its profitability and ensure its sustainable management." Reorganization proceedings are commenced by the court and the relevant prerequisites are that (RA § 8(1)): "(1) the undertaking is likely to become insolvent in the future; (2) the enterprise requires reorganisation; [and] (3) the sustainable management of the enterprise is likely after the reorganisation." "Reorganisation proceedings shall not be commenced [if, inter alia,] bankruptcy proceedings have been brought against the undertaking" (RA § 8(2)(1)).

In reorganization proceedings, a claim, including a secured claim, may be transformed by: "(1) extension of terms for the performance of obligations; (2) fulfilment of a financial claim in instalments; (3) reduction of the amount of debt; [or] (4) replacement of an obligation with the holding of shares of a legal person" (RA § 22(1)). If a secured claim is transformed, the original claim is "frozen" and a new claim is established next to it. The security will continue to secure both claims, but if the company enacts its reorganization plan, the frozen claim is also regarded as having been satisfied.[16] It is not possible to transform a pledge right in reorganization proceedings, but by transforming a secured claim, it is possible to restrict the

[16] Judgment No. 3-2-1-25-11 of May 19, 2011 by the Civil Chamber of the Supreme Court, para 60.

realization of a pledge right. A pledgee cannot be forced to waive a pledge right without compensation. Reorganization of the claim does not affect the right of the pledgee to get satisfaction for his claim if the debtor does not satisfy the reorganized debt.

For natural persons, the possibility of restructuring the debtor's financial obligations in accordance with the Debt Restructuring and Debt Protection Act (DRDPA) is made available in order to overcome solvency problems and avoid bankruptcy proceedings. A debt can be restructured "by way of extension of the term of performance of an obligation, by way of performing the obligation in instalments or by way of reducing the obligation" (DRDPA § 2(1)). As a rule, "[a] claim secured by a pledge may be restructured only if the creditor consents to it, even if the pledgor is a third party" (DRDPA § 24(6)). "This does not preclude or restrict the restructuring [...] of the claim remaining after selling the [pledged object]." In certain cases, the consent of the pledgee is not required for termination of a credit contract (*Ibid*).

7.2 *Transfer of IP Rights as Security*

7.2.1 Outside Insolvency

Enforcement depends on the terms of the transfer agreement. For example, the parties can agree that if the debtor/transferor fails to perform his/her obligations, the creditor/transferee is entitled to permanently keep the IP right and exercise the rights of an owner of a right. Alternatively, the parties can agree that the creditor is obliged to sell the IP right under certain conditions to get satisfaction for his/her claims and give any excess revenue to the debtor.

7.2.2 In Bankruptcy Proceedings

There are no special provisions in the Bankruptcy Act on providing securities through the transfer of IP rights or through the assignment of any other rights. Such transfers/assignments have not been considered equal to securing a claim with a pledge. Thus, if an IP right has been transferred to a creditor as security for a debt, it is regarded as an object belonging to a third person and is not included in the bankruptcy estate (see BA § 123(1)). The secured claim, however, can be presented in the bankruptcy proceedings.

7.2.3 In Reorganization or Debt Restructuring Proceedings

There are no special provisions on providing securities through the transfer of IP rights or through the assignment of any other rights which would apply in reorganization or debt restructuring proceedings. If an IP right has been properly transferred to a creditor as security for a debt, it is not regarded as part of the debtor's property. The secured claim, however, can be transformed or restructured in the proceedings.

8 Costs

8.1 Establishment and Registration Costs

8.1.1 Pledge Over IP Rights

Registered Security

Costs for legal advice are typically incurred when encumbering an IP right with a registered security. In addition to the contract from which the secured debt arises, the pledgor (i.e. owner of the IP right) and the pledgee (typically, the creditor of the secured debt) need to conclude a real right contract to establish the registered security (i.e. the pledge contract). In addition, they must conclude a contract in which they determine the claims secured by the registered security (i.e. the security contract). They may also conclude an agreement whereby they subject the pledgor to immediate enforcement of the secured object. All these contracts are typically prepared by lawyers. The average hourly fee for a leading law firm in Estonia is 150–200 euros, plus taxes.

In the case of trademarks, the TMA requires that the pledge contract be notarized. Other IP laws do not establish a notarization requirement. The notary fee for the establishment of a pledge depends on the transaction value, which is two thirds of the amount of the pledge (§ 9(1) of Notary Fees Act (NFS)). However, if the agreement on the establishment of the security is concluded together and in the same document with the agreement from which the secured obligation arises, a single notary fee is paid and the transaction value is determined on the basis of the transaction with the higher value (NFS § 9(3)). Table 1 shows examples of transaction values and corresponding notary fees.

A state fee must be paid for registering a pledge contract and entering a registered security in the relevant register of IP rights. The amount of the state fee depends on the transaction value. The transaction value corresponds to the monetary value of the security to be registered (§ 343(1) and Annex 2 of the SFA). Table 2 shows examples of transaction values and corresponding state fees.

Pledge of Rights

In case copyright or related rights are encumbered with a pledge of rights, the pledgor (i.e. the owner of the economic rights in the work) and the pledgee must

Table 1 Notary fee for establishing a pledge

Transaction value (EUR)	Notary fee (EUR)
5753–6391	24.90
19,174–20,452	37.70
95,871–102,260	160.40
498,511–511,300	773.95
639,121–1,278,235	958.65 + 0.14% of the amount of the transaction value exceeding 639,120
Over 6,391,165	5,368.55 + 0.02% of the amount of the transaction value exceeding 6,391,165

Table 2 State fee for registering the security

Transaction value (EUR)	State fee (EUR)
5761–6400	10
9181–20,460	25
95,871–102,260	110
498,521–504,910	755
More than 639,120	0.16% of the amount of the transaction value, but not more than 2560

conclude a pledge contract and a security contract, which can be part of a single document. Thus, legal costs are typically incurred. There is no requirement of notarization of the agreements nor of registration of the pledge.

Commercial Pledge

Copyright and related rights can form part of a general commercial pledge of the movable property of a company. In order to establish a commercial pledge, a pledge contract and a security contract must be concluded. The pledge contract has to be notarized (CPA § 4(2)). Thus, legal costs and a notary fee are incurred. The amount of the notary fee is determined on the basis of the transaction value in the same manner as set out above.

"Upon making of an entry concerning a commercial pledge in the commercial pledge register, a state fee shall be paid in the amount of 0.2 per cent of the value of the pledge being applied for but not less than 32 euros and not more than 2560 euros" (SFA § 70(1)).

8.1.2 Transfer of IP Rights as Security

An agreement for the transfer of copyright or related rights, trademarks, patents, European patents valid in Estonia, utility models, industrial designs, or integrated circuits has to be concluded. Such an agreement must be in writing but there is no requirement of notarization. Either in the same or in an additional document, the parties need to agree on the conditional obligation of the transferee to transfer the IP right back to the transferor upon satisfaction of the debt. Thus, legal costs are incurred for preparing these documents.

In the case of registered IP rights, an entry concerning the transfer of the IP right has to be made in the relevant register. "A state fee of 32 euros shall be paid for the submission of an application for making [this] entry" (SFA § 108).

8.2 Enforcement Costs

8.2.1 Costs of Obtaining an Enforcement Instrument

In order to initiate proceedings for the enforcement of a secured claim through the compulsory sale of an object of registered security or a commercial pledge, the pledgee must first obtain an enforcement instrument. First and foremost, enforcement proceedings can be started on the basis of a court judgment which has entered into force (CEP § 2(1)(1)). Legal costs are incurred for obtaining the judgment. The average hourly fee of a leading law firm in Estonia is 150–200 euros, plus taxes. There are three levels to the court hierarchy and the duration of the process and the cost depend on the complexity of the matter and the objections raised by the defendant. For a relatively simple matter, around 20 h of work may be needed for representation in one level of court.

Alternatively, upon conclusion of the pledge contract, the parties may also conclude a "notarized [agreement] which [prescribes] the obligation of the owner of [the IP right] to be subject to immediate compulsory enforcement for the satisfaction of [the secured claim]" (CEP § 2(1)(19)). In that case, there is no need to obtain a court judgment, as the agreement of the parties already constitutes an enforcement instrument.

In the case of a pledge of rights, the pledgee has the option of selling the object of the pledge himself in order to obtain satisfaction for his/her claims from the revenue of the sale. If the pledgee decides to use this statutory right, there is no need to obtain an enforcement instrument through court proceedings.

In the case of a transfer of IP rights as security, there is no need for enforcement proceedings and thus no need for an enforcement instrument. The security right is enforced by the pledgee when the pledgee does not transfer it back to the original owner.

8.2.2 Costs of Enforcement Proceedings

"A bailiff has the right to charge a fee for professional acts and request the compensation of the accompanying costs" (§ 28(2) of the Bailiffs Act). The "[b]

Table 3 Bailiff fees

Amount of claim for payment (EUR)	Bailiff's basic fee (EUR)	Advance payment of Bailiff's fee (EUR)
Up to 500	Up to 130	Up to 30
2500–3000	500	60
12,500–15,000	1100	191
100,000–150,000	4500	191
350,000–500,000	7000	191
More than 500,000	7000	319

ailiff's fee may compose of the fee for commencement of proceedings, basic fee of proceedings and additional fee for enforcement actions" (§ 29(1) of the Bailiffs Act). "In enforcement proceedings, the fee for commencement of proceedings [and the basic fee] shall be paid by the debtor", but an "advance payment shall be made by the person who applies for the making of a professional act" (§ 30(1)–(3) of the Bailiffs Act).

"The fee for commencement of enforcement proceedings in case of proprietary claims depends on the amount of [the] claim and the expenses incurred upon delivery of the enforcement notice to the debtor" (§ 34(1) of Bailiffs Act).

- "If the enforcement notice can be delivered to the debtor with reasonable effort via the address or telecommunications data entered in the population register or the seat or contact data entered in the commercial register or the non-profit associations and foundations register or via the debtor's address specified in the enforcement instrument, the fee for commencement of enforcement proceedings shall be: (1) 15 euros in case of non-proprietary claim; (2) 15 euros in case of a claim up to 51 euros; (3) 30 euros in case of a claim from 51 to 5000 euros; [and] (4) 60 euros in case of a claim over 5000 euros" (§ 34(2) of Bailiffs Act).
- "If the enforcement notice cannot be delivered to the debtor with reasonable effort via the [means described above], the fee for commencement of enforcement proceedings shall be: (1) 30 euros in case of a non-proprietary claim; (2) 30 euros in case of a claim up to 51 euros; (3) 60 euros in case of a claim from 51 to 5000 euros; [and] (4) 120 [euros] in case of a claim over 5000 euros" (§ 34(3) of Bailiffs Act).

The basic fees and the cost of the required advance payments are based on the amount of the claim for payment. Table 3 provides several examples.

9 Practical Use, Difficulties and Law Reform

Encumbering a thing with a pledge is a common way of securing debts, particularly credit debts. However, the most common objects of pledges are immovables (i.e. mortgages) or undertakings' movable property (i.e. commercial pledges).

Granting a security in IP rights is not common in Estonia. It is done more often with industrial property rights in the form of a registered security than it is with copyright or related rights in the form of a pledge of rights. While the assignment of rights as security is rather common in Estonia, it is not often done with IP rights. This is reflected in the lack of disputes in courts.

The taking of a registered security is not very common in Estonia in general, not just for IP rights. One of the reasons for this is probably the fact that legal regulations on registered security over movables were difficult to implement and those that existed contained several gaps until July 2003, when they were thoroughly amended. The use of the pledge of rights and the transfer of IP rights as security are also not common.

It is difficult to estimate the main legal and practical difficulties involved in taking security over IP rights because not many disputes have reached courts.

Some general practical difficulties in establishing pledges are as follows:

- The conclusion of so-called *global* security contracts—these are security contracts in which the claims secured by a pledge are determined globally, i.e. as all future claims against the debtor. The validity and effect of such agreements has been questioned by the Supreme Court, especially in cases of third-party pledgors.[17]
- The bankruptcy of a third-party pledgor—if the debtor of a secured claim has not breached the obligation (i.e. there is no enforceable claim), then the pledgee does not have a claim against a third-party pledgor that the pledgee could file in the bankruptcy proceedings. Due to the lack of a more appropriate legal construction, these claims are filed in bankruptcy proceedings as conditional claims.[18]

The main problem concerning the transfer of IP rights as security is the issue of over-securing the claim. The Supreme Court has held that enabling the pledgee to keep an object whose value is considerably higher than the amount of the secured debt as a security is against the principles of granting securities and thus not allowed. Instead, if the debt is not paid, then the grantor of the security should be compensated for the difference between the amount of the claim and the value of the security transferred to the creditor.[19] An agreement enabling the over-securing of a claim could be found to be void for violation of the general principles of good faith and fair dealings, in which case the transferred objects would have to be returned.

There are currently no proposals for a law reform relating to security over IP rights in Estonia or at the EU level. However, the need for reform in Estonia is expected to be considered at the time of drafting an Industrial Property Code in the near future. The first version of this Code was finished in 2014 and it includes

[17]Judgment No. 3-2-1-64-12 of May 29, 2012 by the Civil Chamber of the Supreme Court, paras 27–35.

[18]Kõve (2014), § 280, Sec. 3.3.5.1.c.

[19]Judgment No. 3-2-1-19-14 of May 12, 2014 by the Civil Chamber of the Supreme Court, paras 17, 19.

provisions specifying the application of the general rules on registered security in the LPA to intellectual property rights. The Estonian Ministry of Justice has decided to continue work on an Industrial Property Code in 2021.

References

Kõve V (2014) §§ 279, 280. In: Varul P, Kull I, Kõve V, Käerdi M, Puri T (eds) Asjaõigusseadus II. Kommenteeritud väljaanne. Juura, Tallinn

Volens U (2014) §§ 297, 298. In: Varul P, Kull I, Kõve V, Käerdi M, Puri T (eds) Asjaõigusseadus II. Kommenteeritud väljaanne. Juura, Tallinn

Security Rights in Intellectual Property in Finland

Teemu Juutilainen

Abstract Finnish law provides for the registrable pledges of patents, trademarks and other registrable intellectual property rights. This part of the legal framework is, by and large, adequate, so that one can reliably obtain fully effective security rights over these types of intellectual property rights. However, statistical data from the Finnish Patent and Registration Office shows that this opportunity is quite rarely used. In turn, copyright and other intellectual property rights that are not registrable under Finnish law are problematic in terms of achieving third-party effectiveness. Solutions proposed in legal literature, such as accepting security transfers of copyright as effective against third parties without any form of publicity, remain disputed and uncertain. Indeed, the most common way of using intellectual property rights as security under Finnish law is through the enterprise mortgage. Enterprise mortgages are frequently used (although often as a supplementary security, due to their limited priority) and they cover all types of intellectual property rights.

1 Introduction

This chapter presents an overview of Finnish law on security over intellectual property rights (IPRs), with the main focus on patents, trademarks and copyright.[1] At the same time, the chapter critically examines this legal framework, identifying its

[1]References to Finnish statutes in the chapter are given with their respective numbers in the Statutes of Finland—e.g., "Patents Act (550/1967)". The latter part of the number indicates the year when the statute was published, which is usually also the year of enactment. Most statutes referred to have been amended on several occasions, but the numbers do not reveal amendments. The statutes can be found in their original form, as well as in their amended and consolidated form with the dates of amendment indicated, in the Finlex database: https://www.finlex.fi/en. While Finnish statutes are official only in the Finnish and Swedish languages, the database provides some unofficial

T. Juutilainen (✉)
Faculty of Law, University of Turku, Turku, Finland
e-mail: teemu.juutilainen@utu.fi

E.-M. Kieninger (ed.), *Security Rights in Intellectual Property*, Ius Comparatum – Global Studies in Comparative Law 45,
https://doi.org/10.1007/978-3-030-44191-3_13

shortcomings and observing how and to what extent IPR security is actually used in Finland.

The chapter proceeds as follows. The relevant types of IPRs and security rights are introduced in Sects. 2 and 3, respectively. Section 4 discusses the structure of secured transactions involving specific IPRs individually, while Sect. 5 deals with questions of priority related to them. Section 6 moves on to enterprise mortgages, which cover all types of IPRs. Section 7 outlines the rights and duties of the parties to an IPR security agreement before debtor default. Section 8 discusses the enforcement of IPR security both outside and in insolvency. For a quantitative perspective on the use of IPRs as security, Sect. 9 looks at statistical data provided by the Finnish Patent and Registration Office. Section 10 concludes the chapter.

2 Types of IPR

In Finland, IPRs have traditionally been divided into two broad categories: copyright on the one hand and so-called "industrial rights" on the other. A leading textbook in the field,[2] sticking with this division, classifies IPRs as follows:

> Copyright: a) copyright ("copyright proper" – that is, rights in literary and artistic works by, for example, a writer, a painter, a composer, an architect, or an author of a computer program), b) rights related to copyright ("neighbouring rights" – that is, rights of a performing artist, a producer of a sound recording, a producer of a video recording, a radio or television organisation, a producer of a catalogue or database, a photographer, or a press agency or correspondent).
>
> Industrial rights: a) patent, b) utility model ("minor patent"), c) protection of industrial designs, d) exclusive right in the layout design of an integrated circuit, e) plant variety right (that is, plant breeder's right), f) trademark, g) protection of geographical indications, h) trade name and i) protection against unfair trade practices.

The main focus of this chapter is on patents, trademarks and copyright ("copyright proper").

The procedure for obtaining a (national) patent is laid down in Chapter 2 of the Patents Act (550/1967). The patent authority, which processes patent applications and grants patents, is the Finnish Patent and Registration Office. According to

---

translations in other languages (mostly in English). English translations, where available and to the extent that they are up to date, have been used in the chapter. The author thanks Professor Taina Pihlajarinne for helpful comments and the staff of the Finnish Patent and Registration Office for making available statistical data on IPR security and enterprise mortgage registrations.

[2]Haarmann (2014), pp. 3–4. Haarmann notes that the division between copyright and industrial rights is based on international conventions and that it is still maintained in Finland although its relevance can be questioned in the light of the current industrial and commercial significance of copyright. This division is also visible in the division of labour between Finnish ministries: copyright matters belong to the Ministry of Education and Culture, while most industrial rights matters belong to the Ministry of Economic Affairs and Employment.

Section 20(2) of the Patents Act, "[a] granted patent shall be recorded in the Patent Register kept by the Patent Authority". For patent protection beyond (but including) Finland, the options consist of applying for a European patent under the European Patent Convention (EPC) or filing an international patent application under the World Intellectual Property Organization (WIPO) Patent Convention Treaty (PCT).[3] Neither of these options creates a supranational IPR.[4]

According to Section 4 of the Trademarks Act (7/1964),[5] one can obtain an exclusive right to a trademark by recording it in the Register of Trademarks. This register, too, is kept by the Finnish Patent and Registration Office (Section 12). Even without registration, an exclusive right to a trademark can be obtained once the trademark has been established, meaning that it has become commonly known in Finland in the relevant business or consumer circles as a distinct mark for the proprietor's goods (Section 4a). For trademark protection beyond (but including) Finland, the options consist of applying for an EU trademark or for international trademark registration under the WIPO Madrid Protocol. Out of these trademarks, only the EU trademark is a supranational IPR.[6] An EU trademark can "be given as security or be the subject of rights *in rem*",[7] but this chapter only discusses security over national trademarks.

Section 1 of the Copyright Act (404/1961) provides that "[a] person who has created a literary or artistic work shall have copyright therein". Unlike patents and trademarks, copyright is not registrable under Finnish law.

---

[3]See Patents Act, Chapters 3 (international patent applications) and 9b (European patent applications).

[4]On the European patent with unitary effect ("unitary patent"), which has not yet become operational, see the European Patent Office website: https://www.epo.org/law-practice/unitary/unitary-patent.html. Accessed Jan 10, 2019. Finland has recently enacted a legislative package enabling its participation in the new European patent system—i.e., the unitary patent and the Unitary Patent Court. This legislation is meant to be put into force by a separate State Council decree, which has not yet been enacted. See Patents Act, Chapter 9c; Government proposal HE 45/2015.

[5]The Finnish Parliament is currently processing a proposal for a new Trademarks Act. See Sect. 4.2 below.

[6]See the European Union Intellectual Property Office website: https://euipo.europa.eu/ohimportal/en/trade-marks. Accessed Jan 10, 2019.

[7]See Articles 22, 26 and 27 of the Parliament and Council Regulation (EU) 2017/1001 of June 14, 2017 on the European Union trade mark (codification) [2017] OJ L154/1 (EU Trademark Regulation). According to Article 28, the same applies to applications for an EU trademark.

3 Types of IPR Security

The Finnish Patent and Registration Office keeps registers for most industrial right-type IPRs, including patents and trademarks, as noted above.[8] A registered IPR can be encumbered by a registrable pledge.[9] This is the primary way of using specific IPRs individually to secure an obligation under Finnish law.[10] While a pledge of this kind generally comes into existence by virtue of an agreement between a pledgor and a pledgee (or through disposition by a pledgor, as the creation of a pledge may alternatively be explained), the pledge has to be recorded in the relevant IPR register in order to achieve (full) effectiveness against third parties, notably the pledgor's other creditors. Put differently, registration of a pledge strengthens (or "perfects") the pledgee's agreement-based legal position in relation to third parties.[11]

In contrast, non-registrable IPRs, such as copyright, are problematic in terms of achieving third-party effectiveness. Indeed, the effectiveness of a security arrangement against the security provider's creditors and certain other third parties generally requires some form of publicity (this refers to registration, possession or notification), but no suitable publicity measure seems to exist in the case of non-registrable IPRs. Some commentators have argued that security transfers of copyright should be accepted as effective against third parties without any form of publicity, although under Finnish law, security transfers (and security assignments) are generally thought to be subject to the same publicity requirements as pledges, in order to avoid security transfers being used to circumvent rules on pledges.[12] However, these arguments are disputed and uncertain in that no binding source of law confirms them.[13]

As discussed in Sect. 6 below, the Finnish enterprise mortgage covers all types of IPRs. In addition, an IPR can be subject to a retention of title clause (or a functionally similar clause not resorting to the terms "title" or "ownership"—that is, a clause on

---

[8]See the Finnish Patent and Registration Office website: https://www.prh.fi/en. Accessed Jan 10, 2019. The division between copyright and industrial rights was explained at the beginning of Sect. 2 above.

[9]Patents Act, Section 44; Act on Utility Model Rights (800/1991), Section 28; Registered Designs Act (221/1971), Section 27; Act on Exclusive Rights to Layout-Designs (Topographies) of Integrated Circuits (32/1991), Section 23; Plant Breeder's Right Act (1279/2009), Section 22; Trademarks Act, Section 33(3). This chapter follows the majority of the translations of IPR acts in the Finlex database, using "pledge" for the Finnish term *panttioikeus* and the Swedish term *panträtt*. *Panttioikeus* and *panträtt* denote both possessory and non-possessory security rights alike. To translate them as "pledge" risks confusion, though, because "pledge" may be associated with possessory security rights. In that light, "charge" might be preferable. See, e.g., Recital 26 of the EU Trademark Regulation (cited in note 7 above), according to which an EU trademark "should be capable of ... being *charged* as security in favour of a third party" (emphasis added).

[10]Trade names cannot be used as security. See Haarmann and Mansala (2012), pp. 148–149.

[11]Tepora (2008), p. 112. See Tepora et al. (2016), pp. 68–70, 373–374. Cf. Sect. 4.2 below on the pledge of a trademark.

[12]See, e.g., Havansi (1992), pp. 513–514.

[13]Tepora et al. (2016), pp. 483–484.

recovery of the sales object or cancellation of the sales contract). Retention of title is effective against third parties without any form of publicity, but this is subject to conditions. For example, the secured obligations must be based on the sales contract in question.[14]

Finally, it should be noted that IPRs can be used to secure an obligation in indirect ways (that is, other than using an IPR, as such, as an encumbered asset). One such way is to use a pledge or security assignment of a stream of income (that is, receivables) generated by an IPR. Another way involves establishing a company to own an IPR, and then pledging the value of the IPR in the shape of the shares of that company.

4 Structure of Secured Transactions: Specific IPRs Individually as Security

4.1 Pledge of a Patent

A pledge of a patent is created by an agreement between a pledgor and a pledgee. This agreement is not subject to form requirements, but a written form is often a practical necessity due to the many details that have to be agreed upon; in addition, it may be necessary for evidential purposes (to facilitate registration, etc.).[15] For effectiveness against the pledgor's creditors and certain other third parties, a pledge of a patent has to be registered—that is, recorded in the Patent Register kept by the Finnish Patent and Registration Office. Section 44(1) of the Patents Act provides as follows: "The transfer of patents and the grant of licences shall be recorded, on request, in the Patent Register. The same shall apply to the pledging of a patent."[16] The ineffectiveness of an unregistered pledge of a patent against the pledgor's creditors in enforcement (that is, debt collection and distraint proceedings) as well as in bankruptcy (that is, collective liquidation proceedings) is confirmed by the Finnish Supreme Court in the judgment KKO 1988:31. This precedent is very clear because the part of the case that is relevant here concerned two pledges of a patent, one of which was recorded in the Patent Register and the other of which was not.[17]

[14]Tuomisto (2007), pp. 191–194. In Tuomisto's view, as a starting point, retention of title clauses over IPRs or other intangibles should be subject to the same rules as retention of title clauses over tangible movables. See the Bankruptcy Act (120/2004), Chapter 5, Section 7(2).

[15]Tuominen (2001), pp. 158–160.

[16]Registration can be requested by the pledgor or the pledgee. If the pledgee does this, it is probably necessary to present a written agreement or other written evidence of the pledging. See Tepora et al. (2016), pp. 69–70; Tuominen (2001), p. 179. Cf. Tammi-Salminen (2015), p. 285.

[17]The Supreme Court based its judgment in part on the earlier, repealed Patents Act (387/1943), which was clearer in terms of third-party effectiveness, especially in enforcement proceedings. The Supreme Court found no reason to assume that the legislator had intended the current Patents Act to

As regards evaluating the security value of a patent, one commentator suggests that the most reliable methods consist of estimating the future net cash flow generated by the patent. However, these methods are also laborious and time-consuming. Other possible methods may be based on the cost of creating or recreating the patented invention, the market price of the patent, or licence payment cash flows. All of these methods come in different variants and can be combined with one another. The time of patent protection is limited to a maximum of 20 years from the application date (Patents Act, Section 40). As a result, the value of a patent, be it for security or other purposes, will generally be declining towards the end of that time.[18]

4.2 *Pledge of a Trademark*

Section 33(3) of the Trademarks Act provides: "If any person wishes to pledge his trademark rights, a written agreement shall be made and entered in the register. No right of pledge shall be valid until such an entry has been made." On the face of it, this wording appears to suggest two differences as compared to the creation of a pledge of a patent: (1) a form requirement of agreement in writing and (2) registration as a condition for validity (in fact, the official Finnish and Swedish texts even speak of "coming into existence" rather than "validity").

However, commentators in legal literature tend to take Section 33(3) less than literally. Some commentators argue that the creation of a pledge of a trademark occurs similarly to the creation of a pledge of a patent, meaning that a pledge of a trademark comes into existence and becomes effective between a pledgor and a pledgee by virtue of their agreement. Recording the pledge in the Register of Trademarks, so the argument goes, is required for third-party effectiveness, particularly against the pledgor's creditors.[19] It is also a common view that an earlier pledgee's first-in-time priority ("first in time, first in right") based on an unregistered agreement of pledge should be upheld against later transferees and pledgees, although only as a starting point—that is to say, subject to the possibility that a later pledgee or transferee takes priority by registering first in good faith.[20] In

change the legal norms in this respect. On the significance of registration, see also the judgment KKO 1993:49.

[18]Tuominen (2001), pp. 91–92, 111–133. According to Tuominen, three questions must be answered in the positive for the evaluation of the value of an industrial right (e.g., a patent or a trademark) to be worthwhile in the first place. First, is the industrial right capable of distinguishing the products or services subject to it from other assets of the enterprise? Second, is the industrial right relevant to a third party (e.g., would a third party be willing to buy or licence the right)? And, third, would a third party be willing to pay licence fees in exchange for a right to use the industrial right?

[19]Tepora (2008), p. 112; Tepora (2004), p. 191. See Tuomisto (1993), p. 119.

[20]Tepora et al. (2016), p. 187; Havansi (1992), p. 298.

addition, it has been suggested that even an oral agreement of pledge is valid and suffices for registration, provided that the agreement is evidenced in writing (for example, through a document signed by the pledgor) or confirmed by a court of law.[21]

As noted in Sect. 2 above, other than by way of registration, an exclusive right to a trademark can be obtained once the trademark has been established (Trademarks Act, Section 4a). However, an established trademark cannot be used as security, unless this trademark is also registered.[22] Unlike applications for EU trademarks, applications for national trademarks cannot be used as security.[23]

The methods of evaluating the security value of a patent discussed in Sect. 4.1 above apply to all industrial right-type IPRs, including trademarks. A significant difference between patents and trademarks here is that trademark registrations can be kept effective for an indefinite time through successive renewals (Trademarks Act, Section 22).[24]

At the time of writing, the Finnish Parliament is processing a proposal for a new Trademarks Act.[25] In terms of pledges of a trademark, the proposed Act involves both autonomous reform of national law and implementation of the EU Trademark Directive.[26] If the Act is adopted, the law on pledges of a trademark will change as described below.

The wording of the relevant provisions will no longer include agreement in writing and registration as conditions for the validity of a pledge.[27] The idea behind this change follows the above-cited legal literature, according to which a pledge is created by agreement between the parties, while the recording of the pledge in the Register of Trademarks is required for third-party effectiveness.[28] Moreover, it will be possible to create a pledge not only with respect to a registered trademark, but also with respect to an established trademark or a trademark application.[29]

However, it will only be possible to register a pledge with respect to a registered trademark or a trademark application, and not with respect to an established trademark.[30] Registration of a pledge will not be mandatory, but it will be a condition for effectiveness of the pledge against third parties. Indeed, an unregistered pledge will be ineffective ("will not bind") against the pledgor's other creditors and, for example, good faith transferees of the trademark or trademark application (that is, transferees who were not aware and had no reason to be aware of the earlier pledge at the time of the transfer). To be exact, third-party

[21]Tepora et al. (2016), p. 70.

[22]*Ibid.*, p. 69; Haarmann and Mansala (2012), pp. 149–150; Salmi et al. (2008), p. 584.

[23]See Salmi et al. (2008), p. 584.

[24]See Tuominen (2001), pp. 91–93. See Haarmann and Mansala (2012), p. 149. Haarmann and Mansala refer to the brand valuation standard SFS-ISO 10668 as helpful in this context. The standard comprises economic, behavioural and legal analysis.

[25]Government proposal HE 201/2018; Economic Committee report TaVM 38/2018.

[26]Parliament and Council Directive (EU) 2015/2436 of December 16, 2015 to approximate the laws of the Member States relating to trade marks (recast) [2015] OJ L336/1.

[27]Section 39(1) of the proposed Act.

[28]Government proposal HE 201/2018, p. 138.

[29]*Ibid.*

[30]Section 40 of the proposed Act; Government proposal HE 201/2018, p. 138.

effectiveness will begin at the moment that a request to register a pledge is recorded in the Register of Trademarks and the relevant information becomes available in the Trademark Database. The actual registration of the pledge may occur later.[31]

4.3 Security Over a Copyright

In Finland, copyright is not recorded in a register. This makes copyright problematic as a security object in comparison to patents and trademarks.[32] As a rule, under Finnish law, the effectiveness of a security arrangement against the security provider's creditors and certain other third parties requires some publicity measure.[33] Generally speaking, the options are: (1) registering the security right (or some aspect of the security arrangement), (2) establishing the creditor's possession of the security object (or at least dispossessing the security provider of the security object, or preventing the security provider from independently exercising control over it) and (3) notifying a certain person of the security arrangement (most typically, the debtor of a pledged or security assigned claim). However, as regards copyright, none of these options seem to be available.[34]

Views presented in legal literature vary on the consequences of the absence of a suitable publicity measure. According to one commentator, a copyright is altogether incapable of being pledged.[35] Another commentator argues that a pledge can be created (by agreement) with effects between the parties, but effectiveness against third parties cannot be achieved.[36] In contrast, a third commentator considers third-party effectiveness achievable if the agreement of pledge effectively prevents the pledgor from utilising the pledged copyright without the pledgee's consent. The proposed stipulation in this regard is that, without the pledgee's consent, the pledgor cannot reproduce the copyright-protected work, distribute copies of it, or independently prohibit others from reproducing or distributing copies of it.[37]

In case it is accepted that a pledge can be validly created, with or without effects against third parties, Sections 28 and 42 of the Copyright Act may complicate matters further. Section 28 provides that "[u]nless otherwise agreed, the person to whom a copyright has been transferred may not ... transfer the copyright to

[31]Government proposal HE 201/2018, p. 139.

[32]If feasible in the first place, any security rights over a copyright are limited to the "economic rights" in Section 2 of the Copyright Act, whereas the "moral rights" in Section 3 (and Sections 36, 52a and 53(1)) cannot be validly disposed of and contain no security value. See Tepora (2004), pp. 184, 187.

[33]Retention of title is an exception.

[34]Tepora (2004), pp. 190–192.

[35]Havansi (1992), p. 86. However, Havansi may have made his comments with a fully effective right of pledge in mind, i.e., including effectiveness against third parties. See *ibid.*, pp. 30–32.

[36]Tepora (2004), pp. 192–193.

[37]Rahnasto (1997), pp. 557–561.

others".[38] This entails that the author (the original proprietor of the copyright) and a transferee of the copyright may be in different positions in terms of competence to pledge the copyright.[39] In turn, according to Section 42, "[c]opyright shall not be subject to foreclosure [distraint] as long as the copyright remains with the author or with a person to whom the copyright has been transferred by virtue of marital right to property, inheritance or will".[40] If interpreted literally, this provision seems to limit the enforceability (realisability) of a pledge in cases where the pledgor is the author or one of the close persons referred to in the provision. That being said, distraint is not the only available method for realising a pledged IPR.[41] Moreover, the provision should probably not be interpreted literally. Indeed, it has been argued that the purpose of the provision is to protect the author and close persons from premature publication of the work—that is, publication earlier than the author had meant the work to be published. Therefore, so the argument goes, an author who voluntarily pledges a work agrees (tacitly, if not explicitly) that in the case of default, the work can be commercially utilised and, to that end, published.[42]

Unfortunately, no case law or other binding legal source confirms or disproves any of the above three views on the consequences of the absence of a suitable publicity measure. Still, the prevailing view in legal literature appears to be that one cannot obtain a pledge of a copyright with (full) effectiveness against third parties. Most notably, according to this view, a pledge of a copyright would not be effective against the pledgor's creditors.[43]

In this light, it has been repeatedly argued that third-party effectiveness should be achievable in an alternate way, without any form of publicity—namely, through the

[38] Yet, according to the same section, "[w]hen copyright is held by a business, it may be transferred in conjunction with the business or a part thereof; however, the transferor shall remain liable for the fulfilment of the agreement".

[39] Tepora (2004), pp. 185–186. See Rahnasto (1997), p. 555. Rahnasto stresses the importance of ascertaining, at the time of pledging, that the pledgor has got a right to transfer the copyright and consents to a further transfer. Cf. Tepora et al. (2016), p. 375.

[40] The unofficial translation of the Copyright Act uses the term "foreclosure" instead of "distraint". This chapter uses "distraint", which is also used on the Finnish Enforcement Authority website: https://oikeus.fi/ulosotto/en/index/velkojanaulosotossa.html. Accessed Jan 10, 2019.

[41] See Sect. 8.1 below.

[42] Tepora (2004), pp. 188–189. See Rahnasto (1997), pp. 555–556. According to Rahnasto, it is typical of "copyright industry" that the rights in a copyright protected work are transferred away from the author. As examples, he names newspapers, advertising, computer programming and, in some cases, film and music industry.

[43] Tepora et al. (2016), pp. 373–376. Tepora et al. note that a pledge of a copyright would not be entirely without third-party effects. Indeed, Section 42 may prevent distraint of the copyright by other creditors. If this is the case, then the copyright also falls outside the author's or close person's bankruptcy estate as provided by the Bankruptcy Act, Chapter 5, Section 3(1). In addition, a pledge of a copyright might remain in force against a subsequent transferee of the copyright, at least if the transferee were aware of the pledge.

security transfer of a copyright.[44] This would be exceptional because under Finnish law, security transfers (and security assignments) and pledges are generally thought to be subject to the same publicity requirements, with pledges invariably requiring some form of publicity.[45] Again, no binding source of law confirms or disproves these arguments.[46]

All in all, the use of copyright as a security object involves a great deal of uncertainty in Finland. What is certain, though, is that copyright is covered by the Finnish enterprise mortgage and that a copyright can be used as security if one establishes a company to own the copyright and then pledges the value of the copyright in the shape of the shares of that company.[47]

5 Priority of IPR Pledges

A registered pledge of an IPR is a "right of pledge" in the sense of Section 3 of the Act on the Ranking of Claims (1578/1992), which applies in bankruptcy (that is, collective liquidation proceedings) and in enforcement (that is, debt collection and distraint proceedings). This entails a top ranking for the secured claim.

As for other questions of priority, the relevant provisions include:

> Patents Act, Section 44(5): "If a person acting in good faith has requested the Patent Authority to record in the Register that a patent has been assigned to him or that he has obtained a licence under a patent or a pledge of a patent, prior assignment of the patent or rights therein shall not be enforceable against him if the other party has not previously requested registration as the assignee or proprietor of rights in the patent."[48]

> Trademarks Act, Section 33(2): "A transfer not recorded in the register shall not affect a third party who has obtained the trademark in good faith."

[44]Tepora (2004), pp. 196–198; Havansi (1992), pp. 513–514. Cf. Kaisto (2006), pp. 62–63. Kaisto suggests that the requirement of a publicity measure in connection with pledging has too lightly been accepted as a dogma when it comes to security objects, such as copyright, for which no suitable publicity measure exists. He calls for discussion on whether a pledge of a copyright could be effective against the pledgor's creditors even without a publicity measure. See Kaisto (2002), pp. 26–28; Tammi-Salminen (2015), pp. 517–518.

[45]In legal literature, this dogma is being increasingly questioned in situations where no suitable publicity measure is available. See Tammi-Salminen (2015), p. 163.

[46]See Tepora et al. (2016), pp. 483–484. As regards IPRs the pledge of which is registrable (i.e., industrial rights), Tepora et al. consider security transfers effective against the transferor's creditors on the basis of registration of the transfer.

[47]Tepora et al. (2016), p. 69. See Tepora (2004), pp. 199–200. As for the company option, Tepora emphasises the role of covenants in monitoring the value of the company and as a risk management tool.

[48]This provision has been slightly amended and moved to Section 44(6) by Act 23/2016. The amending Act will be put into force by a separate State Council decree, yet to be enacted.

Trademarks Act, Section 33(3): "If any person wishes to pledge his trademark rights, a written agreement shall be made and entered in the register. No right of pledge shall be valid until such an entry has been made."

The Trademarks Act provisions in particular are rather unclear and open to interpretation.[49]

As noted in Sect. 4.2 above, notwithstanding Section 33(3) of the Trademarks Act, it is a common view among commentators that an earlier pledgee's first-in-time priority based on an unregistered agreement of pledge should be upheld against later transferees and pledgees as a starting point—that is to say, subject to the possibility that a later pledgee or transferee takes priority by registering first in good faith.

The proposed new Trademarks Act, discussed in Sect. 4.2 above, would clarify the situation by separating effectiveness against third parties from the creation of a pledge and effectiveness between the parties.

6 Enterprise Mortgages

With certain exceptions, the entire movable property of an enterprise (that is, a trader recorded in the Trade Register), including both tangibles and intangibles alike, can be used as a "floating" security by an enterprise mortgage. All IPRs are included, as can be read in Section 3(1) of the Enterprise Mortgage Act (634/1984), which explicitly mentions that an enterprise mortgage covers trademarks, trade names, industrial designs, patents and other IPRs.

Enterprise mortgages must be applied for from the register authority: the Finnish Patent and Registration Office. Perhaps curiously from a comparative perspective, a mortgage application must be appended with a negotiable promissory note (on a designated form), which will be used as the mortgage instrument. The promissory note expresses the maximum amount of money that the mortgage being applied for is intended to cover, but it does not express any actual debt owed by the mortgagor, nor does it relate to any specific debt relation. Once the mortgage application has been made, the register authority makes an entry concerning the mortgage in the Register of Enterprise Mortgages and, importantly, on the promissory note.[50] After these preparations, in order to give rise to a third-party effective security right ("pledge" in the terminology of the Enterprise Mortgage Act), the mortgagor must still conclude a security agreement with a creditor, and the creditor, in addition, has to receive possession of the promissory note containing the register authority's entry concerning the mortgage.[51]

[49] Tepora et al. (2016), pp. 189–194, 202–203. Some priority questions concerning pledges of copyright were mentioned in note 43 above.

[50] Enterprise Mortgage Act, Sections 16–18. The applicable handling fee is currently EUR 170. See the Finnish Patent and Registration Office website, price list: https://www.prh.fi/en/yrityskiinnitykset/palvelut_ja_hinnat.html. Accessed Jan 10, 2019.

[51] Enterprise Mortgage Act, Section 7. See Tuomisto (2007), pp. 9–13.

According to Section 8 of the Enterprise Mortgage Act, the priority of enterprise mortgages is determined by application date: the enterprise mortgage that was applied for earliest takes priority. Meanwhile, enterprise mortgages that were applied for on the same date share the same priority position, unless it is decided otherwise based on the application. Section 4(3) deals with questions of priority between an enterprise mortgage and a competing pledge of a specific object. An earlier pledge of a patent or trademark takes priority over a later enterprise mortgage, whereas a later such pledge is ineffective ("does not bind") against the holder of an earlier enterprise mortgage. The wording of Section 4(3) and its preparatory works is unclear, but according to the prevailing view, the applicable "priority determinant" is the time of the relevant publicity measure (that is, registration of the pledge vs. possession of the promissory note containing the register authority's entry concerning the mortgage).[52]

On insolvency, the priority afforded to claims secured by an enterprise mortgage is limited, as provided by Section 5 of the Act on the Ranking of Claims. First, certain other claims rank higher. These include claims secured by a right of pledge (or charge) or a right of retention, claims arisen in connection with enterprise restructuring proceedings, and child maintenance claims. Second, in bankruptcy (that is, collective liquidation proceedings), claims secured by an enterprise mortgage are entitled to payment with priority over other claims only with respect to 50% of the value of the mortgaged assets. As noted in comparative legal literature, the 50% rule reduces the commercial significance of enterprise mortgages.[53] Because of the limited priority, enterprise mortgages are often used as supplementary security.[54]

7 Rights and Duties Before Default

No IPR security-specific provisions exist in Finnish law on parties' mutual rights and duties before debtor default. All relevant stipulations should be included in the security agreement between the parties. These stipulations may be divided into general content requirements for the security agreement, which concern any IPRs

[52]Tuomisto (2007), pp. 143–51. See Lindberg et al. (2016), pp. 12–13. Lindberg et al. argue that a possibility should be introduced to create a separate pledge of an IPR in addition to an existing enterprise mortgage ("floating charge"). In their view, this could more fully "support exploiting the security potential of IPRs".

[53]Kieninger (2004), p. 650. However, this rule is based on a deliberate policy choice. The rule was introduced as part of a general reform of priority rules in 1993, with the explicit aim of promoting creditor equality by reserving assets to be distributed among unsecured creditors. At the same time, most statutory privileges, including those for tax and wage claims, were abolished. The role of the 50% rule was to keep the priority position of enterprise mortgages similar to what it was when the abolished statutory privileges still existed. See Government proposal HE 181/1992, pp. 17–19. See also Juutilainen (2018), pp. 146–147; Bergström et al. (2004), pp. 276–277.

[54]Tepora (2013), p. 25; Tuomisto (2007), pp. 14–15.

(industrial rights) as security, and specific content requirements for the security agreement, which concern particular types of IPR as security. The general content requirements may concern, for example, income generated by the security object, surrogates to the security object, the course of action if the value of the security object should deteriorate, and the security provider's information duties. In turn, the specific content requirements may concern, for example, the maintenance of the security object (including renewals and related payments) and the defence of the security object (including reactions to infringements).[55]

The proposed new Trademarks Act, discussed in Sect. 4.2 above, would introduce a new provision on the defence of the security object. The provision would allow the pledgee of a trademark to take legal action against trademark infringement if the proprietor of the trademark does not do so within a reasonable period of time after having been informed of the infringement by the pledgee. The exception to this would be a case where the pledgee and the proprietor have agreed that the pledgee has the right to take legal action even without informing the proprietor.[56]

In addition, general principles may play a role, especially in the absence of agreed stipulations. For example, the principle of loyalty and duty of care as regards the security object may require the pledgor to refrain from using the pledged IPR in value-diluting ways, such as "providing a global royalty-free license to everyone, or executing a perpetual and irrevocable exclusive license".[57]

The above discussion focuses on security over specific IPRs, individually. In contrast, IPRs forming part of enterprise mortgaged property are subject to the Enterprise Mortgage Act. For example, according to Section 9(1), an enterprise mortgage does not prevent the enterprise mortgaged property from being transferred and used in ways required for the regular exchange of goods, the necessary replacement of enterprise property, or other normal conduct of business.

8 Enforcement

8.1 Enforcement Outside Insolvency

In the event of debtor default, Section 2 of Chapter 10 of the Trade Code (3/1734) affords pledgees of an ordinary tangible object or negotiable document an independent power of realisation (that is, private enforcement) directly by operation of law. This section is usually understood to cover pledgees of an IPR as well, although its

[55]Tuominen (2001), pp. 160–213.

[56]Section 39(2) of the proposed Act; Government proposal HE 201/2018, p. 138. See Section 68 (2) of the proposed Act.

[57]Lindberg et al. (2016), p. 7.

interpretation is not clear.[58] The section sets out some detailed provisions on the realisation process, including a notification period of at least 1 month before liquidation by sale, but the parties can contract out of most of these provisions. In any case, the pledgee of an IPR can acquire an independent power of realisation through agreement with the pledgor.

The parties' freedom of agreement is the main rule when it comes to alternatives to simple liquidation. Options include assigning licence payments generated by the pledged IPR to the pledgee or vesting the pledged IPR in the pledgee.[59] As regards vesting the IPR in the pledgee, Section 37 of the Contracts Act (228/1929) may cause complications. It provides as follows: "A term under which property pledged as security for an obligation is forfeited if the obligation is not discharged shall be void." This so-called *lex commissoria* prohibition does not mean that a forfeiture term is never possible. In legal literature, Section 37 is generally interpreted as meaning that a pledgee is only entitled to receive the amount of the secured obligation out of the value of the pledged asset, while any surplus belongs to the owner of the asset. Accordingly, vesting ownership in a pledgee through a forfeiture term is considered possible if that vesting is made conditional upon the value surplus (if there is any) being returned to the owner.[60] It has even been suggested that Section 37 may not apply to situations in which forfeiture has been agreed after the security arrangement has been initiated and credit extended. In such situations, the creditor's bargaining power may have weakened to the extent that the pledgor-debtor no longer needs the special protection that Section 37 is supposed to provide.[61]

As an alternative to independent realisation (that is, private enforcement), a pledgee may choose court proceedings. After a final judgment where the court orders the pledgor to pay a certain amount of money out of the value of the pledged IPR, the pledgee still needs to turn to the enforcement authority, which will take care of enforcement in accordance with the Enforcement Code (705/2007).

An enterprise mortgage does not entitle the mortgagee to independent realisation of the mortgaged assets. Instead, a court judgment and enforcement through the enforcement authority (or realisation in bankruptcy proceedings) are required.[62]

---

[58] Tepora et al. (2016), pp. 230–231, 375; Lindberg et al. (2016), p. 4; Tuomisto (2010), pp. 55–56; Tuominen (2001), p. 220.

[59] Tuominen (2001), pp. 221, 224–225.

[60] Tepora et al. (2016), pp. 359–360.

[61] Tepora (2008), pp. 23–24. Tepora makes this argument in discussion of security transfer of ownership (sale and lease-back with a security purpose).

[62] Tepora et al. (2016), pp. 225, 230; Lindberg et al. (2016), p. 5.

8.2 *Effects of Insolvency Proceedings*

The relevant types of insolvency proceedings are: (1) enforcement (that is, debt collection and distraint proceedings), (2) bankruptcy (that is, collective liquidation proceedings), (3) restructuring of an enterprise and (4) adjustment of the debts of a private individual. Security rights over an IPR as discussed in this section are presumed to be "fully developed" as regards protection against the security-provider debtor's other creditors. For example, a pledge of a patent is presumed to be validly created between the parties and registered in the Patent Register. Accordingly, pledges of or other types of security right over a copyright are not discussed, due to uncertainty in terms of achieving third-party effectiveness.[63] It should also be noted that, due to the complexity and detailedness of the insolvency legislation, only a broad outline can be discussed here.

Even if it is subject to a security right, an IPR can be subject to distraint as a part of enforcement proceedings initiated by another creditor; however, the security right will be taken into account in the realisation and distribution of proceeds (Enforcement Code, Chapter 4, Section 44).[64] The secured creditor's priority position is laid down in the Act on the Ranking of Claims.[65] However, an enterprise mortgagee has no right to be paid out of the proceeds if the remaining (that is, non-realised) mortgaged property clearly suffices to cover the mortgagee's secured claim (Enterprise Mortgage Act, Section 14(3)). Before realisation takes place, the enforcement authority must find out whether registered pledges or mortgages exist (Enforcement Code, Chapter 5, Section 29). Depending on the object of distraint, this may require searching the relevant IPR register and the Register of Enterprise Mortgages kept by the Finnish Patent and Registration Office.[66]

According to Section 9(1) of Chapter 3 of the Bankruptcy Act (120/2004), when bankruptcy proceedings begin, claims that have not yet fallen due are generally considered due between the creditor and debtor. Industrial rights, including patents and trademarks, are part of the proprietor's bankruptcy estate. As regards trademarks, this is explicitly stated in Section 35(2) of the Trademarks Act.[67] To begin with, the pledgee of a patent or trademark (but not an enterprise mortgagee) has a "separatist position" in relation to the bankruptcy estate (Bankruptcy Act, Chapter 17, Section 11). This means that the pledgee is entitled to realise the security

[63]See Sect. 4.3 above, especially note 43.

[64]According to the Trademarks Act, Section 35(1), a trademark cannot be distrained unless it is subject to a right of pledge. Section 41(1) of the proposed new Trademarks Act, discussed in Sect. 4.2 above, is a similar provision, but with application for a trademark added in the wording. Government proposal HE 201/2018 clarifies (at p. 140) that "right of pledge" in the provision also covers enterprise mortgage.

[65]See Sects. 5 and 6 above. Importantly, the "50% rule" on enterprise mortgages (discussed in Sect. 6) only applies in bankruptcy, not in enforcement.

[66]Linna and Leppänen (2015), p. 532.

[67]See Section 41(2) of the proposed new Trademarks Act, discussed in Sect. 4.2 above.

object (that is, use the powers of realisation that the right of pledge entails) and to satisfy the secured claim.[68] However, under Chapter 17 of the Bankruptcy Act, the bankruptcy estate can temporarily prevent the realisation to scrutinise the pledgee's rights or to protect the interests of the estate, and, in certain situations, can realise pledged assets (or apply for realisation under the Enforcement Code). Again, the secured creditor's (that is, pledgee's or enterprise mortgagee's) priority position is laid down in the Act on the Ranking of Claims.

Starting to restructure an enterprise or adjust the debts of a private individual (that is, opening rehabilitation proceedings) causes a stay on realisation efforts, including the realisation of security objects. Indeed, realisation falls within the scope of "interdiction of debt collection". The provisions on this interdiction and the grounds on which exceptions can be granted to it are found in Chapter 4 of the Restructuring of Enterprise Act (47/1993) and Chapter 4 of the Act on the Adjustment of the Debts of a Private Individual (57/1993). In the restructuring of an enterprise or adjustment of the debts of a private individual, a claim secured by one or more IPRs (individually or as part of enterprise mortgaged property) may count as a "secured debt", which has a special position. In these proceedings, the court is allowed to alter the content of existing debt relations. Generally, the payment schedule can be altered; it can be decided that payments will primarily amortise the principal amount and only go towards credit costs after that; costs concerning the rest of the credit period can be lowered; and the outstanding principal amount can be lowered. However, the special position of a secured debt entails (in a somewhat simplified explanation) that the principal amount of that debt cannot be lowered (Restructuring of Enterprise Act, Section 45; Act on the Adjustment of the Debts of a Private Individual, Section 26). Section 3(1) of the Restructuring of Enterprise Act and Section 3(1) of the Act on the Adjustment of the Debts of a Private Individual define "secured debt" as follows: a debt where the creditor holds a security right, which is effective against third parties, over property that belongs to or is in the possession of the debtor, insofar as the value of the security object at the commencement of the proceedings would have sufficed to cover the amount of the creditor's claim after the deduction of liquidation costs and claims with a higher priority.

9 Use of IPR Security in the Light of Statistics

Statistical data is available on the registration (or requests for registration) of pledges of patents and trademarks. The following data, provided by the Finnish Patent and Registration Office, is from January 23, 2019.[69] The total number of national patents granted in Finland that may still be in force within the maximum patent protection time of 20 years (that is, patents whose maximum term has not expired, regardless of

[68]Of course, any surplus belongs to the bankruptcy estate.

[69]In file with the author.

whether they are actually in force) is 14,378. Registration of a pledge has been requested with respect to 131 of these national patents.[70] The total number of European patents validated in Finland that may still be in force within the maximum patent protection time of 20 years is 82,497. Registration of a pledge has been requested with respect to 61 of these European patents.[71] Current data for pledges of patents is not available, but the numbers would be even lower than the above-mentioned numbers for requests for registration of a pledge. This is because the above-mentioned numbers for granted and validated patents include patents that have already expired. In addition, some of the registered pledges have come to an end, and some of the requests for registration of a pledge may have been rejected.

More exact data is available on the registration of pledges of trademarks. The number of registered pledges of a trademark (situation of January 23, 2019) is 262, while the total number of registered trademarks or pending applications for trademark registration is 68,096. In sum, pledges of patents and trademarks are rarely used in Finland.

No statistical data exists for security over copyright. As noted above, copyright is not registrable under Finnish law, and consequently neither are security arrangements that concern specific copyright. Due to uncertainty regarding achieving third-party effectiveness,[72] these arrangements are likely to be uncommon. However, they have occasionally been seen in contract and bankruptcy practice.[73]

Enterprise mortgages, in contrast, are frequently used, although their role is often that of supplementary security. Indeed, enterprise mortgages are by far the most common way to use IPRs as security under Finnish law, and they cover both industrial rights and copyright alike. The following data, provided by the Finnish Patent and Registration Office, was collected at the end of February 2019.[74] The number of enterprises that have one or more enterprise mortgages in force is 76,603. The total number of enterprise mortgages in force is 112,942, while the total number of promissory notes with a mortgage entry in force is 249,822.[75] The total principal amount of all promissory notes with a mortgage entry is EUR 164,799,535,559.26.

The nearly negligible use of patents and trademarks as security in Finland (other than through enterprise mortgage) is not easy to explain. The legal framework for pledges of patent and trademark is, by and large, adequate, so that third-party

[70]The total number of national patents in force in Finland is 7167.

[71]The total number of European patents in force in Finland is 44,973.

[72]See Sect. 4.3 above.

[73]Tepora (2004), p. 193. Tepora refers to arrangements where a pledge of copyright is complemented with an agreement aiming to prevent the pledgor from distributing copies of the copyright protected work, e.g., a film or a video.

[74]In file with the author.

[75]As discussed in Sect. 6 above, promissory notes with a mortgage entry are used as mortgage instruments and do not express any actual debt owed by the mortgagor or relate to any specific debt relation. The number of promissory notes with a mortgage entry does not reveal how many of them are currently used in security arrangements and how may remain with the enterprise ready to be used or re-used in a security arrangement.

effective pledges of these types of IPR can reliably be obtained. Therefore, reasons should be sought elsewhere, including in the special characteristics of IPRs.

A study group consisting of practitioners has also recently observed that "IPRs are not as commonly used as a specific subject-matter of a security interest, as they are as a part of a floating charge [enterprise mortgage]".[76] They explain it as follows:

> This is presumably at least partly due [to] the realization and valuation of IPRs being more complex than those of most other forms of movable assets. Valuation of IPRs is inherently subjective, and their commercialization requires specific legal and commercial expertise, which has perhaps not been widely available in Finland, with the exception of certain specific sectors and entities. The rather strong emphasis on IPRs as a part of a floating charge [enterprise mortgage], where assets are usually realized as a whole, may be seen as a logical consequence of this.[77]

This is certainly plausible. Another factor may be the prevalent use of the enterprise mortgage as a blanket security covering almost the entire movable property of an enterprise, given that later pledges of a specific IPR are ineffective against the holder of an earlier enterprise mortgage.[78] Further explanations might be found in the territorial nature of IPRs and the relatively small size of the Finnish market.[79]

10 Conclusion

The question whether one can reliably obtain a third-party effective security right over an asset is a fundamental test of adequacy for any system of security rights. As presented above, the Finnish law of security passes this test in terms of patents and trademarks, but fails it in terms of copyright—other than as part of an enterprise mortgaged property. Then again, the statistical data discussed shows that the actual use of these types of security rights can be nearly negligible even if the legal framework is adequate in this sense.

Although the need for legislative or judicial solutions is greatest in respect of security over copyright, all types of IPR security could benefit from a law reform, provided that this reform would manage to clarify their part of the legal framework for IPR security. This is because Finnish law contains very few provisions

[76] Lindberg et al. (2016), p. 6.

[77] *Ibid.* Lindberg et al. also list aspects of laws on security over IPRs that, in their view, could be improved (at pp. 11–13). Among other things, they call for more provisions or case law on IPR valuations, raising the priority percentage of enterprise mortgage ("floating charge") to 100 and simplifying the system, and limiting a security provider's rights in certain situations.

[78] See Sect. 6 above.

[79] Market size may be a relevant factor, e.g., where a prospective security provider holds different national patents for the same invention and has to choose which of them to use as security. This is so especially if the legal framework for security over patents varies greatly between the relevant states, making it excessively difficult or cumbersome to obtain and manage third-party effective security rights in several states simultaneously.

specifically related to IPR security and it is often unclear how the general legal framework for security—much of which is based on case law and doctrine patching up fragmentary legislation—should be applied in the case of IPR security. The proposed new Trademarks Act promises such clarifications. The crucial impulses for this reform came from outside the national context, as is so often the case.

11 Postscript

The new Trademarks Act (544/2019) was enacted on April 26, 2019 and entered into force on May 1, 2019. It introduced the changes discussed in Sects. 4.2 and 7 and elsewhere in this chapter.

References

Bergström C, Eisenberg T, Sundgren S (2004) On the design of efficient priority rules for secured creditors: empirical evidence from a change in law. Eur J Law Econ 18:273–297

Economic Committee report TaVM 38/2018. Talousvaliokunta: Hallituksen esitys eduskunnalle tavaramerkkilaiksi ja siihen liittyviksi laeiksi sekä tavaramerkkioikeudesta tehdyn Singaporen sopimuksen hyväksymiseksi ja voimaansaattamiseksi

Government proposal HE 181/1992. Hallituksen esitys eduskunnalle etuoikeusjärjestelmän uudistamista koskevaksi lainsäädännöksi

Government proposal HE 201/2018. Hallituksen esitys eduskunnalle tavaramerkkilaiksi ja siihen liittyviksi laeiksi sekä tavaramerkkioikeudesta tehdyn Singaporen sopimuksen hyväksymiseksi ja voimaansaattamiseksi

Government proposal HE 45/2015. Hallituksen esitys eduskunnalle yhdistetystä patenttituomioistuimesta tehdyn sopimuksen hyväksymisestä ja laeiksi sopimuksen lainsäädännön alaan kuuluvien määräysten voimaansaattamisesta ja sopimuksen soveltamisesta sekä patenttilain ja eräiden muiden lakien muuttamisesta

Haarmann P-L (2014) Immateriaalioikeus, 5th edn. Talentum, Helsinki

Haarmann P-L, Mansala M-L (2012) Immateriaalioikeuden perusteet, 2nd edn. Talentum, Helsinki

Havansi E (1992) Esinevakuusoikeudet: panttioikeus, pidätysoikeus, omistuksenpidätys, vakuusluovutus, 2nd edn. Lakimiesliiton Kustannus, Helsinki

Juutilainen T (2018) Secured credit in Europe: from conflicts to compatibility. Hart, Oxford

Kaisto J (2002) Tekijänoikeudesta panttauksen ja ulosmittauksen kohteena. Edilex. Edita, Helsinki

Kaisto J (2006) "Pantti tai muu vakuus": vakuusoikeuden yleisistä opeista erityisesti vakuusluovutuksia ja takaisinsaantilain 14 §:n soveltamista silmällä pitäen. Suomalainen Lakimiesyhdistys, Helsinki

Kieninger E-M (2004) Evaluation: a common core? Convergences, subsisting differences and possible ways for harmonisation. In: Kieninger E-M (ed) Security rights in movable property in European private law. Cambridge University Press, Cambridge, pp 647–673

Lindberg J, Flythström J, Lehtonen K, Lehtimäki M, Sinkkonen J, Tahvanainen J, Toiviainen M, Uusitalo E (2016) Security interests over intellectual property: Finland. AIPPI study report 2016. http://aippi.org/wp-content/uploads/2016/05/2016_Study_Question_General_Security_interests_over_intellectual_property_GroupReport_Finland_28-04-2016.pdf. Accessed Jan 10, 2019

Linna T, Leppänen T (2015) Ulosotto-oikeus II: ulosmittaus ja myynti, 2nd edn. Talentum, Helsinki

Rahnasto I (1997) Tekijänoikeuden panttaus. Defensor Legis 78:553–563
Salmi H, Tommila M, Häkkänen P (2008) Tavaramerkki, 2nd edn. Talentum, Helsinki
Tammi-Salminen E (2015) Esinevakuusoikeuden perusteet. Talentum, Helsinki
Tepora J (2004) Tekijänoikeuden käyttö vakuutena. In: Tammi-Salminen E (ed) Omistus, sopimus, vaihdanta: juhlakirja Leena Kartiolle. Turun yliopiston oikeustieteellinen tiedekunta, Turku, pp 181–203
Tepora J (2008) Johdatus esineoikeuden perusteisiin. Helsingin yliopiston oikeustieteellinen tiedekunta, Helsinki
Tepora J (2013) Rahoitusmuodot ja vakuudet. Lakimiesliiton Kustannus, Helsinki
Tepora J, Kaisto J, Hakkola E (2016) Esinevakuudet, 2nd edn. Kauppakamari, Helsinki
Tuominen M (2001) Teollisoikeudet vakuutena. WSLT, Helsinki
Tuomisto J (1993) Tyyppipakosta aikaprioriteettiin: näkökohtia esineoikeudellisen sivullissuojan perusteista. Suomalainen Lakimiesyhdistys, Helsinki
Tuomisto J (2007) Yrityskiinnitys. Talentum, Helsinki
Tuomisto J (2010) Sopimus ja insolvenssi. CC Lakimiesliiton Kustannus, Helsinki

Security Rights in Intellectual Property in France

Michel Séjean and Nicolas Binctin

Abstract This paper presents the French general law (i.e. ordinary law, *droit commun*) and specific law (*droit spécial*) for security rights in intellectual property. As a general rule, French law transposes European Union law. However, the French legal system has maintained a wide variety of devices to secure rights in intellectual property—the pledge of claims (*nantissement de créances*), fiducia security (*fiducie-sûreté*), assignment of claims (or assignment of credit-claims, *cession de créances*) are only the tip of the iceberg. While this variety of devices may seem complex, it has also provided decent legal certainty to users.

1 Overview of Intellectual Property Rights in France

France has a wide variety of intellectual property rights. The different types of intellectual property and the prerequisites for their creation are as follows:

(a) **Patents**: The creation of a patent depends on novelty and inventive activity, and requires a filing procedure.
(b) **Trademarks:** The creation of a trademark depends on the availability and distinctiveness of the trademark, and also requires a filing procedure.
(c) **Copyright and related rights (including database producer's right)**: The criterion for copyright and related rights is the work's originality. Copyright exists independently of any need for a filing procedure.
(d) **Other**:

M. Séjean (✉)
Université Bretagne Sud, Vannes, France
e-mail: michel.sejean@univ-ubs.fr

N. Binctin
Université de Poitiers, Poitiers, France

E.-M. Kieninger (ed.), *Security Rights in Intellectual Property*, Ius Comparatum – Global Studies in Comparative Law 45,
https://doi.org/10.1007/978-3-030-44191-3_14

(1) Design rights: The creation of a design right presupposes that the design is novel and that it has its own character. A filing procedure is necessary under French law.
(2) Plant variety rights: Reference should be made here to the well-known UPOV criteria.

French law also transposes European Union law. As a result, it incorporates the European Union's trademark and design laws, which are transnational property rights covering the entire EU territory. In addition, it allows the coexistence of national and supranational laws. A French patent is obtained through the patent examination procedure before the European Patent Office (EPO). There are no supranational patents in force in France as of yet.

2 Security Right Categories

In France, a security is possible for all of the types of intellectual property mentioned above in the form of (Sect. 2.1) a pledge, (Sect. 2.2) a clause of reservation of ownership (*clause de réserve de propriété*), (Sect. 2.3) a fiducia security (*fiducie-sûreté*), or (Sect. 2.4) a conventional right of retention. However, it is important to distinguish between a security in the intellectual property itself and the fiducia security mechanisms concerning (Sect. 2.5) *claims from the exploitation of the intellectual property*.

2.1 General Law Pledge of Incorporeal Movables Applied to Intellectual Property

The pledge of incorporeal movables (*nantissement*) is a general-law security concerning incorporeal property (see Art. 2355 et seq. of the *Code civil*). A pledge of incorporeal movables is defined by Article 2355 of France's *Code civil* (Civil Code, henceforth CC) as "the allocation of an incorporeal movable or of a set of incorporeal movables, present or future, as security for an obligation".[1] A pledge of incorporeal movables can be either judicial in origin or voluntarily constituted under an agreement. It gives the creditor, who is the beneficiary of the security, the right over other creditors to receive payment on the property or set of properties pledged.

The CC does not develop the regime of pledges of incorporeal movables any further, since the other provisions only apply to claims. It simply refers to the regime

[1] Art. 2355, para. 1 CC. Unless otherwise specified, all translations of extracts from the CC have been taken from the English translation of the Code Civil, as of July 1, 2013, translated by David W. Gruning, available at https://www.legifrance.gouv.fr/Traductions/en-English/Legifrance-translations.

of pledges of corporeal movables, with the legislator understanding both corporeal and incorporeal properties to mean something other than claims (see Art. 2355, para. 3 and 4[2]). Hence the word "pledge" is used to refer to a security right concerning intellectual property.

The general law of security rights applies to copyright (even if the author as a natural person in the contract pursuant to Article L. 131-2 of France's *Code de la propriété intellectuelle* (Intellectual Property Code, henceforth IPC)), related rights, design rights (Articles L. 513-2 and L. 513-3 of the IPC), patent law (Articles L. 613-8 and L. 613-21 of the IPC), plant variety law (by reference to Article L. 623-14 of the IPC) and trademark law (Article L. 714-1 of the IPC, with the exception of collective trademarks in accordance with the provisions of Article L. 715-2(no 4) of the IPC).

It should be noted that difficulties can arise when a pledge relates to future properties as authorized by the CC. In intellectual property matters, it is risky to consider pledging future properties if the author is the pledgor. As such an act may result in a possible assignment, it would be sanctioned by Article L. 131-1 of the IPC prohibiting the global assignment of future works because the pledge may have this effect in the long term.

2.2 *Reservation of Ownership*

Article 2367 of the CC, which allows ownership of a property to be reserved as security, also applies to intellectual property.[3] Under the clause of reservation of ownership, the debtor will only become the owner once he has paid the price of the property in full. For as long as he has not paid, the debtor retains the use of the intellectual property, and the creditor retains ownership of it.

2.3 *Fiducia Security in Intellectual Property*

A **fiducia** (*la fiducie*) is "the operation by which one or more grantors transfer assets, rights, or security rights, or a set of assets, rights, or security rights, present or future, to one or more fiducia who, keeping them separate from their own patrimonies, act to achieve a specified goal for the benefit of one or more beneficiaries" (Art. 2011 of the CC[4]). A fiducia under Articles 2011 et seq. of the CC can be used as a management tool (referred to as "fiducia management") or as a security right. In the latter case,

[2] Art. 2355, para. 3 and 4 CC.
[3] Art. 2367 CC.
[4] Art. 2011 CC.

Articles 2372-1 et seq. of the CC provide for special rules on property assigned as security rights.

The fiducia security, which can be found in the trust laws of many countries, is a recently introduced solution in French law. For a debtor (the grantor), this consists of transferring in trust the ownership of an asset, including an intellectual property or royalty claims portfolio, to one or more fiduciaries (who must keep this separate from their own patrimony) as a guarantee of the payment of a debt or the fulfillment of an obligation. If the debtor does not repay his debt or fulfill his obligations, the creditor (beneficiary) then receives the assets placed in ficudia. A fiducia security is an assigned patrimony that consists of having property assigned to it as security for a debt until it is paid. The fiduciary must return the assets to the grantor when the guarantee is no longer valid. The beneficiary of the fiducia security is the creditor. However, if the debtor of the debt or obligation pays up in the normal way, the assets transferred in fiducia revert to the grantor. The contract of fiducia may provide that the creditor will only be a beneficiary in the event of non-payment of all or part of the debt or of failure to fulfil the obligation. The contract may also specify that the fiducia will be required to return the property to the settling debtor upon presentation of a receipt from the creditor. It is good policy for the grantor to be registered as a beneficiary so that the fiducia is tax neutral in the presence of capital gains tax. Acceptance by all beneficiaries—including the grantor—also means the agreement cannot be revoked by the grantor.

A fiducia security is highly flexible and seems to be able to adapt to the constraints of the exploitation of intellectual property. Because of its contractual freedom, it extends beyond the scope of the pledge or guarantee while also providing the beneficiary with a high degree of legal security, particularly in the event of collective proceedings by the debtor. It covers both intellectual property and claims from royalties. In addition, compared to instruments that require the transfer of assets for financing or refinancing, the fiducia security allows the grantor to keep the ability to dispose of the rights he intends to reserve for himself. This reservation is necessary for maintaining both the value of the intellectual property portfolio given as security and full legal use of the intellectual property in question.

2.4 *The Conventional Right of Retention*

In the case of the conventional right of retention,[5] either the author retains the commissioned work until he receives the payment due to him in full or the third party retains the work until the author has fulfilled his financial obligations towards this third party. If the retainer voluntarily divests himself of the work, he loses his right of retention.

[5]See Art. 2286 CC.

2.5 *Appropriateness of Certain Security Rights for Intellectual Property*

There are two sides to this issue. One concerns the description of the security and guarantee mechanisms that are particularly suited to intellectual property (Sect. 2.5.1). The other relates to the fact that the proper functioning of security rights depends on how the property in question is valued (Sect. 2.5.2).

2.5.1 Security Interests and Guarantees Suited to Intellectual Property

In addition to the general law of securities, the IP-specific law of securities concerns two specific cases: software (section 'Software Pledge'), and cinematographic and audiovisual works (section 'Cinematographic Pledge'). Patents, on the other hand, are only the subject of a provision that specifies the regime for a French patent coexisting alongside a European patent when both patents are the subject of a security right. However, this provision does not require any specific measures.[6] Another practice that has become increasingly frequent should also be mentioned, namely the fiducia security concerning intellectual property (section 'The Fiducia Security'). Finally, the delegation of revenue for the financing of cinematographic films (section 'The Delegation of Revenue for the Financing of Cinematographic Films') is also a widespread practice.

Software Pledge

Article L. 132-34 of the IPC provides that, without prejudice to the provisions relating to the sale and pledging of business assets, the author's right to exploit software may be the subject of a pledge under specific conditions.[7]

Cinematographic Pledge

The cinematographic pledge[8] is a derogation from general law. Unusually, its system is determined not by the IPC, but by France's *Code du cinéma et de l'image animée*[9] (Cinema and Moving Picture Code, henceforth CMIC). It is based on the model of the pledge without dispossession of the grantor.

---

[6]See Art. L. 614-14, para. 1 IPC.

[7]Art. L. 132-34 IPC.

[8]See Kamina (2014), no. 160 et seq.

[9]Ordinance No. 2009-901 of July 24, 2009 pertaining to the legislative section of the *Code du cinéma et de l'image animée*, *JORF* No. 0170, July 25, 2009, Text No. 39.

This pledge can relate to a number of things: the copyright and related rights attached to the work ("exploitation right" in the CMIC sense); the right of ownership of the medium; or the delegations and assignments, either by way of full transfer of ownership or as security, of all or part of the present or future revenue attached to the cinematographic or audiovisual work.

In essence, these various guarantees are established under general law, either as a tangible movables pledge for the medium of the work or as an incorporeal movables pledge for the intellectual property.

The original CMIC mechanism comes under Article L. 124-2, which provides that, unless otherwise provided for in the contract recorded in the public register, the beneficiary of a security right in intellectual property rights, either over the medium or over the revenue from its exploitation, shall collect the sum of the proceeds from the cinematographic or audiovisual work, whatever its nature, solely and directly. This is notwithstanding any opposition other than that based on a legal privilege, and will be up to the amount of his rights and in the order of his registration. There is no need to notify the assigned debtors, who shall be rightly paid up by this beneficiary.

The Fiducia Security

The fiducia security requires the conclusion of a special agreement through which it is determined that an intellectual property portfolio is assigned as security. Under French law, this fiducia is governed by Articles 2011 to 2030 of the CC. The contract must mention, under pain of nullity, the secured debt and the estimated value of either the intellectual property or the claims from royalties transferred to the fiduciary patrimony.

Under pain of nullity, the contract of fiducia must be registered within one month with the tax authorities of the fiduciary's registered office or with the non-residents' tax authorities if the fiduciary is not domiciled in France.

The Delegation of Revenue for the Financing of Cinematographic Films

The delegation of claims[10] is an interesting transaction to examine in terms of intellectual property in general because it is widely used in one sector in particular, namely the financing of cinematographic films.[11]

This solution can be extended to other types of financing transactions involving intellectual property. Delegation entails a transfer of the existing legal relationship between the debtor and the creditor through a change of debtor.

It is governed by the provisions of Articles 1336 and 1338 of the CC.

---

[10] Billiau (1998), p. 207.

[11] See Kamina (2014), no. 153 and 171.

Article 1336 states that "Delegation is a transaction by which one person (the delegator) obtains from another (the delegate) an obligation in favour of a third party (the beneficiary of the delegation), who accepts him as debtor. Unless otherwise provided, the delegate may not set up against the beneficiary of the delegation any defence arising from his relations with the delegator, or from the relations between the latter and the beneficiary of the delegation."[12] Article 1338 adds: "Where the delegator is the debtor of the beneficiary of the delegation but the latter has not discharged his debt, the delegation provides the beneficiary with another debtor."[13]

Delegation involves either adding a new debtor or substituting a new debtor for the original debtor. It is called "imperfect delegation" when the new debtor (i.e. the delegate) is added to the original debtor (i.e. the delegator), and "perfect delegation" when the new debtor replaces the original debtor.

Both alternatives can be considered in the case of intellectual property claims since they have limited impact on the potential of this transaction to mobilize the resources attached to intellectual property in order to finance a company.

Delegation is not just a simplified payment mechanism; rather, more importantly, it is a means of providing a payment guarantee for the delegate, who benefits from the transaction. It is an alternative way of providing an effective guarantee to secure funding based on the operating revenue of an intellectual property portfolio.

Delegation requires a dual consensus *ad idem* involving an agreement between the delegate and the delegator on the one hand, and the delegate and the delegatee on the other. It is less flexible than the assignment of claims in this respect. Each of the parties must know about the transaction and be aware of its consequences. The delegate's commitment must be firm and unequivocal. Delegation does not entail the transfer of the royalty claim on intellectual property; instead, it involves the creation of a new debt. The delegate's commitment is autonomous from that of the delegator, and they do not share the same cause. Consequently, the delegate may not invoke the defences and exceptions used by the delegator against the delegatee in order to avoid his commitment. This gives effective protection to the beneficiary of the security. For example, the delegate cannot refuse to pay the delegatee on the grounds that the delegator's commitment is null and void, for example due to the nullity of the licensed intellectual property. With a portfolio, the risk that all its components would be cancelled is virtually nil. This protects against a possible challenge of past payments, particularly in the event of the cancellation of property titles.[14]

Such an arrangement allows the owner of the intellectual property portfolio to retain full ownership and free management of its assets. He is only required to provide his licensees with the bank details of the third-party beneficiary of the

[12]Art. 1336 CC. English translation taken from *The Law of Contract, the General Regime of Obligations, and Proof of Obligations: The New Provisions of the Code civil Created by Ordonnance n° 2016-131 of February 10, 2016*, translated into English by John Cartwright, Bénédicte Fauvarque-Cosson and Simon Whittaker.

[13]Art. 1338 CC, *ibid.*

[14]See the Court of Cassation's Plenary Assembly of Feb. 17, 2012, no. 10-24.282: https://www.courdecassation.fr/jurisprudence_2/assemblee_pleniere_22/604_17_22333.html.

delegation of claims. This mechanism is temporary and responds in practice to a need for refinancing.

2.5.2 Valuation of Intellectual Property

Valuation methods must determine the financial value of intellectual property.[15] They are marked by the need to ensure the *transparency* of the process. Valuation techniques can be grouped into two categories: valuation based on the intellectual property's patrimonial value and valuation based on the intellectual property's financial yield.

A good valuation procedure combines techniques from both of these categories. The value is a determining factor because the use of several valuation methods establishes a set of indices. The aim is not to arrive at conclusive valuations, but rather to arrive at acceptable orders of magnitude, obtained using precise and rigorous methods.

Whatever the method used and whatever the intellectual property being valued, the following fundamental aspects must always be taken into account: the quality (technical, commercial, artistic, etc.) of the intellectual property being valued, the relevant existing markets, and the objective advantages provided by the intellectual property.[16]

Valuation methods can be presented using the dividing line between patrimonial value and yield value, distinguishing first between static valuation methods (section 'Static Valuation Methods') and dynamic valuation methods (section 'Dynamic Valuation Methods').

Static Valuation Methods

There are two static methods for valuing intellectual property that achieve the objectives of accuracy and consistency of value (*sincérité et régularité de la valeur*), but neither of them is suited to the legal and economic characteristics of intellectual property.

The "cost-based method"[17] is based on the idea that something's value corresponds to the costs incurred in producing or discovering it. This can lead to prejudicial undervaluation.

---

[15]In this regard, see Decocq (1996), p. 1: "*L'évaluation est une opération intellectuelle que doit opérer l'auteur d'un acte juridique consistant à calculer la valeur de la contre-prestation – bien échangé... – justifiant l'existence d'une dette – prix, droit des associés*" ("Valuation is an intellectual activity that must be carried out by the author of a legal act. It consists of calculating the value of the consideration – the property exchanged, etc. – and justifies the existence of a debt – price, shareholders' rights").

[16]On this subject, see Weinstein (1977), no. 167 et seq., and no. 302.

[17]See Binctin (2015), no. 438 et seq.

The "income-based method"[18] determines the value of intellectual property according to the financial revenues it has generated. Although this analysis of past gains limits the risk of fraud, it can also be a source of under- or overvaluation.

Dynamic Valuation Methods

Dynamic valuation methods define the value of intellectual property according to a yield logic. The more likely the property is to have a high economic and financial yield, the higher its value, because yield is the investor's motivating factor. Yield valuation includes weighting to adjust for future unknowns. Dynamic methods applied to valuing intellectual properties benefit from a theoretical and practical environment that gives them an undeniable legitimacy.

These methods are primarily derived from techniques used in the insurance sector to determine policyholder premiums. Insurance companies use proven valuation models to do this, including in particular actuarial methods. The yield-based valuation of intellectual properties uses the same actuarial techniques.[19]

2.6 *Collateralization of Intellectual Property Proceeds*

It is possible to provide a guarantee on the proceeds generated from the exploitation of intellectual property. This guarantee is economically more attractive and legally more common than that directly related to the intellectual property. Three approaches are possible: (Sect. 2.6.1) the pledge of claims, (Sect. 2.6.2) the assignment of claims, and (Sect. 2.6.3) the delegation of claims.

2.6.1 Pledge of Claims

The pledge of claims attached to the exploitation of intellectual property is made under the general law of the pledge of incorporeal movables, pursuant to Articles 2355 et seq. of the CC.

2.6.2 Assignment of Claims

Instead of providing security over his claims, the owner of intellectual property may choose to transfer ownership of those claims as security. The assignment of claims is made in accordance with general contract law. It is enforceable against third parties

[18]See Binctin (2015), no. 441 et seq.

[19]On dynamic valuation methods, see Binctin (2015), no. 449 et seq.

from the date of the act (Art. 1323 of the CC[20]). The assignment of claims may be carried out according to the tools of commercial law, either through exchange instruments if the owner of the intellectual property is a trader or through the assignment of professional claims ("Dailly assignment," see Art. L. 313-23 f. of France's *Code monétaire et financier* (Monetary and Financial Code)[21]) if the owner is carrying out his professional activity. This allows an inventor—that is, a natural, non-trading person—to use such a mechanism.

2.6.3 Delegation of Claims

The mechanisms of the general law of obligation can also be used in relation to proceeds of intellectual property, meaning that it is possible to execute a delegation in relation to such proceeds.[22]

3 Operational Structure: Perfection

3.1 Perfection of Security Rights in Intellectual Property

Under French law, all security rights encumbering intellectual property rights must have been (Sect. 3.1.1) established in writing and (Sect. 3.1.2) made public in a register. In all cases, the guarantee concerns the right of exploitation rather than the intellectual property as such.

3.1.1 Written Requirement for the Creation of Security Rights Concerning Intellectual Property Rights

Pledges in General and Specific Law

For an act to be perfected, the general law relating to pledges states that both the designation of the secured debt and the quantity, type, and nature of the intellectual property given as a pledge must be established in writing (Art. 2336 of the CC[23]). These provisions, as applied to intellectual property, require that the pledge agreement give a detailed description of the intellectual property or its dismemberment given as security. On this point, the general law also applies to the software pledge.

---

[20] Art. 1323 CC.

[21] Assignment of professional claims.

[22] For applications of this technique in the film industry, see Kamina (2014), no. 153 and 171 and Quiquerez (2013), p. 39.

[23] Art. 2336 CC.

Where the IP-specific law contains provisions relating to pledges, some provisions refer to the "in writing" requirement. For example, Article L. 714-1 of the IPC states that pledges concerning trademarks must be in writing, under pain of nullity.[24] In other specific instances, such as those pertaining to design rights, the "in writing" requirement is not expressly indicated, but the specialist doctrine considers that it exists nevertheless.[25]

Fiducia Security

While public disclosure formalities are required in the vast majority of cases in France in order for the legal act to be opposable, the fiducia must be published *ad validitatem* (as a condition of validity), as indicated in Articles 2018[26] and 2019[27] of the CC.

3.1.2 Publication of Security Rights Concerning Intellectual Property Rights

With regard to third parties, the opposability of a security right presupposes compliance with a public disclosure measure. Disclosure must be made in the register of the intellectual property right in question, provided of course that the encumbered right itself involves a registrable transaction. In the case of **patent** pledges, the opposability of the pledge is subject to publication requirements; these are prescribed by Article R. 613-55 of the IPC for French patents and in Article L. 614-11 of the IPC for EU patents. The opposability of **trademark** pledges depends on compliance with the public disclosure formalities contained in Article R. 714-4 of the IPC (French trademarks) and Article 19 of Regulation No. 40/94 (EU trademarks). **Design** pledges are opposable against third parties if they are published in accordance with Article R. 512-15 of the IPC (French designs) and Article 29 of Regulation No. 6/2002 (EU designs).

The rules for the disclosure of general law, copyright (e.g. of software, cinema) and fiducia pledges concerning intellectual property are laid out below.

[24] Art. L. 714-1 IPC.

[25] See Martial-Braz (2007), no. 118.

[26] Art. 2018 CC.

[27] Art. 2019 CC.

General Law Pledge Concerning Intellectual Property

Regarding public disclosure, the CC provides that a pledge is opposable against third parties by virtue of its public disclosure.[28] The IPC implements this requirement by organizing public disclosure measures through the registration of pledges in the relevant official registers.

Special Law Pledge Concerning the Software Exploitation Right

According to Article L. 132-34 of the IPC,[29] the software pledge is registered, under pain of being unopposable, in a special register held by France's *Institut national de la propriété industrielle* (National Institute of Industrial Property, henceforth NIIP). The registration must precisely state the subject-matter of the security right, and the source code and operating documents in particular. It must also state the identities of the copyright-holder and of the secured creditor, as well as any changes relating to their first names, last names, company names, legal statuses, domiciles or registered offices. It must record any intrinsic elements likely to make the software identifiable, such as its name; trademark or source code designation; operating documents; updates; and any other characteristics of the software, including filing references where applicable. In addition, an original copy of the deed of pledge concerning all or part of the software exploitation right must be shown for registration, as must any subsequent deeds changing who owns or enjoys the exploitation right, or altering the rights of the secured creditor. Finally, the register records legal claims and final court rulings as they relate to the rights covered by the pledge contract.

Cinematographic Films Pledge

Article L. 123-1[30] of the CMIC stipulates that cinematographic and audiovisual works must be entered in France's *Registre public du cinéma et de l'audiovisuel* (Public Register of Cinema and Audiovisual Media) at the request of the first party to act. Registration is purely formal. It may not have the effect of conferring any new privilege on its beneficiary; granting pledges on all or part of the rights; or delegating or transferring all or part of the present or future products of a cinematographic or audiovisual work, either by transfer of full ownership or as a guarantee. Registration does not ensure the deed is effective *between the parties*; rather, it has effect *only with respect to third parties*. If the deed of pledge is not recorded in this register, the resulting rights are unopposable against third parties.

---

[28] Art. 2337 CC.

[29] Art. L. 132-34 IPC.

[30] No English translation of this provision currently exists.

Fiducia Security

Where the fiducia security concerns a claim, its opposability against third parties is established on the date of the contract. Opposability against the debtor of the assigned claim is dependent upon notice being given to said debtor.[31] Article 2020 of the French CC provides that a "national register of fiduciaries is established as provided by decree *en Conseil d'État*."[32] However, this register is not designed to be consulted by third parties. The security trust is therefore not subject to a system of disclosure to third parties.

3.2 *Conditions and Effects of the Registration of Security Rights in Intellectual Property*

Security rights encumbering intellectual property may be recorded in the IP register. This makes the security right effective against third parties and gives the secured creditor priority over competing claimants.

4 Priorities

Several creditors may be registered on the same pledge. Since registration is necessary for the pledge to be opposable against third parties, the rule is that the person registered first takes precedence over all others registered (*prior tempore, potior jure*).

5 Enterprise Charges

There is no floating charge system in France. The only situation in which a security right may encumber a plurality of rights in a single deed concerns the business asset pledge. Article L. 142-2, paragraph 1 of France's *Code de commerce* (Commercial Code) states that the following is likely to be included in the pledging of assets: "corporate and trade name, leasing rights, goodwill, custom and passing trade, commercial furniture, equipment and tools used for the operation of the business, patents, licences, trademarks, industrial drawings and designs, and in general the

[31]Art. 2018-2 CC.

[32]Art. 2020 CC.

intellectual property rights attached thereto."[33] It follows, therefore, that intellectual property rights are only included in the subject-matter for pledging business assets if this is expressly specified in the deed of pledge. Where the parties have contractually opted to include intellectual property rights, they must undertake two series of public disclosures. First, they must publish the business asset pledge, under pain of nullity, at the register of the commercial court of the area in which the business is located. Then, they must publish the intellectual property rights in the NIIP registers corresponding to each right. If this second type of registration is not undertaken, the penalty appears to be that the pledge is unopposable against third parties.[34]

As Borga explains, "a conflict may arise between a creditor secured on the business assets [*nantissement de fonds de commerce*] and a creditor holding a security right in an intellectual property right when that IP-right has incorporated the subject-matter of the two security rights. The existence of a double disclosure does not in itself resolve all difficulties. What should happen when an intellectual property right has incorporated the subject-matter of a business asset pledge [*nantissement de fonds de commerce*], but another creditor has published a pledge on the intellectual property right in question between the two required registrations?"[35] For Borga, "entry in the NIIP registers is retroactive to the day of entry in the commercial court register."[36] It is regrettable that there is no clearly defined solution on this point.

6 Pre-default Rights

6.1 The Intellectual Property Pledge

The pledge remains in effect until the secured claim has been paid in full. If the debtor or owner of the pledged intellectual property fails to preserve the property (Art. 2344 of the CC), the creditor may claim forfeiture of the term of the secured debt or request an additional pledge. In the case of intellectual property, this

[33]Art. L. 142-2, para. 1 *Code de commerce*. Citation taken from the English translation of the *Code de commerce*, as of July 1, 2013, translated by Martha Fillastre, Amma Kyeremeh, and Miriam Watchorn, available at https://www.legifrance.gouv.fr/Traductions/en-English/Legifrance-translations. This text concerns conventional pledges, but judicial pledges are also possible. See. Art. L. 531-1 *Code des procédures civiles d'exécution* (Code of Civil Enforcement Procedures, henceforth CCEP): "A judicial security may be granted as a precautionary measure on buildings, business assets, shares, partnership shares and transferable securities." This and all subsequent citations from the CCEP have been translated from the French (no English translation of this document currently exists).

[34]In this sense, see Borga (2013), pp. 117 et seq., specifically no. 9, for a recent examination of contractual guarantees on intellectual property rights.

[35]Borga (2013), *ibid.*

[36]Borga (2013), *ibid.*

obligation of preservation forces the owner to be proactive in both renewing his title of ownership when necessary and exploiting his intellectual property when failure to exploit would result in a loss of ownership.

6.2 *The Fiducia Security*

The fiducia agreement entails a transfer of ownership from the grantor to the fiduciary. It generates obligations for both of these parties, which in turn affect the rights of third parties—in this case, both parties' creditors. The grantor is not necessarily materially affected by the fiducia security in terms of his enjoyment of the intellectual property involved. The contract may provide that he retain the use or enjoyment of this property. However, from a legal point of view, the grantor is required to transfer the agreed property to the fiduciary, losing all power of administration and alienation over it and retaining only personal (but not real) rights. Once ownership has been transferred, he only enjoys the uses expressly retained under the agreement. Thus, in principle the grantor receives the fruits of the transferred ownership, but it is preferable to specify this in the contract.

The fiduciary is bound not only by a primary obligation to achieve the purpose of the fiducia, but also by duties of diligence and loyalty. The economic value of the fiduciary patrimony does not belong to the fiduciary, who is only responsible for preserving it and potentially growing it. This presents a real problem in intellectual property law, and it is sensible to hand the power of exploiting the intellectual property in question over to the grantor. In his dealings with third parties, the fiduciary is deemed to have the most extensive powers over the fiduciary patrimony, unless it can be shown that the third parties had knowledge of the limitations of his powers. He must act in an official capacity and report on his task to the grantor. He therefore most notably handles infringement actions and defences and takes on the risks associated with such proceedings.

The beneficiary is not immediately affected by the fiducia. His future vocation is only for full and complete ownership of the property affected, subject to his acceptance. In this scenario, the beneficiary is the creditor providing finance to the operator who has transferred his patents to a trust patrimony. The grantor himself is a second beneficiary.

7 Enforcement

7.1 *Default Without Insolvency*

In the event of non-payment of the debt by the pledge grantor, the creditor may, at his discretion, obtain a court order for either:

a. the pledged property to be sold at auction (Art. 2346 of the CC[37]), or
b. the property to remain with him as payment (Art. 2347 of the CC[38]).

The challenge with this option relates to the intellectual property's value. Article 2347 of the CC provides that when the value of the property exceeds the amount of the secured debt, the sum equal to the difference is either paid to the debtor or held in consignment if there are other secured creditors.[39] It is essential that the intellectual property be valued carefully.

The creditor may also enter into a *lex commissoria* (forfeiture clause) with his debtor, whereby the creditor becomes the owner of the secured intellectual property right if the debtor defaults (Art. 2348 of the CC). Article 2348 provides that, where the pledge contract adopts the solution of transferring ownership, the valuation should be carried out on the day of the transfer by an amicably or judicially appointed expert in those cases where no official listing has been made on an organized market for intellectual property.

Either way, the formalities of the seizure and sale of intellectual property rights are carried out by a court bailiff (*huissier de justice*) or public finances bailiff (*huissier des finances publiques*). The seizure of intellectual property is effected by an extrajudicial act served on the owner of the intellectual property, on the NIIP if the property is registered, and on all persons holding rights in the intellectual property. It renders any subsequent modification of the rights attached to the intellectual property right unopposable against the seizing creditor. On pain of nullity of the seizure, the distraining creditor must, within the prescribed period of time, petition the court for validation of the seizure and for the purpose of putting the intellectual property up for sale. The time limit prescribed by paragraph 2 of the aforementioned Article L. 613-21 of the IPC is fifteen days from the date that notice of the seizure provided for in paragraph 1 of said Article is served (Article R. 613-51). In accordance with the provisions of Article R. 613-53(No. 1) of the IPC, subsequent acts affecting the ownership of the patent or the patent application are recorded in France's national patent register. The practical procedures for making an entry in this register are defined in Articles R. 613-53 to R. 613-59 of the IPC.

The only high court in France that is able to hear actions concerning patents for the invention of semiconductor products is in Paris: the *Tribunal de grande instance de Paris*. This court's mission is to verify the claim; validate the seizure; and order and organize the sale of the patent. The CCEP does not provide for a specific mechanism for the seizure of these incorporeal rights; however, Article L. 231-1 of the CCEP states that "any creditor in possession of an enforceable title (*titre exécutoire*) revealing a liquid and due claim may have his incorporeal rights, other than claims, seized and sold by his debtor". In addition, Article R. 112-1 of the CCEP specifies that "all movable or immovable, corporeal or incorporeal properties

[37] Art. 2346 CC.
[38] Art. 2347 CC.
[39] Art. 2347 CC.

belonging to the debtor may be the subject of a forced or protective enforcement action, except in cases where the law prescribes or allows its unseizability". In the absence not only of a general regulatory text applicable to the seizure of such rights but also of specific provisions, it is possible, subject to any necessary adaptations at the enforcement judge's discretion, to transpose the procedure defined in Articles 182 to 194 of the Decree of July 31, 1992 (Art. R. 232-5, Art. R. 232-6, Art. R. 232-7 and Art. R. 232-8 of the CCEP) for the seizure operations and the provisions of Articles 189 to 192 of said Decree (Art. R. 233-5, Art. R. 233-6, Art. R. 233-7 and Art. R. 233-8 of the CCEP) for the sale. This solution was confirmed as the CCEP was being codified. The regulatory provisions governing the seizure of shareholders' rights and transferable securities are grouped together under Title III of Book II of the CCEP (Article R. 231-1 et seq.), entitled *La saisie des droits incorporels* (The Seizure of Incorporeal Rights). They include a new article, which states: "Unless otherwise provided, the seizure of incorporeal rights is governed by the present Title insofar as their specific nature does not prevent it" (Article R. 231-1 CCEP).

The value of intellectual property rights is determined on the day of transfer, either by an official listing on an organized market within the meaning of the French Monetary and Financial Code or, in the absence of such a listing, by an amicably or judicially appointed expert (Art. 2348 of the CC). If the value of the secured right exceeds the amount of the debt, the difference is either paid to the debtor or held in consignment if there are other creditors.

Finally, if the creditor has entered into a retention of title clause concerning the intellectual property, he may request the restitution of the property encumbered by the security right, in accordance with the provisions of Article 2371 of the CC.[40]

As far as the fiducia security is concerned, in the event of non-payment, there are a number of possible scenarios.

If the fiduciary is also the creditor, he acquires full ownership of the transferred intellectual assets, provided that the contract does not state otherwise.

If the creditor is not the fiduciary, he has a personal right against the fiduciary to demand the return of the property in full ownership or, if the contract so provides, the sale of the property and the return of all or part of the price. In the latter case, an expert valuation procedure is provided for, in the case of both the intellectual property and the royalties. If the amount of debt is less than the proceeds of the sale, the beneficiary or fiduciary making the sale pays the difference to the grantor. If the debtor who set up the fiducia has honoured his debt, the fiducia agreement terminates. Where the fiducia security concerns intellectual property, the return of the property to the debtor's patrimony requires a renewal of all public disclosure formalities.

[40] Art. 2371 CC.

7.2 *Default with Insolvency*[41]

When the defaulting debtor is the subject of collective proceedings, the resulting effects may be as described in this section. First, if the creditor is the beneficiary of a reservation of ownership, he can bring an action for specific recovery (*action en revendication*).[42] Second, as soon as the decision to open the collective proceedings has been handed down, the agreement can no longer include a *lex commissoria* (i.e. a clause making it possible to attribute ownership of the property to the creditor in the event of default by the debtor, also called a "forfeiture clause"). If a *lex commissoria* has already been included in the contract, its effects are suppressed by the decision to open collective proceedings.[43] Finally, this decision deprives the fiducia security of its effects.[44] All the potential effects listed above are in accordance with the regulations as set out in the Commercial Code, which are, in the case of collective proceedings, a matter of public order.

8 Typical Costs

The creation of a security right must be distinguished from its registration (i.e. its opposability against third parties in most cases), except in the case of the fiducia security, where public disclosure is required *ad validitatem* (as a condition of validity).

[41]See, specifically, Henry et al. (2016), p. 6 of the report submitted to the AIPPI on June 3, 2016 on the subject of security rights concerning intellectual property rights http://aippi.org/committee/security-interests-over-intellectual-property/. Report authors: Guillaume Henry, Enrico Priori, Virginia De Freitas, Emmanuel Gouge, Romain Viret, Yves Bizollon, Charles Simon, Florence Jacquand, Caroline Levesque, Cécile Joubert, Jules Fabre, Jeanne Mercier, Alexandre Jacquet, Thomas Bouvet, Louis Jestaz and Agathe Caille. It should be noted that the terminology used in the AIPPI report differs from that used here. Where the report refers to 'trust' and 'trustee', we use the terms 'fiducia' and 'fiduciary' in order to be in line with the terminology used in the English translation of the Code Civil that is available on the French government's official website Legifrance.gouv.fr.

[42]See, specifically, Art. L.624-16 para. 2. Comm. Code.

[43]Art. L.622-7, II, para.2 and L.641-3 Comm. Code.

[44]Art. L.622-23-1 Comm. Code.

Table 1 Regulated fees for notaries

Services covered by the fee	Basic bands	Rate applicable
All the preparation of all deeds (fiducia agreement and subsequent deeds)	From €0 to €6500	3.945%
	From €6500 to €17,000	1.627%
	From €17,000 to €60,000	1.085%
	More than €60,000	0.814%

8.1 *Legal Costs Related to the Creation of a Security Right in Intellectual Property*

Pledges can all be made by an act under private signature. With the exception of advisory fees, which vary from one professional to the next, there are no specific creation costs.

The fiducia security, on the other hand, must be created by notarial act under pain of nullity if "the assets, rights, or security rights transferred into the fiduciary patrimony belong to the community existing between spouses or belong to owners in indivision" (Art. 2012, para. 2 of the CC[45]). In this case, the cost of creation is provided for by the Decree of October 28, 2016 on regulated fees for notaries (*Journal officiel* of November 5, 2016) (Table 1).

If the fiducia security is rechargeable, the creation costs are spread out.

8.2 *Legal Costs Related to the Publication of a Security Right in Intellectual Property (as of January 1, 2017)*

The rates listed below apply to the registration of the following security rights:

1. business asset pledges (conventional, protective measure)
2. judicial pledges (only on business assets, not possible for intellectual property rights)
3. incorporeal movable pledges

   – For a claim of less than €20,800 (without postage): €25.20
   – For a claim of less than €20,800 (including postage): €26.81
   – For a claim between €20,800 and €41,600 (without postage): €96.34
   – For a claim between €20,800 and €41,600 (including postage): €97.94

[45] Art. 2012 CC.

Table 2 Number of patents with pledges and patents with written-off pledges by year and by stage in the procedure at the time of registration (Source: NIIP, 2016)

	Pledges			Written-off pledges		
Year	Applications submitted	Applications published	Patents granted	Applications submitted	Applications published	Patents granted
2006	12	25	275	0	4	169
2007	4	22	533	0	1	55
2008	0	37	323	0	2	76
2009	1	47	685	0	4	83
2010	0	16	159	0	1	17
2011	1	37	526	0	9	367
2012	3	57	521	0	23	423
2013	4	107	2690	0	0	69
2014	22	22	2890	0	72	4811
2015	6	56	853	0	0	127

- For a claim of more than €41,600 (without postage): €142.28
- For a claim of more than €41,600 (including postage): €143.89[46]

9 Practical Usefulness

On this point, reference should be made to a report written by Laurence Sekkat and Franck Dazin entitled "*Quand les brevets servent à lever des fonds en France: les constitutions et les radiations de gages dans le Registre national des brevets de l'INPI,*" which was published in October 2016.[47] The following Table 2 is taken from this report (p. 6).

Regarding the ease of raising funds using intellectual property rights, it is also worth mentioning the December 14, 2012 deal made by telecommunications equipment company Alcatel-Lucent with Credit Suisse and Goldman Sachs for multi-year bank loans totalling €1.615 billion. In return, the company pledged its extensive portfolio of approximately 29,000 patents with an indicative value of €5 billion (Table 3).

10 Legal and/or Practical Difficulties

The creation of security rights in intellectual property rights is faced with the challenge of valuing encumbered assets (see the discussion on valuation above). This is a practical difficulty with significant legal consequences, since legal certainty requires carrying out a valuation where the rules are not clearly defined.

[46] http://www.greffe-tc-paris.fr/fr/privileges-et-nantissement/tarifs_privileges_nantissements.html.

[47] https://www.inpi.fr/sites/default/files/quand_les_brevets_servent_a_lever_des_fonds_en_france_1.pdf.

Table 3 Summary table of the pledges registered over the last 4 years

Fields of activity	Rights pledged	Types of transaction
Pharmaceutical	Patents	Bond issue agreement through a venture capital fund
Pharmaceutical	Patents and trademarks	Bond issue agreement through a venture capital fund
Pharmaceutical	Patents and trademarks	Bank financing
Video games	Trademarks and software	Bank financing
Medical devices	Patents and software	Bond issue agreement through a third-party company specializing in R&D

11 Reform of the Law

There is currently no proposal for reform concerning security rights in intellectual property rights. The reform of the security rights law by the ordinance of March 23, 2006 created a general law relating to pledges without dispossession that seems able to address most of the issues related to security rights in intellectual property rights.

References

Billiau M (1998) La délégation de créance : essai d'une théorie juridique de la délégation en droit des obligations. Dissertation. coll. Bibliothèque de droit privé

Binctin N (2015) Stratégie d'entreprise et propriété intellectuelle. LGDJ-Lextenso Éditions, Paris

Borga N (2013) In: Bruguière J-M (ed) Les contrats de propriété intellectuelle. Dalloz, Paris

Decocq G (1996) Essai sur l'évaluation. Dissertation. Paris II

Henry G, Priori E, De Freitas V, Gouge E, Viret R, Bizollon Y, Simon C, Jacquand F, Levesque C, Joubert C, Fabre J, Mercier J, Jacquet A, Bouvet T, Jestaz L, Caille A (2016) Security Rights Concerning Intellectual Property Rights. http://aippi.org/committee/security-interests-over-intellectual-property/. Accessed 6 Mar 2019

Kamina P (2014) Droit du cinéma, 2nd edn. LexisNexis, Paris

Martial-Braz N (2007) Droit des sûretés réelles sur propriétés intellectuelles. Dissertation, Université d'Aix-Marseille III

Quiquerez A (2013) Acte de délégation de recettes ou de cession de créances : clauses contraires, note under Cass. com. October 23, 2012. Juris-Classeur Périodique, édition entreprise, 39 et seq

Weinstein Z (1977) Le régime fiscal de la propriété industrielle, 2nd edn. Delmas, Paris

Security Rights in Intellectual Property in Germany

Moritz Brinkmann, David Rüther, and Bianca Scraback

Abstract Intellectually property and collateral are two of the most important areas in commerce and law. Germany is no exception to this. However, the area of security rights in intellectual property is a whole new ball game. In German practice, IP rights are only seldom—if ever—used to secure a loan. This is certainly not because of a lack of options. As this chapter will demonstrate, German law offers a multitude of security rights in IP rights and licences: the pledge of rights, the security assignment, the security usufruct, and the security licence. Rather, there are various legal and practical reasons why IP rights are rarely used as collateral. First, the pledge and security usufruct are both impractical due to enforcement restrictions. Second, a security assignment makes it virtually impossible to create junior security rights in the collateral. Third, the legal character of licences is unresolved, which leads to legal uncertainty, especially with regard to their treatment in insolvency. Practical difficulties further add to these impediments. The main problem is that there is no method to reliably assess the value of an IP right, much less the value the IP right might have at the time of realization. Furthermore, as there is no liquid market for many IP rights, it is very difficult to realize the value of an IP right after default.

1 Introduction

Security rights in intellectual property (IP) have received considerable attention in German legal literature. This academic interest, however, stands in stark contrast to the limited practical importance of security rights in IP.

In preparation for this report, we have interviewed about 120 IP practitioners, corporate lawyers, insolvency trustees, and bankers. The participants were asked

M. Brinkmann (✉) · D. Rüther · B. Scraback
Institut für deutsches und internationales Zivilverfahrensrecht, Rheinische Friedrich-Wilhelms-Universität Bonn, Bonn, Germany
e-mail: Sekretariat.brinkmann@jura.uni-bonn.de; druether@uni-bonn.de; scraback@uni-bonn.de

E.-M. Kieninger (ed.), *Security Rights in Intellectual Property*, Ius Comparatum – Global Studies in Comparative Law 45,
https://doi.org/10.1007/978-3-030-44191-3_15

whether they had any experience with security rights in IP rights. Only a handful of participants indicated that they had even seen a security right in IP, let alone been personally involved in a transaction in which security rights had played a significant role.

Even though our inquiry lacks scientific rigour both in methodology and in scope, it provides anecdotal evidence that IP rights are only seldom—if ever—used to secure a loan. This conclusion is corroborated by the fact that there is no German case law on security rights in IP known to the authors. The participating practitioners offered two explanations for this:

1. It is very difficult to assess the realizable value of an IP right.[1]
2. IP rights are perceived as unreliable collateral because the creditor faces the risks that
   a. a third party may successfully challenge the IP right, or
   b. the grantor is not the true owner of the right as there is no *bona fide* acquisition of security rights in IP rights.

Moreover, the life cycle of a loan can often exceed the duration for which the value of an IP right remains consistent, especially in the technology sector. As *Bill Gates* reportedly said, "intellectual property has the shelf life of a banana."

Furthermore, IP rights, and trademarks in particular, are sometimes only valuable as long as the debtor's business is successful; they become worthless once the debtor's business model is in crisis. As this is exactly the moment when the creditor needs his security most, IP rights offer poor protection in the insolvency of the grantor.

Some participants indicated that they have seen IP rights used as additional collateral in situations where all of the debtor's assets were encumbered, such as in the context of project financing. In such a situation, security rights over IP rights might serve as more of a shield against seizure of the IP right by other creditors rather than as a sword against the debtor.[2] In these instances, the IP rights are not encumbered because the creditor hopes to satisfy his claim by selling or otherwise disposing of the IP rights, but because he wishes to prevent other creditors from seizing the rights. Since foreclosures by other creditors could have ruinous effects on the success of the project, the creditor will try to anticipate such seizures by taking any IP rights as collateral (e.g. by way of a security assignment) and thus frustrate the drastic effects of a third party's foreclosure.

The bottom line is that very little practical experience exists in Germany regarding security rights in IP. If encumbered, they are probably not the main collateral, but are instead utilized when all of the debtor's assets have been encumbered, as may occur in the context of an M&A transaction.

The following report should be read against this backdrop.

---

[1]For details, see Sect. 4.1.

[2]Klein (2004), p. 117.

In this national report on security rights in intellectual property, we will begin with an outline of the existing IP rights in Germany (Sect. 2). In Sect. 3, we will explain how IP rights and/or their corresponding licences can be used in a pledge of rights, security assignment, or usufruct for security. For each of these security rights, we will analyze the requirements for creation and the grantors' and creditors' rights not only before and after default but also in insolvency. Some remarks on the economic aspects of using IP rights as collateral will follow (Sect. 4).

2 IP Rights in Germany

2.1 Patent and Utility Model Law

2.1.1 Patents

German patent law is codified in the Patent Act (*Patentgesetz*, PatG). The Patent Act protects inventions that are new,[3] involve an inventive step,[4] and are susceptible of industrial application[5,6] in all fields of technology.[7]

Patent protection begins with the publication of the patent registration in the Patent Gazette.[8] The publication concludes the registration process, which is initiated by the inventor's application for patent protection.[9] The Patent and Trademark Office reviews the application before it grants patent protection.[10] Finally, the public is invited to oppose the patent within 9 months of the publication.[11] An action to set aside the patent may be filed any time after the 3-month period.[12]

Patent protection ends either 20 years after the date following the filing of the application[13]; when the proprietor surrenders the patent, refrains from paying the annual renewal fee, or fails to abide with sec. 37 Patent Act[14]; or when the patent is revoked or invalidated.[15]

[3]Sec. 3 Patent Act.
[4]Sec. 4 Patent Act.
[5]Sec. 5 Patent Act.
[6]Sec. 1 subsec. 1 Patent Act.
[7]Sec. 1 Patent Act.
[8]Sec. 58 subsec. 1 Patent Act.
[9]Sec. 34, 44 Patent Act.
[10]Sec. 42, 48 Patent Act.
[11]Sec. 59 Patent Act.
[12]Sec. 81 Patent Act.
[13]Sec. 16 Patent Act.
[14]Sec. 20 subsec. 1 Patent Act.
[15]Sec. 21, 22 Patent Act.

A patent grants the inventor or joint inventors—who can only be individuals[16]—exclusive exploitation rights.[17] The infringement of exploitation rights is punishable by injunctions or damage claims.[18] Every inventor also possesses non-transferable moral attribution rights.[19]

Patents may be inherited or transferred.[20] A transfer does not require registration in order to be effective.[21] The registered person is, however, formally legitimized vis-à-vis the Patent and Trademark Office in registry affairs and in legal proceedings.[22] There is also a growing tendency to construe a (rebuttable) presumption of ownership with regard to the registered person.[23] This presumption, however, does not allow a *bona fide* acquisition of a patent.[24] Instead of transferring a patent, the patent holder may also license some or all of his exploitation rights to third parties.[25]

2.1.2 European Patents

The European patent prevails over a German patent of similar priority[26] since German law prohibits dual national and European protection.[27] A German patent is deemed invalid as soon as either the European patent opposition period has run out or an unsuccessful opposition proceeding has taken place.[28] However, the German legislator has recently proposed a draft law that would accept co-existing national and European patents.[29] It is expected to be ratified concomitantly with the projected European patent with unitary effect.[30]

[16]See Kraßer and Ann (2016), p. 5.

[17]Sec. 6, 9 Patent Act.

[18]Sec. 139 Patent Act.

[19]Sec. 63 subsec. 1 Patent Act.

[20]Sec. 15 subsec. 1 Patent Act.

[21]Kraßer and Ann (2016), p. 492; Rudloff-Schäffer (2014), § 30, para 17.

[22]Sec. 30 subsec. 3 s. 2 Patent Act.

[23]BGH, 7. 5. 2013 – X ZR 69/11 – GRUR 2013, 713; OLG Düsseldorf, 24.6.2011 – 2 U 26/10; cf. also Kühnen (2014), p. 137; Ohly (2016), p. 1120; Picht (2018), pp. 221 et seq.; Pitz (2010), p. 688.

[24]Kraßer and Ann (2016), p. 492; Rudloff-Schäffer (2014), § 30, para 17.

[25]Sec. 15 subsec. 2 Patent Act.

[26]See Kraßer and Ann (2016), p. 623.

[27]Art. II Sec. 8 International Patent Treaty Act.

[28]Art. II Sec. 8 International Patent Treaty Act.

[29]See Romandini et al. (2016), p. 555.

[30]At the time of the manuscript's finalization, a constitutional complaint with the German Constitutional Court regarding the legitimacy of the European patent with unitary effect is pending. Whether Germany will ratify the law on the European patent with unitary effect depends on the decision of the Constitutional Court.

2.1.3 Utility Models

The German Utility Model Act (*Gebrauchsmustergesetz*) provides another way to protect inventions. Utility model protection is often perceived as a simplified version of patent protection[31]; hence, this overview will focus on their discrepancies only.[32] Arguably, an invention can be protected under the Utility Model Act if the inventive step is less substantial, which allows for the protection of simple technical improvements.[33] Unlike the Patent Act, the Utility Model Act denies protection to technical processes.[34] Moreover, the understanding of "state of the art" is less strict in the Utility Model Act than in the Patent Act.[35] The protection of utility models begins with publication in the Utility Model Gazette and lasts for only 10 years following the application with the Patent and Trademark Office.[36] The entire application and review process is shorter and less rigorous for utility models.[37]

2.2 *Trademarks*

Signs, commercial designations, and indications of geographical origin may be protected by the Act on the Protection of Trademarks and Other Symbols (*Markengesetz*; hereinafter Trademark Act).[38]

2.2.1 Signs

Signs—which may range from words and designs to non-visual signs such as sound marks—can be protected under the Trademark Act "if they are capable of distinguishing the goods and services of one enterprise from those of other enterprises".[39] The protection of a sign presupposes either its entry in the register at the Patent and Trademark Office, public recognition of the sign as a trademark, or its recognition as a well-known mark within the meaning of Article 6bis Paris Convention.[40]

[31]See Pierson et al. (2014), pp. 151 et seq.

[32]See also Pierson et al. (2014), pp. 151 et seq.

[33]See Kraßer and Ann (2016), pp. 319 et seq.

[34]Sec. 2 no. 3 Utility Model Act.

[35]Compare sec. 3 subsec. 1 Utility Model Act and sec. 3 subsec. 1, 2 Patent Act.

[36]Sec. 11 subsec. 1, sec. 23 subsec. 1 Utility Model Act.

[37]Sec. 8 subsec. 1 Utility Model Act.

[38]Sec. 1 Trademark Act.

[39]Sec. 3 subsec. 1 Trademark Act.

[40]Sec. 4 Trademark Act.

Trademark protection is conferred onto the sign as soon as it is entered into the register at the Patent and Trademark Office.[41] However, third parties may oppose trademarks within 3 months of publication of the registration[42] or file an invalidity action at any time.[43]

A sign may also obtain trademark protection if it has acquired public recognition in a given market sector and does not violate sec. 8 subsec. 2 No. 4-10 Trademark Act.[44] The degree of public recognition necessary depends on the sign's nature, and varies between more than 20–25% and more than 50% in that market sector.[45] The market sector may be geographically limited to a city, region, or province.[46] Trademark protection would then be limited correspondingly.

In Germany, trademark protection of a well-known mark within the meaning of Article 6[bis] Paris Convention requires a degree of public recognition higher than 50% in all relevant national trade circles.[47]

Registered trademarks are protected for 10 years, but can be renewed multiple times.[48] However, a registered trademark that has not been used for 5 consecutive years may be revoked upon request.[49] Publicly recognized trademarks and well-known trademarks exist until they lose their public recognition.[50]

A trademark grants the proprietor the exclusive right to use a sign.[51] Proprietors can be natural persons, legal persons, or partnerships.[52] Trademarks may be transferred or licensed to third parties.[53] The transfer of a registered trademark does not require registration[54]—the amendment of the register is merely declaratory.[55] The registration creates a rebuttable presumption of ownership with regard to the registered person.[56] This means that, unless proven otherwise, the registered person is treated like the holder of the trademark both within and outside of legal proceedings. A third party or an unregistered but materially entitled owner who wishes to sue the material holder has to prove their ownership despite the registration of another

[41]Hacker (2016), p. 29.

[42]Sec. 42 Trademark Act.

[43]Sec. 50, 51 Trademark Act.

[44]Hacker (2014), § 4, para 18.

[45]Hacker (2014), § 4, paras 42 et seq.

[46]Hacker (2016), pp. 101 et seq.

[47]Hacker (2014), § 4, paras 75 et seq.

[48]Sec. 47 Trademark Act.

[49]Sec. 49 Trademark Act.

[50]Hacker (2016), p. 145.

[51]Sec. 14 Trademark Act.

[52]Sec. 7 Trademark Act.

[53]Sec. 27 subsec. 1 Trademark Act; sec. 30 Trademark Act.

[54]See Sec. 27 subsec. 3 Trademark Act.

[55]Hacker (2014) § 27, para 24.

[56]Sec. 28 subsec. 1 Trademark Act.

person as the holder.[57] In registry affairs, only the registered person is allowed to participate.[58]

2.2.2 Titles of Works and Company Symbols

Titles of works and company symbols enjoy protection as commercial designations according to sec. 5 Trademark Act. Business symbols and other signs intended to distinguish the business operation from others are only protected if they are publicly recognized. All other commercial designations are protected from the moment that their trade usage begins.[59] Commercial designations can only be transferred in conjunction with their corresponding works or companies.[60]

2.2.3 Indications of Geographical Origin

Indications of geographical origin are precluded from becoming collateral due to their collective character.[61] Therefore, this overview on the protection of trademarks and other symbols excludes details on indications of geographical origin. The same applies to collective rights classifications, which can be transferred among qualified recipients,[62] but are of little importance.[63]

2.2.4 EU Trademark

An EU Trademark may coexist with a national trademark.[64] A proprietor's sign can be protected under EU and national law. However, provisions on relative obstacles to trademark protection allow proprietors of registered marks to object to third-party registration for EU or national trademark protection.[65]

---

[57]BGH, 22-01-1998 – I ZR 113/95 – GRUR 1998, 699, 701; Kirschnek (2014), § 28, paras 2, 4.

[58]Sec. 28 subsec. 2 Trademark Act, but see sec. 55 subsec. 1 and 4 Trademark Act regarding cancellation proceedings.

[59]Hacker (2016), pp. 304 et seq., 315.

[60]Hacker (2014), § 27, paras 72–74.

[61]See Fezer (2009), § 27, para 13.

[62]Sec. 97 subsec. 2 MarkenG.

[63]Kober-Dehm (2014), § 97, para 2.

[64]See Directive (EU) 2015/2436 of the European Parliament and of the Council of December 16, 2015 to Approximate the Laws of the Member States Relating to Trade Marks (recast) Recital 3. See also Kur (2017), Introduction, para 105.

[65]Kur (2017), Introduction, para 106.

2.3 Copyright

German copyright law is codified in the Act on Copyright and Related Rights (*Gesetz über Urheberrecht und verwandte Schutzrechte*; hereinafter Copyright Act). The Copyright Act protects all works in the literary, scientific, and artistic domains.[66] Sec. 2 subsec. 2 Copyright Act defines "works" as an "author's own intellectual creation".[67] Thus, the term is limited to an author's own creation rather than a creation by nature or a random creation by machine,[68] demanding a certain intellectual depth to the work[69] and at least a small degree of creativity.[70]

The German Copyright Act does not provide any formal requirements for copyright protection.[71] Therefore, copyright law protects all copyrightable works as soon as they are expressed in a perceptible form.

"Copyright protects the author in his intellectual and personal relationships to the work and in respect of the use of the work."[72] Both the moral rights and exploitation rights of copyrighted works expire 70 years *post mortem auctoris*.[73]

Copyright is exclusively granted to the author or joint authors of a work, with the author(s) being the creator(s) of the work.[74] Legal entities cannot become authors, and the German Copyright Act has no provisions containing a "work made for hire" doctrine. Until the death of the author(s), the copyright subsists with them and cannot be transferred.[75] However, the author(s) may license their exploitation rights to third parties.[76]

---

[66]Sec. 1 Copyright Act.

[67]Sec. 2 subsec. 2 Copyright Act.

[68]Schack (2015), pp. 103 et seq.

[69]Schack (2015), pp. 104 et seq.

[70]BGH, 12-03-1987 – I ZR 71/85 – GRUR 1987, 704, 706; see also Schack (2015), pp. 156 et seq.

[71]Schack (2015), pp. 136 et seq.

[72]Sec. 11 Copyright Act.

[73]Sec. 64 Copyright Act. The duration of copyright protection varies for related rights; see Pierson et al. (2014), pp. 373 et seq.

[74]Sec. 7 Copyright Act.

[75]Sec. 29 subsec. 1 Copyright Act.

[76]Sec. 29 subsec. 2 Copyright Act.

2.4 *Other IP Rights*[77]

2.4.1 Registered Designs

The second-most important industrial property right by registration numbers alone is the registered design, which has seen more than 300,000 registrations in total, 50,000 of which were in in 2015.[78] The Act on the Legal Protection of Designs (*Designgesetz*; hereinafter Design Protection Act) codifies the preconditions of design protection. A design is the "two-dimensional or three-dimensional appearance of the whole or a part of a product resulting from the features of, in particular, the lines, contours, colours, shape, texture or materials of the product itself or its ornamentation".[79] A design is protectable "if it is new and has individual character".[80] The formal requirements for registering designs are similar to those for utility models and thus are shorter and less rigorous than those laid down in the Patent Act.[81] Design protection accrues upon registration in the register of the Patent and Trademark Office.[82] The designer, his successor, or his employer owns the exclusive right in the registered design for 25 years.[83] This right may be licensed or transferred.[84] The registration of the transfer is merely declaratory.[85] Community designs and German design rights may protect a design simultaneously.[86]

2.4.2 Semiconductor Products and Plant Varieties

The German Act on the Protection of Topography of Microelectronic Semiconductor Products protects original and non-ordinary three-dimensional semiconductor structures.[87] Its practical relevance has become miniscule, with a total of

---

[77]Know-how and business information (trade secrets) are only partially protected in Germany and are therefore arguably unsuitable for use as collateral. For further information see Picht (2018), pp. 152 et seq.

[78]Deutsches Patent- und Markenamt (2015), *passim*.

[79]Sec. 1 no. 1 Design Protection Act.

[80]Sec. 2 Design Protection Act.

[81]See sec. 11–26 Design Protection Act.

[82]Sec. 27 subsec. 1 Design Protection Act.

[83]See sec. 7 Design Protection Act on ownership of the exclusive right; see sec. 27 subsec. 2 Design Protection Act on the protected term of a design.

[84]Sec. 29, 31 Design Protection Act.

[85]See sec. 29 subsec. 3 Design Protection Act.

[86]Cf. Article 95 Council Regulation (EC) No. 6/2002 of December 12, 2001 on Community Designs.

[87]Sec. 1 Semiconductor Protection Act.

19 registered topographies in 2015.[88] Slightly more relevant is the Plant Varieties Protection Act, with a total of approximately 1800 protected plant varieties as of 2014.[89]

2.5 Licences

An IP right-holder can contractually grant another party the right to exploit the IP right, which is known as a licence.[90] Such a licence is not an IP right in itself.

Licences can be exclusive, in the sense that they allow the licensee to exploit the IP right within the agreed boundaries and they prohibit any other person from using it.[91] Non-exclusive licences, on the other hand, grant the licensee an exploitation right without prohibiting others from using the IP right.[92] Depending on the licence agreement, the licensee may be allowed to transfer his licence or to create sublicences.[93]

The legal character of exclusive licences is highly debated in Germany. Some authors take the view that an exclusive licence is a right in rem with proprietary character.[94] Others see it as merely a contractual right.[95]

Regardless of the classification, a licence will continue to exist even if the IP right is transferred by the licensor to another party (*Sukzessionsschutz*).[96] It is, however,

[88]Deutsches Patent- und Markenamt (2015), p. 93.

[89]Bundessortenamt (2016), p. 9. For further information on the Plant Variety Protection Act, see Pierson et al. (2014), pp. 170 et seq.

[90]Sec. 15 subsec. 2 Patent Act; sec. 30 Trademark Act; sec. 22 subsec. 2 Utility Model Act; sec. 29 Subsec. 2 Copyright Act; Sec. 31 Design Protection Act.

[91]Ullmann and Deichfuß (2015), § 15, paras 89 et seq.; Mes (2015), § 15, para 41; Ingerl and Rohnke (2010), § 30, para 16.

[92]Ullmann and Deichfuß (2015), § 15, paras 99 et seq.; Mes (2015), § 15, para 43; Ingerl and Rohnke (2010), § 30, para 18.

[93]There is no consensus as to whether the licensee has such a right without an express agreement by the parties. In favour of general transferability for exclusive licences: Ullmann and Deichfuß (2015), § 15, para 104; Ingerl and Rohnke (2010), § 30, para 49; Mes (2015), § 15, para 41; BGH, 16.4.2002 – X ZR 127/99 – GRUR 2002, 801, 802. Opposing: Bühling (1998), p. 199; Fezer (2009), § 30, para 24; Hacker (2014) § 30, para 71. Differentiating: McGuire et al. (2006), pp. 687 et seq.

[94]Koziol (2011), p. 88; Pahlow (2006), pp. 340 et seq.; Harke (2015), pp. 99 et seq.; Schulze (2015a) § 31, para 52; Fezer (2009), § 30, paras 6 et seq.; BGH, 26-03-2009 – I ZR 153/06 –, GRUR 2009, 946, 948; OLG Hamburg, 19-12-2003 – 5 U 43/03 – GRUR-RR 2004, 175, 178.

[95]McGuire (2012), p. 476; Sosnitza (2005), p. 195; Hacker (2014), § 30, para 21; Brinkmann (2015), § 47, para 76.

[96]Sec. 30 subsec. 5 Trademark Act; sec. 15 subsec. 3 Patent Act; sec. 33 Copyright Act; sec. 31 subsec. 5 Design Act.

disputed whether sublicences cease to exist upon the termination of the main licence.[97]

3 Security Rights on IP Rights

Under German law,[98] patents,[99] utility models,[100] trademarks,[101] and designs,[102] as well as the respective European IP rights[103,104] and the preliminary stages of all of these,[105] can be the object of a:

- pledge of rights,
- security assignment, or
- security usufruct.

Furthermore, IP rights can be used as collateral when the creditor is granted a licence for security purposes, which is known as a security licence.

Since copyright is not transferable,[106] such a security licence is the only type of security right available with respect to copyright. However, some neighbouring

---

[97] Against automatic lapse: BGH – 9.7.2012 – I ZR 24/11, GRUR 2012, 914 (Copyrights); BGH, 19.7.2012 – I ZR 70/10, GRUR 2012, 916 (Copyrights); Ingerl and Rohnke (2010), § 30, para 49 (trademarks). For lapse: Dammler and Melullis (2013), p. 781 (patents). McGuire and Kunzmann (2014), p. 28, propose a solution using a takeover of the licence contract. Following this approach: Ullmann and Deichfuß (2015), § 15, para 107 (patents). Differentiating: Picht (2018), pp. 177 et seq.

[98] For further information on security rights on IP in a cross-border context, see Drexl (2016), paras 216 et seq.

[99] Sec. 15 subsec. 1 sentence 2 Patent Act.

[100] Sec. 22 subsec. 1 sentence 2 Utility Model Act.

[101] Sec. 27 subsec. 1 Trademark Act. Sec. 29 subsec. 1 no. 1 Trademark Act specifically states the possibility of limited proprietary rights, especially pledges.

[102] Sec. 29, 31 Design Protection Act. Sec. 30 subsec. 1 no. 1 Design Protection Act specifically states the possibility of limited proprietary rights, especially pledges.

[103] By the term "European IP rights," we mean EU IP rights, such as EU trademarks, EU designs, and the European Patent.

[104] For example, Art. 17 subsec. 1 Council Regulation (EC) No. 207/2009 of February 26, 2009 on the Community Trade Mark as amended by Regulation (EU) 2015/2424 (hereinafter EU Trademark Regulation), and Art. 71, 72 Convention on the Grant of European Patents (European Patent Convention) of October 5, 1973 as revised by the Act Revising Article 63 EPC of December 17, 1991 and the Act Revising the EPC of November 29, 2000.

[105] Preliminary stages are, for example, the right to the patent and right to the granting of a patent, sec. 6 subsec. 1 Patent Act. If a full legal right is granted, the security right in a preliminary right continues in the full IP right, BGH, 24-03-1994 – X ZR 108/91 – GRUR 1994, 602, 604; Fitzner (2017), § 6, para 68; Ballestrem (2009), p. 133; Hofmann (2009), pp. 223, 261, 276; Kraßer and Ann (2016), p. 981.

[106] Sec. 29 subsec. 2 Copyright Act.

rights are transferable[107] and can, therefore, be pledged, assigned, or encumbered by a security usufruct or a security licence.

Licences may also be used as collateral. Depending on their transferability,[108] they can be the object of a pledge, security assignment, security usufruct, or security sublicence.

As an alternative to taking a security in IP rights, the parties may either encumber the royalty claims of the IP right-owner against a licensee or encumber the payments resulting from the contract adjustment claim[109] in copyright law.[110] Such a pledge of receivables, however, is widely perceived as impractical, as sec. 1280 of the German Civil Code (*Bürgerliches Gesetzbuch*; hereinafter GerCivC) requires notification of the third-party debtor of the pledge.[111]

3.1 Pledge of Rights (**Pfandrecht an Rechten**)

3.1.1 Creation[112]

A pledge of rights according to sec. 1273 GerCivC is a contractually created limited proprietary right.

A pledge is an accessory security right in the sense that it requires an existing secured claim. The secured claim may also be a future claim.[113] If the claim is assigned or ceases to exist, the pledge automatically expires. The pledge of rights secures the whole claim, as it exists in any given moment, including interests or contractual penalties, unless otherwise agreed upon.[114]

The pledge contract only needs to be in writing if the pledged IP rights are EU trademarks, European patent applications, or Community plant variety rights.[115] In

[107]Sec. 72 subsec. 2 Copyright Act (Posthumous Works); sec. 87 subsec. 2 sentence 1 Copyright Act (broadcasts); sec. 87g subsec. 1 sentence 1 Copyright Act (publishers).

[108]See Sect. 2.5.

[109]Sec. 32 subsec. 1 sentence 2 Copyright Act.

[110]Sec. 1273, 1213 subsec. 1 GerCivC. See Decker (2012), pp. 48 et seq.

[111]Decker (2012), p. 49.

[112]German law does not distinguish between creation and third-party effectiveness. Thus, a right in rem, such as a pledge or a usufruct, is perfected once it is created. The same is true for an outright assignment of an IP right for security purposes (security assignment): if the assignment is effective between the assignor and the assignee, it is also effective against third parties.

[113]Sec. 1204 subsec. 2 GerCivC.

[114]Sec. 1210 subsec. 1 GerCivC.

[115]Art. 17 subsec. 3 EU Trademark Directive; art. 72 European Patent Convention; art. 23 subsec. 2 Community Plant Variety Regulation. See also Decker (2012), p. 39; cf. Grabinski (2012), Art. 72, para 1.

practice, however, pledge contracts are almost always in writing, even if the law does not require it to be done in a specific form.[116]

The priority of a pledge is determined by the time of its creation, even if it is created for a future or conditional claim.[117] Therefore, a pledge has priority over any subsequently created security right, the rights of judgment creditors, and the insolvency trustee in any subsequently opened insolvency proceedings.[118]

While the registration of a pledge of rights with the German Patent and Trademark Office or the corresponding European Register is possible,[119] such registration is not necessary for the creation or perfection of a pledge.[120] This registration lacks any effect vis-à-vis third parties[121]: neither a *bona fide* acquisition of a pledge nor an unencumbered *bona fide* acquisition of a German IP right is possible, regardless of the registration of the pledge.[122] In contrast, the registration of a pledge of European IP rights effectively protects a pledge of rights from a *bona fide* acquisition by a third party.[123]

3.1.2 Rights Before Default

The pledgor remains the owner of the IP right at all times before a default. Correspondingly to the pledgor's remaining ownership, the pledgee holds no exploitation rights with respect to the pledged IP right. This distribution of rights correlates in most instances with the intentions of the parties, since the pledgee is usually not interested in exploiting the right himself. Likewise, an antichresis (pledge of emoluments, *Nutzungspfandrecht*)[124] extends only to the licensing royalties of pledged IP rights and does not give the pledgee the right to exploit the IP right.[125] If the pledgee wishes to exploit the IP right, the parties need to enter into a licence agreement.

Furthermore, the pledgor remains primarily responsible for remedying infringements of the IP right.[126] The pledgee may, however, also remedy infringements of

[116]Klawitter and Hombrecher (2004), p. 1214.

[117]Lwowski (2011), § 2, para 33.

[118]Cf. Tetzlaff (2013), § 170, para 20.

[119]Sec. 29 subsec. 2 Trademark Act; art. 19 subsec. 2 EU Trademark Regulation; art. 23 subsec. 2 EU Trademark Directive; sec. 30 subsec. 2 Design Act; art. 29 subsec. 2 Community Design Regulation; sec. 30 subsec. 2 Patent Act in connection with sec. 29 German Patent and Trademark Office Regulation; see Decker (2012), p. 40 regarding utility models.

[120]Decker (2012), p. 39.

[121]See sec. 27 subsec. 3 Trademark Act; sec. 30 subsec. 3 Patent Act. Hacker (2014), § 27, para 24; Decker (2012), p. 40; Kraßer and Ann (2016), p. 980.

[122]Decker (2012), p. 40.

[123]Decker (2012), p. 40; Fammler (2006), pp. 536 et seq.; Taxhet (2017), Art. 23 UMV, para 10; Hacker (2014), § 27, para 70. But see Schennen (2014), Art. 23, paras 7 et seq.

[124]Sec. 1273 subsec. 2, sec. 1213 GerCivC.

[125]Decker (2012), p. 41; cf. Knüpfer (2003), pp. 126 et seq.

[126]Woeste (2002), pp. 91 et seq.; Decker (2012), p. 41.

the pledgor's IP rights pursuant to sec. 1273 subsec. 2, sec. 1227 GerCivC if his pledged IP rights are impaired.[127]

An alteration or cancellation of the pledged right that would affect the pledge requires the approval of the pledgee.[128] Unless the parties have agreed otherwise, the pledgor must pay the renewal fee to the Patent and Trademark Office.[129] Given that non-payment leads to the termination of a patent and with that the termination of the pledge of rights, the pledgee should consider paying the fees himself as a last resort. The Patent and Trademark Office cannot refuse payment made by the pledgee.[130]

A related issue exists regarding the non-usage of trademarks. Since trademarks expire when the owner refrains from using the trademarks for 5 years, the pledgee might find himself in a situation where he will lose his pledge of rights in the event of the trademark's expiration. Lacking exploitation rights, the pledgee cannot stop the expiration. As a workaround, some authors suggest that the pledgee can sell the pledged IP right in a public auction due to the imminent "spoilage" of the pledged rights (sec. 1273 subsec. 2, sec. 1219 subsec. 1 GerCivC.)[131]

Before default, the pledgee may at any time transfer the pledge by assigning the secured claim, as laid down in sec. 1273 subsec. 2, sec. 1250 subsec. 1 GerCivC.

The pledgor can transfer his ownership of the pledged IP rights irrespective of the pledge.[132] However, the new owner will acquire the IP right encumbered with the pledge, even if he is in good faith regarding the pledge.

Whether the pledgor is also allowed to license the pledged IP right is highly controversial. Given that the licensing of pledged IP rights is detrimental to the value of the pledge, *Klawitter* and *Hombrecher* have argued against the admissibility of licensing.[133] According to them, sec. 1276 subsec. 2 GerCivC prohibits licensing altogether.[134] Others see no fundamental problem with the licensing of pledged IP rights by the pledgor.[135] *Decker*, however, suggests a compromise between the two positions. In his opinion, the pledgor may license the IP rights, but any licences entered into after the pledgor has pledged the IP rights to the pledgee are null and

---

[127]Voß and Kühnen (2014), § 139, para 12. Ambiguous Decker (2012), pp. 41 et seq.; Kraßer and Ann (2016), p. 916; Woeste (2002), p. 92; Berger (1994), pp. 1015–1016; Hacker (2014), § 29, para 4.

[128]Sec. 1276 subsec. 1 sentence 1 GerCivC.

[129]Woeste (2002), p. 92; Decker (2012), pp. 41 et seq.

[130]Woeste (2002), p. 92.

[131]Woeste (2002), pp. 92 et seq. In favour of the applicability of sec. 1219 GerCivC for a pledge of rights: Wiegand (2009), § 1273, para 19; Habersack (2001), § 1273, para 10; Wicke (2017), § 1273, para 2. Against the applicability of sec. 1219 GerCivC: Michalski (2011), § 1273, para 7; Sosnitza (2012), § 1273, para 6; Damrau (2015), § 1273, para 8.

[132]Decker (2012), p. 42.

[133]Klawitter and Hombrecher (2004), p. 1215.

[134]Klawitter and Hombrecher (2004), p. 1215. But see Decker (2012), p. 44; Damrau (2015), § 1276, para 1.

[135]Woeste (2002), p. 90; McGuire et al. (2006), p. 689. Cf. Damrau (2015), § 1276, para 1; Wicke (2017), § 1273, para 1.

void from the moment of the debtor's default.[136] *Decker* argues that the pledgor can only license encumbered IP rights to a third party. Therefore, a third party's licence is tainted with the pledge, and only exists contingent on the non-enforcement of the pledge.[137]

3.1.3 Enforcement Outside Insolvency

Pursuant to sec. 1277 GerCivC, "[t]he pledgee may seek his satisfaction from the right only on the basis of an enforceable judgment in accordance with the provisions governing execution, unless otherwise provided." The pledgee can and should urge the pledgor to enter into an agreement that allows realization of the pledge without an enforceable judgment.[138] However, according to sec. 1277 sentence 2 GerCivC, the parties may not—before default—agree on realization by way of private sale,[139] or enter into a forfeiture agreement (*lex commissoria*).[140]

Absent a post-default agreement of the parties, the pledgee must, according to sec. 857 Civil Procedure Act, enforce the pledge by way of public auction.[141]

3.1.4 Enforcement in Insolvency

Pursuant to sec. 50 German Insolvency Act, "[c]reditors holding a contractual pledge [...] in an object forming part of the insolvency estate [are] entitled to separate satisfaction in respect of the main claim, interest and costs from the pledged object under sections 166 to 173."[142] The pledgee's secured claim has priority in insolvency proceedings in the sense that the value of the collateral is primarily used to satisfy this claim.

For a pledge of IP rights, it is an open and unresolved question as to who may sell or otherwise dispose of the collateral: the trustee or the secured creditor himself. Some argue that the trustee may dispose of the encumbered IP right in analogy to sec. 166 subsec. 1 Insolvency Act, particularly if the IP right is essential to the debtor's business. Others are of the opinion that the secured creditor may dispose of

[136]Decker (2012), p. 46.

[137]Decker (2012), pp. 44 et seq.

[138]Alternatively, the pledgor can subject himself to immediate compulsory enforcement in a notarial record; sec. 794 subsec. 1 no. 5 Civil Procedure Act; Decker (2012), p. 138.

[139]Sec. 1277 sentence 2, sec 1245 subsec. 2, sec. 1235 subsec. 2, sec. 1221 GerCivC. See Knüpfer (2003), pp. 127 et seq.

[140]Sec. 1229 GerCivC.

[141]See Decker (2012), pp. 137 et seq.; Smid (2016), § 857, para. 49. For details regarding all enforcement options, see Picht (2018), pp. 405–422.

[142]Sec. 50 subsec. 1 Insolvency Act. See Brinkmann (2015), § 50, para 5 for the applicability of sec. 50 subsec. 1 Insolvency Act to pledges of rights.

the IP right himself, pursuant to sec. 173 Insolvency Act.[143] In practice, the trustee and secured creditor settle this problem by entering into an enforcement agreement.

In any event, the secured claim will eventually be satisfied up to the amount of the IP right's value. If, however, the collateral is sold or otherwise disposed of in insolvency proceedings by the trustee, 9% of the proceeds will be retained for the estate.[144] If the trustee delays the disposition of the collateral, he must pay interest and compensate the creditor for any resulting loss of the collateral's value.[145]

3.2 *Security Assignment* (Sicherungsübertragung)

3.2.1 Creation

Some of the requirements and effects of a pledge are perceived as burdensome and impractical. To avoid these problems (namely, the restrictions on realization after default[146]) legal practice has taken recourse to a (fiduciary) transfer of the right for security purposes. In contrast to the pledge, which merely creates a limited right in rem on the collateral while the pledgor remains the holder, a security assignment gives the secured party fiduciary title to the IP right.

In order to secure a debt by way of a fiduciary assignment, the parties must enter into a security agreement. The security agreement governs the relationship between the parties for the duration of the security assignment. *Inter alia*, it establishes a fiduciary relationship between them.

The assignment itself only requires an agreement by the parties.[147] Unlike with the pledge, the security right and the secured claim are independent from each other in the sense that the effectiveness of the transfer does not depend on the existence of the secured claim. If the right is transferred to the secured creditor but the secured claim either does not come into existence or subsequently expires, the secured creditor is obliged to retransfer the right to the grantor.

---

[143]In favour of the analogy: Brämer (2005), pp. 367 et seq.; Hirte and Knof (2008), pp. 52 et seq.; Hirte (2008), pp. 239–254, 250; Lüke (2008), p. 356; Picht (2018), pp. 453 et seq.; Dithmar (2017), § 166, para 26; Büchler (2017), § 166, para 20; Flöther (2017), § 166, para 14; Becker (2017), § 166, paras 34 et seq.; Sinz (2016), § 166, para 37; Brinkmann (2015), § 166, para 35 et seq. Opposing the analogy: Ballestrem (2009), pp. 233 et seq.; Decker (2012), pp. 153 et seq.; Woeste (2002), p. 112; Berger (2007), p. 1536; Sessig and Fischer (2011), pp. 623 et seq.; Wallner (1999), pp. 453 et seq.; Landfermann (2016), § 166, para 34; Tetzlaff (2013), § 166, paras 64 et seq.; AG Karlsruhe, 07-02-2008 – 12 C 490/07 – ZIP 2009, 143.

[144]Sec. 170, 171 Insolvency Act.

[145]Sec. 169, 172 Insolvency Act.

[146]See Sect. 2.1.3.

[147]Sec. 398 sentence 1, 413 GerCivC.

Neither the assignment of German IP rights nor the security agreement must be carried out in a specific form[148]; however, a written and signed agreement is required with respect to the transfer of European IP applications.[149] These assignments are only effective if the grantor is the true holder of the IP right, since no *bona fide* acquisition of IP rights exists under German law.[150]

Regarding German IP rights, the security assignment is effective between the parties as well as against third parties once the assignment takes place. While it is not necessary for the effectiveness of the assignment,[151] it is nevertheless possible to register the secured creditor as the new holder in the relevant IP register[152]—either indicating that he is the full owner or indicating the security nature of the transfer.[153] The ***registration*** of the transfer of a patent or trademark, however, has no effect on the substantive legal situation.[154] Third parties cannot acquire the right in good faith from the registered person if that person is not the true owner.[155] However, there are certain procedural and material effects tied to registration.[156]

With regard to European IP rights, registration is possible,[157] but again not necessary for the effectiveness of the transfer.[158] However, until registration has taken place, the transfer is not effective vis-à-vis third parties. Arguably, it is

[148]Sec. 398 sentence 1, 413 GerCivC with sec. 15 subsec. 1 sentence 2 Patent Act, sec. 27 subsec. 1 Trademark Act.

[149]Art. 72 European Patent Convention; art. 17 subsec. 3 EU Trademark Regulation.

[150]Ballestrem (2009), pp. 146 et seq.; Brämer (2005), pp. 155 et seq.; Ullmann and Deichfuß (2015), § 15, para 8; Ingerl and Rohnke (2010), § 27, para 14; Mes (2015), § 15, para 32; Müller (2015), § 27, para 2; BPatG, 06-09-2007 – 10 W (pat) 53/06.

[151]Patents: BGHZ 197, 196, 206; Kraßer and Ann (2016), p. 492; Schäfers (2015), § 30, para. 8; Mes (2015), § 30, para 18. Trademarks: Brämer (2005), p. 154; Fezer (2009), § 27, para 41; Ingerl and Rohnke (2010), § 27, para 26.

[152]Ballestrem (2009), p. 145; Brämer (2005), p. 154; Decker (2012), p. 30; Woeste (2002), pp. 76, 80; Rudloff-Schäffer (2014), § 30, para 24; but see (for patents) Klawitter and Hombrecher (2004), pp. 1216 et seq. with reference to BPatG, 07-02-2000 – 10 W (pat) 113/99. The transfer of a trademark can only be registered if the trademark has previously been registered.

[153]Ballestrem (2009), pp. 145 et seq.

[154]BPatG, 14-08-1974 – 4 W (pat) 117/73, MittdtPatA 1975, 90, 91. But see Enchelmaier (2014), p. 537.

[155]Patents: Ballestrem (2009), pp. 147 et seq.; Kraßer and Ann (2016), p. 980; Ullmann and Deichfuß (2015), § 15, para. 8; BPatG, 06-09-2007 – 10 W (pat) 53/06 – mn. 27. Trademarks: Woeste (2002), p. 80; Ingerl and Rohnke (2010), § 27, para 14.

[156]See Sects. 2.1 and 2.2.

[157]Rule 22 Implementing Regulations to the European Patent Convention; Art. 17 subsec. 5 EU Trademark Regulation.

[158]Patents: Grabinski (2012), Art. 71, paras 8, 14. Trademarks: Fammler (2006), p. 536; Schennen (2014), Art. 17; para 22; Hacker (2014), § 27, para 69; but also see McGuire (2008), p. 11; Zorzi (1997), p. 794.

possible to acquire European IP rights in good faith from a registered party who is not the real owner.[159]

German courts have developed several limits on the effectiveness of fiduciary transfers of assets for security purposes. The most important one is the doctrine of excessive collateralization (*Übersicherung*, or "overcollateralization"), which applies to situations in which the value of the collateral grossly exceeds the amount of the secured claim.[160] An initial overcollateralization renders the security right void. As a rule of thumb, the creditor is initially overcollateralized if at the time of the transfer the prospective realization value of the collateral exceeds the amount of the secured claim by 300%. Excessive collateralization may also occur later on due to either a rise in the value of the collateral or a decline of the secured claim. In case of such subsequent overcollateralization, which is deemed to exist if the collateral is worth more than 150% of the amount of the secured claim, the security right is not void, but the secured creditor has to retransfer part of the collateral.[161] If the collateral consists of only one single IP right, however, he will not be obliged to do so unless the grantor can offer sufficient alternative collateral.[162]

3.2.2 Rights Before Default

The mutual rights and obligations of the parties to a security assignment are governed by the security agreement. This agreement will usually provide for several rights and obligations, discussed below.

If an IP right is subject to a security assignment, the grantor loses all rights in rem in the collateral. Hence, he cannot create any junior rights in rem in that IP right.

The grantor may continue to use the IP right as before. To this end, the secured creditor will license the right back to the grantor[163]; this can be done in the same contract and no particular form is required.[164] The grantor does not have to pay any

[159]Brämer (2005), pp. 477 et seq.; Decker (2012), p. 40; Albrecht and Hombrecher (2005), p. 1693; Fammler (2006), pp. 536 et seq.; Taxhet (2017), Art. 23, para 10; Hacker (2014), § 27, para 70; ambiguous Schennen (2014), Art. 23, paras 7 et seq.

[160]Busche (2012), Einl zu §§ 398ff., paras 78 et seq.; Roth and Kieninger (2016), § 298, paras 119 et seq., 128 et seq.

[161]BGH, 27-11-1997 – GSZ 1 u. 2/97 – NJW 1998, 671, 672.

[162]Ballestrem (2009), pp. 201 et seq.; Brämer (2005), p. 317; Decker (2012), p. 90. Even though some IP rights can be split, the secured creditor does not have to retransfer a partial IP right to the grantor if doing so will endanger the realization of the security right; Brämer (2005), pp. 319 et seq.

[163]Ballestrem (2009), pp. 152 et seq.; Woeste (2002), pp. 94, 98, 107. Brämer (2005), pp. 186 et seq. also identifies other means through which a right of use can be designed for the assignor; Decker (2012), p. 34, has doubts whether this is even necessary, but still recommends contractually agreeing on a licence.

[164]If the collateral is a future patent or trademark, the right may be licensed back to the grantor even before the IP right starts to exist. Ballestrem (2009), p. 160; Brämer (2005), pp. 214 et seq.; BGH, 14-11-1968 – KZR 1/68 – BGHZ 51, 263, 264; BGH, 17-03-1961 – I ZR 94/59 –, GRUR 1961, 466, 467.

licence fees.[165] In order to ensure the full effect of the security right in case of default, the parties will adopt either a condition linking the duration of the licence to the time of default[166] or a right for the secured creditor to terminate the licence.[167]

An exclusive licence will arguably also give the grantor the right to create sublicences.[168] These sublicences are, again arguably, subject to the effectiveness of the main licence[169] and will therefore cease to exist in case of default, making them less valuable for the interested parties.[170] It is possible for the secured creditor to authorize the grantor to create independent licences, which will not be affected by a default.[171] The parties may also agree that such authorization depends on the assignment of the resulting third-party licence fees.[172] Absent any express or implied assignment of licence fees, the secured creditor is not entitled to the fees of licences that were granted by the grantor before or after the security assignment.[173] The security assignment does not affect any pre-existing licences (*Sukzessionsschutz*).[174]

The grantor is obliged to use the IP rights[175] since a lack of use may endanger not only the value of these IP rights but also their very existence.[176] It could also result in compulsory licences.[177] Under the security agreement, the grantor will usually have to pay the renewal fee to the Patent and Trademark Office.[178] If he is still registered as the holder of the right, he is formally legitimized to do so.[179] If the secured creditor has been registered, the grantor may still pay the fee as an interested

[165]Ballestrem (2009), p. 153; Brämer (2005), p. 190.

[166]Ballestrem (2009), pp. 155 et seq.; Brämer (2005), p. 194; Decker (2012), p. 34; according to Woeste (2002), pp. 94, 98, the security agreement has to be interpreted as to include such a provision in cases of doubt.

[167]Albrecht and Hombrecher (2005), p. 1693; Brämer (2005), p. 194.

[168]For patents: Ullmann and Deichfuß (2015), § 15, para 104; Mes (2015), § 15, para 41; BGH, 07-11-1952 – I ZR 43/52 – GRUR 53, 114, 118; BGH, 16-04-2002 – X ZR 127/99 – GRUR 2002, 801, 803. For trade marks: Brämer (2005), p. 195 et seq.; Ingerl and Rohnke (2010), § 30, para 49; Woeste (2002), p. 98; but see Fezer (2009), § 30, para 24.

[169]See Sect. 2.5.

[170]Ballestrem (2009), pp. 157 et seq.; Decker (2012), p. 37.

[171]Sec. 185 subsec. 1 GerCivC; Ballestrem (2009), p. 158 et seq.; Woeste (2002), pp. 73, 95, 99; Albrecht and Hombrecher (2005), p. 1693; cf. RG, 01-11-1933 – I 119/33 – RGZ 142, 168, 170.

[172]Woeste (2002), pp. 73 et seq., 95; Albrecht and Hombrecher (2005), p. 1694; cf. also Koziol (2011), p. 112. A detailed explanation of how such an agreement works (regarding sales) can be found in Kieninger (2004), p. 304.

[173]Ballestrem (2009), pp. 136 et seq.; Brämer (2005), pp. 149 et seq.; Woeste (2002), pp. 71 et seq.; Albrecht and Hombrecher (2005), p. 1694.

[174]Sec. 15 subsec. 3 Patent Act; sec. 30 subsec. 5 Trademark Act; sec. 33 Copyright Act.

[175]Ballestrem (2009), p. 163; Brämer (2005), pp. 223 et seq.; Woeste (2002), pp. 96, 100; Albrecht and Hombrecher (2005), p. 1695.

[176]Sec. 26 subsec. 1, sec. 49 Trademark Act.

[177]Sec. 24 subsec. 5 Patent Act.

[178]Ballestrem (2009), pp. 163 et seq.; Brämer (2005), p. 235; Woeste (2002), pp. 96, 99.

[179]Woeste (2002), pp. 96, 99.

party.[180] As he is the legal owner of the IP right, the secured creditor may also pay the fee even if the transfer has not been registered.[181] Furthermore, the grantor is also obliged to defend the IP right extra-judicially and in court.[182] Patent or trademark infringement claims can be pursued by a licensee,[183] and thus the grantor can, by virtue of his licence, pursue them regardless of whether the security assignment has been registered. If the grantor does not fulfill these obligations, the secured creditor can use the IP right himself, claim damages, and/or terminate the licence agreement.[184] Under the security agreement, the secured creditor may demand information relevant to the IP right from the grantor.[185]

As the secured creditor is merely the fiduciary owner of the IP right, he is therefore not allowed to use the IP right or to create licences of his own.[186] However, being the legal owner of the right, he has the power to validly grant licences or a pledge. The grantor in turn only has contractual remedies against the secured creditor.[187] Likewise, even though it is prohibited, it is technically possible for the secured creditor to transfer ownership of the IP right to a third party.[188] While a licence previously granted to the grantor remains effective despite such a transfer,[189] the secured creditor who has transferred the IP right to a third party is unable to return the full IP right to the grantor. Therefore, the grantor has a dilatory plea against the secured claim until the secured creditor is able to return the IP right unimpaired to him.[190] He may also claim damages.[191]

[180] Brämer (2005), p. 234; Woeste (2002), pp. 96, 99.

[181] Woeste (2002), pp. 96, 99.

[182] Ballestrem (2009), pp. 164 et seq.; Brämer (2005), pp. 240 et seq. (differentiating between different kinds of defence mechanisms); Woeste (2002), pp. 97, 101.

[183] For patents cf. RG, 16-01-1904 – I 373/03 – RGZ 57, 38, 40; BGH, 20-12-1994 – X ZR 56/93 – GRUR 1995, 338, 340. For trademarks: Sec. 30 subsec. 3 Trademark Act, which requires the authorization of the holder of the trademark. This authorization is usually implicitly included in the security agreement; cf. Brämer (2005), p. 238; Woeste (2002), p. 101; Lwowski and Hoes (1999), p. 773.

[184] Ballestrem (2009), pp. 189 et seq.; Brämer (2005), pp. 286 et seq.

[185] See Ballestrem (2009), p. 169.

[186] Ballestrem (2009), p. 190; Brämer (2005), p. 280.

[187] Ballestrem (2009), p. 190; Brämer (2005), pp. 280 et seq.; Decker (2012), pp. 36 et seq.

[188] Brämer (2005), pp. 266 et seq.

[189] Sec. 15 subsec. 3 Patent Act; sec. 30 subsec. 5 Trademark Act; sec. 33 Copyright Act; sec. 31 subsec. 5 Design Act.

[190] Ballestrem (2009), pp. 192 et seq.

[191] Brämer (2005), pp. 275 et seq.

Once the secured claim has been paid, the secured creditor is obliged under the security agreement to reassign the right to the grantor.[192] This reassignment does not have an effect on any licences granted to third parties.[193]

3.2.3 Enforcement Outside Insolvency

As a consequence of default, the grantor's licences and any sublicences created by him will (subject to the licence agreement) cease to exist.[194]

Before realization commences, the grantor has to be informed of the imminent enforcement so that he has the chance to settle the debt and thereby avoid the loss of the IP right.[195]

The secured creditor can choose between different ways of getting satisfaction out of the encumbered IP right.[196] He remains, however, bound by the security agreement and must therefore take into consideration the interests of the grantor.[197] This pertains in particular to the realization method: the secured creditor must choose the one that promises the highest proceeds,[198] given that the grantor is entitled to any surplus over the secured claim.[199] The secured claim only ceases to exist up to the amount that the secured creditor is actually satisfied. The most promising method is the private sale of the encumbered right.[200] Since the secured creditor is already the legal owner, he does not need the grantor's cooperation for the sale. Registration of the purchaser can be carried out without previous registration of the secured creditor.[201]

---

[192]Ballestrem (2009), pp. 209 et seq.; Brämer (2005), p. 386; Decker (2012), p. 123; Albrecht and Hombrecher (2005), pp. 1689–1695; Lwowski and Hoes (1999), p. 773. Theoretically, the parties may also provide for an automatic retransfer, but this option is rarely used in practice.

[193]Ballestrem (2009), pp. 213 et seq.; Brämer (2005), pp. 388 et seq.

[194]Ballestrem (2009), pp. 216 et seq.; Brämer (2005), p. 401; Decker (2012), p. 126. Whether the sublicences cease to exist has recently been called into question (cf. Sect. 2.5). The agreement of the parties usually has to be understood as granting the grantor (and any sublicensees) a right to discharge any remaining products linked to the IP right until the time of full realization; Ballestrem (2009), pp. 216 et seq.; Brämer (2005), p. 406.

[195]Brämer (2005), p. 400; Decker (2012), p. 125.

[196]Ballestrem (2009), p. 217 et seq.; Brämer (2005), p. 433; Woeste (2002), p. 123; but see Decker (2012), pp. 132 et seq.

[197]Ballestrem (2009), pp. 217 et seq.; Brämer (2005), p. 433; Decker (2012), p. 125; Woeste (2002), p. 123; Albrecht and Hombrecher (2005), p. 1693.

[198]Decker (2012), p. 125; Woeste (2002), p. 123; Klawitter and Hombrecher (2004), p. 1217.

[199]Brämer (2005), p. 411; Decker (2012), p. 137.

[200]Ballestrem (2009), pp. 217 et seq.; Brämer (2005), p. 412; Decker (2012), p. 126; Woeste (2002), p. 123. In case of trademarks, a partial sale may be considered if it will yield enough for the satisfaction of the secured creditor's claim. Brämer (2005), pp. 413 et seq.; Decker (2012), p. 128; Lwowski and Hoes (1999), p. 773; Rohnke (1993), p. 563.

[201]Brämer (2005), p. 442; Woeste (2002), p. 124; but see Decker (2012), p. 127.

As the *lex commissoria* is not forbidden in the context of a security assignment,[202] the secured creditor may also assume the full IP right in order to exploit it himself.[203] The secured claim ceases to exist at the amount of the proceeds of a fictional sale.[204]

Granting licences to third parties is another option for the secured creditor. The secured creditor may either create new licences and use the licence fees to satisfy his claim,[205] or seek satisfaction from pre-existing licences, provided that the grantor has assigned him the licence fee claims.[206] In both alternatives, the encumbered IP right has to be transferred back to the grantor once the secured debt is paid.[207]

3.2.4 Enforcement in Insolvency

In insolvency proceedings, pursuant to sec. 50, 51 no. 1, alt. 2 Insolvency Act, a creditor who is secured by an assignment will be treated not in the same way as the owner of the right, but in the same way as a pledgee.

Therefore, the secured claim has priority in insolvency proceedings. However, it is disputed whether the creditor or insolvency trustee may sell the IP right. Regardless of this dispute, the secured claim will be satisfied up to the amount of the IP right's value.[208]

*3.3 Usufruct for Security Purposes (*Sicherungsnießbrauch*)*

3.3.1 Creation

Another possible way to secure a claim is by creating a usufruct for security purposes. A usufruct is a right in rem that entitles the beneficiary to the civil fruits of the right covered by the usufruct, i.e. to any revenues of this right, such as licence

[202]See Brinkmann (2011), p. 121, para 178; Picht (2018), p. 426.

[203]Ballestrem (2009), pp. 220 et seq.; Brämer (2005), p. 416; Decker (2012), p. 128.

[204]Brämer (2005), p. 416. The amount of the proceeds will, however, be very difficult to estimate.

[205]Brämer (2005), p. 419; Decker (2012), p. 131; Woeste (2002), p. 123.

[206]This is not truly a form of realization from the security assignment of the IP right; cf. Brämer (2005), p. 424; Decker (2012), p. 137; according to BGH – 9. 7.2012 – I ZR 24/11 – GRUR 2012, 914 and BGH, 19. 7.2012 – I ZR 70/10 – GRUR 2012, 916, the secured creditor might even have a right to demand the assignment. However, whether these rulings can be applied to licences on IP rights other than copyright and whether they can be applied in a security context is uncertain.

[207]Brämer (2005), pp. 419, 423; Decker (2012), pp. 131, 137.

[208]For details, see Sect. 3.1.4.

fees.[209] A usufruct can be established with regard to any right that is transferable.[210] It encompasses all fruits and benefits of the object,[211] including indirect benefits.

Like a security assignment, the security usufruct requires two agreements: an agreement on the creation of the usufruct and a security agreement that establishes the link between the usufruct and the secured claim. With regard to German IP rights, neither agreement must be carried out in a specific form.[212] For European IP rights, a written agreement on the creation of the usufruct is necessary.[213] It is possible to register a security usufruct on German and EU trademarks and on European patents.[214] Registration is, however, not required for the usufruct to become effective.[215]

Some scholars[216] argue that the usufruct may also be used to protect the licensee from the risk of the licence being rendered void by the insolvency trustee in the licensor's insolvency proceedings.[217]

As with pledges, the priority of a usufruct is determined by the time of its creation, so the usufruct takes precedence over any subsequent right.[218]

3.3.2 Rights Before Default

The relationship between the parties is governed by the security agreement. The parties will usually adopt either a suspensory condition for the usufruct, to the effect that it will only become effective after default, or an obligation for the usufructuary to abstain from using his rights until that time.[219] Pursuant to sec. 1030, subsec. 2 GerCivC, the parties can agree to restrict the usufruct to specific means of use.

Thus, the owner of the IP right may still use the full right himself, create licences,[220] or even transfer it,[221] the usufruct notwithstanding. A transfer of the right to a third party does not impact the validity of the usufruct. However, an

---

[209] Sec. 1030 subsec. 1 GerCivC.

[210] Sec. 1069 subsec. 2 GerCivC.

[211] Sec. 100 GerCivC.

[212] Sec. 1069 subsec. 1, sec. 413, 398 GerCivC with sec. 15 subsec. 1 sentence 2 Patent Act, sec. 27 subsec. 1 Trademark Act.

[213] Art. 17 sec. 3 Community Trademark Regulation; Art. 72 European Patent Convention.

[214] Sec. 29 subsec 2 Trademark Act; art. 19 sec. 2 EU Trademark Regulation; cf. § 29 Verordnung über das Deutsche Patent- und Markenamt (DPMAV).

[215] Decker (2012), p. 49; Fezer (2009), § 29, para 13; Rudloff-Schäffer (2014), § 30, para 17.

[216] Berger (2004), p. 20; but see Heim (2008), p. 339.

[217] The treatment of licences in insolvency proceedings is highly disputed; see *infra*, Sect. 3.3.3.

[218] Lwowski (2011), § 2, para 33.

[219] Decker (2012), p. 48; Frank (2009), § 1030, para 66.

[220] Decker (2012), p. 48; Fezer (2009), § 29, para 13.

[221] Decker (2012), p. 48, Fezer (2009), § 29, para 13; Frank (2009), Anh § 1068f., para 8.

alteration or cancellation of the encumbered right by the grantor requires the approval of the usufructuary (i.e. the secured creditor) if it affects the usufruct.[222]

The security agreement will usually provide that, contrary to sec. 1047 GerCivC, the owner of the IP right is obliged to defend the IP right and pay the necessary renewal fees.[223] However, the usufructuary may also do this if the owner does not comply with his duties under the security agreement.[224] As the usufruct automatically ceases to exist if the encumbered right is terminated, the IP right can only be altered or terminated with the consent of the usufructuary.[225]

The usufruct cannot be transferred.[226] If the secured claim is transferred, the former creditor is obliged to terminate the usufruct.[227] The new creditor acquires the claim as an unsecured claim and needs the grantor's consent in order to create a new usufruct.

Once the secured claim has been paid, either the usufruct ceases to exist pursuant to a resolutory condition or the usufructuary is obliged to agree to its termination.[228]

3.3.3 Enforcement

In case of default, the usufructuary has the right to exploit the IP right.[229] This includes personal use, creation of licences, and collection of licence fees.[230] Once the claim has been fulfilled, the usufruct is terminated. This arguably means that the licences cease to exist.[231]

In insolvency proceedings, the right of usage is separated from the insolvency estate (sec. 47 Insolvency Act).[232] The usufructuary can exploit the secured IP right as if the default occurred outside insolvency. He may satisfy his claim by using the right himself or by licensing it to third parties and collecting the licence fees.

[222]Sec. 1071 subsec. 1 sentence 1 GerCivC.

[223]Decker (2012), p. 48; Berger (2004), p. 22; such an agreement is only void in special circumstances due to public policy concerns; cf. Frank (2009), vor §§ 1030 ff., para 38.

[224]Ingerl and Rohnke (2010), § 29, para 8; Frank (2009), Anh § 1068, paras 14, 17. He doesn't even need the owner's consent as a licensee would according to sec. 30 subsec. 3 Trademark Act, cf. Hacker (2014), § 29, para 10.

[225]Sec. 1071 GerCivC.

[226]Sec. 1059 sentence 1 GerCivC.

[227]Frank (2009), § 1030, para 70.

[228]Hauck (2015), p. 211; Berger (2004), p. 24; Frank (2009), § 1030, para 67 et seq.

[229]Decker (2012), p. 48; Woeste (2002), p. 75; Fezer (2009), § 29, para 13.

[230]Berger (2004), p. 24; Ingerl and Rohnke (2010), § 29, para 8; Frank (2009), Anh §§ 1068 f., para 17; Hacker (2014), § 29, para 10.

[231]Frank (2009), § 1068, para 6.

[232]Brinkmann (2015), § 47, para 55; Thole (2016), § 47, para 47.

3.4 *Security Rights in Licences*

3.4.1 Creation

The requirements for security assignments, pledges, and usufructs pertaining to licences are by and large the same as for security rights in IP rights.[233] However, a few differences do exist.

Because the licences derive from IP rights owned by third parties, the third parties' consent to a transfer or encumbrance of the licence is required at least in some circumstances.[234] The Copyright Act explicitly requires third-party consent, yet allows for certain exceptions.[235] Even though other legislative acts on IP rights do not explicitly mention a consent requirement, whether consent is needed for the encumbrance of other IP licences is contested among academics.[236]

It is disputed whether the pledge of a licence is treated like the pledge of a claim and therefore requires notification of the debtor/licensor.[237]

3.4.2 Rights Before Default

The rights and duties of the pledgee and pledgor or usufructuary and grantor of a licence are equivalent to the rights and duties that these parties have regarding pledges of and usufructs on IP rights.[238]

Just like with a security assignment of IP rights, the rights and duties held by the parties undertaking a security assignment of licences depend on the security agreement. They tend to be distributed as follows: The grantor will remain responsible for the collateral, i.e. the licence.[239] However, if the grantor does not abide by his duties, the secured creditor may ensure its preservation.[240] The grantor/back-licensee does not owe any licence fees to the secured creditor, but remains responsible for the payment of the licence fees to the initial licensor.[241] Furthermore, the grantor will

---

[233] See Berger (2004), p. 23; Decker (2012), p. 65; Hauck (2015), pp. 341 et seq.

[234] Sec. 34 subsec. 1 sentence 1 Copyright Act; cf. Decker (2012), p. 60; Woeste (2002), p. 86; Schmidt (2003), p. 465 (also regarding the obligation to give consent); Schulze (2015b), § 34, para 7; disputed however by Decker (2012), pp. 61 et seq. Koziol (2011), p. 107 and Bühling (1998), p. 199 require the consent of the holder of the right for the transfer of a licence of a trademark (or patent) as well.

[235] Sec. 34 subsec. 1, subsec. 5 Copyright Act.

[236] Demanding consent of the IP right owner: Decker (2012), pp. 60 et seq.; Koziol (2011), p. 107; Berger (2004), p. 23; Bühling (1998), p. 199. Rejecting a consent requirement at least for exclusive licences: Kraßer and Ann (2016), pp. 987 et seq.; Ingerl and Rohnke (2010), § 30, para 49.

[237] See Wiegand (2009), § 1279, para 7 citing further authorities.

[238] See Decker (2012), p. 65.

[239] Koziol (2011), p. 112.

[240] Koziol (2011), p. 113.

[241] Koziol (2011), p. 111.

usually hold the right to sublicense the IP right[242] and the secured creditor will be contractually prohibited from sublicensing, even though it would legally be possible for him to do so.[243] Hence, any sublicences entered into by the security creditor are effective, but constitute a breach of his obligations.[244]

3.4.3 Enforcement

Outside insolvency, the procedures and limitations mentioned above also apply to the enforcement of security assignments and pledges of licences, as well as to the enforcement of usufructs on licences.

It is largely unclear what effects the insolvency of the licensor has on the rights of the licensee under German law. Two distinctions may, however, be helpful in order to assess how a German court might treat and enforce encumbered licences in insolvency. The first is the distinction made in the Insolvency Act between executory and non-executory contracts,[245] and the second is the distinction made by the courts between exclusive/proprietary licences and non-exclusive licences.

If either of the parties has fulfilled their part of the licence agreement, the insolvency trustee cannot refuse the licence.[246] Any pledges of or usufructs on the licence continue to exist together with the licence, irrespective of the licensor's insolvency, and can be enforced similarly to encumbered IP rights: either by way of separation in accordance with sec. 47 Insolvency Act (usufructs), or through separate satisfaction in accordance with sec. 50 Insolvency Act (pledges).[247] Any security assignment of the licence remains valid as well. A security assignment can be enforced in insolvency proceedings according to sec. 51 Insolvency Act.

If the licence used as collateral is based on an executory licence agreement that none of the parties has yet fulfilled, the insolvency trustee may **refuse the licence agreement** pursuant to sec. 103 subsec. 2 Insolvency Act.[248]

The **consequence of** such a **refusal** depends on the—heavily debated[249]—question whether a licence is a right in rem (i.e. whether it has proprietary character).[250]

---

[242]But cf. Decker (2012), p. 66 for copyright licences.

[243]Koziol (2011), p. 111. But see sec. 35 subsec. 1 Copyright Act for copyright licences, for which the possibility of sublicensing will usually be stipulated; see sec. 35 subsec. 2, 34 subsec. 5 sentence 2 Copyright Act.

[244]Koziol (2011), pp. 111 et seq.

[245]See sec. 103 Insolvency Act.

[246]Brinkmann (2015), § 47, para 76. But see Koziol (2011), p. 120; McGuire (2009), p. 21.

[247]Cf. Huber and Kreft (2013), § 103, para 76.

[248]In most cases, courts seem to consider a licensing agreement as having been fulfilled, rather than not; cf. BGH, Urteil v. 21-10-2015 – I ZR 173/14 – BGH NZI 2016, 97 (a one-time payment for a trademark suffices for contract fulfillment by the licensee).

[249]McGuire (2012), p. 476.

[250]Huber and Kreft (2013), § 103, para 76; see Thole (2016), § 47, para 59; Homann (2017), § 47, para 32; cf. Decker (2012), pp. 162 et seq. But see Brinkmann (2015), § 47, para 76.

The preponderant view is that the exclusive licence at least is not just contractual in nature; rather, it has a proprietary or absolute character.[251] According to this view, the exclusive licence continues to exist irrespective of a refusal by the trustee to fulfill the licence agreement.[252] Consequently, if the secured creditor is the licensee of an exclusive licence—either because of a security licence or because of a security assignment of a licence—he will not be affected by the refusal. Whether the encumbered licence is an exclusive licence is just as important to the pledgee or usufructuary of a licence because the insolvency trustee's refusal to perform the licence agreement would then not affect the encumbered licence. Security rights on exclusive licences would also be enforced in insolvency proceedings according to sec. 47, 50, 51 Insolvency Act.[253]

Others argue that all licences, including exclusive licences, are **contractual in nature**.[254] Hence, a refusal of the trustee to continue the licence agreement would render the licence as well as the security right attached to it void. Some scholars try to protect licences in insolvency proceedings by an analogous application of sec. 108 subsec. 1 Insolvency Act.[255] The prevailing opinion, however, disapproves of this.[256]

Non-exclusive licences and any security rights attached to them are not insolvency-proof as long as the licence agreement remains executory.[257]

[251] Koziol (2011), p. 88; Pahlow (2006), pp. 340 et seq.; Harke (2015), p. 99 et seq.; Schulze (2015a), § 31, para 52; Fezer (2009), § 30, para 6 et seq.; BGH, 26-03-2009 – I ZR 153/06 –, GRUR 2009, 946, 948; OLG Hamburg, 19-12-2003 – 5 U 43/03 – GRUR-RR 2004, 175, 178.

[252] Huber and Kreft (2013), § 103, para 76; cf. Thole (2016), § 47, para 59; Decker (2012), pp. 162 et seq.

[253] Decker (2012), p. 169.

[254] McGuire (2012), p. 476; Sosnitza (2005), pp. 183–196, 195; Hacker (2014), § 30, para 21; Brinkmann (2015), § 47, para 76.

[255] See Koziol (2011), pp. 129 et seq.; Fezer (2004), p. 793; Koehler and Ludwig (2007), pp. 81 et seq.

[256] See exemplary Decker (2012), p. 160; Berberich (2016), pp. 154–157. Cf. BGH, 17-11-2005 – IX ZR 162/04 – NJW 2006, 915, where the court does not even mention an analogy to sec. 108 subsec. 1 Insolvency Act as an option.

[257] See LG München I, Urteil v. 21-08-2014 – 7 O 11811/12 (2) – BeckRS 2014, 16898. A few academics, cited by the court in its decision, even disagree with this general understanding. To them, non-exclusive licences are also proprietary and hence are insolvency-proof. Also disapproving of the German treatment of non-exclusive licences was the Virginia Eastern Bankruptcy Court in In re Qimonda AG, 462 B.R. 165, 185 (Bankr. E.D. Va. 2011), that held § 103 Insolvency Act to be "manifestly contrary to U.S. public policy."

3.5 Security Licences

3.5.1 Creation

A licence grants the licensee a right to use the IP right,[258] whereas the licensor always keeps at least bare title[259]; this differs from a security assignment, where the grantor loses his IP right or licence.

In a security licensing scheme, the grantor grants the creditor either a licence—generally an exclusive one—on an IP right or a sublicence.[260] This licence has a fiduciary character established by a security agreement. The secured creditor will sublicense the right back to the grantor,[261] so that he may use the right in accordance with the terms of the security agreement.[262]

The registration of patent licences[263] and European IP right (sub)licences[264] is possible, but is unnecessary for the effectiveness of the licence.[265] In contrast, licences on German trademarks, utility patents, or designs cannot be registered.[266] Unregistered EU trademark and Community design licences become void if a *bona fide* third party acquires the IP rights.[267]

[258] Kraßer and Ann (2016), p. 984; Taxhet (2017), § 30, para 6; Ullmann and Deichfuß (2015), § 15, para 54, 56; Schulze (2015a), § 31, para 56; Ingerl and Rohnke (2010), § 30, para 12 et seq.; BGH, 25-01-1983 – X ZR 47/82 – GRUR 1983, 237, 238.

[259] Decker (2012), p. 63.

[260] See Koziol (2011), pp. 107 et seq.

[261] Ballestrem (2009), p. 79. See Koziol (2011), p. 110 on whether the back-license requires the consent of the IP-right owner.

[262] Cf. Decker (2012), p. 64.

[263] Sec. 30 subsec. 4 Patent Act; Rudloff-Schäffer (2014), § 30, paras 57, 64. It is, however, unclear whether non-exclusive licences can be registered. In favour of such a possibility: Rudloff-Schäffer (2014), § 30, para 14; Schäfers (2015), § 30, para. 7. Against such a possibility: Feuerlein (2017), § 30, para. 47.

[264] Art. 22 subsec. 5 EU Trademark Regulation; art. 32 subsec. 5 Communiy Design Regulation; art. 87 subsec. 2 lit. f) Community Plant Variety Regulation. Sublicences regarding European IP rights can be registered according to Rule 23 subsec. 2 Implementing Regulation to the European Patent Convention; Art. 22a subsec. 3 EU Trademark Regulation (effective 01-10-2017, Art. 4 Regulation EU 2015/2424). There is, however, no equivalent provision for sublicences as regards Community Designs and Community Plant Varieties.

[265] Sublicences regarding German IP rights cannot, however, be registered. Decker (2012), pp. 67 et seq.

[266] Cf. Decker (2012), p. 67.

[267] Art. 23 subsec. 1 EU Trademark Regulation; Art. 33 subsec. 2 Community Design Regulation. See Decker (2012), p. 67; ambiguous Schennen (2014), Art. 23, para 10 et seq.; see also Sect. 3.2.1.

3.5.2 Rights Before Default

The parties' rights and duties regarding security licences emanate from the security licence agreement. They are usually distributed in that agreement in the manner discussed above for the security assignments of IP right licences.[268]

3.5.3 Enforcement

Outside insolvency, security licences operate similarly to security assignments of licences. Upon default, the secured creditor of a security licence can personally use the licence, transfer the licence, or sublicense unless the parties have limited the options in the security agreement.[269]

As discussed above, the treatment of licences in insolvency proceedings is highly disputed. If the security licence agreement is executory, the security licence is valid regardless of the insolvency proceeding and will be enforced pursuant to sec. 51 Insolvency Act. If the licence is based on an executory licence agreement that none of the parties has yet fulfilled, the insolvency trustee may refuse the licence agreement pursuant to sec. 103 subsec. 2 Insolvency Act.[270] Therefore, the treatment of licences depends on whether they are viewed as contractual or not.

---

[268] See Koziol (2011), pp. 110 et seq.

[269] Ballestrem (2009), pp. 77 et seq. Koziol (2011), p. 108 mentions only the latter two options.

[270] In most cases, courts seem to consider a licensing agreement as having been fulfilled, rather than not; cf. BGH, 21-10-2015 – I ZR 173/14 – BGH NZI 2016, 97 (a one-time payment for a trademark suffices for contract fulfillment by the licensee); see also Brinkmann (2012), pp. 739–740; Rüther (2016), pp. 103–104.

3.6 Summary (Table 1)

Table 1 Overview on security rights under german law

	Pledge of rights	Security assignment	Security usufruct	Security rights on licences	Security licences
Creation					
Existence of Secured Claim Requirement	Yes	No	No	Only for pledge of licence	No
Specific Form Requirement	Only for European IP rights: writing	Only for European IP rights: writing	Only for European IP rights: writing	No	No
Registration in IP Register (If Existent)	Possible, but not necessary for effectiveness	Possible, but not necessary for effectiveness	Possible, but not necessary for effectiveness	Not possible	Possible for some, but not necessary for effectiveness
Effectiveness	As of conclusion of pledge agreement	As of conclusion of assignment	As of conclusion of usufruct agreement	Generally with conclusion of agreement; consent by third-party owner may be necessary	Generally with conclusion of licence agreement; consent by third-party owner may be necessary
Rights Before Default					
Exploitation Rights	Remain with grantor	Grantor receives exploitation rights by power of back-licence	Remain with grantor	Like respective security right in IP right	Grantor receives exploitation rights by power of back-licence
Defence and Maintenance of IP Right	Obligation of grantor	Obligation of grantor	Obligation of usufructuary according to sec. 1047 GerCivC, unless otherwise agreed	Like respective security right in IP right	Obligation of grantor
Power of Grantor to Grant Licences and Transfer the Collateral	Licences: disputed; transfer: yes	Arguably yes	Yes	Like respective security right in IP right	Yes

(continued)

Table 1 (continued)

	Pledge of rights	Security assignment	Security usufruct	Security rights on licences	Security licences
Power of Secured Creditor to Create Licences	No	Legally yes, but contractually prohibited	No	Like respective security right in IP right	Legally yes, but contractually prohibited
Enforcement Outside Insolvency					
Means of Realization	Public auction unless post-default otherwise agreed upon	Free choice: private sale, third-party licences, or personal use	Personal use, creation of licences, or collection of licence fees	Like respective security right in IP right	Free choice: private sale, third-party sub-licences, or personal use
Licences Granted by Grantor After Security Right Creation	Possibility of creation debated	Arguably cease to exist	Remain valid	Like respective security right in IP right	Arguably cease to exist
Enforcement in Insolvency					
Entitled to Separate Satisfaction/ Separation	Separate satisfaction	Separate satisfaction	Separation	Separate satisfaction: no; separation: debated	Separate satisfaction: no; separation: debated
Disposal Right	Debated: trustee or secured creditor	Debated: trustee or secured creditor	Secured creditor	Debated	Debated

For European patents, however, see Rule 23 Implementing Regulations to the European Patent Convention

4 Economic Aspects

4.1 Mechanisms to Evaluate the IP Rights Used as Collateral

German law does not provide for a formal mechanism to assess the value of an IP right.[271] In practice, the methods mentioned below—or a combination of them[272]—are used.[273]

Assessing the value of an IP right is (relatively) easy when the grantor has recently purchased the IP right in a transaction at arm's length. In that case, the

[271]There are, however, attempts to standardize valuation methods, e.g. ISO 10668, DIN 77100, IDW standard 5; see also Decker (2012), pp. 499 et seq.

[272]Brämer (2005), pp. 86 et seq.; Decker (2012), p. 496; Repenn (1994), pp. 13–15.

[273]An extensive overview is provided by Wurzer (2006), pp. 14–19, 18.

current value of the IP right can be equated with the purchase price.[274] Similarly, the value can also be easily ascertained if a comparable IP right has recently been transferred for a known price.[275] The current value, however, may differ greatly from the future realization value. Furthermore, the secured creditor will have to factor in any uncertainty regarding the grantor's title to the IP right, which may be questionable, since a transfer does not require registration.[276]

Absent any market transactions regarding the IP right or comparable rights, the valuation of an IP right is more difficult. The problems and uncertainties associated with valuating IP rights seem to be one of the major reasons why IP rights are rarely used as collateral.

If there is no ascertainable market price, the value may be calculated either based on the costs that were incurred during the creation of the innovation or based on the costs that would be incurred for it to be recreated. The sum of all of the costs is presumed to be the (minimum) value of the IP right.[277] This method, however, is criticized on the grounds that it does not account for profits that can be made in the future.[278]

Other methods focus on possible returns from the IP right, e.g. by comparing the value of a company with the IP right to its value without it.[279] For the purposes of secured transactions, however, this approach can also be unsuitable as an IP right may be vital for one company but largely useless in the hands of another. Hence, this method may only be used to assess the realization value of an IP right as collateral if a going concern sale of the debtor's business is the most likely form of realization.[280] Alternatively, parties may try to estimate a fictional licence fee,[281] which may be very difficult and hence yield unreliable results.

More recent methods empirically evaluate the effect that certain factors of IP rights have on the value of these rights and determine the value of the IP right in question as an outcome of the combination of these factors.[282]

274 Woeste (2002), p. 61 et seq.

275 Ballestrem (2009), pp. 111 et seq.; Brämer (2005), pp. 83 et seq.; Decker (2012), p. 495; Woeste (2002), p. 60.

276 Woeste (2002), p. 64; sceptical Brämer (2005), p. 90.

277 Ballestrem (2009), p. 109; Decker (2012), pp. 490 et seq.; Woeste (2002), p. 63.

278 Ballestrem (2009), p. 110; Decker (2012), p. 491.

279 Ballestrem (2009), p. 110, Brämer (2005), pp. 85 seq.; Decker (2012), pp. 493 et seq.; Woeste (2002), p. 62.

280 Cf. Ballestrem (2009), p. 229; Brämer (2005), p. 86.

281 Ballestrem (2009), pp. 110 et seq.; Brämer (2005), pp. 84 et seq.; Woeste (2002), pp. 61 et seq.

282 Picht (2018), pp. 76 et seq.; Busche (2006), pp. 19 et seq.

4.2 Legal Costs & Fees

The assignment or encumbrance of IP rights does not have to be carried out in a specific form. There are no fees for registering the transfer or encumbrance of a German trademark or patent. The fee for registering an exclusive licence on a patent is €25. The fees for European IP rights are significantly higher; for example, the fee for registering a licence on an EU trademark is €200, and the registration of a licence on or the transfer of a European patent costs €100.

The costs associated with the creation of a security right in an IP right are mainly costs for legal advice. These costs and the costs for enforcement vary greatly. They depend on the type of security, the method of realization, and the value of the collateral.

5 Conclusion

Even though there are numerous types of security rights that can be created in IP rights and licences, they are rarely (if ever) used as collateral for both legal and practical reasons.

Each type of security right described involves difficulties[283]:

- A security assignment makes it virtually impossible to create junior security rights in the collateral.[284]
- The pledge and security usufruct are impractical because of the legal restrictions on enforcement.[285]
- The legal character of licences is unresolved, which leads to legal uncertainty, especially with regard to their treatment in insolvency.[286]

Despite these difficulties and the discussed solutions in legal literature,[287] there are currently no official initiatives for reform that would affect the law or practice regarding IP rights as collateral.

Practical difficulties further add to these impediments. The main problem is that there is no method to reliably assess the value of an IP right, much less the value the IP right might have at the time of realization.[288]

Furthermore, as there is no liquid market for many IP rights, it is very difficult to realize the value of an IP right after default.[289]

[283]For a more detailed summary of these and other difficulties, cf. Decker (2012), pp. 210 et seq.

[284]Decker (2012), p. 210.

[285]Decker (2012), p. 210; Albrecht and Hombrecher (2005), pp. 1690 et seq.

[286]Decker (2012), p. 210.

[287]Ahrens and McGuire (2012); Picht (2018), pp. 239 et seq., 439 et seq., 479 et seq.

[288]Decker (2012), pp. 486 et seq., 501 et seq.

[289]Decker (2012), pp. 489 et seq.

One should also take into account that in some instances, the value of IP rights strongly correlates with the economic success of their owner: if the debtor's business flourishes, his IP rights, and trademarks in particular, will most likely be valuable. In such a situation, however, the default of the debtor is very unlikely. If, in contrast, the debtor's business is in crisis and his default is likely, his IP rights will often be worthless or at least not very valuable. Consequently, IP rights are often poor collateral because their value depends on the debtor's success. They are valuable as long as they are not needed to serve as security; the moment they are needed, they are worthless.

Acknowledgements The authors wish to thank Prof. Dr. Peter Picht, University of Zurich, for his valuable comments on an earlier draft of this paper as well as for providing them with the manuscript of his post-doctoral thesis, which is now published as (2018) *Vom materiellen Wert des Immateriellen*. Mohr Siebeck, Tübingen.

References

Ahrens H-J, McGuire M-R (2012) Modellgesetz für Geistiges Eigentum: Normtext und Begründung. Sellier GRUR, Munich

Albrecht C, Hombrecher L (2005) Aspekte der Vertragsgestaltung bei der Kreditsicherung mit Markenrechten. WM:1689–1695

Ballestrem J (2009) Die Sicherungsübertragung von Patent- und Gebrauchsmusterrechten. RWS, Cologne

Becker C (2017) § 166 InsO. In: Nerlich J, Römermann V (eds) Insolvenzordnung. C. H. Beck, Munich

Berberich M (2016) Anmerkung zu BGH, Urteil v. 21.10.2015 – I ZR 173/14. ZInsO:154–157

Berger C (1994) Anmerkung zu BGH, Urteil v. 24.03.1994 – X ZR 108/91. JZ:1015–1016

Berger C (2004) Der Lizenzsicherungsnießbrauch: Lizenzerhaltung in der Insolvenz des Lizenzgebers. GRUR:20–25

Berger C (2007) Die Verwertung verpfändeter Aktien in der Insolvenz des Sicherungsgebers. ZIP:1533–1538

Brämer A (2005) Die Sicherungsabtretung von Markenrechten. Mohr Siebeck, Tübingen

Brinkmann M (2011) Kreditsicherheiten an beweglichen Sachen und Forderungen. Mohr Siebeck, Tübingen

Brinkmann M (2012) Schiedsverfahren über Lizenzen in der Insolvenz des Lizenzgebers – eine Gleichung mit drei Unbekannten. NZI:735–741

Brinkmann M (2015) §§ 47, 166 InsO. In: Uhlenbruck W, Hirte H, Vallender H (eds) Insolvenzordnung, 14th edn. C. H. Beck, Munich

Büchler O (2017) § 166 InsO. In: Schmidt A (ed) Hamburger Kommentar zum Insolvenzrecht, 6th edn. Carl Heymanns, Cologne

Bühling J (1998) Die Markenlizenz im Rechtsverkehr. GRUR:196–200

Bundessortenamt (2016) Das Bundessortenamt: Schutz und Zulassung neuer Pflanzensorten. https://www.bundessortenamt.de/internet30/fileadmin/Files/PDF/BroschuereBSA.pdf. Accessed 30 June 2017

Busche J (2006) Arbeitspapier zum Workshop Patentbewertung, Düsseldorf. http://www.gewrs.de/fileadmin/redaktion/Fakultaeten/Juristische_Fakultaet/CIP/Arbeitspapier-apud.pdf. Accessed 21 Dec 2018

Busche J (2012) Einl zu §§ 398ff. In: Staudinger J (founder) Kommentar zum Bürgerlichen Gesetzbuch mit Einführungsgesetz und Nebengesetzen, Buch 2, Recht der Schuldverhältnisse, §§ 397–432. Sellier – de Gruyter, Berlin

Dammler M, Melullis K-J (2013) Störung in der patentrechtlichen Lizenzkette: Folgen für die Unterlizenz im Patentrecht. GRUR:781–789

Damrau J (2015) § 1273 BGB. In: Säcker F-J, Rixecker R, Oetker H, Limpberg B (eds) Münchener Kommentar zum Bürgerlichen Gesetzbuch, Band 7: Sachenrecht, 6th edn. C. H. Beck, Munich

Decker M (2012) Geistiges Eigentum als Kreditsicherheit. Mohr Siebeck, Tübingen

Deutsches Patent- und Markenamt (2015) Jahresbericht 2015. https://presse.dpma.de/docs/pdf/jahresberichte/jahresbericht2015.pdf. Accessed 30 June 2017

Dithmar T (2017) § 166 InsO. In: Braun E (ed) Insolvenzordnung, 7th edn. C. H. Beck, Munich

Drexl J (2016) Internationales Immaterialgüterrecht. In: Säcker F-J, Rixecker R, Oetker H, Limpberg B (eds) Münchener Kommentar zum Bürgerlichen Gesetzbuch, Band 11: Internationales Privatrecht II, Internationales Wirtschaftsrecht, Einführungsgesetz zum Bürgerlichen Gesetzbuche (Art. 25-248), 7th edn. C. H. Beck, Munich

Enchelmaier S (2014) Übertragung und Belastung unkörperlicher Gegenstände im deutschen und englischen Privatrecht. Mohr Siebeck, Tübingen

Fammler M (2006) Die Gemeinschaftsmarke als Kreditsicherheit. WRP:534–540

Feuerlein F (2017) § 30 PatG. In: Fitzner U, Lutz R, Bodewig T (eds) Beck'scher Online-Kommentar Patentrecht, 4th edn. C. H. Beck, Munich

Fezer K-H (2004) Lizenzrechte in der Insolvenz des Lizenzgebers: Zur Insolvenzfestigkeit der Markenlizenz. WRP:793–809

Fezer K-H (2009) Markenrecht, 4th edn. C. H. Beck, Munich

Fitzner U (2017) § 6 PatG. In: Fitzner U, Lutz R, Bodewig T (eds) Beck'scher Online–Kommentar Patentrecht, 4th edn. C. H. Beck, Munich

Flöther L (2017) § 166 InsO. In: Kübler B, Prütting H, Bork R (eds) InsO: Kommentar zur Insolvenzordnung. RWS, Cologne

Frank J (2009) § 1030 BGB. In: Staudinger J (founder) Kommentar zum Bürgerlichen Gesetzbuch mit Einführungsgesetz und Nebengesetzen, Buch 3, Sachenrecht, ErbbauRG, §§ 1018–1112. Sellier – de Gruyter, Berlin

Grabinski K (2012) Artt. 71, 72 EPÜ. In: Benkard G (founder) Europäisches Patentübereinkommen, 2nd edn. C. H. Beck, Munich

Habersack M (2001) § 1273 BGB. In: Soergel H-T (founder) Bürgerliches Gesetzbuch mit Einführungsgesetz und Nebengesetzen, Band 16: Sachenrecht 3, 13th edn. Kohlhammer, Stuttgart, Berlin, Cologne

Hacker F (2014) § 4 MarkenG. In: Ströbele P, Hacker F, Kirschnek I, Knoll H, Kober-Dehm H (eds) Markengesetz, 11th edn. Carl Heymanns, Cologne

Hacker F (2016) Markenrecht, 4th edn. Carl Heymanns, Cologne

Harke J-D (2015) Dingliche Rechtsverschaffung und schuldrechtliche Überlassung. ZfPW:85–101

Hauck R (2015) Nießbrauch an Rechten. Mohr Siebeck, Tübingen

Heim S (2008) Lizenzverträge in der Insolvenz: Anmerkungen zu § 108a InsO–E. NZI:338–345

Hirte H (2008) Die Verwertung "besitzloser" Gegenstände in der Insolvenz des Sicherungsgebers. In: Ganter G (ed) Haftung und Insolvenz. Festschrift für Gero Fischer zum 65. Geburtstag. C. H. Beck, Munich

Hirte H, Knof B (2008) Das Pfandrecht an globalverbrieften Aktien in der Insolvenz – Teil II. WM:49–57

Hofmann F (2009) Immaterialgüterrechtliche Anwartschaftsrechte. Mohr Siebeck, Tübingen

Homann S (2017) § 47 InsO. In: Ahrens M, Gehrlein M, Ringstmeier A (eds) Insolvenzrecht. Kommentar, 3rd edn. Luchterhand Verlag, Cologne

Huber M, Kreft G (2013) §103 InsO. In: Kirchhof H-P, Eidenmüller H, Stürner R (eds) Münchener Kommentar zur Insolvenzordnung, Band 2: §§ 80–216 InsO, 3rd edn. C. H. Beck, Munich

Ingerl R, Rohnke C (2010) Markenesetz: Gesetz über den Schutz von Marken und sonstigen Kennzeichen, 3rd edn, C. H. Beck, Munich

Kieninger E-M (2004) Motor cars supplied and resold. In: Kieninger E-M (ed) Security rights in movable property in European private law. Cambridge University Press
Kirschnek I (2014) § 28 MarkenG. In: Ströbele P, Hacker F, Kirschnek I, Knoll H, Kober-Dehm H (eds) Markengesetz, 11th edn. Carl Heymanns, Cologne
Klawitter C, Hombrecher L (2004) Gewerbliche Schutzrechte und Urheberrechte als Kreditsicherheiten. WM:1213–1219
Klein M (2004) Projektfinanzierung. Nomos, Baden-Baden
Knüpfer T (2003) Marken als Kreditsicherheit. Frankfurt am Main
Kober-Dehm H (2014) § 97 MarkenG. In: Ströbele P, Hacker F, Kirschnek I, Knoll H, Kober-Dehm H (eds) Markengesetz, 11th edn. Carl Heymanns, Cologne
Koehler P, Ludwig D (2007) Die Behandlung von Lizenzen in der Insolvenz. NZI:79–84
Koziol G (2011) Lizenzen als Kreditsicherheit: Zivilrechtliche Grundlagen in Deutschland, Österreich und Japan. Mohr Siebeck, Tübingen
Kraßer R, Ann C (2016) Patentrecht: Lehrbuch zum deutschen und europäischen Patentrecht und Gebrauchsmusterrecht, 7th edn. C. H. Beck, Munich
Kühnen T (2014) Patentregister und Inhaberwechsel. GRUR:137–143
Kur A (2017) Introduction. In: Kur A, von Bomhard V, Albrecht F (eds) Beck'scher Online-Kommentar: Markenrecht, 10th edn. C. H. Beck, Munich
Landfermann R (2016) § 166 InsO. In: Kayser G, Thole C (eds) Insolvenzordnung, 8th edn. C. F. Müller, Heidelberg
Lüke W (2008) Zu den Folgen von rechtswidrigen Verwertungshandlungen bei zur Sicherheit abgetretener Forderungen. In: Ganter G (ed) Haftung und Insolvenz. Festschrift für Gero Fischer zum 65. Geburtstag. C. H. Beck, Munich, pp 239–254
Lwowski H-J (2011) § 2. In: Lwowski H-J, Fischer G, Langenbucher K (eds) Das Recht der Kreditsicherung, 9th edn. Schmidt, Berlin
Lwowski H-J, Hoes V (1999) Markenrechte in der Kreditpraxis. WM:771–779
McGuire M-R (2008) Die Funktion des Registers für die rechtsgeschäftliche Übertragung von Gemeinschaftsmarken. GRUR:11–19
McGuire M-R (2009) Nutzungsrechte an Computerprogrammen in der Insolvenz. Zugleich eine Stellungnahme zum Gesetzentwurf zur Regelung der Insolvenzfestigkeit von Lizenzen. GRUR:13–22
McGuire M-R (2012) Die Lizenz. Eine Einordnung in die Systemzusammenhänge des BGB und des Zivilprozessrechts. Mohr Siebeck, Tübingen
McGuire M-R, Kunzmann J (2014) Sukzessionsschutz und Fortbestand der Unterlizenz nach "M2Trade" und "Take Five" – ein Lösungsvorschlag. GRUR:28
McGuire M-R, von Zumbusch L, Joachim B (2006) Verträge über Schutzrechte des geistigen Eigentums (Übertragung und Lizenzen) und dritte Parteien (Q 190). GRUR Int.:682–697
Mes P (2015) Patentgesetz, 4th edn. C. H. Beck, Munich
Michalski L (2011) § 1273 BGB. In: Westermann HP, Grunewald B, Maier-Reimer G (eds) Erman: Bürgerliches Gesetzbuch, 13th edn. Schmidt, Cologne
Müller U (2015) § 27 MarkenG. In: Spindler G, Schuster F (eds) Recht der elektronischen Medien, 3rd edn. C. H. Beck, Munich
Ohly A (2016) Wirkung und Reichweite der Registervermutung im Patentrecht. GRUR:1120–1124
Pahlow L (2006) Lizenz und Lizenzvertrag im Recht des Geistigen Eigentums. Mohr Siebeck, Tübingen
Picht PG (2018) Vom materiellen Wert des Immateriellen – Immaterialgüterrechte als Kreditsicherungsmittel im nationalen und internationalen Rechtsverkehr. Mohr Siebeck, Tübingen
Pierson M, Ahren T, Fischer K (2014) Recht des geistigen Eigentums: Patente, Marken, Urheberrecht, Design, 3rd edn. Nomos, Baden-Baden
Pitz J (2010) Aktivlegitimation im Patentstreitverfahren. GRUR:688–692
Repenn W (1994) Ermittlung des Verkehrswertes von Marken: System Repenn. MittdPatA:13–15
Rohnke C (1993) Warenzeichen als Kreditsicherheit. NJW:561–564

Romandini R, Hilty R, Lamping M (2016) Stellungnahme zum Referentenentwurf eines Gesetzes zur Anpassung patentrechtlicher Vorschriften auf Grund der europäischen Patentreform. GRUR Int.:554–560

Roth GH, Kieninger E-M (2016) § 298 BGB. In: Säcker FJ, Rixecker R, Oetker H, Limpberg B (eds) Münchener Kommentar zum Bürgerlichen Gesetzbuch, Band 2: Schuldrecht – Allgemeiner Teil, 7th edn. C. H. Beck, Munich

Rudloff-Schäffer C (2014) § 30 PatG. In: Schulte R (ed) Patentgesetz mit Europäischem Patentübereinkommen, 9th edn. Carl Heymanns, Cologne

Rüther D (2016) Anmerkung zu BGH, Urteil vom 21.10.2015 – I ZR 173/14 – ECOSoil. NZI:103–104

Schack H (2015) Urheber- und Urhebervertragsrecht, 7th edn. Mohr Siebeck, Tübingen

Schäfers A (2015) § 30 PatG. In: Benkard (founder) Patentgesetz, 11th edn. C. H. Beck, Munich

Schennen D (2014) Art. 23 GMV. In: Eisenführ G, Schennen D (eds) Gemeinschaftsmarkenverordnung, 4th edn. Carls Heymanns, Cologne

Schmidt H (2003) Urheberrechte als Kreditsicherheit nach der gesetzlichen Neuregelung des Urhebervertragsrechts. WM:461–473

Schulze G (2015a) § 31 UrhG. In: Dreier T, Schulze G (eds) Urheberrechtsgesetz, 5th edn. C. H. Beck, Munich

Schulze G (2015b) § 34 UrhG. In: Dreier T, Schulze G (eds) Urheberrechtsgesetz, 5th edn. C. H. Beck, Munich

Sessig F-J, Fischer P (2011) Das Verwertungsrecht des Insolvenzverwalters bei beweglichem Sicherungsgut. ZInsO:618–625

Sinz R (2016) § 166 InsO. In: Schmidt K (ed) Insolvenzordnung, 19th edn. C. H. Beck, Munich

Smid S (2016) § 857 ZPO. In: Krüger W, Rauscher T (eds) Münchener Kommentar zur Zivilprozessordnung, Band 2: §§ 355 – 945b, 5th edn. C. H. Beck, Munich

Sosnitza O (2005) Gedanken zur Rechtsnatur der ausschließlichen Lizenz. In: Ohly A (ed) Perspektiven des geistigen Eigentums und Wettbewerbsrechts: Festschrift für Gerhard Schricker zum 70. Geburtstag. C. H. Beck, Munich, pp 183–196

Sosnitza O (2012) § 1273 BGB. In: Bamberger HG, Roth H (eds) Kommentar zum Bürgerlichen Gesetzbuch, Band 2: §§ 611–1296, 3rd edn. C. H. Beck, Munich

Taxhet M (2017) Art. 23 UMV. In: Kur A, von Bomhard V, Albrecht F (eds) Beck'scher Online-Kommentar: Markenrecht, 10th edn. C. H. Beck, Munich

Tetzlaff C (2013) §§ 166, 170 InsO. In: Kirchhof H-P, Eidenmüller H, Stürner R (eds) Münchener Kommentar zur Insolvenzordnung, Band 2: §§ 80–216 InsO, 3rd edn. C. H. Beck, Munich

Thole C (2016) § 47 InsO. In: Schmidt K (ed) Insolvenzordnung, 19th edn. C. H. Beck, Munich

Ullmann E, Deichfuß H (2015) § 15 PatG. In: Benkard G (founder) Patentgesetz, 11th edn. C. H. Beck, Munich

Voß D, Kühnen T (2014) § 139 PatG. In: Schulte R (ed) Patentgesetz mit Europäischem Patentübereinkommen, 9th edn. Carl Heymanns, Cologne

Wallner J (1999) Sonstige Rechte in der Verwertung nach den §§ 166 ff. InsO. ZInsO:453–457

Wicke H (2017) § 1273 BGB. In: Palandt O (founder) Bürgerliches Gesetzbuch mit Nebengesetzen, 76th edn. C. H. Beck, Munich

Wiegand W (2009) § 1273 BGB. In: Staudinger J (founder) Kommentar zum Bürgerlichen Gesetzbuch mit Einführungsgesetz und Nebengesetzen, Buch 3, Sachenrecht, ErbbauRG, §§ 1018–1112. Sellier – de Gruyter, Berlin

Woeste C (2002) Immaterialgüterrechte als Kreditsicherheit im deutschen und US-amerikanischen Recht. Osnabrück

Wurzer A (2006) Methoden der Patentbewertung. In: Busche J (ed) Arbeitspapier zum Workshop Patentbewertung, pp 14–19. http://www.gewrs.de/fileadmin/redaktion/Fakultaeten/Juristische_Fakultaet/CIP/Arbeitspapier-apud.pdf. Accessed 21 Dec 2018

Zorzi N (1997) Die Verkehrsfähigkeit der Marke im italienischen Recht und in der Gemeinschaftsmarkenverordnung. GRUR Int.:781–795

Security Rights in Intellectual Property in Greece

Dionysia Kallinikou and Pierrina Koriatopoulou

Abstract Intellectual property includes both copyright and industrial property. The national legislation is harmonized with the international conventions and European directives. Intellectual property (IP) rights can be used to provide security if they are transferable. The main security rights over IP are pledges and fiduciary agreements. Evaluating IP rights presents difficulties, mainly because the value of IP rights does not generally appear in financial records. In case of bankruptcy and/or insolvency, the priorities of security rights are generally directed by the principle of time priority. The costs involved are legal and registration costs. The harmonization of security rights over IP rights is desirable.

1 Overview of IP Rights

Intellectual property includes both copyright (and related rights) and industrial property, such as patents and trademarks (art. 8, par. 18 of L. 2557/1997).[1] The main statutory sources of intellectual property law in Greece are the following: L. 2121/1993 for copyright and related rights; L. 1733/1987 for patents and utility models; and Articles 121–196, 330 L. 4072/2012 for trademarks. Further acts brought amendments, including the implementation of the European Community Directives. Greece has also ratified many international conventions regarding IP rights. IP rights can be used to provide security if they are transferable.

Copyright protects the work as an intangible object, not the physical object in which the work is embodied. Greek copyright legislation contains an indicative enumeration of the works and within this context any original intellectual creation can be protected. The prevailing criteria concern the form and originality of the

[1]For the analysis of IP rights in English see Kallinikou et al. (2019), passim.

D. Kallinikou (✉) · P. Koriatopoulou
National and Kapodistrian University of Athens, Athens, Greece
e-mail: kallinikoudionysia@yahoo.gr

E.-M. Kieninger (ed.), *Security Rights in Intellectual Property*, Ius Comparatum – Global Studies in Comparative Law 45,
https://doi.org/10.1007/978-3-030-44191-3_16

work. No formalities (i.e. publication, fixation, or registration) are needed for the acquisition or the exercise of copyright. The principle of protection without formalities is valid for all kinds of works. Art. 1(1) of L. 2121/1993 provides that "authors shall have, with the creation of the work, the right of copyright in that work", while art. 6(2) stipulates that economic and moral rights "shall be vested in the author of a work without resort to any formality". Depositing copies in the National Library, the Parliament Library, and public libraries is a purely administrative procedure that aims to preserve cultural heritage and enrich national archives, but it does not constitute a requirement in order to obtain or safeguard copyright.

Patents are granted to inventions that are new, involve an inventive step, are capable of industrial application, and do not fall within any of the specific categories of subject matter that is considered to be non-patentable. A number of procedural requirements have to be complied with. L. 1733/1987 applies only to patented inventions and inventions for which an application has been filed. Non-patented inventions do not enter into the scope of the Law. The boundary is marked by the issuance of the patent as an administrative act. For patents, Greece has adhered to the formal system.[2] For the granting of a patent, the competent patent office (i.e. the Industrial Property Organization, hereinafter referred to as "OBI" (*Organismos Biomixanikis Idioktisias*)) examines only whether the relevant application contains the elements required by law and whether the subject matter is in principle allowed to be protected by patent. If those formal requirements are met, the OBI is obliged to grant the patent.

Where supranational IP rights exist, such as under the European Patent Convention, the two patents are legally independent of each other as far as their existence, function, and validity are concerned. This means that any decision, assessment, or legal order concerning the European patent does not affect the validity of the national patent and does not provide a legal basis to contest the existence or validity of the latter patent.[3] The aforementioned Convention does not establish a separate European industrial property right (as was the purpose of the Community Patent); instead, it establishes a bundle patent that splits into several national rights after grant, with effect in those Member States for which the applicant has requested protection. The owner of a European patent enjoys the same rights and protection in Greece as the owner of a Greek patent that was granted by the national patent office.

Trademarks are acquired through registration and are used in connection with goods or services. They have origin, quality guarantee, and advertisement functions.[4] Marks are registrable if they are distinctive and can be represented graphically. In this context, all types of traditional, two-dimensional marks can be registered. This includes, among others, words, drawings, figurative elements, slogans, abbreviations, colour combinations, or even colours as such. Three-dimensional marks are also registrable if they can be represented graphically.

[2]Kallinikou et al. (2019), p. 102.

[3]CA of Athens 5111/2012, unreported.

[4]Kallinikou et al. (2019), p. 147.

Collective trademarks are also recognized and protected under Greek law. Law 4072/2012 introduced the Greek mark to indicate the national origin of goods and services. The General Secretariat of Commerce of the Ministry of Development and Competitiveness is the relevant trademark authority. Greek law on trademarks is based on Directive 2008/95/EC, amended by Directive EU 2015/2436, which is to be implemented into national legislation by January 2019. The process of registration before the local trademark authority is similar to the process used by the European Union Intellectual Property Office.

Current Greek law has been fully harmonized with the European directives on IP rights.

2 Categories of Security Rights

The main security rights[5] over IP are pledges and fiduciary assignments.

Pledges over IP rights are governed by the relevant provisions of the Greek Civil Code. Pursuant to Article 1214 of the Greek Civil Code and according to the provisions of Law 2844/2000, a non-possessory pledge may be constituted over IP rights. A pledge may be constituted without possession being ceded by the debtor for the benefit of the creditor. The establishment of such a pledge requires the conclusion of a pledge agreement in written form. Registration of the relevant pledge agreement with a public registry (called *enechyrofylakio*) is required. According to Article 1247 of the Greek Civil Code, a pledge may also be set up in a right if it is transferable.

Concerning pledges over film productions,[6] the specific provisions of Legislative Act 4208/1961 and Article 10 of Law 1597/1986 are abolished by Article 20(e) of Law 2844/2000. The conclusion of pledges in relation to film productions is governed by Article 1 of Law 2844/2000, regarding the film as a material object. Concerning the economic rights over film productions, Article 1247 of the Greek Civil Code and Article 15 of Law 2844/2000 are applied. The consent of the audiovisual authors is necessary. A moral right is not assignable and cannot be used to provide security. Pledges over films insure banks' claims.

For trademarks, Article 133(1) of Law 4072/2012 contains a specific provision, as follows: "A trademark may be given as security or be the subject of rights in rem". The establishment of a pledge of a trademark requires a written agreement before a notary public. The pledge agreement should be registered with the Trademark Office of the Ministry of Development. Article 133(2) and (3) allows the civil enforcement and liquidation of trademarks.

[5]For security rights over IP, see Koumantos (2002), p. 206; Rokas (2004), p. 142; Marinos (2007), p. 273; Ballas et al. (2012/13), p. 92; Kontizas et al. (2012), p. 4.

[6]For pledges over films, see Patrinos (1968), pp. 184–190.

Fiduciary assignments are concluded under the legal requirements and restrictions applicable to the relevant type of IP right assigned. Fiduciary assignment is applied to copyright collective management organizations as regards the management of authors' rights.

3 Structure of Transactions: Attachment and Perfection

IP rights serve as security for credit. The encumbered assets are the economic rights of the owner, licensor, or licensee. The evaluation of IP rights presents difficulties, mainly because the value of IP rights does not generally appear in financial records.

The following steps must be taken to make security rights effective:

a) Identification of the IP rights, taking into consideration the different types of intellectual property and whether each type of intellectual property is transferable; for example, under Greek copyright law, only the economic rights may be transferred, not the moral right of the author;
b) Determination of ownership—for example, determining the author, joint authors, or right-holder; the patent owner or co-owner; or the first user or owner of the trademark;
c) Examination of the status of IP rights;
d) Examination of the terms of licences;
e) Identification of infringement proceedings;
f) Determination of royalties; and
g) Determination of the value of the IP right.

For the creation of a pledge, an agreement between the IP right-holder and the creditor is required, either in notarial form or through a private deed bearing an officially certified date. In the case of a pledge of a claim, official notice of the act must be given to the debtor.

A pledge of IP rights may also arise through the forced execution of an executive or authentic document, or through the pronouncement of a provisional measure (judicial right of pledge).

The registration of pledges with a public registry has the effect of making the security right effective between the creditor and the debtor, as well as against parties. The special legislation being considered that establishes the appropriate public records according to Law 2844/2000 applies only to professional and company-related forms of real security.

A security assignment or pledge relating to a community design or community trademark can be registered with the Office for Harmonization in the Internal Market (Trade Marks and Designs).

4 Priorities

In case of bankruptcy and/or insolvency, the priorities of security rights with respect to other parties taking rights in the same IP right are generally regulated by the principle of time priority (prior tempore potior jure), i.e. the first-in-time rule. The rank of the security right depends on the date of the registration.

5 Enterprise Charges

In Greek law, there is no provision corresponding to the "floating charge."

The IP rights considered to be subject of the pledge must be specified in the pledge agreement. Security over IP can only charge specific rights and assets.

6 Rights Before Default

The grantor has the obligation to take reasonable steps to preserve the encumbered IP right (e.g. pursue infringers, renew registration, etc.).

7 Enforcement

The general enforcement regime is applied. The pledgee may seek satisfaction by means of enforcement of the pledged assets. The enforcement procedure provides the issue of a court decision, which enables the seizure of assets in favour of the pledgee, followed by the auction of the assets.

8 Typical Costs

The costs involved are legal and registration costs. For patents, the fees are fixed by decision of the Administrative Council of the Industrial Property Organization.[7]

[7]OBI ¬ www.obi.gr.

9 Practical Usefulness

It is not easy for SMEs to obtain credit by granting a security right over IP rights because they have to prove the value, durability, and marketable power of the IP assets. It is difficult to obtain an objective valuation of IP assets. The potential of IP assets as a source of finance is very important, but should be supported by valuation methodologies.

10 Legal and/or Practical Difficulties

There are difficulties as regards the valuation of IP rights.

11 Law Reform

There are no proposals for law reform relating to security rights over IP rights in Greece. The harmonization of security rights over IP rights at EU and international levels is desirable.

References

Ballas G, Prentoulis N, Volanis N, Spanos M (2012/13) Practical law. Multi-juridictional guide. IP in Business transactions: Greece. www.practicallaw.com/ip-mig. Accessed 4 Mar 2019

Kallinikou D, Athanasiou L, Chrissanthis C (2019) Intellectual property law in Greece. Walters Kluwer Law and Business, New York

Kontizas N, Melegou S, Charaktiniotis S (2012) Security over collateral. Lex Mundi Publication, Greece. www.zeya.com. Accessed 4 Mar 2019

Koumantos G (2002) Greek copyright law. Ant. Sakkoulas Publication, Athens

Marinos M (2007) Trademarks. P N Sakkoulas, Athens

Patrinos S (1968) Problems concerning film pledges. Epitheorisi Emporikou Dikaiou/Commer Law J:184–190

Rokas N (2004) Industrial property. Ant. Sakkoulas, Athens

Security Rights in Intellectual Property in Italy

Marco Ricolfi

Abstract This paper is based on a taxonomy of categories of security rights over IP, depending *first* on whether or not the IP right is registered and *second* on whether the transaction creating the collateral is asset-centric or debtor-centric. After discussing the questions raised by reconciling the security function with the non-rival nature of IPRs, the essay deals in some detail with the question whether security over IP follows the pattern of a pledge or of a mortgage; subsequently, it follows the ramifications of these alternatives for the major open issues in the area. The section focusing on the structure of the transaction intends to clarify the separate phases of the security's creation, attachment, and perfection. The paper ends by looking at enforcement and bankruptcy.

1 Overview of IP Rights

As Italy is a member of both major IP conventions (Paris 1883; Berne 1886), TRIPs (1994), and the EU, the Italian legal system provides protection for intellectual property rights (hereinafter "IPRs") across the board. In view of the limits imposed on a national report in a comparative law initiative, this overview will focus only on the IPRs which are most likely to be used as security. These include:

a) national patent rights;
b) national trademark rights;
c) national design rights,
which, in our domestic legal system, are cumulatively characterized as industrial property rights (hereinafter "IndPRs") and provided for by Artt. 45 ff., 7 ff., and 31 ff. of the Italian Industrial Property Code (Legislative Decree No. 30 of 2005, hereinafter "IIPC"); and

M. Ricolfi (✉)
Turin University, Department of Law, Torino, Italy
e-mail: Marco.ricolfi@weigmann.it

E.-M. Kieninger (ed.), *Security Rights in Intellectual Property*, Ius Comparatum – Global Studies in Comparative Law 45,
https://doi.org/10.1007/978-3-030-44191-3_17

d) copyright-protected works, governed by the provisions of Law No. 633 of 1941 (the Italian Copyright Law, hereinafter "ICL").

The basic principles concerning all of the above IPRs are to be found in Artt. 2563 ff. of the Italian Civil Code (hereinafter "ICC"), upon which the more specialized provisions quoted above build.[1]

For present purposes, special consideration should be given to cases in which a single entity is protected both at the national and at the European level. In patent law, the current European patent is granted and protected as a bundle of national rights in accordance with the European Patent Convention; under Art. 59 of the IIPC, protection granted by the European patent terminates whichever rights the same holder may have originally held over "the same invention" at the national level. A different rule applies to trademarks, where a sign may be simultaneously protected both under national law and under a single EU title encompassing all of the Member States (see the European Union Trade Mark Regulation, EU Reg. No. 2017/1001, hereinafter "EUTMR", Art. 136). Accordingly, the rights over national and EU trademarks may be independent even if they concern the same sign for the same goods. However, the earlier sign may invalidate all subsequent and conflicting trademarks if they come into different hands. The same caveat applies to the relationship between national and Community designs (as protected under Reg. No. 6/2002, the European Union Community Designs Regulation, hereinafter "CDR").

All these rights may be encumbered by a security right in the ways detailed below. It should be noted from the outset, however, that security may also be created in applications filed with a view to obtaining a registered IPR. The equivalence of an application to a registered right for the purpose of a secured transaction is expressly stated in Artt. 22 and 28 EUTMR, as well as in Artt. 29 and 34.2 CDR, but is believed to extend also to applications for other national registered IPRs.[2]

2 Categories of Security Rights Over IP

In the Italian legal system, a party having an interest over intellectual property (IP) is in a position to create a security right over the IP in question contractually—that is to say, through a voluntary arrangement between the parties (i.e. the debtor and the creditor).

The transaction whereby IP is given as collateral may take different shapes depending on two sets of factors: first, whether the IPR is registered or unregistered; and second, whether the transaction creating the collateral is asset-centric or

[1]The implementing regulations for a) to c) can be found in Decree No. 33 of 2010 and those for d) in Decree No. 1936 of 1942.

[2]For this view see Bonomo (2013), Art. 140, pp. 1504 et seq., 1507; Spolidoro (2010), pp. 43 et seq., 45, 47.

debtor-centric. While the first distinction does not need further elucidation, as the divide between registered and non-registered IPRs is well established and depends on a factor which is easy to establish (whether the law does or does not provide for a register where the IPR may be registered), the second one is not current in standard literature[3] and therefore may require some clarification.

For current purposes, asset-centric secured transactions are so named because they concern only one specific IP asset at a time (i.e. an entity which is a discrete and separate portion of the entire estate of the debtor). In contrast, debtor-centric secured transactions in principle concern all the assets of the debtor, so that they may affect one or more IPRs to the extent these are included among the debtor's assets.

Italian legislation provides for debtor-centric secured transactions only in connection with unregistered rights, as shall be seen in greater detail when considering Art. 46 of Legislative Decree No. 385 of 1993 and Art. 1 of Law No. 119 of 2016 (see below Sects. 2.3 and 3.3). As a result, a matrix with only three boxes is generated, which will be henceforth illustrated.

2.1 Security Rights Over Specific Registered IP Assets

Security rights over registered IndPRs (i.e. trademarks, patents, designs, or plant varieties) are specifically provided for by Art. 140 IIPC.[4]

The general provisions of Italian private law foresee two main types of consensually created security rights: the pledge (Artt. 2784 ff. ICC) and the mortgage (Artt. 2808 ff. ICC).[5] It remains unsettled whether the expression "diritti di garanzia" ("security rights") used in Art. 140 IIPC refers to the notion of pledge or to the notion of mortgage. According to part of the literature, the concept used in Art. 140 IIPC should be understood to refer to the notion of pledge on the basis of an argument drawn not from the IIPC itself but from the ICC. There, Art. 2806 deals in very broad

[3]The distinction is developed thoroughly by Brennan (2009), pp. 5 ff. See also Uncitral (2011), pp. 59 et seq.

[4]Art. 140 of the IIPC reads:

Security Rights

(1) Security rights over industrial property rights may be created only as collateral for money credits.
(2) In the event that multiple security rights are granted on the same IndPR, priority is established based on the order of the registrations.
(3) The cancellation of the registration of security rights over intellectual property rights is effected on the basis of the filing of a deed of consent bearing the creditor's certified signature; a court decision ordering cancellation, once this has become final and binding; or proof that the right for which security was given has been fully satisfied as a result of enforcement.
(4) The same fee due for registration is also due for cancellation. [My translation.]

[5]I use here the term "mortgage" rather than "hypothec" because the former term, while less accurate, is more current than the latter.

terms with "pledges of rights other than credits"; it is argued that this provision is to be understood to encompass IPRs and, even more to the point, that Art. 2806 is specifically intended to clarify that also IPRs may be pledged.[6] This view is univocally supported by the *travaux préparatoires*. At the time of the adoption of the Italian Civil Code, the Justice Minister then in office wrote in connection with sec. 2 of Art. 2806: "*by stating that provisions of specialized statutes are left untouched, I mainly intended to refer to copyright and to the statutes providing for industrial property rights which require publicity [in registers*, note of the translator*] for the grant of a security right*".[7]

This view may be reinforced by another argument. While IPRs are non-rival assets (so that a creditor cannot take delivery of them and thereby come into exclusive possession of them, as is normally required in order to pledge an asset), this is not an obstacle for the creation of a pledge over registered IPRs. Indeed, when these are based on the filing of the rights in specialized registers, the transfer of possession may be replaced by the registration of the transaction, which is a device that is a perfect equivalent to delivery for the purpose of giving notice to third parties.[8]

However, the opposing view is also widespread. There are two grounds for arguing that the security provided for by Art. 140 IIPC is closer to the concept of a mortgage than to that of a pledge.[9] The first reason is that efficiency dictates, for the benefit of the parties as well as for the optimal exploitation of the IP asset, that the debtor remain in possession of the IP asset. This feature is characteristic of a mortgage, as shown by Art. 2813 ICC, which, in forbidding the debtor to engage in acts which may imperil the subsistence or the value of the encumbered asset, presupposes that its management remains in the hands of the debtor. It is disputed that this same feature fits in connection with a pledge, where—at least traditionally—the debtor is conceived of as being dispossessed.[10] The second reason offered

[6]For this view, see Auteri (2009), pp. 129 et seq., 137; Gabrielli (2005), p. 208. The classic work by Gorla (1955), p. 384 considered only patents and copyrights, as at the time, trademarks could circulate only along with the underlying business assets.

[7]Grandi (1942a), p. 604; See also Grandi (1942b), p. 1134.

[8]Brennan (2009), pp. 17 et seq. Credits may also be pledged without the necessity of a transfer of possession to the secured creditor by resorting to the equivalent device of a requirement of notice to the third-party debtor. Similarly, shares in private corporations and in partnerships are not represented by a document; however, it is generally held that this fact does not prevent them from being pledged, at least to the extent that proof of possession of the corresponding position within the corporation or partnership can be reliably given. See in connection with this Revigliono (1998), pp. 300 ff.; Desana (2014), pp. 71 et seq.

[9]See Spolidoro (2010), pp. 45, 46.

[10]Spolidoro (2010), p. 45. This view is subject to the counterargument that the transfer of possession is a normal but not a necessary feature of the pledge and that it may be replaced by notice in the case of credits and by registration in the case of IndPRs. The counterargument continues by remarking that even when the secured transaction is categorized as a pledge, there are good reasons to assume that the management of the IP asset remains in the hands of the debtor (see Sect. 3.1(vii)).

by the supporters of this view is that sec. 2 of Art. 140 IIPC deals with the priority of consecutive credits secured on the same asset in a way that mirrors Artt. 2852–2853 ICC in connection with the mortgage. In contrast, a similar treatment of priority is neither foreseen, nor even conceivable in connection with the rules concerning the pledge, as exclusive possession, which is assumed as a normal feature in the provisions concerning the pledge, is conceivable only for the benefit of one creditor at a time.[11]

This divergence of opinions has remained unsettled for a long time now.[12] Even EU law has not contributed to clarification, as the most straightforward provision concerning the matter, Art. 22(1) EUTMR, shies away from taking a definite stand on the issue. Indeed, the Italian text refers to "pegno" ("pledge"), exactly like the German and French versions; however, the English and Spanish texts broadly refer to the notion of "security," which might encompass both the pledge and the mortgage.

This continued uncertainty should not come as a surprise. To begin with, it appears that, except in the very specific sector of motion pictures,[13] resorting to security over IPRs is not very common in the Italian legal environment. Therefore, litigation concerning the interpretation and enforcement of such security is very limited[14] and, as it happens, has not touched on the preliminary issue of characterization. Moreover, the implications of characterizing a security over IPRs as a pledge rather than as a mortgage are, as we shall presently see, not vast,[15] and, more to the point, may be settled in advance contractually.[16]

As indicated above, Art. 140 of the IIPC concerns only industrial property rights and therefore does not apply to copyright-protected works. There is a sub-sector of copyright, however, where a specific and urgent need for the creation of collateral has been felt for a long time: namely, the sub-sector of motion pictures, where the need for project financing is keenly felt. This explains why Art. 22 of Law No. 153 of

[11]It is also argued that, to provide legal certainty, the registration of the transaction in the appropriate IP register is required for the creation of the security as well, and not just for its perfection; this feature, again, is held to be characteristic of a mortgage but not of a pledge by Spolidoro (2010), p. 46 (however, for the opposite view, according to which creation or attachment requires registration in connection with a pledge as well, see Sect. 3.1(iv)).

[12]As acknowledged in the literature: see Mezzanotte (2014), pp. 1180 et seq.; Chianale (2009), pp. 116 et seq.; Nivarra (2009), pp. 107 et seq.

[13]See Sect. 2.1.

[14]Among the reported cases see Trib. Rome November 26, 2008, Settimaluna s.r.l. v Italian International Film s.r.l., in *AIDA 1347* case "La paura degli Angeli" with annotation by A. T [osato] and Trib. Rome September 16, 2008, Merrill Lynch Capital Markets Bank Ltd. v Fall to Mediafiction, in *AIDA 1303*, case "Mediafiction", which both concerned securities over motion pictures.

[15]For a similar view see Auteri (2009), pp. 138–139 and literature quoted therein. See however Sect. 3.1(vii) and Sect. 5.

[16]See Sect. 3.1 (vii).

1994 provides for a special register for motion pictures.[17] According to sec. 2 of Art. 22, all motion pictures intended for movie theatres have to be registered; their registration, as well as the registration of all "deeds that pertain to the establishment or transfer of economic exploitation rights and that create a lien or security right", is a prerequisite (not for creating such transfers and security, but) for making said transfers and securities effective against third parties. It is believed that this specific set of rules follows the mechanism of the general register provided for by Artt. 2643 ff. of ICC rather than the specialized rules of the IIPC.[18]

2.2 Security Rights Over Specific Unregistered IP Assets

The mechanisms which might enable a security right to be granted over specific unregistered assets have been explored particularly in connection with copyright-protected works. The practical results that may be obtained under the current regime are far from satisfactory (with the exception of the specific case of motion pictures, which benefit from the special provision just discussed above).

In other legal systems, this goal has been achieved by resorting to the transfer of title by way of security.[19] This is not the solution adopted in Italy: this route has to a large extent been blocked by Art. 2744 ICC, which invalidates transactions through which a creditor obtains the ownership of an asset given as collateral as a result of the debtor's default. Under this rule, transfer of title by way of security may be invalidated as a transaction in breach of the prohibition established by Art. 2744 ICC.[20]

---

[17]On this provision, which is the successor to Royal Decree No. 1061 of 1938, see Tosato (2009), pp. 560 et seq., 585 et seq.; Maggiolo (2009), pp. 148 et seq.; Auteri (2009), pp. 135–136 and 139; Nivarra (1994), pp. 117 et seq. Also the legislative decree No 518 of 1992 provides for the registration in a special register of computer programs and dealings in them, but falls short of making the corresponding filings effective against third parties; the same applies to the general register established by Art. 104 ICL, which is optional and does not have effects other than providing proof of the date of the registration itself (see Auteri 2009, p. 135).

[18]Nivarra (1994), pp. 129 et seq.

[19]Brennan (2009), pp. 17 et seq., describes these approaches as title-based devices (as opposed to possession-based devices) for establishing secured financing. In Germany, where the grant of a mortgage entails a voluntary transfer of the asset (Brennan 2009, p. 19), the collateral usually takes the form of a mortgage.

[20]The secured transaction based on a transfer was found invalid by Trib. Rome of September 16, 2008, case "Mediafiction," quoted above at note 14. A sale/lease-back transaction has, however, been held valid by Cass. July 21, 2004, No. 13580, Banca Agrileasing s.p.a v N.I. s.r.l., in *Studium iuris* 2004, II, 1581 ff., to the extent that the effective purpose of the transaction could be identified as enabling the leasing of the asset, rather than as creating a security. See also Cass. January 28, 2015, No. 1625, Unicredit Leasing s.p.a. v Fallimento Morettoni s.p.a., in *Giur. It.* 2015, 2341 ff., recognizing the validity of transactions whereby a clause (the so-called "patto marciano") provides that any excess in the value of the asset compared to the debt is handed over to the debtor. The prohibition contained in Art. 2744 ICC is no longer absolute, however: see Art. 48-bis of the

Therefore, it is usually held that the only way to establish security over copyright-protected works is by resorting to a "pledge of rights" under Art. 2806 ICC.[21] The corresponding legal mechanism is rather convoluted and, for analytical purposes, requires being broken down into three separate steps, which correspond to the notions of *creation*, *perfection*, and *priority* that are familiar in the field of secured transactions.

First, it has to be noted that, under Art. 107 ICL, economic rights based on copyright may be assigned, transferred, and granted in all of the ways provided for by law through deeds that comply with the requirement of written form (*ad probationem*) set forth by Art. 110 ICL; under Art. 111 ICL, the pledge is also permitted.[22] As far as secured transactions are concerned, one must recall that in such instances, a pledge cannot be created through delivery of possession, as an intangible IP asset is non-rival (in the meaning adopted in Sect. 2.1) and therefore not amenable to exclusive possession. It also cannot be created by the substitute method of filing with a register, as no register is provided either for copyright-protected works or for dealings in them, with the exception of motion pictures (see above Sect. 2.1). Here, sec. 1 of Art. 2806 ICC comes into play and provides a solution to the conundrum by providing that the *creation* ("costituzione") of the pledge takes place in the form required for the transfer. This may well be a positive answer to the question *whether* a security over copyright is possible. However, difficulties arise when we turn to the *how*, as difficulties crop up when the security is in fact given.

In principle, dealings in copyright are governed by the general provisions of Art. 1376 ICC, whereby mutual consent is sufficient for transferring ownership of a thing; creating or transferring rights *in rem*; or transferring other rights. Therefore, the creation of a security and the attachment of a non-registered IP asset also only require an agreement complying with the written form requirement of Art. 110 ICL. However, as for effectiveness against third parties (i.e. questions concerning the *second* issue: *perfection* of the security), the applicability in this regard of the various possession-based criteria is ruled out on the basis of the recurring rationale that exclusivity of possession cannot be relevant in connection with IPRs, as IP is amenable to simultaneous uses as a result of the feature of non-rivalry which characterizes it.[23] It is therefore generally accepted that conflicting claims over the same work are to be decided by the principle of priority in time, based on the ancient

Consolidated Text of Banking and Credit Laws, adopted by Legislative Decree No. 385 of 1993, as amended by Law No. 119 of 2016.

[21]For a comprehensive treatment of this reasoning, see Auteri (2009), pp. 137–145 (who also gives Art. 2806 ICC an extremely expansive role in regard to the separate question of whether registration is required for the creation of a security, which is dealt with below in Sect. 3.1(iv)).

[22]Insofar as the same rights do not still personally belong to the creator: this proviso clearly has the "paternalistic" aim of protecting the creator from unconsidered dealings in her works (see Fabiani 1958); as such, it does not apply when the copyright has already been assigned or otherwise transferred to a person or entity other than the creator.

[23]In this connection see also the recent work by Mezzanotte (2015), pp. 245 et seq.

maxim that *nemo plus iuris transferre potest quam ipse habet*, in conjunction with Art. 2704 ICC, which additionally requires certainty concerning the date of the deed.[24]

As for the *priority* of claims (that is, the *third* issue: establishment of the sequence in accordance with which multiple subsequent claims may find fulfillment in case of the enforcement of the encumbered asset), the matter is governed by Art. 2787 ICC, which is expressly recalled by the last part of Art. 2806 ICC. According to this provision, for claims exceeding the (in fact symbolic) amount of €2.58, the priority must be established by "a written deed" (required *ad substantiam*) "having certainty of date which must give sufficient indication both of the credit and of the asset".

The resulting regime is far from satisfactory, as it is based on the criterion of proof of priority in time, which is a factor which may remain privy only to the two parties concerned and does not exhibit any feature that makes it publicly accessible to the rest of the world. This regime entails very high transaction costs for secured financing based on copyrighted works. It is true that, once copyright is obtained as collateral, the secured creditor may prevail against claims subsequently obtained by third parties simply on the basis of a written deed meeting the requirement of certainty of date; however, by the same token, the same creditor remains subject to the corresponding adverse effect, which benefits prior claimants, if any, meeting the requirements of form and of proof of time. The point is sometimes made that to rule out this occurrence, a complete due diligence across the whole chain of title over the copyright-protected asset is required; however, even this course of action may still not provide complete reassurance. In the absence of both publicity provided by a register and the inferences which may be drawn from exclusive possession (at least in connection with tangible assets), unpleasant surprises cannot be ruled out except in very special cases.

Unsurprisingly, secured financing based on specific copyright-protected works has never taken off in this country.

Similar difficulties are bound to arise in connection with other unregistered IPRs, such as unregistered trademarks and designs. Also, in this connection, while it is generally admitted that a pledge may be created, it is also well recognized that its effects are limited to the parties concerned (i.e. the grantor and the creditor) for the same reasons explored in connection with copyright. This makes the transaction correspondingly unsecure: as it lacks both the possibility of exclusive possession and the possibility of being filed in a register, the certainty of perfection available in connection with other secured transactions is ruled out.[25]

---

[24]In turn, the rule whereby priority in time requires certainty of date is found in Art. 1380 ICC (see Auteri 2009, pp. 144–145). Other references in Ricolfi (2001), pp. 505 et seq.

[25]See Spolidoro (2010), pp. 48–49 and, incidentally, Mezzanotte (2014), p. 1185 note 80.

2.3 *Security Rights Over All the Assets Belonging to the Debtor's Business, Including IP*

Unregistered IPRs may be among the objects of the debtor-centric secured transactions provided for by Italian law.

A) Debtor-centric secured financing (also characterized as enterprise-centric) is provided for by Art. 46 of the Consolidated Text of Banking and Credit Laws (CTBCL), which was adopted by Legislative Decree No. 385 of 1993 and subsequent amendments.[26] This piece of legislation deals only with medium- and long-term bank financing and enables the collateralization of most business assets other than real estate and industrial plants. While no express mention is made of IP among the assets over which security may be granted, it is usually held that reference to "beni mobili non iscritti in pubblici registri" encompasses unregistered IPRs.[27] The mechanism established by this provision is based on the assumption that the assets used as collateral (i) remain in the possession of the debtor, who employs them in the firm's business cycle; and (ii) may change over time, the older ones being replaced by newer ones as they are from time to time transformed, used, or disposed of, so that the security is evolving and thus also extends to future assets that originally did not exist at the time of the grant of the security.[28] Among the features of the mechanism, the following facts stand out: (i) the creation of the security is based on a voluntary written transaction between the debtor and the creditor that precisely indicates the credit and the goods being given as collateral (sec. 2 of Art. 46 CTBCL); (ii) the perfection of the grant requires the filing of the transaction[29] in an enterprise-centric register, which is the same register that is provided for by sec. 2 of Art. 1524 ICC for the hire-purchase of machinery and is held by the administration of the court that is established where the registered office of the debtor is located (sec. 3 of Art. 46); (iii) the priority over other types of claims is established by reference to sec. 3 of Art. 2777 ICC[30]; and (iv) the legal basis of the preference, which is characterized as a "privilegio speciale convenzionale" (i.e. a floating lien or enterprise charge: Art. 2745 ICC), is to be found not in the characterization of the security chosen by the parties, but in the typical features (i.e. causa) of the transaction—namely, the provision of medium- and long-term financing for businesses.
B) A broader scheme of secured financing was subsequently adopted through Art. 1 of the Law No. 119 of 2016 (formerly known as the "Banks Decree"). In this later piece of legislation, unregistered IPRs are expressly included (sec. 2 of Art.

[26]For commentaries on this provision, see Falcone (2013); Tucci (2003), pp. 662 et seq.

[27]See Auteri (2009), p. 134; Capo (2009), pp. 17 et seq., 21.

[28]Falcone (2013), pp. 448 et seq. On the difficulties faced in the past when, for future credits, one had to resort to an ordinary pledge, see Stella (2003), pp. 3 et seq.

[29]With notarized signature: Tucci (2003), p. 668.

[30]For elucidation, see Tucci (2003), p. 674.

1); financing which may be assisted by security is not limited to medium- or long-term loans, as this legislation encompasses any credit extended "in the course of business" (sec. 1 of Art. 1). The filing, required for the perfection of the security, is again enterprise-centric, but the register is held centrally by the Italian Tax Administration (Agenzia delle entrate) in digital format (sec. 4 of Art. 1). While Art. 1 contains a number of specific provisions (including sec. 5, which provides what could be described as a "cut-through" provision that benefits acquisition financing rights), for all aspects not expressly covered by sec. 10-bis of the same Art. 1, reference is made to the provisions concerning pledges in Artt. 2784–2807 ICC "to the extent they may be compatible". At the time of writing, the decree providing for the setting up of the registry, which was to be adopted by August 2016, was not yet available.

3 Structure of the Different Security Transactions

The section which follows will essentially deal with the main features of the various transactions through which secured financing is put in place: the subject matter given as collateral; the parties to the transaction and their rights and obligations under the applicable legal and contractual rules; the steps leading to the creation and perfection of the security; and the priority derived therefrom.

As the rules vary depending on the type of IPR given as security, we shall deal with registered IndPRs first and with unregistered IPRs later. A shorter comparison with debtor-centric devices will follow.

3.1 Structure of Secured Transactions Over Registered IndPRs

3.1.1 Subject Matter

As noted earlier (in Sect. 1), all registered IndPRs (including patents, trademarks, designs, and plant varieties) may be used as security; the same is true for applications once the filing with the relevant register has been made.[31] From an economic viewpoint, nothing prevents the parties from using a portfolio of different registered IndPRs as security, as opposed to an individual IP asset. As a matter of fact, this can

[31] However, as the original trademark or patent application may be subdivided at a later stage (under Artt. 158 and 161 IIPC, respectively), the question arises whether the security that was originally given on a single right will expand upon the final grant of multiple rights. The answer is likely to be in the affirmative, as the grant does not encompass any subject matter which was not included in the original filing. However, there does not seem to be any precedent for this conclusion, which is unsurprising as the point is indeed very specific.

often be a good idea, as the debtor may be the owner of several IndPRs which may in practice conflict (e.g. a device mark containing a sign which has previously been registered as word mark). From a legal viewpoint, however, a security may only concern one specific, individual, registered IndPR at a time, in accordance with the principle of specialty, which governs both pledges and mortgages.[32]

In addition, it should be noted that in structuring the deal, the parties should consider the fact that the right or the interest which is given as a security might conflict with prior rights belonging either to the same debtor or to an unrelated third party. Thus, as an example, the validity of a registered trademark given as security may be put in question by a senior trade name or domain name belonging to the debtor, or it may be subject to the continued authorization of the person whose effigy or personal name is registered as the sign. Similarly, an earlier EU trademark may invalidate a later national sign, even though they may only partially overlap (for other examples, see Sect. 1). This potential conflict, irrelevant as long as both entities remain in the same hands (i.e. the debtor's), may become fatal to the junior sign should this come into the hands of a third party as a result of the enforcement of the security. In these cases, the stability of the security depends on the appropriate releases being given at its inception.

The *interest* over which the security is granted may be either the right itself in its entirety or one or more of the prerogatives based on the same right. For example, one may consider a security over a given trademark. The trademark owner has the right to prevent third parties from using the sign, as well as the right to authorize them to use it. Therefore, if the trademark owner has granted an exclusive licence, the security given by him may concern his own rights, either excluding or including his rights as licensor under the licence itself, as the case may be,[33] or include just the receivables (i.e. royalties) due under the same licence.[34]

There are limits, however, to the legal feasibility of the corresponding transactions.

It should be considered that a licence is a contractual arrangement. Therefore, the licensor, as a party to the agreement, cannot enter into a transaction whereby, in the event of his default, a third party (i.e. the creditor obtaining the security) may take over the contractual relationship with the licensee unless he obtains the licensee's consent (as required by Art. 1406 ICC), which may be given either at the outset or at some later stage. In contrast, in principle the consent of the debtor is not required for the transfer of a credit under Art. 1260 ICC, unless the parties to the licence have agreed otherwise (e.g. through a contractual anti-assignment provision). Therefore,

[32]See Artt. 2787, sec. 3 and 2809, sec. 1 ICC, and for further detail Galgano (2015), pp. 371 et seq. For the opposite feature in debtor-centric secured transactions, which are general rather than specific, see Sect. 2.3.

[33]An express stipulation to this effect may be required, however, for the reasons detailed in Sect. 3.1.7.

[34]For the separate question whether the owner of an IP right may license it after having granted a security over it, see Sect. 3.1.7.

nothing prevents the licensor from giving the royalties due to him from the licensee as security for credit, in lieu of or in addition to a security over the trademark.

However, it would appear that the obverse phenomenon, whereby the exclusive licensee obtains credit by giving as collateral the rights derived by his exclusivity, is of far greater importance. After all, it is the licensee who may require financial resources in order to make the investments that are necessary to fully exploit the licensed IP.[35] It stands to reason that the consent of the licensor is required here: in case of the default of the licensee, he will have to deal with the possibility that another business may step into the licensee's shoes. Apart from this, the feasibility of the transaction may be questioned, as Italian provisions on the registration of securities concern industrial property titles (Art. 140 IIPC) rather than contractual positions over industrial property titles. It is suggested[36] that this difficulty may also be overcome, but this would be achieved in a rather roundabout fashion, which we will come to later.[37]

In either case, it should be considered that, when an IndPR is given as security, this does not mean that the security automatically extends to the goods (e.g. inventory) incorporating the IndPR itself, as the object of the security here is the right rather than the goods incorporating it. Nevertheless, the secured creditor may, on the basis of the IndPR, exert prerogatives over the IP-incorporating goods; for example, the right to object to acts which would infringe the right in question, such as the resale of the relevant goods. However, the doctrine of first sale or, in EU parlance, of exhaustion of IPRs limits the prerogatives of the right-holder after the IP-incorporating goods have lawfully been put on the market.

As some of the rights belonging to the trademark (or other IndPR) owner may be granted by him to a licensee, so may the licensee be authorized to sublicense the sign. If this is the case, the same considerations would apply to the licensee's rights in regard to his sub-licensees.[38]

There are no reasons to rule out in principle the possibility that a share in an IndPR that happens to be jointly owned by several parties (e.g. the heirs of an inventor) is given as security by one of the co-owners.[39] However, a decision to this effect may require the consent of the other co-owners; whether this is the case essentially depends on the rules that are from time to time applicable to each IndPR.[40]

[35] Mezzanotte (2014), pp. 1169–1170.

[36] By Mezzanotte (2014), pp. 1186–1187.

[37] See Sect. 3.1.4.

[38] On this ramification, see Piepoli (2009), pp. 627 et seq., 638; Troiano (2009), pp. 3 et seq., 8.

[39] Piepoli (2009), p. 638.

[40] In connection with TM law, see Ricolfi (2015), pp. 1651, 1671.

3.1.2 Value of Collateral

The value of assets given as security is considered by Art. 2743 ICC, which deals with the loss of the asset or a decrease in its value. According to this provision, if at some point in time the value turns out to be inadequate, the creditor may ask for additional security over other goods and, failing this, demand immediate payment.[41] The obverse situation, in which the value of the collateral increases, would seem not to have a corresponding impact. Indeed, the provision of Art. 2799 ICC on the indivisibility of the security is understood as a basis for denying the right of the debtor to ask for and obtain a release of part of the collateral given, even though its value has increased after the attachment.[42]

As a matter of fact, it is common (and sometimes advisable) for the parties to give security over a portfolio of IP assets, rather than over an individual IndPR. However, as the abovementioned Art. 2743 ICC is relevant for each asset given as security, its mechanism will be triggered even if only one specific IP asset loses value while all the other assets included in the portfolio more than compensate for the loss due to an increase in value. Therefore, it may be appropriate for the parties to deal with the matter contractually. The parties may wish to establish what we may designate a "pooled assets evaluation mechanism," which would provide for the evaluation (both at the time of attachment and afterwards) of all of the assets included in the portfolio given as a security and might establish a set-off of variations in value, making irrelevant those variations concerning individual IP assets which do not affect the overall value. If the question of the release of specific assets included in the portfolio is dealt with, the arrangement should take into account not only variations of value, but also the (previously mentioned: see (i)) potential for conflict between rights.

3.1.3 Parties

There are normally two parties to a security transaction over IP: the secured creditor and the debtor granting the security. However, nothing prevents a third party from giving security over his IP assets to the creditor in order to guarantee the obligations of the debtor. This is a normal occurrence when the debtor belongs to a group of companies and IP is centrally administered by a holding entity.

In theory, not every type of credit may be secured. Sec. 1 of Art. 140 IIPC indeed provides that "security rights over industrial property rights may be created only as collateral for *money* credits" (italics added). This limitation is in line with the restrictions contained in Art. 2787, sec. 3 ICC for pledges and those in Art. 2809, sec. 1 ICC for mortgages. In practice, however, this does not mean that only

---

[41]On the relationship between Artt. 2742 and 1186 ICC, see Galgano (2015), p. 359.

[42]However, it has been noted that a specific provision concerning goods and services given as security for a loan (Art. 1849 ICC) points in the opposite direction: see Galgano (2015), p. 364.

obligations to pay a given sum of money may be effectively secured. Obligations to deliver certain goods, engage in a certain activity, or abstain from an activity may also be guaranteed, if and to the extent that the damage caused by a failure to perform is quantified, or "liquidated," at the outset. If this is the case, then the security may be structured in such a way as to guarantee the resulting obligation to pay a sum rather than the original, non-monetary obligation.[43]

3.1.4 Creation, Attachment, and Perfection

Conceptually, it is possible to distinguish between the steps which may be necessary for creating security rights over an asset between parties (this refers to the "creation" of the security right, which is described in the American tradition of Art. 9 UCC as "attachment") on the one hand, and the steps which may be required to make the same security effective against third parties (i.e. "perfection") on the other hand. The third parties against whom the security is to be made effective may be licensees or assignees who subsequently intend to acquire a right over the same IP asset or who have acquired—but not registered—the corresponding right at some earlier date.[44] They may also be creditors of the owner of the asset who intend to obtain a security right against their debtor on the basis of their claim against him, or, finally, insolvency administrators who have obtained control over the debtor's assets.

A recurring question concerns the issue whether security can be created (and attached to the asset) at a time prior to perfection. When perfection requires registration in the specialized IP register, as in the case of registered IP assets, the same question can be rephrased as follows: Is registration only "declaratory" ("dichiarativa"), making a transaction that is otherwise already completely binding and final between the original parties also effective against third parties, or is registration "constitutive" ("costitutiva"), constituting an integral part of the initial transaction between the original parties that remains incomplete and inchoate until registration has taken place?

A starting point to deal with the issue can be found in sec. 1 of Art. 139 IIPC, which states that "[t]he deeds", including the ones referred to in lett. b) of sec. 1 of Art. 138 of the same IIPC, that establish, modify, or transfer security rights "have no effect against third parties that have acquired or lawfully maintained rights over the industrial property right until they"—i.e. the deeds—"have been registered".

One possible reading of this provision is that registration is declaratory rather than constitutive—or, in other words, that a security may be created as between the parties and a registered IP asset may be attached even before and in the absence of registration. From this perspective, registration would be required only for

[43]Galgano (2015), p. 363.

[44]*Quaere* what the position is of non-exclusive licensees, whose licences in accordance with the prevailing view cannot be registered.

perfection.[45] This reading would appear to be confirmed by sec. 2 of Art. 22 of Law No. 153 of 1994 concerning the specialized register for motion pictures, which, again, as noted above (in Sect. 2.1), makes registration a prerequisite for effectiveness against third parties (or, in other words, for perfection), possibly suggesting that the security may be created (and the rights over the motion picture attached) even before registration.

However, this reading of the provisions is considered unacceptable by specialized IP literature.[46] It is argued that if one assumes that the guarantee is created and the asset attached even before the registration of the transaction, then the necessary implication of this assumption would be that the principle *nemo dat* (or, in more complete Latin, *nemo plus iuris transferre potest quam ipse habet*) applies and its application is bound to lead to a situation where the party registering first may still end up succumbing as being later in obtaining title. This outcome would, however, run against the principle of legal security that underpins the establishment of title registers.[47]

Therefore, it is suggested that the provision be read in a way that is the opposite of what its literal wording would at first glance appear to suggest: in this view, registration of the transaction is seen as constitutive rather than declaratory as far as the creation of the security right is concerned. To reach this outcome, one must resort to a quite convoluted—and not unchallenged—reasoning.[48] To begin with, it is noted that according to general, non-IP provisions, the creation of a mortgage requires registration (under sec. 2 of Art. 2808 ICC) and that, for the pledge of personal property (i.e. moveable goods), delivery is required (according to sec. 1 of Art. 2786 ICC). It is further remarked that such requirements for creation do not rule out the possibility that the title creating the obligation to provide security may be found in a contract or in another act that is a source of obligations, such as a unilateral promise.[49] However, it is argued, the obligation to provide security as such does not yet entail its creation, even between the parties. Therefore, the general principle whereby the meeting of minds is normally sufficient to produce the final outcome (Art. 1376 ICC) does not apply here. This explains why the contract of pledge is classified as "real" rather than "consensual," as no security is created without the delivery of the goods. This same rule requiring a further formality for

[45]As admitted, but only for argument's sake, by Auteri (2009), p. 138.

[46]See Spolidoro (2010), p. 46.

[47]See, however, the (unpublished) judgment by Trib. Torino October 15, 2013, Esseci s.r.l. v Stoner s.n.c., Gilardino Carlo, Sawing Lda., caso "Gems", which—admittedly in a matter different from the creation and perfection of securities—considers that the subsequent purchaser who is an earlier registrant prevails over the first purchaser who failed to register, by applying Art. 139 IIPC as though this provision contains the same general rule as Art. 2643 ff. ICC, which concern the registration of real estate transactions. The decision clearly states that the validity of the first sale does not prevent the first registrant from prevailing, thereby overriding the *nemo dat* rule.

[48]For a—not unsympathetic, but then also not wholly convincing—account of this argument, see Auteri (2009), pp. 137–138 with further references.

[49]See, for instance, Gazzoni (2001), p. 651.

the creation of a security applies both for the pledge of credit and, more importantly in this context, for the pledge of IP, where notification (for credit) and registration (for IndPRs) are viewed as the functional equivalents of delivery (for goods).[50]

It should be noted that in this second perspective, Art. 2806 ICC is given an extended meaning. This provision is understood as having a double purpose: not only to clarify that IPRs may also be pledged (see above Sect. 2.1), but also to indicate the requirements for the creation of a security. According to this view, reference to "the form required for the transfer of rights" is to be understood as a reference both to the written form and to a formality which is the functional equivalent of delivery in a pledge (i.e. registration of the transaction in the appropriate IP register). Therefore, in accordance with this approach, registration is to be seen as constitutive rather than declaratory, so that the security is not created—and the good is not attached—between the parties until registration has taken place. Accordingly, registration of the security over an IP asset in the appropriate register is deemed to be required for the purposes of both the creation of the security (or attachment of the asset *inter partes*) and the perfection of that same security against all third parties.[51]

Under Art. 140 IIPC, registration of the security concerns industrial property titles, i.e. registered trademarks, designs, patents, etc. It is, however, suggested that Art. 138(1)(b) IIPC has a broader scope and may also enable the registration of contractual rights over these assets and, in particular, over an exclusive licence. If this is the case, the creation and perfection of the security would appear to be simultaneous and to depend on the registration of the security over the right in the appropriate register.[52]

[50]Galgano (2015), pp. 359–360; Trimarchi (2009), p. 523.

[51]It should be noted that, conversely, under sec. 3 of Art. 140 IIPC, the security is still in place even when the creditor has agreed to its release; the release has been ordered by a final and binding decision; or the debt has been extinguished via enforcement proceedings, until cancellation from the register has occurred in actual practice. Understandably, Spolidoro (2010), p. 46 sees this provision as a confirmation of the reading referred to in the text above: indeed, here the final effect depends on the filing in the register rather than on the preliminaries to this filing.

It is worth mentioning that this approach is contradicted by provisions such as Art. 27(1) and (2) EUTMR, which state that even without registration, a transaction may be effective against third parties who acquired their right subsequently and who have knowledge of the prior transaction and in the case of a transfer of business (see Ricolfi 2015, p. 1577). This contradiction may also have an impact on national rules, as in the long run, case law tends to adapt national solution to EU principles. On a different note, it may be interesting to see which rules are applied when the transaction concerns an entity which is protected by a registered IndPR and an unregistered IPR at the same time. For an example, see the Vespa case (Trib. Torino April 6, 2017, Zhejiang Zhongneng Industry Group e Taizhou Zhongneng Import and Export Co. v Piaggio s.p.a., caso "Vespa"), where the same vehicle was deemed to be protected under both trademark and copyright law.

[52]Mezzanotte (2014), pp. 1186–1187 and 1181.

3.1.5 Priority

According to sec. 2 of Art. 140 IIPC, "if multiple security rights are granted on the same IndPR, then priority is established based on the order of the registrations". While sec. 1 of Art. 139 IIPC deals with all third parties who may have a competing claim over the same IP asset (and therefore also with prior and subsequent purchasers and licensees, as well as prior and subsequent creditors), sec. 2 of Art. 140 IIPC embodies a specialized rule: it applies when competing claims are all credits that originated from consecutive secured transactions that are all registered. The provision, which mirrors Artt. 2852–2853 ICC in connection with mortgages, clarifies that the controlling factor is not the dates on which the relevant deeds were entered, but the dates of their registration. Therefore, even a registrant who happens to be aware of a security granted at an earlier stage would still prevail over a prior secured creditor if the latter failed to promptly register.

3.1.6 The Mechanics of Filing the Registration

The registration of a deed granting a security right over an industrial property right requires the filing of an application pursuant to Art. 138, sec. 3 IIPC. The details to be given in the application (including the names of the parties, the nature of the deed or legal title for which registration is requested, and the identification of the industrial property right affected) are indicated in Artt. 195–196 IIPC. An original or a copy of the deed granting the security, either in notarized form or bearing notarized signatures, must be attached.[53] In principle, the order of the registrations is determined by the order in which the applications were filed (Art. 138, sec. 4 IIPC). However, the registration is subject to the payment of a fee (Art. 138, sec. 2 IIPC); in the event of failure to pay the fee, the filing will be considered to have been made only at the date on which the failure has been remedied (Art. 148, sec. 3 IIPC). The filing may be made online (Art. 147, sec. 1, IIPC). Both the application and the attachments to it must be in Italian; if the attachments are in a foreign language, a certified translation is required.[54]

[53]Artt. 138, sec. 3 and 196, sec. 1. For deeds formed abroad, the legalization takes place in accordance with the *apostille* procedure pursuant to the Hague Convention of October 5, 1961. No legalization is required for those countries (such as Germany) where a bilateral convention with Italy on the recognition of notarized certification is in place.

[54]Art. 148, sec. 5 IIPC; Art. 40 of the implementing regulation of the IIPC, Ministerial Decree No. 33 of 2010. Art. 40, sec. 5 of the same implementing regulation also requires that a copy of the foreign deed be deposited with an Italian notary or in an Italian notarial archive.

3.1.7 Rights and Obligations of the Parties to a Secured Transaction Over Registered IP

As long as the security is in place—that is, in the period of time starting with the creation and perfection of the security itself and ending with the grantor's default or the discharge of the debt—the rights and obligations of the parties are established by a set of rules which are derived either from the provisions concerning mortgages or pledges, depending on the preferred characterization (on the choice between the mortgage and the pledge, see above Sect. 2.1), or from the specific rules concerning the IP asset given as security. As most of the issues dealt with by both sets of rules do not involve public policy matters, ample room is left for the parties to resort to contractual autonomy.

A starting point for the required drafting exercise has to do with the question about the identification of the party who has to make the decisions that concern the management of the asset in the ordinary course of trade. As noted earlier,[55] efficiency dictates that the debtor retain control of the management of the IP asset. We may add here that the creditor is usually in the business of lending, so he has neither the interest nor the managerial and technical expertise required to take over the exploitation of the asset. If we characterize the security as a mortgage, the desirable outcome of leaving the management of the IP asset in the hands of the debtor derives automatically from the applicable rules. This outcome would be questionable, however, in the event that the characterization of the security as a pledge is preferred, as—at least in a traditional view—the pledgor is seen as typically deprived of possession and therefore of management powers over the asset.

It should, however, be noted that the dispossession of the debtor is no longer mandated when the security has been filed in a public register.[56] In a similar vein, it may be pointed out that the general duty of the debtor to optimally manage and protect the asset given in security is implied in the final part of Art. 1186 ICC, which establishes the debtor's obligation to not decrease the value of the security, and that this provision applies to all kinds of securities, therefore including not only mortgages but also pledges.[57]

Furthermore, it should be considered that IP assets are particularly vulnerable. If a trademark is not used for a period exceeding five years, it becomes subject to cancellation (Art. 24 IIPC); in turn, failure to exploit a patent may make it subject to compulsory licensing (Artt. 69 and 70 IIPC). It stands to reason that the actions that are required for the optimal exploitation of the asset and to avoid the negative

---

[55] See Sect. 2.1.

[56] Which, as noted in Sect. 2.1, may replace the transfer of possession.

[57] Art. 1186 ICC reads: "(Loss of benefit of time limit). Even if the time limit is established in favour of the debtor, the creditor can immediately demand performance if the debtor has become insolvent or has by his own act reduced the security which he had furnished or has failed to furnish the security he had promised".

events foreshadowed by these provisions are left to the party who is a position to do it best, for the benefit of both parties and of society at large.

It is therefore suggested that, whatever characterization is adopted for the security, the management of the asset should be understood to be left to the debtor. In any event, nothing prevents the parties from clarifying contractually, for the avoidance of doubt, that the management of the asset will remain in the hands of the debtor.

Who has the standing to sue third-party infringers? From the perspective adopted here, the reply is straightforward: the standing belongs to the debtor. In case of infringement, the debtor has not only the corresponding power, but also, in certain circumstances, the duty to sue. Failure to do so might in fact erode the value of the asset and run counter to the debtor's duties under Art. 2813 ICC, which is specific to mortgages, and under Art. 1186 ICC, which, as just indicated above, applies to all guarantees across the board. In any event, the debtor should have a certain discretion in deciding whether to sue infringers. After all, the most frequent counterclaim raised by infringers is the invalidity of the IP on which the action is based. Therefore, a certain flexibility would appear appropriate. On the one hand, the holder of the asset is in the best position to balance the cost of failure to protect his IP and the risk of seeing it invalidated. On the other hand, if the failure to act does not have a reasonable and objective basis, the secured creditor should have a remedy. This is to be found in Art. 2900 ICC, which allows the secured creditor to step into the shoes of debtor through subrogation and to act in his place against infringers.[58]

The existence of the debtor's positive duty to maintain the legal existence of the IP asset is confirmed by those provisions (Art. 78, sec. 2 IIPC; Art. 57(3) EUTMR) which require the consent of the secured creditor in order for the trademark holder to be able to surrender his right.

Are there limits to the management prerogatives which, according to this view, belong to the debtor? The question becomes relevant in determining whether the debtor may license (e.g. exclusively) the IP asset he has given as security. In principle, the answer should be in the affirmative.[59] However, it should be noted that the royalties owed by the licensee to the licensor/debtor are to be seen as "fruits" which, in accordance with the rules concerning pledges (Art. 2791 ICC), accrue to the creditor. The mortgagee, in contrast, has a claim over improvements to and increases in the mortgaged asset, but not over its fruits (Art. 2811 ICC). Here once again resurfaces the uncertainty deriving from the still unsettled characterization of security over IP as a pledge or as a mortgage (above, Sect. 2.1). Again, the difficulty may be easily resolved through appropriate contractual arrangements between the

[58]This opinion is widely followed; for variations on this theme, see Spolidoro (2010), p. 45; Piepoli (2009), pp. 644–645. On the question whether damages accrue to the debtor or to the creditor, see Art. 2742 ICC (which may apply only by analogy).

[59]For this view, see also Galli (2009), pp. 182 et seq., 193. On the (germane but separate) question whether a pre-existing licence may be given as collateral, see Sect. 3.1.1; in either case, the licensee's consent is, as already noted, required.

parties (e.g. providing that the creditor's security extends to royalties due to debtor/ licensor).[60]

If the corresponding stipulation is not in place, then room for controversy remains. This risk may be generalized, except for issues which are governed by rules which do not depend on the characterization of the transaction. For example, it is undisputed that the secured creditor of a licensed IP should retain certain control rights over the IP-incorporating goods; therefore, should the debtor/licensor of a trademark fail to engage in quality control of the production undertaken by the licensee in a way which risks leading to the cancellation of the trademark for deceptiveness, this failure is not going to remain unaddressed, as it may trigger the right to immediate repayment under Art. 1186 ICC.

Some registered IP assets may require the payment of a fee to the IP office, either to preserve their protection (for patents), or to extend their life (up to a maximum of 25 years for registered designs and without any limitation for trademarks). If the debtor fails to pay this fee, the question arises whether the creditor may step in to make the payment and then ask for reimbursement. There is no definite answer to this.[61] If the security is over a portfolio composed of several complementary IP assets, it may be up to the debtor to determine which assets he will keep protecting and which assets he will abandon. Also, subrogation under Art. 2900 ICC is hardly the appropriate tool to use for the creditor to step into the debtor's shoes in this specific regard, as this provision enables the creditor to do so in connection with the debtor's claims against third parties and not in connection with his business conduct in general.[62]

What happens if the IP asset given as a collateral is declared invalid or cancelled? No doubt this event will affect the security, which will be extinguished as far as that specific IPR is concerned.[63] Whether this event will in turn trigger repayment of the debt depends on the circumstances. It may well be that the security concerns an entire portfolio of IPRs. In this case, the deficiency may be compensated by the value of the remaining collateral. Also, Art. 2743 ICC may come into play, particularly if

---

[60]A separate question concerns the issue whether the licensee's consent is required for the contractual extension of the security to the royalties due by the licensee. From this perspective, it should be considered, as indicated earlier, that the enforcement of the guarantee would lead to the replacement of the current licensor/debtor with the creditor, an event which might require the consent of the third-party licensee under Art. 1406 ICC. Even apart from this contingency, an anti-assignment provision in the licence contract might prohibit the licensor from transferring his credit and have an impact on the contractual extension of the security over the IP to the royalties due. On this cluster of issues, see Uncitral (2011), pp. 41 et seq., 59 et seq.; Brennan (2009), pp. 30 et seq. The licensor of an IP right may create a separate security over the royalties due to him as receivables, rather than have them treated as mere incidents to the security over the IP asset itself. This situation should be visualized as a security over a credit rather than as a security over an IP asset; nevertheless, even so, some of the issues referred to in this footnote are likely to resurface.

[61]For a discussion of the issue, see Spolidoro (2010), pp. 47–48.

[62]For this point, see Nivarra (2009), p. 112.

[63]Spolidoro (2010), p. 48.

the parties have contractually resorted to a "pooled assets evaluation" mechanism as envisaged above (Sect. 3.1(ii)).

3.2 Structure of Secured Transactions Over Unregistered IPRs

Some time may be spent as well in dealing with secured transactions concerning unregistered IPRs. Here, we mainly refer to copyrighted works, as security over unregistered trademarks, trade names, and designs is unusual, at least from an asset-centric perspective. However, it should be kept in mind that the most frequent secured transactions concerning copyright-protected works concern motion pictures, which, as indicated earlier (Sect. 2.1), enjoy the remarkable privilege of having a specific register dedicated to them.

In working from this circumscribed perspective, the following should be noted:

3.2.1 Interests and Parties

Only economic rights, to the exclusion of moral rights, may be given as security. Even in connection with economic rights, Art. 111 ICL provides a significant limitation: economic rights may not be given as security by the author, as long as these belong to her personally. It is therefore necessary for a third party—an heir, or, more likely, an assignee or other transferee—to have become a right-holder before the work may be given as security.[64]

3.2.2 Additional Parties

When a right-holder other than the original author or creator gives the work as a security, practical convenience may suggest that, if the circumstances so allow, the original author or creator be personally involved in the transaction. This might minimize subsequent challenges that might be based on moral rights grounds.

3.2.3 Divisibility

Copyright is governed by the principle of divisibility, whereby each stick in the bundle of rights belonging to the right-holder is separate from all of the other sticks (Art. 19 ICL) and dealings over copyrighted works never cover all of the possible exploitations of that work; instead, they are restricted to the object, time, and space

[64]Fabiani (1958), *passim*.

that the parties had in mind at the time of the agreement (see Art. 119 ICL). This feature applies also to the granting of collateral: the security cannot extend beyond the specific types of exploitation that the parties envisaged at the time of the grant.[65]

3.2.4 Creation, Perfection, and Priority

We have gone through the sad story whereby, in our legal system, the creation of a security over a non-registered IP asset does not require anything more than a written deed, which, when meeting the additional requirement of certainty of date, is also effective against later, competing claims. In other areas of law, Italian torpedoes have been discussed.[66] The expression refers to litigation, but might turn out to be especially appropriate here.[67] A secured creditor may at any time find out that his claim has been subordinated to an as-of-yet unknown secured creditor or competing claimant, just as a later acquirer of a copyright may have the surprise of finding out that the work he purchased was encumbered. No wonder copyrighted works other than motion pictures are rarely accepted as collateral.

3.3 Structure of Secured Transactions Over All of the Assets Belonging to the Debtor's Business, Including IP

The debtor-centric secured transactions contemplated by Italian law have already been briefly illustrated (in Sect. 2.3). To avoid duplication, a few remarks will here suffice. As to the *parties* to the transaction, it should be noted that initially, the benefits of this device were restricted to banks engaged in medium- and long-term financing, by way of what were described as "crediti speciali"[68]; later, they were restricted to banks engaged in any kind of medium- or long-term financing under Art. 46 CTBCL, and finally they were provided for any financing extended by any kind of lender (Art. 1, sec. 1 of Law No. 119/2016).

[65] Auteri (2016), pp. 701 et seq.; Auteri (2009), p. 130.

[66] See Véron (2004), pp. 638–641; Franzosi (2002), pp. 154 et seq.

[67] I am not aware of any other writing which uses this metaphor; however, I submit that the expression is most appropriate here, as the earlier, competing claim may have until then remained submerged like a submarine. Italian torpedoes are pre-emptive strikes in Italian courts, which have the effect of greatly delaying effective remedies to the detriment of claimants intending to act before a foreign court having jurisdiction; however, in this situation there is at least the advantage that notice must be served to the other party, making him aware of the fix he is in. This advantage is not a given in transactions over copyright-protected works.

[68] Under this expression, which covers a vast and once-sprawling area, are understood various forms of publicly supported credit initiatives designed to foster specific economic sectors; see Tucci (2003), pp. 662 et seq.

It is therefore arguable that the original idea behind the provision of this sort of floating lien—which, after all, is still a "privilegio," even though it is based on a private covenant rather than on a legal rule in favour of a given category of creditors—has been gradually diluted.

As to the rights and obligations of the parties to the transaction, it seems safe to assume that the management powers of the debtor under Art. 46 CTBCL and Art. 1 of Law No. 119/2016 are even more expansive than is normally assumed in asset-centric secured transactions. Sec. 2 of Art. 1 of Law No. 119/2016 clearly authorizes the debtor to replace encumbered assets with others of the same kind; the evolving character of the security was already established under Art. 46 CTBCL.[69] It is suggested that there is a limit to this freedom, however: the total value of the secured assets should not go below the sum agreed between the parties.[70] Provided that this total value is preserved, the debtor would seem to have a free hand in most decisions that might affect the individual assets under security, including the decision of whether to directly exploit the IP assets included in the security at the relevant time or to license them; whether or not to sue infringers; and whether or not to register an IP asset.[71]

Finally, it would appear that there is also ample space here for the secured creditor and the debtor to shape their relationship, as long as the few mandatory provisions contained in legislation (e.g. sec. 4 of Art. 1 of Law No. 119/2016, concerning "cut-through provisions" that benefit acquisition financing rights) are not affected.

4 Default and Enforcement

However auspicious the initial secured transaction and harmonious the ongoing relationship between the debtor and the creditor, things may come to head at any time, either because the debtor defaults on his repayment obligations or because he is otherwise in breach of his duties (including the ones detailed in Sect. 3.1.vii above). This event opens up the next chapter—or rather, paragraph—in our enquiry: What rules apply to the enforcement of a secured transaction concerning registered IP? The legal practitioner might find himself in some embarrassment to reply to this question, if we were left with the conundrum we explored—and left open—in Sect. 2.1. In

[69]Falcone (2013), pp. 447–450.

[70]While sec. 2 of Art. 46 CTBCL refers to the secured sum of money as one of the items to be established in the agreement, sec. 3 of Art. 1 of Law No. 119/2016 refers to the "*maximum* guaranteed sum" (italics added). It would, however, appear to be against the principle of good faith interpretation of contracts under Art. 1375 ICC to assume that the debtor is authorized to substantially decrease the value of the collateral below this threshold.

[71]Thus, the debtor cannot be accused of taking an IP asset away from the pool of IP assets going into the collateral by registering it (it should be remembered that registered IPRs are not included in the collateral—see Sect. 2.3). The important issue is whether this decrease in the value of the collateral is set off by the inclusion or appreciation of other items.

fact, the choice between characterizing the security in question as a pledge or as a mortgage would be an especially difficult one, considering that the difference between the respective sets of rules is here quite significant.

According to Artt. 2796 and 2797 ICC, the pledgee may have the pledged asset auctioned off and obtain the proceeds of the sale up to the amount of his outstanding credit. Art. 2798 ICC also contemplates the possibility that the pledgee himself may acquire the asset if the asset's value is assessed by an independent expert.

The rules concerning the enforcement of mortgages are much more complex, as they are suited not for the rather straightforward case of the sale or attribution of an item of personal property, but for the much more complicated—and typically high-stake—matter of disposing of real property. Accordingly, the very detailed provisions concerning the foreclosure of real estate contained in Artt. 555 of the Italian Civil Procedure Code (ICPC) come into play. If the initiative is taken by a creditor other than the secured creditor, Artt. 498 ICPC will also apply.

Therefore, choosing between the two sets of rules would pose a formidable challenge. Fortunately enough, once more we are spared the task. Indeed, Art. 137 of the IIPC offers a comprehensive body of rules for the enforcement of claims concerning registered IndPRs.[72] The provisions contemplate both the case in which the initiative is taken by the secured creditor himself (secc. 1–9) and the case where it is taken by another competing claimant (sec. 10), who then has the duty to notify the secured creditor. The initial stage of foreclosure on the registered IP asset, which has to be registered with the Patent and Trademark Office (hereinafter "Office") (sec. 6), leads to the auctioning off of the IP asset. After the proceeds have been distributed in conformity with each creditor's level of priority (sec. 11), the purchaser acquires the asset free of all third-party claims, including the claims of any secured creditors (sec. 12). A certification of this is filed with the Office.

The rules we have dealt with in this paragraph specifically concern registered IndPRs. A specialized rule concerns copyrighted works: under Art. 111 ICL,[73] economic rights cannot be subject to individual enforcement as long as they belong to the individual creator personally. Therefore, enforcement at the request of a secured creditor (in accordance with the general rules set out in the ICPC[74] and, as far as the law of securities is concerned, in the ICC, rather than in Art. 137 IIPC, which applies only to registered IndPRs) is limited to situations where the right-holder is an heir or assignee of the creator.

For debtor-centric devices, the enforcement of the security in case of the default of the debtor takes a particular shape. More specifically, secc. 7 to 7*quater* of Art. 1 of Law No. 119/2016 provide for a mechanism whereby the secured creditor is

---

[72]On this provision, see Ferrari (2016), pp. 77 et seq. (who at 80 highlights the similarity of these provisions to the rules applicable to real estate rather than to personal goods) and Bonomo (2013), Art. 137, pp. 1481 et seq. Sec. 2 of Art. 137 refers to Artt. 513–542 of the ICPC for matters not directly dealt with by Art. 137. For a more general look at the enforcement of security rights over IP, see Pagni (2009), pp. 194 et seq.; Biffi (2012), pp. 374 et seq.

[73]On this, see Sects. 2.2 and 3.2.1.

[74]As suggested by Ferrari (2016), p. 77.

entitled to obtain physical possession of the items of collateral (sec. 7*ter*) and to proceed directly to their sale, applying the proceeds to the debt (lett. a) of sec. 7). Alternatively, he may even be entitled to "appropriate" (i.e. directly acquire title over) the item (lett. d) of sec. 7), to the extent that this occurrence is stipulated in the secured transaction and accordingly registered. A reference to the general provisions of the ICPC can also be found here, but, as enforcement is conceptualized as taking physical delivery of the goods, the provisions incorporated by reference are Artt. 605–611 ICPC, which concern the enforcement of the obligation to deliver specific goods. It remains to be seen how this mechanism, which is conceived for tangible physical property and is in part adapted to the enforcement of credit (lett. b) of sec. 7), may be actually implemented when the security consists of IPRs.

5 Insolvency[75]

Under Art. 42 of the Italian Bankruptcy Act (Royal Decree No. 267 of 1942, hereinafter "IBA"), the debtor in default is dispossessed of all of his assets, which are administered by a receiver. In accordance with the standstill provisions in Art. 51 ff. IBA, individual enforcement over the insolvent debtor's assets is in principle stayed from the day of the declaration of insolvency and all creditors' claims have to be processed through the insolvency administration. Acceleration clauses, according to which repayment of the debt is triggered by default, are declared ineffective by Art. 72, sec. 6 IBA. Therefore, as the result of a debtor's insolvency declaration, secured creditors are also prevented from proceeding to the enforcement of their claim. There are exceptions to this regime, however. One concerns pledged goods (Art. 53 IBA) and the other concerns mortgaged goods (Art. 54 IBA). Neither provision enables individual enforcement. The former, however, provides for a preferential channel for auctioning off pledged goods for the benefit of pledgees, while the latter provides for a regime of advance payments for the benefit of mortgagees. In the absence of a provision specifically concerning IPRs in insolvency proceedings,[76] we are once again faced with the recurring question whether secured transactions over IP may be characterized as pledges or as mortgages.

Not all secured transactions survive an insolvency declaration. Some acts, including the grant of security, may be revoked under Art. 64 ff. IBA at the initiative of the insolvency receiver, particularly on the basis of the rationale that such a grant is liable to create unjustified preferential treatment to the benefit of a specific creditor and may also show that at the time of the transaction, the same creditor, aware of the impending insolvency, was seeking that advantage.[77]

[75]For essential reading, see Ferri (2016), pp. 837 et seq.

[76]Such as Art. 137 IIPC, just mentioned above, for individual enforcement.

[77]See Art. 67, sec. 1(3) and (4) and sec. 2 IBA.

If the security holds and the encumbered IP asset is eventually sold under the ordinary proceedings in the IBA (Art. 105 ff.) or under the specialized provisions of Artt. 53 or 54,[78] then the somewhat enigmatic provision of Art. 108*ter* applies, which provides that the transfer of some IPRs (but not all of them) is governed by special legislation.[79]

As we saw earlier, a security may be given not only over an IP asset, but also over the licence of the IP asset belonging to the debtor and over the receivables which the licensee of that IP asset may owe the licensor/debtor. What is then the impact of the insolvency of either the licensor/debtor or of the licensee on these arrangements and on the security they provide to the creditor of the licensor?

If the insolvency concerns the licensor, Art. 80, sec. 1 IBA is held to apply: the licence agreement continues between the receiver and the licensee.[80] In this context, the licensee, who remains solvent, is likely to pay the royalties into the hands of the receiver administering the assets of the licensor/debtor. Under sec. 2 of Art. 80 IBA, the same receiver may opt to terminate the licence. This choice makes sense from the perspective of the insolvent estate if and to the extent that the sale to third parties of the unencumbered asset is likely to fetch a higher sum than the sale of an asset which has a string attached (i.e the right to a contractually predetermined cash flow). The interesting question is whether the secured creditor, who is the party who will be ultimately affected, favourably or otherwise, by the decision, has any say in it.

From the perspective of the secured creditor, another question also arises: whether the royalties paid by the licensee into the hands of the receiver of the licensor/debtor as long as the contract continues ultimately benefit the creditor himself. The answer is in the affirmative if and when the security concerns the licence proceeds as receivables. The same applies when the security is given both over the IP asset and over the licence of the IP asset. Such a conclusion is much more doubtful if the security concerns only the IP asset. To the extent that royalties are considered to be "fruits" of the licensed IP asset, they benefit the pledgee but not the mortgagee.[81]

If the insolvency affects the licensee instead, the receiver may at any time terminate the licence by paying equitable compensation to the licensor/debtor (in accordance with Art. 80, sec. 3 IBA). Here, the creditor having received security over the licensed IP from the licensor/debtor is on the receiving end of whatever decision the receiver of the licensee's estate may make. The secured creditor is likely to want the agreement to be terminated, freeing the asset to the advantage of both the licensor/debtor and the creditor himself. This secured creditor may also hope to

---

[78]For the mechanics of the bankruptcy proceedings and for the necessary coordination with Art. 111 IBA concerning relevant costs, see Zanichelli (2014), pp. 79 et seq.

[79]For a (rather awkward) attempt to reconcile the conflicting norms in Art. 137 IIPC and Art. 105 IBA, see Spiotta (2014), pp. 391 et seq.

[80]See in connection to this Spolidoro (2002), pp. 604 et seq.

[81]See Sect. 3.1.7, but also see Art. 54, sec. 2 IBA (providing for the entitlement to interest of all creditors having priority).

derive some benefit from the equitable compensation. Whether he has any say in either matter is an open question.[82]

Law No. 119/2016 provides a specialized rule for debtor-centric devices in connection to insolvency as well. Sec. 8 of Art. 1 provides that in the event of bankruptcy, the secured creditor may avail himself of the provisions concerning individual enforcement only after his credit has been acknowledged through the general procedure of credit verification and is found to have priority over the other credits.

6 Typical Costs

A register tax of 0.5% of the value of a secured transaction is established under Law No. 131/1986. As most of the deeds necessary for the creation and perfection of a security require the intervention of a notary public, a notarial fee will also be due. Also, registration in the Patent and Trademark Office entails the payment of a fee, which normally runs to a few hundred euros. Translations and certifications may entail additional costs.

7 Legal and Practical Difficulties, Law Reform

While no statistics are available, anecdotal evidence suggests that security over copyrighted works other than motion pictures is very rare; security over motion pictures is frequent and considered to be a normal occurrence when outside financing is needed. Secured transactions over registered IndPRs remain in the middle of these two extremes.

Therefore, the question arises whether it is possible to think of alternative ways to obtain the practical result of creating a security over IP assets without incurring the difficulties that are faced when copyrighted works are given as a collateral. It is conceivable for rights over copyrighted works to be transferred to a special purpose vehicle (SPV) and for shares in the SPV to be given as collateral (typically by means of a pledge) instead of the works themselves. This is a possibility. However, it should be considered that the transaction would require the creditor to place at least one person on the board of the SPV, to make sure that the transfer is not undone while the debtor remains in possession. Moreover, if the security is enforced as the result of a default by the debtor, the creditor will find himself in a position where he is forced to run the company whose shares were given as security. This is, again, an

[82]Which may possibly be dealt with contractually in the agreement between the secured creditor and the licensor through a clause requesting that the latter avail himself of the right to secure a decision from the receiver under Art. 72, sec. 2 IBA.

occurrence which would not be in line with the typical interests and technical expertise of the creditor.

A way out has been proposed in the past decade: to set up a global digital register for all copyrighted works for which right-holders intend to have full copyright protection. One of the goals of this global digital register would be to finally enable the registration of all transactions concerning copyrighted works, including securities, and this registration would be conditional for the creation and perfection of secured transactions. The technical feasibility of the project has been endorsed by the UN agency responsible for IP.[83] The idea is finding support from research institutions operating in the field.[84] Whether it will eventually be adopted is still very much an open question.

References

Auteri P (2009) Il pegno del diritto di autore: costituzione e opponibilità nei confronti dei terzi. AIDA, pp 129–147

Auteri P (2016) Diritto d'autore. In: Auteri P, Floridia G, Mangini V, Olivieri G, Ricolfi M, Romano R, Spada P (eds) Diritto industriale. Proprietà intellettuale e concorrenza. Giappichelli, Torino, p 701 et seq

Biffi L (2012) L'esecuzione forzata sulle privative. In: Giussani A (ed) Il processo industriale. Giappichelli, Torino, p 374 et seq

Bonomo V (2013) Artt. 137, 140. In: Vanzetti A (ed) Codice della proprietà industriale. Giuffrè, Milano, pp 1481–1448

Brennan L (2009) International intellectual property financing. An overview. In: Information meeting on IP Financing organized by WIPO. Geneva, March 10, 2009. http://www.wipo.int/edocs/mdocs/copyright/en/wipo_ip_fin_ge_09/wipo_ip_fin_ge_09_7-main1.pdf. Accessed 6 Mar 2019

Capo G (2009) I finanziamenti bancari garantiti da IP. AIDA, pp 17–28

Chianale A (2009) La funzione dei registri pubblicitari nella costituzione di garanzie reali su privative titolate. AIDA, pp 116–128

Desana E (2014) La partecipazione sociale e la sua circolazione. In: Cottino G, Cagnasso O (eds) Le nuove società di persone. Zanichelli, Bologna, pp 67–98

European Law Institute (2014) Response to the European Commission's Public Consultation on the review of the EU Copyright Rules. http://www.europeanlawinstitute.eu/uploads/media/Statement_on_EU_copyright_rules.pdf. Accessed 6 Mar 2019

Fabiani M (1958) Esecuzione forzata e sequestro delle opere dell'ingegno. Giuffrè, Milano

Falcone G (2013) Art. 46. In: Costa C (ed) Commento al Testo Unico delle leggi in materia bancaria e creditizia, d. lgs. 1° settembre 1993, No 385, T. 1. Giappichelli, Torino, pp 437–458

Ferrari F (2016) Il sequestro dell'anima. Natura e funzione del sequestro in materia di proprietà intellettuale. Giappichelli, Torino

Ferri GB (2016) Manuale di diritto commerciale. In: Angelici C, Ferri GB (eds). Torino, Utet

Franzosi M (2002) Torpedoes are here to stay. IIC 33(2):154–157

Gabrielli E (2005) Il pegno. In: Sacco R (ed) Trattato di diritto civile. Torino

---

[83]See the speech made by WIPO's Director General Gurry (2011), *passim*.

[84]See European Law Institute (2014), p. 9.

Galgano F (2015) Trattato di diritto civile, Vol. III. Gli atti unilaterali e i titoli di credito. I fatti illeciti e gli altri fatti fonte di obbligazioni. La tutela del credito. L'impresa. Cedam, Padova
Galli C (2009) Marchi comunitari e diritti di garanzia: problemi e prospettive. AIDA, pp 182–193
Gazzoni F (2001) Manuale di diritto privato. ESI, Napoli
Gorla G (1955) Del pegno. Delle ipoteche, in Commentario del cod. civ. Scialoja A, Branca G (eds) Libro VI, Della tutela dei diritti (Artt. 2740-2899). Zanichelli, Bologna
Grandi D (1942a) Relazione al duce, in Lavori preparatori del codice civile 1939–1941. Roma
Grandi D (1942b) Relazione al codice civile del Guardasigilli, ministro di stato per la grazia e giustizia, alla Maestà del Re Imperatore. Roma
Gurry F (2011) The future of copyright. Sydney, February 25, 2011. http://www.wipo.int/about-wipo/en/dgo/speeches/dg_blueskyconf_11.html. Accessed 6 Mar 2019
Maggiolo M (2009) Le garanzie nel credito cinematografico. AIDA, pp 148–162
Mezzanotte F (2014) Garanzie del credito e proprietà industriale. Riflessioni sulla collateralization delle licenze esclusive. Riv. dir. civ.:1168–1198
Mezzanotte F (2015) La conformazione negoziale delle situazioni di appartenenza. Numerus clausus, autonomia privata e diritti sui beni. Jovene editore, Napoli
Nivarra L (1994) Osservazioni sulla nuova disciplina del pubblico registro cinematografico. AIDA, pp 117–134
Nivarra L (2009) Le garanzie reali su privative titolate. AIDA, pp 107–115
Pagni I (2009) Competenza ed esecuzione in presenza di garanzie su diritti di proprietà intellettuale: problemi interpretativi e difficoltà con la disciplina (riformata) del processo esecutivo. AIDA, pp 194–207
Piepoli G (2009) Autonomia privata e garanzie reali sulla proprietà industriale. Contratto e impresa 25:627–648
Revigliono P (1998) Il trasferimento della quota di società a responsabilità limitata. Il regime legale. Giuffrè, Milano
Ricolfi M (2001) Il diritto d'autore. In: Abriani N, Cottino G, Ricolfi M (eds) Diritto industriale. Trattato di diritto commerciale. Cedam, Padova, pp 335–517
Ricolfi M (2015) Trattato dei marchi. Diritto europeo e nazionale, 2nd edn. Giappichelli, Torino
Spiotta M (2014) La liquidazione dell'attivo: profili sostanziali. In: Jorio A, Sassani B (eds) Trattato delle procedure concorsuali. Vol. III, Il Fallimento. Giuffrè, Milano, pp 391–395
Spolidoro MS (2002) Fallimento e diritti di proprietà intellettuale. Riv. dir. ind.:604 et seq
Spolidoro MS (2010) Il pegno e altri strumenti giuridici di garanzia su diritti di proprietà industriale. Il dir. ind.:43–49
Stella G (2003) Il pegno a garanzia di crediti futuri. Cedam, Padova
Tosato A (2009) Garanzie "reali" e diritti IP: per un censimento dei materiali. Il Diritto d'autore, pp 560–601
Trimarchi P (2009) Istituzioni di diritto privato. Giuffrè, Milano
Troiano O (2009) Le garanzie sui diritti IP: spunti problematici in prospettiva comparatistica. AIDA, pp 3–16
Tucci G (2003) Finanziamenti alle imprese: costituzione di privilegio. In: Belli F, Contento G, Porzio M, Santoro V (eds) Commento al d. lgs. 1° settembre 1993, No 385 Testo Unico delle leggi in materia bancaria e creditizia. Zanichelli, Bologna, pp 662–675
Uncitral (2011) Legislative guide on secured transactions. Supplement on Security Rights in Intellectual Property. https://www.uncitral.org/pdf/english/texts/security-lg/e/10-57126_Ebook_Suppl_SR_IP.pdf. Accessed 6 Mar 2019
Véron P (2004) ECJ restores Torpedo power. Int Rev Intellect Prop Compet Law 35:638–641
Zanichelli V (2014) Gli effetti del fallimento per il fallito e per i creditori. In: Jorio A, Sassani B (eds) Trattato delle procedure concorsuali, vol 3, Il Fallimento. Giuffrè, Milano, pp 79–82

Security Rights in Intellectual Property in Japan

Megumi Hara and Yuriko Haga

Abstract Although using intellectual property rights as collateral for obtaining credit has gained attention, it is far from being widespread in Japan. In this chapter, the types of security rights in intellectual property rights under Japanese law are examined, particularly their creation, perfection, and enforcement. Together with a description of the practical use of intellectual property rights as collateral and an overview of the financing environment, this chapter provides an assessment of intellectual property financing in Japan.

1 Introduction

In Japan, promoting businesses in the software and information fields has been a particular focus of government policy, especially since 2002, when the idea of the so-called "nation built on intellectual property" was launched by the prime minister of the time. Issues concerning intellectual property rights (hereinafter IP or IP rights) were regarded as being of primary importance, which led to the adoption of the Intellectual Property Basic Act[1] in 2002. Based on this Act, in March 2003, the

---

[1]The Act came into effect in 2003. The purpose of the Act is as follows: "Article 1 The purpose of this Act is, for the objective of realizing a dynamic economy and society that is based on the creation of added values through the creation of new intellectual property and effective exploitation of such intellectual property in light of a growing necessity for intensifying the international competitiveness of Japanese industry in response to the changes in the social and economic situations at home and abroad, to promote measures for the creation, protection and exploitation of intellectual property in a focused and systematic manner by stipulating the basic principles on the creation,

M. Hara (✉)
Gakushuin University, Tokyo, Japan
e-mail: Megumi.Hara@gakushuin.ac.jp

Y. Haga
Kanazawa University, Kanazawa, Japan
e-mail: y-haga@staff.kanazawa-u.ac.jp

E.-M. Kieninger (ed.), *Security Rights in Intellectual Property*, Ius Comparatum – Global Studies in Comparative Law 45,
https://doi.org/10.1007/978-3-030-44191-3_18

Intellectual Property Strategy Headquarters was created in the Cabinet. Since then, every year, the Headquarters publishes the Intellectual Property Strategic Program for promoting the creation, protection, and exploitation of IP.

One important aspect of this program is the use of IP rights as collateral for credit. Generally, since the businesses operating in the software and information fields do not own real estate, their IPs are essentially their only valuable collateral.[2] To facilitate IP financing, amendments such as the 2004 amendment of the Trust Business Law have been made. This particular reform enabled trust business to include intellectual property as the objects of a trust; before the reform, this had not been allowed. However, the use of IP rights as collateral is yet to become the norm in Japan.[3]

2 Overview of IP Rights

In Japan, IP is defined as "inventions, devices, new varieties of plants, designs, works and other property that is produced through creative activities by human beings (including discovered or solved laws of nature or natural phenomena that are industrially applicable), trademarks, trade names and other marks that are used to indicate goods or services in business activities, and trade secrets and other technical or business information that is useful for business activities".[4] Paragraph 2 of the above-mentioned article enumerates the following as types of intellectual property: (1) patent; (2) utility model right; (3) plant breeder's right; (4) design right; (5) copyright; (6) trademark right; (7) others (i.e. "right that is stipulated by laws and regulations on other intellectual property or right pertaining to an interest that is protected by acts"). Each right is explained below.

(1) Patent A patent protects new technology born from invention, which is described under the law as "the highly advanced creation of technical ideas utilizing

protection and exploitation of intellectual property and the basic matters to achieve the principles, clarifying the responsibilities of national government, local governments, universities, etc. and business operators, establishing the Intellectual Property Strategy Headquarters, and providing stipulations on the development of a strategic program on the creation, protection and exploitation of intellectual property."

[2]The Intellectual Property Strategic Program 2018, focusing on venture companies, summarizes the situation as follows: "as IP is the main asset of many venture companies, it is important to promote insights into the IP that they have and provide them with swift support in acquiring and utilizing IP. However, some have pointed out that, although there is a great deal of support on the menu for SMEs, the support available is not fully applicable to the unique challenges faced by venture companies, such as the difficulty of procuring finance and the paucity of accumulated know-how."

[3]Data provided by the Patent Office show that for example, number of cases of creation of pledge (including transfer of pledge) on patent was, 120 (2012), 165 (2013), 109 (2014), 81(2015), 47 (2016), 193 (2017).

[4]Article 2(1), Intellectual Property Basic Act.

the laws of nature".[5] In order to obtain a patent, the inventor must apply to the Japan Patent Office and have their invention examined to determine whether the application fulfils all the necessary requirements.[6] The requirements for a patentable invention are: (i) industrial availability, (ii) novelty, and (iii) inventiveness. When different applicants apply to patent the same invention, the earliest applicant will acquire the patent (this is the first-to-file system). The duration of a patent is 20 years.

(2) Utility Model Right The utility model right is granted for the "creation of technical ideas utilizing the laws of nature".[7] The way in which a device is used is not relevant for this right and inventiveness is not required. The Japan Patent Office is also in charge of utility model rights. The duration of the right is 10 years after registration.[8] The first-to-file principle is also applied to utility model rights.[9]

(3) Plant Breeder's Right The plant breeder's right is a guaranteed prerogative of breeders of "agricultural, forestry and aquatic plants".[10] A breeder who has bred a new variety of plant may to apply to register the variety (Article 4) with the Ministry of Agriculture, Forestry, and Fishery.[11] Whether a variety can be registered is determined through what is known as "DUS testing": testing for distinctness, uniformity, and stability.[12] The duration of a breeder's right is in principle 25 years.[13] The first-to-file principle is also applied to the plant breeder's right.[14]

(4) Design Right Design right is a right against "design". Design is defined as the following. First, the design must be "the shape, patterns or colours, or any combination thereof, of an article (including a part of an article), which creates an aesthetic impression through the eye".[15] In addition to this, designs must be (i) industrially applicable and (ii) novel and without precedent when compared to pre-existing designs. The only reasons for refusal of an application are if the proposed design

---

[5] Article 2, Patent Act.

[6] The steps are mentioned on the website of the Japan Patent Office (JPO) (2018). https://www.jpo.go.jp/tetuzuki_e/t_gaiyo_e/pa_right.htm.

[7] Article 2(1), Utility Model Act.

[8] The steps for application are published in the website of the JPO. https://www.jpo.go.jp/tetuzuki_e/t_gaiyo_e/model.htm.

[9] Article 7, Utility Model Act.

[10] That is, spermatophytes, pteridophytes, bryophytes, multicellular algae, and other plants specified by the Cabinet Order that are cultivated for the production of agricultural, forestry, and aquatic products (Article 2(1), Plant Variety Protection and Seed Act).

[11] The steps for application are published in the leaflet of the MAFF: Plant Variety Protection (PVP) office at Ministry of Agriculture, Forestry and Fisheries (2011a): http://www.hinshu2.maff.go.jp/en/about/contents/3-4.pdf.

[12] Plant Variety Protection (PVP) office at Ministry of Agriculture, Forestry and Fisheries (2011b) http://www.hinshu2.maff.go.jp/en/about/contents/5.pdf.

[13] For perennial plant such as fruit tree, it is 30 years (Article 19(2)).

[14] Article 9, Plant Variety Protection and Seed Act. Exception exists when the plant is registered in foreign country (Article 11).

[15] Article 2(1), Design Act. By definition, design only covers visible matter.

contravenes public order or morality, can be confused with another design, or is purely functional with no aesthetic nature. The first-to-file principle is also applied to the design right.[16]

(5) Copyright A copyright guarantees the rights concerning a creative work—that is, a "production in which thoughts or sentiments are expressed in a creative way and which falls within the literary, scientific, artistic or musical domain".[17] The author of a work enjoys moral rights as well as copyright (in a narrow definition). The moral rights protect the moral interests of the author and include the right to make the work public, the right to determine whether and how the author's name is indicated, and the right to maintain the integrity of the work.[18] The moral rights "shall be personal and exclusive to the author and cannot be transferred".[19] In contrast, copyright, which guarantees the economic interest concerning the works, can be transferred. Copyright includes the rights of reproduction, performance, screen presentation, public transmission, recitation, exhibition, distribution or rental, and more.

Registration is unnecessary for copyright to be effective.[20] At the time of the creation of a work, the author automatically acquires the copyright. The duration of the right is 50 years after the death of the author of the work.[21]

(6) Trademark Right A trademark refers to any mark "any character(s), figure(s), sign(s) or three-dimensional shape(s), or any combination thereof, or any combination thereof with colours"[22]:—that is used in connection with a specified good or service.[23]

The duration of a trademark right is 10 years from the date of registration (it can be renewed every 10 years). The first-to-file principle is also applied to trademark.[24]

---

[16]Application steps are published on the JPO website. https://www.jpo.go.jp/tetuzuki_e/t_gaiyo_e/de_right.htm.

[17]Article 2(1), Copyright Act.

[18]Articles 18-20, Copyright Act.

[19]Article 59, Copyright Act.

[20]"Enjoyment of the moral rights of author and copyrights shall not be subject to any formality", Article 17(2).

[21]Article 51(2), Copyright Act.

[22]Article 2(1), Trademark Act.

[23]The following marks cannot be registered as trademarks:

(i) Marks that cannot be differentiated from others' goods or services (e.g. a common or customarily used name for a good/service; a common surname or name for a legal person; or any simple, common mark);
(ii) Marks that are used officially (e.g. the Japanese national flag or imperial chrysanthemum crest; a decoration, medal, or foreign national flag; a mark indicating the United Nations or any other international organization; or a famous mark indicating a state, local government, state/local government agency, non-profit organization, or non-profit enterprise); and
(iii) Marks that are against the public order. https://www.jpo.go.jp/tetuzuki_e/t_gaiyo_e/tr_right.htm.

[24]Article 8, Trademark Act. There is an exception when there is right to use trademark arising from prior use. Article 32 (1) states the following. "(1) Where a trademark identical with, or similar to, the

(7) Others Other IP rights include the following:

- the layout-design exploitation right (in the Act on the Circuit Layout of a Semiconductor Integrated Circuits);
- trade names (in commercial law);
- "name[s], . . . container[s] or package[s], or any other indication of goods or trade pertaining to a person's business" (in the Unfair Competition Prevention Act); and
- geographical indications (in the Act on Protection of the Names of Specific Agricultural, Forestry and Fishery Products and Foodstuffs).

3 Categories of Security Rights

As Japan has not adopted the unitary approach to security rights, the various types of security rights, including mortgage,[25] pledge,[26] right of retention,[27] and lien,[28] are provided for in the Civil Code. The enforcement of security rights is regulated under the Civil Execution Act. Some important security rights are left out of the Civil Code, the most notable of which is the security assignment, *joto-tanpo* (i.e. assignment by way of security), which will be explained further below. Accordingly, there is no comprehensive law on secured transactions.

One must also keep in mind that many movables, such as cars, aircraft, ships, and heavy equipment, are governed by special laws under which they may be mortgaged.

---

trademark for which the application is filed by another person has been used in Japan in connection with the designated goods or designated services of the trademark for which the application is filed, or in connection with goods or services similar thereto, without any intention to be engaged in unfair competition, from the time prior to the filing of such other person's application for the said trademark registration, and as a result, at the time of filing of the application for trademark registration (at the time of filing of the original application for trademark registration or the submission of a written amendment, if the application for trademark registration is deemed to have been filed at the time of submission of a written amendment under Article 9-4 of this Act or Article 17-3 (1) of the Design Act as applied mutatis mutandis under Article 17-2 (1) or 55-2(3) of this Act (including its mutatis mutandis application under Article 60-2 (2))), such trademark has become well known among consumers as that indicating goods or services pertaining to the business of the person, the person shall have the right to use the trademark in connection with such goods or services as far as the said person continuously uses the trademark for the goods or services. The same shall apply to those by whom such business is succeeded."

[25]Mortgage is provided for in Articles 369 through 398 of the Civil Code. The object of a mortgage is limited to immovables.

[26]Pledge is provided for in Articles 342 through 367 of the Civil Code, and in other special laws. The subject matter of a pledge may be any asset that is transferable, such as movable, immovable or rights.

[27]Rights of retention are provided for in Articles 295 through 302 of the Civil Code and Article 521, etc., of the Commercial Code.

[28]Liens are provided for in Articles 303-341 of the Civil Code and in various special laws. These two security rights are created by statute and are not subject to alteration by agreement of the parties.

Security rights in IP can also be governed by different laws and security devices, including (i) the pledge of IP, which is governed by the respective laws on IP rights, and (ii) the security assignment, which is governed by case law.

This section will only deal with the principal types of IP rights, and will illustrate the application of the secured transactions framework on these types of rights.[29] Furthermore, it will focus on the use of IP as collateral.[30]

3.1 Registered Rights (Patents, Designs, Utility Models, Trademarks)

(1) Pledge One type of security right over IP is the pledge. Not only can an IP right itself be the object of a pledge, but one can also pledge its exclusive or ordinary licenses.[31] However, the right to obtain a patent cannot be the object of a pledge.[32] In cases where several people own a patent (i.e. jointly owned patents), a pledge on one's share of the patent is possible, but only provided that all of the owners give their consent.[33]

Additionally, royalties or other monetary compensation for such rights can also be the object of a pledge.[34]

(2) Security Assignment Another type of security right over IP is the security assignment ("*Joto- tanpo*"). The security assignment has been developed through case law. It is frequently used in practice.[35] There have been many court rulings on the nature of security assignments for immovables, tangible movables (including inventory financing), and receivables. However, there has not been a case in the

[29]In subsequent sections, we focus on pledges and security assignments, which are the two typical types of security rights over IP.

[30]In Japan, financing methods based on IP, such as usage of co-ownership, where creditor receives a share of the IP and holds the IP as joint owner, or forming joint-business (such as partnership under civil law or limited liability partnership under Limited Liability Partnership Act), or creation of trust are all considered as effective ways of finance. However for the purpose of this book, which is focused on creating security rights on IP, such ways are excluded from the scope of this chapter.

[31]It is possible to create a pledge of a plant breeder's right and its exclusive and ordinary licenses (Article 30, Plant Breeder's Act).

[32]Article 33, Patent Act. Rights deriving from an application for a trade mark and registration and rights deriving from a design registration are also excluded as object of pledge.

[33]Article 73(1), Patent Act.

[34]Article 96, Patent Act; Article 66(2), Copyright Act; Article 35, Design Act; Article 25, Utility Model Act.

[35]"A security assignment takes the form of a transfer or a pre-contract for the transfer of title (ownership, a real right such as an IPR), which serves as security (collateral) in effect. The details of such security rights have been clarified in judicial precedents and partially codified in law (the Act on Contract for Establishment of Security Rights by Use of Provisional Registration, Act No. 78 of June 20, 1978)." Japan Group (Honda et al.) (2016), p. 238.

Supreme Court where the security assignment of an IP right has been disputed, so we do not know if, in the case of the security assignment of IP rights, there is any divergence from the established general nature of security assignments. The Supreme Court says the following regarding security assignments in general:

(i) A transfer of title has effect only to the extent necessary to achieve the purpose of securing claims[36]; and
(ii) Even if the transaction takes the form of an assignment with a repurchase option, as long as it does not involve a transfer of possession, it should be regarded as a security assignment unless the circumstances are exceptional.[37]

This type of security is important in practice especially for tangible movables since only the pledge is recognized under the Civil Code as security for tangible movables and there is no non-possessory security right over tangible movables.

Third-party effectiveness for security assignments over tangible movables or receivables can either be achieved through the civil law method (i.e. fictitious possession for tangible movables and notification of the debtor on a certified date for receivables), or it can be done through registration (both for tangible movables and receivables).[38] The registration system is stipulated by a special law - the Act on Special Provisions of the Civil Code regarding Registration on Transfer of Tangible Movables and Receivables ('Act on Registration'). As the name of the Act suggests, this registry is specific for tangible movables and receivables, and it does not include IP rights. Both the civil law method and the registration method under the Act on Registration have equal standing, so the priority is decided on a first-come basis, regardless of the method chosen. Note that fictitious possession is where the grantor simply indicates their will that, from then on, they be in possession of the object as an agent of the creditor. This means that there is no actual change of possessor and the grantor can continue to use the object.

For security interest over IP rights, registration is always necessary, since a special registry for IP is stipulated as either a condition for transfer (for a patent) or as a requirement for third-party effectiveness (for copyright).[39] Other methods, such as the civil law methods, are not available.

There are two competing approaches to understanding the nature of the security assignment. One is the form approach, which puts more importance on the form than on the substance and considers a security assignment to still be a veritable title transfer, even if it is for the purpose of security. The other is the functional approach, which puts the substance over the form and holds that a security assignment should be considered a security. It is not clear which approach is taken by the court. As stated above in (i), the court considers a security assignment to be a "transfer of title"

---

[36]Supreme Court decision of September 28, 1982 (Hanrei Jiho No. 1062, p. 81).

[37]Supreme Court decision of February 7, 2006 (Minshu Vol. 60, No. 2, p. 480).

[38]Both a security assignment and a pledge over claims or tangible movables can be perfected against third parties by registration at the Tokyo Legal Affairs Bureau, if the grantor is a corporation (Articles 4(1) and 14, Perfection Act). For details, Kozuka and Fujisawa (2009).

[39]It will be further explained in the following section on attachment and perfection.

to the creditor, but only to the extent necessary for the purposes of a security. It is widely understood that since the Supreme Court considers there to be a transfer of title, it takes the form approach, where there is an actual transfer of ownership from the grantor to the creditor.[40] However, there have been obvious applications of the functional approach on case-by-case bases. For example, there are some cases where the court approved of subrogation,[41] and other cases where the court approved of subordinate security assignments.[42] This signifies that the court does take the security right aspect into account rather than the ownership aspect.

As for the object of a security assignment, it is possible for this to be the right to obtain a patent. This is in contrast to a pledge. However, inalienable rights are excluded from security assignments. Thus, the moral rights of copyright law cannot be the object of a security assignment.

(3) Enterprise Mortgage The enterprise mortgage is security over the whole of the enterprise's property and is regulated under a special law: The Enterprise Mortgage Act (enacted in 1958). Intellectual property is naturally included within this property.[43] This will be explained further later on.

(4) Factory Mortgage To the extent that industrial property rights are included in the list of assets covered by a factory mortgage,[44] they can be the objects of a factory mortgage.

3.2 Copyright

(1) Pledge A copyright in a technical/narrow definition of the term can be the object of a pledge; however, moral rights cannot. The effect of the pledge extends to monetary interests such as royalties arising from the pledged copyright.[45]

(2) Security Assignment The abovementioned statement in the Sect. 3.1 on general security assignments also applies to copyright.

(3) Enterprise Mortgage Copyright may also be part of an enterprise's property and can be the object of an enterprise mortgage.

---

[40]Commentary written by Judicial research official of the Supreme Court states that the supreme court takes after the form-approach and considers security assignment as transfer of title (Masumori T., Commentary on the Supreme Court decision of October 20, 2006 [2004 (Ju) No. 1641] Minshu Vol. 60, No. 8, p. 3098, Saikosaibansho, hanreikaisetsu, Minjihen [Commentary of the Supreme Court decision, civil affair, p. 1103].

[41]Supreme Court decision of December 2, 2010 (Minshu Vol. 64, No. 8, p. 1990).

[42]Supreme Court decision of July 20, 2006 (Minshu Vol. 60, No. 6, p. 2499).

[43]Article 2(1), Enterprise Mortgage Act. For more on enterprise mortgage, see Sect. 4.

[44]Article 11(5), Factory Mortgage Act.

[45]Article 66(1), Copyright Act.

(4) Factory Mortgage Copyright is not classified as industrial right and thus cannot be included in a factory's property. Therefore, it cannot be the object of a factory mortgage.

4 Enterprise Mortgage

Under the Enterprise Mortgage Act, it is permitted to take the entirety of an enterprise's assets as collateral. However, the Act only applies to cases where the debtor is a stock company and the secured claim is a corporate bond (Article 1). This Act is influenced by the English floating charge.

It was possible to take the entirety of an enterprise's assets as collateral even before the Enterprise Mortgage Act, thanks to foundation mortgages. Foundation mortgages derived from the German system and are limited to certain industries, with immovable property being the main collateral and accessories of the property being included in the mortgage.[46] Industrial property can be included as part of the foundation, but goodwill cannot.[47]

The Enterprise Mortgage Act includes all assets of the enterprise, including not only all types of IP but also goodwill. However, the Act is directed at very large companies and enterprise mortgages are only used as collateral in the hope of increasing the chances of recovering after default.

Looking at the number of registrations under the Enterprise Mortgage Act, the peak was in the latter half of the 1960s with around 250 per year; however, after that, the number began to decrease, finally reaching zero in the late 1990s.[48] In addition, enterprise mortgages are always subordinate to other security rights (e.g. statutory liens, pledges, and mortgages), even if they are registered first. Since the creditor of the enterprise mortgage only has priority against unsecured creditors, there is not much merit in using this security right.

---

[46]The idea of land being the central element of the foundation mortgage is seen in Factory Mortgage Law Article 14, where it is stated as follows: "A factory foundation shall be deemed as an immovable as whole".

[47]Factory Mortgage Law article 11 explicitly states the following as composition of the factory foundation: (1) land and structure belonging to the factory; (2) machines, implements, electric poles, electric wire, various tubes placed, rails and other attachments; (3) Superficies, (4) lease of things, if lender consents, (5) industrial property; (6) right to use dam.

[48]Editorial Division (2007), pp. 8–9. Statistic of registration is published by Ministry of Justice. http://www.moj.go.jp/housei/toukei/toukei_ichiran_touki.html.

5 Structure of Transactions: Attachment, Perfection, Cost and Priorities

There are two typical ways to use IP as collateral to secure an obligation. One is the security assignment, whereby the IP right that is the object of this assignment is transferred to the creditor, and the other is the pledge. Security assignments are considered to be more favourable, since the registration fees for pledges can be much greater than those for security assignments.

5.1 Attachment and Perfection

(1) Pledge When an IP right is pledged, it is not transferred and the pledgee does not become the IP right-holder. The law clearly states that the right-holder continues to exercise the right. However, it does not prevent the pledgee from exercising the right if the parties explicitly agree to this.[49] The pledge of a patent must be registered to take effect.[50]

(2) Security Assignment The transfer of title has effect only to the extent necessary to achieve the purpose of securing claims. Thus, under the contract of a security assignment, the IP that is the object of the security assignment is transferred to the creditor, but the grantor retains the right to use the IP.[51]

For patents, the patent itself is born when it is registered.[52] Registration is also required for a transfer to occur.[53] This means that for a security assignment to occur, registration is necessary.

For copyright, the situation is different. Copyright itself does not have to be registered, but for a security assignment to be effective against a third party,[54]

[49]Article 95, Patent Act; Article 66, Copyright Act. Article 95 of Patent Act states that "Unless otherwise agreed upon by contract, where a right of pledge is established on a patent right, exclusive license or non-exclusive license, the pledgee may not work the patented invention."

[50]Article 98(1)(iii), Patent Act; Article 77, Copyright Act.

[51]A book written by law firm on financing technique states that although there is no established understanding on whether there needs a license contract between the creditor and the grantor, the author has never encountered a case where such license contract was concluded between the creditor and the grantor separate from contract of security assignment. Nishimura and Asahi (2015), p. 252.

[52]Article 66(1), Patent Act.

[53]Article 98(1)(i), Patent Act.

[54]Article 77, Copyright Act. The "third party" in this article is limited to the third party who has the "legitimate interest" to claim the absence of the registration, such as double assignment. The registration is also necessary to take the effect against the licensee who received the license from the former copyright owner, according to lower court cases (Tokyo High Court decision of May 28, 2003 (Hanrei Jiho no. 1831 p. 135, Tokyo District Court decision of March 28, 2013) and majority opinion. Handa and Matsuda (2015), pp. 921–922.

registration is necessary.[55] Upon registration, since the security assignment transfers the patent to the creditor, the creditor appears to be the patent holder. There is no distinction made between an outright transfer and a security assignment in the registry (for both patents and copyright). Consequently, if the creditor transfers the IP right in breach of the security assignment contract, the grantor cannot oppose this on the basis that the IP right has only been transferred by way of a security assignment.

5.2 *Cost*

The costs involved in a typical transaction, particularly the legal costs, are hard to determine since there is no public record or data. For registration, the fees are outlined below.

(1) Pledge The registration fee is 0.4% of the amount of the secured claim. In cases where several IP rights are acting as security for a single claim, the registration fee is calculated as though there were only one pledge over one IP right. However, in cases where these IP rights were registered separately, and not at the same time, the registration fee will be calculated separately each time. As a result, the cost of registration will add up and, in the end, if the grantor's IP rights come into existence afterwards, and they are necessary to set a pledge on, then the cost of registration can become excessive.[56] Since registration fees are calculated differently for pledges and security assignments, the ultimate cost of registration is one element to consider when choosing between these two types of security interests.

(2) Security Assignment The registration fees are: (1) 15,000 yen for a patent; (2) 9000 yen for a utility model right; (3) 9000 yen for a design right; (5) 18,000 yen for copyright; and (6) 30,000 yen for a trademark right.

5.3 *Priorities*

Where there is a series of patent or copyright pledges, which one takes priority is determined by the date of registration.

In general, the Supreme Court has recognized that multiple security assignments may be created over a single asset.[57] However, it is likely impossible to do this with a patent. Given that there is no difference between the outright transfer of a patent and the security assignment of a patent, once it is registered, and given that registration is

[55] Article 98(1)(i), Patent Act.
[56] Nishimura and Asahi (2015), p. 279.
[57] Supreme Court decision of July 20, 2006 (Minshu Vol. 60, No. 6, p. 2499).

essential for a transfer to occur, it is impossible to register a subsequent security assignment once an initial registration has been made. As for copyright, the transfer of title occurs through a contract; registration is only for the purpose of achieving third-party effectiveness. Thus, competing security assignments could exist for copyright. In such a case, the person first-to- register will take priority.[58]

6 Rights Before Default

With both the pledge and the security assignment, the grantor generally retains the right to use the encumbered IP right. The creditor may, however, decide to collect the earnings generated from the use of the IP and may notify the account debtors accordingly.

6.1 Pledge

Authorization for the pledgee to use the pledged IP right must be provided by contract.[59] There is no restriction on the pledgor's right to use the IP right unless the contract stipulates otherwise. A pledgor may also assign their encumbered right (s) to a third party.

The relevant statutes provide that pledges automatically extend to royalties.[60] This is based on the fact that the pledge of IP extends to the fruits of this IP through subrogation. Given this subrogation, it is necessary to attach the royalties before the pledge is paid off.

6.2 Security Assignment

For security assignments, the allocation of rights and the use of the collateral depend on the individual contractual arrangement. Thus, there is wide range of possibilities

[58]There is neither explicit approval nor restriction in the copyright law on registration of subsequent security assignment. The explanation here is deduced from the general nature of security assignment.

[59]Article 95(1), Patent Act; Article 34(2), Trademark Act; and Article 35(3), Design Act.

[60]Article 96, Patent Act; Article 34(3), Trademark Act. For example, Article 96 of the Patent Act stipulate as follows; "A right of pledge on a patent right, exclusive license or non-exclusive license may be exercised against any consideration to be paid for the patent right, exclusive license or non-exclusive license or any money or goods to be received by the patentee or the exclusive licensee for the working of the patented invention; provided, however, that the pledgee have to attach the consideration, money or goods prior to the payment of money or delivery of goods."

available to the parties. However, a great deal of legal uncertainty exists for security assignments in general in the absence of both a statutory law and well-developed case law.

Depending on the approach adopted,[61] the treatment of the parties' rights differs. Under the form approach, a licence contract concluded between the grantor (licensor) and a third party (licensee) will need to be amended so that the creditor becomes the licensor. This will enable the creditor to receive royalties. Under the functional approach, where the grantor remains the right-holder, there is no need to amend the licence agreement.[62] Also, it is likely that the security right will extend to royalties by way of subrogation, since the Supreme Court approves of fruits being the object of a security assignment by way of subrogation.[63]

Given that a security assignment is actually a transfer, the creditor is the actual right-holder and so can file a request for damages and/or injunctions against infringement.

6.3 Right to Dispose of the Collateral

The pledgee may only dispose of the pledged IP after default. However, for security assignments, if the creditor assigns the IP to a third party before default (constituting a breach of the contract with the grantor), such a transfer is recognized as being fully valid since an assignment of interest from the debtor/grantor to the creditor is considered to be an absolute transfer with respect to third parties.[64]

7 Enforcement

7.1 Pledge

When the debtor defaults, the pledgee can execute the right of pledge by selling the IP rights through a court-supervised auction,[65] the proceeds of which are applied towards the outstanding obligation. In addition, after the pledgor defaults, the

[61]See Sect. 3.1(2).

[62]There is no dominant and consistent understanding of nature of security assignment, causing this to be another barrier in using security assignment.

[63]Although the court is careful in generalization of subrogation for security assignment, it is understood that by Supreme Court decision of December 22, 2010 (Minshu Vol. 64, No. 8, p. 1990) admitted subrogation for movable assets, in this case, inventory.

[64]Supreme Court decision of September 25, 1920 (Minroku Vol. 26 p. 1389) and September 3, 1959 (Minshu Vol. 13, No. 11 p. 1357).

[65]Article 167, Civil Enforcement Act. See Hirano (2004), p. 101. For the right to obtain patent, see Umemoto (2013), pp. 5 et seq.

pledgee becomes entitled to receive royalties.[66] Private sale is possible after default. Once the creditor has enforced their pledge, they must remit the surplus, if any, to the grantor. However, in the event of a private sale, a joint application with the grantor is required in order for the transfer of rights to be registered. Thus, without the cooperation of the grantor, the creditor will have to file an action in court.

A pledge is classified as a "right of separate satisfaction" in case of the debtor's bankruptcy,[67] so the pledgee can enforce the pledge outside of (and unaffected by) the bankruptcy procedure.

7.2 Security Assignment

There is no written rule governing the enforcement of security assignments, and so security assignments are enforced privately and extrajudicially. The creditor may choose between two methods of enforcement: selling the collateral, or becoming the definitive right-holder of the IP (once it has been appraised). The latter is the accepted method of enforcement if the method to be used has not been agreed upon. The creditor must remit the surplus, if any, to the grantor (this is another element of the aforementioned functional approach[68]).

A security assignment is classified as a "right of separate satisfaction" in case of the debtor's bankruptcy[69] and the security-taker is not affected by the bankruptcy procedure.

8 Practical Usefulness

In the absence of data, it is difficult to discern trends in the practical usefulness of IP rights as collateral. However, Development Bank of Japan (DBJ), which took initiative in supporting IP financing, considers the possibility of using IP as collateral in instances where the prospective borrower lacks immovable property that may be used to secure a loan.[70] For DBJ to consider accepting an IP right as collateral, the following conditions must be met: (1) the IP right is recognized as a right by the relevant law, (2) the law does not restrict the use of the IP right as collateral, and (3) the value of the IP right can be readily established.[71] As for determination of which IP rights are qualified as collateral, since it is important to factor in how much

---

[66] Articles 362(2), 371(2) and 372(3), Civil Code.

[67] Article 2(9), Bankruptcy Act.

[68] See Sect. 3.1(2).

[69] Supreme Court decision of April 28, 1966 (Minshu vol. 20 no. 4 p. 900).

[70] Ministry of Economy, Trade and Industry; Intellectual Property Policy Office (2007), p. 46.

[71] Kobayashi (2004) p. 26.

value the IP will generate, any IP that is not generating revenue is not accepted as collateral. Businesses that are the potential beneficiaries of such IP financing are ones that are considered to be higher risk than normal corporate financing, but lower risk than start-up companies.

There are some transactions where IP plays an important role, such as copyright for the financing of movies.[72] The reason is simple: such copyright can be sold in single units without any need to construct a complex pool of IP rights, making the transaction easy to accomplish. Following this line of thinking, theoretically, pharmaceutical products would be suitable for collateralization, as they can also be sold in single units as individual patents. However, practically, IP rights in pharmaceutical products are unheard of. This is because, realistically, just the transfer of a right is not enough, since there is no facility to produce the product. In addition, clinical trials of drugs would have to be restarted from scratch with every new right-holder.[73] Thus, from a practical point of view, it is easier to simply buy an entire business together with the associated IP rights, clinical trials, personnel, etc.

9 Legal and Practical Difficulties

In Japan, generally speaking, the most common collateral used for financing is the real estate. If the company in need of credit does not own real estate, it is more likely that the financial institutions will provide equity financing and acquire its shares.[74] They will not rely on any IP that the company may own as collateral against which advances will be calculated. The reasoning is as follows: In determining whether or not financing will be provided, potential lenders rely on self-assessments to determine the expected expense (provisions) for bad debts. If an obligation is supported by collateral or a guarantee, the provisions are reduced. To that end, under the practice that was mandated by Financial Service Agency's Inspection Manual,[75]

[72]Ministry of Economy, Trade and Industry; Intellectual Property Policy Office (2007), pp. 44, 48 et seq.

[73]For approval of pharmaceutical products, it is necessary to turn-in clinical trial data that the applicant has conducted. The data that are turned in are protected for 8 years under the Pharmaceutical Affairs Act (Article 14), and new comers are prohibited to refer to this data. The reasoning behind such restriction on the new comers are to protect the pharmaceutical company that have first produced this product from generic to be created. The cost of development of such pharmaceutical products could be up to tens of billion dollars (Rademacher 2015, p. 83). For explanation on the value of clinical trial, see Ishino (2018), passim.

[74]For percentage of collaterals used in Japan, see Ono (2015), pp. 191–214.

[75]The supervision manual of Financial Service Agency, "Inspection Manual for Deposit-Taking Institutions", spells out in detail, how collaterals should be evaluated by the financial institutions. This Inspection Manual provided for a checklist of items that banks must comply with. The Manual was abolished for a number of reasons, but one main reason was due to the fact that because of the existence of the Inspection Manual, the banks had excessively relied its lending decision on collateral and guarantees than by presenting bankers' own views on borrowers' future business

which was abolished at the end of March 2019, the collateral was categorized as "good collateral" (such as deposits, government bonds, or electronically recorded loans) or "general collateral" (such as immovables and movables that are registered and monitored). IP was not classified as either good or general collateral. Therefore, for regulated financial institutions, it was costlier to take a security right over IP rights since such collateral is not factored in when calculating the provisions. The result of the abolishment of the Manual and how this may affect IP as collateral is yet to be seen.

Also, another problem for IP financing is that more than 90% of regional financial institutions lack the human resources to determine the value of their borrowers' IP rights,[76] indicating the need for capacity building.

There is no specific law reform project underway concerning IP rights as collateral. However, it is worthwhile to point out that the Financial Service Agency is recommending to regional banks (as opposed to megabanks) to consider a lending practice where the focus is on the assessment of the borrower's business as a whole. In such business assessments, the evaluation of IP rights in relation to how it is relevant to borrower's business, is considered as a crucial element for the banks to understand and value the business for lending purposes.[77]

References

Editorial Division (2007) Houkatsu Tanpohousei no Kento-jyokyo [in English: status of examination of Enterprise Mortgage Law]. Bank Law J 1792:8–9

Financial Services Agency (2014) Publication of the financial monitoring policy for 2014–2015. http://www.fsa.go.jp/en/news/2014/20141225-1/01.pdf. Accessed 14 Jan 2019

Handa M, Matsuda M (2015) Chosakuken-ho Commentaire [in English: Commentary on Copyright Act], 2nd edn. Keiso Shobo Publishing, Tokyo

Hirano K (2004) Chiteki Zaisan Ken no Kinyu Tampo no Kinkyu Tampo Ho Jo no Ichiduke [in English: IP security rights in finance security legislation]. Kawasaki Med Welfare J 14 (1):99–108

Ishino M (2018) Rinsho Shiken Data no Chizai-teki Katsuyo wo Meguru Giron [in English: Discussion on the IP utilization of clinical trial data]. J Ind Acad Gov Collab 14(2):16–20

Japan Group (Honda H et al.) (2016) Study question (General). AIPPI Yearb 2016(3):237–249

prospects. By abolishing the Manual, the Financial Service Agency is expected to inspect the banks by focusing more on the individual bank's overall governance, which should facilitate the banks to explore its own best practices to evaluate borrowers' business prospects.

[76]Mitsubishi UFJ Research and Consulting (2017), p. 21.

[77]"Financial institutions should facilitate the growth of companies and industries based on an assessment of borrower companies business profiles and growth potential (evaluation of customers business potentials), providing financing and advice without overly relying on financial data, collateral and guarantees. In addition, financial institutions should continue supporting small and medium enterprises (SMEs) carefully and endeavor to smoothly facilitate access to finance." Financial Services Agency (2014), p. 3.

Japan Patent Office (JPO) (2018) Procedures for obtaining a patent right. https://www.jpo.go.jp/tetuzuki_e/t_gaiyo_e/pa_right.htm. Accessed 14 Jan 2019

Kobayashi T (2004) Chitekizaisan Finance [in English: Intellectual property financing]. Seibunsha Publishing, Tokyo

Kozuka S, Fujisawa N (2009) Old ideas die hard?: an analysis of the 2004 reformation of secured transactions law in Japan and its impact on banking practices. Thomas Jefferson Law Rev 31 (293):315

Ministry of Economy, Trade and Industry; Intellectual Property Policy Office (2007) Chitekizaisan no Ryutsu/ Shikinchoutatsu Jirei Chousa Houkoku [in English: Intellectual property distribution and fundraising examples survey report]. http://www.meti.go.jp/policy/intellectual_assets/guideline/list8.html. Accessed 14 Jan 2019

Mitsubishi UFJ Research and Consulting (2017) Heisei 29 Nendo Chizai Kinyu no Jittai ni Kansuru Enquete Chosa Kekka [in English: Result of fiscal year 2017 on IP finance]. http://chizai-kinyu.go.jp/reference/docs/reference05.pdf. Accessed 14 Jan 2019

Nishimura & Asahi (2015) Atarashii Finance Shuho [in English: The technique of new finance], 2nd edn. Kinzai Institute for Financial Affairs, Inc, Tokyo

Ono A (2015) A new look at bank-firm relationships and the use of collateral in Japan: evidence from Teikoku databank data. In: Watanabe T, Uesugi I, Ono A (eds) The economics of interfirm networks. Springer, Tokyo, pp 191–214

Plant Variety Protection (PVP) office at Ministry of Agriculture, Forestry and Fisheries (2011a) Plant breeder's right procedures for application. In: The outline of Plant Variety Protection System. http://www.hinshu2.maff.go.jp/en/about/contents/3-4.pdf. Accessed 14 Jan 2019

Plant Variety Protection (PVP) office at Ministry of Agriculture, Forestry and Fisheries (2011b) Examination. In: The outline of Plant Variety Protection System. http://www.hinshu2.maff.go.jp/en/about/contents/5.pdf. Accessed 14 Jan 2019

Rademacher C (2015) Iyaku Tokkyo no Arikata ni Okeru Tokkyo-ho, Gyosei-jo no Shomondai: Nichi Bei In no Shiten kara [in English: Legal and administrative problems on medical patent: comparison between Japan, US and India]. Project Res 11:65–85

Umemoto Y (2013) Chiteki Zaisan Ken ni taisuru Shikko: "Tokkyo wo Ukeru Kenri" oyobi Know-How wo Chushin ni [in English: Compulsory Execution against Intellectual Property Right]. Patent Stud 56:5–19

Security Rights in Intellectual Property in Mexico

Laura Murguía-Goebel

Abstract The use of intellectual property as a security interest is relatively new in Mexico, and it is mainly used to promote access to credit for small and medium-sized enterprises. For this usage to be applied, it has been necessary to undertake important reforms in Mexican intellectual property rights legislation (1) and to create a modern framework of security rights (2). Despite these important efforts, there are still some obstacles that must be overcome and some practical aspects that need to be improved in order to make the creation of security rights over intellectual property in Mexico both efficient and successful (3).

1 An Overview of Intellectual Property Rights in Mexico: Legal Framework

According to Articles 3 and 28 of the Mexican Constitution, the Mexican state supports scientific and technological research and does not consider monopolies to be privileges allowed to authors and inventors.[1] In Mexico, intellectual property law is divided into two important areas. One is industrial property law, which is regulated by the Law on Industrial Property of 1991 (*Ley de la Propiedad Industrial*)[2] and its Regulation of 1994 (*Reglamento de la Ley de la Propiedad Industrial*).[3] These regulations establish the protection of patents, utility models, industrial designs, trademarks, commercial advertisements, trade names, appellations of origin, and industrial secrets.[4] The other is copyright law, which is governed by the Federal Law

[1]Mexican Constitution, Official Journal (OJ) 05.02.1917.

[2]Industrial Property Law (IPL) OJ, 27.06.1991. Last Amendment: OJ, 18.05.2018.

[3]Regulations of the Industrial Property Law OJ, 23.11.1994. Last Amendment: OJ, 16.12.2016.

[4]IPL Art. 2 section V.

L. Murguía-Goebel (✉)
Faculty of Law of the Julius-Maximilians-Universität Würzburg, Würzburg, Germany
e-mail: laura.murguia@jura.uni-wuerzburg.de

E.-M. Kieninger (ed.), *Security Rights in Intellectual Property*, Ius Comparatum – Global Studies in Comparative Law 45,
https://doi.org/10.1007/978-3-030-44191-3_19

on Copyright of 1996 (*Ley Federal del Derecho de Autor*)[5] and its Regulation of 1998 (*Reglamento de la Ley Federal del Derecho de Autor*).[6] These federal laws and regulations are applicable throughout the Mexican Republic and their administrative enforcement falls to the federal executive branch. The federal authorities responsible for administering and applying the rights of industrial property and copyright in Mexico are the *Instituto Mexicano de la Propiedad Industrial* (known by its Spanish acronym, IMPI),[7] the *Instituto Nacional del Derecho de Autor* (known by its Spanish acronym, INDA),[8] and the *Registro Público del Derecho de Autor* (Public Copyright Registry).

In addition to these national regulations, intellectual property rights are also governed by a multiplicity of international treaties for the protection of industrial property and copyright to which Mexico is a party.[9] Mexico is also a member of the World Trade Organization and is a signatory to the WTO Agreement on Trade-Related Intellectual Property Rights (TRIPS). The country has also concluded several free trade agreements that contain rules related to intellectual property, such as the North American Free Trade Agreement (NAFTA) with Canada and the United States (chapter XVII of which pertains to intellectual property).[10]

1.1 Industrial Property Rights

The protection of industrial property is the responsibility of the Mexican Institute of Industrial Property (IMPI). This federal institution of the executive branch is a decentralized public agency with a legal identity and assets. The IMPI is competent to protect industrial property rights and promote the transfer and development of technology. It administers the legal procedures for obtaining patents on inventions and manages their publication, renewal, and transfer.[11]

In accordance with the IPL, an individual (or his assignee) who invents something or creates a utility model or industrial design shall have the exclusive right to exploit it for his benefit, either personally or through others with his consent.[12] The IPL defines an invention as "any human creation that enables matter or energy existing in nature to be transformed to be used by man, in order to satisfy his needs."[13] The Mexican regulation accords the inventor and the designer of the utility model or

[5]Federal Law on Copyright (FLC) OJ, 24.12.1996. Last Amendment: OJ, 13.01.2016.

[6]Regulations of the Federal Law on Copyright (OJ, 22.05.1998). Amended in: OJ, 14.09.2005.

[7]Instituto Mexicano de la Propiedad Industrial (2016), *passim*.

[8]Instituto Nacional del Dercho de Autor (2016), *passim*.

[9]Zamora et al. (2004), pp. 64, 661.

[10]For further information about the international legal framework for IP in Mexico, *see* Annex II.

[11]IPL Art. 6.

[12]IPL Art. 9.

[13]IPL Art. 15.

industrial design the right to obtain a patent or a registration, as well as the right to transfer this patent or registration. This right may be transferred through *inter vivos* transaction or through succession.[14]

To be patentable, inventions must be new, the result of an inventive step, and industrially applicable.[15] To get a patent in Mexico, the inventor or someone representing the inventor must apply for and receive a patent through the legal procedures administered by the IMPI.[16] The period of validity of the patent is 20 years, is renewable, and begins on the date of the filing of the application, upon payment of the filing fee.[17] Once a patent is granted, the IMPI must publish it in the IMPI Gazette, and the patentee enjoys the right to file claims for damages against third parties who exploit the patented product or process without his consent. This is possible even if the exploitation occurred before the patent was granted, as the patentee's rights are established on the date of publication of the patent application in the monthly Gazette of the IMPI.[18]

The owner of the patent also enjoys the right to prevent other persons from manufacturing, using, selling, marketing, or importing the patented product, or any product obtained directly from the patented process, without his prior consent.[19] He has also the right, by virtue of an agreement, to encumber or transfer the rights conferred by a patent or registration, or the rights derived from a pending application. In order to be binding on third parties, the transfer or encumbrance of rights shall be registered with the IMPI.[20] According to the IPL, it shall be sufficient to register the transfer of a patent and to make the appropriate request in the manner specified in the Regulations of 1994.[21] Unless provided otherwise, the granting of a licence shall not prevent the owner of the patent or registration from granting other licences, or from making use of the patent at the same time. In addition, the patentee shall be entitled, unless stipulated otherwise, to institute legal proceedings in defence of the patent rights as if he were the actual owner of those rights. The use of the patent by the person to whom a licence registered with the Institute has been granted shall be considered to be the same as a use by the patent owner, except in the case of compulsory licences.[22] The IPL determines the rules when an applicant has already

[14]IPL Art. 10-10 BIS.

[15]The IPL (Art. 16) considers the following to be non-patentable: essentially biological processes for obtaining, reproducing, and propagating plants and animals; biological and genetic material as found in nature; animal breeds; the human body and the living matter constituting it; and plant varieties.

[16]IPL Art. 38.

[17]IPL Art. 23.

[18]IPL Art. 24.

[19]IPL Art. 24 – 25.

[20]IPL Arts. 62 – 63.

[21]Regulations of the IPL Arts. 5 – 12.

[22]IPL Arts. 67 – 69.

filed for a patent in another country[23] and when several inventors have made the same invention independently of each other.[24]

With respect to other categories of industrial property, protection is available under the IPL for rights in utility models[25]; industrial designs[26]; trade secrets[27]; trademarks[28]; collective marks[29]; well-known and famous marks[30]; advertising slogans[31]; trade names[32]; appellations of origin[33]; and the layout designs of integrated circuits.[34] The IPL and its Regulations of 1994 set the requirements and procedures that must be fulfilled and followed, respectively, in order to obtain and transfer[35] industrial property rights.

In accordance with the IPL, a mark is "any visible sign that distinguishes products or services from others of the same type or category on the market".[36] The registration of a trademark is valid for 10 years, starting from the date of the application, and may be renewed for periods of the same duration.[37] For the registration of

[23]In accordance with IPL Art. 40, the filing date in the country of first filing may be recognized as the priority filing date, provided that the filing in Mexico falls within the periods stablished by international treaties or, failing that, within 12 months of the application for a patent in the country of origin.

[24]In that case, according to IPL Art. 42, the patent rights shall belong to the inventor whose application bears the earliest filing date or recognized priority date, as the case may be, provided that said application is not rejected or abandoned.

[25]IPL Arts. 27 – 30. According to Art. 29, rights in utility models last for 10 years starting from the filing date of the application and cannot be renewed.

[26]IPL Arts. 31 – 37. According to Art. 36, industrial design registration lasts for 15 years starting from the filing date of the application and cannot be renewed.

[27]IPL Arts. 82 – 86 Bis – 1.

[28]IPL Arts. 87 – 98 Bis 9.

[29]IPL Arts. 96 – 98.

[30]IPL Arts. 98 Bis – 98 Bis 9.

[31]IPL Arts. 99 – 104. According to Art. 103, the registration of an advertising slogan shall have a term of 10 years starting from the filing date of the application and may be renewed for periods of the same duration.

[32]IPL Arts. 105 – 112. According to Art. 110, the effects of the publication of a trade name shall last for 10 years starting from the filing date of the application and may be renewed for periods of the same duration. If they are not renewed, the effects shall cease.

[33]IPL Arts. 156 – 178. According to Art. 167, the Mexican state shall be the owner of the appellation of origin. It may be only used by virtue of authorizations issued by the IMPI. However, pursuant to Art. 174, the right to use an appellation of origin may be transferred by the authorized user in accordance with the provisions of ordinary legislation. According to Art. 172, the effects of the authorization to use an appellation of origin shall have a duration of 10 years starting from the date on which the application is filed with the IMPI and may be renewed for equal periods.

[34]IPL Arts. 178 Bis – 178 Bis 9. According to Art. 178 Bis 3, the registration of a layout design shall have a non-renewable term of 10 years, starting from the date on which the application is filed with the IMPI.

[35]The licensing and assignment of rights is regulated by IPL section VI Arts. 136-150.

[36]IPL Art. 88.

[37]IPL Art. 95.

trademarks with the IMPI, the principle that the filing date shall determine precedence between applications prevails.[38] Regarding the licensing and assignment of trademarks, the IPL entitles the owner of a registered or pending trademark, by agreement, to license one or more persons to use the mark in relation to all or some of the goods or services to which the mark applies. In order to be binding on third parties, the licence shall be registered with the IMPI.[39] Moreover, the rights deriving from an application for the registration of a mark or those conferred by a registered mark may be encumbered or transferred in the manner of and according to the procedures set by the ordinary legislation. In order to be enforceable against third parties, such encumbrance or transfer of rights shall be registered with the IMPI.[40]

Finally, the IPL has established several administrative procedures,[41] as well as criminal and civil actions,[42] to enforce industrial property rights in Mexico.

1.2 Copyright

Copyright in Mexico is governed by the abovementioned Federal Law on Copyright of 1996 (*Ley Federal del Derecho de Autor*) and its Regulation of 1998 (*Reglamento de la Ley Federal del Derecho de Autor*), whose purpose is the safeguarding and promotion of the cultural heritage of the nation and the protection of copyright.[43] This legislation is a matter of policy and in the interest of society, and it is applicable throughout the Mexican territory.[44] Other important legislation affecting copyright in Mexico includes the abovementioned Industrial Property Law, as well as the Federal Penal Code,[45] the Federal Law of Administrative Proceedings,[46] and the Federal Code of Civil Proceedings.[47]

In accordance with the copyright legislation, the rights of authors, performers, publishers, producers, and broadcasting organizations in relation to their literary or artistic works (in all forms); performances; publications; phonograms; videograms; or broadcasts, as well as other intellectual property rights, shall be protected.[48] The

[38] IPL Art. 121.

[39] IPL Art. 136.

[40] IPL Art. 143.

[41] IPL Title VI: Administrative Procedures. This title provides the general Rules of procedure (chapter I), the administrative declaration procedure (chapter II), and the appeal for reconsideration (chapter III).

[42] IPL Title VII: Inspection, Administrative Infringements and Sanctions, and Offenses.

[43] FLC Art. 1.

[44] FLC Art. 2.

[45] Código Penal Federal OJ, 14.08.1931 and amendments OJ, 05.12.1996.

[46] Ley Federal de Procedimiento Administrativo OJ, 04.08.1994 and subsequent amendments.

[47] Código Federal de Procedimientos Civiles OJ, 24.02.1942 and subsequent amendments.

[48] FLC Art. 1.

works protected by the FLC are originally created works that can be disclosed or reproduced in any form or medium. The recognition of copyright and neighbouring rights shall not require registration or documentation of any kind, or be subject to compliance with any formality. The protection shall be accorded to works from the time at which they are fixed in a material medium, regardless of their merit, intended purpose, or form of expression.[49] Copyright is the recognition given by the state to the creator of any of the literary or artistic works specified by the FLC[50] to grant protection and allow the enjoyment of exclusive prerogatives and privileges that have a personal or economical character.[51]

It should be noted that Mexican legislation makes a distinction between moral rights and patrimonial rights. Moral rights[52] are inalienable, imprescriptible, unrenounceable, and unattachable. They are considered to be inherent to the author, who is the sole, original, and perpetual owner. Only he and his hires have the right to decide the form of disclosure of the work[53] or whether it will remain unpublished; to demand recognition of his authorship or decide that the work is to be disclosed as an anonymous or pseudonymous work; to demand the respect for the integrity of his work; to amend or withdraw the work from the market; and to object to a work not created by the author being attributed to him.

As for patrimonial rights,[54] these rights grant the author the exclusive privilege to exploit his works or to authorize others to exploit them in any form in accordance with the FLC. The Law recognizes the author, his heir, or the person who has acquired the rights on any grounds to be the owner of the rights. However, by law, only the author shall be considered the original owner of the economic rights; his heirs or successors in title on whatever grounds shall be considered secondary owners. Owners of economic rights are entitled to the reproduction, publication, editing, transmission, distribution, or sale of the work or derived works, and to any other form of transfer of ownership, importation, or disclosure of the work or derived works. They are also entitled to any public use of the work. Patrimonial rights remain

[49]FLC Art. 5.

[50]According to FLC Article 13, the following works are copyrightable: literary works; musical works (with or without words); dramatic works; dance; pictorial works or drawings; sculptures and three-dimensional art; caricatures and short stories; architectural works; cinematographic and other audio-visual works; radio and television programs; computer programs; photographic works; works of applied art, including works of graphic or textile design; compilations consisting of collections of works (e.g. encyclopaedias, anthologies, etc.) and works or other elements like databases, provided that these collections constitute intellectual creations by reason of the selection or arrangement of their contents or subject matter; and other works which may by analogy be considered literary or artistic works.

[51]FLC Art. 11.

[52]FLC Arts. 18 – 23.

[53]It should be mentioned that according to FLC Article 20, in absence of any heirs of the author, or in case of works in the public domain, anonymous works, or works protected by the FLC, the state shall exercise the moral rights in accordance with Article 21 insofar as the works concerned are of interest to the national cultural heritage.

[54]FLC Arts. 24 – 29.

in force for the entire life of the author, for 100 years after his death, and for 100 years following the disclosure of the work. When the work belongs to two or more co-authors, the 100 years shall be counted from the death of the last living co-author. Once these terms have expired, the work shall fall into the public domain.

According to the FLC,[55] patrimonial rights may be transferred through contracts allowing others to exercise the economic rights or to grant exclusive or non-exclusive licences for use. However, these rights shall be assigned in accordance with specific rules that set a high level of protection for copyright. Thus, any transfer of economic rights shall be onerous and temporary. The right of the author or of the owner of the economic rights to receive either a proportional share in the proceeds of the exploitation concerned or a predetermined, fixed remuneration amount is unrenounceable. The following rules shall be observed regarding the acts, agreements, and/or contracts through which economic rights are transferred or licenced: they shall invariably be concluded in writing, failing which they shall be null and void; they shall be entered in the Public Copyright Register in order to be binding on third parties; contracts that have been executed by a notary, public broker, or any authenticating official and entered in the Public Copyright Register shall create enforceable rights (*títulos ejecutivos*); and in the absence of any express provision, any transfer of economic rights shall be deemed to last for a term of 5 years.[56] In addition, the global transfer of future works shall be null and void, and future production may only be carried out pursuant to a contract in the case of a specific work. The FLC allows the granting of licences affording exclusive rights.[57] According to Mexican legislation, copyright shall not be bound to the ownership of the physical object in which the work is embodied. Thus, the alienation of a material medium containing a work shall not constitute the transfer to the acquirer of economic rights. It should be noted that, although economic rights in Mexico may not be either attached or pledged, the benefits and products derived from the exercise of such rights may be used in such manners.[58]

In order to allow the transfer of copyright, the FLC has established six types of contracts: the contract for the publication of a literary work, the contract for the publication of musical works, the stage performance contract, the broadcasting contract, the audiovisual production contract, and the advertising contract.[59]

The FLC considers the author of the work to be the person whose name or pseudonym, either known or registered, appears as the author. In the absence of

---

[55]FLC Arts. 30 – 41.

[56]According to FLC Art. 33, in exceptional cases where dictated by the nature of the work or the scale of the required investment, a term of more than 15 years may be agreed upon.

[57]According to FLC Arts. 35 – 36, licences affording exclusive rights shall: be expressly granted as such; give the licensee the right to exploit the work to the exclusion of any other person, unless otherwise agreed; and give the licensee the right to grant non-exclusive authorizations to third parties. For his part, the licensee shall take whatever action is necessary for the licensed exploitation to be effective.

[58]FLC Art. 41.

[59]FLC Arts. 42 – 76.

proof to the contrary, any actions brought by that person for the violation of his rights shall consequently be entertained by the competent courts.[60] Several rules have been established by the Law to protect all kinds of copyright. Thus, derived works such as arrangements, compendia, expanded editions, translations, adaptations, paraphrased versions, compilations, collections, and transformations of literary or artistic works shall be protected.[61] In addition, full protection is allowed by the FLC for photographic, three-dimensional, and graphic works[62]; cinematographic and audiovisual works[63]; computer programs and databases[64]; and neighbouring rights.[65]

In accordance with Mexican legislation, literary and artistic works and neighbouring rights shall be protected even if they are not registered. However, registration is mandatory in the case of non-literary or artistic works in order for the author to be entitled to claim rights of protection.[66] The Public Copyright Register (Registro Público del Derecho de Autor), as part of the National Copyright Institute (Instituto Nacional del Derecho de Autor), is the federal agency in charge of ensuring the legal security of authors, owners of neighbouring rights, holders of the economic rights concerned, and their successors in title. It is also responsible for affording sufficient publicity to works, instruments, and documents through registration.[67] In accordance with the FLC, it is not only literary or artistic works that are required to be registered with the Public Copyright Register, but also several instruments concerning copyrights, such as agreements or contracts that in any way confer, alter, transfer, encumber, or cancel economic rights.[68] It should be noted that,

---

[60]FLC Art. 77.

[61]According to FLC Art. 78, the abovementioned derived works shall be protected with respect to their original content, but they may only be exploited when this has been authorized by the owner of the economic rights in the original work.

[62]FLC Arts. 85 – 93.

[63]FLC Arts. 94 – 100.

[64]FLC Arts. 101 – 114. Art. 103 provides that unless otherwise agreed, the patrimonial rights concerning a computer program that has been created by one or more employees in the course of their duties or on instructions from their employer shall belong to the employer. It should be noted that, as an exception to both the 5-year term established by Art. 33 and the exceptional term of 15 years that can be accorded where dictated by the nature of the work or the scale of the required investment, the period of the assignment of rights in connection with computer programs shall not be subject to any limitation. Furthermore, Art. 104 sets forth that the owner of the copyright in a computer program or database shall retain the right to authorize or prohibit the lending of copies thereof even after the sale of said copies, except when the copy of the computer program does not in itself constitute an essential element of the licence for use. This regulation is an exception to the provisions of Article 27 (IV) concerning the economic rights of owners to authorize or prohibit the distribution of the work, including sale or other forms of transfer of the ownership of the physical material in which the work is embodied, and also to authorize or prohibit any form of transfer of the use or exploitation of the work.

[65]FLC Arts. 115 – 146 concerning the protection of literary and artistic works.

[66]Zamora et al. (2004), p. 669.

[67]FLC Art. 162.

[68]FLC Art. 163 (V).

under the FLC, entries in the register shall be based on the assumption that the facts and circumstances provided are true in the absence of any proof to the contrary. Any registration shall be subject to third-party rights. In case of dispute, the effects of registration shall be suspended until such time as a final decision is handed down by a competent authority.[69]

The Public Copyright Registry shall register appropriate works and documents submitted to it and provide requested information about registrations. It may, in certain cases, refuse to register works, as determined by the Federal Law on Copyright.[70]

The National Institute of Copyright[71] is competent to investigate administrative infringements; request the practice of tours of inspection; prevent or end the infringement of copyright and related rights through preliminary injunctions; and impose appropriate administrative sanctions. It has other functions as provided for by legislation in this area.[72]

The FLC provides for three types of proceedings in copyright violation cases. First, there is the procedure before the judicial authorities.[73] The Federal Law on Copyright empowers the federal courts to be competent for copyright violation litigation. The state courts and the Court of the Federal District can also be competent in such cases, but only if particular interests are affected. Regarding the applicable law, any civil action brought in connection with copyright and neighbouring rights shall be prepared, conducted, and ruled upon in accordance with the provisions of the FLC and with the Federal Code of Civil Procedure as subsidiary legislation. Only the federal courts shall have jurisdiction to hear appeals involving the contestation of records and registrations in the Public Copyright Register. The INDA shall take part in these proceedings. The Federal Courts shall also have jurisdiction over offences related to copyright in accordance with the Federal Criminal Law.[74] The judicial authorities shall inform the INDA of the commencement of any process that involves copyright and shall send it a copy of all binding resolutions that affect copyrights. The INDA shall record all provisional or final annotations.

Second, the FLC introduces two alternative dispute resolution options. One involves an administrative arrangement proceeding (i.e. conciliation procedure) before the INDA, held at the request of either of the parties, to amicably settle a dispute that has arisen out of the infringement of copyright. The conciliation agreement signed by the parties and the INDA shall be considered *res judicata*

[69]FLC Art. 168.

[70]FLC Art. 164.

[71]Title X about the National Institute of Copyright.

[72]FLC Art. 210.

[73]Title XI of the FLC.

[74]These offences are set forth in the Federal Criminal Code in Title XXVI, OJ, August 14, 1931. Amended in OJ, 18.07.2016.

and enforceable.[75] The other is an arbitration procedure[76] governed by the FLC, which is supplemented by provisions of the Commercial Code.[77]

Third, the FLC provides for administrative proceedings: an administrative infringement proceeding for copyright infringements[78] and an administrative proceeding for trade-related infringements.[79] As sanctions, the FLC provides for different types of fines. There is also the possibility of an administrative appeal, during which the acts and decisions of the INDA are reviewed. Administrative appeals are governed by the Federal Law on Administrative Procedure.[80]

2 An Overview of Security Rights in Mexico: Towards the Creation of a Modern Legal Framework for Security Transactions in Mexico

The modern and efficient regulation of secured transactions, which increases access to credit and reduces its cost, is an important national development tool.[81] In the past two decades, the Mexican government had revised, amended, and harmonized a large part of its commercial legislation to implement a legal system to promote access to credit, mainly for small and medium-sized enterprises, and to ensure the creation, protection, publicity, and enforcement of secured transactions in Mexico.

The new Mexican legislation attempts to reflect the developments made in this area worldwide. Louise Gullifer summarizes this evolution by dividing it into in three important aspects.

The first aspect is the type of collateral available, which has evolved from immovable property to movable property and, very recently, to goods, equipment, and intangible property (i.e. receivables, intellectual property, and securities). The second aspect concerns the ability to process and access data, which has turned paper registration systems into electronic filing systems. The third aspect is the unification and harmonization of national and transnational regulations on security transactions worldwide, which is necessary due to the recent dramatic increase in international transactions and global markets.[82]

With this aim, the Mexican government, in cooperation with delegates, academics, lawyers, and businessmen from Mexico and the United States of America,

[75] FLC Arts. 217 – 218.

[76] FLC chapter III of Arbitration.

[77] Commerce Code Arts. 1415 – 1463.

[78] FLC Arts. 229 – 230.

[79] FLC Arts. 231 – 236.

[80] Federal Law on Administrative Procedure (Ley Federal de Procedimiento Administrativo), (OJ, 04.08.1994).

[81] *See* Gullifer (2016), Introduction.

[82] *Idem.*

have executed a series of studies and tasks with the intention reforming and modernizing Mexican secured transactions regulations to turn Mexico into a more competitive partner within the framework of NAFTA.[83]

2.1 The 2000 Amendments

Unprecedented reforms were carried out in 2000[84] to increase the range of eligible security interest assets. These amendments introduced the non-possessory-pledge,[85] the purchase money security interest,[86] and the guarantee trust.[87]

To support companies that finance their activities with working capital, the area of collateral extends to all rights and assets currently owned by the debtor at the moment of the granting of a non-possessory pledge, inclusive of intellectual property, as well as the assets acquired in the future by the debtor, the assets considered to be products of the pledge, and all assets obtained as a result of transactions of the assets and goods. It also extends to all of the rights and assets that the debtor receives as payment for the sale to third parties of the pledged assets or as indemnification in the event of damages or losses of such assets.[88]

Furthermore, the reforms allow the debtor to transfer his goods through sales of the collateral in due course,[89] but only with the consent of the creditor.[90] Other important contributions in the procedural field are the introduction of two procedures of execution, a judicial proceeding, and some extrajudicial foreclosure mechanisms that are applicable for the non-possessory pledge and the guarantee trust.[91] Despite these efforts, these regulations have some deficiencies. First, it is impossible for

---

[83]North American Free Trade Agreement, U.S., Canada, México. 17.12.1992. The agreement entered into force among the parties on January 1, 1994. https://ustr.gov/trade-agreements/free-trade-agreements/north-american-free-trade-agreement-nafta.

[84]*See* Decree that amends, adds, and repeals various provisions of the General Law of Negotiable Instruments and Credit Operations (GLNICO), the Commercial Code, and the Law of Credit Institutions, OJ, May 23, 2000.

[85]Arts. 355 – 380 of the GLNICO.

[86]Art. 358 of the GLNICO According to this provision, even if the debtor pledges all of the movable assets that he uses for his activities to the creditor without transfer of possession, he is able to pledge to other creditors the assets he receives from the monies provided by these new creditors. The first creditor has priority in relation to the goods that the debtor has pledged to him, with the exception of those assets acquired from the monies of the new creditor that will serve as security to the new creditor. Due to the new creditor's purchase financing, his priority is secured with respect to other creditors, including the first.

[87]Arts. 395 – 407 of the GLNICO.

[88]GLNICO Art. 355.

[89]GLNICO Art. 356 section III.

[90]GLNICO Art. 357.

[91]These reforms were introduced into Title III of the Fifth Book of the Commercial Code (Art. 1414 BIS-1414 Bis 20).

creditors to sue for a deficiency if the value of the property securing the loan is less than the amount of the debt.[92] Second, creditors can only foreclose on their security interests through judicial proceedings, unless the debtor does not contest either the amount of the debt or the fact that it was due and payable.[93]

Finally, the new provisions regarding the Public Registry of Commerce facilitate the implementation of electronic archives through pre-codified forms; this is coordinated nationally through the Integrated Registry Management System (known by its Spanish acronym, SIGER).[94] The development of SIGER began in 1997 and it was introduced in 2000 through the Program of Registry Modernization to ensure completeness of information (in coordination with the 32 Mexican states) and the implementation of the Updated electronic signature (*Firma Electrónica Actualizada*).[95]

The important reforms of 2000 were consolidated with the creation of the Model Inter-American Law on Secured Transaction, which was accomplished within the framework of the OAS (Organization of American States) and with the active participation of the United States and Mexico.[96]

Various provisions of the model law had a decisive influence on the subsequent legislation reforms carried out by the Mexican Government and other Latin American countries.[97]

2.2 The 2003 Amendments

A new package of amendments was launched in 2003[98] to modify the General Law of Negotiable Instruments and Credit Operations in relation to the non-possessory pledge and the guarantee trust,[99] and the following laws in relation to secured

[92]GLNICO Art. 379. This Article was abrogated by the amendments of 2003.

[93]Rogers et al. (2014), *passim.*

[94]Regarding the modernization of the Public Registry of Commerce, *see* the Secretaria de Economía (2013), *passim.*

[95]Sistema Integral de Gestión Registral (2016), *passim.*

[96]Barry (2012), p. 297.

[97]Rogers (2016), *passim.*

[98]*See* Decree to reform, add, and repeal a number of provisions of the General Law of Negotiable Instruments and Credit Operations (GLNICO); the Commercial Code; the Law of Credit Institutions; the Securities Market Law; the General Law on Credit Institutions, Business Companies, and Insurance Companies; the General Law on Mutual Insurance Institutions and Companies; the Federal Law on Bonding Institutions; and the General Law on Credit Organizations and Auxiliary Activities (OJ, 2003-06-13).

[99]In accordance with Article 1 of the Decree of 2003-06-13, Articles 346, 348, 353 paragraph 1, 361 paragraph 1, 373, 374 paragraph 1, penultimate, and last paragraphs, 375, 381 to 385, 386 paragraph 2, 387, 392 section V, 393 paragraph 1, 394 section III, and 395 to 407 were reformed; Articles 346 paragraph 2, and 393 paragraphs 2 and 3 were added; and Articles 379 and 408 to 414 of the GLNICO were repealed.

transactions: the commercial law concerning commercial lawsuits,[100] the Law of Credit Institutions,[101] the Securities Market Law,[102] the General Law on Insurance Companies,[103] the Federal Law on Bonding Institutions,[104] and the General Law on Credit Organizations and Auxiliary Activities.[105]

One of the most important goals for the 2003 Amendments was to replace the deficiencies of the regulations amended in 2000 and to remove the provisions that did not allow the creditor to sue because of a deficiency.[106] Despite this attempt, the 2003 Amendments did not improve the 2000 Amendments concerning the procedures for assuring creditors of the efficacy of extrajudicial foreclosure mechanisms.[107]

To complete the reforms of 2003, a new Regulation of the Public Registry of Commerce was passed in October of 2003,[108] establishing important provisions for implementing the SIGER, as well as rules of registration of security interest.[109]

Despite these new endeavours, it should be noted that the new Article 30 of the 2003 regulations refers uniquely to the registration of the non-possessory pledge,

---

[100]In accordance with Article 2 of the Decree of 2003-06-13, Articles 1054, 1063, 1070 paragraph 1, 1373, 1391 section II, 1393, 1401 paragraph 3, 1414, 1414 Bis 7 paragraph 1, 1414 Bis 8 paragraph 1, 1414 Bis 17 sections I and II, 1414 bis 18, and 1414 Bis 19 were reformed; and Articles 1055 Bis, 1070 paragraphs 2, 3, 4, and 5, 1070 Bis, 1376 Bis, 1395 the last three paragraphs, 1412 Bis, 1412 Bis 1, and 1414 Bis 17 section III of the Commercial Code were added.

[101]In accordance with Article 3 of the Decree of 2003-06-13, Articles 47 paragraph 1 and 2, 66 section II, 67 paragraph 1, 68 paragraph 2, 85, and 106 sections II and XIX (b) and (c) were reformed; Articles 46 Bis, 68 paragraph 3, and 106 section XIX (d), (e), (f) and (g) were added; and Article 68 section I and II and Article 72 of the Credit Institution Law were repealed.

[102]In accordance with Article 4 of the Decree of 2003-06-13, Articles 22 section IV (d), 99 paragraph 1 and sections II, III, and IV, and 103 sections I, II, VII, VIII, IX (a, b, c and d), and X were reformed; Articles 99 paragraph 3 and 103 section IX (e), (f), (g) and (h) were added; and Article 103 section VI of the Securities Market Law was repealed.

[103]In accordance with Article 5 of the Decree of 2003-06-13, Articles 34 section IV and 35 section XVI Bis (a) and (b) were reformed; the last 2 paragraphs of Article 34 section IV, paragraph 2 of (a), (b) Bis and (b) Bis 1, paragraph 2 of (d), (h) of Article 35, and section XVI, section VI with (a), (b), (c), (d), (e), (f), (g) and (h) of Article 62 were added; paragraph 4 of section IV of Article 34 of the General Law on Mutual Insurance Institutions and Companies was repealed.

[104]In accordance with Article 6 of the Decree of 2003-06-13 Article 16 section XV and (a), (b), (d) and (e) were reformed; Articles 16 section XV (h) and 60 section VI Bis with (a), (b), (c), (d), (e), (f) and (g) of the Federal Law on Bonding Institutions were added.

[105]In accordance with Article 6 of the Decree of 2003-06-13, Articles 33 and 48 paragraph 1 were reformed; paragraphs 2 and 3 of Article 48 of the General Law on Credit Organizations and Auxiliary Activities were added.

[106]According to Barry, these provisions stated that if the realization of the collateral did not cover the amount stipulated as due and owing to the creditor, the creditor could not assert a claim against the debtor for the amount of the deficiency. *See* Barry (2012), pp. 320–321.

[107]*Ibid.* p. 321.

[108]*See* the Regulations of the Public Commercial Registry OJ, 24.10.2003.

[109]*See* chapter V of the Public Commercial Registry.

which is effective against third parties following registration,[110] but it does not include other types of security interests.

2.3 The 2009 Amendments

It took several years to continue the modernization of the Mexican secured transactions framework. Thus, another series of significant reforms of the Commercial Code and the Public Registry of Commerce took place in 2009,[111] 2010,[112] and 2014.[113] These reforms implemented the RUG (Unified Electronic Registry of Movable Property Collateral), which contributed significantly to the modernization of the Mexican legal framework for secured transactions.

It should be noted that relevant international instruments, such as the abovementioned 2002 Model Inter-American Law on Secured Transactions of the OAS, the 2008 Legislative Guide on Secured Transactions,[114] and the 2009 OAS Model Registry Regulations,[115] had a significant influence on the creation of the RUG.[116]

By means of the regulations of 2009, Mexico unified its registration system on a national level. With the RUG, Mexico has implemented an electronic system that is modern, universal, exclusive, and applicable throughout the whole territory. This is an important contrast to the United States, where the registry systems are operated separately and more than 50 different iterations of the UCC (Unified Commercial Codes) exist. In addition, there are separate province-by-province filing or registry systems in Canada.[117] Because of this, Harry C. Sigman considers the RUG the best registry in Latin America.[118]

The RUG is an institution overseen exclusively by the Ministry of Economy. It is a section of the Public Registry of Commerce that is available to the public 24 h a day, 365 days a year and that operates through a digital system with national-level

[110]GLNICO Art. 366.

[111]*See* Decree that amends and adds various provisions of the Commercial Code OJ, 27.08.2009.

[112]*See* Decree that amends and adds various provisions of the Public Commercial Registry Regulations OJ, 23.09.2010.

[113]*See* Decree that amends and adds various provisions of the Commercial Code and the General Law of Negotiable Instruments and Credit Operations, OJ, 13.06.2014.

[114]United Nations Commission on International Trade Law (2007), *passim*.

[115]Organization of American States (2009), *passim*.

[116]Rogers et al. (2014), *passim*.

[117]Rogers et al. (2016), *passim*.

[118]In noting some of the most relevant improvements of the RUG, Sigman mentions how the RUG is an all-electronic system, available 24/7 for both searching and registering. It provides a single nation-wide secured transactions database, accessible and free of cost, for registering and for searching for security rights. It has a substantially all-inclusive scope for security rights that are required to be registered at the RUG and it is very user-friendly. Sigman (2013), pp. 393–396.

data.[119] The aim of the RUG is to provide certainty and transparency to secured transactions. Registered in the RUG are security interests; their modifications, transfers, or cancellations; and all related acts. In addition, under the reforms of 2009, registration responsibility falls to the creditors, eliminating the obligation of registrars to revise registration information.[120]

It should be observed that, although the amendments of 2009 took significant steps in establishing the RUG, the 2009 regulations provided, in a general way, that security interests and commercial juridical acts which found, modify, transfer, or cancel a special privilege or a retention right on mobile assets in favour of third parties were "capable to registration." In other words, the term "susceptible" introduced by the amendments of the Commercial Code did not make it obligatory for the registration of security transactions to be effective against third parties.

2.4 The 2010 Amendments

Another series of amendments of the Public Registry of Commerce Regulations, enacted in 2010, introduced relevant improvements.

First, they implemented an operative procedure for the SIGER. Second, for the first time, a concept of "security interest" was introduced in Mexican regulations. It is defined as "the effect of a juridical act through which collateral is created, modified, transferred, or cancelled, as well as a special privilege, or a retention right in favour of third parties, under movable assets to secure the enforcement of an obligation". Other important contributions include the criteria introduced by the regulations—absent in the reforms of 2009—to classify both security interests and movable assets under security. Thus, according to the regulations of 2010,[121] security interests are classified as: (1) non-possessory pledges; (2) the derivatives of equipment credits or operating credits; (3) the derivatives of industrial mortgages; (4) rights in aircrafts or vessels; (5) the derivatives of financial leasing; (6) title reservation clauses in commercial purchase and sale agreements covering movable assets which are capable of being indubitably identified; and (7) the derivatives of guarantee trust agreements, rights of retention (i.e. possessory liens), and other special privileges in accordance with the Code of Commerce and the other commercial laws.

For their part, the movable assets listed by the reforms of 2010 are: (1) machinery and equipment; (2) motor vehicles; (3) stock; (4) agricultural products; (5) consumables; (6) inventory; (7) shares and obligations, gratifications, option contracts, and futures; (8) rights, including the rights of claim; and (9) others.

[119] Registro Único de Garanías Mobiliarias, Secretaría de Economía (2016), *passim*.

[120] Isunza (2016), p. 128.

[121] *See* Decree of 2010 Art. 32.

However, it should be observed that the named list of legal devices subject to registration in the RUG excludes some security mechanisms, such as the possessory pledge and factoring.[122] In addition, the 2009 reforms, as well as these of 2010, did not harmonize the several existing laws governing security transactions. For example, the GLNICO does not mandate the registration of financial leasing,[123] while the RUG regulations of 2010 require that it be registered.[124]

2.5 The 2014 Amendments

Several reforms of the Commercial Code, the GLNICO, and the Organic Law of the Judicial Branch of the Federation that were implemented on January 10, 2014 and June 13, 2014 consolidated the modernization process of the secured transactions framework that had been undertaken by Mexico over the previous two decades.

First, the reforms of January 2014 of the Commercial Code concerning commercial proceedings allow the lender to get an order immediately for the provisional sequestration of assets without the possibility of the debtor's opposition.[125]

Second, the amendments to the Organic Law of the Judicial Branch of the Federation set up special federal district courts to settle on commercial matters more quickly and efficiently.[126]

Third, there were significant amendments to the Commercial Code Article 32 Bis in June 2014. In contrast to the Regulations of the Public Registry of Commerce of 2003, which only provide for the registration of the non-possessory pledge, and the 2009 regulations, which provide (generally) that security interests are "susceptible to registration" in order to be effective with respect to third parties, the amendments of June 13, 2014 list all security transactions and establish the "obligation of their registration" in the RUG. Thus, the following security mechanisms shall be registered: the non-possessory pledge; the commercial pledge when the pledging creditor will not maintain possession of the goods; the equipment credit or the operating credit; and the industrial mortgage. Furthermore, Article 32 Bis includes a new list of juridical commercial acts by which a right of retention may be created in favour of a creditor who does not have possession of the movable assets. The list also includes any other acts, encumbrances, or liens on personal property or movable assets used to secure loans where the creditor does not have possession of the collateral. It also lists other credit mechanisms like financial leasing; factoring; commercial sales contracts when the seller does not have possession of the movable assets but retains

---

[122] *See* RUG Regulations Art. 32 amended on OJ, 23.09.2010.

[123] *See* GLNICO Art. 408. This provision was amended and harmonized with the RUG Regulations through the reforms of the GLNICO OJ, 13.06.2014.

[124] Isunza (2016), p. 128.

[125] Isunza (2016), p. 129.

[126] *Idem.*

any ownership or rescission rights; security trusts; and judicial or administrative rulings affecting movable assets, including those related to attachment orders. Moreover, the June 2014 reforms pursue the harmonization of the RUG Regulations with the GLNICO, stipulating the obligation of registration of financial leasing found in the RUG, as well as other similar provisions concerning security mechanisms such as the pledge, non-possessory pledge,[127] and security trust.[128]

It shall be mentioned that this reform had an important impact on the Mexican economy. Isis Isunza[129] summarizes the results according to statistics of the RUG. First, the impact on the increase of secured transactions: over 13,000 registrations in the period of 2009/10; 45,000 in the period of 2010/11; more than 69,000 registrations by November 2011, including initial registrations, modifications, and cancellations of security transactions; and more than 400,000 registrations in the RUG by November 2014.[130] Second, there has been increased access to credit by small and medium-sized enterprises (known by the Spanish acronym PYMES). Third, there has been a major increase in access to credit by farmers, since agricultural products, followed by machinery and equipment, represent the majority (41%) of assets registered as collateral in the RUG. Fourth, there has been a drastic decrease in the number of registrations made by intermediaries (such as notaries public or lawyers), since 97% of current registrations are made by creditors directly.[131]

Despite these relevant efforts undertaken by Mexico in the past two decades, the modernization process of the Mexican framework of secured transactions has not yet been fully completed. Unlike Article 9 of the UCC, implemented by all of the States of the American Union, the Mexican regulations concerning security mechanisms are fragmented into several laws, including the Civil Codes of the Mexican States, the Federal Commercial Code, and other commercial laws.[132]

Consequently, no unified legislation exists that encompasses all secured transactions, nor is there a single regulatory mechanism. Instead, there are different legal institutions contemplating transactions that include personal property or movable property, which are regulated by the variety of abovementioned laws like the Commercial Code,[133] the General Law of Negotiable Instruments and Credit

[127]GLNICO Art. 376 amended on OJ, 13.06.2014.

[128]GLNICO Art. 389 amended on OJ, 13.06.2014.

[129]Isunza (2016), pp. 130–134.

[130]According to the Ministry of the Economy, Mexico has climbed in the rankings for access to credit by seven positions compared to last year, reaching fifth place. *See* Ministry of Economy, accessible through a government webpage: https://www.gob.mx/se/articulos/conoce-que-es-el-registro-unico-de-garantias-mobiliarias-rug.

[131]It should be observed that, according to the amendments of 2009 of Commerce Code Art. 32 bis 4, the following are entitled to register with the RUG: notaries and commercial notaries public; judges; authorities allowed by the Ministry of Economy; financial institutions; public officers; and other persons allowed by the Ministry of Economy.

[132]Rogers et al. (2014), *passim*.

[133]Commercial Code OJ, 13.12.1889. Last Amendment: OJ, 25.01.2017.

Operations,[134] the Law of Credit Institutions,[135] the several valid Civil Codes in Mexico,[136] and the Regulations of the Public Registry of Commerce and Property. Contrary to Civil Law, in Mexico the local Congress of the Federal States is responsible for the regulation in the commercial sphere. Article 73—X of the Mexican Constitution vests power in the Federal Congress alone to legislate on commercial matters, which means that the commercial law is of general application throughout the Republic of Mexico. While this provides uniformity, the Mexican Security Instruments are regulated by various different legal and regulatory institutions, which makes the study and the practical application of them difficult. For instance, Mexican law regulates pledge and mortgage agreements through the Civil Codes of the 32 federal states.[137] The commercial pledge; the non-possessory pledge[138]; the pledge on equipment credits or operating credits; and certain commercial legal acts involving the transmission of privileges or rights of retention of chattels such as the security trust, financial leasing, and factoring are regulated by the General Law of Negotiable Instruments and Credit Operations. The industrial mortgage, meanwhile, is regulated by the Law of Credit Institutions.[139] The registration of security interests in the RUG is regulated by the Commercial Code, as are commercial proceedings in cases of non-compliance. Furthermore, other important laws managing security interests can be found in the Regulations of the Public Registry of Commerce.

Although in the last two decades Mexico has made much great progress by implementing a modern, transparent, and secure system for security transactions, there are still some efforts to be made to complete this process. Among the most important issues, it would be preferable for the extensive lists of security interests that have until now been governed by different federal and state regulations to be regulated by a single piece of legislation, much like Article 9 of the UCC.[140] This

[134]General Law of Negotiable Instruments and Credit Operations (GLNICO) (OJ, 27.08.1932). Last Amendment: OJ, 13.06.2014.

[135]Law of Credit Institutions OJ, 18.07.1990. Last Amendment: OJ, 17.06.2016.

[136]It has to be observed that in addition to the Civil Codes of the 32 federal states of the Mexican Republic, the Federal Civil Code also applies in federal matters throughout the Republic. *See* Federal Civil Code OJ, 26.05.1928, 14.07.1928, 03.08.1928 and 31.08.1929. Amended in OJ, 24.12.2013.

[137]Art. 2856 of the Federal Civil Code defines the pledge as "a right in a movable asset that secures the performance of an obligation and its payment priority". For its part, Art. 2893 defines the mortgage as follows: "The mortgage is a security right in assets that are not delivered to the creditor and it gives him the right in the case of non-compliance with the obligations to be paid from the value of the assets according to the priority provided by law".

[138]In Title II on credit operations, the GLNICO regulates the possessory pledge (section VI of chapter IV) as well as the non-possessory pledge (section VII).

[139]Law of Credit Institutions OJ, 18.07.1990, Art. 67.

[140]According to López-Velarde and Wilson, before the implementation of Article 9, there were several mechanisms for creating security interests, making the decision as to which legal device was best suited to create a security interest difficult. *See* López-Velarde and Wilson (2004), p. 7.

would simplify harmonization and prevent confusion and difficulties for lenders when they must choose and implement a security interest.

3 Security Rights Over Intellectual Property Under Mexican Law

Creating security rights over intellectual property is possible under Mexican law, but it is not commonly done. Intellectual property is governed by Mexican Law as intangible goods. Copyright is considered to be a movable asset by Civil Code Art. 758. In addition, according to the Mexican IPL, patents, trademarks, and designs are intangible goods and can be granted as security interests. As mentioned above, Art. 62 contemplates the possibility of encumbering or transferring the rights conferred by a patent. Moreover, Art. 143 states that the rights deriving from an application for the registration of a mark or those conferred by a registered mark may be encumbered or transferred.

3.1 Typical Structures of Secured Transactions Over IP Rights in Mexico

Security transactions over IP rights under Mexican law are typically structured as the commercial pledge, the non-possessory pledge, and the security trust.

Pursuant to Civil Law,[141] the pledge is a right *in rem* created over a movable asset to secure the performance of an obligation and its priority for payment. The commercial pledge is governed by the General Law of Negotiable Instruments and Credit Operations (GLNICO). It is a security mechanism applicable to all types of rights and movable assets. To constitute a pledge, a pledgor (i.e. debtor) transfers a right or an asset to a pledgee (i.e. creditor) to secure a debt. Upon default of the secured obligation, the pledgee can request foreclosure on the pledged good before a judicial court to get payment from the proceeds resulting from the sale of the good. The GLNICO regulates two kinds of commercial pledge: the possessory pledge (*prenda con transmisión de posesión*)[142] and the non-possessory pledge (*prenda sin transmisión de posesión*).[143] By means of a possessory pledge, the pledgor is dispossessed of the movable assets and rights by the pledgee to secure the performance of the obligation. By means of a non-possessory pledge, the debtor maintains possession and operation of the pledged rights or assets.[144]

[141] Civil Code Art. 2856.

[142] GLNICO Arts. 334-345.

[143] GLNICO Arts. 346-380.

[144] *See* Castillo et al. (2016), *passim.*

According to the GLNICO,[145] the non-possessory pledge is a right *in rem* over movable property for the purpose of securing both compliance with an obligation and priority in payment, with the debtor maintaining physical possession and operation of the property.[146] In exceptional cases, it may be agreed that the creditor or a third party will maintain physical possession of the collateral. A security interest in the form of a Mexican non-possessory pledge may cover all types of rights and movable assets,[147] unless the assets are considered to be personal assets according to law.[148] The encumbered assets shall be identified individually, either by category of goods or in a generalized way. Pursuant to the GLNICO,[149] the following movable assets can be encumbered with a non-possessory pledge: all assets and rights belonging to the debtor, including trademarks and commercial advertisements; the property acquired by the debtor after the creation of the security agreement (i.e. after-acquired property); and the property derived as fruits of the aforementioned assets or rights, or of their proceeds. Under a non-possessory pledge mechanism, the pledgor may, with prior authorization from the pledgee, assign encumbered IP rights to third parties.[150]

By means of a security trust (*fideicomiso de garantía*), the grantor or trustor/creditor (*fideicomitente*) transfers ownership or title of the rights and movable assets constituting the collateral to the trustee (*acreedor/institución fiduciaria*)[151] to guarantee the performance of an obligation and its priority for payment.[152] The advantages of the security trust are that title to the collateral remains with the trustee (and not with the debtor), and special summary and out-of-court proceedings are available, in case of a foreclosure, to make the entire foreclosure process efficient.[153] Pursuant to the GLNICO,[154] the same trust can be used to secure several simultaneous or successive obligations engaged by the debtor with the same or different security trustees pursuant to the rules and priorities applicable. Moreover, the parties to the trust may agree that the grantor may use movable assets affected by the trust,

---

[145] Art. 346.

[146] According to GLNICO Art. 356, the pledgor (i.e. debtor) has the right to: use the pledged assets; receive and use the assets considered to be products of the pledge; and sell or transfer the pledged assets for his commercial activities.

[147] GLNICO Art. 352.

[148] GLNICO Art. 353.

[149] Art. 355.

[150] GLNICO Arts. 358 and 261.

[151] Pursuant to GLNICO Art. 395, the trustee for a guarantee trust must be one of the following types of institutions: a credit institution; insurance institution; securities institution; brokerage firm; social purpose financial institution that has been duly registered before the National Commission for the Protection and Defence of Financial Services and Customers; public bonded warehouse; credit union; and mutual fund management company that fulfills the requirements established in the Mutual Funds Law.

[152] GLNICO Arts. 381 and 395.

[153] *See* García (2010), *passim*.

[154] GLNICO Art. 397.

combine them with other assets, or instruct the trustee to sell them within the usual course of the activities of the grantor.[155]

It should be emphasized that the non-possessory pledge and the security trust are the most appropriate mechanisms for creating security transactions over IP in Mexico.

3.2 *Steps to Be Taken to Make Such Security Rights Effective*

The commercial pledge over IP must be set forth in a contract in writing and must be registered with the IMPI[156] to be effective against third parties.[157] This pledge will be perfected once the assets or rights are held by the pledgee.

A written agreement on the creation of a non-possessory pledge over IP is also required.[158] A contract in which a non-possessory pledge is created is deemed to be a commercial contract for all of the parties involved.[159] The pledge agreement should be executed or ratified before a notary public if the amount of the secured obligation is equal to or higher than the peso equivalent of 250,000 Investment Units (known by its Spanish acronym, UDI).[160] To be effective against third parties, the non-possessory pledge must be registered with the RUG[161] and before the IMPI. A non-possessory pledge registered with the RUG has priority over any acts or liens recorded afterward.[162] The legal acts creating, modifying, extinguishing, or transferring the non-possessory pledge, as well as its cancellation by legal resolution, must be registered with the RUG or before a special registry such as the IMPI[163] or the National Copyright Institute,[164] depending on the procedure.[165]

The security trust must be also perfected in a written agreement. It must be ratified before a notary public if the value of the IP is equal to or higher than the peso equivalent of 250,000 Investment Units (known by its Spanish acronym, UDI).[166] To be effective against third parties, the security trust agreement regarding IP must also be registered with the RUG, as well as with the IMPI or the National Copyright Institute, depending on the type of IP. It must be observed that, according to

[155]GLNICO Art. 398.
[156]IPL Art. 62.
[157]*See* Castillo et al. (2016), *passim*.
[158]GLNICO Art. 365.
[159]GLNICO Art. 347.
[160]GLNICO Art. 366.
[161]GLNICO Art. 367.
[162]GLNICO Art. 371.
[163]IPL Art. 62.
[164]FLC Art. 32.
[165]GLNICO Art. 376.
[166]GLNICO Art. 404.

Regulation of the Public Registry of Commerce Art. 31 Bis, in case of security transactions that are capable of being registered in a special registry, this registry shall make the entry automatically in the RUG.

3.3 Mechanisms to Evaluate the IP

Mexican legislation on secured transactions does not establish general mechanisms for assessing IP rights. However, GLNICO Art. 399, which concerns security trusts, allows the parties to state in the contract how the assets will be evaluated.

Therefore, the grantor and the secured creditor generally hire an independent firm or appraiser (*perito o tasador*) to assess the IP. They also may engage a commercial broker (*corredor público*), who is allowed by the Federal Law of Public Brokerage[167] to act as an expert appraiser.

The following internationally recognized mechanisms are the methods most commonly used by the experts mentioned above to evaluate IP in Mexico[168]:

- the income-based method
- the cost-based method
- the market-based method
- the option-based method

Another relevant reference is the International Accounting Standards Board (IASB). These rules have been substantially improved in Mexico over the last few years, and now allow IP to be included as an intangible asset in financial statements.[169] International Accounting Standard C-8 in particular establishes rules for the recognition and assessment of intangible assets in Mexico.[170]

Finally, another useful tool used in Mexico for the valuation of intangible assets is chapter VI of the OECD guidelines, which introduces important concepts for estimating market value in transactions related to intangible assets.[171] Vicente Torre summarizes the following OECD considerations to be taken into account for the valuation of intangibles[172]:

- Existence (check whether this is an intangible that is actively identifiable in a clear way and that represents a competitive advantage);

[167]Federal Law of Public Brokerage Art. 6-II, OJ 29.12.1992. Last Amendment: OJ, 09.04.2012.

[168]UNCTAD, OMC, OMPI (2003), *passim.*

[169]*See* Morales Lechuga (2004), *passim.*

[170]*See* CINIF (2008), *passim.*

[171]*See* Torre Delgadillo (2012), pp. 308–310.

[172]*Idem.*

- Transfer (the transfer or sale of property rights in intangible goods, and the transfer of the right to use or temporarily exploit an intangible good by means of the payment of a royalty through a licence contract);
- Characteristics of the operation (to know the contractual conditions of the transaction involving the transfer of the intangible);
- Perspective of the parties involved in the operation (to determine if the estimated value corresponds to the price that an independent would have been willing to pay in a comparable transaction);
- Proportionality between consideration and future benefits (the proportionality between the value given in return for the transfer or license of an intangible asset and its capacity to generate future economic benefits);
- No duplication of the consideration (the agreed consideration for the transfer of the intangible asset should not be doubled);
- Individual analysis (the market value of each intangible asset transferred together with other goods, services, or intangibles must be determined on an individual basis).

Even though in recent years Mexico has improved its legal framework to facilitate security transactions over IP, it would be suitable to establish general rules for valuating IP.[173] This would simplify and promote the implementation of intangible assets as collateral, providing more transparency and security to grantors and secured creditors.

3.4 Priorities

Pursuant to the provisions of the Civil Code in relation to pledges, the following rules must be observed:

I. Tax debts must enjoy priority[174];
II. Mortgage creditors and pledgees must have priority over others creditors and be payed from the collateral's value[175];
III. To have priority, the creditor/pledgee must keep the pledge in his possession[176]; and
IV. The following expenses and credits must be paid in this order[177]:
    a. Trial expenses and expenses incurred by the sale of the goods;
    b. Expenses for conserving and administrating the goods;

[173] Astudillo and Mancilla (2014), p. 19.
[174] Federal Civil Code Art. 2980.
[175] Federal Civil Code Art. 2981.
[176] Federal Civil Code Art. 2984.
[177] Federal Civil Code Art. 2985.

c. Expenses for insuring the goods; and
d. Mortgages, creditors, and pledgees in accordance with the date of their creation.

The validity of the non-possessory pledge[178] and the security trust agreement[179] must be determined by when the pledge or agreement was created. To enjoy priority against third parties, these mechanisms must be registered before the RUG[180] or with a special registry like the IMPI or the National Copyright Institute. Priority for both mechanisms is determined by the time of registration.

Other relevant rules govern the non-possessory pledge. According to the GLNICO, a security created with a non-possessory pledge of movable assets has priority over other guarantee mechanisms (such as mortgages, equipment, credits, or security trusts) when the registered non-possessory pledge of the movable asset adheres to secured immovable property, unless the pledgee agrees that the second guarantee has priority over the security interest. The priority between non-registered securities shall be determined by the chronological order of the contracts. The non-possessory pledge registered with the RUG shall have priority over recordable and non-recordable acts and encumbrances and over acts and encumbrances that are registered later on. The priority created by a non-possessory pledge may be modified with the agreement of the affected pledgee and the new priority established by the parties shall be effective at the moment of its registration.[181]

In addition, the Insolvency and Bankruptcy Law (*Ley de Concursos Mercantiles*)[182] provides a list showing priorities of payment in case of insolvency, classifying the creditors in the following categories according to the nature of their credits[183]:

- Singularly privileged creditors (such as the creditors for the funeral expenses of the merchant and the creditors for the expenses related to the illness that has caused the death of the merchant (provided, in both instances, that the commercial insolvency ruling is after the merchant's death));
- Creditors with collateral (e.g. mortgagees and those with a pledge)[184];
- Creditors with special privileges (e.g. creditors who, according to the Commercial Code or other related laws, have a right of withholding);

[178]GLNICO Arts. 365-366.

[179]GLNICO Art. 404.

[180]Regulation of the Public Registry of Commerce OJ, 24.10.2003 amended on OJ, 30.12.14. *See* Art. 31.

[181]GLNICO Arts. 367-372.

[182]The Insolvency and Bankruptcy Law (IBL) was published on the OJ, 12.05.2000 and amended on 10.01.2014.

[183]IBL Art. 217.

[184]According to IBL Art. 219, creditors with collateral will receive the payment of their credits from the proceeds of the assets, subject to their liens; creditors with special privileges, common creditors, and subordinated creditors shall be completely excluded in accordance with the applicable regulations regarding the registration date of the guarantee mechanism.

- Common creditors (i.e. those who do not fall under the above paragraphs; their common credits will be paid ratably without regard to the dates of their credits); and
- Subordinated creditors.

It should be underlined that labour credits other than preferential labour credits (i.e. wages and severance payments owed for the 2 years preceding the insolvency declaration)[185] and tax credits have priority and shall be paid once the credits against the estate, singularly privileged credits, and credits with collateral have been paid, but before credits with special privileges and common credits.[186]

Concerning the security trust, in order to perfect this mechanism, the debtor's assets shall be transferred to the trustee and shall not form part to the debtor's estate.[187]

3.5 *Enterprise Charges*

As explained above, the debtor is allowed to encumber all inventories and receivables (these can be described in general terms, rather than described by referring to specific items[188]) by means of the non-possessory pledge or the security trust. These security mechanisms enable present and future assets to be subject to a security interest. They can be granted over all[189] or part of the assets (tangible or intangible) used in the ordinary course of business by a debtor for his primary activities. These are designated by practitioners as "blanket liens"[190] or "Mexican floating liens"[191] and are compared with the floating lien granted under Article 9 of the UCC of the United States of America.[192] To create a Mexican floating lien, the same requirements described above with respect to non-possessory pledges and security trusts

[185]It shall be mentioned that the Mexican Labour Law protects the rights of workers in the event of insolvency. Thus, according to Federal Labor Law Art. 113, "the salaries earned during the last year and the indemnity owed to the workers have priority over any other credit, including credits that benefit from "in rem" guarantees, tax credits, and credits for the Mexican Social Security Institute, and over all of the assets of the employer."

[186]IBL Art. 221.

[187]Nevertheless, Chadbourne & Parke LLP observe that because the assets remain on the debtor's books for accounting and tax purposes, the bankruptcy of the debtor could result in challenges to the transfer from third parties based on discrepancies and the favourable treatment of certain creditors, and one should consider whether a court could conclude that such a transfer is a fraudulent transfer or priority. *See* Chadbourne & Parke LLP (2009), *passim.*

[188]*See* Alford (2016), *passim.*

[189]GLNICO Art. 358.

[190]Goebel Caviedes designates these mechanisms as "Blanket Liens". *See* Goebel Caviedes (2005), pp. 72–73.

[191]*See* Alford (2016), *passim.*

[192]Baker & McKenzie (2008), pp. 70–71.

must be met. They may be summarized as follows: one must identify the assets subject to the pledge, enter into a non-possessory pledge or security trust agreement, formalize this agreement before a notary public, and register the security agreement with the RUG or a special registry (i.e. the IMPI or the National Copyright Institute, depending on the IP).

It shall be underlined that, although floating liens based just on IP are envisaged by Mexican legislation, this practice is unusual in Mexico. The Mexican financial system still continues to favour tangible assets and immovable property or the combination of these with IP for securing loans.[193]

3.6 Rights Before Default

The mutual rights and obligations of the debtor/grantor and the creditor in transactions are determined by the GLNICO, according to the type of security mechanism.

Concerning the commercial pledge (possessory pledge), pursuant to the GLNICO,[194] the creditor/pledgee is entitled to: (I) keep possession of the movable assets or rights; (II) exercise all rights inherent in them (the expenses to be placed on the account of the debtor); (III) sell the goods when the value of the rights or the movable assets goes down and is not enough to cover the debt; and (IV) ask the judge to authorize the sale of the goods or rights when the guaranteed obligation expires or when the debtor does not comply with the obligation to provide the necessary funds in time to cover the debt. The pledgee may not retain ownership or possession of the pledged assets or rights without the express consent of the debtor.[195] According to the Civil Code, the pledgee must indemnify the debtor for deterioration and damages that are the pledgee's fault and return the asset to the pledgor upon the full repayment of the debt, together with any interest or charges for maintenance expenses.[196] The pledgor may object to the sale of the movable assets; repay the debt; improve the collateral; or increase the number of goods given in pledge or for reduction of the debt.[197]

Regarding the pledge without transfer of possession (non-possessory pledge), the GLNICO[198] enables the pledgor to make partial payments to decrease the collateral in proportion to the payments made, provided that the rights of the creditor are guaranteed and the parties do not agree otherwise. If the debtor is subject to a

[193]This conclusion was reached by the Director of the Regional Office of the Mexican Institute of Industrial Property at the Bajío, Alejando Salas Domínguez.

[194]GLNICO Arts. 338- 342.

[195]GLNICO Art. 344.

[196]Federal Civil Code Art. 2876.

[197]GLNICO Art. 342.

[198]GLNICO Arts. 349-351.

bankruptcy process, the secured credit will be required from the date of the bankruptcy declaration and the stipulated interest will continue to accrue to the extent of the collateral value. In the event of bankruptcy, the secured creditor may proceed with the foreclosure of his collateral security with the bankruptcy judge, who must order the enforcement of the collateral without further processing. Pursuant to Art. 361 of the GLNICO, the pledgor, in his capacity as the possessor of the assets, must: (I) pay the necessary expenses for the maintenance of the encumbered assets; (II) provide the pledgee other collateral or the full repayment of the debt, even before the agreed deadline, in case of loss or deterioration of the encumbered assets; (III) and allow the pledgee to inspect the encumbered assets to determine their maintenance status. In addition, pursuant to Arts. 364 and 376 of the GLNICO, after credit, interest, and other expenses have been fully paid, the pledgee must release the non-possessory pledge by means of registration with the RUG or with a special registry (i.e. the IMPI or the National Copyright Registry).

Finally, concerning the security trust, according to the GLNICO, the grantor is entitled, based on the agreement of the parties, to: (I) make use of the assets; (II) perceive and use the fruits and products of the assets or rights guaranteed by the trustee; and (III) inform the trustor about the disposal of the assets or rights in accordance with the trust and in the grantor's normal course of activities.[199] Moreover, the parties are entitled to agree on[200]: (I) the place where the guaranteed assets should remain; (II) the minimum amount of compensation that the trustee should receive for the selling or transferring of the assets; (III) the persons (designated by the trustee) to whom the trustee may sell or transfer the assets or rights; (IV) the information that the trustor should give to the trustee concerning the transformation, sale, or transfer of the assets or rights; (V) the way in which the assets or rights are to be assessed; and (VI) the reassessment of the assets, if their value increases. In the event of non-compliance, the secured credit may be declared expired in advance.

The parties are also permitted to agree on the following: (I) the possession of the assets or rights by third parties or by the grantor (in such cases, these parties are responsible for the assets and for the cost of maintenance); (II) the creditor having the right, in the event of loss or deterioration of the assets or rights, to request the transfer of other assets or rights, or the amortization of the debt before the stipulated term; (III) expenses being borne by the party who is in possession of the assets or rights in the event of their loss or damage, or the deterioration of their value; (IV) the party that is in possession of the assets or rights allowing the other party to inspect and verify their maintenance status; (V) the debtor providing additional assets to meet the original value in the event that the market value of the assets decreases and is not sufficient to meet the principal amount and related debts; and (VI) credit being stopped in advance in the event that the debt is not reconstituted, in which case the creditor must notify the debtor before a court or a notary public. In addition, the parties are entitled to agree on the way in which the trust institution will proceed to

---

[199] GLNICO Art. 398.

[200] GLNICO Arts. 399-401.

dispose of the assets and rights (out of court) in case of non-compliance with the secured obligation. Pursuant to the GLNICO, secured creditors with a non-possessory pledge[201] or a security trust[202] will see their right to claim expire after 3 years, starting from the date of the guaranteed obligation.

3.7 *Enforcement*

Security rights over IP can be enforced in Mexico both outside insolvency and in insolvency.

3.7.1 Outside Insolvency

Enforcement and foreclosure procedures will depend on the type of security interest.

Commercial Pledge (Possessory Pledge)

Art. 34 of the GLNICO allows the creditor to request that the judge authorize the sale of collateral when the secured obligation expires. The judge will summon the defendant, who will receive a term of 15 days to raise objections. The judge must then decide within 10 days. If the debtor accepts the facts of the claim, the judge will allow the selling of the assets.

Non-possessory Pledge and Security Trust

Pursuant to the GLNICO,[203] the enforcement of a non-possessory pledge or security trust must adhere to the provisions of the Commercial Code, which provides for two types of proceedings, described below.

Non-judicial Procedure

Payment of the defaulted obligation or the delivery of the collateral can be requested under the extrajudicial foreclosure mechanism,[204] provided the following requirements are met: (I) there are no disputes as to the enforceability of the credit or the amount claimed; and (II) there is agreement regarding the delivery of the collateral.

[201]GLNICO Art. 375.
[202]GLNICO Art. 405.
[203]GLNICO Arts. 346 and 402.
[204]Commercial Code chapter II Arts. 1414 Bis – 1414 Bis 6.

This procedure follows the following steps: (I) the extrajudicial foreclosure starts with the formal requirement of the delivery of the property, which the debtor performs for the secured creditor or the trustee before a notary public; (II) once the goods have been delivered, the pledgee or the trustee will be designated as the official receiver; (III) the sale of the collateral will follow, and the debt will be settled when the value of the collateral is equal to the amount of the debt; (IV) when the value of the collateral is less than the amount of the debt, the creditor may freely dispose of the collateral and may sue for the difference that has not been covered.

Judicial Procedure

Pursuant to chapter II of the Commercial Code,[205] if the procedure provided for in Art. 403 of the GLNICO has not been observed, there shall be a judicial procedure that is intended to pay a certain liquid and enforceable credit and award material possession of the assets or rights being used as security in case of a non-possessory pledge or guarantee trust.

This provision regarding a guarantee trust makes it possible for the parties to agree on the manner in which the trustee will proceed to dispose—extrajudicially and on an onerous basis—of the assets or rights in trust while observing the following requirements: (I) the fiduciary institution must initiate an out-of-court sale of the collateral if it receives written communication from the creditor requesting such a sale and specifying the breach of the secured obligation; (II) the fiduciary institution must notify the debtor in writing of the request for an out-of-court sale and the debtor may only object if he repays the debt, complies with the obligation, or presents a document proving the extension of the repayment period or the novation of the obligation; (III) the text containing the extrajudicial sales agreement shall be included in a special section of the guarantee trust with the signature of the settlor. In the absence of an agreement, the procedure of the Commercial Code regarding the sale of the assets and rights in trust and the processing of a trial to oppose the implementation of the trust shall be followed.

During the judicial procedure provided by the Commercial Code, the following requirements shall be observed: (I) the secured credit shall be recorded in a public or private document in accordance with the provisions of the GLNICO; (II) the written request shall be accompanied by the relevant agreement, the determination of the balance, and, in the case of a credit institution, the corresponding balance certification; (III) the judge will accept the lawsuit, requiring payment from the defendant and summoning him to trial; if not, the defendant or the depositary of the assets will transfer material possession to the creditor or a party whom he designates, who shall become a legal depositary; (IV) if the defendant does not deliver the assets or the rights, the judge may use whatever means of enforcement he deems appropriate; (V) for his part, the defendant can invoke procedural defences pursuant the rules of Art. 1414 Bis 10 of the Commercial Code; (VI) if the defendant accepts the facts of

[205] Commercial Code Arts. 1414 Bis. 7-1414 Bis 20.

the lawsuit, the final decision will be pronounced; (VII) the evidence will be presented in court before the judge, who shall act on the judgment; (VIII) the sale, if chosen by the plaintiff party, will be made before a judge or notary public pursuant to the procedure established by the Commercial Code; (IX) when the value of the assets or rights is greater than the amount of the compiled debt, the plaintiffs, having deducted the credit, interest, and expenses generated, will give the defendant the remainder of the value of the goods; and (X) in this procedure, no procedural issues may be raised and the pronounced decisions will only be appealable in devolutive effect; furthermore, in no case, the procedure will be suspended.

3.7.2 In Insolvency

Reorganization and bankruptcy proceedings are governed by the abovementioned Mexican Insolvency and Bankruptcy Law (the IBL). The IBL is a federal law that has been in force since May 12, 2000; it replaced the Law of Bankruptcy and Suspension of Payments (*Ley de Quiebras y Suspensión de Pagos*, known by its Spanish acronym, LQSP), which had been enacted in 1943. Chadbourne and Parke LLP note that, unlike the old LQSP, which had an adversarial approach that focussed on liquidation rather than reorganization, the IBL of May 2000 promotes cooperation and agreement, and involves court-appointed officials in the process.[206] Moreover, under the LQSP, cases were assigned to local or federal judges who, in most cases, were not specialized in bankruptcy matters, whereas under the IBL, cases are assigned to a federal district court which is assisted by a specialist appointed by the Federal Institute of Reorganization Specialists (*Instituto Federal de Especialistas de Concursos Mercantiles*, known by its Spanish acronym, IFECOM). This institute was introduced by the IBL to advise civil judges on the bankruptcy process.[207]

The Mexican IBL organizes insolvency proceedings (*concursos mercantiles*) in two stages,[208] each of which is supervised by the IFECOM. The first stage is the conciliation or reorganization stage (*conciliación*), whose purpose is to preserve the operation of the debtor's business and prevent the debtor's bankruptcy, while reaching a binding agreement between the debtor and his creditors in the form of a restructuring plan. The second stage, which comes into effect if reorganization is not achieved, is the bankruptcy or the liquidation stage (*quiebra*), whose purpose is to liquidate the business to repay the creditors.

---

[206] *See* Chadbourne & Parke LLP (2009), *passim.*

[207] *Idem.*

[208] IBL Art. 2.

Reorganization Stage

The purpose of the reorganization stage is to verify whether the debtor is in general default on his obligations. Reorganization cases are commenced by the filing of a claim in a federal district court. According to the IBL, the following parties are empowered to file insolvency claims[209]: the debtor (in a voluntary case, he files a *solicitud*),[210] any creditor, and the Attorney General (in an involuntary case, they file a *demanda*).[211] A guarantee must be posted with the petition filed by the debtor or the creditors to guarantee payment of the examiner's fees.[212]

Once the request for bankruptcy has been accepted by the court, the judge must file a request with the IFECOM for the appointment of an examiner (*visitador*). The examiner must report to the court if the debtor is insolvent and can be declared bankrupt (*en concurso*).[213] Once the petition for bankruptcy is filed by the debtor or admitted by the court, the merchant may request authorization from the judge to contract the credit needed to maintain the ordinary operations of the company and the necessary liquidity during the insolvency proceeding.

Once the examiner's report has been received, the debtor, the creditors, and the Attorney General are allowed to review it, file any request for modification, and submit any evidence they deem appropriate.[214] Within 5 days after the last petition, the court must determine whether or not the debtor is insolvent.

Pursuant to the IBL, a merchant can be declared insolvent if he has generally failed to perform his obligations as follows[215]: (I) the debtor has failed to comply with his contractual obligations in respect of two or more different creditors; (II) the obligations of the debtor that have been due for at least 30 days represent at least 35% of the debtor's payment obligations as of the date of filing; and (III) the debtor does not have sufficient liquid assets (e.g. cash and demand deposits; term deposits and investments; accounts receivable; securities; or negotiable instruments) to perform at least 80% of the obligations that are past due as of the date of filing.

If the court determines the solvency of the debtor, the bankruptcy procedure ends.[216] If the court finds that the debtor is legally insolvent, the judge will issue the order of relief (*sentencia de concurso mercantil*), which begins the conciliation stage. The goal of this stage is to come up with a creditors' agreement or reorganization plan (*convenio de restructuración*) between the debtor and the creditors through the mediation of a conciliator, who will be designated by the IFECOM.[217]

[209]IBL Art. 9.

[210]IBL Art. 20.

[211]IBL Art. 21.

[212]IBL Art. 24.

[213]IBL Art. 29.

[214]IBL Art. 41.

[215]IBL Art. 10.

[216]*See* Sainz (2016), *passim*.

[217]IBL Art. 147.

The mission of the conciliator is to prepare and present to the court a list of the debtor's creditors and to determine the amount, order, and level of priority of his creditor payments. The reorganization agreement must provide for the payment of the following categories of claims/creditors, in the following order of priority[218]: (I) special labour claims; (II) claims related to the administration of the estate (including attorney's fees); (III) specialists' fees and expenses (i.e. fees and expenses charged by the examiner (*visitador*), conciliator (*conciliador*), and/or trustee in bankruptcy (*síndico*) and their assistants in the performance of their duties); (IV) singularly privileged creditors (i.e. the creditors for funeral and medical expenses that were incurred with respect to an illness that led to death (when the debtor is a natural person)); (V) secured creditors (i.e. creditors with a mortgage, pledge, or other security right covering property belonging to the debtor[219]); (VI) labour and unsecured tax claims; (VII) creditors with a special privilege (i.e. statutory privilege); and (VIII) general unsecured creditors (who will be paid only if all superior classes of creditors have been fully paid).

The conciliation stage is designed to be completed within 185 calendar days, although two 90-day extensions may be granted by the court. Under no circumstances may the reorganization stage be extended beyond 365 days.[220] According to the IBL, the conciliation stage will conclude and the debtor will be declared bankrupt in the following cases[221]: (I) the debtor asks to be declared bankrupt; (II) the term for conciliation has elapsed; and (III) the conciliator requests the debtor's bankruptcy and the court agrees to grant it. The reorganization agreement will, with the approval of the court, becoming binding on: the merchant; all common recognized creditors and subordinates; all secured and priority creditors; and all secured and priority creditors whose claims are to be paid in full, subject to certain legal rules concerning quantification.[222]

Liquidation Stage

The order of liquidation has the following effects[223]: (I) the suspension of the legal capacity of the debtor to manage his business; (II) the debtor and his administrators, managers, and employees must pass possession and administration of the property and rights forming the bankruptcy estate on to the trustee in bankruptcy; (III) the debtors of the bankrupt debtor must not make any payments without the approval of

[218]*See* Chadbourne & Parke LLP (2009), *passim.*

[219]Chadbourne & Parke LLP observe that secured creditors' claims are satisfied from the collateral to the extent of the collateral's value; however, if the claim is greater than the value of the collateral, the resulting deficiency claim will be considered an unsecured claim. *Idem.*

[220]IBL Art. 145.

[221]IBL Art. 167.

[222]IBL Arts. 164-165.

[223]Backer McKenzie (2016), *passim.*

the trustee (with the observation that they must pay twice in the case of non-compliance); and (IV) the IFECOM must appoint the conciliator or someone else as trustee to administer the debtor's company. Once the order of liquidation has been given, the trustee in bankruptcy must, within 60 days of his appointment, file with the court an inventory, accounting, and balance sheet. According to the IBL, the trustee is responsible for selling the assets and rights that make up the estate of the debtor for the highest price possible in a public auction.[224] It is important to point out that creditors with security interests in the assets being auctioned off will be paid out of the collateral, subject only to the payment of qualified labour claims.[225] For the payment of credits, the Order of Recognition, Ranking, and Preference of Claims must be respected.[226] In the event that the assets or rights are not sufficient to satisfy all claims, there will be a pro-rata distribution to the holders of claims.[227]

Finally, it is interesting to mention that, to ensure greater cooperation in Mexican/American cross-border insolvencies, Title 12 of the IBL adopts the UNCITRAL Model Law on Cross-Border Insolvency.[228]

3.8 Some Practical Issues

Other practical issues concerning security rights over intellectual property in Mexico are their cost, their practical usefulness, their legal and/or practical difficulties, and the need for reforms to the legal framework.

The costs involved in a typical transaction concerning secured transactions over IP rights in Mexico consist of notarial fees and registration fees. Notarial fees vary according to the value of the assets and the type of document or security interest being notarized. In most cases, notarial fees have a ceiling, but they can be high.[229] Notarial fees can also vary according to the place of the transaction: they are regulated locally depending on the state and can be quite expensive in some states.[230] Concerning registration fees, registering personal property in the RUG is free of charge. The registration of IP is handled by the IMPI or the Mexican Institute

---

[224] IBL Arts. 197-198.

[225] *See* Chadbourne & Parke LLP (2009), *passim*.

[226] *Idem*.

[227] *Idem*.

[228] *See* Phelan et al. (2012), *passim*.

[229] *See* Rivero Andere (2017), *passim*.

[230] According to Machorro JC notary fees and registration are quite expensive in Mexico particulary where registration duties are based on the value of the secured debts. *See* Machorro and Santamarina y Steta SC (2010), *passim*.

of Copyright. The IMPI rates[231] and National Institute of Copyright fees are available online.[232]

As for the practical usefulness of security rights over IP, unfortunately, there are no available statistics that can show the frequency of transactions involving IP as a security interest in Mexico. However, it is possible to assert that such transactions are not common in this country.[233]

Regarding legal and/or practical difficulties, despite major reforms undertaken by Mexico in recent years, using intellectual property as a security interest is not a common business practice. One of the causes for this is the lack of knowledge in this area. Many SMEs (*PYMES*) do not record or recognize their intellectual property due to the cost of doing so or due to an ignorance of the benefits of using it as a security interest. There is also a lack of knowledge concerning how IP should be valued. In Mexico, banks still prefer immovable property and tangible movables such as machinery, cars, equipment, etc. for guaranteeing loans. Finally, we can mention that the Civil Law tradition of Mexico imposes various requirements when formalizing security interests, such as the creation of the security interest before a notary or public broker and its registration in several registries. This formalism, together with the cost and time that it requires, is often seen as excessive and discourages the use of security interests.

Finally, as we have noted throughout this study, since 2000, Mexico has been implementing a series of unprecedented reforms in all areas related to security interests. This country is currently, in the context of its recent legislative reforms, seeking to establish mechanisms to promote and consolidate the use of security interests with the goal of achieving greater financial inclusion of SMEs (*PYMES*).[234] However, there are currently no proposals for any reforms relating to security transactions over IP rights in Mexico.

References

Alford K (2016) The RUG: floating lien, preventive filing and is the RUG the better than the UCC. NCS Blog. http://home.ncscredit.com/rug-floating-lien-preventive-filing-and-rug-better-ucc. Accessed 15 Nov 2018

Astudillo M, Mancilla ME (2014) La valuación de los bienes intangibles en México. Actualidad Contable FACES 17(28):5–20

Baker & McKenzie (2008) Doing business in Mexico. Juris Publishing, Inc., New York

Backer McKenzie (2016) Global restructuring and insolvency guide. https://www.bakermckenzie.com/-/media/files/expertise/banking-finance/bk_globalrestructuringinsolvencyguide_20170307.pdf?la=en. Accessed 15 Nov 2018

[231] Instituto Mexicano de la Propiedad Industrial (2018), *passim*.

[232] Instituto Nacional del Derecho de Autor (2017), *passim*.

[233] This is the view taken by Alejando Salas Domínguez, Director of the Regional Office of Mexican Institute of Industrial Property at the Bajío.

[234] *See* Devolder (2016).

Barry J (2012) Secured transactions reforms in Mexico: in pursuit of a uniform system. Houston J Int Law 34:289–343

Castillo E, Mendez JJ, Michaus M (2016) Security interest over intellectual property. AIPPI Study Report. http://aippi.org/wp-content/uploads/2016/07/2016_Study_Question_General_Security_interests_over_intellectual_property_GroupReport_Mexico_12-07-2016.pdf. Accessed 15 Nov 2018

Chadbourne & Parke LLP (2009) Guide to Mexican bankruptcy law. http://www.nortonrosefulbright.com/files/chadbourne/publications/mexican%20bankruptcy%20law%20guide.pdf. Accessed 15 Nov 2018

CINIF (2008) Norma de Información Financiera C-8 Activos intangibles. www.cinif.org.mx. Accessed 15 Nov 2018

Devolder M (2016) Garantías mobiliarias, una ruptura para la inclusión financiera. Forbes México, IFC. https://www.forbes.com.mx/garantias-mobiliarias-una-ruta-para-la-inclusion-financiera/. Accessed 15 Nov 2018

García JA (2010) The Mexican Trust (fideicomiso). https://www.mdtlaw.com/images/uploads/The_Mexican_Trust_Fideicomiso1.pdf. Accessed 15 Nov 2018

Goebel Caviedes H (2005) Current techniques for secured financing of negotiated acquisitions in Mexico, including analysis of effective use of guarantee trust and pledges without possession. U S Mexico Law J 13:71

Gullifer L (2016) Introduction. In: Gullifer L et al (eds) Secured transactions law reform: principles, policies and practice. Hart Publishing, London

Instituto Mexicano de la Propiedad Industrial (2016) IMPI. http://www.gob.mx/impi. Accessed 16 Oct 2018

Instituto Mexicano de la Propiedad Industrial (2018) Servicios que ofrece el IMPI. https://www.gob.mx/impi/acciones-y-programas/servicios-que-ofrece-el-impi-tarifas-tarifas-marcas-avisos-y-nombres-comerciales. Accessed 16 Oct 2018

Instituto Nacional del Dercho de Autor (2016) INDA. http://www.indautor.gob.mx/. Accessed 16 Oct 2018

Instituto Nacional del Derecho de Autor (2017) Primera Solicitud ISBN - Persona Física (Autor-Editor). http://indautor.gob.mx/isbn/p_fisica_primera.html. Accessed 29 Nov 2018

Isunza I (2016) The impact of secured transactions reforms in Mexico and Colombia. Ariz J Int Comp Law 33:126–138

López-Velarde A, Wilson JM (2004) A practical point-by-point comparison of secured transactions law in the United States and Mexico. Uniform Commercial Code Law J 36(4):7

Machorro JC, Santamarina y Steta SC (2010) Country Q&A Mexico finance 2010. PLC cross-border finance handbooks. Practical Law Company, London

Morales Lechuga VM (2004) Los activos de propiedad industrial y mecanismos para facilitar en los sectores productivos nacionales capacidad efectiva de constitución, mantenimiento y observancia de estos activos, tanto a nivel nacional como en los mercados nacionales de exportación. El papel de los agentes de la propiedad industrial. http://www.wipo.int/meetings/es/details.jsp?meeting_id=6062. Accessed 15 Nov 2018

OAS (2002) Ley Modelo Interamericana sobre Garantías Mobiliarias. http://www.oas.org/es/sla/ddi/docs/garantias_mobiliarias_Ley_Modelo_Interamericana.pdf. Accessed 22 Nov 2018

Organization of American States (2009) Model registry regulations under the model Inter-American law on secured transactions. http://www.oas.org/dil/cidip-vii_doc_3-09_rev3_model_regulations.pdf. Accessed 18 Oct 2018

Phelan RE, Beckham CA, Haynes and Boone, LLP (2012) Cross-border insolvency with Mexico. III Second annual international insolvency conference Fordham University Law School, New York, p 21. https://www.iiiglobal.org/sites/default/files/3-_Cross_Border_Insolvency_with_Mexico.pdf. Accessed 15 Nov 2018

Registro Único de Garanías Mobiliarias, Secretaría de Economía (2016) RUG. https://www.rug.gob.mx/Rug/home/inicio.do. Accessed 18 Oct 2018

Rivero Andere JI (2017) Lending & secured finance 2017—Mexico. https://iclg.com/practice-areas/lending-and-secured-finance/lending-and-secured-finance-2017/mexico. Accessed 27 Feb 2017

Rogers JE (2016) Mexico's unified secured transactions registry offers new opportunities for secured lending. http://www.strasburger.com/mexicos-unified-secured-transactions-registry-offers-new-opportunities-secured-lending/. Accessed 22 Dec 2016

Rogers J, Pérez Ortega FJ, Villegas Guillot CA (2014) Recent improvements in Mexican secured transactions law. http://www.strasburger.com/wp-content/uploads/2014/11/Recent-Changes-in-Mexican-Secured-Transactions-Law.pdf. Accessed 12 Nov 2016

Rogers JE, Pérez Ortega FJ, Villegas Guillot CA (2016) Recent improvements in Mexican secured transactions law. Law360. https://www.law360.com/Articles/814084/the-state-of-secured-lending-in-mexico. Accessed 9 Feb 2017

Sainz A (2016) Restructuring and insolvency in Mexico: overview. Thomson Reuters Practical Law. https://cervantessainz.com/descargables/Restructuring_and_insolvency_in_Mexico.pdf. Accessed 15 Nov 2018

Secretaria de Economía (2013) El Registro Público de Comercio. http://www.cofemer.gob.mx/imagenesUpload/201310281756Registros%20P%C3%BAblicos%20del%20Comercio%20y%20Garant%C3%ADas%20Mobiliarias%20-%20Elsa%20Ayala%20G%C3%B3mez.pdf. Accessed 16 Oct 2018

Sigman HC (2013) Security over movable in Mexico: Mexico's new Registro Único de Garantías Mobiliarias (RUG). UNAM, Mexico City, pp 387–400. https://archivos.juridicas.unam.mx/www/bjv/libros/8/3581/30.pdf. Accessed 22 Nov 2018

Sistema Integral de Gestión Registral (2016) SIGER. http://www.siger.gob.mx/. Accessed 16 Oct 2018

Torre Delgadillo V (2012) Precios de transferencia. Trillas, Ciudad de México

UNCTAD, OMC, OMPI (2003) La Clave de la Propiedad Intelectual: Guía para pequeños y medianos exportadores. http://www.wipo.int/publications/es/details.jsp?id=294. Accessed 15 Nov 2018

United Nations Commission on International Trade Law (2007) UNCITRAL, legislative guide on secured transactions. http://www.uncitral.org/uncitral/en/uncitral_texts/security/Guide_securedtrans.html. Accessed 18 Oct 018

Zamora S, Cossio JR, Pereznieto L, Xopa JR, Lopez D (2004) Mexican law. Oxford University Press, Oxford

Legal Provisions

Annex I: National Legal Framework for Security Transactions and IP in Mexico

Commercial Code, "Código de Comercio", Official Journal 13.12.1889. (Last Amendment 02.05.2017)

Federal Civil Code, "Código Civil Federal", Official Journal 31.08.1928 (Last Amendment 24.12.2013)

Federal Labor Law, "Ley Federal del Trabajo", Official Journal 01.04.1970 (Last Amendment 12.06.2015)

Federal Law of Administrative Procedure," Ley Federal de Procedimiento Administrativo", Official Journal, 04.08.1994. (Last Amendment 02.05.2017)

Federal Code of Civil Proceedings, "Ley Federal del Procedimientos Civiles", Official Journal, 24.02.1943. (Last Amendment 09.04.2012)

Federal Law of Copyright, "Ley Federal del Derecho de Autor", Official Journal, 24.12.1996. (Last Amendment, 13.01.2016). The full text in English may be found at: http://www.wipo.int/wipolex/en/details.jsp?id=3079
Federal Law of Public Brokerage, "Ley Federal de Correduría Pública", Official Journal, 29.12.1992. (Last Amendment in OJ 09.04.2012)
Federal Penal Code, "Código Penal Federal", Official Journal, 14.08.1931. (Last Amendment 26.06.17)
General Law of Negotiable Instruments and Credit Operations, "Ley General de Títulos y Operaciones de Crédito", Official Journal, 27.08.1932. (Last Amendment, 13.06.14)
General Law on Credit Institutions and Auxiliary Activities, "Ley General de Organizaciones y Actividades Auxiliaries del Crédito", Official Journal, 14.01.1985. (Last Amendment 10.01.2014)
Insolvency and Bankruptcy Law, "Ley de Concursos Mercantiles", Official Journal 12.05.2000. (Last Amendment 10.01.2014)
Law of Credit Institutions," Ley de Instituciones de Crédito", Official Journal, 18.07.1990. (Last Amendment 17.06.2016)
Law on Industrial Property, "Ley de la Propiedad Industrial", Official Journal, 27.06.1991. (Last Amendment 18.05.2018). The full text in English (amended version, 25.01.2006) may be found at: http://www.wipo.int/edocs/lexdocs/laws/en/mx/mx029en.pdf
Mexican Constitution, "Constitución Política de los Estados Unidos Mexicanos", Official Journal, 05.02.1917. (Last Amendment 24.02.2017)
Securities Market Law, "Ley de Mercado de Valores", Official Journal 18.10.1990. (Last Amendment 10.01.2014)

Regulations

Regulation of the Public Registry of Commerce, "Reglamento del Registro Público de Comercio", Official Journal, 24.10.2003. (Last Amendment 20.12.2016)
Regulations of the Industrial Property Law, "Reglamento de la Ley de la Propiedad Industrial", Official Journal, 23.11.1994. (Last Amendment 16.12.2016)
Regulations of the Federal Law on Copyright, "Reglamento de la Ley Federal del Derecho de Autor", Official Journal, 22.05.1998. (Last Amendment 14.09.2005)

Model Laws

OAS, Model Registry Regulations under the model Inter-American Law on Secured Transactions, 09.10.2009
UNCITRAL, Legislative Guide on Secured Transactions, adopted by the General Assembly on December 11, 2008

Annex II: International Legal Framework for IP in Mexico

IMPI:https://www.gob.mx/impi/acciones-y-programas/temas-de-interes-asuntos-internacionales-marco-juridico-internacional-en-propiedad-intelectual?state=published
Lisbon Agreement for the Protection of Appellations of Origin and their International Registration. OJ 11.07.1964. In force since 26.01.2001
Convention Establishing the World Intellectual Property Organization. OJ 21.01.1975. In force since 14.06.1975

Paris Convention for the Protection of Industrial Property. OJ 27.07.1976. In force since 26.07.1976

Nairobi Treaty on the Protection of the Olympic Symbol. OJ 02.08.1985. In force since 16.05.1985

North American Free Trade Agreement, "Tratado de libre Comercio de América del Norte", 17.12.1992. In force since 01.01.1994

Patent Cooperation Treaty (PCT). OJ 25.07.1994. In force since 01.01.1995

Agreement on Trade-Related Aspects of Intellectual Property Rights (TRIPS) (Annex 1C of the Marrakesh Agreement Establishing the World Trade Organization). OJ 30.12.1994. In force since 1994

International Convention for the Protection of New Varieties of Plants (UPOV). OJ 07.12.1995. In force since 1997

Regulation of the Patent Cooperation Treaty. OJ 31.12.1995. In force since 01.01.1995

Regulation of the Lisbon Agreement for the Protection of Appellations of Origin and their International Registration. In force since 1966.

Marrakesh Agreement (establishing the WTO). OJ 30.12.1994. In force since 01.01.1995

Vienna Agreement Establishing an International Classification of the Figurative Elements of Marks. In force since 26.01.2001

Locarno Agreement Establishing an International Classification for Industrial Designs. In force since 26.01.2001

Nice Agreement Concerning the International Classification of Goods and Services for the Purposes of the Registration of Marks. In force since 21.03.2001

Strasbourg Agreement Concerning the International Patent Classification (IPC). In force since 26.10.2001

Security Rights in Intellectual Property in the Netherlands

Th. C. J. A. (Dick) van Engelen

Abstract The topic of security rights over IP rights is not well developed in The Netherlands. In practice, such rights are generally asked for in financing and investment agreements. In the absence of a central chapter in the Dutch Civil Code, dealing with security rights over IP rights, vesting security rights requires checking the applicable specific IP statutes, which have different provisions, and the general provisions for security rights in the Dutch Civil Code and is this a relatively cumbersome exercise. There is not much case law on the topic, which seems to indicate that as a practical matter security rights over IP rights seem to be effective.

1 Overview of IP Rights in the Netherlands

International Perspective The Netherlands is a Member State of the European Union and of TRIPS. Therefore, Dutch law has the intellectual property rights that are required under these international regimes.

1.1 Patents

Under the Dutch Patent Act ("*Rijksoctrooiwet*") ("*DPA*"), two kinds of patents exist: European patents in which the Netherlands is a designated state and national Dutch patents.

European Patents European patents for which the Netherlands is a designated state exist under Dutch law once they are granted by the European Patent Office. A Dutch translation of the claims is required. If a European patent is granted in a language

Th. C. J. A. (Dick) van Engelen (✉)
Maastricht University, Maastricht, The Netherlands
e-mail: dick.vanengelen@maastrichtuniversity.nl

E.-M. Kieninger (ed.), *Security Rights in Intellectual Property*, Ius Comparatum – Global Studies in Comparative Law 45,
https://doi.org/10.1007/978-3-030-44191-3_20

other than English, a Dutch translation of the patent needs to be filed with the Dutch national patent office. Upon grant of the patent, the Dutch part of a European patent is subject to Dutch law and is treated in the same manner as a Dutch national patent.

National Dutch Patents National Dutch patents are granted after a national application is filed with the national patent office ("*Octrooicentrum Nederland*"). The application will be followed by (a) a search report regarding the state of the art and (b) an opinion on novelty and inventiveness. However, the applicant is free to disregard the opinion and to obtain the patent as the applicant pleases; the patent office is unable to refuse to grant the patent in such cases.

Supplementary Protection Certificates In accordance with the two European regulations on supplementary protection certificates ("SPC") for (i) medicinal products and (ii) plant protection products, SPCs for such products can be obtained for the Netherlands. These certificates are governed by the property law provisions of the Dutch Patent Act that also apply to patents (Article 97 DPA).

1.2 Trademarks

Trademark rights that are enforceable in the Netherlands find their basis either in EU trademarks or Benelux trademarks.

EU Trademarks EU trademarks as granted under the EU Trade Mark Regulation ("EUTM Regulation") are valid and enforceable in the Netherlands. These are supranational trademark rights that only exist if and when granted, upon application, by the European Union Intellectual Property Office ("*EUIPO*"). Article 16 of the EUTM Regulation provides that, as objects of property, these rights are—in in their entirety, and for the whole area of the Union—dealt with as national trademarks, unless Articles 17 to 24 of the regulation provide otherwise. That same article also indicates which national trademark law applies, which is, simply put, the national law of the seat, domicile, or establishment of the trademark proprietor, provided that this seat, domicile, or establishment is in an EU Member State. If that is not the case, then Spanish law, being the national law of the seat of the EUIPO, applies.

Benelux Trademarks In 1970, the Netherlands ceased to have national trademarks; instead, it only has supranational trademarks for the combined territories of Belgium, the Netherlands, and Luxembourg ("*Benelux*") as provided for in the Benelux Convention on Intellectual Property (Trademarks and Designs) ("Benelux IP Convention"). These rights are truly supranational in that they are only granted or invalidated for the Benelux territory as a whole. They need to be granted, upon application, by the Benelux Office for Intellectual Property ("*BOIP*"). The Benelux Convention contains some provisions on property law aspects for Benelux trademarks. In addition, the national property law of the individual Benelux countries may apply, or the national property law provisions that apply to the trademark proprietor may apply. The Benelux Convention does not contain any specific private international law provisions (contrary to the EU Trade Mark Regulation).

1.3 Copyright

The Dutch Copyright Act ("*Auteurswet*") applies to copyright in the Netherlands. In line with the requirements of the Berne Convention, a copyright comes into existence by operation of law once a work is created.

1.4 Other

In the category of "other" IP rights, the Netherlands has the following IPRs:

1.4.1 Neighbouring or Related Rights

The Act on Neighbouring Rights ("*Wet op de naburige rechten*") provides for four specific IPRs for (i) performers of copyright protected works; (ii) producers of phonograms; (iii) producers of films; and (iv) broadcasting organizations. The legal regime that applies to these specific IPRs is generally in line with copyright law.

1.4.2 Database Rights

Following the EU Database Directive, the Database Act ("*Databankenwet*") provides for a specific intellectual property right for producers of databases. The legal regime for database rights is similar to the regime for copyright law.

1.4.3 Design Rights

Design rights that are enforceable in the Netherlands find their basis in either (a) Community designs or (b) Benelux designs. The regimes relating to these rights very much mirror the legal framework that applies to trademarks, as described above.[1] Design rights come into existence after a granting procedure, although the Community Design Regulation also provides for an unregistered Community design that lasts a limited period of time (namely, 3 years). There are therefore three kinds of design rights that can exist in the Netherlands in practice: (i) an unregistered Community design, (ii) a registered Community design, and (iii) a registered Benelux design.

[1] See Sect. 1.2.

1.4.4 Semiconductor Designs

The Netherlands has an act providing for a specific IPR for original topographies of semiconductors as required under the EU Semiconductor Directive. The right is vested upon the creation of the design, but registration is required within 2 years from the date of first exploitation. The legal regime very much mirrors that of the Copyright Act. The practical relevance of this right seems to be negligible.

1.4.5 Trade Names

The Trade Names Act ("*Handelsnaamwet*") provides for an intellectual property right for trade names. No registration or granting is required. Merely using a trade name in commerce creates the right.

1.4.6 Plant Variety Rights

Plant variety rights exist in the Netherlands either under (a) the Dutch Plant Variety Act ("*Zaaizaad en Plantgoedwet*") or (b) the Community Plant Variety Rights Regulation. These rights are granted upon application.

1.4.7 Other IPRs

It is subject to debate among scholars whether Dutch law also has certain common-law intellectual property rights that are not governed by a particular statute or EU regulation. Case law, for instance, gives protection to portraits of celebrities and also prohibits the slavish imitation of products. Trade secrets are also protected by case law, but their status does not seem to amount to that of an actual property right. However, all of these IP-like "rights" are not relevant for the subject at hand, given that security rights cannot be vested in such rights in the absence of a statutory provision allowing for their transferability.[2]

1.5 General

It can be noted that patents, trademarks, trade names, and copyright tend to be the IPRs that are the most relevant for the creation of security rights, given their commercial value and given that copyright and trademarks are relevant assets for almost all companies, while patents are relevant assets for technology companies.

[2]See Sect. 2.1.1.

All businesses have trademarks, trade names, and copyright that are in effect protecting their marketing properties, including advertising materials and codified knowledge. Database rights are only of relevance for those businesses that exploit information in some way. Neighbouring rights tend to be of relevance mostly for the entertainment industry. Plant variety rights are only relevant in the agricultural sector.

2 Categories of Security Rights

2.1 Security Rights in IPRs

Consensual security rights to secure obligations can be created in all statutory IP rights (described under Question 1) by the proprietor of those rights.

2.1.1 Transferability Requirement

As a matter of Dutch law, security rights can be created in any right that is transferable, as follows from Article 3:81(1) of the Dutch Civil Code ("*Burgerlijk Wetboek*") ("DCC").[3] Article 3:83(3) DCC, which applies to IPRs (among other rights), provides that a right is only transferable if there is a statutory provision that determines that the right is transferable.[4] It is generally assumed by scholars that such a "statutory" provision can also be a provision in an international treaty or an EU regulation, but there is no case law in which this is specifically addressed or confirmed. In this report, the term "statutory" must be deemed to also include international treaties and EU regulations.

2.1.2 Other IPRs

In the absence of any broadly defined statutory provisions regarding the transferability of IPRs, only those IPRs that have a statutory basis are transferable as a matter of Dutch law and can be subject to the creation of any security rights. Consequently, any and all "common-law" kinds of protection for certain achievements existing in and acknowledged by the cases of Dutch courts (such as the right to publicity of famous people, the right to be protected against the slavish imitation of commercial products, or the right to trade secret protection) are not transferable and therefore cannot be subject to the creation of security rights.

[3] Article 3:83(1) DCC: "*Ownership rights, limited property rights and debt-claims are transferable, unless their nature or the law opposes to this.*".

[4] Article 3:83(3) DCC: "*All other property rights are only transferable where the law indicates so.*".

2.1.3 Rights Other Than Exclusive Exploitation Rights

In addition, it has to be noted that the various statutory provisions dealing with the transferability of IPRs tend to expressly provide that intellectual property rights as such are transferable. This concerns the exclusive right to exploit the protected subject matter or, put differently, the exclusive right (i) to use the trademark; (ii) to reproduce, distribute, communicate to the public, or publicly perform a copyrighted work; or (iii) to apply the patented technology. However, any other kinds of rights that the proprietor of an IPR may have—in particular, any other rights related to the application for or registration of a trademark or patent, such as priority rights—are usually not expressly addressed in a specific provision that explicitly stipulates that such a right is transferable. The transferability of such rights generally seems to be assumed in international treaties and EU regulations, but as matter of Dutch law, such rights are probably not separately and independently transferable. Consequently, any security created in an IPR is, generally speaking, deemed to be limited to the commercial exploitation right conferred by statute and to not also encompass any other related or accessory rights. This issue is relevant under Dutch law with regard to, for instance, Dutch patent applications; the right to a European patent (Article 60 European Patent Convention); the application for or registration of an international trademark under the Madrid Arrangement or Protocol; and priority rights for patents and trademarks.

2.1.4 Moral or Personal Rights

In addition, rights of a personal nature, such as the moral rights of the author of a copyrighted work or the right to be named as the inventor in a patent, are also not transferable as a matter of Dutch law because there are no statutory provisions to that effect and also because such rights are deemed not to be transferable due to their nature. Consequently, any security rights created in an IPR also do not encompass such moral or personal rights.

2.2 Right of Pledge

The type of security right available for IPRs under Dutch law is the right of pledge ("*pandrecht*"), as provided for in Article 3:227 DCC.[5] Such pledges create a right in

[5]Article 3:277 DCC: *"(1) A pledge and a mortgage are both real security rights on an asset of someone else, granting their proprietor ('pledgee' and 'mortgagee') the title to recover his financial debt-claim from the sale proceeds of the encumbered asset prior to all other creditors of the person to whom the encumbered asset belongs. When such a real security right is established on immovable property or on a registered ship or airplane, it is called a mortgage; when it is*

rem in the IPR concerned and, simply put, allow the pledgee to sell the pledged IPR in case of a default under the secured obligation.

2.2.1 Right of Mortgage

With regard to registered IPRs, the question has been raised in legal literature whether under Dutch law security rights in such IPRs should be created by way of a right of mortgage (Article 3:227 DCC). The practical implication of this would be that a security right could only be created by (i) the execution of a notarial deed and (ii) registration in the relevant IP register. However, case law (namely, three separate judgments by three different courts of appeal in the Netherlands) indicates that such IPRs do not qualify as assets for which a right of mortgage is required instead of a right of pledge.[6] Although there is no judgment by the Dutch Supreme Court on this issue, it is generally assumed that the position taken by the courts of appeal is correct.

2.2.2 No Other Security Rights

Article 3:84(3) DCC[7] makes it clear that any agreement (i.e. "title") to the transfer of an asset with the sole objective of creating a security interest in that asset is null and void. Consequently, any security rights other than those provided for in the Dutch Civil Code (that is, the right of pledge and the right of mortgage) are not available under Dutch law.

2.3 *Security Rights on IP Licences vs. Royalties*

As a matter of Dutch law, one cannot create a right of pledge of an agreement as such as it constitutes the entire contractual arrangement, including all of the collective rights and obligations belonging to the parties to the agreement. Consequently, a licence agreement cannot be pledged. However, any claims originating from a licence agreement, such as a royalty claim, can be pledged as a claim, provided that the (licence) agreement that provides the basis for that claim does not state that such a claim is not assignable. A pledge of a claim originating from a licence

---

established on any other property, it is called a pledge. (2) A pledge or mortgage on a thing is vested on all that is covered by the right of ownership of that thing.".

[6]See: Court of Appeals Amsterdam, October 4, 2011, *Ventoux v Van Engelen* (IEPT20111004); Court of Appeals The Hague, July 24, 2012, *Spirits v FKP* (IEPT20120724) and Court of Appeals Leeuwarden-Arnhem, March 18, 2014, *Waarschip* (IEPT20140318).

[7]Article 3:84(3) DCC: *"A juridical act performed with the intention to transfer property merely to provide security for a debt or performed without the intention of bringing the property into the patrimony (capital) of the acquirer, is no valid legal basis for a transfer of that property."*.

agreement is subject to the regime of the Dutch Civil Code that applies to pledges of claims in general. The fact that the claims find their basis in intellectual property rights does not make any difference. The various intellectual property statutes also do not contain any specific provisions for such claims or for any pledges of such claims.

3 Structure of Transactions: Attachment and Perfection

3.1 Attachment and Perfection

For a right of pledge to be legal, valid, and binding, it is required that (i) there is a legally valid obligation to create a right of pledge of the IPR concerned (i.e. "title"); (ii) a written deed creating the right of pledge ("pandakte") is executed by and between the pledgor (i.e. the IPR proprietor) and the pledgee; and (iii) the pledgee has legal power to dispose of (is "*beschikkingsbevoegd*" with regard to) the IPR concerned—that is to say, the pledgee is not bankrupt ("*failliet*") or in "receivership" ("*surseance van betaling*").[8] Provided these three requirements are fulfilled, the right of pledge is created by the mere act of executing the deed of pledge and no further steps are necessary for such a pledge to be legal, valid, and binding between the pledgor and the pledgee.[9]

3.2 Third-Party Effect

Only with regard to those IPRs that are registered in IP registers (such as trademarks, patents, design rights, and plant variety rights ("registered IPRs")) is the registration of the pledge relevant, but only to obtain third-party effect. The various statutes all contain provisions that stipulate that registration is a requirement for any third-party effect of such a pledge, such as vis-à-vis any successors, the IPR proprietor, or any third-party infringers.[10]

---

[8]This follows from the fact that the provisions of Article 3:84(1) DCC that apply to the transfer or property also apply to the creation of so-called "limited property rights" (e.g. security rights) according to Article 3:98 DCC. Article 3:84(1) DCC: "*The transfer of property requires a formal delivery pursuant to a valid legal basis by the person with power of disposition over that property.*" Article 3:98 DCC: "*All the provisions of this Section that relate to the transfer of property apply accordingly to the transfer, encumbrance and waiver of a limited property right in such property, unless the law stipulates otherwise.*".

[9]Article 3:236(2) DCC: "*A pledge on other property is established in the way as determined by law for the delivery of the to be pledged assets.*".

[10]According to the judgments of the Court of Justice of February 4, 2016, (C-163/15), *Hassan v Breiding* (IPPT20160204) and June 22, 2016, (C-419/15) *Thomas Philipps v Grune Welle*

3.3 Typical Structure

Typically, a secured transaction with regard to IPRs is structured as an overall financing agreement with one party (e.g. a bank or investor) providing some kind of loan and another party being financed; the latter party usually also owns the IPRs that are used as collateral. Under Dutch law, one can also provide a security interest in one's own assets to secure an obligation of a third party. In these situations, the typical structure will be that of a transaction between three (or more) parties. This is usually the case where certain companies belonging to a particular group of companies are to provide security for the financing of the group.

3.4 Contractual Rights

The contractual and proprietary rights of the parties are generally no different from those that are common in financing transactions. In most transactions, IPRs are used as collateral because the party being financed is under a general obligation to create security rights in all of their assets or possessions. In these cases, the deeds will be simple and the general terms of the bank concerned will usually apply; little attention will be paid to what these terms actually provide or require. In case of "IP-driven companies" (companies whose assets predominantly consist of IPRs), more attention will be paid to the creation of these security rights and substantial due diligence may be conducted. In such situations, it is customary for the documents to also contain more specific provisions regarding these IPRs. These will usually concern specific representations and warranties regarding (all or particular) IPRs and pertaining to their validity and ownership. These provisions may concern, for instance, whether and how it is to be decided (i) that certain IPRs are to be applied for or are to have their registration terminated, and (ii) whether and how IPRs are to be enforced against infringers and who needs to be involved in any decisions regarding the commencement or continuation of legal proceedings against infringements and the defence against any counterclaims (in particular regarding validity issues).

(IPPT20160622), such registration is with regard to EU trademarks or Community designs not required for third-party effect of a licence vis-à-vis an infringer; however, it is required for effect vis-à-vis a successor in title. The same is likely to apply with regard to the registration of pledges on these EU IPRs as a matter of EU law. The same approach was taken by the Benelux Court of Justice in its judgment of January 28, 2008 (*Dreentegel*) (IEPT20030228) as a matter of Benelux law. There is no case law on this issue with regard to Dutch law.

3.5 Evaluation of IPRs

There are no specific legal provisions regarding the evaluation of IPRs and as a practical matter, the actual appraisal of the commercial value of IPRs being pledged is not specifically addressed; however, the decision to finance will be based on an overall appraisal of the business as a whole.

3.6 Steps to Be Taken

As indicated above, the mere execution of a deed of pledge between the parties concerned is sufficient to create a right of pledge between the pledgor and the pledgee. As a formal requirement, a deed needs to be a written document signed by the parties. As a result of Article 9 of the E-Commerce Directive,[11] a deed can also be concluded through electronic means, but in practice, this is rare. The involvement of a notary is not required and it is also not required to register the deed with any governmental authority. With regard to registered IPRs, registration of the pledge is necessary to give the pledge third-party effect vis-à-vis any third parties who derive their rights from the IPR proprietor, such as successors of the IPR, creditors seizing the IPR, or receivers in the event of bankruptcy of the pledgor.

4 Priority of Security Right

4.1 Priority

The priority of a right of pledge is determined by the date of its creation, i.e. the date of the execution of the deed of pledge on the basis of a valid legal obligation to do so by a pledgor who has legal authority to dispose of the IPR (i.e. who is not bankrupt). The priority of subsequent rights of pledge created on the same IPR will be determined by the date of execution of the deed only. In case of registered IPRs, the priority of subsequent pledges will be determined by the date of registration of the IPRs in question, unless a subsequent pledgee knew of the existence of an unregistered pledge that was created earlier.

[11] Directive 2000/31/EC of the European Parliament and of the Council of June 8, 2000 on certain legal aspects of information society services, in particular electronic commerce, in the Internal Market ('Directive on electronic commerce'). Article 9(1): "*Member States shall ensure that their legal system allows contracts to be concluded by electronic means. Member States shall in particular ensure that the legal requirements applicable to the contractual process neither create obstacles for the use of electronic contracts nor result in such contracts being deprived of legal effectiveness and validity on account of their having been made by electronic means.*".

5 No Enterprise Charges

Dutch law does not have the concept of an enterprise charge or a security right over all of the assets of a company or enterprise, like floating charges under English law.

6 Rights Before Default

6.1 Right to Protect the Pledged Asset

Article 3:245 DCC[12] gives the pledgee a general right to commence legal proceedings against third parties to protect the pledged asset. Consequently, legal literature holds that the pledgee is entitled to sue third parties who infringe the IPR to cease and desist from further infringements; the pledgee can also sue for damages and to obtain declaratory judgments regarding the validity of the IPR concerned. There seems to be no case law demonstrating the execution of such rights of a pledgee with regard to IPRs.

6.2 No Other Rights

Other than the above right to protect the pledged asset, the pledgee has no other rights prior to default.

7 Foreclosure of Pledge

7.1 Execution of the Pledge

In case the debtor of the secured obligation is in default, the pledgee can simply execute the right of pledge by carrying out a foreclosure sale of the pledged asset (i.e. the IPR) by means of a public auction and using to proceeds to pay the outstanding obligations of the debtor (Article 3:250 DCC).[13] The pledgee can

[12] Article 3:245 DCC: *"The pledgor and pledgee are both independently entitled to file lawsuits or to lodge applications against someone else in order to protect the pledged property, provided that he ensures that the other is called to the legal proceedings in time."*.

[13] Article 3:250 DCC: *"(1) The foreclosure sale is held in public in accordance with local practice and on the usual terms and conditions. (2) Where the pledged asset is marketable on a commodity market or exchange, the public sale may take place on that market with assistance of an intermediary who is active on this market or exchange, under conditions and usages that apply to an ordinary sale on that market or exchange. (3) The pledgor is allowed to bid too."*.

auction the pledged asset once the debtor is in default; no further court order to that effect is required unless it is otherwise expressly agreed by and between the pledgor and the pledgee. This is referred to as the right of "*parate executie*" of the pledgee. If the pledge is of a patent or plant variety, the auction needs to be administered by a notary. The pledgee requires specific court authorization to use any other means of selling the pledged asset or to take possession of it (Article 3:251 DCC).[14] In case there is a surplus value of the pledged asset compared to the secured obligation, the surplus goes to the proprietor of the pledged IPR or, in case of bankruptcy of the IPR proprietor, to the receiver in the bankruptcy of the IPR proprietor. In case the proceeds are not sufficient to fully repay the outstanding debt, the remainder of the debt will remain outstanding and due and the creditor will join the ranks of unsecured creditors of the debtor for the remainder of the amount still outstanding.

7.2 *Insolvency*

In case of insolvency, the pledgee is entitled to execute the right of pledge without any authorization or interference from the receiver. In that way, the pledgee can ignore the insolvency (i.e. be a "separatist") and foreclose on the pledged IPR.

8 Typical Costs

The costs involved in a typical transaction, such as legal costs (for legal advice, documentation, or notarial deeds, if applicable), are hard to determine, since there is no public record of them. These costs simply follow the actual costs incurred for legal advice and for the drafting and negotiating of such transactions and of the security documents. Generally speaking, it seems that these costs tend to be marginal if a pledge of an IPR is simply part of a right of pledge of all assets of the debtor that is being created. However, if the IPRs are the major or sole assets that secure the creditor, the costs tend to become quite substantial (meaning above € 10,000 or more) relatively easily.

[14] Article 3:251 DCC: *"(1) Unless the contrary has been stipulated, the provisional relief judge of the District Court may, upon the request of the pledgee or pledgor, order that the pledged asset is sold by foreclosure in a different way than the one meant in the previous Article, or he may order, upon the request of the pledgee, that the pledged asset will be transferred to the pledgee, as being the buyer, for a purchase price that is determined by this judge. (2) After the pledgee has become entitled to start a foreclosure procedure, the pledgee and pledgor may agree to sell the pledged property in another way than the one mentioned in the previous Article. When the pledged asset is burdened with a limited property right or when it has been seized by another creditor, then also the limited proprietor or, respectively, the seizor needs to co-operate in this agreed alternative sale by foreclosure."*.

9 Practical Usefulness

9.1 *Frequency*

There is no public information available on the frequency of transactions in which IPRs are used as collateral. In general, any transaction in which a bank finances a company will contain a standard provision stipulating that the company's IPRs also need to be pledged, and this is usually actually done. However, in most of these transactions, the creation of pledges of IPRs is predominantly done for "defensive" reasons—that is, to make sure that the interests of the bank/lender are protected. The creation of such pledges means that these IPRs cannot be used as collateral for a third party, nor can a third party acquire better rights with regard to such IPRs than the bank. In addition, together with standard pledges of the other business assets, it gives the bank/lender a good position to be able to actually auction off—or at least control the sale of—the various business assets and effectively be able to get a price for the business (or at least for a substantial part of it). For instance, in case of a bankruptcy, these pledges will make it possible for the bank/lender to effectively ignore the receiver, since the bank can execute the rights of pledge. They will at least make it almost impossible for the receiver to actually be able to sell the business as a going concern without the consent of the bank/lender.

9.2 *Possible Better Terms*

In most transactions, rights of pledge of IPRs are seen as a "must-have" for the reasons described above and will play a role in the general credit analysis of the bank/lender. In practice, the number of cases in which rights of pledge of IPRs may actually have been critical to obtaining credit on better terms seems to be marginal and such instances are certainly the exception to the rule. The rule seems to be that having IPRs as collateral is seen as a necessity, but it is only one of many factors that a bank/lender takes into consideration when deciding whether or not credit will be given and on what terms (i.e. at what interest rates).

10 Legal and/or Practical Difficulties

10.1 *National Considerations*

The reason why security rights over IPRs do not play a more distinct role seems to be that the creation of valid, binding, and enforceable pledges of IPR portfolios tends to be relatively costly. Generally speaking, arranging for proper security rights over IPRs tends to be relatively expensive compared to arranging for security rights over other assets given that specialized knowledge is required for the former and this knowledge is not readily available among practicing lawyers or notaries. This is one of the reasons why using IPRs as commercially relevant and meaningful collateral for financial transactions is a somewhat underdeveloped area.

10.2 International Aspects

The abovementioned cost problem is even more pressing when these rights of pledge of IPRs also need to be valid, binding, and enforceable in a number of foreign jurisdictions, given that most IPR portfolios tend to be of relevance not only in one national jurisdiction but probably also in a number of foreign jurisdictions. Taking into consideration that IPRs are principally governed by national (i.e. property/ commercial) law and because of the *lex protectionis* principle, specialized advice under each relevant national law is required, the cost of this transaction will be dramatically high. This would only be different under what one might refer to as the "*lex proprietas*" regimes provided for in (i) the EU Trademark Regulation (Article 19 EUTM-Regulation), (ii) the Community Design Regulation (Article 27, CDR), and (iii) the Community Plant Variety Regulation (Article 22, CPVR-Regulation).

11 Law Reform

There are at present no proposals for law reform relating to security over IP rights in the Netherlands. The subject has been discussed and revisited in legal circles since the introduction of a new civil code in 1992. The draft of that civil code envisaged that there would be a Book 9 that would deal with IPRs in general, but not so much as a draft for such a Book 9 has ever been made.

Security Rights in Intellectual Property in Poland

Beata Giesen

Abstract In Polish law, there are two important types of security for claims that may be established over rights to intangible assets, namely the ordinary pledge and the registered pledge. The ordinary pledge is regulated in the Polish Civil Code (Art. 306–335); in the case of intangible assets, it is hardly ever used in practice. The registered pledge is regulated in Art. 7 Section 1 of the Act of December 6, 1996 on Registered Pledge and the Register of Pledges (ARPRP); it is more frequently applied in the case of intangible assets. Both rights are, as a general rule, accessory rights. However, the Act on Registered Pledge and the Register of Pledges provides some exceptions to the accessoriness principle. For instance, according to Art. 18 Section 2 of ARPRP, under special conditions, a registered pledge is not extinguished even if the claim it secures expires.

1 Intellectual Property Law: Overview

In Polish law, intellectual property rights constitute a separate category of subjective rights.[1] They are used in the context of intangible assets of various kinds and are absolute in nature. Effective *erga omnes*, they are most often economic rights.[2] Their sources are found in a variety of legal acts, for instance the right to a work is rooted in the provisions of the Act of February 4, 1994 on Copyright and Related Rights (hereinafter referred to as the Copyright Law).[3] The very existence of copyright is not contingent on any formal conditions (Art. 1 Section 4 of the Copyright Law), as

[1]See more in: Pyziak-Szafnicka (2007), pp. 727–729.

[2]Careful characteristics of rights in intangible assets in Poland is offered by Skubisz (2012), pp. 44 et seq.

[3]Act of 4.02.1994 on Copyright and Related Rights, Journal of Law (J. of. L.) 2006 No. 90, item 631.

B. Giesen (✉)
Faculty of Law and Administration, University of Lodz, Department of Civil Law, Lodz, Poland
e-mail: bgiesen@binar.pl

E.-M. Kieninger (ed.), *Security Rights in Intellectual Property*, Ius Comparatum – Global Studies in Comparative Law 45,
https://doi.org/10.1007/978-3-030-44191-3_21

copyright comes into being upon the creation of a work that is characterised by certain features stipulated in Art. 1 of the Copyright Law. Such a work is required to be "established", but "fixing" the work in a material medium is not indispensable. Polish law does not introduce the notion of a register of works. Instead, the dualistic concept of Polish copyright law is based on the distinction between two categories of author's rights, namely economic and moral rights. The former may be subject to both *inter vivos* and *mortis causa* transactions. Contractual disposal of economic copyrights is conditioned by a number of prerequisites, determining in particular the form of a contract and certain provisions that are indispensable for contract validity. In view of the focus of this paper, Art. 41 Section 2 seems to be of particular significance to these considerations, as it introduces the obligation to list explicitly the fields of exploitation. On the other hand, moral copyrights are non-waivable and non-disposable. Due to the very special nature of copyright, it is often emphasised in the literature on the subject that it is not copyright in general, but only certain specific author's rights that can be pledged.[4] In order to establish a pledge on author's economic rights it is irrelevant that—pursuant to Art. 18 Section 1 of the Copyright Law—these rights are not enforceable as long as they are vested in the author, as the said provision does not apply to due and payable receivables. The fact that it is not possible to conduct enforcement against a right does not preclude establishing a pledge on this right.[5] As a matter of fact, the non-executory procedure of satisfying the claims of a pledgee (i.e. the person entitled to the claim encumbered with a pledge) is also available.

Polish Industrial Property Law[6] (hereinafter referred to as IPL) is another act that covers and governs a variety of rights which may be used to secure a claim. These rights include in particular: right to a patent,[7] right under a patent (patentee's right),

---

[4]Expressly so in: Preussner-Zamorska and Traple (1992), p. 49.

[5]Expressly so in: Karasek (1998), p. 468, and also in: Żelechowski (2011), pp. 178 et seq.

[6]Act of June 30, 2000, Industrial Property Law, J. of. L. 2001 No. 49, item 508.

[7]As per judicial decicions, a patent is "an absolute subjective civil right which gives the person on whom it is conferred the authority of the exclusive use of an invention both for profit or for occupational/professional purposes and as an object of legal transactions," (judgment of the Provincial Administrative Court WSA in Warsaw of 23.05.2006, VI SA/Wa 43/06). Pursuat to Art. 24 of IPL, "Patents are granted for inventions that are new, involve an inventive step and are susceptible of industrial application." The following prerequisites for the patentability of an invention are formulated in the literature on the subject: (1) its technical character, (2) newness, (3) inventive step (non-obviousness), (4) applicability of the solution invented; The author of an invention is the original person that is entitled to obtain a patent. The territorial scope of the patent right is confined to the area of Poland. The patent is granted for 20 years of the date of filing a patent application with the Patent Office. The material scope of a patent is shaped by patent claims included in the so-called patent description. Due to the limited admissibility of enforcement against a patent right to an invention in relation to which an application has not been filed with the Patent Office, certain reservations are voiced in the literature as to whether such a right may be pledged. Cf. more about it in: Żelechowski (2011), pp. 228 et seq., and also in: Szewc (2011), pp. 73 et seq., and also in: Sieńczyło-Chlabicz (2015), pp. 421 et seq.

right to obtain a utility model and right to a utility model (Art. 94)[8] and right to a trademark[9] (Art. 120–121), to an industrial design[10] (Art. 102–104), to integrated circuit topographies (Art. 196),[11] to new varieties of plants, and the right protecting medicinal products and plant protection products (Art. 75[1]).

A pledge can also be established on a right to a trademark in relation to which an application has already been filed with the Patent Office, but which has not been granted a protection certificate yet (i.e. the so-called unregistered trademark, also referred to as the right under a trademark application). Pursuant to Art. 162 Section 6 of ILP the right under a trademark application is transferable and it has a specific economic value.

At present, Community industrial designs[12] and Community (EU) trademarks[13] are also protected in Poland. Moreover, Poland signed the European Patent Convention on 1.03.2004.[14]

Even when analysed from a very broad perspective, the industrial property rights introduced above are clearly very different from one another, mainly due to the distinct character of assets to which they appertain. Therefore, the substance and content of each individual right have been shaped separately. However, apart from these differences, they do share certain features. Their common characteristics

[8]Art. 94 Section 1 of IPL defines a utility model as "a new and useful technical solution concerning the shape, construction or specification of an object with a permanent form". New and creative combination of an already existing and known construction and technical elements into a completely new and useful solution is the essence of a utility model. Cf. more about it in: Szewc (2011), pp. 98 et seq.

[9]A trademark may be any marking which can be represented graphically if it can be used to distinguish the goods or services of one undertaking from those of another.

[10]Pursuant to Art. 102 of IPL "an industrial design is a new appearance of a product or part thereof, such an appearance being of individual character and resulting from the features of, in particular, the lines, contours, shapes, colours, texture and/or materials of the product itself and/or its ornamentation." An industrial design should be characterised as follows: (1) it must refer to a form of a product or part thereof; (2) it must be new; (3) it must have individual character (i.e. be original); (d) it must be fit for repeatable reproduction in production of objects. Pursuant to Art. 102 Section 2 of IPL, those forms of a product which are conditioned solely by "technical or functional aspects" may not be registered as utility designs. Moreover, such utility models the use of which would be against public order or good moral conduct, or such utility models which include markings/indications to which protection cannot be granted are also not patentable (Art. 106 PrPW).

[11]In Polish law, integrated circuit topography is understood as "the internal (three-dimensional) structure of such a circuit, conceptualised and fixated, or recorded, as a model which enables copying (reproducing) such a circuit," see: Szewc (2011), p. 111. Only original topographies are registrable.

[12]The principles of their protection are specified in the Council Regulation (EC) No. 6/2002 of December 12, 2001 on Community designs (Official Journal L 003, 05/01/2002).

[13]Council Regulation (EC) No. 40/94 of December 20, 1993 on the Community Trademark (Official Journal L 011, 14/01/1994).

[14]As a result of the ratification of the European Patent Convention, the Act of March 14 the Filing of Europan Patent Applications and Effects of the European Patent in the Republic of Poland was introduced.

include: the fact that all the rights that fall with this category are absolute subjective rights, they all guarantee a certain extent of monopoly to the person in whom they are vested. Their existence is contingent upon an administrative decision of a competent patent office and requires the completion of the registration procedure and fee payment. Except for a right under registration of a geographical indication, which—as it should be duly emphasized here—may not be encumbered with any sort of security, all other industrial property rights are limited in time, which means they expire upon the lapse of the period specified in the act.[15] It should be added that this effect occurs *ex lege*, i.e. by law. The IPL Act determines precisely the guaranteed monopoly framework for each of the assets listed. First and foremost, this monopoly encompasses the economic interest of the person in which a given right is vested, and it is expressed in the right to exploit these assets, which is why these rights are unanimously deemed to be economic rights. Moreover, they are transferable, which means that they can be disposed of. They are categorised as independent rights, as their existence is not contingent upon the existence or validity of any other rights. It should also be emphasised that all the rights to industrial property assets are limited in terms of a territory and they are effective only in Poland. However, their protection may be extended internationally, mainly based on a European patent, the International Trademark System, registration of a Community Trademark and Community Industrial Design. Obtaining one of those titles guarantees the effectiveness of the said rights within the European Economic Area. It should also be mentioned while describing Polish industrial property rights that even when the statutory conditions are satisfied, these rights may be annulled under an administrative decision, effective *ex tunc*. In consequence, all the transactions on such an annulled right are also deemed absolutely void.[16]

Apart from the industrial property rights listed above, one more category of intangible assets should be specified. There is an ongoing academic dispute whether they are the object of exclusive subjective rights or not. This group includes, in particular, all kinds of confidential information of economic value, with confidential know-how being the most significant asset.[17] The exclusivity of using unregistered trademarks and indications to identify an undertaking also guarantees certain factual monopoly. Such exclusivity is guaranteed to this entity which started actually using them as the first one. The monopoly as defined here is restricted to the shared group of clients, and proving that there is a risk of misleading consumers is a prerequisite for its protection. Some doctrine experts find the source of absolute rights for the said exclusivity areas in the provisions of the Act of April 16, 1993 on Combating Unfair

[15]IPL Act—specifies the duration of individual rights. The periods stated in the Act my not be extended, except for the protection of a trademark, which lasts for 10 years of the application date, but may be prolonged without any limitations.

[16]Jasińska (2014), p. 974.

[17]To learn more about the manner in which Polish law protects *know-how* and how confidential information may be deemed as the object of absolute subjective rights, see: Sołtysiński and Gogulski (2013), pp. 451 et seq., and also: Promińska (2010), pp. 777 et seq.; Giesen (2014), pp. 278 et seq.

Competition.[18] More often than not, opinions are voiced that the position of those in whom the rights to use identification markings and unregistered trademarks are vested consists in much more than just the factual monopoly in terms of using these assets. The disputes on the legal character of those two types of assets brought about another discussion, namely the one focusing on the admissibility of contractual disposal of such assets. Obviously, those authors who tend to base such monopoly on absolute subjective rights also allow such person's ability to contractually dispose of those assets with a dipositive effect. Seen from such a perspective, these assets or rather rights to these assets, may also be used to secure claims.[19]

2 Types of Transactions Aimed at Securing a Claim by Way of Encumbering Intangible Property Rights

In Polish law, two forms of security for claim which may be established against rights to intangible assets are important to be named, namely ordinary pledge and registered pledge.[20] In theory, rights to intangible assets can also be the object of a transfer of title made in order to secure a specific claim.[21] Not regulated directly by the Act, this type of a contract is used in practice mainly for the purpose of securing movables by a transfer of title. Obviously, a right to a specific intangible asset may just as well be the object of a title of transfer performed as a form of security, but as it is pledge that is most often applied in practice, transfer of title of rights to intangible assets shall not be further analysed in this paper.

2.1 Ordinary Pledge

This form of securing receivables is regulated in the Polish Civil Code (Art. 306–335).[22] In its most basic structure, a pledge is a way of securing a claim. It is established on a movable and grants a limited real right upon the pledgee. Its essence consists in pledgee's right to seek satisfaction of his claim from a thing (or, accordingly, from a right), regardless of whose property it has become and with priority over the personal creditors of the owner of the thing (or, accordingly, the

[18]The rights to a business secret are discussed by: Sołtysiński and Gogulski (2013), pp. 453 et seq.; Wojcieszko-Głuszko (2002), pp. 146 et seq; Giesen (2014), p. 228.

[19]For more, see: Widło (2008), pp. 399–400.

[20]For more about the registered pledge on rights in Polish law, see: Żelechowski (2011), pp. 136–177.

[21]See e.g.: Niemirka (1995), p.15.

[22]Act of 23.04.1964, J. of. L. 1964 No. 16, item 93, as amended.

person holding the right), save for those who under the law hold special priority (Art. 306 § 1 of the Civil Code).

During the period of a pledge, the pledgor, who is indeed the person holding the right to a thing (or, accordingly, to a right) that has been encumbered with a pledge, may freely dispose of this thing (or right). In fact, Art. 311 of the Civil Code states expressly that a stipulation whereby a pledgor commits to the pledgee not to dispose of or encumber a thing (or, accordingly, a right) before the pledge expires is invalid.

A pledge is an accessory right which is closely connected to the claim it secures. There are some important consequences of this feature of a pledge, for instance a pledge may not be established without any claim to secure, nor may it be transferred without this very claim being transferred at the same time (Art. 323 § 2 of the Civil Code), and if the claim is transferred without the pledge, the pledge is extinguished. It also follows from the accessoriness principle that the scope of security provided by a pledge is contingent on the actual status of the claim that it secures. A pledge also secures claims that are related to the principal claim it secures, for instance claims for interest (Art. 314 of the Civil Code).

However, there are certain exceptions to the applicability of the accessoriness principle to a pledge. For instance, a pledge may be established for the purpose of securing a future or contingent claim. It is believed that in such a case a future claim does not need to be specified.[23]

Although in practice a pledge is most often used to encumber things, the law admits expressly the possibility to establish a pledge on transferable rights (Art. 327 of the Civil Code). In such cases, provisions on pledge on movables apply accordingly (Art. 328 of the Civil Code).

An ordinary pledge may be used to secure both pecuniary and non-pecuniary claims, but in the latter case the creditor can seek satisfaction of his claim from the pledge only if a compensatory claim comes into being in the place of the non-pecuniary claim.[24]

A pledge may secure both an existing claim and any claim that may arise in the future (Art. 306 § 2 of the Civil Code). A contingent claim may also be secured by way of a pledge.

Establishing an ordinary pledge requires a contract between the creditor (called the pledgee), whose claim is to be secured in this manner, and a person entitled to dispose of the right that is to be encumbered with a pledge (called the pledgor). Their contract should also indicate the personal debtor of the claim that is to be secured by a pledge, unless he himself is the pledgor. Moreover, the content of a pledge transaction should specify the claim that is secured by way of a pledge and the object of a pledge, i.e. the right on intangible assets. To this end, the parties have to clearly name the asset. For instance, in the case of a pledge on a copyright, such features of the work will have to be determined that distinguish it from other works.

[23]Gołaczyński (2002), pp. 149–150.

[24]Expressly so in: Żelechowski (2011), pp. 142–143.

As a rule, a pledge contract must be executed in writing, with an authenticated date (Art. 329 § 1 of the Civil Code). Moreover, Art. 329 § 1 of the Civil Code also requires that the provisions on the transfer of a right be applied accordingly to the establishment of a pledge on this right. Consequently, the requirements related to the transfer of certain types of rights in intangible assets have to be respected. For instance, in the case of a pledge on an author's economic rights, Art. 41 Section 2 of the Act on Copyright and Related Rights is of fundamental importance, as it stipulates that the fields of exploitation must be clearly indicated, i.e. a clearly defined part of the copyright must be separated from the whole.

2.2 Registered Pledge

The rights to intangible assets specified above can also be encumbered with a registered pledge (Art. 7 Section 1 of the Act of December 6, 1996 on a Registered Pledge and the Register of Pledges, hereinafter referred to as ARPRP). Any person can be the pledee in a registered pledge contract. A register pledge can only be used to secure a monetary claim. Such a claim does not need to exist at the moment of establishing a pledge, but in such a case the contracting parties must indicate the source of such a future claim and they must also determine the maximum amount secured.

In order to establish a registered pledge, a pledge contract must be executed in writing and the pledge must be entered into the register of pledges, otherwise it shall be void (Art. 2 Section 1 in connection with Art. 3 Section 1 of ARPRP).

The possibility of establishing a registered pledge on a patent is stipulated expressly in Art. 67 Section 4 of IPL. Its validity is contingent on the entry into the register of pledges. At the same time, a registered pledge does not need to be entered into the register of patents in order to be valid, although the fact it was established should be revealed there.[25] On the other hand, the register entry is in fact necessary in order for the pledgee to be able to exercise his rights towards third parties.[26]

Registers are public. Revealing the rights under a pledge is a prerequisite for the effectiveness of a pledge in relations with third parties. The public character of a pledge justifies the assumption that such third parties are familiar with the data revealed in the register. There is a dispute in the literature on the subject whether an authenticated date is required for a contract document in the case of a registered pledge—the relationship between the norms shaped by the Civil Code and the regulations included in the Act on a Registered Pledge and the Register of Pledges seems to be ambiguous. It is worth emphasising here that a registered pledge can also be established on the object to which the pledgor will obtain rights in the future. In

[25] So stated in: Szczepanowska-Kozłowska (2014), pp. 123–124.

[26] Expressly so in: Gniewek (2007), p. 726. So stated in: Szczepanowska-Kozłowska (2014), p. 124.

such a case, a registered pledge becomes effective upon the pledgor obtaining the object that is to be encumbered with the pledge (Art. 7 Section 3 of ARPRP).

Similarly, as in the case of an ordinary pledge, a registered pledge is an accessory right. However, the Act on Registered Pledge and the Register of Pledges provides for many more exceptions from the accessoriness principle in the case of this right. For instance, Art. 18 Section 2 of ARPRP stipulates the circumstances in which a registered pledge is not extinguished even if the claim it secures expires.

3 Priority to Satisfy the Creditor

The pledgee has a limited *quasi* real right to the object of the right on which a pledge was established. In consequence, he has the priority to be satisfied from the object of a pledge before personal creditors of the person who holds the right encumbered with a pledge. However, the priority privilege is far more extensive. Pursuant to Art. 316 of the Civil Code, the pledgee can seek satisfaction from the object of a pledge regardless of any limitation on debtor's liability under the inheritance law. Similarly, Art. 20 of the Act on Registered Pledge and the Register of Pledges stipulates that the claim that is secured with a registered pledge shall be satisfied from the object of the pledge prior to any other claims, unless there is a specific provision which provides otherwise.

4 Pledge on a Variable Set

It is generally accepted as a principle that only one, individualised right can be encumbered by a pledge.[27] Therefore, a question arises as to whether it is allowed by Polish law to establish a pledge on a variable set, – and if so, to what extent. It is rather uncomplicated in the case of a registered pledge. It can be concluded from Art. 10 Section 1 of ARPRP that unless the parties to a pledge contract agree otherwise, the surrogacy principle also applies to the pledged right or elements of the set of rights. The changed object of a registered pledged is revealed in the register of pledges at the request of the pledgor or pledgee. However, it remains vague whether an ordinary pledge may be established on a variable set. The Civil Code does not refer to this question directly. The systemic interpretation of Art. 332 of the Civil Code, which refers only to a pledge on a claim, shows that it may be concluded that this principle also applies to other pledges established on rights whose objects are "naturally" converted into other rights.[28] One example of the application of the provision mentioned above is the case of acquisition of a patent right as a result of

[27]Fore more on this subject, see in particular: Gołaczyński (2012), p. 488.

[28]Widło (2018), pp. 399–400.

the pledge on the patent right established earlier.[29] Without focusing too much on intricacies, it should be stated here that Polish law seems to allow both ordinary and registered pledges, whose object may by assumption change during the pledge term. In such a case, formal requirements have to be respected that are stipulated for the acts in law concerning disposal of assets, in this case, a particular kind of right. Their significance may become apparent especially in the case of future rights, which do not exist at the moment of establishing a pledge. For instance, in the case of copyright, the following principle is accepted: a copyright transfer contract related to a future work shall be deemed valid only if the parties agree in it to transfer the right onto the purchaser once the work is created and, moreover, no additional transaction concerning disposal of assets shall be necessary for this effect to occur.[30] According to *argumentum a maiori ad minus*, the same principle applies to a pledge which is established on a right.

Another question arises here, whether it is admissible to establish a pledge on a set of rights. Art. 7 of ARPRP seems to admit this possibility, but the idea of a pledge on a set of rights is the object of much theoretical controversy. It is a rather common opinion that a pledge on a set of rights encumbers each single right included in this set. Therefore, it also encumbers a given individualized right at all times, even when it is disposed of.[31]

The parties may settle this issue in another manner. Moreover, Art. 10 of ARPRP excluded the surrogacy of the object of *pledge* if it would lead to pledgee's harm. For instance, in relation to a patent it is assumed that extending the legal effect of a *registered pledge on a right to a patent* onto the patent itself does not lead to pledgee's harm.[32] Unless a pledge contract stipulates otherwise, a registered pledge encompasses all the compensatory claims to which the pledgor is entitled in relation to loss, damage or lowering the values of the object of the registered pledge.

5 Mutual Rights and Obligations of Parties to a Pledge Contract

The pledgor, i.e. the person who is entitled to the right which is encumbered by a pledge, is always a limited debtor in relation to the creditor (pledgee). Of course, the fact of establishing a pledge does not exclude the possibility—which, importantly, is by no means a requirement—of the pledgor also being a personal debtor in relation to the creditor of the secured claim.

The fact of establishing a pledge, whether ordinary or registered, on a right gives rise to the following consequences in terms of pledgor's liability: the pledgor has the

---

[29] Żelechowski (2011), p. 239.
[30] Targosz (2015), p. 626.
[31] Gołaczyński (2012), p. 488.
[32] So stated in: Żelechowski (2011), pp. 151–154.

obligation of tolerance (*pati*) towards creditor's actions aimed at obtaining satisfaction from the object encumbered with a pledge right. Therefore, the pledgee is entitled to seek satisfaction from the encumbered right, regardless of who is the current holder of that right, and he comes with priority before other creditors of the holder of such a right, except for those creditors who have special priority.

The positive (*facere*) obligation to act does not stem directly from the Act, although some theoreticians suggest it should be adopted.[33] Restricting the liability of a limited debtor to the obligation of tolerance does not mean that he himself is not allowed to perform the obligation and in this way have the pledge extinguished. Contractual modification of the principles of limited debtor's responsibility is also possible.[34]

Encumbering a right on an intangible asset does not deprive the pledgor of the right to use and exploit such an asset. Accordingly, the pledgee has no right to exploit or use the intangible asset encumbered with the pledge.[35] In consequence, for instance, it is the pledgor that will have the exclusive right to use an invention or a trademark.[36] However, it is the subject of discussion whether the parties themselves can, decide—when entering into an ordinary pledge agreement—that it is the pledgee that shall have the right to use the intangible asset protected by the right that is encumbered with a pledge.[37]

In addition, the pledgor has the right to authorise other persons to use the object of a *pledge* (e.g. by granting a licence, renting/hiring, etc.) or to dispose of the *right* in an intangible asset (e.g. by establishing a usufruct or leasehold on it).[38]

At the same time, it is assumed that in the case of a pledge on intangible assets the pledgee can undertake—without pledgor's consent—any and all actions aimed at retaining the right encumbered with a pledge.[39] This opinion becomes particularly noteworthy in the context of the so-called register rights which are related to the obligation and payment of periodical fees for keeping the pledged right in force. The pledgee can also pursue claims related to the violation of the pledged *right* (Art. 330 of the Civil Code). Certain doubt arises in relation to the application of the principle stipulated in Art. 319 of the Civil Code to a pledge on rights. According to this principle, unless the contract stipulates otherwise, the pledgee should—which means he is obliged to do so—collect the profits brought by the thing and credit the towards the receivable and any claims related thereto. After the pledge expires, he is obliged to present accounts to the pledgor. In this respect, the opinion expressed by Ł. Żelechowski is particularly convincing. He rejects the possibility of applying this

---

[33] Contradicted by Żelechowski (2011), p. 406.

[34] Zoll (1937), pp. 8–9.

[35] Szewc and Jyż (2011), p. 257.

[36] Expressly so in: Żelechowski (2011), p. 410.

[37] This solution is advocated by Kopff (1973), p. 204, but contradicted by Żelechowski (2011), pp. 410–411.

[38] Szewc and Jyż (2011), p. 257.

[39] Sołtysiński (2012), p. 521; Szewc and Jyż (2011), p. 256.

principle to an ordinary pledge on industrial property rights, but at the same time he allows the idea of contractual stipulation of the said rule.[40] As a result, in the case of an ordinary pledge the parties should determine unambiguously in their pledge contract whether during the term of pledge on a right to intangible assets the pledgee should seek satisfaction from the profits they bring (Art. 319 of the Civil Code), otherwise the profits from the right shall be vested in the pledgor. The prevailing opinion found in the literature on the subject is that the pledgee can collect profits from the object of the pledge only when entitled to do so under the pledge contract.[41] However, another question arises here, namely the issue of pledgee's right—in the case of an ordinary pledge—to collect fruits from the pledged right, such profits being e.g. licence fees. There is no unambiguous answer to that doubt either.

In the case of a registered pledge, unless the contract stipulates otherwise, the pledgor can use the object of a pledge in accordance with its social and economic purpose (Art.11 Section 1 Point 1 of ARPRP). Therefore, for this type of a pledge, the pledgor preserves the right to exploit the pledged right on an ongoing (current) basis. It also seems that the parties may not agree to the contrary in their contract.[42] In the case of profit collection under a registered pledge, it is generally accepted that the pledgor is entitled to such profits.

6 Enforcement, Execution

Pursuant to Art. 312 of the Civil Code the pledgee's claim is satisfied in line with the provision on court execution procedure. This means that the pledgee has to obtain an enforcement title which will provide grounds for execution. Enforcement title is understood as an enforcement order accompanied by a writ of execution (Art. 776 of the Code of Civil Procedure). Art. 777 § 3 of the Code of Civil Procedure stipulates that a notarial deed in which a person other than a personal debtor, whose property, clam or right is encumbered with an ordinary or registered pledge, submits to enforcement with respect to the pledged property in order to satisfy pledgee's claim can also be considered an enforcement order. In practice, the so-called bank enforcement orders are also very important.[43]

As the pledges discussed in this paper may only encumber transferrable rights, it is usually obvious that enforcement may be undertaken with respect to them. Nevertheless, there is one significant exception in this respect, which results from Art. 18 of the Copyright Law and was discussed above. In principle, the enforcement

[40]Żelechowski (2011), pp. 414–415.

[41]Preussner-Zamorska and Traple (1992), p. 56.

[42]So stated in: Żelechowski (2011), pp. 416–417.

[43]Pursuant to Art. 96 Section 1 of the Act of August 29, 1997—Banking Law, banks may issue bank enforcement titles only on the basis of bank books or other documents related to banking activities.

of a pledge of rights is governed by the same rules as the enforcement of monetary claims. In some cases, the legislator took the specific character of individual industrial property rights into account and introduced certain additional rules. For instance, Art. 910^1 of the Code of Civil Procedure stipulates that the court enforcement officer who conducts the attachment of patent rights, utility model rights, rights to registered decorative designs, rights to registered trademarks, or rights to registered topographies of integrated circuits shall apply to the Patent Office of the Republic of Poland for the attachment to be recorded in the relevant register. The rights listed are deemed to be attached once notice of the attachment has been given to the debtor (Art. 910 § 3 of the Code of Civil Procedure). Notifying the relevant register of the attachment does not affect the attachment's effects, but due to the public character of registers and the presumption of the accuracy and reliability of register entries, recording such information in the register may be important for the application of Art. 911^5 of the Code of Civil Procedure. This provision stipulates that if an attached right involves a due claim, the court enforcement officer shall request that the obligor of the attached debt perform his obligation to the benefit of the creditor of the court enforcement officer.[44]

The principle related to the satisfaction of creditors is included in Art. 911^6 of the Code of Civil Procedure. According to this provision, if a right is attached, the creditor shall be satisfied from the earnings generated by that right (if any) or from the proceeds obtained from the sale of the right. Pursuant to Art. 911^6 § 3 of the Code of Civil Procedure, the sale of economic rights other than receivables—meaning that industrial property tights are also included here—is performed by way of an auction held in accordance with the provisions on the enforcement of movables, subject to specific regulations.

7 Costs Related to Establishing a Pledge and Enforcement from Its Object

In practice, the costs related to pledging a right and to enforcing such a pledge vary to a large extent. They mostly depend on the value of the claim that is secured by the pledge. This value is significant for the establishment of a pledge, as it directly influences not only the fee of the lawyer who is entrusted with the task of performing all the necessary legal acts, but also other costs that are related to satisfying the pledgee from the object of the pledge. In order to obtain satisfaction in such a way, the pledgee needs to get an enforcement order with a writ of execution. If a judgement ordering performance is necessary, the plaintiff is obliged to pay a court fee[45] in the amount specified in the Act on Court Costs in Civil Law

[44]For more on this subject, see: Pietrzkowski (2009), pp. 404–405.

[45]At present it is equal to 5% of the disputed or appealed amount, but not less than PLN 30 and not more than PLN 100,000.

Cases.[46] Furthermore, if enforcement by the court enforcement officer is necessary, then, pursuant to Art. 770 of the Code of Civil Procedure, the debtor is obliged to bear any related costs.[47]

8 Legal Difficulties

Although it is possible in order to secure a claim under Polish law by way of encumbering rights on intangible assets, this form of security is hardly ever used in practice. Several reasons contribute to this situation. Firstly, trading in this sort of rights is not as popular as in other, economically developed countries. The potential hidden in such assets seems to be still underappreciated in Poland. However, recent years have brought some slight change in this area. Secondly, significant difficulties in estimation of the economic value of such rights should be emphasised. Obviously, *in abstracto* the rights of this kind are economic by nature, so they are also assumed to have certain economic value. It is highlighted in the literature on the subject that the fact that these rights—in particular industrial property rights—are designed to be formal and limited in time and territory, as well as the fact that their effectiveness it statutorily limited result in their economic value being often just illusory.[48] Thirdly, the law includes a number of provisions which to some extent undermine legal certainty that is so important when it comes to deciding about the manner of securing claims. For instance, in the case of author's economic rights legal uncertainty comes from author's moral rights, such as in particular the right to the authorship of the work, to attribute author's name or pseudonym to the work, or the right to the inviolability of the content and form of the work (Art. 17 of the Copyright Law). Although it is possible to dispose of economic rights only, moral rights usually constrain the freedom of copyright exploitation to some extent, if somebody else that the author himself is entitled to them. Similarly, Art. 8 Section 1 of ILP stipulates the moral right of the creator of an invention, utility model industrial design and topography of an integrated circuit to have his authorship acknowledged although it is clear that the significance of this right is far weaker than it is in the case of the copyright law. It is often emphasised in the literature on the subject that exercising one's moral authorship right with respect to an invention by does not prevent enforcement in any way, although it is clear that the said right has to be respected by the person who obtains the patent.[49] Similar remarks may also be valid in the context of a right to a trademark. Although Polish academia categorises it as an economic right, its character is modified to some extent if such a trademark includes

[46]Act of July 28, 2005 on court costs in civil cases, J. of L. 2005 No. 167, item 1398.

[47]They are determined by Art. 49 of the Act of August 29, 1997 on court enforcement officers and enforcement, J. of L. 1997 No. 133, item 882.

[48]Cf. Promińska (2017), pp. 634–635.

[49]Expresly so in: Żelechowski (2011), p. 186.

the name of a natural or legal person.[50] It is because these assets all with the category of personal rights/interest/moral rights of a natural (Art. 23 of the Civil Code) and legal person (Art. 43 of the Civil Code). In consequence, enforcement in the by means of attachment of such a right or its sale in the public auction will not be possible.

References

Giesen B (2014) In: Kępiński M (ed) System Prawa Prywatnego, Prawo konkurencji, vol 15. C.H. Beck, Instytut Nauk Prawnych PAN, Warszawa, pp 278–306
Gniewek E (ed) (2007) System Prawa Prywatnego, vol 3, Prawo rzeczowe. C.H. Beck, Instytut Nauk Prawnych PAN, Warszawa, pp 726–728
Gołaczyński J (2002) Zastaw na rzeczach ruchomych. C.H. Beck, Warszawa
Gołaczyński J (2012) In: Gniewek E (ed) System Prawa Prywatnego, vol 4, Prawo rzeczowe. C.H. Beck, Instytut Nauk Prawnych PAN, Warszawa, pp 459–544
Jasińska K (2014) In: Kostański P (ed) Prawo własności przemysłowej. Komentarz. C.H. Beck, Warszawa, pp 300–340
Karasek I (1998) Przedmiot zastawu rejestrowego. Kwartalnik Prawa Prywatnego 3:458
Kopff A (1973) Przejście autorskich praw majątkowych. In: Grzybowski S, Kopff A, Serda J (eds) Zagadnienia prawa autorskiego. PWN, Warszawa, pp 287–290
Niemirka B (1995) Prawne formy zabezpieczania kredytów – przewłaszczenie na zabezpieczenie. MoP 10:10–15
Pietrzkowski H (2009) In: Ereciński T (ed) Kodeks postępowania cywilnego. Komentarz, part 3, Postępowanie egzekucyjne, vol 4. Wolters Kluwer, Warszawa
Preussner-Zamorska J, Traple E (1992) Zastaw na prawach w prawie polskim i niemieckim ze szczególnym uwzględnieniem problematyki praw na dobrach niematerialnych (zagadnienia wybrane). KSP XXV:41–59
Promińska U (2010) In: Katner WJ (ed) System Prawa Prywatnego, vol 9, Prawo zobowiązań – umowy nienazwane. C.H. Beck, Instytut Nauk Prawnych PAN, Warszawa, pp 635–640
Promińska U (2017) Dobra własności przemysłowej jako przedmiot wkładu do spółek handlowych. In: Kostański P, Podrecki P, Targosz T (eds) Experientia Docet. Księga jubileuszowa ofiarowana Pani Profesor Elżbiecie Traple. Wolters Kluwer, Warszawa, pp 629–642
Pyziak-Szafnicka M (2007) In: Safjan M (ed), System Prawa Prywatnego, vol 1, Prawo Cywilne – część ogólna. C.H. Beck, Instytut Nauk Prawnych PAN, Warszawa, pp 727–729
Sieńczyło-Chlabicz J (2015) Prawo własności intelektualnej. Wolters Kluwer, Warszawa
Skubisz R (1997) Prawo znaków towarowych. Komentarz. Wydawnictwo Prawnicze, Warszawa
Skubisz R (2012) In: Skubisz R (ed) System Prawa Prywatnego, vol 14A, Prawo własności przemysłowej. C.H. Beck, Instytut Nauk Prawnych PAN, Warszawa, pp 40–45
Sołtysiński S (2012) System Prawa Prywatnego, vol 14A, Prawo własności przemysłowej. C.H. Beck, Instytut Nauk Prawnych PAN, Warszawa
Sołtysiński S, Gogulski S (2013) Ustawa o zwalczaniu nieuczciwej konkurencji. Komentarz. C.H. Beck, Warszawa, pp 451–495
Szczepanowska-Kozłowska K (2014) In: Nowińska E, Promińska U, Szczepanowska-Kozłowska K (eds) Własność przemysłowa i jej ochrona. LexisNexis, Warszawa, pp 124–130
Szewc A (2011). In: Szewc A, Jyż G (eds) Prawo własności przemysłowej. C.H. Beck, Warszawa, pp 36–40

[50]Expresly so in: Skubisz (1997), p. 133.

Szewc A, Jyż G (2011) Prawo własności przemysłowej. C.H. Beck, Warszawa
Targosz T (2015) In: Flisak D (ed) Prawo autorskie i prawa pokrewne. Komentarz. Wolters Kluwer Polska, Warszawa, pp 626 et seq
Widło J (2008) Zastaw rejestrowy na prawach. LexisNexis, Warszawa
Widło J (2018) In: Fras M, Habdas M (eds) Kodeks cywilny. Komentarz, vol 2. Wolters Kluwer Polska, Warszawa, pp 50–56
Wojcieszko-Głuszko E (2002) Ochrona prawna know-how w prawie polskim na tle porównawczym. ZNUJ PWiOWI 81, Kraków
Żelechowski Ł (2011) Zastaw zwykły i rejestrowy na prawach własności przemysłowej. Wolters Kluwer Polska, Warszawa
Zoll F (1937) Prawa zastawnicze, według źródeł prawa obowiązującego w Małopolsce i na Ziemi Cieszyńskiej. Księgarnia Powszechna, Kraków

Security Rights in Intellectual Property in Romania

Răzvan Dincă and Radu Rizoiu

Abstract This chapter presents the current status of the Romanian regulation of security interests in IP rights. While Romanian law follows a functional approach (being largely based on the UCC Article 9 blueprint), it fails to address specific problems raised by the very nature of IP collateral. Friction between the regulation of IP rights and secured transactions (especially in the areas of perfection and enforcement) are prone to generate difficulties in practice.

1 Overview of IP Rights

Romanian laws provide for various intellectual property rights.

1.1 Inventions

Inventions[1] may be protected either by patents, in accordance with Law No. 64/1991 on Patents (hereinafter "Patents Law"), or by utility models, in accordance with Law No. 350/2007 on Utility Models (hereinafter "Utility Model Law"). Based on the European Patent Convention to which Romania adheres through Law No. 611/2002, a European patent that designates Romania and was issued by the European Patent Office produces in Romania the same effects as a national patent. As for the uniform European patent, Romania signed the Agreement on a Unified Patent Court in 2013, but it has not yet ratified this agreement.

[1]See Macovei (2010), pp. 45–170; Mihai (2002), *passim*; Ştrenc et al. (2005), *passim*; Eminescu (1997a), *passim*; Eminescu (1982), *passim*; Petrescu and Mihai (1987), *passim*.

R. Dincă · R. Rizoiu (✉)
University of Bucharest, Law School, Bucharest, Romania
e-mail: rizoiu.radu@drept.unibuc.ro

E.-M. Kieninger (ed.), *Security Rights in Intellectual Property*, Ius Comparatum – Global Studies in Comparative Law 45,
https://doi.org/10.1007/978-3-030-44191-3_22

A patent may be granted by the State Office for Patents and Trademarks (hereinafter "OSIM") on an invention if it is new,[2] involves an inventive step,[3] and is capable of industrial application.[4]

Under art. 8 (1) of the Patents Law, patents shall not be granted in respect of:" (a) inventions the exploitation of which would be contrary to public order or morality, including inventions harmful to the health or life of persons, animals or plants, and which are likely to seriously harm the environment, provided that such exception from patentability shall not depend merely on the fact that exploitation is prohibited by a legal provision; (b) plant varieties and animal breeds, as well as the essentially biological processes for the production of plants or animals. This provision shall not apply to microbiological processes or products obtained thereby; (c) the inventions having as a subject-matter the human body in its various stages of formation and development, as well as the mere discovery of one of its elements, including the sequence or partial sequence of a gene; (d) methods of treatment

---

[2]Arts 9 and 10 of the Patent Law: Art. 9: "(1) An invention shall be considered to be new if it does not form part of the state of the art. (2) The state of the art shall be held to comprise all knowledge that has been made available to the public by means of a written or oral description, by use, or in any other way, before the date of filing of the patent application. (3) The state of the art shall be also held to comprise the content of the patent applications filed with OSIM and international applications that have been entered the national phase in Romania or European patent applications designating Romania, as filed, provided that their filing date is prior to the date referred to in paragraph (2) and they were published on or after that date, according to the Law. (4) The provisions of paragraphs (2) and (3) shall not exclude the patentability of any substance or composition comprised in the state of the art, to be used in a method referred to in Art. 8, paragraph (1) d), provided that its use in any such method is not comprised in the state of the art. (5) The provisions of paragraphs (2) and (3) shall not exclude the patentability of any substance or composition referred to in paragraph (4), for any other specific use, in any method referred to in Art. 8, paragraph (1) d), provided that its use in any such method is not comprised in the state of the art."

Art. 10: "(1) For the application of Art. 9, the disclosure of the invention shall not be taken into consideration if it occurred within the six months preceding the filing of the patent application, and if was due to or in consequence of: (a) an evident abuse in relation to the applicant or his legal predecessor; (b) the fact that the applicant or his legal predecessor has displayed the invention at an official or officially recognized international exhibition falling within the terms of the Convention on international exhibitions signed at Paris on November 22, 1928 with the subsequent revisions. (2) The provisions of paragraph (1) b) shall be applicable only if the applicant states, when filing the patent application, that the invention has been actually displayed and if he files a document supporting his statement within the time limit and under the conditions provided for by the implementing regulations concerning this Law."

[3]Art. 11 of the Patent Law: "(1) An invention shall be considered as involving an inventive step if, having regard to the state of the art, it is not obvious to a person skilled in the art. (2) Patent applications referred to in Art. 9, paragraph (3), although included in the state of the art, are not to be considered in deciding whether there has been an inventive step."

[4]Art. 12 of the Patent Law: "(1) An invention shall be considered as susceptible of industrial application if it can be made or used in any industry, including agriculture. (2) The industrial application of a sequence or partial sequence of a gene must be disclosed in the patent application."

concerning the human or animal body, by surgery or therapy and methods of diagnosis applied to human or animal body."

During the procedure of granting a patent, OSIM examines if the patentability conditions mentioned above are met or not. In principle, the duration of a patent is 20 years from the filing date. During this period, with certain exceptions provided by the Law, if the patented subject matter is a product, then the patent owner can "prevent third parties not having the owner's consent from the acts of: making, using, offering for sale, selling, or importing for these purposes that product". In case the patented invention is a process, the patent owner can "prevent third parties not having [his] consent from the act of using the process, and from the acts of: using, offering for sale, selling, or importing for these purposes at least the product obtained directly by that process."[5]

The requirements for the registration of a utility model[6] are less severe than for patents, simply because instead of the inventive step, any invention surpassing mere professional skill suffices.[7] The other requirements of patentability apply to utility models as well.[8] However, a chemical or a pharmaceutical product, as well as a process or method of any kind, cannot be protected by a utility model. During the registration procedure, OSIM will not examine the substantive conditions for the registration of a utility model,[9] which means that there will be a weaker presumption of validity for this type of registration than there will be for a patent. The rights granted by the utility model certificate are similar to those granted under a patent for product inventions, but their duration is shorter: 6 years from filing, which may be extended for a maximum of two times, with 2 years for each extension.

[5] Art. 31(2) of the Patent Law: "(2) It is prohibited to perform, without the owner's consent, the following acts: (a) manufacturing, using, offering for sale, selling or importing for the purpose of using, offering for sale or selling, where the subject-matter of the patent is a product; (b) using the process and using, offering for sale, selling or importing for those purposes the product directly obtained by the patented process, where the subject-matter of the patent is a process."

[6] See Macovei (2010), pp. 211–235.

[7] Art. 1(1) of the Utility Models Law: "The utility model shall protect, under this law, any technical invention, provided that it is new, it exceeds the framework of mere professional skill and it is susceptible of industrial application."

[8] *Ibidem.*

[9] Art. 17(3) of the Utility Model Law: "OSIM shall not examine the subject-matter of the utility model application to assess if the conditions of being new, exceeding the framework of mere professional skill or being industrially applicable are met."

1.2 Trademarks

Trademarks[10] protected in Romania may be registered by following one of the following procedures:

- Filing an application for trademark registration with OSIM which, if approved, will result in the registration of a national Romanian trademark, submitted to the effects provided for by Law No. 84/1998 on Trademarks and Geographical Indications (hereinafter "Trademarks Law");
- Filing an application with the European Union Intellectual Property Office (EUIPO) which, if approved, will result in the registration of a European Union trademark, as per European Union Trademark Regulation No. 207/2009; or
- Filing an international application based on the Madrid Agreement Concerning the International Registration of Marks, ratified by Romania pursuant to Decree No. 1176/December 22, 1968; if Romania is a designated state and the registration is not refused by OSIM, this will entail in Romania the same effects as a national trademark.

Even if it is not registered, a trademark may be protected in Romania if it is well-known to the relevant Romanian public.

In order to be protected, a trademark should comply with both absolute conditions and relative conditions.

The absolute conditions basically require that the trademark be a distinctive sign, capable of being graphically represented. As part of the latter requirement, irrespective of whether the sign is to be perceived visually or through other senses, its graphical representation should be clear, precise, self-contained, easily accessible, intelligible, durable, and objective.[11] The requirement that it be distinctive means that the sign should be able to indicate to the average consumer the commercial origin of the product or service to which it is applied. In order to accomplish this basic trademark function, the sign should not be generic, customary, in the shape necessary for achieving a technical result, or exclusively descriptive of one of the objective features of the product or service to which the trademark is applied.[12] Also, the trademark should not be contrary to public order or to official, historic, religious,

---

[10]See Macovei (2010), pp. 307–396; Roş et al. (2003), *passim*; Eminescu (1997a), *passim*.

[11]CJEU, December 12, 2002, *Ralf Sieckmann v Deutsches Patent- und Markenamt.*

[12]Art. 5(1)(b)-(e) of the Trademarks Law: "Registration shall be refused or, if registered, shall be deemed to be cancelled, for the following absolute grounds: (b) trademarks which are devoid of any distinctive character; (c) trademarks which consist exclusively of signs or indications which have become customary in the current language or in the *bona fide* and established practices of the trade; (d) trademarks which consist exclusively of signs or indications which may serve, in trade, to designate the kind, quality, quantity, intended purpose, value, geographical origin or the time of production of the goods or of rendering of the service, or other characteristics of the goods or services; (e) trademarks which consist exclusively of the shape of the product which results from the nature of the goods themselves or which is necessary to obtain a technical result or which gives substantial value to the goods."

or cultural symbols; in addition, it should not be deceptive, meaning that it should not mislead the average consumer concerning the objective features of the product or service to which it is applied.

The relative conditions require that the trademark not infringe on any previous right of a third party, including a copyright, design right, name right, and so on.[13] In

[13]Art. 6 of the Trademarks Law: "(1) Besides the grounds provided in Art. 5 paragraph (1), registration of a trademark shall also be refused or shall be susceptible of being cancelled, as the case may be, for the following relative grounds: (a) if it is identical with an earlier trademark, and the goods and services for which registration is applied or the trademark has been registered are identical with the goods and services for which the earlier trademark is protected; (b) if, because of its identity with or similarity to the earlier trademark and because of identity or similarity of the goods or services covered by the two trademarks, there exists a likelihood of confusion in the public perception, the likelihood of association with the earlier trademark included. (2) Within the meaning of paragraph (1), earlier trademarks mean trademarks with a date of application for registration earlier than the date of application for registration of the trademark concerned or of the priority claimed in respect thereof, as the case may be, and contained in the following categories: (a) Community trademarks; (b) trademarks registered in Romania; (c) trademarks registered under international agreements and having effects in Romania; (d) Community trademarks for which seniority is duly claimed, in accordance with the provisions of Community Trademark Regulations, in respect of a trademark covered by letters (b) or (c) , even where the latter has lapsed or surrendered; (e) application for registration of the trademarks covered by letters (a)–(d), under the condition of subsequent registration thereof; (f) trademarks which, on the date of the application for registration of the trademark or on the date of the claimed priority, as the case may be, are well-known in Romania, within the meaning of Art. 6 bis of the Paris Convention. (3) Registration of a trademark shall also be refused or, if registered, it shall be susceptible of being cancelled if it is identical with or similar to an earlier Community trademark, within the meaning of paragraph (2), and if it was intended for registration or it is already registered for goods and services which are not similar to those for which the earlier Community trademark is registered, where the earlier Community trademark has a reputation in the European Union and where, by the use of the subsequent trademark, unfair advantage would be taken of the distinctive character or the reputation of the earlier Community trademark. (4) Registration of a trademark shall also be refused or, if registered, shall be susceptible of being cancelled if: (a) the trademark is identical with or similar to an earlier trademark registered in Romania, within the meaning of the paragraph (2) and it is intended for registration or it is already registered for goods and services which are not similar to those for which the earlier trademark is registered, where the earlier trademark has a reputation in Romania and where, by the use of the subsequent trademark, unfair advantage would be taken of the distinctive character or the reputation of the earlier trademark or if such a use would be detrimental to the distinctive character or reputation of the earlier trademark; (b) rights arising from an unregistered trademark or another sign used in the commercial activity were acquired prior to the date of the application for registration of the subsequent trademark, or prior to the priority date claimed by the application for the registration of the subsequent trademark, and if that unregistered trademark or used sign confer to its owner the right to prohibit the use of the subsequent trademark; (c) there is an earlier right, other than those covered by paragraph (2) letter (d), in particular, a right to name, to image, a copyright, an industrial property right; (d) the trademark is identical with or similar to an earlier collective mark conferring a right which expired 3 years, at the most, before the date of application; (e) the trademark is identical with or similar to an earlier certification mark the validity of which lapsed 10 years, at the most, before the date of application; (f) the trademark is identical with or similar to an earlier trademark registered for identical or similar goods or services, conferring a right which expired for failure to renew 2 years, at the most, before the date of application, provided that the owner of the earlier trademark had given permission for the

respect of earlier individual trademarks, a new trademark should not be identical to an earlier trademark registered for similar products or services, and it should not be similar to a trademark registered for identical or similar products or services if such similarity could result in confusion for average, relevant members of the public, including a risk of association with the earlier trademark. If the earlier trademark is well-known, either at an EU level or at a national level, and if the new, similar trademark would dilute the distinctiveness of the earlier, well-known trademark or if the owner of the new trademark would gain undue benefit from the prestige or the distinctive character of the earlier, well-known trademark, then the new, similar trademark should be rejected or, if already registered, cancelled, no matter what products or services it is registered for.

The certificate of trademark registration is valid for 10 years from the filing date and may be extended without limit for successive periods of 10 years each. During its validity period, the certificate of trademark registration allows the owner to prohibit any third party from using in commerce any signs for products or services identical to the ones for which the trademark is registered, as well as similar signs for identical or similar products or services and identical signs for similar products or services if such similarity might create confusion for average, relevant members of the public, including any association with the owner of the trademark. Moreover, the owner of the well-known trademark may also ban third parties from using identical or similar trademarks for dissimilar products or services if such use would dilute the distinctiveness of the well-known trademark or would result in the new trademark gaining undue benefit from the prestige or the distinctive character of the well-known trademark.

1.3 Copyright

In the field of copyright,[14] Romanian law is influenced by the personalist tradition of continental law. Therefore, a literary, artistic, or scientific work is protected by copyright if it is an intellectual creation of some form, providing that it is original—that is, that it expresses the personality of the author. All kinds of works are

registration of the subsequent trademark or had not used the trademark; (g) there is likelihood of confusion between the trademark and a trademark which was in use abroad and continues to be used there, where the application was made with bad faith by the applicant. (5) Furthermore, the registration of a trademark shall be refused where the registration is applied for by the representative of the trademark owner in his own name and without the permission of the trademark owner, except when said representative can prove that he has the right to apply for such a registration. (6) Registration of a trademark shall not be refused or cancelled, as the case may be, where the owner of the earlier trademark or of the earlier right agrees with the registration of the subsequent trademark. (7) Registration of a trademark can be refused or susceptible to be cancelled, as the case may be, under the conditions set forth by Art. 6 septies of the Paris Convention."

[14]See Roş et al. (2005), *passim*; Roş (2016), *passim*; Macovei (2010), pp. 417–554; Eminescu (1997b), *passim*.

included, including pleadings; speeches; cinematographic, audiovisual, and multimedia works; architectural sketches, plans, and edifices; sculptures; paintings; musical works; choreographies; and so on and so forth. Meanwhile, with the EU law influence in introducing copyright of subject matter such as photographs, software, and databases, the criterion of originality has been reduced to the "expression of intellectual creation of its author".[15] The protection of the work is not dependent upon merit or artistic value. Also, it results from the mere fact of creation, irrespective of the subject matter and without the need for any registration or formality. The Romanian law on copyright protection applies in Romania whether the covered work was created in Romania or abroad. The main instrument containing the rules of this protection is Law No. 8/1996 on Copyright and Neighboring Rights (hereinafter "Copyright Law").

The personalist concept of copyright also stretches to protection. The rights recognized for the author fall into two categories: economic rights and moral rights. Moral rights, which are a kind of right of the personality (i.e. personal non-pecuniary rights), concern the legal protection of the link between the author and the work that is the expression of his personality. Some authors believe[16] that since moral rights protect the basic function of copyright, which is to promote personal expression through creation, they are the main prerogatives of copyright and the economic prerogatives have only an ancillary function. The moral rights are[17]: (a) to decide whether, how and when the work will be disclosed to the public; (b) to demand recognition of his authorship of the work; (c) to decide under what name the work will be disclosed to the public; (d) to demand respect for the integrity of the work and to oppose any modification or any distortion of the work if it is prejudicial to his honor or reputation; (e) to withdraw the work, subject to indemnification of any users of the rights who might be prejudiced by the exercise of the said withdrawal right. All of these rights are a function of the author's personhood; thus, they cannot be transferred or waived. While the rights mentioned above under letters (a), (b), and (d) transfer to the author's heirs as prerogatives of the right to memory, the rights mentioned under letters (c) and (e) cease with the author's death.

Economic rights derive from the economic exploitation of the work. They are expressly provided by the Copyright Law, which enumerates some exclusive rights (which can be assigned) as well as the resale right (which cannot be assigned). The resale right is the right of the author of a work of art to receive a percentage of the

---

[15]CJEU, Case C-5/08, *Infopaq International A/S v. Daske Dagblades Forening,* Fourth Chamber, July 16, 2009.

[16]See Ionașcu (1961), pp. 35–40; Eminescu (1969), pp. 140–141.

[17]Art. 10 of the Copyright Law: "The author of a work shall have the following moral rights: (a) to decide whether, how and when the work will be disclosed to the public; (b) to demand recognition of his authorship of the work; (c) to decide under what name the work will be disclosed to the public; (d) to demand respect for the integrity of the work and to oppose any modification or any distortion of the work if it is prejudicial to his honor or reputation; (e) to withdraw the work, subject to indemnification of any users of the rights who might be prejudiced by the exercise of the said withdrawal right."

price of any sale of the original version of that work.[18] The exclusive rights include the right of the author to authorize or prohibit the reproduction, public communication, distribution, broadcasting, cable transmission, rental, lending, importation for trade, and adaptation of the work.[19] Generally, these rights last for the life of the author and 70 years after his death.[20]

Unlike moral rights, economic rights may be exclusively or unexclusively assigned. Therefore, since there is no specific prohibition against it, these prerogatives may also serve as collateral for movable hypothecs.

---

[18] Art. 21 of the Copyright Law: "(1) The author of an original work of graphic or plastic art or of a photographic work benefits from a resale right representing the right to collect a share from the net selling price obtained at any resale of the work, after the first alienation by the author, as well as the right to be informed of the work's whereabouts. (2) The right provided for under the paragraph (1) applies to all acts of resale of an original work of graphic or plastic art or of a photographic work that involves, as sellers, buyers or agents, art exhibitions, art galleries as well as any trader of works of art. (3) For the purposes of the present law, the copies or the original works of art or photographic works that have been made in a limited number by their author himself or with his consent, are considered to be original works of art. (4) The amount owed on the grounds of paragraph (1) is computed according to the following shares, without exceeding EUR 12,500 or the equivalent in Lei: (a) from EUR 300 to EUR 3,000 – 5% (b) from EUR 3,000.01 to EUR 50,000 – 4% (c) from EUR 50,000.01 to EUR 200,000 – 3% (d) from EUR 200,000.01 to EUR 350,000 – 1% (e) from EUR 350,000.01 to EUR 500,000 – 0.5% (f) over EUR 500,000 – 0.25%. (5) The seller shall convey the information referred to in paragraph (1) to the author, within two months as of the date of sale and he shall be responsible for withholding from the net selling price, without adding other fees and for paying to the author of the amount owed according to the provisions of paragraph (4). (6) The beneficiaries of the resale right or the representatives thereof may request, within 3 years as of the date of resale, to the persons provided for under paragraph (2) the necessary information in order to insure the payment of all owed amounts according to the provisions of paragraph (4). (7) The resale right cannot be waived or alienated."

[19] Art. 13 of the Copyright Law: "The use of a work gives rise to distinct and exclusive economic rights of the author to authorize or to prohibit: (a) reproduction of the work; (b) distribution of the work; (c) import for trading on the domestic market, of copies of the work made with the author's consent; (d) rental of the work; (e) lending of the work; (f) communication to the public, directly or indirectly, of the work, by any means, including by making the work available to the public, in such a way that members of the public may access them from a place and at a time individually chosen by them; (g) broadcasting of the work; (h) cable retransmission of the work; (i) making of derivative works."

[20] Art. 25 of the Copyright Law: "(1) The economic rights provided for in Articles 13 and 21 shall last for the author's lifetime, and after his death shall be transferred by inheritance, according to civil legislation, for a period of 70 years, regardless of the date on which the work was legally disclosed to the public. If there are no heirs, the exercise of these rights shall devolve upon the collective administration organization mandated by the author during his lifetime or, failing a mandate, to the collective administration organization with the largest membership in the area of creation concerned. (2) The person who, after the copyright protection has expired, legally discloses for the first time a previously unpublished work to the public shall enjoy protection equivalent to that of the author's economic rights. The duration of the protection of those rights shall be 25 years, starting at the time of the first legal disclosure to the public."

1.4 Other Rights

Under Law No. 129/1992 on the Protection of Designs (hereinafter "Design Law"), design rights[21] may be obtained on the exterior aspect of a product, consisting of its ensemble of shapes, colours, and textures, and are gained through a certificate of registration that is issued by OSIM following an examination procedure. In order to achieve this certificate, as of the filing date, the design must be new to the world in respect of the products for which it is registered, of an individual character according to the informed consumer,[22] not contrary to public order and morals,[23] and not exclusively determined by a technical function.[24] In addition, the registration must

---

[21] See Eminescu (1993), *passim*; Macovei (2010), pp. 236–280.

[22] Arts. 6–7 of the Design Law: Art. 6: "(1) The subject of the application may be registered to the extent in which it constitutes a design, within the meaning of Art. 2, it is new and has individual character. (2) A design shall be deemed to be new if no identical design was rendered available to the public prior to the date of filing the application for registration or, if priority was claimed, before the priority date. (3) The designs shall be deemed to be identical if their characteristic features differ only in immaterial details. (4) A design shall be deemed to have individual character if the overall impression it produces on the informed user differs from the one produced on such a user by any design rendered available to the public prior to the date of filing the application for registration, or prior to the priority date, if priority was claimed. (5) In assessing the individual character, the degree of freedom of the author in developing the design shall be taken into account. (6) If a design applied to a product or incorporated in a product constitutes a component of a complex product, this shall only be deemed to be new and have individual character, if the following conditions are fulfilled cumulatively: (a) once incorporated into the complex product, the component part remains visible during the normal us e of the product; normal use means the use by the end user, excluding the maintenance and repairs; (b) the visible component part characteristics fulfil themselves the conditions concerning the novelty and the individual character."

Art. 7: "(1) Within the meaning of Art. 6, a design is deemed to have been rendered available to the public if it has been published or disclosed in any other way, exhibited, employed in the commerce, except for the case where such actions could not reasonably become known in the normal course of the activity of the circles specialized in the sector concerned within the European Community, prior to the date of filing the application for registration, or prior to the priority date, if a priority has been claimed. However, a design shall not be deemed to have been rendered available to the public for the sole reason that it has been disclosed to a third party in explicit or implicit confidentiality conditions. (2) For the purpose of applying Art. 6, paragraphs (2) and (4), disclosure shall not be deemed to have occurred if the design for which protection is claimed has been rendered available to the public: (a) by the author, the successor in title thereof or a third party, as a consequence of the information offered by the author, or of the actions performed by him or by his successor in title; (b) within twelve months before the date of filing the application for registration or the priority date, if a priority has been claimed. (3) The provisions of paragraph (2) shall also apply if the disclosure of the design was made through an abuse to its author or to his successor in title."

[23] Art. 9 of the Design Law: "Designs contrary to public order and morality shall be excluded from protection."

[24] Art. 8 of the Design Law: "(1) Designs determined exclusively by a technical function cannot be registered. (2) A design which must be reproduced in the exact shape and dimensions in order to allow the product it is incorporated in or the product to which it applies to be mechanically connected or placed in, around or on another product, so as to allow either product to perform its

not infringe upon earlier rights (for example, the copyright of the author of the design).[25] Once it has been obtained, the design right provides for an exclusivity of use in trade of the respective design for the products for which it was registered; it will last for 10 years and may be renewed for a maximum of three successive periods of 5 years each.[26] This exclusivity of use includes reproducing, manufacturing for trade, offering for sale, putting on the market, importing, exporting, or using a product to which the design has been applied, or stocking such a product for these purposes.[27] EU design rights applying *inter alia* in Romania may be granted by EUIPO based on similar criteria under European Union Design Regulation No. 6/2002.

Under Romanian law, other specific exclusivity rights may be obtained, as follows:

- On commercial names and commercial emblems as per Trade Registry Law No. 96/1990;
- On topographies of semiconductor products[28] as per Law No. 16/1995 on the Protection of Topographies of Semiconductor Products;
- On new varieties of plants[29] as per Law No. 255/1998 on the Protection of New Varieties of Plants; and
- On collective or certification trademarks and geographical indications under the Trademarks Law or on geographical indications under EU Regulation No. 1151/2012 on Quality Schemes for Agricultural Products and Foodstuffs.

function, cannot be registered either. (3) Designs allowing multiple assemblies or connections between interchangeable products within modular systems can be registered."

[25] Art. 22(3)(c) of the Design Law: "(3) The application for the registration of a design shall be refused or registration shall be invalidated if: c) it incorporates, without the holder's permission, a work protected by the Law No. 8/1996 on Copyright and Related Rights, with the subsequent amendments and completions, or any other protected industrial property rights."

[26] Art. 35 of the Design Law: "(1) The term of protection of a certificate of registration of the design is of ten years counting from the date of constituting the regular deposit and it may be renewed for three successive five-year periods. (2) Throughout the period of validity of the certificate, the holder of the certificate has the obligation of payment of the corresponding maintenance fees. (3) OSIM shall grant a period of grace of maximum six months for the payment of the maintenance fees, for which increased fees shall be levied. (4) Failure to pay these fees shall entail the forfeiture of the holder's rights. (5) The forfeiture of the holder's rights shall be published in the Official Industrial Property Bulletin of OSIM. (6) In case of forfeiture of the holder's rights, the holder may request OSIM to revalidate the certificate of registration for justified reasons, within six months from the date when the forfeiture occurred."

[27] Art. 30 of the Design Law: "Throughout the period of validity of design registration, the holder has the exclusive right to use the design and to prevent any third party not having his consent from using it. The right holder has the right to prohibit third parties from performing, without his permission, the following acts: reproducing, manufacturing, marketing or offering for sale, putting on the market, importing, exporting or using a product having the design incorporated or applied thereto or storing such a product for the above-mentioned purposes."

[28] See Macovei (2010), pp. 283–306.

[29] See Macovei (2010), pp. 182–208.

As may be noticed, the Romanian law system for the protection of intellectual property rights is rather complex. However, the economic prerogatives of these rights follow certain uniform features which are relevant in respect of the subject matter of this national report. All of these rights are exclusive rights which entitle their owners to prohibit third parties from certain specific activities which are set down in the law and concern the subject matter of those rights. However, their purpose is not to absolutely prohibit third parties from performing these activities; rather, it is to provide incentives whereby the owner can allow them to participate in exploitation of the right and to share the benefits with him, as it was his creativity or investment that led to the economic success of this exploitation. Therefore, the characteristic feature of these rights is to entitle their holder to be indemnified for the economic exploitation of their subject matter.

In the continental conception of right of ownership, this entitlement corresponds to *ius fruendi*, the owner's entitlement to civil fruits and revenues; in other words, the right to obtain benefits from the exploitation by others of the subject matter of the ownership. For intellectual property rights specifically, the subject matter of this ownership is intangible. It has the nature of a real right (*jus in re*), but this is not expressed by direct action of the owner in relation to its subject matter; rather, it is expressed by the owner's actions in relation to third-party interference with the right. Based on the initial entitlement granted by an intellectual property right, each act of exploitation covered under the law as being exclusive to the holder that is accomplished by a third-party user gives the holder in principle a right to be indemnified for that exploitation. This secondary right is a personal right, corresponding to an obligation for the user to pay a certain amount of money established either by the (licence or non-exclusive assignment) contract or, if such a contract (i.e. holder's agreement on exploitation) is lacking, by the tort liability rules. The intellectual property right is the real (primary) right which leads to one becoming a creditor of such a (secondary) personal right.[30]

Expressed in terms of the classical concepts of continental law, IP rights are rights related to incorporeal assets where the underlying value is captured in an intangible good.[31] While the right itself is no longer an asset[32] (although it continues to encapsulate the monetary value[33]), it receives legal treatment similar to that of any asset.[34] In classifying the assets, such rights should be regarded as similar to movable intangible assets,[35] as under Law No. 287/2009 regarding the New Civil

[30]See Dincă (2007), pp. 76–120.

[31]Art. 535 NCC: "Assets are the goods, tangible or intangible, that are subject to a patrimonial right."

[32]See Rizoiu (2015c), pp. 128–178.

[33]Art. 31(1) NCC: "Any individual or legal person is the holder of a patrimony that includes all the rights and debts that can be valued in money and belong to him."

[34]Art. 542 NCC: "(1) Unless otherwise stated, the rights *in rem* over the immovable assets are subject to the rules regarding the immovable assets. (2) The other patrimonial rights are, within the limits provided by the law, subject to the rules regarding the movable assets."

[35]See Rizoiu (2017b), pp. 285–298.

Code (hereinafter "NCC") any asset which is not declared under the Law to be immovable or which does not have an immovable as an object will be considered movable.[36] These rights are generally limited in time and space by the subject matter that is their object and by the activities that are included by the Law under the scope of exclusivity. They are economic rights, both patrimonial and assignable, which allows them to serve as the collateral for a movable hypothec.

2 Categories of Security Rights

Romanian law on security interests underwent a major transformation in 2011 with the enactment of the NCC.[37] Together with Law No. 71/2011 for the enactment of the NCC (hereinafter "LPA"), it constitutes the general legal framework for secured transactions under Romanian law. Under the NCC, all non-possessory security interests[38] are called "hypothecs,"[39] whether the collateral is movable or immovable and whether the structure is tangible or intangible.[40] Hence, all security interests in IP rights would be qualified as (movable) hypothecs (*ipoteci mobiliare* in Romanian).[41]

While the NCC maintained the pledge as a possessory security interest in movable assets, it limited its scope to tangible assets and instruments only.[42] Therefore, the pledge is ill-suited for use with IP collateral.

The only type of security (in intangibles) outside of the NCC general regulations is security interests in financial collateral, regulated by Directive 47/2002 EC (implemented in Romanian law as Government Ordinance No. 9/2004). However, as the scope of this regulation is limited to financial instruments, IP rights do not fall within its scope.

Therefore, the only (consensual) security interest that could be created in IP is a movable hypothec. Apart from this, the NCC allows various financing techniques to be structured in any way the parties see fit (in general, through using different types

[36] Art. 539(1) NCC: "Assets that are not considered immovable by the law are movable assets."

[37] For a brief history of this legal change, see Rizoiu (2019), pp. 145–149.

[38] Art. 171 LPA: "By 'movable hypothecs' within the meaning of Title XI of the fifth Book of the Civil Code are designated all non-possessory security interests on personal property, irrespective of the time and legal basis of their conclusion."

[39] Art. 2343 NCC: "The hypothec is a right *in rem* over a movable or immovable asset that is affected to the enforcement of an obligation." For an explanation of the scope of this concept, see Rizoiu (2015a), pp. 37–40.

[40] Art. 2350 NCC: "(1) The collateral may be movable or immovable, tangible or intangible. (2) It may be determined or determinable assets or *universitas facti*."

[41] Art. 2389(e) NCC: "The collateral may be: e) intellectual property rights and any other intangible goods."

[42] Art. 2380 NCC: "The hypothec that bears upon a future estate cannot be recorded, but only provisionally registered in the land register, according to the law."

of reservation of title or conditional assignment techniques).[43] All such structures will have a legal treatment similar to that of the hypothec when it comes to their registration, perfection, ranking, and enforcement.[44] They are called "operations assimilated to a hypothec" (*operatiuni asimilate ipotecii* in Romanian).

As a general rule, the NCC allows for any IP right to be used as collateral under a movable hypothec.[45] Hence, a movable hypothec can be created in any IP right. Also, such rights could be subjected to operations assimilated to a hypothec. It must be specified that only patrimonial rights corresponding to the IP rights can be used as collateral,[46] while moral rights are not subject to (legal) trading. Also, IP rights that cannot be separated of the personhood of their holder, such as the rights in a commercial name, cannot be transferred and therefore cannot be used as collateral for a hypothec other than within the enterprise to which they belong.[47]

A specific problem arises in respect of the possibility to create a movable hypothec in contractual rights regarding IP. Such rights can be created through industrial property licence contracts, software licences, or non-exclusive copyright licences. Despite a certain doubt that might persist on this point in Romanian legal literature,[48] in the opinion[49] of the authors of this report, all of these rights share the same nature and we will call them "licensee rights." These rights entitle the licensee to require the licensor to guarantee him a certain type of exploitation of an IP right in exchange for remuneration. Therefore, the licence contracts that generate such rights are a variety of lease contract over an intangible movable asset. As such, unless otherwise provided for by the specific IP laws, they are subject to the legal regime provided by the NCC for lease contracts.

In the field of lease contracts, art. 1805, last paragraph of the NCC provides that, if such a lease is concluded for a movable asset, the sublease or the assignment of the lease can be concluded only upon the written agreement of the lessor. The rationale behind this rule is that the movable lease contract is considered concluded *intuitu personae*—that is, in consideration of the lessee's identity. Therefore, it might result

[43]To learn more about these devices, see Rizoiu (2013a), pp. 181–220.

[44]Art. 2347 NCC: "(1) The contracts that have the effect of preserving or constituting a right over an asset in order to ensure the performance of an obligation, whichever their number, their nature or their denomination, cannot be opposed to third parties which acquired rights regarding that asset unless they are registered in a public register, according to the rules regarding the hypothecs. (2) The reservation of title clauses, buy-back agreements or assignments of receivables concluded for security purposes are operations assimilated to a hypothec. (3) The provisions of this chapter regarding the ranking and enforcement of hypothecs shall apply accordingly to the contracts referred to in paragraph (1)."

[45]Art. 2350 NCC: see fn. 40.

[46]Art. 2351 NCC: "(1) Inalienable or unseizable assets cannot be mortgaged. (2) A mortgage created in these types of collateral will be considered a mortgage over future assets, if the inalienability or unseizability is of a conventional nature."

[47]Art. 42 of the Trade Registry Law: "The commercial name cannot be transferred without the enterprise to which it belongs."

[48]See Roş (2016), pp. 398–400.

[49]See also Dincă (2016), p. 372.

that the lessee's rights under such a contract are granted in consideration of his identity. This observation bears relevance in the context of Article 1573(2) of the NCC, under which a relative right (including a contractual right) can be assigned only with the consent of the assigned debtor if that right is essentially linked to the identity of the creditor. This means that the licensee's rights or the licence contract can only be assigned with the consent of the licensor. In other words, the licensee's rights are inalienable.

As a rule, art. 2351 NCC provides that inalienable assets cannot be hypothecated. However, paragraph 2 of the same article provides that such a hypothec can be valid as a hypothec over a future asset if the inalienability is contractual. The reason for this exception stems from the rule provided by art. 627 NCC, according to which a contractual inalienability is not valid if it is temporary.[50] The hypothec on a temporarily inalienable asset becomes effective only after the inalienability ceases. Thus, this mechanism cannot apply to a licensee's rights, as they are inalienable as long as they exist. Therefore, as a principle, licensees' rights cannot serve as collateral for a hypothec.

However, the parties may deviate from the last paragraph of Article 1805 NCC. For example, the licensor can expressly agree through the licence contract to any assignment that the licensee might conclude in the future in respect of his licensee's rights or of licensee contract. Alternatively, the licensor might grant approval for a specific hypothec in the licensee's rights or even in the licensee contract (which, in this case, would serve as collateral as a legal universality). In all of these cases, the licensee's rights can validly be used as collateral. This is so even if the hypothec secures a right that the licensor himself has against the licensee. In this case, the enforcement of the hypothec will result in the termination of the licensee's rights and of the licence contract due to fact that the licensor would be both creditor and debtor in the legal relationship created under this contract.

As for foreign or international security devices, the NCC specifies (in the chapter on conflict of laws[51]) that IP rights are subject to the laws of the state where they were published and/or registered for the first time.[52] Also, in case of security interests created in intangible collateral, the governing law of the security device shall be the law of the state in which the securing debtor is located.[53]

[50]On the essentially temporary duration of conventional inalienability, see Stoica (2013), pp. 45–46.

[51]To see the conflict of laws rules (under the former but similar regulation), see Sitaru and Sitaru (2000), pp. 58–66.

[52]Arts. 2624–2625 NCC: Art. 2624: "(1) The birth, content and extinguishment of copyrights are subjected to the law of the state where the work was made available to the public for the first time by publication, representation, exposure, broadcast or in any other proper way. (2) Undisclosed works are subjected to the national law of the author."

Art. 2625: "The birth, content and extinguishment of industrial property rights are subjected to the law of the state where the application was registered or filed."

[53]Art. 2628 NCC: "(1) By way of exception from the provisions of art. 2627, the law of the state where the debtor is located in shall apply in the case of: (a) a movable tangible asset that is used,

3 Structure of Transactions: Attachment and Perfection

3.1 Typical Structure and Attachment

Typically, a secured transaction in IP under Romanian law shall be based on the conclusion of a (valid) security agreement.[54] This is the sole requirement for the attachment of a security.[55]

The security agreement must be in written form in order to be valid.[56] It should identify the parties, offer a reasonable description of the collateral, and indicate both the criteria for determining the secured amount and the source of the secured obligation.[57] Future assets are an accepted type of collateral.[58] Future (or even potential) claims may be used as valid types of secured obligations.[59] Variable monetary claims (e.g. the claim derived from a revolving facility) are also acceptable.[60] Therefore, the attachment can occur even if the collateral and/or the secured obligation do not yet exist. While the law requires that the securing debtor have

according to its destination, in several states, unless otherwise stated by special provisions; (b) a movable intangible asset; (c) a negotiable instrument that is not in the possession of the creditor. However, in the case of shares or bonds shall apply the law of the organic status of the issuer, excepting the case when these securities are traded on a regulated market, when shall apply the law of the state in which the market operates. (2) The location of the debtor is considered to be in the state in which he has his usual residence or, where appropriate, its headquarters at the date of the conclusion of the movable hypothec contract."

[54]Art. 2387 NCC: "The movable hypothec is valid on the conclusion of the security agreement, but it is effective from the date when the secured obligation takes birth and the securing debtor acquires the rights in the collateral."

[55]For the general legal regime of the security agreement, see Rizoiu (2015a), pp. 66–154.

[56]Art. 2388 NCC: "The security agreement shall be drafted and acknowledged by a Civil Law Notary or concluded as a document under private signature, under the pain of contract's absolute nullity."

[57]Art. 2372 NCC: "(1) The security agreement is not valid unless the secured amount is reasonably determinable under it. (2) Under the pain of nullity, the security agreement shall identify the securing debtor and the secured creditor, shall indicate the source of the secured obligation and shall offer a reasonable description of the collateral. (3) It is not considered a reasonable description within the meaning of paragraph (2) the stipulation according to which the mortgage covers all assets of the debtor or all present and future assets of the debtor."

[58]Art. 2387 NCC, see fn. 54.

[59]Art. 2370 NCC: "When the mortgage secures a future claim, the ranking will be granted as from the date of the registration in a public register."

[60]Art. 2371 NCC: "(1) If the security agreement is concluded to secure a monetary claim, the mortgage is valid even if, at the time of conclusion, the debtor did not receive or he only partially received the consideration for which the mortgage is to be granted. (2) If the creditor refuses to provide this consideration, the debtor may obtain the reduction or termination of the mortgage, on the creditor's expense, by paying him the amount owed at that time. The creditor, however, owes damages."

rights in the collateral,[61] such rights may be conditional or voidable; this means that the security shall be subject to the same limitations.[62]

The parties to a security agreement[63] are the secured party (i.e. the creditor) and the securing debtor. The latter will not necessarily be the debtor of the secured obligation as well—this could be a third party (i.e. a person who is not involved in the underlying relationship giving rise to the secured obligation). In this case, the transaction will continue to be treated as a security interest rather than a surety.[64]

There are no special conditions for the nature of the parties—they could be either individuals or legal entities. Both parties must have full capacity in order to conclude the security agreement[65] since it is considered an act creating a right *in rem*. It is important to note that the security could attach to any right (either contractual (i.e. *ad personam*) or proprietary (i.e. *in rem*)) and, therefore, the securing debtor is not required to be the owner of the asset; he only has to be the holder of certain (even potential) rights in the collateral. Of course, the security will attach only to the extent of these rights. This means that the licensee of an IP right could give a security over his licence (provided that it is assignable).

As for the securing party, it is generally the creditor of the secured claim. However, in case of multiple-creditor structures (e.g. a syndicated lending), the secured party in the security agreement could be a security agent (who is either one of the lenders or a third party) who will act on behalf of the lenders' pool.[66] Hence, the capacity required for the validity of the security agreement shall be verified with respect to the security agent rather than with respect to each lender.

---

[61] Art. 2365 NCC: "The security agreement can be concluded only by the holder of the rights in the collateral and who can dispose of it."

[62] Art. 2367 NCC: "One who has a conditional or voidable right in the collateral can only conclude a security subjected to the same voidance or condition."

[63] For more on the parties to the security agreement and their capacities, see Rizoiu (2015a), pp. 156–168; Moise (2015), pp. 382–389.

[64] Art. 163 LPA: "If the security is concluded by a third party, it shall have the rights and obligations of a securing debtor, without being subjected to the legal regime of sureties."

[65] Art. 2365 NCC, see fn. 61.

[66] Art. 164 LPA: "(1) The movable hypothec can be concluded in favor of the creditor of the secured obligation or in favor of a third party designated by the creditor. (2) When the secured party is a third party, it shall exercise the rights of the creditor and shall be bound by his obligations. (3) The conventional movable hypothec can be concluded in favor of one beneficiary or several beneficiaries at the same time. (4) When there are several beneficiaries of the same movable hypothec, they will have the same rank either by simultaneously registering the movable hypothec in the public registers or by designating an agent. (5) The agent can exercise all the rights of the secured creditors who designated him. He can ensure, by himself, the perfection of the movable hypothec and the maintaining or modification of its registration. (6) The agent shall answer in front of the beneficiaries of the movable hypothec for the actions taken."

In case the IP rights are associated with a business operation (as they are in most cases), the collateral could consist of a pool of assets (i.e. *universitas facti*).[67] In such cases, the security will function similar to an English floating charge, meaning that the security attaches to each component.[68] As a result, the transfer of any of the assets in the pool will be made clear of the security.[69] The proper attachment begins once the enforcement is started by way of a "crystallization" process on the assets found in the pool at the time. Fraudulent transfers of assets in the pool are, of course, voidable.

There are no special rules for valuing IP collateral, since the value has no impact on the validity of the security agreement. Nonetheless, the collateral should be identified in the security agreement in a reasonable manner.[70]

Sometimes the specific IP laws require certain validity conditions for the assignment contract. Thus, for copyright, the contract of assignment should provide the duration, the territorial scope, and the modalities of exploitation of the assigned rights.[71] One might question the applicability of these requirements for the security agreement over the respective IP rights. The answer that these requirements are applicable is supported by the observation that any hypothec can cause a forced assignment of the collateral during the hypothec enforcement procedure. Therefore, any hypothec agreement may be analyzed as a conditional assignment agreement.[72]

---

[67]Art. 2368 NCC: "The conventional hypothec over a collateral consisting in a pool of movable or immovable, present or future, tangible or intangible assets can only be concluded regarding the assets used by an enterprise."

[68]Art. 2357 NCC: "The hypothec over a collateral consisting in a pool of assets attaches on every asset thereof. (2) The hypothec survives over the pool of assets even when such assets have perished, if the securing debtor replaces them in a reasonably amount of time, taking into consideration the quantity and nature of the assets."

[69]Art. 160 LPA: "(1) In the case of a hypothec over a collateral consisting in a pool of assets, if an asset is transferred, it will be made clear of the security. (2) The provisions of art. 1562–1565 of the Civil Code remain applicable."

[70]Art. 2391 NCC: "The security agreement shall comprise a reasonable description of the collateral. (2) The description is reasonable, even if the collateral is not individualized, as long as it can be reasonably identified. (3) The description can be made by compiling a list of the collaterals, by determining the category to which they belong, by indicating the quantity, by establishing a determination formula and by any other means of reasonable identification of the collateral. (4) When the hypothec bears upon a pool of assets, the security agreement shall describe the nature and content of the pool of assets. (5) It is not considered a reasonable description within the meaning of paragraph (1) the stipulation according to which the hypothec bears upon all assets of the debtor or upon all present and future assets of the debtor. (6) If the hypothec bears upon a bank account, it shall be distinctly individualized in the security agreement." For an analysis of the evolution of this requirement in Romanian case law, see Rizoiu (2015b), pp. 137–180.

[71]Art. 41 of the Copyright Law: "(1) The contract for the transfer of the economic rights shall specify the economic rights transferred and, for each of them, the forms of exploitation, the duration and scope of the transfer as well as the remuneration payable to the copyright owner. The absence of any of these elements shall entitle the interested party to apply for cancellation of the contract. (2) Any transfer of the economic rights in all of the author's future works, whether designated or not, shall be null and void."

[72]See Sect. 7.

In our view, the matter should be solved based on Article 2347 of the NCC,[73] which expressly provides that the assignment for security purposes is assimilated by the hypothec only in respect of certain specific aspects of the legal regime: opposability, publicity, and enforcement. In other regards—for example, in respect of the validity condition of the assignment contract—the assignment for purposes of security is not subject to the hypothec regime; therefore, it is not a hypothec. In other words, the legislator distinguished between security agreements and assignment agreements by avoiding applying the specific requirements of validity of one of those agreements to the other. Therefore, in case of the specific requirements for the validity of IP assignment, they will not apply to the security agreement, but they will apply to the assignment agreement that might eventually be concluded within the enforcement of the hypothec in the IP right in question.

3.2 Perfection

In order to be perfected, a security interest should meet two supplementary conditions in addition to attachment: effectiveness and publicity.[74]

The *effectiveness* of the security occurs once (i) the securing debtor has (or obtains) the rights in the collateral *and* (ii) the secured obligation is born.[75] This means that once both conditions are met, the security is enforceable. Since the security is meant to be a secondary means of achieving realization of the secured obligation, the secured obligation should already exist. In addition, since the security affects certain collateral, this collateral should already exist and the securing debtor should have rights in it.[76]

The *publicity* of the security is ensured by a mix of formalities that are generally structured around specialized registers.[77] Before publicity formalities are dealt with,

[73] Art. 2347 NCC, see fn. 44.

[74] Art. 2409 NCC: "(1) The hypothec is perfected when it is effective according to the provisions of art. 2387 and the publicity formalities required by law are met. (2) The publicity of movable hypothecs is ensured by registration in the archive, unless otherwise provided by law. (3) The perfected hypothec is opposable to the other creditors of the securing debtor, to those who acquire rights over the collateral and as well as to every other third party." The Archive is now replaced by the RNPM (see fn. 85 below).

[75] Art. 2387 NCC, see fn. 54.

[76] For a discussion on whether a security interest is enforceable if it is created by a person who does not hold (valid) rights in the collateral (but appears to hold them), thus making the secured party a holder in due course, see Rizoiu (2015a), pp. 482–484; Moise (2015), pp. 519–521.

[77] See Sect. 3.3.

the security is enforceable only against the securing debtor and it is not opposable to third parties,[78] except for those having actual knowledge that it exists.[79]

The unsecured creditors could therefore ignore the security, as could the insolvency administrator (i.e. the trustee in bankruptcy).[80] The latter shall ignore any security that was not made public before the opening of the insolvency proceedings and can also disregard any security that was made public within the last 6 months before the proceedings.[81]

3.3 *Registration Formalities*

In order to be opposable to third parties, the security interest must be registered in certain public registries. Once this formality has been performed, the security will become opposable to third parties.[82] If the law or laws require the security interest to be registered in different registries, only the fulfillment of all of the required registration formalities shall constitute a true registration which gives the effect of opposability towards any third parties.[83]

---

[78]Art. 2409 para (3) NCC *a contrario*: see fn. 74.

[79]Art. 22 NCC: "(1) If the publicity formality is not met and it did not have constitutive character, the rights, acts, facts or legal relations subjected to publicity are not opposable to third parties, except for those having actual knowledge of them. (2) When the law provides that the mere knowledge does not cover the lack of publicity, its absence can be invoked by any interested person, including the third party who actually knew the right, act, fact or legal relation subjected to publicity. (3) In all cases, the mere knowledge of the right, act, fact or legal relation subjected to publicity does not cover the lack of publicity towards other persons besides the third party who had actual knowledge of them." However, unless properly published, the movable hypothec is imperfect [art. 2409 (1) NCC] and, as such, it is not opposable to (any) third parties [art. 2409 (3) NCC].

[80]Art. 88 of Law No. 85/2014 ("LPI"): "If at the time of the opening of the insolvency proceedings a right, act or legal fact was not opposable to third parties, enrollments, transcripts, tabulation and any other specific formalities required for this purpose, including those disposed during a criminal trial for special and/or extended confiscation, performed after the opening of the proceedings are not effective towards the creditors, excepting the case when the request or notification, legally filed, was received by the court, authority or competent institution at the latest on the day before the decision to open the proceedings. Registrations performed in violation of this article will be automatically annulled."

[81]Art. 117 para (2) letter (e) LPI: "concluding a security for an unsecured claim, within the last 6 months before the opening of the proceedings."

[82]Art. 2346 NCC: "Unless otherwise provided by law, the hypothec is opposable to third parties from the day of registration in the public registers."

[83]Art. 23 NCC: "If a right, act, fact or any legal relation is subjected at the same time to different publicity formalities, the performance of one formality does not cover the lack of other."

As a general rule, any movable hypothec should be registered in a special (electronic) database[84] called[85] the National Registry for Publicity of Rights in Personal Property (*Registrul National de Publicitate Mobiliara*, in Romanian; hereinafter "RNPM").[86] The registration process is a filing one (as opposed to a recordation system). It is not the security agreement itself that is registered, but a filing statement (*aviz de ipoteca*, in Romanian) signed by either party and providing information on the parties to the security agreement and the type of security, as well as a description of the collateral. The filing service is a private one, conducted by various authorized agents. Therefore, the filing agent cannot and should not censor the filing, unless the filing statement does not indicate all of the required data.

Of course, since the filing agent is not provided with a copy of the security agreement, this filing cannot validate an otherwise invalid security agreement.[87] Also, the third parties are bound only by the information that was made public through the filing. For example, if the description of the collateral differs between the security agreement and the filing statement, only the description in the filing statement will be relevant to third parties.[88]

The filing has two different effects: (i) it ensures the opposability of the security towards third parties and (ii) it provides the basic rule for determining priorities.

The RNPM is an electronic database to which only authorized agents can add information but which can be searched by anyone at any moment[89] and from anywhere access to the Internet is available. Once a filing statement has been entered into the RNPM, all subsequent secured creditors are considered to have knowledge of the previously filed security interests.[90] In addition, all perfected security interests are considered to be opposable to any third party.[91]

---

[84]Art. 2409 para (2) NCC, see fn. 74. Until 2018, this registry was called the Electronic Archive for Security Interests in Personal Property (hereinafter "Archive").

[85]As per Law No. 293/2018 (enacted in December 2018), the Archive was renamed "RNPM," while the rules for the perfection of security interests were kept unchanged. The change in designation was due to the fact that, in addition to security interests in personal property, other rights in personal property could be also recoded. Since December 2018, all references to the Archive in earlier regulations shall be considered to refer to the RNPM.

[86]Art. 18 para (2) NCC: "The publicity is performed through the land register, the Electronic Archive for Security Interests in Personal Property, hereinafter referred to as the archive, the Trade Registry and through any other public registers provided by law." To read about the functioning of the Archive, see Rizoiu (2013b), pp. 114–175. For the new designation of the Archive, see fn. 85 above.

[87]Art. 2414 NCC: "The registration does not validate an invalid hypothec."

[88]Art. 2416 NCC: "If there are inconsistencies between the information in the filing statement and the information in the security agreement, between third parties and between the parties of the security agreement and third parties shall prevail the information in the filing statement."

[89]For the practical limitations of these searches, see Moise (2012), pp. 128–141.

[90]Art. 2415 NCC: "The secured creditor who registers a hypothec over collateral is alleged to have knowledge of all other previously registered hypothecs over the same collateral. The proof to the contrary is not allowed."

[91]Art. 2409 para (3) NCC, see fn. 74.

When a filing statement is registered in the RNPM, it automatically receives a time stamp provided by the system. This time stamp is accurate to the millisecond and the system shall make sure that no two statements have the same time stamp. Therefore, each filing statement has a unique time stamp and can be arranged in perfect chronological order. This unique time stamp associated with each filing statement is the basis for the priority rules,[92] the most important of which is *prior tempore, potior jure*.[93]

While registration in the RNPM is in principle sufficient to ensure the opposability of security interests in copyright, hypothecs in industrial property rights require special registration in the industrial property registries held by OSIM. The relevant laws provide this formality only in respect of the transfer of industrial property rights, a category which is considered to include licence agreements.[94] However, the

---

[92] See Sect. 4.

[93] Art. 2420 para (1) NCC: "(1) The rank of the perfected hypothecs is granted accordingly to the order of the registrations or the perfection, with the exceptions provided by law. (2) The perfected hypothec is always preferred to other hypothecs that have not been perfected."

[94] See art. 42(3) of the Patents Law, art. 28(e) of the Models of Utility Law, arts. 42(3) and 43(4) of the Trademarks Law, art. 38(3) of the Design Law, art. 38(7) of the Plant Varieties Law, art. 30 of the Semiconductor Topographies Law; art. 42(3) of the Patents Law: "Transfers shall produce effects in respect of third parties only as from the date of publication in the Official Industrial Property Bulletin of the mention of the transfer registered with OSIM."

Art. 28(e) of the Models of Utility Law: "The provisions of the Patent Law no. 64/1991, as republished, concerning: e) transfer of rights."

Art. 42(3) of the Trademarks Law: "Upon request by person concerned and on payment of the prescribed fee, OSIM shall enter the assignment in the Trademark Register and publish it in the Official Industrial Property Bulletin. Assignment may be invoked against third parties as from the date of its publication."

Art. 43(4) of the Trademarks Law: "Licenses shall be entered in the Trademark Register on payment of the prescribed fee and shall be published in the Official Industrial Property Bulletin. A license may be invoked against third parties as from the date of its publication."

Art. 38(3) of the Design Law: "The transfer shall be recorded with OSIM, in the Register of designs, and shall produce effects in respect of the third parties only starting on the date of publication of the notice of transfer in the Official Industrial Property Bulletin."

Art. 38(7) of the Plant Varieties Law: "The transfer of rights shall be entered in the National Register for Variety Patent Applications or in the National Register of Variety Patents, as appropriate, shall be published in the Official Industrial Property Bulletin and become opposable to third parties starting on this date."

Art. 30 of the Semi-conductor Topographies Law: "The transfer of rights provided by Art. 28 and 29 shall have effects for third parties only starting with the date when the mention of the transfer registered with the State Office for Inventions and Trademarks has been published in BOPI."

secondary legislation for the application of these laws provides, usually in a rather unclear way, that the registration procedures also apply for security interests in industrial property rights.[95]

---

[95] Art. 86 of Government Decision No. 547/2008 for approving the rules on the application of the Patent Law; art. 20 of Government Decision No. 1457/2008 for approving the rules on the application of the Models of Utility Law; art. 35 of Government Decision No. 1134/2010 for approving the rules on the application of the Trademarks Law; art. 86 of Government Decision No. 547/2008: "(1) The request for registration of a license shall be made in writing and signed by the owner or the beneficiary of a licence and shall contain the following elements: (a) express request for the registration of the license; (b) number of the patent or patents referred to in the license; (c) name and address of the owner; (d) name and address of the beneficiary of the license; (e) indication of the exclusive or non-exclusive character of the license or other indications relating to the kind of license; (f) denomination of the State in which the beneficiary of the license has a real and effective industrial or a commercial enterprise as provided for in Art. 3 of the Paris Convention; (g) date of granting and duration of the licence. (2) The request is considered to be filed only after the payment of the legal fee. (3) The provisions of paragraphs (1) and (2) shall apply mutatis mutandis to: (a) requests for registration of the setting up of a guarantee referring to a patent application or patent; (b) the request for canceling the registration of a licence or of the setting up of a guarantee concerning a patent application or a patent. (4) The request for registration of the license shall be accompanied by the copy of the license contract or the copy of an excerpt thereof, certified by a notary public for compliance with the original. (5) When the license is granted on the basis of a decision of the court or it results by the effect of the law, the request for registration of the license shall be accompanied by the final and irrevocable decision mentioned above. (6) When a guarantee is set up, the request for registration shall be accompanied by the legalized copy of the act for setting up the guarantee. (7) The fee for the registration of a guarantee is the same in respect of the amount and time limit as the fee to be paid for registration of licenses. (8) The request for compulsory license, formulated according to Art. 46 paragraphs (1) and (2) of the Law shall be accompanied by the justification of the fact that the person requesting license could not obtain an exploitation license from the patent owner and that he is capable of exploiting the invention seriously and effectively. (9) The provisions of paragraphs (8)–(10) of Art. 85 shall also apply mutatis mutandis in the case of registration of the licenses and of setting up the guarantees. (10) Upon request by one of the parties, the licenses, sub-licenses, the setting up of a guarantee as well as the measures for compulsory execution, as the case may be, shall be entered in the National Register of Filed Patent Applications or in the National Register of Patents and shall be published in BOPI in the month immediately following to the month when the registration was made. (11) The provisions of the present article are also applicable to the registration of the licenses and setting up of a guarantee concerning patents."

Art. 20 of Government Decision No. 1457/2008: "Mutatis mutandis application of provisions of the Implementing Regulations to the Patent Law 64/1991, approved by Government Decision No. 547/2008. In application of Art. 28 of the Law, the following provisions of the Implementing Regulations to the Patent Law 64/1991, as republished, shall apply mutatis mutandis: Art. 2–10, Art. 14–16, Art. 18, except paragraph (15), Art. 19–24, Art. 26–31, Art. 33–34, Art. 38, Art. 44–46, Art. 48, except paragraph (2), Art. 49, Art. 52–54, Art. 55 wherein the phrase 'request for revocation' shall be replaced by the phrase 'request for cancellation', Art. 56, except paragraph (1), letter b), Art. 57, except paragraph (4), and wherein the phrase 'request for revocation' shall be replaced by the phrase 'request for cancellation', Art. 58 wherein the phrase 'request for revocation' shall be replaced by the phrase 'request for cancellation', Art. 59, except paragraph (2) and wherein the phrase 'request for revocation' shall be replaced by the phrase 'request for cancellation', Art. 60, Art. 63, Art. 64, except paragraph (4), Art. 65, except paragraph (3), (5) and (6), Art. 80, except letter a), Art.81, except paragraph (13), Art. 82 and Art. 84–91."

This secondary legislation raises numerous uncertainties. First, there is no uniformity in respect of industrial property rights. Specific provisions exist only in respect of patents, utility models, and trademarks. Second, the scope of these provisions is defined by different wording (if any exists); for example, for inventions, the wording refers to security interests over the rights in the invention, while for trademarks, it refers to real rights in general. Third, no specific provision provides for opposability once these registration procedures have been completed.

Based on this last observation, we take the view that complying with these formality requirements relating to publicity is not a requirement for the opposability of the hypothecs in industrial property; instead, the formality requirements merely allow the third parties to be informed. Only when an actual transfer of industrial property rights is concluded as part of the enforcement of such a hypothec will the registration of this transfer in the specific industrial property registry be required for it to be opposable to third parties.

Art. 35 of Government Decision No. 1134/2010: "(1) The request for recording a license or for constituting a real right in respect of a trademark shall contain the following: (a) name or denomination and address or registered office of the owner; (b) if the owner has a professional representative, name or denomination and address or registered office thereof; (c) name or denomination and address or registered office of the licensee or of the user of the real right; (d) if the licensee has a professional representative, name or denomination and address or registered office thereof; (e) where appropriate, indication of the state of which the licensee is a national, indication of the state wherein the licensee has his residence/ registered office or an establishment within the meaning of Art. 3 of the Paris Convention; (f) where the owner is a legal entity, the statutory form thereof as well as the name of the State the legislation of which served as a legal framework for the organization of the legal entity; (g) registration number of the trademark which is the object of recording the license or the real right; (h) list of goods and services represented by the trademark which is the object of the request for recording the license or the real right; (i) period for which the license is granted; (j) territory for which the license is granted; (i) signature of owner or of his representative. (2) When the trademark is the object of a license for a part of goods and services in respect of which the trademark is registered or when the license has territorial limits or is a temporary license, the request for recording the license shall indicate: (a) the goods and services which the license refers to; (b) the part of the territory of Romania for which the license is granted; (c) the period for which the license is granted, as the case may be. (3) At the time of filing the request for recording the license, proof of payment of the legal fee shall also be filed, otherwise the request shall produce no effects. (4) The request for recording a license shall be filed with OSIM by the owner of the registered trademark or the licensee and shall be accompanied by a certified copy of an excerpt from the license contract indicating the transferred rights. (5) When the requirements provided for in paragraphs (1) and (2) are not fulfilled, OSIM shall grant the person having filed the request for recording the license a 3-month time limit for remedying the deficiencies. Where the deficiencies are not remedied within the granted time limit, OSIM shall decide to reject the request. (6) An exclusive license relating to a trademark shall be entered in the Trademark Register under the mention "exclusive license" if the owner and the licensee expressly requested this mention. (7) A single request may be submitted for two or more trademarks, provided that it relates to the same owner and the same licensee and the numbers of all trademark registrations concerned are indicated in the request and the legal fee for recordal of licenses is paid for each of the said trademarks."

The solution is different in respect of European uniform titles. Under both the European Union Trade Mark Regulation[96] and the European Union Design Regulation,[97] the opposability of a security over a right granted under these regulations is conditional upon its registration in the relevant EU registries. By correlating these specific provisions with the general rules on publicity and on the opposability of movable hypothecs, we can determine that in order for a hypothec in an EU title to be opposable to third parties subsequently acquiring rights in that title under Romanian law, it is necessary either for the third party to have known at the moment of acquisition that the hypothec had been created or for the respective hypothec to have been registered both in the RNPM and in the EU relevant industrial property registry.

---

[96] Arts. 19 and 23 of the European Union Trade Mark Regulation: Art. 19: "(1) A Community trade mark may, independently of the undertaking, be given as security or be the subject of rights in rem. (2) On request of one of the parties, rights mentioned in paragraph 1 shall be entered in the Register and published."

Art. 23: "(1) Legal acts referred to in Articles 17, 19 and 22 concerning a Community trade mark shall have effects vis-à-vis third parties in all the Member States only after entry in the Register. Nevertheless, such an act, before it is so entered, shall have 24.3.2009 effect vis-à-vis third parties who have acquired rights in the trademark after the date of that act but who knew of the act at the date on which the rights were acquired. (2) Paragraph 1 shall not apply in the case of a person who acquires the Community trade mark or a right concerning the Community trade mark by way of transfer of the whole of the undertaking or by any other universal succession. (3) The effects vis-à-vis third parties of the legal acts referred to in Article 20 shall be governed by the law of the Member State determined in accordance with Article 16. (4) Until such time as common rules for the Member States in the field of bankruptcy enter into force, the effects vis-à-vis third parties of bankruptcy or like proceedings shall be governed by the law of the Member State in which such proceedings are first brought within the meaning of national law or of conventions applicable in this field."

[97] Arts. 29 and 33 of the European Union Design Regulation: Art. 29: "(1) A registered Community design may be given as security or be the subject of rights in rem. (2) On request of one of the parties, the rights mentioned in paragraph 1 shall be entered in the register and published."

Art. 33: "(1) The effects vis-à-vis third parties of the legal acts referred to in Articles 28, 29, 30 and 32 shall be governed by the law of the Member State determined in accordance with Article 27. (2) However, as regards registered Community designs, legal acts referred to in Articles 28, 29 and 32 shall only have effect vis-à-vis third parties in all the Member States after entry in the register. Nevertheless, such an act, before it is so entered, shall have effect vis-à-vis third parties who have acquired rights in the registered Community design after the date of that act but who knew of the act at the date on which the rights were acquired. (3) Paragraph 2 shall not apply to a person who acquires the registered Community design or a right concerning the registered Community design by way of transfer of the whole of the undertaking or by any other universal succession. (4) Until such time as common rules for the Member States in the field of insolvency enter into force, the effects vis-à-vis third parties of insolvency proceedings shall be governed by the law of the Member State in which such proceedings are first brought under the national law or the regulations applicable in this field."

4 Priorities

The order of priority is provided by rules mentioned in the law.[98] Therefore, the parties to the security agreement are not allowed to set their own priority system. However, it is possible for the creditors to conclude private agreements on certain subordination arrangements.[99] Also, it is possible for the secured creditors to assign their security independently from the secured claim,[100] or even switch the ranking of their respective security interests.[101]

Another important consequence of the legal nature of priorities is that the ranking system is relative—that is to say, there is no absolute ranking. For example, a second-ranking security will automatically become a first-ranking one once the first-ranking security has been discharged. Similarly, if a super-priority security is created, the original first-ranking security shall automatically become a second-ranking one.

It is important to specify that all types of encumbrances share the same set of priorities. Therefore, a movable hypothec could be placed in the same ranking as an immovable hypothec,[102] a pledge,[103] a lien,[104] or even an asset freeze (whether civil,

[98]Art. 2420 para (1) NCC, see fn. 93.

[99]Art. 2326 para (1) NCC: "The price obtained from enforcement sale of the asset is divided between the creditors *pro rata* with the amount of their claims, except when there are legal preferences or private subordination arrangements."

[100]Art. 2358 NCC: "(1) The hypothec or its rank can be transferred independently of the secured claim only if the secured amount is determined in the security agreement. (2) In the case referred to in paragraph (1), the transfer is performed by written form between the secured creditor as the assignor and another creditor, as an assignee, while notifying the debtor. (3) The law provisions regarding the land register or, as the case may be, regarding the movable hypothec's opposability towards third parties remain applicable."

[101]Art. 2427 NCC: "(1) The secured creditor can transfer to an unsecured creditor the hypothec of his secured claim. Also, the secured creditors can agree between themselves to swap their ranks, provided that the publicity formalities are met. (2) If between the hypothecs whose ranks are swapped were other security interests or other encumbrances and their holders did not agree to the swap, the swap agreement is opposable to them only inasmuch the higher ranked hypothec was also opposable to them. (3) In all cases, the rank assignment is performed within the amount of the secured claim whose rank was assigned and the rank swap is performed within the amount of the higher ranked secured claim. (4) If the collateral is auctioned, the secured creditor who acquired the rank of a conditional claim may give up the rank swap benefit, while the secured conditional claim resumes to its former rank."

[102]Art. 2422 NCC: "When the same asset acts as collateral for both a movable hypothec and an immovable hypothec, shall prevail the secured creditors who first filed their hypothec. However, the immovable hypothec registered on the same day as a movable hypothec shall prevail."

[103]Art. 2423 NCC: "The secured creditor who filed the registration of his hypothec shall prevail over the pledgee creditor, even if the latter acquired the detention of the collateral prior to the hypothec's registration."

[104]Art. 2342 NCC: "(1) In case of competing claims between liens or liens and hypothecs, the claims are enforced as following: 1. the claims secured by a lien over a movable collateral, referred to in art. 2339; 2. the claims secured by a hypothec or a pledge. (2) The creditor secured by a special

fiscal, or criminal[105]). In addition, the assimilated operations shall also be ranked as encumbrances in the same system of priorities.[106] While pledges cannot encumber IP rights and it is likely that immovable hypothecs also cannot,[107] only movable hypothecs can be created over intellectual property.

The main rule for determining priority is the timing when the filing statement is filed in the RNPM.[108] It is irrelevant whether the security was perfected (i.e. effective) at the time of filing or not. The same rule applies to security over *universitas facti*.[109] However, before perfection, an unperfected security shall be subordinated to every perfected security (even if filed later).[110]

The only (relevant) exception to the rule of "first in time, first in right" is the purchase money security interest ("PMSI").[111] Under this exception, the creditor who offered credit (either as a vendor postponing payment or as a lender financing the acquisition) for the securing debtor to acquire a new asset can create a security in the acquired asset. The PMSI exception states that such a security shall have super-priority (i.e. it shall come first, irrespective of any encumbrances filed earlier on the same collateral) provided that the PMSI is filed before the securing debtor obtains possession of the collateral *and* the PMSI secured creditor notifies the other

---

lien shall prevail over the creditor secured by a perfected movable hypothec, if he filed the lien prior to the perfection of the hypothec. Also, the lien creditor shall prevail over the creditor secured by an immovable hypothec, if he filed the registration in the land register prior to the registration of the hypothec." See Moise (2015), p. 95.

[105]For competing claims between a hypothec and freezing measures, see Rizoiu (2016), pp. 129–161. The opinion presented in that article was later used as a basis for the decision of the Romanian High Court of Cassation and Justice ("ICCJ") to make it mandatory to interpret the law in the sense that a criminal asset freeze is nothing more than a statutory lien that cannot hinder the secured creditor from enforcing their hypothec over the frozen asset, provided that the hypothec was registered before the freezing was registered. See ICCJ, *Decision (RIL) No. 2/2018*, available at www.scj.ro. Accessed Dec 29, 2018.

[106]Art. 2347 para (3) NCC, see fn. 44.

[107]Yet immovable hypothecs are not necessarily out of the picture, since they can extend over any accessory. For example, if an IP right is considered an accessory for a building (e.g. an industrial construction implying certain patents), the immovable hypothec could cover the IP right as well. Art. 2356 NCC: "(1) Movable assets which become accessories for an immovable asset, without losing their individuality, can act as a collateral either alongside the immovable asset or separately. (2) The movable asset still acts as a collateral even if it becomes an accessory. However, can no longer act as a movable collateral the building materials or any other such assets used in an edifice or any other land improvement."

[108]Art. 2420 para (1) NCC, see fn. 93.

[109]Art. 2424 NCC: "Between a hypothec over a collateral consisting of a pool of movable assets and a hypothec over a collateral consisting of individual movable assets shall prevail the hypothec which was registered or perfected first."

[110]Art. 2420 para (2) NCC, see fn. 93.

[111]Art. 2425 para (1) NCC: "The hypothec concluded in favor of the vendor or the lender financing the acquisition prevails over a prior hypothec if, before the debtor obtains possession of the collateral, the filing registration was filed and the vendor or, as the case may be, the lender notifies in written form the prior secured creditor about the sale and the registration."

(i.e. earlier) secured creditor(s). In case of IP rights, the concept of possession is difficult to pin down, but it is acknowledged[112] that having control over an intangible asset is equal to having possession (or quasi-possession) of the asset.[113]

In case of insolvency, the priority structure is not affected. However, the insolvency administrator shall disregard security interests filed after the start of the insolvency proceedings and may ignore any security interests filed in the 6 months prior to the start of the proceedings.[114]

5 Enterprise Charges

Under Romanian law, the concept of enterprise (*fond de comert*, in Romanian) is generally[115] considered to be a type of *universitas facti*.[116] The IP rights of a business are included in the enterprise as a going concern. Therefore, the rules for the security in *universitas facti* apply to the IP rights included in such a security as well.[117]

This means that the security over the enterprise shall function like an English floating charge and will crystallize only at the time of enforcement, covering whatever the enterprise comprises at that time.

---

[112] See Popa (2010), pp. 85–104.

[113] Art. 916 NCC: "(1) The possession is the exercising of ownership interests by the person who controls the asset and acts like its owner. (2) The provisions of this Title apply accordingly in the matter of the holder who acts like the owner of another right *in rem*, excepting the security interests."

[114] Please note that there is still debate on whether a criminal asset freeze will be enforceable against the insolvency estate, since art. 91 para (1) LPI states *in fine* that any liquidation sale made by the insolvency administrator shall not impede the freezing measure. This means that the frozen asset could be sold in a liquidation sale, but the buyer will acquire it together with the freezing lien. Of course, such encumbrance will cause this kind of sale to be avoided in practice, since nobody will want to assume such a risk.

[115] The debate is still open, since a former legal definition of the concept of enterprise (*fond de comert*, in Romanian) was repealed back in 2014 and the change is being analysed in legal literature. However, case law is still using the concept based on the legal literature continuing to treat the enterprise as the main example of *universitas facti*.

[116] Art. 541 NCC: "(1) A *universitas facti* is comprised of assets belonging to the same person and that have a common destination set by her will or by law. (2) The assets comprising the *universitas facti* can, together or individually be subjected to distinct legal relations." See Cărpenaru (2009), pp. 134–137.

[117] See Sect. 3.1.

6 Rights Before Default

As a general rule, before default occurs, the secured party only has rights meant to preserve the value (i.e. usefulness) of the security.[118] This means that the securing debtor retains (almost) all of the prerogatives related to the collateral. The securing debtor will continue to deal with the collateral as if it were not encumbered, meaning that he can use it, benefit from its proceeds, and even dispose of it.[119]

Nonetheless, the security will continue to adhere to the collateral irrespective of any transfer occurring after the security was created in (i.e. attached to) the collateral.[120] There are two exceptions to the rule that the security follows the collateral. The first is that in some cases the security will extend to the proceeds of the (original) collateral instead. The second is that the security will cease to encumber the collateral in the event of particular transfers.

The concept of "proceeds" is extensive and covers not only the fruits and products of the collateral,[121] but also any asset to which the value of the collateral was transferred.[122] Thus, the security may extend its scope while remaining attached to the initial collateral. The extension is automatic, but it requires registration in order to be effective against third parties. In case the initial filing was not sufficiently descriptive so as to encompass the proceeds, the secured party needs to file an additional statement describing the resultant proceeds within 15 days after their occurrence.[123] However, monetary proceeds are not required to be registered,[124] since money is always considered to be a type of proceed (provided it can be traced). Thus, the monetary royalties for IP rights, as well as damages for infringement by third parties, will be covered in the description of IP collateral.

A specific proceeds problem may arise when an industrial property right has been requested but not yet granted. In principle, in such cases, the applicant provisionally holds the exclusive right that will result from the title from the moment the

---

[118] See Rizoiu (2011), pp. 558–566.

[119] Art. 2373 NCC: "The securing debtor is free to use, administrate and dispose of the collateral without prejudice to the secured creditor's rights."

[120] Art. 2360 NCC: "The secured creditor can pursue collateral irrespective of any transfer, notwithstanding any real right created or registered after the hypothec's registration."

[121] Art. 547 NCC: "The proceeds of assets are the fruits and products."

[122] Art. 2392 NCC: "(1) The hypothec extends over the fruits and products of the collateral, as well as over every asset acquired by the securing debtor as a result of an administrative or disposal act regarding the collateral. (2) It is considered to be a proceed of the movable collateral any asset that replaces it or acquires its value."

[123] Art. 2412 para (1) NCC: "In case the initial filing was not sufficiently descriptive as to encompass the proceeds, the hypothec maintains its rank over the proceeds only if the secured creditor files an additional statement describing the resulted proceeds within 15 days since their occurrence."

[124] Art. 2412 para (2) NCC: "When the proceeds are traceable amounts of money, the hypothec maintains its rank over them without filing an additional statement."

application for title is published.[125] This right is subject to the dismissal or withdrawal of the application for title. If the title is granted, it will produce retroactive effects from the filing date of the application,[126] even if it is only directed against the infringing acts committed by a third party after the publication of the application or, if such acts are prior to publication,, after the notification sent by the applicant requesting that the third party cease the infringing acts.[127] This means that, in principle, for the period between the publication of the application and the granting of the title, two different rights with the same object will overlap in the estate of the holder.

In our opinion, a hypothec constituted in either of these two rights will also automatically exist in the other one. Thus, if the hypothec is created in the provisional exclusive right, then once the title is granted, the title will be a proceed of the provisional right and the hypothec will be in the value of the title. If the hypothec is created in the right granted by the title, then it should be noted that, in relation to the definite exclusive right, the provisional exclusive right is an accessory.[128] Thus,

---

[125] Art. 32 of the Patents Law, art. 34(1) of the Design Law, art. 30(1) of the Trademarks Law; art. 32 of the Patents Law: "Starting from the date of its publication under Art. 22, paragraphs (1)-(3), the patent application shall provisionally confer on the applicant the protection laid down in Art. 31."

Art. 34(1) of the Design Law: "Starting on the date of publication of the application, the natural person or legal entity entitled to be granted the certificate of registration shall temporarily enjoy the same rights conferred according to the provisions of Art. 30, until the issuance of the certificate of registration, except for the cases when the application has been rejected or withdrawn."

Art. 30(1) of the Trademarks Law: "The registration of a trademark shall take effect on the date of the regular filing of the trademark and shall subsist for a period of 10 years."

[126] Art. 30(1) of the Patents Law, art. 35(1) of the Design Law, art. 37(1) of the Trademarks Law; art. 30(1) of the Patents Law: "Patent duration shall be 20 years as from the date of filing the application."

Art. 35(1) of the Design Law: "The term of protection of a certificate of registration of the design is of ten years counting from the date of constituting the regular deposit and it may be renewed for three successive five-year periods."

Art. 37(1) of the Trademarks Law: "The applicant for trademark registration may only request the prohibition referred to in Art. 36 paragraph (2) after publication of the trademark."

[127] Art. 57 of the Patents Law, art. 34(2) of the Design Law, art. 37(2) of the Trademarks Law; art. 57 of the Patents Law: "Where the acts referred to in Art. 31, paragraph (2) continue to be done after notification, the court may, upon request, order such acts be discontinued until OSIM makes a decision on the patent application. Said measure may be ordered subject to payment by the applicant of a security fixed by the court."

Art. 34(2) of the Design Law: "Violation of the provisions of paragraph (1) shall entail the infringers' liability of paying the damages, according to the general rules of law; the title for the payment of damages may be enforced only after the issuance of the certificate of registration of the design."

Art. 37(2) of the Trademarks Law: "The applicant may claim damages for the acts referred to under paragraph (1), committed subsequently to trademark publication, under the general provisions of law. A decision ordering payment of damages shall be enforceable only as from the date of trademark registration."

[128] Art. 546(1) NCC: "An asset that was intended, in a stable and exclusive way, for the economic use of another asset is considered an accessory as long as it satisfies this use."

considering the mechanism of the condition subsequent, the single purpose of the provisional right is to anticipate the entitlement to enforce the definitive right to the strict extent to which it will result from the title. Therefore, unless otherwise specifically provided for by the parties, the provisional accessory right recognized from the publication of the application will be covered by the hypothec created in the main definitive exclusive right issued from the title as it is granted.[129]

In case the collateral is disposed of by the (professional) securing debtor in the ordinary course of his business, the security in the original collateral will cease[130] and will automatically be transferred to the proceeds of the sale.[131] The monetary proceeds should be segregated by the securing debtor in a separate bank account and the secured party should be informed of this fact. This rule could also apply in the case of a professional entity engaged in dealing with IP rights (such as patent pools). It may also be discussed whether a holding company managing all of the intellectual property of a corporation can have this status. Also, a motion picture company dealing with the copyright of its movies could fall within this category if it manages these IP rights as a stock.

Before default, the secured party has the right to inspect the collateral[132] in order to make sure that its value is preserved. The securing debtor is required to maintain this value and not allow it to decrease beyond what it would with the normal wear and tear of using the collateral.[133] Lack of diligent care concerning the value of the collateral from the securing debtor will result in damages to be paid to the secured party, even if the secured claim has not yet matured.[134] In addition, the secured party may accelerate the secured claim when he reasonably believes that the value of the collateral is in jeopardy or the prospects of enforcement have been affected.[135] Even if there is no default under the main contract, these issues related to the value of the

[129] Art. 546(3) NCC: "Unless otherwise stated, the accessory asset follows the legal status of the main asset, including its alienation or encumbrance."

[130] Art. 2393 para (1) NCC: "The asset acquired in the ordinary course of business of an enterprise alienating assets of the same kind no longer acts as a collateral for the securing debtor even if the hypothec is perfected and the acquirer had knowledge of it."

[131] Art. 2393 para (2) NCC: "In this case, the hypothec transfers to the proceeds of the sale."

[132] Art. 2394 NCC: "The secured creditor has the right to inspect the collateral. He must not hamper the activity of the holder."

[133] Art. 2374 NCC: "The securing debtor cannot destroy or damage the collateral and cannot diminish its value unless it occurs during a normal usage of the collateral or during a state of emergency."

[134] Art. 2375 NCC: "The secured creditor may demand, within the amount of his claim, damages for the prejudice caused by the destruction, damage or diminution of the collateral, even if the secured claim is not matured. Such damages are deducted from the secured claim."

[135] Art. 2396 para (1) NCC: "The secured creditor may accelerate his secured claim and enforce the hypothec when he finds the lack of a proper maintenance of the collateral or other events attributable to the securing debtor affecting the prospects of enforcement, as they were determined by the security agreement."

collateral could trigger a default. The right to accelerate is limited to the case of insolvency of the securing debtor.[136]

The debtor's duty to maintain the value of the collateral has specific aspects in case the collateral is an IP right. If the respective right results from a patent, the patent owner shall pay the annuities in order to prevent foreclosure on the patent rights.[137] He will have also to ensure that the invention is sufficiently exploited in order to provide the market with a reasonable supply in relation to demand; this will prevent requests for the granting of compulsory licences.[138]

If the collateral is a trademark right, the trademark owner will have to prevent the foreclosure of such right by using his trademark seriously and effectively in trade in such a manner that the trademark does not lose its distinctiveness and does not

---

[136] Art. 123 para (1) LPI: "Contracts in progress are maintained at the opening of the insolvency proceedings, the provisions of art. 1417 of the Civil Code not being applicable. Any contractual clauses that stipulate the cease of the contract, the decay from the benefit of the term or the declaring of anticipated maturity for the reason of opening the insolvency proceedings are null and void. [. . .]"

[137] Art. 40(3) of the Patents Law: "Failure to pay such fees shall cause the patent owner's loss of his rights arising from the patent. The loss of said rights by the owner shall be entered in the National Register of Patents and published in the Official Industrial Property Bulletin. Maintenance fees may also be paid in advance, under the conditions laid down by the regulations for implementing this Law, for a period not exceeding 4 years."

[138] Art. 43 of the Patents Law: "(1) Upon request by any interested person, the Bucharest Tribunal may grant a compulsory license after 4 years have elapsed from the patent application filing date or after 3 years have elapsed from the grant of the patent, whichever period expires later. (2) The provisions of paragraph (1) shall only apply where the invention has not been exploited or has been insufficiently exploited on the territory of Romania, and the patent owner cannot justify his inaction, and where no agreement has been reached with him regarding the conditions and commercial methods for applying the invention. (3) The Bucharest Tribunal shall authorize the compulsory license, if it considers, based on given circumstances, that, in spite of all efforts made by the interested person, no agreement could be reached within a reasonable time period. (4) Besides the cases referred to in paragraph (2), a compulsory license may be authorized by the Bucharest Tribunal: (a) in national emergency cases; (b) in other cases of extreme emergency; (c) in cases of public use for non-commercial purposes. (5) The grant of the compulsory license, for one of the reasons provided under paragraph (4), shall not require the fulfilment of the conditions mentioned under paragraph (2). Nevertheless, the licensee shall inform the applicant or patent owner about the authorization given by the Tribunal, within the shortest delay. (6) In cases of public use for non-commercial purposes, the Government or third parties authorized by the Government, if they know or have demonstrable reasons to know that a valid patent is or will be used by the Government or the third parties, shall inform the patent owner accordingly, within a reasonable time. (7) In cases where a patent cannot be exploited without infringing the rights conferred by other patent granted for an application having a prior regular national filing date, a compulsory license for exploiting the subsequent patent may only be authorized if the following additional conditions are cumulatively fulfilled: (a) the invention claimed in the subsequent patent involves an important technical advance of considerable economic significance as compared with the invention in the earlier patent; (b) the owner of the earlier patent is entitled to a cross-license on reasonable terms for using the invention claimed in the subsequent patent; (c) the use authorized in respect of the earlier patent shall be non-transferable, except for the transfer with the subsequent patent."

mislead consumers in respect of the objective features of the product.[139] In addition, because the trademark value is dictated by its notoriety and reputation, the trademark owner is bound to maintain the quality of the products and services to which the trademark is attached; adapt the quality to the technological and perceptual evolutions of the market[140]; maintain the volumes of trade targeting a certain number of consumers; and introduce in his licence contracts obligations and legal tools to effectively allow him to control and direct the participation of the licensee towards those objectives.[141]

For all IP rights, if the title has not been granted at the moment that the hypothec contract is concluded, the applicant debtor is required to take all necessary steps within the examination procedure to obtain a title as extended in scope as possible as soon as is reasonably possible. Also, even if the title has already been granted, if the

---

[139] Art. 46(1)(a)-(c) of the Trademarks Law and art. 15 of the EU Trademarks Regulation; art. 46 of the Trademarks Law: "(1) Any concerned person may apply to the Bucharest Tribunal, at any time during the term of protection of the trademark, for revocation of the owner of the rights conferred by the trademark: (a) if, within a continuous period of 5 years, as from the date of its entry in the Trademark Register, the trademark has not been put to genuine use on the territory of Romania in connection with the goods or services in respect of which it is registered or if such use has been suspended for a continuous period of 5 years, and there are no proper reasons for non-use; (b) if, after the date of registration, the trademark has become, in consequence of acts or inactivity of the owner, the common name in the trade for a product or service in respect of which it is registered; (c) if, after the date of registration and in consequence of the use made of it by the owner or with his consent, the trademark is liable to mislead the public, particularly as to the nature, quality or geographical origin of the goods or services in respect of which it is registered."

Art. 15 of the EU Trademarks Regulation: "(1) If, within a period of five years following registration, the proprietor has not put the EU trade mark to genuine use in the EU in connection with the goods or services in respect of which it is registered, or if such use has been suspended during an uninterrupted period of five years, the EU trade mark shall be subject to the sanctions provided for in this Regulation, unless there are proper reasons for non-use. The following shall also constitute use within the meaning of the first subparagraph: (a) use of the EU trade mark in a form differing in elements which do not alter the distinctive character of the mark in the form in which it was registered; (b) affixing of the EU trade mark to goods or to the packaging thereof in the EU solely for export purposes. (2) Use of the EU trade mark with the consent of the proprietor shall be deemed to constitute use by the proprietor."

[140] The essential function of a trademark is to identify the commercial origin of the goods or services to which it is attached: it allows the public to identify the undertaking which controls whether the goods or services are put on the market and which guarantees their quality. See CJEU, June 18, 2002, *Koninklijke Philips Electronics NV v Remington Consumer Products Ltd.l*

[141] Art. 43(2) of the Trademarks Law and art. 22(2)(e) of the EU Trademark Regulation; art. 43(2) of the Trademarks Law: "The owner of a trademark may invoke the rights conferred by that trademark against a licensee who contravenes the provisions of his licensing contract with regard to its duration, the form of the trademark and the nature of the goods or services for which the license is granted, the territory in which the trademark may be used, or the quality of the goods manufactured or of the services provided by the licensee under the trademark for which the license has been granted."

Art. 22(2)(e) of the EU Trademark Regulation: "The proprietor of an EU trade mark may invoke the rights conferred by that trade mark against a licensee who contravenes any provision in his licensing contract with regard to: (e) the quality of the goods manufactured or of the services provided by the licensee."

collateral is a trademark, utility model, or design, the obligation to maintain the value of the collateral implies that the owner has a duty to renew the registration as long as the hypothec is in place, to the maximum extent possible. The same goes for patent rights on pharmaceutical or plant treatment product inventions for which an up-to-five-year additional protection period may be obtained upon request by the patent holder.[142]

For all IP rights, this duty involves a licensing policy that is reasonably oriented towards increasing both the IP exploitation value and active use to prevent and sanction infringements, including by bringing court actions for injunction and damages.

If the security agreement provides for this structure, the secured party can collect the proceeds of the collateral, including IP royalties and damages, before default. Such proceeds will be applied against the main claim. However, this mechanism should be carefully detailed in the security agreement.[143]

The securing debtor, in turn, has the right to ask the secured party to provide updated information related to the remaining value of the secured obligation and the list of collateral still subject to the security.[144] It is to be noted that the security interest is indivisible, meaning that it will continue to cover the entire collateral, irrespective of the amount of the remaining secured obligation, until this obligation is discharged.[145]

[142]See EU Regulation No. 469/2009 concerning the creation of a certificate of supplementary protection for medicines and EU Regulation No. 1610/1996 concerning the creation of a supplementary protection certificate for plant protection products.

[143]Art. 2395 NCC: "The stipulation by which the secured creditor collects the proceeds of the collateral against the main claim is not valid unless it carefully details the manner and proportion of the proceeds' deduction from the main claim."

[144]Art. 2397 NCC: "(1) The securing debtor has the right to ask the secured creditor in writing: (a) to issue a statement regarding the remaining value of the secured claim; (b) to confirm or, as the case may be, to modify the list of collaterals still subject to security in the securing debtor's opinion; (c) to confirm or, as the case may be, to modify the value of the claim that, in the securing debtor's opinion, is still secured at a certain moment. (2) The secured creditor is obliged to inform the securing debtor within 15 days from receiving the request referred to in paragraph 1, as the case may be: (a) a written statement indicating the remaining value of the secured claim; (b) the confirmation or rectification of the securing debtor's statement regarding the collateral and the remaining amount; (c) a statement according to which he is no longer the holder of the hypothec, providing the name and address of his successor. (3) The securing debtor has the right to obtain such statements every 6 months, free of charge. (4) The secured creditor can charge the securing debtor for issuing an additional statement to the one referred to in paragraph (3)."

[145]Art. 2344 NCC: "The hypothec is, by its nature, accessory and indivisible. It subsists as long as the secured claim and it bears entirely upon all collateral, upon each one of them and upon every part of them, even when the ownership is divisible or the obligations are divisible."

7 Enforcement

7.1 General Issues

As a general observation, the enforcement of the security shall occur only after default under the secured obligation.[146] It is to be noted that "default" refers to any irregularity related to the full, exact, and timely performance of the obligation.[147] The default should refer to the secured obligation, but it may be triggered by default under another obligation (i.e. "cross-default") or even by failure to maintain the collateral.[148] The default could refer to the main obligation or to an accessory thereof, since the accessories are considered to be implicitly covered by the security.[149] The default should originate from the debtor of the secured obligation (if this is a different person from the securing debtor).

Enforcement of the security requires the (secured) obligation to be certain, liquid, and matured.[150] This means that the secured obligation should exist and its value should be determined. The criteria for determining the existence and the amount of the secured obligation should be referred to in the security agreement.[151]

The security agreement is a writ of execution,[152] meaning that it can be enforced without a trial of the merits. It was recently determined that the security can be enforced even when the main agreement is not a writ of execution.[153] In all cases, the enforcement process requires an order allowing the enforcement procedure to start to be obtained first from the court.[154]

---

[146] Art. 2429 NCC: "If the securing debtor does not willingly perform his obligations, the secured creditor can enforce the hypothec, according to the provisions of this Chapter."

[147] Art. 1516 NCC: "(1) The creditor has the right to a full, exact and timely performance of the obligation. (2) When, without justification, the debtor does not perform his obligations and he is formal noticed, the creditor may choose, without losing the right to ask for damages, if he is entitled to: 1. to ask or, as the case may be, to enforce the performance of the obligation; 2. to obtain, if the obligation is contractual, the resolution or resilience of the contract or, as the case may be, the reduction of his own correlative obligation; 3. to use, when appropriate, any other means provided by law to accomplish his right."

[148] Art. 2396 NCC, see fn. 135.

[149] Art. 2354 NCC: "The same rank of the hypothec is granted to the capital, interests, fees, penalties and reasonable expenses made with the recovery or conservation of the collateral."

[150] Art. 2430 NCC: "The hypothec can be enforced only by a writ of execution and if the secured obligation is certain, liquid and matured."

[151] Art. 2372 para (1) NCC, see fn. 57.

[152] Art. 2431 NCC: "The valid security agreements are, according to the law, writs of execution."

[153] Until 2018, this was a debatable argument. See Rizoiu (2017a), pp. 109–127. However, the Romanian High Court of Cassation and Justice settled the issue based on the arguments presented in the scholarly article cited. See ICCJ, *Decision (HP) No. 60/2017*, at www.scj.ro. Accessed Dec 29, 2018.

[154] Art. 666 NCPC: "(1) Within maximum 3 days from the filing, the enforcement agent shall request an order of execution from the court, submitting, in a certified copy of the original, the

There are several methods of enforcement: (i) private enforcement of the collateral under the security; (ii) regular enforcement of the collateral; or (iii) regular enforcement of all of the debtor's assets. The choice lies with the secured party,[155] who also retains the rights of an unsecured creditor. This analysis will focus only on specific enforcement of the collateral, since this is the true enforcement under the security (*actio hypothecaria*),[156] unlike the general enforcement of claims (*actio personalia*).

In all cases, the enforcement should follow the rules laid down by the law and the parties are prohibited from providing in the security agreement that the collateral is automatically transferred to the secured party in case of default (*lex comissoria*).[157]

7.2 Enforcement Outside Insolvency

While the NCC provides for a US-inspired self-help remedy in the case of security interests in personal property,[158] this procedure is not applicable to intangible property such as IP rights. Special provisions in the NCC meant for the enforcement of a security in commercial paper or receivables are also not applicable.

However, it is possible to benefit from the special procedure allowing the secured party to manage the collateral in order to apply the proceeds of this use against the secured obligation.[159]

Therefore, the main tool for enforcing the security in IP rights is to use the general enforcement procedure laid down by the New Code of Civil Procedure[160] (hereinafter "NCPC").[161] This process starts with the sequestration of the collateral by the

---

creditor's request, the writ of execution, the conclusion referred to in art. 665 (1) and the proof of the stamp tax payment. [. . .]"

[155] Art. 2432 NCC: "The provisions of this Chapter do not affect the possibility of the secured creditor to enforce his claim by the way of a personal action or to take any measures deemed necessary for the enforcement of the hypothec, according to the Civil Procedure Code."

[156] For details regarding this remedy under Romanian law, see Rizoiu (2018), pp. 266–270.

[157] Art. 2433 NCC: "Any clause according to which the collateral is automatically transferred to the secured creditor or he can dispose of it without meeting the formalities provided by law, in order to secure his claim, is considered unwritten."

[158] Art. 2438 NCC: "The secured creditor has the right to: (a) take over the collateral with its accessories, (b) without moving them, to take the necessary actions that the equipment and other similar assets can no longer be used and to subsequently dispose of them according to the provisions of art. 2447."

[159] Art. 2468 NCC: "If the collateral belongs to an enterprise, the secured creditor can take it over for management purposes if he notifies the persons referred to in art. 2450 and he files an enforcement notice accordingly to the provisions of arts. 2449–2451. (2) The takeover of the collateral is temporary, at most until the performance of his secured claim."

[160] Law No. 134/2010 regarding the Code of Civil Procedure.

[161] Art. 731 et seq. NCPC: "To fulfill his claims, the creditor may pursue the movable assets of his debtor, placed in his possession or in others'. The creditor may indicate the movable assets to be

enforcement agent.[162] The freezing of the collateral should be recorded in the RNPM.[163] Once the collateral is frozen, the securing debtor no longer has the right to deal with the collateral.[164]

The collateral shall be sold by the enforcement agent either in an amiable manner[165] (provided that the securing debtor agrees to this) or through a forced procedure.[166] In case the secured debtor does not agree to a negotiated sale, the enforcement agent shall organize a public auction. The collateral shall be appraised by the enforcement agent or by an authorized valuator at its market value.[167] The auction shall use the appraised value as the starting price and shall go upwards until

---

pursued. If the enforcement agent assesses that they are not sufficient to fulfill the creditor's claims, he may pursue other assets too."

[162] Art. 732 NCPC: "(1) If within 1 day from the notice followed by the court order allowing the enforcement procedure to start the debtor does not pay the owed amount, the enforcement agent shall sequester the debtor's movable assets, in order to sell them, even if they are held by a third party. (2) If there is obvious jeopardy of concealing the assets, at the creditor's request, the court may order their sequestration at the same time with the notification. In this case, the appropriate mention will be made in the order of execution."

[163] Art. 742 NCPC: "(1) The sequester will be registered, at the enforcement agent's request, in the Trade Registry, the Electronic Archive for Security Interests in Personal Property, the Inheritance Register held by the Chamber of Notaries or in other public registers, as the case may be. (2) From the filing date, the freezing measure is opposable to everyone who later acquires a right in the asset." For the new designation of the Archive, see fn. 85.

[164] Art. 745 NCPC: "Once the assets are frozen, the debtor can no longer deal with them for as long as the enforcement procedure lasts, under the penalty of a judicial fine from 2.000 lei to 10.000 lei, if the act is not a crime. The provisions of arts. 189–191 remain applicable."

[165] Art. 754–755 NCPC: Art. 754: "(1) The enforcement agent may allow the debtor, if the creditor agrees, to sell himself the frozen assets. In this case, the debtor shall inform the enforcement agent, in writing, about the offers received, indicating the name of the potential buyer and the deadline for the payment. (2) If the buyer does not pay the agreed price within the deadline referred to in paragraph (1), the enforcement agent shall proceed to a sale at a public auction, according to art. 759."

Art. 755: "(1) The enforcement agent may sell the assets directly to the buyer who offers at least the price referred to in art. 758, if both parties agree. (2) The deadline for the direct sale will be set by mutual agreement. The debtor and the creditor will be notified about the day, the time and the location of the sale, as well as about the offer made by the potential buyer. (3) After the sale, the enforcement agent will draw up the minute referred to in art. 773, while the provisions of this article apply accordingly. If a party is absent, the enforcement agent will send a certified copy of the minute."

[166] Art. 756 NCPC: "If the parties do not agree or the direct or amiable sale does not complete, the enforcement agent shall proceed to a sale at a public auction."

[167] Art. 758 NCPC: "(1) While freezing the assets, the enforcement agent shall identify and valuate each one, unless he is unable to. The assets shall be valuated at their market value, related to the average market price in the respective town. (2) Apart from the price, the enforcement agent shall valuate the real rights of use, using the criteria shown in paragraph (1); if it is not possible, an authorized valuator shall be named. (3) At the interested party's request or if the enforcement agent cannot valuate the frozen assets, he will name an authorized valuator for this purpose. (4) The enforcement agent shall order the authorized valuator to deliver a written report with the determined price at least 5 days ahead of the sale. [. . .]"

the best price is achieved.[168] In case the starting price is not offered, a new round shall begin, starting at 75% of the initial price. If this round is also unsuccessful, a new auction shall be organized later on where the starting price shall be 50% of the initial price. If this will also not be tendered, the collateral shall be sold at any price.

In case the movable hypothec was created in the licensee's rights rather than in property IP rights, it must be discussed whether the enforcement can follow the special rules laid down by the NCC for the enforcement of security interests in receivables.[169] Since the licensee's rights are not merely receivables and require certain actions from the licensee in order to be preserved, it is hard to conceive of an enforcement mechanism where the secured creditor will obtain the rights but not the obligations of the licensee.

However, it is possible (provided this is allowed by the security agreement) for the secured creditor to take over the management of the IP rights and to apply the proceeds of this management against the secured obligation.[170]

---

[168] Art. 769 NCPC: "(1) The auction shall be held public by the enforcement agent, who will offer the assets for sale through 3 consecutive shouts. (2) The starting price is the one provided in the publications or announcements, accordingly to art. 762 (2). (3) The assets will be sold together or separately, according to their nature or destination, taking care not to be depreciated. (4) If the enforcement agent collected amounts of money, he will proceed to the sale of the other assets only if the amounts are not sufficient for the claim, its proceeds and enforcement expenses. (5) The asset is sold to the buyer who offered the highest price after 3 consecutive shouts, made at sufficient time apart to allow overbids and options; if there is only one buyer, the asset will be sold to him if he offers the starting price. (6) If the asset is encumbered by a real right of use, acquired subsequent to any registration of a hypothec, the starting price will be the highest bid or the one provided in the announcement, diminished by the value of these rights determined accordingly to art. 758 (2). (7) If the price was not sufficient for the prior registered secured claims due to the existence of the rights shown in paragraph (6), the enforcement agent will resume the same day the auction, disregarding said rights; in this case, the starting price shall be the one provided in the announcement, without the diminution shown in paragraph (6). (8) If the starting price is not offered, the auction will be resumed the same day with a starting price of 75% of the initial price and the asset shall be sold to the highest bidder. (9) If the price referred to in paragraph (8) is not offered, the auction will be postponed and the publicity formalities referred to in art. 762 will be performed again. The second auction cannot be later than 20 days from the first auction and shall start from 50% of the initial price. If this price is not offered, the assets will be sold, at the same auction, to the highest bidder, even if there is only one buyer. (10) In all cases, if two bidders offer the same price shall prevail the one who has a preemption right in the asset. (11) The provisions of paragraphs (8) and (9) do not apply if the assets are perishable. In this case, the sell shall be done irrespective of the price and the number of bidders. (12) The enforcement agent shall draw up a list of the sold assets and their selling price."

[169] Art. 2465 NCC: "(1) If the collateral is a claim, if the secured claim is enforceable, the secured creditor can take over the title of claim, can ask for the payment or can sell it and deduct the price, all within the length of the secured claim. (2) Regarding the sale referred to in paragraph (1), the provisions referring to the transfer of debts apply accordingly."

[170] Art. 2468 NCC, see fn. 159.

7.3 *Enforcement in Insolvency*

Insolvency affects the enforcement if it refers to the securing debtor. It has little effect if it affects the secured party and no effect if it concerns a debtor of the main claim who is not the securing debtor.[171] Once the insolvency procedure is started against the securing debtor, all claims against him as well as any enforcement still pending shall be suspended.[172] Automatic stay in insolvency occurs once the insolvency proceedings are declared opened by the court.

The stay can be lifted by the syndic (i.e. insolvency) judge if (i) the collateral is not essential for the reorganization of the debtor *and* (ii) the sale of the collateral covers the secured claim in full.[173] Also, it can be lifted by the syndic judge in certain cases if the value of collateral is in danger of decreasing below the secured obligation value.[174]

In all other circumstances, the secured party should participate in the insolvency proceedings as a (secured) creditor. While his claim will remain secured during the proceedings and it may continue to accrue interest,[175] he should wait until the

[171] Art. 75 para (2) letter (b) LPI: "(2) Are not bound by the automatic stay referred to in paragraph (1): [. . .] b) judicial actions against joint debtors and/or sureties."

[172] Art. 75 para (1) LPI: "From the opening of the insolvency proceedings, all judicial or extrajudicial actions and enforcement procedures against the debtor shall be suspended. The performance of the claims shall be obtained only within the insolvency proceedings. Said actions could be reopened only if the opening decision was abolished or revoked or the proceedings were closed accordingly to art. 178. If the opening decision is abolished or revoked, the judicial or extrajudicial actions against the debtor can be reopened and the enforcement procedure can be resumed. When the opening decision becomes final, the suspended judicial or extrajudicial actions and the enforcement procedure cease."

[173] Art. 78 para (1) letter (A) LPI: "(1) The secured creditor may request the syndic judge, while notifying the creditors' committee, the special administrator and the judicial administrator, to lift the stay referred to in art. 75 (1) and enforce the security over the collateral within the insolvency proceedings, accordingly to arts. 154–158, provided that he pays from the obtained price the expenses referred to in art. 159 (1) 1, in the following cases: A. when the value of the collateral, determined by an authorized valuator according to the international valuation standards, covers to the full extent the secured claims, if: (a) the collateral is not essential for the reorganization of the debtor; (b) the collateral is part of a functional sub-assembly and by its detachment the sub-assembly's value does not diminish."

[174] Art. 78 para (1) letter (B) LPI: "(1) The secured creditor may request the syndic judge, while notifying the creditors' committee, the special administrator and the judicial administrator, to lift the stay referred to in art. 75 (1) and enforce the security over the collateral within the insolvency proceedings, accordingly to arts. 154–158, provided that he pays from the obtained price the expenses referred to in art. 159 (1) 1, in the following cases: B. when there is no real security of the claim in relation to the collateral due to: (a) the diminishing of the value of the collateral or the presence of a real danger of significant diminution; (b) the diminishing of the security of a lower ranked claim as a result of accumulation of proceeds of a higher ranked claim; (c) the lack of an insurance of the collateral against destruction or damages."

[175] Art. 80 and art. 103 LPI; art 80: "(1) No proceeds may be claimed if the debt is prior to the opening of the insolvency proceedings, with the exceptions provided by art. 103. (2) If a reorganization plan is confirmed, the proceeds accrued after the opening of the insolvency proceedings are

insolvency administrator decides to sell the collateral. At that time, his claim will have priority over those of most creditors (depending on his ranking before insolvency); however, it will have a lower priority than the insolvency costs, utility fees, and loans granted after the insolvency was started.[176]

8 Typical Costs

Since security agreements in IP rights are not subject to any formality except that they be made in writing, there are no notarial costs. If the parties choose to turn it into a notarial deed, the notarial costs are about 0.1% of the secured obligation.

Filing of the security statement with the RNPM costs approximately EUR 15, but if multiple collateral descriptions are used, then this amount will be multiplied.

9 Practical Usefulness

In practice, security interests in IP rights are quite commonly used, but not as an independent device. They are generally employed as part of a more comprehensive security package where the debtor offers more of his enterprise's assets. Frequently, the security agreement itself is structured to address IP rights together with other assets used by the business (in different sections).

As part of the security package, security interests in IP rights have a certain influence in promoting access to credit by SMEs.[177] They certainly have an impact on the cost of the credit, since secured credit is cheaper than unsecured credit.

---

payed accordingly to the relevant documents and the reorganization plan. If the plan fails, the proceeds are owed until the opening of the bankruptcy."

[176] Art. 159 para (1) LPI: "The amounts of money acquired from the sale of the collateral shall be distributed as follows: 1. the taxes, stamps and any other expenses in relation to the sale of the collateral, including the expenses incurred for their preservation and management, as well as the expenses incurred by the creditor in the enforcement proceedings, the claims of the utilities suppliers born after the opening of the insolvency proceedings, as stated in art. 77, the remunerations owed to the personnel employed in the common interest of the creditors, as stated in arts. 57 (2), 61 and 63, which shall be borne by the creditors proportionally in relation to the value of all debtor's assets; 2. the secured claims born within the insolvency proceedings. These secured claims comprise of capital and proceeds; 3. the secured claims comprising of capital and proceeds, including expenses, as well as those referred to in arts. 105 (3) and 123 (11) a)."

[177] See Fleisig and de la Peña (1999), passim; Fleisig et al. (2006), pp. 1–11.

10 Legal and/or Practical Difficulties

There are few (if any) legal difficulties in creating a security in IP rights under Romanian law. The main areas of uncertainty are related to parallel registries (the IP Registry versus the RNPM) and the lack of any specific enforcement procedures. This is obvious when considering that this security device is often employed for financing, but not on a stand-alone basis.

However, the main practical difficulty is uncertainty concerning how the enforcement process will result in meaningful proceeds for the secured party.

11 Law Reform

There are no (publicly available) projects for reforming this area of law. As mentioned above, the legal devices are quite flexible and in line with best industry practices. Despite some inconsistencies in the areas of registration and enforcement, there are no major legal drawbacks. However, there is hesitation to use security in IP rights as a stand-alone device because of the practical difficulty of appraising the value of the IP rights by themselves. While the Romanian parliament passed a reshaped regulation dealing with the registration of security interests in personal property in December 2018, the new law establishing the RNPM failed to address the issue of multiple recordation formalities for hypothecs over IP rights.

Romania is expected to ratify the Agreement on a Unified Patent Court, signed in 2013. However, in the context created by Brexit, the future of this instrument is still subject to doubt.

References

Cărpenaru SD (2009) Tratat de drept comercial român. Universul Juridic, Bucharest

Dincă R (2007) Natura juridică a drepturilor de proprietate intelectuală. Revista Romana de Drept Privat 1(3):76–120

Dincă R (2016) Legal regime of free software in Romania. In: Metzger A (ed) Free and open source software (FOSS) and other alternative license models. A comparative analysis. Springer, Cham, pp 371–385

Eminescu Y (1969) Dreptul de inventator. Editura Academiei RSR, Bucharest

Eminescu Y (1982) Tratat de proprietate industrială. Creații noi. Editura Academiei RSR, Bucharest

Eminescu Y (1993) Protecția desenelor și modelelor industrial. Drept român și comparat. Lumina Lex, Bucharest

Eminescu Y (1997a) Regimul juridic al creației intelectuale. Comentariul Legii brevetelor de invenție. Lumina Lex, Bucharest

Eminescu Y (1997b) Dreptul de autor. Legea nr. 8 din 14 martie 1996, comentată. Lumina Lex, Bucharest

Fleisig HW, de la Peña N (1999) Romania: Creating a Legal and Institutional Framework to Promote Access to Credit by the Poor. http://www.ceal.org/papers/RomaniaAccesstoCreditbythePoor(cealp057)CovPage&ExecSum.htm. Accessed 29 Dec 2018

Fleisig HW, Safavian M, de la Peña N (2006) Reforming collateral laws to expand access to finance. The World Bank, Washington, DC

Ionaşcu A (1961) Dreptul de autor în legislaţie. JN 17(6):35–40

Macovei I (2010) Tratat de drept al proprietăţii intelectuale. CH Beck, Bucharest

Mihai L (2002) Invenţia. Condiţiile de fond ale brevetării. Drepturi. Universul Juridic, Bucharest

Moise A-A (2012) Observaţii referitoare la efectuarea de căutări în Arhiva Electronică de Garanţii Reale Mobiliare potrivit legislaţiei în vigoare. Dreptul 23(9):128–141

Moise A-A (2015) Regimul juridic al privilegiilor şi al ipotecilor imobiliare. Universul Juridic, Bucharest

Petrescu A, Mihai L (1987) Drept de proprietate industrială. Introducere în dreptul proprietăţii industriale. Invenţia. Inovaţia. TUB, Bucharest

Popa I (2010) Sunt bunurile incorporale susceptibile de posesie? Revista Romana de Drept Privat 4 (5):85–104

Rizoiu R (2011) Garanţiile reale mobiliare. O abordare funcţională. Universul Juridic, Bucharest

Rizoiu R (2013a) Operaţiunile asimilate ipotecii – unitate în diversitate. Revista Romana de Drept Privat 7(1):181–220

Rizoiu R (2013b) Publicitatea mobiliară prin Arhiva Electronică de Garanţii Reale Mobiliare. Revista Romana de Drept Privat 7(6):114–175

Rizoiu R (2015a) Contractul de ipotecă în Noul Cod civil. Universul Juridic, Bucharest

Rizoiu R (2015b) Când nu ştii ce garantezi: despre cauza cauţiunii reale. In: Bob MD, Trandafir A-R (eds) Creditori versus debitori – perspectiva Hexagonului. Universul Juridic, Bucharest, pp 137–180

Rizoiu R (2015c) Ipoteca asupra bunurilor incorporale: Cum urmăreşti ceea ce nu vezi? Revista Romana de Drept Privat 9(4):128–178

Rizoiu R (2016) I se spunea "Buldozerul": Despre concursul dintre sechestru şi ipotecă. Revista Romana de Drept Privat 10(2):129–161

Rizoiu R (2017a) Chiar poate fi pus în executare un contract de ipotecă? Oricum? Oricând? In: Oprina E, Bozeşan V (eds) Executarea silită. Dificultăţi şi soluţii practice, vol 2. Universul Juridic, Bucharest, pp 109–127

Rizoiu R (2017b) Universul invizibil şi economia sa. Ipoteca asupra bunurilor incorporale şi ipoteca asupra drepturilor patrimoniale. Revista Romana de Drept Privat 11(3):285–298

Rizoiu R (2018) O fantomă bântuie Noul Cod civil: Acţiunea ipotecară. Revista Romana de Drept Privat 12(4):244–286

Rizoiu R (2019) 20 ans après: L'unification du droit des sûretés réelles en Roumanie. In: Popescu CL (ed) Colloque Franco-Roumain : «20 ans et le temps du droit». Actes du colloque. Hamagiu, Bucharest, pp 144–157

Roş V (2016) Dreptul proprietăţii intelectuale. Dreptul de autor, drepturile conexe şi drepturile sui generis, vol 1. C.H. Beck, Bucharest

Roş V, Spineanu-Matei O, Bogdan D (2003) Dreptul proprietăţii intelectuale. Dreptul proprietăţii industriale. Mărcile şi indicaţiile geografice. All Beck, Bucharest

Roş V, Bogdan D, Spineanu-Matei O (2005) Dreptul de autor şi drepturile conexe. Tratat. All Beck, Bucharest

Sitaru D-A, Sitaru C (2000) Regimul de drept internaţional privat al garanţiilor reale mobiliare conform prevederilor Legii nr. 99/1999. RDC 10(10):58–66

Stoica V (2013) Clauza voluntară de inalienabilitate. Revista Romana de Drept Privat 7(1):33–56

Ştrenc A, Ionescu B, Gheorghiu G (2005) Dreptul brevetului. Lumina Lex, Bucharest

Security Rights in Intellectual Property in Scotland

Patrick Masiyakurima

Abstract Scottish law permits the taking of security over intellectual property rights. Such security takes several forms including assignation. According to Scottish Law, an assignation creates a personal right. A real right can only be created if the assignation is intimated. Apart from this, trade marks and patents can be charged. It is also possible for a trust over intellectual property rights to be created. However, there are problems with such security rights in relation to their creation, priorities and certainty.

1 Overview of IP Rights

Britain‘s Copyright Designs and Patents Act 1988 governs copyright protection in Scotland. That statute protects various prescribed works. A work is protected by copyright if it falls into one of the prescribed categories[1]; it qualifies for British protection[2]; and its term of copyright has not expired. The United Kingdom is a signatory to The Berne Convention (1886) as amended, The Rome Convention (1961), The WIPO Copyright Treaty (1996), and The WIPO Performances and Phonograms Treaty (1996). As a Member State of the EU, British copyright law is influenced by EU Directives. It must be noted that copyright protection is automatic.

British law also protects patents.[3] Unlike copyright, patent protection is not automatic. A patent application has to be filed with the Intellectual Property Office.

[1]Note the effect of Case C-5/08, *Infopaq Int'l A/S v. Danske Dagblades Forening* [July 19, 2009] ECR I-6569 which suggests that the closed list of protected subject matter is no longer tenable. A work can be protected as along as it is its author's own intellectual creation. See also Rosati (2013), passim.

[2]Sect. 153 Copyright, Designs and Patents Act 1988 (CDPA).

[3]See Patents Act 1977.

P. Masiyakurima (✉)
University of Leicester, Leicester, UK
e-mail: p.masiyakurima@abdn.ac.uk

E.-M. Kieninger (ed.), *Security Rights in Intellectual Property*, Ius Comparatum – Global Studies in Comparative Law 45,
https://doi.org/10.1007/978-3-030-44191-3_23

To be patentable, an invention must be new and it must involve an inventive step.[4] This means that the invention must not simply be an obvious development of something that is already known. In addition, the invention must be capable of industrial application.[5] Lastly, the invention must not fall within an excluded category.[6] Patent protection is territorial. However, applications for patent protection in several countries at once may be made via the European Patent Convention (EPC) or the Patent Cooperation Treaty (PCT). Once obtained, a patent is an absolute monopoly which restricts making, using or selling an invention without the patentee's permission for a limited period.

There is also a registered design regime which protects objects with eye appeal.[7] A registered design excludes others from using, selling, importing and exporting any product embodying the design irrespective of whether it is copied. To obtain a United Kingdom registered design an application must be filed with the Designs Registry which is a part of the UK Intellectual Property Office.[8] The design must be novel and possess individual character. These criteria are judged by reference to designs which have been made available to the public before the effective filing date of the application. If granted, the registration endures for 25 years. However, the registration must be renewed every 5 years. Britain also has an unregistered 'Design Right' which provides automatic protection for 15 years from the date of creation.

In general, a trade mark can be a name, word, phrase, logo, symbol, design, image, sound, shape, signature or any combination of these elements which reduces consumer search costs by distinguishing the source or quality of goods or services. The current UK legislation on the subject is the Trade Marks Act 1994, which implements the European Trade Marks Directive into national law. In order to obtain a trade mark, an application should be made to the UK Intellectual Property Office. Trade marks are registered for specific goods or services within individual classes. They should not be descriptive and must not include common surnames, geographical names, registered company names or anything implying royal patronage.[9] The registration of trade marks in the UK is achieved through the UK Intellectual Property Office. Trade marks can also be registered in other Member States of the European Union. Applications are filed at the Community Trade Marks office (the Office of Harmonisation in the Internal Market). If granted, a Community Trade Mark (CTM) registration is valid in all Member States of the European Union. It is a statutory right governed by the Community Trade Mark Regulations. A trade mark gives its owner the right to prevent unauthorised use of the mark on products that are identical or similar to the registered mark.[10] Unregistered trade marks can be

---

[4]Sect. 1(1)(b) Patents Act 1977.

[5]Sect. 1(1)(c) Patents Act 1977.

[6]Sect. 1(1)(d) Patent Act 1977.

[7]Sect. 1B Registered Designs Act 1949.

[8]Sect. 3 Registered Designs Act 1949.

[9]Sect. 4 (1) Trade Marks Act 1994.

[10]Sect 10 Trade Marks Act 1994.

protected by the law of passing off which governs misrepresentations of the source or quality of goods or services which harm another's goodwill.[11]

2 Categories of Security Rights

Scottish law permits the taking of security over intellectual property rights.[12] Several examples are pertinent. Firstly, section 90 of the Copyright, Designs and Patents Act provides that copyright in an existing or future work can be assigned. A valid assignation must be expressed in writing and it must be signed by the copyright owner.[13] It follows that merely purchasing a work from its owner or author does not transfer copyright to the buyer. The same argument is equally relevant to licensing of copyright. A buyer would require the copyright owner to assign copyright in her work. As will be observed below, according to Scottish Law, an assignation creates a personal right. A real right can only be created if the assignation is intimated.

Secondly, the security interests in unregistered designs broadly correspond to those in copyright. For example, it is the case that registered designs can be assigned. Once again, a valid assignation must be in writing. Apart from this, in common with patents, a registered design can be the subject of a charge. The charge itself must be registered within the prescribed time.[14] Because, in common with copyright, an unregistered design is protected automatically, questions regarding real rights arising from assignations of unregistered designs arise.

As far as patents are concerned, section 31(3) of the Patents Act 1977 provides that "[a]ny patent or any such application, or any right in it, may be assigned and security may be granted over a patent or any such application or right". From that provision, one can detect two distinct possibilities. Firstly, in common with copyright, a patent can be assigned. Such assignations can embrace patent applications and patents. Once again, Scottish Law postulates that the assignation should be in writing. Moreover, the assignation must be registered with the Intellectual Property Office. The second possibility is that a patent or patent application can be the subject of a floating charge. Floating charges must be registered with the Registrar of Companies. From the point of view of the inventor, a charge or assignment over a patent application facilitates raising of the capital needed for developing the invention.

Similar considerations apply to trade marks. The Trade Marks Act 1994 provides that a mark can be assigned. Apart from this, provided that the relevant requirements are met, a trade mark can be the subject of a charge.[15] However, great care ought to

[11]See *Reckitt and Colman Products Ltd v Borden Inc & Ors* [1990] WLR 491.

[12]Guthrie and Orr (1996), p. 597; Scottish Law Commission (2011), p. 65.

[13]Guthrie and Orr (1996), p. 597.

[14]See sections 878 to 892 of the Companies Act 2006.

[15]See sect. 24 Trade Marks Act 1994.

be exercised in this area. Assignation of trade marks might raise non-use problems. Essentially, a trade mark may be revoked if it is not used by its owner. The effect of an assignation is to transfer property rights (in this case the mark) to the assignee. The implication of that argument is that the cedent ceases to own the mark but continues to use it in order to distinguish its goods and services from those of its competitors.

It is also possible for a trust over intellectual property rights to be created. Under such an arrangement, the intellectual property owner does not part with the valuable intangible as such.[16] Instead, the owner holds the property in trust and for the benefit of the creditor. The intellectual property owner would be a trustee and the creditor would be the beneficiary. In the event of insolvency or other enforcement, the beneficiary's claim is preferred over other creditors.

3 Structure of Transactions: Attachment and Perfection

In general, an assignation is a tripartite transaction.[17] The parties to an assignation are usually the debtor, the new creditor and the original creditor. Assignation of intellectual property is different from assignation of other moveable property because it involves two parties, namely copyright owners and creditors. In our context, copyright, trade marks, patents or registered designs form the collateral for the loan. The effect of an assignation is to transfer copyright to the creditor. That transfer is subject to the copyright owner's right to have the intellectual property right transferred back upon payment of the debt. An assignation gives the assignee a personal right over the moveable property.[18] It must be noted, however, that an assignation can only bind third parties if it is a real right. An assignation can be converted from being a personal into a real right by notifying the debtor.

A floating charge is capable of securing all or a part of a company's assets. A floating charge contemplates that a borrower can deal with the secured assets in the ordinary course of business. In our context, a patentee can work the invention or use the charged trade mark, for example. Because a floating charge embraces inventory, the charged assets can change. A floating charge usually crystallises on the occurrence of a specific event e.g. insolvency. In addition, a floating charge can be contained in a debenture. A debenture is an acknowledgment of debt. If a floating charge is contained in a debenture then it should cover all of the debtor's assets.[19]

A valid trust arises from a declaration of trust by a trustee.[20] For our purposes, an intellectual property owner can declare that they are holding a particular work,

[16] Guthrie and Orr (1996), p. 597.

[17] See Anderson (2008), passim.

[18] Anderson (2008), passim.

[19] Section 882 Companies Act 2006.

[20] Guthrie and Orr (1996), p. 597.

invention, mark or design for the benefit of a particular creditor. Usually, a declaration of trust is supplemented by a letter delineating the beneficial ownership of the trust assets. The beneficiary must be notified about the trust. There is no requirement for registration. While it is theoretically possible for a trust covering intellectual property rights to be created for the benefit of creditors there is no evidence suggesting that trusts are readily used for that purpose.

In Scotland, an assignation has to be intimated to third parties in order for it to be complete.[21] In the case of patents, trade marks and registered designs, registration of the assignation in the appropriate register completes the assignation. A different regime applies to copyright, however. Because copyright protection is automatic, an assignation of copyright can be completed if the assignation documents are delivered to the assignee.

In the case of charges over intellectual property rights, such instruments must be registered within 21 days of their creation.[22] Failure to register a charge makes it void against creditors and the liquidator.[23]

As detailed earlier security interests in patents, trade marks,[24] registered designs[25] can all be registered. In the absence of registration, the holder of the interest retains a personal right in the collateral and such personal rights have little value in the event of the debtor's insolvency.

4 Priorities

Floating charge holders are paid out after fixed charge holders, preferential creditors and the prescribed part (a maximum sum of £ 600,000 which is ring-fenced for unsecured creditors). A floating charge crystallises into a fixed charge on the occurrence of a limited number of insolvency events.

5 Enterprise Charges

Can IP rights be part of a security right over all assets of a company or enterprise (such as, for example, a floating charge under English law)? What are the prerequisites and the costs involved? What priority does an all asset charge have with respect to third parties and the debtor company's insolvency administrator?

[21]Guthrie and Orr (1996), p. 597.

[22]See sect 859A Companies Act 2006.

[23]Sect 874 Companies Act 2006.

[24]Section 25 (2) and 25 (3) Trade Marks Act 1994.

[25]Section 19 Registered Designs Act 1949.

As indicated above, Scottish law contemplates that patents, copyright, registered designs and trade marks are capable of being embraced by a floating charge. The pre-requisites for obtaining a floating charge are described above. A floating charge covers the whole or a part of a company's inventory and it has to be registered. The costs that are associated with a floating charge include drafting the instrument and registering the charge. There are also costs involved with enforcing the charge once it crystallizes.

6 Rights Before Default

A valid assignation transfers the intellectual property right from the owner to the creditor. The intellectual property owner has the right to have the work, invention, mark, or design transferred back to her if she discharges the debt.

With respect to a floating charge, the debtor can use the assets subject to the charge in the ordinary course of business. The creditor's rights under a floating charge become crucial once an event, which crystallizes the charge, occurs. Usually, the charge crystallizes if the debtor becomes insolvent. The charge can be discharged once the debt has been paid.

7 Enforcement

A floating charge will crystallise on the appointment of a receiver. It may also crystallize on the commencement of the winding up of the debtor. Alternatively a floating charge may crystallize if an administrator chooses to do so in order to effect a distribution of the debtor's assets. A receiver is usually appointed to the whole assets charged by a floating charge. This is also the case for administrators.

8 Typical Costs

There are legal costs associated with drafting the relevant security instruments. Other costs pertain to registration of charges. The costs of enforcement once the debtor has defaulted include legal advice, drafting an application to declare a debtor insolvent if necessary, finalizing legal proceedings, and administering the insolvent debtor's estate.

9 Practical Usefulness

Transactions involving granting security over intellectual property rights are likely to be low. There are significant uncertainties especially in relation to patents. There are problems for, example, in connection with security interests in patent applications. The nature of the rights that attach after the patent has been granted are uncertain.[26] Moreover, because copyright protection is automatic, notice of the security interest might not be available with the result that personal rights only can be conferred on a creditor.

10 Legal and/or Practical Difficulties

There are uncertainties regarding the rights of innocent third parties who buy intellectual property rights without notice of pre-existing security interests. A similar problem arises in connection with trusts. A person who purchases a trust asset in good faith acquires title in the asset irrespective of others' security interests with the result that the beneficiary of the trust would be disadvantaged.[27] Besides, a trust asset cannot form the debtor's estate.[28]

11 Law Reform

The Scottish Law Commission has grappled with aspects of security rights in intellectual property rights[29] and at present, there is a bill in the Scottish Parliament, which is meant to improve these matters.[30]

References

Anderson RG (2008) Assignation. Edinburgh Legal Education Trust, Edinburgh

Guthrie T, Orr A (1996) Fixed security rights over intellectual property in Scotland. Eur Intellect Prop Rev 11:597–603

Rosati E (2013) Originality in EU copyright law. Edward Elgar, Cheltenham

Scottish Law Commission (2011) Discussion paper on moveable transactions. https://www.scotlawcom.gov.uk/files/6113/1057/2523/dp151.pdf. Accessed 4 Mar 2019

[26]Scottish Law Commission (2011), p. 65.

[27]Guthrie and Orr (1996), p. 597.

[28]Guthrie and Orr (1996), p. 597.

[29]Scottish Law Commission (2011), p. 65.

[30]Bill on Moveable Transactions. See https://www.scotlawcom.gov.uk/news/consultation-on-draft-moveable-transactions-scotland-bill.

Security Rights in Intellectual Property in South Africa

Sadulla Karjiker

Abstract This chapter contains an overview of the forms of statutory IP rights (namely, copyright, trademarks, registered designs, patents, and plant breeders' rights) in South Africa, and the statutory provisions concerning the creation of security interests over statutory IP rights. The legal position in South African law concerning IP rights is found to be underdeveloped. The legal nature of the statutory security interests over IP rights is considered, together with the common-law methods of obtaining real security rights over statutory IP rights.

1 Overview of IP Rights

Intellectual property (IP) rights in South Africa are protected by legislation and pursuant to the common law. Copyright, trademarks, designs, patents, and plant breeders' rights are established by statutes,[1] while unlawful competition (including passing off) is grounded in the common law.[2] South African legislation and the common law are subject to the Constitution,[3] which is the supreme law of land.[4]

[1]Copyright Act 98 of 1978; Trade Marks Act 194 of 1993; Designs Act 195 of 1993; Patents Act 57 of 1978; and Plant Breeders' Rights Act 15 of 1976.

[2]Webster and Morley (2015), para 15.1.

[3]The Constitution of the Republic of South Africa, 1996 (the "Constitution").

[4]Section 2 of the Constitution, which states:

> This Constitution is the supreme law of the Republic; law or conduct inconsistent with it is invalid, and the obligations imposed by it must be fulfilled.

S. Karjiker (✉)
Anton Mostert Chair of Intellectual Property Law, Stellenbosch University, Stellenbosch, South Africa
e-mail: skarjiker@sun.ac.za

E.-M. Kieninger (ed.), *Security Rights in Intellectual Property*, Ius Comparatum – Global Studies in Comparative Law 45,
https://doi.org/10.1007/978-3-030-44191-3_24

Although IP rights are not expressly protected in the Constitution, they have been recognized as constituting property,[5] which is protected under the constitutional property clause.[6] In addition, the Constitutional Court has held that both natural

[5]See *Laugh It Off Promotions CC v South African Breweries International (Finance) BV t/a Sabmark International* 2005 (2) SA 46 (SCA) 53; and *Laugh It Off Promotions CC v SAB International (Finance) BV t/a Sabmark International (Freedom of Expression Institute as Amicus Curiae)* 2006 (1) SA 144 (CC) 172–3.

[6]Section 25 of the Constitution which reads as follows.

(1) No one may be deprived of property except in terms of law of general application, and no law may permit arbitrary deprivation of property.
(2) Property may be expropriated only in terms of law of general application—
  (a) for a public purpose or in the public interest; and
  (b) subject to compensation, the amount of which and the time and manner of payment of which have either been agreed to by those affected or decided or approved by a court.

(3) The amount of the compensation and the time and manner of payment must be just and equitable, reflecting an equitable balance between the public interest and the interests of those affected, having regard to all relevant circumstances, including—
  (a) the current use of the property;
  (b) the history of the acquisition and use of the property;
  (c) the market value of the property;
  (d) the extent of direct state investment and subsidy in the acquisition and beneficial capital improvement of the property; and
  (e) the purpose of the expropriation.

(4) For the purposes of this section—
  (a) the public interest includes the nation's commitment to land reform, and to reforms to bring about equitable access to all South Africa's natural resources; and
  (b) property is not limited to land.

(5) The state must take reasonable legislative and other measures, within its available resources, to foster conditions which enable citizens to gain access to land on an equitable basis.
(6) A person or community whose tenure of land is legally insecure as a result of past racially discriminatory laws or practices is entitled, to the extent provided by an Act of Parliament, either to tenure which is legally secure or to comparable redress.
(7) A person or community dispossessed of property after June 19, 1913 as a result of past racially discriminatory laws or practices is entitled, to the extent provided by an Act of Parliament, either to restitution of that property or to equitable redress.
(8) No provision of this section may impede the state from taking legislative and other measures to achieve land, water and related reform, in order to redress the results of past racial discrimination, provided that any departure from the provisions of this section is in accordance with the provisions of section 36 (1).
(9) Parliament must enact the legislation referred to in subsection (6).

and legal persons may be holders of constitutionally-protected property, which includes IP.[7]

South Africa is not party to any supranational or regional system of registration of IP rights.

The discussion regarding the various forms of security interests below assumes that the transactions do not result in the applicability of any consumer-protection legislation. In other words, the discussion is confined to transactions in commercial arrangements in which neither party is protected by any form of consumer-protection legislation.

1.1 Trademarks

In South Africa, trademarks are protected through legislation and under the common law.[8] Owners of trademarks may choose whether to register their trademarks. If a trademark is registered, the trademark is protected under the Trade Marks Act 194 of 1993 ("Trade Marks Act") and by the common law, specifically the law of passing off.[9] Unregistered trademarks enjoy limited protection, with only passing off as an available remedy.[10]

The Trade Marks Act defines a trademark as "a mark[11] used or proposed to be used by a person in relation to goods or services for the purpose of distinguishing the goods or services in relation to which the mark is used or proposed to be used from the same kind of goods or services connected in the course of trade with any other person."[12]

The statutory definition of a trademark emphasizes the distinguishing function of a trademark. When consumers are confronted with different products and services, trademarks function to identify a specific product or service and distinguish it from similar products or services.[13] If a trademark is unable to fulfill this distinguishing

[7] *First National Bank of South Africa Ltd t/a Wesbank v Commissioner, South African Revenue Service; First National Bank of South Africa Ltd t/a Wesbank v Minister of Finance 2002 4 SA 768 (CC) 790 with reference to section 8(4) of the Constitution, which provides that "[a] juristic person is entitled to the rights in the Bill of Rights to the extent required by the nature of the rights and the nature of the juristic person."*

[8] Webster and Morley (2015), para 15.1.

[9] Webster and Morley (2015), paras 12.1–12.2.

[10] Webster and Morley (2015), paras 12.1–12.2.

[11] Section 2(1) of the Trade Marks Act defines a "mark" as "*any sign capable of being represented graphically, including a device, name, signature, word, letter, numeral, shape, configuration, pattern, ornamentation, colour or container for goods or any combination of the aforementioned.*"

[12] Section 2(1).

[13] Webster and Morley (2015), para 3.16.

function, then registration of the trademark will not be possible.[14] Case law, however, emphasizes that the principal function of trademarks are to fulfill their roles as

[14]Section 9 of the Trade Marks Act requires that a trademark be distinctive: either inherently capable of distinguishing goods or services, or capable of distinguishing goods or services due to prior use. Section 10 disqualifies trademarks for registration if they lack this ability to distinguish, with reference to section 9.

Section 9—Registrable trade marks:

(1) In order to be registrable, a trade mark shall be capable of distinguishing the goods or services of a person in respect of which it is registered or proposed to be registered from the goods or services of another person either generally or, where the trade mark is registered or proposed to be registered subject to limitations, in relation to use within those limitations.
(2) A mark shall be considered to be capable of distinguishing within the meaning of subsection (1) if, at the date of application for registration, it is inherently capable of so distinguishing or it is capable of distinguishing by reason of prior use thereof.

Section 10—Unregistrable trade marks:

The following marks shall not be registered as trade marks or, if registered, shall, subject to the provisions of sections 3 and 70, be liable to be removed from the register:

(1) A mark which does not constitute a trade mark;
(2) a mark which—
    (a) is not capable of distinguishing within the meaning of section 9; or
    (b) consists exclusively of a sign or an indication which may serve, in trade, to designate the kind, quality, quantity, intended purpose, value, geographical origin or other characteristics of the goods or services, or the mode or time of production of the goods or of rendering of the services; or
    (c) consists exclusively of a sign or an indication which has become customary in the current language or in the bona fide and established practices of the trade;
(3) a mark in relation to which the applicant for registration has no bona fide claim to proprietorship;
(4) a mark in relation to which the applicant for registration has no bona fide intention of using it as a trade mark, either himself or through any person permitted or to be permitted by him to use the mark as contemplated by section 38;
(5) a mark which consists exclusively of the shape, configuration, colour or pattern of goods where such shape, configuration, colour or pattern is necessary to obtain a specific technical result, or results from the nature of the goods themselves;
(6) subject to the provisions of section 36 (2), a mark which, on the date of application for registration thereof, or, where appropriate, of the priority claimed in respect of the application for registration thereof, constitutes, or the essential part of which constitutes, a reproduction, imitation or translation of a trade mark which is entitled to protection under the Paris Convention as a well-known trade mark within the meaning of section 35 (1) of this Act and which is used for goods or services identical or similar to the goods or services in respect of which the trade mark is well-known and where such use is likely to cause deception or confusion;

badges of origin. The Supreme Court of Appeal stated that the function of a trademark was to indicate the origin of goods or services and that the registrability

---

(7) a mark the application for registration of which was made mala fide;

(8) (a) a mark which consists of or contains the national flag of the Republic or a convention country, or an imitation from a heraldic point of view, without the authorization of the competent authority of the Republic or convention country, as the case may be, unless it appears to the registrar that use of the flag in the manner proposed is permitted without such authorization;

(b) a mark which consists of or contains the armorial bearings or any other state emblem of the Republic or a convention country, or an imitation from a heraldic point of view, without the authorization of the competent authority of the Republic or convention country, as the case may be;

(c) a mark which consists of or contains an official sign or hallmark adopted by the Republic or a convention country, or an imitation from a heraldic point of view, and which indicates control and warranty, in relation to goods or services of the same or a similar kind as those in relation to which it indicates control and warranty, without the authorization of the competent authority of the Republic or convention country, as the case may be;

(d) a mark which consists of or contains the flag, the armorial bearings or any other emblem, or an imitation from a heraldic point of view, or the name, or the abbreviation of the name, of any international organization of which one or more convention countries are members, without the authorization of the organization concerned, unless it appears to the registrar that use of the flag, armorial bearings, other emblem or imitation or the name or abbreviation in the manner proposed, is not such as to suggest to the public that a connection exists between the organization and the mark, or is not likely to mislead the public as to the existence of a connection between the organization and the proprietor of the mark:

Provided that—

(i) paragraphs (b), (c) and (d) shall apply to a state emblem and an official sign or hallmark of a convention country and an emblem, the name, or the abbreviation of the name, of an international organization only if and to the extent that—

(aa) the convention country or international organization, as the case may be, has notified the Republic in accordance with Article 6ter of the Paris Convention that it desires to protect that emblem, official sign or hallmark, name or abbreviation, as the case may be;

(bb) such notification remains in force; and

(cc) the Republic has not objected to it in accordance with Article 6ter of the Paris Convention or any such objection has been withdrawn;

(ii) paragraph (b), (c) or (d) shall apply only in relation to applications for registration made more than two months after receipt of the notification referred to in paragraph (i) (aa);

(iii) paragraph (b) or (c) shall not prevent the registration of a trade mark by a citizen of any country who is authorized to make use of a state emblem or official sign or hallmark of that country, notwithstanding the fact that it is similar to that of another country;

(9) a mark which contains any word, letter or device indicating State patronage;

(10) a mark which contains any mark specified in the regulations as being for the purposes of this section a prohibited mark;

of a trademark should be determined by examining whether the trademark fulfills this function.[15]

The Trade Marks Act recognizes trademark infringement through dilution; this serves to protect the advertising function of a trademark. As part of its advertising

---

(11) a mark which consists of a container for goods or the shape, configuration, colour or pattern of goods, where the registration of such mark is or has become likely to limit the development of any art or industry;
(12) a mark which is inherently deceptive or the use of which would be likely to deceive or cause confusion, be contrary to law, be contra bonos mores, or be likely to give offence to any class of persons;
(13) a mark which, as a result of the manner in which it has been used, would be likely to cause deception or confusion;
(14) subject to the provisions of section 14, a mark which is identical to a registered trade mark belonging to a different proprietor or so similar thereto that the use thereof in relation to goods or services in respect of which it is sought to be registered and which are the same as or similar to the goods or services in respect of which such trade mark is registered, would be likely to deceive or cause confusion, unless the proprietor of such trade mark consents to the registration of such mark;
(15) subject to the provisions of section 14 and paragraph (16), a mark which is identical to a mark which is the subject of an earlier application by a different person, or so similar thereto that the use thereof in relation to goods or services in respect of which it is sought to be registered and which are the same as or similar to the goods or services in respect of which the mark in respect of which the earlier application is made, would be likely to deceive or cause confusion, unless the person making the earlier application consents to the registration of such mark;
(16) a mark which is the subject of an earlier application as contemplated in paragraph (15), if the registration of that mark is contrary to existing rights of the person making the later application for registration as contemplated in that paragraph;
(17) a mark which is identical or similar to a trade mark which is already registered and which is well-known in the Republic, if the use of the mark sought to be registered would be likely to take unfair advantage of, or be detrimental to, the distinctive character or the repute of the registered trade mark, notwithstanding the absence of deception or confusion, unless the proprietor of such trade mark consents to the registration of such mark:

Provided that a mark shall not be refused registration by virtue of the provisions of paragraph (2) or, if registered, shall not be liable to be removed from the register by virtue of the said provisions if at the date of the application for registration or at the date of an application for removal from the register, as the case may be, it has in fact become capable of distinguishing within the meaning of section 9 as a result of use made of the mark.

[15] *Beecham Group plc v Triomed (Pty) Ltd* 2003 (3) SA 639 (SCA); *AM Moolla Group Ltd v The Gap Inc.* 2005 (6) SA 568 (SCA).

function, which is also highlighted in case law, a trademark generates goodwill and promotes the sale of goods or services.[16]

The registration of a trademark ensures that the owner of the trademark has statutory remedies against trademark infringement.[17] Registration of a trademark under the Trade Marks Act does not exclude the protection afforded by the common

---

[16]In *Verimark (Pty) Ltd v BMW AG* 2007 (6) SA 263 (SCA), the advertising function of a trademark is underlined. The advertising function is protected by way of section 34(1)(c) of the Trade Marks Act, the so-called "anti-dilution provision."

[17]Section 34 of the Trade Marks Act.

Section 34—Infringement of registered trade mark:

(1) The rights acquired by registration of a trade mark shall be infringed by-

(a) the unauthorized use in the course of trade in relation to goods or services in respect of which the trade mark is registered, of an identical mark or of a mark so nearly resembling it as to be likely to deceive or cause confusion;
(b) the unauthorized use of a mark which is identical or similar to the trade mark registered, in the course of trade in relation to goods or services which are so similar to the goods or services in respect of which the trade mark is registered, that in such use there exists the likelihood of deception or confusion;
(c) the unauthorized use in the course of trade in relation to any goods or services of a mark which is identical or similar to a trade mark registered, if such trade mark is well known in the Republic and the use of the said mark would be likely to take unfair advantage of, or be detrimental to, the distinctive character or the repute of the registered trade mark, notwithstanding the absence of confusion or deception: Provided that the provisions of this paragraph shall not apply to a trade mark referred to in section 70 (2).

(2) A registered trade mark is not infringed by—

(a) any bona fide use by a person of his own name, the name of his place of business, the name of any of his predecessors in business, or the name of any such predecessor's place of business.
(b) the use by any person of any bona fide description or indication of the kind, quality, quantity, intended purpose, value, geographical origin or other characteristics of his goods or services, or the mode or time of production of the goods or the rendering of the services;
(c) the bona fide use of the trade mark in relation to goods or services where it is reasonable to indicate the intended purpose of such goods, including spare parts and accessories, and such services;
(d) the importation into or the distribution, sale or offering for sale in the Republic of goods to which the trade mark has been applied by or with the consent of the proprietor thereof;
(e) the bona fide use by any person of any utilitarian features embodied in a container, shape, configuration, colour or pattern which is registered as a trade mark;
(f) the use of a trade mark in any manner in respect of or in relation to goods to be sold or otherwise traded in, or services to be performed, in any place, or in relation to goods to be exported to any market, or in any other manner in relation to which, having regard to any conditions or limitations entered in the register, the registration does not extend;
(g) the use of any identical or confusingly or deceptively similar trade mark which is registered:

law against unlawful competition, or, more specifically, passing off.[18] Passing off must be relied upon when a trademark owner does not own a registered trademark.[19]

1.2 Patents

Patent law, as governed by the Patents Act 57 of 1978 ("Patents Act"),[20] grants a statutory monopoly for the protection of an invention.[21] The Patents Act states that a patent may "be granted for any new invention which involves an inventive step and which is capable of being used or applied in trade or industry or agriculture."[22]

Provided that paragraph (a) shall not apply to the name of any juristic person whose name was registered after the date of registration of the trade mark: Provided further that the use contemplated in paragraph (a), (b) or (c) is consistent with fair practice.

(3) Where a trade mark registered in terms of this Act has been infringed, any High Court having jurisdiction may grant the proprietor the following relief, namely—

(a) an interdict;
(b) an order for removal of the infringing mark from all material and, where the infringing mark is inseparable or incapable of being removed from the material, an order that all such material be delivered up to the proprietor;
(c) damages, including those arising from acts performed after advertisement of the acceptance of an application for registration which, if performed after registration, would amount to infringement of the rights acquired by registration;
(d) in lieu of damages, at the option of the proprietor, a reasonable royalty which would have been payable by a licensee for the use of the trade mark concerned, including any use which took place after advertisement of the acceptance of an application for registration and which, if taking place after registration, would amount to infringement of the rights acquired by registration.

(4) For the purposes of determining the amount of any damages or reasonable royalty to be awarded under this section, the court may direct an enquiry to be held and may prescribe such procedures for conducting such enquiry as it may deem fit.
(5) Before a person institutes proceedings in terms of this section he shall give notice in writing of his intention to do so to every user concerned whose name is recorded in the register, and any such registered user shall be entitled to intervene in such proceedings and to recover any damages he may have suffered as a result of the infringement.

[18] Section 33.
Section 33—Registration a condition precedent to an action for infringement:

No person shall be entitled to institute any proceedings under section 34 in relation to a trade mark not registered under this Act: Provided that nothing in this Act shall affect the rights of any person, at common law, to bring any action against any other person.

[19] Webster and Morley (2015), paras 12.1–12.2.

[20] The South African Patents Act is based on the Paris Convention for the Protection of Industrial Property and on the TRIPS Agreement.

[21] Burrell (2016), pp. 1–2.

[22] Section 25(1) of the Patents Act.

The definition of an "invention" used in section 25(2) of the Patents Act lists that which is not considered to be an invention, rather than that which is an invention.[23] Therefore, in determining patentability, it is necessary to determine whether any aspect of an invention falls within the exclusions that are not considered to be inventions.[24] The list of exclusions largely consists of subject matter worthy of protection by other IP rights, or subject matter excluded from being patented due to public policy considerations.[25]

A requirement for patentability is that the invention must be new. The Patents Act in section 25(5) states that "[a]n invention shall be deemed to be new if it does not form part of the state of the art immediately before the priority date of that invention." In turn, the "state of the art" (or prior art) is defined as "[comprising] all matter . . . which has been made available to the public (whether in [South Africa] or elsewhere) by written or oral description, by use or in any other way."[26] Determining whether an invention is novel requires examining the claims made for that particular invention. A comparison between the claims made for an invention and the prior art will determine whether the requirement of novelty is fulfilled.[27]

According to the Patents Act, "an invention shall be deemed to involve an inventive step if it is not obvious to a person skilled in the art".[28] When determining

---

Section 25(1):

> A patent may, subject to the provisions of this section, be granted for any new invention which involves an inventive step and which is capable of being used or applied in trade or industry or agriculture.

[23]Section 25(2):

> Anything which consists of—
>
> (a) a discovery;
> (b) a scientific theory;
> (c) a mathematical method;
> (d) a literary, dramatic, musical or artistic work or any other aesthetic creation;
> (e) a scheme, rule or method for performing a mental act, playing a game or doing business;
> (f) a program for a computer; or
> (g) the presentation of information,
>
> shall not be an invention for the purposes of this Act.

[24]Burrell (2016), p. 29.

[25]Burrell (2016), pp. 29–30.

[26]Section 25(6):

> The state of the art shall comprise all matter (whether a product, a process, information about either, or anything else) which has been made available to the public (whether in the Republic or elsewhere) by written or oral description, by use or in any other way.

[27]*Gentiruco A.G. v Firestone South Africa (Pty) Ltd* 1971 BP 58 (A).

[28]Section 25(10):

> Subject to the provisions of section 39 (6), an invention shall be deemed to involve an inventive step if it is not obvious to a person skilled in the art, having regard to any matter

whether an invention is inventive, courts will consider whether the inventive step goes beyond, or differs from, the current and relevant state of the art.[29]

For an invention to be patentable, it must be "capable of being used or applied in trade or industry or agriculture."[30] Determining whether an invention is capable of being used or applied in trade, industry, or agriculture is a factual question and will be evident, based on the invention itself.

Upon registration of the patent, the patentee will have the exclusive right to "[make, use, exercise, dispose or offer to dispose of, or import] the invention".[31] The duration of patent protection is 20 years from the date of application for the patent.[32]

1.3 Design Rights

South Africa, pursuant to the Designs Act 195 of 1993 (the "Designs Act"), provides protection for registered designs, which may be aesthetic or functional in nature. These rights do not subsist automatically, and only come into existence upon the registration of the particular design.[33] Design protection (more specifically, that concerning aesthetic designs) protects the visual appearance of an article of

---

which forms, immediately before the priority date of the invention, part of the state of the art by virtue only of subsection (6) (and disregarding subsections (7) and (8)).

[29] *Ensign-Bickford (South Africa) Pty Ltd v AECI Explosives & Chemicals Ltd* 1998 BIP 271 (SCA).

[30] Section 25(1) of the Patents Act.

[31] Section 45—Effect of patent:

(1) The effect of a patent shall be to grant to the patentee in the Republic, subject to the provisions of this Act, for the duration of the patent, the right to exclude other persons from making, using, exercising, disposing or offering to dispose of, or importing the invention, so that he or she shall have and enjoy the whole profit and advantage accruing by reason of the invention.
(2) The disposal of a patented article by or on behalf of a patentee or his licensee shall, subject to other patent rights, give the purchaser the right to use, offer to dispose of and dispose of that article.

[32] Section 46(1):

The duration of a patent shall, unless otherwise provided in this Act, be 20 years from the date of application therefor, subject to payment of the prescribed renewal fees by the patentee concerned or an agent.

[33] Section 20(1) of the Designs Act:

The effect of the registration of a design shall be to grant to the registered proprietor in the Republic, subject to the provisions of this Act, for the duration of the registration the right to exclude other persons from the making, importing, using or disposing of any article included in the class in which the design is registered and embodying the registered design or a design not substantially different from the registered design, so that he shall have and enjoy the whole profit and advantage accruing by reason of the registration.

manufacture, that is, those features "which appeal to and are judged solely by the eye".[34] While the line between aesthetic designs and functional designs is not always easy to draw, functional designs protect the features of an article that are "necessitated by the function which [it] is to perform".[35] Articles are often registered for both aesthetic and functional design protection.

Aesthetic designs must be new and original to be registrable,[36] and functional designs have to be new and "not commonplace in the art in question".[37] Another important requirement is that the articles must be intended to be manufactured through an industrial process.[38] Designs are registered in various classes, corresponding to the Locarno Agreement establishing an International Classification for Industrial Designs,[39] and give the registered proprietor the exclusive right to manufacture, "[import, use, or dispose] of any article included in the class in which the design is registered" that is "not substantially different from the registered design".[40] Aesthetic designs are protected for a maximum of 15 years from the date of registration, and a functional design is protected for a maximum of 10 years

---

[34]Section 1 sv "aesthetic design" ("*means any design applied to any article, whether for the pattern or the shape or the configuration or the ornamentation thereof, or for any two or more of those purposes, and by whatever means it is applied, having features which appeal to and are judged solely by the eye, irrespective of the aesthetic quality thereof*") and "article" ("*means any article of manufacture and includes a part of such article if manufactured separately*").

[35]Section 1 sv "functional design" ("*means any design applied to any article, whether for the pattern or the shape or the configuration thereof, or for any two or more of those purposes, and by whatever means it is applied, having features which are necessitated by the function which the article to which the design is applied, is to perform, and includes an integrated circuit topography, a mask work and a series of mask works*") and "article".

[36]Section 14(1)(a).
Section 14(1):

> The proprietor of a design which—
>
> (a) in the case of an aesthetic design, is—
>
> (i) new; and
> (ii) original,
>
> (b) in the case of a functional design, is—
>
> (i) new; and
> (ii) not commonplace in the art in question,
>
> may, in the prescribed manner and on payment of the prescribed fee, apply for the registration of such design.

[37]Section 14(1)(b).

[38]Section 14(4):

> Designs for articles which are not intended to be multiplied by an industrial process shall not be registrable under this Act.

[39]Designs Regulations GN R844 in *GG* 20256 of July 2, 1999 (as amended).

[40]Section 20(1) of the Designs Act.

from the date of registration.[41] Importantly, if an article "is in the nature of a spare part for a machine, vehicle or equipment," no functional design protection exists for such an article.[42] Moreover, it is not possible to circumvent this limitation by seeking to protect an article by way of an aesthetic design if the protected feature is "necessitated solely by the function which the article is intended to perform" or a method of construction.[43]

1.4 Copyright

Copyright, a branch of IP rights, is governed by the Copyright Act 98 of 1978 ("Copyright Act"). Copyright protection in the specified categories of work subsists automatically and does not require any form of registration or other formalities.[44] The owner of the copyright is given the exclusive right to perform certain acts in relation to the copyright work and has the right to restrict others from performing such acts. These restricted acts give the owner of the copyright the opportunity to exploit and profit from the specific work, which serves to motivate innovation and creativity.[45]

---

[41] Section 22(1):

The duration of the registration of—

(a) an aesthetic design shall be fifteen years;
(b) a functional design shall be ten years,

from the date of registration thereof or from the release date, whichever date is earlier, subject to the payment of the prescribed renewal fee.

[42] Section 14(6):

In the case of an article which is in the nature of a spare part for a machine, vehicle or equipment, no feature of pattern, shape or configuration of such article shall afford the registered proprietor of a functional design applied to any one of the articles in question, any rights in terms of this Act in respect of such features.

[43] Section 14(5):

No—

(a) feature of an article in so far as it is necessitated solely by the function which the article is intended to perform; or
(b) method or principle of construction,

shall afford the registered proprietor of an aesthetic design any rights in terms of this Act in respect of such feature, method or principle.

[44] Dean and Karjiker (2015), para 1.6.

[45] Dean and Karjiker (2015), para 1.2.

The restricted acts are specified for each of the categories of work protected by the Copyright Act.[46]

The Copyright Act provides protection to nine categories of work, provided that they are original,[47] and exist in a material form.[48] In addition, the author of the copyright work must be a national of (or domiciled, resident, or incorporated in) South Africa or a Berne Convention country. Failing this, the place of first publication of the work must have been in South Africa or a Berne Convention country.[49]

---

[46]Sections 6–11B of the Copyright Act provides for, inter alia, reproduction, publishing, performing, broadcasting, transmission, adaptation, recording, communicating, letting, and distribution of a specific category of work as restricted acts.

[47]Section 2(1):

> Subject to the provisions of this Act, the following works, if they are original, shall be eligible for copyright—
>
> (a) literary works;
> (b) musical works;
> (c) artistic works;
> (d) cinematograph films;
> (e) sound recordings;
> (f) broadcasts;
> (g) programme-carrying signals;
> (h) published editions;
> (i) computer programs.

[48]Section 2(2) of the Copyright Act requires that the work must be written down, recorded, represented in digital data or signals, or otherwise reduced to a material form to be eligible for copyright. This section reads as follows:

> A work, except a broadcast or programme-carrying signal, shall not be eligible for copyright unless the work has been written down, recorded, represented in digital data or signals or otherwise reduced to a material form.

[49]Sections 3(1) and 4(1) of the Copyright Act.

Section 3(1):

> Copyright shall be conferred by this section on every work, eligible for copyright, of which the author or, in the case of a work of joint authorship, any one of the authors is at the time the work or a substantial part thereof is made, a qualified person, that is—
>
> (a) in the case of an individual, a person who is a South African citizen or is domiciled or resident in the Republic; or
> (b) in the case of a juristic person, a body incorporated under the laws of the Republic:
>
> Provided that a work of architecture erected in the Republic or any other artistic work incorporated in a building or any other permanent structure in the Republic, shall be eligible for copyright, whether or not the author was a qualified person.

Section 4(1):

> Copyright shall be conferred by this section on every work which is eligible for copyright and which—
>
> (a) being a literary, musical or artistic work or a sound recording, is first published in the Republic;

Originality, which is the primary requirement for the subsistence of copyright, is not defined in the Copyright Act. Case law on the subject provides guidance as to the requirement of originality, and it is clear that the amount of effort required to obtain copyright protection is not very great, given that South Africa still applies the sweat-of-the-brow standard for originality.[50] In other words, the requirement of originality will be satisfied if the author of the work has expended independent knowledge, skill, or labour in creating the work and has not slavishly copied from other sources. Intellectual novelty and innovation are not required, although the resulting work cannot be merely commonplace.[51]

The Copyright Act also requires that a work be in material form. Copyright does not vest in ideas, facts, or concepts, but rather in the material embodiment thereof. Therefore, a work does not come into existence until it is reduced to a material form, which makes the subsistence of copyright possible.[52]

Copyright is of limited duration. The term for copyright protection varies according to the specific category of the work, but, as a general rule, in the case of a work authored by a natural person, copyright exists for the lifetime of the author and for a further 50 years thereafter.[53] When the term of copyright expires, the work falls into the public domain and is free to be used by anyone.

(b) being a broadcast, is made in the Republic;
(c) being a programme-carrying signal, is emitted to a satellite from a place in the Republic;
(d) being a cinematograph film, is first published or made in the Republic;
(e) being a published edition, is first published in the Republic;
(f) being a computer program, is first published or made in the Republic,

and in respect of which copyright is not conferred by section 3.

[50] Dean and Karjiker (2015), para 3.3.

[51] *Waylite Diaries CC v First National Bank Ltd* 1993 (2) SA 128 (W) 133; *Waylite Diary CC v First National Bank Ltd* 1995 (1) SA 645 (A) 649–50; *Klep Valves (Pty) Ltd v Saunders Value Company Ltd* 1987 (2) SA 1 (A) 22.

[52] Dean and Karjiker (2015), para 3.4.

[53] Section 3(2) of the Copyright Act states:

The term of copyright conferred by this section shall be, in the case of—

(a) literary or musical works or artistic works, other than photographs, the life of the author and fifty years from the end of the year in which the author dies: Provided that if before the death of the author none of the following acts had been done in respect of such works or an adaptation thereof, namely—

(i) the publication thereof;
(ii) the performance thereof in public;
(iii) the offer for sale to the public of records thereof;
(iv) the broadcasting thereof;

the term of copyright shall continue to subsist for a period of fifty years from the end of the year in which the first of the said acts is done;

(b) cinematograph films, photographs and computer programs, fifty years from the end of the year in which the work—

1.5 Plant Breeders' Rights

Much like patents provide protection for inventions, the Plant Breeders' Rights Act 15 of 1976 ("Plant Breeders' Rights Act") provides protection for new plant varieties following registration. The requirements for obtaining a plant breeder's right in a plant variety are that the variety must be "new, distinct, uniform and stable."[54] Each of these requirements has a technical meaning and these are defined in the Plant Breeders' Rights Act.[55]

An applicant for a plant breeder's right must be a citizen of (or domiciled in) one of the following countries: South Africa, a country which is a member of the International Convention for the Protection of New Varieties of Plants, or a country with which South Africa has a bilateral agreement concerning plant breeders' rights.

(i) is made available to the public with the consent of the owner of the copyright; or
(ii) is first published,

whichever term is the longer, or failing such an event within fifty years of the making of the work, fifty years from the end of the year in which the work is made;

(c) sound recordings, fifty years from the end of the year in which the recording is first published;
(d) broadcasts, fifty years from the end of the year in which the broadcast first takes place;
(e) programme-carrying signals, fifty years from the end of the year in which the signals are emitted to a satellite;
(f) published editions, fifty years from the end of the year in which the edition is first published.

[54]Section 2(1) of the Plant Breeders' Rights Act reads as follows:

This Act shall apply in relation to every variety of any prescribed kind of plant if it is new, distinct, uniform and stable.

[55]Section 2(2):

A variety referred to in subsection (1) shall be deemed to be—

(a) new if propagating material or harvested material thereof has not been sold or otherwise disposed of by, or with the consent of, the breeder for purposes of exploitation of the variety—

(i) in the Republic, not more than one year; and
(ii) in a convention country or an agreement country, in the case of—
(aa) varieties of vines and trees, not more than six years; or
(bb) other varieties, not more than four years,
prior to the date of filing of the application for a plant breeder's right;

(b) distinct if, at the date of filing of the application for a plant breeder's right, it is clearly distinguishable from any other variety of the same kind of plant of which the existence on that date is a matter of common knowledge;
(c) uniform if, subject to the variation that may be expected from the particular features of the propagation thereof, it is sufficiently uniform with regard to the characteristics of the variety in question;
(d) stable if the characteristics thereof remain unchanged after repeated propagation or, in the case of a particular cycle of propagation, at the end of each such cycle.

Alternatively, if the applicant is a juristic person, it must have its registered office in one of the aforementioned countries.[56]

The holder of plant breeder's rights has the exclusive right to sell, import, export, produce, or reproduce the particular plant variety.[57] In fact, it is possible for an applicant to obtain similar provisional protection from the time the details of the application are published, following which objections to the application may still be lodged.[58] The term of plant breeders' rights is 25 years in the case of vines and trees, and 20 years in all other cases, calculated from the date upon which a certificate of registration is issued.[59]

---

[56] Section 6(2):

An application referred to in subsection (1) may only be made by a person who—

(a) is a citizen of, or is domiciled in, the Republic or a convention country or an agreement country; or
(b) in the case of a juristic person, has a registered office in the Republic or a convention country or an agreement country.

[57] Section 23(1):

The effect of the protection given under this Act by the grant of a plant breeder's right shall be that prior authority shall during the currency of the plant breeder's right be obtained by way of licence under section 25 or 27 by any person intending to undertake the—

(a) production or reproduction (multiplication);
(b) conditioning for the purpose of propagation;
(c) sale or any other form of marketing;
(d) exporting;
(e) importing;
(f) stocking for any of the purposes referred to in paragraphs (a) to (e), of—

 (i) propagating material of the relevant variety; or
 (ii) harvested material, including plants, which was obtained through the unauthorised use of propagating material of the relevant variety.

[58] Section 15 (as read with sections 13 and 14).
Section 15:

While a protective direction is in force, the variety in respect of which it was issued shall be protected as if a plant breeder's right had been granted in respect thereof, and anything that would constitute an infringement of a plant breeder's right or would be actionable in proceedings by the holder of such right, shall, if it is done with reference to a variety so protected, be actionable.

[59] Section 21:

A plant breeder's right shall be granted for a period of—

(a) 25 years, in the case of vines and trees; and
(b) 20 years, in all other cases,

calculated from the date on which a certificate of registration is issued under paragraph (a) of section 20(2).

2 Categories of Security Rights

In South African law, personal security and real security serve as important devices in the extension of financial credit. Both mechanisms secure a creditor's claim should a debtor default or become insolvent.[60] In the case of personal security, a person other than the debtor undertakes liability on the debtor's behalf if the debtor defaults in his obligations to the creditor. In the case of real security, property belonging to the debtor (or another party) is encumbered to satisfy the creditor's claim in the event of the debtor's default.[61]

While the legislation dealing with certain types of IP rights (more specifically, trademarks, patents, and designs) makes express provision for these rights to be offered as a form of real security, such provisions may not exclusively determine the means by which these rights can be provided as real security. Therefore, it is necessary to indicate possible alternative methods by which IP rights can serve as a form of real security. In particular, there is the possibility that real security may be obtained by way of a security cession of the relevant IP rights (in terms of the common law) or—to a very limited extent—through registering a general or special notarial bond over the IP rights.

Even where there are specific statutory provisions concerning the use of certain IP rights as real security, this security's form is analogous to one of the established forms of real security pertaining to movable corporeal property, namely, the pledge. This is expressly the case in respect of registered trademarks.[62] Depending on the nature of the property—whether it is immovable or movable—different forms of real security are available. Immovable property can be encumbered by a registered mortgage bond.[63] Movable property can serve as security either by being pledged, in which case the asset is delivered to the creditor,[64] or by having a notarial bond registered over the asset.[65]

Whether IP as intangible property is of an immovable or movable nature will determine the category of real security available (in the absence of statutory measures providing a mechanism for the creation of a security right). Legislation does not expressly indicate whether trademarks, patents, designs, or plant breeders' rights are of an immovable or movable nature, but it explicitly states that copyright is

---

[60]Lubbe (2008), para 324.

[61]In para 324. For the purposes of this work, it will be assumed that the real security is being provided by the debtor.

[62]Section 41(4) of the Trade Marks Act.

[63]Lubbe (2008), para 327. Even though the terms "mortgage" and "hypothec" are sometimes used interchangeably, a hypothec refers to a specific type of real security that differs from a mortgage bond with regard to its creation, operation, and effect.

[64]In Lubbe (2008), para 406.

[65]In Lubbe (2008), para 399; Brits (2016), pp. 197–198. A distinction can be made between a general notarial bond and a special one: a general notarial bond is registered against all of the debtor's movable assets, while a special notarial bond is limited to only certain movable assets.

movable property.[66] Statutory provisions regarding security rights over trademarks (as well as over the other forms of IP rights) indicate that the hypothecation of a trademark will have the same effect as a pledge.[67] This suggests that trademarks (and, indeed, other forms of IP rights) are property of a movable nature.[68] The statutory provisions relating to the hypothecation of registered trademarks, patents, and registered designs resemble those for ships and aircraft—that is to say, there are special registries in which their ownership is recorded and in which hypothecation is recorded.[69]

2.1 Trademarks

The Trade Marks Act expressly provides for the hypothecation of a registered trademark only; it does not provide for the hypothecation of an application for the registration of a trademark (in contrast to the situation in respect of patents and designs).[70] Hypothecation of a registered trademark is achieved by endorsing the trademark register, following the lodging (or filing) of a deed of security (or security agreement).[71] Endorsement of the register has the legal effect of a pledge of the trademark.[72] Therefore, to the degree possible, the rules of pledge will be applicable.[73] Accordingly, the creditor will have a preferent right to the proceeds of the trademark when it is sold in execution.[74] Unlike with the hypothecation of patents and designs, a hypothecated trademark can be assigned, provided that the creditor in whose favour the trademark has been hypothecated gives written consent for such an assignment.[75] In addition—and, once again, in contrast to the hypothecation of

[66]The Patents Act, Designs Act, Plant Breeders' Rights Act, and Trade Marks Act do not specify the nature of each specific category of intellectual property. However, section 22(5) of the Copyright Act states that copyright shall be transmissible as movable property.

[67]Section 41(4) of the Trade Marks Act.

[68]Du Plessis et al. (2012), p. 364. In the context of determining whether a South African court would have jurisdiction to decide matters relating to foreign copyright infringement, the Supreme Court of Appeal held that IP rights, including copyright, are immovable incorporeals (*Gallo Africa Ltd & Others v Sting Music (Pty) Ltd & Others* 2010 (6) SA 329 (SCA) [19] and [24]. It is proposed that this finding, if correct, must be considered to be confined to the narrow issue of the jurisdiction of the court.

[69]Brits (2016), p. 266.

[70]Section 41(1) of the Trade Marks Act.

[71]Section 41(3). Trade Mark Regulation 43 GN R578 in *GG* 16373 of April 21, 1995, requires that an application for endorsement be served on the registered proprietor and any other person recorded in the register as having an interest in the trademark.

[72]Section 41(4).

[73]Brits (2016), p. 269; Webster and Morley (2015), para 11.29.

[74]Webster and Morley (2015), para 11.29; Section 41(2) of the Trade Marks Act.

[75]Section 41(5) of the Trade Marks Act.

patents and designs—there is no explicit statutory prohibition on the granting of licences by the proprietor of a registered trademark that has been hypothecated.

As already mentioned above, in addition to the express statutory provision, a right of real security may be created by way of a security cession of the trademark[76] or, to a more limited extent, through the registration of a general or special notarial bond over the trademark.[77]

2.2 *Patents*

The Patents Act provides that a real security right (described in the legislation as a "hypothecation") may be registered against a patent, or against an application for a patent, to provide security for a creditor's claim.[78] The formalities relating to the registration of such real security are provided for in the Regulations to the Patents Act ("Patent Regulations").[79] If there is a registered hypothecation of a patent, or of an application for a patent, the patentee, or applicant for the patent, is prohibited from alienating or encumbering the hypothecated patent or patent application.[80] The Patents Act, furthermore, prohibits the patentee or applicant for the patent from granting a licence in respect of the hypothecated patent or patent application.[81] However, a compulsory licence may possibly still be granted in respect of a hypothecated patent or patent application.[82] The Patent Regulations prescribe the

[76]See Sect. 3.1.2 'Security Cession'.

[77]See Sect. 3.1.2 'Notarial Bonds'.

[78]Section 60(5) of the Patents Act, together with section 1, states that the hypothecation of a patent or application for a patent may be entered in the register kept at the Patent Office by the Registrar of Patents.

[79]Patent Regulations 64 and 65, published in GN R2470 in *GG* 2709 of December 15, 1978 ("Patent Regulations"). Patent Regulation 64 requires that an application be made on the prescribed form and brought to the Registrar of Patents, together with a deed of hypothecation (both the original deed and a certified true copy) and a power of attorney. If the original deed is not in English or another official South African language, an English translation must also accompany the application. Should the applicant be made by a party other than the patentee or patent applicant, the application should be served on the patentee or patent applicant, as well as on any other party who has an interest in the patent or patent application.

[80]Section 60(6) of the Patents Act.

[81]Section 60(6).

[82]Du Plessis et al. (2012), pp. 367–368. Section 60(6) Patents Act corresponds with section 30 (6) Designs Act. While the former does not mention the granting of a compulsory licence, the latter makes provision for the granting of a compulsory licence in case of an abuse of rights. Therefore, the assumption is that a compulsory licence may be granted in respect of a hypothecated patent or patent application.

manner in which a patent, or application for a patent, may be attached and sold in execution to fulfill a creditor's claim.[83]

As already mentioned above, in addition to the express statutory provision, a right of real security may be created by way of a security cession of the patent[84] or, to a more limited extent, through the registration of a notarial bond over the patent.[85]

2.3 Designs

Formalities similar to those prescribed for registering a right of real security (described in the legislation as a "hypothecation") against a patent, or an application for a patent, are provided for in the Designs Act in respect of registered designs or applications for registered designs.[86] The formalities relating to the registration of the real security are specified in the Regulations to the Designs Act ("Designs Regulations").[87] As with patents, once there is a registered hypothecation of a design or of an application for a registered design, the registered proprietor of the design or the applicant for the registered design will not be allowed to alienate or encumber the design or the application for registration.[88] Even though the Designs Act prevents the proprietor of a registered design or the applicant for a registered design from granting licences, the granting of compulsory licences may still be possible.[89] Similar to the situation with patents, the Designs Regulations prescribe the manner in which a registered design or an application for a registered design may be attached and sold in execution should the debtor be unable to perform his obligations.[90]

As already mentioned above, in addition to the express statutory provision, a right of real security may be created by way of a security cession of the registered design[91] or, to a more limited extent, through the registration of a notarial bond over the registered design.[92]

[83]Patent Regulations 60 and 61 require that a warrant or a writ of execution or attachment be served at the address for service of the patentee or patent applicant and that a copy, together with the prescribed form, be filed with the Registrar of Patents.

[84]See Sect. 3.2.2 'Security Cession'.

[85]Section 3.2.2 'Notarial Bonds'.

[86]Section 30(5) of the Designs Act.

[87]Design Regulation 40 GN R587 in *GG* 16383 of April 28, 1995 ("Design Regulations").

[88]Section 30(6) of the Designs Act.

[89]Section 30(6).

[90]Design Regulation 38.

[91]See Sect. 3.3.2 'Security Cession'.

[92]See Sect. 3.3.2 'Notarial Bonds'.

2.4 Copyright

The Copyright Act does not contain any provisions relating to the creation of a statutory right of real security over a copyrighted work. As an unregistered form of IP, copyright also has no register within which a security right can be recorded.[93] This complicates the use of copyright as real security.[94] However, the Copyright Act makes provision for the transfer of copyright by way of an assignment and provides that it is transmissible as movable property.[95]

Given the fact that the Copyright Act does not contain any explicit method by which copyright can be provided as real security, the only possible means by which a security right may be created in respect of a copyrighted work is by way of a security cession of copyright[96] or, to a more limited extent, through the registration of a notarial bond over the copyright.[97]

2.5 Plant Breeders' Rights

As is the case with the Copyright Act, the Plant Breeders' Rights Act does not contain any provisions relating to the creation of a statutory right of real security over a plant breeder's right. However, unlike copyright, a plant breeder's right is a registered form of IP. Therefore, it may be possible to note or record a security right in the register. The Plant Breeders' Rights Act also makes provision for the transfer of a plant breeder's right,[98] but it does not indicate whether such a right is considered to be movable or immovable property. As with copyright, this complicates the use of plant breeders' rights as real security.

Similar to the case with copyright, given the fact that the Plant Breeders' Rights Act does not contain any explicit method by which a plant breeder's right can be provided as real security, the only possible means by which a security interest may be created in respect of a plant breeder's right is by way of a security cession of the right[99] or, to a more limited extent, through the registration of a notarial bond over the right.[100]

---

[93]The only exception to this is the register of copyright in cinematograph films established under the Registration of Copyright in Cinematograph Films Act 62 of 1977. It is not compulsory for cinematograph films to be registered for copyright protection to subsist in such works; registration simply facilitates the enforcement proceedings in relation to cinematograph films. See Dean and Karjiker (2015), para 15.2.

[94]Dean and Karjiker (2015), para 12.17.

[95]Section 22 of the Copyright Act.

[96]See Sect. 3.4.2 'Security Cession'.

[97]See Sect. 3.4.2 'Notarial Bonds'.

[98]Section 29(1) of the Plant Breeders' Rights Act.

[99]See Sect. 3.5.2 'Security Cession'.

[100]See Sect. 3.5.2 'Notarial Bonds'.

3 Structure of Transactions: Attachment and Perfection

Before proceeding to describe the typical structures used to establish real security over IP rights, it is necessary to make some preliminary comments. A real security right is always of an accessory nature, that is, the security right has to relate to a lawful obligation (i.e. the principal obligation) owed by the debtor (for these purposes, the debtor is assumed to be the grantor of the security interest over its IP rights) to the creditor (i.e. the holder of the security interest).[101] If the principal obligation is extinguished, the security right is extinguished.[102] However, it is not required that the principal obligation exist or be enforceable at the time of the creation of the security interest. A security interest may be created over a possible future obligation and in such circumstances the security will be suspended until the obligation arises.[103]

3.1 *Trademarks*

3.1.1 Typical Structures of Secured Transactions Over IP Rights

The use of IP rights as a form of security is underdeveloped in South African law. In any event, the structures (or requirements) of the various ways in which a security right may be obtained over a registered trademark are discussed below in relation to each of the forms of security right.

3.1.2 Creation of Effective Security Rights

Statutory Hypothecation (Pledge)

The Trade Marks Act provides for the possible hypothecation of a registered trademark once a deed of security has been lodged (or filed) in the prescribed manner and the registrar has endorsed the register of trademarks regarding the hypothecation.[104] Furthermore, the Trade Marks Act provides that a statutory hypothecation shall have the effect of a pledge of the relevant trademark.[105] Unlike with the

[101]Brits (2016), pp. 114–116; Sharrock (2007), p. 567; Nagel (2011), para 27.04.

[102]Brits (2016), pp. 115–116; Sharrock (2007), p. 567.

[103]Sharrock (2007), p. 568.

[104]Sections 41(1) and 41(3)(a) of the Trade Marks Act.

[105]Section 41(4). It is not clear whether the pledge takes effect from the date that the application is lodged for the endorsement of the register regarding the hypothecation, or from the date the endorsement is entered in the register.

statutory provision for the hypothecation of patents and registered designs,[106] the Trade Marks Act does not provide for the possible hypothecation of an application for a registered trademark; it only provides for the hypothecation of trademarks that have actually been registered.[107]

Pledge Under South African Law Given the fact that the statutory hypothecation of a trademark is stated to have the effect of a pledge, it is necessary to consider the law relating to pledges in South Africa. However, before discussing the legal structure of a pledge under South African law, it is necessary to make some preliminary comments. First, as previously mentioned, the law relating to the use of IP rights as real security is particularly underdeveloped in South Africa; thus, the legal position set out below is of a general nature. Second, given the incorporeal nature of IP rights, the application of the law of pledge under South African law must be understood as applying by analogy (subject to the necessary changes required by the context), given the fact that the principles relating to pledges are based on the application of the pledge in connection with *corporeal* movable property. In order to avoid uncertainty due the application of the principles of pledge to IP rights, parties could seek to contractually provide for matters concerning the practical aspects of the implementation of the security arrangement where necessary.

A pledge is a form of real security which may be granted over movable property for the fulfilment of an obligation. In a typical pledge transaction, there are two parties: the party providing the property over which the security right is being granted is the pledgor (or debtor), and the party whose rights are secured by the real security provided over the property by the pledgor is the pledgee (or the creditor).

Besides the fact that pledges are of an accessory nature, that is, the security is provided in respect of an obligation (i.e., the principal obligation) owed by the pledgor to the pledgee, there are three other important aspects of pledge: first, the security (or pledge) contract (or agreement); second, the type of property that may be pledged; third, the creation of the real security by way of a real agreement (i.e., the property law aspect), namely, that is, the physical aspect of the pledge, which is the delivery of the pledged asset to the pledgee.[108]

The pledge takes place pursuant to a contract, namely, the security agreement (also referred to as the pledge contract or agreement to pledge). Pursuant to the pledge contract, the pledgor agrees to provide specific property as real security by

[106]See section 60(2) of the Patents Act; and section 30(2) of the Designs Act.

[107]While it may not be possible to create a statutory hypothec over an application for a registered trademark, as discussed below in this Sect. 3.1.2 ‘Security Cession’, it may be possible to effect a security cession of the application. Alternatively, a deed of security with a condition subsequent may be entered into, where the condition subsequent is registration; thus, the deed takes effect upon the registration of the trademark. Furthermore, the security agreement may provide that the debtor (that is, the applicant for registration) is obliged to hypothecate the trademark in favour of the creditor if it is registered.

[108]Brits (2016), pp. 108 and 111.

way of pledge for the principal obligation, and the pledgee agrees to accept the same property as security for the obligation owed to him.[109] The security agreement does not itself give rise to the pledge, but it creates personal rights and obligations, which, if given effect to, result in a pledge.[110] The security agreement will determine the circumstances in which the pledgor will have breached his obligations and the pledgee will be entitled to foreclose (or enforce) the pledge.[111] The statutory provision requires the lodging of a deed of security[112] and the security agreement serves that purpose.

As for the type of property that may be pledged, any movable asset which is capable of being traded may be pledged. While pledges may have traditionally been confined to corporeal movable property, it is now well-established that incorporeal movable property may be pledged by means of a cession *in securitatem debiti* (or a "security cession").[113] In other words, despite some doctrinal difficulties, South African law has combined principles of property law (namely, the pledge) and contract law (namely, cession) to provide a pragmatic solution for the need to allow incorporeal assets to be used as real security for financing purposes.[114] However, given that the statutory provision explicitly states that the hypothecation of a registered trademark has the effect of a pledge, it is, strictly speaking, unnecessary to use a security cession as a legal device for pledging a trademark (although this will, in any event, be discussed below). There may be a valid security (or pledge) contract in respect of property which is still to come into existence; however, the actual pledge will only come into existence when the property comes into existence and is delivered to the pledgee.[115] The security right will cease to exist if the pledged property is destroyed.[116]

While a security right created by way of pledge of a corporeal movable asset is created upon the delivery of the asset to the pledgee, this delivery serves a more important underlying objective. The pledge itself, that is, the creation of the limited real security, is constituted by giving the pledgee legal control (or possession) over the specified property and divesting the pledgor of such control. Typically, the pledgee acquires legal possession over the pledged asset by being given physical control of it, to the exclusion of others.[117] The delivery of the pledged property to the pledgee also serves to publicize the pledgee's legal control over the relevant property in order to prevent third parties from being deceived by the pledgor.[118] Given the

[109] Brits (2016), p. 117.
[110] Brits (2016), pp. 118–119.
[111] Brits (2016), pp. 159 and 162.
[112] Sections 41(1) of the Trade Marks Act.
[113] Brits (2016), pp. 111 and 300.
[114] Brits (2016), pp. 273–274.
[115] Brits (2016), p. 112.
[116] Brits (2016), p. 113.
[117] Brits (2016), pp. 121–122 and 139.
[118] Brits (2016), pp. 122–123 and 139.

incorporeal nature of IP, such as, registered trademarks, it is not possible to accomplish any form of physical delivery so as to satisfy the need to publicize the pledgee's security right. However, as indicated above, the Trade Marks Act makes provision for the endorsement of a hypothecation in the register,[119] which provides publicity for the security arrangement. Furthermore, a hypothecated trademark can only be assigned with the written consent of the holder of the security,[120] which gives the holder of the security legal control over the trademark. The pledgee's security interest is strengthened by section 39(3) of the Trade Marks Act, which provides that the assignment or transmission (that is, the transfer by operation of law) of a registered trademark will be subject to any hypothecation. However, as mentioned above, unlike with the statutory hypothecation of patents and designs, there is no express statutory prohibition on the granting of licences by the proprietor of a registered trademark that has been hypothecated. This type of restriction could, of course, be imposed contractually on the debtor through the deed of security (or security agreement).

Security Cession

Given that there is a statutory provision explicitly enabling the hypothecation of a registered trademark, this should be the preferred way to obtain real security over a registered trademark. However, there may, at least theoretically, be other possible means of obtaining a security right over a registered trademark (or, indeed, any other type of IP right). The first of these other possible means is a security cession (cession *in securitatem debiti*, or a pledge of claims). Another possible alternative is the registration of a notarial bond.

As indicated above, a security cession (cession *in securitatem debiti*, or a pledge of claims) combines principles of property law (namely, the pledge) and contract law (namely, cession) and serves as a means by which incorporeal assets may be used as security for financing purposes.[121] The principles of the law of pledge, referred to above, are therefore also applicable to security cessions (as far as is possible, depending on the context).

Cession involves the consensual transfer of a personal right or claim from one party (the cedent) to another party (the cessionary).[122] Unless there is a specific legal exception (such as a common-law or statutory restriction) or a contractual prohibition (or restriction), any personal rights or claims that have a monetary value (such as amounts receivable, the proceeds of an insurance policy, and even IP rights) are cedable and can serve as objects of real security.[123] These forms of assets are

[119] Section 41(3)(a) of the Trade Marks Act.

[120] Section 41(5).

[121] Brits (2016), pp. 111 and 273–274.

[122] Lubbe (2013), para 128.

[123] Brits (2016), pp. 273–274 and 316.

regarded as incorporeal movables and may be provided as security by way of a security cession.[124] A security cession is legally characterized as having the nature of a pledge, even though the particular subject of the cession is incorporeal.[125] The personal rights or claims are hypothecated by the cedent (or debtor), who cedes the personal rights or claims to the cessionary (or creditor), giving the latter a limited real right (that is, real security) in the ceded rights.[126]

A cession requires a *causa*, which can be satisfied by the intention to provide security to the cessionary (or creditor) by way of a pledge of claims.[127] This requirement is typically satisfied by a security (or pledge) agreement, which creates the contractual obligation to transfer the specified rights through cession. This contractual obligation does not by itself give effect to the actual cession (that is, the pledge of claims), which is a juristic act distinct from the contractual obligation under the security contract. It may be possible for the cession to take place simultaneously with, and by way of, the security agreement, but it is important to note that is the actual cession, which is a distinct juristic act that vests the cessionary (or creditor) with the required legal control over the personal rights or claims.[128]

Subject to any special legislative requirements, or within the terms of the transaction which created the particular personal right or claim, there are no formal requirements for a valid cession other than the parties' respective intentions to proceed with the cession of the right in question.[129] There is no publicity requirement for a cession to be valid,[130] nor is there a general requirement to notify the "original" debtor (that is, the third party against whom the claim being ceded may be enforceable) that the claim against it is being ceded.[131] The physical delivery of a document is only required where such a document can be said to be constitutive of the right being transferred (that is, in a situation where the right is inseparable from the document and cannot be enforced without it). In other words, where the existence of the right is constituted by the document, the document has to be delivered to the cessionary.[132] While the existence of IP rights is not constituted by any such documents, the prudent cessionary (or creditor) would probably stipulate in the security agreement that the proof of registration (where applicable) be delivered to him upon the cession of the right.

As already mentioned, while the general principles of pledge are impliedly (*ex lege*) applicable to security cessions, the parties may seek to cater for possible

---

[124] Brits (2016), pp. 273–274.

[125] Brits (2016), pp. 142 and 192.

[126] Brits (2016), pp. 324–325 and 327.

[127] Scott (1991), p. 79; Brits (2016), pp. 303–304; Lubbe (2013), para 155. However, the invalidity of the *causa* will not affect the transfer of the rights that results from the cession (see para 155).

[128] Brits (2016), pp. 277–278.

[129] Brits (2016), pp. 308–309.

[130] Brits (2016), pp. 298, 303 and 304.

[131] Brits (2016), pp. 307 and 313.

[132] Brits (2016), pp. 311–312.

uncertainties concerning the practical aspects of the cessionary's (or creditor's) control and disposition of the right (e.g. in case of foreclosure) through contractual stipulations. There may be issues that must be addressed, depending on the type of personal right or claim that is the subject of the security cession.[133] For example, the parties may wish to regulate the situation relating to the payments made by licensees of the IP rights during the subsistence of the security cession.

Security Cession Distinguished from Out-and-Out Cession There is an alternative form of cession—the so-called "out-and-out cession" (or "absolute security cession")—through which it may be sought to provide a creditor a security interest in respect of IP rights, such as a registered trademark. However, for reasons which will become clear, this form of cession does not create a limited right of real security. In an out-and-out cession, the debtor cedes (that is, transfers) the relevant rights in full to the creditor, until the debtor's obligations are discharged.[134] In other words, the debtor completely divests itself of the rights, which are then owned by the creditor. Thus, this does not create a real security right in the relevant rights; rather, it constitutes a transfer of those rights. The only right which the cedent (or debtor) has against the creditor (or cessionary) is a personal right (a *pactum fiduciae*) in terms of the security agreement, which obliges the creditor to transfer the rights back to the debtor after the debtor has discharged his obligation to the creditor.[135]

Significantly, in the case of a security cession, the relevant rights continue to be owned by the debtor (i.e. he retains *dominium*), which is of vital importance if the creditor becomes insolvent. In contrast, where there is an out-and-out cession, in case of the creditor's insolvency, the rights will form part of the creditor's insolvent estate.[136] Insolvency law does not make any provision for the fact that an out-and-out cession may be used to provide a creditor with security so as to prevent the rights from falling into the creditor's insolvent estate.[137] The pledge construction of the security session thus corresponds more closely to the general principles of real security and insolvency law.[138]

Notarial Bonds

Subject to what is stated below, the third possible way in which a right of real security can be established over IP rights is through the registration of a notarial bond. A notarial bond is a formal instrument containing the agreement under which a

[133]Brits (2016), pp. 150, 192, 296–297, 301, 327–328 and 330–331.

[134]Brits (2016), pp. 274 and 277.

[135]Brits (2016), pp. 279–280, 287 and 289.

[136]Brits (2016), p. 279.

[137]Brits (2016), p. 283.

[138]Brits (2016), p. 280.

debtor agrees to hypothecate movable property in favour of its creditor (or bondholder) as security for the repayment of a debt.[139] Importantly, notarial bonds can also be registered over incorporeal movable property, such as, personal rights or claims.[140]

Insofar as IP rights are concerned, there are two possible types of notarial bonds: first, a general notarial bond, which may be registered over both corporeal and incorporeal movable assets;[141] and second, a special notarial bond which is registered over specific IP rights and which does not comply with the Security by Means of Movable Property Act ("SMMPA").[142] It is important to note that, unlike with a notarial bond registered according to SMMPA terms, these two forms of notarial bonds do not automatically confer a real security right on the bondholder.[143] A real security right is only obtained when the bondholder gains control over the relevant property via a perfection (or attachment) court order.[144] Perfection is the process through which the bondholder gains control over the bonded property and thereby obtains a right of pledge of this property.[145] In other words, before perfection, the bondholder's rights are, in essence, contractual rights.[146]

3.1.3 Can Security Rights in IP Be Registered in the IP Registry?

Statutory Hypothecation

The Trade Marks Act provides for the endorsement of the hypothecation of a trademark in the register of trademarks.[147] While the security interest should be effective against third parties upon the endorsement of the register (there is no case law on the matter), the question remains whether it may already be effective from an earlier date, namely, from the conclusion of the deed of security (that is, the security agreement) or from the lodgement of the application for endorsement. As indicated above, a distinction has to be drawn between the contractual undertaking, pursuant to which the obligation to create the security interest is agreed upon in terms of the

[139] Brits (2016), p. 193.

[140] Brits (2016), pp. 242 and 305; Lubbe (2013), para 403.

[141] A general notarial bond is one which seeks to hypothecate all of the movable property (without any exceptions) that is owned by the debtor at the time of the bond's creation *and* all of the movable property that may be owned by the debtor at the time the security is enforced; this includes IP rights. Brits (2016), pp. 194 and 199–200.

[142] Security by Means of Movable Property Act 57 of 1993. A special notarial bond which complies with the requirements of this act is limited to corporeal movable assets (section 1(1)). See Brits (2016), pp. 262–263.

[143] Lubbe (2013), paras 400 and 405; Brits (2016), pp. 231–232; Du Plessis et al. (2012), p. 368.

[144] Brits (2016), pp. 198, 202, 206 and 231–232.

[145] Brits (2016), p. 213.

[146] Brits (2016), p. 271.

[147] Sections 41(1) and 41(3)(a) of the Trade Marks Act.

security agreement, and the hypothecation itself—namely, the creation of the real security, constituted by giving the pledgee legal control over the specified property (the so-called "real agreement"). Given the fact that a statutory hypothecation is meant to have the effect of a pledge, it is unlikely that the security interest would be created simply through a contractual undertaking pursuant to the deed of security (or security agreement). In other words, the real security is probably only obtained on the endorsement of the register, and not on the mere conclusion of the deed of security.

Security Cession

There is no registration required, or provided, for security cessions.

Notarial Bonds

If a notarial bond is to provide any real security over movable assets—bearing in mind the fact that the two relevant types of notarial bonds give a bondholder no immediate real right of security over the assets—it has to be registered.[148] However, such registration is not in the register of trademarks, but in a separate registration system administered under the Deeds Registries Act 47 of 1937.

3.2 *Patents*

3.2.1 Typical Structures of Secured Transactions Over IP Rights

As indicated above, the use of IP rights as a form of security is underdeveloped in South African law.

3.2.2 Creation of Effective Security Rights

Statutory Hypothecation

Section 60(5) of the Patents Act[149] provides for the possible hypothecation of a patent or of an application for a patent by way of an entry, made in the prescribed

[148] Brits (2016), pp. 193–194. A notarial bond must be registered in a deeds registry within the period of three months after its execution or within such extended period as the court may have allowed (s 61(1) Deeds Registries Act 47 of 1937).
[149] Patents Act 57 of 1978.

manner, in the register at the Companies and Intellectual Property Commission.[150] However, unlike the Trade Marks Act, the Patents Act (like the Designs Act) does not indicate what the nature of the real security right is. For example, it does not state that the nature of the real security right is like that of a pledge. It is submitted that, based on the statutory provisions concerning the hypothecation of registered trademarks, the nature of the security interest is in the nature of a pledge. The only other possible established types of real security that this real-security right may be analogous to are a security cession (the so-called "cession *in securitatem debiti*") or a notarial bond. As indicated previously,[151] the accepted nature of the security cession is, in any event, considered to be like that of a pledge.[152] Furthermore, as already noted,[153] notarial bonds do not automatically confer real security on the bondholder;[154] hence, little purpose would be served by characterizing such a registration as either of the two aforementioned forms of notarial bond. In any event, even the only form of notarial bond that does create an immediate right of real security (namely, a special notarial bond registered over corporeal movable assets pursuant to the Security by Means of Movable Property Act 57 of 1993) amounts to a form of non-possessory pledge.[155] Hence, it is suggested that the security interest created pursuant to a statutory hypothecation is in the nature of a pledge, and the law relating to pledges[156] must be understood as applying by analogy (subject to the necessary changes required by the context).

As previously indicated,[157] there are two parties to a pledge transaction: the party providing the property over which the security interest is being granted is the pledgor, and the party who obtains real security over the property is the pledgee. The position is, furthermore, as indicated in Sect. 3.1.2 'Statutory Hypothecation (Pledge)', subject to the necessary changes required by the context.

The four aspects of pledge (i.e., its accessory nature, the security (or pledge) contract, the type of property that may be pledged, and the vesting of legal control over the pledged property in the pledgee) as indicated in Sect. 3.1.2 'Statutory Hypothecation (Pledge)' will also apply to the statutory hypothecation of patents. Again, as with registered trademarks, the pledgee acquires the necessary legal control, thanks to the endorsement of the hypothecation of the patent in the register, as provide for in the statutory provision.[158]

---

[150]Unlike with the hypothecation of registered trademarks, there is no requirement that the deed of security (or the security agreement) be included with the application. A record of the agreement to hypothecate the patent is sufficient.

[151]See Sect. 3.1.2 'Security Cession'.

[152]Brits (2016), p. 297.

[153]See Sect. 3.1.2 'Notarial Bonds'.

[154]Lubbe (2013), paras 400 and 405; Brits (2016), pp. 231–232.

[155]Brits (2016), pp. 59–60.

[156]See Sect. 3.1.2 'Statutory Hypothecation (Pledge)'.

[157]See Sect. 3.1.2 'Statutory Hypothecation (Pledge)'.

[158]Section 60(5) of the Patents Act.

Section 60(6) of the Patents Act strengthens the legal control of the pledgee as it provides that once a hypothecation has been entered in the register, the patentee or applicant for a patent is prohibited from alienating or encumbering the hypothecated patent or application for a patent, and from granting any licences under the patent. Unlike the Designs Act, the Patents Act does not expressly deal with the granting of compulsory licences pursuant to section 56 of the Act. In the absence of an express statutory prohibition, it is submitted that the hypothecation of a patent does not prevent a compulsory licence from being granted pursuant to section 56 of the Patents Act.[159]

Security Cession

Given that there is a statutory provision explicitly enabling the hypothecation of a patent, this should be the preferred way to obtain a real security right over a patent. However, as with registered trademarks and registered designs, it may be possible to obtain a security interest in a patent through a security cession, as indicated in Sect. 3.1.2 'Security Cession', subject to the necessary changes required by the context.

Notarial Bonds

Again, as with registered trademarks, the third possible way in which a real security right may be established over IP rights is through the registration of a notarial bond, as indicated in Sect. 3.1.2 'Notarial Bonds'.

3.2.3 Can Security Rights in IP Be Registered in the IP Registry?

Statutory Hypothecation

The Patents Act provides for the endorsement of the hypothecation of a patent in the register.[160] For the same reasons as those applicable to the hypothecation of registered trademarks,[161] the security interest created according to the rules on statutory hypothecation is likely to only be effective upon the endorsement of the hypothecation in the register.

---

[159] Du Plessis et al. (2012), p. 368.

[160] Section 60(5) of the Patents Act.

[161] See Sect. 3.1.3 'Statutory Hypothecation (Pledge)'.

Security Cession

There is no registration required, or provided, for security cessions.

Notarial Bonds

As stated in relation to registered trademarks,[162] the relevant notarial bond has to be registered, but this registration does not take place in the relevant IP register.

3.3 *Registered Designs*

3.3.1 Typical Structures of Secured Transactions Over IP Rights

As indicated above, the use of IP rights as a form of security is underdeveloped in South African law.

3.3.2 Creation of Effective Security Rights

Statutory Hypothecation

Section 30(5) of the Designs Act[163] provides for the possible hypothecation of a registered design or of an application for a registered design through registration with the Companies and Intellectual Property Commission in the prescribed manner.[164] However, unlike the Trade Marks Act, the Designs Act (like the Patents Act) does not indicate what the nature of the security right is. For the same reason as that stated in respect of the statutory hypothecation of patents,[165] it is submitted that the nature of the security right is like that of a pledge, and the relevant parties and principles that have been described in relation to patents are also applicable to registered designs.

Section 30(6) of the Designs Act strengthens the legal control of the pledgee as it provides that once a hypothecation has been entered in the register, the registered proprietor of the design or applicant for the design is prohibited from alienating or encumbering the hypothecated design or application for the design, and from granting any licences under such registration. However, the Act expressly provides

[162]See Sect. 3.1.3 'Notarial Bonds'.

[163]Designs Act 195 of 1993.

[164]Unlike with the hypothecation of registered trademarks, there is no requirement that the deed of security (or the security agreement) be included with the application. A record of the agreement to hypothecate the registered design is sufficient.

[165]See Sect. 3.2.2 'Statutory Hypothecation'.

that the aforementioned prohibition on the granting of licences does not apply to the granting of compulsory licences pursuant to section 21 of the Act.

Security Cession

Given that there is a statutory provision explicitly enabling the hypothecation of a registered design, this should be the preferred way to obtain a real security right over a registered design. However, as with registered trademarks and with patents, it may be possible to obtain a security interest in a registered design through a security cession, as indicated in Sect. 3.1.2 'Security Cession', subject to the necessary changes required by the context.

Notarial Bonds

Again, as with registered trademarks, the third possible way in which a real security right may be established over IP rights is through the registration of a notarial bond, as indicated in Sect. 3.1.2 'Notarial Bonds'.

3.3.3 Can Security Rights in IP Be Registered in the IP Registry?

Statutory Hypothecation

The Designs Act provides for the endorsement of the hypothecation of a registered design in the register.[166] For the same reasons as those applicable to the hypothecation of registered trademarks,[167] the security interest created according to the rules on statutory hypothecation is probably only effective upon the endorsement of the hypothecation in the register.

Security Cession

There is no registration required, or provided, for security cessions.

Notarial Bonds

As stated in relation to registered trademarks,[168] the relevant notarial bond has to be registered, but this registration does not take place in the relevant IP register.

[166] Section 30(5) of the Designs Act.

[167] See Sect. 3.1.3 'Statutory Hypothecation (Pledge)'.

[168] See Sect. 3.1.3 'Notarial Bonds'.

3.4 Copyright

3.4.1 Typical Structures of Secured Transactions Over IP Rights

As indicated above, the use of IP rights as a form of security is underdeveloped in South African law.

3.4.2 Creation of Effective Security Rights

Statutory Hypothecation

The Copyright Act makes no provision for the hypothecation of, or creation of a right of real security in, copyright.

Security Cession

Given the fact that there is no express statutory provision enabling the hypothecation of copyright, it is necessary to consider other legal devices to obtain a right of real security in copyright. However, as with registered trademarks, registered designs, and patents, it may be possible to obtain a real security right over copyright through a security cession, as indicated in Sect. 3.1.2 ‘Security Cession’, subject to the necessary changes required by the context.

Nevertheless, it appears that in practice, an out-and-out cession may be the preferred method for creating a form of security right.[169] However, as indicated above,[170] an out-and-out cession does not create a real security right over the relevant rights; rather, it constitutes a transfer of those rights.

Notarial Bonds

Again, as with registered trademarks, the third possible way in which a real security right may be established over IP rights is through the registration of a notarial bond, as indicated in Sect. 3.1.2 ‘Notarial Bonds’.

[169] Dean and Dyer (2014), p. 385.

[170] See Sect. 3.1.2 ‘Statutory Hypothecation (Pledge)’.

3.4.3 Can Security Rights in IP Be Registered in the IP Registry?

Statutory Hypothecation

As the Copyright Act makes no provision for the hypothecation of copyright and there is no general registration system for copyright, the security rights cannot be registered in an IP register.

Security Cession

There is no registration required, or provided, for security cessions.

Notarial Bonds

As stated in relation to registered trademarks,[171] the relevant notarial bond has to be registered, but this registration does not take place in the relevant IP register (particularly as there is no general copyright register).

3.5 Plant Breeders' Rights

3.5.1 Typical Structures of Secured Transactions Over IP Rights

As indicated above, the use of IP rights as a form of security is underdeveloped in South African law.

3.5.2 Creation of Effective Security Rights

Statutory Hypothecation

The Plant Breeders' Rights Act makes no provision for the hypothecation of, or creation of a right of real security in, a plant breeder's right.

[171] See Sect. 3.1.3 'Notarial Bonds'.

Security Cession

As with copyright, given the fact that there is no statutory provision explicitly enabling the hypothecation of a plant breeder's right, it is necessary to consider other legal devices to obtain a right of real security in a plant breeder's right. However, as with other IP rights, it may be possible to obtain a real security right over a plant breeder's right through a security cession, as indicated in Sect. 3.1.2 'Security Cession', subject to the necessary changes required by the context.

Notarial Bonds

Again, as with registered trademarks, the third possible way in which a limited real right of security can be established over IP rights is through the registration of a notarial bond, as indicated under Sect. 3.1.2 'Notarial Bonds'.

3.5.3 Can Security Rights in IP Be Registered in the IP Registry?

Statutory Hypothecation

As already noted above, the Plant Breeders' Act makes no provision for the hypothecation of a plant breeder's right, although there is a register of plant breeders' rights.

Security Cession

There is no registration required, or provided, for security cessions.

Notarial Bonds

As stated in relation to registered trademarks,[172] the relevant notarial bond has to be registered, but this registration does not take place in the relevant IP register.

[172] See Sect. 3.1.3 'Notarial Bonds'.

4 Priorities

In terms of insolvency law, strictly speaking, a "preferent"[173] creditor refers to a creditor paid out of the free residue,[174] ahead of concurrent creditors. In other words, in a strict sense, this term would not include secured creditors, as the free residue is that part of the insolvent estate which is free of any security right (or real security). However, in a broader sense, a holder of real security (or secured creditor) can be regarded as a preferent creditor, as it is also paid ahead of concurrent creditors.[175]

A secured creditor is a creditor who holds some form of real security.[176] Pursuant to sections 89(1) and 96(4) of the Insolvency Act, certain costs relating to the administration of the estate and costs associated with the secured asset (collectively, the "initial costs") will rank ahead of a secured creditor's claim.[177] Subject to the payment of the aforementioned costs (and any higher-ranking secured claim[178]), a secured creditor is entitled to payment out of the proceeds of the property over which he holds security.[179] If the secured assets are insufficient to discharge the initial costs, the secured creditor will have to make a contribution to the initial costs. A secured creditor has a choice: it may choose to rely solely on the proceeds from its real security, or it may choose to also participate in the free residue for any amount which remains outstanding, should the proceeds from the secured property be insufficient to satisfy the amount owing to him.[180] In the latter case, he will rank after the concurrent creditors, and just ahead of the preferent creditors for the non-preferent balance of their claims.[181] However, if it elects to participate in the free residue for any shortfall, the secured creditor may have to make a contribution to the costs of administering the insolvent estate.[182]

---

[173] Section 2 of the Insolvency Act 24 of 1936 sv "preference" ("preference," in relation to any claim against an insolvent estate, means the right to payment of that claim out of the assets of the estate in preference to other claims; "preferent" has a corresponding meaning).

[174] Section 2 sv "free residue" ("free residue," in relation to an insolvent estate, means that portion of the estate which is not subject to any right of preference by reason of any special mortgage, legal hypothec, pledge, or right of retention).

[175] Sharrock et al. (2012), pp. 183–184.

[176] Section 2 of the Insolvency Act sv "security" ("security," in relation to the claim of a creditor of an insolvent estate, means property of that estate over which the creditor has a preferent right by virtue of any special mortgage, landlord's legal hypothec, pledge, or right of retention). See also Lubbe (2013), paras 406 and 430.

[177] Sharrock et al. (2012), pp. 186–187.

[178] Section 95(1) of the Insolvency Act.

[179] Sections 95(1) and 89(1).

[180] Section 89(2).

[181] Section 83(12). See Sharrock et al. (2012), p. 192.

[182] Section 106 of the Insolvency Act. See Sharrock et al. (2012), pp. 195–196.

4.1 Statutory Hypothecation

As already stated above, a statutory hypothecation has the effect of a pledge. Generally, when the pledgor has defaulted on its obligations to the pledgee, enforcement involves two actions: first, the obtaining of a court order establishing the indebtedness of the pledgor; and second, the realization of the pledged property (that is, selling it in execution).[183] In the case of a non-possessory pledge, such as, a notarial bond or a security cession, the property will have to be secured via an attachment (or perfection) order.[184] Perfection is, thus, necessarily part of the enforcement process.[185] It is not clear whether the statutory hypothecation may be regarded as a form of non-possessory pledge or if the creditor may, by virtue of the endorsement of the register, be regarded as having possession of the relevant registered IP rights (namely, registered trademarks, patents, and registered designs). It would be advisable for the holder of the real security to seek a perfection order to avoid any doubt as to its perfection of the security as a secured creditor.

Before insolvency, the pledged asset may only be realized through a court order approving such an action, unless the security agreement between the parties makes provision for a summary execution (or *parate executie*) or a quasi-conditional sale.[186] Unless otherwise agreed, the property must be sold by the sheriff of the court by way of a public auction, to the highest bidder.[187] In case of a summary execution, the pledgee may realize the pledged asset by way of a public auction or on a market where the particular asset is normally traded.[188] In case of a quasi-conditional sale, the pledgee has an irrevocable right to acquire the pledged property at a fair value (or reasonable price), determined after the pledgor's default.[189]

In terms of insolvency law, the pledge gives the pledgee a preferent right to the proceeds of the subject matter of the real security and a secured right to the proceeds of the sale of the pledged asset in case of insolvency of the pledgor.[190] Also, from an insolvency perspective, ownership of the pledged property remains with the pledgor—that is to say, it remains in the pledgor's estate and does not form part of the pledgee's estate.[191]

---

[183] Brits (2016), pp. 159 and 162.

[184] Brits (2016), p. 159.

[185] Brits (2016), p. 160.

[186] Lubbe (2013), para 183; Brits (2016), p. 331.

[187] Brits (2016), pp. 159–160.

[188] Brits (2016), p. 331.

[189] Brits (2016), pp. 162, 166, 169 and 331.

[190] Section 2 of the Insolvency Act sv "security" ("security," in relation to the claim of a creditor of an insolvent estate, means property of that estate over which the creditor has a preferent right by virtue of any special mortgage, landlord's legal hypothec, pledge, or right of retention). See also Lubbe (2013), paras 406 and 430.

[191] Brits (2016), p. 106.

4.2 Security Cession

Given that a security cession is analogous to a pledge, as indicated in Sect. 3.1.2 'Security Cession', the legal position is as described in Sect. 4.1. In the case of a security cession, the cedent retains ownership (*dominium* or bare *dominium*) of the asset (that is, the asset remains in the cedent's estate), but legal control over the claim is passed to the cessionary.[192]

If the cedent becomes insolvent, the trustee of the cedent's estate will be entitled to enforce the right that was provided as security through the security cession, but the cessionary will have preference to the proceeds from the asset.[193]

4.3 Notarial Bonds

4.3.1 General Notarial Bond

The bondholder of a general notarial bond does not automatically obtain a real security right. He only obtains a real security right (that is, becomes a secured creditor) once he has gained physical control over the property that is the subject of the bond (i.e., upon perfection).[194] Following perfection, the bondholder gains a right of pledge over such property,[195] and the legal position is then as described in Sect. 4.1.

Following the insolvency of the debtor, if the bondholder did not perfect the bond prior to insolvency, a general notarial bond does not amount to a "special mortgage" (and, hence, real security); however, the bondholder does have a preferent right to the value of the proceeds of the subject matter of the bond in respect of the free residue of the estate.[196] In other words, the bondholder will be paid just ahead of the concurrent creditors of the insolvent estate. If a perfection clause in the bond allows the bondholder to gain possession of the property pursuant to a court order, pursuant to which it has perfected the security prior to insolvency of the debtor, it will have a real right of security and will have the same position as a pledgee.[197]

[192] Brits (2016), pp. 324–325, 328 and 337.

[193] Brits (2016), pp. 342–343 and 343–344.

[194] Brits (2016), pp. 198, 202 and 206.

[195] Brits (2016), pp. 185 and 213.

[196] Section 102 of the Insolvency Act; Brits (2016), pp. 184 and 221–222.

[197] See Sect. 4.1; Brits (2016), pp. 142, 185 and 227.

4.3.2 Special Notarial Bond

As a special notarial bond over specific IP rights will not comply with the Security by Means of Movable Property Act,[198] it will provide no real security to the bondholder.[199] However, the bondholder of a non-compliant special notarial bond can obtain a real security right by gaining physical control over the relevant property (i.e. by way of perfection).[200] If the bond has been perfected, the bondholder will have the rights of a pledgee and the legal position will be as described in Sect. 4.1.

Following the insolvency of the debtor, if the bondholder did not perfect the bond prior to insolvency, the bond provides no real security right to the bondholder, nor does it provide any preference to the free residue of the insolvent estate (unlike in the case of a general notarial bond).[201] If a perfection clause in the bond allows the bondholder to gain possession of the property pursuant to a court order, pursuant to which it has perfected the security prior to insolvency of the debtor, it will have a real right of security and will have the same position as a pledgee.[202]

5 Enterprise Charges

As indicated above in Sect. 3.1.2 'Notarial Bonds', a general notarial bond may be registered over both the corporeal and incorporeal movable assets of a debtor, which will have an effect similar to that of a floating charge under English law. A general notarial bond does not confer a real right of security to the bondholder. The bondholder only gains a real security right (that is, becomes a secured creditor) once he has gained control over the property that is the subject of the bond via a perfection (or attachment) court order (that is to say, through perfection).[203] Following perfection, the bondholder obtains a right of pledge of the property[204] and the legal position is as described in Sect. 4.1.

As already indicated in Sect. 4.3.1, following the insolvency of the debtor, if the bondholder did not perfect the bond prior to insolvency, then the bondholder is not a secured creditor. However, the bondholder does have a preferent right to the value of the proceeds of the property covered by the bond in the free residue of the insolvent estate.[205] If a perfection clause in the bond allows the bondholder to gain possession of the property pursuant to a court order, pursuant to which it has perfected the

[198] Security by Means of Movable Property Act 57 of 1993.

[199] Brits (2016), pp. 239 and 262.

[200] Brits (2016), p. 240.

[201] Brits (2016), pp. 239 and 262.

[202] See Sect. 4.1.

[203] Brits (2016), pp. 198, 202 and 206.

[204] Brits (2016), pp. 185 and 213.

[205] Section 102 of the Insolvency Act; Brits (2016), pp. 184 and 221–222.

security prior to insolvency of the debtor, he will have a real right of security and will have the same position as a pledgee.[206]

6 Rights Before Default

Real security is generally provided pursuant to a contract, which also provides the *causa* for the provision of the security. This contract can generally be referred to as a "security agreement," although other names may be used for certain security arrangements. For example, in the context of a pledge, the pledge may be said to take place pursuant to a "pledge contract" (also sometimes referred to as a "security contract" or "agreement to pledge"). In the case of a security cession, the *causa* may be provided for in an "obligationary agreement."[207] Similarly, in the case of a statutory hypothecation of a registered trademark, the security agreement may be called a "deed of security," and in the case of a notarial bond, it may be referred to as the "bond document."

It is important to note that the security agreement does not *per se* create a right of real security; rather, it creates personal rights and obligations which may result in a pledge if given the necessary effect.[208] Moreover, and importantly for this issue, the security agreement will generally also impose obligations on the debtor concerning what it may do in relation to the relevant property. In addition, it will also stipulate the circumstances under which the debtor will be regarded as having defaulted on its obligations, thereby entitling the creditor to enforce his rights of security.

6.1 Trademarks

6.1.1 Statutory Hypothecation

Following the entry of the endorsement on the trademark register, once a deed of security has been lodged (or filed), the hypothecation has the legal effect of a pledge of the trademark.[209] As indicated above, unlike the regulations covering the hypothecation of patents and designs, the Trade Marks Act expressly provides for a hypothecated trademark to be assigned, subject to the provision of written consent for such assignment from the creditor in whose favour the trademark has been

---

[206] Brits (2016), pp. 142, 185 and 227.

[207] Scott (1991), pp. 8–9.

[208] It is, of course, possible that an obligationary agreement may also constitute a cession; see Scott (1991), p. 8.

[209] Section 41(4) of the Trade Marks Act.

hypothecated.[210] In addition—and, once again, in contrast to the situation with the hypothecation of patents and designs—there is no express statutory prohibition on the granting of licences by the proprietor of a registered trademark that has been hypothecated. Thus, subject to the provisions of the security agreement, the registered owner of a hypothecated trademark appears to be free to license or use the trademark.

Although a statutory hypothecation is stated as having the effect of a pledge, it is not clear to what extent the creditor would be considered to be in possession of the registered trademark (that is, whether such hypothecation amounts to a non-possessory pledge). The reason why this is important is because in case of the pledge of a corporeal movable asset, the pledgee has a duty to take reasonable care of the pledged property and is entitled to recover any reasonable costs relating to such care from the pledgor.[211] To avoid uncertainty concerning any of the legal and practical aspects, such as the debtor's use of the IP rights or the creditor's control and disposition (i.e. foreclosure) of the rights, it is advisable to regulate these matters by way of contractual stipulations. There may be particular issues which need to be addressed. For example, the parties may wish to regulate the future licensing of the IP rights and the payments made by licensees of the IP rights during the subsistence of the hypothecation.

6.1.2 Security Cession

As indicated in Sect. 4.2, the principles of the law of pledge are also applicable to security cessions, as far as is possible. However, due to the incorporeal nature of IP rights and the fact that the exact nature of the creditor's "possession" of those rights is unclear, the parties may wish to add contractual stipulations to address possible uncertainties concerning the practical aspects of both the debtor's use of the IP rights and the creditor's control and disposition (i.e., foreclosure) of the rights. There may be particular issues that may be advisable to address.[212] For example, the parties may wish to regulate the debtor's use of the IP rights, arrangements concerning future licensing of the IP rights, and payments made by licensees of the IP rights during the subsistence of the security cession.

Out-and-Out Cession

Importantly, if the security arrangement is structured as an out-and-out cession of the IP rights, rather than a security cession, the relevant IP rights will be acquired by the creditor,[213] subject to the debtor's personal right to require that the creditor transfer

[210]Section 41(5).

[211]Brits (2016), pp. 142 and 145–146.

[212]Brits (2016), pp. 150, 192, 296–297, 301, 327–328 and 330–331.

[213]Brits (2016), pp. 274 and 277.

the rights back to the debtor after the debtor has discharged its obligation to the creditor.[214] In other words, in the case of an out-and-out cession, the IP rights belong to the creditor and the debtor will have no right to use the IP rights. From a commercial perspective, this is, of course, fundamentally problematic, as the debtor generally needs to use the IP rights. Thus, the security agreement must regulate the debtor's right to use the IP rights and must put limits on what the creditor can do with the IP rights before any default. For example, the debtor would probably want to prohibit the creditor from granting third parties any rights to the IP rights without the debtor's consent.

6.1.3 Notarial Bond

As indicated in Sect. 4.3, both a general notarial bond and a special notarial bond over incorporeals confer no immediate right of real security to the bondholder. A real security right is only obtained when the bondholder gains control over the relevant property through a perfection (or attachment) court order.[215] In fact, in the case of a general notarial bond, the bond covers movables that the debtor may own or have acquired at the time the security is enforced.[216] Thus, it means that the pool of movable assets may change, as the debtor may alienate property that was covered by the bond prior to perfection.[217] If the creditor wants to restrict the ability of the debtor to alienate specific property, it will have to do so by imposing a contractual obligation to that effect on the debtor in the security agreement.[218] However, as there is no specific legislative provision for a special notarial bond over incorporeals, it is not clear what the effect of such a bond would be prior to perfection. It is unclear whether the law will prohibit the debtor from alienating the specific IP rights that are covered by the bond.

Accordingly, the security agreement relating to a general notarial bond or a special notarial bond should regulate the debtor's rights to use the IP rights and limit what the creditor can do with the IP rights before any default by the debtor. For example, the creditor would want to prohibit the debtor from alienating the IP rights to third parties without the creditor's consent.

[214] Brits (2016), pp. 279–280, 287 and 289.

[215] Brits (2016), pp. 231–232.

[216] Brits (2016), pp. 194 and 199–200.

[217] Brits (2016), p. 201.

[218] Brits (2016), pp. 201–202.

6.2 *Patents*

6.2.1 Statutory Hypothecation

As indicated in Sect. 3.2.2 'Statutory Hypothecation', although the Patents Act does not indicate the nature of the security right that is created by a statutory hypothecation, it is likely in the nature of a pledge. Section 60(6) of the Patents Act strengthens the legal control of the pledgee as it provides that once a hypothecation has been entered in the register, the patentee or patent applicant is prohibited from alienating or encumbering the hypothecated patent or application for the patent, or from granting any licences under the patent in question. Unlike the Designs Act, the Patents Act does not expressly deal with the granting of compulsory licences pursuant to section 56 of the Act. In the absence of an express statutory prohibition, it is submitted that the hypothecation of a patent does not prevent a compulsory licence from being granted pursuant to section 56 of the Patents Act.[219]

For the same reasons that were stated in relation to trademarks,[220] to avoid any uncertainty regarding any of the legal and practical aspects concerning the nature of a pledge, it is advisable to regulate matters by way of contractual stipulations in the security agreement.

6.2.2 Security Cession

The position is the same as that set out in Sect. 6.1.2.

6.2.3 Notarial Bond

The position is the same as that set out in Sect. 6.1.3.

6.3 *Registered Designs*

6.3.1 Statutory Hypothecation

As indicated in Sect. 3.3.2 'Statutory Hypothecation', although the Designs Act does not indicate the nature of the security right that is created by a statutory hypothecation, it likely in the nature of a pledge. Section 30(6) of the Designs Act strengthens the legal control of the pledgee as it provides that once a hypothecation has been entered in the register, the registered proprietor of the design or applicant for the

[219] Du Plessis et al. (2012), p. 368.

[220] See Sect. 6.1.1.

design is prohibited from alienating or encumbering the hypothecated design or application for the design, or from granting any licences under such registration. However, the Designs Act expressly provides that the aforementioned prohibition on the granting of licences does not apply to the granting of compulsory licences pursuant to section 21 of the Act.

For the same reasons that were stated in relation to trademarks,[221] to avoid any uncertainty regarding any of the legal and practical aspects concerning the nature of a pledge, it is advisable to regulate matters by way of contractual stipulations in the security agreement.

6.3.2 Security Cession

The position is the same as that set out in Sect. 6.1.2.

6.3.3 Notarial Bond

The position is the same as that set out in Sect. 6.1.3.

6.4 Copyright

6.4.1 Statutory Hypothecation

As stated in Sect. 3.4.2 'Statutory Hypothecation', there is no statutory provision for the hypothecation of, or creation of a security right in, copyright.

6.4.2 Security Cession

The position is the same as that set out in Sect. 6.1.2.

6.4.3 Notarial Bond

The position is the same as that set out in Sect. 6.1.3.

[221]See Sect. 6.1.1.

6.5 Plant Breeders' Rights

6.5.1 Statutory Hypothecation

As stated under Sect. 3.5.2 'Statutory Hypothecation', there is no statutory provision for the hypothecation of, or creation of a security right in, a plant breeder's right.

6.5.2 Security Cession

The position is the same as that set out in Sect. 6.1.2.

6.5.3 Notarial Bond

The position is the same as that set out in Sect. 6.1.3.

7 Enforcement

Given the fact that the various forms of real security discussed either constitute pledges, or will result in a pledge if perfection occurs prior to the insolvency of the debtor, it is only necessary to consider the realization of pledged property (as opposed to any other form of real security). Prior to insolvency, enforcement generally involves two actions: first, the obtaining of a court order establishing the indebtedness of the pledgor (or debtor); and second, the realization of the pledged property. In the case of a non-possessory pledge (as would be the case with a security cession or either of the two notarial bonds that may be used in respect of IP rights), control over the property will have to be established via an attachment (or perfection) order and will be realized by the sheriff following the execution of the court order.[222]

Even in cases where the relevant statute provides that the IP rights may be hypothecated and that such hypothecation functions as a pledge, it is not clear whether this constitutes a genuine example of a non-possessory pledge,[223] and, therefore, to what extent the creditor can be considered to be in possession of the relevant IP rights, such as, registered trademarks. Thus, until the legal position has

[222]Brits (2016), pp. 159–160.

[223]A specific notarial bond over corporeal movables that is in accordance with the Security by Means of Movable Property Act 57 of 1993 is a non-possessory pledge. The bondholder does not have to perfect the bond as it already has a real right of security. The bondholder can simply gain control over the property covered by the bond pursuant to the provisions in the bond instrument that detail the circumstances in which he may do so (i.e. pursuant to the perfection clause); then, he can realize the property in accordance with the terms stipulated (i.e. in accordance with the execution clause). See Brits (2016), pp. 260–261.

been clarified, it is advisable for the creditor to establish control over the hypothecated IP rights via an attachment (or perfection) order.

Generally, execution (that is, the realization of the pledged property) can only be effected pursuant to a court order.[224] Whether a pledgee is entitled to realize the property without a court order will depend on two things: first, whether there is a contractual entitlement in the security agreement allowing the pledgee to do so; and second, whether the pledgor has objected to the sale of the property.[225] There are two types of contractual provisions through which pledgees seek to avoid having to ask for court approval for a sale in execution of the pledged property: a right of summary execution (*parate executie*) and a quasi-conditional sale.[226] These contractual provisions do not offend against the prohibition of forms of self-help remedies.[227] Unless otherwise agreed, the property must be sold by way of a public auction, to the highest bidder.[228]

A summary execution provision (*parate executie*) is a contractual stipulation giving the pledgee the right to sell the pledged property without a court order approving such an action.[229] Summary execution provisions are not *per se* unlawful. Their legality depends on their effect in each particular case. For example, reliance on such a provision would be unlawful in situations where the amount owing by the pledgor is in dispute, the pledgor is prevented from approaching the court, or the provision causes prejudice to the pledgor.[230] In case of summary execution, the pledgee acts as the pledgor's agent in effecting the sale to a third party.[231]

A contractual term providing for a quasi-conditional sale gives the pledgee an irrevocable right to acquire the pledged property at a fair value (or reasonable price) as determined at the time of acquisition (that is, after the pledgor's default).[232] The purchase price paid by pledgee will be set off against the amount owed by the pledgor.[233] The pledgee becomes the owner of the pledged property when this set-off takes place.[234]

If the pledgor is insolvent, the pledgee becomes a secured creditor in terms of the Insolvency Act due to the fact that a pledge falls within the definition of

[224]Brits (2016), p. 162.
[225]Brits (2016), p. 160.
[226]Brits (2016), pp. 162 and 166.
[227]Brits (2016), pp. 172–174.
[228]Brits (2016), p. 160.
[229]Brits (2016), pp. 162 and 170.
[230]Brits (2016), pp. 171 and 174.
[231]Brits (2016), pp. 163 and 177.
[232]Brits (2016), pp. 162, 166, 169 and 331.
[233]Brits (2016), p. 166.
[234]Brits (2016), p. 170.

"security."[235] Accordingly, the pledgee will be entitled to the proceeds from the sale of the pledged property once certain specified costs have been deducted.[236]

8 Typical Costs

8.1 Trademarks

8.1.1 Statutory Hypothecation

The legal fees charged by lawyers in respect of the drafting and finalization of the security agreement and ancillary documentation will be time-based. As a result, these costs will vary, depending on the particular issues that have to considered; at present, the costs of preparing the necessary documentation may range from ZAR 20,000 to ZAR 30,000.

The official fee for the registration of the hypothecation of a registered trademark is ZAR 150 for the first trademark and ZAR 26 for every subsequent registration. As far as professional fees that may be charged are concerned, they may be in the following ranges: ZAR 2500 to ZAR 3000 for the registration of the hypothecation of the first trademark, ZAR 1000 to ZAR 1500 for the registration of the hypothecation of the second to tenth trademarks, and ZAR 250 to ZAR 300 for the registration of the hypothecation of the eleventh trademark onwards.

8.1.2 Security Cession

As indicated in Sect. 8.1.1, the professional costs for the drafting and finalization of the security agreement and ancillary documentation may range from ZAR 20,000 to ZAR 30,000.

8.1.3 Notarial Bonds

The fees for notarial bonds are based on the amount of the secured debt and the value of the property secured. The office fees range from ZAR 392 (for capital amounts less that ZAR 150,000) and ZAR 6380 (for capital amounts greater than ZAR 30,000,000). For bonds securing an amount up to and including ZAR 200,000, the basic recommended legal fee is ZAR 1200; and for bonds securing an amount over ZAR 200,000, the basic fee is ZAR 1000. In addition, there is a fee that is payable on a sliding scale based on the value of the property. This is set out in Table 1 below:

---

[235] Section 2 of the Insolvency Act. See also Lubbe (2013), paras 406 and 430.

[236] See Sect. 4; Brits (2016), p. 161.

Table 1 Recommended legal fees

Value of property or bond	Recommended fee
ZAR 100,000 or less	ZAR 5000
Over ZAR 100,000, up to and including ZAR 500,000	ZAR 5000, plus ZAR 770 per ZAR 50,000 or part thereof above that
Over ZAR 500,000, up to and including ZAR 1,000,000	ZAR 11,600 for the first ZAR 500,000, plus ZAR 1540 per ZAR 100,000 or part thereof above that
Over ZAR 1,000,000, up to and including ZAR 5,000,000	ZAR 18,860 for the first ZAR 1,000,000, plus ZAR 1540 per ZAR 200,000 or part thereof above that over ZAR 5,000,000
Over ZAR 5,000,000	ZAR 49,660 for the first ZAR 5,000,000, plus ZAR 1925 per ZAR 500,000 or part thereof above that

8.2 *Patents*

8.2.1 Statutory Hypothecation

As indicated in Sect. 8.1.1, the professional costs for the drafting and finalization of the security documentation may range from ZAR 20,000 to ZAR 30,000.

The official fee for the registration of the hypothecation of a patent is ZAR 70 for the first patent and ZAR 26 for every subsequent registration. The professional fees that may be charged for the registration of hypothecations are as set out in Sect. 8.1.1.

8.2.2 Security Cession

As indicated in Sect. 8.1.1, the professional costs for the drafting and finalization of the security documentation may range from ZAR 20,000 to ZAR 30,000.

8.2.3 Notarial Bonds

The recommended fees for notarial bonds are as indicated in Sect. 8.1.3.

8.3 *Registered Designs*

8.3.1 Statutory Hypothecation

As indicated in Sect. 8.1.1, the professional costs for the drafting and finalization of the security documentation may range from ZAR 20,000 to ZAR 30,000.

The official fee for the registration of the hypothecation of a registered design is ZAR 75 for the first registered design and ZAR 24 for every subsequent registration.

The professional fees that may be charged for the registration of hypothecations are as set out in Sect. 8.1.1.

8.3.2 Security Cession

As indicated in Sect. 8.1.1, the professional costs for the drafting and finalization of the security documentation may range from ZAR 20,000 to ZAR 30,000.

8.3.3 Notarial Bonds

The recommended fees for notarial bonds are as indicated in Sect. 8.1.3.

8.4 Copyright

8.4.1 Statutory Hypothecation

As already noted in Sect. 2.4, there is no provision for the statutory hypothecation of copyright.

8.4.2 Security Cession

As indicated in Sect. 8.1.1, the professional costs for the drafting and finalization of the security documentation may range from ZAR 20,000 to ZAR 30,000.

8.4.3 Notarial bonds

The recommended fees for notarial bonds are as indicated in Sect. 8.1.3.

8.5 Plant Breeders' Rights

8.5.1 Statutory Hypothecation

As already noted in Sect. 2.5, there is no provision for the statutory hypothecation of a plant breeder's right.

8.5.2 Security Cession

As indicated in Sect. 8.1.1, the professional costs for the drafting and finalization of the security documentation may range from ZAR 20,000 to ZAR 30,000.

8.5.3 Notarial Bonds

The recommended fees for notarial bonds are as indicated in Sect. 8.1.3.

9 Practical Usefulness

The use of IP rights—namely, patents, registered designs, copyright, and plant breeders' rights—as a form of real security is at present far from being a common commercial or financing practice. The case of a creditor being granted or seeking a security right over specific IP rights is particularly uncommon. If IP rights are provided as a form of real security, it is likely that this will be as part of a more general right granted by the debtor, such as, a security cession or notarial bond. Nevertheless, the number of hypothecations of registered trademarks is increasing.

It is very unlikely that a borrower will be able to obtain credit on better terms by granting a security right over its IP rights, especially if that borrower is an SME.

10 Legal and/or Practical Difficulties

As indicated above, there is no express statutory provision for the creation of a right of real security over copyright or a plant breeder's right. This is a situation which needs to be specifically addressed.

Besides the fact that IP rights are probably simply overlooked as assets that could serve as security for financing purposes, there are practical difficulties in determining their value, both at the time they are offered as security and when they must be realized under the security right.

It is important to note that if a right of real security over IP rights is created by a South African resident in favour of a non-resident, this requires Treasury approval under the Currency and Exchanges Act 9 of 1933 (the "CEA"). Regulation 10(1)(c), in particular, of the Exchange Control Regulations[237] (the "Regulations") issued under the CEA prohibits the export of "capital" by a resident to a non-resident without Treasury approval. With effect from June 8, 2012, the Regulations were amended to provide that "capital" for the purposes of Regulation 10(1)(c) includes

[237]GN R1111 in *GG* 123 of December 1, 1961 (as amended).

any IP right, whether registered or unregistered (see reg 10(4)).[238] In addition, the scope of transactions which could constitute an "export" from South Africa has been extended well beyond the assignment or transfer of IP rights to a non-resident and includes the creation of a security right over any IP rights in favour of a non-resident.

11 Law Reform

Currently, there are no proposals to reform the law relating to security over IP rights in South Africa.

References

Brits R (2016) Real security law. Juta, Cape Town
Burrell TR (2016) Burrell's South African patent and design law. LexisNexis, South Africa
Dean OH, Dyer A (2014) Dean & Dyer: introduction to intellectual property law. Oxford University Press, Oxford
Dean O, Karjiker S (2015) Handbook of South African copyright law. Juta, Cape Town
Du Plessis ED, Kotzé GS, Brown SB, Moerdijk M, Thompson K-M, Pienaar J, Garnett N, Phaswana N (2012) Adams & Adams: practitioner's guide to intellectual property law. LexisNexis, South Africa
Lubbe GF (2008) Mortgage and pledge. In: Joubert W, Kuhne M (eds) Law of South Africa. LexisNexis, South Africa
Lubbe GF (2013) Cession. In: Joubert W, Kuhne M (eds) Law of South Africa. LexisNexis, South Africa
Nagel C (2011) Commercial law, 4th edn. LexisNexis, South Africa
Scott S (1991) The law of cession, 2nd edn. Juta, Cape Town
Sharrock R (2007) Business transactions law, 7th edn. Juta, Cape Town
Sharrock R, Smith AD, Van der Linde K (2012) Hockly's insolvency law, 9th edn. Juta, Cape Town
Webster C, Morley G (2015) Webster and Page: South African law of trade marks, 4th edn. LexisNexis, South Africa

[238] GN R445 in *GG* 35430 of June 8, 2012.

Security Rights in Intellectual Property in Spain

Iván Heredia Cervantes

Abstract With a few exceptions, Spanish law does not have specific rules relating to securities over IP and most of the issues concerning attachment and perfection requirements; priorities; and enforcement proceedings (both in an insolvency scenario and outside of one) must be resolved using the general rules relating to security rights. A chattel mortgage is the only type of security interest over IP rights that is explicitly recognized by Spanish law. Accordingly, the requirements for making a security interest effective against third parties; the priority to be given to the security interest; and the enforcement of this security interest are similar to those applied to the rest of the chattel covered by the mortgage, although some additional requirements must be met. The effectiveness of the security right against third parties and the priority of the secured creditor over competing claimants is conditional upon the registration of the mortgage in the Registry of Movable Goods. Registration in "special registries" (i.e. the Intellectual Property Registry and the Spanish Patent and Trademark Office) is merely for informative purposes. Outside of insolvency, enforcement of the mortgage must be undertaken through the public sale of the mortgaged rights, which is normally implemented through an auction procedure that is supervised by a judge or (subject to strict conditions) by a notary public. This chapter surveys and analyses the regulation of security interests over IP rights in Spain; identifies the main challenges posed by the current legislation; and attempts to better understand why IP rights are not seen as suitable collateral to be used within the framework of secured transactions.

This chapter has been produced within the framework of the research project "Financiación internacional: función de las garantías mobiliarias" (DER2017-85585-P).

I. H. Cervantes (✉)
Universidad Autónoma de Madrid, Madrid, Spain
e-mail: ivan.heredia@uam.es

E.-M. Kieninger (ed.), *Security Rights in Intellectual Property*, Ius Comparatum – Global Studies in Comparative Law 45,
https://doi.org/10.1007/978-3-030-44191-3_25

1 IP Rights in Spain: A Short Overview

Under Spanish law, the term "intellectual property" comprises two different concepts: industrial property rights (e.g. patents, commercial names, and trademarks) and so-called "intellectual property rights" (copyrights and neighbouring rights). In the current work, both terms will be distinguished insofar as they are governed by different legal frameworks and, although there are similarities in the requirements for the creation of security interests over each kind of right, there are also some relevant differences. In some cases, however, the term "IP rights" will be used to encompass both kinds of rights.

The Spanish national regulations on IP rights are set out in specific rules for each right:

> Consolidated Text of the Law on Intellectual Property, Regularizing, Clarifying and Harmonizing the Applicable Statutory Provisions (approved by Royal Legislative Decree No. 1/1996 of April 12, 1996, and amended to Royal Decree-Law No. 2/2018 of April 13, 2018) (IPA); Law No 24/2015 of July 24, 2015, on Patents; (PA)[1]; Law No. 17/2001 of December 7, 2001, on Trademarks (as amended up to Royal Decree-Law No. 23/2018 of December 21, 2018 (TMA); Law No. 20/2003 of July 7, 2003, on Legal Protection of Industrial Designs (as amended up to Law No. 24/2015 of July 24, 2015, on Patents) (IDA); Law No. 11/1988 of May 3, 1988, on the Legal Protection of Topographies of Semiconductor Products (as amended up to Law No. 39/2010 of December 22, 2010) and Law No. 3/2000 of January 7, 2000, governing the Protection of Plant Varieties (as amended up to Law No. 3/2002 of March 12, 2002) (2002); In addition, as Spain is a European Union Member State, the EU rules on IP rights are in force in Spain and internal rules have incorporated the provisions contained in the European regulations.[2] Finally, the major international conventions on IP rights are also in force in Spain and internal rules have been adapted to them.

The requirements for the creation of the different IP rights regulated by Spanish law and the duration of these rights depend on the asset to be protected.

As regards intellectual property rights, Spanish law distinguishes between moral and economic rights. Moral rights are recognized for authors and performers and are inalienable, do not expire, cannot be waived, cannot be encumbered, and accompany the author or performer throughout his life. Moral rights include the right to recognition of the authorship of the work or recognition of the artist's name in their performances, as well as the right to demand respect for the integrity of the work or performance and to object to any alteration. Economic rights include rights related to the exploitation of the work and compensatory rights (for instance, compensatory remuneration rights for private copies). The exploitation rights

---

[1]The Spanish Official State Gazette published the text of the Act on July 25, 2015, but it has only been in force since April 1, 2017.

[2]Note, however, that Spain decided not to join the European Unitary Patent and Unified Patent Court System because of the exclusion of Spanish as an official language of the system.

conferred on authors last for the life of the author and for 70 years after his death.[3] There are other terms for moral rights as well as rights for the works of authors who died before 1987.[4]

The General Registry of Intellectual Property is the public body responsible for the registration of copyright. However, registration in this registry is voluntary. Intellectual property rights are protected in Spain from the very moment of their creation and the holders receive the full protection of the law from that time without having to comply with any formality, including registration in the Intellectual Property Register, although it is convenient to indicate the reservation of rights and use the © symbol in the case of a work or service or, in the case of phonograms, the ® symbol.

According to the IPA, Spanish intellectual property rules protect literary, artistic, or scientific creations expressed in any medium, such as books, writings, paintings, musical compositions, plays, audiovisual works, sculptures, choreography, drawings, models, maps, photographs, computer programs, and databases. They also protect artistic interpretations, phonograms, audiovisual recordings, and broadcasts. However, mutually exclusive ideas, procedures, methods of operation, and mathematical concepts are excluded from the protection of Spanish law (although the expression thereof is not). Legal or regulatory provisions and their corresponding projects; court decisions; and the acts of public bodies, as well as translations of such texts, are also excluded.

The Spanish Patent and Trademark Office (*Oficina Española de Patentes y Marcas*) is the authority that registers recordable industrial property rights. In contrast to the situation with intellectual property rights, the registration of inventions, plant varieties, and designs with the Spanish Patent and Trademark Office is constitutive in nature. As for trademarks, although Article 2.1 TMA provides for the general principle of the constitutive nature of registration, it is assumed that Spanish law has a mixed system that combines this principle with the principle of trademark notoriety.[5]

According to Spanish law, an invention is patentable when it is new, involves an inventive activity, and is capable of industrial application.[6] Spanish law does not consider "inventive activity" to exist for and excludes from patent protection: (a) discoveries, scientific theories, or mathematical methods; (b) literary, dramatic,

[3]Article 26 IPA. There are specific calculation rules for posthumous, pseudonymous, and anonymous works (Article 27); works of joint authorship and collective works (Article 28); and works published in parts (Article 29).

[4]Transitional Disposition 4 IPA. The exploitation rights conferred on performers run for 50 years starting from January 1 of the year following that of the performance.

[5]The owner of an unregistered well-known mark has the right to: file (a) an opposition to an application for registration of a sign that is identical or confusingly similar to its own, for identical or similar goods; (b) a civil action to invalidate an identical or similar trademark registered for identical or similar goods; and (c) a civil action against the unauthorised use of the unregistered mark for identical or similar goods.

[6]Article 4.1 PA.

musical, or artistic works or any other aesthetic creations whatsoever; (c) computer programs or schemes, rules, or methods for performing a mental act, playing a game, or doing business; and (d) presentations of information.[7] In addition, the following are not considered patentable: (a) an invention whose publication or exploitation would be contrary to public order or morality (processes for cloning human beings, processes for modifying the germline genetic identity of human beings, uses of human embryos for industrial or commercial purposes, processes for modifying the genetic identity of animals that are likely to cause them suffering without any substantial medical benefit to man or animal, as well as any animal resulting from such processes); (b) any variety of animal or plant or any essentially biological process for the production of animals or plants—this does not include micro-biological or other technical processes or the products of such processes; (c) the human body in its various stages of formation and development and the simple discovery of one of its aspects, including the sequence or partial sequence of a gene; and (d) the simple discovery of a DNA sequence without indication of a function.[8]

The protection of patent rights lasts for 20 years, starting from the moment the patent application is filed. The period of protection cannot be extended.[9]

As regards trademarks, the legal requirement for registration is that the mark is capable of graphical representation and is distinctive in character.[10] Spanish law distinguishes between absolute and (upon opposition) relative grounds for refusing the registration of the mark.

The first group contains[11]: (a) signs which do not comply with the definition of a trademark; (b) signs devoid of any distinctive character; (c) signs consisting exclusively of words or signs used in trade to designate the price, quantity, value, geographical origin, production date, or other characteristics of the good or service; (d) signs consisting exclusively of signs or indications which have become customary in everyday language or in the bona fide and established practices of the trade; (e) signs consisting exclusively of the form imposed by the nature of the good itself or by the form of the good necessary to obtain a technical result, or by the form which gives substantial value to the good; (f) signs contrary to the law, public policy, or morals; (g) signs which may mislead the consumer, for instance, as to the nature, quality, or geographical origin of the good or service; (h) signs used to identify wines or spirits and which contain or consist of indications of geographical origin which identify wines or spirits that do not have such an origin; (i) coats of arms, emblems, flags, and denominations of the Spanish state or the Spanish regions, provinces, or localities, as well as signs excluded from protection by virtue of Article 6 *ter* of the Paris Convention or by public interest, unless the applicant has been duly authorized by the respective authorities to use and register such signs as a trademark.

---

[7]Article 4.4 PA.

[8]Article 5 PA.

[9]Article 58 PA.

[10]Article 4 TMA.

[11]Article 5 TMA.

The second group includes: (a) signs that are identical to an earlier trademark, where registration is sought for identical goods or services, and signs that are identical or similar to an earlier trademark, where registration is sought for identical or similar goods or services and there is a likelihood of confusion on the part of the public, including the likelihood of association with the earlier trademark[12]; (b) signs that are identical to an earlier trade name designating activities which are identical to the goods or services for which registration is sought, and signs that are identical or similar to an earlier trade name, where registration is sought for goods or services identical or similar to the activities designated by the earlier trade name and there is a likelihood of confusion on the part of the public, including the likelihood of association with the earlier trade name[13]; and (c) signs that conflict with identical or similar earlier registered trademarks and trade names that are famous in Spain.[14] Additional grounds for denying registration are provided in case of rights related to the name or surname of a person; copyright; application for a protected designation of origin or a protected geographical indication; and unauthorized registration by an agent or representative.[15]

The protection of trademarks starts on the date of the publication of the grant by the Spanish Patent and Trademark Office and lasts 10 years, although it may be renewed in perpetuity for 10-year periods.

2 Categories of Security Rights

A chattel mortgage ("*hipoteca mobiliaria*") is the only type of security interest over intellectual and industrial property that is explicitly recognized by Spanish law art. 12 Law of December 16, 1954, on Chattel Mortgage and Non-dispossessory Pledges—henceforth CMNDPA—and art. 53 IPA). In a chattel mortgage, the debtor mortgages certain types of assets owned by him in favour of the creditor to secure his own obligations or those of a third party. It is true that the wording of the specific rules on industrial property (Art 82 PA, Art. 46.2 TMA, and Art. 59.1 IDA) looks to be much more flexible and states that industrial property may "be given in security" and refers to chattel mortgages only by way of example. However, the dominant interpretation is that, in such cases, a chattel mortgage is the only admissible kind of security interest.[16] As with all other mortgages, Spanish law requires the precise

[12]See Article 6.1 TMA. The term "earlier trademark" is defined in Article 6.2 TMA.

[13]See Article 7 TMA.

[14]See Article 8 TMA.

[15]See Articles 9–10 TMA.

[16]See Lobato (2007), p. 789; Martín (2008), p. 785.

identification of the collateral, parties, and secured credit for mortgages of IP rights.[17]

Chattel mortgages of intellectual property rights can only be created with alienable rights which are transferable *inter vivos*.[18] This includes exploitation rights (e.g. the right of reproduction, right of distribution, right of communication, right of transformation, right of making a collection, etc.) and the other patrimonial rights.[19] It excludes moral rights. There is also a specific and exhaustive provision on mortgages of cinematographic works in Royal Decree 3837/1970 regarding chattel mortgages of cinematographic works.[20]

According to Article 46.2 CMNDPA, intellectual property rights can be mortgaged by the author, the owner of the rights as a result of a mortis causa transfer, or the (exclusive or partial) assignee of the rights. In this last case, it is required that the assignee have the power to dispose of the rights. Spanish law does not distinguish between main and accessory intellectual property rights. Consequently, each intellectual property right must be mortgaged separately and the mortgage of one right does not imply the mortgage of the rest of the rights.[21]

The parties can agree that the creditor shall appropriate any fruits or proceeds arising out of the encumbered right as they are generated ("*anticresis*"). In this case, the creditor would have to allocate the sums received to the payment of the mortgaged credit, with consequent reduction of the debt.[22,23] Although the CMNDPA does not include a detailed provision on such agreements ("*pacto*

[17]Article 13 CMNDPA. In the case of intellectual property rights, this identification may consist of the enumeration of the specific rights which will be encumbered or of a simple statement that all of the exploitation rights contained in Article 17 and following LOPI are encumbered. Article 43.2 IPA includes a "delimitation rule" of the mortgaged rights for cases where the parties did not provide this identification. It is possible to mortgage several of the exploitation rights of a single work or of several works. In the latter case, it is necessary to identify the share of the debt that corresponds to the exploitation rights of each encumbered right.

[18]Article 46.1 CMNDPA.

[19]Although according to Article 1 CMNDPA the constitution of mortgages of patrimonial rights that are not exploitation rights is allowed, in practice, this possibility involves serious uncertainties. First, it is doubtful whether a compensatory remuneration right for private copies can be mortgaged. Some authors rule out this possibility for these cases, and as the collateral is a receivable, accordingly the rules on pledges of receivables should be applied. See Marco (2017), Art. 53, pp. 958–959. Other scholars consider that even in these cases, the mortgage extends to the receivables; see Carrasco (2015), Ch. 24, 19. Secondly, some scholars reject the constitution of mortgages of the resale right with the argument that, according to Article 6 Ley 3/2008, the resale right can only be transmitted by means of mortis causa acts; see Carrasco (2015), Ch. 24, 19.

[20]See in detail Cobos (1975), pp. 9–64; Diéguez (2006), pp. 123–168.

[21]Article 46.4 CMNDPA and Articles 23 and 57.2 IPA. See Jiménez (2018), p. 59.

[22]Article 49 CMNDPA.

[23]The economic justification for such an agreement is found in the gradual reduction of the intellectual property right's value.

anticrético"), an exhaustive provision can be found in Royal Decree 3837/1970,[24] which can be extended to mortgages of other intellectual property rights.

As for industrial property rights, one can create chattel mortgages of all of the rights protected by the legislation on industrial property (e.g. patents, trademarks, trade names, industrial designs, topographies of semiconductor products, plant varieties, etc.).[25] The mortgage extends to rights arising out of additions to, modification of, or improvement of the registered rights.[26] Spanish law allows the creation of chattel mortgages not only of the right itself, but also of the application of the right. It is only possible to mortgage industrial property rights that can be disposed of separately (Art. 1 CMNDPA). This excludes collective marks, for instance.[27] In contrast, and in spite of the difficulty in determining the mortgage responsibility, a chattel mortgage can secure a pooled debt against several debtors or, conversely, a pooled credit belonging to several creditors.[28] According to Article 45.2 CMNDPA, non-patrimonial and non-transferable rights cannot be mortgaged.

In contrast to intellectual property rights, where the collateral is not the ownership of the work but the patrimonial rights over it, when it came to industrial property rights, it was traditionally assumed that the mortgage was created over the ownership of the very same right (i.e. patent, trademark, etc.). Accordingly, scholars thought that it was not possible to mortgage the right to use or to exploit the industrial property right separately (art. 1857 CC. and 1.II CMNDPA) and that a licensee could not mortgage his right. However, a contested recent reform of CMNDPA prevents one from maintaining such view. According to the new version of Article 45.2 CMNDPA, a mortgage can be created both by the owner and by a (exclusive or non-exclusive) licensee who has the power to dispose of the right or of some of the privileges derived from the right.[29]

3 Attachment and Perfection Requirements

The typical structure of secured transactions over IP rights in Spain involves financing transactions that include IP rights (particularly industrial property rights in combination with securities and other movable assets (e.g. pledges of receivables, shares, etc.). However, it must be kept in mind that, as stated above, floating charges are not regulated by Spanish law and Spanish law does not provide for a security right over all of the assets of a company.

[24]See Articles 13–21.

[25]Article 45.1 CMNDPA.

[26]Article 45.4 CMNDPA.

[27]Article 62.4 MA. See also Carrasco (2015), Ch. 24, 21.

[28]See Lobato (2007), p. 789.

[29]See Jiménez (2018) p. 36; Martín (2015), p. 352.

The chattel mortgage of intellectual and industrial property rights must be recorded in writing and in the corresponding public deed issued by a notary (art. 3.1 and 47 CMNDPA). A public deed is an essential requirement and non-compliance entails the nullity of the contract. According to Article 47 CMNDPA, in addition to the general requirements for chattel mortgages, in the case of mortgages of intellectual or industrial property rights, the public deed must include the following specific information:

1. Complete information about the mortgaged rights;
2. The date or registration, renewal, restoration, or extension number in the relevant special register (i.e. Intellectual Property Registry or Spanish Patent and Trademark Office);
3. Licences, authorizations, and concessions granted by the holder of the right to a third party;
4. Certification of being up-to date with the canon payment (if any).[30]

In order for a chattel mortgage to be effective against third parties, public deeds must be registered in the Registry of Movable Goods (Sect. 4). In cases where all or several of the exploitation rights are mortgaged, an independent document is not required for each one.[31] The Registry of Movable Goods evaluates ("*califica*") the public deed in order to check whether it fulfills the legal requirements for registration. If the registry finds that the public deed has rectifiable defects, the registration is suspended until such defects are corrected. The term fixed for the evaluation of the public deed is 15 days from the date of filing for registration.

For mortgages of intellectual property rights, although, as stated above,[32] registration in the Intellectual Property Registry is not required for the existence and protection of such rights, the holder will have to register his rights in this registry prior to creating the mortgage.[33] It must be kept in mind that the record of the mortgage in the Registry of Movable Goods does not have constitutive or third-party effects when the mortgagor is not the true owner of the mortgaged right ("*hipoteca a non domino*"). The Registry of Movable Goods is not an entitlements registry; rather, it is a charges registry and accordingly it does not guarantee the entitlement of the mortgagor to the mortgaged right.[34]

Once the mortgage has been registered in the Registry of Movable Goods, either the Intellectual Property Registry or the Spanish Patent and Trademark Office must

[30]According to Article 8 Royal Decree 3837/1970, in the case of the chattel mortgage of cinematographic works, the public deed must also include additional information to help in identifying the works (e.g. title, footage, the name of the director and the screenwriter, etc.).

[31]Carrasco (2015), Ch. 24, 19.

[32]See Sect. 1.

[33]Article 46.3 CMNDPA.

[34]See Rodríguez (2005), pp. 126–127; Pau (1997), pp. 1770–1771. As for the specific case of the chattel mortgage of cinematographic works, legal scholars consider that the mortgagor must have the right to dispose of the negative, the internegative, or the copy. See Marco (2017), p. 960.

be notified, so that it is registered in the relevant special registry.[35] As mentioned above, the effectiveness of the security right against third parties and the priority of the secured creditor over competing claimants is conditional upon registration of the mortgage in the Registry of Movable Goods. Registration in these special registries does not have constitutive purposes, merely informative ones.[36]

4 Priorities

4.1 Insolvency Scenario

The Spanish Insolvency Act (hereinafter "IA") does not expressly regulate the effect of insolvency on mortgages of IP rights and the general insolvency rules relating to security rights within the framework of insolvency proceedings must be applied.[37]

According to Spanish law, mortgage creditors are considered "specially privileged creditors" (*"acreedores con privilegio especial"*).[38] In broad terms, specially privileged credits are those secured by a specific asset or right and are senior rights as regards the proceeds obtained from the foreclosure of the asset. If the value of the asset is not sufficient to satisfy the credit, the remaining amount shall be paid pro rata with the ordinary credits.[39] In other words, a secured creditor, while preserving his full claim against the rest of the assets of the debtor, will have a privileged right enforceable against the relevant asset. However, during the stay, in some specific cases the insolvency administrator may serve notice on the mortgage creditor that the payment of his claims shall be settled from the assets of the estate without foreclosing on the secured rights.[40]

---

[35]Articles 76.2 CMNDPA, 26 RHMPSD, 46.3 TMA and 82.7 PA.

[36]Although Article 46.3 TMA provides that "*The legal acts envisaged in the previous paragraph shall be binding on third parties acting in good faith only after entry in the Register of Trademarks*", nevertheless, a considerable number of scholars and some judgments (Supreme Court Judgment of 6 June 2007) also think that the moment at which the mortgage becomes effective erga omnes is upon registration in the Registry of Movable Goods.

[37]Due to its indefeasible nature, patrimonial rights over Intellectual Property rights cannot be included within the insolvency estate in cases where the insolvency debtor is the author. However, such rights can be included within the estate when they have previously encumbered by a chattel mortgage See Carbajo (2009), p. 356.

[38]Article 90 Insolvency Act.

[39]Article 157.2 Insolvency Act.

[40]Article 155.2 Insolvency Act.

4.2 *Non-Insolvency Scenario*

Registration of the mortgage in the Registry of Movable Goods implies that a subsequent transfer of the encumbered asset will not affect the creditor. According to the "*prior in tempore, potior in iure*" principle, a better or higher ranking of the mortgage is directly linked to an earlier date of registration. In other words, the mortgage is binding on any third party who buys or registers a new burden or encumbrance on the mortgaged asset. Registration gives priority over the rest of the creditors of the debtor for the collection of his debt up to the value of the encumbered asset and the right to enforce the relevant security in case of default by the debtor, which implies the right to be reimbursed with the amount obtained through the different enforcement proceedings described below.[41]

5 Enterprise Charges

Although there are several security interests seldom used in Spain that have some similarities with floating charges (e.g. the mortgage of industrial or business premises, including machinery, movable assets, and labour instruments in cases where an express agreement exists), Spanish law does not provide for a security right over all of the assets of a company. Floating charges are not regulated by Spanish law and the creation of a "floating" or "adjustable" encumbrance is not admitted, except in some cases relating to immovable property. According to Spanish law, the substitution of collateral from time to time will be considered a new security. It implies that the previous security must be cancelled and that the new guarantee must comply with the same requirements as the original. The only exception to this rule is Article 569.17 of the Catalonian Act 5/2006 of May 24, on in rem rights, which allows for the parties to agree to the substitution of all or part of the fungible assets given as collateral.

6 Mutual Rights and Obligations of Debtor/Grantor and Creditor

The owner of the encumbered right is obliged to maintain it. Accordingly, he cannot waive it, either expressly or implicitly (e.g. by not applying for the renewal; not paying the fees for trademarks and designs; or not paying the granting fees and annuities of patents and utility models, as the case may be), without the secured

[41] See Sect. 7.

creditor's authorization.[42] The CMNDPA provides for two means of safeguarding the creditor's rights against a possible waiver by the owner of the mortgaged right. First, Article 18 allows the creditor to request judicial administration of the encumbered assets in the event of depreciation of the encumbered rights. This implies that a judge must authorize any act made by the owner concerning the rights. Second, with the aim of preventing the right from expiring, Article 50 allows the mortgagee to request the right's renewal, prorogation, etc. and to pay the fees. The protection provided for in this article is developed from specific rules regulating mortgages over industrial property rights[43] and aimed at avoiding the negative consequences of the debtor's inactivity. According to Article 50 CMNDPA, the expiry of the right due to lack of renewal or of payment of the corresponding fees cannot be declared unless the mortgage creditor has previously been notified in order to allow him to carry out the payments or renewals. However, it must be kept in mind that in the case of intellectual property rights, nowadays Article 50 CMNDPA has a very limited scope, given that the end of the term of protection is the only reason for cancellation of the right. In addition, it must also be noted that the prohibition of waivers is very attenuated in the case of intellectual property rights as a result of the right of withdrawal contained in Article 14.6.1° IPA, which allows the author to withdraw his work from the market due to changes in his intellectual or moral convictions once he has paid compensation to the holders of the exploitation rights.

Spanish law forbids the total or partial assignment of the use of the encumbered rights or the exploitation of these rights without the authorization of the creditor. It is unclear whether violation of this prohibitive rule implies the nullity of the assignment or merely contractual liability and, if appropriate, the early maturity of the credit.[44]

In case of default of the obligation secured by the mortgage, the creditor may deem the obligation to have expired and realize it.[45] Furthermore, unless otherwise agreed, the creditor may also deem the secured obligation to have expired in those cases where the debtor does not pay the maintenance fees, does not exploit the patent for a period exceeding 6 months, or does not use the mark during 4 consecutive years.[46]

Unless otherwise agreed, the creditor cannot bring legal actions intended to defend the encumbered rights against third parties (particularly infringement actions). The right to exercise such actions corresponds exclusively to the owner[47] and, in the case of patent rights, to the exclusive licensee.[48]

---

[42] Article 48.1 CMNDPA.

[43] Article 109.4 PA, Article 55.2 TMA, and Article 73.2 IDA.

[44] The doctrinal debate on this question is thoroughly explained in Rodríguez (2005), pp. 172–178.

[45] See Sect. 7.1.

[46] See Article 51.2 CMNDPA.

[47] Article 40 TMA, Articles 52–53 IDA, and Article 71 PA.

[48] Article 117.2 PA.

7 Enforcement

7.1 Outside Insolvency

As a general rule, Spanish law prohibits what is known as "pacto comisorio" (any agreement whereby, in the event that the debtor fails to make the payment as agreed, the creditor would have an automatic right to appropriate for himself or otherwise dispose of the assets granted as collateral), except in certain specific cases (e.g. financial collateral arrangements and pledges of credit rights by way of set-off). This implies that enforcement of the mortgage must be made through the public sale of the mortgaged rights, implemented normally through an auction procedure supervised by a judge or notary public.

Spanish law does not have specific procedural rules relating to the foreclosure of intellectual and industrial property rights. Consequently, the general rules relating the enforcement of mortgages must be used. According to Spanish law, in addition to the so-called "declarative proceeding," the creditor is entitled to choose between several enforcement proceedings:

(a) The "ordinary" executive proceeding ("procedimiento de ejecución forzosa,") governed by Articles 538 and following of the Spanish Civil Procedure Act (CPA). In addition to the auction of the rights,[49] the CPA sets forth two other ways to realize the encumbered right. In the first, the party seeking enforcement, the party subject to enforcement, and whoever may prove a direct interest in the enforcement request that the court clerk in charge arrange a hearing in order to reach agreement on the most efficient manner of realizing the mortgaged, pledged, or attached assets subject to enforcement ("*convenio de realización*").[50] The agreement must be approved by the court clerk. In the second way, the court clerk responsible for the enforcement agrees, at the request of the party seeking enforcement or of the party subject to enforcement (with the consent of the party seeking enforcement) and where the characteristics of the attached asset render it advisable, that the asset be realized by a specialized person or organization having knowledge of the market in which such assets are bought and sold and who meets the legal requirements to operate in the market in question.[51]

(b) A "fast track" special enforcement court proceeding ("*procedimiento especial de ejecución hipotecaria*"), governed by Articles 681-698 CPA. For secured parties to enforce a mortgage through this fast-track proceeding, the following requirements must be met: (i) the mortgage must have been executed in a public deed; (ii) the deed of mortgage must set out the price at which the parties valued the property or mortgaged property, so that this might serve as a minimum bid rate at the auction; (iii) the deed must include an address for the grantor for the purposes

[49]Rules relating to the auction of moveable property are contained in Articles 643–654 CPA.

[50]See Article 640 CPA.

[51]Articles 641–642 CPA.

of summons and notification, to guarantee that he is promptly informed about the enforcement of the mortgage and is able to receive any relevant court documents; and (iv) the grantor must be notified of the intention to enforce the mortgage and be given a period of at least ten working days to satisfy the amount of the debt that is in default and that triggers the right of the secured party to enforce the mortgage.

According to Article 693.2 CPA, the mortgagee is entitled to declare early termination of the loan on the grounds of non-payment of money due if this has been provided for in the loan agreement. Such an agreement must be included in the corresponding public deed issued by a notary and recorded in the Registry of Movable Goods. In the absence of an early termination clause which complies with these requirements, the mortgagee is only entitled to claim the principal and interest overdue, not the whole amount of the loan. Early termination of the mortgage loan cannot be declared (and therefore the mortgage may not be enforced) unless the default in payment extends to three monthly installments (or the equivalent amount, if payments are not made on a monthly basis or if the default corresponds to payment obligations other than debt service). If the mortgaged property is transferred before the payment of any overdue installment and there are other installments that are not yet due, the property will be transferred subject to the mortgage corresponding to the part of the loan pending payment.

Once the court has published a date for auction, the debtor will only be able to object in limited circumstances, such as the prior extinction of the mortgage, full payment of the secured obligation, or the existence of a material mistake.

(c) In those cases where this is provided for in a separate clause in the public deed of mortgage, the creditor can initiate an out-of-court procedure before a Spanish notary which takes place by means of an electronic public auction. This is regulated, fundamentally, by Articles 86–88 CMNDPA, Article 129 of the Mortgage Act, Articles 235–236 of the Mortgage Regulation, and Articles 72–76 of the Notaries Act. This territorially competent notary is the notary of the place where the asset is located or of an adjoining district.[52] The debtor (or the non-debtor mortgagor) must designate in the public deed of mortgage a representative who represents him in the sale of the encumbered assets.[53] Spanish law is not clear with regard to the maximum number of auctions that can be conducted, but it is generally assumed that only one single electronic auction is allowed. In most cases, the terms and conditions of this procedure are not entirely regulated by the law and hence they usually follow the provisions agreed upon by the parties in a relevant security document. In the absence of a specific agreement, notaries tend to follow the equivalent provisions applicable to judicial enforcements. Although none of these enforcement procedures provide a legally predefined deadline for carrying out the enforcement, under

[52] Article 87.1 CMNDPA.

[53] Article 86 CMNDPA.

normal circumstances, a notarial enforcement procedure is faster than a judicial one.

7.2 *In Insolvency*

Spanish law does not have specific rules relating to the foreclosure of mortgages of IP rights during insolvency. This implies that the general rules on the enforcement of security rights within the framework of insolvency proceedings will be applied. According to Article 56.2 of the Insolvency Act, once the debtor is declared insolvent, the enforcement of security interests over assets owned by the debtor and used for his professional or business activities will be stayed until one of the following circumstances occurs: (a) a creditor's composition agreement is approved, although its content does not affect the exercise of the enforcement (when the content has been approved with the favourable vote of the secured creditor, it will be bound by whatever has been agreed in the composition agreement); or (b) one year elapses following the declaration of insolvency without liquidation proceedings being initiated. Spanish courts have generally adopted a broad interpretation in determining which assets of the debtor are used for his professional or business activities and IP rights are likely to be included.

Enforcement will be stayed even if at the time of the declaration of insolvency, the notices announcing the public auction have been published.[54] The stay will only be lifted when (a) the court hearing the insolvency proceedings determines that the asset is completely irrelevant for the debtor's professional or business activities, or (b) it is demonstrated that the insolvent person is the owner but not the debtor of the mortgage or another secured credit; in this case, the foreclosure or enforcement will be completely independent from the insolvency. In general, when a foreclosure action is commenced or resumed within the framework of the insolvency proceedings before the winding-up phase has begun, this action shall be dealt with by the insolvency court in a separate procedure, according to the general provisions set forth in the CPA. As a general rule, the disposal of property, goods, and assets that secure claims with special preferences (including security rights) at any stage of the insolvency proceedings shall be performed at auction. Once the winding-up phase has commenced, creditors who did not exercise a foreclosure action prior to the insolvency being declared shall lose the right to do so in a separate proceeding.[55] However, the secured creditor will maintain his privilege over the value of the security.[56]

In addition, Spanish law has adopted different pre-insolvency or "hybrid" mechanisms that can also imply an automatic stay of enforcement actions with regard to

[54] Article 56.2 IA.

[55] Article 57.3 IA.

[56] See Sect. 4.1.

assets that are necessary for the insolvency debtor to continue in the ordinary course of his professional or business activities. In particular, the insolvency debtor can apply the stay when he serves an "Article 5 bis Insolvency Act Notice," which enables him to negotiate a pre-insolvency solution to financial distress within a four-month period. There are different criteria when calculating the stay of enforcement actions, but in general terms, it lasts for a three- or four-month period. Any enforcement action conducted by the holders of financial claims may be stayed if the debtor obtains a standstill supported by 51% of the financial claim holders.[57]

8 Typical Costs

As mentioned above, a chattel mortgage of intellectual and industrial property rights must be documented in a corresponding public deed issued by a notary. Notary fees vary according to the secured liability (they are approximately 0.03% of the secured liability), although in transactions with an aggregate value higher than €6 million, they can be reduced if negotiated with the notary. It has also been indicated above that in order for a chattel mortgage to be effective vis-à-vis third parties, public deeds must be registered in the Registry of Movable Goods. Consequently, in addition to notarial fees, registry fees must be paid (approximately 0.02% of the secured liability). Moreover, the creation of a chattel mortgage of IP rights also implies the payment of stamp duty tax (varying from 0.5 to 1.5% of the secured liability (i.e. the principal, interest, and any related costs), depending on the Spanish region where the collateral is located).

9 Conclusion

In general terms, IP rights are not seen in Spain as suitable collateral to be used within the framework of secured transactions. This is particularly clear in the case of chattel mortgages of intellectual property rights. With the exception of cases where the encumbered assets are rights over cinematographic works, chattel mortgages of these rights are extremely rare in Spain. The situation is a little better for industrial property rights, which are used as collateral in Spain in cases where the rights have a relevant market value. In fact, in recent years, there have been relevant transactions where the debtor's trademark has been considered one of the most important assets in financing or refinancing him.

But, beyond the specific problems indicated earlier, the law in force in Spain provides adequate regulation of securities over IP rights with regard to identifying

[57] See Article 5 bis (4)(iv). Security interests subject to the special regime on financial collateral will always escape this automatic stay.

the rights that can be used as collateral; the specific kind of guarantee that can be used (i.e. the chattel mortgage); the formal requirements for the constitution of the mortgage; and the rights and obligations of both the debtor and the mortgage creditor. Moreover, although the specific rules regulating securities over IP rights are not particularly numerous, the general rules on chattel mortgages ensure adequate levels of legal certainty. It is assumed by Spanish scholars and legal practitioners that the majority of the difficulties involved in taking security rights over IP rights do not arise out of legal malfunction; rather, they arise out of the "quality of the collateral." In this respect, it is striking that the most frequently invoked objections to the use of IP rights as collateral are the difficulty of valuing the rights and the rapid depreciation of the value of the rights, particularly in the case of intellectual property rights.

However, despite the fact that, to date, there are no concrete proposals for in-depth law reform relating to security over IP rights in Spain, there are some aspects that could be improved. For instance, it would be advisable to allow mortgage creditors to take legal actions against infringements of the IP right—currently, this possibility is limited to cases where it has been expressly agreed. Moreover, it would be advisable to clarify the consequences of the assignment of the encumbered rights without the authorization of the creditor, as well as to rethink the duality of registries (i.e. the Registry of Movable Goods and special registries) that exists at the moment.

References

Carbajo F (2009) Hipoteca, embargo de los derechos de autor y situaciones concursales. In: Esteve A (ed) Propiedad Intelectual: Doctrina, jurisprudencia, esquemas y formularios. Tirant lo Blanch, Valencia

Carrasco A (2015) Tratado de los Derechos de Garantía, vol 1, 3rd edn. Aranzadi, Cizur Menor

Cobos F (1975) Garantías reales sobre películas cinematográficas. Revista Crítica de Derecho Inmobiliario 506:9–64

Diéguez M (2006) La hipoteca mobiliaria sobre obra cinematográfica. In: Fayos A (ed) La propiedad intelectual en la Era Digital. Dykinson, Madrid, pp 123–168

Jiménez ZBS (2018) Las garantías reales sobre derechos de propiedad industrial e intelectual en Derecho internacional privado. Doctoral Thesis, Universidad Complutense de Madrid, p 59

Lobato M (2007) Comentario a la Ley 7/2001, de Marcas. 2nd edn. Cívitas, Madrid, p 789

Marco J (2017) Art. 53. In: Bercovitz R (ed) Comentarios a la Ley de Propiedad Intelectual, 4th edn. Tecnos, Madrid, pp 958–959

Martín P (2008) Art. 46. In: Bercovitz A (ed) Comentarios a la Ley de Marcas, 2nd edn. Thomson Aranzadi, Cizur Menor

Martín P (2015) Chapter XV: Transferencias, licencias y gravámenes. In: Bercovitz A (ed) La nueva Ley de Patentes: Ley 24/2015 de 24 de julio Thomson Aranzadi, Cizur Menor, p 352

Pau P (1997) La hipoteca de propiedad intelectual. Revista Crítica de Derecho inmobiliario 642:1770–1771

Rodríguez A (2005) La hipoteca de propiedad intelectual. Reus, Madrid, pp 126–127

Security Rights in Intellectual Property in Taiwan, Republic of China

Su-Hua Lee

Abstract In recent years, the importance of security transactions over IP rights has been recognized in Taiwan, and the government has initiated to draft the Floating Charge Act. Currently the provisions and principles set forth in the Civil Code, Compulsory Enforcement Act, IP laws are applied while establishing a pledge of IP rights, since the draft of the Floating Charge Act has not passed by the parliament. In practice, creditors are generally not very interested in securing debts with IP rights, because IP rights do not represent a sufficiently liquid form of security and that valuating the secured object is a challenge.

1 Overview of IP Rights

1.1 Legal Framework of IP Protection

In Taiwan, the legal protection of IP can be divided into the following categories[1]:

(A) Industrial property rights: Industrial property rights include patent rights on inventions, utility models, and designs, as well as circuit layout rights,[2] and plant variety rights.[3]

[1]Shieh (2016), p. 9; Tsai (2000), p. 25.

[2]Integrated circuit layouts are protected through the Integrated Circuit Layout Protection Act introduced in 2002. The proprietor of a circuit layout right enjoys 10 years' protection commencing from the earlier of the following: (1) the filing date of the circuit layout registration application; or (2) the date of the first commercial exploitation (Integrated Circuit Layout Protection Act, s 19).

[3]Plant varieties are protected by the Plant Variety and Plant Seed Act, introduced in 1988. The competent authority is the Council of Agriculture under the Executive Yuan. The term of a plant variety right for a tree or a perennial vine plant is 25 years from the date of approval. The term of a

S.-H. Lee (✉)
College of Law, National Taiwan University, Taipei, Taiwan
e-mail: leesh@ntu.edu.tw

E.-M. Kieninger (ed.), *Security Rights in Intellectual Property*, Ius Comparatum – Global Studies in Comparative Law 45,
https://doi.org/10.1007/978-3-030-44191-3_26

(B) Copyright and culture-related rights: In addition to copyright, Taiwan introduced the Protection Act for the Traditional Intellectual Creations of Indigenous Peoples in 2007, to provide protection for the traditions and cultures of indigenous peoples.
(C) Rights related to unfair competition: This kind of IP right covers trademarks and the protection of trade secrets.[4]

Since Taiwan acceded to the WTO in 2002, the requirements for the protection and enforcement of IP rights are principally in compliance with the TRIPS Agreement and other international treaties.

The following discussion about Taiwan's IP laws focusses on the patent, copyright, and trademark laws.

1.2 Patent[5]

Taiwan's Patent Act was enacted and came into effect in 1944. Over the past seven decades, the Patent Act has been amended 14 times; its most significant revision was the amendment of January 3, 2003, when Taiwan acceded to the WTO.[6]

With the goal of promoting industrial development, the Patent Act "encourage[s], protect[s] and utilise[s] the creation of inventions, utility models and designs". That is to say, inventions, utility models, and designs are all protected through patent rights.[7] Under the Patent Act, the protection period for the invention patent is 20 years, while that of the utility model patent is 10 years and the design patent's protection period is 12 years.[8]

---

plant variety right for all other plant species is 20 years from the date of approval (Plant Variety and Plant Seed Act, s 23).

[4]Taiwan's Trade Secrets Act came into effect in 1996. In 2013, Trade Secrets Act introduced the provisions for criminal sanctions against economic espionage.

[5]Liu and Lee (2014), pp. 401–420; Shieh and Lee (2015), pp. 349–381.

[6]The requirements for patent applications under Taiwan's Patent Act are no different from those of other countries, including in the areas of eligibility of invention (Patent Act, s 21) and subject matter excluded from patent protection (Patent Act, s 24). Also, patentable inventions should meet the requirements of industrial application, novelty (Patent Act, s 22(1)), and inventive step (Patent Act, s 22(2)). Furthermore, the description of the invention should disclose sufficient information about the invention to enable persons with ordinary skill in the art to make the invention (Patent Act, s 26 (2)). The patentee enjoys the exclusive right to prevent others from exploiting the invention without the patentee's consent, including through the acts of making, offering for sale, selling, using, or importing the subject matter of the patent (Patent Act, s 58(1), (2), (3)).

[7]Sections 21 to 103 of the Patent Act contain provisions governing the protection and utilization of invention patents. Provisions for utility model patents are found in ss 104 to 120, and those for design patents are in ss 121 to 142.

[8]The provisions on invention patents are the most important part of the Patent Act, and many of these provisions apply *mutatis mutandis* to utility model patents and design patents (Patent Act, ss 120 and 142). From July 2004 onwards, utility model patents have been subject only to a formality

The nature of patent right is economic and it can be inheritable and transferable. In contrast, the right to attribution of inventorship for a patented invention, utility model, or design is a moral right, which is exclusive, non-inheritable, and non-transferable.

1.3 Copyright

Taiwan's Copyright Act was enacted and came into effect in 1928. Over the past nine decades, the Copyright Act has been amended 19 times, with an average life cycle of 4.7 years for each amendment. Rapid developments in technology and social changes contributed to the frequent amendments; however, the main reason for these amendments was pressure from trade partners like the USA and Japan.[9] For example, under the influence of the USA, neighbouring rights are not recognized as such in Taiwan. Instead, all kinds of creative works, including databases, photographic works, audiovisual works, sound recordings, and performances, are protected by copyright.

Copyright protection covers works from literary, artistic, scientific, or other intellectual domains which are the result of the creative work of the author (Copyright Act, 3(1)(i)), provided that the work in question fulfills the requirements of originality (independent creation) and minimum degree of creativity.[10] Furthermore, the work should not constitute those subject matters excluded from copyright protection, like the constitution, acts, regulations, or official documents.

The bundle of rights that make up copyright consist of rights that can be of an economic or moral nature, and the protection terms of these are different. Economic rights endure principally for the life of the author and 50 years after the author's death (Copyright Act, s 30). However, there are some exceptions laid out in sections 30 (2) and 32 to 34 of the Copyright Act. Economic copyright is inheritable and transferable.

The author enjoys moral rights, including the divulgation right (Copyright Act, s 15), the right to attribution of authorship (Copyright Act, s 16), and the integrity right (Copyright Act, s 17). It is worth noting that moral rights are not only non-inheritable and non-transferable, but also protected forever in Taiwan.[11]

---

examination (Patent Act, s 111(1)). In contrast, the patentability conditions and requirements for the protection of invention patents and design patents come under close scrutiny by the TIPO through substantive examinations.

[9]For example, the Copyright Act has been substantially revised since 1992 under the threat from Section 301 of the U.S. Trade Act.

[10]Shieh (2016), pp. 96–97.

[11]Copyright Act, s 18 states: "The protection of moral rights of an author who has died or been extinguished shall be deemed to be the same as when the author was living or in existence and shall not be infringed upon by any person; provided, the act shall not constitute an infringement where it

In addition to copyright, section 79 of the Copyright Act provides for the plate right, which is protected for 10 years.

1.4 Trademark

Taiwan's Trademark Act was enacted and came into effect in 1930. Over the past nine decades, the Trademark Act has been amended 15 times; its most significant revision was the amendment of May 28, 2003, when Taiwan acceded to the WTO.

The proprietor of a registered trademark[12] enjoys an exclusive right in the trademark in relation to the designated goods or services for a period of 10 years (Trademark Act, s 35(1)). The term of a trademark right may be renewed and the duration of each renewal period shall be 10 years (Trademark Act, s 33 (2)). The nature of a trademark right is economic and it can be both inheritable and transferable.

In addition to the trademark, the certification mark, collective mark, and collective trademark are regulated by the Trademark Act (ss 80–94). In principle, they are all subject to the provisions relating to the trademark.[13] However, the right of a certification mark, collective mark, or collective trademark shall not be transferred, licensed, or made the subject of a pledge right unless such transfer or licence is unlikely to damage the interests of consumers or contravene fair competition and has been accepted by the TIPO (Trademark Act, s 92).

2 Attachment and Perfection of Security Right

Principally transferable and inheritable economic IP rights can serve as security and the principle of freedom of contract set forth in the Civil Code is applied in such instances.

---

can be considered that the author's intent has not been contravened given the nature and degree of the act of exploitation, social changes, or other circumstances."

[12]Any sign which may consist of words, devices, symbols, colours, three-dimensional shapes, motions, holograms, sounds, or any combination thereof can form a trademark (Trademark Act, s 18(1)). The distinctiveness requirement (Trademark Act, s 6(2)) and the absolute and relative grounds for refusal of registration set forth in section 30(1) of Taiwan's Trademark Act are no different from those of other countries. The issues of whether the application for trademark protection fulfills the distinctiveness requirement and whether absolute or relative grounds for refusal of registration exist are substantively examined by the TIPO.

[13]Trademark Act, s 94 states: "Unless otherwise prescribed in this Chapter, the provisions of this Act in relation to a trademark shall apply *mutatis mutandis* to a certification mark, collective mark or collective trademark."

2.1 *Eligibility of Establishment of Security Right*

2.1.1 Eligible Subject of Security Right

IP rights can be divided into economic rights and personal rights, which are subject to civil law. Economic rights are inheritable and transferable and personal rights are exclusive, non-inheritable, and non-transferable. According to Section 900 of the Civil Code, transferable and inheritable economic IP rights can generally serve as security and parties can enter into a contract, to create either relative rights (obligations) or proprietary rights (rights in rem). Also, the IP laws explicitly stipulate that patents,[14] utility models,[15] designs,[16] copyright,[17] trademarks,[18] circuit layout rights,[19] and plant variety rights[20] can all be the subject matter of a pledge.

IP laws like the Patent Act, Trademark Act, and Copyright Act merely regulate eligibility for establishing a pledge right and/or the registration of such a right. Apart from that, security rights in Taiwan are regulated by the Civil Code, from ss 900 to 910.[21] However, the Civil Code does not provide sufficient instruction or guidance on the pledge rights of IP.

---

[14]Patent Act, s 62(1) states: "The assigning, entrusting, licensing, or establishing of a pledge on a patent right by the patentee shall have no *locus standi* against any third party unless it is registered with the competent authority."

[15]According to section 120 of the Patent Act, section 62(1) concerning the creation of a pledge on an invention patent right applies *mutatis mutandis* to the utility model patent.

[16]According to section 142 of the Patent Act, section 62(1) concerning the creation of a pledge on an invention patent right applies *mutatis mutandis* to the design patent.

[17]Copyright Act, s 39 states: "Where economic rights are the subject of a pledge, unless otherwise stipulated at the time the pledge is created, the economic rights holder may exercise the economic rights to the work."

[18]Trademark Act, s 44(1) states: "A creation, change, or extinguishment of a pledge made by the proprietor of a registered trademark shall have no *locus standi* against any third party unless it is registered with the competent authority."

[19]Integrated Circuit Layout Protection Act, s 22(1) states: "For any of the following events related to circuit layout rights, parties concerned shall jointly sign and apply for registration, accompanied by contracts or other documentary evidence, with the competent authority of circuit layout affairs; otherwise, these parties shall have no *locus standi* against third parties who have no notice of the following: (1) assignment; (2) license; or (3) creation, transfer, alteration or extinguishment of a pledge."

[20]Plant Variety and Plant Seed Act, s 27(2) states: "The license of a plant variety right to others or the creation of a pledge on a plant variety right shall not be binding as against a bona fide third party, unless it is registered with the competent authority."

[21]Civil Code, s 900 states: "A pledge of rights is a pledge and the subject of which is a transferable claim or other transferable right."

Section 901 states: "Unless otherwise provided in this section, the provisions concerning pledges of personal property shall apply *mutatis mutandis* to pledges of rights."

Section 902 states: "The creation of a pledge right shall be made in accordance with the provisions concerning the transfer of such rights, as well as with the provisions of this section."

Section 903 states: "A pledger may not, by means of a juristic act, cause a right that is the subject of a pledge to be extinguished or modified without the consent of the pledgee."

Section 904 states: "If the subject of a pledge is a claim, the pledge shall be created in writing (para 1). If there is any document evidencing a claim referred to in the preceding paragraph, the pledgor is obligated to deliver it (para 2)."

Section 905 states: "If a claim that is the subject of a pledge is a pecuniary claim with a maturity earlier than the maturity of the claim it secures, the pledgee may demand that the debtor lodge the payment for the pecuniary claim, and may exercise its pledge against the thing lodged (para 1). If a claim that is the subject of a pledge is a pecuniary claim with a maturity later than the maturity of the claim it secures, then at the maturity of the claim secured by the pledge, the pledgee may demand payment of the amount of the claim secured by the pledge (para 2)."

Section 906 states: "If a claim that is the subject of a pledge is a claim for payment by delivery of personal property other than money, then at the maturity of that claim, the pledgee may demand that the debtor delivers the personal property, and the pledgee will hold a pledge over the thing delivered."

Section 906*bis* states: "If a claim that is the subject of a pledge is a claim for payment by the creation or transfer of rights in rem in real property, then at the maturity of that claim, the pledgee may demand that the debtor creates or transfers such rights in rem in the real property in favor of the pledgor, and the pledgee will hold a mortgage on the rights in rem in the real property (para 1). At the time of the creation or transfer of the rights in rem in the property in favor of the pledgor, the mortgage referred to in the preceding paragraph shall be registered together therewith (para 2)."

Section 906*ter* states: "When a pledgee has not received payment upon maturity of the claim secured by a pledge, in addition to taking measures under the preceding three articles, the pledgee may enforce its pledge in accordance with the provisions of section 893(1), or section 895."

Section 906*quarter* states: "When a claim that is the subject of a pledge may be caused to reach maturity by the exercise of a certain right, the pledgee may exercise that right when the pledgee has not received satisfaction upon maturity of the claim secured by the pledge."

Section 906*quinquies* states: "When a debtor makes a lodgment or a payment in accordance with section 905(1), section 906, or section 906*bis*, the pledgee shall notify the pledgor but need not obtain the consent of the pledgor."

Section 907 states: "If the subject of a pledge is a claim, and its debtor has been notified of the creation of the pledge, that debtor, when making any payment either to the pledgor or the pledgee, shall first obtain the consent of the other of those parties. In the absence of such consent the debtor shall lodge the thing given as payment."

Section 907*bis* states: "If the subject of a pledge is a claim, and its debtor, after having been notified of the creation of the pledge, obtains any claim against the pledgor, that debtor may not assert offset of that claim against the claim that is the subject of the pledge."

Section 908 states: "If the subject of a pledge is securities for which no rights holder is named, the creation of the pledge becomes effective by the delivery of the securities to the pledgee. If the subject is any other type of securities, endorsement is also required to be made (para 1). The endorsement referred to in the preceding paragraph may include a notation as to the purpose for which the pledge is created (para 2)."

Section 909 states: "If the subject of a pledge is securities for which no rights holder is named, a negotiable instrument, or any other securities transferred by endorsement, the pledgee may collect payments receivable on such securities even if the claim secured thereby has not matured. If to do so it is necessary to cause the securities to reach maturity, the pledgee shall also have the right to bring about the maturity by giving notice or by other means. And the debtor may make payments only to the pledgee (para 1). The provisions of section 905, paragraph 1, or section 906 apply to payments collected pursuant to the preceding paragraph (para 2). The provisions of section 906*ter* and section 906*quarter* apply mutatis mutandis to pledges the subject of which is securities (para 3)."

Section 910 states: "If the subject of a pledge is securities, the effect of the pledge further extends to attached interest coupons, fixed-payment securities, or any other attached securities, provided they have been delivered to the pledgee (para 1). Unless otherwise stipulated, if attached securities

Table 1 Statistics of security transactions over IP rights (2011–2018)

Year	Patent	Copyright	Trademark
2011	20	1	361
2012	73	2	38
2013	49	1	71
2014	4	0	104
2015	17	0	39
2016	11	0	35
2017	56	0	24
2018	15	0	77

Resource: TIPO's statistics (unpublished)

2.1.2 Ineligible Subject of Security Right

Certain types of IP rights cannot serve as the object of a security right.

Exception of Transferable Economic Right

As mentioned above, economic IP rights are generally eligible to be the subject matter of a security right, since they are inheritable and transferable. However, there are some exceptions. The plate right set forth in the Copyright Act, for example, is a transferable economic right and it can be the subject matter of an assignment or placement in trust (Copyright Act, s 79(4)).[22] With regards to the question whether a plate right can be pledged, however, the abovementioned provision is silent on this issue. Yet since this provision does not mention the establishment of a pledge, the answer should be given in the negative.

Some IP laws explicitly forbid the right to apply for IP protection to be used as the subject matter of a pledge. That is to say, the right to file for protection, including the right to apply for patent (Patent Act, s 6(2))[23] and right to apply for plant variety protection (Plant Variety and Plant Seed Act, s 7(1))[24] cannot be pledged, even though these economic IP rights are transferable.[25] The rationale behind these provisions is the guarantee of transaction security, since the final outcome of the application and the scope of the right are still pending.

are issued after the creation of the pledge, the pledgee may demand their delivery from the issuer or the pledgor (para 2)."

[22]Copyright Act, s 79(4) states: "Assignment or placement in trust of plate rights shall not be effective against third parties unless it has been registered."

[23]Patent Act, s 6(2) states: "The right to apply for a patent shall not be taken as the subject of a pledge."

[24]Plant Variety and Plant Seed Act, s 7(1) states: "The right to apply for a plant variety right shall not be taken as the subject of a pledge."

[25]Patent Act, s 6(1) states: "The right to apply for a patent or the patent right is both assignable and inheritable."

With regard to the right to file for protection, it is worth noting that there is no similar provision in the Trademark Act or the Integrated Circular Layout Protection Act dealing with ineligibility for a pledge, and it seems unclear whether these rights could serve as the subject of a pledge. The author is of the opinion that the same provisions in the Patent Act and the Plant Variety and Plant Seed Act should have analogous application to the right to apply for trademark and circular layout protection.

Trade secret protection is another exception. As mentioned above, in Taiwan, trade secret protection falls into the category of IP and it may be assigned in whole or in part (Tract Secrets Act, s 6(1)).[26] However, the protection of trade secret is to a certain extent different from patent rights, copyright, and trademark rights, since trade secret protection is merely the right to protection against unfair competition. Therefore, trade secret protection cannot be the subject matter of a pledge (Trade Secrets Protection Act, s 8).[27]

Exceptions of Non-transferable Economic Right

Some economic intellectual property rights are non-inheritable and non-transferable. Thus, they cannot be pledged. Examples include the right of a certification mark, collective mark, or collective trademark (Trademark Act, s 92).[28] The same rule applies to the exclusive right of the traditional intellectual creations of indigenous peoples (Protection Act for the Traditional Intellectual Creations of Indigenous Peoples, s 11).[29]

Moral Right

As mentioned above, personal IP rights are exclusive, non-inheritable, and non-transferable. In accordance with the principal set forth in section 900 of the Civil Code, personal rights are ineligible for the establishment of a security right. Therefore, the right to attribution of authorship of a copyrighted work or

[26]Tract Secrets Act, s 6(1) states: "Trade secret may be assigned in whole or in part, or jointly owned."

[27]Tract Secrets Act, s 8 states: "Trade secret shall not be used as the subject matter of a pledge or compulsory enforcement."

[28]Trademark Act, s 92 states: "The right of a certification mark, collective mark or collective trademark shall not be transferred, licensed, or be the subject of a pledge, unless such transfer or license is unlikely to damage the interests of consumers or contravene fair competition and has been accepted by the competent authority."

[29]Protection Act for the Traditional Intellectual Creations of Indigenous Peoples, s 11 states: "The exclusive right to use intellectual creations shall not be assigned or be the subject matter of a pledge or compulsory enforcement."

inventorship of a patented invention, utility model, or design cannot serve as the subject of a security right.

2.2 *Attachment of Security Right*

The creation of a pledge follows the principle of freedom of contract. The details are as follows.

2.2.1 Effective Conditions for Creating a Pledge Right

Section 902 of the Civil Code provides that "[t]he creation of a pledge right shall be made in accordance with the provisions concerning the transfer of such rights, as well as with the provisions of this section." The Civil Code is silent on the effective conditions for creating a pledge and refers to the provisions concerning the transfer of the right governed by IP laws.

With regard to the transfer of an IP right, the Patent Act, Copyright Act, Trademark Act, Integrated Circular Layout Protection Act, and Plant Variety and Plant Seed Act do not stipulate a formality requirement concerning effective conditions in light of the principles of private autonomy and freedom of contract. Therefore, there is no formality requirement concerning any effective conditions for creating a pledge right. To be effective, a lien agreement and a pledge agreement do not need to be in written form or require registration. When the parties agree on the essential elements of the lien agreement or the pledge agreement, the agreement is constituted and effective (Civil Code, s 153).[30]

2.2.2 Joint Ownership of IP Rights

When joint ownership is involved, the IP laws stipulate the statutory effective condition of creating a pledge. That is, in the event of joint ownership, a pledge on an IP right or a pledge on its share should not be created without the unanimous

[30]Civil Code, s 153 states: "When the parties have reciprocally declared their concordant intent, either expressly or impliedly, a contract shall be constituted (para 1). If the parties agree on all the essential elements of the contract but have expressed no intent as to the non-essential elements, the contract shall be presumed to be constituted. In the absence of an agreement on the above-mentioned non-essential elements, the court shall decide them according to the nature of the affair (para 2)."

consent of all of the joint owners (see sections 64,[31] 65(1)[32] of the Patent Act, section 40*bis*(1) of the Copyright Act,[33] section 46(1) of the Trademark Act,[34] and section 21(1), (2) of the Integrated Circular Layout Protection Act[35]).

Remarkably, section 28 of the Plant Variety and Plant Seed Act takes a slightly different position. That is, instead of requiring the unanimous consent of all of the joint owners, it only requires the consent of the owners who have at least two-thirds of the shares in a plant variety right.[36]

Section 40*bis* (1) of the Copyright Act explicitly stipulates that a joint owner shall not refuse consent without a legitimate reason. This principle should apply *mutatis mutandis* to patent rights and other IP rights.

2.2.3 Original and Derivative Design

Concerning design patents, section 138(1) of the Patent Act stipulates that a derivative design patent right shall be pledged along with its original design patent due to the relative connection between the original design and derivative design.[37]

---

[31]Patent Act, s 64 states: "Where a patent right is jointly owned, except for exploitation by each of the joint owners, it shall not be assigned, entrusted, licensed, pledged, or abandoned without the consent of all the joint owner(s)."

[32]Patent Act, s 65(1) states: "Where a patent right is jointly owned, no joint owner may assign, entrust or establish a pledge on his/her own share without the consent of all the other joint owner (s)."

[33]Copyright Act, s 40*bis*(1) states: "Joint economic rights in a work shall not be exercised except with the consent of all the joint economic rights holders; no economic rights holder shall transfer its share to another person or establish a pledge of its share in favor of a third party without the consent of all other joint economic rights holders. A joint economic rights holder shall not refuse consent without a legitimate reason."

[34]Trademark Act, s 46(1) states: "Any license, sub-license, transfer, abandonment of, or creation of pledge on the right in a jointly owned trademark or any transfer of or creation of pledge on the share in a jointly owned trademark shall have the consent of all joint proprietors, unless such right or share is transferred by succession, compulsory enforcement, a judgment of the court or operation of other law."

[35]Integrated Circular Layout Protection Act, s 21(1), (2) states: "For circuit layout rights jointly owned by two or more parties, any assignment, grant of license or creation of pledge of the circuit layout rights shall have the unanimous consent of all joint owners (para 1). Without the consent of all joint owners of circuit layout rights, no single joint owner shall assign, license or create a pledge in the joint owner's share of the ownership; no joint owner shall refuse consent without proper reasons (para 2)."

[36]Plant Variety and Plant Seed Act, s 28 states: "Without the consent of the holders of two-thirds or more of the interested shares in a plant variety right, no joint owner shall assign his or her own share, license others to exercise such share, or create a pledge on such share; provided, however, that if the parties have agreed otherwise, the terms of such agreement shall govern."

[37]Patent Act, s 138(1) states: "A derivative design patent right shall be assigned, entrusted, inherited, licensed or pledged along with its original design patent."

2.2.4 Enterprise Charges

The ability to have a security over all of the assets of a company or enterprise is not yet recognized in Taiwan. However, the government is now drafting the Floating Charge Act, following the UNCITRAL Legislative Guide on Secured Transactions, the Supplement on Security Rights in Intellectual Property, and the Draft Model Law on Secured Transactions.[38]

2.3 *Perfection of Security Right*

As mentioned above, the creation of a pledge follows the principle of freedom of contract. However, when patent rights, trademark rights, circular layout rights, or plant variety rights are involved, a pledge agreement can be registered with the competent authorities. This registration is not an effective condition of the agreement; rather, it is a condition for asserting the pledge agreement against a third party, according to section 62(1) of the Patent Act,[39] section 44(1) of the Trademark Act,[40] section 22(1) of the Integrated Circuit Layout Protection Act, and section 27(2) of the Plant Variety and Plant Seed Act. Therefore, a pledge agreement that has not been registered still binds the parties (i.e. pledgor and pledgee), but it cannot be asserted against a third party.

Another important function of registration is to decide the ranking of the pledge rights. Section 62(4) of the Patent Act[41] and section 44(2) of the Trademark Act[42] stipulate that in the event that multiple pledges are established on the same IP right for the purpose of securing multiple lienors' rights, the ranking of these pledges shall be determined according to the order in which they were registered.[43]

It is worth noting that the formality of registration does not apply to a pledge agreement targeted at a copyright since for the existence of copyright it is not

---

[38]See the explanation under Sect. 5.

[39]Patent Act, s 62(1) states: "The assigning, entrusting, licensing, or establishing of a pledge on a patent right by the patentee shall have no *locus standi* against any third party unless it is recorded with the Specific Patent Agency."

[40]Trademark Act, s 44(1) states: "A creation, change, or extinguishment of a pledge made by the proprietor of a registered trademark shall have no locus *standi against* any third party unless it is entered in the Register by the Registrar Office."

[41]Patent Act, s 62(4) states: "Where a patentee establishes multiple pledges on the same patent for the purpose of securing multiple creditors' rights, the ranks of these pledges shall be determined according to the order of their registration."

[42]Trademark Act, 44 (2) states: "Where a proprietor creates multiple pledges on his/her trademark right for the purpose of securing multiple creditors' rights, the ranks of these pledges shall be decided by the order of the entry in the Register."

[43]Even though there is no similar provision in the Integrated Circular Layout Protection Act or the Plant Variety and Plant Seed Act, the same principle should be applied *mutatis mutandis*.

necessary to follow the application and registration procedure. However, for public notification, it is possible to register a pledge on copyright with the TIPO.

2.4 *Method of Assessing Value*

The value of a pledged IP right is assessed by the general methods of asset valuation. However, valuating an intangible asset, particularly IP, is one of the most serious challenges in Taiwan, not only in the circumstances of creating a pledge, but also for the purposes of calculating compensatory damages.

Since pledge agreements are rare, methods of assessing the value of a pledged IP right (e.g. establishing an expert mechanism to carry out the valuation) still need to be developed in Taiwan in the near future.

2.5 *Typical Costs*

Legal advice, documentation, notarial deeds, and even registration are not obligatory to create a pledge of an IP right. However, it is possible to register a pledge of an IP right with the competent authorities.

The cost of registering a pledge is relatively low in Taiwan. For example, it takes only TWD[44] 2000 to register a pledge of a patent or trademark with the TIPO.[45] The cost of registering a pledge of a copyright or circuit layout right with the TIPO is TWD 3000,[46] and the cost of registering a pledge of a plant variety right with the Council of Agriculture under the Executive Yuan is only TWD 500.[47]

3 Legal Effect of Security Right

After the establishment of security right, it is important to clarify the right and obligation of parties, priorities of satisfaction of a claim and the enforcement.

---

[44] At the time of writing, USD 1 is almost equal to TWD 30.

[45] https://www.tipo.gov.tw/ct.asp?xItem=203067&CtNode=7390&mp=1; https://www.tipo.gov.tw/ct.asp?xItem=155854&ctNode=7566&mp=1.

[46] https://www.tipo.gov.tw/ct.asp?xItem=332353&ctNode=7011&mp=1; https://www.tipo.gov.tw/ct.asp?xItem=207004&ctNode=6748&mp=1.

[47] http://www.rootlaw.com.tw/LawArticle.aspx?LawID=A040270040006700-0940629.

3.1 Relationship Between Parties

3.1.1 Right to Exercise the IP Right

After establishing a pledge, the proprietor of the IP right (i.e. the pledgor) may continue to enjoy and exercise the IP right unless otherwise stipulated in the pledge agreement (see section 6(3) of the Patent Act,[48] section 39 of the Copyright Act,[49] section 44(3) of the Trademark Act,[50] section 23 of the Integrated Circular Layout Protection Act,[51] and section 7(2) of the Plant Variety and Plant Seed Act).[52] This means that, in general, the pledgee is not allowed to exercise the IP right.

The most frequently used form of security transaction in IP is the lien (Civil Code, s 900). Generally, this transferable economic right is the result of a pledge. The lien is a security right of an absolute nature and is adhered to a pledge, regardless of whether or not it has been transferred. For this reason, the pledgee does not enjoy a statutory right to restrict the proprietor with regard to the transferability of the pledged IP right. Also, consent from the pledgee is not required, unless otherwise stipulated in the pledge agreement.

3.1.2 Obligation to Maintain Existence of IP Right

On the basis of the principle of private autonomy, the proprietor has the right to dispose of the asset freely (i.e. to abandon it). However, if the IP right is the object of a pledge, the pledgor is obligated to maintain the existence of the legal protection and to refrain from anything that might impair the pledge for the duration of the pledge agreement. For example, the pledgor must take the proper actions if the validity of the pledged IP right is challenged by third parties through revocation or invalidation proceedings. Also, in the event that an IP right is pledged, the proprietor is not free to abandon the IP right without the consent of the pledgee, according to sections 69

[48]Patent Act, s 6(3) states: "In the case of taking a patent right as the subject of a pledge, the pledgee shall not be allowed to exercise the patent right, unless it is otherwise provided for in an agreement."

[49]Copyright Act, s 39 states: "Where economic rights are the subject of a pledge, unless otherwise stipulated at the time the pledge is created, the economic rights holder may exercise the economic rights to the work."

[50]Trademark Act, s 44(3) states: "A pledgee in respect of right in a registered trademark shall not use such trademark unless otherwise licensed by the proprietor thereof."

[51]Integrated Circular Layout Protection Act, s 23 states: "For a creation of a pledge in circuit layout rights, the pledgee shall not make use of the circuit layout unless otherwise provided by a contract."

[52]Plant Variety and Plant Seed Act, s 7(2) states: "If the plant variety right is used as the subject of a pledge, the pledgee shall not exercise such plant variety right, unless an agreement between the parties otherwise specifies."

(1)[53] and 140[54] of the Patent Act, section 45 of the Trademark Act,[55] section 26(1) of the Integrated Circular Layout Protection Act,[56] and section 29 of the Plant Variety and Plant Seed Act.[57]

It is worth noting that there is no similar provision in the Copyright Act. Instead of following the "monistic theory," the legal framework of copyright law in Taiwan follows the dualistic theory. Thus, although the Copyright Act and scholars are silent on this issue, theoretically, a proprietor of copyright could abandon the economic right. When a pledge of copyright is involved, the same rules stipulated in the Patent Act, etc. shall have analogous application. That is, the proprietor of copyright must get the consent of the pledgee before abandoning the pledged economic right.

With regard to patent rights, a post-grant amendment to delete or narrow the scope of any claim is allowed provided that the pledgee give consent, according to section 69(1) of the Patent Act.[58] The rationale behind this provision is that this kind of amendment has a negative impact on the pledgee's right.

3.2 Priorities

In the event that the debtor fails to satisfy the debt properly and in due time, the lienee (i.e. the pledgee) can sell the pledged IP right. The pledge of an IP right is the "preferential right of a creditor to receive satisfaction of a claim from the proceeds

[53]Patent Act, s 69(1) states: "A patentee shall not abandon the patent right, or apply for a post-grant amendment as stated in subparagraph 1 or 2, paragraph 1 of section 67 without the consent from the licensee(s) or pledgee(s)."

[54]Patent Act, s 140 states: "A design patentee shall not abandon the design patent right without consent from the licensee(s) or pledgee(s)."

[55]Trademark Act, s 45 states: "The proprietor of a registered trademark may abandon the trademark right. However, if a license or a pledge has entered and registered with the competent authority, the proprietor shall get the consent of the licensee(s) or the pledgee(s) (para 1). The abandonment referred to in the preceding paragraph shall be made in writing to the competent authority (para 2)."

[56]Integrated Circular Layout Protection Act, s 26(1) states: "The proprietor of circuit layout rights shall not abandon the circuit layout rights without obtaining the consent of the licensee(s) or the pledgee(s)."

[57]Plant Variety and Plant Seed Act, s 29 states: "The proprietor of a plant variety right shall not abandon the right without the consent of the licensee(s) or the pledgee(s)."

[58]Patent Act, s 69(1) states: "A patentee shall not abandon the patent right, or apply for a post-grant amendment as stated in subparagraph 1 or 2, paragraph 1 of section 67 without the consent from the licensee(s) or pledgee(s)."

Section 67(1) states: "The patentee filing a request for amending the description, claim(s) or drawing(s) of a granted invention patent shall only conduct the following: (i) to delete claim(s), (ii) to narrow down the scope of claim(s), (iii) to correct errors or translation errors, and (iv) to clarify ambiguous statement(s)."

from sale of [the pledged subject matter]" (Civil Code, s 884[59]). That is to say, a creditor's claim that is protected by a pledge right is given priority.

The ranking of secured creditors in relation to the same secured asset is principally determined by when the security rights were created. However, if a registered pledge right is involved, the ranking of the pledges shall be determined according to the order in which they were registered (see section 62(4) of the Patent Act[60] and section 44(2) of the Trademark Act[61]).[62]

If a creditor's claim protected by a pledge right, mortgage, or right of retention is not fully satisfied by the secured asset, the claim will no longer enjoy priority and may be satisfied by the debtor's other assets if anything remains, according to section 109 of the Insolvency Act.

With regard to insolvency proceeding concerning the debtor's assets, there is no special rule on IP rights or on pledges targeted at IP rights. Section 108 of the Insolvency Act provides simply that a creditor's claim protected by a pledge right, mortgage, or right of retention is a priority claim (para 1), which can be satisfied through the secured asset, regardless of the insolvency proceedings (para 2). It is unclear how this provision applies to a creditor's claim that is protected by a pledge right of IP. Judicial practice is silent on this issue, since there has not yet been a remarkable case or dispute involving it.

3.3 Enforcement

In the event that the debtor fails to satisfy the debt properly and in due time, the lienee (i.e. the pledgee) can sell the pledged IP right (Civil Code, s 893(1)[63]). The Compulsory Enforcement Act sets out the procedure for public auctions. The public auction of real property, personal property, vessels, airplanes, and creditors' claims

---

[59]Civil Code, s 884 states: "A pledge of personal property is a preferential right of a creditor to receive satisfaction of a claim from the proceeds from sale of personal property the possession of which has been transferred by a debtor or a third party as security for the claim."

According to section 901, the provisions concerning pledges of personal property shall apply *mutatis mutandis* to pledges of rights, including pledges of IP rights.

[60]Patent Act, s 62(4) states: "Where a patentee establishes multiple pledges on the same patent for the purpose of securing multiple creditors' rights, the ranks of these pledges shall be determined according to the order of their registration."

[61]Trademark Act, 44 (2) states: "Where a proprietor creates multiple pledges on his/her trademark right for the purpose of securing multiple creditors' rights, the ranks of these pledges shall be determined according to the order of their registration."

[62]Even though there is no similar provision in the Integrated Circular Layout Protection Act as well as the Plant Variety and Plant Seed Act, the same principle should be applied *mutatis mutandis*.

[63]Civil Code, s 893(1) states: "A pledgee who has not received payment upon maturity of the claim may sell the object pledged by auction and receive payment from the proceeds of the sale."

As mentioned above, the provisions concerning the pledge of personal property apply *mutatis mutandis* to the pledge of rights.

is covered by the Compulsory Enforcement Act. However, there is no specific provision governing the auctioning of IP rights. Section 117 of the Compulsory Enforcement Act provides that the provisions concerning the auctioning of a creditor's claim apply *mutatis mutandis* to other types of property rights; nevertheless, the details are unclear. Also, there has not yet been a significant case in judicial practice.

Apart from public auction, the parties (i.e. the debtor and the creditor) may agree to have the ownership of the pledged object transferred to the pledgee if the debtor fails to satisfy the debt properly and in due time (Civil Code, s 893(2)). However, this agreement should be registered with the competent authorities. Without registration, it only binds the parties and can't be asserted against a third party.

4 Practical Usefulness

4.1 Difficulties in Practice

Even though there are some security transactions over IP rights in practice, creditors are generally not very interested in securing debts with IP rights.

That is to say, security transactions over IP rights are not a common business practice in Taiwan. The main reasons for this might be that IP rights do not represent a sufficiently liquid form of security and that valuating the secured object is a challenge. It is particularly difficult for an SME or an innovative company to obtain credit by granting a security right in its IP.

4.2 Statistics of Security Transactions Over IP Right

In line with the practical difficulties mentioned above, the statistics of security transactions over IP rights provided by the TIPO[64] show that the trademark right is the most popular object of a security right (see Table 1). With regard to copyright, few security transactions are registered. This might be due to the fact that following the application and registration procedure is not necessary in order for copyright to exist. Also, the Copyright Act is silent on the registration of a pledge agreement targeted at a copyright.

5 Law Reform

In recent years, the government and industries in Taiwan have recognized the importance of security transactions over IP rights, particularly floating charges. For this reason, the government has initiated to draft the Floating Charge Act,

[64]TIPO (2017), The Security Transactions over the IP in Taiwan (power point), January 20, 2017 (unpublished); TIPO (2019), TIPO's statistics (unpublished).

following the UNCITRAL Legislative Guide on Secured Transactions, the Supplement on Security Rights in Intellectual Property, and the Draft Model Law on Secured Transactions.

Since February 2016, the draft of the Floating Charge Act has been under discussion and the author was invited to participate in the discussion. However, it is still unclear whether it will be enacted or not, since the method of assessing value the secured IP right is a challenge and needed to develop. The Financial Supervisory Commission and experts in banking are concerned about the potential negative impacts on transaction security. Till now, the draft of the Floating Charge Act has not passed by the parliament.

References

Liu K-C, Lee S-H (2014) The patent system in Chinese Taipei. In: Ganea P, Luginbuehl S (eds) Patent law in Greater China. Edward Elgar Publisher, Frankfurt, pp 401–420

Shieh M-Y (2016) Intellectual property rights, 6th edn. Angel Publishing, Taipei

Shieh M-Y, Lee S-H (2015) Patent enforcement in Taiwan. In: Heath C (ed) Patent enforcement worldwide: writings in honour of Dieter Stauder, 3rd edn. Hart Publishing, Oxford, pp 349–381

Tsai M-C (2000) Researches about patent law, 3rd edn. Tsai M-C, Taipei

List of Laws

Civil Code, English version is available at http://law.moj.gov.tw/Eng/LawClass/LawAll.aspx?PCode=B0000001

Compulsory Enforcement Act, English version is available at https://law.moj.gov.tw/ENG/LawClass/LawAll.aspx?pcode=B0010004

Copyright Act, English version is available at http://law.moj.gov.tw/ENG/LawClass/LawAll.aspx?PCode=J0070017

Insolvency Act, Chinese version is available at http://law.moj.gov.tw/LawClass/LawAll.aspx?PCode=B0010006

Integrated Circular Layout Protection Act, English version is available at http://law.moj.gov.tw/Eng/LawClass/LawAll.aspx?PCode=J0070027

Patent Act, English version is available at http://law.moj.gov.tw/Eng/LawClass/LawAll.aspx?PCode=J0070007

Plant Variety and Plant Seed Act, English version is available at http://law.moj.gov.tw/Eng/LawClass/LawAll.aspx?PCode=M0030024

Trade Secrets Act, English version is available at http://law.moj.gov.tw/Eng/LawClass/LawAll.aspx?PCode=J0080028

Trademark Act, English version is available at http://law.moj.gov.tw/Eng/LawClass/LawAll.aspx?PCode=J0070001

Security Rights in Intellectual Property in Turkey

Ergun Özsunay and Murat R. Özsunay

Abstract Although intellectual property rights are still not commonly used as security in Turkey, this usage does occur. Turkish law enables and, as of recently, even encourages the use of such rights as security, especially in the field of commerce. Two relatively new laws—namely, the *Law on Industrial Property*, No. 6769 of December 22, 2016 (Sınai Mülkiyet Kanunu) and the *Law on Movable Pledge in Commercial Transactions,* No. 6570 of October 20, 2016—are based, in general, on recent global developments and are in harmony with foreign and international legislation. *Law on Movable Pledge in Commercial Transactions*, No. 6750 has not introduced the system and solutions of the *UNCITRAL Model Law on Secured Transactions.* Nevertheless, *Law No. 6750* has indeed expanded the possible practical uses of security rights over movables (including, inter alia, IP rights) that were formerly prescribed by the *Turkish Civil Code* and the relevant legislation. Accordingly, while the functions of the Registry (SMS) of the Turkish Patent and Trademark Office have been maintained, a second, quasi-parallel registry (TARES) has been established for certain commercial purposes. As mentioned before, the expanded possibilities provided by the new Turkish law do not include *the Model Law* concepts "registration of a notice", "registration of an amendment or cancellation notice", "search criteria in the Registry", etc. The authors of this paper are of the opinion that Turkish lawmakers should eventually adopt the *UNCITRAL Model Law on Secured Transactions* and *relevant UNCITRAL texts*.

E. Özsunay
Istanbul University Law Faculty (Em.), Istanbul, Turkey

M. R. Özsunay (✉)
Istanbul Bar Assoc. Apprentice Training Center (SEM), Istanbul, Turkey
e-mail: murat@ozsunay.com

E.-M. Kieninger (ed.), *Security Rights in Intellectual Property*, Ius Comparatum – Global Studies in Comparative Law 45,
https://doi.org/10.1007/978-3-030-44191-3_27

1 Overview of IP Rights in Turkish Law

1.1 Legal Terminology

For a long time, two terms were used in Turkish intellectual property law to express different kinds of intellectual works: "intellectual rights" (fikri haklar) and "industrial property" (sinai mülkiyet).

The first term, "intellectual rights," was used to define the author's rights, such as copyright, moral rights, financial rights, and neighbouring rights on intellectual and artistic works. The second term, "industrial property," was used for rights on inventions (i.e. patents), utility models, industrial designs, geographical designations, and trademarks.[1]

The new Turkish doctrine today prefers to use a single term to express all kinds of intellectual and industrial rights. The new term is "intellectual property" ("fikri mülkiyet"). It is used to encompass not only the abovementioned intellectual and industrial rights, but also computer programs, databases, chips, and plant variety rights. In the *UNCITRAL Legislative Guide on Secured Transactions*, "intellectual property" means "copyright, trademarks, patents, service marks, trade secrets, designs, and any other assets considered to be intellectual property under the domestic law of the enacting State or under an international agreement to which the enacting State is a Party".[2]

Likewise, it is observed that the term *"intellectual, industrial and commercial property"* was used in the Council decision dated March 6, 1995 in relation to a common position held by the Community on the EC-Turkey Association Council's implementation of the final phase of the Customs Union.[3]

In law school curricula, the term "intellectual law" (fikri hukuk) is used in the narrow sense and usually covers the *author's rights*.

Within the broadest sense of the term "intellectual property" (fikri mülkiyet) employed in recent doctrine, "the law on intellectual and artistic works" and the "law on trade names, undertaking names (i.e. enterprise or business names), and geographical indications" are sometimes distinguished from one another. The first

[1]*See* Tekinalp (2012), pp. 1–5; Brown Keyder (1996), pp. 25 et seq.

[2]*See* UNCITRAL Legislative Guide on Secured Transactions, New York, 2010. Further see UNCITRAL Legislative Guide on Secured Transactions, Terminology and Interpretation, paragraphs 15–20, and UNCITRAL Legislative Guide on Secured Transactions-Terminology and recommendations, Vienna, 2009, and UNCITRAL Legislative Guide on Secured Transactions-Supplement on Security Rights in Intellectual Property, New York, 2011. The reference to international agreements is intended to refer to agreements such as the "Convention Establishing the World Intellectual Property Organization" and the "Agreement on Trade-Related Aspects of Intellectual Property Rights" (TRIPS).

[3]*Cf.* The Decree of the Council of Ministers dated March 19, 2001 on 'Turkey's National Program for Adoption of the Acquis of the EU' and 'Decree concerning the Implementation, Coordination and Following-up of the Turkey's National Program on the Adoption of the Acquis of the EU' (Official Gazette, No. 24352 (Mük.) of March 24, 2001).

category usually comprises the author's rights, patents, and trademark rights, as its subject matter is "works of intelligence." Regarding the second category, it is obvious that trade names, undertaking names (i.e. enterprise, business names), and geographical indications are only distinctive signs. They are not "works of intelligence." They only distinguish one owner of an undertaking from another, or the goods and services of an undertaking from others.

Moreover, some "intellectual works" are distinguished from others. Normally, pure rights in intellectual works do not need to be registered for their protection, while registration is required for the other kinds (e.g. patents, utility models, etc.).[4]

Recently, *Law on Industrial Property*, No. 6769 (Sınai Mülkiyet Kanunu), enacted on December 22, 2016, used the term *"industrial property right"* (sınai mülkiyet hakkı). This term only covers the areas of *"trademark, geographical indication, design, patent and utility model"*. Under this new Law, -as under the previous relevant legislation- a "Registry" for industrial property rights (Sınai Mülkiyet Sicili: SMS) has been established. This Registry represents a recording milieu in which the information on industrial property rights and traditional product names is kept (Article 2(1)(i): Definitions).

1.2 *Categories of Intellectual Property Rights*

Protection of intellectual property is not new to Turkey. In the early days of the foundation of the Republic of Turkey, the Government took steps to protect intellectual property (the Republic's first government instituted a program on September 5, 1923 relating to the "development of arts and national creation").

1.2.1 Copyright

The first endeavour to draft a law for the protection of intellectual and artistic works can be found in the early 1940s ("Hirsch's Draft").[5]

Since its enactment in 1951, the *Law on Intellectual and Artistic Works* (Fikir ve Sanat Eserleri Kanunu: FSEK) No. 5846 has been amended and updated several times. A major amendment Draft is currently being examined. Over the decades, the emergence of new technologies, rapid technological changes, and innovations (e.g. transistor radios, stereo FM transmissions, tape/cassette recorders, digital/Internet audio broadcasting, widespread commercial use of color TV, etc.)

[4]Likewise, "moral rights" are peculiar only to intellectual and artistic works. Compulsory licensing is peculiar to patents in spite of some restrictions regarding "intellectual and artistic works" for public interest. *See* Tekinalp (2012), pp. 1–5.

[5]Despite considerable efforts, the first Law on Intellectual and Artistic Works (Fikir ve Sanat Eserleri Kanunu, FSEK) was enacted on December 5, 1951 (Official Gazette, No. 7931 of December 13, 1951).

necessitated amendments to FSEK. On the other hand, EU-Turkey relations have considerably affected modernization endeavours in the field of copyright law.[6]

Turkey is a party to the following conventions: the Berne Convention for the Protection of Literary and Artistic Works (Paris Revision 1971) (Law No. 4711); the Stockholm Convention Establishing the WIPO (1968); the Rome Convention for the Protection of Performers, Producers of Phonograms and Broadcasting Organizations (1961); the Agreement Establishing the WTO, Annex 1/C: Agreement on Trade-Related Aspects of Intellectual Property Rights (TRIPS).

Under Turkish copyright law, protected works are works that are any kind of intellectual and artistic creation carrying characteristics of their authors. FSEK has distinguished several categories of intellectual and artistic works: (i) scientific and literary works; (ii) musical works; (iii) artistic works; (iv) cinematographic works; and (v) adaptations and compilations.

Under the FSEK, author rights are separated into two groups: (i) moral rights, and (ii) economic rights. FSEK protects the author in his/her rights to exploit the work (e.g. right of reproduction, right of distribution, right of performance, etc.)

1.2.2 Trademarks

Previously, Turkish trademark law was regulated by the *Decree Having the Power of Law [Decree-Law] for Protection of Trademarks* (Markaların Korunması Hakkında Kanun Hükmünde Kararname, KHK/556) of June 24, 1995.[7]

KHK/556 was replaced by *Law on Industrial Property* (Sınai Mülkiyet Kanunu), No. 6769 of December 22, 2016, (Articles 4–31).[8] As explained below, the new Law No. 6769 has a catch-all approach, and accordingly replaces various Decree-Laws which previously covered specific matters.

---

[6] Since its enactment, several amendments have been made to FSEK (in 1983 by Law No. 2936 of November 1, 1983, Law No. 4110 of June 7, 1995, and Law No. 4630 of February 21, 2001) as the result of new technical developments and international agreements relating to the protection of industrial property. These amendments were followed by other amendments relating to new issues and solutions in intellectual property law (Law No. 5101 of March 3, 2004, Law No. 5217 of July 14, 2004, Law No. 5571 of December 28, 2006, Law No. 5718 of November 27, 2007, and Law No. 5728 of January 23, 2008). Thus, provisions protecting computer programs, databases, and neighbouring rights were included in Law No. 5846. (For Law No. 2936: Official Gazette, No. 18210 of November 3, 1983; Law No. 4110: Official Gazette, No. 22311 of June 12, 1995; and Law No. 4630: Official Gazette, No. 24335 of March 3, 2001.)

[7] Although now replaced by the new *Law No. 6769*, it should be noted that KHK/556 has introduced the following features into Turkish intellectual property law: protection of service marks; protection of guarantee and collective marks; absolute and relative grounds for refusal; exhaustion of rights conferred by the registered trademark; publication of applications; opposition by third parties; strong and satisfactory remedies for infringements; and specialized courts for intellectual property law matters.

[8] *See* Official Gazette, No. 29944 of January 10, 2017.

1.2.3 Patents

Turkish patent law was previously regulated by the *Decree Having the Power of Law [Decree-Law] on the Protection of Patent Rights* (Patent Haklarının Korunması Hakkında Kanun Hükmünde Kararname, KHK/551) of June 27, 1995.[9]

KHK/551 was replaced by *Law on Industrial Property* (Sınai Mülkiyet Kanunu), No. 6769 of December 22, 2016. This Law regulates, inter alia, *patents* together with *utility models* (faydalı model) (Articles 82–145).

1.2.4 Designs

Until recently, *designs* (tasarım) were regulated in Turkish law under the title *"industrial design"* (sınai tasarım) by the *Decree Having the Power of Law [Decree-Law] for Protection of Industrial Designs* (Sinai Desenlerin Korunması Hakkında Kanun Hükmünde Kararname, KHK/554) of June 27, 1995.[10] KHK/554 was replaced by *Law on Industrial Property* (Sınai Mülkiyet Kanunu), No. 6769 of December 22, 2016 (Articles 55–81).

1.2.5 Geographic Indications and Traditional Products Names

Previously in Turkish law, the *Decree-Law No. 555 of June 27, 1995 on the Protection of Geographical Indications* (Coğrafi İşaretlerin Korunması Hakkında Kanun Hükmünde Kararname, KHK/555) regulated geographical indications. The system of KHK/555 was based on the TRIPS Agreement. It was also drafted in light of the recent developments in this field.[11]

---

[9]The important novelties brought by KHK/551 to Turkish patent law were: regulation of utility models; introduction of a patent system based on examination and non-examination; criteria for patentability (novelty, inventive step, and susceptibility of industrial applicability); publication of applications; opposition by third parties; protection terms (7 years for non-examined patents, 10 years for utility models, and 20 years for patents granted upon examination); employee inventions; compulsory licensing compatible with the TRIPS Agreement; a system of satisfactory protection against infringements; and a specialized court for patent infringements.

[10]KHK/554 was drafted in light of the TRIPS Agreement as well as EC legislation. KHK/554 introduced the following points into Turkish industrial property law: a system for industrial designs based on registration; non-examination as to the substance; publication of industrial designs; deferment of publication; possibility of multiple applications; opposition by third parties; better protection against infringements on the rights of industrial design; and specialized courts for cases relating to industrial designs.

[11]The following should be mentioned as the major significant points brought by KHK/555 to Turkish law: protection of designation of origin and geographical indications; publication; opposition by all interested parties; relation of geographical indications with trademarks; better protection against infringements; and specialized courts.

KHK/555 was later replaced also by *Law on Industrial Property* (Sınai Mülkiyet Kanunu), No. 6769 of December 22, 2016, Articles 33–54. This Law regulates not only "geographical indications," but also "traditional product names" (geleneksel ürün adı).

1.2.6 Chip Protection

In Turkey, *integrated circuit topographies* are protected by *Law on the Protection of Integrated Circuits Topographies*, No. 5147 of April 22, 2004. The aim of this Law is not only to protect integrated circuit topographies, but also to encourage the development of industry and technology in this field. This Law covers the principles, rules, and requirements for the protection of registered layout designs (topographies) (Article 1).

1.2.7 Plant Variety Protection

In Turkey, *breeder's rights on new varieties of plants* are protected by *Law No. 5042 of January 8, 2004*.

1.3 Law on Movable Pledge (Security) in Commercial Transactions, No. 6750

1.3.1 In General

Movable security in the form of pledge, related to commercial transactions is regulated by *Law on Movable Pledge*[12] *in Commercial Transactions,* No. 6750 of October 20, 2016 (Ticari İşlemlerde Taşınır Rehni Kanunu).[13] This Law has been amended by *Law Amending Certain Laws to Improve Investment Environment (Yatırım Ortamının İyileştirilmesi Amacıyla Bazı Kanunlarda Değişiklik Yapılmasına Dair Kanun)*, No. 7099 of February 15, 2018.[14]

Regarding movable pledge, *Law No. 6750* introduced several new solutions to Turkish law, particularly to the *Turkish Civil Code*, No. 4721 (TMK).

Under the *Turkish Civil Code*, with certain exceptions provided for by law, movables can only be given as security through delivery/transfer of possession to

[12]Although it may be argued that the legal term "pledge" alone is sufficient to describe its nature, scope and contents, we, the writers, chose to use the term "movable pledge" as observed recently in similar papers in English.

[13]*See* Official Gazette, No. 29871 of October 28, 2016.

[14]*See* Official Gazette, No. 30356 of March 10, 2018.

the creditor. No security can be constituted as long as the debtor/grantor retains exclusive control over the movable (Article 939).

Law on Movable Pledge in Commercial Transactions, No. 6750 on (Ticari İşlemlerde Taşınır Rehni Kanunu) has introduced several exceptions into the *Turkish Civil Code*. The most important exception introduced by this Law is the exception to the *principle of delivery/transfer of possession* (*Turkish Civil Code*, Article 939(1)). For certain commercial transactions, entry in the special Registry for Movable Pledge (explained below), rather than transfer of possession, is enough for the creation of a security right over a movable asset (Article 4.1).

Another exception was introduced regarding the principle of lex commissoria. Under the *Turkish Civil Code*, it is prohibited for the creditor to become the owner of the pledged movable (Article 873(2)). *Law No. 6750* introduced an exception to this prohibition in certain commercial transactions (Article 14.1).

The creation of a security right over movables in commercial transactions is further regulated by the *Bylaw on Creation of Security Right and Enjoyment of Post-Default Rights in Commercial Transactions* of December 31, 2016 (Ticari İşlemlerde Rehin Hakkının Kurulması ve Temerrüt Sonrası Hakların Kullanılması Hakkında Yönetmelik).[15]

The establishment and organization of the Registry for Movable Pledge is provided for in the *Bylaw for Registry for Movable Pledge* of December 31, 2016 (Rehinli Taşınır Sicili Yönetmeliği).[16]

1.3.2 Registry for Movable Pledge

Under *Law No. 6750*, the Registry for Movable Pledge (Taşınır Rehin Sicil Sistemi: TARES) shall be established by the Ministry of Customs and Trade (Article 8). However, a protocol was signed on December 23, 2016 between the Ministry and the Union of Public Notaries of Turkey (Türkiye Noterler Birliği). Accordingly, the establishment, organization, management and operation of this Registry have been entrusted to the Union. The organization, administration, and function of TARES are regulated by the *Bylaw for Registry for Movable Pledge* of December 31, 2016 (Rehinli Taşınır Sicili Yönetmeliği). This Bylaw covers the requirements for making an entry in the Registry, the formalities for registration, the basis for the rejection of an application for entry, amendments in the registration, access to registry services, search requests, the removal of records from the Registry, etc.

[15] *See* Official Gazette, No. 29935 (3. Mükerrer) of December 31, 2016.

[16] *See* Official Gazette, No. 29935 (3. Mükerrer) of December 31, 2016.

1.3.3 The Scope of Law on Movable Pledge in Commercial Transactions

The scope of *Law No. 6750* is limited to *certain categories of parties* and *assets* mentioned as "movable" in the Law (Article 5).

1.3.4 Parties to Security Agreements

Under this specific Law, the *parties* to such security agreements can only be *credit institutions*, *merchants* (tacir), *tradesmen/craftsmen* (artisan; esnaf), *farmers* (çiftçi), *producers' organizations* (üretici örgütü), or *self-employed professionals* (serbest meslek erbabı).

Moreover, security agreements can be concluded between *merchants*; between *a merchant and a tradesman*; and between *tradesmen/craftsmen* (artisans; esnaf) (Article 3.1). Parties to security agreements can be physical persons or legal entities.[17]

Credit organizations are *banks* and *finance organizations* under *Law on Banking*, No. 5411 of October 19, 2005 (Bankalar Kanunu). These include public and private credit institutions that carry out activities under *Law on Financial Leasing, Factoring and Finance Corporations*, No. 6361 of November 21, 2012 (Finansal Kiralama, Faktoring ve Finansman Şirketleri Kanunu) (Article 2.1.e). The term *merchant* (tacir) is described by the *Turkish Commercial Code* (Türk Ticaret Kanunu, Article 12), No. 6102 of January 13, 2011. The term *farmer* means the person who is active under *Law on Agriculture* (Tarım Kanunu), No. 5488 of April 18, 2006. *Tradesmen* (esnaf) are persons who carry out a business under *Law on Professional Organizations on Tradesmen and Craftsmen* (artisan; Esnaf ve Sanatkarlar Meslek Kuruluşları Kanunu), No. 5362 of June 7, 2005.

1.3.5 Movable Assets Over Which a Security Right Can Be Established

Under *Law No. 6750*, movable assets that may be encumbered are as follows: receivables; trees that bear fruit for years; intellectual and industrial rights; raw materials; animals; rights to proceeds; proceeds from lease agreements; compensation for goodwill ("droit au bail"); machines; equipment; electronic communication devices; stock; agricultural products; tradenames; company names; commercial enterprises (businesses) (ticari işletme); tradesmen businesses (esnaf işletmesi); commercial projects; wagons; and any similar assets and rights (*Law No. 6750*, Article 5.1.a-p.).[18]

---

[17]For details, see the *Bylaw on Creation of Security Right and Enjoyment of Post-Default Rights in Commercial Transactions* of December 31, 2016, Article 10.

[18]For details see the *Bylaw on Creation of Security Right and Enjoyment of Post-Default Rights in Commercial Transactions* of December 31, 2016, Article 11.

1.3.6 Security Agreement

Under the said Law, security agreements over movable assets must be concluded *in writing* or *electronically* (Article 4.2. See also *Law on Electronic Signature* (Elektronik İmza Kanunu), No. 5070 of January 15, 2004.[19] In order for an agreement to be entered in the Registry (TARES), the signatures of the parties must be notarized or the security agreement must be signed before a Registry officer (Article 4.4).[20]

Security agreements must:

(a) identify the secured creditor and the grantor, in one of the following ways:
   (i) if the party to the security agreement is a commercial company, its trade name and the first and last name of its authorized representative must be provided, together with the representative's signature;
   (ii) if the party is an ordinary physical person or tradesman/craftsman, their identification number, first name, last name, and signature must be provided;
   (iii) if the party is a farmer, their identification number, first name, last name and signature must be provided; and
   (iv) if the party is a producers' organization (üretici örgütü), its licence for production and the first and last name of its authorized representative must be provided, together with the representative's signature;

(b) describe the secured obligation, the amount that the obligation is for, the currency of the payment, and the maximum amount for which the security right may be enforced; and

(c) describe the encumbered asset, identifying features such as the serial number, brand, production date, licence plate, etc. (Article 4.6 a-c).

Under *Law No. 6750* (Article 4.1), a *right of pledge* is created by *the entry* of the pledge (security) agreement in the Registry for Movable Pledge (TARES).

1.3.7 Rights and Obligations of the Parties

The rights and obligations of the parties to a security agreement are described in Articles 12–13 of *Law No. 6750*.

[19] *See* Official Gazette, No. 25355 of January 23, 2004.

[20] For details, see the *Bylaw on Creation of Security Right and Enjoyment of Post-Default Rights in Commercial Transactions* of December 31, 2016, Article 18.

1.3.8 Effectiveness of the Security Right (Movable Pledge) Against Third Parties

The security right (movable pledge) is effective *against third parties* as soon as the security agreement is entered in the Registry (Article 9.1). *Law No. 6750* provides a *degree system* under which the security provided by the security right is limited to the secured amount and degree indicated in the Registry (TARES). Therefore, in determining the priority between multiple secured parties, the mutually agreed degree of the specific security can be more relevant than the time of its entry in the Registry. Under *Law No. 6750, differently ranking security rights* can be created. Comparable to rights in mortgages over immovable property under the *Turkish Civil Code*, under *Law No. 6750* the parties may stipulate in their security agreement the right *to move up to free (empty) degrees* (Article 10.1-2).[21]

1.3.9 Priority Rights

If several security rights have been established over the same movable asset without any indication of priority in the security agreement, the priority rights of creditors are determined at the time of TARES registration (*Law No. 6750*, Article 11.1).[22]

1.3.10 Post-default Rights

Law No. 6750 has introduced several alternatives for secured creditors with regard to the *enforcement of security rights* in *case of default by the grantor* (Article 14.1.a). The new solutions introduced in Turkish law are described below.

Under Article 14.1.a of *Law No. 6750*, the secured creditor may request *transfer of title of the encumbered movable asset* in accordance with the *Code of Enforcement and Bankruptcy* (Icra Iflas Kanunu), No. 2004 of June 9, 1932 (as amended) (Article 24).[23]

Under *Law No. 6750*, the secured creditor is entitled to *assign its receivables to an asset management company* operating under *Law on Banking*, No. 5411 (*Law No. 6750*, Article 14.1.b).

The secured creditor may apply to pursue their *debt in accordance with general rules* (*Law No. 6750*, Article 14.1.ç).

---

[21] For details, see the *Bylaw on Creation of Security Right and Enjoyment of Post-Default Rights in Commercial Transactions* of December 31, 2016, Articles 24–26.

[22] See also the *Bylaw on Creation of Security Right and Enjoyment of Post-Default Rights in Commercial Transactions*, of December 31, 2016, Article 33.

[23] For details, see also the *Bylaw of December 31, 2016 on Creation of Security Right and Enjoyment of Post-Default Rights in Commercial Transactions*, Articles 30–41.

In some circumstances, the secured creditor may use *rental or licensing rights* with respect to secured assets that are not subject to transfer of possession (Article 14.1.c).

1.3.11 Extinguishment of Security Rights

A security right is extinguished when all secured obligations have been discharged. In such a case, the secured creditor subject to Turkish law shall apply to the Registry to have the security deleted within 15 days following the date of extinguishment of the receivable (Article 15.1). Creditors subject to foreign law can apply within 30 days (Article 15.1).

1.3.12 Legal Situation of Security Rights Over Intellectual and Industrial Property Rights

If the security right is to be created over an intellectual or industrial property right within the scope of *Law No. 6750* as part of a *"commercial transaction"* between the *parties specified by this Law*, the entry of the security agreement in the Registry for Movable Pledge (TARES) is enough for its creation (Article 4.1; *Bylaw on Creation of Security Right and Enjoyment of Post-Default Rights in Commercial Transactions* of December 31, 2016, Articles 2; 19).

Where the parties to the security agreement are not the parties specified by *Law No. 6750* (Article 3), a security right over intellectual and industrial property can be established in accordance with the specific legislation on security rights: Security rights over intellectual and artistic works are subject to *Law on Intellectual and Artistic Works*, No. 5846 (Fikir ve Sanat Eserleri Kanunu: FSEK). The security agreement must be in writing and the subject matter of the security right must be specified in the agreement (Article 62/II).

Regarding security rights over industrial property rights, the requirements pertaining to the security agreement and its entry in the Registry maintained by the *Turkish Patent and Trademark Office* (Türk Patent ve Marka Kurumu) are specified by *Law on Industrial Property* (Sınai Mülkiyet Kanunu), No. 6769 of December 22, 2016, Article 148. *Security agreements* must be in *written form* like other transactions on such rights (Article 148.4). They are entered in the Registry (SMS) and published in the *Bulletin* ("Bülten": a publication for all industrial property rights) (Article 148.5.)[24]

[24]See also *Law on Patent Attorneys and Trademark Attorneys and Some Regulations*, No. 5000, previously named *Law on Formation and Duties of Turkish Patent and Trademark Office* (Patent ve Marka Vekilliği ve Bazı Düzenlemeler Hakkında Kanun, Türk Patent ve Marka Kurumu Kuruluş ve Görevleri Hakkında Kanun (as last amended on July 9, 2018 by KHK/703), Official Gazette, No. 25294 of November 6, 2003.

The Registry for Movable Pledge (TARES)[25] is notified of *records of security rights* in the Registry for Industrial Property Rights (SMS).[26]

In short, since the new *Law on Movable Pledge in Commercial Transactions*, No. 6750 came into force, two different registries (TARES and the Registry (SMS) of Turkish Patent and Trademark Office) exist for the registration of particular security rights under Turkish law. Specific security rights between certain parties are covered by the new *Law No. 6750*. Others outside the scope of this specific Law continue to be registered only at the Registry (SMS) of the Turkish Patent and Trademark Office. These two different registries are not to be confused with each other.

2 Categories of Security Rights

According to the *Turkish Civil Code* (TCC), No. 4721 (Articles 954 et seq.) and *Turkish Code of Obligations* (TCO), No. 6098 (Article 1), a party with an interest in intellectual property (IP) may create *a consensual security right* to secure of an obligation (TCC Article 954 et seq.).[27]

An IP right can be given as a security right to secure the debtor's own obligation or another person's obligation. Moreover, IP rights can be the subject matter of fiduciary transactions. The ownership of an IP right can be transferred for security purposes as a fiduciary transaction (German: "Sicherungsübereignung").

Security transactions in IP rights which create a security right are explained below.

---

[25]Website: https://www.tares.org.tr/nbsweb-tasinirRehinSorgu-app/public/main.xhtml.

[26]See the *Bylaw on Implementation of Law on Industrial Property* of April 24, 2017 (Sınai Mülkiyet Kanununun Uygulanması Hakkında Yönetmelik), Article 127.2,Official Gazette, No. 30047 of April 24, 2017.

[27]Under the *UNCITRAL Legislative Guide on Secured Transactions*, *"secured transaction"* means a "transaction that creates a security right". *"Security right"* refers to all types of property right in a movable asset that are created by agreement to secure payment or other performance of an obligation, irrespective how they are nominated. The term "security right" covers the right of a pledgee or mortgagee of intellectual property (as well as of a transferee in a transfer for security purposes). *"Security agreement"* means an agreement, using whatever form or terminology, between a grantor and a creditor that creates a security right. *"Secured obligation"* means an obligation secured by a security right. As regards *"encumbered asset,"* it means a tangible or intangible asset that is subject to a security right. The term also covers a receivable that has been the subject of an outright transfer. For all these concepts, see *UNCITRAL Legislative Guide on Secured Transactions*, pp. 12–13. Further, see *UNCITRAL Legislative Guide on Secured Transactions – Terminology and recommendations,* pp. xiv–xv, *UNCITRAL Legislative Guide on Secured Transactions-Supplement on Security Rights in Intellectual Property,* pp. 11–13.

2.1 Security Transactions Related to Copyright

Security transactions on copyright are regulated by the *Law on Intellectual and Artistic Works* (FSEK), No. 5846 (as amended).

The aim of FSEK is to protect intellectual and artistic works and the rights of authors. Under FSEK, authors' economic rights can be the subject of a security right.

2.1.1 Permitted Cases

Copyright as the Subject Matter of a Security Right

Under FSEK, the following may constitute the subject of a legal or contractual security right (or a forced execution or retention):

- drafts or originals of a work made public;
- reproduced copies of a published work;
- economic rights of the author over a work that has become public (provided the author's moral rights are not affected prejudicially); and
- money debts due to the author as a result of legal transactions concerning economic rights (Article 62/I).

Form of Security Agreement

Security agreements concerning either intellectual and artistic works or economic rights must be in writing, and the subjects of the security right must be specified in the agreement (FSEK Art. 62/II).[28] Under *Law on Movable Pledge in Commercial Transactions*, No. 6750 security agreement shall be made in written form or electronically (elektronik ortamda) (Article 4(2)).

2.1.2 Prohibited Cases

Under FSEK, the following may not constitute the subject of a legal or contractual security right (or a forced execution or retention):

[28]Under FSEK, moulds and other devices used to reproduce artistic works may be temporarily seized from their holders (possessors) if they are considered necessary to execute enforcement of collection of a debt relating to economic rights (Article 62/III). Likewise, with the exception of architectural works, originals of artistic works and drafts of musical, scientific, and literary works belonging to the author or his/her heirs may be temporarily seized from their holders (possessors) if this is deemed necessary to execute enforcement of collection of a debt relating to economic rights (Article 62/IV).

- drafts or originals of a work not yet made public, which are the property of the author or one of his heirs;
- the economic rights of such works, except for cinematographic works; and
- debts due to the author, other than money resulting from legal transactions concerning economic rights (Article 61).

It should be noted that in the cases mentioned above, Articles 24 and 30 of the *Code of Enforcement and Bankruptcy* (Icra ve Iflas Kanunu, IIK), No. 2004 (as amended) are reserved.

2.2 Security Transactions on Patents

Under *Law on Industrial Property*, No. 6769, all industrial property rights can be transferred, inherited, and considered the subject matter of a licence agreement. They may constitute the subject of a forced execution or retention. They can also be the subject matter of a security agreement, which creates a security right (Article 148/I). Secured transactions and security agreements on a patent or patent application should be in writing. The patent can independently be the subject matter of a security agreement associated with the undertaking.

All transactions relating to industrial property rights are entered in the (Industrial Property Rights) Registry (SMS) and announced in the *Bulletin* upon the request of one of the parties; payment of the fee, and implementation of the other requirements are indicated in the Bylaw. Rights arising out of legal transactions not entered in the Registry cannot be put forward to third parties in good faith, except for those contained in the provisions of Article 115 (Article 148 of *Law on Industrial Property*, No. 6769).

2.3 Secured Transactions on Trademarks

Under *Law on Industrial Property*, No. 6769, trademarks can be the subject matter of a security agreement independently from the related enterprise and can also be the subject matter of other transactions mentioned in Article 148.

Like secured transactions of patents, security agreements relating to trademarks are subject to written form and, in accordance with the same requirements for other industrial property rights, they are registered in the Registry (SMS).

2.4 Designs

As an industrial property right, *"designs"* may be the subject matter of secured transactions like trademarks and patents. They can be the subject matter of a security agreement, which creates a security right. On the request of one of the parties, they are entered in the (Industrial Property Rights) Registry (SMS) and announced in the *Bulletin*. The payment of the fee and the implementation of other requirements are indicated in the Bylaw.

Rights arising out of legal transactions that are not entered in the Registry (SMS) cannot be put forward to third parties in good faith, except for those contained in the provisions of Article 115 (Article 148 of *Law on Industrial Property*, No. 6769).

2.5 Geographical Indications and Traditional Product Names

Under *Law on Industrial Property*, No. 6769, geographical indications and traditional product names may neither be the subject matter of legal transactions such as licenses, transfers, successions, attachments etc. nor can they be provided as colleteral for securities (Article 148/I).

3 Structure of Transactions: Attachment and Perfection

3.1 Form of Security Transaction

Under *Law on Intellectual and Artistic Works*, No. 5846 (FSEK) (Article 52) and *Law on Industrial Property,* No. 6769 (Article 148), security transactions relating to copyright and industrial property rights are subject to *written form*, as explained above. Under *Law on Movable Pledge in Commercial Transactions*, No. 6750, security agreements shall be made either in written form or electronically (elektronik ortamda) (Article 4(2)).

4 Priorities

4.1 The Right of Priority and Its Effects on Third Parties

As formulated in *the UNCITRAL Legislative Guide on Secured Transactions*, priority means "the right of a person to derive the economic benefit of its security right in preference to the right of a competing claimant." "Competing claimant means a creditor of a grantor that is competing with another creditor of the grantor having a security right in an encumbered asset of the grantor and includes:

(a) Another creditor with a security right in the same encumbered asset [. . .];
(b) Another creditor of the grantor that has a right in the same encumbered asset;
(c) The insolvency representative in the insolvency proceedings in respect of the grantor; or
(d) Any buyer or other transferee (including lessee or licensee) of the encumbered asset"[29]

4.2 Priority Rights Regarding Selected IP Rights

4.2.1 Priority Rights Relating to Trademarks

Persons eligible for the priority rights relating to the protection of a trademark are defined under *Law on Industrial Property*, No. 6769. The following categories of persons may benefit from protection: (a) nationals of the Republic of Turkey; (b) persons or legal persons who are domiciled or have an active industrial or commercial business within the territory of the Republic of Turkey; (c) persons having the right to application in accordance with the Paris Convention or the Agreement Establishing the World Trade Organization of April 15, 1964; and, (d) in accordance with the principle of reciprocity, nationals of foreign States that recognize industrial property rights for Turkish nationals (Article 3).

As regards the right of priority, we can distinguish between "priority right under international conventions" and "exhibition priority."

Priority Rights Under International Conventions

According to *Law on Industrial Property,* No. 6769 "(i) natural or legal persons or their successors in title (i) *who are nationals of any State party to the Paris Convention or Agreement Establishing the WTO*; or, (ii) *if not, nationals who are domiciled or have an active business in these States"* may, from the date of filing a valid application for registration of a trademark with the authorized bodies of these States, enjoy a right of priority of six months for the purpose of filing an application for a registration certificate in Turkey in respect of the same trademark. To enjoy this priority right, a priority document should be obtained from the authorized body of the State to which the first application has been made (Article 12.1).[30]

[29]*See UNCITRAL Legislative Guide on Secured Transactions*, pp.185 et seq. Further, see *UNCITRAL Legislative Guide on Secured Transactions –Terminology and recommendations, pp. xiv; UNCITRAL Legislative Guide on Secured Transactions-Supplement on Security Rights in Intellectual Property,* pp. 77 et seq.

[30]Any priority right not exercised within this period is forfeited (Article 12.1).

Moreover, if *a natural or legal person who is a national of the State which is a party to the Paris Convention or the WTO Agreement* has filed a valid application *in a State not party to these Conventions*, he/she/it may enjoy a priority right in respect of that filing (Article 12.2).

Exhibition Priority

Natural or legal persons specified in Article 3 (i.e. persons eligible for the protection of trademarks) who have displayed the goods or services for which the trademark has been applied (either at national or international exhibitions in Turkey or at official or officially recognized national or international exhibitions in those States party to the Paris Convention or WTO Agreement) may claim a right of priority for registration of the trademark in Turkey if the application of priority is filed within a period of six months from the date of the first display of the goods (Article 12.3).

Effect of Priority Rights

The effects of priority rights under Article 12 arise as of the date of the application for which the priority is declared. An applicant wishing to benefit from his right of priority should file a declaration of priority with his application for registration of the trademark. If the document relating to the right of priority has not been submitted within three months after the date of filing, the applicant does not benefit from this right anymore (Article 13.1).

4.2.2 Priority Rights Relating to Designs

According to the Paris Convention on the Protection of Industrial Property, designs enjoy the right of priority of six months (Article 62.1).[31]

A distinction between *"priority rights under international conventions"* and *"exhibition priority"* can be made with regard to designs.

Priority Rights Under International Conventions

Under *Law on Industrial Property*, No. 6769, "(i) natural or legal persons or their successors in title who are nationals of any State party to *the Paris Convention* or *Agreement Establishing the WTO*; or, (ii) if not, nationals who are domiciled or have an active business in these States" may, from the date of filing with the authorized

[31] *Cf. Directive 98/71/EC of the European Parliament and of the Council of October 13, 1998 on the legal protection of designs* (Article 6).

bodies of these States, enjoy a right of priority of six months for the purpose of filing an application for a registration certificate in Turkey in respect of the same design. To enjoy this priority right, a priority document should be obtained from the authorized body of the State to which the first application has been made (Article 62.1).[32]

Furthermore, if a natural or legal person who is a national of the State which is a party to the Paris Convention or the WTO Agreement has filed a valid application in a State not party to these Conventions, he may enjoy a priority right in respect of that filing (Article 62.2).

Exhibition Priority

Natural or legal persons specified in Article 3 (i.e. persons eligible for the protection of trademarks) who have displayed the design or the product for which the design has been applied (either at national or international exhibitions in Turkey or at official or officially recognized national or international exhibitions in those States party to the Paris Convention or WTO Agreement) may claim a right of priority for registration of the design in Turkey if the application of priority is filed within a period of six months from the date of the first display (Article 62.5). If the product has been displayed at the exhibition before the official opening date, the right of priority starts from the date on which the product was first displayed at the exhibition (Article 62.6).

Effect of Priority Rights

The effects of priority rights under Article 62.1 arise as of the date of the application for the priority right. An applicant wishing to benefit from his right of priority should file a declaration of priority with his application for registration of the design (Article 63.1).

5 Enterprise Charges

Under Turkish law, IP rights can be part of a security over all the assets of a company enterprise.

[32]Any priority right not exercised within this period is forfeited (Article 62.1).

6 Rights Before Default

Under Turkish law, the provisions of the *Turkish Civil Code* relating to *security agreements on movables and claims* apply *mutatis mutandis* to security agreements on IP rights (Articles 954/II and 959, 961, and *Bylaw on Implementation of the Law on Industrial Property* (Sınai Mülkiyet Kanununun Uygulanmasına Dair Yönetmelik), Article 127). The mutual rights and obligations of the parties to a security agreement can be summarized as follows:

- The principle of party autonomy applies to security rights in IP, subject to any limitations specifically laid down by law relating to IP.
- The secured creditor may exercise some of the rights of the owner/grantor (e.g. renew registrations or pursue infringers).
- The secured creditor must take reasonable steps to preserve the IP right (i.e. the asset) and its value.
- The secured creditor may collect royalties owed to the owner/grantor as licensor even before default on the part of the owner/grantor.
- The secured creditor must return the encumbered IP right (i.e. the asset) if the security right has been extinguished through full payment or otherwise.
- The owner/grantor may not grant licences (in particular, exclusive licences).[33]

7 Enforcement

7.1 In Case of Default

In case of default, the encumbered IP right is enforced under the *Code of Enforcement and Bankruptcy,* No. 2004 of June 9, 1932 (Icra ve Iflas Kanunu: IIK). Before enforcement, the value of the IP right should be evaluated as prescribed under IIK. Several criteria and methods exist regarding this evaluation. According to IIK, it can be carried out by an expert (Article 87). Nevertheless, in practice, the evaluation is also carried out by expert institutions. In respect of encumbered trademarks and patents, the following points must be noted.

With regard to the assessment of trademarks, the sector in which the trademark is used, the number of years it has been used, the proceeds earned by the use of the trademark, the advertising costs for the trademark, the influence of the trademark upon sales, etc. are taken into account.

Regarding the assessment of patents, the provisions of *Communique No. 5.14.4.1.1* published in the Official Gazette, No. 29333 of April 21, 2015 apply. According to these provisions, there are several assessment methods that

[33] *Cf. UNCITRAL Legislative Guide on Secured Transactions - Supplement on Security Rights in Intellectual Property*, UN., New York, 2011, Nos. 222 et seq.

are taken into consideration: methods based on owning costs, on marketing, and on proceeds from the patent.

After the assessment of an IP right, the encashment of the right is carried out in accordance with Article 121 of the *Code of Enforcement and Bankruptcy,* No. 2004. In such cases, the Enforcement Director (Icra Müdürü) should ask the *Enforcement Court* (Icra Mahkemesi) to decide how the sale of the encumbered IP right is to be carried out. For instance, the Enforcement Court may decide, after the relevant persons are heard, that the sale shall be made in accordance with the rules relating to *public auction* (açık artırma) and that the sale price shall be given to the creditors. It may also appoint *a specific sale officer to carry out the encashment procedure* or take other *relevant measures* (Article 121). *Sale through bargaining* (pazarlık yoluyla satış) is another significant option that may be chosen by the Enforcement Court.

In case of a public auction, ownership of the IP right passes to the buyer as a result of the Enforcement Director's decision on the tender bid.

7.2 In Case of Bankruptcy

If the grantor becomes insolvent and bankruptcy proceedings are initiated against him, the encumbered IP right (e.g. trademark or patent) is covered by the mass of bankruptcy (iflas masası); however, the secured creditor's priority rights remain as before, they are not affected. The encumbered IP right is then encashed by the *bankruptcy administration* (iflas idaresi) and, after the deduction of maintenance and sales costs, the value of the IP right is paid to the creditor (*Code of Enforcement and Bankruptcy*, No. 2004, Article 185/1).

8 Typical Costs

This section covers the minimum costs related to several transactions on IP rights.

Legal Counselling/Assistance Bar Associations of various Turkish cities annually update their own recommendations for local minimum attorneys' fees. Moreover, *Minimum Fees for Attorneys* are announced by the *Union of Turkish Bar Associations (TBB).* These fees are made public on their official websites on the Internet.

Note that attorneys-at-law (avukat) are not licensed to represent clients before the *Turkish Patent and Trademark Office* (Türk Patent ve Marka Kurumu). Representation in administrative procedures before this office (e.g. during registration) can only be carried out by licensed patent attorneys (Patent Vekili) or licensed trademark attorneys (Marka Vekili), who are not necessarily attorneys-at-law. They also charge their own fees for their services.

Notarial Costs Regarding *notarial costs*, the following items must be considered:

- Notarization of a security agreement and registration,
- Notarization of the amendment of a security agreement and registration,
- Notarization of the deletion of a security,
- Notarized documents (per page), etc.

The above fees are relatively reasonable and are calculated by an official software used by public notaries. Since the fees and especially foreign currency exchange rates may change in time, it is advisable for foreigners to have then roughly calculated as they stand at the relevant time.

Costs for Application and Registration These formalities are carried out by the *Turkish Patent and Trademark Office* (Türk Patent ve Marka Kurumu). As of mid 2020, the security transaction registration fee (Rehin İşlemi Kayıt Ücreti) for patents and trademarks is TRY 590 (ca. USD 85.00) if this is done *online*. All fees (and if needed, current exchange rates) should be double-checked at the relevant time.

9 Practical Usefulness

In practice in Turkey, it is rather rare to obtain credit from a bank or financial institution through security over IP rights. It is important to note that this is due to the ambiguity regarding the assessment of IP rights.

Nevertheless, following the enactment of the above-mentioned *Law on Movable Pledge in Commercial Transactions*, No. 6570 of October 20, 2016 (Ticari İşlemlerde Taşınır Rehni Kanunu), security transactions on movable property are expected to increase in the near future. Under this Law, "intellectual and industrial property rights" are specified inter alia as "movable property" (Article 5/c). They can be the subject matter of a security transaction through registration in the Registry for Movable Pledge (TARES) (Article 1/1).[34]

It is expected in relevant circles that small and medium-sized enterprises (SMEs) will be able to obtain credit from financial institutions (e.g. banks, etc.) through this type of security.

10 Legal and/or Practical Difficulties

As explained in the previous paragraph, the main difficulty regarding security transactions on IP rights is caused by *inexperience with the relevant business circles and ambiguity relating to the assessment of intellectual property rights*.

[34]This law entered into force on January 1, 2017 (Article 20). *See* Official Gazette, No. 29871 of October 28, 2016.

11 Law Reform

As explained above, *Law on Industrial Property*, No. 6769 of December 22, 2016 (Sınai Mülkiyet Kanunu) and *Law on Movable Pledge in Commercial Transactions,* No. 6570 of October 20, 2016 are rather recent legislative acts. These two laws are based, in general, on recent developments in these fields of law and are in harmony with foreign and international legislation.

Law on Movable Pledge in Commercial Transactions, No. 6750 has not introduced the system and solutions of the *UNCITRAL Model Law on Secured Transactions.* Nevertheless, as explained above, this Law has introduced some exceptions to the classic security rights over movables laid down by the *Turkish Civil Code* and the relevant legislation. These exceptions added to the practical use of these type of securities and made them commercially more attractive than before.

Under *Law No. 6750* regarding commercial transactions between the parties specified by this Law, security rights over "movables" as defined in this Law can be created by entering a security agreement into the Registry (TARES) established by this Law. For a certain category of commercial transactions, the transfer of possession of these movables is no longer a legal requirement.

Moreover, *Law No. 6750* has introduced another exemption to the principle of prohibition of lex commissoria. Within the scope of this Law, a secured creditor is entitled *to request transfer of title of the encumbered movable* (Article 14.1.a). The solutions relating to post default rights of *Law No. 6750* are new for the Turkish security law.

As regards the registry system of *Law No. 6750*, the Registry (TARES) to be established under this Law has not been inspired by the registry system specified by the *UNCITRAL Model Law on Secured Transactions* (Article 28 et seq. of Model Law). Turkish *Law, No. 6750* does not adopt the concepts "registration of a notice", "registration of an amendment or cancellation notice", "search criteria in the Registry", etc.[35]

The authors of this paper are of the opinion that regarding the law reform in this field of law Turkish lawmakers should also consider *UNCITRAL Model Law on Secured Transactions* and *relevant UNCITRAL texts* and eventually introduce the UNCITRAL system of secured transactions to the Turkish law ("de lege ferenda").

[35] *Cf. UNCITRAL Guide on the Implementation of a Security Rights Registry.*

Turkish Legal Sources

Codes, Laws, Bylaws, Presidential Decrees, and Other Regulations

Select Codes and Laws

- Turkish Civil Code (TCC), No. 4721 of November 22, 2001 (Türk Medeni Kanunu: TMK), Official Gazette, No. 24607 of December 8, 2001.
- Turkish Code of Obligations (TCO), No. 6098 of January 11, 2011 (Türk Borçlar Kanunu: TBK), Official Gazette, No. 27836 of February 4, 2011.
- Turkish Commercial Code (TComC), No. 6102 of January 13, 2011 (Türk Ticaret Kanunu: TTK), Official Gazette, No. 27846 of February 14, 2011.
- Turkish Penal Code (TPC), No. 5237 of September 26, 2004 (Türk Ceza Kanunu: TCK), Official Gazette, No. 25611 of October 12, 2004.
- Law on Intellectual and Artistic Works (Fikir ve Sanat Eserleri Kanunu: FSEK), No. 5846 of December 5, 1951 (as amended several times), Official Gazette, No. 7981 of December 13, 1951.
- Law on Industrial Property (Sınai Mülkiyet Kanunu), No. 6769 of December 22, 2016, Official Gazette, No. 29944 of January 10, 2017.
- Law on Movable Pledge in Commercial Transactions (Ticari İşlemlerde Taşınır Rehni Kanunu), No. 6570 of October 20, 2016, Official Gazette, No. 29871 of October 28, 2016.
- Code of Civil Procedure (CCP), No. 6100 of January 12, 2011 (Hukuk Muhakemeleri Kanunu: HMK), Official Gazette, No. 27836 of February 4, 2011.
- Code of Enforcement and Bankruptcy (CEB), No. 2004 of June 9, 1932 (Icra ve Iflas Kanunu: IIK, as amended several times. Last amendments entered into force on March 15, 2018), Official Gazette, No. 2128 of June 19, 1932.
- Act (= Law) on Private International Law and Procedural Law, No. 5718 of November 27, 2007 (Milletlerarası Özel Hukuk ve Usul Hukuku Hakkında Kanun: MÖHUK), Official Gazette, No. 26728 of December 12, 2007 (APIL).
- Law on Press (Basın Kanunu), No. 5187 of June 9, 2004, Official Gazette, No. 25504 of June 26, 2004.
- Law on Evaluation, Classification and Support of Cinematographic Works (Sinema Filmlerinin Değerlendirilmesi ve Sınıflandırılması ile Desteklenmesi Hakkında Kanun), No. 5224 of July 14, 2004, Official Gazette, No. 25529 of July 21, 2004.
- Law on Protection of Breeder's Rights on New Varieties of Plants, No. 5042 of January 8, 2004 (Yeni Bitki Çeşitlerine Ait Islahçı Haklarının Korunmasına İlişkin Kanun), Official Gazette, No. 25347 of January 15, 2004.
- Law on the Protection of Integrated Circuit Topographies, No. 5147 of April 22, 2004 (Entegre Devre Topografyalarının Korunması Hakkında Kanun), Official Gazette, No. 25448 of April 30, 2004.

Other Regulations

- Bylaw on Commercial Registry (Ticaret Sicili Yönetmeliği), Official Gazette, No. 28541 of January 27, 2013.
- Bylaw on Registry for Movable Pledge (Rehinli Taşınır Sicili Yönetmeliği), Official Gazette, No. 29935 of December 31, 2016.
- Bylaw on Creation of Security Rights and Enjoyment of Post-Default Rights in Commercial Transactions (Ticari İşlemlerde Rehin Hakkının Kurulması ve Temerrüt Sonrası Hakların Kullanılması Hakkında Yönetmelik), Official Gazette, No. 29935 of December 31, 2016.
- Bylaw on Recording and Registration of Intellectual and Artistic Works (Fikir ve Sanat Eserlerinin Kayıt ve Tescili Hakkında Yönetmelik), Official Gazette, No. 26171 of May 17, 2006.
- Bylaw on Implementation of the Law on Industrial Property (Sınai Mülkiyet Kanununun Uygulanmasına Dair Yönetmelik), Official Gazette, No. 30047 of April 24, 2017.
- Bylaw on Protection of Breeder's Rights on New Varieties of Plants (Yeni Bitki Çeşitlerinin Korunmasına Dair Yönetmelik), Official Gazette, No. 25551 of August 12, 2004.
- Bylaw on Protection of Integrated Circuit Topographies (Entegre Devre Topografyalarının Korunması Hakkında Kanunun Uygulanma Şeklini Gösterir Yönetmelik), Official Gazette, No. 25686 of December 30, 2004.

International Legal Sources

- Under the current Turkish Constitution, No. 2709 (Art. 90), international agreements ratified by the Turkish Grand National Assembly are constituent parts of Turkish law.
- In the field of international intellectual property, Turkey has signed and ratified various multilateral agreements. The following multilateral agreements are of most importance:
  - Convention Establishing the World Intellectual Property Organization (WIPO) of July 14, 1967, as amended in 1979. It was ratified by Turkey (Official Gazette, No. 15417 of November 11, 1975).
  - Paris Convention for the Protection of Industrial Property of March 20, 1883, revised at Brussels (1900), Washington (1911), The Hague (1925), London (1934), Lisbon (1958) and Stockholm (1967), and amended in 1979. It was ratified by Turkey (*see* Official Gazette, No. 15418 of November 20, 1975). Turkey has renounced the reservation relating to Arts. 1-12 through Governmental Decree No. 94/5903 (Official Gazette, No. 22060 of September 23, 1994).

- Madrid Agreement for the Repression of False or Deceptive Indications of Source on Goods of April 14, 1891, revised at Washington (1911), The Hague (1925), London (1934), Lisbon (1958), and supplemented by the Additional Act of Stockholm (1967). It was ratified by Turkey (Official Gazette, No. 9529 of February 7, 1957).
- Madrid Agreement Concerning the International Registration of Marks of April 14, 1891, revised at Brussels (1900), Washington (1911), The Hague (1925), London (1934), Nice (1957), and Stockholm (1967), and amended in 1979. Turkey had ratified The Hague's version (1925) of the Madrid Agreement (Official Gazette, No. 1506 of May 29, 1930). However, it set aside this agreement in 1955 through Decree, No. 4/5215 (Official Gazette, No. 9059 of July 20, 1955).
- Protocol relating to the Madrid Agreement Concerning the International Registration of Marks (as signed at Madrid on June 28, 1989). Turkey adhered to this protocol through Decree No. 97/9731 of August 5, 1997 (Official Gazette, No. 23088 (Mük.) of August 22, 1997).
- Implementing Bylaw Concerning the Madrid Agreement and Related Protocol for International Registration of Marks (Markaların Uluslararası Tesciline İlişkin Madrid Anlaşması ve Bu Anlaşmaya İlişkin Protokolün Uygulanmasına Dair Yönetmelik), (Official Gazette, No. 23637 of March 12, 1999).
- Nice Agreement Concerning the International Classification of Goods and Services for the Purposes of the Registration of Marks of June 15, 1957, revised at Stockholm (1967) and at Geneva (1977), and amended in 1979. It was ratified pursuant to Decree No. 95/7094 of July 12, 1995 (Official Gazette, No. 22373 of August 13, 1995).
- Vienna Agreement Establishing an International Classification of the Figurative Elements of Marks of June 12, 1973 and amended on October 1, 1985. It was ratified pursuant to Decree No. 95/7094 of July 12, 1995 (Official Gazette, No. 22373 of August 13, 1995).
- Trademark Law Treaty (adopted at Geneva on October 27, 1994). Turkey ratified this Treaty pursuant to Law, No. 5118 of April 7, 2004. It entered into force in Turkey on January 1, 2005.
- Hague Agreement Concerning the International Deposit of Industrial Designs of November 6, 1925, revised at London (1934) and The Hague (1960), supplemented by the additional Act of Monaco (1961), the Complementary Act of Stockholm (1967), and the Protocol of Geneva (1975), and amended in 1979. Turkey ratified this agreement pursuant to Law, No. 5117 of April 7, 2004. It entered into force on January 1, 2005.
- Locarno Agreement Establishing an International Classification for Industrial Designs of October 8, 1968, as amended on September 28, 1979. Turkey adhered to this agreement through Decree, No. 97/9731 of August 5, 1997 (Official Gazette, No. 23088 (1. Mük.) of August 22, 1997).

- Patent Cooperation Treaty (PCT) of June 19, 1970 (Washington), amended in 1979 and modified in 1984. It was ratified pursuant to Law, No. 415 of July 7, 1995 (Official Gazette, No. 22341 of July 12, 1995).
- Implementing Bylaw Concerning the Patent Cooperation Treaty (Patent İşbirliği Antlaşmasına Dair Yönetmelik). This Bylaw was in force as of July 1992 (Tutanak Dergisi [Review for Protocols, Period 19, Legislative Year 3. No. 665]).
- Convention on the Unification of Certain Points of Substantive Law on Patents for Invention of November 27, 1963.
- Convention on the Grant of European Patents (European Patent Convention) of October 5, 1973 as amended on December 21, 1978; December 17, 1991; December 13, 1994; October 20, 1995; and December 5, 1996. This Convention and its protocols were ratified by Turkey pursuant to Law, No. 4504 of January 27, 2000 (Official Gazette, No. 23948 of January 29, 2000).
- Act Revising the Convention on the Grant of European Patents (European Patent Convention) of November 29, 2001. EPC 2000 entered into force on December 13, 2007. This Convention was ratified by Turkey pursuant to Law, No. 5598 of March 13, 2007 (Official Gazette, No. 26465 of March 17, 2007).
- Implementing Bylaw Concerning the Validation of European Patents Related to European Patent Convention in Turkey (Avrupa Patentlerinin Verilmesi İle İlgili Avrupa Patent Sözleşmesinin Türkiyede Uygulanma Şeklini Gösterir Yönetmelik) (Official Gazette, No. 24282 of January 9, 2001) and Amending Implementing Bylaw of this Bylaw (Official Gazette, No. 26883 of May 22, 2008).
- Strasbourg Agreement Concerning the International Patent Classification of March 24, 1971, as amended on October 2, 1979. It was ratified pursuant to Decree, No. 95/7094 of July 12, 1995 (Official Gazette, No. 22373 of August 12, 1995).
- Budapest Treaty on the International Recognition of the Deposit of Microorganisms for the Purposes of Patent Procedure of April 28, 1977, modified in 1980. Turkey adhered to this treaty through Decree, No. 97/9731 of August 5, 1997 (Official Gazette, No. 23088 (Mük.) of August 22, 1997).
- International Convention for the Protection of New Varieties of Plants of December 2, 1961, revised at Geneva (1972 and 1978), and revised again at Geneva in 1991.
- Berne Convention for the Protection of Literary and Artistic Works of September 9, 1886, completed at Paris (1896); revised at Berlin (1908); completed at Berne (1914); revised at Rome (1928), at Brussels (1948), at Stockholm (1967), and at Paris (1971); and modified in 1979. The Paris version of the Convention was ratified by Turkey pursuant to Law No. 4117 of July 7, 1995 (Official Gazette, No. 22341 of July 12, 1995).
- Universal Copyright Convention of September 6, 1952, revised at Paris (1971).
- International Convention for the Protection of Performers, Producers of Phonograms and Broadcasting Organizations (Rome Convention) of October

26, 1961. It was ratified pursuant to Law No. 4116 of July 7, 1995 (Official Gazette of July 12, 1995).

- Convention for the Protection of Producers of Phonograms Against Unauthorized Duplication of Their Phonograms of October 29, 1971.
- Agreement Establishing the World Trade Organization (List of Annexes 1–4); Annex 1/C: Agreement on Trade-Related Aspects of Intellectual Property (TRIPS Agreement). WTO Agreement was ratified pursuant to Law No. 4067 of January 26, 1995 (Official Gazette, No. 22213 of February 25, 1995).

References

Brown Keyder V (1996) Fikri Mülkiyet Hakları ve Gümrük Birliği (in English: Intellectual Property Rights and Customs Union). Intermedia, Istanbul

Tekinalp Ü (2012) Fikri Mülkiyet Hukuku (in English: Intellectual Property Law), 5th edn. Vedat Kitapcilik, Istanbul